Stuart's Tarheels
Second Edition

STUART'S TARHEELS

*James B. Gordon and His
North Carolina Cavalry
in the Civil War*

Second Edition

Chris J. Hartley

McFarland & Company, Inc., Publishers
Jefferson, North Carolina

The present work is a reprint of the illustrated case bound edition of Stuart's Tarheels: James B. Gordon and His North Carolina Cavalry in the Civil War, *first published in 2011 by McFarland.*

LIBRARY OF CONGRESS CATALOGUING-IN-PUBLICATION DATA

Hartley, Chris J.
Stuart's tarheels : James B. Gordon and his North Carolina cavalry in the Civil War / Chris J. Hartley.— 2nd ed.
p. cm.
Includes bibliographical references and index.

ISBN 978-1-4766-6798-0
softcover : acid free paper ∞

1. Gordon, James B. (James Byron), 1822–1864.
2. Generals — Confederate States of America — Biography.
3. Confederate States of America. Army of Northern Virginia — Cavalry.
4. North Carolina — History — Civil War, 1861–1865 — Cavalry operations.
5. United States — History — Civil War, 1861–1865 — Cavalry operations.
I. Title.
E467.1.G65H37   2016   973.7'455 — dc22   2011016556

BRITISH LIBRARY CATALOGUING DATA ARE AVAILABLE

© 2011 Chris J. Hartley. All rights reserved

No part of this book may be reproduced or transmitted in any form or by any means, electronic or mechanical, including photocopying or recording, or by any information storage and retrieval system, without permission in writing from the publisher.

Front cover: Union and Confederate cavalry clash at Brandy Station, Virginia, 1863 (painting by Don Troiani, www.historicalimagebank.com); background © 2011 Shutterstock

Printed in the United States of America

McFarland & Company, Inc., Publishers
Box 611, Jefferson, North Carolina 28640
www.mcfarlandpub.com

For Laurie, my wife; Jim and Ann, my parents

Acknowledgments

It has been a decade and a half since the first edition of *Stuart's Tarheels* appeared, and it is an honor and a privilege to introduce a second edition. The work of a researcher is, it seems, never done, as perhaps the surest thing about publishing a book on a historical topic is that new information will appear after the presses run. So, this new volume has been, the author hopes, improved with the inclusion of some additional source material that has indeed come to light in the intervening years. Plus, this volume includes a roster of the regiment that Gordon loved so much: the 1st North Carolina Cavalry.

The people who helped to make this second volume possible includes not only those I thanked back in 1996, but also many more individuals. In the summer of 1989 I began this endeavor, and now my journey is finished. It has been possible to produce this book only through the help of many, starting at home. I would like to extend thanks and love to Laurie, my wonderful wife; to my father and mother, Mr. and Mrs. James S. Hartley; and to my extended family. I am blessed to be a part of the Hartley-Triplett-Connor-Marion clan.

My appreciation is first and foremost due to my original publisher, Jim McLean of Butternut & Blue, who made this possible. I also express thanks to McFarland & Company, for the opportunity to create a second edition. On Gordon's behalf, I must also thank several writers and historians. The late J. Jay Anderson, Wilkes County's historian, showed me key sources and also gave me a valuable, hard-to-find publication. Robert E. L. Krick painstakingly read the entire thing and through his extremely helpful critiques saved me from glaring errors. Horace Mewborn focused his professional eyes on this manuscript with verve and made it better, and he even went out of his way to provide missing photographs. Robert K. Krick offered priceless suggestions, first regarding research and again after reading part of the "Gordon-Hartley" opus. Clark B. Hall carefully critiqued my Brandy Station chapter and pointed me to important sources. Bob O'Neill thoroughly examined the Aldie, Middleburg, and Upperville section of my manuscript. He and Horace Mewborn even gave me a fabulous tour of those battlefields. Robert J. Trout offered a willing hand in tracking down information. With a few questions and kind words, Burke Davis also sparked the early stages of this work. Thanks also to Butch Barringer, John Divine, Whit Joyner, Michael Musick, Donald Pfanz, Doug Pitts, Gordon C. Rhea, Herbert Schiller, and Richard J. Sommers.

This list must also include the descendants. The late Annie Finley Winkler, great-granddaughter of Gordon's sister Sarah Ann Gordon Finley, shared family stories, memories, and folklore. Peter W. Hairston has become not only a link to the past but also a man I am proud to call a friend. So too is Rufus Barringer, grandson of Gordon's fellow cavalryman, who willingly provided important sources. Archibald Craige, grandson of Gordon's aide, graciously supplied information and a wonderful photograph. J.E.B. Stuart IV provided his support just as General Stuart once did to General Gordon. Alfred T. Adams, son and nephew of "Old First" troopers, gave typescripts of family letters, and also a lot of fun on the golf course. Meneta W. Proffit Henderson loaned a diary detailing her family's wartime experiences. My gratitude is also due to Billy Dawn Auciello, Beverly Barrier Troxler, J. L. Meem, Jr. (Aurelia Halsey's grandson), and Sidney S. Bost (a grandson of William H. H. Cowles).

The organizations, publications, and institutions (and their staffs) to which I am indebted include the *Appalachian Journal*, Duke University's Perkins Library, Emory and Henry College, the Georgia Department of Archives and History, J. Stephen Catlett and the Greensboro Historical Museum, the *Journal-Patriot,* The Library of Congress, Guy Swanson and the Museum of the Confederacy, the National Archives, the North Carolina Collection at UNC–Chapel Hill, the North Carolina Division of Archives and History, the Southern Historical Collection at UNC–Chapel Hill, the University of Virginia, Michael J. Winey and the U.S. Army Military History Institute, the Valentine, the Virginia Historical Society, the Virginia State Library and Archives, Wake Forest University's Z. Smith Reynolds Library, and the Winston-Salem/Forsyth County Public Library. I also wish to recognize Gary Coffey, Steve Daye, Frank E. McKenzie, Scott Mauger, Nancy R. Petree and the James B. Gordon Chapter of the United Daughters of the Confederacy, Dick Underwood, and Peggy Vogtsberger.

I reserve emphatic gratitude for two organizations and one person in particular. Old Wilkes, Inc. first gave me the opportunity to share my work. The J.E.B. Stuart Birthplace Preservation Trust, Inc. provided many additional forums. Then there is Tom Perry, would-be Virginian and founder of the Stuart Birthplace Preservation Trust. Frankly, I should have dedicated this book to him, because I could not have finished it without his help, but I will not do that until the Hokies beat the Tar Heels on the hardwood.

For the second edition, I would also offer my thanks to Elizabeth Bennett of Historic Cabarrus, Inc., Kathryn Bridges and the Charles A. Cannon Memorial Library Staff, Susan Carpenter-Smith (great-granddaughter of Daniel Penninger), Buddy Colvard, Randall Crews (ancestor of Thomas N. Crumpler), Mrs. R. E. Davis, W. Robert C. Deal (great-great nephew of Sidney Deal), Bonnie Emmert of the Warren County Memorial Library, the staff of the Forsyth County Library, Sanna Gaffney of the Genealogical Society of Watauga County, Dr. Dallas Herring of the Duplin County Historical Society, Harold E. Howard, Robert E.L. Krick, Horace Mewborn, Dr. James H. McCallum, Jr., Kent McKoury, George F. and Joyce McNeil, Henry Mintz, Janet Morrison (ancestor of Martin Van Buren King), the late Whit Joyner, Tom Perry (yes Tom, the Hokies have come a long ways in hoops and they are still pretty darn good in football too), Zoe Rhine of the Asheville-Buncombe Library System, Tom Smith, Jeff H. Stepp of the North Carolina Confederate Burial Locator Project, and Mr. Ray Smith (grandson of Caleb Smith).

The old, errant historical marker in Wilkes County still stands, but perhaps James B. Gordon and his North Carolina cavalrymen have not been forgotten after all. They still ride, if only in these pages.

Above all, I thank God for the opportunity.

Contents

Acknowledgments	vii
Preface	1
Prologue: Near Yellow Tavern, Virginia, May 11, 1864	5

PART I: GORDON AND HIS CAVALRY

1. Overmountain Men	7
2. "A High Sense of All That Is Honorable"	15
3. A Hole in Your Hide	33
4. Back to Carolina	52
5. Wholesome Lessons	63
6. *Petite Guerre*	78
7. A Season of Raiding	93
8. Spent and Recovered	111
9. "General, There Comes the First North Carolina"	126
10. With the 5th	139
11. "Now, Gordon, Is Your Time!"	163
12. One Needful Thing	189
13. "Every Man Must Be a Hero"	207
Conclusion: "Muffled Drums"	231

PART II: THE ROSTER

Abbreviations	241
Roster of the 1st North Carolina Cavalry Regiment (9th Regiment North Carolina State Troops)	247

Appendix I. J.E.B. Stuart's Brigade and Divisional Commanders   389
Appendix II. Gordon and His Farm   390
Appendix III. Gordon's Printed House Documents   391
Notes   397
Bibliography   425
Index   431

Preface

And the gallant Gordon! how well I knew him, and how we all loved him! Tall, elegant in person, distinguished in address, with a charming suavity and gaiety, he was a universal favourite. Of humor how rich! of bearing how frank and cordial! of courage how stern and obstinate! Under fire, Gordon was a perfect rock; nothing could move him. In camp, off duty, he was the soul of good-fellowship. His bow and smile were inimitable, his voice delightful. He would present a bouquet to a lady with a little speech which nobody else could approach; and, at the head of the 'Old First' North Carolina cavalry, he would have charged McClellan's massed artillery at Malvern Hill. We used to tell him that his rapid rise to the rank of General was the result of his 'personal, political, and pecuniary position;' but that alliterative accusation was only a jest. He won his rank by hard fighting and hard work; he gave the South all he had — his time, his toil, his brain; she demanded his life, and he gave that, too, without a murmur. Peace to that brave!
— John Esten Cooke, *Wearing of The Gray*, 512–13.

THE OLD HOUSE HAS BEEN GONE for over fifty years, but you would not know it from reading a nearby historical marker. According to that iron gray sign, the home of James B. Gordon stands three hundred yards to the north. Instead, a busy hospital stands there on a steep hill. Even so, the marker's silent falsehood draws little attention. Only an occasional motorist, waiting at a neighboring stoplight, actually reads it. Few wonder about the missing house and its long-deceased owner, a Confederate general. Most passers-by do not recognize the general's name.

With a simple signal change, cars pass and the marker is forgotten — like the memory of the general. Resurrecting that memory would, however, bring to light a man who made his mark in a pivotal time in American history. James Byron Gordon lived traditionally, in the way of the South, in the way that all but died in the nation's growth. Living in a small prewar North Carolina town, he was a prominent leader and citizen. A member of an agricultural society, he farmed, ran a business, served his political party, and filled church leadership positions. Friendly, aristocratic, and a gentleman, he often offered a helping hand to his neighbors. His agrarian methods and political beliefs linked him with the South, secession, and slavery. In war, Gordon sided with the Confederacy to defend his land, his home, and his way of life. Though not a professional soldier, he rose to lead an infantry company, a cavalry regiment, a cavalry brigade, and (temporarily) a cavalry division. The troopers who served under Gordon came to consider him "every inch a soldier."[1] But what has happened to the memory of this man? Why have so few heard of him? Why is the marker that is meant to memorialize him incorrect?

In history, Gordon has been understandably overshadowed by the talented men he served with. Some students have even confused him with his more prominent first cousin, Confederate

Major General John Brown Gordon of Georgia. Yet Gordon's story is one worth telling, for the efforts of men such as Gordon helped bring success to Stuart's Confederate cavalry. These men played their part in tactics, not strategy; in fighting, but not often in planning battles. Gordon, for example, was largely responsible for Stuart's last battlefield victory.

Consider the fact that only three men served as brigadier generals of cavalry under Stuart without the benefit of pre-war military experience or training. Gordon was one; Wade Hampton and Matthew C. Butler were the others. Of the three, Gordon was perhaps the most subordinate, but he did play an interesting role as the leading North Carolina horse soldier in Stuart's cavalry. Indeed, at the time of his death, James B. Gordon was the best cavalryman produced by North Carolina. Perhaps he was North Carolina's best cavalryman ever. Whatever the case, one thing is apparent: the history of the Old North State's cavalry in the Confederacy is the history of James B. Gordon.

Since Stuart, Robert E. Lee, and Jefferson Davis preferred professional training for command, Gordon's accomplishments become more impressive. Examine the speed of Gordon's promotions. Stuart's valued staff officer, Major H. B. McClellan, described the rise of this "capable officer" as exhibiting "unparalleled rapidity."[2] In just over two years, Gordon rose from lieutenant to brigadier general. That is a jump of no less than five grades. Other men enjoyed equally rapid advancement, but few did so with as little military background as Gordon.[3]

This rise may be less surprising when one remembers how Gordon's men saw him. "He was the Murat of the Army of Northern Virginia," wrote one veteran North Carolina cavalryman. Gordon was not the only Southern soldier who received this sobriquet, but it speaks volumes that Gordon's cavalry skills have been compared with Murat, the legendary leader of Napoleon's cavalry.[4] Another witness, Gordon's aide-de-camp, wrote, "He was recognized as a brave, daring, and skillful officer.... As a brigade commander Genl Gordon ranked among the bravest and best." The Virginian Chiswell Dabney, Gordon's adjutant and inspector general, wrote of Gordon, "He was a noble gentleman and a most gallant and accomplished officer."[5] General William Paul Roberts of North Carolina served under Gordon before being promoted to brigadier general. "I beg to state here that the South furnished no grander or more glorious soldier to the cause of Southern liberty," he wrote. According to another Confederate, Gordon was nothing less than a "genius of war, a 'veritable god of battle.'" D. H. Hill grouped Gordon with the Confederacy's best horsemen: "The deeds they performed justly entitle them to high repute, and fully vindicate their arm of the service from all reproach," he wrote.[6]

The testimony does not end there. "When he fell," recorded cavalryman-writer John Esten Cooke, "he left behind him no braver soldier or kindlier gentleman." A trooper from the 5th North Carolina Cavalry called Gordon "that great cavalry leader." One of J.E.B. Stuart's staff officers, Theodore S. Garnett, remembered, "He was a fine soldier, brave and true, and much beloved and admired by Gen. Stuart."[7] Edward L. Wells, a veteran who became an admiring biographer of Wade Hampton, delivered his own brief eulogy of Gordon. He described Gordon as "an excellent officer" who lost his life in an unequal contest, "fighting stoutly in the front, as was his wont." Daniel Coltrane, also one of Gordon's men, said of May 18, 1864: "The South lost a great and courageous fighting general that day." William H. Cheek, one of Gordon's officers, said that his commander "proved himself a soldier of extraordinary capacity."[8]

This is high praise, yet in many ways Gordon was like other soldiers in that he simply did his duty. His superiors never criticized him for a poor performance but did occasionally complement him for gallantry. Yet more often than not, officials did not single Gordon out because he did his work quietly and as expected. His job was to lead cavalrymen, and he did that with increasing skill. Thanks to his leadership, his cavalrymen earned a place in military history. His men said "a hole in your hide" was the fate of any man who held a commission in one of units Gordon commanded. Gordon himself proved this true.[9]

Today, one can still enjoy the same countryside that Gordon once called his. In Virginia the remains of his battlefields survive. In North Carolina, the house where one of his sisters lived still stands. Westward from and in plain view of that house is the site of Gordon's hilltop home, overlooking the land he once cultivated. To see the land today is to wonder what it was like then. To see the land today is to wonder about a single, stubborn, errant sign...

Over the dark sea's ebb and flow,
   Marching with stately tread
'Neath a spotless banner waving low
   Is the hero we call dead.

Far up the slopes of that beautiful shore,
   By the side of the musical river,
His cares, his sorrows, his last fight o'er,
   He has stacked his arms forever.

He has struck his tent in the morning land,
   In the sphere without shadow or sin,
Where the sentries on guard no longer stand,
   And the pickets have all come in.

And journeying on to the distant spires,
   To the ruby and diamond wall,
No more he lights the old camp fires,
   Or lists for the bugle's call.

'Tis there mid the long sweet sunny hours,
   He has won a Christian's crown,
And among the radiant fadeless flowers,
   He has flung his sabre down.

'Tis there where light and music blend,
   That Gordon, the hero, waits,
And his last long furlough will never end,
   For he leans on the golden gates.

—Anonymous
(Finley, "Address to the James B. Gordon Chapter
of the United Daughters of the Confederacy")

Prologue

Near Yellow Tavern, Virginia, May 11, 1864

"Would to God that Gordon were here."[1]

These words lingered on the lips of James Ewell Brown Stuart as he surveyed the battlefield before him. Outnumbered at least two to one, his cavalry had weathered Federal demonstrations and assaults for four hours. Soon, he hoped, it would be his turn to dictate the battle, but his plan required James B. Gordon's North Carolina Cavalry Brigade. It was possible that the two horse brigades Stuart had with him would not be enough to stop the next Union attack, so in the soft afternoon sunlight he waited impatiently for his friend Gordon. Unfortunately, the North Carolinian was busy fighting elsewhere.

Just two days before, as the Army of Northern Virginia fought near Spotsylvania Court House, Stuart had received grim information. A thirteen-mile long column of Union cavalrymen was moving south, around Lee's flank, toward Richmond. General Philip H. Sheridan, commander of the cavalry corps of the Federal Army of the Potomac, led the column, which consisted of more than ten thousand men. The incursion was the result of orders from Ulysses S. Grant, who had given Sheridan permission to slide past Lee's army, destroy anything of value, and challenge the highly-regarded Confederate cavalry.

Undismayed, Stuart pursued immediately with only about five thousand cavalrymen, or roughly half his force. As Sheridan cruised southward, capturing and destroying Lee's advance base on the Virginia Central Rail Road, Stuart split his forces. Gordon's Brigade harassed Sheridan from behind; the brigades of generals Lunsford Lomax and Williams C. Wickham tried to block Sheridan's way. Finally, at an abandoned stagecoach inn called Yellow Tavern, Stuart and Fitz Lee placed Lomax and Wickham between Richmond and the Federal advance while Gordon continued to snap at Sheridan's heels.

That suited "Little Phil" Sheridan just fine. The Yankee general, veteran of battles in the West, was quite sure he could handle Stuart. He got his chance to find out when the Federals began arriving at Yellow Tavern, only six miles from Richmond. It was about 11:00 A.M. on May 11. The battle began soon thereafter and lasted late into the afternoon. Probing, charging, and skirmishing of a vicious nature characterized the fight as Sheridan's men kept Stuart on the defensive. About 3:00 P.M. a lull fell over the field; Sheridan had apparently spotted a weak link in Stuart's defenses and was designing an attack to exploit it. Meanwhile, Stuart sat talking with members of his staff, his horse-soldiers ready and waiting for the enemy. It was probably about this time when Stuart muttered the words, "Would to God that Gordon were here."

But Gordon was not. Under Stuart's orders, he and his Tarheels were still involved in rearguard action near the South Anna River. Admired and beloved "for his courage and skill and kindliness," Gordon was a big-boned man who stood about six-foot-three-inches tall. His chin sported a "long, flowing silky" beard. Even in this trying situation, he held himself with a "fine military carriage." That day, Gordon looked as magnificent as ever. He directed his early morning battle with skill and forced the Yankees to relinquish both Goodall's Tavern and Ground Squirrel Church. Yet when the fighting ended, he was still several miles away from Stuart and Yellow Tavern.[2]

Four o'clock came, and with it the sight and sound of enemy cavalrymen pounding down against Stuart's position. At full gallop, Federal troopers, mostly from General George A. Custer's brigade, pressed Stuart's left and left center. Other Federals struck the Confederate right. Gray-clad soldiers fired at the charging Federals as fast as they could, and held until the pressure grew intolerable. Stuart just did not have enough men. Would Phil Sheridan next try for Richmond? Stuart didn't think so, but the city's defenses were being stoutly readied just in case.[3]

Before long, the left side of the gray line gave way completely. The Confederates fell back about four hundred yards to a defensible ravine. Stuart himself dashed to the Telegraph Road in time to see the Federals charge past him in pursuit of his reeling line.[4] The general watched the tide of battle turn against him, punctuated by the cheers of the Federals. He listened to the firing, the whiz of minie-balls, and the booming of artillery that signaled his enemy's success.

As Stuart's pistol flamed in defiance, the Michigan regiments suddenly turned back. Behind the Yankees, Confederate troopers formed their own driving pursuit. Rebel yells replaced Yankee hurrahs. A last-minute counterattack had slammed the Federals and driven them back, temporarily robbing the Stars and Stripes of victory. Encouraged by the turn of events, Stuart turned and yelled, "Steady, men, steady. Give it to them." All was confusion as the Confederates rallied and the Yankees struggled to preserve what they had won.[5]

In the midst of the pandemonium, a lone Federal trooper fired a shot that struck Stuart's right side. The Virginian realized through his pain that he had been badly, perhaps mortally, wounded. While being hurried from the field, Stuart yelled to his disorganized force, "Go back! go back! and do your duty, as I have done mine, and our country will be safe. Go back! go back! I had rather die than be whipped."[6]

Would to God that Gordon were here...

PART I: GORDON AND HIS CAVALRY

1

Overmountain Men

TOGETHER, GEORGE AND CHARLES GORDON walked up Kings Mountain. The dust of a hundred-mile journey clung to their clothes; their weary bones cried for rest. The steep, forested hill seemed endless, but at that moment the two brothers ignored all else. They readied their weapons for the task at hand.

Ahead, on top of Kings Mountain, an army of Tories waited. It was October 1780.

On either side of the Gordons, almost one thousand Patriots dotted the tree-filled landscape. Three of Charles's sons walked with them, including Chapman Gordon, who had married into the family that owned Kings Mountain. George Gordon's brothers-in-law also were there. So too were some of the leading members of the Gordons' home community. Locals called them Lenoir's Rangers; now, they formed part of the makeshift army of "Overmountain Men" that had come over the mountains of Tennessee, Virginia, and North Carolina to fight the Tories. Like a ring of hunters closing in on a rabbit, they surrounded their quarry.[1]

British Major Patrick Ferguson, commanding the one thousand man-plus Tory army, held Kings Mountain beneath the autumn sun. He had confidence in his position, but entertained little respect for his backwoods enemies. That, he would learn, was a mistake.

George Gordon and his older brother Charles Gordon were typical Overmountain men. They hailed from a rugged northwest North Carolina river valley. In another time, Native Americans had hunted buffalo, panther, and bear in the valley's forests. They had carved paths in the foothill country, which bristled with both gentle and rugged hills. They had farmed the fertile banks of the Yadkin, a river that split the valley roughly in half. Although the Indians spent their winters in warmer climates, they had loved the valley and had raised their families there. They felt safe there, shielded from the north and west by the mighty Blue Ridge Mountains and from the south by the modest Brushy Mountains. That changed in about 1750, however, when Englishmen began arriving, at first to enlist Indians into the King's service. Christopher Gist, an Indian scout and surveyor, built a home along the Yadkin River with that in mind. Daniel Boone was another such pioneer; he lived with his family near a Yadkin River ford during the 1750s before he moved to Kentucky. Yet where Gist came as a friend, others did not. As more settlers came to the valley, the Indians retreated.[2]

These newcomers, also servants of the crown, secured new homes by buying land in the valley that had once belonged to a Lord Proprietor. The story behind the Lord Proprietor's lands concerned a century of tangled politics. In 1660, King Charles II of England had returned to the British throne in debt from the English Civil War. Money being scarce, gifts of land represented the only way he could repay his partisans. The King thus dubbed eight of his closest supporters "the true and absolute Lords and Proprietaries" of colonial land in Carolina.[3] As time passed, however, the administrative capabilities of the Lords Proprietors fell under suspicion. The crown eventually asked the men or their families to sell their land back to the crown. Only John, Lord Carteret, refused to return the proprietorship he had inherited from Sir George Carteret. Instead, the man later known as Earl Granville chose to sell his land in North Carolina to incoming settlers through agents.[4]

Still more Englishmen came from the east and northeast, purchased grants, and planted their roots. Strength, not gentility, was the requirement here, and the lineage of George and Charles Gordon echoed both qualities. The two had been born into a hardy family of proud heritage and tradition. Scottish in stock, the family came from a land where hardship and violence were commonplace. Law and order were often anything but a feature of Scotland's early history; instead, the Scots had known constant war with many peoples, as well as themselves. Many members of the Gordon family were government and military leaders, so the name was well known in Scotland. The family tree held many branches and wound in several directions, but all who bore the name did so proudly.[5]

The promise of the New World proved to be a siren's song that many Scots could not resist. In 1724, John George Gordon came to America. Sailing from Aberdeen, he landed in Charleston, South Carolina.[6] He was one of thousands of Scotch and Irish persons who emigrated to America after 1717. In doing so, they bore the danger and expense of the transatlantic journey to escape financial hardships and religious persecution. Settling in Maryland, John Gordon's "good looks and prepossessing appearance were too much for the heart of the fair young Mary Chapman...." Despite the opposition of her wealthy uncle, Dr. James Chapman, "the course of true love proved too strong...." The two soon married.[7]

So began an American branch of the Gordon family. John and Mary Gordon started their new life together by following the tendencies of their people: as one sociologist has noted, Scotch-Irish were known for pulling up roots and moving at least twice. Soon after their marriage, the Gordons moved to Spotsylvania County, Virginia. Settling near Fredericksburg, John and Mary had children and strove for a better standard of life. Then, in the 1770s, the Gordons' sons, George and Charles, sought land of their own. They migrated to North Carolina.[8]

George and Charles Gordon came to the Northwest North Carolina river valley and obtained a former Earl Granville grant. (The grant had first been purchased in 1752 and passed through other hands before the Gordons bought their portion.) Charles's wife and children joined him in the river valley. Sarah Herndon Gordon came to be with her husband, George. As Gist had, George Gordon's family built a home near the Yadkin River. They worked hard and reaped the benefits of the land, and in doing so emerged as one of the prominent, aristocratic families of the valley.

Government followed the pioneers. In 1778, their valley was named Wilkes County, North Carolina. Charles Gordon was appointed coroner of the first county government; John Brown became register and ranger; and Benjamin Cleveland, a justice of the peace. For a county seat, the new government began to build a settlement. Just a few months later, George Gordon served on a committee that selected the site on which to "erect a Court House, Prison, Pillory and Stocks." Thus was born the town of Wilkesborough.[9]

None of this changed the fact that the Revolution approached like a distant thunderstorm. Tories and Loyalists were already skirmishing in the mountains on occasion. Then, in 1780, the war came closer. British leadership decided that the key to ending the rebellion in the colonies was to subdue the South. After reestablishing royal rule in most of South Carolina and Georgia, the British dispatched troops to North Carolina. To guard the flank of Lord

1. Overmountain Men 9

Cornwallis's main army, British Major Patrick Ferguson led a column of Loyalists into the western Piedmont. Threatening to ravage the countryside unless the Rebels surrendered, Ferguson began punishing his opposition. By late September, this threat infuriated the locals. Mountain men gathered and set out to find Ferguson. In Wilkes County, the rotund Benjamin Cleveland sounded his great hunting horn from the top of Rendezvous Mountain. Legend has it that his horn echoed through the valley, calling 450 Wilkes men to war. The Gordons were among those who heard the call. Cleveland then marched the volunteers to join the rest of the Overmountain Men.[10]

They found Ferguson at Kings Mountain on October 7. Surrounding the Tories, the makeshift army slowly scaled the mountain. Cleveland led his column of Wilkes Countians to the summit. Isaac Shelby, John Sevier, and William Campbell directed other frontiersmen. Soon, the fight was on. From the shelter of rocks and trees, the Overmountain Men fired their muskets at the foe. Ferguson's army suffered more than three hundred casualties in the savage fight, and Ferguson himself fell dead. Charles Gordon also paid a price as he received a wound. The Tories, though they repulsed their attackers more than once, ultimately had no alternative but to surrender. With that, the tide of war in the South began shifting.[11]

For years afterward, the story of the Overmountain Men passed from generation to generation. Descendants took pride in their forefathers' role in securing American Independence. The Gordon family was no different; after all, the family had done its part. Even though the years passed and family members moved away, this mountain pride, this tradition of resistance, lived on in the sons and daughters of the Overmountain men. Four of Charles's sons moved to Georgia. George Gordon's children, among them six daughters, took to their own roads. One son, John, moved to Mississippi. Only one son, Nathaniel, who had been born on May 1, 1784, chose to remain in Wilkes County to start his family.[12]

James Byron Gordon was born on November 2, 1822. The town of Wilkesborough that greeted him had grown little since his grandfather had helped select its location. The designated spot, near the site of an old Indian village, was on the southern side of a hill that seemed to rise out of the Yadkin. The town's nineteen dwellings, courthouse, and jail, along with a few other buildings, did not come close to filling the available land. Baby James's home sat just across the river.[13]

James's proud parents were the first Gordons in three generations to

In this Garl Browne portrait of James B. Gordon, it is easy to see what an observer called his "expression in which resolution of mind and kindliness of heart were happily blended" (courtesy North Carolina Museum of History).

raise their family in a single place. Already the parents of a baby girl when James was born, Nathaniel and Sarah were good and respected people. When James was born in Nathaniel's thirty-eighth year, Nathaniel had already lived a life of accomplishments. As inheritor of his father's land, Nathaniel was one of the wealthiest and most prominent men in the county. His spacious farmland, which stretched hundreds of yards south to the Yadkin, east to the Reddies River, and west toward rising hills, made him one of the largest landowners in the county. "Oakland," his hilltop home that dominated the surrounding countryside, was probably the closest thing to a plantation that could be found in those parts. It was a fitting residence for a proud veteran and successful politician. Nathaniel had fought as a cavalryman in the War of 1812. He had also served in the North Carolina General Assembly and as a local justice of the peace.[14]

Nathaniel's wife, twenty-four-year-old Sarah, was an attractive, well-bred woman. The daughter of Richard R. and Martha Lenoir Gwyn, Sarah had caught the eye of more than one man in her lifetime, but it was Nathaniel whom she married on March 30, 1820. She was a deeply committed Christian, "her living religion a better sermon in her Master's cause than the most eloquent words that man can speak."[15] Later in life, she would continue to see to her children's religious education, advising them to read their Bibles daily. Her personal creed was simple but penetrating: "Without religion, [there is] no happiness, the aim of our being is to live wisely, soberly, and righteously." Sarah proved to be a good wife and a caring mother. From the cradle, the young mother displayed a tender love for James. Gordon became devoted to his mother as he grew. He would never go on a trip without his mother and not feel sad.[16]

With such parents, it is no surprise that the first few years of James's life passed in the setting of a happy, growing family. Martha Lenoir was James's older sister. Martha had been named for Sarah's mother, Martha Lenoir Gwyn, who at the age of twelve had negotiated the release of her imprisoned father by appealing to General Charles Lord Cornwallis himself. Two girls, Sarah Ann and Caroline Louisa, were born in 1826 and 1828 respectively. James and his three sisters were lucky to be raised by caring, well-off parents. They had plenty of food, and the slaves handled most of the work. Mother, and father when politics did not call, could spend lots of time with their children. The days passed quickly.

In 1829, illness wracked Nathaniel. The happiness of the young family, and the sheltered life of James and his sisters, came to an abrupt halt. It seemed unfair; Nathaniel's father and grandfather had worked so hard to give their children better opportunities. Now, it appeared Nathaniel was to be robbed of a long life in which to flourish. Helpless family members could only watch him decline. As Nathaniel's condition worsened, Sarah realized that she faced the future without her husband. The former cavalryman, even in his sickness, knew it too. Lying on a homemade feather bed, Nathaniel determined to provide for his family.

On a wintry January day in 1829, Nathaniel Gordon fought off the chills and aches of illness and dictated his last will and testament to a friend. He directed "that all my estate real and personal of whatever nature or kind soever ... shall be and remain under the control and management" of Sarah, "until my son James shall attain the age of 21 years...." Furthermore, Nathaniel said, each of his four children should be provided with a "good English education" above and beyond the normal "support and maintenance" the family required.[17]

Nine days after he wrote his will, pneumonia took the life of Nathaniel Gordon. They buried him beneath a monument that bore the words, "The glory of man is as the flower of grass. But the word of the Lord endureth forever." In their mourning, his family and friends remembered his love, accomplishments, and hard work. They also comforted themselves with the fact that Nathaniel had won one last victory. He had provided for his family.

The winter of 1829 got no easier for the Gordons. Martha Lenoir Gwyn, James's maternal grandmother, died less than a month later. The two deaths were a lot for a six-year-old to deal with, but James apparently bore it well. The most significant results of these tragedies, save the memories, were the inheritances. These eventually meant everything to James. If nothing else, Mrs. Gwyn blessed her grandson with the feisty spirit of the Overmountain Men, while Nathaniel left not only an inheritance but also a legacy and a place in society. It was not in passing that Nathaniel stressed education in his will. It was not a side note that James was to be given the land, the home, and even "the negro boy named Henry" when he came of age.[18] James had only lived with Nathaniel for a scant six years, and never got the chance to grow up learning from him, but he was without a doubt his father's son. He inherited a Southern way of life; he had in his blood the ambition, the talent, and the characteristics of his father. Because of his father's untimely death, James was forced to grow up quickly and take on more responsibility than most young men his age. He did not have the same opportunities educationally or in growing up that he would have had if Nathaniel had lived. Still, the early end of Gordon's childhood was the foundation of his future. Gordon would become the farmer, landowner, businessman, public servant, and cavalryman that his father had been. Friends, neighbors, fellow churchgoers, and politicians would come to respect his personality, manners, and disposition. Finally, Gordon's life would climax in the midst of civil war as he defended his home and his convictions. Even General J. E. B. Stuart would desire Gordon's help in his own darkest hour. Grandma and Dad would have been proud.

Just as Nathaniel had wanted it, Gordon's mother and his appointed guardian, Samuel F. Patterson, continued to provide for the youngster's education. About a year before Nathaniel's death, Gordon had started his education at the Wilkesborough Academy, where Nathaniel was a trustee. Perhaps to ensure his attendance, the Gordons had sent James to school with a young neighbor, Calvin Miller. With a little boy's reluctance, James would walk with Calvin to the top of a hill about half a mile from town, where the log academy sat in the midst of a forest. There he would sit down to work. The academy, under the direction of the Reverend Abner Gay, offered its students a classical situation, "exactly such that Apollo and the Muses are represented as loving to haunt...." Tuition was reasonable for a five month session: ten dollars for Latin and Greek and seven dollars for English grammar and geography. Mrs. Gordon hoped that Reverend Gay would live up to his promise to "pay strict attention to the improvement of the youth intrusted to his care." She truly wanted James to receive a "healthy constitution" and "have [his] mind improved."[19]

Gay did his best, but it was not enough for Mrs. Gordon. When James turned ten, Mrs. Gordon sent him to the school of Peter S. Ney in the Mocksville area. Prominent families of the area also sent their children to the school, so to her it was only logical that James should go. Locals knew Ney, a former soldier, as a "remarkable man, of scholarly attainments and soldierly bearing." A muscular man who stood about six feet tall, Ney always held himself formally erect. Though slightly bald, his remaining hair showed a reddish-blonde hue, and his eyes flashed a dark blue that verged on gray. Ney's habit of being gentle, indulgent, and obedient with studious pupils and strict with problem students was the right technique for Gordon.[20] Under the tutelage of this impressive man, James began to enjoy his studies and to admire his splendid professor. "My teacher is the best scholar I ever saw," he wrote his mother in September 1833. "Mr. Ney makes my class write letters every Friday afternoon. Am pleased with the school...."[21]

An aura of mystery surrounded Peter Ney. Some whispered that he was none other than Marshal Michel Ney, one of Napoleon's leaders. For one thing, Ney often wore a long blue coat that had a military air about it. He had a long deep scar on the left side of his head that gave him the look of a fugitive European leader and military man. Ney himself, in his slight foreign accent, even claimed he was the Marshal — when he was drunk. Another rumor said that Ney humbled a French fencing master in swordplay before the gaze of some pupils.[22]

When James was not at school, he boarded with Samuel Young, who lived nearby. There, James undoubtedly began to exhibit the "patriotism and martial pride and ambition" that Ney was teaching him. In letters home, James also wrote excitedly about his lessons. His favorite was geography. Ney's classes on the subject fascinated him, James said, because he "does not teach it in the common way, as men of learning say." Gordon also proudly displayed how to calculate the distance between the earth and the sun.[23]

In Nathaniel Gordon's absence, Peter Ney was the first man to substitute as James's father. Ney's "great personal magnetism" drew in the youthful Gordon. His "courtliness of manner," kindness, helpfulness to people, appreciation for education, and especially his military bearing left marks on James that were to be seen again.[24]

In 1834, James had to say good-bye to Peter Ney and Samuel Young. Mrs. Gordon was concerned about James because his health had not been "robust;" the youngster had even suffered through a bout with the measles. As a result, she removed him from school and brought him home. Besides, an extra hand was always needed around "Oakland." Thus came the next step in James's education: the school of hard work. Gordon's mother immediately put him to work on the farm. There, "in the performance of such light labor as was suited to his age and strength, he grew up, developing into a finely formed young man."[25] For seven years, Gordon labored in the fields below "Oakland." No longer did the young man play beneath the oak trees around "Oakland," as he had loved to do. From the plantation's overseer and from his own experiences, Gordon learned to farm and to manage the extensive property and its people. This knowledge would serve him well one day.

Gordon also learned from his stepfather. On October 6, 1830, Mrs. Gordon married Hamilton Brown, a prominent citizen of Wilkesborough and ancestor of an Overmountain Man. Brown, a farmer, veteran of the War of 1812, ex-sheriff, and former justice of the peace, had apparently tried to court Sarah Gwyn before. Those first attempts proved unsuccessful as Sarah "sassily" ignored Brown and chose to wed Nathaniel Gordon. Yet Brown, who lived above Brown's Ford on the Yadkin River, never gave up. After Nathaniel died, he called on Sarah again. As the courtship led to marriage, Hamilton could tell his fiancée with all honesty, "I was waiting."[26]

After James returned from Ney's school, the newlyweds decided to have children. On January 14, 1835, Hugh Thomas Brown joined the family and became half-brother to the Gordon children. On September 25, 1837, five days before Hamilton's fifty-first birthday, Hamilton Allen Brown was born. Mr. Brown was proud to have sons of his own, but he seemed even happier to have future farm-hands in the fold. James welcomed them with love, eagerly stepping into the role of big brother. James determined that he would be a role model for Tom and Allen.

To be sure, Hamilton Brown had little time to raise his boys. Brown helped take care of "Oakland" and its twenty-three slaves until Gordon came of age, and he had land of his own to tend.[27] Pulled in all directions, Brown failed to be the perfect family leader. He commanded respect but evidently gave little affection to his children, as Tom later intimated. "How strangely I have been raised," he wrote. "My Father was always willing to furnish me with money sufficient to go to school [while] at the same time abusing me like a dog. He is a strange man, and I believe his treatment of me was all with the best intention. O that I had had in my early youth a father who was a congenial [one], that would have encouraged the too timid boy to put forth all his efforts."[28]

From 1835 to 1841, while farm life fashioned the catalyst for physical development, Gordon was on his own to grow mentally. Work in "Oakland's" fields allowed little time for the pursuit of knowledge. This disturbed Gordon, and he let his parents know it. In 1841, not long after he turned eighteen, the family decided that James should return to school. It was the best time, because when he turned twenty-one the responsibility of "Oakland" would beckon. Gordon did not hesitate.

The motto of the southwestern Virginia college Emory & Henry promises students *Macte Virtute*, an "Increase in Excellence." That, in a phrase, summed up Gordon's education goals. In 1841, Gordon applied and was admitted to Emory & Henry. After kissing his mother and sisters good-bye and shaking Mr. Brown's hand, he migrated to the headwaters of the Holston River, between the Clinch and Iron Mountain Ranges in Virginia. There he returned to the pursuit he loved.

Riding up the lane from the Lynchburg-Knoxville stage road, Gordon arrived at the new school — it had only opened its doors to students in 1838 — and moved in. Before him, he saw two main campus buildings. One, the college building, contained classrooms, housing for 150 students, and faculty apartments. The other building, a boarding house, which stood 150 yards to the west, was fronted by a wooden porch and housed the college's kitchen, dining room, study hall, and a few student rooms.[29]

James, one of four roommates, set to studying. Given his limited background, he was behind from the start. Incoming freshmen had to be familiar with, among other things, Colburn's or Emerson's arithmetic, English grammar, Latin grammar and literature, ancient and modern history, and Cicero's orations.[30] Since he was not as prepared as other freshmen, he was not allowed to take the regular course. Ney's influence kept its grip, however. Gordon applied himself to his studies and took part in the college's other activities, such as daily devotions and chapel.[31] He even had the chance to learn more about farming since Emory & Henry was a manual labor institution where students could work on the college's farm to pay for their education.

Only family emergencies, such as the death of his grandmother Sarah Herndon Gordon in March 1842, interrupted Gordon's education. In the end, the knowledge he gained at Emory & Henry completed the maturation that had begun with Nathaniel Gordon's death. The things Gordon learned, the people he met, and the experiences he enjoyed affected his life as only college can.[32]

James would long remember his days at Emory & Henry as proof of the value of higher education. Later, Gordon corresponded often about his days at Emory & Henry, and kept up with the friends he made there. One fellow student recalled "the pleasant hours we spent in college." Another remembered a more difficult time, but Gordon never frowned on his experience.[33] There was much to remember: strolling the campus's walkways; studying by candlelight; attending religious services; and even trips to nearby Abingdon, where there was a girl's college. Gordon definitely improved himself spiritually, physically, and mentally. And, although it was true that his schooling fell short of what other men of like status enjoyed, Gordon made more out of his education than most. Only responsibility caused him to leave education behind.

When his irregular course ended in 1843, James took the dirt and plank roads of Virginia toward home. That was where his land and future beckoned, so he must have thought often about what lay ahead. Home, however, was not as pleasant as he had hoped to find it. The winter had been harsh, so the returning scholar found lingering sickness and disease in Wilkesborough. The population struggled with measles, smallpox, and other illnesses. Possibly at his mother's urging, Gordon again left home. He turned his brief trip into something of an adventure.[34]

It became his final fling, a moment that marked the end of his youth. As "Oakland" passed out of sight, Gordon made for the mountainous sections of Wilkes County. There he joined in the popular nineteenth century quest of gold-mining, but to no avail. Instead, he discovered the marvelous beauty of the Blue Ridge. The frills and formalities of Society, he mused, were far away, but nature was everywhere "arrayed in her most glorious robe."[35]

James B. Gordon returned from the mountains a man.

2

"A High Sense of All That Is Honorable"

> *Here the whiskered gentleman ... strode across the room twirling his mustachios, and came up to the table where we sate, making a salutation with his hat in a very stately manner, so that Hoskins himself was, as it were, obliged to bow....*
>
> — William M. Thackeray
> *The Newcomes: Memoirs of*
> *a Most Respectable Family*

ANYONE SITTING ON "OAKLAND'S" FRONT PORCH could see Buzzard's Roost in the distance. A tall clump of "dead, ghost-like sycamore trees" clustered around the junction of the Reddies and Yadkin rivers, the roost was a Gordon landmark. George Gordon had left those trees standing when he cleared land for his new home. As the years passed, the trees earned their moniker by attracting buzzards in large numbers.[1] If nothing else, this strange place formed a boundary of sorts. Each owner of "Oakland" could claim the land that stretched northward from those trees to the large white house on the hill as his own.

When he turned twenty-one in November 1843, Gordon became the legal owner of "Oakland" and its environs. That included the main house, the surrounding farmland, and even Buzzard's Roost. It was all according to the provisions of Nathaniel Gordon's will. Happily, Gordon claimed the home of his youth as his own.

His grandfather had built the house in the 1770s, then willed it to Nathaniel in 1800. It was a home to be proud of. The main building faced south toward the Yadkin River. The Reddies River curled around the house's hill from left to rear before turning northward again. Two tall stone and brick chimneys, one at the house's eastern end and one at its western end, looked like bookends. A porch of almost fifty feet in length wrapped around the front of the house; the chairs there offered comfort during many summer afternoons. From that perch, one could look beyond the house's six pine columns and enjoy the view of the Brushy Mountains.

Pine trees must have been plentiful around "Oakland" at the time of its construction. The house's interior was made mostly of that material, including the walls and the floors. Hardwood pegs held the floor's heavy pine planks in place. From the main entrance a central hallway led to a narrow staircase, whose plain spindles and heavy railing served a more functional than aesthetic purpose. The main room, situated near the front door, was probably where the Gordons entertained. It measured eighteen feet by eighteen feet. Behind the first floor's western front room was the dining room, where over three generations of Gordons took their meals. A small butler's pantry adjoined the dining room so the slaves could quickly serve their master and his guests. Two other rooms, including a "shed room," stood on the eastern

"Oakland," circa 1900. Built in the 1770s, Oakland sat atop a high hill overlooking the Yadkin and Reddies rivers. From its fifty-foot long porch, one could enjoy a view of the Brushy Mountains (courtesy Annie Finley Winkler).

side of the house. The colonial-style fireplaces that were located at each end of the house provided the warmth that made "Oakland" feel like home.

At the top of the stairs, a large room — sized about eighteen feet by eighteen feet — evidently served as the master bedroom. Two low-ceilinged bedrooms also waited upstairs; Gordon and his sisters probably slept in those rooms as children. Topping it all off was the attic, a place a little boy would have enjoyed. However, adults used it for more mundane purposes.

Out back, small porches were attached to either side of the dining room. A storage room sat behind the back porch, within easy reach of the house. For other supplies, "Oakland's" inhabitants accessed the main cellar through a trapdoor on one of the back porches. If extra storage space was needed, a root cellar had been dug near the barns. Several outhouses stood behind the porches, including four slave quarters, a carriage house, a spinning and weaving house, smoke houses, a blacksmith shop, and the kitchen. Depending on the amount of trading Gordon did, the barns held about six horses and a mule or two. About eight cows also stayed in the barns for milking. The Gordons also used storage space of a more secluded variety a few hundred yards from "Oakland": a cave had been carved out of the steep banks that rose out of the Reddies River. If Gordon ever wanted privacy, that was the place to find it.[2]

From the house, a road circled down the steep hill to the surrounding land. There Gordon began tending to the endless work of his 1,800 acre farm. With his overseer Crowden at his side and slaves at his call, Gordon planted, cultivated, harvested, and marketed a myriad of crops, including corn, wheat, oats, rye, potatoes, and tobacco. He also kept a variety of livestock ranging from turkeys and chickens to cows, sheep, and swine, while his four oxen kept the plows moving. Under Gordon's direction, the large fields of "Oakland" regularly yielded enough to satisfy the needs of the plantation's occupants and also provide a surplus for Gordon to market.[3]

Specifically, in the summer of 1850, Gordon reckoned that "Oakland" had produced 190 bushels of wheat, 150 bushels of rye, 3,635 bushels of corn, two hundred bushels of oats, ten bushels of Irish potatoes, and forty bushels of sweet potatoes during the previous twelve months. His livestock during that time included forty-two cows, thirty-five sheep, eighty pigs, and even bees. Within ten years, Gordon began raising more corn, wheat, oats, and Irish potatoes. He also discovered the value of raising tobacco as he readied fourteen thousand bushels of tobacco for market.[4] However, despite this strong output, Gordon constantly faced the problem of getting his crops to market. The inadequate roads of the area dictated Gordon's economic success in agriculture as much as the type of crops he raised.

Slave labor also directly affected "Oakland's" output. Gordon was accustomed to the peculiar institution, liked it, and found it profitable. During times of heavy work loads, he hired extra slaves to assist him. However, since farming did not require intensive year-round labor, Gordon worked his slaves at other duties. When necessary, he had them perform chores or general maintenance work. In addition, Gordon probably employed his slaves in helping to run and making goods for the store he and his brother-in-law operated.[5]

Whatever the task, Gordon was one of the largest slave owners in the county even though he apparently never owned more than twenty-odd slaves. As a rule, slave-owning in Wilkes County and western North Carolina was not as common as in eastern North Carolina. Slaves constituted about 10.2 percent of the population of the state's westernmost counties, but only 8.3 percent of Wilkes's population. According to the U.S. Census of 1850, there were only 1,112 slaves in Wilkes. The small farms dotting the hilly landscape simply did not need the amount of labor required by eastern plantations. Gordon's land, however, was unusually large and flat, so it did require the extra hands. One other factor also set Gordon apart: unlike most of his fellow mountain farmers, he had the means to buy slaves.[6]

An average of eighteen slaves lived and worked on the Gordon property during the 1850s. Gordon apparently liked to keep a balanced number of male and female slaves. Some of them were babies who had been born at "Oakland." Others were very old, probably having served the family for years. Gordon did not hesitate to sell or trade when he thought it necessary, and the work was hard, but he realized the value of caring for his slaves. The four buildings behind the main house that served as slave quarters were small, but comfortable. Family tradition has it that the slaves dearly loved Gordon. They referred to him as "the kind young master of whom they were proud." One family member later recalled, "if you could talk with them today they would tell you that 'they would do anything for Marse James.'"[7]

The family for which the slaves toiled meant everything to James B. Gordon. The Brown/Gordon clan was an aristocratic family in a crude, western North Carolina way, and as he matured Gordon became as much of a family leader as the aging Mr. Brown. He paid equal attention to his half-brothers and his sisters. As "one who realized the great necessity of a thorough and accomplished education," Gordon acted the part of big brother and tried to advise his younger siblings. Mrs. Brown looked to Gordon to help her raise the boys and often asked him for his opinion. In this, Gordon had two primary goals. He wanted Allen and Tom to get the most from their education, and he wanted them to mature as gentlemen.[8]

Since the youngster's birth, Gordon had taken his baby half-brother Hamilton Allen under his wing. He loved him as only a big brother could. Allen developed into a "great talker, and sometimes a tease," much to the family's enjoyment. When Mr. Brown sent Allen to attend school at Tennessee's Jackson College, it was only natural that the family missed him.[9]

Early on, Allen proved to be an intelligent but somewhat indifferent student. Both Mrs. Brown and Gordon worried about him and constantly gave him advice. In 1855, Mrs. Brown told Allen that Gordon "seems pleased with your success so far, thinks there is no danger of your future prosperity if you only will be diligent." In counseling Allen, Gordon carefully chose his words, offering his own personal philosophy of life. He urged the fifteen-year-old to follow his example and "make early efforts to gain at least a respectable if not prominent position in society. Well it may be enquired how that is to be done; one of the principal means is intelligence, sustained by a high sense of all that is honorable, just and degrading, treating all associates with courtesy and politeness, and demanding the same in return.... Allen, let diligence and industry mark your course."[10]

One lecture, even by letter, never seemed to be quite enough to get the point across. Gordon kept after Allen:

> I have ... a deep anxiety for your success and standing in the world. As you are now forming a platform for your future position and standing in the world, it is all important you should form the basis of your future operations with a great deal of care and judgment. I have always had great hopes of you, 'cause 1st you have a great deal of latent energy which with proper direction will lead to a very respectable position in anything you undertake. Secondly, you have pride of character sufficient to protect you from the devices and contamination of bad company and vices. 3rdly I hope you are fully impressed with the great advantages that a high position in society gives to any one who strives to acquire it and endeavors to maintain it.... You should always have the highest respect for the good opinions of the good and intelligent citizens of the country where you stay.[11]

Despite his worrisome lecturing, Gordon was quite proud of Allen. "I am very much pleased to see him improving his mind," he told Caroline.[12]

Gordon did more to help his half-brother. During a business trip, Gordon met with James C. Dobbin, secretary of the Navy, and asked that an appointment to the Naval Academy be awarded to Allen. He did so in the hopes that Annapolis would provide Allen with a fine education and a basis for that "high position in society." It would also offer "a young man an opportunity of seeing the world that no other situation does." Dobbin, who had met Gordon in the North Carolina legislature, agreed. Allen jumped at the chance and, although his mother was not exactly pleased with the idea, became a midshipman in 1854.[13]

Allen went, but soon found that Annapolis was not everything he had hoped. A summer cruise along the east coast to Portland, Boston, and Plymouth was sobering enough. "Felt very sick in the morning; lost my dinner over the port gangway," Allen recounted. He even considered resigning from the academy, but in the end decided to stick it out. He graduated on time.[14]

Gordon looked out for Tom, too. He considered himself protective of Tom's reputation and as anxious for his success as he was his own. As it was, Gordon believed that "Tom really ought to be in college," especially since he had such a "fine intellect."[15] Mr. Brown agreed and took steps to send Tom to study, first to Emory & Henry and later to law school at the University of North Carolina. Though a sickly person, Tom managed to succeed. On one occasion, for example, a brief visit to a cousin turned into a three-week stay when he fell gravely ill. Tom's poor constitution made law school a struggle. Besides long hours of studying, one stumbling block he faced was a weak throat with which he could "scarcely speak more than 15 minutes at a time." Even so, the problem did not curtail Tom's ambition. Once he decided against entering the ministry, Tom drove himself to study Blackstone and absorb his lessons.[16]

To support Tom in his studies, Gordon regularly sent him money. The law student dutifully recorded each gift. During the fall session of 1857, for example, Gordon sent Tom a total of $83.00. Gordon also supported Tom in other ways, such as with occasional visits. While on a business trip in the fall of 1857, Gordon stopped in Chapel Hill. he came bearing gifts of "some very nice clothes." Tom thought a lot of his half-brother. When Gordon's visit ended, Tom admitted he had "been feeling rather lonesome since the departure of Brother J. whose genial disposition cheered me very much while here." He confided to his diary that "he is one of the best and most open hearted kind men I ever knew, and although he has more knowledge of the world, yet he puts me very much in the mind of old Col. Newcome, as Thackeray describes him. He goes home to be welcomed by a family of awaiting relations."[17]

Tom completed his graduate work in 1858. His proud half-brother was there for the commencement. After being accepted to the bar, Tom moved to Van Buren, Arkansas, where he became a reputable attorney. He quickly became involved in highly visible cases. On one occasion, he prosecuted a man for murder after confiding to Gordon that he would not "have touched the fee [of $100] if I was not thoroughly convinced of the defendant's guilt." Tom also hoped to find in Van Buren the one thing that had eluded him in Chapel Hill: a woman to be his wife.[18]

While the menfolk made their way in life, Gordon watched his sisters achieve their place in society. Not one faced the same courting problems; each married prominent men who also became some of Gordon's closest friends and associates. In March 1842, Gordon's older sister Martha married Augustus Washington Finley. Eight years Martha's senior, Finley was a Wilkesborough merchant, tradesman, and cattleman. He and Martha built their home, "Fairmount," out of a structure that had once been used for fighting Indians. They kept sixteen slaves at Fairmount, which rested on a hill within sight of "Oakland."[19]

Caroline — or Carrie, as Gordon called her — tended to her education before she settled down. Gordon's letters, which found Carrie at Salem College, held counsel typical of him. "You ought to devote a portion of every day to reading, and let it be in well selected books and read not only to while away the time but for information," Gordon wrote. "All other accomplishments without intelligence, are vain and transitory...." In 1859, after she left Salem, Carrie married Dr. Robert F. Hackett. Since Carrie and Gordon had always been close, Carrie's suitor had to be an outstanding man. Hackett fit the bill. He had studied at Philadelphia's Jefferson Medical College and returned to practice in the Wilkes area. Hackett also held several town and county government positions and served as a steward for the Wilkes Circuit of Methodist Episcopal Churches.[20]

Ann also received her education at Salem College, located about sixty miles from Wilkes. As a student, she studied subjects like German and French. After college, she married John Tate Finley and joined him in a home in Wilkesborough east of the courthouse. There they began a family. Although their children were spoiled rotten by "Uncle Jim," John, a Presbyterian, came to like and respect Gordon.[21]

Gordon's responsibilities prevented him from spending much time with his Georgia cousins. His sisters, however, did their best to maintain those relationships despite the distance. Gordon's grandfather had chosen to settle in Wilkes, but the family of his brother, Charles — one of North Carolina's six largest landholders and a representative to the Provisional Continental Congress in 1775 — decided to settle in northwest Georgia. Situated near Chickamauga Creek, the family's property was named Gordon Springs because of nearby natural mineral springs. The area became something of a summer resort that centered around a hotel owned by the Gordons. Gordon's sisters, especially Carrie, visited there often, mostly with their aunt Caroline Gwyn Gordon.[22]

Among Charles Gordon's descendants was the Reverend Zechariah Herndon Gordon, who also had been born in Wilkes in 1796 before his family moved to Georgia. When James B. Gordon was ten, Zechariah and his wife, Melinda, had a son. John Brown Gordon grew up to achieve great things: he fought as a general officer in the Army of Northern Virginia, served two terms as Georgia's governor, and became a U.S. Senator. John and James apparently never knew each other personally, but John renewed his relationship with the Wilkes Gordons around the turn of the century.[23]

Then there was the extended family of Gordon's stepfather. The Browns owned a large amount of property near Columbia, Tennessee, because Hamilton Brown's father had received land grants there after negotiating Indian treaties. Tom and Allen visited their cousins on a regular basis. Somehow, Gordon managed to visit the Browns more often than the Georgia Gordons. Allen lived with his Uncle Allen while briefly attending Columbia's Jackson College, so it was all the more reason for Gordon to visit. Allen liked Tennessee enough to move to a "magnificent estate" in Columbia after the war.[24]

It was at times a widespread family, so Gordon did his best to keep track of his sisters and half-brothers as they traveled and visited. When he wrote, he not only told them news from Wilkesborough but he also gave them travel advice. But Gordon's active life was the most demanding, and that kept him on the road more than his relatives. As a result, Gordon wrote only sporadically. Tom once accused Gordon of composing short letters when he did write — usually because he wrote only before he went to bed or attended church. That gave Gordon an excuse to stop writing.[25]

James Gordon operated a 1,800-acre farm, ran a mercantile business, and played a prominent role in local and state politics (courtesy Annie Finley Winkler).

Despite his long list of pursuits, Gordon felt somewhat lonesome. When everything went well at "Oakland," he had extra time on his hands. However, Gordon learned that John Finley had a similar amount of extra time. As a result, the two brothers-in-law decided to open a mercantile business in Wilkesborough.

The hard-working Gordon soon became "probably the most successful businessman in [Wilkes] county in his day." He had a grasp of financial thinking and a knack for supplying what his customers wanted. The success of his store belied his modest education but meshed with the reputation that people of Scottish heritage have for business canniness.[26] While Finley or the hired help ran the store, Gordon handled bookkeeping and purchasing. He kept meticulous, careful records. Gordon also traveled frequently to large cities like New York and Philadelphia to acquire goods. He supplemented those sources by dealing with local companies such as the Elkin Manufacturing Company and Eagle Mills. To fill the shelves of the store back home, he bought everything from coffee, sugar, and spirits to dishes, trays, and rulers.[27]

Since transportation to and from Wilkes was restricted, the logistics of keeping the business supplied were complicated. Once the goods Gordon purchased were packed in shipping boxes or trunks, they were usually shipped by steamer to Southern ports such as Charleston or Portsmouth. At the ports, a local railroad agent would place the goods on a train bound for Charlotte. The businessmen would arrange for someone to pick up the goods and transport them to the store, or have an express company forward the goods to Wilkesborough by way of Salem.[28]

A business trip Gordon took in April 1861 might be seen as typical. While in Philadelphia, a visit to George W. Reed & Company, Wholesale Clothiers, proved worthwhile for the store back home. In examining the merchandise, he found many products that he thought would sell. Gordon placed an order for eighty-nine coats, forty-one vests, and twenty-one pairs of pants. He then asked the clerk to bill him for the total cost of $341.54. The goods would be transported to him by steamer and railroad.[29]

Gordon had to learn some business lessons the hard way. In the fall of 1858, he traveled to Philadelphia to buy goods. At one store, he bought a marketable sewing machine from a salesman who had set up a display. The man promised to send Gordon a machine from his inventory. After Gordon returned to Wilkesborough, several weeks passed and no sewing machine arrived. Perturbed, he wrote to the Philadelphia store. A store clerk replied that the man "had a sample from which he took orders and received the money for them, with the promise to deliver them, but in no instance can we find that he even delivered a machine.... He was not [our] agent, although he represented himself as such.... We are sorry we cannot aid you to recover the amount."[30]

Such losses were not isolated. The following April, a trunk full of items Gordon had bought from Atwood & Company of Philadelphia was reported missing before the company could ship it. Employees searched depots and steamer wharves without luck, but finally the trunk turned up. The problem was that the recovered trunk was empty. Its contents had been removed and hidden. Two "young men," the alleged thieves, were arrested and placed on trial. Unfortunately, a store representative wrote, "the whereabouts of the goods would have been revealed by them but for the obstacle interposed by their counsel...."[31]

Despite such frustrations, the store remained a fulfilling part of Gordon's life. Mrs. Brown knew that her son enjoyed the challenges and bustle of business more than the life of a farmer. She once wrote, Gordon "can't rest contented without a store, says he is so lonesome at home."[32] More than once, Gordon even considered giving up farming, probably so he could concentrate on business full-time. However, when he once offered to sell his land to his stepfather, Brown refused to buy it. Neither did he have success interesting cousins in the land.[33]

The work and travel appealed to Gordon. When possible, he traveled with friends and enjoyed their companionship, taking every opportunity to sample fine living. While on a five-day business trip to New York City in March 1859, Gordon lodged at the St. Nicholas Hotel on Broadway. During business hours, he priced and purchased goods from establishments like Daters & Company and Sackett, Belcher & Company. At night, the city offered much to an eligible Southern bachelor; things that were topped off by a bottle of champagne. The hotel bill of $17.85, champagne included, was well worth the cost for a little luxury. Of course, a little fun on business trips was not an unusual occasion. Hotel bills with champagne prices figured in were not uncommon in Gordon's ledgers.[34]

Gordon learned that there were other ways a good businessman could profit. Witness the day in the late 1850s when "Robinson's show" came to Wilkesborough. After the entertainers set up and opened for business, a local resident visited a booth to buy candy. To the man's outrage, the showman charged three times what the resident usually paid for candy in local stores. A fracas ensued, and before long a Wilkesborough contingent was fighting a Robinson's show contingent. With considerable effort, Sheriff Esley Staley broke up the fight (twice) and arrested the main participants. That night, the incarcerated showmen appeared at a preliminary trial before Dr. Hackett, who was then serving as Justice of the Peace. Gordon had somehow gotten involved in the legal proceedings, so the showmen paid him $500.00 to stand surety for their final appearance in court the next morning. When time for court came, the showmen did not appear, meaning Gordon could pay the fine and the case would be closed. Since the total fine was $130, Gordon walked away with a $370 profit.[35]

Politics absorbed as much of Gordon's time as anything. Although a Democrat in a county of Whigs, Gordon was popular in Wilkes County circles. Perhaps Gordon's similarity to author William M. Thackeray's Colonel Newcome created this popularity. In the novel *The Newcomes: Memoirs of a Most Respectable Family,* Thackeray portrayed Newcome as a simple, gallant, distinguished, kind, and generous man. What was more, Newcome was a former cavalryman who had been schooled by an old soldier. Indeed, just as "Oakland" was a salient feature of the landscape, Gordon was a prominent and visible community leader. "Tall and well-proportioned ... [and] singularly handsome," he was a confident man with "great common sense and [a] warm personality." If Gordon and Newcome were of the same mold, then Gordon was a gentleman of the highest honor.[36]

While Colonel Newcome may not have been a politician, at a relatively young age Gordon chose to serve in that capacity. Ultimately, as he became a part of state and national politics, contemporary political thinking colored his life as much as his fatherless childhood had. Gordon was a member of the elite planter class that tended to oppose active government because of fears that socioeconomic and political change would curtail rights and freedoms. However, since Gordon hailed from an undeveloped area that contained much belief in government intervention, he was not always decidedly a Democrat in thinking. One thing was certain: Gordon stood for the way of life that had been his since birth. As national events deteriorated, Gordon became a quiet champion of state's rights and secession.[37]

Serving on Wilkes County's Board of Superintendents of Common Schools was Gordon's first political step. He could not envision a better way to improve his community. In keeping with his Scottish heritage, he saw education as an incomparable asset. Gordon helped manage the educational system in a way that would benefit the white children of Wilkes. The school board's business included appointing committeemen for school districts; keeping school district lines logically arranged by either altering current boundaries or creating new districts; and overseeing the disbursement of the county school fund. Gordon initially served on the board while still in his twenties. He served several terms beginning in the late 1840s.[38]

Whether by design or accident, education was just the beginning. Gordon continued dabbling in county politics "when his services were required by his party or friends." He even rose to the leadership of the Wilkes County Democratic Party. That was a more visible platform for the budding young politician, and a post that served as a springboard for greater things.[39]

In 1849, an official-looking letter arrived at "Oakland." The correspondence read: "At a large and respectable meeting of the democracy at Taylorsville Alexander County it was unanimously resolved that you be the first and only choice of the democrats of this Co. to represent them in the next Legislature of N. Carolina in this Senatorial District." A committee had been appointed, the letter continued, to seek the cooperation of Wilkes and Iredell Democrats. There was an exciting letter for a young man with Gordon's sense of adventure! With that, the campaign began.[40]

Success crowned their efforts. In 1850, the twenty-eight-year-old Gordon was elected to the House of Commons of the North Carolina General Assembly. Gordon's wealth, popularity, and ties with area notables probably influenced his election. Bickering within the Whig party had also been known to help Wilkes Democrats win at least one past campaign, and it may also have contributed to Gordon's victory.[41]

On September 27, 1850, Gordon checked into Lawrence's (City) Hotel in Raleigh. The state capitol was buzzing in anticipation of the legislature's opening. Gordon did not go unnoticed in the crowd. None would deny that he looked like a leader; or, at least, his appearance was what many expected from their leaders. He was a "model of manly beauty, tall, well formed, with erect, manly bearing, handsome features, eyes of dark gray or hazel, with an expression in which resolution of mind and kindliness of heart were happily blended." Before the assembly began its work, Gordon divided his time between partaking of gentlemanly diversions found in the capital city and preparing for lawmaking. He evidently gained the reputation of an agreeable person to invite to parties. Though a bit homesick, he soon had invitations to visit several "*respectable houses.*" He even attended an oyster supper at which the governor-elect was present.[42]

At noon on Monday, November 18, the two houses of the legislature assembled in their respective halls at the capitol. Gordon, who had moved to the Yarborough House the day before, took his seat among the representatives in the House of Commons. Soon, the crack of the gavel sounded from the podium. Silence fell over the room. After Wake County's justice of the peace administered the "usual oaths of qualification" to the representatives, the group nominated and voted on candidates for various legislative offices. Gordon's choice for speaker of the house, James C. Dobbin of Cumberland County, won that election.[43]

Two days later, the body completed its organization by placing representatives on various standing committees. Gordon was assigned to the Propositions and Grievances Committee.[44] Being the consummate small-businessman, he also joined the Committee of Finance. He quickly discovered the duties of those committees to be "very laborious."[45]

The lawmakers now turned to the work at hand. In his message to the assembly, Governor Charles Manly described their duties in the context of "spirit of disunion" then affecting the nation. The challenges facing the state, Manly said, required the state to reorganize certain public offices, examine its financial condition, and consider constitutional reform. State suffrage policies, internal improvements, education, and common schools also required their attention. How did his listeners respond? In a Democratic fashion that led Whig newspapers to state that the legislature, like many local banks, "dealt largely in small bills" of an often spurious nature.[46]

For his part, armed with the knowledge of life in Wilkes, Gordon executed his personal agenda. With his first bill, he tried to improve educational opportunities for the children back home. According to Governor Manly, money for common schools, which came in part from the state's Literary Fund, was not being distributed fairly. The fund was then being issued to counties according to Federal population figures. That number included both blacks and whites. As such, counties with many slaves and fewer whites received more money than sparsely populated counties with more whites than slaves. Of course, easterners liked this arrangement since slavery was more common toward the coast.[47]

Gordon introduced his bill on November 26, 1850. Officially an amendment to an 1841 act, Gordon suggested that the Literary Fund "be distributed among the several rural counties of this State according to their white population." After he read the bill debate ensued, prompting the body to print its text for later consideration. When it was read a second time in late January, Gordon rose to reiterate his case. He asked his fellow lawmakers: Is it justice when nine hundred white children in Craven County receive the same amount of money for education as three thousand in Wilkes? His oration fell on deaf ears. In a subsequent vote the bill was rejected, 68–42.[48]

Another proposal from Gordon's pen smacked of his business and bookkeeping background. From personal experience, he recognized that cash flow was critical to any organization—especially a poor western county. He designed "A Bill To Facilitate the Collection of the Public Revenue and Economize the Mode Thereof." The bill was passed at the first reading and referred to the Committee on Finance. After it was reviewed on 27 December, the bill was laid on the table and ordered to be printed.[49]

As Manly had hoped, transportation became a focus of debate during the 1850–51 session. That topic received Gordon's due consideration as well. From his own experience, he knew that a lack of good transportation systems had curtailed economic growth in Wilkes. He reasoned that the quickest solution was to use the Yadkin River, the best route the county had. One of his ideas was to appropriate money to link trade on the Yadkin with the Central railroad, but it was discarded.[50] A more reasonable proposal was his "Bill to incorporate Yadkin Navigation Company." It was Gordon's most detailed piece of legislation. He spent hours considering, writing, rewriting, and studying it. The bill was not a masterpiece of lawmaking, but his hard work showed that he tried to represent the interests of his county.

Introduced on December 12, 1850, the bill provided for the establishment of a company to effect "a communication by Steamboat navigation upon the Yadkin River from that point where the North Carolina Rail Road shall pass over the said River to the town of Wilkesboro' in the county of Wilkes...." Gordon specified that the company would have the power to charge up to six cents a mile per passenger and up to ten cents a ton per mile for freight. The bill also authorized the company to build works in and upon the river to allow for navigation to and from Wilkesborough.[51]

Soon after introducing it, Gordon grew pessimistic about the bill's chances to receive appropriations, despite verbal support from others. After the Committee on Internal Improvements reported its position on the bill, Gordon moved to amend his own work. Standing before the house, he proposed that the state subscribe $100,000 to the company after individuals raised an initial $100,000. A reporter wrote that Gordon "advocated the amendment at length, and stated the importance of the amendment." Like his speech on school funds, this amendment was not well received. A majority of assemblymen believed that the state could not afford it. The body rejected the amendment, seventy-eight to twenty-eight. However, despite the amendment's failure, the bill itself passed.[52]

Whatever proposal was on the floor, interesting and controversial debate could often be heard. That was especially true concerning transportation. One proposal to establish a public road in Wilkes County met with enough resistance that Gordon, although not the proposal's author, made the motion to table it. Gordon tried another tack in late December, presenting a memorial from some citizens of Wilkes praying the establishment of a public road from Church's Store in Wilkes to Lewis Fork Gap. It met with less opposition. The memorial was referred to the Committee of Propositions and Grievances for further study.[53]

The legislature also wrestled with the need to form a new county in the northwest. Again, this raised the question of power. Historically, eastern counties had controlled the legislature because of their numerical superiority over western counties. As a result, western political needs were often slighted. Like many western Carolinians, Gordon believed that new counties would bring equality to the assembly. He addressed this issue personally, soliciting the views of prominent citizens of Wilkes. "I wish you would write me immediately and let me know your views about making a new county on the north side of the [Yadkin] river out of parts of Surry and Wilkes," he wrote Lytle Hickerson. Several petitions in Raleigh suggested that very thing, but Gordon predicted that members from Surry would be opposed to giving away portions of either their county or Wilkes. Gordon also mentioned the legislature's discussions of "the free suffrage doctrine" and Constitutional amendments. "We are getting on very slowly. I think it likely it will be a long session," he added.[54]

Such efforts notwithstanding, Gordon's personal ideas for the formation of new counties enjoyed little approval. At one point, he "presented a memorial praying" that a new county, to be named Williams, be formed from parts of Iredell, Wilkes, and Surry counties. Floor debate killed Williams County, and it was subsequently voted down, eighty to nineteen. Not one to give up, Gordon also proposed the formation of Blue Ridge County, but it eventually went the way of Williams County. In the end, only one new county emerged. With an eighty-eight to twenty-four vote margin, the legislature formed Yadkin County. Gordon, who voted for Yadkin, was happy to see at least one new county added to the west's representation.[55]

As the holidays approached, the assembly remained embroiled in work. Since Gordon was working on a memorial concerning a militia unit, he decided to stay in Raleigh during Christmas. On Christmas Eve, as a sort of compensation, the House of Commons provided holiday entertainment by staging an informal session for "fun and glee."[56] Such events made the holidays bearable, but the young assemblyman would have preferred to be at home. Instead, Gordon had to stay in touch with his family by letter. One missive, from Carrie, demonstrated

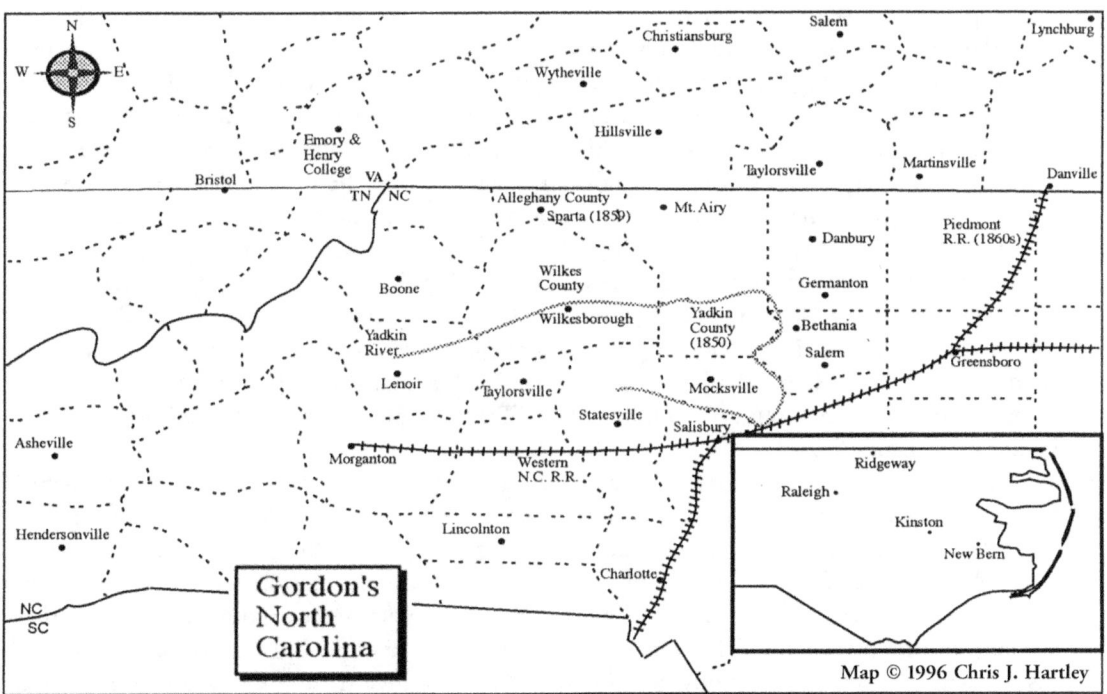

how much he was missed. Writing late at night, Carrie described how busy she had been "with the festivities of Christmas, which altho' not calculated much to disturb the even tenor of one's life, still, were fraught with enjoyment, which fashion and gayety [sic] might fail to awaken." Her description of the holidays, which the family began celebrating at John and Ann Finley's on Christmas Day and concluded on New Year's Day, must have caused some homesickness. Other news included the spread of smallpox in the area, and Wilkesborough's precautions. Mostly, though, Carrie wanted her brother home soon. "I am getting impatient to see you, and am in hopes your desire for public life will cease with the termination of the legislature.... The family all join in love, or would if they were awake."[57]

At least Gordon was not miserable. He liked the capital city. He found the "society in Raleigh very pleasant, more so than I expected, quite a number of young ladies in the place, many interesting and pretty; though not more intelligent than our mountain ladies." Gordon was not shy, so he made the most of each social gathering. One evening before Christmas, he attended a dance at a home of a prominent citizen. Arriving at 8:00 P.M., he socialized and anticipated the dancing, which began at 10:00 P.M. He danced cotillions and waltzes for hours. Then he dined on oysters and champagne. Soon, he could not help declaring how much he enjoyed the party. What was more, he could look forward to another one in two days![58]

The new year saw the inauguration of David S. Reid, a Democrat, as state governor. Gordon met him at a local party and noted that a smile never left the man's face. Reid entered office on his free suffrage platform, which proposed awarding senatorial voting rights to all white citizens, regardless of the amount of land they owned. Yet during Reid's first days in office, the assembly's debate swirled around slavery and the doctrine of secession along opposing party lines. These issues were dominating national politics. The late compromises and agreements were considered, and discussed. Political theories were argued. One thing, at least, emerged: "Among the few subjects which could possibly induce a state to withdraw from the Union," one House Document claimed, "negro slavery stands preeminent."[59] All hoped that the legislature would draw up a clear resolution detailing North Carolina's stance on secession and slavery, but it did not happen.[60]

Slavery was a question Gordon had lived with for a long time. For him, the controversy began in 1845, not long after he inherited "Oakland," when Congress had resolved to admit Texas into the Union after considerable debate over whether or not it would be a slave state. Then, a few weeks after the Texas annexation, Mexico broke off diplomatic relations with the United States. Negotiations ultimately failed and Mexico and the United States went to war.

This stirred the martial ambitions of slave-owner and Democrat Gordon. Moreover, he had an even deeper personal stake in the war. His neighbor and friend, Montford Sidney Stokes, was one of the locals who marched off to war. Born in Wilkes County on October 6, 1810, son of a former North Carolina governor, Stokes was a graduate of the Naval Academy. He had served in the Navy for ten years before returning to Wilkesborough to become a farmer. The younger Gordon admired and respected this man who had driven herds of cattle, on foot, from Wilkes County to Philadelphia. The two men held similar opinions on the issues of the times.[61]

After volunteering for duty, Stokes was elected major in his North Carolina regiment. His unit joined Brigadier General Zachary Taylor's army. Through Stokes's letters from the front, Gordon read stories of Taylor that were enough to make a young man want to join the army. According to Stokes, Taylor's presence saved the Americans from defeat. "I heard an officer of some distinction say that he believed that if every volunteer and regular cavalry and all had run off and left the field Genl Taylor would have sat there crosslegged, as he did, on his old white horse with his body guard and *hollered* out give them *grape*. He is as firm as a rock and won't be whipped by Mexicans in any condition on any ground."[62] That was indeed the case on February 22 and 23, 1847 at Buena Vista, a victory that marked the beginning of the war's end.

Just as Gordon had been influenced by his Scottish military heritage, by the soldierly bearing of Ney, by stories of his grandfather at Kings Mountain, and by tales of his father the cavalryman in the War of 1812, Gordon was fascinated by the Mexican War. He imagined the "hot and dry and very dusty" weather, and wondered what it was like to have "seen the elephant."[63] However, his time had not yet come; for now, his battlefield was a political one, where he had to grapple with the issues with words.

The Mexican War might have been a warning, but Gordon did not see it. His position in the General Assembly is proof of that. Secession and the "slavery question" were now linked to Gordon's future. Already common knowledge locally, his personal stance was now a matter of state record. He believed that secession was a constitutional right and that slavery was a viable economic alternative. Gordon's inheritance of land and slaves, and his application of those resources, had made him who he was. He had no way of knowing what his beliefs would cost him, and the South, in the long run.

Short-term, Gordon's Democratic opinions and votes probably cost him his seat in the legislature. By supporting his party's agenda, he alienated his constituents. The election of the state treasurer was one example. When the Whig candidate lost to his Democratic opponent, Whig newspapers pointed out that Gordon and a few other legislators from Whig counties had voted for the Democratic candidate. What made that especially galling to Whigs was that the votes of those men could have changed the election's outcome. As a result, an anonymous correspondent to the *Register* charged that Gordon and the other legislators were not representatives but "mis-representatives." A writer for The *Carolina Watchman* hoped that, in the future, the voters would apply the "same test of unfitness for office" to the "mis-representatives" that the lawmakers themselves had used.[64]

After seventy-two days of lawmaking, the General Assembly of North Carolina adjourned. In summation, Dobbin told the house, "patriotism and State pride have triumphed." How the body had emerged victorious was never made clear, but Dobbin did hint that the session had been one of debate and controversy. Then, that February morning, the lawmakers parted. "In a few hours," the *Raleigh Register* reported, "a large majority of the members were on their homeward way."[65] Gordon bundled up against the cold and joined the westward travelers.

Gordon never returned to Raleigh as a lawmaker, but his "desire for public life" was not diminished. The ideals of the Democratic party, particularly those of North Carolina Democrats, remained the hook on which he hung his political hat. From 1851 to 1861, he remained a faithful reader of William W. Holden's *North Carolina Standard*, the party's leading newspaper.[66] In that turbulent decade, he continued to serve the county school board and to work with county and state Democrats. Naturally, Gordon absorbed more of the thinking that revolved around the rights of slavery and secession. To him, the issue concerned not the morality of slavery but how the abolitionist challenge to the peculiar institution violated state's rights.

Five years after the end of his legislative term, Gordon again found himself in the midst of political debate. When the state party convention selected him to be a delegate to the 1856 Democratic Presidential Convention, Gordon left his fields behind. Traveling northward from Wilkesborough in late May, he arrived in Washington, D.C., where he joined the rest of North Carolina's twenty delegates. Gordon considered his fellow convention-goers to be "quite a respectable ... set of men."[67] One delegate, Thomas Clingman, hailed from a neighboring county. Clingman was destined to become a Confederate general and a postwar Democratic leader who would also give his name to one of North Carolina's highest peaks. Another delegate, Francis Burton Craige, was to play a special part in Gordon's future. Born March 13, 1811 near Salisbury, Craige was a graduate of the University of North Carolina. He had worked as the editor of the *Western Carolinian* before earning his lawyer's license at twenty-one. A towering man who stood six feet six inches tall, Craige had just begun serving in Congress the year before. Gordon became good friends with the Craiges. One day, Gordon would choose Burton's son, Kerr, to be his aide-de-camp.[68]

From Washington, the contingent set out for Cincinnati. En route, Gordon estimated that the convention, which he called the largest ever assembled in the United States, would probably "take a week or nearly so ... to decide upon a candidate." The North Carolinians resolved to give their support to President Franklin Pierce. Gordon had met Pierce during an 1854 trip to Washington, and that meeting apparently left Gordon with a favorable impression. "I think Pierce ... will get the nomination," Gordon wrote home.[69]

Gordon met Burton Craige while serving as a delegate to the 1856 Democratic Presidential Convention. The lawyer and congressmen would play an important role in Gordon's life (North Carolina Collection, University of North Carolina at Chapel Hill Library).

On a hot and dry June Saturday, Gordon and the North Carolina delegation arrived. His first impression of Cincinnati was favorable: "Great city this," he wrote. The gathering of hundreds of Democrats there, however, gave him a different feeling. When Gordon saw that the town was "running over with delegates and camp followers," he decided that North Carolina was making only "a tolerable showing."[70] Whatever their "showing," the men realized the convention's importance. The problem was that Southern Democrats were increasingly at odds with Northern causes.

At noon on June 2 the convention was called to order. Their meeting place was "a sort of den, approached by a long, narrow passage, barricaded by three doors." "Armed bullies" stood guard. Inside, the hall was small and featureless. The only windows, a row of pivoting glass panes about thirty-five feet above the floor, resembled "steamboat skylights." It was a dark, uncomfortable place. One reporter likened it to the black hole of Calcutta. There was so little room there that one of the convention's first resolutions proposed to limit the number of delegates allowed in the hall at one time.[71]

Gordon was listening to the opening ceremonies when he heard an uproar. At the sound, many turned to see what was happening. Some even jumped on their chairs for a better view.

The delegation from Missouri had caused the ruckus by crashing the gate. The Missourians knocked down several doorkeepers, including Sterling Price, a former governor of Missouri. Although order was soon restored and properly credentialed Missourians gained entrance, the struggle symbolized the deterioration of unity among the Democrats. If men who held similar political beliefs could not have peaceful disagreements among themselves, then the party was headed for tough times. Gordon, perhaps embarrassed at the growing dissension in his party, chose not to record the event for his family.[72]

The convention elected officers and committee members next—Gordon was appointed to the Committee on Organization—and then focused on the matters at hand. On June 4, a platform was adopted and resolutions were considered. The platform affirmed the principles of the Kansas-Nebraska Act "as embodying the only solution of the slavery question consistent with non-interference by congress with slavery in the states and Territories...." Gordon thought the 1854 Kansas-Nebraska Act, the legislation that had given the Kansas and Nebraska territories the freedom to answer the slavery question by referendum, was a solid basis for a platform.[73]

With its platform established, the convention considered its presidential nominee. Delegates from the Old North State supported Pierce vigorously. With his fellow Carolinians, Gordon voted for Pierce fourteen times.[74] Other delegates, however, saw the president in a different light. After all, while Pierce was the country's leader, the Kansas-Nebraska Act had led to "Bleeding Kansas," a border war fought between pro- and anti-slavery elements. Pierce's part in that quagmire made him too controversial. North Carolina delegates next threw their support behind Stephen A. Douglas. Douglas was the leading advocate of the doctrine of popular sovereignty on which the Kansas-Nebraska Act was based.[75]

Although it became a close race between Douglas and James Buchanan, Gordon soon detected how the convention was leaning. While the North Carolinians publicly cast two votes in favor of Douglas, Gordon privately predicted that "Old Buck will be nominated." He was right. When the entire delegation became convinced of the outcome, they placed their final vote for Buchanan.[76]

On Saturday night, June 7, the convention adjourned. Gordon said his good-byes and began packing. He was glad for the experience but fed up with political wrangling. The next morning, delegate Gordon headed east, "tired of conventions" and eager to return home. In North Carolina, the *Raleigh Register* summed up the state's part in convention. "It appears that the delegation from this State were literally dragged into the support of Buchanan — by the strength of party discipline and by that alone."[77]

Happily, Gordon enjoyed other political duties. The decade before the Civil War saw the creation of seven counties in western North Carolina. During the 1858–59 session of the North Carolina legislature, that body formed Alleghany County from land north of Wilkes County. A supplementary act was also passed appointing five men as commissioners to survey the county, locate a county seat, and lay out the town's lots.[78]

Gordon, along with two men from Ashe County and two from Surry County, was appointed to this task. Learning of his selection in the spring of 1859, Gordon accepted and met with the other men to work out the details of Alleghany County. After setting the county's boundaries, the commissioners chose a beautiful spot for the county seat. The town eventually became known as Sparta. Just as his grandfather had done, Gordon had become a founding father of a North Carolina town.[79]

Hard times require spiritual strength. Due in part to his mother's Christian influence, Gordon became a member and leader of a local church. In 1836, the Episcopal Church held

Gordon was a member of the vestry of St. Paul's Episcopal Church in Wilkesboro and was one of the largest contributors toward its construction (author's photograph).

its first service in the valley. The church drew new members as occasional services were held in private homes. The Bishop of the Diocese would come to town and lead the tiny congregation in preaching, baptism, and confirmation. Gordon became involved with the group. He attended services when possible and helped the church grow by lending his support.

As the congregation expanded, the church's faithful organized and planned. One step they took was to select vestrymen to give central guidance to the church. In March 1858, in recognition of his faithful service, his standing, and his talents, the congregation elected Gordon to the vestry of St. Paul's Episcopal Church. As a member of the vestry, Gordon joined five other men in making business decisions for the church.[80]

The greatest task facing the vestry was the construction of a permanent house of worship. Toward the end of 1847, some members had become distressed because there was not a good facility in which they could meet regularly. To correct this, a "subscription was commenced for the building of a church. In spite of a bitter opposition which originated with the coming of the missionary, a sufficient amount was collected to warrant the commencement of the building." Gordon did his part; his $30.00 contribution was one of the largest amounts of money given by any member of the original congregation. Thanks to his generosity and that of his fellow churchgoers, the opposition gave in. As a result, a builder "took the contract for erecting [the church] in May, 1848. The work was commenced in October of the same year...."[81]

One July day in 1849, construction of the church was completed. Gordon and his fellow Episcopalians now had a place in which to worship. "On the morning of the fifth Sunday after Trinity," wrote the Diocesan Bishop, "consecrated in the Town of Wilkesborough, a church by the title of St. Paul's Church; preaching on the occasion and administering the Holy Communion. This is a beautiful Gothic structure of brick, erected at small expense, with free sittings and without debt; showing what may be effected by a few churchmen with small means, applied with zeal."[82]

Building the most expensive church in the county was an accomplishment of which Gordon and the congregation could be proud.[83] The steep-roofed red brick church, which bore a squat white steeple topped off with a cross, would later stand as sentinel over the final resting place of James B. Gordon.

Through it all — watching over his family, farm, business, and politics — Gordon remained a bachelor. Folks expected him to choose a wife and settle down, but it never happened. Neighbors may have attributed it to his busy schedule and constant traveling, but there was more to it than that. Gordon believed he had often been wronged by the opposite sex. Frustration discouraged any thoughts he had about marriage. "Devil take the women for their fickleness," he once told Carrie.[84]

To be sure, Gordon enjoyed the bachelor's life. Hamilton Brown's brother recalled spending a "fun day of social intercourse and spirit with [him] with grate pleasure." On another occasion, Gordon boasted to his brother-in-law that during a trip to Salisbury — one of his favorite places for calling on ladies — he had experienced "quite a gay time with the ladies." A cousin of Gordon's testified to his good looks, and saw the effect he had on the opposite sex. When in the company of seven young ladies one day she received a likeness of Gordon. For a while she passed him off as her sweetheart, to the envy of those present. She decided not to tell Gordon their complimentary comments "for fear you deem it flattery." All the while, she fondly recalled the flash of his "*mischievous* eye," and the teasing he had focused on her in their youth.[85]

Gordon's marital status was largely of his own doing. He broke quite a few "fond hearts" in his day. Certain members of Gordon's family, however, had every intention that he should not stay a bachelor any longer than necessary. In a letter to Carrie, Gordon's aunt told how yellow fever in Georgia caused many people to seek refuge near Gordon Springs. The result was an increase in the number of young ladies to court. "Tell James," she wrote, "that if he had been here he could have suited in a wife...." His mother had similar thoughts. She lamented, "I fear he never will do better any where els if he could only be contended and get a good wife and settle himself on his farm."[86]

Gordon often confided his deepest feelings on the subject to Carrie. He once noted to Carrie with a hint of disgust that "there seems to be a considerable disposition to marry amongst some of our acquaintances." She wrote to him after a holiday celebration, "you will be ready to turn away in disgust at the idea of a dining party in Wilkes being pleasant, with no one but married people for guests."[87]

With age, his feelings about marriage mellowed. The spring of 1860 proved that the right girl at the right time had a chance of breaking through his "defenses." Although he kept the woman's identity a secret, he soon was telling Tom of his plans to devote the summer to courting. He even advised his half-brother to be ready to come to the wedding. Tom replied, "I have heard the cry of '*wolf*' so often that nothing could convince me now but my own eyes." Tom knew his brother. Something happened between Gordon and "the object of his affections." Not long after he wrote Tom, Gordon told his brother-in-law that he was "tired of [women], done no courting and don't think I ever will."[88]

That attitude was short-lived. According to family tradition, Gordon did sire a daughter out of wedlock, but there is no documented evidence to support this. Whatever his feelings about matrimony, Gordon figured that his hometown was anything but an exciting place for a person, married or otherwise. "I find Wilkes very dull," he complained once to Carrie. "I think the town is growing worse daily, it is the last place in the world[;] the population is worse than I ever knew it."[89] Gordon's disposition to immerse himself in every possible pursuit was his attempt to drown his boredom and to curb the resulting blues. It was a plan that did not always work. "Brother James has abandoned all hope of ever removing from Wilkes,"

Tom lamented. "I suppose the thought of spending the balance of his days in that poor old county makes him moody and sad enough."[90]

Still, a man of Gordon's means had ample opportunity to enjoy himself, and so he did. Gordon valued his free time, whether he called on ladies, visited friends, or stayed at home for a quiet evening of reading. He was well read. He perused volumes of history and literature for information purposes, not for whiling the time away. He also took a number of journals and newspapers, among them the *Western Democrat*, the *Home Journal*, and *Thompson's Bank Note and Commercial Reporter*.[91] Other pastimes proved as diverse. He joined in sleigh rides, went skating, and helped to put up ice in the winter. He went swimming in the Reddies in the summer. When visiting larger cities, Gordon enjoyed the theater. He also loved to eat. He could put away several helpings before calling it quits, especially when his favorite, cornbread and buttermilk, sat on the table. Most of all, he enjoyed spending time with his family or with friends such as Rufus L. Patterson, a prominent resident of Caldwell County. Since Patterson's Dad, Samuel, had been Gordon's guardian, Gordon had essentially grown up with Rufus. The two became so close that Patterson asked Gordon to be the best man at his wedding. On the Patterson's honeymoon, Mrs. Patterson (the daughter of former North Carolina governor John M. Morehead) sent Gordon a sprig of boxwood in appreciation. It had been plucked especially for him from the grounds of Mount Vernon.[92]

In any event, Nathaniel Gordon would have been proud of his only son. The man had excelled at almost everything he became involved in. He was successful financially; by the summer of 1860, he could estimate his real estate worth $26,200 and his personal estate worth $33,000. The farm alone, which consisted of 325 improved and 1,650 unimproved acres, was worth $15,000. That was almost double what it had been worth in 1850.[93] In addition, Gordon's property included land in St. Louis County, Missouri, and possibly some land in the Northwest.[94] He was well liked by his neighbors. A giving and protective man, he loved his family and they loved him back. One example of that was evident even in his stepfather. Old Mr. Brown, at the age of seventy-four, had gone blind despite a recent eye operation. Instead of moving to Tennessee to live with his brother, Brown decided to remain in Wilkes so he could be near Gordon. From then on, Gordon often sat down with Mr. Brown and read the mail to him.[95]

Restlessness has been marked as a trait of Scottish heritage.[96] Gordon displayed that trait. He lived a busy and demanding life, but part of him yearned for more. It may have been his home county, which was isolated; it could have been his personality, for Gordon was the type of person who could not sit still for a moment; or it might have been a touch of loneliness, for although Gordon knew many people, and had a good family and close friends, he never managed to find contentment. Whatever the reason, Gordon certainly wanted to do something more with his life. He knew he could succeed given the opportunity. He wanted the honor, as a Southern gentleman, of being involved in some great venture or adventure. Having traveled extensively, he knew that there was a big world out there for the taking. It was evident that he had done just about everything he could do in Wilkes, yet his roots were deep in the soil of Happy Valley and securely held him there. He had a sentimental attachment to the place as well. From Arkansas, Tom wrote Carrie, "I hoped to see brother James out here in the spring, but Allen says he has purchased another stock of goods, and I suppose come to the settled conclusion to spend the balance of his days in old Wilkes. There is certainly some cohesive power about that old county, being the poorest and the worst to be found, yet very few of its citizens move away."[97]

It would take something quite extraordinary to wrench James B. Gordon away from his roots and give him new chances to flourish. Such an occurrence was not long in coming. In December 1860, the most extraordinary event of the century began when South Carolina left the Union.

3

A Hole in Your Hide

As OTHER SOUTHERN STATES FOLLOWED South Carolina's lead, the Gordon/Brown family wondered what North Carolina would do. Gordon saw secession as the state's only option. "From the first," remembered a friend, "Gordon was in favor of North Carolina taking her position with the South, and opposed to any neutral ground.... His opinion was that should North Carolina attempt to maintain a neutral position, her soil would be drenched with the blood of both sides, and her own precious heart would be torn out by contending factions of her own people." Tom Brown shared his half-brother's view. "I am afraid," he wrote, "that under the leadership of such men as Holden and others she will disgrace herself for all time to come. I will hang my head in shame for her if she does not act *now*."[1]

As Tom feared, state politicians avoided secession while secession fever marched across the South. Then came April 1861; shells rocked Fort Sumter. The Federal government subsequently called for seventy-five thousand men to suppress the Southern "insurrection." To many North Carolinians, the issues of states' rights and slavery did not warrant secession, but the prospect of having to fight their fellow Southerners all but required it. As a result, Governor John W. Ellis replied to President Abraham Lincoln's call for troops with an emphatic no. "I can be no party to this wicked violation of the laws of the country, and to this war upon the liberties of a free people. You can get no troops from North Carolina," Ellis wrote. Presently, on May 20, a convention in Raleigh passed the ordinance of secession and ratified the provisional Constitution of the Confederate States of America. Gordon's fellow delegate to the 1856 Presidential Convention, Burton Craige, proposed the secession ordinance to the state convention.[2] Rufus Patterson, one of Gordon's best friends, was present as a delegate to vote on it.[3] Like that, North Carolina joined the Confederacy.

Meanwhile, in Wilkesborough, Gordon did not bother to wait on the state government. In April, before the state seceded, Gordon and Montford Stokes began planning to raise a company of soldiers. On May 1, their efforts culminated with a search for manpower. According to a Wilkes merchant, the search created a "wild day in this place. Major Stokes is beating for volunteers ... and some half dozen others made speeches.... about 30 persons in all have volunteered." One of Gordon's cousins, James Gwyn, also saw the day's thrilling events. "Went to Wilkesboro to attend a general convention of the People of the County to adopt measures for the protection of the country and to get up volunteers — a large collection of people and a great deal of excitement, most everybody now for the South," he wrote.[4]

Twenty-two-year-old W. Harrison Proffit, a local teacher, became one of those volunteers. After proudly dubbing themselves the Wilkes Valley Guards, Proffit wrote, the men elected their officers. They appointed Stokes captain and Gordon first lieutenant. They also elected

Gordon's half brother, Allen Brown, first sergeant in recognition of his Naval Academy background. Thus promoted, Captain Stokes and Lieutenant Gordon continued to search for volunteers. Since the process required publicity and even something of a business proposition between recruits and organizers, Gordon had the opportunity to apply his selling skills. Within two weeks, Stokes and Gordon had culled 96 would-be soldiers.[5] When North Carolina officially seceded on May 20, Governor Ellis's call for volunteers prompted a few more local men to join. Now 110 men strong, the group made "altogether a fine-looking company." To some, however, it was a disappointing turnout. Gwyn hoped that the draft would be instituted to fill the ranks.[6]

Since their typical recruit had no military background, Stokes, Gordon, and the other officers had to create a military unit out of the rawest material. Stokes, with Allen Brown's help, used his military background to drill the men. Gordon, though he too had to learn about soldiering, applied his business and political skills to organize and motivate. Gordon even took it upon himself to equip the unit, using his own money to buy items like cloth for the men's uniforms. He hoped that the county and state would share this pecuniary burden. "I send you an account of the expenses of equipping the Wilkes Valley Guards," Gordon wrote one citizen. "The cloth I bought I expected the state to pay, but the Quarter Master General refused to pay by order of the Adjutant General. Therefore had to pay it myself. I have bills for all accounts rendered.... I do hope the county will make some arrangement to pay the amount due immediately as every county in the state has equipped their troops and companies well, and I do hope Wilkes will not forget her boys who are in the field."[7]

Gordon on the eve of the Civil War. As South Carolina and other states seceded from the Union, Gordon was in favor of North Carolina doing the same. North Carolina Museum of History.

It was an interesting time that did not foreshadow events to come. The atmosphere had a holiday flavor to it, as well as a hint of adventure. Feeling like fearsome warriors, the men camped on a hill just outside town, above the old tan yard.[8] There, in the cool, cloudy weather, they played soldier and learned about camp life. Except for a gentle shower on May 6, rain remained scarce. The men spent the first of many nights in tents, or under the stars. They laughed over miscues such as password confusion.[9] Undisciplined and careless, they often lost equipment about the hill. Years later, residents of the area would find rusty items that had been misplaced by the soldiers.

Soon the time came to join other volunteer soldiers who were massing near Raleigh. On

May 27, after nearly a month of recruiting, organization, and "soldiering," Gordon, Stokes, Brown, and the Wilkes Valley Guards said good-bye to Wilkes. Each man made final preparations; for his part, Gordon arranged for family members to look after his finances and property during his absence. Then, the contingent broke camp and formed ranks, heads held high, and set off. Friends and family watched and cheered admiringly as the unit stirred up the dust and disappeared into the distance. They walked a few miles before darkness fell and forced them to choose a campsite. At their first bivouac "in the field" along the banks of Moravian Creek, the men rested and wondered what the future held. For many, it would be their last moment in Wilkes.[10]

The amateur soldiers greeted the dawn the next morning. A long journey lay ahead. Shouldering their equipment, they moved out. Marching the entire day, the Wilkes Valley Guards crossed the Brushy Mountains, walked through Taylorsville, and camped for the night at Salem Church near Mr. A. Sharp's. On May 29, the unit resumed its march at an early hour, and reached Statesville by noon. After a few hours of waiting they took the evening train to Salisbury, where they were hailed as "one of the finest companies in the state." One soldier recorded: "The Brass Band and many spectators were assembled at the depot. We were escorted through the town in elegant stile [sic], the Brass Band sending forth its most sweet and fascinating notes."[11]

The next morning, the North Carolina Railroad took the Wilkes Valley Guards away from Salisbury. Many of the men, sore from the march, doubtless felt glad to be riding. The train chugged across the state, past villages and towns where others prepared for war. At last, the locomotive pulled the cars into the station of their destination, the state capital of Raleigh. Gordon and the men moved to a bivouac in the Baptist Grove near the capital.[12]

On May 31, the company's journey to war gained official status: the unit was sworn into state service as Company B of the 1st Regiment of North Carolina State Troops. On June 4, Gordon was promoted to captain and assumed command of the company, while Allen became First Lieutenant. Stokes, in view of his Mexican War and military experience, was appointed colonel of the regiment.[13] In the midst of these changes, Gordon wrote his mother:

> I write to merely inform you that we are getting along pretty well. We are assigned to the First Regiment of State Troops. We will remain in No Carol. some two or three months ... 16 of our men have left us, unwilling to go in the regular service. We have gone for the war, and as soon as that is ended we are disbanded. It is now raining and we are sitting in the tents some singing some playing the violin some writing love letters. I received a letter from Tom this morning which I enclose [for] you. My love to Carrie and her little babe and all the other dear relations. I have ordered my portrait to be taken by a splendid artist which I will send to you. So should you not see me again it will remind you of former scenes and associations. Majr. Stokes is Col of the regiment. I am captain and Allen, 1st Lieut Allen, is doing remarkably well and is quite a favorite with the men ... I will write you again soon.[14]

A week later, the company moved to Camp Edwards at the Warrenton Race Paths near Warrenton, North Carolina. There, Stokes completed the mustering of his regiment and whipped it into fighting trim. Company B's new commander did his part, working hard to improve his unit's efficiency. Gordon scrutinized the company's organization, administration, and equipment needs. He kept an eye on the well-being of his troops and he helped his men deal with personal problems. He also trained the men in earnest. Proffit explained that Gordon kept them hopping: "Very little time spent in idleness as we drill hard almost every day." Captain Gordon also personally visited with each man in the company. Instructed to enlist his soldiers for the entire war instead of the obligatory year's service, he encouraged his men to fight the war to the finish. Nearly one hundred men chose to remain with the company, making it the largest unit in the forming regiment.[15]

Time off came on Sunday, when many chose to attend church or relax. Gordon found Camp Edwards to be a "very pleasant place" for a camp. As he had several acquaintances in Warrenton, his tent rarely lacked visitors. Food was plentiful and the water clear and good. A nearby house provided comfortable shelter for the regiment's officers and staff. Bragged Samuel Ginnings, the regiment's commissary sergeant, "i git to stay in the House all the time if i choose i never have to stand guard nor to drill only when i choose." Yet Ginnings paid his dues. As commissary sergeant, he fed about five hundred men a day. There were times when he did not have to prepare food, however, because the men occasionally received adulation and honors from neighboring communities. One soldier told his family about a "celebration at Warrenton, N.C., which was, indeed, a grand exhibition. A No. 1 dinner was gratuitously bestowed upon the officers and soldiers of Col Stokes' Regiment by the patriotic and noble ladies and gentlemen of Warrenton."[16] Thanks to this care, Gordon could report home that "we are all getting along very well and in fine health."[17]

Because of their proximity to a major rail line, the men had no difficulty in keeping abreast of events. "We get the news here every day from Richmond, Petersburg & other points in Va.," one soldier wrote. "There are many rumors and reports being circulated and many of them are not reliable." One true piece of bad news concerned Governor Ellis, who died on July 7. Gordon, who knew Ellis well, mourned his passing.[18] Officials expected Ellis's remains to pass through Warrenton, giving the men an opportunity to pay their respects. Another reliable piece of intelligence concerned the war's first big fight. Proffit wrote, "I suppose a severe battle was fought ... at or near Manassas Junction, General Beauregard commanding the Southern forces, who were victorious."[19]

When Gordon learned of the Battle of Manassas from these news reports, it doubtless sparked a touch of jealousy in his breast. On July 21, Federal General Irvin McDowell descended upon the Confederate forces of generals P. G. T. Beauregard and Joseph E. Johnston along Bull Run. McDowell's flank attack found early success, but Confederate reinforcements from the Shenandoah Valley turned the tide and sent the Federals reeling back to Washington. The Confederate army's bloody victory was, thought many observers, the first step in what would be a brief and successful war for Southern independence.

Gordon was now learning to be the soldier his grandfather, father, and teacher had been, but the frustrating part was that the war was being fought elsewhere. Characteristically, Gordon wanted to be in the thick of things. The hours he spent experiencing camp life and conducting drill had gotten old quickly. Those slow times gave him the opportunity to reflect on his current position and consider options. Turning it over in his mind, Gordon decided to do something about it. What could he do to be a part of the times, to play a role in the unfolding drama? Where was the best place for a man of his abilities? One thing was certain: he wanted more responsibility and more challenge. He decided that the infantry was not the answer. The place for him, Gordon believed, was the cavalry, where he could use his skill as a horseman in battle, just as his father had.[20]

Not long after Bull Run, Gordon learned that a cavalry unit was forming nearby. It was in the process of recruiting men and officers. This was the opportunity he had been looking for, so he worked out a transfer. Called the Ninth Regiment North Carolina State Troops (1st Regiment North Carolina Cavalry), the state's first cavalry unit was organizing at Camp Beauregard near Ridgeway, North Carolina. Enlistments for the unit had begun during May and June in the western part of the state. The men had assembled in July in Asheville and on August 1 moved to Camp Beauregard.[21] Gordon joined his new comrades there, but his thoughts went with the Wilkes Valley Guards. In late July, that old company of hometown friends started moving toward the front. Most of all, Gordon had hope for Allen, who was turning into a fine infantry officer. Not only had he overcome a problem with stuttering, but the men had persuaded the Naval Academy graduate to put aside any thoughts of joining the navy.[22]

Located three-fourths of a mile from the railroad, Camp Beauregard was a fitting place for Gordon to begin his new career. Wrote one witness, it was "a beautiful place for an encampment, being on [a] large and extensive farm, and in sight and almost fronting [another] large and magnificent dwelling." A newspaper reporter agreed. "The encampment is situated in one of the most lovely and quiet groves in the whole country, with several very fine springs of water quite accessible, and two small creeks near, where the horses are usually taken to water."[23]

Governor Henry T. Clark, Ellis's successor, "took special interest" in the selection of the officers and staff of the 1st North Carolina Cavalry. He awarded the commissions himself.[24] One of Clark's first moves was to appoint Gordon senior major of the regiment.[25] In that post, Gordon could learn from the vantage point of a regimental field officer. It complemented his brief but informative experience as a company commander. Gordon's date of entry into the state service with the regiment was August 12, the same date of the official organization of the 1st North Carolina Cavalry.[26]

Gordon reported to Colonel Robert Ransom, Jr., the regiment's commander. Bob Ransom had been born on February 12, 1828 along Bridle Creek, not far from Camp Beauregard. After graduating from West Point in 1850, he became a lieutenant in the regular army. At the Military Academy, and after graduation, Ransom "was distinguished for splendid horsemanship and the practical qualities of a soldier." As his career progressed, Ransom returned to West Point to teach. During Robert E. Lee's tour as academy superintendent, Ransom was instructor of cavalry. His pre-war career also included service in the West with the 1st United States Cavalry.[27]

At war's onset, Ransom had traveled east to offer his sabre to the chivalric Governor Ellis. "Should my state at any time need me," Ransom had said, "command me." Ellis was "on the brink of the grave" when he welcomed Ransom. Nonetheless, he proved that he was an able judge of talent by placing Ransom in charge of

Robert Ransom, Jr., was the first colonel of the 1st North Carolina Cavalry and a friend and mentor to James Gordon (Military Order of the Loyal Legion of the United States — Massachusetts Commandery Photograph Collection, U.S. Army Military History Institute, Carlisle Barracks, Pennsylvania).

the 1st North Carolina Cavalry. After Ellis's death, Governor Clark concurred in that choice. For his part, Gordon became quite fond of both Ransom and his wife. Gordon and the Ransoms laid the foundations for a lasting friendship during those August days.[28] With a man like Ransom in command and the promise of responsibility and honor in his new assignment, Gordon felt proud to be a major in the 1st North Carolina Cavalry. He wrote home:

> It has been some time since I wrote to you. I have been changing my location, and am at last settled down for a few weeks. I came into this camp regularly on Saturday last and I am very well satisfied and pleased though it was very hard for me to give up my old company. I regret so much to leave Allen believing that I could be of great service to him in many ways. But I find he is doing very well succeeding in commanding the company finally. I learn the Regt left Richmond on Thursday. I expect there is some hard work before them but hope they may be equal to the task. My present position is one of more responsibility and danger than the former one but I feel confident of my determination to discharge all the duties required of me. The Col. of this Regt. is [a] true military man, gallant and generous, and we are getting along finely. The Col. and myself had a delightful ride into the country yesterday to call on the wives of some of the officers. If you had seen the rapid headlong riding you'd have thought we could have charged any battery. He is a splendid rider and you know I am. It is understood that a cavalry officer never rides any way only in a race. I think there is more danger of some of our men getting their necks broken than being killed.... Tell Mr. Brown that he must keep up his spirit and be ready to hear the news of peace after the cavalry gets into a fight.[29]

Though plagued by poor health,[30] Ransom applied his cavalry experience well during the organization. Gordon paid close attention, and also did a lot to add to the unit's efficiency.[31] Ransom meshed the regiment's ten companies, designating them A–K (without a "J" company). Each company, filled with recruits from Ashe, Northampton, Mecklenburg, Watauga, Warren, Cabarrus, Buncombe, Wayne, Duplin, and Macon counties, contained between sixty-four and one hundred men. With the companies consolidated under a single command structure, designated men filled the remaining field and staff positions, including adjutant, sergeant major, regimental surgeon, and regimental chaplain. Meanwhile, elections in the ranks selected company commanders and squad positions such as "drill master."[32]

While Ransom concentrated on organization, state officials worked to supply the unit. In theory, the state was to provide the uniforms, equipment, and horses for enlisted men. (Officers had to furnish their own mounts.) In practice, problems arose in equipping the regiment. Ransom and his wife were at times forced to help outfit the company themselves.[33] The state government bought horses from Kentucky easily enough, but neither the state nor the Confederate government could furnish the regiment with enough sabres and saddles. A state agent finally managed to find enough saddles in New Orleans, but sabres were still scarce. At last, North Carolina officials asked the 2d North Carolina Cavalry to give up their sabres so that the 1st could be completely equipped. The 2d Cavalry's troopers reluctantly consented. They would be furnished with new sabres when the government found a source for them.[34] Ransom even had trouble finding enough buglers, which forced him to post an ad in a Richmond newspaper.[35]

Ransom and his staff could only have been frustrated with such problems. One of Gordon's duties was to oversee the issuing of equipment. As he worked, it became apparent that the regiment was lacking. While the men filed by to draw equipment, Gordon carefully recorded which company received what. On August 13, for example, Captain W. H. Cheek's company was issued ninety rifles and additional equipment such as wipers, corks, screw balls, and bullets; Captain Thomas Ruffin's company received ninety rifles and similar equipment; Captain T. N. Crumpler's company received twenty-nine of those precious sabres; and Captain

J. M. Miller's company drew eighty pistols, twenty-seven wrenches, forty-five saddles, and nine bridles. During the coming days, as supplies trickled in, the officers continued to issue equipment. One company was lucky enough to receive Colt revolving rifles. The regiment also secured servants; regulations specified that four could serve in each company.[36] Gordon's personal servant, Burt, joined him in the field.

Regardless of their equipment, Ransom and his staff drilled the men in cavalry tactics daily. The only let-up came on Sunday because Ransom attended church regularly. Of the drills and exercises, one remembered that "no troops ever went thru a severer ordeal." Individuals bonded into a unit during the harsh training. The troopers "bore the severity of the service with patriotic fortitude, and enjoyed the ups and downs of the drill and the jests and jeers of camp-life with infinite humor." However, the cavalrymen did not always endure quietly. "At times and on occasions," a trooper remembered, "there were loud complaints against Colonel Ransom for the rigid rules and harsh measures adopted." Harvey Davis, a cavalryman in Captain George Folk's Company D, agreed that Ransom was strict. However, he added that "we [would have] fared quite well, if we had been better cooks, but at first altho rations were abundant, it was badly cooked, nearly all being new hands at the culinary art, and as a result much suffering among the troops was the results."[37] Another man sampled firsthand how tough Ransom could be. During a drill, the colonel spotted a loafing trooper and yelled, "Close up there, you man on the black horse! Close up! You are not paying any attention to this drill! You are studying about some of the good things your mother has at home!"[38] Ransom struck a chord with that statement; all the men longed for the comfort of hearth and home. All the same, these experiences proved to be a strong and valuable foundation for the regiment.

In this atmosphere, Gordon formed strong friendships. One new friend was Laurence S. Baker, Ransom's second in command. Born in May 1830, Baker had a sad face that featured a full mustache and a bushy beard cropped off just below his chin. A man with a taste for spirits, Baker was the son of a respected doctor and the grandson of a representative to the Continental Congress.[39] Officials valued Baker's talents. That fall, they sent him to Asheville to inspect several new cavalry companies. Baker discharged the unfit from those units. Gordon would come to know Baker well, and would learn from him in many ways. Another close friend was Lieutenant William Henry Harrison Cowles. Cowles, twenty-one, the son of a tinware maker and postmaster, was from Hamptonville, not thirty miles east of Wilkesborough. Before the war, Gordon had occasion to know young Cowles when Cowles's brother courted a friend of Gordon's. A tall and athletic man, Cowles wore his hair parted and had a lengthy beard. He was a fine horseman who was fond of the outdoors.[40]

By summer's end, the regiment was ready. Ransom had molded the 1st North Carolina Cavalry into a proud unit of about nine hundred men, one thousand horses, plus wagons.[41] Gordon was no closer to the fighting, but at least he was a field officer in an efficient, well trained, and proud regiment.

He certainly shared the sentiment a fellow soldier expressed to a Richmond newspaper. "I trust a field of usefulness and glory awaits us — one that will gratify the whole regiment in getting 'pops' at Yankees, showing our bravery, distinguishing or extinguishing ourselves, &c., &c," the man wrote.[42]

In Arkansas, "the rolling drums and squeaking fife" prompted Hugh Thomas Brown to postpone his impending marriage and rush to the service of the Confederacy. Along with about eighty other Van Buren recruits, Tom boarded a boat bound for Little Rock to join up.

Like his brothers, Tom held himself "in readiness for immediate service." He was confident in the "power of Southern arms."[43]

It was not long until the Federals tested that power. On August 10, 1861, Captain Brown commanded a company of the 3d Arkansas Infantry Regiment in the Battle of Wilson's Creek. Brown led his Frontier Guards well until a bullet pierced his heart and stifled his cry, "Onward! Onward, my brave boys!" General N. Bart Pearce, who had considered Brown a rising star, noted the death of the "chivalrous and gentlemanly Captain Brown" with sorrow.[44]

About a week later, back in North Carolina, Gordon and Colonel Baker found a few extra minutes and sat down with the Richmond papers. As Baker read an account of Wilson's Creek, he came across Tom's name in the casualty list. Shocked, Gordon tried to confirm the report by contacting Burton Craige. Craige was then a member of the Provisional Confederate Congress, supporting measures to strengthen the central government for the war effort.[45] After talking with Craige and others, Gordon decided that the report was accurate. He broke the news to Allen as easily as he could. "It was to me my dear Brother," Gordon wrote, "the most terrible shock I ever experienced; to think he has fallen by the hands of an invading foe on the plains of Missouri far from home and kindred, and God alone knows where his remains may now be." Gordon encouraged his brother to bear his grief in a way becoming a soldier, but he admitted that "it really seems impossible to reconcile one self to the belief that we shall never again behold that manly form imbued with all the impulses of a noble and generous heart whose many virtues and high toned bearing won him the esteem and high regard of all who knew him." The two brothers also worried about the effect of the news on their parents. Gordon had not had the heart to tell them yet, so unless fighting was imminent, Gordon advised Allen to go home and comfort them.[46]

Gordon next went to Richmond to learn more. There he met Hugh F. Thomason, a member of Congress from Van Buren who knew Tom well. Thomason apparently knew the facts. "Oh! do I regret to say that the account is too true," Gordon later wrote. While there, Gordon also happened to see Stokes. He told the colonel about Tom's death, and asked about a furlough for Allen. Stokes, who was very distressed at the news, said he would take care of the furlough. Finally, Gordon telegraphed to Little Rock.[47]

With that, the war hit home. It was devastating to learn of a loved one's death in such a callous way, but Gordon bore it. With Tom dead, Camp Beauregard seemed to have lost some of its beauty. The war was no longer something that only hurt others but could not touch the Gordon/Brown family. Gordon channeled his grief into drill and instruction. In the back of his mind, he also hoped for another outlet through which to vent his sorrow: specifically, a chance to strike back.

As the leaves began to turn, the wheels of bureaucracy that would send the regiment to war began working. Initially, it looked as if the cavalry unit would not be sent to Virginia. The Confederate government had decided that the regiment could best be used in North Carolina. A September 14 dispatch from Samuel Cooper, Adjutant and Inspector General of the Confederacy, to Governor Clark, read: "The cavalry regiment from your State under Colonel Ransom had better be retained in the State for purposes of defense until further advised."[48] Governor Clark, worried more about problems within the boundaries of his state than beyond, was doubtless pleased with that news.

Three days later, Cooper wired Governor Clark a new message. The "further advisory" had come quicker expected. The September 17 correspondence read: "The President desires that you will direct Col. R. Ransom to proceed, with his regiment, to this city." Clark read the message with surprise. Reluctant to release the regiment from the state's defense, the governor dragged his heels and delayed the unit's departure. Richmond, however, was persistent. On the first Monday in October, the Confederate government ordered Colonel Ransom to march to Richmond "with as little delay as possible."[49]

Governor Clark would have to make do without the 1st. At least, as he told the war department, it would be fairly easy for him to raise more cavalrymen. For his part, Ransom directed his staff and the company commanders to prepare the regiment. The colonel also assembled the men to give them the news. On October 3, he told them that the regiment would leave for Virginia the following week. Making this announcement, Ransom said, was the most pleasant thing he had done since the formation of the regiment. The men responded with nothing short of joy. They raised three cheers for Ransom, three cheers for Gordon, and three for the impending departure.[50]

The regiment's training came to a formal end a week later with a farewell review for state officials. General James G. Martin, adjutant general and leading organizer of all North Carolina troops, and Governor Clark conducted the festivities. Several hundred visitors came from miles around to see the troopers execute their crisp drill. Some of those who watched, like Mrs. Robert Ransom, were family or friends. Splendidly mounted, the cavalrymen brandished their sabres and demonstrated their skills as their horses pranced about the grounds. The men held themselves proudly because they knew they were the state's best. It was a thrilling sight.[51]

Following the display, the regiment's officers provided dinner for their guests. Over the food, the air buzzed with excited conversation as everyone talked about what lay ahead. When everyone had their fill, the meeting place resounded with patriotic speeches and presentations. The state attorney general, representing Warren County, gave Colonel Ransom a handsome charger—the finest animal that could be purchased in the state—to carry him into battle. A proud Mrs. Robert Ransom presented a beautiful battle flag to the regiment. Governor Clark delivered his best speech and gave the troopers a banner. The speeches and the presentations made it clear that expectations of the regiment were high. After all, "competent judges" said it was now the finest cavalry unit on the continent.[52]

On Sunday, October 13, the 1st North Carolina Cavalry Regiment left Camp Beauregard.[53] As they turned their horses toward Virginia, color bearers proudly unfurled their new banners. Two newspapers estimated that 850 men and 950 horses were in the column that marched north; another said 970 men and one thousand horses.[54] The regiment took "ordinary roads" and made no attempt to hide the movement from Union spies. Ransom set an easy pace as they rode toward the northeast. At dusk, they camped just five miles north of Warrenton.[55]

The next day, the troopers made better time. Pushing their horses a bit harder, the cavalrymen covered twenty miles before bivouacking near the Roanoke River. At about noon on the trip's third day, they crossed the state line and entered Virginia. Gordon had been out of his native state often, but for many of the men it was their first trip outside North Carolina. They gave three cheers for the Old North State as they crossed the border. Later, the cavalrymen bedded down at Bellfield in Sussex County.[56]

After two more days of riding, the North Carolinians filed into Petersburg. Their 1:00 P.M. entrance caused a stir despite the rainy weather. Most of Petersburg's citizens had never seen a full regiment of cavalry, so they opened their windows or crowded into the streets to watch. The Carolinians came into town by way of Halifax Street, traveled down Market Street, turned onto Bank Street, and then rode along Sycamore Street until they reached the "poplar lawn." There, Gordon and the men camped. Before long, they had about 150 tents sprawled across the grass and the regiment's horses quartered in the square across the street.[57]

Locals visited the camp throughout the day, complimenting the men and officers. The hospitality and kindness extended by the citizens of Petersburg made Gordon's first few days in Virginia pleasant. William Barrier recalled that the men, having eaten nothing since an early snack, arrived hungry. They ravenously "devoured the good things which had been prepared for our reception. I drank five cups of good coffee and a gentleman present insisted on my taking more but I positively declined as I thought I had done justice to the good cause."[58] Harvey Davis's stay was just as enjoyable:

> The people of Va. and especially of Petersburg were very kind to us and set a public table for the whole regiment, both supper and breakfast. It was hugely enjoyed, after subsisting on such tough hard bread as we were wont to Bake, the fine bread & the nice delicasis [sic] were a boon not to be despised.[59]

On Saturday morning, October 19, the cavalrymen broke camp and rode to Richmond. The 126-mile trip from Camp Beauregard had taken a toll — four horses had died during the march — but the men looked surprisingly fresh and spirited. Reaching the capital city at about 3:00 P.M., the long line of cavalrymen crossed Mayo's Bridge and wound its way up the town's main street. The regiment's arrival created a "marked sensation" among the town's citizens.[60] Gordon, dressed in an orange-trimmed uniform of dark gray cloth that bore a single gold star on the jacket collar, nodded or tipped his gray fatigue cap as citizens greeted the regiment. A correspondent with a Richmond newspaper observed that the regiment "attracted general admiration by their really imposing appearance. Its members were evidently of the best blood of the Old North State."[61]

Once they reached Reservoir Hill, Ransom ordered them to camp and had rations issued. The well-drilled men pitched their tents in an organized and efficient fashion, and then some began cooking rations. Later, if any troopers were given the opportunity, the forty-four dollars that the enlisted men had been paid eight days previously disappeared in Richmond stores.[62]

The regiment's stay in the Confederate capital was brief. Even as the North Carolinians camped, Confederate officials were preparing the unit's orders. The assignment: "Colonel Robert Ransom will proceed," read Special Orders Number 184, "with his regiment of North Carolina cavalry as soon as he can reach there with due regard to the good condition of his command and report for duty to General Joseph E. Johnston, commanding the [Confederate] Army of the Potomac." Johnston himself had eagerly anticipated these orders. When he heard of the regiment's arrival in Virginia, he wired Cooper: "Cannot Ransom's regiment of North Carolina cavalry be ordered to report to me forthwith?" Cooper quickly assured him, "Ransom's regiment leaves here tomorrow to join you by route march."[63]

Ransom was asked to show his regiment to President Jefferson Davis before leaving for the front. It was an opportunity any soldier would jump at. On Tuesday, October 22, "the people turned out *en masse* to see the parade."[64] Other members of the Confederate government, as well as many local ladies, were also in the audience. On a field near Hollywood Cemetery, the 1st North Carolina Cavalry marched and played to the crowd. Gordon rode proudly with the regiment's leadership. They gave their best effort; to be reviewed by the commander-in-chief required it. Witnesses commented on the unit's impressive training and its fine horses and equipment. The grand finale, a thunderous charge across the field by the entire regiment, was, said a correspondent, "A sight worth going a long way to see." President Davis "expressed himself highly pleased with the efficiency and unexceptionable appearance of the command." One Tarheel cavalryman bragged, "All agreed that, up to this time, no such trained cavalry had been seen in Virginia."[65]

One stirring moment remained. "On leaving our camp in Richmond," recalled one trooper, "we passed through the city in a rather winding way. We passed through the capital square where we saw the Father of our prosperous and happy country sitting high in the air upon his snorting steed directing his men forward, as it appeared, to that victory which so gloriously obtained. There too we saw Henry Clay standing as it were in the senate chamber staying the storms which so often hung over us. There too we saw others standing around seeming to listen to the warning voice of the immortal Washington. The scenes were calculated to sadden and to cheer a soldier's heart. We saw, also, the residence of President Davis."[66]

Leaving these statues behind, the regiment left town via the Brook Turnpike, a macadamized road that led northward through green fields and cultivated farms. One tragic event marked their departure; a horse, spooked by a dog, bolted and ran over a 13-year-old boy near the intersection of Brook Avenue and Leigh Street. The boy's leg was broken and had to be amputated. Otherwise, unlike the exciting reviews of the past days, the ride was dull. It was punctuated by only a few events noteworthy enough for veterans to remember. After covering seventeen miles, they stopped in Ashland on the Richmond, Fredericksburg, and Potomac Railroad. From that point, the cavalrymen rode thirty-eight miles in two days and reached Massaponax Church. Considering the amount of baggage they carried, progress was often slow. The regiment's cumbersome train consisted of forty-odd wagons, each of which needed the pulling power of four stout horses.[67]

Sunday, October 28, was a bright, beautiful day ready-made for weary travelers. The column traversed another eighteen miles of Virginia countryside, and drew nearer to the war. During the morning hours of that march, the 1st passed through Fredericksburg. The *Fredericksburg Recorder* veered from editorial policy to describe the 1st North Carolina Cavalry as the "best looking set of men and horses that we ever witnessed." Townspeople turned out to see the regiment. A number of ladies seemed "perfectly carried away" with the scene. Observers remarked that the large number of "colored gentlemen" accompanying the regiment, including Burt, looked "as intent upon the war as their masters."[68]

The excitement generated by the 1st did not confine itself to the streets. In a nearby hospital, a nurse was reading to a bedridden patient when shouting interrupted them. Learning that a column of Southern soldiers was passing, the sick man begged the nurse to raise his head so that he could see the "boys." When the patient could see the Tarheels, he became so excited that he tried to get out of bed. "It's Harry! Harry's with that column!" the man protested. The puzzled nurse, who knew that her patient was not from North Carolina, figured he was suffering from sickness-induced confusion. She administered a "composing draught" to relax him, but tragically the man had known what he was talking about. The patient died on Monday, soon after the nurse learned that the man's brother had indeed been marching with the 1st. The soldier had been on his way to the front to join another regiment.[69]

Just as these brothers parted ways forever, the 1st soon crossed a symbolic line of departure. The noise of the Fredericksburg crowds had hardly died down when the men heard another sound in the distance: cannon-fire. It was the first concrete evidence that fighting lay ahead.[70]

The rest of the march passed without incident. Manassas Junction was the last stop. There, on the night of October 31, the men camped on the Manassas battlefield and paid silent homage to the dead. The quiet battleground must have made for an eerie welcome to the war. Meanwhile, Colonel Ransom went about his business by riding ahead and reporting to army headquarters. There, Ransom learned that his regiment was assigned to J. E. B. Stuart's cavalry brigade. Directed to the cavalry camps, Ransom next called on Brigadier General James Ewell Brown Stuart for orders. Stuart, the twenty-eight-year-old cavalryman, was an 1854 graduate of West Point who knew Ransom from their pre-war service together.[71] A former Indian fighter, Stuart doubtless was glad to have Ransom's regiment.

Stuart was working with a new command. On the same day President Davis reviewed the 1st North Carolina, Stuart was appointed to command all the cavalry forces in Johnston's Army of the Potomac. Promoted to brigadier general on September 24, Stuart was then best known for leading a key cavalry charge at Manassas against a Federal regiment of Zouaves.[72]

As cavalry commander, one of Stuart's first actions was to order the 1st North Carolina Cavalry into the picket lines before Centreville. The day's order was a milestone in Gordon's life. From that point to the day Stuart died, the events of Gordon's and Stuart's lives would be strikingly intertwined.

Ransom led the 1st from the battlefield to Camp Johnston, just past Centreville. After a few days there, the regiment moved to Camp Ashe, their home for the next few weeks. The outpost was located one and one-half miles outside Centreville. Named for William Ashe, the North Carolina native who was assistant quartermaster general of the Confederate army, the camp offered an unusual life for the green troopers. Camp Ashe was in front of the main infantry lines and exposed to enemy attack.[73] Although the front then was relatively quiet, picket duty and scouting was tense duty. Both the Confederates and the Federals wondered when the other side would do something. Yankee drums thumped ominously in the distance. One Carolinian remembered that those first days at the front were tempered with "a constant round of alarms, surprises, and distant picket shots, often attended with amusing incident and personal adventure."[74]

Stuart's orders required the 1st North Carolina Cavalry to keep a strong picket on duty at all times. That meant constant work of the sort that few were prepared for, especially in the winter weather. The cavalrymen became so busy that the only time they had for drill was while they rode to and from the picket lines. The average trooper rode to the picket lines every five days and stayed for three. Outposts were usually extended seven or eight miles from camp — far enough forward that the enemy occasionally came within rifle shot. One common position was located about nine miles out along Difficult Run.[75]

Whatever the location, Harvey Davis of Company D described picketing as an uncomfortable chore:

> This we found to be the most difficult and hard task of a soldier. Being compelled to stand 2 hours of each 6 hours on picket alone in the most dismal storms of cold[,] snow[,] rain[,] hail[,] or sleet[,] often miles from the camp & expecting the enemy any moment tried the courage of the stoutest, for altho such petty attacks hardly can be said to expedite the termination of the war, yet it is allways [sic] practiced....[76]

Picket duty could also be harrowing. The regiment's first night on the lines was especially tense for Private Henry Fisher of Company F. Spooked by some unidentified sound in the dark, Fisher just knew that the Yankees had come. He opened fire, but only managed to hit fellow trooper Henry Dellinger. If the regiment did not wake at the sound of his gunfire, it surely did when he started yelling, "They are coming! The Yankees are upon us!" Then the hapless Fisher could stand it no more; he fainted dead away. It all turned out to be a false alarm. Fisher went on to serve with distinction, but his comrades never let him forget that night. Dellinger did not forget it either, for the gunshot crippled him for life.[77]

Gordon's assignment as regimental major showed him war's toll on horses as well as men. Given the constant use, many of the regiment's horses became crippled or sorebacked. The use of old-fashioned "shafter" saddles, a type that often gave horses saddle galls, exacerbated the situation. All steeds suffered from a lack of food. According to one cavalryman, by December many of the regiment's horses were so thin that "you can almost see the sun shine through them." Stuart's solution was to establish a camp near Groveton where worn-out horses could recover. The rest area, which became known as Camp Cripple, soon had plenty of visitors from the 1st.[78]

The unceasing field duty required creativity to make life easier for both man and beast. Gordon was used to having hay readily available whenever he wanted it, but at the front he had to learn how to forage. Once a hay stack was found, a trooper would line out his halter or surcingle on the ground, pile hay on top of it, and bring the ends together tightly. The ends were then tied together so that when the bundle was thrown on the horse's back behind the rider, the long end would pass over the rider's shoulder. That helped horse and rider keep their balance. A trooper could carry as much as fifty pounds of hay in this fashion.[79]

But minds were bent on war. Lt. Jacob A. Fisher had a good reason for telling his parents that picket duty was very dangerous. Once, he saw one hundred Yankees come within three or four hundred yards of his post, not far from Difficult Run. Two of Fisher's men "took deliberate aim" and opened fire, but missed. Fisher decided the distance was too far and his strength was too little, so he ordered a cease fire. The Federals kept on going, and soon came within about seventy-five yards of Lt. W. H. H. Cowles's outpost. Although vastly outnumbered, Cowles brazenly ordered the Federals to halt. They ignored him, and kept marching toward the village of Vienna. Then Cowles ordered his men to open fire, which prompted the Unionists to wheel and flee. "Such running you never saw and seldom heard of, those behind spurring there horses with all there might, charging against those in front" Fisher wrote. Later, the Confederates learned that they had wounded at least one of the Federal troopers and possibly two, plus a horse.[80]

As a matter of course, Stuart's cavalry brigade was required to send out a daily scout to watch for enemy movements. Fisher's and Cowles's skirmish occurred the day before the 1st North Carolina Cavalry was to execute this scout. On the morning of November 26, Colonel Ransom hand-picked 120 men and moved north from Camp Ashe. The scout, composed of twenty-man contingents from Companies B, D, E, G, H, and K, had Major Gordon as its second in command. Ransom left Baker in charge of the camp.[81]

The unit hoped to see something of Federal positions and intentions. Beneath them, the ground was still white from a heavy snow that had fallen two days before. When they reached Hawkhurst's Mill on Difficult Run, about twenty-five men who had just come off picket duty joined the scout.[82] The contingent then passed beyond the front lines and rode westward "by a small path through the thick pines and oak woods near where the Dranesville road crosses the railroad, then followed said road to a lane nearly opposite and to the right of [a] dwelling...." The riders looked and listened. Some may even have noticed Federal balloons, which were hovering about the area.[83]

Continuing on, the troopers reached an old brick mill. Inquiring at a nearby home, they learned that about 150 enemy cavalrymen had passed by one or two hours before.[84] The discovery of tracks confirmed the information. Gordon slowly realized that the enemy was near, and that the war was closer to him than ever before.

The troopers remounted and followed the tracks. After about a mile, the trail veered left. Locals said that an enemy force of between five and ten thousand men was camped in that direction, near the Old Court House. To avoid that superior force, Ransom directed his troopers toward Vienna. The colonel also made a mental note to report the enemy position to headquarters.[85]

A few hundred yards outside Vienna, the troopers came to a road junction. The joining road showed every indication that another enemy force had just passed. The Confederates knew they were immediately in the Yankees' rear. At that, the rookie troopers "brightened up with lively expectation." The colonel ordered a brief halt and rode along the column. "And now, boys," he said, "I want you to show them the stuff you are made of. They are between us and our camp, and we must put them through, no difference what their numbers are!" Almost every trooper responded, "We are ready."[86]

Ransom expected to be upon the enemy almost instantly. He formed his men into column of fours and ordered them after the Federals. Quietly, the men urged their horses forward. They trotted through the deserted town of Vienna, turned right toward the picket line and Hawkhurst's Mill, and began ascending a hill just south of Vienna. In moments, the advance guard discovered an unknown number of enemy soldiers. They were marching in column of twos just on the other side of the hill. These were the first Yankee soldiers most of the men had ever seen, and now they blocked the regiment's route to safety.[87]

When they reached the hill's summit, Confederates at the head of Ransom's column found the entire Union rear guard below them. Woods surrounded the road on which the Yankees marched. The road itself was sunken from years of use. With his enemy at last before him, Ransom made his decision. After designating men from Rufus Barringer's Company F as a reserve, he ordered his advance guard to open fire and then yelled, "Charge, boys, charge! I know you won't disgrace yourselves!"[88] The move was a gamble. Ransom had no way of knowing the size of the force before him, and other Federals were likely to be nearby. Surprise would be the key.

The report of the Confederate weapons, along with what Gordon remembered as "yelling and firing and reckless riding," scared Captain Charles A. Bell's Federals out of their wits. In the confusion, some Confederate troopers' horses had to leap over a fence because the dismounted advance guard blocked the road.[89] Ahead, one Federal yelled, "Run for your lives; they're on us!" Blue-clad officers tried to halt the mass exodus, but to no avail. The Yankees' blue overcoats spread out in the November air as their horses galloped away at full speed. The retreat was on. "I don't much blame the poor creatures for running," Gordon later said.[90]

Ransom, his eyes flashing and his bald pate shining, yelled for Gordon to lead the chase. He did so "most gallantly," proving himself a candidate for promotion.[91] In moments, Gordon was far ahead because his horse outpaced the others. As he directed the Confederate pursuit, Gordon "felt calm and quiet ... though most of the time in close proximity to the enemy and firing at them."[92] Gordon's shooting proved accurate. His fire killed at least one Federal and wounded several others. Gordon also captured several Yankees when he charged a group of about forty Federal cavalrymen, firing as he rode, and ordered them to surrender. Many did, and the major proudly led them away.[93]

The rest of the Confederate horsemen, still yelling and firing, chased Gordon and the Federals for about three miles. As they ran, the Federals wheeled right and headed for the safety of their camps. Along the route, they came across a hill that served as a rallying point. Ransom, Gordon, and the other officers saw their enemy take position there. Concerned that enemy reinforcements were nearby, the Confederate officers blocked the road to halt the chase. A few brave North Carolinians avoided them, however, and dashed up the hill, exchanged fire with the enemy, and then charged. The Federals broke again.[94]

Ransom decided his men had done enough so he ordered the rally sounded. The "wild notes of the bugles" echoed across the countryside. Reluctantly, the Confederates reassembled and collected their prisoners. Counting noses, they estimated that the Federal force — a part of the well-trained 3d Pennsylvania Cavalry out on a regular patrol — had lost one dead, six wounded, and twenty-six prisoners, while the Confederates had suffered no casualties. The loss of seventeen horses, twenty-six sabres, twenty-five revolvers, and fifteen Sharp's carbines made things worse for the Yankees. (Later, Stuart wrote that the Carolinians would have captured more Federals but for "the difficulties of the road.")[95] Ransom's gamble had paid off.

At camp, the men celebrated their "brilliant little affair." (For their part, the surviving Yankees were chewed out during dress parade that night.) Certainly, the battle had not been much; but it was an introduction to war. They had seen their first Yankees and had whipped them. News of Gordon's personal exploits made the Richmond papers, and became known as far west as Arkansas.[96] Best of all, Jeb Stuart was proud of his North Carolinians. The cavalry commander summed up the real significance of the affair in this endorsement: "Colonel Ransom's report speaks well and deservedly of the gallantry of his officers and men in this their first meeting with the enemy. It remains for me to call attention to the admirable management of Colonel Ransom himself, to whose untiring zeal and unceasing efforts this regiment owes that efficiency and discipline which will always ensure its success. The result of this our first engagement with the enemy's cavalry is, I doubt not, highly satisfactory to the General-in-Chief."[97] Also, it was the first time Stuart noticed Gordon's talents. It would not be the last.

The men tried to make the best of camp life. Gordon described Camp Ashe as "a very pleasant camp in a thicket of pines and cedars all small and scrubby so that we are well protected from the wind. The ground is rolling so as to drain the camp and we have to cut out roads to pop from our row of tents to the others." Gordon personally enjoyed fine health and was feeling "quite comfortable," but the "very cold weather" affected the thinly-clad pickets. "We have 120 men of the regiment sick and a death about once a week," he wrote. And since the camp was situated on a high hill and exposed to the elements, there was little prospect for improvement.[98]

With troops traipsing everywhere, Gordon also saw how the countryside itself suffered. From nearby hills a man could see the picturesque Blue Ridge Mountains in the distance, but far-off beauty could not cover up the devastation of war. He wrote, "Such desolation you can't imagine. The whole country seems laid waste. But such is the desolation of war."[99]

Talk in the tents and around the camp fires centered, as usual, on the Yankees. "We have been expecting an advance of the enemy for some weeks," Gordon wrote in early December, "but they have not yet arrived. It is now believed by our Generals that a fight is inevitable within a short time but [they] don't know where the main attack will be ... and [they] are desirous for our regt. to find out where it will be." Besides, Gordon thought, "we have a large number of troops near here and if the attack is made at this point I have no fear of the result." At any rate, General Johnston readied his troops "for active service by diligent instruction" so they would be ready when an attack came from Union General George B. McClellan's Army of the Potomac.[100]

Preparations continued throughout December. The expected attack did not develop, save for an insignificant raid on the regiment's supply depot at Stony Creek. Instead, other facets of army life drew Gordon's attention. The month's highlight was the December 15 visit of General Pierre Gustave Toutant Beauregard. Beauregard toured Camp Ashe and met many of the regiment's officers and men. He apparently impressed few of the onlookers, including Gordon. There is no extant evidence that Gordon took to the hero of Fort Sumter and victor of First Manassas. As another trooper told his father, "There is nothing very striking about him except his eye."[101]

Little else occurred of note. There was some discussion of moving the camps to a better site, but that was all. However, the regiment's oldest, most familiar problem remained unsolved. The day after Beauregard's visit, after a routine night's sleep with their clothes and arms stashed under their beds, Gordon and Ransom were reminded of supply problems. As the weather grew colder, the officers expected the state to forward overcoats. When the shipment arrived, it contained only "old rotten things" that looked like anything but military coats. Enraged, Ransom cursed the state authorities and swore that he would never again claim North Carolina as his native state.[102]

The monotony of winter days, and the despair of Christmas far from home, was soon broken. Gordon received orders to assist in a foraging expedition. The men always found food worth fighting for. On December 20, "for the purpose of covering an expedition of all the wagons of our army that could be spared (after hay)," General Jeb Stuart marched four infantry regiments, an artillery battery, and 150 cavalrymen to the area west of Dranesville, Virginia.[103] Gordon was the ranking cavalryman selected to join the expedition, suggesting that Stuart had been impressed by Gordon's performance at Vienna.

The Carolinians were roused at 1:00 A.M. and instructed to prepare two days' rations. At daylight, Stuart, who knew the location of the enemy's advance posts, sent Major Gordon and one hundred North Carolina cavalrymen, along with Captain Andrew L. Pitzer and fifty Virginia cavalrymen, before the infantry. The cavalrymen were to cover the turnpikes, which led directly to the Federal posts, to prevent news of Confederate movements from reaching the Federals. Stuart followed with 1,600 infantrymen up the Leesburg-Georgetown and Leesburg-Alexandria turnpikes. He hoped to form a strong position on high ground contiguous to the roads' intersection. From that point, Stuart would be able to protect the wagons while they foraged.[104]

As Gordon and the cavalrymen rode ahead, a rocket arced into the sky. It signaled that the enemy knew the Confederates were coming. In confirmation, Captain Pitzer discovered a strong Federal presence on a ridge ahead. (The brigade of Brigadier General E. O. C. Ord, reinforced by the 1st Pennsylvania Reserve Rifles, some cavalry, and a battery of artillery, constituted the Union force.) Pitzer summoned Stuart, who galloped ahead to see for himself. There, Stuart saw Federals in his front. They were entrenching and receiving reinforcements. The gray-clad general suspected that the Federals were "either marching upon Leesburg or had received intelligence through a spy of our intended forage expedition and was marching upon it." Fearing his wagons would be easy prey, Stuart decided to attack the enemy rear and left flank.[105] From his vantage point, Gordon's snap judgment was merely that "the meeting was accidental, both parties out foraging."[106]

Stuart immediately ordered his troops, who were three-fourths of a mile away, to drop their blankets and hurry forward. He then sent Captain Pitzer's detachment "to gain the roads toward Leesburg, give notice to our wagons to return at once to camp, and keep between them and the enemy, threatening his front and flank."[107] Finally, looking about them, Stuart and Gordon considered the heavy pine thickets that hindered effective deployment and maneuver. Accordingly, Stuart decided to hold Gordon and his detachment in reserve.

Blue-clad skirmishers were by this time moving up; grayback infantrymen had also begun to arrive. The Confederate units—the 11th Virginia, the 6th South Carolina, the 10th Alabama, and the 1st Kentucky, supported by the Sumter (Ga.) Flying Artillery—straddled the road and faced their enemy. While the infantry formed, artillery and sharpshooters of both sides started banging away at each other. Because of the terrain, Stuart's artillery had to settle for a poor position that offered scant protection and little opportunity for effective firing.[108]

Stuart proceeded with his plan and ordered the Confederate right wing forward. The 10th Alabama "rushed with a shout in a shower of bullets," and charged until it reached a position along a fence. There, the regiment opened up on the Federals. A bit to the right and rear, the well-covered 11th Virginia suffered little as it added fire and lead. In the center, the 6th South Carolina inched ahead as well, but it was in an exposed position and began taking

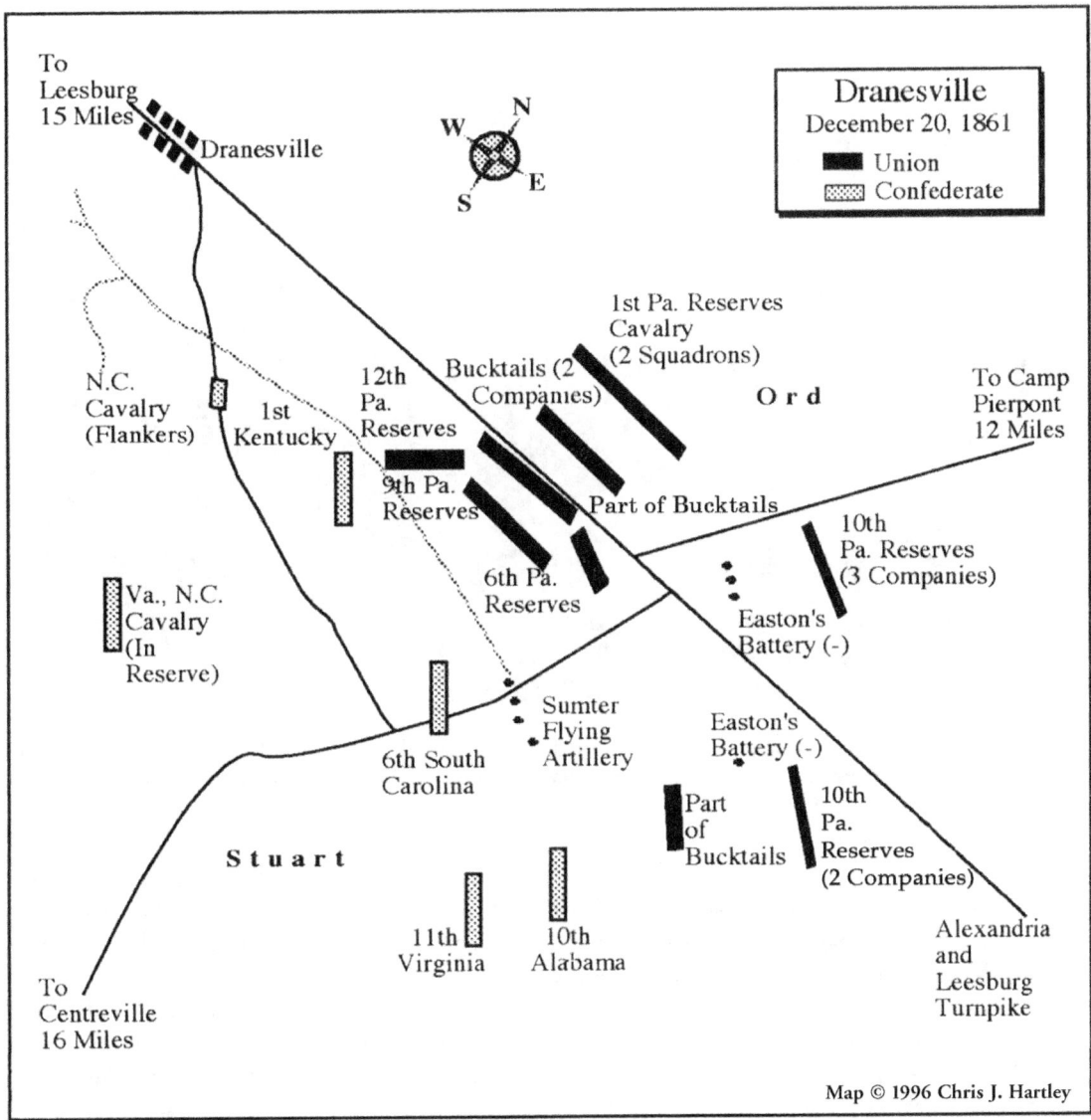

casualties. On the extreme left, the 1st Kentucky and some South Carolina troops became confused in a dense thicket and began firing at each other.[109]

Gordon, still in reserve, was nonetheless exposed to the fighting. He was moved by what he witnessed. This was Gordon's first taste of serious combat. For the first time, Confederates died before his eyes. For the first time, the terrible roar of cannon and the crack of several thousand muskets stung his ears. He watched the battle, frustrated that he could not join in, and cringed as several cannon shots landed nearby. All he could do was send out pickets to protect the flanks.[110]

Gordon's greatest lesson that day was what weapons could do to people. From his vantage point, he saw "two men standing near each other and both men's heads were taken off with a cannon shot. Many [others] were badly mutilated." Some of those shots passed near him.[111] If Gordon had any remaining notions of war's nobility, they died at Dranesville.

Gordon watched as the Confederates pressed their attack, and even achieved some success,

Gordon saw shocking carnage at the 1861 Battle of Dranesville, but that did not hinder his solid performance leading the Confederate rear guard (*Frank Leslie's Illustrated newspaper,* January 11, 1862, Library of Congress).

but they could not continue much longer. After less than two hours of fighting, Federal reinforcements began to arrive. Stuart decided to withdraw. By now, he reasoned, the battle should have bought the wagons enough time to escape. The guns fell back first, followed by the caissons that still had horses. The infantry withdrew next.[112]

Stuart ordered Gordon to come up and cover the retreating guns, caissons, and men. Accordingly, Gordon formed his horsemen in the road in column of fours. He then told them they had an "opportunity of showing what we were and hoped that every man would fall before he dishonored his native state." Happy to be moving at last, the troopers went to work. Gordon thought it a very trying time, but his men obeyed his commands without hesitation. Gordon then ordered his own slow retreat, instructing the men to round up stragglers where possible. The Federals, who "seemed very willing to end the fight," only briefly threatened the withdrawal.[113] Once Gordon broke contact, he moved his men to Fryingpan Church and then back to Camp Ashe, where they collapsed into their quarters. It had been a near thing, but Stuart's men had preserved the army's wagons, including the wagons of the 1st North Carolina Cavalry. The regimental wagon-master, Jacob Dove, reported to Ransom: "Yes; Jacob Dove not only brought out his teams, but brought them loaded, and even made them jump fences."[114]

Afterward Stuart defended his soldiers, saying victory had been theirs, but his forty-three dead and 143 wounded compared unfavorably with the Federals' seven dead and sixty-one wounded. Confederate ambulances worked until late on Saturday bringing off the hurt. Even though the Confederates saved their wagons, and filled them in many cases, the Federals had punished them. Still, the soldiers credited Stuart with getting them out of a tight spot.[115]

Overall, it did not amount to much. Dranesville had been a small battle for small stakes. Only about five thousand men had been engaged. Gordon, however, had seen something more of war. After all, it was the largest fight he had ever witnessed, and it made its impression. He had no way of knowing that coming battles would be much larger.

Barely a week after Dranesville, the cavalrymen began constructing winter quarters. Gordon sent Burt to cut logs for their "log cabbin"; hopefully, the structure would ward off the winter chill. Another trooper planned to "erect a *little mansion* of nine poles, eight feet by twelve, with a chimney in one end and a family bed in the other sufficiently large for six boys to sleep in." Once his quarters were finished, Gordon occupied himself by writing letters and conducting occasional business transactions. He used portions of his pay to buy goods by mail and direct them to the store.[116]

Gordon celebrated Christmas of 1861 in the camps of the 1st North Carolina Cavalry. Instead of family, the cavalrymen observed the Yuletide with each other. As they saw no change in their routine, the men mumbled to each other, "What a dull Christmas." Gordon, however, had a lot on his mind as the year drew to a close. He could look back on his short experience as a Confederate cavalry officer with mixed feelings. He had fought in two skirmishes and performed well for a man without formal military training. The men were beginning to love and respect him. His superiors were becoming increasingly impressed with his abilities. Inside, however, he had hardened. Tom's death was an "incomparable loss" that still hurt. "But then knowing he fell gallantly and in his countries cause consoles us in some degree for his loss," he wrote.[117]

Death had first taken loved ones from Gordon when he was young. Now Death was back, and the great adventure was over. Only the cause remained. He would do whatever he could to ensure that Tom Brown had not died in vain.

James B. Gordon had become a soldier.

4

Back to Carolina

IDLE WAS THE BEST WORD FOR IT. Pulling back from Camp Ashe after New Year's Day, Gordon spent most of January and February 1862 doing little near Centreville. The regiment's winter quarters, which the men called Cantonment W. N. Edwards, was located near the stone bridge made famous in the Battle of Manassas.[1] While there, Gordon and his men only engaged in occasional picketing, drilling, or patrolling. The rotation went like this: a squadron would go on picket every tenth day and remain there for two days. Back at camp, they built stables and housing, rested, talked, and wrote letters. In one missive home, a Company D trooper could not even fill up a single page of stationery. "There is very little to write," he told his family.[2]

Because their quarters were then simply crude shelters, many suffered constant exposure to the harsh winter weather. January mustered only two days of sunshine; hail, sleet, and snow ruled the skies. "Our camp is one continuous mudhole," Gordon wrote. As a result, illness spread. In a vain attempt to turn away the effects of the cold, at least one company requisitioned seventy new pairs of pants, shoes, drawers, shirts, socks, and jackets. Gordon worried as the sick list lengthened to two hundred names.[3] Pneumonia, mumps, and measles soon claimed more lives than all the regiment's skirmishes put together. Even Burt, Gordon's servant, fell ill.[4] There was hope, though. Trooper George F. Adams told his family that as time passed, "a great many others have recovered from severe spells."[5] Perhaps the harsh training and conditioning the men had endured in the fall helped.

The regiment's only real action that winter, insignificant as it was, happened on February 7, 1862. A detachment from the 5th Pennsylvania Cavalry initiated it by harassing some of Ransom's pickets. Passing through Vienna, the Federals first torched a barn known to be a notorious hiding place for pickets. Then the Unionists, guided by a local sympathizer, discovered several Tarheels from Company H in a house near the picket lines. The Federals unhesitatingly charged. Confederates inside and in the surrounding woods turned their Colt repeaters on the attackers, but that did not stop the Federals from breaking through the door. When the smoke cleared, the 5th Pennsylvania men had killed one Confederate and captured four more. They collected three horses and five revolving rifles for their troubles. Finally, before returning to their lines, the Union troopers captured five more men from Company H. The entire 1st North Carolina Cavalry Regiment pursued, but it was too late.[6]

This tiny skirmish stung Confederate pride and robbed families of loved ones but changed nothing. One must look elsewhere to find the winter's key event in relation to the 1st North Carolina Cavalry. The same day of the skirmish, over two hundred miles away, Brigadier General Ambrose E. Burnside landed an amphibious force on Roanoke Island, North Carolina, and captured it the next day. Gordon had been in eastern North Carolina before on business so he could probably imagine the significance of this invasion. The farther inland a Yankee force moved, the more of a threat it posed to Norfolk and vital supply lines to Virginia — and Burnside was already planning a move on New Bern. With the Federals already occupying Northern Virginia, food must come to Richmond from elsewhere; much of it was delivered by the threatened Weldon railroad spur. Worse, mail that traveled that line was also Gordon's primary means of communication with home. This gave the state's sons, from Gordon to Baker to Cowles, plenty of reasons to resent the thought of Yankees occupying North Carolina. They wished for the chance to defend their native soil.

Two North Carolinians with ties to Gordon were already on hand to do just that. Lieutenant Colonel William Morgan Barbour, a fellow St. Paul's vestryman of Gordon's, was one. Barbour was a native of Rowan County who, like Gordon, had studied under Peter Ney. At New Bern, Barbour awaited the expected Union advance as a member of the 37th North Carolina Infantry Regiment.[7] Also in New Bern was Confederate general Lawrence O'Bryan Branch. As commander of the town's defenses, Branch hoped to hold the town with only four thousand troops and some elaborate fortifications. Branch's daughter would one day marry 1st North Carolina Cavalry trooper Kerr Craige, Gordon's future aide-de-camp.[8]

In March, Burnside made the expedition's second amphibious landing and then launched a three-column attack on New Bern. The Confederates, dug in deep, held until the Federals found and exploited a weak spot in Branch's line. (Barbour and Branch escaped to fight again.) As would be expected, New Bern's fall sparked more concern in both Richmond and Raleigh, and also bred rumors in the Virginia camps of the 1st North Carolina Cavalry. Some said the regiment would be reassigned to North Carolina! The scuttlebutt was not far off the mark. Confederate officials recognized the threat Burnside posed to Southside Virginia and Richmond's supply lines. Something had to be done. Secretary of War Judah P. Benjamin soon reassured Major General Benjamin Huger, commander of the Department of Norfolk, that the government was "using every effort to strengthen your command."[9]

Ten days after Roanoke fell, the 1st North Carolina Cavalry was ordered to Suffolk, Virginia to temporarily reinforce Huger. From that point, the regiment could assist in either the defense of Norfolk or of eastern North Carolina, depending on Burnside's next move. Confederate officials thought it proper that the Tarheel regiment should handle this role.[10] Yet even as Benjamin assured Huger that "one of the finest" cavalry regiments "in any service" was on its way, events brought about a change in plans. The Confederates began thinking about evacuating Norfolk, so it soon made little sense to use the regiment at Suffolk. For his part, Stuart also held Ransom's men back. The cavalry general balked at letting the North Carolinians go until the expected replacement unit arrived.[11] Finally, before Ransom could move the regiment anywhere, General Joseph E. Johnston canceled the mission.

Johnston had other plans: he wanted to withdraw his entire army to a better defensive position. General McClellan's large Army of the Potomac looked very menacing, and Johnston thought it unlikely that his own force could cover all the routes of attack McClellan could use. So as Federal activity increased along the Potomac in early March, Johnston ordered all Confederate forces in Virginia east of the Blue Ridge back to the line of the Rappahannock River. The first infantry units to march south were those that held the flank.[12]

Stuart's cavalry was assigned to cover the withdrawal, and the 1st North Carolina Cavalry had to stay to do its part. Plans for Suffolk were put on hold. To ensure a quick exit, Ransom ordered Gordon to take command of the regiment's wagons and begin the retreat. The remainder of the regiment would stay until Johnston's entire force had pulled out. When the time came for the speedy retreat, the wagons would not be around to slow the 1st down.

Gordon began packing. Preparing for retreat was not a morale-building, positive state-of-mind experience. Still, he believed the retreat would be temporary; eventually, a battle would be fought to settle the matter. Anything would be a welcome change from the cold, illnesses, and dying of the last few months. When everything was ready, Gordon took a few minutes to write home and tell his mother the news. The words he set down on paper showed his resignation toward the future:

> This is the last letter I shall write you from this point. The army of the Potomac falls back in a day or two. I start in the morning at day light in command of the train, the principal part of the regiment will remain a day or two longer. I do not know where [we] will make a stand between this and Richmond some place. I think under all the circumstances it will be for the best. I may have no opportunity of writing you again soon. We will not have a fight for some days, but it must come ere long, no one but he who rules and controls the destiny of nations can tell the result. I will write you when I have an opportunity. In the mean time give yourself no more anxiety than possible. Burt is quite sick. I take him with me but he is unable to ride horseback; ... I wish much he was at home he is very frail. The Yankees will get him.... Well my dear mother should any fatality befall me, I believe I expressed in a former letter my wishes. My destiny is in the hands of he who rules the universe and he will do all things for the best. My love to all.[13]

As Friday night became Saturday morning, Gordon apparently felt too anxious to get much sleep. In the darkness, he stumbled about the regimental tents to ensure that all was ready. He checked on Burt. Neither the Yankees nor home wandered far from his thoughts. At 3:00 A.M., Gordon added a postscript to his letter. As he wrote, the bustle of a cavalry camp coming to life reached his ears:

> The bugles are now sounding and summoning our men to prepare for the march. In a few hours more, the camp with its little town of log cabbins [sic] will be as quiet as though it were in a primeval forest. How changed and changeable the events of life. I had hoped very much to have gone home about the 1st of this month and fully expected to have done so.... Burt is slightly better this morning.[14]

After sealing the letter, Gordon turned to the work at hand. Before long, the column was ready. He gave the order. Wagon wheels began churning up the muddy road that led to Warrenton, Virginia. Most cavalrymen detested the slow, onerous duty of escorting trains, but Gordon's men accomplished their duty.[15]

On Sunday morning, while Gordon's column trudged slowly southward, Johnston's remaining infantry divisions began falling back. These were the units stationed on the old Manassas line, so their withdrawal marked a turning point in the war. Things were already going badly in the West and in North Carolina; now, Southern troops were abandoning Manassas. The Confederacy was on the retreat. Stuart's cavalry was the last to leave. His units remained in position until 10:00 A.M. on March 10. Stuart drew the duty of torching what the army could not carry.[16]

Like the other regiments in Stuart's command, the 1st fired everything that could not be moved. Cantonment W. N. Edwards went up in smoke. The stone bridge was blown up.[17] Supplies that could not be packed in wagons or carried on horses were burned. It was sad to see those valuable supplies destroyed, but it was a military necessity. With columns of smoke reaching skyward behind them, Stuart's cavalrymen rode south. Ransom looked forward to a junction with Gordon and the regiment's trains.

Gordon had already arrived in Warrenton and was waiting when the rest of the regiment reached the town on March 10. There, Ransom received fresh orders. The instructions made such an impression on him that he announced them to the entire regiment: they had been ordered to North Carolina. Given Burnside's continued success, the regiment was to forget Suffolk and move by slow marches to Weldon. The news that they were returning to the Old North State brought resounding cheers from the entire regiment.[18]

General Stuart, already saddened at having to abandon Northern Virginia, hated to see the regiment go. He rode past the ranks — according to one source, Stuart knew every man in his brigade by name — and "[gave] each man good bye."[19] The cavalry commander, who was quickly becoming close to Gordon, doubtless had a special farewell for the major who had shared the trial of Dranesville with him.

The next morning, the 1st North Carolina Cavalry began its trek to Weldon. New Bern fell while Gordon and the regiment marched south.

Threatened by multiple armies in Virginia, North Carolina, and elsewhere, the Confederacy was in such a predicament that even the placement of a regiment became controversial. Civilians and reporters became armchair generals. Some Virginians pointed to McClellan's army and warned the government that the 1st North Carolina Cavalry was needed in Virginia; dissenting North Carolinians, citing Burnside's invasion, pleaded for more help. Ransom could only follow his orders from Robert E. Lee, military adviser to President Davis. The 1st North Carolina Cavalry, several regiments from Norfolk, and two brigades from Johnston were to assist in the defense of North Carolina. Major General Theophilus Holmes, a North Carolina native, was to take command in the Old North State. The detachment represented ten percent of the strength of the main Confederate army in Virginia, so officials considered matters grave indeed. After all, it was said that a decisive battle could be expected at Kinston and Suffolk any day.[20]

The 1st's march to Weldon was a wet one. Davis recorded in his diary that "it rained abundance." Through Culpeper County and over the Rapidan and Rappahannock rivers, cold, mud, and rain became Gordon's constant companions and worst obstacles. One problem was Kelly's Ford, where the river flowed too high and too fast for the wagons. After a frustrating halt there, the North Carolinians pressed on. The men put in a few more days as mud travelers before arriving in Richmond on March 21. Camping on Reservoir Hill, they enjoyed two days of rest in the capital — there were no reviews and no grand welcomes this time — before taking to the road again. By way of Drewry's Bluff, the Rebel cavalrymen rode south. At Petersburg, the *Petersburg Express* "could scarcely refrain from comparing the worn and weary condition of the horses with the splendid appearance they presented in their passage through town some months ago." With its long train of baggage wagons in tow, the unit rode on, passing Stony Creek, Bellfield, and Boston before crossing the state line.[21] It had been five months since Gordon had last been in North Carolina.

Like the rain, it seemed as if the slow, tedious trip would never end. On March 29, after crossing the Roanoke River railroad bridge, the regiment finally arrived in Weldon, a tough place also known as "Hell's half acre." The North Carolinians found orders waiting on them there. General Holmes, who hoped to "authorize the commanding officer of that department to use [the regiment] if the enemy makes his appearance in that direction," instructed the regiment to pause in Weldon for a few days.[22] Camping between Weldon and Halifax, the men took a well-deserved break. As General Lee noted, the regiment's "horses were so much reduced that it was thought advisable to halt it temporarily at Weldon, for the purpose of recruiting."[23]

On April 1, Gordon saw another reason to fight for the Weldon line: ease and speed of travel. Ordered unexpectedly to Kinston, the cavalrymen climbed aboard railroad cars instead of horses. Leaving a detail to escort the regiment's horses to Kinston, the locomotive chugged southward toward the state's coastal plains. The men inside the cars were glad to be traveling with a minimum of effort. On April 2 the train arrived at its destination, five days before the horses.[24] The railroad's impact on Civil War troop movements proved valuable even in Gordon's service, if only to keep men rested.

The 1st North Carolina Cavalry had a new commander directing its movement south: Laurence Simmons Baker. Baker, promoted to colonel, assumed command of the 1st North Carolina Cavalry in early March when Ransom was promoted to brigadier general. Baker was a thirty-two-year-old native of Gates County. Following early education in North Carolina and at the Norfolk Academy, Baker had attended West Point. While at the military academy, a clerk erroneously altered the spelling of his name to "Lawrence." His name is still recorded that way in many sources. After graduating last in his 1851 class, he was commissioned second lieutenant in the 3d United States Cavalry. On the frontier he took part in Indian scouting and fighting. Rising to captain by the time North Carolina seceded from the Union, Baker resigned from the U.S. Army without hesitation and tendered his services to his native state. On March 16, 1861, he was commissioned lieutenant colonel in the Confederate army. Leaving his "delicate looking" wife behind, he had joined the 1st North Carolina Cavalry as Ransom's second in command.[25]

Ransom's and Baker's promotions left an opening in Baker's staff. Gordon was promoted to fill the position, and soon donned the two gold stars of a lieutenant colonel. His commission, which dated from March 1, was formally executed on April 3 in Raleigh.[26] While a major for nearly a year, Gordon's leadership abilities, management skills, and his way with the troops had evidently impressed his superiors. He would now be the regiment's second in command and assist Baker in administrative and military duties. One of Gordon's first tasks as lieutenant colonel was to assist in transferring the regiment from their first Kinston camp, situated in a pine forest along the railroad about six miles below Kinston, to a new position in the town's immediate defenses.[27] Located on Dibbles Field in east Kinston, two miles from the railroad, the men named it Camp Ransom to honor the balding yet inspiring leader who had made the regiment what it was.[28]

There the 1st North Carolina Cavalry found other Tarheel horse soldiers, many from units that Gordon would one day command. The 2d North Carolina Cavalry (Nineteenth Regiment North Carolina State Troops), and the several detached companies that would later form the 3d North Carolina Cavalry (Forty-first Regiment North Carolina State Troops) played a part in the Confederate defenses. The 2d, the regiment that had surrendered its sabres to the 1st the previous fall, was then still waiting for a supply of suitable arms. Making do with "almost every kind of arms (except the newest patterns) known to the warrior or sportsman," the unit had been serving in eastern North Carolina since October and had even fought at New Bern. They did have one thing over their rivals: troopers from the 1st had became discouraged by comparing their worn-out horses with the mounts of the 2d.[29]

General Holmes meshed the operations of these cavalry forces with his existing and newly-arrived infantry units. The reinforcements strengthened his force to four brigades of infantry and one of cavalry, totaling over 25,000 men. Holmes placed his men so they could defend both Kinston and Goldsboro because, as Sergeant J. M. Pugh of the 1st wrote, the Rebels expected "a battel [sic] here before long."[30]

Surprisingly, Burnside did not advance. On April 20, Federal General George B. McClellan warned Burnside about Confederate reinforcements sent from Virginia. He estimated that the force consisted of thirteen or fourteen infantry regiments, one horse regiment—which he identified as "Ransom's regiment of North Carolina cavalry"—and four light artillery batteries. McClellan further cautioned Burnside that he should entertain no thought of an offensive

Kinston, North Carolina, was one of the communities the 1st North Carolina Cavalry was sent to help defend in the spring of 1862 (Military Order of the Loyal Legion of the United States — Massachusetts Commandery Photograph Collection, U.S. Army Military History Institute, Carlisle Barracks, Pennsylvania).

movement until he freed his rear by capturing Fort Macon, the remaining Confederate-held entrance through the Outer Banks. After Burnside reduced Fort Macon on April 26, McClellan told Burnside to postpone his offensive until the fighting around Yorktown, Virginia concluded.[31]

In reality, McClellan was so completely fixed on his Yorktown battle that he ignored other opportunities. McClellan's march there had begun on March 17 when the "Young Napoleon" moved his army over water to Fort Monroe and then began marching up the Peninsula between the York and the James rivers — toward Richmond. McClellan moved slowly and deliberately; the Confederate troops on hand harassed the advance. That gave Johnston's army time to leave its Rappahannock River positions and rush to Richmond's defense. Facing such resistance with care, McClellan ordered Burnside to postpone the North Carolina offensive. That, coupled with the fact that Burnside had his own misgivings about the strength of his force, was the reason Gordon saw no real fighting that spring. Patrols and expeditions were the only offensive actions Burnside could take in the interim.[32]

So, as the Confederates awaited Burnside's attack, Burnside waited on McClellan and reinforcements. The 2d North Carolina Cavalry and the other area cavalry companies skirmished here and there, but the days passed with no significant fighting. Pugh told a friend that "there [are] plenty of yankees about here but they will not come close enough from New

Bern for to fight." Likewise, Gordon's view of the situation in North Carolina gradually changed. He became disillusioned with the transfer of his unit to Kinston: "I think there will be no advance of the enemy on this road. I regret much having left the enemy in Virginia."[33] (Holmes agreed, writing Lee that "there appears to be no disposition on the part of the enemy to advance in this direction.") Kinston, Gordon lamented, was not where he wanted to be. He wrote, "there will be much fighting [in Virginia] during the next 2 months, [but] I think we will have little to do here on this line." On a personal level, there was more to complain about. For one thing, Gordon was in a bad way for towels, drawers, and kid gloves. Could Frank Hackett arrange for him to receive some? Gordon also bemoaned the absence of his servant. Burt was in Wilkesborough, recovering from his illness. Gordon hoped that Burt could return soon, but only if his health were restored completely.[34]

Gordon was not the only grumbler in the 1st. As second in command, Gordon circulated the camps and listened to complaints. He got an earful. The troopers worried, Gordon said, that "it will be exceedingly hot here this summer, and nothing to eat but bread and bacon." Still, because he listened, Gordon's visibility improved morale and made an impression. One veteran remembered, "I saw Gordon standing under a large hickory tree.... He was a handsome soldierly looking man and reminded me of General [John B.] Gordon of Georgia."[35]

Off duty, Gordon relaxed and thought about home. He wondered how the family was getting along, especially Carrie and her new baby. He had the chance to spend a day with Colonel Barbour, who told Gordon he was pleased with his position in the service. He joined in campfire debates with the men. The recent Conscription Act, one topic of discussion at Dibbles Field, was affecting life even in Wilkes. In April, the Confederate government decided that all able-bodied white males between the ages of eighteen and thirty-five who were not in the service (with specified exemptions) were to be conscripted. Their service to the Confederacy would be for three years or the duration of the war. "How did the draft fall upon our people (in Wilkes)?" he wrote his brother-in-law. "The Conscription Act I think is the very thing for the occasion. It will bring into the service many men who have been shirking the cause."[36]

Yet the bottom line was that Gordon was frustrated. While Gordon was in Virginia, the action had been in North Carolina; while he was on duty in North Carolina, the action moved to Virginia. Except for moving their camps a few miles closer to Kinston, to an outpost named Camp Mars,[37] Gordon believed he was doing little that contributed to the war effort. What he did do often proved unpleasant. Baker was absent sick at the time so regimental duties fell to Gordon, including that of reviewing, approving, and forwarding certificates of disability. One case concerned Company K's James Anderson, a twenty-year-old trooper who suffered severely from hemorrhoids. "Anderson is badly gotten up," Gordon wrote. So what did that mean to the cavalry? In a characteristically blunt fashion, Gordon called Anderson a "worthless sort of a man." Another discharged from the service the same day was John Anderson, also of Company K. In Anderson's certificate, Gordon cited the man's age and the fact that he suffered from "acute rheumatism in damp weather," and declared that he was generally inefficient.[38]

Although he deplored the loss of any man, all in all it amounted to routine work, which Gordon had little use for. It meant only that the winter's idleness had returned:

> I received yours of the 3d a few days since we have fallen back to Kinston four miles from our former camp. No news here, no prospect of a fight, but we have just heard certainly that because [Confederate General Edward Johnson] has driven [Federal General Robert Milroy] back seven miles, repulsed him, and met Jackson in the valley of Virginia at McDowell's, gained a brilliant victory of the enemy, pursuing him with great

vigor, compelling him to leave his dead upon the field. This one received officially by telegraph, had it read to the troops on inspection this Sunday morning. If our army on the Peninsula can defeat McClellan I think that hostilities will soon close. Our regiment is chaffing here in idleness, all anxious to go to the scene of action. I would dislike for the war to end without ever having the pleasure of one proud charge upon an open plain at the enemy. But for the sake of our country's quiet I would forego it. We are still living very hard here but I can get along. You know I don't care much for anything besides cornbread and buttermilk which I can't get here. I am now the only field officer with the Regt. [since] Col. Baker [is] absent sick.... Tell Crowden not to plow the land too wet. I will write to him soon. I saw Allen on Friday. He is quite well and his company looks finely. I learned that Col. Stokes has been appointed to Brigadier Gen.; also Z.B. Vance.[39]

The regiment may have been chaffing in idleness, but the absence of fighting did help one thing. Their mounts, worn out from the hard winter of picket duty and the recent movement to North Carolina, gained valuable rest in Kinston. The result was that "our horses are improving rapidly," the new Lieutenant Colonel said.[40] There was much less need for a "Camp Cripple" in North Carolina than there had been in Virginia. Given the improvement of the horses, Baker and Gordon decided the regiment could increase picket duty and patrolling.

That was the case during the next few weeks. Like the 2d Cavalry's patrols, various parts of the 1st covered about four hundred miles of the Carolina countryside to parry Burnside's patrols and raids.[41] They scouted and picketed to divine enemy intentions. They patrolled and guarded against attack. Many of these nameless actions and expeditions have been lost to history, but they were significant to the men who fought them. Although a man or two would be killed and a few wounded in most of these outings, details were rarely recorded.

In mid–May, in an assault on Pollocksville, the regiment showed that no amount of training can prevent troopers from making mistakes. Baker, who had recovered from his illness, sent a dismounted detail of 150 men through a cane break to bypass Pollocksville and take up position behind it. There, Baker hoped, the detail would catch any Federals who retreated when the main part of the regiment advanced through town.

Under normal conditions the plan may have worked. In practice, problems arose. Harvey Davis of Company D served with the detail. "Those who have [not] tried to penetrate a cane break can have no idea of the undertaking," he wrote. "The reeds from 15 to 20 feet high and almost as thick as an ordinary wheat or rye field, with plenty of soggy boggy ground, progress is almost impossible." After the men floundered about in the thicket for a while, an officer figured they had gone far enough. The detachment turned to the right so as to strike the road back to town.[42]

Baker gave the detail what he thought was enough time to get into position before he ordered the regiment forward. As the main body moved on Pollocksville, Gordon and others saw soldiers exit the cane break about four hundred yards away. It was the detail, defeated by the cane break, but the Confederates did not know it. They thought their comrades were on the other side of Pollocksville. Baker identified them as the enemy and gave the order to charge. With guns ablaze, the regiment gave a rebel yell and pounded across the muddy ground toward the "foe." Ahead, Davis and his comrades escaped harm by hiding behind trees. The troopers only realized their mistake when they reached the detail. Although no one was hurt, the Yankees in Pollocksville saw the "hullabaloo" and prepared their defenses accordingly. Surprise being no longer possible, the regiment returned to camp.[43]

The regiment's movement on Pollocksville was an anomaly. Most of the 1st's cavalrymen, rather than advancing *en masse* on enemy positions, served in small detachments that spring, picketing or patrolling. On May 25, for example, one detachment, consisting of Companies

A and B, was ordered to the Roanoke River to defend against a supposed Federal advance on the railroad bridges at Weldon.[44] That advance never materialized. The Federals did, however, raid towns such as Washington and Plymouth but made no real advances on Holmes's main force. This became especially apparent one May evening. Near 11:00 P.M., the alarm sounded in the 1st's camps. A Federal attack was imminent! The troopers were ordered to be in the saddle in fifteen minutes; but the news of the enemy's advance turned out to be a hoax.[45] It was obvious that the war's focus was in Virginia.

The story was the same with the other North Carolina cavalry regiments around Goldsboro. A new commander, Colonel Solomon Williams, took over the 2d Horse in June after Colonel Spruill resigned and his replacement died. As they had since March, Spruill's and Williams's troopers continued to fight various small skirmishes with the Yankees.[46] The results of such fights were not always favorable, either. Poor performance at Gillet's Farm even brought charges that "the engagement was not creditable to the regiment."[47]

The hardships the 2d and the other cavalry units endured counted for good experience. However, before these units could be top-notch cavalry units like the 1st, they needed real fighting experience in Virginia under experienced leaders such as Stuart. The bad showing by the 2d at Gillet's gave evidence of that. Gordon could attest that those horse-soldiers had not seen the kind of war he had.

Gordon's fate to be away from the action continued to hold, but things were happening in Virginia that eventually changed that. McClellan continued his slow trudge up the Peninsula toward Richmond. A separate Union force under Irvin McDowell was near Fredericksburg, preparing to join McClellan. Simultaneously, another Federal army under Nathaniel P. Banks marched in the Shenandoah against a smaller force commanded by Stonewall Jackson. These multiple threats pressured the Confederate government to begin searching for reinforcements to help defeat the Northerners. In retrospect, the Virginians who had protested the transfer of the 1st North Carolina Cavalry to North Carolina had been right.

As Johnston's army began arriving on the Peninsula, it initially proved stubborn to McClellan's advance on Richmond. At Yorktown, Confederate General John B. Magruder's troops marched and countermarched. They feinted and moved. They made noise at every turn. Magruder's idea was to convince McClellan that the Confederate forces at Yorktown were large enough to stand and fight. The ploy worked. Rather than attacking such a "numerous" foe, McClellan took the time to besiege the Confederates. After lengthy preparations, McClellan finally got his siege train into position only to find that Magruder had withdrawn and joined the rest of Johnston's army. The Confederates had won time but still needed help.

McClellan's 100,000-man war machine began plodding toward Richmond again. Under the Army of the Potomac's pressure, Johnston decided to defend Richmond from the city's outskirts. In effect, after a rear-guard action at Williamsburg on May 5, and a few smaller such stands, Confederate defense of the lower Peninsula ceased. By May 17, Johnston's Confederate army had withdrawn to the suburbs of Richmond. The Federal army followed slowly.[48]

While thousands of blue-clad soldiers drew nigh Richmond, some events worked in Johnston's favor. As Gordon had announced to the men, Stonewall Jackson (with Lee's guidance from Richmond) conducted a masterful campaign in the Shenandoah Valley that befuddled the larger forces of Banks and John C. Fremont. At one point, Jackson even briefly threatened Washington. Jackson's presence at the northern end of the Valley worried Federal politicians enough to recall McDowell. Ultimately, Jackson and his men would escape from the Valley, beating up various Federal units in the process, and move to join the Confederate forces defending Richmond. Thus Jackson, while ensuring that McClellan would not be reinforced, would be around to strengthen the Richmond defenses.

For his part, Johnston could not wait for Jackson. He tried to alleviate the grim situation he faced with his own counter-offensive. He hoped to prevent the junction of McDowell and McClellan and the threat they posed to the Confederacy. He thought it necessary to attack the Federals and draw attention away from McDowell. When Stuart's cavalry scouts reported that McDowell had returned to Fredericksburg, however, Johnston decided to delay his planned assault until May 31. That allowed time for the troops of Major General Huger, the former defenders of Norfolk, to arrive and join in Johnston's attack. Johnston also redesigned the attack itself. He decided that the Federal southern flank, divided from the Federal northern flank by the Chickahominy River, was the most vulnerable. The gamecock general made that flank his target.

In Richmond, the Confederate government did what it could to support Johnston's offensive. Aware of their precarious position and of the value of the interior lines, officials began funneling other forces to reinforce Johnston. They looked everywhere for troops, including North Carolina.[49] As Burnside remained relatively quiet, the 1st North Carolina Cavalry became a candidate for duty in Virginia. Stuart, as Johnston's eyes and ears, could always use cavalry reinforcements. In late May, officials ordered the 1st North Carolina Cavalry to Johnston's aid. The 2d Horse and the various detachments of what would become the 3d North Carolina cavalry were left to handle the cavalry duties in eastern North Carolina on their own.

To get troopers to Richmond as quickly as possible, the regiment moved in increments. On May 27, Lieutenant Colonel Gordon took companies E, G, and K of the 1st and began the trek to Richmond. He led the unit toward his nation's capital with all dispatch. Colonel Baker and the rest of the regiment stayed on for a couple of days to break camp and pack equipment.

A Tarheel cavalryman later expressed the sentiment of the regiment over the whole expedition: "The capture of New Bern ought not to have occurred — at least it need not have taken place in 1862 ... if the authorities at Richmond had given it help with half the troops it uselessly sent down afterwards."[50]

Gordon was still urging his detachment over roads toward Richmond when fighting began anew outside Richmond. Johnston's attack, which resulted in the Battle of Seven Pines or Fair Oaks, was fairly sound in conception. It ended up little more than an organized mess that earned the Confederacy nothing. One Confederate cavalryman wrote that "the temporary success of the Confederates early in the engagement had been more than counterbalanced by the reverses they sustained on the second day...."[51] Several critical mistakes ruined any chance of Confederate success. The Federals, in turn, inflicted heavy casualties and kicked their enemy back to their original positions.

One of those Confederate casualties was Joseph E. Johnston. In an ironic way, the mismanaged battle of Seven Pines changed the course of the war. Because of Johnston's wound, Jefferson Davis named Robert E. Lee to command the Confederate army before Richmond on June 1.

While Lee began planning his first move and McClellan wondered what to do, the two armies "lay passively watching each other in front of Richmond."[52] On June 15, Lieutenant Colonel James B. Gordon, having retraced the route the regiment had taken in March, reached Richmond with his detail. He attached his three companies to General J. E. B. Stuart's command.

The remainder of the regiment did not ride directly to Richmond. Instead, Baker moved them around the northeastern part of the state to confuse the Federals. Leaving Camp Mars on May 29, the regiment marched northward via Snow Hill, Sparta, Tarboro, and Halifax. When they arrived in Halifax on June 2, Baker sent a detail to Wilkesborough to obtain fresh horses. (If Gordon heard of this detail and its destination, he was certainly disappointed not to be a part of it.) The regiment then moved to Clarksville, marked time there for a few days, countermarched to Tarboro, and again marched through Halifax. When the detail at last returned with the horses, the regiment rode for Richmond.[53]

Companies A and B, however, only watched as their comrades rode away. At the last moment, they had been ordered to stay and help defend against an expected Federal advance on the Weldon railroad bridges. It turned out that the real struggle these troopers, would face, save picketing and patrolling, was one unequal fight with gunboats along the Roanoke River.[54] The remainder of the regiment meanwhile plodded toward Richmond. Except for their arrival in their camps near Richmond, Baker's return to Virginia was uneventful. Traveling now familiar roads through Pleasant Hill Depot, Jarret's, and Petersburg, they rode by forced march.[55] The hard, fatiguing ride did not stop the men from their usual catcalling and talking. One trooper, Thomas N. Crumpler, spoke on a more serious topic: he told a correspondent that he was proud to be a member of the 1st and that he was especially looking forward to meeting the enemy. (That was certainly a change for Crumpler; he had been a proponent of the Union until Lincoln's 1861 call for men to put down the Southern rebellion.)[56] Soon, Crumpler and his fellow troopers would have their opportunity.

On Friday, June 28, the North Carolinians reached the capital and rejoined Gordon's detachment.[57] Years later, veterans would recall little about this trip to Richmond, but few ever forgot what it was like to ride into a city at war. When they dismounted that summer morning, the men heard cannons roaring in the distance.[58] The fight for Richmond had begun.

5

Wholesome Lessons

"If our army on the Peninsula can defeat McClellan," Gordon had written, "I think hostilities will soon close." The time had come to see if he was right. On June 15, Lieutenant Colonel Gordon and the three companies under his command joined the embattled army. After passing through Richmond, which was packed with the wounded, the drilling, and preparing citizens, they camped on the east side of the James River about one mile from the Capitol. The very tension in the air told Gordon that he had found the war.[1] McClellan was knocking on the gates of Richmond, and Lee was planning to keep him out.

As Gordon and his men began setting up their tents, one thing became evident: a scarcity of cavalrymen, save the sick and an occasional unit or two.[2] It turned out that a large portion of the Confederate horse was in the field, riding around the enemy's army. Just five days before, Stuart had met with General Lee. As they talked, Lee told Stuart that he had plans to assault McClellan's right flank, north of the Chickahominy River. For the attack to succeed, information about that flank was vital. Securing that information was Stuart's job. Stuart gladly accepted the assignment and expanded on it with an idea of his own. Perhaps, once he learned the exact position of the Federal right, he would continue to ride until he circled completely around McClellan's army. Such a move would mislead the enemy, who would expect him to return the way he came. It would also enhance the reputation of the Confederate cavalry. Enjoining caution, Lee did not restrain Stuart's creativity.

Stuart's first large raid in the Union rear became the blueprint for his later raids — the ones Gordon would participate in. Into the unknown the troopers went. The command, composed of 1,200 men from the 1st, 4th, and 9th Virginia regiments, the Jeff Davis Legion, and the horse artillery, rode by day and night. They moved north up the Brook Turnpike, turned east at the South Anna River, and then searched for the Federal flank while thoroughly studying the features of the countryside. On a couple of occasions the Rebels met Yankee resistance, and there were collisions of horse and man, steel and flesh. Each time the bluecoats melted away, but the price they extracted was the life of Captain William Latane. News of Latane's death spread so quickly that Gordon heard of it when he arrived in Richmond. According to the scuttlebutt, Latane had been shot through with two balls. One infantryman, a Virginian who had grown up with Latane, confided to his diary that "a more noble, brave, generous, correct, man never lived." Latane's death was an event that at once symbolized both the pride and the tragedy of Stuart's cavalry: the pride of young cavaliers and brave deeds, and the tragedy of a dying generation.[3] For years after the war, a painting of Latane's burial would hang in Gordon's "Oakland."

As he had suggested to Lee, Stuart continued his ride around the Union army. While it was the route the enemy did not expect him to take, Stuart also wanted to chance "having to swim the Chickahominy and make a bold effort to cut the enemy's lines of communication."⁴ If Stuart had known that Federal efforts to capture the raiders, directed by his own father-in-law, General Philip St. George Cooke, were meager, slow, and ineffective, it would have made his decision even easier. Onward they rode, passing completely around McClellan's army. At last, the exhausted troopers dashed to the Chickahominy River and the protection of friendly forces. Only then did an enemy contingent really challenge the cavalrymen. By building a makeshift bridge over the Chickahominy, the grayclad cavalrymen escaped from Federal controlled territory.⁵

On June 16, the weary but triumphant troopers filed into camp. There, amid the admiration of the entire Confederacy, they found legend growing around their exploits. One who rode with Stuart remembered that "the country rang out with praises of the men who had raided entirely around General McClellan's powerful army, bringing prisoners and plunder from under his very nose." R. E. Lee called it a "signal success" and expressed "his admiration of the courage and skill so conspicuously exhibited throughout by the general and the officers and men under his command."⁶

Before the raid, Lee had ordered Stuart to leave behind enough cavalry "for the service of [the] army." As late arrivals, Gordon's men became part of the horse reserve. The duty was not rigorous, so Gordon found time on his hands. At one point, he may have tried to track down an old family member. The story is told that an old, feeble man, dressed in homespun, squirrel rifle in hand, appeared at General D. H. Hill's tent. The man was searching for Colonel Alfred H. Scales's 13th North Carolina so he could replace his dead son. "We must whip those yankees," he told Hill. Since it was near sundown, Hill invited the man to spend the night in his tent. The next morning he continued on his mission as Hill could not dissuade him. As it turned out, the man's name was Gordon and he was from Milton, North Carolina. Hill wrote that J. B. Gordon took "quite an interest in him, and we believe, traced up some sort of relationship."⁷

In any event, Gordon only had to wait a day for the return of Stuart's raiders. There was plenty of makeshift celebration for the Carolinians to join. With the raid's successful conclusion, pride and *esprit de corps* became real weapons for Stuart's cavalry. The praise that was heaped on the veterans of Stuart's raid caused Gordon to hope for action all the more. As one of his troopers said, the boys are in good spirits and anxious to "have a hand in it."⁸

Having armed Lee with knowledge of the position of the enemy's flank,

A native of Gates County and a graduate of West Point, Laurence Baker became the 1st North Carolina Cavalry's second commander (Library of Congress).

Stuart now readied his cavalry brigade to assist the infantry's planned offensive. Baker and the remainder of the regiment reached Richmond on June 28 after their countermarching between Halifax, Clarksville, and Tarboro.[9] Including the 1st North Carolina Cavalry, Stuart's cavalry was then the equivalent of a large brigade, containing the 1st, 3d, 4th, 5th, 9th, and 10th Virginia Cavalry Regiments, the Georgia Legion, the 15th Virginia Battalion, the Hampton Legion, the Jeff Davis Legion, and the horse artillery.[10] As of July 20, these units boasted 5,277 men as "aggregate present." Adding those troopers who were absent on other duties, wounded, or sick, the brigade totaled 6,724 men.[11]

Meanwhile, McClellan moved his army little during June. Rather than take the opportunity to deal the Confederacy a heavy blow, the Federal general soon talked himself out of attacking at all. Instead, he decided to disengage his army from Richmond and move it to the James River, where he would be protected by the guns of the United States Navy. His opponent, the new commander of the Army of Northern Virginia, meanwhile did have attack in mind. Based on the knowledge gained from Stuart's ride, Lee's design called for Jackson to swoop down from the Valley and outflank the Federals from their strong defensive positions. Simultaneously, the bulk of the Confederate army would drive along the Chickahominy's north bank and rout McClellan. This would provide Richmond breathing room and give Lee a fighting chance to destroy much of his adversary's army.

The larger part, and by implication the best part, of the Confederate cavalry, directed by Stuart, was to serve as the eyes, ears, and guides of Lee's north-bank attack.[12] Meanwhile, Lee ordered Colonel Baker to take command of those troopers operating south of the Chickahominy.[13] Those units were the 1st North Carolina, the 3d Virginia, the 5th Virginia, and a squadron from the Hampton Legion that was attached to the 5th. With Baker coordinating, the 1st North Carolina and Tom Rosser's 5th Virginia were to observe the Darbytown, Varina, and Osborne roads, while the 3d Virginia Cavalry patrolled the Charles City Road. If any Federal movement toward the James River or along the Chickahominy was detected, the regiments were to notify the nearest commander and then harass and hinder the enemy until reinforcements arrived.[14] Any Federal attempts to move across the White Oak Swamp toward the James River had to be spotted, for there was the vulnerable part of Lee's plan. While most of the Confederate army was on the offensive north of the Chickahominy, only a thin defense guarded the direct approach to Richmond. A determined westward thrust there could easily have punched through the Southern defenses. Or a Federal withdrawal to the James River would offer new problems and opportunities and force a change in Confederate strategy. As such, the southside cavalry had drawn an important, though inglorious, assignment.

On June 26 the infantry battle began, but not as set down on paper. As Lee's plan unfolded, the unexpected happened. Stonewall Jackson failed to complete his assignments. As a result, the Union troops on the river's north bank were waiting in prepared defensive positions when Lee attacked. Thus, after capturing Mechanicsville, the Confederates smacked head-on into General Fitz John Porter's Federals along Beaver Dam Creek. The Confederates were subsequently slaughtered in a miscoordinated attack. The carnage touched thousands of families throughout the South. Miles Cowles, a brother of William H. H. Cowles, was one who died of wounds received at the Battle of Mechanicsville.[15]

That day, Gordon could have changed his mind about cavalry service being more dangerous than infantry service. Gordon's old unit, Company B (Wilkes Valley Guards) of the 1st North Carolina Infantry Regiment, was one of the units that charged the tough Federal positions near Beaver Dam Creek. The Unionists crushed the Confederate advance and mauled the regiment, which lost 142 men.[16] Gordon's half brother Allen, commanding Company B, survived the battle unwounded but had many a narrow escape. Afterward, he was promoted to colonel and assumed command of the regiment because Colonel Stokes fell mortally wounded. Stokes spent his last moments as he had lived his life:

> [Stokes's] surgeon stood mournfully by. [Stokes's] cheek had the pallor of death; his eye had lost its luster, and his hands had the clammy coldness of dissolution. He needs stimulants, the doctor suggested.... [Stokes said,] "Yes, I should be glad to have some, but the other boys here need it as much as I, and we cannot get enough for all. I am very thankful, but do not wish that you should trouble yourself for me."[17]

Losing a friend like Montford Stokes hurt Gordon. He had always looked up to Stokes. He had taught Gordon everything about the basics of being a soldier. Calling up memories of the pre-war days around Wilkesborough or of the founding of the Wilkes Valley Guards, Gordon thought about his friendship with Stokes and mourned his passing. That war was death had become all to clear. Yet that was not all he had to mourn. The same day, the fourteen-year-old daughter of Augustus and Martha Finley—Gordon's niece—died in Wilkesborough.

The next day, Porter's Federals fell back to another strong position near Gaines's Mill. The Confederates followed, attacking with a plan similar to that of the previous day. Again, however, something went wrong with Jackson's flanking mission. Lee's assault on the Federal center suffered as the Confederates again found their enemy stoutly entrenched. Only Herculean efforts—paid for dearly—gained the Confederates a victory of sorts.

By now, Lee had begun to suspect that McClellan was retreating toward the James River and not just reeling from Confederate blows. Columns of dust rising from the south, intelligence from his commanders, cavalry reports, and even the reactions of the enemy at Beaver Dam Creek and Gaines's Mill were indications, if not proof.[18] Solid proof did come on June 29 when Stuart found that McClellan's Chickahominy base had been abandoned. Other scouts discovered empty Federal trenches before Richmond.

With grim purpose, Lee quickly revised his strategy and began shifting his troops to the south bank of the Chickahominy. At Savage's Station, on June 29, the Confederates took another swing at McClellan; but again, problems prevented Lee from striking with effect. Given the weak pursuit, not to mention stubborn Federal resistance, the battle gained Lee nothing. On June 30, Lee had one last chance to catch his prey. In an attack near Glendale, the Confederates fought gallantly, charging through confusing terrain. They hoped to cut off at least half of the Federal army with converging columns that would close a three-sided box around the retreating Federals. If Lee's forces cut that road, McClellan would be in trouble. The Confederates managed to push the Federals back until they only held a portion of their previous line, but McClellan still escaped from Lee's trap. Try as he might, Lee found himself unable to wield the Army of Northern Virginia efficiently. "Under ordinary circumstances," he later reported, "the Federal army would have been destroyed."

Stuart's horse-soldiers served in this struggle, yet the troopers' performance also fell short of expectations after the stunning success of their "ride." Late on June 25, Lee ordered Stuart to move out. Under orders to guide Jackson to the Union flank, Stuart set out with Fitz Lee's 1st Virginia, William Wickham's 4th Virginia, "Rooney" Lee's 9th Virginia, W. T. Martin's Jeff Davis Legion, Thomas R. R. Cobb's Georgia Legion, and Captain John Pelham's horse artillery. Stuart skirmished with the enemy while successfully conducting Jackson to the Federal flank. After the battle at Gaines's Mill, Lee ordered Stuart to leave the main army and ride eastward to the nearest point of the York River Railroad. There he could cut McClellan's line of communications and intercept his retreat.[19] Skirmishing, snipping telegraph wires and tearing up tracks as they went, the horse soldiers reached McClellan's base on June 29. There, they found what Lee had suspected — that McClellan was retreating. Stuart's men enjoyed the lavish remnants of McClellan's supply base, taking time out only to destroy excess supplies and to chase off a Federal gunboat with artillery.

Meanwhile, the 1st North Carolina Cavalry and the other horse units south of the Chickahominy found life a bit harder. One of the unit's earliest challenges came near an insignificant run on the Peninsula when, with the 9th Virginia and the Cobb Legion in support, the 1st prepared to charge an obstinate enemy force. The plan went awry, however, when the Virginians mistook the movements of the Tarheels for the advance of the enemy and retreated. The charge never took place, leaving some horse artillerymen to fire away at the enemy the rest of the day.[20] On the night of June 28, after General Lee placed him in command of all cavalry south of the Chickahominy River, Baker directed his cavalrymen to pinpoint the Federal army's location. Lee wanted a "cordon of troops and vedettes extending completely around McClellan's army," and to Baker's men fell a large part of the responsibility. Baker's force represented the only cavalry with the army at the time.[21]

Southern cavalrymen spread about the countryside. Scouts were dispatched and couriers raced from commander to commander to report any new intelligence. Patrols kicked up the dust of the Peninsula roads and suffered in the summer heat. When the men paused to gnaw on their rations of hard bread and bacon, the rumbling of cannon could be heard in the distance. Then they would continue, struggling through terrain that was anything but hospitable for cavalry.[22]

Stuart believed that a Union victory would be worse than anything the Peninsula offered. He instructed the cavalrymen south of the Chickahominy to remember "that it is our first duty to whip the enemy, and to effect that no necessary sacrifice is too great, no hardship too severe."[23] Gordon agreed. He, like the rest of the cavalrymen, bore the hardships and continued to manage his search of the countryside.

They examined every inch of the area. Colonel Goode's 3d Virginia and parts of the 1st North Carolina Cavalry rode the Charles City Road. Gordon and Rosser employed their units along other routes, such as the Darbytown and Osborne roads, watching for Federal movements across the Chickahominy toward the James River. Learning of a camp of retreating Federals near Willis Methodist Church on Willis Church Road (Quaker Road), Baker decided to drive in the Federal pickets there to see for himself.[24] He took the 3d Virginia Cavalry as well as five companies of 1st, even though those tired men had only arrived in Virginia the day before by way of forced marches.

R. E. Lee did not know for sure which roads McClellan was using in his retreat, so he hoped that Baker would find out. Baker did his best. At about 9:00 A.M. on Sunday, June 29, Baker's graybacks approached the Willis Church area and ran into a strong patrol of infantry and cavalry.[25] Their chance for a fight having finally come, the Carolina cavalrymen charged a group of Union pickets and sent them reeling, killing one and wounding one. This provided little information, however, so the cavalrymen kept going.[26] They rode through a patch of woods and entered a field, at the end of which was the Willis Church Road (Quaker Road) itself. Turning onto the lane in column of fours,[27] Baker's eager force ran straight into the foe. "In an instant," Rufus Barringer remembered, "artillery and infantry of the enemy opened upon our devoted heads, all huddled up in the lane, where orders and maneuvers were alike impossible." Barringer's Cabarrus County company rode in the column's center. Baker gave the order to retreat, but Barringer did not hear it. He told his men to stay put even as the rest of the column tried to get out of the trap.[28] "Attention, Company F! Stand firm! I will myself ride to the front and see if the orders (to retreat) are correct!" Barringer yelled. After

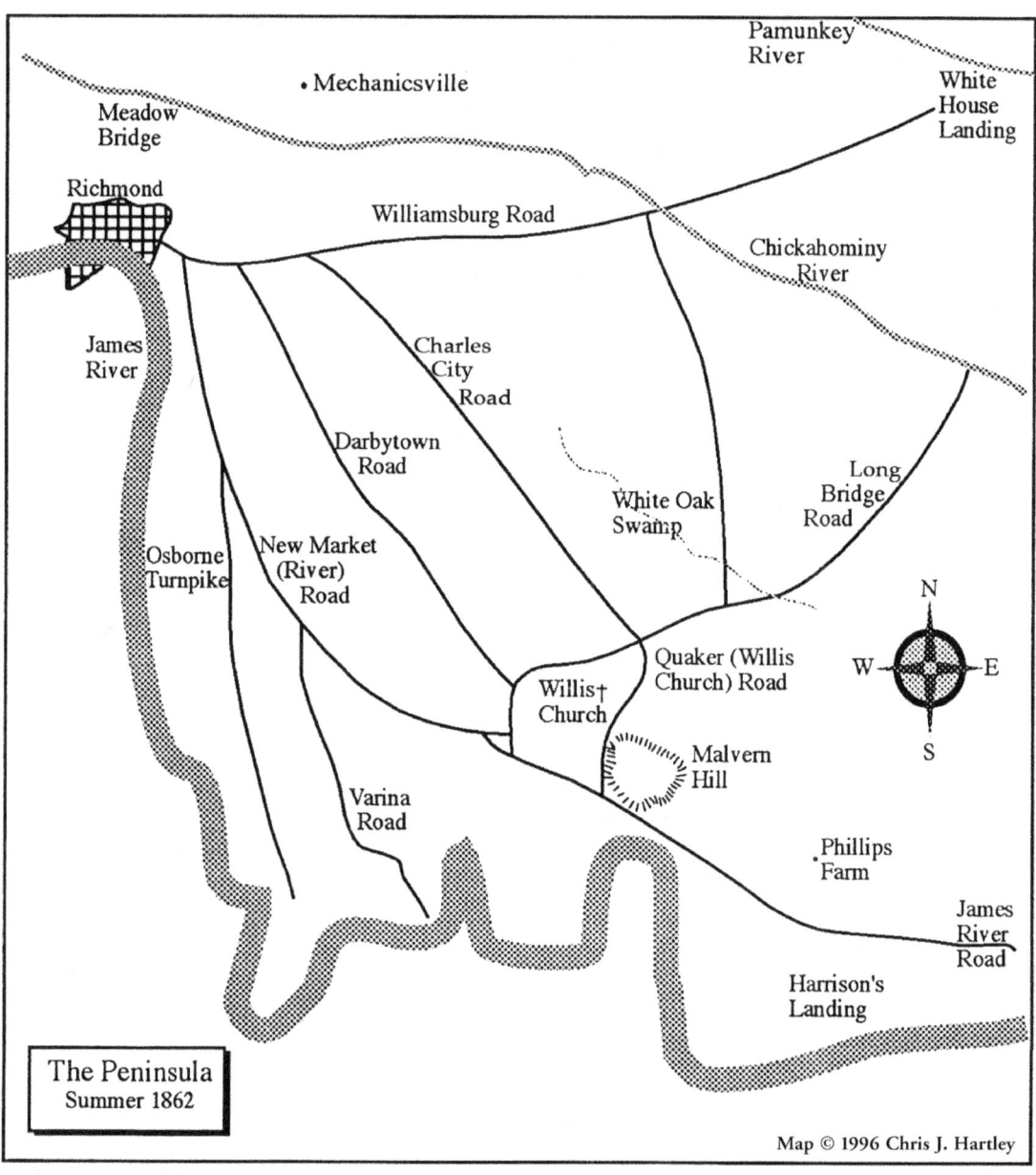

The Peninsula
Summer 1862

Map © 1996 Chris J. Hartley

a quick check, he came galloping back and ordered, "Company F! The orders are correct. By fours, left a-bout wheel, and *run like the devil!*"[29]

It was too late for most of them. Metal tore into the exposed cavalrymen, unhorsing them by the dozen. The volleys killed or wounded more than sixty North Carolinians and several horses.[30] One who fell dead was Baker's courier, Private M. L. White. Another was Thomas N. Crumpler, who during the march to Richmond had expressed his readiness to fight. Marching at the head of the column, Crumpler was struck fifteen times, at least once in the torso by a minie ball. When the Yankees later found him, however, Crumpler was still alive. As he expired, the man boasted about killing a Yankee, and then cursed the North. Those Confederates who survived "fled in great disorder toward Richmond," even at the price of leaving their casualties on the ground. W. W. Averell, a friend of Baker's in the pre-war army, was the commander of the victorious Federal cavalrymen. His troopers chased the retreating graybacks for two miles, collecting a few more prisoners in the process.[31]

As it turned out, Baker had accidentally led his men straight into a Federal position defended by the 2d Rhode Island and the 7th Massachusetts infantry regiments, 2 artillery batteries, and a squadron of cavalry. In fact, it was later rumored that Baker had been careless because of "too much whiskey."[32] From the Federal standpoint, the success had been due to either chance or fortuitous planning. At least two witnesses — Rebel Harvey Davis and Federal General Darius Couch — called the fight an accident. Averell later credited the victory to a Yankee trap, but that is suspect because he did not mention it in his after-action report.[33]

Ironically, the Federal force included troopers from the 3d Pennsylvania Cavalry — the same unit routed by Ransom and Gordon at Vienna. Revenge came sweet to the Federals. They talked over the Vienna fight with their prisoners, who acknowledged that Willis Church had "fully squared accounts." At the same time, the whipping was hard on the Tarheels who had escaped. One later wrote, "This disaster served as a wholesome lesson in making mounted charges." And as if to rub salt into their wounds, scouts from the 5th Virginia searching along the Quaker Road recaptured fifteen of the 1st's horses. That was prominently reported to Stuart, as if to say the Carolinians could not have done it themselves.[34]

The 1st North Carolina Cavalry, having suffered more battle casualties in five minutes than it had during the first ten and a half months of its existence, returned to Confederate lines to recover. They stayed on Lee's right to monitor McClellan's movements. The unit's primary mission was to insure that the Unionists did not cross to the south bank of the James.

Willis Church today. Near here, Federal forces gave the 1st North Carolina Cavalry a "wholesome lesson in making mounted charges" (author's photograph).

On June 30, while the guns of Frayser's Farm roared ominously in the distance, Baker kept his cavalry to the army's right, watching Federal movements. His men may have been involved in the cavalry skirmish that played out before the advance of Longtreet's and A. P. Hill's divisions along the Long Bridge Road.[35]

On July 1, a Tuesday, McClellan concentrated his army near the James River on a hill called Malvern. His troops occupied yet another strong position; Malvern Hill, he said, "could justly be regarded as impregnable." His trains were well on their way to Harrison's Landing, where they would be protected by powerful naval guns. He also could easily withdraw the rest of his army — as he intended to do — to where the gunboats would protect them. With all the odds stacked in his favor, he allowed his army to make a stand. Ostensibly, fighting it out on the slopes of Malvern Hill would check the Confederate pursuit, gaining more time for the trains to escape.[36]

Colonel Thomas Rosser of the 5th Virginia Cavalry had informed General Lee of the Federal retreat across Malvern Hill. So with recent failures nagging him, Lee came up. Confederate troops probed the Federal defenses during the morning hours. The two sides commenced an artillery duel that afternoon, the Confederates hoping to break up the overwhelming Union artillery advantage. Though the Federals won the long-range fight in short order, the Confederates soon launched their first full-scale attack. A Federal volley easily shattered Lee's mid-afternoon infantry thrust. After two hours of relative silence, the Confederates came again. This time, McClellan remembered, their charges were desperate. "They were always repulsed with the infliction of fearful loss, and in several instances our infantry awaited their approach within a few yards, poured in a single volley, and then dashed forward with the bayonet."[37] Repeated Confederate attacks — all unsuccessful — continued until dark.

The 1st North Carolina Cavalry joined the Confederates on the scene, but played no part in the battle. For most of the day, the regiment, along with the attached 3d and 5th Virginia cavalry regiments, was posted on the left of Stonewall Jackson's corps, east of the Quaker Road. There the men searched for prisoners.[38] As the hot day progressed and they took few prisoners, Gordon would often stand near his mount — his favorite was an iron gray charger he called Pigeon — and try to watch the action.[39] Before his eyes, the infantry lines surged up Malvern Hill toward the smoke-wreathed crest, fought, and then came streaming back in shambles. Considering their recent "lesson" Gordon knew that the cavalry had no business attacking, but his thoughts ran to the contrary. Gordon wanted to charge. He had seen the dead and felt the cruel impact of war; he had lost people close to him. Other friends had also been killed, wounded, or were missing, mostly from Willis Church. The thought that his other half brother, Allen, was somewhere on the field, perhaps on the hill itself, did not help. In such a state of mind, "he would have charged McClellan's massed artillery" without hesitation.[40] Yet at that moment, there were plenty of Confederates swarming up the hill to charge Federal positions, and they were being slaughtered.

Gordon's desire to charge the Federal guns, although misdirected, was perhaps not far from the mark. One Federal cavalryman believed that "it was a discredit to Stuart's cavalry" that it had attempted no reconnaissance of the Federal center and right on July 1. Had the horse soldiers scouted, he said, they probably would have discovered that the Federal center and right were more vulnerable to attack than the left.[41] Stuart, the man who could have ordered such a reconnaissance, was not at Malvern Hill. He was still trying to reach the battle, delayed because he had been posted along the Chickahominy for too long. Lee was perhaps so wrapped up in learning how to wield his new army that he did not properly use all the resources he had on hand.[42] Gordon, although in no place to authorize an attack, knew the cavalry had to do something to help. He voiced his desire to help so loudly that one man who was several miles away would hear of it and remember it after the war.[43]

When the sun at last set — albeit slowly to those who had to watch or fight — it was serenaded by the spattering of musket and artillery fire. At last the battle, and with it Lee's last real chance to catch McClellan, ended. Leaders considering their troops' performances saw that they had much to learn. Lee looked to his army and Stuart to his cavalry to make adjustments or reflect on how troops reacted in the fighting. As for the Tarheels, one Federal prisoner provided qualitative evidence of their fighting abilities. "Give N. Carolinian's a barlow knife and they will charge h — l for a canteen and a haversack," he wrote.[44] The 1st North Carolina Cavalry displayed this attitude and came through the Seven Days battered but wiser, although its commander did not emerge from the Seven Days battles without blemish.

Gordon impressed his superiors with a solid performance, much of it while commanding independently. He had proven himself a leader by his work with the detachment. He had led his unit admirably from North Carolina to its Seven Days operations. Thanks to his management, the unit had covered the distance without incident and arrived in time to assist Lee in patrolling and picketing. Yet all was not perfect with him; like most of Stuart's cavalrymen, Gordon had failed to secure timely and valuable information. Indeed, the Confederate campaign had suffered from a great lack of intelligence, and the blame for that belonged in part to Stuart's cavalry.[45] Gordon was learning, though. His state of mind at Malvern Hill showed that his imagination in command and grasp of cavalry tactics and strategy were improving.

On the evening of July 1, with the dead of the battle still strewn across the grassy fields, McClellan began withdrawing to Harrison's Landing. Meanwhile, at the foot of Malvern Hill, Stuart arrived with the bulk of the cavalry. The next day, near Gatewood's on Jackson's left, Baker formally reunited his cavalrymen with Stuart. The 1st was placed in reserve. It spent that rainy day reconnoitering, rounding up Federal stragglers and abandoned equipment, and burying the dead. Afterward, they camped a few miles east of Malvern Hill near Phillips's Farm.[46]

If the Seven Days had proven anything, it was that Gordon was not a prognosticator. Although Lee's army had inflicted a defeat of sorts, hostilities did not end. Instead of a victorious celebration, Stuart's cavalry kept after McClellan until they were turned away in a controversial skirmish at Evelington Heights.[47]

On July 10, Stuart assigned a portion of his cavalry to picket duty on the Charles City Road. The 1st North Carolina Cavalry was one of the units that drew the assignment. Their Phillips's Farm camp was close enough for the work, and their familiarity with the area also proved beneficial. Besides, the troopers needed work to get their minds off the events of July 9, when a trooper from Company F, W. A. Blackwelder, had accidentally been shot. Baker and Gordon placed the pickets carefully and directed their attention toward the James. Through these dispositions, Stuart was able to keep tabs on McClellan in the unlikely event that he should venture forth from Harrison's Landing.[48]

Meanwhile, the remainder of Stuart's cavalry was ordered to rest and recruit "in the fresh country" near Hanover Court House. Initially, cavalry headquarters were established north of Richmond on a farm near Atlee's Station on the Virginia Central Railroad. While there, Stuart took the opportunity to show off his troops by staging a cavalry review. On July 21, cavalry headquarters moved to Hanover Court House. Stuart planned to resume the drilling of his men and continue regular duties there, including picketing and patrolling to the north. Stuart again reviewed his might while at Hanover.[49]

The cavalrymen around Hanover Court House rested, cleaned their uniforms and themselves, cared for their mounts, and sought pleasant pursuits.[50] In contrast, the 1st's picket duty near Harrison's Landing did not bring the same amount of relaxation, but at least there was time for talk. In the midst of such banter, Gordon may have mentioned that he felt like he would survive the war. According to one fellow trooper, who observed this feeling in Gordon, "He often spoke hopefully and happily of his future and the prospect that awaited him on the return of peace." Whatever the subject of conversation, the act of watching proved monotonous and tiring,[51] compounding the effects of the recent travels and the hard campaign. Stuart recognized that. On July 22, he relieved the regiment and sent it to Hanover Court House. Gordon looked forward to a few days of rest in the warm weather. It was not to be, however. The regiment had hardly arrived at Hanover when, on July 24, new orders came down: the regiment was to go on scout. They were given only fifteen minutes to cook three days' worth of rations, but boots and saddles sounded before the men could even collect enough wood for cooking fires. The "hungry[,] grumbling" and tired soldiers were again in the saddle. Baker and Gordon led them away from camp.[52]

The regiment moved toward Fredericksburg by way of Hanover Junction and Massaponax Church. It was the same route they had taken in October 1861, but this time there were no cheering crowds to meet them. Instead, just thirteen miles outside Fredericksburg, the advance guard met and drove off a Federal picket. The troopers paused and "fed on the corn that the yankees had intended for their stock." It was not as extravagant as the food Stuart's men had enjoyed at McClellan's abandoned base, but it was good enough. When they at last moved ahead, scouts saw a Federal force too strong for the regiment to handle. Baker apparently decided that he had learned enough, so he and Gordon led the regiment back to its Hanover camp. The only other incident of note occurred when a gunboat (probably in the James River) fired on part of the regiment, wounding a horse in the mouth; but that was all.[53]

Hanover Court House was an old brick structure that was the site of a famous Patrick Henry speech. An "ancient tavern," and a few other buildings with "modest roofs," sat nearby. The whole was surrounded by "fertile fields waving with golden grain...." The summer sun warmed the men of the 1st in this picturesque setting. They enjoyed the band music of nearby enemy forces, rested, "cooked and ate, drank, and [were] merry."[54] The men apparently did this with relish. Soon, one Tarheel trooper wished for a regimental chaplain "for if wickedness is a criterion by which to judge we certainly stand very much in need of one."[55]

In the meantime, Confederate military leadership applied the lessons of the Seven Days by reorganizing the army. General Lee thought the cavalry needed centralized direction, so the horse units were included in the reorganization. On July 28, while the 1st resumed drilling, Jeb Stuart was promoted to major general.[56] As for the cavalry's reorganization, Special Orders Number 165 realigned the expanding cavalry into a division of two brigades. Wade Hampton and Fitzhugh Lee were promoted to command the brigades. The 1st North Carolina Cavalry was assigned to the unit of the senior brigadier, Hampton, along with the Cobb Legion, the Jeff Davis Legion, the Hampton Legion, and the 10th Virginia. "Fitz" Lee's Brigade consisted of the 1st, 3d, 4th, 5th, and 9th Virginia Regiments.[57]

Of the two new brigadier generals, one was Gordon's junior in age. Fitzhugh Lee, nephew of Robert E. Lee, had been born in Fairfax County, Virginia, on November 19, 1835. In 1856, he graduated forty-fifth in a class of forty-nine at West Point. (His uncle, the academy superintendent, had at one time strongly considered dismissing him for his unruly behavior.) "Fitz" Lee's first assignment was as instructor in the cavalry school at Carlisle, Pennsylvania. Afterward, he rode the Texas frontier with the 2d U.S. Cavalry. During a battle with Comanche Indians, he was shot through the lungs with an arrow. After recovering, he again served as a cavalry instructor, this time at West Point, until the Civil War broke out. Resigning his commission and offering his services to Virginia, Lee was commissioned first lieutenant in the Confederate cavalry and quickly rose to colonel. Lee's strong cavalry background and his staff experience with Beauregard and with Richard Ewell at Manassas served him well as a leader of horse soldiers. However, given his family connections to the commanding general, his appointment was attended with some grumbling.[58]

In joining the brigade of Wade Hampton, Gordon became subordinate to a man who was not unlike himself. A rich South Carolinian, Hampton was the first man to attain brigade command under Jeb Stuart without any prior military training — a testimony to his natural abilities. Born in Charleston, South Carolina on March 28, 1818, Hampton graduated from South Carolina College and went on to study law. Also a plantation owner, he was anything but a vigorous proponent of the economy of slave labor. He worked to counteract some of the policies of the "fire-eaters" in the state legislature. Hampton, his large frame often draped with a worn, faded, plain gray coat, was a man who inclined toward the serious; he smiled more often than he laughed. His "face was browned by sun and wind, and half covered by dark sidewhiskers joining a long moustache of the same hue; the chin bold, prominent, and bare. The eyes were brown, inclining to black, and very mild and friendly; the voice low, sonorous, and with a certain accent of dignity and composure."[59] In his youth, Hampton had passed many pleasant summers in western North Carolina. The summer of 1861, however, was a violent one for the South Carolinian. He won distinction as commander of the Hampton Legion at First Manassas, and later fought well on the Peninsula. By the time Gordon met him in the cavalry brigade, Hampton had already been wounded twice. The man was a fighter.[60]

The men Hampton now commanded, and the men Gordon joined, had much in common. They were, one witness said, "An impulsive youth, most of them brought up in the lap of luxury and ease — fresh from college and schools. Men of worth and standing, from the desk, the shop, the office, and the farm, had been transformed into the hardy and dashing trooper."[61] There was little time for such transformations, however. The Confederate cavalry, thanks to scouts from Hanover Court House like the one Gordon had participated in, learned of a new Federal threat. On July 12, General Lee discovered that the enemy had occupied Culpeper Courthouse, which threatened the capital's only direct line of rail communication with the Shenandoah Valley.[62] The key danger came from a newly organized fifty thousand-man force, Major General John Pope's Union Army of Virginia. In Washington, Lincoln had tired of hearing McClellan's demands for reinforcements and decided to combine them with Pope's army for a new offensive, so on August 3 the administration ordered Harrison's Landing evacuated. Lincoln hoped that Pope, a commander fresh from victories in the West, would defeat Lee where others had failed. Lee, however, anticipated this move, and also remembered that Burnside's army, which had arrived from North Carolina and stood poised for action at Fortress Monroe, constituted a separate threat. Clearly, Lee had to do something before these Federal forces could unite and overwhelm him.

In mid–July, Lee accordingly ignored McClellan, who was still at Harrison's Landing, and ordered Jackson to move north to deal with Pope. Reinforced by A. P. Hill in early August, Jackson felt strong enough to strike Pope's advance. At Cedar Mountain on August 9, Stonewall did just that and defeated a portion of Pope's army. The bad news, of course, was that McClellan's Federals were thought to be on the way.

A bloody summer it was, and to make matters worse Gordon had to worry about his family as well. By late July, death and illness rampaged through his clan. Gordon's sister Martha wrote that Mrs. Brown "is still very low with fever, we fear very much, that she will never recover, Carrie is getting better slowly, has had a very severe attack, my own health is feeble it seems difficult for me to get over our terrible affliction in the death of my dear child [14-year-old Ann]."[63] Fortunately, his mother and sisters shook off their illnesses in time.

Gordon maintained the delicate balance between home and duty as best as he could. Certainly he wanted to be at home, but he remained in Virginia to fight. His next lesson in command could have been entitled "cooperation and coordination" or "intelligence gathering." After a few more days of rest and training at Hanover Court House, the troopers of the 1st North Carolina Cavalry marched back to the Malvern Hill area for picket duty around Harrison's Landing. As they traveled, the soldiers saw the debris of the Seven Days: abandoned clothing and equipment lay strewn everywhere. The Carolinians even happened across an abandoned boat, resting in the middle of a field far from any water. By Tuesday, July 30, their journey ended as Baker's cavalrymen took position on the upper part of the line, near the junction of the Quaker and the Charles City roads.[64]

Less than a week later, the rattling of artillery wagons and the tramp of horses echoed again across the Peninsula.[65] Baker's pickets raised the alarm. It was about 9:00 P.M. on August 4, and the Carolinians had discovered that an enemy force had advanced to the Gatewood field. Sensing an opportunity to trap the enemy, Baker notified P. M. B. Young and the Cobb Legion and then marched the 1st to Gatewood's. Once he was satisfied that the information was correct, Baker sent another note to Young. He also dispatched an officer — probably Gordon — to General Roswell S. Ripley with the news that the Federals would likely advance along the road to Malvern Hill. Arriving at Ripley's headquarters at 3:45 A.M., the officer asked Ripley for support so Baker could attack. Ripley, who had previously told Baker to call on him whenever he needed help, authorized Baker to call up some nearby artillery and infantry units.[66]

By 6:00 A.M. the next morning, the time had come. Just as Baker had predicted, the Federals — infantry, cavalry, and artillery under General Joseph Hooker — continued moving along the road toward Malvern Hill.[67] Baker called for the infantry. Critical moments passed while the cavalrymen waited. The Federal troops moved closer to the impregnable hill by the minute, but still no infantry arrived. Between 7:00 and 8:00 A.M., Wade Hampton came up and joined in the frustrating vigil. Hampton, too, saw the opportunity and hoped to attack when infantry support arrived, but Ripley's infantry never came. General Lee had decided to handle the Confederate infantry in person, so Baker's ideas were negated.[68] The North Carolinians even tried to stem the advance themselves, but they could not. The blue soldiers reached Malvern Hill, chased off the meager Confederate forces guarding it, and then formed in their old positions of July 1. Unionists shouted victoriously while the cavalrymen saw their chance slip away.[69] Baker and Hampton would have agreed that, through no fault of their own, their first "action" together was a failure.

As it turned out, Baker and Hampton could not have done anything about the Federal advance; it was too strong for the cavalrymen and a small force of infantry to handle. General Lee, worried that it was a general advance by the enemy, had sent the infantry divisions of Longstreet, McLaws, and Ripley to the hill after Baker's information reached him.[70] The soldiers moved carefully as a unit, skirmishing with enemy pickets and cavalry as they marched. To threaten the routes that led to the Federal rear, Lee extended his left toward the Quaker (Willis Church) Road. Baker's Carolinians waited nearby throughout the intensely hot day, skirmishing occasionally with the enemy as they hoped for a change in the situation. To be ready, Baker kept his men in the saddle constantly, even at night, but the opportunity to attack never materialized. Late on August 6, a Rebel reconnaissance drove in a few pickets before discovering that the Federals had withdrawn. All Baker had to show for his efforts were thirty-three prisoners.[71] The infantry arrived too late to be of any effective use. General Lee was simply satisfied that it had not been a general advance of the enemy.[72]

5. Wholesome Lessons 75

Gordon learned two things from his commander during the operation. One was that cooperation and coordination between cavalry and infantry is a delicate thing that needs constant attention. The other was a textbook lesson in cavalry picketing. Hampton later praised the "watchful and energetic" Baker for the "very efficient manner in which [he] maintained his picket line and to the timely information he furnished as to the movements of the enemy."[73] The colonel had redeemed himself before the stigma of the Willis Church defeat could take hold. Now all Baker had to do was stay away from the bottle.

Gordon's regiment received the news of the Battle of Cedar Mountain with delight. Meanwhile, Robert E. Lee told President Davis that he believed McClellan was withdrawing by water, probably toward a junction with Pope.[74] With that thought in mind, the Confederate general began shifting the rest of his army north to link up with Jackson and A.P. Hill, leaving a few infantry and cavalry units to watch McClellan. Stuart's camps were also soon unoccupied; the troopers once more went north, toward the enemy. Their job was to screen the Army of Northern Virginia and to divine Federal intentions.

Instead of marching with his entire force, however, Stuart chose to leave Hampton's Brigade "in observation on the Charles City border, where the enemy's demonstrations left us in some doubt as to his intentions."[75] Doubtless part of the reason they were earmarked for that duty was because the 1st North Carolina Cavalry had suffered ninety-one percent of Confederate cavalry casualties during the Seven Days. (The regiment also lost eight more men in early August, most of them captured while on picket duty near Malvern Hill.[76]) In effect, Lee needed confirmation that the Army of the Potomac was definitely gone, and Stuart knew Hampton's Brigade needed time to rest and refit. Lee left Hampton and a few infantry units with instructions to "keep out scouts and to use every means in their power to ascertain General McClellan's movements."[77]

Baker began doing just that. On August 15, a scout ventured down the Charles City Road and found evidence that the Yankees were definitely withdrawing.[78] As a result, Baker decided that it was time to check out first-hand the Federal camps along the James. General Lee had to know what McClellan was up to; if he attacked instead of withdrawing to join Pope, it would mean disaster for the Confederacy. On August 17, the 1st North Carolina Cavalry gladly left camp. For some reason, they had been bivouacked in the midst of the carnage of the Peninsula battles, where "half buried men and horses cause a great many flies which mainly eat up both men and horses." The troopers marched along the roads that led south and east of Malvern Hill toward Harrison's Landing. Wade Hampton was interested enough to join them. Cautiously, the horsemen advanced through the thickly wooded terrain. Deserted camps stood here and there, offering commissary treasures to the Rebels. No sign of an enemy presence could be found until the sun began sliding below the horizon. Federal pickets were spotted in a distant cornfield. Quickly, Hampton formed the 1st into squadron-sized detachments while the advance dispersed the pickets. Then, in a clear, calm voice, the South Carolinian told his North Carolinians, "Charge them!" Sabres leaped from scabbards; hooves pounded the Peninsula. In a wheatfield beyond the cornfield, the Rebels chased off a contingent of enemy horsemen. The excitement continued until dark, when the officers called a halt.[79]

The men slept fitfully for one or two hours while scouts checked the countryside. The night's only noise came from the nearby James, where an occasional bell sounded from Federal gunboats. When the scouts returned with news that the enemy army had gone, Hampton and Baker decided to make sure. Having skirmished with the enemy the previous evening, it all but required verification. The troopers marched again, over broken bridges and through more deserted camps until daylight, then after a short halt marched again. Along the way, one trooper recalled, they found a Yankee message tacked to a board:

> Farewell, Rebels, we will leave you a while to your salubrious clime, and if you follow us up, we will give you a repetition of Williamsburg, Fair Oaks, Mechanicsville, Gain's [sic] Mill, and Malvern Hill. We intend to conquer and restore you to the [U]nion yet. We will then hang Jeff. Davis, Beauregard, and Co., and take your men for a standing army to defend the Union for all time.[80]

At noon, outriders along the James River and Charles City roads again reported that the Federals had withdrawn beyond reach. Still Baker and Hampton wanted confirmation, so they dispatched a force that could quickly examine McClellan's works at Coggin's and Maycock's points. This unit silently arrived at its objective near dusk. Just enough light remained to illuminate enemy sentinels standing guard on the breastworks.[81] Perhaps McClellan was not gone after all; if so, General Lee had to be informed.

At daylight, Gordon and the men were in their saddles. Baker knew what he had to do; he turned to the bugler and directed him to sound the charge. At that, the men spurred their horses toward the enemy's defensive positions. Rebel yells rose above the sound of the pounding of hundreds of horses' hooves. The men gritted their teeth and waited for the inevitable volley of musket and artillery fire. Horses leaped over the Federal breast-works as the horsemen saw that the Yankee sentinels spotted in the dark had been scarecrows holding large sticks or old guns. Stove-pipe "cannons" pointed mockingly out of the works.[82] McClellan was gone.

Now Lee could prosecute his action against Pope. After Cedar Mountain, the two armies — Lee moving north from Richmond, Pope threatening south — drew opposite each other along the Rappahannock River, where Lee began probing the Federal lines to find a weak spot. Stuart raided Pope's headquarters near Catlett's Station and found further confirmation that Federal reinforcements from the Peninsula were on the way to join Pope. With this and intelligence from the 1st, Lee could be certain that his time was running out. He planned to divide his already outnumbered forces and send Jackson and Stuart after Pope's line of communications.

The Confederate flanking movement began on August 25. Jackson reached the Federal supply depot at Manassas the next day and destroyed everything in sight. Longstreet, after holding position while Jackson sneaked around Pope's flank, followed Jackson's route on August 26. Pope realized what was happening in his rear and sent Federal troops northward to trap the "flanking" portion of Lee's divided army. When Federal units stumbled across Jackson's troops, Pope threw his men at them, but Jackson managed to fight off the determined blueback attacks. Soon, Longstreet and the rest of the army arrived and positioned themselves ominously on the Pope's flank. The next day, August 30, while Pope renewed his assaults on Jackson, Longstreet's troops attacked and caved in Pope's flank. The result was decisive. The Federal army ran for Washington.

The 1st North Carolina Cavalry did not reach the front in time to see this fight. For his part, Gordon simply enjoyed a brief stay in Richmond after the embarrassing incident at Harrison's Landing. Thereafter, the 1st returned to their camps at Hanover Court House and began drilling anew. Like Ransom, Baker worked the men hard. Gordon knew the constant drilling would pay off; he, too, learned a lot from more instruction in the art and science of being a cavalryman. In a sense, it was Gordon's own memorial to Colonel Montford Stokes. The unit as a whole became more cohesive and professional with each day of practice. The regiments' officers knew they were doing their job when the men began to call Hanover "Camp Discipline."[83] Although the troopers grumbled, the practice would prove invaluable in the coming days.

While they drilled, the regiment returned to full strength for the first time since May when Companies A and B returned from North Carolina.[84] The addition of the companies made good the 1st's losses during the Seven Days. The regiment continued to keep the required watch for the Federals, but it was obvious that they were gone for good. The fact of the matter was that the war was to the north, and that was where Gordon wanted to be. He was not alone in that; many cavalrymen had resented being left behind while the Virginians were at the front.

Toward the end of August, Gordon's wish was fulfilled when fresh orders arrived at brigade headquarters. Lee wanted Stuart to have all his horse-soldiers on hand for the pending operations. The regiment — already earning the new nickname "The Bloody First"— left Camp Discipline on August 23 and rode toward the war.[85]

6

Petite Guerre

IN THE WAKE OF HIS LATEST VICTORY, Robert E. Lee decided to take the war to the North. Because the Confederate general set lofty goals, his proposed invasion of Maryland and beyond was nothing short of a gamble — especially since the army had been weakened by straggling and by the fighting at Second Manassas. Lee hoped to give the people of Maryland the chance to ally themselves with the Confederacy; to cause Federal troop withdrawals from threatening positions elsewhere in the South; to exacerbate further the anti-war movement afoot in the North; and to collect supplies, horses, and recruits from north of the Potomac, thus relieving Virginia from the burden of war's destruction. It was a tall order to Lee's liking.

To accomplish his objectives, Lee needed every man he could get, meaning infantrymen, artillerymen, and cavalrymen alike. Even before he decided to enter Maryland, Lee had begun the process of obtaining more troops by writing President Davis, "The whole army, I think, should be united here as soon as possible."[1] He based his reasoning on intelligence that twelve thousand Federals under General Jacob D. Cox were being withdrawn from the Kanawha Valley. Since Cox's move left western Virginia exposed, Lee toyed with the idea of pushing in that direction. "In the event of the information ... about the withdrawal of Cox proving true, Hampton's cavalry I particularly require," he wrote. It was only a thought, however; after further reflection and analysis, Lee decided Maryland was the proper goal.[2]

In any event, Lee needed more cavalry. Focusing on Maryland, Lee continued to push for reinforcements, especially Hampton's Brigade. President Davis hesitated; the idea of leaving Richmond unprotected concerned him. Lee's argument was compelling, however. "Cavalry is very much need in this region; the service is hard, and the enemy strong in that arm," he wrote. Davis gave in. On August 26, the president wrote Lee that Hampton's Brigade and the infantrymen of D. H. Hill, Lafayette McLaws, and others were on their way to rejoin the Army of Northern Virginia.[3]

Thankful for the chance to do some real fighting, Hampton's cavalrymen sped toward a junction with Stuart. The 1st North Carolina Cavalry left Camp Discipline quickly, but took a circuitous route to scout for stray enemy forces. Initially the North Carolinians rode toward Fredericksburg, a town Gordon could trace his roots to since his grandfather had been born and raised there. Next, Baker directed his men to Orange Court House before turning them northward to the Rapidan River, Culpeper Court House, across the Rappahannock, and to Warrenton. The regiment's officers stopped the men there and ordered them to cook three days' rations. At 2:00 A.M. on September 1, the 1st North Carolina Cavalry left Warrenton by way of the Warrenton Turnpike, reaching Bull Run next. On the battlefield itself the dead still covered the field. Some wounded Yankees also remained, and they begged for food and water. That night, with the memory of Bull Run's dead and wounded probably plaguing his sleep, Gordon rested with the regiment near their old winter quarters, Cantonment W. N. Edwards.[4]

The next morning, Tuesday, September 2, the 1st North Carolina Cavalry and the other two regiments and two legions of Hampton's Brigade rejoined Stuart's cavalry division. The meeting was a proud moment not only for Gordon but also for all of Hampton's men. Heros Von Borcke remembered how the cavalrymen were so happy to see Hampton's "splendid" brigade that they let loose with a shout. "Our loud cheering," the staff officer continued, "was heartily responded to by the dashing horsemen of the Carolinas and Mississippi, who had long been anxious to meet the enemy under the lead of Stuart."[5]

The arrival of Hampton's Brigade, plus the addition of another brigade, raised Stuart's strength to a new high. The new brigade, which boasted four regiments and a battalion of Virginians under Brigadier General Beverly H. Robertson, came from "Stonewall" Jackson in mid–August when Special Orders #183 placed all the Army of Northern Virginia's cavalry under Stuart's command.[6] Including Fitz Lee's brigade of five Virginia regiments, that gave Stuart a trio of brigades supported by John Pelham's three batteries of horse artillery. With morale soaring, Stuart's 6,400 cavalrymen were ready and willing to take on whatever task was assigned them.[7]

Specifically, Stuart's troopers were to screen the army from the Federals while the Confederates prowled the soil of Maryland. Lee's plan called for the cavalry division to stay between the Army of Northern Virginia and the Army of the Potomac, hold key passes in the Catoctin and South mountains, and watch the Federals carefully. Meanwhile, Lee would rest and recruit his forces west of the mountains and plan for battle.[8] When Lee felt ready, he would lure McClellan westward to stretch Federal supply lines, then fight the Federals on grounds of his choosing.

Not long after Hampton arrived at the cavalry division's camps, which were located in a dense pine grove near Chantilly, Stuart began wielding his bolstered organization to clear Northern Virginia. That was a prerequisite to any move into Maryland. Colonel Thomas T. Munford's 2d Virginia Cavalry, for example, rode to Leesburg "to capture the party of marauders ... which had so long infested that country and harassed the inhabitants." As for Hampton, Jeb directed the South Carolina general to take the advance and move his brigade, along with the horse artillery, toward Flint Hill, near Fairfax Court House. Flint Hill was reported to be held by the enemy, probably a detachment from General Edwin V. Sumner's 2d Corps which was covering the Federal army's retreat.[9] Stuart himself led Hampton's Brigade toward the enemy with a smile on his face.[10]

Baker's scouts soon pinpointed the location of Federal troops in the Fairfax Court House area. Reaching Flint Hill late on September 2, Hampton and Stuart surveyed the enemy position from a knob near a woodline. Hampton, glass in hand, called for two guns from the horse artillery. The Confederate cannoneers eagerly unlimbered their weapons and opened fire. Sharpshooters added their accurate lead. Together, the gunners achieved the desired result when the Federals quickly made off. It was a quick and easy victory, but it almost ended in tragedy. In the confusion, a North Carolinian came within a whisker of shooting Hampton before he recognized the general.[11]

To follow up their success, the men of Hampton's Brigade spurred their mounts after the Federals. There was no denying the gray-clad troopers, especially the cavalrymen of the 1st North Carolina Cavalry who still remembered the sting of Willis Church. Before long the fleeing Federals came within range, and the gallant John Pelham unlimbered. He began thundering away with his artillery piece, "scattering them [the Federals] in every direction." The

Confederate horsemen then pounced, taking prisoners wherever they could find them. Gordon helped direct the operation.[12]

Reassembling his men, Hampton continued the sweep in the gathering dusk. The 1st North Carolina Cavalry took the advance as the brigade traveled a tree-lined road. Pelham's detachment moved off on other duties and left the brigade without artillery support, so the troopers rode more cautiously. The wisdom of this soon bore out. Before long, the brigade stumbled onto yet another enemy position — this one complete with artillery commanding the road. Heavy enemy musketry flashed in the twilight and forced the column to halt. Hampton, wearing a broad-brimmed black felt hat that bore a simple Palmetto device, steadied his men with cool and encouraging tones. Then Federal artillery opened, and the Confederates found themselves in a hornet's nest of shells whizzing and crashing among their horses. Hampton ordered a withdrawal, which was executed quickly. Somehow, the Federal fire only wounded one horse-soldier who died the next day. It turned out that the Yankees were shooting too high. At first in the form of shell and then grape and canister, their fire harmlessly struck trees on either side of the road. This errant shooting caused much amusement in the 1st North Carolina Cavalry. One Company D trooper called out, "Listen at their grape shot. They make just like a gang of horses passing over a bridge."[13] Gordon probably smiled at the jokes but knew that the Yankees had the stronger position. The brigade's advance was over for the day.

While the 1st camped and raided a cornfield for food — much to the chagrin of the field's owner — other Rebel cavalrymen occupied Fairfax Court House. Civilians joyously greeted them. The Federals opposite Gordon withdrew during the night, apparently satisfied with their evening's work. Stuart later learned that the Federals had been "thrown into considerable confusion" by Hampton's attacks.[14] Stuart's men had successfully swept away all resistance in the area. As one of Stuart's staff wrote, "I don't believe there is a yankee in Virginia, this side of Alexandria."[15]

Early the next morning, Hampton's Brigade continued its northward trek by way of the Leesburg and Alexandria turnpike. They passed two places of interest to Gordon: Vienna and Dranesville. Unlike the latter village, the former elicited no memories of defeat. Almost nine months had passed since Gordon had first tasted the horrors of war at Dranesville, but the memories were still fresh. This march near Dranesville thankfully proved less eventful. The gray-clad troopers only picked up a few stragglers along the way. Stuart, who rode with Hampton's troopers during that march, likewise thought about the Dranesville struggle. He even took a member of his staff, the Prussian Heros Von Borcke, on a quick tour of the battlefield. As they examined the terrain, Stuart pointed out the positions of both sides and evaluated the decisions he had made during the fight.[16]

After a restful but hungry night spent on the banks of the Potomac "in a little hole of a place," Gordon and the troopers scouted near Georgetown and skirmished with enemy horsemen. They next pointed their mounts toward Leesburg, where the army was gathering. The troopers halted for a few hours of rest on the outskirts of town. Dust clouds, stirred up by thousands of marching soldiers, floated everywhere. George Neese of the horse artillery wrote, "There are thousands of soldiers camped around Leesburg this evening, and all seem to be in joyous gayety, caused, I suppose, by bright anticipations of crossing the Potomac and entering Maryland. As I am writing I hear soldiers shouting, huzzahing all around us. Just now a brass band has struck up, which helps to swell the cheer of the merry throng."[17] Truly, the cavalrymen anticipated that their next stop would be the Potomac River.

The advance sounded near sunset. Hampton's men mounted and rode through the streets of Leesburg. After a dusty march of about two hours, the cavalrymen reached the river and paused near Ball's Bluff, scene of another 1861 battle. Then, in the early evening hours of

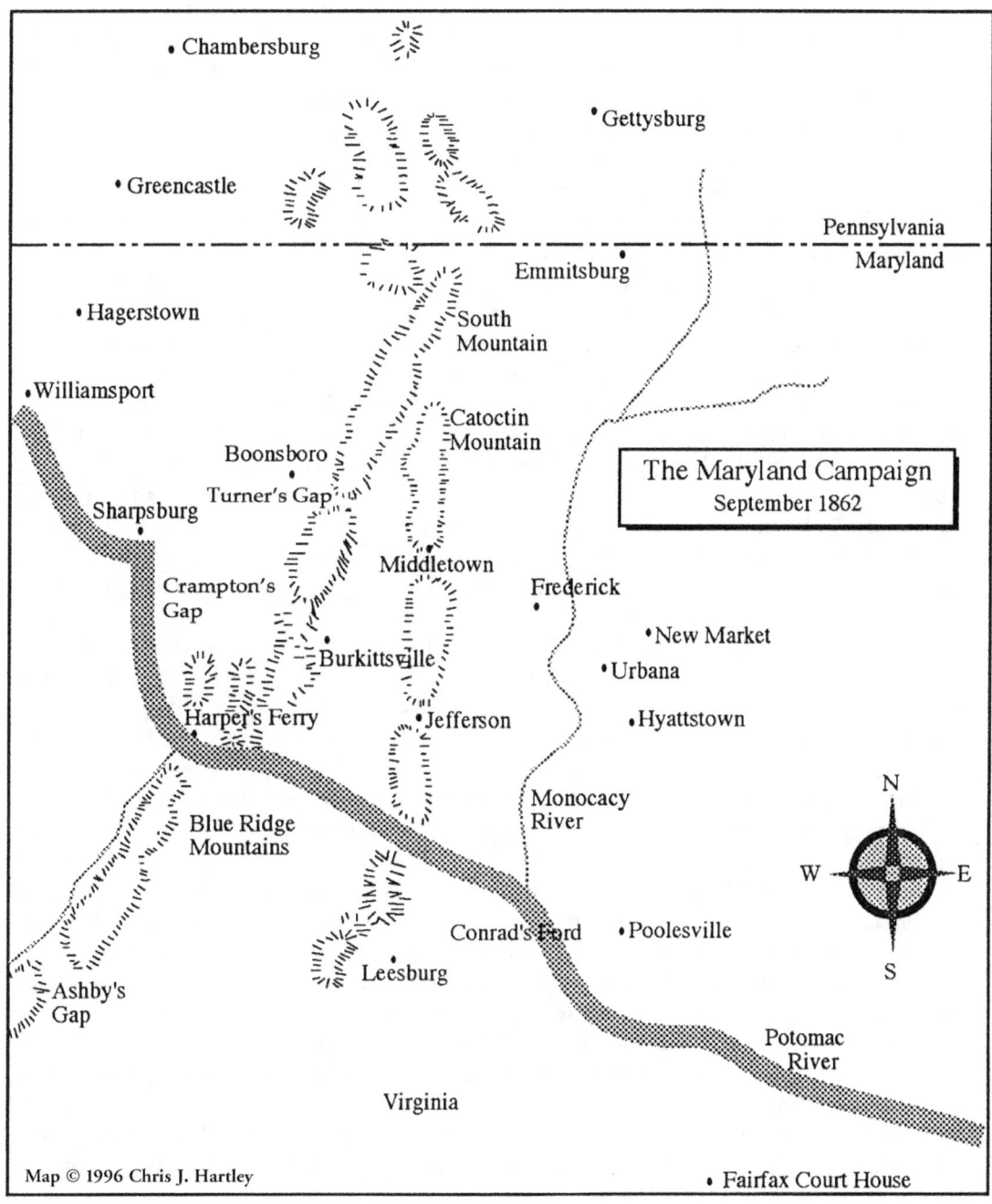

September 5, they left Virginia behind. The waters of the Potomac had seemed so far away to these men, as if in a foreign land, when the shadow of McClellan's great army had menaced Richmond. Now, the river's waters flowed at their feet thanks to hard fighting and wise generalship. The Potomac, said one witness, was their Rubicon. The Confederate cavalry, the men of the 1st North Carolina Cavalry among them, crossed the Potomac River at Conrad's Ford and began their invasion of the North. Gordon urged his horse to wade the great North-South barrier as darkness covered this panorama of invasion. Bands on either bank played stirring music, while the moon and stars above "never shown more brightly on the placid rolling waters of this classic stream."[18] It was an ironic moment for Gordon. He was preparing to fight for freedom and Southern independence in Maryland, the same land his great-grandfather had come to 138 years before in search of similar liberties.

Gordon had been a part of a tactical offensive before, but this was his first glimpse of an army on the strategical offensive. It began with little excitement. Forward elements skirmished briefly with Federal cavalry across the river, but that was the only sign of enemy resistance. Leaving the cool waters of the Potomac behind, the men marched about eight miles to the Poolesville area and camped for the night.[19]

The next morning, the 1st North Carolina Cavalry formed the brigade's advance guard. They moved on Urbana, Maryland and occupied it, capturing a Union "signal corps" in the process. The brigade stayed in Urbana "for several days, having various little skirmishes with the enemy near Hyattstown, driving them back on every occasion."[20] The cavalry's task here was to cover the front toward Washington. Hampton's Brigade constituted Jeb's center near the Urbana-Hyattstown area; Fitz Lee's Brigade covered the left near New Market and the Baltimore and Ohio Railroad; and Robertson's Brigade, under Colonel Munford because Robertson had been transferred, hovered on the right between Sugar Loaf Mountain and Poolesville.[21] The skirmishes Gordon witnessed were the result of Federal cavalry efforts to ascertain Lee's whereabouts; but thanks to the vigilance of Stuart's cavalry screen, the Federals learned little. Gordon may have taken note of the fact, though, that the Unionists grew more inquisitive as the days passed.[22]

The official reports do not tell the whole story of the brigade's stay near Urbana, "a pretty village of neat white houses ... in the midst of a smiling and prosperous country." Located a few miles southeast of Frederick and a mere forty miles from Washington, Urbana became to the troopers "an oasis in the war-worn desert of our lives." Another recalled the good time they had with the local inhabitants, especially the ladies.[23] The village was well situated geographically so that the troopers had nothing to do but sit back and watch for a Federal advance while Lee concentrated the army around Frederick. Stuart, whose headquarters sat "in a nice grassy yard in the village," even saw to the morale of his men by hosting a grand ball in a local female academy. They decorated the dance hall with roses; they sent invitations to local young ladies and to selected Confederate officers; and they asked a band from the 18th Mississippi to provide music. Dancing halted only once when a dusty courier dramatically arrived, saying to Stuart in a loud voice that the Federals were attacking. As small arms fire sounded in the distance, the gallant Confederate officers left swooning ladies behind and sped to the fight. The Yankees were soon disposed of; they had run smack into the waiting guns of the 1st North Carolina Cavalry and were quickly turned back, Pelham's artillery pieces barking at their backs.[24] Although some of the 1st's men were "in poor fix for fighting" because they were under the influence of whiskey, a contingent of the regiment chased the Yankees until after midnight. The 1st's work enabled many officers to return to the more pleasing company of the ladies.[25]

This warm reception in Urbana gave Stuart reason to believe that Marylanders would flock to the Southern banner. General Lee hoped it would be so since that had been a goal of the invasion, but privately he told President Davis, "I do not anticipate any general rising of the people in our behalf."[26] At any rate, the question of Maryland's loyalties was only a sidelight while the Army of the Potomac remained a threat. So regrettably for Gordon and the men, Lee's army left the Frederick area and continued its thrust into Maryland by dividing its forces. Parts went north. Others moved on Harper's Ferry, requiring Stuart to inch his own way north and west to cover the various Confederate movements. On September 11 Stuart withdrew his horsemen. They had "maintained the ... front even longer than was contemplated," Stuart wrote, while the army tried to capture Harper's Ferry, the lone Federal outpost remaining in Lee's rear. From Urbana, Hampton's troopers were ordered to hold Frederick until the infantry passed through. Lee's Brigade fell back across the Monocacy River to near Liberty, while Robertson's Brigade withdrew toward Jefferson. Gordon mounted his horse and, in a steady rain, rode northwestward along the Frederick pike.[27]

The next morning in Frederick was quiet. The silence did not indicate that the nature of the campaign was changing. Hampton, diligently picketing key roads leading to Frederick, was rewarded with fresh intelligence of McClellan's army. Shortly after noon on September 12, a trooper galloped up to Hampton's headquarters with the ominous news that the Federals were advancing westward in heavy force by way of the National Road. Orders went out for the Confederates to again fall back, but to slow the Federal advance as much as possible.[28]

The Federals belonged to Brigadier General Jacob D. Cox's Kanawha Division, specifically the brigades of Colonel Augustus Moor and Colonel Eliakim P. Scammon. The infantrymen marched along the National Road and approached a stone bridge outside Frederick. They were merely on reconnaissance, but gave roving Confederate horsemen the impression of a Federal advance in strength.

Hampton reported:

> Having two squadrons on picket at the bridge over the Monocacy (on the road from Urbana) and near that point, it was of the utmost consequence that I should hold the approaches to the city by the National road until these squadrons could be withdrawn. With this object in view, I took one rifled gun to the assistance of the two guns that were on the pike, and placed a squadron of the Second South Carolina Regiment to support the battery.... The enemy opened fire on the squadron, killing 2 of the men. Finding that my other squadrons were coming in, I withdrew slowly to the city, sending my guns to occupy a position which would command the road from the city to the foot of the mountain.[29]

The Kanawha Federals, part of Burnside's 9th Corps, reacted strongly. Cox deployed Moor on both sides of the pike and advanced toward Frederick. Scammon moved in support. This done, they posted a gun on the outskirts of Frederick, allowing the blue-clad soldiers to fire into the city "along its crowded streets" while an attached cavalry troop drove back Rebel pickets and advanced into town.[30] Moor, responding to criticism from a nearby staff officer, rashly led the cavalry troop in a head-long charge. The portly colonel waved his sabre and yelled, "Come on boys, let's give 'em h — l."[31]

Hampton saw this thrust and decided that he had to repulse it to secure his own line of retreat. He ordered a South Carolina squadron to countercharge. It was supported by other squadrons, including one from Gordon's regiment. Cox watched the fight develop. "Just at the outskirts of town the road turns to the left among the houses, and cannot be seen. While we were wondering at the charge by the brigade commander and his escort, he came to the turn of the road: there was a quick, sharp rattling of carbines, and [the Confederates were] atop of the little party. There was one discharge of the cannon, and some of the brigade staff and the escort came back in disorder." Hampton's counterattack scattered the Federals with a headlong rush. Cox quickly sent Scammon to Moor's aid, but it was too late. Hampton reported, "So successful was the charge and so complete the repulse of the enemy that no further attempt to molest me was made, and I withdrew the brigade, at a walk, from the city, bringing off my prisoners." Cox arrived at the scene to find that Hampton had escaped, learning only that "Moor had been ridden down, unhorsed, and captured. The artillerymen had unlimbered their gun, pointed it, and the gunner stood with lanyard in his hand, when he was struck by a rushing of horse; the gun was fired by the concussion, but at the same moment it was capsized into the ditch by the impact of the cavalry column." Cox was also right about Moor; a North Carolinian had captured him by parrying a saber thrust and then yanking the man off his horse by his uniform collar.[32]

Leaving Frederick to the enemy, Hampton's Confederate troopers continued their journey. After placing Lieutenant Colonel William T. Martin's Jeff Davis Legion as rear guard at the gap in the Catoctin Mountains, the main body halted along the Catoctin Creek in Middletown. Hampton spent time looking over his new mount, a splendid black charger that had recently belonged to Colonel Moor. Gordon, who was also with the main body, joined the rest of the men as they unhorsed and pitched camp. At Middletown, a "dingy mountain hamlet," the day's tension surfaced.[33] Baker made some offhand negative comment about the performance of the Cobb Legion. Lieutenant Colonel P. M. B. Young, the legion's young, brash leader, heard the remark and bristled. He immediately challenged Baker to mortal combat on the spot, "on horseback or on foot, with sabre or pistol, or any way he would fight."

Baker realized he had overstepped his bounds. "Why, Pierce," Baker said, "you are nothing but a boy, you forget yourself; I came here to fight Yankees, not as good a soldier as you."[34]

Reason and cooler heads prevailed, and the episode passed. As Baker had intimated, there were more important things to attend to. Rest would be very important during the coming days of conflict, so Hampton's cavalrymen had to get some sleep. Gordon probably stressed as much to his men. Yet as he bedded down, Gordon might have wondered which there were more of: stars in the sky or Union soldiers coming for the Confederate army. He might have worried even more if he had known that the next day Federal soldiers would find a copy of Robert E. Lee's orders for the campaign.

Special Orders No. 191, dated September 9, 1862, directed portions of the Confederate army to converge from three directions on Harper's Ferry. While Stuart stood forward of and in the passes in Catoctin and South mountains and kept the highlands between the two armies, General John Walker's division was to return to Virginia, swing westward, and move on Harper's Ferry from the south; General Lafayette McLaws, with two divisions, was to cross South Mountain and approach Harper's Ferry from the north; and General Thomas J. Jackson was to move west, recross the Potomac at Williamsport, push through Martinsburg, and invest Harper's Ferry from the west. General James Longstreet was to hover west of South Mountain and watch Lee's flanks.[35] When on September 13 Federal soldiers found a copy of the order at an old Confederate campsite, Lee was in big trouble. At that moment, Stuart's cavalry screen and Longstreet's infantry rear guard were the only defenders standing between the Army of the Potomac and the piece-by-piece destruction of Lee's scattered army.

Fortunately for Lee, it somehow took the methodical McClellan another eighteen hours to put his first troops in motion. The Federal general made his plans carefully. While he planned, September 13 passed with most of the Federal army resting in bivouac. At last, McClellan decided to send the bulk of his army, close to seventy thousand men, through Turner's Gap and after Longstreet while Franklin's left wing of three divisions, 19,500 men in all, moved through the Crampton's Gap area, south of Turner's, to relieve the garrison at Harper's Ferry.[36] The major offensive movements were slated to begin on September 14.

On the day the Lost Order was found, the only significant fighting pitted Confederate cavalrymen and infantrymen against the continuing Union probe that had forced Hampton back to Middletown. The Union cavalry, now under Brigadier General Alfred Pleasonton, who had just reorganized his blue units into a more centralized five-brigade structure, added their weight to the probe.[37] They worked to confirm the Confederate dispositions revealed in the Lost Order.

For Gordon, these combinations ensured that the coming day would be a tough one. If there was a benefit, it was an educational one. Again, he was about to sit in the classroom of reality and study the various facets of cavalry tactics and strategy: dismounted skirmishing, scouting, coordination with infantry, and fighting withdrawals. The techniques were ones he would use when he commanded cavalry units later in the war. Specifically, Gordon's task as a lieutenant colonel, like the duties of the major and regimental staff, was to actively assist Baker in commanding the regiment. According to a document Stuart wrote later, that meant helping Baker supervise the unit's movements, checking "any wavering by prompt support," coordinating squadron offensive and defensive actions, and superintending rallying and returns to action.[38]

Gordon's "class" began that Saturday when Stuart moved Hampton's men to support Colonel Martin. Stuart hoped to hold the Catoctin pass against the Federal advance, be it a reconnaissance or a general advance.[39] The blue-clad infantrymen in Frederick had other ideas as they began reaching toward the gap and Middletown with the hope of learning something of Confederate dispositions. Skirmishing started early.

By 4:00 A.M., Hampton's cavalrymen — led by the 1st North Carolina Cavalry — had joined Martin's men. They came together at the highest point of the Middletown Path, along a wooded spur of the Blue Ridge Mountains. "The Gap through which the Turn Pike passes," wrote one witness, "is approached by a gentle acclivity nearly on a straight line from the base to the summit. The extreme summit of the Gap is overlooked by high ridges rising on the right and left of the road — still running up to loftier proportions as it recedes from the pass." Some troopers dismounted and posted themselves as sharpshooters along the cliffs overlooking the road, while artillery pieces unlimbered nearby. The 1st took position on the right.[40] From there, Gordon watched as the overwhelming numbers of Cox's Kanawha Division and other units drew closer. Stuart saw to it that "every means was taken to ascertain what the nature of the enemy's movement was; whether a reconnaissance feeling for our whereabouts, or an aggressive movement of the army." In notifying D. H. Hill, commander of Lee's rear-guard, about the Federal advance, Stuart suggested that Turner's Gap in South Mountain would serve as a strong defensive position. That message prompted Hill to send two infantry brigades to the South Mountain pass.[41]

While Hill fortified the main South Mountain pass, it was up to the cavalrymen to buy time by defending Catoctin and the approaches to Turner's Gap. As the Federals came on, it looked more and more as if they were launching a major attack. Blue cavalry led the way, while Federal artillery and infantry arrayed some distance to the rear in support. For the first time since Willis Church, Laurence Baker's 1st North Carolina Cavalry was going to be severely tested. It was 9:00 A.M.[42]

Burnside's forward elements approached the cavalrymen's position warily. As they came into range, the Jeff Davis Legion and the 1st North Carolina Cavalry opened fire, driving back the Federal advance guard with little trouble. Confederate Blakely pieces belched away as well. The Federals called for support and brought up artillery, which they posted on the turnpike. The big guns then opened up on the Confederates' mountain crest position. A section of Rebel rifle guns fired back with such effect that the blue battery changed its position several times.[43] Shells thickened the Maryland air and left their mark wherever they impacted. As the fighting intensified, the noise from muskets and artillery grew from a spattering to a roar.

While the artillery duel continued, Federal officers commanded their skirmishers to feel out the Confederate positions. The Confederates, knowing it was critical to conceal that they were only cavalry, countered with their own line of dismounted skirmishers and again checked the Federals. The enemy also tried to flank the Confederate right with a line of skirmishers, but the 1st beat back the maneuver with accurate carbine fire. Gordon was one of the fighting troopers who conducted himself with "the utmost gallantry, and sustained a hot fire of artillery and musketry without flinching or confusion...."[44] Just as the Gordons of Scotland had done in epic battles such as Bannockburn and Flodden Field, the Gordon from North Carolina gave his all.

The fight remained a stalemate until about 1:00 P.M. when Cox decided to turn up the pressure. He ordered two brigades of infantry to attack. Once foot soldiers pitched into dismounted cavalry, it was purely mathematical; the infantry's firepower overwhelmed the carbines of the Confederate cavalry. The blue brigades stepped forward, flags flying. The gray horsemen wielded their carbines and artillery pieces with some effect, but not enough. Things got so hot that Stuart's troopers "were obliged to abandon the crest" of the Catoctins.[45] It was about 2:00 P.M. when the withdrawal began.[46]

A contingent of skirmishers remained on the mountain as a rear guard, abandoning the crest only grudgingly to buy more time for D. H. Hill. As for the overall picture, Stuart's officers decided that the Federals were pushing the cavalry "for the purpose of relieving the garrison of Harper's Ferry."[47] As a result, Stuart was not quite ready to relinquish the whole area. He readied a delaying action on the backside of Catoctin Mountain near Middletown. The 1st North Carolina Cavalry, supported by two pieces of artillery, was called on to fill this need. It took position in front of Middletown, directly in the path of the enemy. The other regiments and guns fell back to the other side of the village, behind Kitochtan Creek.[48]

At 4:00 P.M., the Yankees "came teeming through the pass we had just evacuated and with exulting shouts, came pouring down the slopes." The squadron commanded by Captain Thaddeus P. Siler bore the brunt of the assault, while Baker and Gordon managed the regiment against the heavy odds. Through the smoke and dust of the battle, and the thunder of cannon, the Federals avoided a frontal assault and began to work around Baker's flanks. Soon, a fierce cross-fire raked the North Carolinians' flanks.[49] From the pass above, heavy artillery fire pounded Baker's position. Many Tarheels fell wounded, including Captain Siler, whose thigh was shattered by a ball.[50] With nothing else to gain, Stuart finally decided to pull back. He later cited Baker and the regiment for bravery:

> A spirited engagement took place, both of artillery and sharpshooters, the First North Carolina, Colonel Baker, holding the rear and acting with conspicuous gallantry. This lasted for some time, when, having held the enemy in check sufficiently long to accomplish my object, I withdrew slowly toward the gap in the South Mountain, having given General D. H. Hill ample time to occupy that gap with his troops.[51]

Withdrawing from Middletown, Hampton sped his forces to the South Mountain gaps. Gordon probably breathed a sigh of relief because it had been a near thing. He had escaped the withering enemy fire unscathed.

As the North Carolinians joined the retreat toward South Mountain, things continued to turn against the Confederacy. More than half of the Army of Northern Virginia remained two days' march away, while the rest of the army was no closer than thirteen miles distant.[52] Meanwhile, as the Confederates soon learned, well over forty thousand men in blue could be found just a short walk away; twice that many Unionists were not far behind. The fate of the Army of Northern Virginia now hinged on the defense of South Mountain.

Late on September 13, in yet another twist of fate, Lee probably learned from Stuart that a civilian informer, during a visit to Federal headquarters, had seen McClellan receive the lost Confederate plans.[53] The Virginian quickly notified his infantry commanders of the developments, urging them to hasten their already behind-schedule operations. To Stuart and Harvey Hill fell the task of delaying the Federal advance until the army captured Harper's Ferry and reunited. Hill, who already had forces at Turner's Gap, was formally charged with conceiving a practicable defense of South Mountain with Stuart. Lee wrote Stuart: "The gap must be held at all hazards until the operations at Harper's Ferry are finished. You must keep me informed of the strength of the enemy's forces...."[54] The Confederates drew the line at South Mountain.

Stuart, having withdrawn from Middletown, reached the vicinity of Turner's. He found a portion of Hill's troops already in place. Believing the position relatively secure, he thought his troopers could be more effective elsewhere since the gap "was obviously no place for cavalry operations, a single horseman passing from point to point on the mountain with difficulty." Surely, he surmised, the enemy would not confine its westward movement to only one gap. Stuart reported, "As General Jackson was then in front of Harper's Ferry, and General McLaws, with his division, occupied Maryland Heights, to prevent the escape of the Federal garrison, it was believed that the enemy's efforts would be against McLaws, probably by the route of Crampton's Gap." As such, Stuart reinforced other weak links in the South Mountain lines by sending Rosser and the horse artillery to Braddock's Gap and Hampton to reinforce Munford's cavalry and the small infantry force that had been placed at Crampton's Gap.[55] (The Jeff Davis Legion did not go with Hampton because it was detached for service at the Boonsboro Gap.[56]) Harvey Hill arrived with the remainder of his rear guard at Turner's Gap on the morning of the fourteenth and began bolstering the defenses there.

As Hampton's troopers wearily made their way to Crampton's Gap late on September 13, they encountered a Union cavalry regiment riding on a parallel road. The South Carolinian set his forces into line of battle and ordered his freshest unit, P. M. B. Young's Cobb Legion, to charge. The orders were carried out with skill and "remarkable gallantry." Wade Hampton's son did his share in the fight. When his father threw his overcoat to his son to hold during the battle, young Preston Hampton threw the coat into a fence corner and followed his father to the fight. When he was later asked to explain his actions, Preston said, "I've come to Maryland to fight Yankees and not to carry Father's overcoat." Gordon, who had already done his share of fighting that day, watched Young's troopers cross sabers with the Yankees, killing or wounding thirty of them. The Confederates lost thirteen men, including four dead.[57] Lieutenant Colonel Young, a lovable man who was becoming a close friend of Gordon's, was one of the wounded; a ball shattered his leg.[58]

The skirmish over, darkness closed in on Hampton's tired cavalrymen when they at last drew near Crampton's Gap. Although the fight had helped relieve the pressure on Munford's men at the gap, the day almost ended in disaster for them. Colonel Munford, awaiting reinforcements, mistook Hampton's approaching unit for the enemy. He ordered his artillery to prepare to fire. The quick-thinking Hampton noticed the activity in the gap, displayed a white flag, and dispatched a courier in time to stop the firing.[59] Saturday, September 13, perhaps the longest day Gordon had yet experienced in the war, finally ended.

Stuart rode to Crampton's Gap early the next morning. The sun, burning off an early fog, appeared bright in the cloudless sky. Pondering the situation, Stuart considered the three regiments of infantry and two cavalry brigades then on hand. Learning that there had been no major thrust toward Crampton's, "and apprehending that [the enemy] might move directly from Frederick to Harper's Ferry," Stuart decided to send Hampton toward the Potomac River. He figured Munford could hold until reinforcements arrived.[60] Hampton accordingly struck off for the Knoxville area, at the lower end of South Mountain, and began picketing the roads toward Point of Rocks and Frederick. This protected against an approach to Harper's Ferry by way of the roads next to the Potomac. As for the gap, Stuart requested more infantry to help Munford. However, even as Hampton rode south, William Franklin's 6th Corps, 12,300 strong, moved on Crampton's Gap.[61] If the Federals threw the bulk of the corps against the gap and pierced its inadequate defenses, McLaws's rear would be exposed to Franklin. The 6th Corps could then attack McLaws — who was on Maryland Heights, still trying to take Harper's Ferry along with the bulk of Lee's army — and drive him into the Potomac. The rest of the Confederate army would be equally vulnerable. Just after noon, Franklin arrived before Crampton's Gap. Defiantly, Confederate artillery banged away at the Federals. The gap's defenders made all the noise they could. As he ordered his forward division to deploy, Franklin lost his courage and decided that the pass was too strongly held, but division commander General Henry Warner Slocum proved him wrong and captured the gap.[62] The Confederates broke and ran, halting a few miles down the Harper's Ferry Road about dusk with the assistance of Stuart.

Crampton's Gap did not fall alone. North of Crampton's, at Turner's Gap and Fox's Gap, guns thundered and men died. Cox's Federals, reinforced by the rest of Jesse L. Reno's 9th Corps, and by elements of Joseph Hooker's 1st Corps, fought for control of South Mountain. Hill, reinforced by Longstreet, had fought off most Union attacks, but as evening came on, the Confederates were forced to withdraw. Fitz Lee's cavalry covered Hill's withdrawal with great skill.[63]

The last natural barrier between McClellan and Lee's divided army had fallen. Stuart's cavalry had fought well. Harvey Hill's infantry had also done their part. Stuart and Hill could only hope that they had given Lee enough time.

As soon as it was light the next morning, September 15, Gordon and the men of the 1st could plainly see Federal troops pouring over South Mountain and marching in their direction. The sight had become a familiar one. While Hampton's men continued picketing south and west of South Mountain, reinforcements arrived. Major General Richard H. Anderson came up to take command in the area west of Crampton's.[64] He set up a defensive line in Pleasant Valley; but it was only a thin line compared with what the Federals could bring to bear. As the blue host could now flow westward toward a still divided Confederate army, and the Federal garrison at Harper's Ferry continued to hold on, Lee even considered withdrawing from Maryland.[65] Timely good news from Harper's Ferry helped the Virginian decide to stand in Maryland.

Events at the old arsenal town had been moving slowly. While it was true that Dixon S. Miles, the garrison commander, could count only twelve thousand noses in a place not easily defended, the rough terrain around Harper's had considerably complicated the Confederate advance. Finally, on September 15, once the grayback soldiers reached the best positions from which to end the matter, Harper's Ferry fell. Only a cavalry force under Colonel Benjamin Franklin Davis managed to escape. This ensured that Davis and his 8th New York Cavalry would meet Gordon in battle two months later.

With his rear cleared, Lee turned his entire force to deal with McClellan. He ordered his wide-spread troops to assemble around a small Maryland town called Sharpsburg along the banks of a creek known as the Antietam. This decision was bold because Lee faced an enemy almost twice his size. Worse, the nearby Potomac River flowed frighteningly across the Confederate line of retreat. Then again, the whole campaign had been a gamble; Lee had faith in his soldiers.

To cover the withdrawal to Sharpsburg, the cavalry occupied the infantry's existing battle lines. Hampton's command took position confronting Franklin's troops in Pleasant Valley while Anderson's and McLaws's troops disengaged and marched to Sharpsburg. Late in the evening, Hampton's Brigade followed McLaws into Harper's Ferry. Pickets kept a close watch on the roads leading to Maryland Heights. One member of the 1st described the feelings of most of the regiment's men at the time, including Gordon. He wrote home, "I have been through many dangerous battles.... We ride day and night and get no sleep hardly."[66] That day turned out to be no exception, although one good thing did come out of the brigade's time in Harper's Ferry. As one witness described it, the troopers foraged their hungry horses on the "vast Quartermaster Garners" found there. On the morning of the seventeenth, the brigade crossed the river at Shepherdstown and joined the rest of the army at Sharpsburg, where they took position on the extreme left. The horse-soldiers supplemented Lee's line, extending it in a westerly direction toward the Potomac. Stuart reported, "The cavalry was held as a support for the artillery, which was very advantageously posted so as to bring an enfilading fire upon the enemy's right."[67] Another trooper described the position thusly: "the cavalry was posted along a line closing the entrance to the peninsula formed by Antietam Creek and the Potomac, with its left resting on the river and its right connecting with our infantry left flank." The terrain's combination of open space and rising ground made it an important position, so Stuart was "ceaselessly active" in its defense.[68]

McClellan followed Lee's army to Sharpsburg and brought the two armies face-to-face. The Federal general had been as methodical as always in bringing his troops up. When battle at last became imminent, Gordon had a ringside seat for the drama. Dawn, September 17, brought blood.

"As the sun rose," wrote one of Gordon's men, the Federals' "gay blue uniforms and bright and glittering weapons contrasted strongly with the dusty thread-bare apparel and unpolished weapons of Lee's 'Rebel Army.'" This pageantry died as the fighting exploded into a test of humanity. "No battle of the war," wrote a member of Stuart's staff, W. W. Blackford, "displayed the indomitable pluck of our army more conspicuously than Antietam, and in none were the odds more fearfully against us."[69] McClellan massed his troops for the assault, which hammered first the Confederate left, then the center, and finally the right. The Rebels fearfully contested each attack. Casualties mounted. On the left, around Dunker Church, the blue-clad soldiers gained ground, and stumbled through a gruesome and bloody cornfield. Their advance forced Stuart to withdraw "more to the rear of the Confederate left" so that his horse artillery could continue firing without endangering Confederate units.[70] Eventually, reinforcements, with the help of Stuart's artillery, pushed the Federals back. The center had its Bloody Lane where bodies stacked up like cordwood, but again the Confederates somehow dodged catastrophe. By the end of the day, the Confederates had repulsed all attacks and held or reclaimed their positions — but only after General A. P. Hill came up with reinforcements from Harper's Ferry in the nick of time, saving the Southern right flank from the attack of Burnside's men. The butcher's bill was grim: September 17, 1862 became the bloodiest single day in the history of American warfare.

No man who was a part of that day and that campaign, including James Gordon, ever forgot the hellish cauldron of Antietam. The day belonged to the infantry and the artillery, for the cavalry had already done its work well; as Stuart wrote, "During the Maryland campaign, my command did not suffer on any one day as much as their comrades of other arms, but theirs was the sleepless watch and the harassing daily *petite guerre*." Gordon and the 1st North Carolina Cavalry spent most of their day rounding up stragglers, caring for the wounded, and burying the dead, but were often where they could keep an eye on the fighting.[71]

Just as he had at Malvern Hill, Gordon wanted to do more to help win the battle, but he could not. The tragic panorama of smoke, noise, blood, and death moved the horse-soldiers. Stuart himself had a narrow escape during the fighting. At one point, while crossing an open field under the fire of a Union battery, a Southern regiment mistook him for a Yankee. The unit was a bloodied one that had just been rallied, and in their haste to redeem themselves its men fired a volley at the cavalry commander. Bullets struck Stuart's horse but somehow missed him.[72]

All the while, the Confederate command wanted to go over to the offensive, for such was their nature. Jeb Stuart, at day's end — even as A. P. Hill was saving the Confederate right — put together seven regiments of cavalry, the 48th North Carolina Infantry Regiment, and supporting artillery, with the hopes of leading a back-door attack on the Federal rear.[73] The sight of McClellan's still-formidable position on the Union right caused the Virginia cavalry leader to rethink his plans. The battle groaned to a conclusion.

The next day, Lee continued to look for an opportunity to attack the Federals, who remained in their positions. He found none. H. B. McClellan remembered September 18 vividly, writing, "the scene can never be forgotten by those who rode along Jackson's attenuated line. There appeared to be hardly one man to a rod of ground, and it seemed that a compact regiment must pierce such a line at any point, should the attempt be made."[74] Later that day, with his battered army thus wedged between the Army of the Potomac and the Potomac River, Lee came to the only remaining conclusion: the Army of Northern Virginia must return to Virginia.

Gordon, however, prepared to renew the fight in Maryland. That was because of Lee's concerns about withdrawing in the face of the Army of the Potomac. In a meeting with Stuart, Lee decided that Brigadier General Fitz Lee's cavalry should cover the withdrawal of the main army across the Potomac. Meanwhile, Stuart was to take Hampton's Brigade and return to Virginia, swing westward, re-cross the Potomac, and thrust into Maryland to make some noise.[75] Hopefully, Stuart's diversion would cause McClellan to worry more about his flanks than the enemy forces in his front.

Blackford, who had found an obscure yet suitable ford from which to begin the diversion, guided Hampton's Brigade as they silently retired from their Sharpsburg position. They reached the Potomac River crossing after nightfall on September 18. The ford — "just below a fish trap where a shallow dam had been built of loose stones over which the water poured"— was so far off the beaten path that Stuart had directed Blackford to post men along the route so Hampton's men could find their way in the dark.[76] The precaution worked, and the South Carolinian's troopers made good time.

Gordon made his way through the darkness toward the crossing point. Once at the ford, he discovered that their problems had just begun. In fact, as one of Gordon's men remembered, the night-time river crossing was a nightmare. "This was even worse than fighting," he lamented. Stuart wrote, "As the ford was very obscure and rough, many got over their depth and had to swim the river."[77] It made for an eerie night as the men crossed the flowing Potomac by way of the unfamiliar ford. The night itself radiated a solid, almost impenetrable blackness due to a heavy fog rising from the river. Gordon could barely see the man in front of him, let alone the way across the river. "The place was very rough and the water swift, but it was the best that could be had," Blackford added.[78]

The horse soldiers braved the conditions and the darkness, and their numbers on the far bank grew. The crossing, at last, was completed, but not without loss. Back in Virginia, they turned their horses westward and rode along the river. Ahead, a detachment from Company I of the 1st North Carolina Cavalry searched for another ford.[79]

By late afternoon on Friday, September 19, Stuart and Hampton's troopers, supported by an infantry battalion, some artillery, and a few smaller detachments, had moved about fifteen miles, re-crossed the Potomac at Mason's Ford, and occupied Williamsport, Maryland.

There, they took position along the ridges overlooking the town. Working on only an hour's rest, Gordon was across the Potomac and in enemy territory for the second time in a month.[80]

From this threatening position on McClellan's flank, the horse soldiers made active demonstrations and patrols. As part of the ruse, they spread rumors among civilians that Lee and the Army of Northern Virginia were close behind. Stuart decided to expand his noise-making activities the next evening by dispatching Hampton toward Hagerstown to wreak havoc deeper in the Federal rear. Prior to that movement, however, Hampton's forward scouts had captured Federal soldiers from several divisions, sparking worries that there were more enemy troops about than thought. Despite that information, Stuart — still believing that Hampton would face little resistance — ordered the brigade forward. Hampton obeyed but told a comrade, "Good-bye, my dear friend; I don't think you will ever see me or a man of my brave brigade again."[81]

Hampton's scouts were right: Federal troops were closing in on Williamsport. The cavalry's demonstrations and rumors of the nineteenth had worked to a degree, prompting investigation from elements of the Army of the Potomac. By September 20, Union troops under Major General Darius N. Couch were probing toward Confederate-held Williamsport. Fighting erupted as Hampton pressed toward Hagerstown and met a large force of cavalry supported by a division of infantry. In fact, his troopers ran into strong resistance on every road leading out of Williamsport. Hampton did not have the chance to move on Hagerstown because he could not even get out of the Williamsport area. Stuart recalled Hampton.[82]

At dark, Stuart gave the order to return to Virginia. Hampton personally delivered the 1st's withdrawal orders to Baker. Gordon looked on as Colonel Baker received his instructions and, "pulling his long muchtache [sic] and smiling ... gave orders 'by fours, forward march[']', 'trot march,' 'Jallop March [sic].'" The North Carolinians made for the ford with all dispatch, except for Captain W. H. H. Cowles who remained with a rear guard.[83]

Later, the Prussian Heros Von Borcke would remember the cavalry's exit as a "magnificent spectacle." Wrote Von Borcke, "The whole landscape was lighted up with a lurid glare from the burning houses of Williamsport, which had been ignited by the enemy's shells. High over the heads of the crossing column and the dark waters of the river, the blazing bombs passed each other in parabolas of flame through the air, and the spectral trees showed their every limb and leaf against the red sky."[84]

Although this river crossing went much smoother than the one on the eighteenth, the diversion itself fell short of expectations. Stuart did draw enemy response his way, but not enough to keep another Federal force from crossing the Potomac and striking Lee's rear-guard hard.

By about 11:00 P.M. on September 20, Gordon was back in Virginia and glad of it. He and his fellow cavalrymen rode about six miles from the Potomac, toward Martinsburg, and camped near a large plantation. There they found plenty of corn and hay for their tired and hungry horses, and a place to pitch tents so they could get their own rest. The next day dawned clear and beautiful and provided a refreshing backdrop for the troopers' arrival in Martinsburg at about noon. Gordon was with the bulk of the cavalry there, but parts of the 1st remained near the Potomac and picketed for a few days. The entire regiment was reunited at Martinsburg by September 28.[85]

Meanwhile, in the halls of government, Gordon began to receive recognition for his solid if not distinguished service. Zebulon B. Vance, North Carolina's new governor, heard that a new regiment of North Carolina cavalry was being organized. It was a move of which Vance "heartily approved," as long as it did not siphon men from North Carolina's defenses. Vance also was "anxious to have [the regiment] officered in the best possible manner and by North Carolinians," so he wrote George W. Randolph, the Confederate Secretary of War, to recommend candidates. Gordon was Vance's choice for colonel and commander of the regiment. Vance told Randolph that Colonel Gordon was known to be a most excellent officer: "Col. Gordon has service with distinction for 12 months, under Col (now Gen) Ransom." Vance added that the appointment of Gordon and the other officers he recommended "would be gratifying not only to myself, but to the North Carolina public generally."[86] Vance's recommendation said a lot about Gordon's growing reputation back home. However, for some unrecorded reason, Randolph instead selected John A. Baker of New Hanover County to be colonel of the new regiment. At the time, Baker was serving on the staff of General Samuel G. French, commander of the Department of Southern Virginia and North Carolina. Baker's regiment, designated the 3d North Carolina Cavalry (41st Regiment North Carolina State Troops), was organized at Kinston that autumn but actually did not concentrate until 1863.[87]

In Northern Virginia, Gordon knew nothing of such correspondence. Instead, he helped keep a close watch on McClellan as Stuart's cavalry occupied the line of the Potomac from opposite Williamsport to Harper's Ferry. The men of the 1st North Carolina Cavalry settled into their camps near Martinsburg and enjoyed good food, recreation, and the chance to change their linen.[88] Of course, they also resumed normal picketing, despite the loose clothing and tattered boots that many of them wore. One Tarheel, hoping to retire southward, wished that Stuart and Hampton would grow "as tired uv [sic] these ere [sic] parts as I am."[89]

Gordon and Baker, who had become friends in the midst of war, indulged in a little recreation of their own. Heros Von Borcke recalled spending time with the two North Carolinians and the artilleryman John Pelham on Monday, September 22:

> In the evening, Pelham and I, mounting our mules, rode very proudly over to the camp of the 1st North Carolina regiment, where we had been invited by its officers, Colonel Baker and Major Gordon, to join them — rare luxury indeed — in a bowl of punch, and where we had a very pleasant symposium, laughing and talking over the adventures of our recent campaign.[90]

Gordon had obviously not lost his nose for refreshments. Baker, who had served his country by staying away from liquor, figured he deserved it. Sadly, this celebration may have renewed Baker's alleged drinking problem, which in turn spotlighted nepotism in the regiment. According to trooper William M. Barrier, Baker soon "returned to his drink and our quarter master and commissary are both considered swindling scoundrels. They were appointed by Col. Baker to their positions because they were his near relatives." In addition, some sort of a personality conflict developed between Baker and Captain Rufus Barringer. A chagrined Barrier told his father what it all meant. "I am sorry to say," he wrote, "that our regiment is going to sticks very fast." Snow would come before something could be done about the situation.[91]

7

A Season of Raiding

WADE HAMPTON SET THE PACE. He rode at an easy trot, as if he planned to look over his cotton fields, but he had other ideas in mind. So did the men behind Hampton: Jeb Stuart, astride his favorite dark bay, and a few hundred Confederate troopers from Hampton's Brigade. These cavalrymen matched Hampton's gait and followed him in a strange direction. Though the Maryland campaign had ended barely three weeks ago with the ejection of the Army of Northern Virginia from Northern soil, they marched *toward* the Potomac River.[1]

Hampton's Rebels, most of whom did not know the purpose of the movement, bivouacked at Hedgesville as October 9 grew old. As the first of Stuart's forces to arrive, they prepared the camp for detachments to come.[2] Once all had assembled, Jeb Stuart released a published address that gave his curious troopers a glimpse of the future. Without revealing their exact destination, he described their task as "an enterprise" which would require "coolness, decision, and bravery; implicit obedience to orders without question or cavil, and the strictest order and sobriety on the march and in bivouac." This, of course, only piqued the soldiers' interest. What could the General be planning? Rumors quickly spread throughout the camps. Some said that the raid would venture into the enemy's backyard, perhaps Pennsylvania. Stuart's secrecy held, however, and his address gave no more hints. He mentioned nothing else save his confidence in his men.[3]

There was one clue as to the mission's importance: the best horse-soldiers of the cavalry division had gathered. Stuart had personally culled 1,800 men and four guns. That number included Hampton, whom Stuart chose as the mission's second-in-command, and 650 of Hampton's men, including 175 from the 1st. Gordon was asked to command the North Carolinians.[4]

Since the morrow would tell all, the men reluctantly turned in. The rushing waters of the Potomac River roared in the distance, coaxing many to sleep, but doubtless the anticipation and perhaps fear of the unknown kept others awake. Even Hampton appeared concerned. At one point, he was seen standing alone on the banks of the Potomac, probably deep in thought.[5]

Hampton already knew what his men did not. General Lee's orders had been received just two days before. The army commander had told Stuart to penetrate Yankee territory, gather intelligence, and damage his means of transportation. The Cumberland Valley Railroad bridge over the Conococheague Creek was to be destroyed, along with anything else of military value in Stuart's path. As for Stuart's route, Lee wanted him to cross the Potomac above Williamsport and proceed to the Chambersburg area, keeping Hagerstown and Greencastle to his right. How the raiders returned to Virginia was up to Stuart.[6]

Stuart placed his own spin on the expedition's tactics and dictated his thoughts to Channing Price, his assistant adjutant general. Orders No. 13 reflected the government's desire that the troops handle the Marylanders with kid's gloves in case there remained any hope of swinging the state's loyalties. Capture of horses and other property required command approval. A receipt was to be given to civilians in return for property seized. While on the march, one-third of the troopers from each brigade were to procure and lead any captured and spare horses. While those troopers traveled in the column's center, the rest of the brigade was to make up the advance and rear. Should fighting occur, attacks were to be "vigorous and overwhelming, giving the enemy no time to collect, reconnoiter, or consider anything except his best means of flight." As a final touch, once in Pennsylvania the troopers were authorized to capture government officials.[7]

All too soon, "the earliest streakings of light" pierced the cold darkness of October 10. Men left their bed rolls to brush and curry horses, clean weapons, and cook rations.[8] Lieutenant Colonel Gordon and his 175 picked men began making their preparations as well. As his hazel eyes scanned the scene, Gordon's thoughts may have been of the preparations, but more likely they focused on the task he and the men faced. Whatever their destination, he doubtless figured it would be a tough mission. Stuart and Hampton would certainly expect much from Gordon's North Carolinians. Given his personality, Gordon was ready to fight. Problems in the 1st notwithstanding, his inclusion in this raid was an honor, and he wanted to live up to it.

Once animals and equipment were ready, the men went to work. Daylight was not yet strong, but the air held a strong hint of fall. The leaves were turning and the first frosts had just touched the landscape. With that as a backdrop, Hampton's command turned toward the Potomac.[9] A section of the Washington Horse Artillery rode in support of Hampton. Colonels William Henry Fitzhugh "Rooney" Lee and William E. "Grumble" Jones, the former a son of Robert E. Lee and the latter, like Gordon, an Emory & Henry man, ordered their forces to fall in behind Hampton's 650. The raid had begun.

Hampton directed a detachment of Carolinians to wade the river and chase off any pickets before the whole column tried the Potomac. Part of the detachment came from the 1st; Sgt. William L. Barrier led the Tarheel contingent. Then, about 175 men from the 2d South Carolina Cavalry, commanded by Colonel Matthew C. Butler, followed to establish a bridgehead. The plan went well until a bull terrier appeared out of nowhere. It leaped at one Southerner, snarling and barking. With the "alarm" sounded, the Confederates charged and the Yankees ran. Gunfire and muzzle flashes broke the dark stillness. "Kill them! Kill them!" Rebels shouted. "Here goes the damned blue-backed rascals!" Soon it was over; the picketing Federals lost only one man wounded and several horses thanks to the loyal dog. The Rebel column then splashed across the river and entered Maryland for the third time in the past thirty-odd days. Surviving Union pickets scattered to spread the word of Stuart's invasion.[10]

Once across, one of Hampton's first actions was to dispatch twenty men to capture a nearby signal station.[11] The bulk of Hampton's Brigade, followed by the rest of the 1,800, moved for the National Turnpike. Upon reaching the road, Hampton's advance guard collared ten more Federal pickets. The Federals belonged to one of six westward-bound regiments and two batteries, under the command of Jacob Cox, which had just passed an hour before. Nearby citizens confirmed this. Given such intelligence, Stuart opted to head for Chambersburg, Pennsylvania by way of Mercersburg. It was not easy for him to ignore Hagerstown and its supplies, but the proximity of Cox's infantry dictated it.[12] Jeb knew better than to tangle with infantry.

Northward rode the troopers, guided by Confederates from western Maryland who knew the country. Gordon bounced along with the rest of them, the smells of leather and horse pervading his senses. During the early morning hours, he could not see much of the terrain because a heavy fog hung about them. While the fog lasted, however, it obscured their movements.[13]

With the column compact and moving with singular purpose, the ride through Maryland passed quickly and without event. Only the weather threatened to dampen morale. Though the fog burned away, the day remained dim. The sun's vague outline rarely peeked through the thin, white, vapory clouds that owned the skies. Below, distant ridges sat shrouded in a sad, misty blue. Leaves rustled underfoot. Still the Confederates remained intent on other portents. They enthusiastically watched for the Pennsylvania border "across which the fun would begin." Stuart was perhaps the most excited man in the column; as his assistant adjutant general wrote, Stuart had "long-expressed [his] desire to pay a visit to Pennsylvania and especially Chambersburg." Soon, with Hampton still leading, the Confederates crossed into Pennsylvania. As a preliminary, the column halted around 10:00 A.M.[14] Gordon listened as fresh orders were read. "We are now in enemy country. Hold yourselves ready for attack or defense, and behave with no other thought than victory," the directive admonished. "If any man cannot abide cheerfully by the order and the spirit of these instructions, he will be returned to Virginia with a guard of honor."[15]

There was a cheer, and the men rode on by way of a private country road.[16] According to Stuart's orders, one "brigade" led the way, a second "brigade" covered the rear, and detachments from the middle "brigade" now began roaming the countryside. They started cutting wires and collecting horses. The Confederates rudely interrupted farmers who had taken advantage of the cloudy, rainy day to work in their barns or thresh wheat. From each farm, the troopers took powerful draft horses — "great, fat Conestoga horses of the Norman breed, most valuable animals for artillery purposes but wholly unfit for cavalry mounts" — and also captured a number of citizens and interrupted Federal communications in the area. Some also managed to eat their fill of foods such as bread, turkey, ham, beef, brown rolls, cream, and butter.[17] To Gordon's amusement, the Pennsylvanians were shocked to see Rebel cavalry visiting their own farms. Price remembered: "It was ludicrous in the extreme to see the old Dutchmen as their horses were taken in every variety of circumstances, from the stable, the threshing machine, wagons, etc." One farmer, learning that Jefferson Davis's Confederates had captured his animals, protested, "Sheff Tavis! Mine Got! Vot ish Sheff Tavis got tu du mit mine hosses! Mine Got! He vill never send tem pack!"[18]

As they passed through the countryside, the men encountered surprised locals. In one town, Butler's advance guard requisitioned boots and shoes from a merchant. The merchant did not realize who his customers were until he was given a receipt. Another man, once his sorrel mare was pressed into Confederate service, refused to believe that the offenders were Rebels. He protested loudly and uselessly that the Federal government had forbidden the impressment of horses. Stuart's men treated the people generally well, especially the ladies of the area. The chivalrous and flirtatious Gordon supported Stuart's orders to allow ladies to pass the column without being inconvenienced.[19]

Following a halt to feed on "liberated" corn, the detachment rode into Mercersburg at noon. The local home guard, probably warned by a farmer's loud horn, made a stand there. On Hampton's approach, several armed civilians ran to the far end of town, took shelter in a wood shop, and opened fire. The Confederates charged and captured every defender, save one who was shot and killed when he attempted to escape through a window.[20] Leaving Mercersburg at 2:00, the troopers next took Bridgeport, Clay Lick, and Saint Thomas. The weather had worsened as rain now fell "in torrents." In Saint Thomas, Hampton's troopers again met minor opposition from home guardsmen. A few shots were fired, but no one was hurt. By the time the Confederates finished rounding up the overmatched Pennsylvanians, it was about 5:00 P.M. Gordon had been in the saddle for about twelve hours.[21]

The horse-soldiers next set their sights on Chambersburg. It was after nightfall when they took position on a hill about three-fourths of a mile outside the village. The rain only made the tired troopers more miserable after their long, tense day of riding.[22] "When we discovered the lights of the town," Hampton reported, "it was so dark that no reconnaissance could be made." With no way of finding out if the town was defended, Stuart and Hampton decided to demand Chambersburg's surrender before resorting to assault. After training the Washington Artillery's guns on the place, Hampton sent Lieutenant Thomas C. Lee and an escort "to demand that the town should be given up." Lieutenant Lee carried with him a promise that the town would be shelled if the Pennsylvanians resisted.[23]

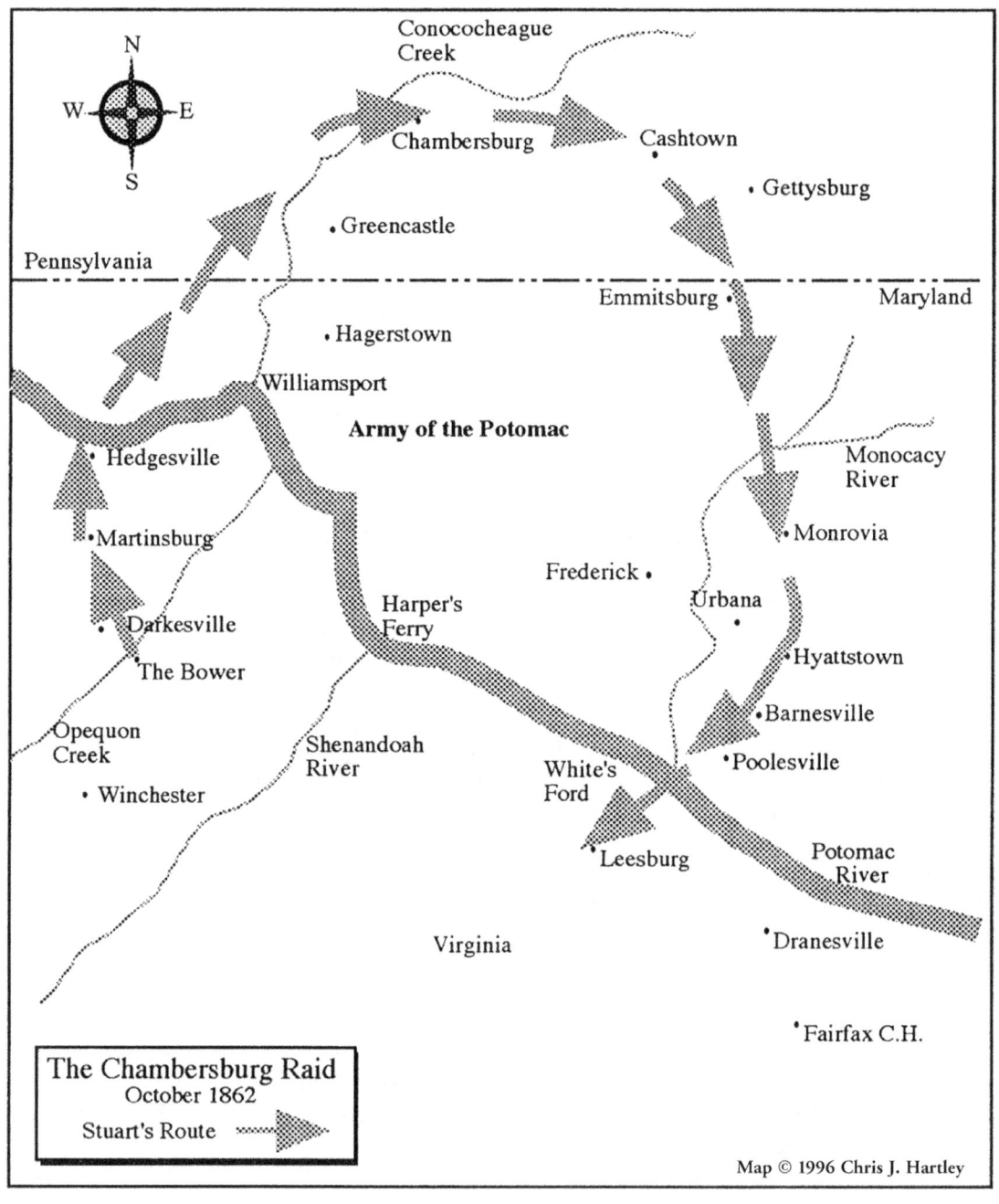

Gordon kept his men ready as the detachment rode down the hill and disappeared into the darkness. Earlier, the cavalrymen had heard drums beating in the town, probably calling civilians to arms; the moments must have been tense as they waited. Soon, three citizens approached the Confederates. They asked Hampton for terms of surrender. Hampton "demanded the unconditional surrender of the town, assuring them at the same time that private persons should be protected and private property unmolested, except such as should be needed for the use of our army."[24] The cowed citizens agreed.

Triumphantly, Gordon joined the raiders as they entered Chambersburg. It was about 8:00 P.M. Closed-up houses and horses attired in "gay Yankee trappings" seemed to be the only witnesses as the column was drawn up in the large public square in central Chambersburg.[25] Two troopers from the 1st hauled down "a genuine specimen of the star and stripes, which was flung to the breeze" under "very amusing circumstances" that are unfortunately lost to history.[26] There, Stuart named Hampton military governor and gave orders to the provost guard. The cavalry commander also asked Butler to relieve the town's bank of its funds. Although Butler's errand was in vain since the money had been whisked away, the bank's cashier provided food for many horse-soldiers.[27]

Hampton wanted his men to remain gentlemen during their stay in Chambersburg. The senior brigadier established a "rigid" provost guard to keep order. In his own way, Hampton also personally ensured that the locals would not suffer needlessly. Soon after entering Chambersburg, he approached a Main Street dwelling and knocked on the door. The person answering the door must have looked wide-eyed at the large, bearded officer in the faded gray coat standing on the doorstep. Hampton gave the home's occupants permission to shoot any private who attempted to enter their house unless he was accompanied by an officer.[28]

Dressed in "rags and filth," the cavalrymen combed the town. Thanks to the provost guard, they caused few problems for the locals. Politely, the men sought food, drink, and other amenities, as well as supplies and mounts. The cavalrymen also searched for hostages, but most of the town's officials had fled. The Southerners were only able to "capture" and parole about 275 sick and wounded Federal soldiers in the town's hospital.[29]

Meanwhile, Colonel "Grumble" Jones's command moved to destroy the railroad bridge over the Conococheague Creek. Jones reached the bridge without incident, only to find that it was made of solid iron. Unable to destroy the bridge, he tried to block the railroad.[30] This failure gave Jeb another reason to dislike Jones.

Back in Chambersburg, Gordon and his men bivouacked as directed by Hampton; Stuart had sent the South Carolinian's detachment through Chambersburg. They camped a short distance east of town, while Lee stayed on the opposite side.[31] For their part, Stuart and his staff bedded down outside town at the tollgate on the Gettysburg Road. Stuart's sleep was troubled as he worried about the Potomac River fords he hoped to gain. Would the fords be swollen, barring the raiders' escape? Rain continued to fall, making the night uncomfortable for all.[32]

The eleventh day of October 1862 was a Saturday. Gordon woke early. As he led his detachment into town to begin the day's work, someone discovered a large Union flag floating on top of a house. Two of Gordon's North Carolinians unceremoniously removed it. Then the troopers began withdrawing, save a detachment that was to destroy military stores that could not be removed. A correspondent noted that the Confederates "went away like gentlemen — that is, if good, new clothing will entitle a man to be called gentleman, for the stores and two car loads of new clothing was seized and distributed among the party...."[33]

"Gentlemen" may not be a good term for those who destroy, but such was the task of several of Gordon's Tarheels. Gordon's young friend from Hamptonville, twenty-two-year-old Captain William H. H. Cowles, drew the duty of firing the stores. When he mounted his horse and sped to join the rest of the brigade, Cowles left "blackened and smoldering remains" in an eight hundred square yard area.[34] Gordon was proud of Cowles's thorough job.

The cavalrymen did not know their next objective until Stuart turned the column eastward. It was an unexpected move. Yet Gordon, in the column of Cashtown-bound riders on the Gettysburg Road, trusted Stuart's judgment. His feeling was a universal one. To a man, they believed in their leader and were ready to follow him anywhere. At Cashtown, where they turned south toward Emmitsburg, Stuart's intentions became clear. Once again, he was riding around McClellan's army. The cavalry general had decided to cross the Potomac in the Leesburg area "particularly as Cox's command would have rendered the direction of the Cumberland, full of mountain gorges, particularly hazardous." Stuart also chose that route because the Federals would not expect him to return to Virginia by the longer, more dangerous way.[35] Still, as a precaution, Stuart did try to deceive scouts and civilians as to his destination.

Time pressed down on the column, but Gordon and his men remained steady. The sun marched across the sky; the Rebels covered the miles from Fairfield to the state line. They also continued to scour the region for fresh mounts. Along the way, they raided the "ample stalls" of the abolitionist Thaddeus Stevens. Gordon personally destroyed Stevens's furnace, and helped as the men "gobble[d] up some of the fine stock of [Stevens's] ... friends then domiciled in their Pennsylvania homes." After crossing into Maryland, however, Stuart closed up his formation and called in the details that were searching for horses.[36] Stuart wanted his men together and ready for whatever lay ahead.

The sun sank below the horizon when Stuart's troopers rode into Emmitsburg, "a pleasant and handsome little village." Thirty-one miles lay between them and Chambersburg; forty-five miles separated them from the Potomac River. With such a long journey remaining, the cavalrymen could only briefly enjoy the salutations of the town's citizens. At least one of Gordon's men, D. B. Rea, was wide-eyed at their reception. "Clusters of fair women and bevies of sparkling maidens," not to mention the old and the young, brought expressions of welcome and refreshments to the riders, he wrote.[37] Yet news that 150 Federal lancers had just passed meant the march must continue, even in the darkness.[38]

Aiming toward Frederick, the entire column increased its speed at Stuart's request. The rapid trot only made the men feel colder in the chilly night air. Beyond Emmitsburg, the column captured a Federal courier who carried messages bound for area commanders. Stuart reported, "... We intercepted dispatches ... which satisfied me that our whereabouts was still a problem to the enemy." Still, the dispatches made it clear that Union troops held Frederick, and that General Alfred Pleasonton and eight hundred Federals were just over four miles to the west and closing.[39] The enemy was in position to make the night a long one. The noise of Rebel horses' hooves slapping the road had a sense of urgency.

Bending southeastward to skirt Frederick, the column crossed the Monocacy River above Frederick and kept moving. As they began to pass landmarks familiar from their earlier trip to Maryland, Stuart and Blackford decided to pay a quick visit to Urbana. Before leaving, Stuart turned to Gordon's 1st North Carolina Cavalry and asked for a detail of ten men to guard them.[40] Once Captain Rufus Barringer — a former state senator Gordon had known from the North Carolina legislature — was selected to lead the detail, the party set off. They rode familiar trails and roads into Urbana and stopped at a house where they found a dear friend of Stuart's, a lady known as 'The New York Rebel.' After reminiscing with her and the other women who were present, the men sped to rejoin the march. Barringer, the bearded forty-year-old Cabarrus County native and organizer of Company F, doubtless enjoyed the diversion. He was in the service out of sympathy for his section. A brother-in-law of D. H.

Hill and "Stonewall" Jackson, Barringer loved the cavalry so much that he had previously declined an invitation to serve as Jackson's quartermaster general.[41]

The bulk of the column continued onward, through Liberty, New Market, and Monrovia. Led by guides familiar with the area, the troopers kept their horses at a trot during the long night. While the confident Stuart visited friends in Urbana, all Gordon could do was ride, manage his detachment's scouting efforts, and be an example to his men. Small unit leadership was critical in the darkness. Without proper guidance, men could become disoriented quickly. Stuart trusted that his subordinates would keep the column closed up and moving steadily and as noiselessly as possible. Stuart's trust in Gordon and the other commanders was well-placed. Still, there were problems that neither Gordon nor his fellow officers could solve. The march had to continue, but the tiring men began to sleep in their saddles. Moreover, the column's horses were becoming "jaded almost beyond endurance." The horse artillery had been forced to change horses three or four times during the night; only two horses in the entire column had made the whole trip. When the column crossed the Baltimore and Ohio Railroad in Monrovia, the horses were at least given a short rest while the cavalrymen cut telegraph wires and damaged tracks.[42]

At daybreak, the cavalrymen occupied Hyattstown, a town on McClellan's line of communication with Washington. The Confederates, artillery and all, had traveled the sixty-five miles from Chambersburg to Hyattstown in twenty hours.[43] Stuart, still escorted by Barringer's Tarheels, rejoined the column there and found their fellow troopers just as tired and frazzled as themselves. Stuart was also disappointed to find only a few Federal wagons at Hyattstown, forcing him to move on with few prizes. Empty-handed, they also felt the need to move fast. With the bulk of McClellan's army now only ten miles or so distant, the avenue of escape could close. The troopers could at least thank the previous evening's rain, for the wet ground gave up no clouds of dust to show the column's location.

Blackford remembered, "the march was the longest without a halt I have ever experienced." It did not seem like a Sunday morning to Gordon while the cavalrymen struggled to reach safety. As he fought off the ache of sore muscles and the desire to nod off, Gordon probably wished he was worshipping at St. Paul's Episcopal Church, back on the hill above Wilkesborough. Many cavalrymen became demoralized, but the spirit of the first ride around McClellan kept them going. The last twelve miles from Hyattstown to the river slowly slipped past.[44]

They were not safe yet, though. When the front of the five-mile long column reached Barnesville, they discovered that a company of Federal cavalry had just passed through. Ahead, Stuart learned, General George Stoneman had several thousand Yankees guarding Potomac River fords. A Union signal station was said to be atop Sugar Loaf Mountain, parallel to Stuart's planned line of march. And Pleasonton was still out there, somewhere.[45]

Hampton's command was the last to arrive in Barnesville. In town, the South Carolinian received new orders. Accordingly, he placed one artillery piece to command the Poolesville Road. His other gun and two regiments were to cover Stuart's rear as he led the way to the Potomac. The artillery piece was not challenged, but Federal pickets did appear in the area at about this time. From his defensive position along the Poolesville Road, Gordon began to hear firing from the direction of the Potomac.[46]

The firing Hampton's men heard was the result of Stuart's latest decision. He had concluded that he had no choice but to force his way through to the Potomac. The cavalry leader, after hearing news of Stoneman and assigning Hampton as rear-guard, had feinted south with the rest of his troopers toward Poolesville before angling southwestward through "a large body of woods which enveloped his command and concealed his movement." Their plunge into the trees not only left occupied Poolesville some two or three miles distant but also led Stuart to an old, disused road his guide had told him about. On the other side of the woods, the old trace joined another road that stretched from Poolesville to the junction of the Monocacy River and the Potomac. Throwing down a few fences, Stuart led his column along the old road and then turned it northward onto the Poolesville-Monocacy Road. He also sent word for Hampton to move his command toward the Potomac. It was about 8:00 A.M.[47]

At that moment, Alfred Pleasonton and four hundred enemy cavalrymen were riding from the mouth of the Monocacy toward Poolesville. With so many soldiers crisscrossing the land between Barnesville, Poolesville, and the Potomac and Monocacy rivers, it was surprising that the opposing forces had not met. A collision was inevitable. The Confederate advance had just cleared the woods and was riding north along the same road when Pleasonton's Union cavalry came into view. The Federals hesitated, unsure of the approaching soldiers' identity. Stuart did not balk; he ordered the charge "which was responded to in handsome style by the advance squadron ... of Lee's Brigade, which drove back the enemy's cavalry" to their main body. Rooney Lee's sharpshooters dismounted and peppered the Federal force, while "the gallant Pelham," with a single gun, unlimbered and opened fire. Pelham also turned his attention to Unionist batteries posted on the far side of the Little Monocacy, a stream below the Monocacy.[48]

Two miles to Stuart's left waited a little-known Potomac River ford. Captain B. S. White, the column's current guide and a native of the area, had told Stuart enough for the commander to select the ford as his way out. Leaving Pelham and Hampton's rear-guard to cover the withdrawal, Stuart ordered his men to dash for that point before the Federals closed the bottleneck. The ford was accessed by a farm road that joined the Poolesville-Monocacy Road. Spurring their tired horses on, Rooney Lee's Brigade led the way. Jones's cavalrymen followed.[49] Virginia lay ahead, and the Southerners were determined not to let the Yankees detain them. They could only hope that the recent rains had not swelled the river to render the ford impassable.

At last, the ford was before them. Stuart's advance, along with the led horses and wagons, approached. The river looked passable, but the Yankees seemed ready to prevent it. Two hundred Federal infantrymen were posted along cliffs on the other side of the Little Monocacy that overlooked the ford. Despairing of assaulting such a strong position, Colonel Lee demanded the Federals' surrender. Lee hoped to bluff his way out of his predicament, but the message went unanswered. With no alternative, the Confederates opened fire. Artillery unlimbered and sharpshooters brought their weapons to bear. Regiments stepped off. It looked as if the Southerners would have to earn their safety with blood. At the next development, the cavalrymen broke into wild cheers: the Federals on the bluff began withdrawing. "Is it possible!" some yelled. "They are retreating! They are retreating!" With that, Stuart reported, "the crossing of the canal and river was effected with all the precision of passing a defile on drill."[50]

Hampton's troopers, in positions on the farm road and on the Poolesville-Monocacy Road, provided cover while Lee's and Jones's men splashed across the river. Ignoring Union fire and the efforts of some officers, thirsty horses stopped in mid-stream and drank. Stuart, ever confident, directed the crossing while Pelham occupied the Federal artillery's attention. He moved his piece from place to place as he fired, each time a bit nearer the river.[51]

When Lee and Jones finished crossing, Hampton sited Pelham's gun to command the approaches to the ford. Then, Hampton began his own withdrawal. The South Carolina general called in his skirmishers and ordered the 10th Virginia and Gordon's North Carolinians to hurry to the river. The Phillips Legion was also nearby, and it, too, dashed for the waters. Butler's South Carolinians, the rearmost guard, were summoned. To be certain, Stuart also hurried couriers to Butler.[52]

The Confederates added more lead to cover the withdrawal. By the time Hampton's leading regiment, the 10th Virginia, was across, W. H. F. Lee had been able to set up some batteries on the Virginia side of the river to cover the withdrawal. The Phillips Legion enjoyed the extra support lent by the artillery.

Somewhere in the confusion, Gordon ordered his men to cross the river. Since Cowles and a small detachment were still with Butler's South Carolinians in the rear-guard, Gordon had fewer than 150 men with him. Gordon's men trudged hurriedly through the cold waters of the rugged ford. Soon, all were across except for Pelham, Butler, and Cowles.

Gordon shouted orders and fired his weapon as his detachment, and every other cavalryman on the Virginia side, supported Pelham in his courageous fight. More Federal infantrymen and cavalrymen were appearing by the minute, but Pelham's work deterred Federal attacks. As he fired his piece, Pelham changed directions often because the enemy approached from all sides.[53]

No one had heard from Butler. Stuart grew worried as the moments ticked by. Gordon likewise began to wonder about

J.E.B. Stuart was quite fond of Gordon. Kindred spirits, the two men grew closer as the war continued (Library of Congress).

Cowles. If the Carolinians did not come soon, they would be lost. Pelham could not keep the ford open indefinitely. After four couriers failed, W. W. Blackford volunteered to fetch them. He recrossed the river, dashed along the farm road, and raced back onto the Poolesville-Monocacy Road. He had ridden more than three miles before he found Butler's men. They were still fighting Pleasonton along the Poolesville-Monocacy Road. Butler had been moving down the farm road toward the ford when Cowles and the rearmost elements, still on the Poolesville-Monocacy Road, were overtaken by the Federals. Butler had been forced to turn and help Cowles fight off this attack.[54]

Breathlessly, Blackford explained the situation. The cavalrymen broke off the fight and galloped for the ford. After three miles of frantic riding, Butler saw that Pelham still held open the way of retreat. The artilleryman even increased his rate of fire to give an impression of strength.[55] Butler's troopers splashed through the waters with dispatch. The brave Cowles, grandson of a Revolutionary War soldier, also finished his day's admirable work. He followed Butler across the river, as did Pelham with his lone artillery piece.[56] Stuart, hat in hand, met Butler in the river. "Well done, my brave boy," he said.[57] The last men in the column were still in the river when the Federals swarmed about the just-abandoned bank, firing on their retreating foes.

Stuart was joyous; none of his men had been severely hurt in the crossing.[58] The belligerent Federals, still swarming about the ford on the Maryland side, did not pursue. The weary Confederates turned their backs on Maryland, Pennsylvania, and invasion, and headed south. They rode for a few more miles until they reached Leesburg. Amid shouts and congratulations, the exhausted raiders dismounted and rested. Lieutenant Colonel Gordon lay down on the grass after caring for his horse.[59]

Stuart's second, and perhaps most daring, ride around McClellan was over. Later, Stuart reported to Lee the information his troopers had gleaned and the damage they had caused. Although they failed to destroy the iron railroad bridge, the cavalrymen had left in ruin public and railroad property worth $250,000. Moreover, the Southerners brought with them thirty hostages and 1,200 horses. Only two men were missing, one of whom was rumored to have been so drunk they had to leave him behind.[60]

The cavalrymen had added luster to the reputation of Stuart's Cavalry Division, and Gordon was proud to be a part of it. Hampton called it a "well-managed affair," but also worried that "Stuart will as usual give all the credit to his Virginia Brigades. He praises them on all occasions, but does not give us any credit." Memories of being left behind during the march toward Maryland apparently still stung. However, Stuart did publicly commend Gordon for his service in the raid.[61]

When they returned to their positions in the Martinsburg area, Hampton's troopers enjoyed a short but well-deserved rest. Gordon, however, did not enjoy as much rest as he would have liked. Baker was absent on detached service, so Gordon assumed command of the regiment.[62] First, he ensured that the men who had not participated in the raid stayed busy picketing. Paperwork also waited. One of his assigned chores was to prepare a statement tracking the number and fate of horses furnished by the state of North Carolina. It was evidently a monthly report that was forwarded to the state government. Gordon's work revealed that between October 1 and 31, 1862, the regiment had 688 state-furnished horses in its employ. Company A had the most with 93 horses, and Company I had the fewest mounts with 46. The report indicated that the enemy had captured six of the regiment's horses, each valued at $150.00 a head. Otherwise, the horses of the 1st had enjoyed a casualty-free month.[63]

While not working, Gordon saw to his men's welfare by being a leader in relaxation. "In camp," remembered one of Stuart's staff-members, "off duty, [Gordon] was the soul of good fellowship." Expeditions like the one in Maryland certainly gave the men plenty to celebrate, but they needed no victory for spirited singing, talking, and joking. One favorite tale in the camps of the 1st concerned a "cavalry charge" that had been executed earlier in the war. The occasion had been tense because the enemy was dug in and ready. Baker had sized up the situation and decided to charge. Unfortunately, a misunderstanding of orders resulted in a charge of only three horsemen. Baker, his bugler, and Charles D. Malone were unable to take the position. Malone, a courier for both Hampton and Stuart who was known as "Little C. D.," did not mind hearing the tale told again.[64]

Gordon also liked to pick on his fellow officers. John Esten Cooke told the story of a "merry and light hearted" ride with Gordon and staff-officer Andrew Reid Venable. One day, the three men were trotting along with a column of horse-soldiers on a monotonous journey that left time for talk. Soon the discussion turned to the "propriety of kissing." With side winks at Cooke, Gordon supported kissing. Venable was "horror struck and indignantly virtuous." Firing in the distance ended the joke, apparently with Venable none the wiser.[65]

The remainder of October passed with little incident save one more pleasant affair. On Sunday, October 26, the troopers of Hampton's Brigade staged a grand review. Among others, the Confederates invited ladies to come see the show. Ladies came "from far and near, and as the day was lovely, it proved a fine military spectacle." Afterward, officers from Hampton's and Stuart's staffs watched the "trial of a diminutive one-pounder gun, which turned out to be of very little account." Equestrian sports such as horse racing and fence jumping were also enjoyed.[66] The day brought a renewal of strength and confidence, even though Hampton still wondered if his men had received enough credit for their service.

While Gordon marched in review, McClellan's war machine lurched into motion again. Lincoln had tired of suggesting a new offensive and summarily ordered McClellan to take advantage of the favorable fall weather. McClellan listened, but dragged his feet until October 26. On that day, the Northern army stepped on Virginia soil once more. This time, McClellan aimed toward Warrenton, taking roads between the Blue Ridge and Bull Run Mountains. By November 3, the entire Federal army stood on the Virginia side of the Potomac. General Pleasonton's cavalry brigade led the way south.[67]

The Confederates pulled back, reluctantly leaving a countryside still full of hay and forage.[68] Lee characteristically divided his forces by sending Jackson up the Shenandoah Valley and Longstreet by way of Front Royal to Culpeper. He took precautions so that the detachments could not be attacked in detail and so that Richmond would never be uncovered. That meant preparing a defense along the Rappahannock River. As his infantry moved, Lee wondered what McClellan was up to.

Gordon's days of rest ended abruptly because of these events. The regiment had spent an unusually long time camping in a single location, so Gordon was probably not surprised when the movement orders came. On October 30, Stuart drew the assignment of watching Union movements and delaying their progress. On a hazy, rainy autumn day, Stuart told Hampton to withdraw from Martinsburg and move his brigade to Upperville by November 3.[69] From that point, not far from Ashby's Gap in the Blue Ridge, the brigade would be in position to assist the cavalry in its mission. "Grumble's" men moved to guard Jackson's rear. Fitz Lee's thousand troopers — under the temporary command of Colonel Williams C. Wickham as Lee was sick — screened Longstreet's move. Rearguard action became the order of the day.[70]

Those early days of November, one trooper recalled, featured "an endless series of skirmishes." Obscure villages like Mountsville, Union, and Paris became the scenes of this vicious mini-war. While the Federals plodded southward toward their objectives, the blue cavalry blazed the way, often supported by infantry and artillery. Stuart barred the way by standing, and then falling back; standing, and falling back; and again.[71] Each stand, they hoped, would delay McClellan's advance and give Lee more time to prepare a reception. Beyond that, the Confederates hoped to extract a price for every bit of ground their enemy gained.

As he harassed the oncoming foe, the cavalry commander tried to predict the enemy's designs. He sent Blackford with a reconnaissance party to the Blue Ridge to take an elevated look at what was coming. Blackford saw trains and men pouring southward from Leesburg, confirming beyond any doubt McClellan's route of invasion.[72] The Confederate cavalry worked hard to slow the Federal storm, and even lent a hand to Jones — by way of Ashby's Gap — in covering Jackson's retreat up the Shenandoah.

Gordon celebrated his fortieth birthday on November 2 at Martinsburg. It was the second he had passed as a soldier, yet if the cynicism of a veteran had touched him he may have wondered how many birthdays he had left. This was not the same man who had turned thirty-nine way back in the war's early days. Indeed, life had continued to change for Gordon as the war worsened: more responsibility, more fighting, more hardship, more death, and the sufferings of family and friends. Yet even in the midst of such a morbid existence, life could take positive turns. On November 6 Augustus and Martha Finley gave birth to Gordon's newest nephew, Thomas Brown Finley. R. F. and Carrie Hackett added a niece, Florence, on the twenty-eighth. That was reason enough to celebrate. As for Thomas Finley, who was named after Gordon's deceased half brother, he would one day keep his Uncle James's memory alive with speeches and research. Of course, the war did not stop for the cries of babies or the celebration of a birthday. Leaving Martinsburg on November 3, Gordon's regiment rode with Hampton's Brigade toward a junction with the cavalry by way of Bunker Hill and Berryville.[73]

In the Valley, Hampton's Brigade "met nothing of special interest save the wishful looks of many a longing old man or fair maiden as we passed along." The warriors simply rode with urgency, toward the Shenandoah River and Upperville. Late on November 3, Hampton's Brigade reached Millwood, near Ashby's Gap in the Blue Ridge, where Jackson had his headquarters. Hampton reported to Stuart there since the latter was still assisting Jackson.[74] Early the next morning, Stuart changed Hampton's destination and ordered him to Markham's Station, astride Manassas Gap, to assist Fitz Lee's Brigade. That unit was now under Thomas L. Rosser as Wickham had been wounded in the neck by a shell fragment. Soon, Stuart also moved the rest of the cavalry toward a junction there.[75]

During the march, Stuart, who had found Ashby's Gap occupied by the enemy, met Hampton at Linden and moved with him toward Markham. That night they discovered that the Federals had arrived at Markham first and forced Munford to retire. Despite Blackford's description of thousands of Yankees pressing southward, Stuart decided around midnight to make yet another stand at Barbee's. "I am determined not to retire without fighting, and shall give battle to the Yankees tomorrow," he said. Accordingly, he made his dispositions there, and had the troopers barricade the road. He posted Fitz Lee's (Rosser's) Brigade of five regiments, barely 900 strong, on the right (east).[76] Hampton's he sent to the left, astride the crossroads, with a portion of both commands in reserve. A detachment of the 1st North Carolina Cavalry formed part of that reserve on the left. Completing his arrangements, Stuart dispatched artillery and sharpshooters to a hill crest north of Barbee's where it could rake the enemy's column as it moved up the road. More artillery, supported by a squadron of the 1st, unlimbered at the crossroads. Thus aligned, Stuart awaited the inevitable Federal advance.[77]

Lieutenant Colonel Gordon spent the night in position with the 1st in fields about one mile behind Barbee's Crossroads. The hamlet was nothing more than an old store house and a few dilapidated buildings surrounded by undulating, open fields. Rough stone fences could be seen here and there, but the terrain was otherwise unremarkable. As if to avoid this, Stuart and Hampton slept in a house in the nearby town of Sandy Hook. Ironically, Pleasonton would enjoy sleeping in the same room the following night.[78]

Gordon woke early on Wednesday morning in his regiment's bivouac. Since Baker was still absent, Gordon was in command. As the men stirred, they boiled coffee and prepared breakfast. Gordon saw to it that they were ready for action. Little did Gordon suspect that the day would bring one of the greatest tests of his life: regimental command in a losing battle.[79] Hampton, however, knew that a fight was in the offing. He sent a courier to the nearest infantry camp, that of D. H. Hill, to inform him of the impending fight. Hampton also requested that all exposed parties be alerted so that they might seek safety. Finally, in preparing his command, Hampton had to confront the fact that no more than three-fourths of his men were fit for duty.[80]

At 9:00 A.M. that November 5, the Federals came as Stuart and Hampton thought they would. It was Brigadier General Pleasonton and the cavalry's 2d Brigade, supported by a battery of artillery. They rode not knowing what awaited them. The Confederates gave Pleasonton a fierce welcome to the strategic crossroads with artillery and carbine fire. The Federals,

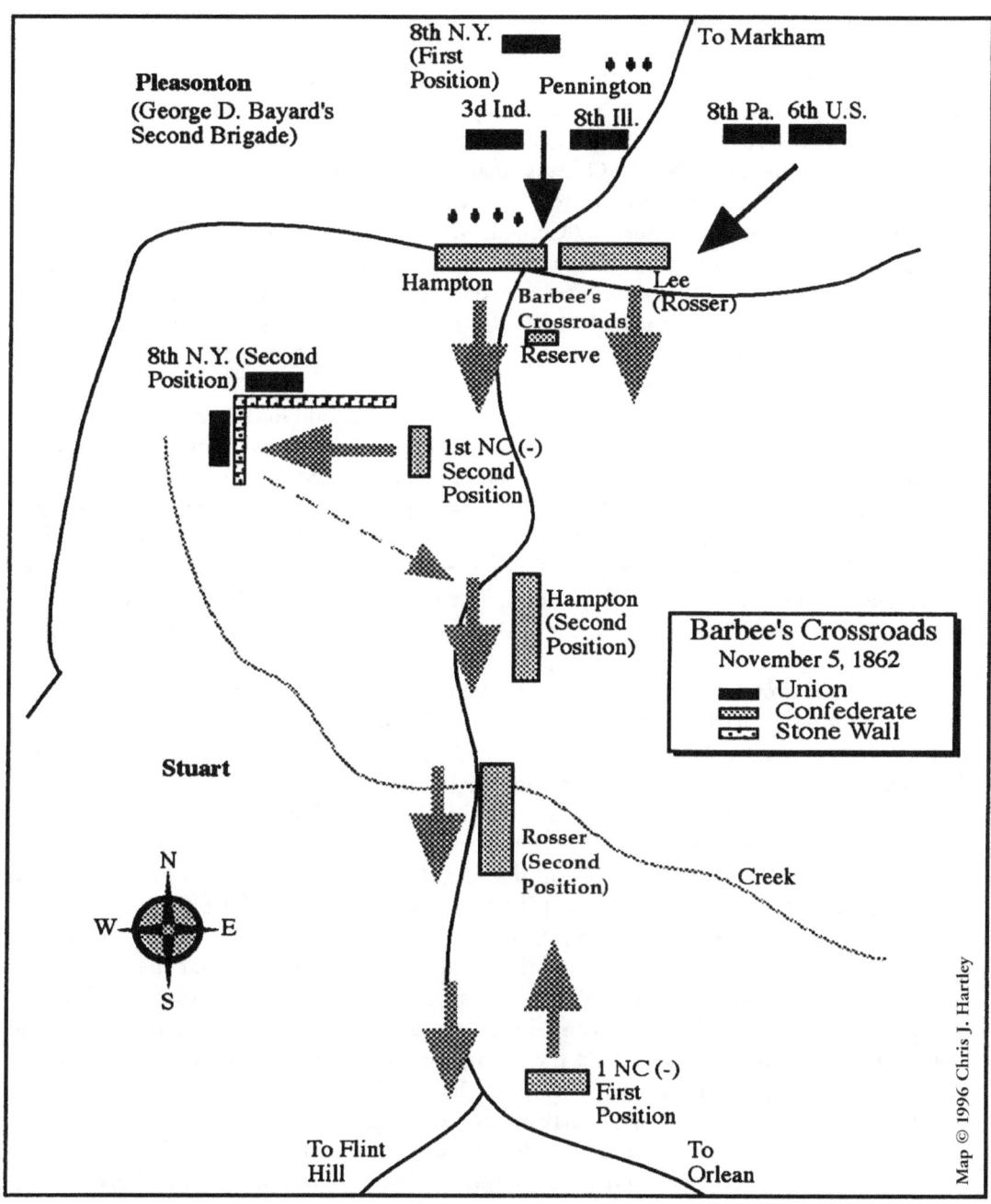

somewhat surprised, accordingly deployed. Federal troopers moved along the road and on either side of it.[81] They answered Pelham with their own battery. The 8th Illinois and 3d Indiana cavalry regiments took up positions in the center, while an artillery battery moved to the right of the road, supported by the 8th New York. Pleasonton then dispatched Colonel David Gregg with the 8th Pennsylvania Cavalry and the 6th U.S. Cavalry toward the east where some ravines and woods offered cover and flanking possibilities.[82]

Gordon listened as artillery and small-arms fire crackled in the chilly November air. He waited for a call to come to the crossroads.

While the Federals moved to their left to flank the enemy, Jeb received disturbing news: a Federal force had been spotted in Warrenton, in his rear. Stuart — at that point unaware that the Federals were moving up through the ravines — decided that he was dealing with a diversion, and the real Federal move was via Warrenton. Citing the "delay and lack of vigor in the enemy's attack at this point," the general ordered Hampton to withdraw by way of the Flint Hill Road and Rosser by the Orleans Road. He used both roads to prevent bunching up. It was well that Stuart had decided to withdraw, for the Federals' flanking movement was close to being in position.[83] Thus, the Confederates began falling back from their positions about the crossroads, and the Federals followed down the main road, which was lined with a stone wall to the west. Von Borcke remembered one chilling sight of the retreat. A Confederate horseman, killed by a bullet through the brain, stiffened so quickly that he remained bolt upright in his saddle, his horse still jogging with the others. It was several minutes before his comrades realized the man was dead.[84]

It was about noon. A courier dashed into the 1st's camp and Gordon met him. The man handed Gordon a dispatch from Hampton, which ordered the North Carolinian to send a squadron to the crossroads to act as sharpshooters. Gordon gave the order. A few minutes later, he looked up and saw General Hampton himself approaching. Hampton ordered Gordon to take the remainder of his command — four squadrons of 275 men, or eight companies — to support the Cobb Legion's withdrawal. Gordon nodded and shouted the appropriate orders, spurring his men toward the legion's position. The legion was posted three-fourths of a mile away on the left where it was in support of the horse artillery. The Bloody 1st was going to war again.[85]

Up the road toward Barbee's the Rebels rode. As they covered the ground toward the fighting, Gordon glanced westward, to his left, and hesitated. "I saw the enemy in a large body...," he reported, "on the opposite side of the field, some 600 yards across. I discovered that I could be flanked and cut off in moving farther up."[86]

As the commander on the scene, Gordon made his decision quickly. He reined in his horse and shouted new orders. This force had to be dealt with to ensure the safety of the Confederate retreat. Seeing a low place in the field that would offer cover from Federal fire, Gordon directed his men to move toward the enemy and halt in the depression. The men of the 1st turned and spurred their mounts; small-arms fire continued to pop and crack. Gordon's faithful Pigeon led the way. From his saddle, Gordon took a careful look at the terrain and considered his next move. In front of the depression, the ground rose toward the Yankees. Riding to the top of the hill, Gordon could make out a stone wall that seemed to mark where Confederate-held territory ended and the enemy's began. To the north (Gordon's right) — toward Barbee's Crossroads — was another stone fence.[87]

Beyond the wall ahead, the Federals saw the Confederates and reacted, sending mounted skirmishers toward Gordon's column. Gordon, in response, turned and yelled for the first set of fours to dismount and move to the crest of the hill. While one man held their horses, three other men jumped from their mounts, ran to the hill-crest, and opened fire. As the Federal skirmishers turned tail, Gordon sent a courier in search of Hampton to report the situation.[88] He deployed his troopers while awaiting further orders.

Hampton reached Gordon's side in minutes. Things were happening quickly, and not going the Southerners' way. As Hampton rode up, across the field a squadron of Federal cavalry darted up and took position along the stone fence. Gordon also thought he saw more enemy troopers to his right, toward Barbee's, diving behind the cover of the fence in that direction. The Confederates did not know it, but they were troopers from Colonel Benjamin F. Davis's 8th New York Cavalry regiment moving up behind the retreating Confederates.[89]

Gordon turned to his commanding officer. Shouting above the noise, he asked, "Should I charge them? There is also a large body of Yankees to my right, behind a stone fence, and they have posted sharpshooters there."

Hampton's deep voice came back, dismissing the possibility of any activity to the north. "No, there is no stone fence there. I was there this morning, and it is open. You may charge."[90]

Gordon fixed his hazel eyes on the general. His ears, covered partially by his brown hair which curled only at its ends, heard his men as they yelled and fired at the Yankees. "Shall I charge in squadron form?" he asked.

"Yes," the burly South Carolinian said. "I will support you with the Second South Carolina."[91]

Gordon swung about and ordered his bugler to sound the charge. As if shot out of a gun, the 1st pointed their lathered horses up and over the hill and bounded toward the stone wall in front. They rode "rapidly at the men we could see." Gordon tried not to worry about what he thought he had seen on his right. The Federals, looking up, saw the North Carolinians pounding down on their position, firing as they came. The mental effects of the sight caused the blue-coats in front to flee through a narrow opening in the fence and up over a hill behind the fence.[92]

The charging Confederates neared the fence in the Federals' wake. Suddenly, Gordon heard the squeal of horses and shouts of some of his men. Looking to see what was happening, Gordon was surprised to see a broad ditch, until now concealed by grass and weeds, squarely across their path. Several of the Tarheels who had not seen the ditch in time rode directly into it, crashing into the weeds and falling off their mounts. Due to this obstruction, the charge slowed while the Confederates struggled to recover their formation.[93]

When he saw that the charge had lost momentum, Gordon shouted for troopers in the advance to lunge through the fence opening and pursue the enemy. Several troopers did so, but not one of them glanced at the fence to the north which formed something of a right angle with the one in front. If they had, it would not have mattered much, because by then it was too late to do anything about what was there. About 150 Federals from Davis's 8th New York were still there. The ditch disaster gave them their chance. As the North Carolinians floundered about, the blue-clad horse soldiers — all dismounted — pointed their weapons at the chargers and pulled the triggers. An artillery piece added its deep-throated boom to the volley.[94]

Lead flew into Gordon's ranks, unhorsing several men. Gordon, as he turned his weapon on the enemy, quickly surveyed the situation. He looked in vain for the promised support from the 2d South Carolina Cavalry, but as he learned later, that regiment was blocked in the road by the retreating Cobb Legion. "Seeing no chance to get at the enemy, and being exposed to a terrible fire from the sharpshooters and artillery (which were nearby), I ordered the regiment to retire from that position by the left-about wheel." In this manner, Gordon hoped to turn his troopers away from the stone wall and reach safety quicker; but instead, he exposed it to more destruction.[95]

As the Confederates wheeled, Gordon's gallant charge received its last blow. "To my surprise," he reported, "I saw a large body of cavalry charging upon us from the right, which had been concealed from view by a hill."[96] The Union cavalry pounded Gordon's flank, horses screaming, men shouting, and weapons firing. That did it; the Confederates broke and galloped out of there. Pleasonton reported the flank attack sent the Confederates "flying in all directions."[97] Alabama-born Benjamin F. "Grimes" Davis, an 1854 West Point graduate and experienced Indian fighter, had won his battle with great skill. When Gordon's charge had reached the stone wall, Davis recognized the flanking opportunity afforded by the fence and sent a detachment to hit Gordon's right. Then, as the flanked Confederates turned to escape and again exposed their flank, Davis finished off his fight by ordering the remainder of his regiment to charge. Davis did not even need the help of the 3d Indiana, which had come up to his support.

Gordon's troopers fell back with some impetus. Legend has it that Gordon soon met Pelham, whose guns had supported Gordon's charge with solid shot. According to a part-fiction part-history account by Cooke:

> The fine face of the North Carolinian was flushed with rage; his eyes glared; he could ill brook such a repulse.
> Pelham met him with a calm smile. "Don't annoy yourself, Colonel," he said, "they won't ride over me." And, turning to an officer, he said coolly: "Double-shot all the guns with canister."[98]

On that field, the respect and admiration that the men had for Gordon was evident when he somehow managed to rally most of his troopers back at the depression. Yet some, despite Gordon's efforts, "Went into the road against orders." Ignoring these, Gordon readied his men to beat off the enemy as they followed up their success; but the Federals apparently reeled and hesitated under Pelham's fire. The Old 1st's exceptional recovery was rewarded, in a small way, when they captured or killed three stray Federals.[99]

At that point, Major William G. Delony galloped up with reinforcements from the Cobb Legion. Joining with the ever-bold Captain Cowles and the gallant Lieutenant Jesse W. Siler, Delony's small band "made a dash at the enemy," that forced the Federals back. The enemy pressure ended momentarily, and the artillery duel intensified.[100]

The way out was now clear. After about two more hours of Pelham's cannonading, the Confederates completed their withdrawal. Hampton directed Gordon to fall back to Warrenton, where Rosser's Brigade was headed. It was about 3:00 P.M. By nightfall, citizens passing through D. H. Hill's camps spread the word that Hampton's Brigade had suffered greatly but still distinguished itself.[101] Gordon could attest to that: he had lost four men killed and seventeen wounded or captured. Most of the missing men had been dismounted at the ditch and captured there. Pleasonton reported that the Confederates lost thirty-seven men killed at Barbee's, "and more than that number of arms, horses, and prisoners were captured." The Federals lost five men killed and eight wounded.[102]

Whatever their actual loss, the Tarheels had fought hard against the odds — odds that made Barbee's Crossroads another crimson stain on the record of the Bloody 1st. Again, the North Carolinians had been taught a lesson in cavalry tactics. This time, it seemed, Hampton was as much at fault as anyone; Gordon had, after a fashion, pointed out his exposed right flank, but that did not change the outcome. The 1st had charged under orders, was flanked twice, and beaten soundly. The shock of these attacks — and doubtless the cries of his men as they fell dead or wounded — taught Gordon more about being a cavalry commander than any West Point class could have. Never again would James B. Gordon expose his flanks with such recklessness.

At the same time, Gordon's decision to attack the stray Federal force back of Barbee's may have prevented a larger disaster. If the Federals had established a strong position, they could have pounded the retreating Confederate columns. Moreover, Stuart himself might also have paid closer attention to the skirmish; it was a sign that the Union cavalry was making great strides, and would soon be the Confederate cavalry's equal.[103] Although Barbee's Crossroads remained an insignificant event, it paid dividends toward the development of James Gordon as a cavalry officer.

Later, Stuart ironically found no enemy troops in Warrenton. The 2d North Carolina

Cavalry Regiment, recently arrived from the Old North State, had repulsed the Federals there.[104]

In Washington, the tiny victory at Barbee's Crossroads went unnoticed. Abraham Lincoln only saw that McClellan had taken ten days to move his army fifty miles. The president had had enough. On November 7, he relieved McClellan and replaced him with Ambrose Burnside. Burnside formally assumed command two days later.[105]

The Confederate cavalry underwent change as well that November. Since the Battle of Sharpsburg, several new arrivals had increased the number of units in the cavalry division. With that in mind, General Robert E. Lee decided it was time for a reorganization to balance the size of each brigade. Dated November 10, 1862, Special Orders Number 238 added a brigade, to be commanded by the newly promoted W. H. F. "Rooney" Lee. The 5th, 9th, 10th, and 15th Virginia regiments, plus the 2d North Carolina Cavalry, joined his brigade. Another new brigadier, William E. "Grumble" Jones, had assumed command of Robertson's old brigade in December. His unit, consisting of the 6th, 7th, and 12th Virginia Regiments, the 17th Virginia Battalion, and Colonel Elijah White's 35th Virginia Battalion, operated in the Valley at that point. Fitz Lee's Brigade was composed of the 1st, 2d, 3d, and 4th Virginia Regiments, and Hampton's Brigade of the 1st and 2d South Carolina Cavalry Regiments, the 1st North Carolina Cavalry, and the Cobb and Phillips Legions. Returns showed that Stuart's cavalry division contained 479 officers and 6,697 men present for duty, with a total aggregate present and absent of 12,107 troopers.[106]

The day after the Barbee's fight was not a happy day for either Jeb Stuart or James Gordon. The necessity of retreat was enough to displease both men, but on top of that Stuart learned that his daughter had just died after a short illness. It was a blow from which he would never recover.[107] Gordon struggled with his own problems. The defeat at Barbee's had been a blow to his confidence. Would he overcome it? The answer was not long in coming.

On November 6, Federal pressure forced Rosser out of Warrenton. As a result, Stuart had to relinquish the territory north of the Rappahannock to the advancing enemy army. He had not yet finished with retarding that advance, however. His next line of resistance centered on Jeffersonton, where Fitz Lee's Brigade reined in. Outposts spread out along the Rappahannock. Hampton's Brigade began covering Sperryville, on the left, from advance posts at Gaines's Crossroads and Amissville. The 1st North Carolina Cavalry, in the advance, camped for the night in a patch of thick timber near the crossroads. The woods, nestled behind a line of hills, deflected the evening breeze but did not completely deter the bitter cold. Worse, the Carolinians had no axes so they had difficulties procuring firewood.[108] In this frigid camp, Gordon confronted his troubled memory of November 5.

Snow began falling on the morning of November 7 and continued into the afternoon. No orders came from headquarters, so Gordon's men did little besides huddle around makeshift campfires. The Yankees, however, decided to pay a visit. Near 3:00 P.M., carbine-fire sounded from the direction of Gordon's picket line. A courier soon appeared with news of the enemy's approach. By the time the Carolinians found their weapons, the Federal advance drew near. A large body of dismounted blue cavalry came into view on the right, while a second column of enemy troopers advanced along the main road. The odds loomed large, especially with the rest of Hampton's Brigade camped too far away to be of any help. Baker had not returned; it was up to Gordon. First, he placed his men in a defensive position to hold the road. Then he considered the flanking column, and dispatched Lieutenant Jesse Siler and a dismounted force to the right. While the bulk of the 1st held the road, Siler's men drove the Federals against their supports, ruined the flanking maneuver, and ended the fight. This repaired Gordon's reputation, but Siler, a promising and popular officer from Macon County, paid for it with his life. The men wept over Siler's body while his blood reddened the fresh snow.[109]

Here the matter ended for the time being. The Federal army, which now occupied the Warrenton area in strength, pushed outposts toward the Rappahannock. Stuart skirmished with the Federal advance at Amissville, and kept his cavalry along the Rappahannock and around the forks of the Hazel and Aestham rivers to protect Longstreet's Culpeper camps.[110] As the initiative remained with the Federals, the Confederate cavalry kept alert.

The Army of the Potomac, like the winter weather, now held a large portion of Virginia in its grasp.

8

Spent and Recovered

Gordon knew horses. His first ride came early in life, and he grew to rely on the beasts more when he turned to farming and business. After spending years in the saddle, the Wilkes Countian considered himself a fine equestrian. He held a special love for horses, and had a good idea of how much strain they could take. Little of this really prepared him for duty as a cavalry officer, for managing the well-being of a thousand horses was a different task altogether. Still, he knew that exhausted, broken down horses resulted in a useless cavalry unit. Thus, as the winter of 1862 settled in, one key question emerged: could the officers and men of Hampton's Brigade keep their means of transportation, and their unit, in fighting condition?

Winter would provide no break from fighting, and therein lay the problem. The Union army was on the move again, marching south under its new commander. General Ambrose E. Burnside, conqueror of Roanoke Island and New Bern, officially assumed command of the Army of the Potomac on November 9. Remembering his adversary's audacity, he ignored the separated pieces of Lee's army (Longstreet still waited in Culpeper County and Jackson held the Valley). Instead, the reluctant Yankee chose a cautious strategy. By taking Fredericksburg, Burnside believed he could protect Washington and the army's supply lines. He would also be astride the most direct route to Richmond. Although it was not what Lincoln had in mind, he approved Burnside's plan.

Lurching forward on November 15, the Federal army marched quickly toward their goal in the hopes they could capture Fredericksburg before Lee could establish a defense. Herded before the advancing Federals, the Confederate cavalry continued its prying ways. Scouting, patrolling, and skirmishing with the Federals, they learned what they could. At times, the Federals proved inhospitable. During one November action, a Union bullet clipped Stuart's beloved mustache in two.[1]

Undeterred, the first Federal troops reached the Rappahannock about forty-eight hours after leaving Warrenton. Burnside's plan then fell apart because promised pontoon trains failed to arrive. General Lee perceived his adversary's intentions, and Stuart's patrols confirmed the Federal menace to Fredericksburg.[2] In response, Lee directed his army to converge there. By November 24, Burnside had the bulk of his army, as well as the pontoons, on hand, but by then the sound of digging Confederates filled the air. Robert E. Lee exploited the terrain, posting Longstreet's corps behind the town along a towering ridge called Marye's Heights. Lee concentrated Stonewall Jackson's troops south of town, and left a detachment of butternut infantry in the town itself to hinder any crossing attempts. The gauntlet had been thrown down. Burnside, however, could not decide how to react. Should he cross here and attack

Lee head-on, or should he cross the river elsewhere and outflank the Confederates? Or was it time to prepare a completely different plan? Stuart tried to make his decision harder.

The Confederate cavalry commander pulled his troopers back before Burnside's advance and established headquarters on Telegraph Road, five miles from Fredericksburg. Extending his cavalry lines along the river about twenty miles below and thirty miles above the town, the Virginian kept his troopers on the lookout for flanking movements. Fitz Lee's (Rosser's) Brigade covered the Spotsylvania Court House area, while the second son of the commanding general, twenty-five-year-old William Henry Fitzhugh "Rooney" Lee, took position near Port Royal.[3] The intelligent and talented "Rooney," a Harvard graduate, prepared to draw on his experience as a second lieutenant in the Utah campaign or as a cavalry commander in Western Virginia and with Stuart earlier in the war.[4]

Gordon, as always, was in the middle of it. He bundled up against the cold and trudged through the persistent snow as Hampton's Brigade took position east of Culpeper near the upper Rappahannock. The 1st North Carolina Cavalry set up beside a saw mill near Germanna Ford on the Rapidan.[5] Like the rest of the brigade, the 1st dispatched pickets to cover Rappahannock River crossing-spots like Freeman's Ford, Beverly Ford, Kelly's Ford, and Fields's Ford. Ordered to watch diligently for signs of Federal flanking attacks, they saw none.

The single enemy activity in Stuart's front presented an opportunity, not a threat. North of the Federal and Confederate battle lines, the Telegraph Road trailed between the divergent courses of the Rappahannock and Potomac rivers. The road and the terrain between the rivers carried some strategic value. Although the Army of the Potomac at Fredericksburg received most of its supplies by water via Aquia Creek, various cavalry reinforcements, sutlers' wagons, and trains traveled the Telegraph Road.[6] They made attractive targets, but would bold winter raids in the Federal rear be worth the potential cost to the cavalry?

On November 27, Wade Hampton began exposing his enemy's vulnerability. Taking a two-hundred man reconnaissance mission over the Rappahannock, Hampton crossed at Kelly's Ford, moved through Morrisville, and rode cross-country toward White Ridge Road.[7] The move put Hampton in the mouth of the funnel and in Burnside's rear.

As they rode little-traveled country roads, the Confederates learned of a Federal regiment stationed at Hartwood Church, about eight miles from Falmouth. The area around that Presbyterian church was also known as Hartwood because deer were in abundance there — but Hampton hunted no deer. Pleased with the chance to hit a large enemy force, Hampton attacked the Federal camp the next morning. At dawn, Major John H. Whitaker of the 1st North Carolina Cavalry led an irresistible charge into the camp and captured every along with several nearby pickets. Hampton's total take equaled eighty-seven privates and non-commissioned officers, two captains, three lieutenants, two colors, about one hundred horses, and approximately one hundred carbines. The Confederates reported no losses.[8]

Back at the river, Hampton felt satisfied with the results. As Channing Price wrote, the best part of the victory was that it had come against elements of one of the Northern army's best units, a regular U.S. Army regiment.[9] Also, Hampton now knew more about the countryside in the Federal rear. He began considering ways to follow up his success.

General Lee called the Hartwood Church skirmish a "handsome affair" and suggested to the Secretary of War that Hampton and his men deserved "high commendations." Lee also sent the two captured Federal guidons to the secretary as a souvenir. Hampton's Confederates could be proud that theirs was the first Virginia operation carried out by troops from states other than Virginia.[10]

Less than two weeks passed before Hampton decided to raid the Federal rear again. The date was December 10, a Wednesday, and the Confederates at Fredericksburg expected an attack at any moment. A diversion, courtesy of Hampton, could disrupt Federal plans and perhaps cause troops to be siphoned off. For the Confederates, it would also present an opportunity for foraging.[11]

Hampton called his commanders together and issued orders. Gordon got the nod; he was to lead a detachment from his regiment on the raid. Joining him were detachments from the 1st South Carolina Cavalry, under Lieutenant Colonel J. D. Twiggs; from the 2d South Carolina Cavalry, under Colonel M. C. Butler; from the Jeff Davis Legion, under Lieutenant Colonel Will Martin; and from the Cobb Legion, under Captain Jerry E. Rich. The carefully selected force numbered 520 men. For better tactical control on the ride, General Hampton placed Butler, who ranked all other detachment commanders, in charge of a "brigade" comprised of Gordon's troopers, the 2d South Carolina Cavalry detachment, and the Cobb Legion detachment. Martin, the next ranking officer, was to oversee a "brigade" containing the Jeff Davis Legion detachment and the 1st South Carolina Cavalry detachment. Butler and Martin were to report to Hampton. This done, the Confederates went to work. Gordon, in the regiment's new camps just two miles from Raccoon Ford on the Rapidan, collected his gear and mounted his horse.[12]

After splashing through the icy waters of Rappahannock, the raiders took much the same route as the one taken in the last raid: toward the White Ridge Road. This time, however, Hampton wanted to capture Dumfries, a town along the Potomac River. From there, he planned to ride up the Telegraph Road to Occoquan.[13] To carry out such a raid so far behind enemy lines meant that the cavalrymen must ride hard and fast, and strike hard and fast, or they would pay dearly.

Gordon spent most of the tenth and the eleventh in the saddle. It was cold. Several inches of snow blanketed the ground, making travel difficult.[14] At first they saw no sign of the enemy, either from the column or through scouting. Nights also came and went quietly; the troopers got what rest they could. The cold and snow made that difficult for the men and the horses, especially for some of Gordon's men. It was not uncommon to see members of the 1st "half-naked and barefooted."[15]

The cavalrymen rose very early on December 12. After breaking camp and saddling up in the quiet, cold post-midnight darkness, the raiders rode the last sixteen miles to Dumfries. By dawn, Gordon could make out the town in the distance. There was no sign of the enemy, but that might have been because of the early hour. To be certain, Hampton ordered Butler's command to swing around and enter Dumfries from the north while Hampton held Martin in reserve.[16]

Minutes passed. Horses' hooves clapped on the frozen soil. Men turned their heads back and forth, their eyes darting about. Where was the enemy? Butler's men rode into Dumfries. At last, the enemy appeared. A challenge rang out as a small enemy detachment opened fire. Gordon and the others, still mounted, wielded their weapons and fired back. Then, Butler ordered the obligatory charge, and Federal resistance crumbled. Blue-clad soldiers came out of their positions, surrendering. The Confederates counted heads and found they had captured more than fifty Federals.[17]

Veterans of Stuart's cavalry would have called it a typical small-unit action: locate the enemy, charge the enemy, and rout the enemy. The action was also characteristic of Butler's performance as a cavalry leader. Twenty-six-year-old Matthew Calbraith Butler was a favorite of Hampton and a rising star in the cavalry. He was known for his narrow escape at the end of Stuart's Maryland raid. A native of Greenville and a graduate of South Carolina College, Butler had been a lawmaker before the war. In 1861 he had resigned from the South Carolina legislature and joined the Hampton Legion. Butler's wife, the daughter of South Carolina governor Francis Pickens, then watched her husband march to war. A veteran of First Bull Run and Antietam, Butler often carried a silver riding whip during battle. He was big-hearted, gentle, courteous, and handsome.[18] Gordon deferred to the younger South Carolinian and doubtless enjoyed the opportunity to get to know him better.

Next came the search for spoils. Gordon's detachment joined in as the Rebels scoured the town for enemy supplies. They found twenty-four sutlers' wagons, which were undoubtedly on their way to Burnside's army. The wagons sat parked in vacant lots with their teams. One sutler, who had recently immigrated to America, watched with disgust as the Rebels helped themselves to his supplies. "Vot for is our army vort?" he complained. "Can't keep von tam leetle rebel hoss off mine goots pehind de place de fights."[19] The Rebels destroyed those wagons that would not travel well and kept the others. They also cut the town's telegraph wires. By 8:00 A.M., Dumfries was secure.[20]

Hampton brought Martin's command into town and then sized up the situation. Telegraph Road led north to Occoquan, and Hampton guessed more targets could be found there. Yet scouts reported that Federal General Franz Sigel's corps was moving on Dumfries from Fredericksburg. (Gordon might have been interested to know that Sigel had fought at Wilson's Creek, where Tom Brown had been killed.) Hampton realized that Sigel would approach along Telegraph Road, directly on his own line of retreat. That intelligence ruled out any notion Hampton had of moving on Occoquan. Reluctantly, he ordered a retreat.[21]

By dark, the Confederate cavalrymen were back at the White Ridge Road. Resistance had again been non-existent, but the raid and exposure to the severe winter weather had taxed the strength and endurance of the men. They spent one more winter's night in the field before recrossing the river on December 13.[22]

As Hampton's men settled back into camp later that day, the Battle of Fredericksburg raged. At last, Burnside had made up his mind. His decision: to cross the Rappahannock and force Lee out of his defenses. The Federals first attacked Lee's right; Stonewall Jackson's Confederates received them with weapons afire. The fight was hard, and some Federals found a gap in the Confederate line, but they were repulsed. Next, Burnside tried attacking Marye's Heights, but Confederate weapons cut down the Federals like wheat before a razor-sharp scythe. After far too many fruitless charges, Burnside called off the attack. He withdrew his troops from Fredericksburg on the night of December 15, leaving the dead in his wake. Later, Hampton would tell his North Carolinians about the carnage. When touring the battlefield, he came across an ice house that had been turned into a makeshift morgue. Inside, no fewer than six hundred bodies lay stacked like cordwood.[23]

Except for Hampton's Brigade, the bulk of Stuart's cavalry had been in position on Lee's extreme right during the battle. They had a ringside seat for the Confederate victory. John Pelham and the horse artillery did their part in the fight; Pelham all but immortalized himself by taking on an attacking Federal column with but a few pieces of artillery. Other than that, the cavalry only carried messages, gathered intelligence, and dodged shells.

Meanwhile, from their position, Hampton's newly returned raiders could do nothing to help the fight at Fredericksburg, so they rested and kept their eyes open. They bore the freezing temperatures and snow as best as they could. Food remained scarce, and the condition of the horses grew worse. The entire brigade had begun suffering from the almost constant activity of the past weeks. Gordon would have given a lot for an evening at the St. Nicholas Hotel on Broadway and a bottle of his favorite champagne.

In a few days, someone decided it was time for another raid. The Confederates hoped more of these raids would force Burnside to send troops from Fredericksburg to protect his army's rear. Stuart also hoped the rides would keep his cavalry alert.[24] The missions certainly

8. Spent and Recovered   115

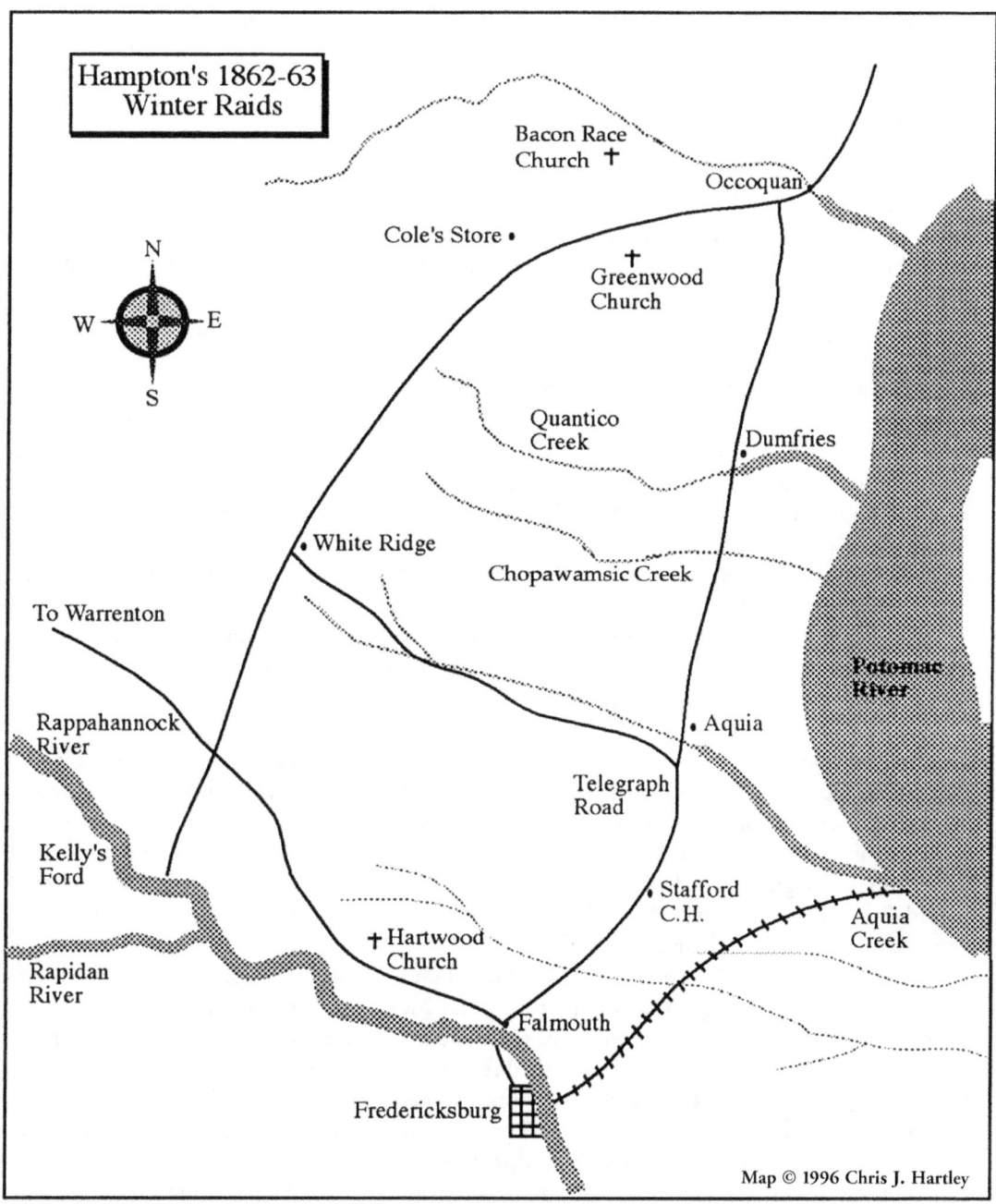

did the latter, but if they were successful in the former it did not matter. Lee had things quite well in hand at Fredericksburg since Burnside recrossed the Rappahannock. At least, some of the cavalrymen would have the chance to get warm by moving about.

This time, Hampton selected 465 troopers from his regiments. Crossing the Potomac on December 17, Hampton tried for Occoquan again. Reaching Telegraph Road, the cavalrymen rode north and swept away Federal picket posts, capturing wagons and supplies. At Occoquan, the Confederates seized a wagon train belonging to Sigel's corps. Finally, Federal cavalry from Alexandria pressured Hampton to retire. The Confederates brought back 150 prisoners and twenty wagons from this their third winter raid in a month. Hampton sent some of the raid's spoils to his commander, including cheese, champagne, and a new pair of boots. In Richmond, the War Department took special notice of Hampton's activities and filed them away for later consideration.[25]

Most of the cavalry's officers spent Christmas eve at Stuart's tent. They ate chicken, turkey, ham, sweet potatoes, and eggs collected from the countryside. Someone even managed to produce apple brandy, but it was concealed from the teetotalling Stuart. The band played festive music while the luckier officers enjoyed the company of their wives. Stuart made sure that his "family" passed the holiday eve pleasantly. Large detachments of Stuart's men camped nearby and enjoyed similar festivities.[26]

Once Christmas celebrations ended, Stuart turned his troopers' thoughts from the holiday season by embarking on a fourth raid. He wanted to send off 1862 with a bang by taking the Telegraph Road and capturing everything Federal in sight. Stuart decided to make this raid the largest of the four by compiling detachments from each of his brigades for a total of 1,800 men and four pieces of horse artillery. The men called it the Dumfries Raid, even though the Confederates ultimately failed to capture that town. Hampton did manage to seize Occoquan, with the help of 175 men from the 1st North Carolina Cavalry under Major John Whitaker, victor of Hartwood Church.[27]

At the cost of one killed, thirteen wounded, and thirteen missing, the Confederates returned from the raid with a number of horses, mules, wagons, saddles, bridles, pistols, and sabres, as well as over two hundred prisoners. A trooper from the 1st added that the cavalrymen obtained "all sorts of Christmas good things." Harvey Davis wrote, "It was unusual to see our men making Rio coffee and eating fine cake, chees[e], oranges, lemons, and nuts of all kinds and strutting in fine yankee boots."[28] In the haul, another Tarheel remembered a wine bottle labeled in fancy letters, "A Christmas present to Gen. A. E. Burnside." Despite such treasures, Stuart admitted that his expedition was not as successful as hoped thanks to enemy units stationed along Telegraph Road. Still, the raids were not without benefits. The Rebels had disrupted Burnside's telegraphic line of communication with Washington, and they had also drawn enemy troops in their direction.[29]

Stuart overlooked the worst result of the constant raiding. Hampton, however, dutifully reported it. "I regret to say," Hampton wrote, "that I lost several of my horses, broken down by the long march, and that very many of them are rendered unfit for service from the same cause."[30] Hampton's Brigade had been pushed so hard that it would not be an effective fighting force until spring. Broken down and hungry horses, spent equipment, tired and hungry troopers: the commanders of the brigade had to get their units in shape. Gordon and his fellow North Carolina troopers faced a tough road to recovery.

Gordon did not participate in this raid. He remained at the Rappahannock, resting and caring for his mounts and equipment: a good saddle and bridle, a saddle blanket and other blankets, a sabre and pistol, a hat and yellow-trimmed uniform, cavalry boots and spurs, a valise, comb, and many other items. Additional duties fell to him as well, since Baker was absent periodically from January to April that year, in part to command the brigade while Hampton was away. That left the regiment to Gordon.[31] The work did him good and built confidence but did little to compensate for being left behind.

After the raid, there were other things to worry about. A New Year's letter from Wilkesborough detailed the condition of Gordon's store back home. The war, it seemed, was even affecting life back in Wilkes County. Local businessmen saw a number of changes in the economy.

Prices went through the ceiling. Shortages of goods were frequent. As a lieutenant colonel of cavalry Gordon made $185.00 a month, but his pay did little to ease personal business matters.[32] The inflation caused businessmen, farmers, and politicians alike, including Gordon, to pause and ponder their futures.

Politically, the situation was no better. The unionist Calvin J. Cowles, half brother of W. H. H. Cowles, had written at the start of the war, "Patriots all over the land groan in agony — our worst fears seem near realization — the men of '76 had not a more fearful struggle than seems to be in store for us."[33] As the weeks and months passed, Wilkes patriots groaned louder and the political situation became even more unsettled. In fact, Unionist feelings spread even in that county. The Conscription Act continued to take farmers away from their land, leaving fewer hands to till the soil. Families had less to eat. The lengthening casualty lists exacerbated the hardships. With many Confederate supporters in the army, disenchantment with the war grew. Investment in the economic growth and development of Wilkes County had never been a priority of the antebellum state government, so the people wondered if the Union's strong central government would not offer a better life.

Confederate deserters hid in the hills and mountains of Wilkes, sheltered by the Unionist feelings of its citizens. More than once, Governor Vance sent troops there to clear out dissension. Some of those Confederates often behaved no better than the deserters, stealing food and causing trouble. Gordon's land and handsome home were prime targets for such visitors. Indeed, perhaps the only thing that had not changed in Wilkes was the church bell that hung in the steeple of Gordon's church, St. Paul's. Somehow, the congregation kept it from being melted down for use in the war effort.

Then there was the war for Gordon to think about. As a cold rain pelted his Culpeper County quarters, Gordon shared his thoughts on home and the war with brother-in-law Augustus:

> I am just in receipt of your letter of the 1st Jany giving statements of sales etc. It was unusually delayed someway. I was surprised at the price of negroes, but astonished at the price of the land. I think the best thing you could do would be to sell your place and mine if it can be done at such prices and leave the country.
>
> If you could sell all my tobacco for 25 or 30 cents per pound I think you had better do so. You must be the judge of that. It may bring more but the danger of its burning up etc. is a consideration. I think the price of everything will decline wonderfully after six or 8 months; negroes will not. They will be high when peace is made. But lands in the mountains will never be so low as formerly.
>
> I would like exceedingly to go home for a short time. I am worn out and a short respite would very much renovate me. I expected to have you [as a guest] in February but the prospect of another fight at Fredericksburg will prevent it. The enemy are bound to fight sometime soon. I think the war will not last another year. The people at the north are getting very tired of it and are clamoring for peace. Burnside's army is very much dissatisfied and a great many are deserting from it.
>
> I hope that you have been relieved from that Va. Cavalry. State to those officers if they are still there that I have their names and they shall be reported to the proper authorities if they are guilty of any inconsistencies with the regulations, and not to take another ear of my corn. Say to Crowden to cultivate what land he cultivates well, and manure it, to plant as much tobacco as he can cultivate, not neglecting the corn.[34]

After a fashion, Gordon was right about the war. Although the Federals were somewhat demoralized, they planned to renew their offensive soon. Most Confederates saw it coming. A Federal cavalry reconnaissance in early January, aimed at Catlett's Station and Rappahannock Station, indicated that Burnside might be considering an advance against the Confederate left along the Upper Rappahannock. Patrols discovered more evidence of this move, including a concentration of Federal troops around Hartwood Church. Lee instructed Hampton to "direct your picket to be on alert everywhere, and be in readiness for whatever may occur."[35]

Readiness was actually unnecessary in the rain that drenched the countryside that January. Even as Gordon sealed and mailed his letter to Augustus, in the rain, Burnside's plans fell apart. On January 20, a storm turned the Virginia countryside into a mud pit. Another one struck a week later, before the land dried from the first storm. Burnside's flanking maneuver floundered about in the muck for a few days before he called it off, further discouraging that army. This "Mud March" signaled two things: it was Burnside's curtain call as commander of the Army of the Potomac, and it marked an end to offensive action for the winter.

The "Mud March" aside, was the cavalry ready for more action if it came? That February, Stuart's muster rolls reported 403 officers and 5,912 men present for duty. Its twelve artillery pieces were polished and ready for action. Yet almost the same number of men remained absent for one reason or another, many due to illness. To make matters worse, the morale of the entire cavalry command ebbed.[36] The Confederate cavalry was lucky the mud ended the Federal offensive before it got started because Hampton's Brigade — not to mention the rest of the cavalry command — needed time to recover from the physical and mental hardships of the winter war.

Once all quieted down, Hampton's commanders saw little improvement in their units. Winter quarters had been erected along the upper Rappahannock, with brigade headquarters at Culpeper Court House, and 1st North Carolina Cavalry headquarters near Stevensburg. Much of the regiment camped on a hill, the men along the north side and the officers on its peak. Though a grove of chestnuts and oaks shielded most tents from the winter wind, the men still had to rig the dwellings themselves in various and ingenious ways against the chill.[37] Unfortunately, better shelters alone could not improve the unit's condition. January brought wintry weather in full fury. Back in North Carolina, it had been so cold that ice on mill ponds was between three and four inches thick. Worse, when it did not snow in Virginia it usually rained, making it miserable for the men and the horses. The food was hardly fit to eat. The beef was tough and the bacon rancid. If it was possible, the horses got worse. Not long after Gordon wrote Augustus, Heros Von Borcke inspected Hampton's Brigade. "It was a mournful sight," he recalled, "to see more than half the horses of this splendid command totally unfit for duty, dead and dying animals lying about the camp in all directions. One regiment had lost thirty-one horses in less than a week."[38]

Hampton knew the stakes and strove to do something about the situation. Embittered, he spent much of his time "quarrelling with Stuart, who keeps me here doing all the hard work, while the Virginia Brigades are quietly doing nothing. His partiality towards those Brigades is as marked as it is disgusting and it constantly makes me indignant. I do not object to the work, but I do object to seeing my command broken down by positive starvation.... Unless Genl. Lee, to whom I have appealed, interferes. Stuart will certainly have my Brigade out of the field before very long."[39]

Soon after an early February snow storm, a skirmish offered more evidence of the brigade's condition. A Federal cavalry regiment, supported by infantry, moved to destroy the Orange and Alexandria railroad bridge over the Rappahannock. Their mission stirred up Hampton's pickets and brought on a fight for the bridge. There, on the night of February 6–7, Hampton's pickets stood their ground, firing from rifle-pits, and somehow repulsed the Yankees (with a little help from the snow-rain-mud weather pattern). In his brief report of the action, Hampton wrote, "I regret that the condition of my horses did not allow me to follow them."[40]

In view of such events, it was recommended to Stuart that Hampton's Brigade be relieved from outpost duty. In mid–February, Stuart visited brigade headquarters to see for himself. Culpeper, "a pleasant village of several hundred inhabitants," and the outlying areas were also bogged down with mud, but Stuart still made his tour. Convinced, on February 12 he relieved the brigade and replaced it with Fitz Lee's Brigade. As if in celebration of the decision, Stuart staged a dance and minstrel show at Culpeper.[41] Hampton's officers enjoyed the festivities all the more because they could now concentrate on getting the brigade back into shape.

The first step was to obtain fresh horses, and that was each man's responsibility. The 1st continued to receive state government assistance in this, but by this point in the war horses were so scarce that the Tarheel troopers had to help scrounge. For that purpose, and to collect absentees, many of the brigade's members, including Gordon, received furloughs. He could not have been happier when army headquarters cleared his twenty-five-day leave beginning February 10.[42] No records detail Gordon's movements during his leave, but as he had indicated to Augustus, he surely traveled home through the snow and mud to recruit his own mounts.[43]

It was three months short of two long years since Gordon had been home. Only his service in the state legislature twelve years before had kept Gordon away for any similar length of time. The long, boring journey to Wilkes was ready-made for reflection. Since the Wilkes Valley Guards had left Wilkes County, Gordon had served his country well. His rise to the rank of lieutenant colonel could not quite be described as meteoric, but it could be characterized as steady and deserved. His commission made him one of North Carolina's ranking cavalrymen in the Army of Northern Virginia. Gordon had learned — sometimes the hard way — what being a cavalryman meant. Every time Gordon unsheathed his sword or wielded his revolver, he had been "among the foremost" of the ranks. As a leader, Gordon was "beloved and respected by the men and with the confidence of his superior officers." A fellow cavalryman and friend wrote of him after the war: "That Gordon led was enough for every man to be willing to follow."[44]

The man that came to Wilkes County in February 1863, tattered uniform and all, must have been proud and excited to ride into town. He relaxed, had the tears in his uniforms mended, cared for his horses, and especially visited his family. He also saw firsthand the shortages and inflation that Crowden and the store had endured in his absence. Wilkes County was not a happy place during the Civil War.

The days passed quickly, too quickly; it was soon time to go back to the war. The end of a furlough is not an easy thing in wartime, but the leave refreshed Gordon immeasurably. His comrades experienced similar rejuvenation. They came back to Virginia confident and ready to prosecute the war to its fullest now that the Federals were thought to be demoralized and struggling to recover from their latest defeats.

Gordon returned to the camps of the 1st North Carolina Cavalry in mid–March. His journey back was shorter because the regiment and the brigade had been sent away from Culpeper to rest and recruit. During March and April, the First moved to from place to place in the Shenandoah Valley and later to Lynchburg. "After two years of almost incessant duty, we needed [the break]," a cavalryman wrote.[45] It also proved to be a more convenient marshaling location for troopers trickling back from furlough in the Carolinas, Georgia, and Mississippi. The change of location, however, had not been easy. As Sergeant Pugh wrote, to get there they had to march "through snow and mud 2 feet deep and half the time not one bite to eat for myself or horse."[46]

Fresh horses in tow and a mended uniform on his back, Gordon found the regiments of the brigade still struggling to recover. Though miles from the front, winter, war, and bad news still marred the unit's condition and morale. Bad news from the front kept spirits low, and the worst news was that John Pelham, a favorite in the army, was dead. Gordon had known Pelham well. He recalled the day that he, Baker and Von Borcke had enjoyed punch and conversation with the "gallant Pelham." The young man's tragic death had occurred during a fight with enemy cavalry near Kelly's Ford. Stuart, hearing the news, said, "Our loss is irreparable!" John Esten Cooke, of Stuart's staff, remembered that he saw "no face over which a sort of shadow did not pass at the announcement, 'Pelham is dead!'"[47] Gordon was not an exception. He joined the army and the nation in mourning Pelham's death. One of Stuart's best was gone.

The March 17 Union cavalry attack across the Rappahannock that resulted in Pelham's death had been aimed at the camps of Fitz Lee and Hampton near Culpeper. It showed how much respect Federal forces had for the Confederate cavalry. All winter long, they had diligently tried to track their foe, looking for any opportunity to strike or glean intelligence. True to form, Stuart still kept the Federals frustrated with occasional raids like Fitz Lee's successful expedition in the Hartwood Church area in late February. General Joseph Hooker, Burnside's replacement as commander of the Army of the Potomac, lamented, "Can no one tell where all the enemy's cavalry come from?"[48]

Far away from the frustrated Joe Hooker, the troopers of Hampton's Brigade and Baker's 1st North Carolina Cavalry had extra time on their hands. Gordon's friend Rufus Barringer was one example. Barringer solicited duty in a sphere where he could make use of his legal abilities. Stuart planned to use him on a military court he tried to set up the winter. Dr. William D. Jones, the 1st's regimental surgeon, meanwhile monitored the health of the men. No amount of sickness or wounds seemed to dampen his hope in the cause. Gordon kept busy as the regiment's inspector and mustering officer. In that position, he kept a close watch on the progress of the regiment's recovery and oversaw mustering as men returned from furlough. He also prepared a report to update the state government on the condition of the 1st's horses. The document showed that as of April 30 the regiment had 727 state horses in its employ. Of that number, 190 horses had been sent to the Roanoke River to be recruited during the previous thirty days.[49]

Most certainly, Gordon also knew of another, darker problem that confronted the regiment. After the incursion into Maryland, it will be recalled, Baker had allegedly taken up with the bottle again. Sometime after that, it is reported, an unidentified subordinate accused Colonel Baker of drunkenness. This was a serious charge indeed. Stuart did not want to lose Baker, a brave and hard fighter, nor did Stuart want the reputation of his cavalry tarnished. As such, Stuart moved swiftly to end the scandal. The cavalry commander required Baker to pledge that he would give up drinking for the duration of the war. That was enough for Stuart. Often, between January and April of 1863, Stuart even entrusted him with brigade command in Hampton's absence. (Baker also stayed away from the regiment during parts of September and November 1862 for unknown reasons.)[50]

The tension of Baker's situation must have affected regimental morale as much as the harsh winter did. What better way to improve morale than to enjoy the humble pastimes of camp life? In their spare time, many of Stuart's cavalrymen built makeshift theaters. Others enjoyed music, played games, and wrote letters. Still others rested and thought about the spring when the fighting would resume. Many attended religious meetings as a revival swept through the army. Gordon partook of these diversions too, and found others more characteristic of his nature. One April evening, he joined Major Whitaker, Captain Cowles, and Lieutenant

Jesse Person at a party in the Campbell County home of a Mr. Dillard. Dillard, a friendly, wealthy gentleman, provided good food and wine for his guests. Dillard's seventeen-year-old-daughter and three of her lady friends held the soldiers' attention more than the food and spirits.[51]

Gordon made a particularly strong impression on another resident of Campbell County, Mrs. Elizabeth Dabney. This particular lady spent the spring caring for about one hundred members of the 1st who were recuperating in Lynchburg. She told her unmarried daughter that all the Tarheels behaved like respectable gentlemen, especially the officers. What was more, Mrs. Dabney knew that most of the brigade's officers were unmarried. "Col. Gordon and Col. Cheek were particularly fine looking and agreeable," she wrote.[52] Ironically, Mrs. Dabney's son would later serve on Gordon's staff.

As always, the men kept up with the news. A leading topic of discussion was Abraham Lincoln's Emancipation Proclamation. Issued the previous September, the decree went into effect on January 1, freeing on paper slaves in rebellious parts of the nation. Slave-holders like Gordon paid close attention to how their own servants reacted. In the main, Hampton's unit lived only "the unrelieved routine of camp life in all its dull and listless monotony." As much as furloughs helped, camp life hindered the brigade's return to effectiveness. Some cavalrymen again built crude winter quarters of huts or log houses, complete with fireplaces and chimneys, to shield themselves from the elements. Others lived in tents or anything they could find. Most shelters were imperfect. Diseases like smallpox were not uncommon, while food for the men and horses remained scarce. The regiment had to move every three or four days to find food. The wheat harvest was expected in early June and the Irish potato crop would be ready at about the same time, but that was still weeks away.[53]

Laurence Baker, then in temporary command of the brigade, did make an appearance in camp that April. In doing so, he inspected the regiment, and doubtless noted that the unit's horses were improving slowly. The high command of the Army of Northern Virginia likewise saw that the cavalry unit was still struggling. In early April, General Robert Lee told a fellow officer: "As far as I can learn, [Hampton's Brigade] requires complete restoration." Still, with spring weather approaching, General Lee hoped that Hampton's Brigade would soon be ready. Its services would be needed to help Stuart discern the Federal army's intentions. As a precaution, Lee informed President Davis that he needed other cavalry reinforcements soon. Although he hoped Hampton would soon rejoin the army, Lee wrote, the Confederate cavalry was becoming deficient in numbers.[54]

General Joseph Hooker prepared the Union army for the coming campaigning season in a way that would affect the lives of every Confederate cavalryman. Hooker, a Massachusetts native and West Point graduate, was a veteran of the Army of the Potomac who knew its ailments. Assuming command of the army in late January 1863, one of his first actions was to reorganize the army's cavalry into a corps. The new Federal cavalry corps, under General George Stoneman, boasted three divisions of over 11,000 men. In one Confederate cavalryman's opinion, the reorganization improved the "heretofore worthless cavalry a great deal and from this time on we were to have more trouble with it, partly from its improvement, and partly from our declining efficiency owing from our inability to supply remounts." Lee also perceived an approaching change in the enemy's cavalry. He told President Davis that "every expedition will augment their boldness and increase their means of doing us harm, and they will become better acquainted with the country and more familiar with its roads."[55]

While he readied his army, "Fighting Joe" also authored a battle plan that promised success. Having inherited Burnside's positions opposite Fredericksburg, he opted to flank and surprise Lee. The idea was to feint at Fredericksburg and hold Lee in place while a large part of the army crossed the Rappahannock and Rapidan in the Confederate left and rear. A simultaneous cavalry raid in Lee's rear would supposedly hinder anything the Army of Northern Virginia tried — especially since Hampton and now Longstreet were detached for other duties.

The passage of time made the difference in Hampton's Brigade, for the unit recuperated with great speed. Rejuvenation came just in time, for soon May arrived and with it the Battle of Chancellorsville began. It fell to units not immediately with Lee's army to deal with one feature of Hooker's plan, Stoneman's cavalry raid. Ultimately Stoneman had little effect on the campaign's outcome, but he did spark concern in the Confederate War Department. Boldly risking his communications in favor of keeping his intelligence-gathering horsemen nearby, General Lee decided not to send the main body of Stuart's cavalry after Stoneman. Thus, as thousands of "finely equipped and well-organized" Federal horse-soldiers rode south, telegraphs in Lynchburg clacked out messages.[56] Ready or not, the government needed Hampton's Brigade to help repel the raiders.

As the fight raged around Chancellorsville, officials in the war department worked to sort the situation out. On May 3, Secretary of War James Seddon wired Hampton at Lynchburg: "Besides the advance on Columbia, detachments of the enemy are reported to be advancing by two roads toward Richmond, from 12 to 17 miles distant." Hampton knew Richmond was not immediately accessible, but he prepared his troopers to move as he awaited further direction. Accordingly, the 1st, then bivouacked twenty-one miles away, marched to Lynchburg.[57]

Urgency was thick in the next dispatch. The war department addressed it to the commander of the post at Lynchburg: Hampton, or if Hampton was unavailable, Baker; or anyone of authority. If necessary, a courier was to be dispatched. According to the wire, "the enemy's cavalry on their raid have left the railroad ... and are moving ... either toward the canal on the Petersburg and Lynchburg Rail Road, or toward Charlottesville. Endeavor, on the best information you can get, to aid in meeting or intercepting them."[58] Fortunately, Hampton was nearby when the message arrived. He quickly reassured Richmond that he would "make every disposition to carry out your instructions. Do keep me advised. My Brigade is in motion."[59]

The wires did not fall silent. In its next message, the Confederate War Department shared the latest news and clarified events somewhat. Seddon informed the South Carolinian of "a decisive victory near Fredericksburg. Jackson and [A. P.] Hill wounded; the former severely, the latter slightly. The enemy's cavalry in detached bodies near this city, but believed to be passing down the Peninsula." The news of the army's victory was welcome, but news of Jackson's and Hill's wounding was not. However, since Stoneman's cavalry force was thought to be moving down the distant Peninsula, Hampton knew his cavalrymen could not help. With the previous orders apparently countermanded, he held his forces back and awaited additional instructions. The men in the ranks had also heard about the Yankee raid below Gordonsville and the brigade's pending countermove, and wondered when they did not leave as expected.[60]

At midnight, Seddon updated Hampton's orders. "I do not think Farmville or Lynchburg threatened," he wrote. "The enemy have, I learn, turned down the river on the north side, either for a daring dash on this city, or, more probably, to escape by the Peninsula to Yorktown or around Port Royal." Seddon ordered the cavalry brigade to "concentrate toward Gordonsville" and, apparently, to Farmville.[61] From that point, the unit could support Lee if necessary.

Bugles blared and officers shouted orders. Breaking camp took several hours, but by morning, the brigade said farewell to "resting and recruiting." Yesterday had been confusing for the unit's commanders, but the marching orders for May 4 were clear. Hampton confirmed to Seddon, "Two regiments ordered to Farmville, three to Gordonsville. I leave to-day for Gordonsville; have no information; would be glad to hear from Fredericksburg."[62]

At the front, the army's leaders continued to worry about Stoneman. Now that Hooker had been defeated, maybe Stuart could help fight Stoneman. Lee hoped that when Hampton reached the front the cavalry would be in position to hit the Federal raiders as they returned to their lines. On May 9, Lee counseled Stuart, "Hampton has probably joined you. Get your cavalry together, and give them breathing time, so as when you do strike, Stoneman may feel you." By then, however, it was all over. Buford's column passed within two miles of Richmond before reaching Federal lines on the Peninsula on May 8. Averell's column was already through; it had been recalled a few days earlier and its commander replaced with Alfred Pleasonton. Hampton later wrote, "Many of the citizens whom I have seen express great regret that my brigade was not here when the Yankees came and I hear that the people of Culpeper said that 'if old Hampton had been here, the Yankees never would have crossed the river.'"[63]

Stuart was pleased to be reinforced by the 178 fit officers and 2,032 effective men of Hampton's Brigade. Hampton brought with him. That made the cavalry division the largest unit Stuart had ever fielded. In terms of effectives, it had 453 officers and 5,763 men, but overall, the division contained 11,306 men and 646 officers. For a change, Hampton's Brigade was now in better shape than any unit in the division, and the 1st North Carolina Cavalry was in better shape than any unit in the brigade. As the troopers approached the camps of the cavalry division, Gordon knew that the 1st North Carolina Cavalry had been rejuvenated by the winter's rest. By late May, its roster boasted of thirty-four effective officers and five hundred effective (mounted) men. Only 151 men and five officers were still poorly mounted, and seven officers and 176 men were absent. (Most of the latter were sick; the regiment had been subsisting on a diet of meat and bread without vegetables.)[64]

Stuart's roster had a new look for the coming campaign season. Davis had heard Lee's complaints of the cavalry's size. His answer was to scrape together a few units to bolster Stuart's roster. One addition was the Laurel Brigade of "Grumble" Jones. A farmer before the war, William Edmonson Jones was a West Pointer and army veteran who had also studied at Gordon's alma mater, Emory & Henry. Stuart and the profane drillmaster did not get along, but Lee made sure the two put the cause before personal feelings. The veteran brigade, fresh from the Shenandoah Valley, joined Stuart at Culpeper in early June. A second addition was the guerrilla unit of John D. Imboden. The forty-year-old graduate of Washington College, a former lawyer and legislator, had established a reputation as an accomplished partisan fighter. Imboden's men, many of whom were recruits, had recently returned from a fairly successful raid in western Virginia. It was thought that they could assist Stuart in any pending offensive movements.[65]

That was not all. Other reinforcements were three regiments and one battalion under Brigadier General Albert Gallatin Jenkins. A graduate of Harvard Law School and a former congressman, Jenkins had joined the cavalry as a captain in 1861. He was remembered for leading his large brigade on a five-hundred-mile raid through West Virginia and into Ohio. The man was a proven combat veteran with untested administrative abilities. Even though they were home guardsmen and guerrillas unfamiliar with the ways of regular cavalrymen, Stuart needed Jenkins and his cavalrymen.[66]

From North Carolina and Southern Virginia came some of Gordon's fellow Tarheels, the 4th and 5th North Carolina Cavalry Regiments. The 4th had been organized in the summer and the 5th in the fall of 1862, both in Garysburg, North Carolina. Neither unit had much fighting experience outside of skirmishing and picket duty in eastern North Carolina. Along with the 2d North Carolina Cavalry, which had joined Stuart in the fall of 1862, Stuart now commanded four Tarheel cavalry units. Unfortunately, the 4th and 5th carried Enfield rifles; in future engagements with Spencer rifle-armed enemy cavalry, the advantage would go to the repeaters.[67]

Beverly Robertson commanded the 4th and 5th North Carolina Cavalry Regiments. Robertson had been with Stuart's cavalry before he was reassigned to other duties in September 1862. During his absence from the Army of Northern Virginia, he drilled the gathering cavalry units in North Carolina and directed some of their operations. Some said Robertson's 1862 reassignment to North Carolina had been because of ineptitude. Earlier in the war, Stuart himself had called Robertson "by far the most troublesome man I have to deal with...." When Robertson was relieved and sent south, Stuart had written his wife, "Joy's mine."[68] In the spring of 1863, when Robertson rejoined Stuart, the event caused surprise. Robertson's troopers, however, had a better opinion of their commander. Jeb even thought better of Robertson as an organizer. By May's end, he wrote army headquarters that Robertson was "eminently fitted" to command a "reserve camp for recuperation and remounting" cavalry since Robertson was "a good disciplinarian, an excellent instructor and organizer of cavalry...."[69]

Overall, the cavalry was organized into six brigades, not counting Imboden's command. With Hampton, as always, were the 1st North Carolina Cavalry, the 1st and 2d South Carolina Cavalry, Cobb's Legion, the Jeff Davis Legion, and the Philips Legion. With W. H. F. Lee were the 2d North Carolina Cavalry and the 9th, 10th, 13th, and 15th Virginia regiments. With Fitz Lee were the 1st, 2d, 3d, 4th, and 5th Virginia Regiments. Jones had the 6th, 7th, 11th, and 12th Regiments plus the 35th Virginia Battalion. Since Stuart's proposal for a reserve camp was not acted on, Robertson continued to command the 4th and 5th North Carolina Cavalry. Jenkins had his three regiments and one battalion. Two battalions were listed as unassigned.[70]

After plugging the reinforcements into his organization, Stuart gave some thought to shuffling his regiments. In late May, he proposed this to army headquarters. Lee read the plan with great interest. Stuart wanted to increase the number of brigades and commanders in the division, but Lee balked at that. "I do not see what good will be accomplished ... without adding something to the effective strength of your commands." One portion of the plan that did strike Lee as advantageous was the idea of equalizing brigades. By dispatching the 5th Virginia from Fitz Lee's Brigade to operate along the Rapidan, and by sending White's battalion from Jones's command to Loudoun and Faquier, the four old brigades would average 1,500 effectives. That number would include the reattachment of the two Virginia regiments, the 4th and 15th, to their original brigades.[71]

Moreover, Lee saw value in Stuart's idea of forming a brigade of North Carolina cavalry regiments from the 1st, 2d, 4th, and 5th North Carolina Cavalry regiments. Potential commanders would be Robertson — "though some objection might be made to him because he is not a North Carolinian" — or better, Baker. Promoting a Tarheel might ease ill feelings at the lack of general officers from the state in Lee's army. The new brigade and the equalization of regiments might also provide opportunity "to see brigadiers and colonels promoted who have served the country long and well...."[72] Gordon, maturing as a commander of cavalry, could vault to regimental command under such a scenario.

This thinking would ultimately affect Gordon, but more pressing things required attention. Lee and Stuart tucked these ideas away for later use. In the meantime, planning for the spring campaign cranked up. As he plotted strategy in his tent, Lee believed that the time had come again to seek victory on Northern soil. A bold move would encourage Northern peace movements and impress European governments. As such, he planned marching routes to the Potomac and beyond. Perhaps, in a long shot, an invasion would draw Federal troops away from threatened Southern cities such as Vicksburg. If nothing else, the incursion would relieve the Virginia countryside from the burden of war.

The men of war emerged from their camps and began preparing for the coming campaign. Some thought that Hooker might move first, so the cavalry increased its vigilance. Instructed to keep his horsemen together, Stuart moved his headquarters toward the Rappahannock in stages.[73] Pickets watched the line of the Rappahannock while the main body of the cavalry gathered again in the Orange Court House-Culpeper area. Hampton's troopers came from Gordonsville and Farmville and had a happy reunion with their comrades. The cavalry camp there was in a valley overlooking the village itself, in a land of growing crops that war had not yet ruined. There, the men cleaned weapons, foraged, tended their horses, and sharpened their sabres. Stuart enjoyed a visit from Mrs. Stuart at Orange, and reviewed the brigades of the Lees and Hampton. Days later, on June 7, he established headquarters on a hill near Brandy Station.[74]

In anticipation of the fighting, Gordon returned his servant, Burt, to Wilkesborough, and addressed some financial matters as well[75]:

> I received your letter two days previous. I was pleased to hear from you. I suppose I will have [$]6000.00 value in corn to sell, which I hope Gwyn will take away as soon as possible. I expected to have gone to Richmond about this time and got yours and your father's bonds, and sent them to you, but the advance of the enemy will preclude me from doing so. I will send you broker's receipts, and you can come or send to Richmond for them. Old notes and solvent ones — I would prefer your not taking Confederate money with its present depreciation for all doubtful notes and accounts.
>
> The battle of Chancellorsville was a terrific fight. Our loss was between one and ten thousand. The enemy's loss was between 20 and 30 thousand. Longstreet's Corps and others did not get there in time for the fight. There will be another fight along this line in the course of two or three weeks. If we Confederates can end this fighting on this line for the summer I will write to you when I wish Burt to return.
>
> General Jackson died on the 10th of this month. It is a great national calamity. His loss was equal to 20,000 men. His wife was with him when he died.
>
> The impressment act will allow you the neighborhood price for your corn.... The impressing officer will make a stated price.[76]

The question, implied in Gordon's letter, turned in everybody's mind that spring. Could the army carry its war to the North successfully without Jackson? Perhaps; time would tell. The army, strengthened to 89,000 men, would surely try. Besides obtaining cavalry reinforcements, Lee also brought Longstreet back as well as three new infantry brigades. To improve control, Lee reorganized the army into three corps, commanded by Longstreet, A. P. Hill, and Richard S. Ewell. Although casualties and promotions meant the army would march with some inexperienced commanders, the soldiers were ready for the test.

Thus, Gordon and the 1st North Carolina Cavalry went back on picket duty at the front. It quickly became apparent that Hampton had not changed over the winter. He itched to get at the Yankees. Because of Hooker's improving cavalry, Stuart was already having trouble learning what was happening on the north side of the river, but Hampton tried. In an early June reconnaissance along the Rappahannock, he discovered an exposed Federal infantry division. The South Carolinian proposed to capture it. Perhaps the winter's boredom and the recovery of his brigade heightened Hampton's audacity; whatever it was, Lee complimented the bold and daring idea but ruled it out as too risky. Besides, the Confederate commander wrote, Hampton's and Stuart's latest reports suggested that the enemy was contemplating no aggressive movements.[77]

Or so Stuart and his cavalry thought.

9

"General, There Comes the First North Carolina"

GENERAL LEE WATCHED INTENTLY as the troopers of Stuart's cavalry division marched past him, their horses at a walk. Here and there, the summer breeze lifted hats off men's heads and tumbled them across the grass.[1] A proud Jeb Stuart, sitting his horse beside Lee, ignored the hats but occasionally pointed out items of interest to his commander. General Longstreet and other officers from the army's First and Second Corps joined in review. Filling out the audience was General John Bell Hood's division of infantry. They were present by way of Fitz Lee's invitation: earlier, Lee had casually told Hood, "Come and see the review, and bring any of your people," and Hood had taken Lee quite literally.[2]

This was the second review of Stuart's cavalry in the past week. Three days earlier, on June 5, the troopers had put on a show of the like never seen before under the Virginia sun. Breathlessly, hundreds of spectators (including a number of ladies) watched in awe. Officers shouted orders and the cavalry charged an imaginary foe. Several thousand horses pounded the ground at full gallop. Battle-flags fluttered in the breeze; the standards of the 1st North Carolina Cavalry flew as proudly as any. According to a witness, one could easily distinguish Hampton's Carolinians: "They rode with military primness and were mounted on steeds of delicately-shaped limbs with glistening eyes full of fire and motion." In support, bugles blared, bands played, and the horse artillery fired blank charges, pouring forth "volley after volley of thunder and smoke...." One Tarheel said the artillery fire and "the yelling of the men and rising clouds of dust gave every appearance of a real battle...."[3] Probably the only bad part of the review was that General Lee had been unable to attend, so Stuart gladly obliged when Lee ordered a repeat performance.

The second review was held on June 8. It was, one said, more of "a business affair." For one thing, the men were not thrilled about it because they had to clean and polish their equipment again.[4] For his part, Stuart had no time to issue invitations, so he had to settle for an audience that included Hood's infantrymen.[5] On the plus side, dignitaries, officers, and infantrymen alike had a superb view of the spectacle. After a ride of six miles past the cavalry's ranks — three miles by the first line and, returning, three miles by the second — the dignitaries took position on ground that "was admirably adapted to the purpose, a hill in the centre affording a reviewing stand from which the twelve thousand men present could be seen to great advantage." This spot was near Inlet Station, just west of the Orange and Alexandria Railroad, three miles south of Brandy Station.[6]

Filing by General Lee, the moving mass of men marched across grassy fields. The horse column contained the bulk of Stuart's five brigades: Fitz Lee's, Rooney Lee's, "Grumble" Jones's, Beverly Robertson's, and Wade Hampton's. The Virginians marched with the pride they had earned in the war. Robertson's North Carolinians were as fresh as they looked; the recently arrived units were, unlike the veteran regiments, at or near full strength.[7] Jones's Brigade marched as professionally as any unit present, although Jones carried himself with a "disdainful air" because he disliked parading.[8] Among the troopers of Hampton's Brigade were the men of the 1st North Carolina Cavalry Regiment, their horses trampling grass as they marched. Colonel Baker rode at the regiment's head. Nearby, Gordon sat his horse and followed Baker's lead. Behind Baker and Gordon, the men held themselves erect as if to demonstrate to Lee that the 1st North Carolina Cavalry had recovered from its winter ordeal.

The 1st North Carolina Cavalry drew near to the reviewing officers. They looked better than could be expected after such a long winter. Before marching, all the men had polished their sabres, guns, and revolvers, rubbed and curried their horses, and even dusted their blankets and saddles. The result was impressive: for the first time in months, they looked less like bloodied warriors and more like soldiers on parade. Stuart saw Baker and Gordon with the regiment; Baker, the West Pointer who was a solid tactician, and Gordon, who was growing ever closer to Stuart. Why only a few days before the two men had traveled together to Rosser's wedding at Hanover Court House. Stuart also saw the men, who were almost resplendent with their unusually clean uniforms and polished equipment. At that, Stuart turned to Lee and pointed at the 1st. "General," Stuart said, "there comes the First North Carolina Cavalry, than which there is not a better regiment in either army."[9] Lee's reply was not recorded, but Stuart's words were repeated throughout the regiment's camps later. Nearly every trooper of the 1st remembered Stuart's comment to his dying day.

Afterward, General Lee was pleased. Though he was disappointed in the quality of the cavalry's Richmond-made carbines and saddles, the review satisfied him that the men and horses had recuperated from the winter.[10] The rejuvenation of his cavalry was a necessity because the wheels of invasion were even then beginning to turn. When Stuart's festivities ended, the cavalry was ordered to commence packing. Lee, who had already positioned the First and Second Corps around Culpeper, planned to march the army to the Potomac and beyond beginning on June 9. Stuart's cavalry was to push into Fauquier and Loudoun Counties to cover the movement.[11]

Stuart was confident that his men were ready. The division was the largest it had ever been: more than nine thousand cavalrymen filled the ranks. Staff-member W. W. Blackford later wrote, the cavalry was "at its zenith of power and efficiency."[12] Reconnaissance reports indicated that the Federals were not planning any aggressive movements, so the Confederates thought it was their turn to attack. Stuart's thousands were eager for the work. Almost to a man, they were sure of victory. Sergeant Pugh of the 1st wrote home, "Direct your letters to Richmond, Va., and I will be shore to git it for by the time this gits to you I will [be] somewhere in Maryland or Pennsylvania."[13]

After dark, Stuart settled down to a night's rest on Fleetwood Hill, a two-mile-long eminence that was the site of an old plantation residence. As for his headquarters, everything but two tent-flies was packed in the wagons. The men in the ranks returned to their respective bivouacs, some of which were moved closer to the Rappahannock in anticipation of the next day's move.[14] A few troopers went on picket duty, but most concentrated on preparations for the march. Fitz Lee's Brigade (commanded by Munford as Lee was ailing from rheumatism), and James Breathed's battery of the horse artillery, camped north of the Hazel River, near Oak Shade Church. Munford took charge of picketing on the upper Rappahannock. W. H. F. Lee's Brigade came to rest at Dr. Robert Welford's Plantation on the road to Welford's Ford, west of where the Hazel and Rappahannock rivers joined. Except for a picket near the river crossing, Jones's Brigade and four batteries of the horse artillery bedded down near a church up the road from Beverly's Ford. Robertson's Brigade took position between the Botts and Barbour farms, with a picket stationed at Kelly's Ford. Hampton's Brigade spread out between Fleetwood Hill and Stevensburg, and encamped on Mountain Run. There, many of the men of the 1st North Carolina Cavalry heard of Stuart's words to General Lee for the first time.[15]

That night, most of the men slept soundly, without fear of their enemy, while across the Rappahannock Union soldiers prepared for a move of their own.

After the war, one of Stuart's staff-members described how Gordon handled himself in combat. "Under fire," John Esten Cooke wrote, "Gordon was a perfect rock; nothing could move him."[16] The ninth day of June 1863 brought perhaps the heaviest fighting Gordon ever experienced, and gave him ample opportunity to demonstrate his bravery. Yet when Gordon woke early that morning, he did not suspect that he was about to participate in the largest cavalry battle ever fought in North America. What he did know was that the cavalry was supposed to start its march north at an early hour. He prepared to move out.

A heavy bank of fog hung over the Rappahannock River valley, waiting for the rising sun to burn it away. Stuart, at his headquarters on Fleetwood Hill, heard a noise slice through the fog even as he rubbed sleep out of his eyes: the sharp sound of firing. It came from the direction of Beverly's Ford. There, it turned out, pickets from Jones's Brigade had met the enemy. Although rudely awakened, in minutes General Jones had his men up and riding to the support of his embattled pickets, his wagons heading toward the rear, and a courier galloping to Stuart with news of the situation. Surprised, Stuart directed Robertson, Hampton, and Rooney Lee to assist Jones, and instructed Munford, commanding Fitz Lee's Brigade, to come up in support. The cavalrymen shook off their sleepiness and obeyed. In the confusion, Munford's troopers did so slowly.[17]

The courier who carried orders to Hampton did so in vain because Hampton's Brigade was awake and already at work. Like Stuart, Hampton had also heard "heavy firing on the picket line."[18] The South Carolinian did not wait for orders. As bugles blared "boots and saddles," Gordon neglected his breakfast to break camp while Hampton went to find Stuart. When they met, Stuart told Hampton to leave one regiment in reserve to protect Brandy Station and to take the rest of his command to support Jones. Hampton ordered Butler's 2d South Carolina Cavalry into reserve where he would picket the roads leading to Carrico's Mills and Kelly's Ford. Then, Hampton turned the rest of his horse soldiers toward the action. Gordon's breakfast went unfinished as the troopers followed the line of the railroad toward the northeast.[19]

Jones, in his shirtsleeves and bootless because of the haste with which he had mounted, needed the help. His pickets had fallen back from the river with the enemy close behind. The horse artillery and its new commander, Major Robert F. Beckham, were encamped on Beverly's Ford Road only one and one-half miles south of the river crossing, so they were in great peril. Luckily, portions of Jones's unit arrived and counterattacked, while the artillery turned and pumped canister at the Yankees. In Beckham's opinion, the makeshift defense saved his artillery from capture.[20] Still, the enemy pressure grew so strong that Jones and Beckham retreated toward new position near a brick church.[21]

So far, the only significant blow the Union forces had absorbed was the death of Gordon's nemesis from Barbee's Crossroads, Benjamin F. "Grimes" Davis. Otherwise, almost eleven thousand blue-clad soldiers were pushing ahead with victory on their minds. Hooker was ultimately responsible for the attack that was at that point a success. He had ordered Alfred Pleasonton, the new commander of the Federal cavalry corps, to "disperse and destroy" the Rebel cavalry thought to be around Culpeper.[22]

Pleasonton, who had assumed command on May 22, divided his force into two detachments for the attack. General John Buford's right wing, consisting of a cavalry division, a cavalry brigade, an infantry brigade, and four artillery batteries, crossed at Beverly's Ford and moved toward Brandy Station. Brigadier General David M. Gregg's left wing, consisting of two horse divisions, an infantry brigade, and one battery, crossed at Kelly's Ford and likewise

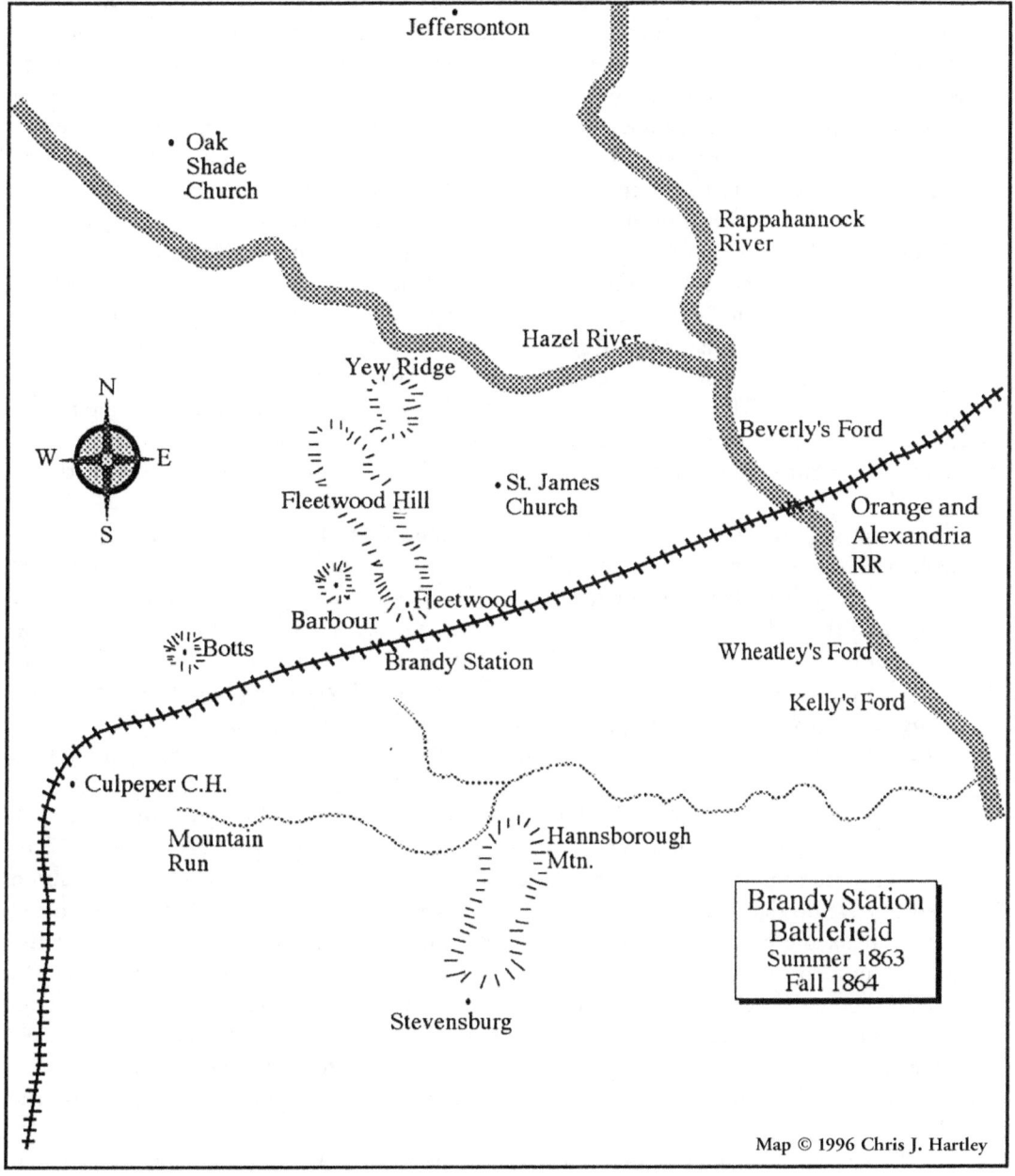

aimed for Brandy. Finally, Colonel Alfred Duffie's cavalry division and one battery approached Culpeper by way of Stevensburg.

Ultimately, the columns were to unite at Brandy and then attack toward Culpeper Court House. Pleasonton, whom John S. Mosby has called the ablest cavalry chief in the history of the Army of the Potomac, had expected to find Stuart in force near Culpeper. Instead, he was surprised to find the enemy along the Rappahannock River.[23]

Jones's Brigade and the horse artillery met the Federals again in the fields around St. James Church. The house of worship, just two miles behind Beverly's Ford and two hundred yards west of Beverly's Ford Road, became the scene of anything but the Lord's work.[24] The Federals marched along the road and attacked the Confederate center, but the Southern defenders stiffened — in part because of arriving reinforcements. One such force was Rooney Lee's Brigade, which took position on a ridge of the Yew Hills facing east. By hooking to Jones's left, Lee made a right angle of the two lines and menaced the Federal flank and rear.[25]

Gordon's fellow Tarheels in the 2d North Carolina Cavalry marched with Lee. The majority of the regiment had been in Virginia since October 1862, but they had never been in a fight like the one confronting them on June 9. Their day had begun with "Boots and Saddles" around 6:30 A.M., followed by "To horse-lead out" at 7:00 A.M. The popular Colonel Solomon Williams had ordered his men to action when he was notified of the Yankees' crossing. In column of fours, the 2d Horse moved out and accessed a road leading toward Beverly's Ford. Then they formed platoons and galloped about a mile, where they found Jones's position. There a Unionist shell rudely greeted them when it hurtled over their heads and sliced off the top of a nearby tree. Though the projectile hurt no one, it persuaded most of the regiment's servants to flee. The Tarheel regiment took position behind a knoll so it could support two horse artillery guns. Sharpshooters then dashed to the front for a long-range duel with the enemy.[26]

Hampton's brigade also came up, with one exception. Colonel John L. Black's 1st South Carolina Cavalry Regiment went toward Kelly's Ford to help Robertson handle a supposed Federal crossing there. Hampton's remaining units — the 1st North Carolina Cavalry, the Cobb Legion, and the Jeff Davis Legion — took a central post between the roads to Beverly's and Kelly's Fords and to the right of Jones's Brigade and Beckham's horse artillery. (Beckham had positioned his batteries between Saint James Church and Mary Gee's house, which was on the opposite side of the road from the church.) The Cobb Legion formed in support of Baker's troopers. When the 1st South Carolina Cavalry completed its mission, the regiment rejoined the brigade there.[27]

While the brigade deployed in the area east of Beverly's Ford Road, Gordon could see the enemy in "a considerable grove of trees" to their front. It was part of the Federal left, which consisted of four regiments under the command of Colonel Thomas Devin. Hampton hoped to envelop that flank, but he started the task with little success.[28] He underestimated their numbers and ordered only one hundred dismounted men to clear them out. After discovering his error, he reinforced his forward sharpshooters with one hundred fresh men. In the sharpshooters' wake, Hampton's line formed and advanced at the double-quick. As Gordon and other officers exhorted the men, the Confederates forced their enemy back a bit. Heavy musketry, and then a Union cavalry charge, retarded the Confederate advance. In counterattack, Hampton threw in the Jeff Davis Legion to support the sharpshooters. The enemy back-peddled.[29]

The woods fighting was only peripheral to the main struggle around the church, but

9. "General, There Comes the First North Carolina" 131

Gordon evidently saw plenty of confusing and hot action. Although projectiles whizzed among the trees and the ringing in his ears grew louder because of the noise, Gordon fired at the enemy and shouted orders. Like a rock, he did not waver; instead, he concentrated on the work at hand. Some of Gordon's men paid the price. P. A. Lefler, struck square in the forehead with a ball, died without a struggle. A Tarheel officer, Captain Rufus Barringer, took a hit in the back of his upper jaw and lost most of his upper teeth. Opposite Gordon, while Devin grappled with Hampton, Buford directed the main effort of his forces elsewhere. When his push against the Confederate center failed, Buford ordered an attack on Rooney Lee's Yew Ridge position beginning at 8:30 A.M.[30]

Fiercely engaged in this fighting was the 2d North Carolina Cavalry. To help repel Buford's attack, the regiment charged a Federal position along a stone wall three hundred yards away. The Tarheels took casualties, but managed to capture the wall along with eighteen prisoners. Rooney Lee and a few members of his staff watched the fight from the shade of a large hickory tree. Though Yankees and their horses fell in great numbers, the brigade commander was not safe from the enemy there. At one point, a shell struck the tree and showered all standing nearby with splinters.[31]

With Confederate attention directed toward Saint James Church, the Federals enjoyed more success at Kelly's Ford. Gregg's Federal force, having met little opposition, was marching toward Stevensburg and Brandy Station. Robertson knew something of the Federal movement, but he was torn as to his duty. "Had I pursued the flanking party," he later reported, "the road I was ordered to defend would have been left utterly exposed. I acted according to orders and the dictates of judgment." Stuart described Robertson's actions by saying he "kept the enemy in check on the Kelly's Ford Road, but did not conform to the movement of the enemy

A war-time photo of Brandy Station on the Aquia Creek and Fredericksburg Railroad. Library of Congress.

to the right, of which he was cognizant, so as to hold him in check or thwart him by a corresponding move of a portion of his command in the same direction." The regimental historian of the 4th North Carolina Cavalry described the result. Though occasionally exposed to enemy artillery fire, the unit — like the whole of Robertson's command — "was held mostly in reserve and its casualties were small."[32] Gregg slid past Robertson and gained Stuart's rear without firing a shot.

Stuart believed that Robertson still held the line and therefore shielded Fleetwood, but he also understood that the Federal crossing at Kelly's threatened Stevensburg. To bolster the defense in that area, Stuart committed his reserve. He ordered Williams C. Wickham's 4th Virginia to follow up the 2d South Carolina Cavalry. One artillery piece, "and the promise of more force, if ... needed," went with Wickham. These actions suggest that Stuart was still convinced that the main Federal advance was at Beverly's. In fact, around 8:00 A.M. he rode toward Beverly's to watch the action there, discounting a contrary opinion from Jones about Kelly's Ford.[33]

Around midday, Stuart became a believer.[34] It was almost too late. When the cavalry leader had gone to watch the fight at Beverly's Ford, he had left Major Henry B. McClellan, his adjutant-general, at Fleetwood to accept and forward dispatches. Except for couriers and the leather pouch slung over his shoulder, McClellan was alone; even Stuart's two tent-flies and camp equipment had been hustled off to Culpeper Court House. Near noon, a courier from one of Robertson's regiments rode up the hill. The North Carolinian told McClellan that the Federals were advancing on Fleetwood, unopposed, from Kelly's Ford. McClellan was disinclined to believe the courier. Surely Robertson would have stopped the Yankee advance from Kelly's! Minutes later, McClellan saw the Federal column himself[35]:

> And so it was! Within cannon shot of the hill a long column of the enemy filled the road, which here skirted the woods. They were pressing steadily forward upon the railroad station, which must in a few moments be in their possession. How could they be prevented from also occupying the Fleetwood Hill, the key to the whole position? Matters looked serious![36]

Alarmed, the adjutant sent courier after courier to notify Stuart of this ominous development. The desperate McClellan also rounded up a howitzer from Chew's Battery that happened to be nearby. It seemed a useless gesture, but it was all McClellan could do. Though short on ammunition, the men who served that six-pounder howitzer were grimly determined to hold the hill until reinforcements came. Their slow shelling bought the Confederates extra time by causing the Federals to pause and return the fire.[37]

Stuart had not listened to Jones, and he at first questioned even McClellan's judgment. When the first courier told him McClellan's news, the cavalry leader turned to one of his officers and said, "Ride back there and see what all that foolishness is about." Then Stuart heard the sound of shelling in the distance and finally understood the danger. Now, Stuart chose his course of action quickly and wisely. He called Hampton's, Robertson's, and Jones's brigades to Fleetwood to fight the approaching Federal force. General W. H. F. Lee was notified "to rejoin the command on the left."[38]

Stuart's orders meant that the Confederates had to break off the fight at St. James Church. They did just that. The surprised Federals watched as their foe disappeared with the suddenness of a summer thunderstorm. Jones fell back toward the southern end of Fleetwood while Lee fell back from Yew Ridge to Fleetwood's northern end. Colonel Devin was as shocked as anyone to see Hampton's Confederates break off their two-hour-long fight, wheel into column, and ride off.[39]

Hampton, whose path of withdrawal was similar to Jones's, had again anticipated Stuart's orders. While his troopers were still fighting in the woods near the church, Hampton had seen a frightening sight: enemy in his rear. They were headed for Fleetwood and Stuart's headquarters. Since Hampton's only line of retreat led across that hill, and the Federal advance focused on the hill, Hampton ordered a withdrawal. One staffer, bearing a message from Stuart, said, "All things considered it was the speediest all round movement I ever remember." One by one, Hampton's regiments fell back. The sharpshooters acted as rear guard. Gordon and his fellow North Carolinians were probably reluctant to give up the woods fight, but they responded to a man. They urged their horses into column.[40]

It turned into a race for the hill, and a close one at that. The Union 1st New Jersey and 1st Pennsylvania cavalry regiments climbed Fleetwood Hill from the southwest while the 1st Maryland skirted the hill's southern base. The Confederates came from the northeast. Jones made good progress, as did Hampton. Stuart ordered Hampton to send a regiment at the gallop "as the enemy had possession of his headquarters." Hampton chose the 6th Virginia, which Jones had left under Hampton's direction, to carry out the mission.[41]

The 12th Virginia Cavalry, also from Jones's Brigade, won the race. Thanks to McClellan's frantic efforts, it arrived at Fleetwood just fifty yards ahead of the Yankees, even as Chew's gun was withdrawing. Immediately the 12th Virginia attacked and stalled the Federal advance up the hill, but the Unionists tossed reserves into the fray. This added strength repulsed the 12th. Stuart, who reached the hill around this time, was later critical of the 12th Virginia's performance. He charged that the regiment's retreat was unnecessary and only resulted in confusion, harder fighting, and heavier losses.[42]

Fresh Confederate units arrived: the 35th Virginia Battalion of Jones's Brigade, the 6th Virginia, and elements of the Confederate horse artillery. These units stemmed the Federal advance, but become disorganized after galloping to the hill and getting mixed up with the 12th.[43] The tide of battle rolled back and forth across the hill as the Confederates and the Federals took turns at attacking and defending. It was a hard fight: pistols popped, carbines cracked, cannons boomed, and swords clanked. A veritable rain of bullets marked some parts of the field; in others, swordplay was the more common. Because of the close quarters, artillery and guns often could not be fired without endangering one's own comrades. The screams of men and horses echoed across the field. The air thickened with smoke and deadly missiles. If a man was dismounted, he was probably either wounded or dead.[44]

Stuart later called it a "critical moment," and he was right; the issue hung in the balance. The Yankees weathered Stuart's patchwork counterattacks with surprising tenacity, placing Confederate control of the hill in jeopardy. When commanders tossed more reinforcements into the enlarging, swirling battle, it was like adding wood to a fire.

Hampton, who was still en route to Fleetwood, followed up the 6th Virginia with units from his own brigade. Their Beverly's Ford position between the two roads complicated the move somewhat since the brigade had to move cross-country. Hampton moved them briskly in column of squadrons. Baker and Gordon worked their men hard in the effort to reach Fleetwood, but it was difficult to keep an organized group moving cross-country in the tension of a fight going wrong. Somehow, the brigade commanders managed to move their men in "magnificent order."[45]

Hampton needed the best efforts of every man in this situation. He got just that from Colonel Baker, Gordon's latest mentor. Just over a week before the cavalry battle, Stuart had evaluated Baker for army headquarters as "the best colonel in Hampton's Brigade" and deserving of promotion because of the way he kept his regiment disciplined and efficient. Although "perhaps not as dashing an officer as Butler," Stuart wrote, Baker had provided faithful service, "and since his affair which called forth his pledge, his conduct has been admirable."[46]

Wade Hampton was proud of his troopers' performance at Brandy Station. "I have never seen troops display greater coolness, bravery, and steadiness," he wrote (Edwin Forbes, "Cavalry Charge Near Brandy Station, Va.," Library of Congress).

As they neared Fleetwood, Gordon saw Baker in his element: commanding his regiment in a tense situation. Throughout their service together, Baker's leadership methods and tactical decisions had been useful examples for Gordon. This day was no different. In the distance, the noise from the fighting rose to a crescendo. Gordon got ready to fight.

About a mile from the base of Fleetwood hill, a courier from Stuart found Hampton and relayed fresh orders. With that, Hampton ordered the Cobb Legion toward Fleetwood at the gallop, and dispatched the 1st South Carolina Cavalry to their support. The 1st North Carolina Cavalry and the Jeff Davis Legion continued their measured pace toward the hill with the intention to turn the Federal right. The ground beneath the horses held firm; neither fence nor forest barred their way because the war had ravaged the landscape.[47] The sun's heat beat down.

"It was a thrilling sight," Blackford later wrote, "to see these dashing horsemen draw their sabres and start for the hill at a gallop." Reaching the hill, the Cobb Legion and the 1st South Carolina Cavalry struck the flanks of the 10th and 2d New York regiments, causing those Yankees to "float off like feathers on a wind." The brigade commander of the New York regiments, Colonel Hugh Judson Kilpatrick, saw his men "float off" and turned to the 1st Maine Cavalry. "Men of Maine," he yelled, "you must save the day!" These Federal cavalrymen responded with a charge that broke Young's and Black's regiments. Then the men of Maine kept on going, away from Fleetwood Hill and toward a higher hill where the Barbour House stood.[48]

The 1st North Carolina Cavalry came next, with Lieutenant Colonel Joseph Waring's Jeff Davis Legion in support. These cavalrymen charged down the eastern face of the hill. Ahead, the ground was covered with Federal cavalry, so Baker's attack became a decisive one.[49] William H. H. Cowles's company led the attack. Preston Hampton, General Hampton's son, rode near Cowles. Baker, displaying his "soldierly qualities," commanded this second wave. Gordon, adrenaline pumping, fought and led and did his duty in the two distinct charges executed by the regiment. The 1st swept around Pierce Young's left, faced south, and "made a series of charges most successful and brilliant."[50] Foe met foe "with a shock that made the earth tremble." The North Carolinians kept riding over the hill, down the slope, and across the Orange and Alexandria. There, they found a retreating column of the enemy and sliced through them. The North Carolinians captured several prisoners and a stand of colors from the 10th New York.[51]

Gordon was fighting in the midst of what Blackford described so admirably: "Acres and acres of horsemen sparkling with sabres, and dotted with brilliant bits of color where their flags danced above them, hurled against each other at full speed." The perfume of early June roses had once scented that soft summer day. Now, it "was dispelled by the sulphurous fumes of the battle smoke" which "rolled in great clouds over the battle scarred fields." Dust mixed with the smoke.[52] In the midst of it all, Baker later reported, the men of the 1st North Carolina Cavalry "behaved admirably." Rufus Barringer remembered that the 1st was "in the thickest of the fight and the longest in the field." Evidently, the Tarheels bore the brunt of their part of the fight; the Jeff Davis Legion lost only four men wounded. An observer called the brigade's charge "as gallantly made and gallantly met as any ... ever witnessed during nearly four years of active service on the outposts."[53] It was an attack that Joachim Murat, Napoleon's great cavalry leader, would have admired.

It was a nightmare illuminated by smoke-filtered sunshine. According to one account, "The whole plain was covered with men and horses, charging in all directions, close in hand to hand encounters, with banners flying, sabers glittering, and the fierce flash of fire arms, amid the din, dust and smoke of raging battle."[54] This was the perfect time for Gordon to draw from the family grit his grandmother had shown in confronting Cornwallis. Soldiers of both sides saw amazing and often unspeakable things as men fought and died. Troopers from Robertson's Brigade, who came up from the direction of Kelly's Ford late in the fight, were repulsed by the sight of the death of a Federal battery commander. When struck by a shell, the Union man and the white horse he was riding exploded into "fragments." Even the unscathed suffered, but theirs was more of the soul than the body. One Tarheel was riding across the grass when he threw his arms up and fell to the ground. His comrades thought he was wounded, but "developments proved that his distress was purely mental." Von Borcke was not specific about it in his memoirs, but it may have been during this battle when Stuart saw a similar incident. When a North Carolinian was knocked off his horse by artillery fire, Stuart asked him if he was hurt. The stunned cavalryman answered, "Oh, General, I shall soon be all right again, but I am dreadfully demoralized by a bomb-shell." With good reason: the cannon ball had passed so close to him that its windage had unhorsed him.[55]

Hampton said of his men that day: "I have never seen any troops display greater coolness, bravery, and steadiness." The 1st North Carolina Cavalry provided evidence for Hampton's statement. Before his wound, Barringer "acted as field officer" and "bore himself with marked coolness and good conduct." Nicholas P. Tredenick was handling some spare horses when he saw his lieutenant fall exhausted to the grass. Tredenick ignored heavy enemy fire, dashed to the man's aid, and dragged him to safety.[56] Baker's adjutant, Lieutenant J. L. Gaines, was partly responsible for the regiment's success that day. He coolly assisted his colonel by helping reform the regiment in the midst of the charges. He also played a part in keeping the men in order during the fighting. Major John H. Whitaker remained in the fray all day despite being listed on the sick report. Cowles displayed his usual "marked gallantry" by leading the charge that overwhelmed the 10th New York.[57] The colors of that regiment remained in Tarheel hands.

It had taken about two hours, but the Federals were finally beaten back. Some retreated toward Brandy Station. While Hampton regrouped, the still fresh 11th Virginia of Colonel Lunsford L. Lomax chased them. The horse artillery tried to encourage the retreat with shelling, but that only hampered the pursuit. The artillerymen could not differentiate friend from foe because of the smoke, dust, and the distances to various targets. Many an errant shell fell among Confederate units. After cleaning out Brandy Station and chasing the Federals toward Stevensburg and Kelly's Ford, Lomax had to retire.[58]

After reforming, Hampton also had the opportunity to cut off a large Federal force. However, indiscriminate Confederate artillery fire discouraged him as well. Only Cowles enjoyed some success in pursuit. He had been quite a hunter before the war; at Brandy Station he proved an efficient hunter of men. After charging completely through the ranks of the 10th New York, Cowles ignored the artillery fire and continued the chase. He and his North Carolinians were soon all alone, but Cowles did not stop until he captured sixty Federals and a *New York Herald* reporter. Preston Hampton, who had been riding with Cowles until his horse was shot, saw that Cowles was cut off. Hampton even reported to headquarters that Cowles had been captured. Cowles escaped by riding cross-country and crossing a deep stream where there was no ford. It was, Baker said, "The most brilliant part of the day's work performed by the regiment."[59]

As the pursuit petered out, Stuart directed the 1st South Carolina Cavalry and the Cobb Legion to reform in the flat near Fleetwood to support the artillery. Hampton, who had hoped to continue the pursuit once the artillery realized its error, could do little without those two regiments.[60]

The two Confederate regiments near Stevensburg had a rough time of it. They did stave off the Federal advance there,[61] but enemy fire knocked Butler off his chestnut sorrel, tearing away his right foot. The same shell mortally wounded Stuart's chief scout, Captain Will Farley.[62] Yet in the afternoon of Brandy Station, Stuart had little time to wonder about Butler because Fleetwood Hill remained the focal point of fighting. This time, the enemy came from the north and northwest. Federal cavalry and infantry, supported by artillery, was spotted near George Thompson's House and St. James Church. It was Buford, who had been realigning his forces while the fight raged on Fleetwood. Stuart ordered Blackford to ride to Longstreet's headquarters with this intelligence. Infantry might be needed to help defend the hill.[63]

Wisely, Stuart respected the combat power of the approaching force and recalled the men pursuing the Federals retreating toward Kelly's. New orders were shouted, sounded, or sent. The horse-soldiers turned north, reloaded, and steeled themselves for more fighting. Sharpshooters rode off to ply their trade. Stuart created a new line. Jones's Brigade took position behind Fleetwood, probably to cover Stuart's rear. The artillery, although low on ammunition, set up on the heights to fire northward. Hampton moved to the right. Rooney Lee's Brigade, just arrived from Yew Ridge, took position on the left. Robertson's Brigade, which had also just arrived, was split up to fill in gaps. The 5th North Carolina Cavalry rode to the left to help face the Federal advance, while the 4th North Carolina Cavalry joined Hampton and began supporting a battery just behind the Fleetwood House.[64]

John Buford's troops were close behind Rooney Lee. In just one month Buford would help win the Battle of Gettysburg and in six months he would be dead from a severe illness, but on this day the Kentuckian was more intent on ejecting Stuart from northern Fleetwood Hill. Gregg's defeated forces soon joined him in that.

Union artillery pounded the hill. It served as cover while blue-clad soldiers maneuvered to within three hundred yards of Stuart's position. On Stuart's right, the men of the 1st North Carolina Cavalry weathered the Union artillery fire without confusion. After the artillery barrage, Hampton reported, the brigade's work ended for the day except for an incident "when we drove a small party across the river, below the railroad bridge."[65]

Down the line, Rooney Lee withstood the attacks of Lincoln's legions and began counterattacks of his own. The Confederates charged, Lee handling his men in a "handsome manner."[66] The Federals recovered from the initial shock and repelled the grayback horsemen. With the command, "Forward, draw sabre; charge!" Colonel Williams hurled his 2d Horse into the fray and helped drive the Federals back about one-half mile. He had received complimentary dispatches from General Lee during the struggle, so he fought with added confidence. Moments later, however, a shout was on Williams's lips when a bullet crashed through his head and killed him. (Only two weeks before, Williams had married the daughter of R. B. Pegram, commander of the CSS *Nashville*.) General Rooney Lee also had a bad time of it, though the Confederates stood their ground. After 4:00 P.M., he was severely wounded in the leg. The army commander, who was coming up to see about the fight, was shocked to see his son being carried from the field.[67]

Munford's (Fitz Lee's) Brigade, slow in coming to the field, made up for it by appearing in a timely fashion in this last stage of the battle. The brigade struck Buford in the flank near the Welford House. This gave the Federals, who had already begun to fall back because Pleasonton had ordered a withdrawal, added incentive. Munford's sharpshooters kept the air alive with bullets, and skirmishing continued until the Federals retired across Beverly's Ford.

At last, the battle was over. Silence fell over the field, but it was almost foreign in comparison to the noise generated by the sunrise-to-sunset fight. Stuart reestablished his picket line along the river, but his headquarters had to be moved off Fleetwood. The bodies of dead horses and men still lay thickly across the hill, and flies swarmed around them. It seems the men of Gordon's regiment would scarcely have noticed it, however. One trooper wrote home that the men fed their horses in the dark and then "laid our weary bodies down to rest."[68]

Roll-call was always depressing after a battle. The morning of June 10, though a "fine" one, was no different. In almost every bivouac, cavalrymen saw gaps in their ranks. Baker and Gordon studied the 1st North Carolina's roster and reported five killed, twelve wounded, and fifteen missing. Hampton put brigade losses at fifteen killed, fifty-five wounded, and fifty missing.[69] Among the dead was Lieutenant Colonel Frank Hampton, Wade's brother.

Stockpiling captured enemy equipment and counting prisoners were more pleasant tasks. All told, Hampton's Brigade had captured 216 Yankees, eighty-two carbines, sixty-four pistols, thirty-five sabres, and thirty-five sabre belts, with Baker's 1st capturing approximately 137 Federals, nineteen horses, nine saddles, thirty-six guns, twenty-eight pistols, and twelve sabres. Two stands of colors could be credited to the 1st's efforts as well. As the pile of equipment grew, it was no wonder that Hampton acknowledged his indebtedness to Baker, Black, Young, and Waring for their service.[70]

Brandy Station has been called a turning point of the Civil War because it marked the ascendancy of the Federal cavalry. That thinking can be traced to the days immediately after the battle when military and civilian critics complained about Stuart's performance.[71] Stuart had been surprised and nearly beaten, they said. The Virginian disagreed, pointing out that his men had fought superbly and had won in the end. At that point, the important thing was that Stuart owned the field after the fight, which meant he had accomplished his first responsibility: that of shielding Lee's infantry — and Lee's plans of invasion — from the enemy. For Gordon, that was a lesson worth learning.

Gordon's part in the twelve-hour fight is undocumented as to his specific involvement. Neither Baker nor Hampton singled out the lieutenant colonel for either gallantry or mistakes. The absence of his name in reports suggests that Gordon did his duty at Brandy Station: nothing more, nothing less. Yet in a real sense, the day's battle was also a turning point for Gordon. The largest cavalry battle ever fought on the continent, and the "hardest day's duty" faced by Stuart's cavalry, was a test for every cavalryman present.[72] Tarheel trooper Kerr Craige, for one, never forgot the fight. One day, Craige and his son took a train trip to Washington. When the train passed the fields around Brandy Station, Craige simply looked out the window and said nothing.[73] The day remained with Gordon for a long time, too. He passed the test, learned from it, and emerged with increased confidence in his abilities and in his men. Before June 9, Gordon had shown much potential, but in a way that earned him recognition in his current position rather than as a man ready for more responsibility. During the fighting on that Virginia hillside near the Rappahannock, something clicked. Something fell into place. During the coming weeks and months, Gordon would enter into a rhythm of consistently good performance that elevated him beyond all expectations.

10

With the 5th

As a businessman, Gordon had traveled to Pennsylvania often to buy goods. Philadelphia was one of his favorite markets. He established a close business relationship with at least one of the city's merchants, a man by the name of Campbell. Gordon had liked and trusted Campbell. He occasionally asked Campbell to make purchasing decisions for him when he was unable to go to Philadelphia himself.[1] But in the summer of 1863, there were no friends awaiting Gordon in Pennsylvania; there were only foes. The Army of Northern Virginia was bent on invading the North. The "Campbells" Gordon had known before the war were now the Yankees who were trying to kill him. The situation had an irony that may not have escaped an intelligent man like Gordon.

Yet in those days of nation-making and nation-saving campaigns, men gave ironies little thought. Instead, Gordon and his comrades — and the "Campbells" of the opposing army — watched, and joined, in events. The day after the Battle of Brandy Station, General Richard S. Ewell started his infantry for the Potomac River. Ewell, Jackson's successor and the new commander of the Second Corps, led his men down the Shenandoah Valley, with Lieutenant Colonel Elijah White's Thirty-fifth Virginia Battalion from Jones's Brigade employed as cavalry support. Later, about 1,500 horsemen under General Albert Jenkins came from southwest Virginia and joined Ewell. On June 15, after the Confederates defeated Federal forces at Winchester, Jenkins's cavalry led Ewell's corps across the Potomac and toward Pennsylvania. Simultaneously, back at the Rappahannock, Longstreet's corps started its northward march along a predetermined avenue, which was to be just east of the Blue Ridge. The only momentary exception was A. P. Hill's corps, which briefly held its position to cover the advance and to deceive the enemy.[2]

The Army of Northern Virginia's latest offensive was under way, but for once Stuart did not lead the way. Like Hill's and Longstreet's commands, the cavalry division had not marched with Ewell. Instead, the horse soldiers rested, reorganized, and buried the dead from their fight. Lee did not consider the Brandy Station battle a serious threat to his plans, but it did keep him from placing his cavalry where he wished — in the army's vanguard. He could only make the best of the situation. Afterward, Lee put his cavalry back to work by directing them to guide and screen Longstreet's and Hill's advance, in part by holding mountain gaps east of the infantry's routes of march. Chagrined in reputation and delayed in movement by the Union stroke at Brandy, Stuart was overjoyed to be in the saddle again. Surely, this offensive would bring many chances for retribution.[3]

On June 15, the same day Jenkins splashed across the Potomac, Stuart's cavalry division began crossing the Rappahannock. Fitz Lee's Brigade (still under Munford) forded the waters first in advance of Longstreet. The next day, the brigades of W. H. F. Lee (commanded by its senior colonel, John R. Chambliss) and Beverly Robertson established a moving screen on Longstreet's right flank. Jones's Brigade was detached for picket duty along the Aestham River. Finally, Stuart ordered Hampton "to remain with his brigade on the Rappahannock, in observation of the enemy during the movement of our forces...."[4] The order was reminiscent of the one given to Hampton before the Maryland campaign, but it did not keep Gordon away from fighting long.

Stuart's screening horsemen did get into a scrape before the 1st North Carolina Cavalry left its position near Beverly Ford. On Wednesday morning, June 17, while Stuart's other forces shielded the army, Munford directed Fitz Lee's Brigade toward Aldie, a village astride a gap in Bull Run Mountain. Aldie was situated in a strategically significant area. From Aldie, a road led through Middleburg and Upperville to Ashby's Gap in the Blue Ridge. A second road coursed northwestward through Mountsville to Snicker's Gap. Mostly west of Ashby's and Snicker's gaps were the northward-bound troops of the Army of Northern Virginia. Control of the countryside between Ashby's Gap, Snicker's Gap, and Aldie Gap was the key to protecting Lee's men as they marched. To that end, Stuart planned to separate his command at Upperville and approach the Potomac along several avenues. He could cover more territory that way.[5]

Pleasant was the "rich and beautiful county of Fauquier" through which Munford marched. As of yet, the landscape showed few signs of war's ravages, but the summer heat was quite evident.[6] Munford's men quickly tired and their horses became hungry, but they still managed to reach Aldie. At Aldie, progress halted when pickets had a brush with Federal cavalry. The enemy gained the advantage and occupied the town.[7] Quickly the Confederates established defensive positions on a hill overlooking the Snickersville pike. Persistent Federal charges began thundering against Munford's men; the Confederates resisted mightily with volleys and countercharges. Some fought along a stone wall, while others battled among haystacks. The affair evolved into a bloody stalemate that cost Munford 119 casualties.[8]

Late in the day, Stuart withdrew Munford toward cavalry headquarters at Middleburg. He also directed Robertson and Chambliss, the former near Rectortown and the latter around Thoroughfare Gap, to hasten to Middleburg. News of a Federal advance had motivated Stuart to assemble his men. "A large force" of Lincoln's horse-soldiers was said to be marching toward Middleburg. Stuart worked quickly, but the Federals — in actuality only the 1st Rhode Island Cavalry — captured Middleburg before Confederate reinforcements arrived. They did it so quickly that Stuart and his staff were "compelled to make a retreat more rapid than was consistent with dignity and comfort."[9] Behind the skedaddling Confederates, the Unionists barricaded the streets. They planned to hold until reinforcements came.

Reinforcements galloped into Middleburg about 7:00 P.M., but the unit did not carry the Stars and Stripes. It was Robertson's Brigade, full of fight. A squadron from the 4th North Carolina Cavalry led the brigade toward the enemy. Some dismounted Yankees, hidden by a stone fence just outside town, saw the Confederates under the darkening sky and let loose a volley. The fire shattered the Carolina squadron. The rest of the 4th, along with the 5th North Carolina Cavalry and some arriving Virginia units, heard the ruckus and responded. Three separate charges thundered against the Yankees along the fence.[10] "With a terrific yell," each successive charge bore down on the foe. Blazes of rifle fire issued "out on the darkness and into those charging Carolinians." The fighting became fierce; the third charge gained the stone fence, where the Confederate troopers dismounted, vaulted the barricade, and took their enemy in the flank.[11] Other barricades blocked the town's streets, but the Confederate cavalrymen, who were "yelling and swinging [their] sabres" and "charging like madmen and with pistols blazing," could not be stopped. According to Stuart, Robertson's attack ejected the enemy from Middleburg and scattered them.¹²

Chambliss iced the victory by cutting off the Yankee retreat. The Rhode Island regiment emerged so decimated that it would not see action for two months. Stuart must also have been encouraged by the performance of Robertson in the battle; only time would tell if the man belonged with the cavalry division.

The next day, with Middleburg in his possession, Stuart consolidated his position between

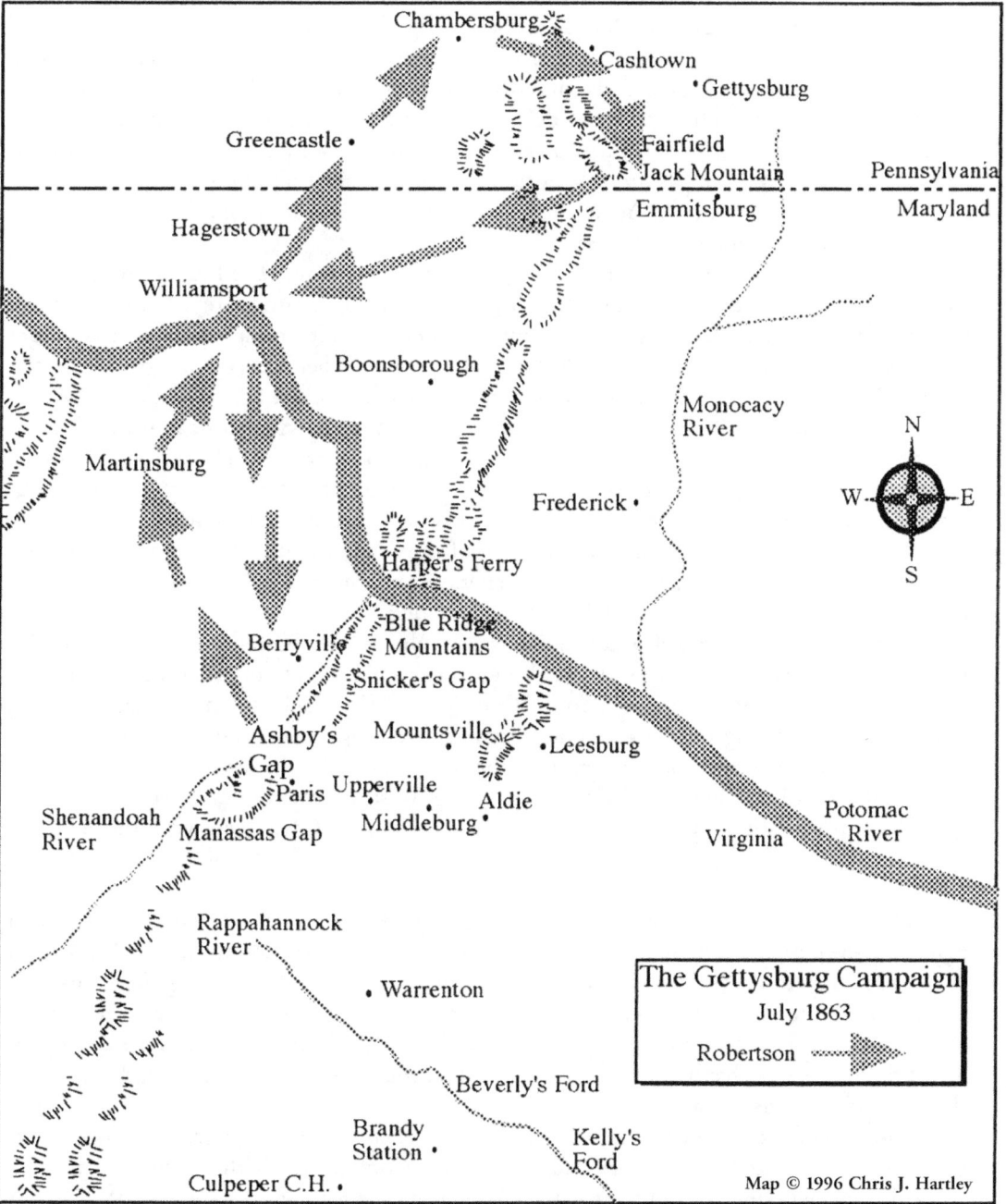

the Blue Ridge and Bull Run Mountain, and pushed pickets, scouts, and patrols out to develop enemy movements. As the day wore on, skirmishing again swirled around Middleburg. Robertson's Tarheels became engaged; at one point, Lieutenant Colonel Edward Cantwell of the 4th North Carolina Cavalry was cut off from his comrades. Unabashed, he refused to surrender and yelled to his men to keep fighting. Blue-clad soldiers silenced him only by snatching the sword from his hand. Ultimately, Robertson's Brigade lost fifty-seven casualties, and the Federals forced Stuart out of Middleburg.[13]

Gordon's journey from the Rappahannock to the front — begun on June 17 after A. P. Hill began marching down the Shenandoah Valley — was over familiar ground. When Burnside had marched on Fredericksburg seven months before, the cavalry division had retreated over that area. Gordon's bloodiest personal defeat had come at Barbee's Crossroads during that retreat. With the exception of Tom Brown's and Nathaniel Gordon's deaths, that had been perhaps the worst event of his life. Memories, and the anticipation of a successful offensive, made Gordon's ride a vivid one. Yet as the brigade approached Warrenton, the time for reflection ended and the time for war arrived.[14]

Hooker knew the Army of Northern Virginia was on the move. The Federal countermove was to keep troops between Lee and Washington with a northward march. In conjunction, blue cavalry had begun reaching toward Aldie and beyond to learn more about Confederate intentions. That prompted the cavalry fighting. On June 18, when Rebel scout John S. Mosby captured one of Hooker's staff officers, Hooker's movements became equally apparent. Mosby told Stuart, "The skies are bright to-night with the reflection of Hooker's camp-fires."[15] The Southerners also learned that Pleasonton was planning to dispatch a reconnaissance toward Warrenton and Culpeper. Stuart assigned Hampton the job of foiling it. With that in mind, Hampton's troopers crossed the Rappahannock at Beverly's Ford and marched, pausing occasionally for their horses to feast on roadside fields of clover and timothy.[16] Reaching Warrenton, the Southerners camped outside town. The enemy came the next day, and Hampton faced him. Stuart briefly described the night's resulting action:

"Hampton met the enemy's advance toward Culpeper, at Warrent[o]n, and drove him back without difficulty, a heavy storm and night intervening to aid the enemy's retreat."[17]

And so it was. According to a South Carolinian, "We fought in an incessantly falling rain until dark, driving them back some distance. We fought until night, and then in the pitch darkness, we wended our way back to the piece of woods which sheltered us the night before, and went into bivouac, where all night long we strove for comfort, between rail fires and the continual rain."[18] Gordon and the 1st North Carolina Cavalry strove with them.

The next day, June 19, was lovely, a day easily appreciated by those who did not have to fight. It made perfect riding weather for the men of Hampton's Brigade as they left Warrenton and headed toward the front. But at cavalry headquarters outside Middleburg, few paused to enjoy the summer day. The noise of distant cannon-fire kept the war on everyone's mind. Beyond Middleburg, the story was the same: outlying Confederate pickets were driven in. Stuart rightly guessed that his enemy was advancing. Federal General David Gregg was sending three brigades against Stuart.[19]

Robertson's and Rooney Lee's brigades met the enemy around a patch of woods about one mile west of Middleburg. Gregg's Yankees hit the Confederates with carbine and artillery fire and began working around their flanks. This made the Confederate line brittle; Federals

10. With the 5th   143

In June 1863, Gordon assumed temporary command of the 5th North Carolina Cavalry, which was a part of the brigade of Brigadier General Beverly H. Robertson. (Military Order of the Loyal Legion of the United States — Massachusetts Commandery Photograph Collection, U.S. Army Military History Institute, Carlisle Barracks, Pennsylvania)

eventually punched a hole in Stuart's line. Only a Southern countercharge and well-placed artillery fire plugged the gap. Under this pressure, Stuart withdrew to a more defensible position one-half mile to the rear. Gordon's friend Heros Von Borcke was severely wounded during the withdrawal. Von Borcke would neither enjoy punch with Gordon nor ride with the cavalry again.[20]

As if in tribute to the Prussian Rebel, Von Borcke's wounding prefaced the fight's end. That night, Jones's Brigade rejoined the main body. Stuart sent Jones's men to guard the left near Union. He then ordered Munford, who had spent the day along the Snickersville turnpike, to continue watching Snicker's Gap. Robertson and Chambliss settled into their new position.[21] Meanwhile, some miles to the cavalry's rear, the Army of Northern Virginia continued its unobstructed march to the Potomac. Stuart had held off the Federal attacks so far, but he needed Hampton badly.

The cavalry also spent the next day waiting for the South Carolinian's Brigade. The wait under rainy skies was a welcome break for some of the division's horses as many had been hobbled by the area's rough, rocky ground. Stuart thought about recapturing Middleburg, but again he decided to wait until he had sufficient strength. Instead, the cavalry leader maintained his screen and kept tabs on the skirmishing that took place on the left. When Hampton arrived late in the day, the added strength enabled Stuart to improve his spread-out defenses. He placed Hampton on the Ashby's Gap pike, west of Middleburg, and directed Chambliss to strengthen Jones around Union.[22]

Gordon had only a few hours to examine the ground and settle in. Two Federal cavalry divisions, supported by infantry and artillery, came at 8:00 A.M. on June 21. The Battle of Upperville began as the early morning mists cleared. Gordon and the 1st North Carolina Cavalry were in the middle of it. Pleasonton had decided to "take my whole corps ... and throw it at once upon Stuart's whole force, and cripple it up ... [and] seriously impair the enemy's force for offensive operations."[23] Pleasonton marched with enough strength to render Hampton's reinforcements insufficient.

For his primary thrust, Buford endeavored to turn Stuart's left. Chambliss and Jones resisted mightily; the attack ground to a halt. This forced a change in the Federal plan. Their original strategy had called for General David Gregg's cavalry division and a supporting infantry brigade to feint toward Stuart's front. Now, since Buford made no progress, the feint became the main attack. Gregg marched along the pike and aimed straight for Hampton's and Robertson's positions.[24]

Those two Southern cavalrymen fought from what Stuart described as a "position previously chosen, of great strength against a force of ordinary size, or against cavalry alone...." The position, overlooking Kirk's Branch, empowered the Confederates to resist Pleasonton's advance. Baker commanded the 1st and the Jeff Davis Legion in a position south of the pike. The 1st came under particularly strong pressure; Company I's captain, William Houston of Duplin County, fell dead from sharpshooters' fire. As the fight wore on Stuart chose to withdraw toward Upperville. The flash of distant Federal bayonets prompted Stuart to find an even stronger position from which to fight.[25]

When Hampton gave the word, his and Robertson's men pulled back en echelon to a new position, ultimately on the rocky, wooded heights west of Goose Creek.[26] The Federals followed, and battle flared again. Goose Creek now became the focal point of the war's death. Blood tainted the creek's waters. At one spot, five dying artillery horses could be seen crumpled in a heap; elsewhere, wounded men struggled for life, including one who lost half his face to a shell fragment. For several hours, Hampton and Robertson wallowed in this carnage, beating back cavalry and infantry thrusts. With no small effect, Confederates fought dismounted from behind stone walls. Meanwhile, mounted cavalry detachments roamed the flanks, protecting against turning movements and seeking opportunities for attack. These tactics worked for a time, but Pleasonton's numerical superiority won out. The Confederate cavalrymen were bone weary from the fighting, and casualties mounted.[27] Stuart decided to retire toward Upperville again.

North of the Upperville pike, Jones and Chambliss continued their gradual withdrawal. They again became hotly engaged and were soon cut off; the 2d North Carolina Cavalry suffered heavy casualties. Ultimately, these brigades retired toward Ashby's Gap. That left Stuart with only Hampton's and Robertson's brigades to face the advance of a Federal division, and more, along the pike, so Stuart ordered his commanders to pull back through town rather than defend it. Ostensibly, he did so because he thought fighting would endanger the women and children of Upperville, but the move was also for a tactical reason. He had to cover a road junction west of town to protect against flanking maneuvers.[28]

Gregg's Federal cavalry division and its supports followed the Confederates into the town's outskirts. They found Stuart in an unusual situation: he had no Virginia units at his call. Robertson covered the pike and the open fields to the north. Hampton held the right, mostly south of the pike, the 1st North Carolina Cavalry manning the extreme right. Gregg pressed ahead, causing the fighting to become desperate and at times hand-to-hand. When a Union attack threw Colonel Peter G. Evans's 5th North Carolina Cavalry into confusion, the battle became general.[29]

Robertson could do nothing, but Hampton saw the 5th North Carolina Cavalry break and guessed the implications. If the whole line collapsed, defeat and disaster would follow. Worse, if the Union forces broke through, they would discover Lee's movement and probably attack him. The South Carolina general ordered his Jeff Davis Legion to help the 5th North Carolina Cavalry, but the Legion was itself flanked by more enemy troopers. The outcome hung in the balance.[30]

Again, Hampton turned for help. This time, his eyes fell on Gordon. During the withdrawal, Gordon had been in command of the right wing of the 1st, which consisted of five companies. Baker, with the other five companies, was not yet ready, but it did not matter to Hampton. Drawing his sabre and raising himself in his stirrups to his full height, Hampton faced Gordon's detachment and cried, "First North Carolina, follow me!" Gordon and his troopers responded with alacrity, and the North Carolinians rode to rescue the Jeff Davis Legion. The horse-soldiers bore down on the flank of the attacking enemy column. For a brief moment, Gordon was a Confederate Murat, leading a victorious cavalry charge against the enemy. Sabres flashed in the sunlight. Small-arms fire roared. Men clashed and the attack had its effect, but then Union courage offset North Carolina bravery. Gordon came under counterattack only moments after slicing into the Federal flank. His five companies did not have the personnel to force a decision.[31]

By this time, the rest of the 1st was in position. Baker struck the flank of the unit attacking Gordon, but then Baker came under counterattack. With his hoarse, strident voice ringing out, Stuart was a steadying influence; his face was stormy and his eyes burned; but Hampton controlled this fight. Next, the South Carolinian fed the Cobb Legion into the meat grinder. When another Federal attack flanked the Cobb Legion, Hampton sent the regrouped Jeff Davis Legion back in. Then Gordon's troopers took another shot, and so on. Before the smoke cleared, each of Hampton's units charged, attacked, and was counterattacked three times. The fighting was vicious; one of Gordon's Tarheels killed three Yankees and captured a fourth before being shot in the foot himself.[32]

Staff-member John Esten Cooke called it a war of giants. Miles away, Union and Confederate infantrymen listened to the distant roar of the artillery but knew nothing of the magnitude of the fight there.[33] They did not know that the Battle of Upperville swept the terrain like a tornado.

The struggle sputtered to a halt only when Hampton's 2d South Carolina Cavalry came up and provided enough cover to allow the brigade to reform. By salvaging an orderly retreat, the Confederates secured a tactical advantage. Somehow, they even captured eighty prisoners and regained more than a half mile of ground. However, Hampton subsequently had to relinquish the dearly bought terrain. His flank was exposed because the enemy had forced Robertson back, so Hampton retired west of town. The battle paused, but like mosquitoes on a humid summer evening, the "blue-birds" followed their prey down the narrow turnpike leading out of Upperville.[34]

Colonel Peter G. Evans of the 5th North Carolina Cavalry, who had survived the dismantling of his regiment, saw them coming. His fifth squadron, which was then about two hundred yards off the pike, was the only organized body Evans could find. The Chatham County native, known as a true friend and a noble-hearted gentleman, prepared the squadron to take on the Yankees. Stuart joined Evans at about this time, took out his field glass, and watched Federal skirmishers work their way toward a stone fence about two hundred yards away. Stuart sent skirmishers forward in response, but Evans wanted to do more. He asked Stuart for permission to charge with the fifth squadron. Stuart calculated the odds and hesitated, then reluctantly approved.[35]

Evans was disgusted with the performance of Robertson's Brigade, so he was eager to make amends. He formed the fifth squadron into column of fours on a "gentle acclivity." Then he turned and pointed his sabre toward the Yankees and yelled, "Now, men, I want you to understand that I am going through!" At that, confusion set in. One veteran recalled that General Robertson heard Evans's order and countermanded it. Some obeyed Robertson, others obeyed Evans, and the charge commenced. Those that followed Evans's directions pounded across the grass toward the stone fence. Carbines cracked from behind the rock fence and sliced into the Confederate ranks. Terrible Federal artillery fire came from the regiment's left and chewed up men and horses. When the survivors reached the fence, they ran smack into a strong mounted force that absorbed the Confederate charge. This charge somehow halted the enemy advance, but the results were tragic for Evans. The Yankees captured his squadron and shot him in the back. He later died in a Union hospital from a combination of his wound and dysentery.[36]

Evans's forlorn hope marked the end of the battles of Aldie, Middleburg, and Upperville — battles Confederate veterans would never forget. On its fields the 1st North Carolina Cavalry left seven men dead, twenty-three wounded, and eight missing. Hampton's Brigade counted 102 casualties. Robertson's two regiments fared the worst of all, losing 172 casualties. Overall, the cavalry division suffered 510 casualties.[37] Thanks to these sacrifices, Lee's infantry was across the Potomac unharmed, and the enemy still did not have a real grasp of his intentions.[38]

After dark on June 21, the Confederate cavalry division gathered near Ashby's Gap. Stuart, who set up headquarters in Paris, faced several decisions there, not the least of which was the question of the 5th North Carolina Cavalry. With Colonel Evans missing, the 5th needed an experienced leader to take over the regiment. Stuart was sensitive to state pride, so he wanted the man to be a North Carolinian, yet few Tarheels in the division could handle the assignment. Colonel Baker was the ranking Tarheel cavalryman with Stuart, but he belonged with the 1st. The 2d North Carolina Cavalry had no one to offer, either. A Virginian, Lieutenant Colonel William H. F. Payne, had held temporary command of that unit since Colonel Williams's death. The story was the same in the 4th. Colonel Dennis Ferebee, already the 4th's commander, was not a logical choice. Lieutenant Colonel Edward Cantwell, second-in-command of the 4th, might have been a solid candidate, but he had been captured at Middleburg. It was unfortunate, because Cantwell's Mexican War experience and his previous service as aide to General Thomas L. Clingman might have proven beneficial. That left Gordon and Lieutenant Colonel Stephen B. Evans of the 5th. Evans was present and available, but apparently Stuart did not think he was ready.[39]

It is unfortunate that in war one's loss is another's gain, but the loss of Colonel Evans gave Gordon a new opportunity to flourish. At Ashby's Gap, on the night of June 21, Stuart told Gordon that he was assigned to temporary command of the 5th North Carolina Cavalry.[40] For Gordon, it was doubtless a surprising end to a long, exhausting day of fighting.

After taking leave of his friends in the 1st, Gordon found the 5th North Carolina Cavalry camped near Paris. What he saw was not comforting. During the past few days, he learned, the unit had had its first real taste of war. The 5th's Upperville experience had been "somewhat demoralizing." One trooper put it more bluntly: "Upperville was the worst we had faced." The regiment's Company Q — that "conglomeration of men" who were mainly the "shirkers" and "malingerers" of the regiment — was overflowing. Yet Gordon's task was clear: the Army of Northern Virginia was on the offensive, and it needed the services of the 5th North Carolina Cavalry. It was up to Gordon to return the 5th to fighting trim, and the first step in that was to establish himself as the regiment's leader. From the moment he first addressed the men, he began earning the confidence and respect of every man in the regiment.[41]

Gordon added needed experience to the ranks of his new regiment. Known in Raleigh as the 63d Regiment North Carolina State Troops, the 5th had been organized at Garysburg, North Carolina in August 1862. Some of its companies had originally enlisted under the Partisan Ranger Act. The 5th began active service in eastern North Carolina. Except for a skirmish at Plymouth in December 1862, picket duty had been the regiment's main activity before it arrived in Virginia the following May. Five hundred men and thirty-one officers had ridden under the 5th's banner then, but when Gordon took command, the regiment's numbers had been reduced.[42]

Gordon reported to Robertson, his new brigade commander. Like Lieutenant Colonel Payne of the 2d North Carolina Cavalry, Beverly Holcombe Robertson was an aberration: he was a Virginian in command of North Carolinians. He was also controversial, but not because of his background. Robertson was an 1849 West Point graduate with plenty of cavalry experience. As a horse-soldier, Robertson had served in the West and had fought against the Sioux. He had been the acting assistant adjutant general of the department of Utah when he resigned to join his native state. As a Confederate colonel, he commanded the 4th Virginia Cavalry and fought on the Peninsula. Promoted to brigadier general in June 1862, the balding Robertson fought in Virginia and in North Carolina, where he molded the 4th and 5th. Many, including Stuart, formed a low opinion of Robertson. Stuart's opinion may have been influenced by Robertson's courtship of Flora before she married Jeb, but Stuart did recognize Robertson's abilities as a disciplinarian, organizer, and cavalry instructor. After all, Robertson was strict and sometimes "irascible" when it came to military procedure. Daniel B. Coltrane of the 5th agreed after a fashion; he called Robertson "a great drillmaster." The 4th and 5th were fortunate to be brigaded under Robertson, Coltrane said, because the troops were "green country boys" who needed "strenuous drilling." But on social occasions, Robertson added to his complex character by acting as a pleasant, polished gentleman.[43]

To be successful in battle, Gordon's unit would need to cooperate with the other regiment in Robertson's Brigade, the 4th North Carolina Cavalry. The regiment's commander, Dennis D. Ferebee, was a native of Camden County. He had been promoted to colonel on August 10, 1862, so he was Gordon's senior. Ferebee was an 1839 graduate of the University of North Carolina where, it was said, he was "more regular than the college bell." Though trained as a lawyer, Ferebee preferred the life of a planter. He also dabbled in politics, as witnessed by his representation of Camden County at the 1861 state secession convention. He had much in common with Gordon. Ferebee had served in the state legislature on a number of occasions, and he had no military background.[44]

With the command situation resolved, Stuart faced another question: what next? When the mist cleared away on the morning of June 22, it was as if a curtain had been raised on a new act. Jeb Stuart was thinking offensively again. The Federals did their part by relinquishing their newly won gains. On June 21, Pleasonton had told Union headquarters, "I shall return to-morrow to Aldie. My command has been fighting almost constantly for four days, and must have a day or two to rest and shoe up and get things in order." When the Yankees fell back, Stuart reclaimed much of the territory lost in the recent fighting. For his part, Gordon moved the 5th toward Upperville, past discarded cavalry equipment, dead horses, crude graves and makeshift headstones. By the end of Monday, June 22, cavalry headquarters had relocated to Rector's Crossroads. The division's farthest outposts rested near Aldie.[45] With that, the countryside between Ashby's Gap, Snicker's Gap, and Aldie Gap was virtually secure, as was the flank of Lee's infantry. It came so easily that it almost mocked the dead of Aldie, Middleburg, and Upperville.

As for strategic offensive operations, Stuart's mind continued to churn. He reported, "The enemy retained one army corps (5th) at Aldie, and kept his cavalry near enough to make attack upon the latter productive of no solid benefits, and I began to look for some other point at which to direct an effective blow." That blow, Stuart reasoned, should fall in Hooker's rear. If he left enough men to guard the Blue Ridge gaps, the rest of the cavalry could "attain the enemy's rear, passing between his main body and Washington, and cross into Maryland, joining our army north of the Potomac."[46] There was a Yankee army out there, and Stuart wanted to ride around it. He proposed this to General Lee. Late on June 23, in a rainy darkness, a headquarters courier brought Lee's answer: if Hooker moved northward and the raiders met little resistance, Stuart had permission to follow his star. The commanding general advised prudence, stressing that Stuart was to screen Ewell's column after the cavalry crossed the Potomac. The army's right was to be in Stuart's charge during the march toward the Susquehanna River.

Immediately, Stuart made ready. On June 24, he sent instructions to the cavalry that was to guard the gaps in the Blue Ridge. As the infantry commander with the most vulnerable flank, Longstreet wanted Stuart to assign Hampton's veteran brigade to that important duty. Instead, Stuart chose Robertson's and Jones's brigades and two batteries of horse artillery. As Jones's senior, Robertson was given overall command of the force. Stuart felt comfortable assigning them this defensive role. The task was especially suited for Jones, whom Stuart considered the best outpost officer in the cavalry. Jones also had the largest brigade of cavalry in the army, and Robertson the smallest. Ostensibly, this would equalize the sizes of the divided cavalry forces.[47]

Lee had specified that the brigades left behind should "watch the flank and rear of the army, and (in event of the enemy leaving their front) retire from the mountains West of the Shenandoah, leaving sufficient pickets to guard the passes, and bringing everything clean along the valley, closing upon the rear of the army." Accordingly, Stuart told Robertson that his objective was to "cover the front of Ashby's and Snicker's Gaps." The cavalrymen were to establish a picket line stretching across the Shenandoah by Charlestown to the Potomac. This line was to serve as both an observation post and as a base from which to mask Confederate intentions. If Robertson spotted an opportunity to hurt Hooker, he was to do so. If Federals advanced on the gaps or against Warrenton, Robertson was expected to check them.[48]

Stuart rightly figured that the Yankees would follow the Army of Northern Virginia's advance. In that event, Robertson's instructions were explicit. "After the enemy has moved beyond your reach," Stuart ordered, "leave sufficient pickets in the mountains, withdraw to the west side of the Shenandoah, place a strong and reliable picket to watch the enemy at Harper's Ferry, cross the Potomac, and follow the army, keeping on its right and rear."[49] The orders gave Robertson little latitude if operations did not go as planned. If that occurred, it was up to Lee, Longstreet, or Stuart to revise them.

Stuart issued these orders on the premise that he would only briefly be out of touch with Lee's right. The cavalry general expected to regain contact with Lee beyond the Potomac. Then he would assume responsibility for the army's flank. Thus, while Stuart raided, Robertson's cavalry needed only to guard the gaps in the Blue Ridge, watch out for Hooker, and deal with any advances on Warrenton. The orders did not instruct Robertson to keep an eye on the Federals once the action moved north because Stuart expected to take care of that himself.

In any event, the assignment formed an advantage for Robertson's newest regimental commander. Gordon may have been disappointed to miss Stuart's ride, but the defensive task gave him time to get comfortable with his command. After all, for the first time since 1861, Gordon faced tomorrow with a unit other than the "Bloody First."

The horsemen rendezvoused in the early evening of June 24 at Salem Depot, about nine miles south of Upperville. They packed away three days of cooked rations in their saddlebags. They curried and brushed their horses. They readied their weapons. Three brigades of cavalry gathered: Hampton's, Fitz Lee's, and W. H. F. Lee's—perhaps the brigades in which Stuart had the greatest faith. Fitz Lee was back with his brigade after his bout with inflammatory rheumatism. Chambliss retained control of Rooney's unit while Rooney recuperated from his wound.[50]

At one hour past midnight, Stuart gave the order to move out. His mother's Bible tucked away in its usual spot, Stuart ached to pull off a spectacular feat. Except for a few ambulances, no wagons accompanied the column. Only six guns and their caissons bumped along with the cavalry. Stuart stressed silence because the brigades were bound for enemy-held territory.[51]

Historian Douglas Southall Freeman later called Stuart's decision to leave Jones and Robertson behind "a fatal choice, based, I fear, on prejudice against these men, whom he did not want with him on his grand raid." Fatal choice or not, Robertson's three thousand men meanwhile took position around the Blue Ridge gaps to watch the flank and rear of the Army of Northern Virginia.[52] They would not see Stuart again until they drew nigh a crossroads town called Gettysburg.

While Pleasonton's cavalry rested, Gordon's 5th spent a few undisturbed days in the area enjoying local hospitality. It was a time to rebuild, renew, recruit, and restore confidence. Clearly, Gordon's organization and leadership skills made perfect antidotes for the 5th's condition. One trooper wrote, "Gordon was every inch a soldier and his previous experience in Virginia campaigns enabled him to give us many points about taking care of ourselves and horses which were of great value to us."[53]

By June 26 all signs of enemy presence in the area had disappeared, allowing Robertson to withdraw his and Jones's brigades to the Blue Ridge. He posted Jones's Brigade, which consisted of the 6th, 7th, and 11th Virginia regiments, in Snicker's Gap. (The 12th Virginia had been sent to the Harper's Ferry area.) Robertson placed his 4th and 5th North Carolina Cavalry regiments at Ashby's Gap. Evidently, the ever-cautious Robertson decided to stay a few more days to be sure the Federals were gone.[54] After all, Stuart had ordered Robertson to be wary: "Be always on the alert; let nothing escape your observation...." A bolder commander might have followed the army quickly, but Robertson did not want to make a mistake. Moreover, there is no evidence that Jones, a stickler for orders and protocol, disagreed with Robertson's judgment.[55]

Federal pressure toward the Blue Ridge gaps faded not only because of Pleasonton's decision to rest his cavalry but also because the Army of the Potomac was otherwise occupied. Lincoln's army was looking internally. Early on June 28, General George G. Meade was appointed to succeed Hooker as army commander. The change did not immediately affect an oblivious Lee; the Army of Northern Virginia continued its march. Hill and Longstreet reached the Chambersburg area. Ewell, with Jenkins's cavalry, arrived at Carlisle. John D. Imboden's cavalry had also joined in. Having been previously ordered to organize a raid into northwest Virginia, Imboden now hovered in Hampshire County. From there, he watched Ewell's left and operated against the Baltimore and Ohio Railroad.[56] Marked progress it was, but on that day, Lee learned that his enemy was closer than previously thought. (To conform to the Confederate move, Hooker had marched his army to the Frederick area before giving way to Meade.) In response, Lee began issuing orders that eventually concentrated his army around Gettysburg.

Stuart was not the source of the intelligence that prompted Lee to concentrate his army. Lee had not heard from his cavalry leader since Stuart had left Salem. The raiders had silently slid through Glasscock's Gap in Bull Run Mountain with little trouble, only to meet Federal troops near Haymarket. Stuart decided to go on. After dispatching news of the Federals to Lee — the message never reached its destination — Stuart dodged the enemy and rode to the Wolf Run Shoals area. On June 27, the Confederates marched past Fairfax Court House, where Hampton's troopers fought a sharp skirmish with a Federal cavalry column. Major John Whitaker of the 1st North Carolina Cavalry, whom Stuart considered "an officer of distinction and great value to us," was killed.[57] That night Stuart's raiders crossed the Potomac.

According to his orders Stuart should then have marched on to "feel the right of Ewell's troops." Unfortunately, the Virginian could not find Ewell. The cavalry's progress had been painfully slow, and would continue to be so, since the men and horses were tired and hungry and the enemy was proving bothersome. All the column could do was try to find the army and perhaps wreak havoc in Meade's rear in the process. The raiders did the latter with some effect.[58] At Rockville on June 28, Stuart captured an enemy wagon train and a few hundred prisoners, while in Washington Union officials grew worried because of his proximity to the city. Yet try as he might, Stuart did not find Ewell (and the army) until July 2 because Meade blocked his way by moving north.

That meant Robertson was one of two senior cavalry officers who had any chance of keeping the army informed. (The other was Jenkins. Imboden's cavalry was two days' march from Lee.) It was a responsibility Stuart never intended Robertson to have. Due to his interpretation of his orders, Robertson was never in the proper position to handle the responsibility, either. Instead, he concentrated on carrying out his orders to the letter. By the afternoon of June 29, Robertson felt sure that the enemy had withdrawn from his front, and may have informed General Lee of that. (By that time, Pleasonton's cavalry division had been north of the Potomac for two days.)[59] Per Stuart's orders, Robertson moved his command west of the Shenandoah River, where they began making sure that the Valley was swept clear of the enemy. Behind them, a heavy fog hung along the Blue Ridge. The two brigades assembled and camped at Berryville, and then headed north along the Charlestown pike on the morning of June 30.[60]

Thus Gordon, his new regiment, and the rest of Robertson's command marched for the Potomac. Throughout the initial part of the ride, Robertson ensured the well-being of his men and did not press them urgently. Stuart had instructed him to maintain unit efficiency by paying attention to the shoeing of horses and marching off the turnpike. The road to Martinsburg, by way of Bunker Hill, was the only route that allowed compliance with such orders. The Rebels took the usual precautions to protect against attack. During halts, a cordon of mounted pickets kept watch. When the column advanced, a lone horseman rode about a half mile ahead. If he encountered trouble, a squadron-sized advance guard marched at the ready between him and the head of the main body. At every crossroad, lane, or patch of woods, additional pickets bolstered the watch. Once the column passed the danger point, the videttes joined the rearguard, which rode about a quarter of a mile behind the column. Despite such precautions, and sometimes because of them, the march was not without incident. Early one morning, three men trotted ahead to relieve the forward outrider while the main body stopped to eat. As the four returned to camp, talking and laughing, a volley of musketry flew at them from a nearby thicket. The attackers turned out to be nervous Confederate pickets who luckily had bad aim.[61]

Robertson concentrated on events around him. The man had no grasp of the bigger picture. He preferred to err on the side of caution; he had done so at Brandy Station, and in this campaign he did so again. He cannot be condemned for obeying orders — neither Stuart nor Lee later censured him — but Robertson apparently never patrolled Lee's right. Thus, Robertson missed the chance to influence the campaign as he kept his units in the Valley.[62]

A courier from Lee brought Robertson news of the army's concentration, but by then it was too late. The messenger found Robertson at Martinsburg, where the command had camped late on June 30. Lee had learned from a spy of the Federals' advance into Maryland, and had decided to concentrate his units.[63] It was probably the first intimation Robertson had that anything was amiss, so it impressed urgency on the command.

On the morning of July 1, they renewed the march at a quicker pace in the oppressive summer heat. Passing through Martinsburg and accessing the Williamsport pike, the troopers rode until they approached the Potomac. They paused there to listen to a message from Lee.

Gordon formed the 5th North Carolina Cavalry into line of battle. The other Virginia and North Carolina regiments followed suit. Then, with the Potomac as a backdrop, the cavalrymen listened to General Order #73. One passage from that order stuck with Private Daniel Coltrane. "... It must be remembered," the passage went, "that we make war only upon armed men, that we cannot take vengeance for the wrongs our people have suffered without lowering ourselves in the eyes of all."[64]

Once across the river, the Confederates continued their forced march toward Chambersburg. The march was unpleasant, mainly because they were hungry. There was little forage about because the infantry had picked the country clean.[65] Despite empty stomachs, Gordon and his North Carolinians marched in an orderly fashion. In accordance with the general order, they generally respected the private property of non-combatants. Upon entering Pennsylvania, the men felt as "light-hearted and as gay as children on a picnic."[66]

Late in the afternoon of July 1, the command halted near Greencastle, north of Hagerstown. After a night's rest, the Confederates entered the town itself. Greencastle, said one artilleryman,

> is a beautiful clean town of about three thousand inhabitants, situated ... in a rich and fertile country. The streets are wide and straight, the houses nearly all built of brick, and kept in good condition. I saw some beautiful, rosy-cheeked, bonny lassies on the street in Greencastle, but they looked as sour as a crab apple, frowns an inch wide and warranted pure vinegar playing over their lovely faces, like the shadow of a cloud that flits across the blushes of an opening rose.[67]

The pace of July 2 was slower, in part because some horsemen rode out on scouts.[68] Another reason for the lack of speed may have been the wearing rigors of the march. There also may have been sounds of distant battle coming from the direction of Gettysburg. Whatever the reason, the command did not reach Chambersburg until about 6:00 P.M. on July 2.[69]

Gordon's ride had been uneventful until that point, but one of his men found Chambersburg worth remembering. "Here we found the citizens quietly sitting about the public grounds or moving about their homes with anxious looks and wondering expectancy as to what might next occur," the cavalryman wrote. Gordon knew the town from his visit the previous October, and he also knew the Pennsylvanians need not have worried. The Confederates had no time to stay. Urgency took hold of Robertson again. At about 1:00 A.M., "To horse—lead out" sounded, and they were off. The column feinted toward Carlisle, turned right, and began a forced march in the direction of Gettysburg. Having lost time during the day, the column strove to make it up that night.[70]

Gordon's tired and hungry regiment, and the rest of Robertson's column, arrived in Cashtown at 10:00 A.M. on July 3. The Rebels dismounted and rested. The sky was clear and the day hot, driving many to seek shade.[71] After midday, Gordon's men heard a "furious" but brief cannonade from the direction of Gettysburg. The distant artillery, wrote George Neese, "howled and thundered." Curiosity grew. What was happening? Clearly a great battle was being fought nearby. Why had they not been called to the front? Not long after, Gordon ordered his regiment to mount, fall in, and move out. At last! Scuttlebutt said that the distant battle had been a Confederate victory! Surely, the column was on its way to pursue the retreating foe.[72]

The scuttlebutt was wrong. What had prompted the move was an order from General Lee, borne by a courier from Gettysburg. Robertson was to take position near Fairfield, to the right and rear of the Confederate line at Gettysburg. Robertson saw the wisdom behind the orders when outriders reported a Federal cavalry advance from the Emmitsburg area. Their objective was suspected to be the baggage and ammunition trains of the Army of Northern Virginia, parts of which were parked near Fairfield.[73]

The 7th Virginia led the way along a lane that coursed toward Fairfield. Ferebee's 4th and Gordon's 5th brought up the rear. The troopers continued to hear sounds of battle, and at one point, where the road ascended a hill, could actually see Gettysburg. George Neese saw "nothing but a vast bank of thick battle smoke, with thousands of shell exploding above the surface of the white, smoking sea.... The artillery fire at one time was so heavy that the hills shook and the air trembled, and the deep thunder rolled through the sky in one incessant roar like as if the giants of war were hurling thunderbolts at each other in the clouds."[74]

Strong post and rail fences lined either side of the road on which they traveled. Small fields lay beyond the fences. Barriers, similar to the ones along the road, marked off most of them. There were few trees about, so Gordon's men marched in the sun without relieving shade. An old planter like Gordon may have seen the value of such well-kept countryside, but from a military point of view the fences and small fields presented problems.[75]

Two miles outside Fairfield, Jones's advance encountered Confederate wagons out foraging. Unharvested wheat fields sat nearby, ready for gleaning. At this critical moment, Robertson's advance was challenged by the 6th United States Cavalry. The Federals, a regular U.S. Army unit, hovered only a few hundred yards from the foraging wagons.[76]

Robertson's column was strung out; the rear regiments had been marching less than an hour. Jones, who looked more like a tramp on horseback than a general, felt short-handed but figured that "a vigorous assault must put even a small force on a perfect equality with a large one." Accordingly, he ordered the 7th Virginia, his oldest, favorite unit, to charge. The Federal commander, Major Samuel H. Starr, was ready. He placed his "carbineers" to pour flanking fire on the charging Southerners. Many took cover behind post and rail fences. Others sought fighting positions in a nearby apple orchard.[77] The charging Virginians saw this happen, hesitated, and then retreated. Federal fire exacted a stiff price. The regiment lost thirty men, including two brothers: Lieutenant Jacob G. Shoup was killed instantly, while Captain John C. Shoup was desperately wounded.[78]

"Shall one damn regiment of Yankees whip my whole brigade?" Jones roared. The 6th Virginia responded, charging with a "wild yell" in the wake of the 7th's retreat. The Virginians rode past Federal skirmishers, pitched into their foe, and, slashing left and right, knocked them back. Among the Federal wounded was Major Starr, who lost his arm.[79] Gordon's 5th and Ferebee's 4th played a small part in supporting Jones's attacks, but it was not significant enough for Jones to mention it in his report.[80] Most importantly, the Confederate trains were safe—for now.

"The skirmish was a success," recalled one of Gordon's men, "but the question of supper was not so easily solved." Unable to issue rations since Ashby's Gap, Gordon was unable to do so now. The horses would be fine since wheat in nearby fields was ripening, but the troopers had to make do with cherries and raspberries.[81]

A few miles away, the Battle of Gettysburg also came to a conclusion. There, Federal defenses crushed the final Confederate assault. (When they were resting in Cashtown, Gordon's men had probably heard the 1:00 P.M. artillery preparation for the assault on Cemetery Ridge.) Stuart's jaded raiders had also fought a bloody battle at Gettysburg on the Confederate left. Gordon's old unit had been in the midst of the hand-to-hand fighting there. The vicious struggle left Hampton with two sabre cuts in his head and a piece of shrapnel in his body. Brigade command devolved on Baker.[82]

The fireworks of war were mostly silent on Independence Day, 1863, in Pennsylvania. Rain fell on the soldiers and tamed the July heat, but the wet weather and lowering clouds made the day gloomy. In his headquarters tent, Robert E. Lee had already considered his next move and had made his plans; it remained only to execute them. The battle had not ended with a rout, but the Confederates had been repulsed. It was time for the Army of Northern Virginia to go home. Rain in the Keystone State would not stop them.

First, Lee ordered the army's wagon trains and ambulances into motion. The wagons, divided into multiple columns to prevent bunching up, began rolling at about 4:00 P.M. Imboden's cavalry escorted them. One column marched for Williamsport by way of the Cashtown Gap. Another marched down the muddy Fairfield Road, past where Jones had fought his battle, while a third section headed for the Monterey Pass. The length of each column was measurable in miles and drenched in rain. Cavalrymen watching the scene used slang to describe the retreat: "That looks like mice."[83]

The infantry's retreat began at nightfall. A. P. Hill's Corps was the first to pull out of line, fall into column, about face, and march for Fairfield. Longstreet's corps marched next. Ewell's infantrymen came last, guarding the rear. With most of the trains underway, only the remaining baggage wagons and the four thousand unwounded prisoners of war became impediments to their march.[84]

An army was most vulnerable while retreating, so the disposition of the cavalry rearguard was of prime importance. At Lee's bidding, Stuart fixed the details of the cavalry's mission. He set out toward Emmitsburg to guard personally the retreat's southern flank with Chambliss and Jenkins. Fitz Lee, commanding his and Hampton's brigades, brought up the rear on the Cashtown Road. Lastly, Robertson's and Jones's commands received a tough assignment. Stuart directed those North Carolinians and Virginians to hold the two passes on either side of Jack's Mountain: the Fairfield pass and the Monterey Pass. The army needed these passes for its retreat, so Stuart thought it "essentially necessary" to hold the Jack's Mountain line.[85]

Late on July 4, Robertson's brigades left Fairfield for Jack's Mountain. Gordon found the way already crowded with the stragglers and wagon trains that had left Gettysburg at 4:00 P.M. The road was not a good one, being a rough, mountainous route that accessed a narrow

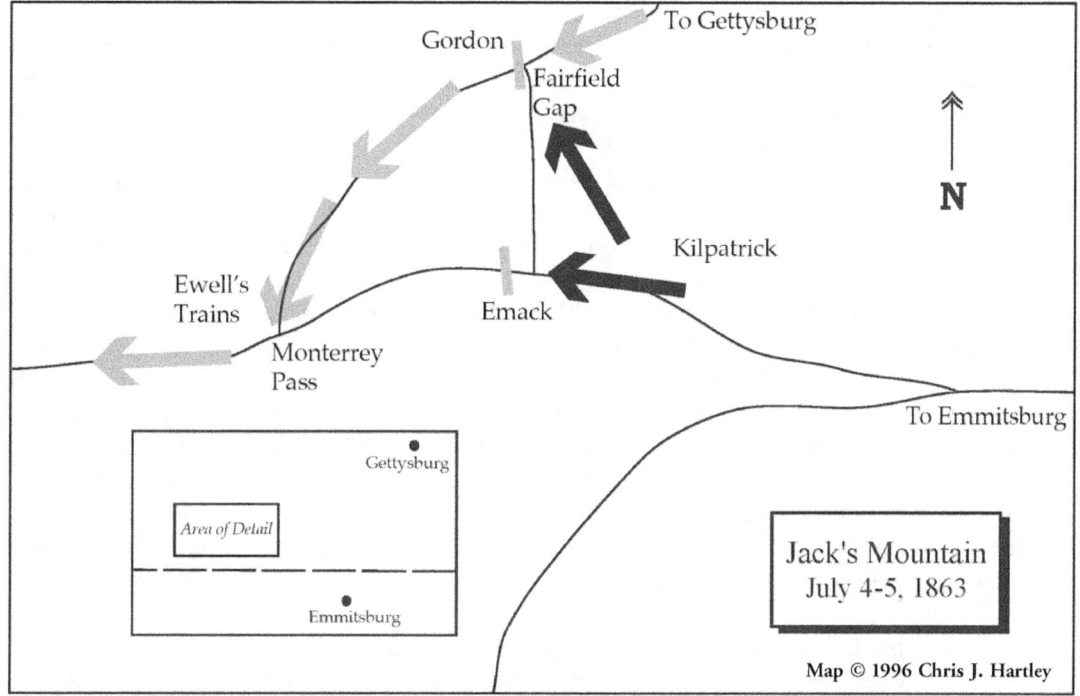

pass. Wagons, ambulances, and dozens of wounded and disabled soldiers were everywhere in the muddy, overused road. The column moved slowly.[86]

Given the noisy retreat, heavy rain, and confusion, the situation was foreboding. To Gordon's men, the withdrawal was already harder than the advance had been. Rumors enlarged the tension. At Emmitsburg, citizens said that Federal cavalry — overestimated at fifteen thousand strong — had passed there en route for Jack's Mountain. A courier delivered a similar report to Robertson. When Jones heard it, he worried about Ewell's trains, which were headed for the Jack's Mountain passes. Jones asked, and received, permission to ride ahead to the Fairfield-Emmitsburg road junction to confirm the report. He took the 6th Virginia Cavalry, the 4th North Carolina Cavalry, and Capt. Roger Preston Chew's battery of artillery.[87]

Jones made his way through the jammed road. It was slow going; the narrow lane could not handle the traffic. Only one horseman at a time could pass. Wagon ruts cut deeply into the mud.[88] Before long, Jones had to leave Chew's battery behind. Worse, the 6th Virginia and the 4th North Carolina Cavalry became strung out. In disgust, Jones abandoned the bulk of his detachment. He figured these to be critical moments, so his staff, and any stragglers they could collect, would have to suffice.[89]

Night had fallen; thunder crashed, and rain pelted the combatants. Federal cavalry even then bore down on the Jack's Mountain passes. For a time, a handful of Maryland cavalrymen and one artillery piece stood at Monterey Pass, keeping General Judson Kilpatrick's cavalry division, plus a reinforcing brigade under Col. Pennock Huey, away from Ewell's trains. Gallant stand though it was, Capt. George M. Emack's brave little force was still driven back several hundred yards. None too soon, Grumble Jones found Emack and saw the long odds. He grabbed every courier and staff officer he could find. He also promised Emack he would get the 6th Virginia Cavalry into position.[90]

Including Jones's reinforcements, Emack matched no more than fifty men against Kilpatrick's onslaught. Do not yield an inch! Emack urged his men. Do not waste ammunition! Briefly the Southerners held, and their shots were well placed. About sixty of Ferebee's men found the battle — with some reluctance, apparently — but the situation remained grim. Emack's lone artillery piece fired its last charge and withdrew. In great number, musket balls whistled past the cavalrymen and toward the Confederate wagons. Since no one could see their foe, Rebels and Yankees aimed at muzzle flashes. When their ammunition ran out, some graybacks resorted to throwing rocks.[91]

No more help came. Back up the Fairfield Road, the bulk of the 4th North Carolina Cavalry and the 6th Virginia remained mired. Farther back, Robertson and the rest of his command advanced; clearly, they could be of no help to the southern Jack's Mountain pass. At about 3:00 A.M., Emack's situation grew worse when Kilpatrick decided to change his tactics. Even in the darkness, Emack saw his enemy advance to a point no more than twenty yards away from his position. "Charge!" was the next order, and the Federals responded in style. Kilpatrick's men galloped through Emack's thin defense and pounded toward the intersection of the Fairfield and Emmitsburg roads. Moments later, the Yankees were running wild among the Confederate wagons. Jones reported, "The led horses, wagons, straggling infantry, and camp followers were hurled down the mountain in one confused mass." One ambulance, its driver shot, careened down the muddied mountain, out of control. The Federals captured dozens of wagons, animals, and more than 1,300 Southerners; what remained of Jones's force scattered. The Confederate cavalry had failed to hold the southern Jack's Mountain pass.[92]

Gordon saw to it personally that the northern pass received ample protection. After Jones had ridden ahead, Robertson's remaining regiments continued marching to the pass, probably with the 5th in the lead. They met the same obstacle course of wagons, stragglers, and back-ups, but somehow Gordon kept his regiment relatively intact. It may have helped that Gordon knew the area from Stuart's October 1862 ride around McClellan. As for the present march, the fact that Gordon's regiment made progress without becoming strung out was a measure of his developing management ability.

To expedite matters, Gordon ordered Company F to ride ahead to the northern Jack's Mountain pass and establish a picket. Company F picked its way past the wagons and ascended toward the pass. They arrived just in time. A second road—not the one on which Emack fought—intersected the Fairfield Road near the northern pass. That road contained what looked like an entire Federal cavalry regiment. In actuality, it was Kilpatrick's right flank, possibly the "strong force of dismounted men and two guns" Kilpatrick had sent toward Gettysburg "to barricade the Road and hold the enemy in check until the [Federal cavalry] column had passed." Company F wheeled to meet the threat, facing a daunting task. While the outnumbered Confederates steeled themselves and opened fire, Company F's commander, Lieutenant William J. Wiley, collared Baxter Caldwell. Wiley, who knew Caldwell was a daring and dependable trooper, looked the youngster straight in the face. Get help from Colonel Gordon, Wiley told Caldwell; get it quick.[93]

Caldwell rushed down the mountain. His was not an easy task because he had to navigate the crowded road in reverse. At last, the cavalryman found his commander. Gordon must have been wide-eyed at hearing that the enemy was one step ahead of him. Realizing the exposed condition of the trains, Gordon reacted with dispatch. He ordered the 5th to the pass, touched the flanks of his own horse, and got things moving.[94]

With Caldwell as a guide, Gordon knew where to go. Getting there was the problem. For seemingly the hundredth time that night, Confederate horsemen struggled through the backed-up road. Frustrated teamsters reluctantly pulled out of the slow, retreating column to make way for the cavalrymen. By the time they reached the pass, the 5th North Carolina Cavalry had gained momentum. Gordon saw the Federals bearing down on Company F and the trains in the pass and ordered a charge. As their horses broke into gallops, the North Carolinians let out whoops and yells that cut through the night air and stunned the Yankees. This was not the same battle-shocked unit Gordon had taken over at Ashby's Gap. Thanks to Gordon's leadership, these troopers were confident, ready, and eager to fight. According to Private Coltrane, Gordon had "put new life in us." Horsemen like John Cahill, a "plain, big, fat country boy," demonstrated this. Atop Jack's Mountain, Cahill saw a "large, grand looking, gallant Federal officer" charging at him with sabre in hand. Cahill, unimpressed, shot him. The men fought like Cahill. All told, these once-cowed troopers forced the Yankees back and held the Fairfield pass.[95]

Night outlasted the fighting. At the battle's conclusion, Gordon directed his men to camp on Jack's Mountain. Some hungry troopers scrounged for food in the rainy darkness. One squad, which bivouacked near a mountain spring and spring house, had more luck than others. In the spring house they discovered a sublime treasure, namely several jars of buttermilk, honey, and apple marmalade. The men quickly devoured these delicacies.[96]

On the morning of July 5, Gordon's staff and field officers roused the 5th. The regiment resumed its march, moving toward Leitersburg. Though Ewell's infantry had left Gettysburg at 2:00 A.M. and, because of the slow march, would not reach Fairfield until 4:00 P.M., the trains had finished passing during the night. Robertson considered his Jack's Mountain mission at an end. He directed his column to fall in with the army's line of march.[97] The Potomac River lay ahead.

The next day, Robertson rejoined Stuart, who had also been battling Federal cavalry thrusts since leaving Gettysburg. The situation facing Stuart was this: the Army of Northern Virginia was concentrating around Williamsport. From there it would recross the Potomac. Many of the army's wagons were then gathering near the river but were unable to cross because the Potomac was swollen. To screen the army against harassing enemy cavalry, Stuart ordered Robertson's North Carolina Brigade to Hagerstown. But even with Chambliss's Brigade, which was also directed to Hagerstown, the two commands boasted few men. In the meantime, Stuart angled toward Boonsboro with Jones's reassembled brigade, and then sent Jones on to Funkstown. While Jones protected Hagerstown's eastern front from that point, Stuart took Jenkins to Hagerstown.[98]

As clock hands turned toward 6:00 P.M., Hagerstown became the focal point of rearguard conflict. General Lee's engineers had previously selected a line behind the town from which to defend their retreat, but in this case it was useless. Chambliss and Robertson ran into Federal fire in Hagerstown. The air filled thickly with projectiles. In the 5th, one man threw up his hand and fell off his horse. His comrades thought him killed, but it turned out later that he had taken "the blind staggers."[99] The uncowed faced Kilpatrick's superior force, which pushed the Confederates back toward the northern end of the town. Brigadier General Alfred Iverson's Confederate infantry brigade, escorting a portion of the trains to the Potomac, pitched into the struggle at an opportune time. Together with Jenkins's and Jones's units, which came up during the fight, Rebel cavalry, infantry, and artillery forces fought to retake Hagerstown. One of Jenkins's men had to forgo "a delicious dinner at the Washington Hotel" to join the battle.[100]

As the enemy's designs became more clear, Stuart resolved to press the attack. It was the only way he could ensure the safety of the trains. Williamsport was an easy trip from Hagerstown; the straight macadamized road that connected the two towns ran through open countryside except for an occasional fence or ditch. Rather than fight the enemy on such indefensible terrain, Stuart's horsemen tried to force the issue at Hagerstown. The cavalry fought coolly, but the foot-soldiers acted differently. One of Gordon's men remembered that in their "sullen, angry mood," the infantry was "ready to take their vengeance." After some time, the Confederates ejected the Federals. Already a veteran of night fighting, Gordon thus became a successful leader in another type of warfare: street fighting.[101]

The problem with the Hagerstown battle was that Lincoln's horsemen escaped toward Williamsport. The fighting had involved only one Federal cavalry brigade. Kilpatrick had left that unit in Hagerstown while he continued pursuing the Confederate trains with his other two brigades. Buford's division doubled the threat by marching on Williamsport from Boonsboro. As if to underscore the danger, Stuart had no sooner secured Hagerstown than he heard artillery from the direction of the Potomac. He pushed Chambliss after Kilpatrick. Robertson and Jenkins's Brigade were also sent on the chase. Supported by the horse artillery, Gordon's horsemen marched to the left of the road, parallel to Chambliss.[102]

The roles were reversed from Upperville. This time, the Confederates gave chase to, and caught, their prey. "We've got them now, boys," Stuart said. Chambliss, with only a few hundred men left in his brigade, "gallantly executed" the initial charge. Stuart hurried the flanking regiments, including Gordon's, to exploit that success with an attack, but post and rail fences hindered the movement. Kilpatrick's Federals used the delay to set up a defensive position along "a crest of rocks and fences." From there, the Yankees raked the Williamsport Road with artillery fire.[103]

At Stuart's bidding, Jenkins's Brigade dismounted and deployed. Those men ignored the artillery fire and set up in a way that rendered the Federal position untenable. Again, commands were shouted, bugles blared, and the Federal forces retreated. Again the Southerners followed. Suddenly, blue-clad cavalrymen turned on their attackers. Gordon saw it coming. With only a fragment of the 5th North Carolina Cavalry, he stood against the tide. It was man against man, firearm against firearm, sabre against sabre. With the confidence of Jack's Mountain, Gordon's 5th beat back this counterattack. Stuart later reported that Gordon exhibited "under my eye individual prowess deserving special commendation." Once Gordon had done his job, the repulse became a rout courtesy of one of Jones's regiments. The men of Lomax's 11th Virginia drew their sabers, charged down the turnpike, and slammed into the enemy.[104]

Despite Confederate intentions, this Hagerstown battle spread perilously close to Williamsport. Harassed by blue cavalry, the army's wagons — still escorted by Imboden and followed by Baker's (Hampton's) Brigade — had reached the town earlier that day. Protection in the form of Confederate infantry and artillery had arrived during the afternoon, and the teamsters had done their part in the defense. It was a good thing; by Buford's account, his division came within one-half mile of the trains before being driven back. Buford did manage to connect his right with Kilpatrick, but to no avail. By the time Confederate cavalry coming up from Hagerstown reached the ridge overlooking Williamsport, the Federal foe had already begun to retire "in hasty discomfiture." The night of July 6 was a safe one for the trains of the Army of Northern Virginia.[105]

The effort around Hagerstown and Williamsport was not without cost. Gordon reported three killed and five wounded in the 5th North Carolina Cavalry, one of the wounded being an officer. They were the first men he had lost as an official regiment commander, and he hated any loss, but eight casualties were acceptable. The 4th North Carolina Cavalry had fared worse: Ferebee reported eighty-four casualties, including seventy-one missing. That was the most of any regiment in the cavalry division.[106]

Nature proved itself a foe when the Army of Northern Virginia found the Potomac River unfordable. A Federal raid had also broken up a bridge below Williamsport, so Lee's army was cut off from Virginia. Soldiers began preparing pontoons with which to vault the rushing river, but until those were ready the army dug in between Williamsport and Falling Waters. And defend they must, for there was little doubt that the bulk of the Army of the Potomac had left Gettysburg and was closing in.[107]

While the army perfected its lines, the cavalry shielded the army from attack. On July 7, Stuart assigned Robertson's small brigade to a quiet area north of Hagerstown. Gordon's 5th took position along the Cavetown Road and began picketing. Roberston's right flank connected with Jones's Brigade, which was also picketing. Jones's men saw as little action as Robertson's that day. The only excitement occurred when a mounted man dressed in Confederate gray created suspicion. He could not name the colonel or captain of his regiment, so Jones's Rebels identified the man as a Jessie Scout — a Federal scout dressed in Confederate garb — and shot him. Elsewhere, Stuart again personally posted Jenkins's Brigade. Commanded by Colonel M. J. Ferguson since Jenkins had been wounded on July 2, the brigade had not performed well recently. Stuart positioned them in Downsville with part of William T. Wofford's infantry brigade. To round out the cavalry's assignments, Stuart dispatched a detachment of Maryland cavalry on a scout toward Greencastle.[108]

On July 8, the Confederate cavalry demonstrated toward Boonsboro to "cover the retrograde of the main body." Although this resulted in "an animated fight" with Federal cavalry, the official report of the action suggests that Ferebee's 4th and Gordon's 5th North Carolina Cavalry, in their weakened conditions, remained on quiet duty along the Cavetown Road.

The next day was strangely quiet, interrupted only by news that the Federal army was certainly marching on Hagerstown. Still, the 1st was at one point drawn up in line of battle and awaiting an attack that never came.[109] Friday the tenth of July was not quiet. The Army of Northern Virginia continued to move, shape, and prepare its lines for the expected attack. General Lee, who was especially anxious, wrote a dispatch urging the army to resist the enemy.[110] The cavalry, supported by infantry and artillery, remained near Funkstown and prepared to renew its efforts. When an enemy advance sparked skirmishing along the Boonsboro Road, Southern infantry forces were placed to cover Funkstown. Cavalry units dismounted and took position covering either flank. Various regiments from the brigades of Jones, Fitz Lee, and Robertson covered the Confederate left. They successfully weathered both infantry and cavalry advances, but Gordon's regiment gave up fifty casualties, including eight dead, during the fighting. That night, to prevent flank maneuvers, Stuart withdrew to the west side of the Antietam.[111]

Though Saturday was as quiet as Thursday had been, it proved just as worrisome. Witness the published circular from Stuart that was read to the men. The cavalry, the circular said, would be posted on the army's flanks and would there take part in the coming battle. Officers and men were to remember that no wavering or giving way would be allowed. With that, Stuart's cavalry resumed its looking, listening, and waiting. Chambliss and Fitz Lee screened part of the army's left near Downsville from the National Road, just west of Hagerstown. Both Jones and Robertson remained toward the right, Jones covering the Funkstown and Cavetown roads while Robertson watched an area about two and a half miles in front of Ewell's lines. The Federals were approaching, but only cautiously.[112]

Gordon might have requested rations for his hungry men that day, but if he did he learned there were little. The army was living day-to-day, hand-to-mouth. Forage was not to be found. The flooded Potomac made it impossible to operate flour mills. Horses had only grass and standing grain to eat. The lack of food took its toll on Gordon's men. The officers suffered more because rations, scanty as they were, were provided only for the men. As a result, the lieutenant colonel himself showed declining health, and cut quite a different figure than he had just a few months before. "My clothes will hardly hang on me I am so thin," Gordon wrote.[113]

On Sunday the army's leaders declared their lines ready to receive attack. Stuart accordingly withdrew the bulk of his division to the left.[114] He initiated reconnaissance from his new position by extending cavalry pickets toward Chambersburg. If they truly wanted the Federals to attack, however, the Army of Northern Virginia faced disappointment. By July 13 all available information suggested that the Northern army was entrenching. In turn, General Lee faced dwindling supplies and worried about reinforcements Meade surely had coming. To the Southern army's rear, the Potomac River continued to flow roughly, but it finally appeared fordable. Further, a satisfactory pontoon bridge was deemed ready for traffic. Lee decided that the time had come to recross the Potomac and close the Gettysburg campaign.

With the cavalry as rear guard, the withdrawal began that night. Stuart's troopers dismounted and occupied the trenches when the foot soldiers pulled back. Fitz Lee's Brigade filed into Longstreet's old position; Baker's (Hampton's) Brigade took Hill's place; and the rest of the cavalry, including Robertson's handful of troopers, assumed Ewell's position. The Potomac was still wide and almost past fording, rain fell heavily, and the mud deepened, making the crossing slow. Wagons often became mired. Torches refused to remain lit. Tempers rose and confusion reigned, and weary soldiers slept at every opportunity. The threat of attack hovered over all, but in the trenches the cavalry saw nothing.[115]

Retreat or not, Gordon had a lot on his mind. Earlier in the day, a courier bearing a dispatch from headquarters found him in line of battle. Reading it, Gordon learned he had been promoted to colonel, to rank from June 18. Along with the commission came an offer to command the 2d North Carolina Cavalry. On June 30 the 2d's commander, Colonel Payne, had been captured at Hanover. The regiment had not made out much better than their commander; one trooper said that the 2d Horse became a "mere shadow of its former self" at Hanover.[116] Captain W. A. Graham was commanding the 2d. Graham was a good soldier, but the regiment needed reorganization and rebuilding — a job for an experienced colonel, not a captain. Gordon was pleased to have been appointed a full colonel, but he was reluctant to take over the 2d. Ordinarily Gordon would have welcomed the challenge, but he was a loyal man who considered himself a member of the 1st and no other regiment. Moreover, with Baker commanding the brigade, the command situation with the 1st was unclear. Perhaps there would be a later opportunity to command the 1st instead. In the muddy positions outside Williamsport, Gordon considered the situation.[117]

His decision had to be postponed, because when the infantry finished crossing it was the cavalry's turn. Except for a portion of Fitz Lee's Brigade, the horsemen marched for the ford at Williamsport. The 5th North Carolina Cavalry was one of the last cavalry units to pull back from the trenches, and perhaps the last to approach the river. Trooper Daniel B. Coltrane knew the withdrawal required wariness and caution, especially since some of Hill's men had already skirmished with the prying enemy. At the same time, Coltrane learned that this dangerous duty could provide nervous levity. Traveling toward the Potomac, Coltrane dodged and ducked as he heard an occasional minie ball whistle past him. Had the Yankees discovered the retreat? Were they already in pursuit? No. After further reflection, he decided there was something strange about the "whistle" of the minie balls. At last Coltrane realized the sound was not coming from whistling minie balls but from a man with a very bad cold. In the nighttime tension, a comrade's "snuffling" had sounded very much like a Yankee ball hurtling past.[118]

Other matters occupied Gordon's attention. At the river, he found cause for concern. The ford he had been assigned to was no more than a narrow, winding ledge of rock just beneath the water's surface. The night's rain ensured that the Potomac was still quite high, and the infantry had left behind a muddy mess. Given the rough river and the tricky ford, and the ford's much-used condition, the crossing proved difficult. Several horsemen drifted off the ledge and were forced to swim for it, but luckily no one was lost in the crossing. Gordon's management of the situation proved effective. The cavalry division, wet saddles and all, was back in Virginia by 8:00 A.M. on the 14th. Unfortunately, it had been an imperfect withdrawal all around. North Carolina's General James J. Pettigrew died in a rear guard action at Falling Waters.[119]

Once across, Stuart reestablished his omnipresent picket line. He ordered Baker to picket the Potomac from Falling Waters to Hedgesville. Except for Robertson's Brigade, the remainder of the cavalry withdrew toward Leetown — near Stuart's favorite headquarters, The Bower — and began picketing. Robertson's 4th and 5th North Carolina Cavalry regiments rode to the fords of the Shenandoah to rejoin Captain L. A. Johnson's picket, the unit Robertson had left in the Valley. (While on detached service, Johnson's troopers — members of the 4th North Carolina Cavalry — had managed to "handsomely repulse" at least one enemy advance on Ashby's Gap.) Gordon, who was becoming "quite sick" from exposure, endured a miserable southward trip.[120]

Following a brief repose near Bunker Hill and Darkesville, General Lee hoped to move the bulk of the army into Loudoun County for more rest. However, the Shenandoah River was unfordable and in worse shape than the Potomac. Lee's plans had to be put on hold. As for Meade, he appeared unsatisfied with the status quo; or at least prodding from the Lincoln administration made it so. As a result, Fitz Lee, Chambliss, and Jones were soon skirmishing with pursuing cavalry units near Shepherdstown. Federal forces crossed the Potomac east of the Blue Ridge, while cavalry rushed for the passes into Loudoun County. Between July 16 and 22, cavalry skirmishes criss-crossed the country between Shepherdstown and Hedgesville. Baker's Brigade figured prominently, and effectively shielded the infantry as it tore up parts of the Baltimore and Ohio Railroad near Martinsburg. Lee's infantry also prepared to retreat.[121]

Meade was not unpopular with Southern soldiers. They considered him a fair and honorable opponent who was not without military ability. It was a good estimate, for Meade often discerned new ways to get at his enemy. During that hot and rainy July, the Pennsylvanian saw opportunity in the swollen Shenandoah River. With Lee boxed in by the rushing waters, Meade thought he could slide his troops between the Army of Northern Virginia and Richmond. On July 19, Lee set Longstreet in motion to prevent that move. The general, with Robertson's cavalry as the advance and A. P. Hill's corps in tow, bridged the Shenandoah with pontoons, marched through Chester Gap, and reached Culpeper Court House on July 24. It must have been a difficult march for Gordon because of his illness, but the move proved successful. By preventing Meade from occupying the Manassas and Chester Gaps, and by establishing a blocking position at Culpeper, Longstreet foiled Meade's designs. The next day, the Confederate army (minus Ewell, who was still in the Valley) took up a new line along the Rappahannock River.[122]

Baker's Brigade went on picket duty along the Beverly's Ford-Kelly's Ford line. Extant records are somewhat contradictory about Gordon's movements, but he probably rejoined the 1st North Carolina Cavalry there if not earlier. He had yet to decide about the 2d, but his job with the 5th was finished. Gordon had done his work well. He had restored the 5th to a confident, quality unit. Officials thought that Lieutenant Colonel Stephen Evans, after "studying" under Gordon, was ready to take over the 5th. Colonel Gordon had set a soldierly example for Evans and the 5th much as Peter Ney had done for Gordon. But for Gordon, the question of the Second remained unanswered. At any rate, while Baker commanded the brigade in Hampton's absence, Gordon assumed temporary command of the 1st.[123]

Gordon continued to ponder his situation. Business affairs diverted his thoughts occasionally, but indecision ruled. While in Martinsburg on July 18, he wrote Augustus Finley of business and of his struggle over the offer of command:

> I received your letter yesterday and was much pleased to hear from home. I also received the one written previously. I would prefer investing the money I have in land or negroes. Negroes are high but not in proposition to bacon and corn. The money in back [the bank?] I wish to remain. The 100 bills drawing 2 cts. per day retain.
>
> We have re-crossed the Potomac — had a terrible battle near Gettysburg — the bloodiest of the war. I saw Allen two days ago. He is quite well and escaped unhurt. I have received the appointment of Col of the 2nd N.C. Cavalry. I don't know yet whether I will accept or not. The officers and men of the 1st N.C. Cavalry are so averse to my leaving I hardly know what to do. My love to all at home.
>
> P.S. If you can buy any negroes anywhere, do so. I wrote to John to buy some for me but haven't heard from him in a long time.[124]

If the content of his letters can be taken as proof, Gordon considered the matter of the 2d often. Everyone offered Gordon their opinion. Stuart urged one course. The troopers in the ranks called for another. In a Culpeper County bivouac, Gordon picked up his pen and wrote his mother about Gettysburg and about his problem:

> I as well as most of the men seem glad to get back after the hard service and campaign in Pennsylvania. I saw Allen since we camped at the Potomac. He is quite well and seems well satisfied. We have both escaped so far through the mercies of a kind providence, endorsed to a great extent by the prayers of a Christian mother. Every thing is quiet here now and I think there will be no battle for a month. I have been appointed Col of the 2 No C. Cavalry. I have been undecided about accepting the appointment. The regt. is in a very bad condition and will require hard work to fix it up and then I am so much attached to the 1st that I dislike so much to go. The officers and men are very anxious for me to remain with them.... But Gen Stuart and others insist I shall take command of [the Second]. I would like so much to go home and rest for a month, to once again recline under the broad and shady Oaks at home to bathe and enjoy the sparkling waters of the Reddies and a good dinner cooked by Aunt Sally would be so acceptable.[125]

Perhaps the answer could be found elsewhere. Until then, other matters required attention. In this, an end of sorts was in the offing. For Gordon and his 1st North Carolina Cavalry, the Gettysburg campaign had begun in the fields around Brandy Station. Now, fittingly, it ended there. Fighting had no appeal to those tired souls, but there was nothing to do about it. As that bloody July ended, Baker received some intimation that the Federals were planning to reconnoiter across the Rappahannock. Indeed they were; Meade, who was then gathering his army around Warrenton, had decided to launch a sizable scout across the Rappahannock. To meet it, Baker marched his dirty, ragged brigade to Brandy Station at 10:00 P.M. on July 31. There they "lay listlessly." Just five hours later, Buford had massed his cavalry division at Rappahannock Station. Because of "mismanagement of some kind," the blue cavalrymen did not cross the river for another eight hours. Yet even without hoped-for surprise, the Federal marched with enough force to gain an advantage. Colonel Baker's pickets met the Federals as they splashed across the river at Beverly's Ford.[126]

Since assuming command of Hampton's Brigade at Gettysburg, Baker had not disappointed. Now, the job before him was ominous. Could Baker's weary brigade of less than one thousand men hold off a well-equipped, well-led division? Could the outnumbered Confederates shield Lee's intentions from prying eyes? These questions were not easily answered. The Federal advance was cautious, but strong and determined. From the initial contact, the Federal horsemen pushed Baker back a mile and more from the Rappahannock Bridge area. Then, near the house of a Mrs. Wise, gray stemmed the Blue tide. For several hours, Baker's men bore repeated enemy charges, and answered in kind. The 1st South Carolina Cavalry, the Jeff Davis Legion, and the Phillips Legion stood right of the Orange & Alexandria Railroad, while the 1st North Carolina Cavalry, 2d South Carolina Cavalry, and the Cobb Legion were to the left. Each regiment, including Gordon's 1st, tested its steel against the foe. Baker was everywhere, directing and exhorting. He fought so hard, and led so admirably, that his men "cheered [him] most lustily." General Lee, who was equally impressed, reported that Baker's men "gallantly resisted" the enemy advance. Even Buford admitted that the foe "made a most obstinate resistance." One correspondent was quite taken with Baker's bravery; he reported that Baker was promoted to brigadier general on the spot. Though the report was incorrect, the day constituted Laurence Baker's brightest moment.[127]

Even so, the Federals had the advantage of numbers. Despite Baker's efforts, the Yankees outflanked the Rebels. The fighting drew nearer Culpeper, perhaps as close as one and one-half miles. However, the Confederates had an advantage of their own. They fell back toward the strength of Lee's main lines, while Buford marched away from his base. Couriers summoned reinforcements. As the hot day wore on, advancing no longer meant winning as far as Buford was concerned. Grumble Jones's cavalry brigade came up in support, as did the infantry brigades of William Mahone and Edward Perry. Easily they drove Buford back, ending the fight. The Federals retired having learned something of value about Lee's whereabouts.[128]

The ranks of Hampton's Brigade suffered a moderate amount of casualties, including the loss of thirty-seven men and fifty horses in the 2d South Carolina Cavalry alone. The brigade's leadership fared worse. Colonel P. M. B. Young, commander of the Cobb Legion, and Colonel John L. Black, commander of the 1st South Carolina Cavalry, had both taken hits. Worse, Baker himself received a particularly nasty wound. The bones of his right arm were completely shattered, rendering the arm useless. Surgeons on the battlefield and in Richmond examined him and operated, but it looked as if Baker was lost to the cavalry for a while. Only praise could truly succor this wound that threatened to separate Baker from his newfound success. In a dispatch to the War Department, Lee said that Hampton's Brigade had performed well and that Baker had "skillfully handled" the unit.[129] Stuart considered Baker's stand worth a congratulatory order. "The gallant and spirited resistance offered by Hampton's brigade," Stuart wrote, "... deserves the highest commendation at the hands of the division commander.... Let the sons of the Carolinas and the Gulf, in Virginia continue to rival the heroism of their noble comrades of Vicksburg and Charleston, remembering that every blow struck at the enemy, no matter where, is a blow for home and its hallowed rights."[130]

Promotion has healing powers for some soldiers. Baker hoped it would be so with him. Stuart, it was said, had sent a message to Baker during the battle that said, "Sir, you are a General." Perhaps with Brandy Station still fresh in his mind, General Lee urged President Davis to make Baker a brigadier general. It was not the first time Lee had requested that move. However, Davis had already seen to it. Though Hampton was expected to return to command his brigade, Baker had been confirmed as brigadier general on July 30, to rank from July 23. Stuart wholeheartedly concurred but privately he admitted that Baker had not been as "dashing" an officer since he had pledged to stay away from whiskey.[131]

This left an opening at the head of the 1st. Gordon got the nod. Clearly, it was a position he wanted; moreover, it was a position he deserved. On August 16, he declined command of the 2d Horse and accepted the appointment as colonel of the 1st North Carolina Cavalry. His rank dated from July 23.[132]

Gordon settled in with the men he considered family, but one man was missing: Laurence Baker. The surgeons, who thought Baker's wound serious, told Baker he would not be able to return to the cavalry anytime soon. There were times when Baker seemed "more dead than alive." To Lieutenant James L. Gaines fell the duty of penning the announcement, which Gordon doubtless had read to the ranks. After thanking the men for "the creditable manner in which each one behaved on 1st instant when engaged by a greatly superior force," Baker made public what had become speculation. "Again he expresses to the brigade feelings of the kindest respect and highest admiration, and reassures them of the reluctance with which he is compelled to sever those ties which are nearest and dearest to a soldier's heart. Farewell is given with the hope and belief that your deservedly high reputation may never be tarnished, and that when we shall have gained our independence it will be a source of pride, as it is now, to say that you belong to Hampton's brigade."[133]

Few in the brigade could have heard or read the announcement without trepidation. Baker lay wounded and would not return. Hampton still nursed his injuries. And for a while at least, two regimental commanders would be out of action. For now, the old brigade had no leader. So while Gordon officially commanded the 1st North Carolina Cavalry, he accepted the additional responsibility of temporary brigade command.[134]

11

"Now, Gordon, Is Your Time!"

FOR THE MOMENT, THE CONFEDERATE high command faced as much uncertainty as did the temporary commander of Hampton's Brigade. While Gordon established picket lines in Culpeper County, to the rear gray-clad foot-soldiers scurried to and fro because Lee was unsure where to place his army. Did the Federal reconnaissance at Brandy indicate an attempt to trap the Rebels between the Rapidan and the Rappahannock? Was it a prelude to another move on Fredericksburg? After reflection, Lee decided to "place the army in a position to enable it more readily to oppose the enemy should he attempt to move southward." By August 4, the Army of Northern Virginia had dug in south of the Rapidan astride the Orange and Alexandria Railroad.[1]

Gordon and his horsemen stayed in Culpeper County. Lee wanted them there to discourage the enemy from advancing to the Rapidan. Characteristically, the Tarheel cavalryman was eager to do whatever the cause required. "Would that war end," he wrote, "But it must never end until we are free and independent."[2] This desire for self-determination and the refusal to quit also emerged in Gordon's men. Sergeant Pugh of the 1st even thought that the army had been victorious in the North. He told his family that the regiment had "been going day and night in Maryland and Pennsylvania and doing some of the hardest fighting that ever poor souls did but thank god we whipped the yankees." Other cavalrymen admitted that Gettysburg had been a setback, and speculated that the fight would lengthen the war, but no Rebel said it would change the outcome.[3]

Now that Lee felt comfortable with his position, he and his officers tried to get the army ready to fight again. For the fought-out men, if food could be found it became one of few available elixirs. Gordon, for one, preferred eating to fighting. He had lost several pounds in Pennsylvania. What he would have given for a plate of piping-hot cornbread and a glass of ice-cold buttermilk! Instead, the horsemen choked down a sort of bread made with water and beef.[4]

Glad tidings from home would also have steeled those soldiers for future battles. Given their position along the railroad, the Confederates received plenty of news. Little of it was good, however, especially for North Carolina natives like Gordon. Back home, many North Carolinians had begun to demonstrate against the war. Defeat at Gettysburg and the fall of Vicksburg had woven a "spell of despondency" over the state. Governor Vance faced a growing number of peace movements. To Gordon's chagrin, Wilkes County had become a focal point of dissension. Its people remained as independent in spirit as the Overmountain Men had been. The county's poorer citizens could not abide the casualties and the lack of farm-hands. More and more men dodged military duty and hid in the backwoods. Home guardsmen and other military units sought to punish them, while still more Confederates roamed about, taking mounts and forage at will. The atmosphere bred dishonesty, disloyalty, and violence. Some whispered that Wilkes had become the strongest Union county in North Carolina. Call it the "Old United States," they said.[5]

Letters and diaries also told the unhappy story. Julia P. Gwyn, a member of a prominent Wilkes family, described the situation. "I am sorry to tell you of the Union sentiment existing in this county, among the women as well as the men," she wrote. "The women write to their husbands to leave the army and come home and that's the reason that so many of them are deserting. They have a regular union company up at Trap Hill! March under a dirty United States rag!" James Gwyn recorded an equally disturbing event. In late August, nearly three hundred deserters marched into Wilkesborough, posted pickets on the roads leading to town, and raised a Union flag. After building a very large fire and several smaller ones, the men made anti–Confederate speeches. "They will rue the day," Gwyn wrote.[6]

Wilkes merchant Calvin J. Cowles was also present, but he had a different point of view. Cowles had only recently been dismissed from his position as local postmaster because he was suspected of disloyalty. On this day, he and about two hundred others watched as the Union flag was "given to the breeze." Later, Cowles spent time in the guard house for his efforts.[7]

Gordon worried about his mother and sisters in this unpatriotic and possibly dangerous atmosphere. However, he had no sympathy for men who shirked duty. Neither did he care for Confederate citizens who demonstrated Unionist sympathies. He said as much to his brother-in-law:

> I regret very much to hear of so gloomy a picture as you represent in Wilkes. The only plan to subdue them is for the government to send a force there to crush out the disloyalty. When they resist the law and enforcement of the conscript act forces will be sent to support it. I would advise you not to excite their animosity by any inflammatory language, better to have nothing to say to them on the subject. The loyal men should be ready to unite and resist any depredations which may be attempted by them. The sentiment of the army is so different — true and loyal. It pains the troops from our state very much to hear these deplorable accounts from home.[8]

True to Gordon's words, events in North Carolina repulsed many Confederate soldiers. James Pugh was but one example. He wrote of Union sympathizers with acid in his pen. "I had rather kill them than the yankees," he seethed, "& I had rather kill a yankee than a snake." Resentment rose to a pitch until many decided to do something. On August 13, Tarheels from the Army of Northern Virginia held a convention at Orange Court House. They adopted a resolution pledging the loyalty of North Carolina to the army and the Confederacy. The resolution also denounced William W. Holden, the editor of the *North Carolina Standard* who was vigorously attacking the war. (Gordon had already made a tiny anti–Holden statement by declining to renew his subscription to the *Standard*.) The 1st, since it was distant from Orange Court House, held its own convention. In doing so, the "Bloody First" expressed regret for conditions at home. To demonstrate their loyalty they trumpeted a new if unoriginal motto: "Victory or Death."[9]

Gordon supported the 1st's creed. His beliefs had not wavered. His letters reflect not only his devotion to Southern independence but also an ignorance of how events were affecting his way of life. Indeed, Lincoln's Emancipation Proclamation, then officially in effect, meant nothing to him. Hearing of a valuable slave in Wilkesborough, Gordon told his brother-in-law, "I would like to own this girl you wrote about. I don't know what price to put upon her by giving a note. I suppose what she would bring in N.C. money. I wish you would buy her. I consider my note better than any money at this time. Negroes I consider cheaper than anything else in proportion. Buy her and make the best trade you can." This was not the first time that summer Gordon thought about investing in slaves. A month before, he had written Augustus, "I would prefer investing the money I have in land or negroes."[10] After all, the war would end one day, and Gordon the businessman wanted to be ready for it.

Whether the war would be renewed soon was also a question of debate in the camps. If it was, the army's leaders intended to be ready. Gordon had the luxury of paperwork to absorb his time and energy—even though paper itself had become scarce. Because the duties of Hampton's Brigade required more labor than the regiment, it suited Gordon. For the first time, he saw more of the workings of higher command, including the planning and analyzing brigadiers must do along with directing and leading. As such, Gordon had been placed in a position to study the strategic situation. In doing so, he showed himself a novice at judging enemy intentions. "In 4 weeks," Gordon wrote, "I think there will scarcely be a Yankee in this section of Virginia. Meade will be driven out. He is very uneasy, fearing Gen Lee will advance upon him. [Meade] commenced falling back three days ago." Under Stuart's tutelage Gordon would learn more about guessing enemy intentions, but the Wilkes Countian certainly knew the minds of his men. "Our troops are anxious for a fight," he continued. "We have no fears of the result if we can overtake the Yankees...."[11]

Gordon was quite wrong about Meade's intentions. On September 13, the Federals advanced and occupied Culpeper County. Since Lee had sent Longstreet's Corps to reinforce Confederate forces in Tennessee, Meade's movement caused concern. However, this turned out to be little more than a change in position. Much cavalry skirmishing, centered around Culpeper, attended this march. James Pugh described how the 1st fared that day in its fighting at the foot of Mt. Pony. The fight, he wrote, "lasted all day and part of the night. The yanks was too [sic] many for us and drove us back but we killed lots of them and we had 30 killed and 40 wounded." After nightfall, Hampton's Confederate horsemen took up a new position around Rapidan Station on the Orange and Alexandria Railroad.[12]

This September fight turned out to be one of few interruptions during that comparatively restful August and September. While the men concentrated on resolutions and resting, Generals Lee and Stuart began to think about the cavalry. Perhaps the most nagging problem centered on the welfare of the arm's mounts. During the summer, the declining quality of horseflesh had become a constant problem. It was as if the harsh influence of Hampton's horrible winter of 1862–63 still lingered. Thousands of horses needed recruiting because recently they had not been shod regularly.[13]

Also chief among the problems was the Confederacy's dwindling corn supply, which caused Lee to fear that many animals would be lost. Though Lee did everything he could to recruit the horses, by mid–October Stuart admitted that his men had been forced to "divide the last crust" of their food with their steeds.[14] The 1st North Carolina Cavalry was among those units facing transportation problems. The state had originally furnished horses for the enlisted men, but its officers had been required to supply their own. The government (when possible) provided feed, a smith to do the shoeing, and forty cents a day for each horse; but if a horse became worn out or was captured, it was up to the owner to replace it.[15] Hungry, tired, and wounded horses, whether government or privately owned, suffered from this system. In early October alone, Pugh took 196 horses to the pastures of "Camp Disabled." The owners of these horses had to find replacements or face transfer. At the same time, partly because of the lack of horses, the number of regimental wagons had to be reduced to three, where in the war's early days the unit had boasted thirty and more.[16]

Gordon, who had spent the war riding his own mounts, also saw his horses suffer. During a summer skirmish, one of his horses had been wounded and permanently disabled. When the horse died, Gordon reported it and asked his due. The government paid him $683.00 the following January, according to the horse's value at mustering.[17]

Generals Lee and Stuart also considered the improving Federal cavalry, as well as the ineffective performance of the Confederate horsemen in Pennsylvania. To help overcome the latter much had to be done in the way of drill and training. As a start, Stuart issued a general order to point out his officers' tactical errors. Then there was the reality of heavy casualties. "We have lost a number of valuable men and officers," Gordon wrote. Another Tarheel put it more dramatically: "[The Federals] have killed up nearly all our regiment."[18] As far as casualties went, the experience of Robertson's Brigade proved instructive. By July 13, that unit had been reduced to "a mere handful." Robertson subsequently confessed that the 4th and 5th North Carolina Cavalry regiments contained less than three hundred men combined. Because of this, Robertson asked to be transferred to a place where his services would be "of more avail." Stuart approved the suggestion, as did Lee. (He ended up commanding the Second District of South Carolina). Those who remained mourned for the lost. When they learned that Colonel Evans had died in captivity, the 5th's leaders passed resolutions of respect to his memory. Someone accepted the responsibility of telling Evans's widow.[19]

Whatever the unit, the cavalry's depleted condition beckoned careful study. What could be done? One solution stood above all others. The possibility of reorganizing the cavalry division had been considered since the previous spring. Now, with the input of Stuart, Lee formally suggested a reorganization of the cavalry and forwarded his ideas to Richmond. That August 1 memorandum from Lee to the president changed Gordon's life by creating an organization that opened the way for his advancement.

To begin with, Lee told Davis that the cavalry brigades were too large for commanders to handle. "Three regiments," he wrote, "if full, would be as much as one commander could properly attend to either in camp, on the march, or in battle. But our regiments, unfortunately, are not full, and I therefore propose four regiments to a brigade." Altering the number of regiments in a brigade, Lee believed, would get more men into the field. Brigade commanders could pay more attention to each regiment, theoretically resulting in less absenteeism.[20]

To reduce the number of regiments in a brigade, Lee continued, it would be necessary to increase the number of cavalry brigades. In turn, Lee suggested the creation of two divisions of cavalry. Each division would be led by newly promoted major generals, Wade Hampton and Fitz Lee, who would report to Stuart. Several other officers would be promoted to fill regimental and brigade vacancies.

Davis agreed. August passed while details were hammered out. In the meantime, those "quiet" days along the Rapidan saw the Army of Northern Virginia recover to some degree. "Our army," Gordon wrote home, "is in fine condition and spirits. It has increased largely in a few weeks." Confidence rose simultaneously; there was even scattered talk in the camps that the war would end before next summer. Then, less than a week before the cavalry fell back to Rapidan Station, the reorganization became official. Special Orders Number 226 fashioned Stuart's cavalry into something resembling a corps structure.[21] Major General Wade Hampton's division contained the brigades of General W. E. Jones (6th, 7th, and 12th Virginia regiments, and the 35th Battalion Virginia Cavalry) and General M. C. Butler (Cobb's Georgia Legion, Phillips Georgia Legion, Jeff Davis Legion, and the 2d South Carolina Cavalry). A North Carolina cavalry brigade, under Baker, filled out Hampton's division. It consisted of Gordon's

1st along with the 2d, 4th, and 5th North Carolina. Fitz Lee's division included the brigades of General W. H. F. Lee (1st South Carolina Cavalry, and the 9th, 10th, and 13th Virginia regiments); General Lunsford L. Lomax (1st Battalion Maryland Cavalry, and the 5th, 11th, and 15th Virginia regiments); and General Williams C. Wickham (1st, 2d, 3d, and 4th Virginia Cavalry regiments).[22]

The reorganization looked good on paper, but in practice several issues had to be dealt with. Jenkins's Brigade, for example, was not included in the reorganization because it did not remain with Stuart. Another question regarded those officers who could not fill their appointed positions. "Rooney" Lee was one. On June 26, while recovering from his Brandy Station wound, he had been captured by Federal forces. Command of his brigade devolved upon Colonel John Chambliss. Similarly, the deserving Calbraith Butler received his September 1 appointment to brigadier general, but his health remained questionable. It became necessary to appoint P. M. B. Young to fill his position.

Pierce Manning Butler Young was destined to become one of Gordon's closest friends. Young, twenty-seven, was a native of Spartanburg, South Carolina. His family later moved to Bartow County, Georgia, after which Young entered the Georgia Military Institute. At eighteen Young had been appointed to the U.S. Military Academy, but war had cut his time there short. He began his Confederate service in the infantry, transferred to the staff of Braxton Bragg in Florida, and then received an appointment as adjutant of T. R. R. Cobb's Georgia Legion. Rising to command the legion as lieutenant colonel and then colonel, he probably came to know Gordon during their service in Hampton's Brigade. A man of splendid manners and great magnetism but a bit spoiled, Young had earned a reputation as a gallant officer. He had suffered a wound near Crampton's Gap and again during the early August Brandy fight, but neither permanently incapacitated him. Stuart wanted to promote him badly, but a lack of Georgia units in the cavalry had made that difficult. Young's commission dated September 28, 1863, but he would not receive it until October.[23]

Other problems arose with William Jones and Tom Rosser. For Jones, it began after his disagreement with Stuart flared anew. The general began grumbling about how he had been left under Robertson's command during the Gettysburg campaign. After complaining to Stuart, Jones found himself under arrest for showing disrespect to a superior officer. A court martial convened, and the disgruntled Jones lost his command. To shore up this widening rift, Lee sent Jones to take over the cavalry in southwestern Virginia. In Jones's stead, Tom Rosser was commissioned brigadier general and assumed command of the unit he would rechristen the Laurel Brigade.[24]

Stuart was fond of Rosser. He described him as "an officer of superior ability, [who] possesses in an extraordinary degree the talent to command and skill to lead with coolness and decision of character." On one occasion, the cavalry commander had called Rosser "my right hand man...." In October 1862, Stuart had even proposed the formation of a new brigade so that Rosser could command it. That had not come about, however, because the twice-wounded, twenty-six-year-old Virginian did not always enjoy Richmond's favor. His West Point background notwithstanding, Rosser had been given to drink in the heartfelt absence of his beloved new bride. Performance in camp, if not in the field, suffered, but by the summer of 1863 he appeared to be regaining control. His more recent service again marked him for advancement, and he was rewarded for it.[25]

It was timely, for Rosser had grown unhappy. To his wife he complained, "I am one of his [Stuart's] oldest Colonels and I feel that I have done my *whole* duty — and feel that I deserve promotion." This feeling affected his view of Stuart. He began disparaging his commander. When Fitz Lee said Rosser deserved promotion, it underscored Rosser's belief that his commander was responsible for the lack of advancement. He wrote: "But Stuart Stuart Stuart! I am done with him!" Of one September skirmish, Rosser wrote: "Gen. Stuart is *badly* whipped, lost three (3) pieces of artillery all their *horses* and *men* This I think is the finishing stroke to Stuart's declining reputation." These feelings culminated when Rosser sought transfer to another unit, but his belated promotion in the cavalry came through instead.[26]

The varied personalities of other new brigadiers helped breathe renewed purpose into the cavalry. Many of the new officers were men Gordon knew well. Lunsford Lindsay Lomax was a Rhode Islander by birth but a Virginian by upbringing. An 1856 graduate of West Point, Lomax had served with the U.S. cavalry on the frontier — where he had met a young J. E. B. Stuart — until civil war persuaded him to resign. Among his more recent experience was staff service with Joe Johnston and other Western generals who had taken him into battles at Pea Ridge, Vicksburg, and others. Promoted to colonel in February 1863, he had come east to assume command of the 11th Virginia Cavalry. A close friend of Fitz Lee, Lomax earned his place in Stuart's cavalry with solid performances at Brandy Station and in the Gettysburg Campaign.[27]

Williams Carter Wickham, whose brigadier general commission dated September 9, was the great-grandson of a Revolutionary War veteran and Declaration of Independence signer. Gordon's elder by two years, Williams Wickham was a graduate of the University of Virginia. Though admitted to the bar in 1842, he opted for the life of a planter and the hand of a North Carolina lady. Wickham had also experienced military life through pre-war service in the Virginia volunteer cavalry. Though initially opposed to secession, he had raised a cavalry company and had led it in battle until he was wounded and captured in May 1862. Returning to the army, he received a commission as colonel of the 4th Virginia Cavalry. Except for a brief interruption because of another wound, Wickham spent the next few months fighting with Stuart's cavalry in almost every campaign. His ambitions included politics, as a result of which Wickham was elected to the Confederate Congress in 1863. Out of a sense of duty, he left his seat vacant until the fall of 1864. Stuart described Wickham as a man of fine administrative abilities who would exercise judicious care for his men and horses.[28]

The promotion of such men, and the creation of the North Carolina horse brigade, evidently was designed to satisfy more than military needs. State rights bred state jealousies, and the War Department confronted that continually. Wade Hampton believed that Stuart credited only Virginians for the cavalry's success, so he often personified this rivalry. At one point, he even campaigned for the creation of a cavalry division for troops from states other than Virginia.[29] Others wanted more publicity for their state's accomplishments; one of the 1st's troopers complained that North Carolina's "deeds of valor will not be found recorded in the columns of the Richmond papers." Governor Vance even thought that many quality North Carolina officers were not receiving deserved promotions.[30] The creation of such units as the Tarheel cavalry brigade did not altogether satisfy the disgruntled, but it did pave the way for men like James B. Gordon to earn three stars and a wreath for their uniform collars.

The birth of the Tarheel brigade had been a slow one, and that led to frustration. In Gordon's view, the changes bred as much confusion as anything. Yet while the cavalry was reorganized, Colonel Gordon watched, waited, and hoped. The wounded Baker was the senior North Carolina cavalryman in the army, but his return to duty would not happen soon, if at all. At the same time, according to rumor the War Department was planning to create a second Tarheel cavalry brigade.[31] If that was the case, then who would command the new brigade? And with Baker's status in question, who would command Baker's brigade? The answer was, at best, a complicated one.

For his part, Gordon wanted promotion. As temporary commander of Hampton's

Brigade, he had again demonstrated his abilities. "Gordon is in command of Hampton's Brigade and commands it well," Stuart told Young. Then came the formation of the North Carolina Cavalry Brigade and the brigading of Gordon's and Ferebee's regiments. Ferebee, as Gordon's senior in rank, became brigade commander. Fortunately no conflict arose here since Gordon drew a new duty; he was ordered to assume temporary command of Butler's Brigade, which awaited Butler's return or the assignment of a new commander. (P. M. B. Young had not yet been selected to fill the position.)[32] Gordon figured this would be short-lived, but it served to whet further his appetite for brigade command, and it demonstrated the faith that officials had in him. Yet despite all this, promotion had not been forthcoming.

A September cavalry fight offered more evidence of Gordon's abilities. It came at a place called Jack's Shop. At 1:00 A.M. on September 22, Ferebee received orders to have his brigade in the saddle by daybreak. "Boots and Saddles" sounded at earliest dawn. A bit later the column struck out. Gordon brought up the available portion of Butler's Brigade and placed it into column with Ferebee. Jones's old brigade also joined the advance. Reconnoitering Federal cavalry had caused Stuart to set his troopers in motion to block the pike near Madison Court House. John Buford was advancing from the courthouse toward Liberty Mills, and Stuart wanted to stop him.[33]

Troopers from the 1st confirmed the reports of Buford's advance. Seeing a mounted enemy picket post in the distance, Stuart turned to Lieutenant Noah P. Foard, commanding Company F. Charge that post, Stuart said, and find out what is behind it. Foard accordingly led his company straight at the foe, driving them handsomely. The Rebels then came to a large field where a sizable force of Federal cavalrymen waited in line of battle. Foard veered left, where woods and rolling ground offered protection. As he vaulted a fence, bullets riddled his horse and killed it, but Foard survived. Before retreating, he drew his knife, cut the saddle's girth and the bridle's throat-latch, and saved his saddle and bridle. He then reported to Stuart what he had seen.[34]

Thus warned, the 1st North Carolina Cavalry was in the advance when the enemy appeared *en masse*. The Rebels in front charged, and those behind prepared to do likewise. Stuart, however, had words of caution for Major William H. Cheek, temporary commander of the 1st. "Be careful, and do not run into an ambush," Stuart said. (Lieutenant Colonel Thomas Ruffin, commander of the regiment in Gordon's absence, was in the rear having a shoe nailed onto his horse.) Cheek heeded Stuart's advice.

"Return sabres! Unsling carbines! Fire on the enemy!" Cheek shouted. The regiment reined in. Lead flew, and the battle was joined. Cheek again consulted Stuart, and soon the 1st was forming into line of battle in an open field "as promptly and perfectly as if there had been no enemy near."[35]

As the 5th North Carolina Cavalry followed suit, Stuart changed his mind and ordered an assault. Driving "fast and hard," the 5th and 1st North Carolina Cavalry regiments charged. Carbine-wielding Yankees shot back from behind fences and fallen pines, but the Carolinians pushed the Federals back with drawn sabres. When the Confederates came upon the main Federal body, however, the advance ended. Private Coltrane of the 5th recalled, "When we saw how many men and guns were there, it looked so awful that we fell back slowly to our own main line. The Federal Cavalry had numbers enough to force us or even to cut us to pieces, but they seemed to be waiting for something."[36]

Indeed they were. Stuart had stepped into a trap. A second enemy column, under Judson Kilpatrick, was marching by way of Wolftown to turn the Confederate left. Worse, a body of dismounted Federal cavalrymen was blocking the Liberty Mills ford road — Stuart's sole line of retreat. (A fourth enemy contingent was heading for Barnett's Ford on Stuart's right.) In front, Buford began pressing his advantage with small arms and artillery fire, while in flank and rear the door to escape was closing. A Southern staff officer began riding along the Confederate lines to inform the men they were surrounded: "Boys, it is a fight to captivity, death or victory."[37]

"Don't worry, we'll get out of here," one Carolina trooper answered.

Another said, "We'll go out of here if there isn't but one of us left." Cheers sounded from the ranks. In front Confederate cavalrymen again charged Buford's numerically superior forces, while in rear Stuart sought an avenue of escape. Gordon brought Butler's Brigade up in support at about this time, throwing sharpshooters forward. Everywhere the enemy forced the Confederates back, but Stuart's men held fast. The battle spread to an open field, which surrounded a small hill. This became a focal point of resistance, a place where no blue-clad soldier could pass. The North Carolina Cavalry Brigade stood there, as did parts of Jones's and Butler's brigades. Unionist shells fell heavily; to curb the enemy shelling, Gordon and the other officers ordered the men to pick off enemy artillerymen. The horse artillery in particular used the hill to advantage. The gunners threw shells in all directions; at times, they fought their pieces back to back. Stuart sat his horse beside the guns, pointing here and there with his right arm to direct the fire.[38]

The drama climaxed when two regiments knocked the Federals aside, opening the way of retreat. The Southerners then withdrew rapidly across the Rapidan at Liberty Mills. It did not end there, however; more Yankees waited on the other side of the river. Linking up with Southern infantry, the cavalrymen charged the enemy again. Over hill and over gully, the charge seemed endless, but the thrust was sure. "The last rays of the setting sun," recorded one participant, "are glistening on our sabres as we raise the war-cry and ply the rowels to our weary steeds."[39] The Federals broke and scattered, and the battle of Jack's Shop came to a close. The Union trap had failed, but it had been a near thing.

According to one solider, Jack's Shop was one of the war's fiercest fights. Gordon had reason to be proud of his performance; with only two unfamiliar units — the Cobb and Phillips Legions — on hand, he "ably" contributed to the battle's outcome.[40] The vicious fight demonstrated Gordon's readiness for brigade command. If there were any remaining doubters as to Gordon's abilities, this fight probably convinced them. Yet Gordon grew impatient in waiting for officials to act. Although he had been a colonel for only two months, Gordon characteristically decided something had to be done. The time had come to apply for promotion.

The politician and businessman in Gordon knew the value of contacts. Robert Ransom came immediately to mind. Ransom had risen through the ranks since leaving the 1st. In 1862, General Lee had awarded Ransom command of an infantry brigade at Kinston. Subsequently, Ransom led his men during the Seven Days and in Maryland. He eventually commanded a division on Fredericksburg's Marye's Heights, against which Federal forces battered themselves in December 1862. In May 1863, following a tour of duty in North Carolina defending the Weldon railroad, Ransom was promoted to major general. He succeeded D. H. Hill as a commander in the department of Richmond. Although struck with illness late that summer, Ransom remained close to his division's Petersburg headquarters.[41]

Gordon figured that Ransom wielded as much, if not more, influence of any of his closest Tarheel friends. Ransom had demonstrated gallantry and military professionalism on almost every occasion, as well as versatility. He had handled both cavalry and infantry in battle, and not without success. His strict West Point way of leading was unpopular with his troops, and his unashamed campaigns for personal promotion were also frowned on, but Richmond surely valued his opinions.⁴² Gordon thought so, anyway. One September day, Gordon wrote Ransom about the North Carolina cavalry brigade's situation. He then asked his old friend a favor: if Ransom would recommend Gordon's promotion to General Samuel Cooper, the Confederacy's chief adjutant and inspector general, it would surely help speed action. Ransom, who expressed his pride in the continued "handsome conduct" and gallantry exhibited by the 1st, eagerly agreed. "Herewith," he answered Gordon, "I send a letter to General Cooper which it has given me great pleasure to write, and I trust it, together with other influences, may obtain the end for which it is written. Wishing you a speedy promotion."⁴³

Bob Ransom was an earnest man not given to speaking with "double-faced meaning." He wrote his letter of recommendation the same day Gordon fought at Jack's Shop:

> Having understood that there would be formed two Brigades of N.C. Cavalry, and as only one Brig Genl, Baker, has been appointed, I presume to recommend Col. *Jas. B. Gordon* of the 1st N.C. Cavalry, as a fit & highly capable officer to fill such position. Col. Gordon entered service at the begginning [sic] of the war as major of 1st N.C. Cavly, of which Regt. I was then Colonel. I had the best opportunities of judging of his capacity, & I am informed that he is held in the highest esteem by the Commander of the Cavalry of Army No. Va. I know no one who would fill the appointment with more ability or credit. I regret that I have been able to see him but once in action, but he *led* our cavly, in the *first* combat of this war when we met that arm of the enemy's service & it was a complete success.⁴⁴

Did Ransom's letter have the impact Gordon hoped for? If nothing else, it achieved one thing by crossing Cooper's desk. Before being placed in Gordon's permanent files, the letter brought the situation to the government's attention. Four days after Ransom wrote, General Lee analyzed the situation for Jefferson Davis:

> The Commission of Genl Baker of N.C. reached me the day that officer was wounded.... Baker is still absent from the effects of his wounds & it is said he will be incapable of duty for some months yet. The command of the Brigade will accordingly devolve upon the senior Col. Ferribee [sic]. This officer though senior in rank has not the experience nor the qualifications for command possessed by the Second Col. Gordon. Col. Gordon has been serving [torn] for some time, his regt. having formed a part of Hampton's brigade, of which until the recent reorganization he has been [torn] was wounded, & has proved capable. There are three regts. of Cav. now in N.C. without a comm. since the departure of Robertson for other duty. To the command of these I recommend Genl Baker on his recovery be [torn]. I also recommend that Col. J. B. Gordon be promoted B. Genl. that I may assign [him] command of the N.C. brigade in this army.... Every brigade should have the best & most experienced commander at this time. As far as I am able to judge the interests of the service will be advanced by the promotion of Col. Gordon.⁴⁵

Lee was not alone in his estimate of Ferebee. "He is a truly gallant man ... [but] a poor disciplinarian & a poor judge of military men," Rufus Barringer wrote.⁴⁶ Davis agreed. On September 28, 1863 Gordon was promoted to brigadier general in the Provisional Army of the Confederate States, to rank from the same day. It was not Lee's normal practice to promote someone while there was a chance his senior would return to the field, but the necessity of maintaining discipline won out. Neither was it Lee's habit to offend anyone, so in some fashion he managed to enact his decision without injuring Ferebee's pride. The official commission instructed Gordon, upon acceptance, to report to Lee "for assignment to Command of the Brigade originally designed for Brig Gen Baker. (disabled by wounds.)"⁴⁷

The joyous Gordon could not contain his excitement. He dashed off a letter of thanks to Stuart:

> I feel very grateful to you for your kindness in sending my commission as Brig. Gen. The interest you have manifested and kindness extended me will ever be recollected with the kindest emotion. I hope to pass through this conflict under thy protecting sagacity and accomplished generalship; and if in the future fortune should bless me with that best of all things, a good wife, the first boy shall be named Jas. E. B. Stuart. Hoping both events may soon happen, I remain most respectfully your friend and obdt. Servant.[48]

Gordon accepted the commission on October 5 and reported to General Lee for assignment. With that, the forty-year-old Gordon became one of the oldest of Stuart's generals (the average age of the cavalry leaders was thirty-three. Only Hampton and Wickham were older than Gordon). Where Pelham had shown that youth had no bearing on cavalry ability, Gordon now set out to prove the same for maturity. In the words of William H. H. Cowles, "Gordon, the peerless, gallant and true" had at last been placed at the head of the brigade. "It was like loosing a cord that had bound an eagle — with his course always upward," Cowles continued, "he at once was accorded a position among the most trusted and competent of the brigade commanders."[49]

As a brigadier, Gordon was entitled to a small staff. The men he retained, many of them members of Baker's staff, were well chosen. Captain Chiswell W. Dabney became the brigade's adjutant and inspector general. If nothing else, Chis Dabney was a respected cavalryman.

On September 28, 1863, Gordon was promoted to brigadier general. "I feel very grateful to you," he told Stuart (Library of Congress).

Earlier in the war, it was said, regulations had prevented his promotion because of his youth; but his comrades called him "Captain" anyway because of his bravery. As essentially the brigade's chief of staff, Dabney's duties included writing orders, dispatches, and reports. Chis, his mother beamed, experienced "constant employment" in his position, and did his work well enough to earn Stuart's praise. Dabney had been born on July 25, 1844 in Campbell County, Virginia. After leaving the University of Virginia to join the army, his performance early in the war, especially at Dranesville, earned him a spot on Stuart's staff. Known as "Young Brown," Dabney was an aide-de-camp for Stuart from January 1862 until November 19, 1863, when he transferred to Gordon's Brigade. Stuart's only complaint of the young man was that he did not sit erect in the saddle. Gordon soon developed a strong liking for Dabney.[50]

Other staff-members were equally valued. Captain James L. Gaines, a twenty-five-year-old native of Buncombe County, was the assistant adjutant and inspector general. Appointed captain on September 2, to rank from July 23, Gaines had joined Baker's staff, but then had to write Baker's retirement announcement. Except for a period following Gaines's wounding in June 1862, Gordon and Gaines had served together in the 1st, of which Gaines had been adjutant. Other brigade staff-members included Major J. C. McRae, an assistant adjutant general, and Paul B. Means, who joined later.[51]

Gordon exercised special care in selecting his aide-de-camp. Knowing his aide must be an intelligent, helpful man whom he could trust with important duties, he selected Lieutenant Kerr Craige, Burton's son, to fill the position. Burton, an ex-member of the Confederacy's Provisional Congress, had played a leading role in North Carolina's secession and in the Confederacy's early efforts; similarly, Kerr had fulfilled his duty to the Confederacy.[52] Lieutenant Craige, who had turned twenty in March, had been a student at the University of North Carolina when war came. Volunteering for duty with the 1st, Craige rose to sergeant before being made lieutenant and joining Gordon's staff. Like his father, Craige was physically impressive. He was a man "of massive frame, with clear-cut features and handsome form and face, agreeable, companionable, and kind. He had a fund of wit and humor in his make-up." In the coming months, Craige and Gordon would grow close as they shared a tent in the field. He would help Gordon transact the business of a brigadier, including that of personal and military correspondence.[53] The youngster's personality and abilities would prove invaluable in the tests ahead.

November came before Gordon's staff was completely in place, but his work began anyway. The general immediately assessed the efficiency of his command.[54] One immediate problem concerned leadership. Of his four regiment commanders, only Ferebee, who had just returned to the 4th, had measurable experience. Thomas Ruffin, a solid soldier but a novice colonel, succeeded Gordon as the 1st's commander. The 2d Horse still lacked appropriately ranked candidates. The unit's proper commander, Lieutenant Colonel William G. Robinson, had been captured in April, but it was hoped he would be exchanged soon. Iredell County-native Major Clinton M. Andrews commanded the regiment in his stead. Lieutenant Colonel Stephen Evans remained at the helm of the 5th.[55] Gordon knew most of these men well but only the coming days would tell if they could fight.

The ranks also needed attention. To begin with, both the 1st and the 5th were battered from the recent campaigning. The 1st mustered only about 130 men.[56] The 2d Horse had also been hurt badly, especially in Pennsylvania. It was said that there was not much of Solomon Williams's old regiment left for Gordon to organize. Ferebee's 4th North Carolina Cavalry (Fifty-ninth Regiment North Carolina State Troops), which had originally been organized and trained at Garysburg in the summer of 1862, was also weak. The 4th had joined the army after serving along the Blackwater and Chowan rivers and in eastern North Carolina. Like the 5th, its real baptism of fire had come during the Gettysburg campaign.[57] Gordon strove to ensure that all his men would be ready.

Given the army's condition, this was a difficult task. However, Gordon's personality, military experience, business skills, and political savvy made him uniquely qualified to handle it. Tom Brown had had no idea of what the future held when he had written: "Brother James has abandoned all hope of ever removing from Wilkes. I suppose the thought of spending the balance of his days in that poor old county makes him moody and sad enough." Now, Tom was more than two years in an Arkansas grave and Gordon was a general officer in an army fighting far away from home. War had brought James Byron Gordon to this, his life's pinnacle. Those Tarheel cavalrymen, those regiments of potential, had become Gordon's men. They would march and fight Gordon's way. In time, Cowles said, the general's skill in organization would bring about "the highest state of reliance among the regiments in each other until their mutual confidence, drill, and discipline became such that the strength of one was the strength of all."[58]

While Gordon worked, the war rumbled on. In the West, Longstreet joined the Army of Tennessee in time to help fight the Battle of Chickamauga near Gordon Springs. Gordon was probably glad Carrie had decided not to visit their relatives there that summer. In the East, the indoctrination period of the North Carolina cavalry brigade and its commander ended when General Lee also decided to renew the war. In early October, Meade made his headquarters in a strong position north of Culpeper Court House. Two of his corps extended to the Rapidan. Though the Army of the Potomac also had been weakened in favor of reinforcing other Federal armies, Jack's Shop signaled the possibility of a Federal attack. Moreover, cavalry outposts often heard the whistles of "Yankee cars" that chugged in the distance.[59] Lee studied this intelligence and decided to turn Meade's right, force a retreat, and attack him in motion. The ranks of the Southern army had yet to fill, many men were poorly clad and barefooted, and Lee himself was unwell, but Lee saw more opportunity than risk. If nothing else, the offensive might keep the Union from sending more men to the West.

On October 9 the plan went into action. Passing Madison Court House and Culpeper, the corps of Hill and Ewell marched toward Warrenton. Ewell used the direct road past Jeffersonton and Sulphur Springs, while Hill traveled a more circuitous route by way of Woodville, Sperryville, Gaines's Crossroads, and Waterloo Bridge. The flanked Meade subsequently began withdrawing along the line of the Orange and Alexandria railroad, leaving his cavalry as rearguard.[60]

While the infantry sought an opening, Stuart fought Meade's rearguard. The cavalry's assignment called for Fitz Lee's division and two infantry brigades to observe the enemy and cover the rear from Raccoon Ford.[61] The other cavalry division, which Stuart would command since Hampton still nursed his Gettysburg wounds, drew the duty of protecting the army's right flank. Stuart also hoped to make a demonstration and divert attention from Lee's advance. Accordingly, on the night of October 9, Gordon bivouacked his brigade near Madison Court House. The rest of Hampton's division joined him there, and pickets were thrown out to Robertson's River.[62] The general had had little time to prepare his brigade for action, but thanks to prior experience he knew his units as well as any new commander could have. He also understood what was expected of him as a brigadier general, but was he ready? Could he fight the brigade effectively? The morrow held the unknown.

At 3:00 A.M. on Saturday morning, October 10, the men of Gordon's Brigade marched. Lines of horsemen stretched everywhere. Jones's old Brigade, under the temporary command of Colonel Oliver R. Funsten during Jones's court martial, joined the infantry's advance toward Woodville. The 2d North Carolina Cavalry also veered off to help the main column, leaving Gordon with three regiments. Then Stuart took Gordon's and Young's brigades to protect Lee's right flank and divert enemy attention. From Madison Court House, Stuart marched toward Russell's Ford on Robertson's River, which was near a bridge leading to Culpeper Court House. With Gordon's Brigade in the vanguard, the Rebels rode into the gathering dawn. The campaign started as envisioned. The advance guard, a contingent from the 4th North Carolina Cavalry, struck the enemy picket line near the ford and pushed it back on its supports at Bethsaida Church, near Thoroughfare Mountain. The Carolinians halted long enough to collect a few prisoners before continuing. Moments later, fresh reports filtered back to Gordon: the advance guard had found a regiment of enemy infantry, supported by cavalry, making a stand near the church. A hot engagement had ensued.[63] Gordon chanced no mistakes, so he halted his brigade and awaited orders.

One of Stuart's staff officers, Theodore S. Garnett, remembered that Rufus Barringer had

11. "Now, Gordon, Is Your Time!"   175

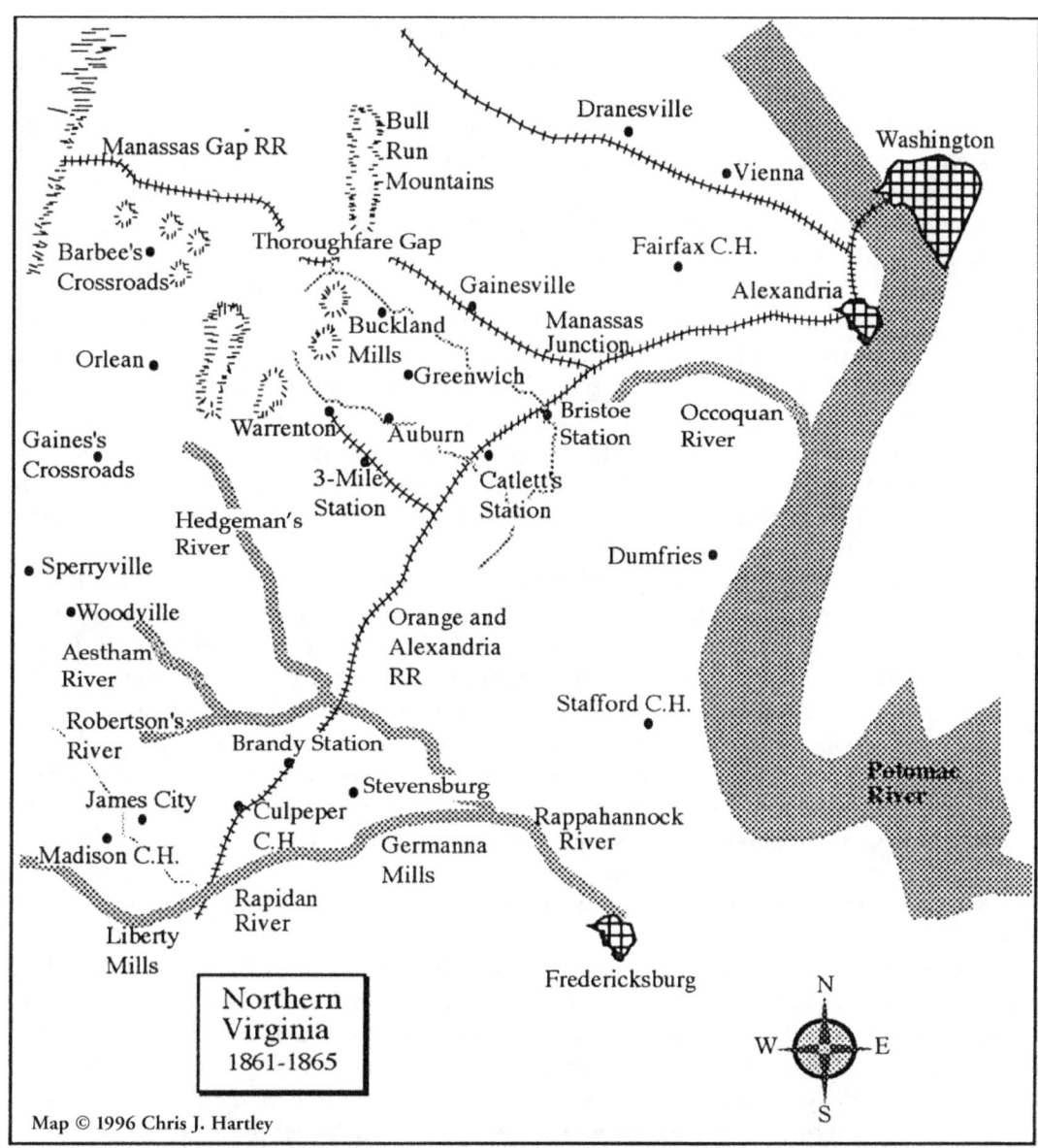

a tough time on this field. Barringer's squadron, under heavy artillery fire, was drawn up on a field awaiting orders. To protect the men, Gordon instructed Barringer to retire to the south side of Robertson's River, which was out of range. Gladly, Barringer rode out in front of his squadron to give the order, but as he did so a Yankee shell "came screaming over and burst just above his head." Barringer went on with his order: "By shells! Right about wheel." The men later got a good chuckle out of this, knowing Barringer had meant to say "By fours!"[64]

When Stuart arrived with Young's (Butler's) Brigade, he ordered Gordon to send "a number" of dismounted men forward. Grayclad horsemen from Gordon's old command, the 5th, dismounted and surged ahead "vigorously." Stuart then directed Gordon to push his command forward while Young flanked the enemy. The terrain was rough and wooded, and the Federals waited in line of battle, but the Confederates carried out their assignments efficiently. A single charge of Young's 1st South Carolina Cavalry combined with Gordon's advance to send the enemy in retreat.[65] Cheers, yells, and the deadly crack of Confederate carbines shattered the morning stillness. The defenders, in their haste, dropped dozens of "the newest, brightest, and handsomest muskets ever handled."[66]

Stuart pursued the Yankees toward James City and found them ready for another fight. Stuart again saw his advance on James City as a diversion "to favor the flank movement," and so far it appeared that the enemy was very much occupied. As the Confederates marched, the Federals took position north of town on a line of hills commanding Stuart's avenue of approach. Gordon figured the defenders to have a "considerable" force on hand.[67] Stuart agreed, estimating that two brigades of Kilpatrick's cavalry division, a division of infantry, and six artillery pieces held the line. Accordingly, reversed the roles of the ford attack, sending Gordon to demonstrate on the left while Young skirmished in front. Brisk firing opened up and sharpshooters advanced, but neither brigade gained much ground. In the interest of the diversion, Stuart chose not to attack. Instead, Young and Gordon consolidated their forces on some hills south of town, with Gordon on the left. They planted Stuart's flag on one hilltop, and it soon floated defiantly in the breeze. James City, in the valley below, sat between the opposing forces. Scattered skirmishing or an occasional artillery shell flying overhead made life tense for the town's inhabitants.[68]

Dusk found the opposing forces still holding their lines. Stuart regretted that the citizens of James City had to suffer war on their doorsteps because of the "peculiarity of the ground," but he knew it could have been worse. Except for skirmishing and shelling, only two incidents had livened the afternoon, and only one had endangered civilians. That was an enemy cavalry charge aimed at two Rebel guns on the edge of James City, but sharpshooters from Young's Brigade had repulsed the attack easily. The other incident threatened Stuart personally. As the cavalry commander and his staff stretched out to await events, an enemy piece sighted on the Confederate flag. A puff of white smoke rose from the enemy gun as it was fired. The percussion shell whistled into the group's midst, exploded, and threw dirt everywhere. Although it landed only five feet from John Esten Cooke, who had been half asleep while holding his horse's bridle, the shell hurt no one. Nonetheless, the men eagerly sought alternative resting spots.[69]

When night took hold, Stuart had his brigades bivouac in line of battle. He established headquarters in the nearby Hill home, and then called his officers to him in the quiet darkness. The gentleman bachelor from North Carolina, whom staff-member Cooke described as "that brave spirit," met with Stuart there, and probably joined them for supper. Gordon's first day had gone well enough, and now he received tomorrow's orders. To keep the army's flank clear, the cavalry would break the stalemate and advance toward Culpeper in the morning.

Once army business was concluded, Gordon's gaze fell on the fair young lady of the house, who had remained with her family despite the battle. Through months of war, the man who had both attracted and eluded the females of northwestern North Carolina had not lost his enjoyment for flirting. In some fashion, he had even developed more respect for the institution of marriage. Prompted by a gift of flowers from the lady, Gordon flashed her a "charming smile" and then voiced an elegant speech that was as good as any he had given to the state legislature almost thirteen years before. As a final touch he gave her a nosegay and his deepest, most elegant bow. Friendly laughter filled the room. Miss Hill also gave Chiswell Dabney a white rosebud, suggesting that he was 'too young to love,' and Cooke a small bouquet.[70]

The next morning, Kilpatrick gave up James City and retired toward Culpeper. Meade marched for the Rappahannock. Leaving Young at James City, Stuart continued with Gordon's Brigade at dawn. Rather than approach Culpeper from the south, Stuart angled his 1,500 troopers westward to stay on the flank of the infantry columns.[71] Funsten, with Jones's Brigade, rejoined Stuart near Griffinsburg at 11:00 A.M. Stuart then ordered Funsten to march down the Culpeper-Sperryville pike and push the enemy away from General Lee's advance. Gordon he sent to the right to hit the pike at Stone-House Mountain, probably to outflank any force contesting Funsten. Leaving Gordon to command at his own discretion, Stuart marched with Funsten. Gordon met little resistance. On both counts, Stuart reported, it was a "rapid pursuit of the enemy" toward Culpeper. The horsemen passed deserted enemy camps along the way, around which were scattered stone chimneys, cabins, tables, magazines, books, empty liquor bottles, coats, shoes, and the like.[72]

The evidence pointed to an enemy withdrawal from Culpeper — exactly what Lee wanted. The roads to the Rappahannock filled with retreating blue soldiers. Nearer Culpeper, the immense infantry camps there were found to be empty.[73] The intrepid William Cowles occupied the courthouse easily, though the thought of the July 3 death of his mother still troubled him. With Culpeper occupied and the cavalry advancing, Stuart decided that all of Meade's infantry had retired beyond the Rappahannock. Only Union cavalry remained. Nearly four thousand of them took up a strong position on "Cumberland George's" hill, east of Culpeper. To confront this threat, Stuart now turned to Gordon. Minus Cowles, Gordon advanced and began demonstrating. Heavy artillery and small-arms fire pounded the North Carolina cavalry brigade's advance.[74] The 4th moved to clear the crossings over Mountain Run, and the 5th moved in support. The 5th's veteran adjutant, J. Turner Morehead, son of a former state governor, received a vicious wound when a bullet crashed into his mouth, broke out his teeth, and passed out the back of his neck. By some miracle Morehead lived, but his bloody mouth clearly warned of Federal marksmanship.[75] Still the Tarheels continued through the storm. Farther right, the 4th charged a stubborn cavalry detachment and drove it across Mountain Run. The gallant Colonel Ferebee fell wounded, depriving Gordon of his sole experienced regimental commander.[76]

Gordon's demonstration descried the strength of Kilpatrick's position. Stuart decided he would gain nothing from attacking across gun–swept fields, so he chose to await Fitz Lee. Stuart had rightly expected that Fitz would have to fight a Federal reconnaissance directed at the fords of the Rapidan. Once the sound of distant fighting signaled that Lee was indeed driving the enemy toward Stevensburg, Stuart began sidling his troopers left, toward Brandy Station. If Stuart could reunite with Fitz Lee on Fleetwood Hill, Kilpatrick's escape would be blocked. With Fitz's help, Stuart did not doubt his ability "to interrupt their retreat and have them at my mercy." While a few artillery pieces occupied Kilpatrick, Funsten's two regiments took the lead. The remainder of the North Carolina cavalry brigade followed. In this way, the Rebels bypassed Kilpatrick.[77]

Stuart sent courier after courier to R. E. Lee to keep him informed of the cavalry's progress, and pressed on as his chief directed.[78] Farm roads, such as the one leading to Rixeyville, served as Gordon's highway toward Brandy Station. It was an area the veterans knew well. Past Chestnut Ford Church they rode, toward the Barbour House and the bloody field of June 9. Because the terrain was open, Kilpatrick discovered Stuart's flanking move and moved to beat it. The force chased by Lee arrived at about the same time. Everywhere, a race for the Fleetwood heights ensued. When Stuart's Confederates reached the open plain near the Slaughter Bradford house, north of the Orange & Alexandria Railroad, they saw a small group of enemy cavalry to their right. Farther on, Kilpatrick's dense columns came into view. These horsemen were trotting along the tracks toward Brandy, parallel to Stuart's march. Beyond the tracks, puffs of smoke marked Fitz Lee's progress and lent hope to a quick junction. At Stuart's order, Gordon dispatched the 1st to strike the first enemy detachment. Ruffin led this assault with ability. The "Bloody First" killed or captured sixty Yankees and reduced this single threat. Elsewhere on the field, however, Kilpatrick's main body pulled ahead in the race for Fleetwood.[79] The Unionists made a great rumbling sound as they rode. According to one witness, "There was no disorder or disorganization in their ranks, as each regiment preserved its own autonomy.... Some regiments were in columns of fours, some in company front, some in squadrons, some actually presenting the regimental alignment."[80]

Already, the enemy's artillery waited on Cumberland George's hill. They shelled the advancing Confederates vigorously, while sharpshooters added more lead. Gordon's column, which Stuart and John Esten Cooke accompanied, came under heavy fire. Hoping to provide some extra protection through maneuver, Stuart told Gordon to move his column along a certain road. Gordon, intending to reply that he would go by a way he knew, said "I'll go by — God!" in a way that made Stuart and Cooke start laughing, even as shells plowed up the ground around them. While the Virginians enjoyed the joke, the Tarheels began to move forward. According to Cooke, "Gordon was superb" in the way he slowly rode at the point of his column, head held high.[81]

Turning leaves had already begun to color the landscape, and now a confused mass of men added more variation. Near Stevensburg, Fitz Lee's gunners fired northward at the distant, indistinguishable masses of moving men. Some of those shells fell among Gordon's and Funsten's troopers. Stuart urged his horsemen in the race, but the shells caused hesitation and confusion. At one point, the 7th Virginia even took the wrong road. Since the 11th Virginia had been detached, that left Funsten with only the 12th Virginia. Next rode Gordon's 4th and 5th, alone because the 1st had been deployed. Last in Stuart's column marched the stray 7th Virginia. The horse artillery had been left behind by the speedy advance. Such was Stuart's order of battle at this critical moment, when Kilpatrick reached the heights near Brandy Station.[82]

The Confederates had to do something quickly. At the column's head, Stuart sent the 12th against Kilpatrick's left flank. To its credit, the understrength 12th managed to cut off more than 1,200 enemy soldiers. Many Unionists broke and ran but most moved on, and still Stuart sought to halt them. The 4th and 5th North Carolina moved along a narrow, sunken farm lane in support of the 12th. Aligned in column of fours, the horsemen followed the road into a field near politician John Minor Botts's house. The large white dwelling, which featured a huge portico on front, stood on a hill about a mile and a half west of Brandy Station.[83]

Below the house, the Confederates stopped, watched the work of the 12th, and waited for orders from Gordon or Stuart. Nobody in gray noticed that their right flank was exposed, but a small, charging force of Lincoln's horsemen did.[84] The tornado came from the right, down a lengthy slope that had shielded the Federals from view; the North Carolinians bolted to the left in what Gordon called "considerable confusion."[85] Shocked, Gordon and Stuart galloped to block the way of the retreating Tarheels. The two made "every effort" to stop the flight, even to the point of drawing their pistols, but the pursuing Federals evinced more persuasive powers. Better than half of Gordon's force scattered.[86]

Even under this onslaught, Gordon's hardiest showed their mettle. At least two troopers, a bugler and a non-commissioned officer from the 5th, had seen the attack coming, but from a distance. At top speed the two men tried to warn their comrades, but were too late. Another Tarheel became a prisoner, but in the act of surrendering he wielded his sabre on his captor. When cavalryman Ham Alexander of the 5th wheeled his horse to retreat, the animal stumbled and fell, trapping Alexander's leg. The grayclad trooper watched the enemy charge past him from this ignominious vantage point. An enemy soldier later moved the horse off his leg— under the cover of Alexander's rifle barrel.[87]

The 7th Virginia stopped the Federal pursuit and evened the score with a flanking charge, but the deed had been done. Because of this disaster, and because of Fitz Lee's misdirected artillery fire, Kilpatrick occupied Fleetwood. Buford came over from Stevensburg and reinforced Kilpatrick. Again, Federal artillery bristled from the Federal position. Fitz Lee's cavalry division, which came up in pursuit of Buford, was likewise unable to prevent the occupation of Fleetwood. Stuart's forces had been reunited, albeit too late.[88]

Above, the sun's journey across the daytime sky neared completion. In the plains below, Stuart resolved to press the action. With charges and countercharges, Lomax's and Chambliss's brigades fought hard. Horseback sharpshooters played the field with eagerness and alacrity. Numerous sabre charges and dismounted advances challenged the Federal defenders. Brandy Station and the woods surrounding it were cleared and a crossfire opened on Fleetwood, but the Federal position stood stoutly. Like the one on Cumberland George's Hill, this position defied the Confederate cavalry. John Esten Cooke described the battle as among the heaviest and most "mixed up" of the war. He remembered seeing nothing but "dust, smoke, and confused masses, reeling to and fro," and hearing nothing but "shouts, cheers, yells, and orders, mixed with the quick bang of carbines and the clash of sabres," and above all "the continuous thunder of the artillery."[89]

In the end, maneuver proved more effective than attack. Fitz Lee's division marched to the left, past the Barbour House and St. James Church, and threatened to cut off the Union avenue of retreat. This persuaded Kilpatrick to withdraw both his and Buford's men across the Rappahannock after nightfall.[90]

With the area south of the Rappahannock cleared, the North Carolina brigade joined Stuart's bivouac near Brandy Station. The Tarheels had done little since the 4th and 5th's disaster. Indeed, while Stuart's other units fought for Fleetwood and then pursued Kilpatrick's retreat, Gordon's Brigade evidently remained in reserve so it could recover. Though many of Gordon's veterans reformed after the break, staff officers still had stragglers to gather. Later, in bivouac, General Gordon's disappointment and sorrow must have been great. The 1st had fought admirably and Ruffin had shown promise, but nothing made up for the performance of the 4th and 5th. Why had the two units broken before a smaller force, when earlier the brigade had served flawlessly? In his report, Gordon made no excuses or offered no explanations; he simply stated the facts. Manifestly the brigade's lack of experienced regimental leadership had taken its toll, as had the battle's confusion. The terrain had played its own tricks by protecting the Federal attackers from detection. Still, in the final analysis, the fault was Gordon's. He had left his brigade's flank exposed, perhaps because of his inexperience as a brigade commander. Nonetheless, he received no censure in Stuart's after-action reports.[91]

This setback notwithstanding, the Rebel cavalrymen had reason to be glad. Stuart had regained the room necessary to maintain his screen. Stuart had coordinated the various elements of assault—horse artillery, cavalry, sharpshooters, and dismounted troopers—with skill.[92] Indeed, though the Confederates had achieved less tactical success, the cavalry's efforts and the army's advance achieved positive strategic results. The army's flank march continued. Because the cavalry scouted and screened with skill, the infantry would have the opportunity to achieve the greater success.

Stuart's first order of business on the morning of October 12 was to ensure the security of his rear and the army's supplies. He first directed Young to Culpeper's depot to guard the unloading of quartermaster's and commissary stores. Further, to protect against an enemy advance toward Culpeper, Stuart established a picket below Fleetwood. This done, Stuart turned Fitz Lee's division, Funsten's Brigade, and Gordon's Brigade to their duties. General Lee wanted Stuart to guard Ewell's flank as he moved toward Warrenton by way of Rixeyville. Funsten assumed the duty of advance guard while Gordon and Fitz Lee took position on Ewell's right and rear. Lee's and Funsten's troopers, as well as those Confederates who remained near Culpeper, fought enemy forces often during the day, keeping them at bay.[93]

The North Carolina Cavalry Brigade, which followed mostly in Ewell's wake, had an uneventful march. Gordon shrugged off the previous day's events and led with confidence. Now that the 2d had rejoined the brigade, Gordon could bring his full strength to bear. The cool weather was pleasant, but the scenery was not. The cavalrymen passed fields in which dead men and horses and abandoned arms lay scattered. One especially sickening sight was the body of a prominent local citizen; a stray bullet had plowed a huge, bloody hole in the man's forehead. Crossing the Hedgeman River at sunset, Gordon's Brigade passed this carnage and joined Funsten in occupying Warrenton.[94]

Early on Tuesday morning, the roads south and west of Warrenton filled with Confederate infantrymen. As a prelude to the next move against Meade, Lee's foot-soldiers were gathering. To shield this concentration from enemy eyes, Stuart's men crawled out of their bedrolls and assumed control of the roads east of Warrenton. About 10:00 A.M., General Lee asked Stuart to reconnoiter toward Catlett's Station on the Orange & Alexandria Railroad. Before marching, Funsten and Gordon paused to replenish their ammunition from brigade ordnance wagons. Lomax meanwhile led his men to Auburn, where he learned that Meade had occupied Warrenton Junction, a mere six miles to the southeast. Stuart, who came up a bit later with Gordon and Funsten, received Lomax's report with great interest. Certainly, this required further investigation. While Lomax held the rear at Auburn and patrols rode southward to check Three-Mile Station on the Warrenton branch of the Orange and Alexandria, Gordon and Funsten prepared to look eastward in force.[95]

It was after 4:00 P.M. when "to horse, lead out" sounded again and the long column of cavalrymen marched for Catlett's Station. Gordon's Brigade brought up the rear, so it was near sunset before the Carolinians crossed Cedar Run, just outside Auburn.[96] The column's leading elements made better progress, however. Not four miles down the road, Rebel scouts found a vantage point from which to survey the countryside.[97] For long minutes Stuart studied the exciting scene: beyond more open fields and woods, countless Federal wagons dotted the landscape between Warrenton Junction and Catlett's Station. Enemy soldiers streamed northward along the railroad, here in detachments and there in dense columns. Plainly, the retreating Meade marched for Manassas. Here, at last, was an opportunity for the army to cave in Meade's flank! An officer galloped off to tell General Lee the happy news, but the man faced a long and difficult road.[98]

What an inviting target that moving mass of unsuspecting enemy soldiers offered Jeb Stuart! He believed he could strike Meade's columns with effect, but decided the infantry could do so with greater success. As such, he resolved to conceal his forces and await Lee's attack. While Stuart waited, events altered Rebel fortunes. Even as Stuart advanced on Catlett's, enemy forces swept Lomax aside and captured Auburn. Through some oversight, Lomax did not inform Stuart of this setback. Instead, scouts told Stuart that both Auburn and Three-Mile Station were in Federal hands. North Carolina scouts confirmed this information. Not long after Gordon's Brigade crossed Cedar Run, one of Gordon's scouts discovered enemy in their rear. Gordon quickly informed his commander.[99] Thus, even as darkness claimed the Virginia landscape, Stuart realized that he was trapped between two Federal columns: one to the south and west, moving by way of Three-Mile Station and Auburn along the Weaverville-Greenwich Road; and the other to the east, along the line of the Orange and Alexandria Railroad. There was no way out.[100]

Stuart left his observation post and rode toward Auburn, a town that consisted of a residence, post–office, and blacksmith shop. Stuart met Gordon along the way and asked for an update on the situation. "Come, and I will show you," Gordon said.[101] They rode to a vantage point and, in the gathering darkness, saw that the path to Warrenton and the main army was indeed blocked. Columns of Federal infantry and artillery marched across their front along a road the led from left to right. This was the Greenwich Road, which intersected with the Auburn Road at a high-banked ford. A glance to the left disclosed Cedar Run, the millrace that trailed across both the Auburn and Greenwich roads and extended into the distance. Blue soldiers were fording this stream and marching toward Greenwich. Only some distant woods, to the right of the Auburn Road, bore no sign of the enemy.[102] The possibility of discovery was real. Gordon, like Stuart, felt the weight of their predicament. "We were surrounded by Yankees in force on all sides," he later wrote. "Our situation seemed critical."[103]

Stuart decided to hide his men until dawn. Stealthily, six separate messengers stole into the night to deliver requests for help to General Lee. That done, Stuart turned to a more present problem. How does one keep two brigades of cavalry quiet and hidden from an enemy in proximity?[104] The answer lay three hundred yards to the right. With surprising alacrity, officers herded troopers, wagons, and seven guns off the road and past a concealing woodline. The ground sloped sharply upward there, creating friendly, sheltering hills. The hills protected something of a valley that was almost within sight of Auburn. Into that hiding place the gray cavalry rode. Just moments after the Rebels gained cover, another column of Federal soldiers trudged by. These men barely missed an opportunity to destroy Jeb Stuart.[105]

As at Jack's Shop, Stuart made the seriousness of the situation known. The night's orders were obvious. Talking must be kept to whispers. All animals must be quieted. Sabres, canteens, and spurs must not rattle. Except for pickets, movement was hazardous, so most remained still. Some sat in their saddles or dismounted and kneeled beside their mounts.[106] Others stood, holding their animals' halters. Many felt hungry, including the animals that had not been fed since morning, and the cold did not help either.[107] One cavalryman remembered standing quietly "almost within a stone's throw" of the enemy. No doubt everyone listened for some hopeful sound. The noise of Meade's army filled the night air: voices of Yankee soldiers and the clopping of horse hooves; the uneven rolling of wheels; and the clanking of equipment. From the little valley nothing could be heard except for an occasional horse's neigh or donkey's bray.[108]

Surely these were the longest hours Gordon had ever endured, but he and his men had "unbounded confidence" in Stuart. The waiting game seemed endless, especially for those Confederates on the hillcrests who could actually see the enemy columns crossing the rocky ford of Cedar Run.[109] Then, toward morning, the situation worsened when a Federal division waded the stream, turned right, placed its batteries on a hill, and stacked arms. They camped not 250 yards away from the Rebel position. A second Yankee division followed and turned left after crossing Cedar Run. They too settled in to prepare breakfast. The roads cleared, but brightly burning campfires showed that Federals were everywhere.[110]

Stuart had heard nothing from General Lee. It looked as if the Southerners would have to cut their way out. Once the Federal corps camped, the Rebels checked their arms and pushed their guns into position on the hillcrest. More slow minutes of waiting brought no change, except for a dense fog that settled in with the dawn. A few enemy soldiers began searching for water close to the Confederate positions. Detection appeared seconds away.[111]

At long last, the sound of musketry drifted through the fog from the west. That must be Lee with the infantry! If the cavalrymen were going to escape, the time was now. Stuart waited until the firing sounded more general, and then gave the order. From the hilltop, the

Horse Artillery began pumping shell and canister into the enemy camps. The resulting surprise, carnage, and confusion, said Private Coltrane, "was wonderful to behold." Coffee and pots spilled into the fires; half-eaten breakfasts crashed to the ground. Shells shrieked and men screamed. Many Federals ran and some died, but more reached for their weapons and prepared to fight back.[112] With the cool efficiency of veterans, the Federals recovered from the initial shock, formed into line of battle, and stepped off. Using the rolling ground as cover, the advance soon threatened the Confederate flanks. Stuart's Horse Artillery turned back one assault, but Unionist cannon fire soon forced the gunners to withdraw. Almost simultaneously, the sound of musketry to the west sputtered and died. This brought a question to every mind: how could an enemy pressed on two sides — here by Stuart and over there by Lee — recover so easily? Was it possible that there had been no Confederate infantry advance? Actually, a portion of Ewell's infantry had marched to Stuart's aid, only to be discouraged by stray shells from the Horse Artillery. This left Stuart's cavalrymen alone, facing what Stuart called "an unequal contest with an army corps."[113]

Stuart summoned Gordon. "For God's sake take the First North Carolina and cut through," he said, and directed Gordon to cover the left, which extended across the Auburn-Catlett's Station Road. Blue troops marched across an open field toward this most critical and vulnerable road, aiming to close Stuart's avenue of escape.[114] Gordon, as he formed the 4th and 5th into a dismounted line to hold the road, understood the threat to the road and turned to the 1st. "Pointing to the glittering bayonets just below, [Gordon] excitedly shouted, 'Charge those fellows!'" The 1st wheeled into column of fours, passed over a ditch and a high rail fence, and pressed on. Spartan-like, the Carolinians thundered down on an infantry regiment, rode over a skirmish line, and took several prisoners.[115] The air thickened with shot, shell, and bullets. The strength of the main Federal enemy line quickly began to tell. "Just then a storm of leaden hail struck the head of the column," a historian explained. "Many men and horses reeled and fell.... The tall form of Ruffin now rose in his stirrups and turning round he exclaimed in soft appealing tones, but heard by all, 'My men, all I ask is — follow me.'" The men could not follow Ruffin for long though, for a bullet crashed into his skull.[116] At that, hesitation and uncertainty gripped the 1st. Would Stuart's cavalry meet its bane on this field? Not if Gordon could help it. Indeed, Stuart later testified that Gordon bravely and ably took and maintained control of the field. The faithful Cowles broke the spell and led Company A in a charge. Barringer, who still walked with a cane because of his Brandy wound, helped rally the rest of the regiment, and personally captured "the whole of" the 126th New York.[117]

The battle swirled around Ruffin's motionless body. Thanks to the 1st's fighting, the enemy paused behind a stone fence. The Carolinians could not, however, overcome the sheer numbers of their foe.[118] Cowles decided that the 1st had done all it could:

> Seeing that we were not supported, and the regiment at this time I do not think amounted to more than two hundred men, while line upon line of the enemy's infantry, in double ranks, was steadily approaching, I ordered the regiment back, which order was executed in style by the commanders of the companies.[119]

Gordon, who had watched the whole affair from a "slight eminence," next met with Cowles to issue further instructions. Shot and shell flew about them while they talked, at least one and possibly two projectiles struck the general. Gordon reeled in his saddle, threw his hand up, and began bleeding profusely from his face. Cowles watched his leader fearfully. William Blackford, who rode up with orders from Stuart, thought Gordon badly hurt. Gordon saw blood on his uniform and, for a moment, could not figure out what had happened. Then he checked himself and discovered that only the surface of his nose was bleeding. With obvious relief, Gordon said, "It is a mere scratch."[120] He then dropped the matter. Cowles's withdrawal had been the proper move, Gordon said. Indeed, the Federal advance had been halted and the avenue of retreat beckoned. "See there," he said, pointing toward the valley of Cedar Run, where Confederate wagons, artillery, and troopers were already making their way toward Auburn and beyond.[121]

Funsten's Brigade, which had been fighting principally as sharpshooters, dismounted and formed the rearguard. While Funsten held the door open and the horse artillery discouraged pursuit, the bloody-faced Gordon and his brigade fell into the column, rode across the run, and headed for Warrenton. Unhindered, they passed a deserted Auburn. The enemy infantry could not pursue; soon, blue stragglers were the only sign that the enemy was near. Once Stuart judged the column safe, he ordered it to halt for feed while he dashed ahead to find Lee. After a short rest, the column moved out in search of the army's right.[122]

Early that same morning, Ewell's and Hill's corps joined Lomax's Brigade and left the Warrenton area. They aimed for Greenwich, beyond which they hoped to find retreating enemy columns along the railroad. Gordon and Funsten soon came up from Auburn and took position on the right of the infantry, but saw no action. That was not the case with General A. P. Hill, who led the way. Before the day's conclusion, he discovered the Federal Third Corps moving northward along the Orange and Alexandria. Here was an opportunity much like the one Stuart had found — and Hill had the infantry Stuart had lacked. Sizing up the scene, Hill figured the enemy on the far side of Broad Run, near Bristoe Station, to be a single corps. Quickly he attacked, and found that another enemy corps was nearby in a strong position behind a railroad embankment. These Federals fired heavily on the exposed Confederate right. Flanked and taking heavy casualties, Hill's men had to fight their way out. It was a disastrous, unhappy moment of lost opportunity for the Army of Northern Virginia. The cavalry might have prevented this disaster, but because of wayward marching Stuart missed the action and his column did not reach Bristoe until after nightfall.[123]

The day ended sadly for the infantry and without result for the cavalry, but it had been a high point in Gordon's life. His men had proven themselves beyond all expectations. With about thirty men, Major Barringer had charged through the Union lines before joining Stuart farther down Cedar Run, but only three officers and twelve men made the entire journey.[124] All told, nearly one hundred men and officers from the First fell in the action, including Private John Carver of Company G, who fought so hard that he absorbed seven wounds. Gordon, by controlling the field at Auburn with Murat-like tenacity, proved himself worthy of his rank. Men took note. Peter W. Hairston, whom Gordon had once recommended to serve on the board of the Yadkin Navigation Company, told his wife that while Gordon "came very near having his nose shot off," he "is gaining a considerable reputation as an officer."[125]

Soon after Bristoe Station, General Lee decided to pull back to the Rappahannock. There were several factors in his decision. Primary was the lack of provisions in the area. Many of the Confederates were also barefooted and coatless, and the weather was not improving. Finally, Meade was growing stronger by retreating toward his Washington base. While withdrawal preparations progressed, Lee directed Stuart to continue watching the enemy, who was entrenching near Bull Run. Accordingly, early on October 15, the Confederate cavalry went to work. Young's Brigade was still coming up from Culpeper, but the rest of Stuart's command had been reunited for the chase. For his part, Gordon continued to be troubled by the pain of his wound.[126] Luckily the bullet had just nicked his nose, but that did not ease his discomfort. The pain came more from the ball's power than anything; its concussion caused blood to settle about Gordon's eyes for several days, and his nose remained sore to the touch. Gordon did not need time for recuperation, however, so his war continued.

At a point near Manassas Junction, the red-eyed general found a Federal picket line and drove it in. Fitz Lee's division, after crossing Bull Run, had a worse time of it when a cavalry and infantry attack forced a vicious fight for McLean's Ford. While that struggle developed, Stuart learned that an enemy wagon train had not crossed Bull Run and was exposed to capture. The North Carolina Cavalry Brigade, being the nearest available unit, rode off in pursuit of this prize. Stuart joined them. With a guide leading, Gordon followed a winding road. He soon came across "quite a force" of enemy cavalry and artillery about two miles below the junction, posted to cover the road on which the trains were traveling. Funsten took a wide circuit to the east to head off the trains, while Gordon attacked the Federals in front near Yates's Ford, below Blackburn's Ford. Beckham's horse artillery dueled with enemy artillery and Gordon's men dismounted and engaged the Federals, who were barricading the road or hiding in dense thickets. The enemy's hot firing, recalled Cooke, made the men nervous, but the Tarheels soon rallied and pressed the Yankees. This "brisk encounter of small-arms" lasted until dark, when the enemy withdrew in the confusion and left their dead on the field. Funsten had little luck in capturing the Union wagons, but in the Confederate view his advance contributed to the enemy retreat.[127]

This fight looked a bit different from the Federal viewpoint. When the struggle began, only the 3d Pennsylvania Cavalry stood between Gordon and the wagons. For most of the day, those Yankee troopers had seen enemy horsemen following them. It was not until 4:00, however, that the rearguard platoon was fired on, probably by Gordon's men. An hour later, when the Federals reached a point two miles from Yates's Ford — the trains were preparing to cross the river there — they had to halt and face the rear. The reason was that a strong cavalry force was "approaching by a road from the west at right angles to the one by which we had been marching, evidently with the intention of cutting us off from the ford and capturing the wagon train, which was plainly visible." The troopers barricaded the road with trees and fence rails, took cover in the woods flanking the road, and called for help. Soon the whole regiment was on hand, while General Buford dispatched more men to cover the wagons.[128]

By this time, Gordon's troopers were forming their battle lines. Primarily positioned in an open field, the brigade made a half-circle around the Federal position. Buford arrived on the scene at about this time and ordered a reconnaissance. The task fell to Corporal Andrew Speese of the 3d Pennsylvania Cavalry. Holding his hand up as if to indicate a truce, Speese rode toward the distant lines. Rain fell lightly. The men in the battle-line ahead wore ponchos, so the corporal could not tell with certainty what color they wore. Reaching a point about fifty yards from the lines, the corporal clearly saw Confederate gray pantaloons between the bottom of the troopers' ponchos and the tops of their boots. Calling out to a mounted officer, Speese indicated that he had a message to deliver. The Southerner dispatched a sergeant to investigate:

The man, hesitating, asked me if I was going to shoot, and upon my replying in the negative, two of them rode out from the ranks with cocked pistols. I asked them what troops they were. The reply came quicker than I had expected: "General Gordon's Brigade of North Carolina Cavalry." At this juncture the officer to whom I had first spoken to rode forward and I asked him where General Gordon was, as I had a message for him. This inquiry threw him off his guard, and raising his hand and pointing to the woods on the left said, "General Gordon is up there placing a regiment in position," and that he would send word to him. He thereupon directed the sergeant to inform General Gordon that a messenger was awaiting him from the Yankee General.[129]

As the men talked, a battery came up, unlimbered, and took position in front of Gordon's line. Speese took this as a cue and suggested to the Rebel officer that he would wait half way between the lines until Gordon arrived. The officer agreed. When the Yankee corporal got close enough to his own lines, he yelled "General Gordon's Brigade of North Carolina Cavalry!" Buford heard him and galloped away, probably to seek reinforcements. Ten minutes later the sergeant rode up to Speese. "General Gordon presents his compliments to General Buford and is ready to receive his communication." Speese told the sergeant that he had no message, and that it was only a ruse to find out who the foe was and whether infantry would be needed. The disgusted sergeant replied, "This is a damned nice story for me to tell General Gordon."[130]

Conversation at an end, the battery opened up and the Rebels began testing the Federal position. Gordon skillfully launched at least three separate charges against the Yankees, as well as a few smaller probes and a flanking attack. Horse artillery fire played havoc on a Federal squadron moving here and there to plug gaps in the line; one shot struck an orderly sergeant square in the body under his bridle arm, tore him to pieces, passed between the head of another trooper and his horse, and finally spent itself after crippling several more horses. A fresh Federal regiment and a battery arrived an hour an a half after the fight began. More than once Gordon's maneuvering nearly won out, but in the end the Yankees saved their trains and safely crossed the stream. It was about 10:00 P.M. before all had done so.[131]

After the fight, Gordon's Brigade bivouacked in a hollow near Manassas, again not far from old Cantonment W. N. Edwards. Rain continued falling that night, making the men cold and wet as well as hungry. On the rainy morning of October 16, Stuart left Fitz Lee at Manassas to guard the rear. He then took Hampton's division northward toward Groveton. Strengthened by Young's Brigade, Stuart hoped to cross Bull Run above Sudley Ford and threaten Meade's right by slicing behind Centreville. The horsemen slopped through muddy roads and across the rushing Bull Run, but Meade's officers had placed their blue soldiers well. A heavy picket challenged Gordon at Groveton. The result was a "warm little affair" in which the North Carolinians drove the enemy. The Yankee presence forced Stuart to detour through Gainesville before he forded the Little Catharpin and bivouacked near Stone Castle. Some skirmishing attended this movement, but the day's torrential rainfall hindered most military operations. Later, Gordon and his staff stopped for the night at a local residence. They found corn and supper and then slept on the floor by the fire. The command moved by Gum Springs toward Frying Pan Church the next day, a Saturday that offered fairer weather. Gordon, Cooke, and another staff officer, Reid Venable, rode along together "merry and light hearted." Parts of Gordon's Brigade and Young's Brigade executed some work near there, but the main diversion came when the men found chinquapins, persimmons, wild grapes, and apples and enjoyed a veritable feast. As a backdrop, fall foliage dressed the whole countryside in splendor.[132]

The Bristoe Campaign now ended in one final blaze of glory. A summons from General Lee, plus the fact that Stuart figured he had accomplished his objective, resulted in the Confederate cavalry's withdrawal from the Frying Pan Church area. Beginning at sundown, the cavalrymen retired the way they had come. Hampton marched toward Gainesville and Haymarket. Fitz Lee rode by way of Manassas Junction and Bristoe Station. On October 18, Kilpatrick's cavalry division and six pieces of artillery, supported by infantry, made it known that Stuart would not withdraw unpursued. Kilpatrick, it is said, remarked over dinner one day that "he would not press Stuart so hard, but he [Stuart] had boasted of driving him [Kilpatrick] out of Culpeper, and he was going to give him no rest." The Federals followed the Confederate rearguard toward Buckland by way of Gainesville. Stuart, realizing his precarious situation, ordered Fitz Lee to come up and monitor his right while Hampton continued toward Buckland.[133]

Fitz Lee had camped near Auburn on the eighteenth, so he had to cover a few miles before he could take position. While he waited, Stuart halted along Broad Run, at Buckland Mills, on October 19. Posting sharpshooters and artillery on the stream's south bank, he hoped to delay the Federals. Several hours worth of skirmishing commenced, in which, Stuart reported, the enemy "was baffled in repeated attempts to force the passage of Broad Run." Gordon's Brigade, which had dismounted, fought fiercely. Late in the morning, when the Unionists gave up the frontal approach and began probing around the Rebel flank, Stuart heard from Fitz. It came in the form of a suggestion. If Stuart would withdraw toward Warrenton and draw Kilpatrick after him, then Lee would strike the exposed Federal left and rear. The brilliant plan delighted Stuart, so he immediately agreed to it. At the sound of Lee's signal gun, Stuart replied, he would turn and attack Kilpatrick to join the fun.[134]

Slowly, Hampton's men began retiring along the broad, straight New Baltimore–Warrenton Turnpike. The withdrawal puzzled Gordon's men, but the brigades of Gordon, Young, and Rosser drew Kilpatrick's cautious Federals after them. Kilpatrick, not suspecting a trap, boasted that he would "catch Stuart before he got to Warrenton." About two and one-half miles northeast of Warrenton, the Confederates reached a low range of hills known as Chestnut Hill. While a weak line of skirmishers offered protection, Stuart stopped and formed his column behind the hills. Gordon dismounted his men in a field alongside the road and told them to be ready to move at a moment's notice. That done, Gordon joined Stuart. The waiting began. By mid–afternoon, the Federal advance caught up and began ascending Chestnut Hill: the column "of splendidly equipped cavalry came marching on with flags fluttering and arms glittering in the bright autumn sunshine," wrote Blackford. They soon reached a point within two hundred yards of Stuart's leading elements. As if on cue, the sound of artillery rolled across the countryside from the direction of Buckland. That was Fitz Lee! The order to mount spread along Gordon's column. A dozen bugles sounded the call "to saddle." The brigade trotted back into the road and began marching up and over Chesnut Hill — toward the enemy.[135]

In column with drawn sabres, Gordon's Brigade manned the center. Young and Rosser took position on either flank.[136] Cowles, second-in-command of the 1st, commanded the column's rear. However, "in the gratification of what I thought would be construed as a pardonable curiosity," he rode to the crest of the hill and saw a "soul-stirring scene":

> Our own column resting in the road with sabres drawn and ready for action, with mounted skirmishers on either flank responding to the enemy's fire; Generals Stuart and Gordon on the right of the road viewing intently the situation; the enemy's column (the pick and flower of the Federal cavalry) confronting us and stretching in column of fours, completely covering the highway in our front as far as we could see, with mounted skirmishers on either flank and evidently in readiness to charge. Not a moment was to be lost; much, as every old cavalryman knows, depended on getting the "bulge on 'em," as Fitz Lee would say.

Stuart turned to Gordon and told him to advance rapidly along the pike. "Now, Gordon, is your time!" he called.[137]

Gordon accordingly rode to the front of his column and sought Rufus Barringer, who still commanded the 1st. "Major Barringer," Gordon said, "charge that Yankee line and break it."[138]

Peter Evans Smith stood nearby. He too saw the Federals drawn up in "splendid array." He also saw Gordon. "Brigadier General Gordown [sic] was a nervous excitable man, but he had the courage and readiness of a born soldier. He had hastily gotten his orders what to do, and what was wanted. He dashed up in person to the front of the 1st, and then said with a calm air that inspired confidence and success, 'Major Barringer, charge those Yankees and break them.'"[139]

Barringer, who "from a sense of duty alone" had recently turned down "numerous solicitations" to become a candidate for the Confederate Congress, accepted the assignment.[140] He ordered his men into a column formation, and then took position at the head of the column with his chief bugler at his side. The rest of the North Carolina brigade formed into column as well, while cavalrymen from other states stretched out on either side of Gordon's flank. Then Barringer gave a command which rang in Southern ears: "Forward, trot, march!" After the men marched a few paces in perfect order, Barringer quickened the pace. "Gallop, March!" he yelled. Then, with the 1st aimed for the enemy, there remained only a single formality. Barringer told the regimental bugler, "Little" Henry Litaker, to sound the charge. The man bore slightly to one side, faced the regiment, and let loose. Bold notes pierced the air. His music

Former state senator Rufus Barringer was destined to lead North Carolina's cavalrymen after Gordon's death (courtesy North Carolina Museum of History).

"fired men and horses to the highest pitch of excitement probably ever seen in battle," a historian later wrote. The men let out a terrific Rebel yell; behind them, bugles from all the division's regiments spread the call.[141] Cowles took an unassigned position at the head of the 1st, yelling "Forward First North Carolina Cavalry; I will lead you!" The smooth, firm ground passed quickly beneath hundreds of horses' hooves. The Confederate brigades bore down on the Federal brigade of General Henry E. Davies.[142] Artillery boomed, sabres flashed, and carbines cracked, and the Federals stood momentarily, but the 1st led the three brigades forward with effective "impetuosity." The 1st drew within fifty yards of the Federal column, with the remainder of Hampton's division not far behind. At that, the blue troopers emptied their pistols and carbines at the Confederates, wheeled, and galloped away in all directions.[143]

Fitz Lee's flank attack struck Brigadier General George A. Custer's Brigade at Broad Run. Unlike Davies, Custer had been ready and was able to keep Lee at bay. Indeed it was Stuart's attack, not Lee's, that really sparked the Federal retreat. Davies's galloping withdrawal uncovered Custer and forced a general retreat, although the Federal fire caused momentary confusion in the 1st. Quickly Barringer reformed his line and resumed the pursuit. The Federals galloped in an orderly fashion for more than a mile, and even wheeled and fired on occasion. Barringer decided to hasten the retreat. At Barringer's command, Cowles and Company A pressed harder and broke the Federal ranks.[144]

At that, Gordon reported, "The enemy fled in great confusion and were pursued for several miles with unrelenting fury." The Confederates pushed their steeds hard, passing riderless horses and running, dismounted blue troopers. Fitz Lee's Brigade chased the enemy more to the right, toward Gainesville. Back through New Baltimore toward Buckland and

Haymarket, Gordon's Brigade enlarged its success. The 5th avenged its Culpeper defeat by routing the 18th Pennsylvania Cavalry; the 1st, 2d, and 4th hunted with glee.[145] Cowles, with what Gordon called "that conspicuous gallantry which always characterizes him," not only helped Barringer lead the chase but also captured five wagons and two enemy ambulances. The haul included Custer's headquarters baggage and papers, as well as discarded weapons. Barringer was perhaps the only man who did not enjoy the chase; near New Baltimore, his horse, Black Shot, became unmanageable and threw him against a house. This aside, the victorious pursuit did not stop until it confronted the lines of Meade's I Corps.[146]

So the Bristoe Campaign ended for the cavalry. Later, Cooke stopped at a Mr. Fletcher's near Rector's Crossroads to get dinner. He enjoyed an excellent free dinner, and then enjoyed the company of four young ladies. The staff-officer found them to be "victims of cavalry charms." One lady, a Miss Eliza, confessed herself to be "a warm admirer of Gen. Gordon." It seemed that the good general had been doing more recently than just beating up on Yankees.[147]

From the infantry camps along the Rapidan to Stuart's bivouacs, Confederates began buzzing about the Buckland fight. A less pleasant sensation plagued the opposing army. Wags called the affair the "Buckland Races," and the name stuck. Ever afterward, memories of the Buckland Races brought smiles to the faces of Stuart's cavalrymen. "It certainly stands alone," Cowles later wrote, "as the *steeple chase* of the war." Lt. Whit Anthony added, "Of all the regular and mounted charges of the war, this was probably the most complete in its success, the most daring and continuous in the onset and the most glorious in the results."[148] Basking in this praise, the cavalry returned to Culpeper on October 20 and established pickets on the south bank of the Rappahannock.

For Stuart, the price of the campaign was 408 killed and wounded, plus exacerbated transportation problems. Overall, however, he viewed his horse-soldiers' performance as superb.[149] Gordon could be pleased with his own work. Consulting with Dabney, he learned that the brigade had captured about five hundred prisoners; in exchange, the brigade had suffered no more than 125 casualties.[150] Stuart later cited Gordon for his "brave example and marked ability" at Auburn, and the cavalry commander might have said more. Beyond the poor showing at Brandy Station, Gordon's North Carolina cavalry brigade had turned in a record unsurpassed by any other cavalry unit. In past battles, Stuart had asked his veteran Virginia units to execute critical duties, but this changed during the Bristoe campaign. In fact, Stuart depended more on Tarheel cavalrymen in this campaign than in any in the Army of Northern Virginia's history. This reflected upon Gordon's leadership. One historian has suggested that none of Stuart's new brigadiers performed any "feat of special brilliance" in the campaign, but James B. Gordon laid claim to the contrary. A short three months ago Gordon had been only a lieutenant colonel, yet these, virtually Stuart's last victories over the Federal cavalry, carried the mark of North Carolina and General Gordon.[151]

Men could not help being impressed with these unheralded Tarheels. When winter came and Stuart began writing his report of the campaign, he thought of his Carolinians. He told his wife: "North Carolina has done *nobly in this army*. Never allow her troops to be abused in your presence."[152] He might have said the same of his friend, the blossoming but still relatively unknown brigadier, James B. Gordon.

12

One Needful Thing

THE BATTLE SMOKE OF THE BRISTOE CAMPAIGN had hardly cleared before Jeb Stuart again decided to show off his command. The date was November 5, a fall day that lent a perfect backdrop for a cavalry review. The place — the sprawling farm of John Minor Botts, near Brandy Station — was well suited. Stuart saw to it that this, like all of his reviews, featured pageantry and drama. At one end of the field, a large Confederate flag fluttered in the breeze. The divisions of Wade Hampton and Fitz Lee arrayed themselves in formation; thousands of men and horses stood proudly beneath their guidons. A reviewing party, which included General Lee and Virginia Governor John Letcher, trotted past the two divisions and admired the hardened warriors. Then Stuart, Lee, Letcher, and the rest of the group stopped to watch. The masses of gray-clad horsemen, as they fell into column and began to march, made an awe-inspiring sight.[1]

Some wondered about the usefulness of this grand display, but the men put on their best. Despite their recent hard service, the troopers were in surprisingly good condition. They had repaired the tears of their uniforms and had polished their weapons. Some had even rubbed their shoes over camp kettles to blacken them. The fighting spirit of these men burned equally as bright. As if in confirmation, bugles blared. Swords leaped from scabbards. On command, the horsemen turned and thundered past the reviewers. They yelled like demons.[2]

It made, wrote Cooke, "A fine spectacle." He noticed General Lee "sitting his horse by the tall flagstaff in his old gray coat and whitening beard." Cooke remembered how "the pretty Mrs. Gen. [John B.] Gordon" watched, and later expressed her delight with the review. This certainly was a moment of which Stuart could be proud. His force, though quite different than the contingent he had led to Pennsylvania, had performed very well in October. The cavalry's newest brigadiers were the main reason for this difference, and perhaps for the solid performance. General Rosser rode at the head of his proud brigade. Elsewhere the youthful General P. M. B. Young sat erect on his horse as he led his Georgians, Mississippians, and South Carolinians forward. On another part of the field marched the tall and handsome General Gordon, whose blooded North Carolina cavalry brigade paraded in its second review in as many days. These men, an observer might say, were Jeb Stuart's students in military and leadership matters, and also his kindred spirits. That made Stuart all the more fond of them. As the cavalry commander told a cousin: "Rosser Young and Gordon are now Brigadiers — also Lomax. Young and Gordon are great beaux."[3]

After the review, Stuart had nothing but praise. "The cavalry is flourishing," he wrote proudly.[4] Behind this positive outlook, however, lurked reality. None present knew it, but the cavalry of the Army of Northern Virginia now faced decline. While the enemy horse improved, Southern supplies and horseflesh continued to dwindle. An admission of defeat was still months away, however, thanks to the men whom Stuart had chosen to lead and to fight.

Almost every time Stuart held a review, fighting followed. In this instance, the Army of Northern Virginia suffered an embarrassing disaster at Rappahannock Bridge on November 7. Only a few of Stuart's horsemen saw action in that fight. Instead, the cavalry corps executed normal duties. Gordon's Brigade, for example, spent November 7 picketing portions of the Rappahannock and Hazel rivers. It took the war a few more days to catch up with Stuart's cavalry. Mine Run, a tributary of the Rapidan River, was the scene of the affair.[5]

As a result of the advantages the Union won at Rappahannock Bridge, the Army of Northern Virginia withdrew to the Rapidan. Gordon's men helped cover the retreat, during which they received a pleasant surprise. At Stevensburg on November 8, the troopers pitched into Meade's cavalry advance to draw them toward the infantry. In the midst of the fight, Wade Hampton appeared for the first time since his wounding at Gettysburg. As the South Carolinian rode his division's battle lines, glad, wild cheers greeted him.[6]

Though he had been out of action for several weeks, Hampton did not miss a beat. He began thinking of raids, not parades. Once the cavalry took up picketing along the Rapidan, Hampton sent Gordon's horsemen to harass the enemy at every opportunity. Lieutenant Colonel Alexander S. (Sandie) Pendleton, assistant adjutant general of the Second Corps, witnessed one such instance. Pendleton told Peter Hairston that he met Gordon's Brigade at midnight on November 18 "going down the river to cross it to surprise a Yankee camp of Cavalry." The North Carolinians ultimately captured about forty prisoners and the wagons of a regiment, some of them belonging to the 18th Pennsylvania.[7]

Some thought the withdrawal to the Rapidan would mark the end of campaigning. For a while, it looked that way; the weather turned colder, and the Confederates started building winter quarters. Soon, however, a construction-stopping report reached headquarters. Federal cavalry had been seen poking about Ely's Ford. Was Meade planning to renew the contest? Hampton's cavalry rode off to investigate.[8] The next day, November 26, Meade showed his hand: he had decided to flank Lee's right. The Mine Run Campaign began when Federal troops crossed the Rapidan at several points, including Germanna and Ely's Fords. Horse scouts saw the movement and sounded the alarm. Not knowing whether Meade's goal was Richmond or his right, Lee sent Ewell's corps (commanded by Jubal Early) and Hill's corps straight at the enemy. Stuart supported the advance. He instructed Fitz Lee, whose division covered the left, to hold the Rapidan west of Clark's Mountain with part of his force. The rest relieved the infantry for the advance. Hampton drew the more active task of delaying the enemy. A relay of couriers found the South Carolinian near Twyman's Store with Gordon, Young, and a detachment of Beckham's Horse Artillery. Initially, Stuart told Hampton to be ready to support pickets at the Rapidan River fords. (Rosser, who was guarding roads leading to Fredericksburg, had to be summoned by telegraph. To his credit, he soon provided excellent intelligence regarding Meade's movements.) Later on the twenty-sixth, Stuart settled on his plan. He ordered Hampton to move his command across the plank road at once.[9]

Before daylight on the twenty-seventh, Fitz Lee was in place, enabling the infantry to move toward the foe. At 9:00 A.M., a tardy Hampton personally arrived at his objective with Gordon's Brigade. The rest of the division was not up yet. Stuart had hoped to contest the Federal advance earlier, but Hampton's late arrival prevented it. Nonetheless, Stuart resolved to do what he could. He ordered Gordon's Brigade forward. Warren County native William

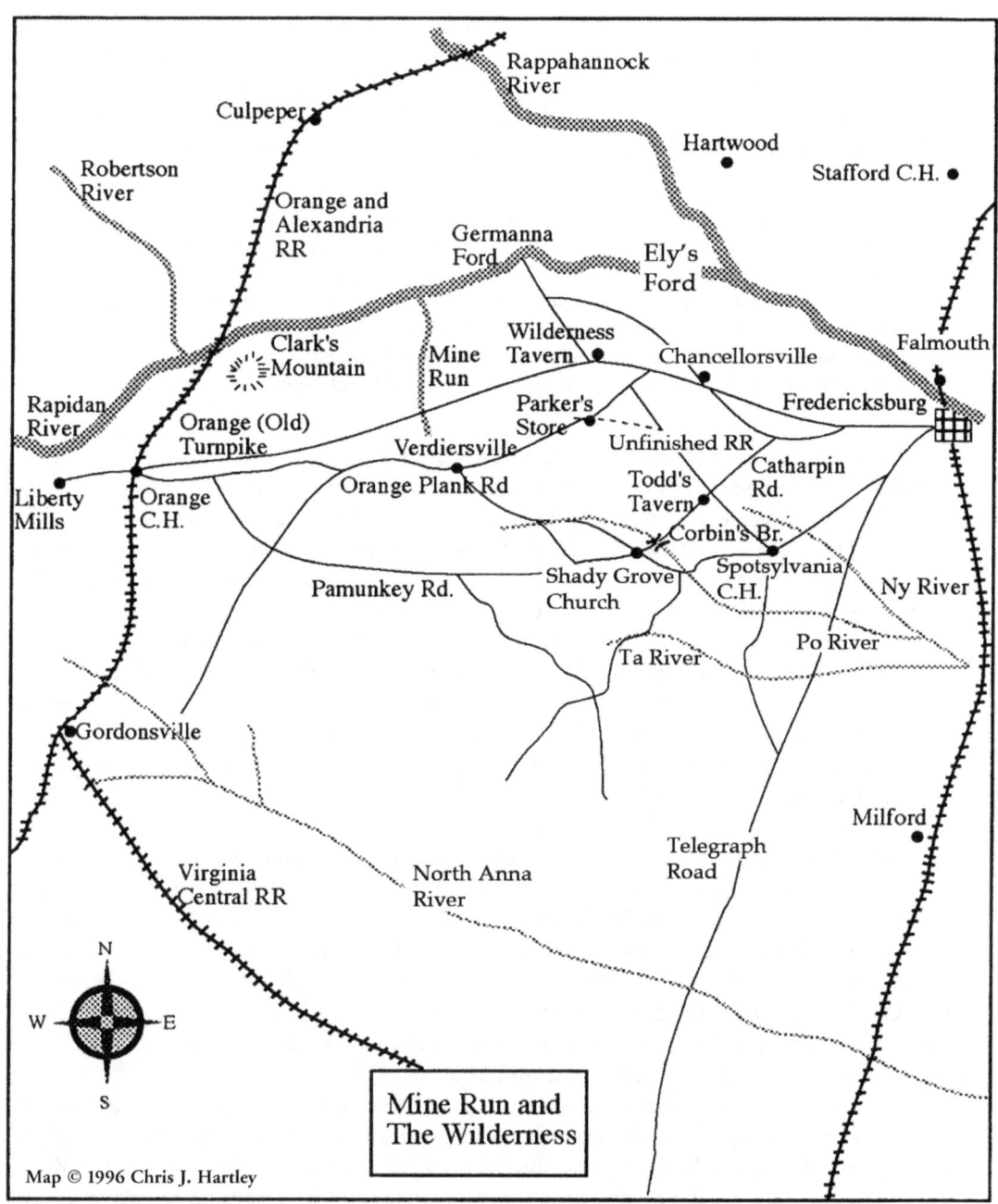

Map © 1996 Chris J. Hartley

Mine Run and The Wilderness

Hayes Cheek, recently promoted to colonel, led the 1st North Carolina Cavalry.[10] Colonel William G. Robinson guided the 2d as they stepped off. Ferebee, still battling his recent wound, nonetheless commanded the 4th North Carolina Cavalry. Lieutenant Colonel Stephen Evans, a tested veteran after surviving the Bristoe Campaign, conducted the 5th. Gordon directed the march along the Orange Plank Road confidently; but he faced a difficult mission. It was up to Gordon to delay the enemy so General Lee could prepare a reception for them.[11]

A division of Confederate infantry fought the enemy hard at Payne's Farm, to Gordon's left, but for the most part Gordon's delaying action prevented a premature general engagement.

At New Hope Church, near 11:00 A.M., the Wilkes Countian made contact with the foe. Stuart described it as "a very unequal contest...." Young had not come up yet; Gordon's men lacked adequate ammunition for their carbines and rifles; and the undergrowth required the Tarheels to fight on foot. Nevertheless, Gordon's Brigade held the Federals at bay long enough for the Rebel infantry to reach suitable defensive positions. Gordon set the example. Said William Cowles:

> He never looked more superb than when ... Stuart was opposing at close quarters the advance of a large body of the enemy's cavalry on the road leading to the right of our lines, and Gordon at the head of the 1st N.C. Cavalry had position in the road and with drawn sabre stood under the fire of the enemy's guns in readiness to charge. Men and horses were shot and fell away from the head of the column, and yet he sat his iron-gray charger with erect bearing amidst the thunder of the guns, determination plainly written in every line of his face as he watched with satisfaction the admirable behavior of the men.[12]

When Hill's corps relieved Gordon's Brigade after 2:30 P.M., Stuart dispatched Gordon to the right. A detachment under Cowles shuttled left, to the turnpike. Hampton, who came up with Young's Brigade at that point, dismounted the bulk of that unit and deployed skirmishers to determine enemy strength. By that time, darkness began to claim the day. The situation stabilized as Meade did not press the issue. In the twilight, the gray-clad infantry fell back to a better defensive line on the west side of Mine Run.[13]

The twenty-eighth day of November, a rainy and windy Saturday, saw the armies square off along Mine Run. Meade deployed his army along hills on the opposite bank and began preparing to advance. General Lee, who expected an attack, prepared his defenses. Confederates dug entrenchments, adjusted and improved positions. Cold weather set in. All the while, the Federals did not budge. That evening, a puzzled Lee ordered Stuart to reconnoiter the Federal left and rear. Stuart told Hampton, whose troopers hovered on the Catharpin Road near Grasty's and Allman's, to be ready to move at an early hour.[14]

Along Mine Run, Sunday remained quiet enough to turn General Lee's mood sour. Gordon and his cavalry, however, saw plenty of action. The day began badly when Stuart and Hampton, by some miscommunication, missed each other. Stuart soon tired of waiting for Hampton and took Rosser's Brigade forward, along the Catharpin Road. He expected Hampton to follow later with another brigade. When the South Carolinian arrived, however, he found Gordon's Brigade already leaving camp under Stuart's orders. Hampton did not know what to do, except to order Young's Brigade to follow. Only a small picket from the Jeff Davis Legion remained behind to protect the army's right flank.[15]

Ahead, Stuart found a Union cavalry camp at Parker's Store. The settlement was surrounded by forest except for a cleared area about two hundred yards to the north and a half mile to the south and southeast. Rosser's Brigade quickly pounced on the enemy there, drove them down the plank road, and captured much of their camp equipage and wagons. Heavy Federal reinforcements rallied their comrades near an unfinished railroad cut. There they adopted a position protected by swamps, heavy timber, and dense undergrowth. Of all the terrain features, the railroad cut posed the greatest tactical problem for Stuart. To prevent the enemy from using the cut as a shield for a flanking maneuver, Stuart deployed Rosser's Brigade to its south. Confederate horsemen fought there for two solid hours, charging and countercharging. Couriers raced back to find Hampton's tardy brigades.[16]

Gordon was three miles back of Parker's Store when Hampton ordered him to advance on the road intersecting the Orange Court House–Fredericksburg plank road. The route brought the North Carolinians up on Rosser's right. Before Gordon could even reach his destination, a courier from Stuart found him. Move up rapidly, the dispatch read; the enemy is forcing Rosser back! The Carolinians urged their horses into a gallop, though the road was muddy and slippery. Gordon soon arrived, his column trailing a single artillery piece. He spotted Rosser's command to the south of the railroad cut, south of and parallel to the plank road, and about eight hundred yards from Parker's Store. He was skirmishing with the enemy and falling back. One of Rosser's regiments could be seen on the plank road about a mile east of the store; it was unengaged and no other friendly troops were in sight. The first thing Gordon did was to help Rosser and Stuart reform Rosser's men. Then Stuart ordered Gordon to attack "on the right of General Rosser." Quickly, Gordon ordered his men to action. He dismounted the 2d North Carolina Cavalry and a portion of the 5th, and directed the 1st to support the artillery and the dismounted contingent. Skirmishers stepped off. A gun of the horse artillery opened up simultaneously, chasing away a column of mounted men. That left a group of Yankee skirmishers near the store.[17] Gordon described what happened next:

> My dismounted men were ordered to charge the Yankee skirmishers, which was done in handsome style, driving them from the railroad cut across the plank road out of their camps, and scattering them through the woods, capturing a number of prisoners, some horses, overcoats, blankets, guns, and their camp equipage. A larger number of prisoners would have been captured (as my right had swung around to the right and rear of the enemy's left) had it not been for a false rumor brought in by courier that a column of Yankee infantry were moving up the plank road in my rear.[18]

Federal bullets flew thickly. One slammed into Gordon's horse and killed it, pitching Gordon roughly to the ground. Few other bullets found their marks, however, and the North Carolinians swept ahead.[19]

Gordon's successful attack diverted pressure from Rosser's front. Rosser wisely took advantage of this by assuming the offensive. Young had been delayed momentarily by a stream, but when he came up on Rosser's left the two brigades joined and pushed forward along the road. In the face of this advance, the enemy fell back. Gordon meanwhile maintained his grip on Parker's Store. Ten of his men marched a short distance to "keep a look out," and were nearly captured by the retreating foe.[20] Nonetheless, in about an hour's time, the fighting ended. There was no further pursuit.

In the throes of this victory, Stuart began receiving reports that the Federals were concentrating against Lee's right, so he decided to call off the reconnaissance. Since Hampton had left only a small picket to cover Lee's right, Stuart warned Lee and then returned the cavalry force to camp.[21]

Stuart's warriors returned to the Mine Run position only to find the armies at rest. Instead of attacking Lee's right as expected, the Army of the Potomac had begun digging in. With no battles to fight, Hampton's troopers simply took position on the right. There, amidst the pines, they awaited a call to action. Daily the Confederates expected attack, and daily nothing happened. Occasional skirmishes broke out as the horsemen scouted Federal positions and the surrounding countryside, but generally all remained quiet. The soldiers of both sides merely suffered through cold days of waiting. Some of the luckier ones ate well and stayed warm. With winter quarters only a few miles away, many servants came to the lines regularly to cook rations and build fires. Gordon's Burt was doubtless among those who came. Others, however, had to scrounge. Troopers from the 2d were spotted exhuming the body of a Federal lieutenant colonel. They relieved the dead man of his boots, overcoat, gloves, suspenders, and socks.[22]

The work of Hampton's troopers almost paid off in another and more important way. On a subsequent scout, horsemen found an exposed portion of the Federal line. Lee decided to attack this vulnerable point. Meade, however, withdrew before the plan was enacted. By December 3, Stuart's pickets walked the banks of the Rapidan. The season of campaigning was over.

For the Confederate cavalry, Mine Run provided an instructive introduction to the winter months. After overcoming the difficulties of Hampton's tardiness, the cavalry had performed well. Gordon's actions in staving off Meade's advance on November 27 and in the battle at Parker's Store two days later ranked among the cavalry's greatest successes of the campaign. Though Mine Run amounted to nothing but a temporary strategic victory for the army, Stuart had good things to say when he wrote his report of the campaign the following April: "The gallantry, energy, and ability displayed by Brigadier-Generals Rosser, Young, and Gordon throughout, and especially at Parker's Store, where Gordon had his horse shot under him, deserve special mention.... These general officers exposed themselves in the most fearless manner, setting the example of individual prowess to their commands." Gordon also earned more respect from the men in the ranks. Wrote J. W. Biddle: "General Gordon is undoubtedly one of the most gallant officers in the service and is always in front seemingly never thinking of his own danger. He had a splendid horse shot under him the other day."[23] Indeed, Gordon's reputation was preceding him on two levels. While some soldiers started calling the dashing bachelor "handsome Jim," others noticed his battlefield performances. "Right nobly [Gordon] has won his spurs," a witness wrote.[24]

Gordon, in writing his own report, ignored his brigade's continuing streak of battlefield successes. He referred only to events without mentioning his personal part in the fight. The general simply ended his report by describing his brigade's losses as "comparatively small," save the deaths of Captain Randall H. Reese and Lieutenant Virginius Copeland of the 2d North Carolina Cavalry. Also unmentioned in Gordon's report, but certainly worth dwelling on, was the loss of W. H. H. Cowles, Gordon's right-hand man. Cowles had led a detachment to the left on November 27 as a result of Ewell's need for a competent officer to take command of the picket lines in his front. At Stuart's suggestion, Cowles was dispatched with a small contingent of North Carolina cavalry. During a skirmish in front of Early's division, a minie ball crashed into Cowles's body. The wound was thought to be fatal, but later proved otherwise. He would need the majority of the winter to recover, however. Stuart sent Cowles a personal note of regret at his wounding, complimenting him for his "services which have won for you a name and a place among the bravest."[25]

James B. Gordon's last winter turned out to be an all-too-short five-month hiatus from fighting. Gordon, who had turned forty-one in November 1863, characteristically packed lots of living into that period. His last days illustrate what may be called the hierarchy of his personality. Duty, his consistent belief in gentlemanly behavior, friendship and camaraderie which imprinted themselves on his brigade, personal improvement through furlough, and love — these were the building blocks of that hierarchy. By winter's end, Gordon would change his mind on the Confederacy's chances for success and then steel himself for his own part in the war.

Duty came first. At the close of the Mine Run Campaign, Gordon's Brigade established winter quarters at Milford Station, along the Richmond, Fredericksburg, and Potomac Railroad in Caroline County. Though more than twenty miles from the Rapidan, the brigade drew a picketing assignment along the river. Though the thermometer often hovered around zero, the Carolinians issued out to river crossings like Jacob's Ford to keep an eye on the enemy. These men saw no threats; they simply endured long and weary work. Other tasks proved just as exhausting, but Gordon and his superiors viewed them as necessary. For example, Gordon's men began leveling the breastworks constructed by Federals during the Mine Run Campaign.[26]

Picketing and the shuttling of troops to this and that point consumed much time, but Gordon managed an occasional foray after the enemy. One of Stuart's officers recalled seeing Gordon's Brigade going out on a scout one snowy January morning.[27] Nothing resulted from this patrol, but a subsequent episode cost Gordon a few men. On January 12, he dispatched a party to raid the railroad and gather information near Accotink, Virginia. To Gordon's chagrin, Federal forces discovered the party, captured two Confederates, and ended the business. Happily, there were more successful outings, such as one that Private Coltrane witnessed. One day a long-range gun opened on the brigade. The brigade's leader asked for a volunteer to shoot the offender. Coltrane, who was armed with a Spencer repeater, stepped forward. Ordered to a nearby log tobacco barn, he maneuvered until he had a clear shot. His mission accomplished, Coltrane returned with Yankee bullets kicking up dust all around him.[28]

Gordon also turned to his administrative tasks. On December 10, he finished his short, terse report of the Bristoe Campaign. He completed his Mine Run report on the twenty-sixth. As an increasingly proficient organizer, he also addressed the demands of his ever-changing organization. Leadership in the brigade stayed fairly constant as the winter began, but there were promotions to be made. In January, B. C. McBride of Watauga County left the ranks to join Gordon's staff as quartermaster.[29] Another change came in the 1st's leadership, where Rufus Barringer received a well-deserved promotion to lieutenant colonel. There had been some consideration of giving Barringer command of a new regiment in North Carolina, but as he preferred the 1st, this promotion suited him. Stuart, who had always considered Barringer to be a good disciplinarian, offered his congratulations.[30] He expressed to Barringer his "high appreciation of that ability and devotion to duty, which has enabled you to raise your Regiment to such a degree of efficiency, that it should be called, 'a pattern for others.'" Stuart hoped that Barringer "may be able to inflict still weightier blows upon our enemy who has so often trembled and fled before the rush of the 1st North Carolina Cavalry."[31] Gordon agreed with his leader's sentiments. In truth, with this promotion, Barringer now joined Cowles as a protégé of Gordon. As Ransom and Baker had done for Gordon, Gordon would try to teach Cowles and Barringer everything he knew about cavalry leadership. The future of the North Carolina Cavalry Brigade rested with these men.

For the cavalry's leaders, there were unpleasant tasks to be handled during those frigid days. Among these was the frustrating, never-ending, almost hopeless job of recruiting the cavalry. According to Robert Lee, "The cavalry of this army, by its hard service, summer and winter, and through the deficiency of forage in the latter season, has become very much reduced." Stuart and the commanding general used every trick, every maneuver, every plan they knew to augment the cavalry. Boards of officers roamed the countryside in search of new foraging places. Fresh reinforcements were sought. Cavalry units were detached or scattered beyond the army's flanks, so man and beast would not exhaust the food in a single area. Yet whatever the measure instituted or requested, and however much time was devoted to repose and reconstitution, Southern horseflesh could not be returned to its heyday. Hunger stalked the stomachs of both man and horse. In many cases, Rebel cavalrymen made do with less than half a prescribed day's ration. Horses gnawed on the bark of trees. The maddening, tiring impact of war continued to increase. Lee wondered whether his army would be effective at all come spring.[32]

What was more, Lee realized that Stuart's two "southern brigades," Gordon's and Young's, enjoyed even fewer opportunities to remount than had the Virginia brigades.[33] Wade Hampton and his subordinates knew it, too, and would have included Butler's Brigade in that list. Not more than five hundred men of Butler's Brigade could mount serviceable horses. Wherever Hampton, Gordon, Young, Rosser, and their fellow officers turned, they saw Confederate cavalrymen wrestling with the difficulties of staying well mounted. Even when dismounted troopers managed to find a replacement horse, high prices forced them into the infantry. For his part, Gordon had the means to keep himself mounted and well clothed. He was also lucky that the gray horse shot at Parker's Store, instead of becoming lame and burdensome, died. As a result, Gordon received $800.00 reimbursement from the government.[34] Gordon was an exception; most had to make do.

To help this situation, Hampton hoped to winter Gordon's brigade in North Carolina, Rosser's in the Valley, and the brigades from distant states along the Roanoke River, where forage and horses were more plentiful. Reorganization would also help. "By these means," Hampton concluded, "Butler's, Young's, and Gordon's could each have a full brigade ready for the spring campaign. But if the horses are kept here this winter on short forage, these brigades will not be in condition for active service, nor will they ever be able to fill up their ranks." Lee did not accept Hampton's plan, however, so the South Carolinian had to expand his efforts in more conventional ways. "How many horses are ready to march?" he would ask. To keep his men suitably fed, he juggled the positions of his various units as best he could. He also ceaselessly sought needed supplies like tents, wagons, and shoes. Hampton knew that his division had to be ready should the enemy threaten.[35]

In overseeing recruitment, Stuart conducted frequent inspections. Toward the end of December, he personally visited Gordon's camps to examine the condition of the North Carolina brigade. He told Hampton afterward, "I desire to express my high gratification at the good order and military discipline in Gordon's and Young's brigades during my recent visit to them." A subsequent inspection turned up equally satisfying results, and proved that Stuart thought a lot of the job Gordon did. In January Stuart took Fitzgerald Ross, a British solider and veteran of the Austrian Hussars, to inspect his troopers. During their three-day tour, the two men visited Young's Brigade, had dinner with the mayor of Fredericksburg, appeared at a ball, toured the Fredericksburg battlefield, attended church, and then visited Gordon's Brigade.[36]

The fact that Gordon maintained his command as well as he did that winter further demonstrates his administrative ability and sensibility. The Wilkes Countian worked with his superiors to find more supplies. He approved furloughs and extensions when appropriate, and forwarded his recommendations up the chain of command.[37] He kept drilling his men to maintain discipline, but did not push them too hard. The results were admirable. The 1st North Carolina Cavalry enjoyed good health for the better part of the winter. The 2d North Carolina Cavalry was "greatly augmented in strength and discipline," and in "fair condition" by spring. On the other hand, situations often contrived against him, and he could do little. Though Gordon did improve the 2d Horse, said William P. Roberts, the regiment never entirely recovered from Hanover.[38] Worse conditions clung to the 4th and 5th as a result of the brigade's winter duty. In January 1864 Gordon told division headquarters that his brigade's picketing assignment was hurting his command. Could something be done to help? Hampton subsequently told Stuart, "The pickets from Gordon's brigade have now to travel 40 miles to their posts. Forage has to be carried to their posts, as none can be obtained near them, and the mere travel is sufficient to prevent any improvement in the horses, if not to break them down." The 4th North Carolina Cavalry especially showed the effects of this duty, counting only 82 effectives by February. When informed of the problem, Lee suggested that Gordon "use videttes on the river, with the reserve camp at Chancellorsville, or other more convenient point [sic] to which forage could be transported."[39] He could do little to help one brigade when his entire army was suffering.

As spring approached, Gordon kept trying to improve the recruiting of his unserviceable cavalry horses; duty was now the cornerstone of who he was. In seeking new solutions, he corresponded with the quartermaster's office in Lynchburg. What can be done to improve recruiting during the winter months? How quickly can horses be restored to the service? Is the current furlough system acceptable? How can better cavalry saddles be obtained? The quartermaster's reply was interesting in that it opposed traditional recruitment methods, like those that Gordon used that very winter. Early in 1864, Gordon assigned Barringer to command the 4th temporarily, while Ferebee recuperated from his wounds. Then he sent the 4th to eastern North Carolina to recruit.[40] Evans's 5th received similar orders in February. Unlike the 1st and 2d, the men of the 4th and 5th had always owned their horses, with more responsibility resulting in keeping mounted. Their condition had declined to the point that Gordon concluded that the Old North State held the best hope for recruiting. The regiments were to disband in North Carolina so that each man could go home to get a new horse or to nurse his old one back to health. According to one of the troopers, the trip proved to be "a great and helpful blessing to our war-wearied men and animals," but Gordon's quartermaster friend had reservations about long furloughs.[41]

In these and other instances, Gordon demonstrated the mental stamina required of leaders. Certainly there was much Stuart's cavalry commanders could not do, but men like Gordon kept at it. For example, a battalion of the Laurel Brigade, try as it might, could only procure about one-fourth of the clothing it needed for the winter. Three hundred members of the 1st South Carolina Cavalry went without blankets until Colonel Black found a charity that could supply him. Gordon personally confronted frustrations of his own — frustrations that did not always concern recruiting. On one occasion, a couple of his men deserted and fled home with stolen horses. Desertion was bad enough, but to take valuable horses was worse. A vengeful Gordon ordered Sergeant J. M. Pugh and two other men to "proceed without delay to Alexander County, N.C., and arrest wherever they may be found Priv. Davidson and accomplices who stole from the Cav. Corps several horses...." Gordon intended to punish those men for their misdeeds.[42]

In 1864, Gordon worked the military courts with persistence. Colonel Joseph Waring of Georgia, who managed the cavalry's courts martial in Milford, could have attested to that. Waring, commander of the Jeff Davis Legion, was a "handsome little officer" who "looked as if he had just jumped out of a bandbox" because of his high-top boots, long black hat plume, the imperial on his chin, and the black mustache over his lip.[43] Gordon spoke often with Waring that winter. The general wanted to apply justice swiftly, and even told Waring that he did not want the court to adjourn "till we get through his cases." Trusted subordinates from the North Carolina brigade helped expedite the matter. William Cheek of the 1st North Carolina Cavalry participated in the trials, and on at least one occasion "managed his case well." Rufus Barringer, who had a reputation in the cavalry as a good lawyer, may have been a part of this court as well. Given such help, the court was able to adjourn on Thursday, January 28.[44]

Court sentences were often harsh. Though it must have pained the gentle Gordon, he knew that the maintenance of discipline had its cost. Examples had to be made. Early that new year, the court sentenced three Tarheels to be shot. Two of them were from the 2d Horse.[45]

By busying himself in many other ways during the winter of 1863–64, Gordon left behind other anecdotal clues as to the hierarchy of his personality. War, it seems, had not changed the outward man. To Gordon, second only to duty was the necessity of being a gentleman. He continued to act with grace and politeness. Tom's comparison of Gordon and Thackeray's unassuming Colonel Newcome still had validity. Consider the fact that Gordon certainly had every reason to be proud of his advancement. His promotion to general went forward when the Confederate Congress returned to work for the first time since he had been awarded his commission. On December 8, Gordon's name was formally submitted to Congress for confirmation to brigadier general, to rank from September 28. After being referred to the Committee on Military Affairs, it was confirmed on February 17. This loftier station did not alter Gordon's friendly personality. One day that winter, Samuel Finley Harper of Lenoir, North Carolina, saw Gordon on a street near Orange Court House. Harper, who thought Gordon did not know him, was surprised when Gordon approached and spoke to him. Harper later described Gordon as "very affable and pleasant, an exceptionally handsome man, and a gallant officer."[46]

Of the few extant stories about James Gordon, a good many of them show the man at parties. That winter had its own example. A lady of the neighborhood invited Gordon, Cheek, trooper Noah Foard, and many majors and captains from the brigade to a huge feast. When they sat down to eat, the hostess said that the dinner was not exactly what she had intended because the main course, a goose, was missing. The lady then turned to Gordon and said, "Some of your soldiers got it night before last." Luckily, the general escaped this embarrassing incident when Foard confessed. He could assure those present that the goose was tasty, thanks to the foraging talents of a trooper from Company F.[47]

Friendship and camaraderie also were important to him. The gentleman was equally liked by his brother officers. One of Gordon's closest friends, the "gay and gallant" P. M. B. Young, spent a lot of time with Gordon that fall and winter. Young was known for his October 12 action at Culpeper during the Bristoe Campaign, when his brigade staved off the advance of a huge enemy force by skirmishing and making a show of force. Magruder-like, Young had fires lighted everywhere and then had his brigade band march to and fro, playing all the while.[48] This bold spectacle not only discouraged attack but also served to underscore his motto, "Here goes for hell or promotion." Young, who was the "beau ideal" of a cavalry leader, with the ability to take his men's hearts by storm, was also a ladies' man. He was known to receive treats such as baskets of vegetables from the local ladies.[49]

Gordon and Young were so much alike that they fell to trading jests. One favorite joke between them was to kid the other about the poverty of their respective states. Young would tell Gordon that Tarheels lived on persimmons; Gordon would fire back that Georgians were overfond of whortleberries. This continued until a certain day when the North Carolina Cavalry Brigade reined in and chose a campsite. Gordon noticed a lovely spot beneath a persimmon tree, so he decided to place his tent there. As he approached, he saw a squad of men drawn up under the tree. Gordon asked, "Who are you and what are you doing?"

Saluting with his sabre, a sergeant who led the squad replied, "I have been ordered by General Young to guard this persimmon tree until General Gordon should come up, and then turn it over to him for the use of his brigade!" Good natured as he was, it was a long time before the proud Gordon got over this well-planned barb.[50]

John Esten Cooke recalled a salvo exchanged by Gordon and Young during the Bristoe Campaign. Near Little River, Young's Brigade came off picket duty and looked for an opening in the cavalry column that was marching past on the turnpike. Rosser passed with his brigade. Next came Gordon's troopers. Either Young did not see the Tarheels or did not care, because he moved anyway, cutting Gordon's column. "Who's brigade is that?" cried Young.

'Gordon's,' came the reply.

"Where is he?"

"Here I am," Gordon said.

"Gordon, if you don't take that thing out of the way, I'll charge it." Young said, but then turned his attention to other "important" matters. "Have you anything to drink?"

"No, have you?"[51]

Another barb directed at Gordon was apparently not unique to Young, but he doubtless made use of it when necessary. "We used to tell him," recalled Cooke, "that his rapid rise to the rank of General was the result of his 'personal, political, and pecuniary position;' but that alliterative accusation was only a jest."[52]

Gordon's quiet charisma touched those who bore weightier responsibilities as well — including one important Virginian in particular. Carolina veterans have said that Gordon was a favorite of Stuart.[53] An indication of that is the amount of time the two men spent together that winter. Waring, when not in the courtroom, campaigned with Stuart and Hampton to have the "Little Jeff" Legion increased to a regiment. Waring often noted Gordon at Stuart's side during such conversations, such as on Friday, January 8, when Waring saw Stuart and Gordon riding the train together to and from Milford. As the winter continued, sightings of the two men together became frequent. Their relationship had its foundation in army business, but Stuart took interest in Gordon's personal affairs.[54] Familiarity also enhanced Stuart's confidence in Gordon's abilities. As of February 1864, the size of the force Gordon commanded equaled one-sixth of Stuart's corps. Later, when Hampton journeyed to South Carolina on furlough, Stuart again entrusted Gordon with temporary command of Hampton's division. In the coming spring, the cavalry leader would give Gordon an independent command of even more importance.[55]

The character of leaders can often be seen in the character of their units. This is certainly true of the men of the North Carolina Cavalry Brigade, who were bold and reckless to a fault, like their leader. Coltrane described how the North Carolinians eased their burden that winter by trading with the enemy. Coltrane rode down to the Rapidan one day and held up a paper, signaling to the Yankees that it was trading time. He then crossed the river, exchanged tobacco for sugar and coffee, plopped on a log, and began talking with the Northerners. Suddenly, one Federal approached and threw a blue overcoat around Coltrane. "The general is inspecting our picket," the man said. "Keep this coat on, and he won't notice you." Sure enough, the Yankee general passed by and Coltrane's incognito escapade proved successful.[56] Had he known of it, Gordon would have grudgingly approved of Coltrane's pluck. His troopers fought as well as they foraged.

Gordon's men had pride and spirit. Much of that can be attributed to Gordon's personality and leadership, and to the *esprit de corps* that he stressed. John Esten Cooke's words ring true here: "In camp, off duty, [Gordon] was the soul of good fellowship." In this, the brigade's actions mirrored their commander's. An anecdote related in an 1898 issue of *Confederate Veteran* demonstrates their ardor. One fall day, a Virginia cavalry officer who was known for his neatness and was often teased about it passed through the camps of the North Carolina Cavalry Brigade. As he sat his saddle in a dignified, soldier-like manner, catcalls greeted him. Cries of "Good morning, General" or "Come out of that hat!" or "Where did you get those boots?" came from all points. An irreverent guard greeted the visitor near the brigade commander's tent. "Don't mind them boys, mister," the guard said. "They are always hollerin' at some fool."[57]

As armies rested, the winter of 1864 left extra time in the hands of the average Civil War soldier. That meant furloughs were forthcoming. As Carolina trooper George Adams wrote his parents, "I think if nothing happens more than I know of, I will get to come home and see you all again. I think there will be furloughs given all winter till the weather gets fit to fight again." By mid–February, as Adams had suspected, furloughs began coming in large numbers. General Lee used great care in issuing such leaves, but hardship cases and the opportunity to relieve pressure on the commissary worked together to deplete the army to thirty-five thousand men.[58]

In February, half of Gordon's brigade was released to recruit in North Carolina. Only the 1st and 2nd North Carolina remained; those regiments were simply in better shape. "The men are in fine spirits, and the horses are in good condition for the season," wrote one trooper. This surprised no one. Since the war began, the regiment had been absent to recruit for only two months. "We will let others give us credit for this, and only say that the old 1st is right side up with care," he added.[59]

Since Gordon now had reduced responsibility, he was one of the glad hundreds who received some time off. Special Orders Number 44 granted him a thirty-day leave of absence as of February 13, 1864. On February 12 he visited Stuart's headquarters, the Wigwam, to pick up his leave papers and say his good-byes. The Wigwam was not an altogether happy place — Sam Sweeney, the cavalry's fabled musician, had recently died of smallpox — but Gordon left his mark. Cooke, who was present, noted not only the unusual beauty of the day but also the character of the departing North Carolinian. "Gen. Gordon here today — a charming man," Cooke wrote. "My heart warms to this jovial, gallant soldier."[60]

Gordon set out on his long journey. Determining not to go home empty-handed, he stopped by Richmond on the way. Remembering how his family slept on homemade beds, he purchased six factory-made beds and hauled them to Wilkesborough. Once his loaded wagon clattered into town, the general made a few stops: one at Dr. Hackett's, to give Caroline and her husband their present; one at Fairmount, to give beds to Martha and Augustus Finley; and last at the John Finleys, where Ann and John received their gift. Gordon doubtless saved his last stop for the Brown house, where he could surprise his beloved mother with a new bed. It was good to be home.[61]

At last! The time had come for a well-deserved rest. He relished moments with family and friends. Unfortunately, not long after he reached Wilkesborough, news from Virginia made headlines. Tarheel cavalrymen had gone into battle without their commander. On February 28, while Federal infantry and cavalry created a diversion, General Judson Kilpatrick led nearly four thousand cavalrymen on a raid to Richmond. After challenging the city's outer defenses, Kilpatrick pulled back because Colonel Ulric Dahlgren and 460 men, who were supposed to attack Richmond simultaneously, could not be located. Hampton and Colonel Cheek, commanding 306 men from Gordon's Brigade, came down from Hanover Junction. Finding Kilpatrick encamped near Atlee's Station, the Carolinians attacked, capturing numerous prisoners, horses, and arms. Kilpatrick accordingly retreated, while Dahlgren's tardy detachment detoured to avoid Hampton and Cheek. Several Virginia units ambushed Dahlgren. The Confederates discovered on Dahlgren's body plans to burn Richmond and to kill President Davis and his cabinet. The Kilpatrick-Dahlgren raid not only ended in disaster for the Union, but also gave Gordon another reason to be proud of his men. President Davis personally thanked Cheek for his service.[62]

Meanwhile, Gordon found depressing political strife in his own home county. The previous fall, Brigadier General Robert F. Hoke had marched more than a regiment of infantrymen into North Carolina's disloyal areas to reestablish Confederate authority. The soldiers rounded up deserters by the thousand. Hoke returned to Virginia in November 1863 and reported success. Peter Hairston agreed with that estimate: "Wilkes is now the truest & most loyal county in the State. He [Hoke] has cleared it of deserters and disloyal men."[63]

As a reminder, Hoke left his men in North Carolina. Those veterans — and squads from other units, including Confederate forces stationed in eastern Tennessee — continued to comb the Carolina landscape. They did not withdraw until about the time Gordon came home on furlough. In their vigor, the troops apparently took undue liberties in foraging. Why should we plant crops, the locals began to wonder, when the harvest will be taken away?[64] When Hoke's infantrymen left, Wilkes reverted to disloyalty. Gordon thus arrived in time to see the home front seethe anew, even to the point of occasional bloodshed. Gordon doubtless compared this reality with what he knew of the war. At Brandy Station, and on every field since, he had seen the enemy come in waves, and fight as well as any Confederate. He had watched the decline in his own force, and had dealt with the myriad of problems that fell to those at his level of responsibility. Now he saw discontent at home. Was a Southern victory possible? Grave was the conclusion at which he arrived.

In the mind of James B. Gordon, the seed of doubt took hold. William H. H. Cowles later remembered how that seed manifested itself on this last furlough.

> In the latter part of the winter of '63 and '64 Gen. Gordon made his last visit home, and those who saw him then — his relatives and friends with whom he was most intimate — noticed and will remember that there was an unwonted expression of sadness that would come into his face, and that his conversation was mingled with a gravity and seriousness which, in the natural joy of reunion with them, he vainly endeavored to throw off.... Gordon knew, as we all did, that the death struggle was coming and near at hand, and that many would be unable to stand this crucial test.

According to tradition, a melancholy Gordon said simply and clearly, "We cannot win."[65] Whether that was the case or not, Gordon had come to believe that he would die in battle, or from wounds received in the line of duty. Carefully, he mentioned how he wished his estate to be distributed should he die.[66] He also put pen to paper, and provided details:

> Mother should anything happen so that I do not return, I wish my debts first paid, most of them due you and Mr. Brown, and then my effects divided equally between my Sisters. The Certificate of Bank Stock in my name belongs to Carrie as well as the bill of sale.... I wish the negroes divided and kept in the family if they should prefer it, and make any division they may think proper. Burt I wish taken care of he has done remarkably well and even in a few miles of the enemy when he could run away and escape if he desired Seems faithfull [sic] and attached to me. I have thought it hardly necessary to make any provision for you my dear mother as you will doubtless be well provided for. If not that is my first wish that bountiful provision should set apart from my effects for you. Allen will be well provided for. I will write a full statement of my wishes and send it to you in the future. I have mainly stated it in this letter to prevent or anticipate any casualty.... My love to all.[67]

All too quickly, the time came to leave Wilkesborough. As he packed his things and looked into his mother's eyes one last time, did Gordon wonder if he would ever see "Oakland" again? Given his apprehension, it is quite possible that Gordon felt as sad as he had at any time in his life. Nevertheless, as the family conveyance carried him to the nearest railroad depot, he knew his future held something better than war. The Carolinian's voyage into war had led him down the most unlikely of paths — the path of love.

Assuredly, the cavalier had not lost his taste for flirting, nor his touch for charming. Kerr Craige, who was ever at Gordon's side, considered Gordon "the most handsome man he ever saw." The faithful aide saw how Gordon used his appearance with the dexterity of an able

Captain Kerr Craige served as Gordon's aide. The son of Burton Craige, Kerr was a witty, handsome, and physically impressive man (courtesy Archibald Craige).

swordsman. How Gordon must have drawn admiring glances at Jeb Stuart's grand cavalry reviews! John Esten Cooke afterward recalled Gordon's gallant way with the fairer sex: "His bow and smile were inimitable, his voice delightful. He would present a bouquet to a lady with a little speech which nobody else could approach." Stuart also saw Gordon impress a Virginia maiden with his pleasantness during a visit to Fredericksburg.[68] As a generation of Carolina women could attest, rare would be the woman who would ensnare this bachelor. Yet in some fashion, in the last few months of his life, Gordon fell deeply in love with Aurelia Cynthia Halsey of Lynchburg, Virginia. Perhaps his fear of a dark future haunted him into love; more likely, the realization of the brevity of life drove him to it. Or maybe Aurelia was simply the right girl at the right time.

They met early in 1864, at a party in Richmond. To seventeen-year-old Aurelia, the occasion was "a bright dream." As the evening passed, she became increasingly attracted to Gordon's personal appearance, his zest for life, and his noble character. From their conversation, she also learned of his "perfect devotion" to his mother. Little did she think at their first meeting "that he whom all considered such an agreeable addition to our gay party in Richmond, was to exercise such an influence upon *my* destiny." Gordon was equally smitten with Aurelia. He later described her face as beautiful, radiant even, with a smile so bright that it impressed his soul "with marks of burning fire."[69]

Gordon often had business in Lynchburg with the quartermaster, or at his Campbell County camps, so he had ample opportunity to call on Aurelia. He did so with persistence. As a gentleman should, he would dispatch a letter ahead requesting permission to visit.[70] Then, upon its arrival, he would ride out to the Halsey farm. The dwelling, known locally as Garland Hills, was located west of town near Blackwater Creek. Aurelia's father, Seth, a sixty-three-year-old "tobacconist," was often among the first to welcome Gordon. Fifty-four-year-old Julia, Aurelia's mother, and two other Halsey children also kept the household lively when the visitor arrived. Three Halsey children were at war: Stephen, a graduate of Emory & Henry, was serving in the 21st Virginia Cavalry as major. Alex was a commissioned officer in Company I of the same unit. Don, the oldest, was an Emory & Henry man who also held law and language degrees from the universities of Virginia and Heidelberg. A veteran of the 2d Virginia Cavalry, Don was then working his way through staff positions with several generals, including Samuel Garland, Jubal Early, Stephen Ramseur, Edward Johnson, and Alfred Iverson.[71]

Gordon quickly charmed the entire family. Soon, his letters were read aloud while the family sat beside the fire after meals.[72] Aurelia had other gentlemen admirers, so she remained discreet about their blossoming relationship. Gordon ached to tell his friends everything; Stuart was especially inquisitive. The shy young woman balked at that. She wrote: "In regards to your Maj. Gen. [Stuart], and the young Brig. [Young], would you object to being a *little secretive?* They are your friends though, and I have too much confidence in you to dictate what you must *tell them.*" Yet Aurelia also had to ward off inquiries about their relationship, so she understood the difficulties of being "secretive." When visitors pressed her, she "received their sayings very quietly and evasively, so that in spite of their persistent teasing, I don't think I committed myself.... They resorted to various means of testing my interest in the State of No. Carolina — made earnest endeavors whether my preference was for the Cavalry or Infantry but were forced at last to confess me incorrigible."[73]

The two held few secrets from each other. As they courted, Gordon and Aurelia talked about many things. Gordon spoke often of his mother, his sisters and nieces, and Allen. Aurelia regularly questioned Gordon about his religious beliefs. A devout churchgoer, she always prayed for the success of the cause, and for her brothers' safety; but Gordon was the primary focus of her petitions. Gordon, it will be remembered, had served the Episcopal Church in Wilkes as a vestryman, and, thanks to his mother, respected Christianity. He often spoke of religion as "one thing needful." He even asked for Aurelia's prayers, but he admitted with regret that he was not a Christian.[74] Aurelia hoped this would change:

> I was more than gratified by your expressions of religious feeling. You have the "deepest respect for Christianity," and now if I could only convince you that it is man's not less than "woman's mission to be good and pious." How happy it would make me to think more of this "one thing needful."[75]

There was hope for him, for Christian influences abounded. A revival swept the Army of Northern Virginia beginning in the fall of 1863. It evidently found its way to Gordon's favored 1st Horse, for Company B became known as "Noisy B" because of the rowdy, "old-fashioned prayer meetings" it held.[76]

Gordon remained preoccupied with the coming campaign. He told Aurelia of a dark premonition he had had: a premonition of evil, defeat, and death. She tried to drive such morbid thoughts away, but later decided that they "made him seek the throne of mercy and pardon. Yes, I have sweet comfort in believing that the loved one died in Christ — that glory, honor, immortality, and eternal life are his." Gordon did tell her that he would pray to be resigned to his destiny, and that "he hoped and felt that he was a better man — that he had determined to endeavor to lead a new life and become a Christian."[77]

In addition to these thoughts of Aurelia, of God and Jesus Christ, and of dark premonitions, one more idea made Gordon's state of mind as jumbled as ever. He returned from furlough with the beginnings of an idea: had the time come for him to marry? Was Aurelia the girl he had always hoped to meet? There was time yet to consider this, but the thought crossed the general's mind more than once as he grew closer to Aurelia.

As his furlough came to a close, Gordon acted in ways that would please Aurelia. On his way to Milford from Wilkes, he paused in Richmond. The date was Sunday, March 14, and the churches of the Confederacy's first city beckoned. Gordon heeded the call, and he was not alone. One worshipper, who saw fourteen generals present at a service, suggested that less piety and more drilling of commands might be appropriate. In addition to Gordon, the congregation included generals R. E. Lee, John Hunt Morgan, James Longstreet, R. F. Hoke, and Braxton Bragg, among others.[78] Gordon and Morgan had never met before, so afterward the two struck up a conversation. Morgan, the famous Confederate raider who had recently escaped from the Ohio State Penitentiary, was in Richmond trying to reorganize a command with which he could resume his Kentucky raids. A talk with Morgan was exactly what Gordon needed to chase away his fears. The conversation of the two men "dispelled all other thoughts save that of duty and war." It was in this frame of mind that Gordon later spoke with the commander of the Army of Northern Virginia, who was in Richmond for a strategy meeting with President Davis.[79] In the company of a few brother officers, Gordon called on the President, and unexpectedly met General Lee. Gordon learned from the resulting conversation that the enemy was expected to begin a new offensive at any time. As a result, Gordon decided to delay any proposal for marriage. The nuptials would have to wait for a more opportune moment.[80]

Generals Morgan and Lee thus reawakened Gordon's martial pride; next his state pride underwent rejuvenation. Hastening back to headquarters, Gordon arrived in time to see Governor Vance, who was visiting the army to bolster the morale of North Carolina troops. Vance began his tour of the camps on March 26. The governor's presence heartened Gordon. It showed that the state still supported the Confederate cause — despite peace meetings and dissension in Wilkes and elsewhere. The men certainly needed the encouragement. One of Gordon's men wrote, "We are almost ashamed of N.C. even now and hate what we were once proud to be called '*Tar Heel.*'" Vance made his rounds of the Tarheel bivouacs, giving speeches by the dozen. Immense crowds, composed of both "fair damsels" and troops from several states, came to listen. Many fell under the spell of Vance's oratory, including Jeb Stuart. One witness said that Stuart "followed him around and seemed to be completely carried away with his speeches."[81] General Lee, who had also returned from Richmond, enjoyed Vance's eloquence as well, and agreed that the speeches made a positive impact. However, the governor's insistence that North Carolina be repaid for its sacrifices made Lee uncomfortable. Administration policy held that brigadiers should command only soldiers from the same state, but Lee sometimes hesitated to comply because he often could not find qualified commanders with the proper birthplaces. The appointment of Baker, and later Gordon, were Lee's ways of maintaining capable leadership while respecting state pride, but it remained an unending problem.[82]

Snow, rain and wind marked the final days of Vance's tour, and threatened to cancel many of his presentations. He was also eager to get back to Raleigh. Still, Vance paused in the camps of the North Carolina cavalry brigade. Gordon had helped welcome the Governor to Virginia, and now he listened as North Carolina's leader exhorted the Tar Heel horsemen. How Gordon wished that Aurelia was there! "Ah!" he wrote. "That you could be there that my Gov my people might see you in your pride and your beauty I know they would love you & be proud of their comd's taste."[83] He had to make do with the anecdotal Vance. On Monday, April 4, after Vance completed his speechmaking and handshaking, he made ready to return home. Waring witnessed what transpired next. "Met Young and Gordon on the train," he wrote. "Gordon was sending off Gov. Vance. Vance is quite a young man and handsome. He had been making a series of addresses to N.C. troops, they say with great effect."[84] Vance, a long-time supporter of Gordon's, would not see the general again.

The brigadier general now could return to his day-to-day duties. Of course, Gordon kept corresponding with Aurelia, for he remained quite smitten; but the work of a brigadier general had not disappeared. At first, Gordon apparently struggled to get back into a routine. On one occasion, he was tardy in furnishing a map of his picket lines to headquarters. When his full attention did focus on duty, it concentrated on the welfare of his men. In mid–April, for example, he considered one man's request for a leave of absence. Both Cheek and Gordon considered the man to be deserving, so they approved the request and forwarded it up the chain of command.[85] Pursuant to Stuart's orders, he also arranged for the Articles of War to be read to each regiment every Monday at dress parade. He again traveled to Richmond, were he learned from Bragg that P. G. T. Beauregard was to assault New Bern. He saw to the court cases that had come up in his absence, particularly those from the 5th. He rode the train to and fro on varied errands; for instance, Stuart asked him to travel to Lynchburg and inspect the arrangements of the quartermaster in caring for disabled horses. On another business trip, he again saw Waring. When their discussion turned to personal advancement, Gordon advised him to apply for promotion. It had worked for Gordon; why not for Waring? He always found fellowship when the day's work was done. On one occasion, he dropped by headquarters and enjoyed a mild mint julep with his brother officers.[86]

In everything, Gordon strove to prepare. He had been unable to give the 1st any respite, but that unit remained reliable. It also received some recruits; six men joined one company in a week's time.[87] The 2d Horse, the brigade's smallest regiment, was ready for action; Gordon had done wonders with the unit. Colonel Clinton M. Andrews, a horse-soldier from Iredell County, stepped forward to command the 2d. As a formality, Gordon worked to bring Andrews before an examining board to confirm his commission.[88] Beyond this, Gordon recalled his absent regiments.[89] The 4th North Carolina Cavalry returned to Virginia with 490 effectives, up from 82. Gordon was glad, and also happy, to see Ferebee return to command that unit around May 1, which also enabled the 4th's temporary commander, Rufus Barringer, to return to the Brigade. (Ferebee never quite shook his wounds. He retired before war's end and died in 1884.) Unfortunately, Gordon soon lost the services of the 4th when it was assigned to a brigade under General James Dearing in the Petersburg defenses.[90]

Slated to replace the 4th was Colonel John A. Baker's 3d North Carolina Cavalry (Forty-first Regiment North Carolina State Troops), the unit Vance had once wanted Gordon to command. The 3d had considerable experience in eastern North Carolina and southeastern Virginia. However, on April 22, while the 3d marched to Virginia, it was redirected to the Kinston-New Bern area. That meant the 3d would not join the North Carolina cavalry brigade until the end of May.[91] The good news regarded Stephen Evans's 5th North Carolina Cavalry, which had halted in Richmond on temporary service. That unit, which was in splendid condition, numbering more than five hundred effective mounted men and officers, would soon rejoin Gordon's Brigade, meaning that Gordon had the 1st, 2d, and 5th at his command.[92]

Even as the spring campaign got underway, an important change resulted from the return of W. H. F. Lee. Lee, in a Federal prison since June 1863, had finally been exchanged in March 1864. He returned to Richmond, to war, and to an empty home as his wife had died in December. Robert Lee coaxed his brokenhearted son to pull together and resume his duties, and that, along with other changes within the cavalry, induced Stuart to reshuffle the structure of his corps. By the end of April, Rooney had received promotion to major general. By reducing Fitz Lee's division to two brigades, a third division of cavalry was created for Rooney.[93] This affected Gordon in a way that neither he nor Hampton reckoned on. Initially, Hampton retained the brigades of Butler, Young, and Gordon, and Fitz Lee kept the brigades of Lomax and Wickham. The brigades of Rosser and Chambliss became parts of Major General Rooney Lee's command. Due to questions of seniority — Gordon was the brigadier with the least seniority next to Chambliss — and equilibrium, Stuart decided the organization needed further modification. The interests of the service would best be served, Stuart thought, if Gordon were transferred to Rooney Lee's division. As a result, on May 5, Hampton's assistant adjutant general, the genial and pleasant Theo Barker,[94] instructed Gordon "to proceed without delay with your command to the vicinity of Shady Grove, where you will concentrate your brigade and report for further orders to Major General Stuart. I am directed by Maj. Gen. Hampton, in communicating the above orders, to express to you, and through you to your whole brigade, the surprise with which he has received the orders and the pain it causes him to execute them."[95]

Hampton had known this might happen, but he rued it anyway. Because of the military situation, the South Carolinian hesitated to carry out the orders. He told General Lee that if Gordon left immediately, he would have only two hundred men on hand.[96] Gordon had a like reaction, as Waring found out when he visited Gordon the day of the transfer. Waring wrote, "He is rather blue about being assigned to Rooney Lee."[97] But the transfer was final. It ensured that Gordon would be fighting along Brook Turnpike a week later.

Once staffers formalized the arrangements, Hampton's division contained the brigades of Young, Rosser, and Butler; Fitz Lee's had the brigades of Lomax and Wickham; and Rooney Lee's division had the brigades of Chambliss and Gordon. This was the organization with which Stuart chose to face the numerous cavalrymen of Ulysses S. Grant. Stuart's ranks were not bursting with manpower, and horseflesh remained a problem, but the troopers would not lack proper organization or solid direction. In terms of leadership, the Confederate cavalry approached the spring in the best shape of any portion of the Army of Northern Virginia — despite the fact that none of Stuart's brigade commanders had held their positions a year before.[98]

In this way, James B. Gordon began the last two weeks of his life. He had done everything he could to prepare his brigade. Though he had but three regiments at hand, he had faith in his men. Thus he saw the spring campaign begin and, with determination, went to work. Inside, however, he felt very different. Despite General Lee's prediction, General Morgan's encouragements, and Governor Vance's exhortations, Gordon could not shake his premonition of death. Neither could he avoid what was inside his heart. There Gordon held his love for Aurelia, and there his love grew till he could hold it in no longer. "I can never express how much I love you," he wrote Aurelia. "The depth of my devotion each moment awakens me to its constant growing consuming influence Its intensity startles me I tremble for its consequences not a hour not a moment of this day has passed without its absorbing influences."[99] In April, he arrived at the most surprising decision of his life. Rather than taking a formal, gentlemanly approach, he hastily proposed to Aurelia by letter. She replied simply, "You wish me to write that 'we may be engaged' at once. You shall not have cause to doubt my affection, but I think it best that I should see you again before I 'pledge myself to thee.'"[100]

With yellow flowers adorning her hair — yellow for cavalry — Aurelia waited for Gordon. Sadly, because of the approaching campaign, Gordon could not come. He would not see Aurelia again.[101]

13

"Every Man Must Be a Hero"

IN THE SPRING OF 1864, a posthumous description of James B. Gordon appeared in a Raleigh newspaper. It represented one last, longing look at the cavalry general. The writer, a longtime friend of Gordon's and a fellow cavalryman, portrayed the "immensely popular" general "as one of the finest looking officers in the whole army — tall and commanding in his personal appearance, he added to it that correct military bearing and character, which distinguishes the educated soldier. He had a powerful and robust frame, sternly set and splendidly muscled, broad shoulders, a massive chest and athletic limbs. He had a faultless physiognomy, his eye blue and large was lustrous with passions of affection and chivalry.... His chin was thickly hidden with heavy auburn whiskers, cut in the Southern style; while a massive rolling mustache hung heavily from his lip, and concealed a broad well carved and expressive mouth." Such was the appearance of Gordon as, only three weeks before, he had faced the spring assault of the Army of the Potomac.[1]

By May 1 that year, spring had definitely come. Horses had shed their winter coats. Tall grass grew around Fredericksburg. Fish beckoned in the Rappahannock. Yet such signs of promise also brought war, so soon after May began the Unionist offensive commenced. Robert E. Lee expected it, so he had his army entrenched along the Rapidan between and behind Barnett's and Morton's fords. Longstreet's Corps, back from the West, played a part in supporting Lee's defenses, while the corps of A. P. Hill and Ewell made ready nearer the river. Stuart's cavalry picketed crossing-points above and below the army's position, with the main body stationed along the Rappahannock below Fredericksburg, where forage was abundant. All along the line, soldiers dreaded what lay ahead. One of Gordon's men, George Adams, predicted carnage. "I am afraid that ... there will be a heap of bloodshed again like last summer. It looks like there has been enough bloodshed to convince the Yankees that they can't whip us, and I am in favor of convincing them if it takes every man in the South, but I hope it can be done without too much killing."[2]

The killing was inevitable as the war was not close to a decision. Lieutenant General Ulysses S. Grant, now commander of all U.S. land forces, put his plan into action. He used a theater strategy similar to that employed by McClellan in 1862. It had not worked then, but this time a persistent man was in control.[3] While other forces worked the Shenandoah Valley and the south bank of the James River, the Army of the Potomac was to make Lee's army its objective. In this way, Richmond lost its importance as a military objective as far as Grant was concerned. Instead, a concerted effort to destroy the Confederate military might became paramount.

Early on May 4, more than one hundred thousand Yankee soldiers marched for the Rapidan River. With a quick march through the tangled Wilderness, General George Meade, the army's commander, hoped to turn the Confederate right. The Federal Second Corps, led by Gregg's cavalry division, crossed at Ely's Ford and moved to Chancellorsville. The Fifth and Sixth Corps followed James H. Wilson's cavalry division across the Rapidan at Germanna Ford and aimed for Wilderness Tavern. Burnside's Ninth Corps hovered nearby, preparing to follow. General Lee, unsure as to his enemy's intentions, looked to his cavalry.[4]

Gordon's Milford headquarters was buzzing with activity. Here came yet another test of his faith in state's rights and the South. He stood as firm militarily as he had politically fourteen years before in the North Carolina House of Commons. He prepared for battle, perhaps with Aurelia's words ringing in his mind: "The very mention of the coming campaign makes me shudder."[5] The 5th North Carolina Cavalry had not yet arrived, so only the 1st and 2d Horse of the North Carolina cavalry brigade were available. Of those two units, only the 1st was in the field; the 2d was in reserve at Milford. Thus, it fell to the river outposts of the 1st North Carolina Cavalry to meet the enemy advance.[6] William H. H. Cowles, who had recovered from his recent wound, was the acting commander of the 1st. As he was among the first to see signs of Yankee activity, he sent a dispatch to Ewell at 9:00 A.M. on May 4:

> I have discovered the enemy's pickets at this point, Mrs. Willis' house, about two miles from Germanna. I have seen some footmen, but they may be only dismounted cavalry; it is evidently a heavy cavalry picket at least, and the moving of their trains on the plank road can be plainly heard. I have sent out dismounted scouts to approach the plank road, and have taken steps to open communication with my detachment on the left.
>
> P. S. My scout of last night has just returned and says that he has already reported information gained to you.[7]

Meanwhile, at Germanna, Nicholas P. Tredenick and eight comrades opened the ball. Spotting an enemy attempt to cross the river, they opened fire. When the Yankees got too close, the men retreated a short distance, stopped, reloaded, and resumed firing. It was thought their fire killed a captain and wounded a few men and horses. Meanwhile, other Tarheels threw up obstacles to retard the enemy advance, but in no way did it slow the Army of the Potomac. Thanks to such work, by 11:00 A.M. Cowles knew more. He wrote Stuart, "The enemy are advancing a half mile below Locust Grove, apparently strong cavalry forces. I will do the best I can with my comparatively small command." Tredenick and his comrades kept up their resistance. Stuart, who dashed forward to supervise his picket lines, left orders to concentrate the cavalry on the right with a view to enveloping the Federal advance.[8]

Other Tarheels, despite their proximity to events, found the day more bearable. William L. Barrier, who was on picket duty, wrote his father, "We have only been skirmishing a little since the fight commenced. I have not fired my gun and have not been shot at." Cadwallader Iredell of the 1st, who had begun the day by informing General Ewell of the Federal movement, even enjoyed himself. Remaining near Germanna on provost duty, Iredell first surmised that the Federals, marching on the plank road, were going toward Chancellorsville. However, such work did not keep him from noticing the day's beauty. The dogwood trees were then in full bloom. Iredell plucked a blossom and enclosed it in a letter home.[9]

Troopers from Fitz Lee's Division also reported the advance. Officers had planned to conduct a division review near Fredericksburg that day, but when the Federals drove in pickets at Ely's and Germanna fords, it had to be canceled.[10]

Alerted by both cavalry reports and lookouts on Clark's Mountain, Lee reacted. Confederate infantry marched ahead to halt the foe. Ewell's and Hill's men stepped off. So too did Longstreet's force. This movement of Southern infantry required speed. If Grant reached the open country beyond the Wilderness, he could bring his dominant strength to bear. Lee had to prevent that. All day the men of both sides pressed forward, but a general engagement did not yet ensue.

On May 5, the Confederates continued their advance toward the Wilderness. Stuart conducted Hill's Corps along the Orange Plank Road. Soon the Federals attacked along that road, and Rosser engaged enemy cavalry on the right near Todd's Tavern. Ewell, whose corps constituted the Southern left, marched east along the Old Turnpike. The 1st North Carolina Cavalry worked to discern enemy movements in Ewell's front. One company formed the advance guard for General Edward Johnson's division. Another scouted Spotswood Road, a trail slanting to the left. With the rest of the regiment, Cowles placed pickets near Germanna and Jacob's Fords and then personally assumed command of the pickets around Germanna. There he saw that bluecoats still poured across the river. Quickly Cowles wrote a dispatch to Ewell, in sight of "a long column moving over the heights beyond the river in the direction of the ford." Clearly, Federal reinforcements were marching from Germanna Ford to the Orange Plank Road, to Ewell's front and right. The head of the Federal columns must be in that direction. Ewell, thus warned, asked for instructions. General Lee wanted to avoid a premature general engagement, but the Federals had other plans. They launched a vigorous assault, and the fight was on.[11]

The harsh, tangled terrain became an equalizer as both Hill and Ewell held fast. On the right the Tapp Farm lent rare open fields to the struggle; on the left, where John Brown Gordon figured prominently, the Lacy House sat silently in the midst of carnage. In places, the Federals gained ground, and then lost it; in others, Confederates advanced a bit, only to withdraw; elsewhere, neither side made headway. Artillery proved all but useless in the undergrowth. The Wilderness hid friend and foe, as well as corpses, of which there were many. Day's end saw little come of the struggle. There would be more fighting tomorrow, though, so Cowles dispatched dismounted troopers to harass the enemy, and sent three trusty scouts to scour the Federal flanks. The regiment's remaining details and detachments continued picketing what Cowles called an "extensive line." All told, from their work in the area, the Tarheel troopers captured nearly two hundred Federals, as well as a "good number" of small arms.[12]

A red dawn announced the next day's fighting. Hampton and Gordon left Milford with the 2d North Carolina Cavalry, aiming for Shady Grove Church.[13] Gordon hoped the 5th would come up from Richmond and join him there. Meanwhile, an early, powerful Union advance found success. Grant wielded his army with skill against the Confederate right. The fight soon hung in the balance there as Hill's corps gave way. In the center, a gap between Hill and Ewell widened, beckoning enemy troops. Without reinforcements from Longstreet, the day would certainly be lost. The fate of the Army of Northern Virginia suddenly rested with him. Lee's Old War Horse did arrive, throwing his First Corps into the fray. The right held, erasing the Federal advantage. The Rebels then assumed the offensive, assaulting Grant's left below the Plank Road. Success crowned their efforts, but on the verge of victory Longstreet fell wounded. Confusion set in as the Federals recovered.

All day on the left, the 1st North Carolina Cavalry continued its vigil from near Germanna westward. The fighting behind them, along Ewell's lines, was not as vicious, but it still had its moments. Early in the day, John Gordon found the enemy right in the air and proposed to attack it. Cowles provided important information to support Gordon's proposal. One Tarheel trooper even accompanied Gordon on a personal reconnaissance of the Federal flank.[14] Ewell balked at the idea until day's end, when General Lee ordered the attack and John Gordon went to work. Only darkness retarded his success. From the right, where the bulk of Stuart's cavalry waited, to the left, where Cowles watched, burning woods lit the night sky.

Saturday, May 7, found the armies still deep in the bloody, fiery Wilderness. Skirmishing sputtered along the lines, but mainly the armies sat quietly. Grant, seeing the formidable position of his foe, had an idea of how to break the stalemate. With a quick move to his left, he hoped to take Spotsylvania Court House and bring the enemy to battle in more open country.[15] Lee anticipated this. While preparing a countermove of his own, he ordered his cavalry to investigate. Colonel Cheek, who had joined Cowles on the picket lines, confirmed the possibility of this move. He told Ewell that the Federals had taken up bridges at Germanna and were moving left toward Ely's. Stuart, skirmishing near key crossroads on the right, discovered more evidence. Fitz Lee, below Todd's Tavern, resisted the advance of Federal cavalry with two brigades. Simultaneously, about two miles away, Stuart maintained Rosser's Brigade on the Catharpin Road near Corbin's Bridge. Large numbers of Federal cavalry advanced in that area as well, threatening Stuart's position.[16]

Near 3:00 P.M., Hampton arrived in the Shady Grove Church area with Gordon's reduced brigade and P. M. B. Young's troopers. Stuart anticipated the approach of these troopers and sent Theodore Garnett to meet Gordon on the Catharpin Road. He found the general dispatching a skirmish line "to feel the enemy." Garnett joined the skirmishers, who moved across open fields and entered a patch of woods. The troopers collided there with another Rebel scouting party, but no one was hurt. An entire Tarheel regiment followed this up by marching on the enemy's barricades, and the Yankees responded by firing two shells that flew overhead without doing any damage. The regiment then dismounted, moved to the side of the road, and prepared to fight on foot. Gordon finally ordered his line forward.[17]

Waring, whose Jeff Davis Legion was present, witnessed Gordon's attack:

> Soon after passing Shady Grove, we found that the Yankees were in our rear. We wheeled around and threw out skirmishers. General Gordon attacked them. The Cobb Legion was sent to aid him. They drove the Yankees.[18]

The 5th North Carolina Cavalry, recently arrived, bore the brunt of this struggle. The regiment (while dismounted) forced the enemy back to some works, but the Yankees proved as obstinate as the Rebels. Eighteen Southerners became casualties, most from the 5th. Darkness brought the conflict to a close.[19]

That night, Garnett again carried orders to Gordon. After withdrawing quietly from the field, the orders read, the brigade was to camp near Shady Grove Church. Garnett rode along the skirmish line and repeated the orders to some of Gordon's colonels, urging silence. To his discomfiture, one trooper disregarded Garnett's advice. The man "perched himself on a pine stump and clapping his arms to his sides in imitation of the lord of the barnyard, uttered a loud, clear crow, which however came near terminating fatally, for at that very same instant a Yankee fired in the direction of the noise, the bullet passing just in front of my horse and striking the stump on which our 'chicken' was sitting." His friends laughed at him when the man was forced to retreat from his stage. The withdrawal began without further difficulty, while the men exchanged cheers, groans, and insults with the enemy.[20]

The fighting around Todd's Tavern and Corbin's Bridge made it clear that the Confederate horsemen faced overwhelming numbers. Thus as the evening wore on, Gordon's hard-fighting brigade became the focus of a tug-of-war between Fitz Lee and Hampton. Lee asked headquarters for the immediate use of Gordon's Brigade. Hampton had an equal need for manpower, so he pleaded to keep it. "Gordon's men will fight none the worse for being with their old comrades and in their old command," he wrote.[21] Fitz won; the unit joined him on May 8. Headquarters did not dawdle over the question because there were many other things to consider. In fact, the cavalry fighting and other intelligence reports brought Robert E. Lee to

13. "Every Man Must Be a Hero"   211

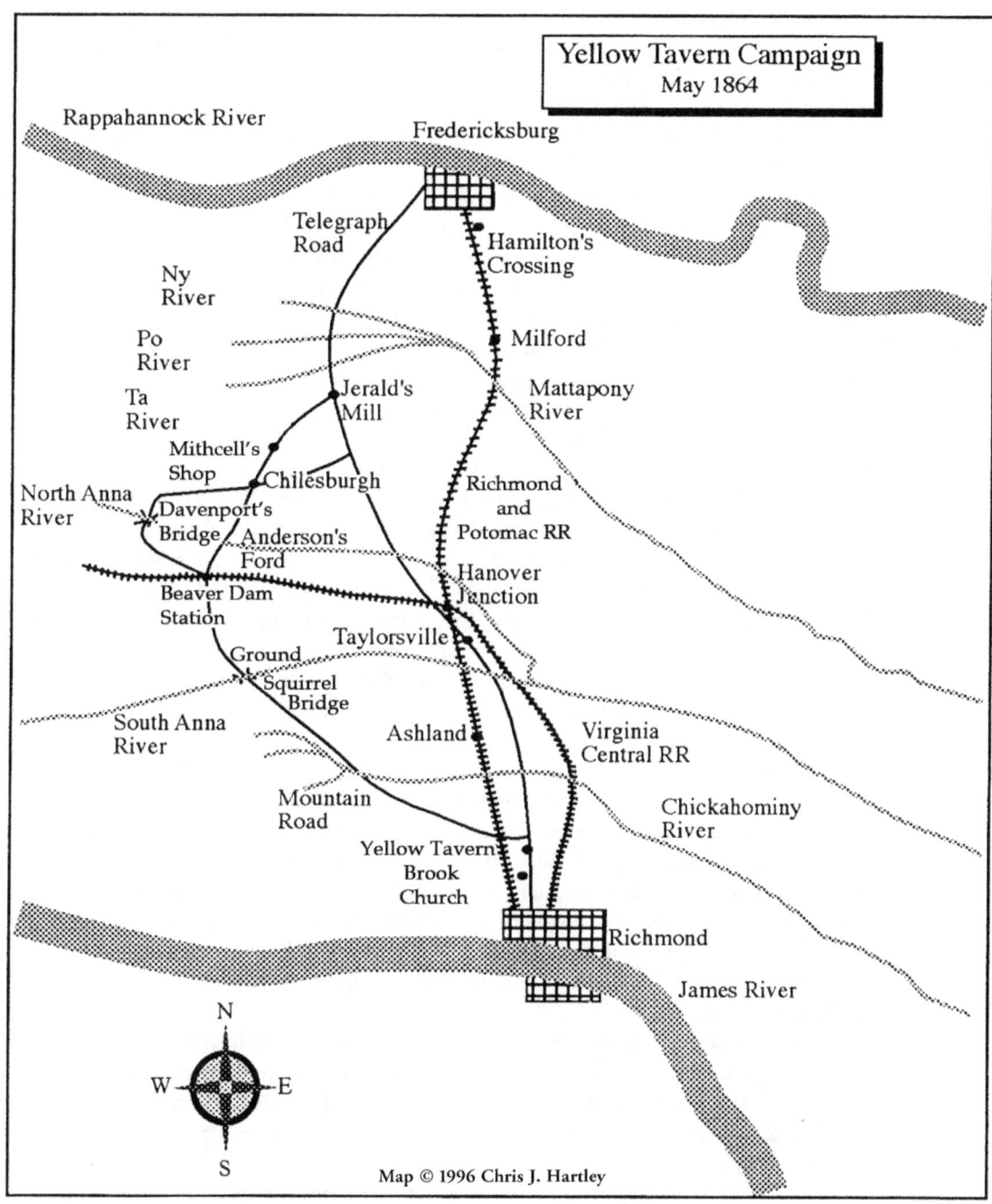

a decision. Now certain that the enemy was moving south, he ordered his infantry to start for Spotsylvania Court House.[22] Stuart was told to locate the best roads to that point.

As it happened, Barringer returned from his brief furlough just as the fight opened. On May 8, Barringer joined Gordon and reported to Fitz Lee. Gordon and Lee, worried about the safety of the cavalry division's trains, placed Barringer in temporary command of all dismounted men and dispatched them to guard the cavalry's wagons.[23]

That same morning, Grant's movement toward Spotsylvania continued bearing down on

Stuart. Clearly, those ragged horsemen had to buy time so Lee could beat Grant to Spotsylvania Court House. The sun was only one hour high when heavy enemy forces renewed the struggle. Federal shells began pounding the Southern positions.[24] Fitz Lee's troopers, dismounted, played the key role in the resistance. Though forced back, they held with surprising tenacity. Thousands of blue-clad soldiers and horsemen strove to reach the Court House, but the cavalry ran invaluable interference.

Given the extra time, Lee's army barely won the race. A portion of the infantry corps commanded by R. H. Anderson, Longstreet's replacement, reached Spotsylvania to Fitz's rear and established a defensive line. Stuart came up and extended Anderson's line with dismounted cavalry. He directed the left portion of the line in person, boldly exposing himself to enemy fire as he did so.[25] The 2d and 5th North Carolina joined the resistance near Spotsylvania Court House, on the army's right flank. Gordon, who "was continuously riding and walking along the lines" of his regiments, did his part with equal vigor.[26] His troopers fought dismounted and held their ground, but as the pressure was overwhelming, Gordon longed for the help of the 1st. That distant regiment began its move to rejoin the brigade, but only after Tredenick and two other men captured three ambulances and several Unionists.[27]

At any rate, the day's battle was tense and the situation desperate. Ewell's infantry arrived late in the day, strengthening the Confederate defenses. The brigades of Rosser, Young, and Gordon, backed by the horse artillery, supported the advance of Ewell's soldiers. Rosser worked the right flank of William Mahone. Young, whose "stentorian" voice could be heard for half a mile, advanced up the slope west of Catharpin Road with Early. Gordon's Brigade approached the Federal line on Catharpin Road. Finding abandoned rations, the hungry Confederates moved to take them, but two Federal regiments opened fire and the Southerners withdrew.[28]

Robert E. Lee's army held. Thanks were due largely to Stuart's cavalry.

A difference over tactics marked the beginning of the end.

Philip Sheridan, new commander of all cavalry forces in the Army of the Potomac, had been unhappy since the beginning of the spring campaign. He disapproved of the fact that his horsemen were being used only to guard trains and to picket. Sheridan wanted to fight, and he told Meade as much. In one version of the incident, which probably occurred on May 8, Sheridan gave Meade information about Stuart's cavalry. Meade interrupted him. "Never mind Stuart," Meade said. "He will do about as he pleases anyhow. Go on and tell what you discovered about Lee's forces."

Sheridan bristled at that. "Damn Stuart, I can thrash hell out of him any day," he said. Such was the essence of the conversation. Other writers give different versions of the confrontation, but the result was the same. When Grant later heard of this conversation, Sheridan got what he wanted: the chance to tangle with Jeb Stuart. Grant ordered Sheridan to go out and engage the enemy's cavalry.[29]

Sheridan turned to planning. He decided to march around Lee's right, "and put my command, before fighting, south of the North Anna, where I expected to procure grain; where I was confident that while engaging the enemy's cavalry no timely assistance from his infantry could be procured, and whence, if not successful, I could proceed west and rejoin our army, swinging around toward Gordonsville and Orange Court-House." Grant projected a return by way of Haxall's Landing on the James River.[30] As for manpower, apparently neither Grant nor Sheridan contemplated using less than the entire Cavalry Corps of the Army of the Potomac. The corps contained three divisions, under brigadier generals Wesley Merritt, David McM. Gregg, and James H. Wilson respectively. Six batteries of artillery, under Captain James

M. Robertson, rounded out the corps. Sheridan felt his men were in "pretty good condition" in terms of health and equipment, "but their horses were thin and very much worn out by excessive, and, it seemed to me, unnecessary picket duty." Blame for the horses' condition also could be attached to February's Kilpatrick-Dahlgren Raid, which may have disabled three or four thousand of the "very flower" of the Northern cavalry.[31]

At any rate, Sheridan had plenty of power with which to execute his orders. At 5:00 A.M. on May 9, between ten and twelve thousand horsemen marched away from Union lines. To avoid Confederate eyes, the Federals rode to Hamilton's Crossing and then turned south on the Telegraph Road. This maneuver did not deceive Stuart's horsemen. The Federal column stretched thirteen miles, so it was a hard sight to miss. Around 8:00 A.M., pickets informed Stuart of Sheridan's move. He dispatched a regiment to "see what it means," and advised Lee that some artillery bivouacked at the cavalry's headquarters might be vulnerable to attack.[32]

Learning that the Federal raid was in force, Stuart sent more troops. The brigade of Williams C. Wickham, being nearest to Sheridan, quickly pursued. Stuart then calmly prepared to follow with reinforcements. Edward Porter Alexander, an artilleryman in Longstreet's corps, saw Stuart sitting under an apple tree at Spotsylvania Court House. The cavalryman, who was cheerful and in high spirits, said Sheridan had gone on a raid toward Richmond, but Southern troopers were already working to stop him. Stuart told Alexander that he was then preparing personally to join the pursuit. That was true; except for the brigades of Young, Rosser, and Chambliss, which were to remain with the army, all of Stuart's units were readying to march. Fitz Lee's division, which was relieved from its Spotsylvania positions at 1:00 P.M. for that purpose, set hoof to road at about 3:00 P.M. Gordon's men likewise received the unexpected marching orders. Since the Tarheels had to wait for the 1st North Carolina Cavalry to rejoin the brigade, Stuart left instructions for Gordon to follow. Then, at the old Spotsylvania Court House, the Tarheels marked time.[33]

The day was bright and breezeless, but aesthetics held no attraction for Sheridan.[34] Instead, his first worry lay in the courses of Ny, Po, and Ta rivers. Each stream sat directly across his line of advance, and any one of them could have been easily defended by the enemy. He need not have worried. The head of the Federal column was a few miles past the Ta River before Confederate horsemen appeared in force. These were Wickham's cavalrymen, who caught up with Sheridan's rear-guard at Jarrald's Mill around 4:00 P.M. Wickham struck the Unionists with some success but failed to impede the Federal advance. While Sheridan's rear-guard held Wickham at bay, "Little Phil" directed his main body to leave the Telegraph Road and angle toward Mitchell's Shop. Wickham continued to follow along the Chilesburg Road and struck the Federal rear-guard again near Mitchell's Shop. Again battle flared. When his initial assault there made no headway, he called for George H. Matthews's squadron of the 3d Virginia. "I know he will go through," Wickham said. Forming column of fours, Matthews attacked the enemy lines, and failed. Five Virginians died, three were wounded, and ten others captured. Matthews also met his end in the charge.[35]

Sheridan, who did not consider this "serious opposition," pressed on. Confederate outposts sounded the alarm. Ominous news of the raid made its way across Virginia. One lookout reported that "the roads are full of [Yankees]." Another scout saw Unionists everywhere, and saw blacks wandering about like lost children. Sheridan paid little attention to the fuss; he was intent only on securing needed forage for his animals. About dark, Merritt led his division, which was in the advance, across the North Anna River at Anderson's Ford. Custer was ordered to take his Michigan brigade to Beaver Dam Station in search of forage.[36]

To the rear, Gordon's Brigade was several hours behind Wickham. After leaving a squadron from the 1st behind, the Tarheels marched along the Telegraph Road. There they noted evidence of the raiders' passing. A trooper from Gordon's 5th remembered, "Devastation and waste characterized the section through which the raiders had passed, and no vestige of a Yankee, save their dead, was seen until our arrival on the North Anna River."[37] Stuart, who came up at dark after Fitz Lee and Lomax's Brigade reinforced Wickham, largely ignored the surroundings while he analyzed the unfolding campaign. Including Gordon's Brigade, Stuart could count on only five thousand or so cavalrymen — about half the size of Sheridan's force — so he had to employ his strength carefully. The cavalryman guessed his opponent was headed for Beaver Dam Station on the Virginia Central Railroad. The station was the site of Lee's advance supply base, so it was a target the South could ill afford to lose. Stuart concluded to re-divide his forces once he rejoined Wickham. When Stuart caught up with this advance brigade, Wickham's men welcomed him with joy. "General Stuart rode up quietly," recalled a witness, "no one suspecting he was there, until a soldier crossed the road, stopped, peered through the darkness into his face and shouted out, 'Old Jeb has come!' In an instant the air was rent with huzzas." Stuart, waving his plumed hat in acknowledgment, replied in a sad-sounding voice, "My friends, we won't halloo until we get out of the woods."[38]

To do just that, Stuart sought Fitz Lee and found him near his skirmish line at a farm house gate. In a short conference, the cavalry commander issued instructions. He gave Fitz Lee the brigades of Wickham and Lomax and sent them to follow Sheridan toward Chilesburg. Stuart also decided to take Gordon's Brigade and dash westward, toward Davenport's Bridge on the North Anna River. With any luck, he could block Sheridan's way and prevent any further advance, and possibly protect Beaver Dam Station. This flanking move also was likely meant to ensure that Sheridan did not turn against the Army of Northern Virginia's rear.[39]

But first Stuart had to find Gordon, who was still marching from his Locust Grove position. Garnett found the Tarheels five or six miles away, near Mud Tavern. When the staff-officer rode up, he learned that Gordon had ordered his men to camp, and had directed his quartermaster to provide corn and forage. (A neighborhood farmer offered his services for this.) Dismounting, Garnett approached the house and asked for Gordon. The general, sitting within earshot on the porch of a small, roadside house, answered for himself.

After taking care of formalities, Garnett got to the point. Stuart had plans for stopping Sheridan, and those plans required Gordon's help. "General Stuart wants you to come right ahead, General," Garnett said.

Gordon knew that his men were bone tired, so the order angered him. "By God, my men shall not move one foot till they feed up," he said. Explaining further, Gordon said that his men had marched over forty miles since daybreak without stopping to feed or water. Then Gordon's anger passed as quickly as it had come, so he invited Garnett to lie down beside him on the porch. In minutes they were asleep. Some time later, Gordon woke up and ordered his brigade to move, and then he woke Garnett. The two men mounted, went to the head of the column, and rode off to find Stuart.[40]

Down the road, Gordon and Garnett approached

During his last leave home, Gordon acted more melancholy and serious than ever before. That is evident in his last photo (courtesy Horace Mewborn).

a picket from the 4th Virginia Cavalry. Garnett rode up to the man to tell him of the advance of the North Carolina Cavalry Brigade. While they talked, a pistol shot rang out and a ball whistled overhead. Five or six other shots followed. Gordon and his staff rode up at about this time. Gordon grew angry over the situation, but the picket checked on his company and found that they had not been the source. No more shots came, and the mystery remained unsolved. No further incident occurred until Gordon met Stuart in the tiny village of Chilesburg. From there, Gordon's column set off for Davenport's Bridge while Fitz Lee, already past Chilesburg, continued on the direct route toward Beaver Dam.[41]

Ultimately, Stuart's attempt to stop the Federals there failed; Sheridan's men had too much of a head start. Two of Custer's squadrons reached the depot near dusk on May 9. The rest of his brigade followed. It took only a few shots to disperse the defenders. The Federals then destroyed what the retreating Rebels had left: two locomotives, one hundred cars, ninety wagons, bacon, flour, meal, sugar, molasses, and other supplies equaling 1,500,000 rations. They also trashed between eight and ten miles of railroad track and telegraph wire and even rescued 378 Yankee prisoners. Confederate records claimed the loss of 504,000 rations of bread and 915,000 rations of meat—a disaster that sent the Confederate commissary scrambling. Stuart could not stop such depredations, but he did his level best to harass the Federals at all points.[42]

Fitz Lee's troopers renewed their skirmish with the foe's rear-guard but made little headway. They struggled late into the night with Gregg and Wilson and then camped on the north bank of the North Anna.[43] Gordon meanwhile approached the North Anna at a ford farther up the river since the bridge was burned. There he discovered less resistance. Only flank-guarding videttes from the 5th Michigan Cavalry held the opposite bank. Heavily timbered hills gave the Federals a defensive advantage, but the odds rested with Gordon. The Wilkes Countian ordered Captain John B. McClennahan to take a dismounted detachment of 5th North Carolina Cavalry troopers and clear the banks. In conjunction with McClennahan, Captain John M. Galloway's fifth squadron of the 5th was instructed to launch a frontal assault against the ford. Supported by McClennahan, Galloway's Tarheels drew their sabres and charged with a yell. The Yankees ran, giving Gordon a bridgehead across the North Anna. The Tarheel brigade then chased the fleeing enemy and advanced close to Sheridan's camps, though it must have been very late before the entire brigade was able to do so. At one point, troopers from the 1st harassed Federals from the 6th Ohio and the 6th New York. A Tarheel officer even managed to cut his way through to an artillery piece. Placing his hand on the gun, he said, "This is my piece." A Federal gunner disagreed quickly, saying "Not by a d____d sight" as he knocked the Confederate off his horse and captured him. This fighting accomplished nothing, however, so Gordon and Stuart called a halt. When the tired brigade camped, the Tarheels could see the raiders' campfires burning in the distance.[44]

The second day of the raid opened with Sheridan still holding a solid hand, and their pursuers trying to change that. Stuart and Gordon did not let up on Sheridan. By 3:00 A.M., The North Carolina Cavalry Brigade was in the saddle. They found enemy outposts a short distance from their camp. Federal skirmishers issued out at Gordon's approach, and Gordon responded with the 2d North Carolina Cavalry. A short skirmish resulted in no apparent advantage for either side. Since Fitz Lee was still north of the river, this may have been the "frequent attempts [made] during the night to drive me from the station" Custer reported. Troopers from the 1st Battalion Maryland Cavalry, based near Hanover Junction, also contributed to this impression.[45] Meanwhile, at the river, the Federal cavalry divisions in Fitz

Lee's front crossed the North Anna, and Fitz Lee's troopers gave them a send-off with artillery and an advance of dismounted men. Nonetheless, the Yankees managed to disengage and take up the march again with full haversacks and fed horses.[46]

In Sheridan's wake, the separated Rebel columns came together at Beaver Dam Station. They paused to survey their foe's handiwork. Gordon's cavalrymen cursed at the sight of burning food and medicine.[47] Stuart sketched the situation for Braxton Bragg, President Davis's military advisor:

> A large body of the enemy's cavalry reached Beaver Dam yesterday at 5 P.M., and is now advancing in the direction of Richmond via Trinity Church. My cavalry have been fighting them all day yesterday and are sill in his rear pushing on. Their rear left Anderson's Bridge at 8 A.M., where they camped last night.[48]

The Rebels collected information from all quarters. One 4th Virginia scout reported that the Unionists had marched southward along the Mountain Road. Stuart wondered. What was the enemy's target now? Why was this huge force continuing its southward march, so far from the support of the Army of the Potomac? Could their goal be the capital of the Confederacy? Memories of the Kilpatrick-Dahlgren raid influenced such thinking. "I think," Stuart surmised, "he will cross between Hanover Junction and Richmond, but it will be well to be prepared for him in the defenses at Richmond."[49]

With that in mind, Stuart again split his command. Fitz Lee, with Wickham and Lomax, drew the duty of blocking Sheridan's route. They headed for Hanover Junction to access the Telegraph Road. Stuart would march with this column. In the meantime, Gordon was asked to follow Sheridan and harass his rear at all hazards "to prevent any delay or depredation on the line of march."[50] Gordon's assignment would require continuous fighting and independent command, so it amounted to a commendation. According to one trooper, Stuart's idea of a compliment was "assignment to extra hazardous or extra fatiguing duty. If he observed some specially good conduct on the part of a company, squad, or individual, he was sure to reward it by an immediate order to accompany him upon some unnecessarily perilous expedition."[51] With that, Gordon and Stuart parted, never again to meet on this earth.

Stuart had not yet experienced his last parting of the day. As chance would have it, Stuart's wife and children were visiting the nearby home of Colonel Edmund Fontaine. The Federals had apparently not molested the Stuarts, but Jeb still wanted to check on them. He asked a staff officer, Major Andrew Reid Venable, to accompany him. Mrs. Stuart greeted her husband of eight and a half years at the front door. The general, still astride his horse, exchanged a few private words with his lady before bidding her "a most affectionate farewell." As they rode away, Venable noticed that his chief became strangely silent. Stuart broke the spell only to say that he never expected to live through the war, and that if the Confederacy ever succumbed he preferred to die.[52]

Sheridan, being mostly unengaged, enjoyed a leisurely pace on May 10. The Federal column covered between fifteen and eighteen miles during the day. Such was not the case with the pursuing Confederate troopers, who put in a full day's march. One of Stuart's favorite expressions, to "go 'a-kiting,'"[53] applied here as Stuart's column took an alternate route from Beaver Dam because enemy outriders left felled trees across the Richmond road. Officers began to worry; one told Stuart that it was impossible for them to overtake and stop Sheridan. Stuart replied, "No, I would rather die than let him go on." Fitz Lee suggested that troops be sent to Tunstall's and Old Church to block Sheridan. Scouts meanwhile kept tabs on the enemy, spotting the head of the Federal column at Ground Squirrel Bridge at 4:15 P.M.[54] Stuart also kept General Lee appraised:

13. "Every Man Must Be a Hero" 217

"Gordon's brigade are rapidly pursuing the enemy toward Beaver Dam. None went toward Gordonsville except a mere picket near Greenbay, which was of the party pursued by Gordon. Lomax is following. The enemy's horses are broken down. They are shooting them in the road. I shall give directions about the railroad."[55]

The day passed uneventfully. Sheridan bivouacked on the south bank of the South Anna late on May 10 after his troopers procured forage. Since the column's head had been at the South Anna since 4:15, some Federals doubtless began reaching in the direction of Richmond, which was less than twenty miles away. Gordon followed somewhere in Sheridan's rear; the delay at Beaver Dam Station evidently prevented him from harassing the enemy that day.[56]

Stuart reached Hanover Junction around 10:00 P.M. He gave some thought to continuing the march, but Lomax's and Wickham's men had had enough. Both men and horses were close to the breaking point. He instructed staff officer Henry McClellan to accompany Lee to his bivouac. McClellan was to see that the column resumed its march at 1:00 A.M. The anxious Stuart then rode on to Taylorsville, two and a half miles south of Hanover Junction, before he allowed himself repose.[57] Even Stuart began to show signs of fatigue. The evening's accommodations, which he shared with Major Venable, consisted of field-glasses for a pillow and a used blanket for cover. Before turning in, however, Stuart sent one last dispatch to his lieutenant from Wilkes County. "Tell Gordon every man must be a hero to-morrow. I know that he will do his duty."[58]

In the first hour or so of May 11, Colonel Bradley T. Johnson arrived in Taylorsville. Johnson was the commander of a collection of Maryland forces guarding the five high bridges over the North Anna, South Anna, and Middle rivers near Hanover Junction. Stuart had requested artillery support from Johnson shortly after midnight. Yet in responding to the request, Johnson was welcomed only by McClellan; the cavalry commander was by that time sound asleep. Both McClellan and Johnson turned Stuart over, but the men could not wake him. Nonetheless, Johnson delivered the finest battery he had and enjoined McClellan to be careful with it.[59]

When the appointed hour came, McClellan turned to the next order of business. As directed, he saw to it that Fitz Lee's troopers were in the saddle. He also gave a wake-up call to Stuart and his staff in Taylorsville, and this time he was successful. After reporting the completion of his duties to Stuart, the major sought rest for himself. When the headquarters party began moving out, someone said to Stuart, "General, here's McClellan, fast asleep. Shall I wake him?"

"No," Stuart said. "He has been watching while we were asleep. Leave a courier with him and tell him to come on when his nap is out."[60]

The next few hours passed quietly. Near 2:00 A.M. on May 11, while Stuart's column renewed its race to gain Sheridan's front, the cavalry commander paused and sent a dispatch to Bragg. Stuart wrote that Unionists had been reported near Ground Squirrel Church and Ground Squirrel Bridge on the Mountain Road, and placed Gordon near Sheridan's camp at the farm of a Mrs. Crenshaw, at the crossing of the South Anna.[61]

As Stuart thought, Gordon had pressed his men hard to catch the Federals. One Tarheel squadron, from the 5th, was so fought-out that its commander asked Colonel Evans to hold it in reserve the next day. By the same token, the brigade's horses were as worn and ill-fed as ever; the men could hardly remember what remounts were. Yet the Tarheels continued their march, hard on Sheridan's heels.[62]

At about the same time, before the curtain came up on the final act, Sheridan decided to wreak more havoc in the countryside. He sent Davies's Brigade east to Ashland. It was still dark when the Federals arrived, chased away a few Rebels, and destroyed government buildings, several miles of track, a locomotive, and a few cars. The bulk of Stuart's cavalry was still just below Taylorsville, but the 2d Virginia Cavalry managed to appear at some point. Fierce fighting flared. The Federals, principally the 1st Massachusetts Cavalry, lost sixteen men and three officers.[63] The opponents broke contact before morning. Davies's Brigade made its way toward Sheridan and rejoined the main Federal column at Allen's Station on the Richmond, Fredericksburg, and Petersburg Railroad. From there, the blue cavalry marched on. Merritt led the way. Wilson came next, and Gregg formed the rear guard.[64]

When Jeb Stuart arrived in Ashland he surveyed the scene of the nighttime battle. At 6:30 A.M. he wrote Bragg, "The enemy reached this point just before us, but was promptly whipped out, after a sharp fight, by Fitz Lee's advance, killing and capturing quite a number. General Gordon is in rear of the enemy.... My men and horses are tired, hungry, and jaded, but *all right*."[65]

As his dispatch indicated, Stuart led his troopers to the intersection of the Telegraph and Old Mountain Roads. McClellan remembered, "As I rode by his side we conversed on many matters of personal interest. He was more quiet than usual, softer, and more communicative. It seems now that the shadow of the near future was already upon him."[66]

So they came to an abandoned stagecoach inn called Yellow Tavern, which stood near the intersection of the Telegraph and Old Mountain Roads. A row of aspen trees stood in front of the building and gave no hint of approaching battle; yet warriors came. The head of Stuart's column reached Yellow Tavern at 8:00 A.M. Stuart arrived two hours later. At long last, he was between the enemy and Richmond. Stuart first alerted his government to the possibility that Sheridan would double back or head in other directions. Then, apparently figuring that Sheridan would continue toward Richmond, he settled down to await Sheridan at Yellow Tavern. Besides his own forces, he counted on the support of two other commanders: Bragg, who commanded Richmond's defense troops, and Gordon, who continued to hang on to Sheridan's rear. Whether Bragg's troops could fight the enemy effectively was questionable, so Stuart sent McClellan to confer with Bragg. Stuart had no such worries about the North Carolina Cavalry Brigade. As if in confirmation, firing from the direction of Ground Squirrel Bridge was heard as early as 7:00 A.M.[67]

Gregg's men began wrestling with Gordon's bulldog tactics early that morning. Sheridan's rear-guard had spent the night around Goodall's Tavern, a country hotel on the old Richmond-Gordonsville stage road (Mountain Road) just eighteen miles from Richmond. Dawn of May 11 found the North Carolina cavalry brigade groping forward, still searching for the enemy rear-guard's exact location. Soon the Tarheels confronted the South Anna.[68] Ground Squirrel Bridge spanned that stream in times of peace, but Yankees had made it into smoking ruins. This, said one witness, "Would have direfully delayed almost any other man than Gordon." Either through prior knowledge or by reconnaissance, Gordon found "an old, steep-banked, almost impassable ford." Knowing the situation and fearing delay, the general took on the ford and its banks, which seemed almost fifteen feet high. Galloping to the river, he pointed to the ford and told all within hearing that this was the only way across. He then yelled "Forward!" and "with a mighty plunge he led the way." The 5th North Carolina Cavalry splashed behind him, and the other regiments followed. The treacherous ford took its toll and injured not a few, some seriously.[69]

After the brigade crossed, the Tarheels charged ahead and took position on a high hill above the river. Unfolding before them was the striking sight of Sheridan's rear-guard waiting in a large clearing around Goodall's Tavern. This was the 1st Maine, one of the finest regiments in the Federal army. The unit was under orders to hold while the rest of Sheridan's column moved on. Bullets from Federal skirmishers already whizzed through the air; the enemy knew of Gordon's approach.[70] From Gordon's vantage point, the sight from the hill must have been daunting. The old hotel, as well as every outhouse, stable, and barn surrounding it, bristled with sharpshooters. The Yankees appeared firmly entrenched, but Gordon resolved to test their position. At his behest, the 1st took its normal place in front and advanced.[71] The 5th dismounted all but one squadron, then followed Company F toward the foe. Up the road they walked in column of fours, braving the storm of enemy fire. Gordon then instructed the 5th to swing out into line of battle to the right of the road. The 5th continued the advance with a "steady step and fire." This continued until 10:00 A.M., by which time dismounted portions of the 1st and 2d were also in place and skirmishing heavily.[72]

The sharpshooters' fight lasted "several hours," and made enough racket for Confederates at Yellow Tavern to hear it. Gordon decided he could not dislodge the enemy in this manner without artillery, so he decided to change tactics. Sending Colonel Cheek to flank the Federal right with the mounted squadron from the 5th, Gordon took personal command of the 1st. Cheek caused enough of a diversion for the 1st to advance safely. The two detachments joined in battle and focused their wrath on the enemy. According to Cheek:

> We had the most desperate hand-to-hand conflict I ever witnessed. The regiment we met was the First Maine, and it had the reputation of being the best cavalry in the Army of the Potomac. Sabre cuts were given thick and fast on both sides. The staff of my colors received two deep cuts while the sergeant was using it to protect himself from the furious blows of a Yankee trooper.

The dismounted Yankees soon withdrew, followed by the North Carolina Cavalry Brigade. One witness described this withdrawal as a rout. Federals called it falling back "with some confusion and considerable loss."[73]

A battery of Federal artillery boomed a greeting as Gordon next approached Ground Squirrel Church. There, in a wood line near the church, a mounted line of fresh Federals waited. The line stretched one hundred yards on either side of the road. Gordon had no artillery with him, but he did not hesitate.[74] Since beginning the pursuit, the general had complimented the 2d North Carolina Cavalry on occasion. Now, on this field, he gave the 2d the task of capturing the battery. Lieutenant Shubal G. Worth of Randolph County, the regimental adjutant, led the attack. He found the Federal artillery well posted and heavily protected. As a result, the attack failed, and Worth died in the attempt. Still, the effort paved the way for the success of the brigade's next move. Gordon afterward told Major W. P. Roberts that the 2d had "covered itself with imperishable glory."[75]

Meanwhile, Cheek led a squadron through the woods to the right. In column of fours, the troopers struck the enemy flank. The ensuing hand-to-hand struggle forced back the enemy, but cost Gordon the services of Cheek. "Here again the sabre was freely used," Cheek wrote, "and here it was that while pursuing a fleeing foe, with the point of my sabre in his back, his companion, with his pistol almost in my face, sent a bullet crashing through my shoulder." Cowles subsequently took command of the 1st.[76]

Paul B. Means of the 5th had a different view of Cheek's flank attack. In the midst of the "rattling fire," Means saw Cheek and Gordon charge past the left of the 5th North Carolina Cavalry. As this Cabarrus County trooper saw it, the two commanders led the entire 1st as well as a squadron of the 5th. At any rate, Means agreed on the hand-to-hand nature of the fight. He described the effect of the close quarters fighting on the enemy: "Men will not stand long the cold steel and clash of the saber."[77]

Major John Galloway commanded the battered squadron for which he had requested reserve duty the evening before. As the battle progressed, his troopers took up a protected position behind thick woods. They listened as the firing became more rapid, and they congratulated themselves on their secure position. Gordon ended this idyllic existence. When he sent a courier to request the squadron's presence on the field. Advancing at the trot, these troopers saw two mounted regiments of Yankees, one of which was grappling hand-to-hand with the 1st. Sharpshooters were everywhere, supporting the fray. Galloway ordered his troopers to charge directly for the second mounted regiment. A rebel yell, a charge, and a vicious fight broke the foe. Gordon arrived in the wake of the charge and told the squadron commander that he had not intended for the squadron to do that. He had only planned on using the cavalrymen for a show of force. But Gordon added that the attack was gallantly executed; it had decided the day.[78]

Reckless exposure to enemy fire could be seen not only in the ranks but also in Gordon's personal staff. Gordon nearly lost the services of his aide-de-camp, Kerr Craige, when enemy fire killed both horses that bore Craige that day, narrowly missing the cavalryman. The second horse did not even belong to Craige. Frustrated at the loss of his first horse, Burton's son acquired a new mount by borrowing one from a trooper he sent to the rear.[79] Luckily, Craige apparently received a third horse from Frank Brown of the 5th. Brown captured four privates and three horses that day, and also personally grappled with an "athletic Yankee Captain." The Federal officer unhorsed Brown with a powerful sabre blow, but the officer's horse fell dead at the same moment. Brown recovered and started to beat the Yankee senseless with his gun-butt before the captain surrendered. Brown drew the honor of escorting his captive to Libby Prison, where he might have been tempted to brag about other heroes of the battle. The bugler of the 1st was worth a story or two. He had sounded the charge on his own bugle, dashed ahead, captured a Federal bugle, and then re-sounded the charge on his new horn.[80]

When the fighting ended, Gordon let his men rest and collect spoils. Among his haul was an entire wagon-load of Spencer rifles and ammunition. Gordon had done his best, but he did not have the strength to overwhelm the Federal foe. Now it was up to Jeb Stuart and Braxton Bragg.

It was decision time for Jeb Stuart. Now that he was ahead of Sheridan, how should he prepare his defense? Should he set his forces directly in front of the Federal advance, or should he place them to assail the Federal flank? Stuart preferred to hit the Federal flank since his cavalrymen were outnumbered, but he could only do so if Richmond were defended with sufficient strength. McClellan, in his errand to Bragg, was charged with confirming this. In the meantime, arrangements had to be made. Stuart compromised. He positioned Wickham on the right, mostly parallel to the Telegraph Road, and Lomax on the left, west of the road and almost at right angles to it. The horse artillery he posted in the center. Together, the units formed an obtuse angle with a two hundred yard interval "between Lomax and the prolongation of Wickham's lines." A portion of the 1st Virginia Cavalry was retained as a mounted reserve. In this wise, Stuart's cavalrymen could deter Sheridan's advance from both front and flank.[81]

Stuart prepared while Sheridan marched down the Mountain Road and drew nigh Yellow Tavern. As the morning grew old, the threat of impending battle hung in the air. Battle sounds reverberated from the rear; in front, Confederates sniped at the Federals and then galloped away. Then, when Sheridan paused at Hungary Station to tear up railroad tracks, troopers from the 6th Pennsylvania Cavalry saw Rebels advancing on the Ashland and Richmond Road. It was time to fight. Merritt ordered the Reserve Brigade to support the 6th Pennsylvania. The raiders reached the abandoned inn at about 11:00 A.M., and skirmishing began.[82]

13. "Every Man Must Be a Hero" 221

The Rebels thought they had Sheridan penned in. Bragg held Richmond, Gordon hovered to the northwest, Wickham sat slightly north of the Yankee advance, and Lomax blocked any eastward movement.[83] The tactical situation never dawned on Sheridan, however. His troopers attempted to drive the Rebels from the Telegraph Road. Custer ordered two regiments to "dismount and drive the enemy" from a thin skirt of woods immediately to his front. Leiper M. Robinson of the 5th Virginia Cavalry recalled the Federal attack. His regiment, in deep ditches along either side of the Telegraph Road, watched the Federals approach in either two or three lines. The fire of Lomax's Brigade did not slow the advance; on the contrary, the brigade suffered at the hands of the enemy. Colonel Henry C. Pate, commanding the 5th Virginia, stood along a bank, waved his hat, and called to his men to stand fast. His men at last stiffened, but Pate fell dead with a bullet in his head.[84]

Staff officer Andrew Reid Venable rode with Stuart that day. Before the Telegraph Road assault, Venable learned, Stuart had ridden over to talk to Pate. The cavalry commander asked him to hold until reinforcements came. Pate rose and said simply, "I will do so." Stuart closed the conversation by complimenting the colonel's gallantry and by extending his hand, repairing their strained friendship. The day after Pate met his fate, Stuart further explained their mended relationship. "You know that Pate and myself have had unkind feelings toward each other," he told Venable. "I want to say that his conduct in holding the line which was the key to our position with a small force against over-whelming numbers was one of the most gallant and heroic acts of the war." Stuart also expressed these thoughts to McClellan.[85]

The Federals enjoyed early success on one part of the battlefield. After the opening shots, Colonel Thomas C. Devin's Brigade came up from Hungary Station to join in the battle. Devin, ordered to drive the enemy from the Brook Turnpike, "swung around on the turnpike, driving the enemy from and seizing the cross-roads leading to Ashland and Hanover Court-House, the point being six miles from Richmond." The 6th New York Cavalry then reconnoitered toward Richmond along the Brook Turnpike. The New Yorkers penetrated the outer defenses of Richmond and rode toward the intermediate defenses. From that vantage point, Devin reported, "The bells could be heard ringing, locomotives whistling, and general alarm and bustling seemed to prevail in Richmond." The way to Richmond lay wide open, but Sheridan chose to stay and fight with Stuart.[86]

Since the Federals maintained their grip on the Brook Road, McClellan did not make it back from Richmond until after 2:00 P.M. The major, compelled to travel through fields to avoid capture, found Stuart south of Half-Sink on the Confederate right, near an artillery battery. Bragg, McClellan reported, counted about four thousand irregular troops. Since three additional brigades were on the way from Petersburg, Bragg thought he could hold. Stuart was pleased with this information, and decided that he could retain his position on Sheridan's flank. At that moment, Wickham's Brigade held the right. Lomax's Brigade, on the left, held the Telegraph Road for a short distance and then crossed it to a hill on the left. A piece of artillery sat on that hill, and two more guns waited immediately in the road. Only a portion of the 1st Virginia Cavalry was mounted, and it was being held as a mobile reserve. With any luck, Stuart thought, infantry from Richmond would strike a blow. Stuart and McClellan, remaining near Half Sink, then talked together for more than an hour.[87]

McClellan did not report it, but Stuart thought about Gordon's Brigade during this time. The unit was probably part of the reinforcements Stuart had promised Pate. Garnett was standing with another officer when a courier from Gordon rode up. The courier's horse was exhausted, but he carried an important dispatch addressed to General Stuart. Garnett took him to Stuart. The message announced Gordon's fight near Ground Squirrel Bridge, and also mentioned a "particularly gallant" charge made by the 1st. Stuart read the dispatch, slapped his right hand on his thigh, and exclaimed "Bully for Gordon!" Then, in a lower tone, he said, "I wish he was here."[88] (Other sources recount Stuart's words as "Would to God that Gordon were here" or "I wish Gordon was here."[89]) That the Virginian was thinking about the North Carolina general is equally evident in a 3:00 P.M. note to Bragg, in which he confidently described his plans. Placing Sheridan's whole force at Yellow Tavern between Mountain Road and Fredericksburg Railroad and Gordon one and one-half miles south of Chile's Tavern, Stuart suggested a combined attack with the cavalry and a brigade from Richmond once Gordon joined his right.[90]

If one takes Stuart's wish statement as evidence, it seems the cavalry commander doubted whether Gordon could join him. If so, that doubt was well founded; Gordon still grappled with the Federal rearguard. At any rate, as clock hands neared 4:00 P.M., the Confederates desperately needed reinforcements. According to Heros Von Borcke, Stuart only had 1,100 men at Yellow Tavern. Though Von Borcke cites Stuart as the source, this figure is extremely unlikely. Since most sources agree that Stuart used between four and five thousand men in the Yellow Tavern campaign, that places upwards of three thousand men in Gordon's ranks if Von Borcke was correct. On the contrary, it seems more logical to credit Gordon's Brigade with around one thousand men. Another more reliable estimate credits Stuart with 2,400 men, as well as ten guns.[91] Either way, Sheridan was much stronger in both men and matériél.

And the strong would wait no longer. Sheridan decided the time had come for his next attack. Custer thought he saw a way to get at the well-sited Confederate artillery on Stuart's left. Around 4:00 P.M., Custer charged with his brigade, mostly mounted; two of the brigade's regiments threatened Breathed's horse artillery frontally to occupy their attention, while a third regiment flanked the position. General George H. Chapman and his brigade struck Stuart's extreme right. Yet another regiment struck the Southern line about fifty or one hundred yards to the left of Custer. Southerners replied with a "brisk fire," and made it hot while the Yankees made their way past fences and over a bridge.[92]

As intended, the gravest danger came on the extreme left. Bradley Johnson's precious guns were there, in advance of Lomax's line and unsupported. Pressured Confederates soon fell back about a quarter of a mile to a ravine, leaving two artillery pieces to attacking Michigan troopers. Stuart and Venable rode over to help. Venable chastised his commander for exposing himself on horseback, but Stuart only laughingly said "I don't reckon there is any danger" before he headed to his broken left. Leaving Venable with Lomax to help prepare a counterattack, Stuart joined Captain G. W. Dorsey of the 1st Virginia Cavalry and about eighty other men on Telegraph Road. There Stuart fought, encouraged his men to hold, and witnessed the release of the Confederate reserve. Part of the 1st Virginia Cavalry had been posted on the extreme left of Wickham's Brigade, but the remainder was still in reserve; now those troopers hurled themselves at Custer's advance and knocked it back. Then the moment came; Stuart was shot.[93]

At Stuart's behest, Fitz Lee took command of the shattered Rebel line. The wounded general, as he was carried off the field, exhorted his men: "Go back! go back! and do your duty, as I have done mine, and our country will be safe. Go back! go back! I had rather die than be whipped," but it was too late. Custer's Michiganders recovered from the counterattack of the 1st Virginia and, Custer wrote, "after a close contest," routed the Rebels from the field. Even Lomax's line fell to pieces before Chapman's assault. As Sheridan described it, his men drove the foe "back toward Ashland and across the north fork of the Chickahominy, a distance of about four miles." Fitz Lee could do nothing but withdraw; he led his remaining troopers across the Chickahominy at Half Sink and moved them to Woolrich's Shop.[94]

Leiper Robinson's experiences illuminate the disorderly part of the Confederate retreat. Simply put, he ran for it. He and the men of the 5th Virginia jumped up from their Telegraph Road positions and scampered past a flank fence. Robinson never forgot the sound of Federal minie balls "plattering against the planks like hailstones." From there the Rebels ran toward a wide-open field. Some surrendered. Others challenged fate and crossed the field under deadly Federal fire. Those who made it joined other retreating Confederates in camp near Atlee's Station that evening.[95]

Overhead, a thunderstorm gathered. Now, only Bragg blocked Sheridan's direct path to Richmond and beyond.[96]

Obviously, Gordon never did find Stuart's right. According to David McM. Gregg, commanding Sheridan's Second Division, Gordon instead focused on the Federal rear-guard after the Ground Squirrel fighting ended. "The attacks of the enemy were repeated during the entire day," Gregg reported, "thus forming a part of the general engagement with the enemy at Yellow Tavern. The Second Brigade of this division was alone engaged, and without difficulty, in every attack, was more than able to drive the enemy at all points, inflicting upon him severe loss." A Richmond newspaper reported that Gordon attacked the Federals three times that day, "using them up badly every time." About the time Stuart fell, Gregg counterattacked Gordon, and the battles of May 11 came to a close.[97]

In the rain, the bulk of the Federal command camped on the battlefield while Sheridan planned. He had heard during the day that General Butler's forces were threatening the south side of Richmond, so he figured a demonstration to Fair Oaks would help Butler. To that end, around midnight the raiders marched. Sheridan marched by way of the Brook Turnpike, hoping to mass his command between the first and second lines of Confederate works on bluffs overlooking the Virginia Central Railroad and the Mechanicsville pike. Sheridan wanted to obtain the Confederate works commanding the Mechanicsville pike so he could use that road for his withdrawal.[98]

Richmond meanwhile braced itself for the worst. Fitzhugh Lee, who was collecting cavalrymen at Atlee's, thought the Confederate capital had never been in such danger of capture. Ben Butler was already knocking on the city gates from the direction of the James River. Generals George Pickett and P. G. T. Beauregard were gathering men at Petersburg and Drewry's Bluff to stave off the foe. Stripped of troops, Braxton Bragg was turning to local forces, many of whom were employees from government offices and workshops. Richmond officials warned of the enemy's approach, called out the militia, and summoned reinforcements from south of the James.[99]

Sheridan, who doubtless would have entered Richmond given the opportunity, decided against forcing an entrance into the city. He instead looked for a way to access the Mechanicsville Pike from Brook Turnpike. Sheridan soon found a military road just suited for the purpose. The east-west road, which sat inside the outer Confederate fortifications, provided a conduit to the Meadow Bridge Road and beyond to the Mechanicsville Turnpike. General James Wilson led the advance; his troopers marched down the Brook Turnpike, turned left onto the military road, and gained the Mechanicsville Turnpike. His march was not without event, however. A Confederate torpedo, which was an artillery shell rigged with a trigger wire, killed several animals and at least one Federal. Wilson got so angry that he used Rebel captives to clear the road. He also left a few torpedoes in the home of a wealthy planter who supposedly had helped place the mines. Wilson met no other trouble until he let his men take a break on the Mechanicsville pike, just north of the second line of Richmond's defenses. At that

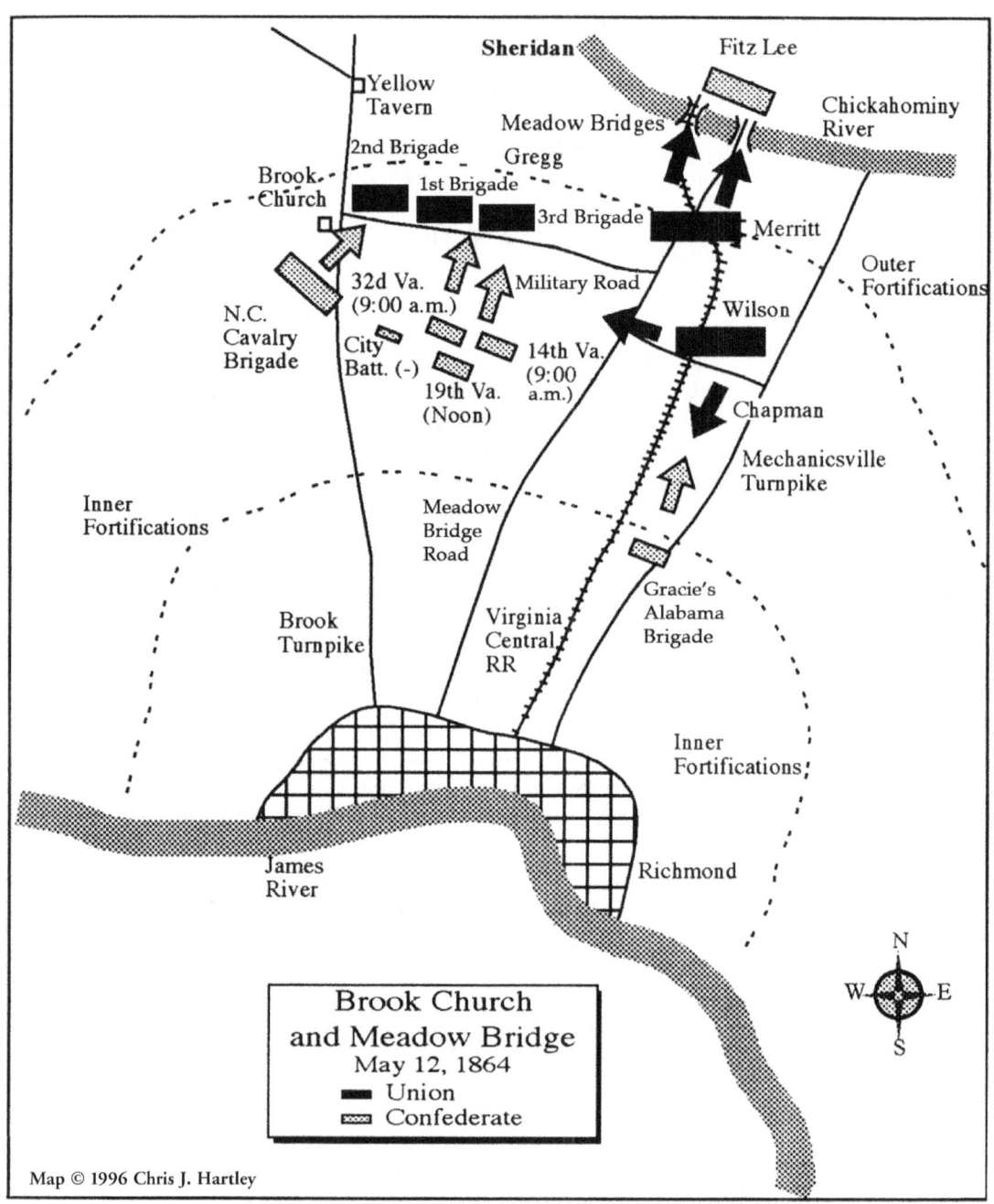

point Confederate artillery, sited so as to sweep the immediate area, pinned Wilson down. This convinced Federal commanders that the Meadow Bridge was the best route of escape.[100]

Unfortunately for the Unionists, Meadow Bridge had been partially destroyed. Nonetheless, Sheridan sent Merritt to explore that route of retreat. Beyond the bridge, the Federals found cavalry, infantry, and artillery that Fitz Lee had scraped together. At Merritt's direction, Custer's Federals crossed anyway. Two regiments outflanked the enemy position by way of a nearby railroad bridge, providing enough cover for engineers to rebuild the Meadow Bridge. That completed, troops crossed the river in strength. Custer reported, "After a hard contest,

13. "Every Man Must Be a Hero"   225

from which we suffered severely, the enemy were driven from his position, leaving his dead and wounded in our hands." Braxton Bragg and President Davis watched the Meadow Bridge fight from a hill in Richmond.[101]

The Meadow Bridge fighting caused delays all along the Federal column, stringing it out back to the Brook Turnpike. Confederates reacted: if Fitz Lee could hold, here was an opportunity to smash Sheridan to bits against the Chickahominy! While he was still pinned down, Wilson turned away one attempt to do just that. It was a sortie by Confederate General Archibald Gracie's arriving brigade of Alabamians. In response, Wilson sent Chapman's Brigade toward Richmond. Southerners in and before the city defenses simply shot too high, so Chapman's advance finished the matter. Sheridan wanted to be sure, though, so he sent Wilson a message. "Go back to General Wilson," Sheridan said, "and tell him to hold his position. He *can* hold it, and he *must* hold it!" Wilson did just that, allowing Sheridan to concentrate on his escape route.[102]

It was still raining as dawn of May 12 approached. David McM. Gregg was known as a steadfast man to his comrades, but being the man in command of Sheridan's rear division, he was in a precarious position. As Gregg put it, "The attack made by the leading division (the First) upon the enemy at the bridge, detained the Second Division, marching in rear, along the Brook turnpike and in front of the second line of the enemy's defenses." In short, Gregg could go nowhere until Merritt captured Meadow Bridge. The flank and rear of the Federal column were thus exposed to Richmond's second line of defenses, and to the North Carolina Cavalry Brigade.[103]

This gave Gordon the time and the opportunity he needed. He caught up with the rear of Gregg's column at a church along the Brook Turnpike, near its intersection with the strategic military road leading to Meadow Bridge. Like so many other Southern places of worship, the church became an unlikely backdrop for battle. This house of worship was known as Brook Church; another church, called Emmanuel, sat nearby. The nearby farm of the ironically-named Mr. Grant, and the sight of the capitol about two or three miles away, completed the scene. On this spot, General Gordon fought his last battle. Gunfire began soon after daylight; the "dull, heavy roar" wakened Richmond and reminded citizens of the days of McClellan.[104]

Gregg was no fool. He positioned his column strongly; several of his artillery pieces viciously swept the approaches to the road with canister. Such fire discouraged initiative, but General Gordon had one advantage: Richmond. He dismounted the 1st and 2d, ordered them into line of battle, and placed the 5th in mounted reserve to the right of the military road. Then, while Cowles oversaw Gordon's right wing, Gordon sent Lieutenant Craige to Richmond in search of artillery support and to coordinate an attack with troops from the city. Troopers from the 5th worried unnecessarily that Gordon was about order the 5th to charge those well-sited Federal batteries. "And that charge," wrote one cavalryman, "which he would have led in person, would have been about the last of our regiment."[105]

Evidently, Gordon planned to charge only in conjunction with support from Richmond. As he awaited Craige's return, the 1st and 2d maintained a heavy fire on Gregg's right, which was held by the Union Second Brigade. Gordon, realizing the power of his enemy, and his own lack of artillery, kept his command disposed "as to completely deceive the enemy with regard to his real strength." In doing so, he exhibited that commanding presence in battle for which he was known. He remained astride his horse, riding up and down his dismounted lines. The return fire was so heavy that an officer urged him to dismount. Gordon demurred. "No, we must set the men an example of gallantry to-day," he said.[106]

The results of Craige's mission were soon evident. In a few minutes, artillery rolled up to the battlefield. Means could not control his emotions: "And oh! such artillery!" he recalled.

This William Waud drawing of the Meadow Bridge area shows the key to Gordon's last battle (Library of Congress).

"It was the most beautiful in all its appearances that we ever beheld. The smoke of battle had never been about it." Gordon placed the pieces to the slight oblique right and front of the 5th, on the slope of some old entrenchments. After hasty preparations, the artillery fired — once — while Federal gunners turned their wrath on the newcomers. Union shells flew over and scattered the Confederate gunners in all directions. Already under stress at hearing of Stuart's wounding, Gordon simply exploded at the sight of soldiers scampering for safety[107]:

> Gordon was furious. He raved and begged. He called it 'Band Box Artillery,' which would have occurred only to him, possibly, under such a fire. But those artillerists "held the trenches faithfully" against Richmond's invaders. Some few of them could not even stand that and came through the woods by us. We laughed at them, ridiculed them, and asked them to go back and man their guns. But they looked at us as if we were surely crazy.[108]

As the general's plans fell apart, a minie-ball struck him in the arm. According to one account, it happened because Gordon was so disgusted that he galloped down the military road, right into the enemy's fire. An earlier account places Gordon in his skirmish lines, where he was trying to set an example for the local troops. Only a single attendant, John Moore of Gaston County, rode with him. Without fanfare, Gordon turned to Moore and said calmly, "I am wounded, bring a surgeon to me *here*, I can not leave my post to go to him." When Moore and the surgeon returned, they found the general abandoned by the skirmishers. He was lying on his back, holding his horse's reins with his unwounded arm. The horse, frightened by the enemy's fire, was wildly plunging about. Together the men calmed the horse, placed Gordon on its back, and held him there as they withdrew. Somehow they made it to safety without further injury, although Moore later counted a dozen balls in his clothing and equipment.[109]

Around them, the fight still swirled. Craige produced infantry support, some of which evidently arrived before Gordon's wounding. Elements of three regular Virginia regiments and three companies from the City Battalion began arriving at 9:00 A.M. Filling in on the right of Gordon's Brigade, these troops assaulted the left of Gregg's Second Brigade and the front of his First Brigade only to find the enemy deeply entrenched in breastworks of logs and rocks. Federal firepower from carbines and artillery, as well as flanking support from Wilson's men, repelled all advances.[110] When Gordon fell, Colonel Clinton Andrews, commander of the 2d, took the reins of the Tarheel brigade. He dismounted the 5th, and then ordered troops under Captain J. R. Erwin to cross the road and form on the Federal left. Erwin calmly turned to his men and said, "Come on, boys." He led his men through the canister-fire, over the road, and into line of battle. They then advanced to a board fence, which had been perforated with rifle balls. A company of sharpshooters under Captain E. F. Shaw added its fire.[111]

The Battle of Brook Church ended at about 4:00 when the Confederates fell back. By that time, Merritt's Federals had repaired Meadow Bridge and secured the crossing. Wilson also managed to disengage, enabling the Federals to continue their withdrawal. From Meadow Bridge, the blue cavalry continued its push, and later completed the raid virtually unchallenged. They generally marched southeast over the next few days, passing Bottom's Bridge and White Oak Swamp. By May 14, they reached a point between Haxall's Landing and Shirley on the James River. At last, they had arrived safely within the protection of General Butler's Union lines.[112]

Rightly so, the Southern press condemned the fighting of May 12 as "timidly managed." Sheridan took a tremendous risk with his force, powerful and mobile though it was. His column was strung out, and his troopers were tired from the Yellow Tavern fighting. On the column's southern flank loomed the Confederate capital and its lightly manned defenses. To the blue cavalry's northern flank and front coursed the Chickahominy. Fitz Lee's battered but game troopers barred the way at Meadow Bridge, and Gordon's Brigade pressed from behind. Yet rather than attack Sheridan's exposed column, many Confederate commanders stayed in the city's fortifications. Only the cavalrymen of the Army of Northern Virginia and a few infantry units carried out an assault. Sheridan's audacity, which paid off, stemmed from two things besides his confidence in his men. One was the discovery of a few uncovered Chickahominy fords—additional escape routes. The other was Grant's massive offensive, which had drawn the bulk of Southern manpower like a magnet.[113]

At any rate, the successful withdrawal of Sheridan from the Confederate "trap" was also a withdrawal of war from the life of James B. Gordon. He never challenged Federal cavalrymen again. Similarly, he never led Confederate horse-soldiers again. Some Tarheel cavalrymen saw their leader being carried from the field after he fell, and others heard of the catastrophe. They rushed to his side. "Gordon spoke cheeringly to them all," one witness remembered, "and said that he was not much hurt, and exhorted them to hold their ground."[114]

They loaded him on an ambulance and made for Richmond, probably by way of the Brook Turnpike. They reached the city around noon or 1:00 P.M. At that moment, Theodore Garnett waited and watched in the home of Jeb Stuart's brother-in-law, where Stuart had been taken after his wounding. Garnett's job was to sit beside Stuart's bed and keep the wounded general's pulse by holding his left hand. As he did so, a loud shout and other noise arose from outside, along Broad Street. Stuart woke at the noise and in an excited voice asked Garnett to find out what was happening. Garnett obeyed and found an ambulance moving slowly through the rain toward the capitol. He learned that it was a Yankee general being driven to the hospital. Garnett didn't believe the story, so he did not tell Stuart, who had fallen asleep. Garnett later found out that the wounded general was actually "our own dear commander of the North Carolina Brigade" on his way to the hospital. Stuart died that evening without knowing of his friend's plight.[115]

Gordon's ambulance at last halted in front of the Officer's Hospital in Richmond. The building was a four-story turreted structure that faced the east side of Tenth Street between Marshall and Clay Streets. Fittingly, the building had once been the home of the Richmond Female Institute. A few ladies there had been among the first to display Confederate flags way back in 1861; later that year, the institute became a hospital. Early in 1863, it was designated an officers' hospital. By the time Gordon arrived, the facility could handle about three hundred patients. Dr. James Bond Read was the surgeon in charge. Now, rain continued to fall as attendants unloaded the general and carried him inside. He was but one of thirty-three casualties brought to the hospital that day.[116]

The surgeon of the North Carolina Cavalry Brigade, who had accompanied Gordon to the hospital, directed the procedures. The hospital's staff also plied their trade. They found his condition to be "feeble, from fatigue, inadequate diet & loss of blood." Further examination revealed the extent of the injury. "The ball had passed through one of the arteries of the fore arm & split off a small portion of the inner condyle of the arm bone above the joint, not injuring this." The doctors operated immediately. "Everything did well," an attendant wrote, "& the prospects for saving the limb were not questioned."[117]

Outside, the press sought details of Gordon's injury. The Richmond *Dispatch* reported that Gordon was "suffering with a musket bullet wound in the left arm, which will have to be amputated. He was holding his bridle-rein when struck. The ball entered the forearm, breaking the bone, and passing through the muscle of the same arm above the shoulder." The *Examiner* noted Gordon's arrival at the Officers' Hospital and described his wound as a severe one "in the left arm above the elbow." Not to be outdone, the *Richmond Daily Whig* printed a list of wounded officers that were received at the Officers' Hospital, adding, "Most of the above, except Gordon, are slightly wounded." The newspaper also speculated that amputation would be necessary. However, at the last moment, the *Whig's* editors heard good news. "We are gratified to learn, just before going to press, that Gen. Gordon's wound is not serious, and that he will save his arm. This comes from his surgeon."[118]

The next few days passed uneventfully as Gordon rested. Of course, he could not attend either Stuart's funeral at St. James Church on May 13 or the interment at Hollywood Cemetery. It remained for him to mourn Stuart's passing in his own private way. He also hoped for the succor only Aurelia could bring. Unfortunately, Aurelia did not learn of Gordon's wounding until Monday, when she saw the announcement in the *Whig*. She had been dreading hearing such news, and saw that his wound was serious, but was thankful that it was "no worse." In a hasty note, she sent her "assurance of the sympathy and great anxiety which you know I feel," and hoped that he was comfortable since "hospitals must be so dreary and cheerless." In closing, she begged him to write soon and often if his wound permitted. After all, Aurelia reminded him, he had promised to notify her at once if anything happened.[119]

This letter never reached Gordon. Kerr Craige, who was at his general's side, saw Gordon's disappointment at not hearing from Aurelia. This troubled him but did not keep him down. The General's wound showed marked improvement over the weekend. A "virulent form of erysipelas" evidently made its appearance on Monday, yet his attendants saw no cause for alarm. By Tuesday, May 17, Gordon felt so well that he got out of bed and made his way downstairs — without permission. He sat in the hospital's doorway for some minutes. One local newspaper even reported that he was seen on the city streets that day. This may have been a warning sign; in some cases, erysipelas has taken hold as quietly as a thief in the night. At least one Civil War–era patient said he had never felt better in his life minutes before the disease showed itself.[120]

Gordon's surgeons doubtless chastised him for his wanderings. In any event, he returned to his room. At some point, probably during the afternoon, a Mr. Gibbon visited him for the first time. Gibbon volunteered to nurse Gordon and sat with him for some hours. When Gibbon rose to leave, Gordon asked him to return the next day. He evidently enjoyed the man's company.[121] Gordon's staff officers were also in and out during the day. Topics of conversation were typical of the general. He spoke "frequently of his attachment and predilection for the Episcopal Church" and also talked of his mother. With Kerr Craige and other staff officers he discussed the condition of his brigade. Gordon urged the officers to "pay particular attention to having horses and men cared for."[122]

Late in the day, he took a turn for the worse. After midnight, Gordon began to realize his condition was critical. Erysipelas set in with some violence. Gordon had difficulty resisting it due to his weakened state. This dangerous skin affliction usually began with a chill and a fever, and was sometimes accompanied by a throat inflammation that would interfere with breathing. A few hours later, the disease's bright red blush would be evident on the skin, and would spread from the point of attack. In cases of great severity, the pain and fever might produce delirium in the patient, as well as nausea and vomiting. Erysipelas, which has also been described as typhus-like, has been called the "scourge of hospital wards." Also known as St. Anthony's Fire, erysipelas can originate from contamination of a surgical wound.[123]

At 9:30 A.M. on Wednesday, May 18, Mr. Gibbon returned to the hospital. Learning that Gordon "had had an uncomfortable night and was not so well," Gibbon hastened to the general's bedside. Gordon greeted him by name and said, "Good morning."[124]

Gibbon found the hospital to be an increasingly busy place because of Grant's offensive. The hospital had admitted more than eighty patients over the last three days. Despite this, the staff's concern for the wounded cavalryman brought a crowd to Gordon's room in the persona of two surgeons. One was Doctor Read. The other was Charles Bell Gibson, who occasionally held consultations with Read. Read and Gibson had only recently examined W. L. Barrier, a trooper from the 1st North Carolina Cavalry who had received an arm wound at Brook Church remarkably similar to Gordon's. The two surgeons examined Gordon, and then said the wound was not doing well. This struck home. After he asked the time, Gordon asked Gibbon "to write to my mother & tell her I am very ill, but hope to recover...." Then, perhaps in the hope that another twenty-four hours would bring improvement, Gordon asked Gibbon to wait until Thursday night to mail the letter.[125]

But that was a vain hope; Gordon, who was forty-two years old, somehow knew the seriousness of his condition. Physically, the general was restless and suffered from a sick stomach. There is also evidence that gangrene had begun to plague his arm. One newspaper reported that the surgeons tried to save his arm at the risk of losing Gordon. Another recorded that Gordon rejected his surgeons' advice to have the arm amputated. Family tradition holds that Gordon prized his looks so much that he refused amputation — much as Joachim Murat had once told his executioners, "Spare my face, aim for my heart." This information is neither confirmed nor disproved by other extant evidence, but it is not far-fetched. Gangrene did develop in some Civil War cases of erysipelas.[126]

At any rate, with Kerr Craige sitting at his bedside, Gordon asked to speak with Dr. Otis Frederic Manson, perhaps in the hope he would receive better news. Gordon asked Dr. Manson what he thought of his case, to which Manson replied that he was very sick. Again, Gordon asked the hour; it was 11:00 A.M. Gordon then turned to Dr. Gibson and asked him if he was a member of a church. Gibbon, realizing where the conversation was going, asked Gordon the same question. Gordon replied, "No, I like the church but am not a Christian."[127]

Gibbon then asked Gordon if he believed in Jesus Christ. "Oh yes," he said, and added that he was willing to die. Gordon called for Craige and instructed him to settle his affairs, and told him that he wanted his remains carried home. At noon, Gordon said, "I am evidently dying, ain't I?"

"Yes," Gibbon replied, "you have but a short time to live. Would you like to see a minister?"

"Yes, I ought to," Gordon said. Gibbon accordingly sent for a minister, and then spoke to Gordon one more time.

"He that believeth shall be saved," Gibbon said. Gordon was quiet for several minutes, and then gave Craige further directions about his affairs.[128]

In some fashion, Elizabeth Maxwell Alsop learned more about Gordon's last moments. Only two weeks had passed since Gordon and Miss Alsop had met on a train trip; now, she confided to her diary what she knew. "A short time before his death, he sent for the matron of the hospital to come to him. When she did so, he told her, 'I am going to die,' & upon her discouraging the idea, said 'No. I am not low-spirited, but I feel my time has come. What would my poor mother say, if she knew I was suffering here?'" It was about 12:45 P.M.[129]

Fifteen minutes later, James Byron Gordon "stretched himself upon the bed" and breathed his last.[130]

Conclusion: "Muffled Drums"

REDUCED TO NOTHING but remains in a box, James Byron Gordon began his last trip home. It was the evening of May 18, just hours after the general had expired. A Congressional delegation, bolstered by Richmond's Public Guard and band, escorted him to the railroad station where he was loaded aboard a waiting train. The locomotive then bore the sad cargo away from the city Gordon had given his all to defend. Southwestward across the Virginia countryside the train traveled, in effect closing a tiny chapter in Civil War history. At the Danville Depot, the Richmond contingent paid its final respects and departed. Kerr Craige, a trooper named Osborne, and a few other staff officers continued their dark journey alone.[1]

In Lynchburg, the eighteenth day of May had dawned with more promise. Aurelia, who awaited word of her wounded general, received a happy message that day. There was no danger, the note said, that Gordon would lose his arm. On Friday, hope vanished; she learned of his death by reading the newspaper. Elsewhere, a friend was shocked at Gordon's death. "Tidings of his death came upon us all unexpected — came to us in an hour when it was most desirable that he should be spared to us, to aid in directing the all powerful movements of our cavalry, since the fall of the lamented Stuart." Meanwhile, in a similar fashion, the cavalry heard of Gordon's death. On May 19, Waring wrote in his diary: "Fitz Lee telegraphs that Gen. Gordon has died of his wounds." Some began to hint that Fitz Lee was to blame for Sheridan's easy escape from the army's front. The Federals, it was said, feinted at Fitz in the Wilderness and started off on their raid before the general realized what was happening.[2]

Richmond newspapers did not touch this rumor, but they did speculate about the cause of Gordon's death. The Richmond *Whig* probably described it best: "General Gordon's wound was not regarded as a dangerous one, but he shrank from the shock superadded to great physical and mental exhaustion incurred during his pursuit of the Yankee cavalry ... and his fierce and repeated engagements with them...." A report of sick and wounded from General Hospital No. 4 — the Officers' Hospital — confirmed Gordon's date of death and listed the disease that killed him as "Vulnus Sclopeticum."[3]

Rumors surrounding Gordon's death were even more popular in the ranks of the Tarheel cavalry brigade. Cavalryman Fred Foard remembered it this way:

> James B. Gordon had received a flesh wound in the arm supposed to be slight, but as he had lost considerable blood, the surgeon advised him to go [sic] hospital in Richmond, where rich nourishing food would be attainable to him to accellerate [sic] the filling of his veins with new blood. He had been there but a short time when he was notified from the War Department that his Commission as Major General had been made out, and as soon as he was able to come and receive it and recommend his successor in the command of his old Brigade. This so exhilerated [sic] him that he went

immediately, walking to the war office and back. He received his promotion and recommended General Barringer for his successor. When he returned to the hospital the surgeons noticed a great change in him, and after examination told him that he had but a few hours to live.

His wound had absorbed the dread piemia from the tainted air of the hospital. He at once made his will and met his death which quickly followed with great calmness and dignity.[4]

Kerr Craige could not dispute such talk because duty took him away from the army. Disheartening though the task was, he could not shirk it because he carried Gordon's sword and his "dying messages." At least one of Gordon's horses, possibly the one he had been riding at Brook Church, also accompanied them to Wilkes.[5]

The countryside through which the contingent passed was already full of reports about the general. A student at the Hillsboro Military Academy expected Gordon's body to pass by that point. Three days after leaving Richmond, the funeral train stopped in Salisbury, Craige's hometown and Gordon's old stomping grounds. The town's Garrison Battalion received the body that evening "with appropriate honors." Gordon was laid in state at the town hall, while a guard of honor watched over him through the night. Early the next morning, a Sunday, Gordon's old friend Burton Craige was one of the pall bearers who took the general back to the train. Reported the local newspaper:

> The quiet of our streets was broken by the solemn cadence of the muffled drums.... All the troops from the Garrison that could be spared, were turned out and formed a beautiful escort for our lamented hero's remains to the Western Rail Road Cars. On the return of the Battalion to the Garrison, the commandant complimented them for their soldierly behavior.... It was remarked by some who were present at that early hour, that they never saw soldiers behave with more decorum."[6]

The next stop down the line was Statesville, where nearly three years before the Wilkes Valley Guards had boarded a train headed for the war. Craige's group left the rails behind there to navigate dusty roads through Taylorsville, over the Brushy Mountains, and down into the Yadkin Valley. It was a journey of at least a day, and its end brought no relief. A sad reception awaited the Confederate contingent in Wilkes. When Craige and company arrived at "Oakland," Gordon's slaves were thunderstruck. "All the colored people," wrote a relative of Gordon's, "went to the brow of the hill and threw themselves on the ground and mourned loudly for 'young Marse,' as his body was carried into the house."[7]

Like the servants, Gordon's family and friends shared their sorrow. Mrs. Brown especially felt the loss of her first-born son. One son was already gone, buried in far-away Arkansas; now, the war had wrenched another from her. If possible, it was harder this time, because she had always been very close to James. Not much can comfort a mother at such a time, but perhaps the visible reminders of his achievements helped. They buried Mrs. Brown's little boy, the general, in the shadow of the church he had helped to build.

Afterward, mourners stated their sympathy to Mrs. Brown and the family, in person and by mail. One letter from a "friend and sincere admirer of your noble son" expressed "profound and heartfelt sympathy" at Gordon's death. "I have watched his course since the beginning of this dreadful war, with great interest, and have felt sincere satisfaction" at Gordon's success, the correspondent wrote. All indications are that the writer was Governor Zebulon Vance.[8]

Gordon's brothers-in-law accepted the sad task of closing out Gordon's affairs. The process began soon after his death; after all, there were many outstanding accounts from his store. Calvin J. Cowles, for example, owed Gordon's estate $9.00 for the hauling of oats, while Gordon owed Cowles money for items such as twenty-eight pounds of beef, socks, indigo, and even an oven lid. The three men were even forced to bring suit on behalf of Gordon against several individuals to recoup principal and interest on land in other parts of Wilkes.[9]

In final tribute, a monument was later erected above Gordon's grave. A Wilkes County man made it out of stone from Wilkes County's Stone Mountain — near where Gordon had spent several days after returning from Emory & Henry. On the south side of the monument he etched powerful words:

> Beneath this stone a Hero martyr sleeps. Of all the offerings laid upon the altar of State Sovereignty and Constitutional Liberty there was none purer than that offered by Jas. B. Gordon, Affable and Courteous in his manners, generous and unselfish in his disposition, kind and indulgent in his nature. The name of this brave man is embalmed in the hearts of his Countrymen and by his courage and devotion he bequeathed to his kindred a legacy of more value than millions of gold and silver.

According to family tradition, the author of these words was Daniel Harvey Hill.[10]

In time, grass began to grow on Gordon's grave, and the grievous war drew closer to its end; and the general's story dimmed. Tragically, Wilkes County had not seen the last of the war. Fresh graves still were dug. Disaffection went unchecked. Then, almost a year after Gordon's death, the war came thundering down on Wilkesborough. Major General George Stoneman, commanding the Cavalry Division of the District of East Tennessee, raided Northwest North Carolina and Southwest Virginia at the direction of General Grant. His six thousand troopers occupied Wilkesborough at the end of March 1865. Gordon's mother and sisters, hearing of the approaching Yankees, hid the family's silver in a riverbank cave along the Reddies. They secured other family treasures beneath loose pine floor boards in "Oakland." When Stoneman's cavalry arrived, the family posted a "sentry" — a little girl playing with her dolls — on top of the boards in the assumption that "even a Yankee" would not bother a child. Even Gordon's horse escaped detection until a Federal bugler passing by "Oakland" blew his horn. The Confederate steed, veteran of so many battles, pranced about to the martial notes in such an obviously military fashion that he was discovered. The Yankees paraded Gordon's horse before "Oakland" for a few hours, as if to celebrate the passing of Gordon and the Confederacy.[11]

Stoneman's Raid was not an altogether pleasant experience for Wilkes County Unionists either, as the Federals intimidated and took what they needed. But the raid underscored one fact for all: the Federals had won. Calvin J. Cowles later thanked one of Stoneman's officers and "your soldiers of the Union who breasted the storm and flood riding the rough mountain roads by day and by night to restore the Old Flag to a people from whom it had been wrested by force and fraud...."[12]

Meanwhile, in Virginia, the war ended badly for the unit Gordon had left behind. The North Carolina Cavalry Brigade fought on until the end; but Phil Sheridan had been right about what his 1864 raid had accomplished. Sheridan listed among his successes the death of Stuart and the severe wound Gordon received. Without those men, the units they had commanded would never be the same. Indeed, when Kerr Craige returned from Wilkes in June 1864, he could already see the effects of Gordon's passing. According to Craige, Gordon's death amounted to "a heavy blow" to the cavalry." The members of the brigade, "all of whom were warmly attached to him," considered Gordon's loss a personal one. William H. H. Cowles agreed:

[Gordon's] death filled the entire command with grief and consternation, and though the brigade sustained its reputation to the last, yet it never recovered from his loss. We fought afterwards like well trained machines, but the *esprit du corps* [sic] was gone, and the croaking of the raven became louder.[13]

The North Carolina Cavalry Brigade did quite a bit of fighting between May 1864 and April 1865. As always, foremost in the brigade was Gordon's pride, the 1st North Carolina Cavalry Regiment; and the unit suffered for it. With the exception of Ransom, who had transferred to the infantry, every field officer of the regiment was either killed or wounded during the war. All but five commissioned officers met similar fates. In fact, after Cheek was hurt during the Yellow Tavern Campaign, Cowles and then Barringer assumed command of that regiment. At other times, Cowles was often called on to do temporary duty.

After Brook Church, the 3d North Carolina Cavalry joined the brigade to replace the 4th. This returned the brigade to its full complement of four regiments. Colonel Clinton Andrews relinquished brigade command to Colonel John A. Baker, commander of the 3d and the senior officer in the brigade. Baker held that post until May 30, when Gordon's friend P. M. B. Young took temporary command. Yankee metal struck Young in a subsequent action at Ashland, and command again devolved upon John Baker.[14]

On June 6, 1864, Rufus Barringer was commissioned brigadier general. Gordon had always thought highly of the man. After Barringer was wounded at Brandy Station, Gordon deplored his absence. He wrote: "Capt. Barringer ... is a most excellent officer and his services are much needed with his command But his wound was serious." Pride would have been the result had Gordon known of Barringer's promotion, as one of Gordon's last acts on earth had been to recommend Barringer's promotion. "Has displayed great skill and valour," Gordon wrote of his friend. "Is one of the best organizers and disciplinarians in the service."[15]

In assuming command of the North Carolina Cavalry Brigade, Barringer became the unit's third and last permanent commander. He led the unit to more laurels, and did much to enhance the brigade's efficiency. Davis's Farm, Blacks & Whites, and Belcher's Hill are but a few of the skirmishes through which the unit passed under his leadership. Barringer's greatest moment came at Reams Station in August 1864, where he led W. H. F. Lee's cavalry division — Rooney being absent sick — in defeating a Federal attempt to cut Richmond's communications with the South.[16] Perhaps Matthew Person sized up Barringer as well as anybody: "He is a slow old fellow but a good officer."[17]

The North Carolina Cavalry Brigade took its first step toward the end at Chamberlain's Run on March 31, 1865. (Stoneman's raiders were that day finishing their work in Wilkes County.) Charging across that stream against Sheridan's entrenched Federals, the brigade lost 120 killed, wounded, and captured, including twenty officers. Afterward, General W. P. Roberts broke down and wept when he saw how his old command, the 2d Horse, had suffered.[18] Thus battered from this fight and the subsequent battle at Five Forks, it is no surprise that the brigade soon collapsed. It happened at Namozine Church during the retreat to Appomattox. Daniel Coltrane heard Fitz Lee order W. H. F. Lee to "put his best brigades at the [Namozine Church] crossroad to protect General R. E. Lee's retreat. The safety of the entire army depended on it, said he." The task fell to the Tarheel cavalry brigade. The Yankee cavalry came, and kept coming, until at last the Tarheels ran out of ammunition and spirit. The enemy overwhelmed the once-proud brigade, tearing it asunder; Barringer was captured. At that point, he later wrote, he had lost control. He did not even know what had become of his adjutant, his headquarters wagons, his black horse, or his brigade. The North Carolina Cavalry Brigade was no more. Only a handful of its troopers escaped to surrender at Appomattox.[19]

How does a family deal with tragedy? For some months after the war, Aurelia Halsey corresponded with Mrs. Brown while they mourned.[20] The impact of Gordon's death apparently stayed with Aurelia, because from all indications she did not become romantically involved for nearly a decade. Finally, at 8:30 P.M. on April 23, 1873, she married General John Gaw Meem, a wartime captain and aide to General Kirby Smith who had been appointed brigadier general of Virginia Militia in 1872. The forty-year-old Meem, a Virginia Military Institute graduate, married Aurelia at St. Paul's Church in Lynchburg. The Rector, Reverend T. M. Carson, officiated.[21]

Aurelia was Meem's second wife. His first wife bore him two boys before she died in 1869. John and Aurelia had four children: Erna Russell, who only lived to age four, and Julia Halsey, Stephen Halsey, and James Lawrence Meem II. The Meems lived at Mount Airy, a beautiful 2,400-acre estate on the North Fork of the Shenandoah River that commanded a marvelous view.[22]

After living a decade at Mount Airy, Aurelia died suddenly on Saturday, August 11, 1883. Hearing the news, the Lynchburg media paid homage to the "unusually fine appearance" of the thirty-six-year-old "noble lady," and her "amiable disposition, easy and gentle" manner. Mrs. General Meem, said another article, "was well known as one of the most beautiful and accomplished ladies of Lynchburg. She was a general favorite among the people of Lynchburg." A railway accident caused a delay in the shipment of her body, but Mrs. Meem was laid to rest at Springhill Cemetery in Lynchburg on August 13. The Reverends T. M. Carson and Ed S. Gregory presided, and "many were the floral tributes laid on the coffin which contained the remains of one who had been so universally beloved."[23]

How does a family deal with tragedy? Old, blind Hamilton Brown probably missed having Gordon at his side as much as anyone. Still, he lived until March 1870, when he died at age 83. Gordon's mother passed away on January 6, 1889 during her ninetieth year. Fittingly, both were buried near James and Nathaniel in the Episcopal Church cemetery. Gordon's older sister, Martha, lived until July 1898, and her husband Augustus died the same year as Mrs. Brown. Carrie always carried her brother's love in her heart, but she faced her final struggle without the support and encouragement Gordon would have given her; she died of cancer in May 1891, not quite five years after her husband. Sarah Ann Finley was the last of the Gordon children to die. She outlived her husband John, who died in February 1896, and survived long enough to see the advent of the twentieth century before passing on in October 1907.

Allen was the last of all. Gordon had invested so much time and worry during Allen's upbringing that he had been like a father to him. Gordon would have been proud had he known of an incident Allen handled in the winter of 1864. Brown, then colonel of the 1st North Carolina Infantry Regiment, requested that his unit's "insolent" doctor be relieved in the interest of harmony. Sounding very much like his half-brother, Brown added his "intention to accommodate myself to circumstance during this war and to submit to everything that is becoming a gentleman and a soldier...." Wounded thirteen times during the war, Brown saw action at Gettysburg, the Wilderness, Spotsylvania, and in the Valley. He was captured during the March 1865 assault on Fort Stedman. Released from Johnson's Island after the war, Brown returned to Wilkes. He helped organize a Ku Klux Klan chapter in Salisbury, of which Kerr Craige was the first member. Afterward Allen moved to the Browns' land in Columbia, Tennessee. He spent the rest of his life on a "magnificent estate" there, although he did visit Wilkes on occasion. He died in April 1917.[24]

Though this marked the passing of the Brown and Gordon name from Wilkes County, the General's memory never quite died thanks to William H. H. Cowles and two of Gordon's nephews, Thomas Finley and James Hackett. Cowles, who deserves further study, never forgot his wartime experiences. Left for dead after receiving a head wound at Chamberlain Run, he survived intact except for his permanently paralyzed right arm.[25] After the war he launched a legal and political career, serving as Reading Clerk of the State Senate, Solicitor of the Tenth Judicial District, and as a United States Congressman from 1885 to 1892. Twice married, he had eleven children, some of whom later joined the military and served in both World Wars. The family lived in Hamilton Brown's old Wilkesborough home, which Cowles purchased following Brown's death.[26] The cavalryman also stayed active in Confederate events. He wrote a few articles detailing the activities of North Carolina cavalrymen, and gave several speeches, including one on Gordon on Memorial Day in 1887. Perhaps his crowning moment as a veteran came when he gave an address at an April 1891 reunion of Wade Hampton's cavalry in Augusta, Georgia. And when Jefferson Davis died, the Confederate Veterans Association of North Carolina selected Cowles to help escort the Confederate leader's remains. Finally, in another way, his efforts are still tangible: a portion of Cowles's personal copies of the war's *Official Records* survive today in the North Wilkesboro library. Cowles died in Wilkesborough in December 1901, and rests there still.[27]

Born in August 1864 to Carrie and R. F. Hackett, James Gordon Hackett was named for his uncle. Although his sister Florence, who had been born in 1862, died at an early age from heart failure, young James flourished. At 18, Hackett received an appointment to West Point from R. F. Armfield, who desired "to do a kindness to an old friend, and because to send to West Point a kinsman of the gallant James B. Gordon who died for his Country and of the equally gallant John B. Gordon who lives for his country."[28] Ultimately educated at Trinity College (today's Duke University), Hackett became a businessman and North Carolina's highway commissioner. He also served as mayor of both Wilkesboro and North Wilkesboro, and postmaster of North Wilkesboro. Before his death in 1952, he did much to maintain the history of his family, including his uncle's letters. Many of these are deposited at various institutions throughout North Carolina.

Another nephew, Thomas Brown Finley, also never forgot. The youngest of Augustus and Martha's eight children, Finley was born one November day in 1862, even as Gordon gazed on Barbee's Crossroads. Finley graduated from Davidson College and a Caldwell County law school and went on to become a lawyer, superior court judge, and first vice president of the North Carolina Bar Association. Ironically, he married Caroline Elizabeth Cowles, a daughter of William Cowles. (This 1893 wedding became the social event of the year in Wilkes County.) Later a founder of North Wilkesboro, Finley died in 1942, but he left memories of his uncle that would not perish. He gave speeches, including one on Gordon to the James B. Gordon Chapter of the United Daughters of the Confederacy, and preserved the history of his family. He even contributed a copy of the poem "Gordon" to the local newspaper. What was more, because of the efforts of the Finleys, North Wilkesboro was almost named Gordon. A hotel and a post office in post-war Wilkes did bear that name for a period of time.[29]

Despite these efforts, Gordon has been an elusive background shadow in Civil War history and Southern history. Indeed, a little-used backstreet in North Wilkesboro is virtually the only thing that still bears his name — save one errant historical marker in Wilkes. In Civil War literature, only occasional mention can be found, but Gordon's name is not as familiar as Barringer's, Ransom's, or even Baker's. In fact, Gordon has been confused with his more famous relative, John Brown Gordon, in more than one book index. John Gordon himself experienced a similar type of confusion. On the bloody fields of Gettysburg, Gordon cared for a wounded Union officer, Francis Barlow. In turn, Barlow entrusted his dying messages to Gordon. After the war, the two men met again. Gordon, of course, supposed Barlow was dead; Barlow, who had seen the announcements of the death of J. B. Gordon in May 1864, assumed John Gordon was dead:

> I asked Barlow: "General, are you related to the Barlow who was killed at Gettysburg?" He replied: "Why, I am the man, sir. Are you related to the Gordon who killed me?" "I am the man, sir," I responded.[30]

At that moment, Gordon was overwhelmed with emotion. The incident may also have kindled emotion for his relative. According to family tradition, John visited "Oakland" near the turn of the century. In renewing his kinship with the North Carolina branch of his family, he is said to have slept in Gordon's chestnut bed in "Oakland." Observed North Wilkesboro's postwar newspaper, *The Chronicle*, "We are glad to see Gordon is almost a Wilkes man. His parents moved from Wilkes, and he has a lot of kinfolks here."[31]

This Barlow-Gordon anecdote suggests how close we came to losing the memory of James Gordon. A primary explanation for this lies in what is known as The Lost Cause. A movement of spirit, it was born in the difficult Reconstruction period. Many Southerners dealt with their troubles emotionally by clinging to the idea that the war had been a noble one. Above all, the sons of the South who had given their all, who had proven themselves the equals of their foe on nearly every battlefield, deserved reverence. Reinforcing these ideals was an 1867 book by Edward A. Pollard called *The Lost Cause*. Pollard admitted that the war decided the issues of secession and slavery, but it did not swallow up everything, including "the right of a people to show dignity in misfortune, and to maintain self-respect in the face of adversity." According to Pollard:

> The war has left the South its own memories, its own heroes, its own tears, its own dead. Under these traditions, sons will grow to manhood, and lessons sink deep that are learned from the lips of widowed mothers.

Other entities and events contributed to The Lost Cause. Late in the nineteenth century, organizations such as the United Confederate Veterans and the United Daughters of the Confederacy sprung up, and they perpetuated the memory of Southern deeds. Even a James B. Gordon chapter of the United Daughters of the Confederacy appeared, in nearby Winston-Salem, North Carolina, in March 1898, while a Sons of Confederate Veterans group was formed in the 1920s in Wilkes in his honor. Memoirs and personal reminiscences of Rebel soldiers appeared regularly. Even as racial tensions and change ruled Southern life, Southerners took solace from memories of courage and made sure that examples of Confederate greatness never died.[32]

However, unlike many Civil War heroes, Gordon's memory was not widely perpetuated by The Lost Cause. Just as Wilkes County had been an antebellum bastion of Whiggery in a state of Democrats, so too did it remain a center of Unionist feeling after the war. In this environment it was simply not fashionable to recall the efforts of a man who fought for the Confederacy, native son or not. The people of Wilkes were ready for change and improvement, so the memory of Gordon began to fade — just as "Oakland," the Gordon landmark, disappeared from the landscape during the twentieth century. Dr. Fred C. Hubbard, the last owner of "Oakland," gave the house and "Oakland's" remaining nineteen acres to the town of North Wilkesboro, which needed a site for a new hospital. In 1952, the Wilkes General Hospital, today the Wilkes Regional Medical Center, opened its doors. The oak trees that Gordon himself had once played beneath lasted in the shadow of the hospital for another thirty-five years.

Gordon's grave in St. Paul's Episcopal Church Cemetery, Wilkesboro, North Carolina, with the church he helped build rising above it (author's photograph).

In 1987, construction began on a new addition for the hospital, and the trees were cut down. Today, even the hill itself is considerably smaller than it once was because of weather and construction.

In his 1887 speech on Gordon, William Cowles laid a task at the doorstep of history. "It has not been possible in the short compass of this address," he said, "to do justice to the life and services of one who in the severe trials of war and amid so many perilous situations, constantly on duty with the van of our army, always bore himself well — many battles, campaigns, 'raids, hot charges, shocks of war,' must be left to the wider field of the biographer or historian."[33] It is this to which this work now attempts to turn.

The majority of James B. Gordon's years passed fruitfully in peacetime. Raised without his biological father to guide him, Gordon still set his goals high. What Nathaniel Gordon had done James Gordon wanted to do better. Family gave stability to the young Gordon's life. Education and farm chores gave maturity. As he grew he cared more deeply for his mother and sisters, and he later tried to set a fatherly example for his half-brothers. Church, community, and friends meant a lot to him, but as an adult he gave most of his time to business, farming, and creating wealth. He was also quite a bachelor, a romantic poet even, who could ensnare almost any lady, although there is a rumor that Gordon carried this pursuit too far. Only in politics did he fall short of complete success. Except for his service on the local school board, Gordon was never asked to repeat a political task.

In 1861, this man faced the American Civil War. Influenced by martial memories and stories — of the Overmountain Men, his father the cavalryman, Montford Stokes and the War with Mexico, and Peter Ney — the North Carolinian rode off to join the army. Within three years, Gordon had established himself as North Carolina's greatest cavalryman. He had become a Confederate Murat. Admittedly, as historian Douglas Southall Freeman once said, it is difficult to compare men who toiled under different circumstances; and there were at least three other Tarheel horse-soldiers of distinction in that war. Take Robert Ransom, the successful organizer of the 1st North Carolina Cavalry. Or Laurence Baker, who was such a solid tactician that he first made a name for North Carolina cavalrymen until, rumors say, the bottle, and then a battle wound, limited his achievements. And Rufus Barringer, Gordon's successor and protégé, fought with even greater success. He was as solid a soldier as ever the state produced, but the dependable Barringer was a product of the desperate days of the war's end, which demanded infantry-like defensive tactics. Gordon was more at home with the headlong charges of the traditional cavalryman. Like Stuart, Gordon was bold, but not normally rash; he was "spirited, quick, prompt, and energetic in his nature, and was sudden and almost irresistible in his attacks on his enemy." Burke Davis has called J. E. B. Stuart America's last cavalier; perhaps James B. Gordon should be known as North Carolina's last cavalier.[34]

Like any person, Gordon had faults; but according to one writer they were few. There is no evidence that he ever considered human slavery to be wrong, but at least there is a hint that he treated his slaves well. Gordon also hid some vanity in his character. Witness his apparent reluctance to have his arm amputated after he received his fatal wound. He was also not above using connections to get ahead, especially when it came to promotion. This practice was not uncommon, but many thought it was not quite proper. For example, when Gordon once advised Joseph Waring to apply for promotion, Waring demurred, telling his diary, "I believe not in that way of doing."[35]

Quite possibly, Gordon might not have become a general without this subtle campaigning. His prewar status and heavy casualties in the ranks helped as well. But to his credit, the more responsibility he received, the better soldier he became. He fell short of having a grasp of the overall strategic picture. He never offered the War Department ideas for prosecuting the war, concentrating only on what was happening in front of his nose. In everything he learned quickly and established himself first as a leader and then as a tactician and fighter. He made great strides in handling troops, especially in battle; contrast his command style at his Brandy Station disaster in the fall of 1863 with his quick-thinking management of the Ground Squirrel Church fighting, where he employed maneuver to pinpoint weak spots. Kerr Craige later wrote a nearly accurate statement about Gordon: "Active[,] alert[,] & vigilant he was never taken by surprise and was always quick to take advantage of any mistakes of his adversary, and to meet any emergency." His primary military weakness was in reconnaissance, which required a more methodical, cautious approach than Gordon was willing to employ. Nonetheless, he improved even in that area, especially at the beginning of the spring 1864 campaign.[36]

An "old man" by cavalry standards, his maturity and experience contributed to his effectiveness. His business experience made him a skillful organizer. His personality and his political background made him a likable, popular person with both his fellow officers and the men in the ranks. Indeed, there is no extant evidence that Gordon endured any personality conflicts with any fellow officer. Rufus Barringer, who spent a lot of time with Gordon, later wrote, "I had no personal difficulties with any except General Baker ... and this was ultimately reconciled." He was a beau of a man with a "charming smile" and "gay humour" who believed in caring for his men, striving in every way to clothe, feed, and rest them where possible.

Witness his angry refusal of Stuart's order to immediately move his men during the Yellow Tavern campaign. In fact, according to his obituary:

> He was one of those men who seem born to command:— his men loved him and fought for him with a spirit that knew no comprehension of danger. Whatever he ordered done, they felt that it was right, and fearlessly dashed at its accomplishment, or sternly stood to its defense, regardless of fate. He had a peculiar faculty or tact for pleasing all whom he met — he was the favorite of his brother officers, and the delight and reverence of his men and subordinates.

But when necessary, he was strict in maintaining discipline. As a result, the North Carolina Cavalry Brigade never suffered from low morale while he commanded, and if his unit lost a fight they bounced back quickly. This suggests that he saw himself as a father to his men — because he had lacked a father himself.[37]

Respected for his administrative abilities, Gordon became something of a fireman who was called on in emergencies. His work in rebuilding the 5th North Carolina Cavalry is the best example of that. This quality had everything to do with why he held temporary command of two regiments, two brigades, and a division, and was recommended to command two other regiments. Later, his work in organizing the Tarheel cavalry brigade set the stage for its success, while his example made possible the achievments of several individuals. Particularly, two of Gordon's protégés — William Paul Roberts and Rufus Barringer — were promoted to brigadier general, while a third man, W. H. H. Cowles, narrowly missed achieving that rank.[38]

And what of Jeb Stuart and James B. Gordon? Stuart's opinion of Gordon might be gauged in a simple way. During the war, the Virginian kept an autograph book. Among those who signed this book — essentially a who's who of the Confederacy — were Joseph E. Johnston, Robert E. Lee, Dick Ewell, Thomas J. Jackson, and D. H. Hill. Gordon's signature was the last.[39] The two men became close friends during the struggle, and were often seen together. It may be said that Gordon provides historians with a civilian parallel of J. E. B. Stuart. Born of fathers with similar backgrounds, they hailed from virtually the same region. Both were of Scottish ancestry. Both attended Emory & Henry. One found his prewar fortune in the military, the other in politics, farming, and business, but from there their paths converged again. During the 1860s, when the younger became the elder's commander, they came together because their personalities were strikingly similar: these kindred spirits shared an affinity for the company of ladies, a desire to be chivalric, and a courage in battle that was unmatched. Finally, their deaths came days apart.

When thinking of General Gordon, take all this into account. Yet to do justice to the life and services of one who always bore himself well in the severe trials of war and peril, remember only this. When he stretched himself out to die in the Officers' Hospital in Richmond, James Byron Gordon was the same man he had always been: popular, fun-loving, a gentleman, dedicated to the cause, and always looking for a way to advance personally. Yet at that moment he was also very different. In the end, he decided what was truly important: his family, his sweetheart, and his God.

That is the most that anyone can say about a man.

Part II: The Roster

Abbreviations

These are used in the Notes and the Roster

Adams	Adams Papers. Copies provided by Mr. Alfred Adams of Boone, N.C.
Alexander	"Roster of Twenty-One Companies Furnished by Mecklenburg County, N.C., in the War of 1861–65," in J.B. Alexander, M.D., *The History of Mecklenburg County, From 1740 to 1900*. Charlotte: Observer Printing House, 1902. Reprint by Southern Historical Press, Greenville, S.C, 1993.
Almsay	Almsay, Sandra Lee. *North Carolina 1890 Civil War Veterans Census*. Joliet, IL: Sandra Lee Almsay with the Kensington Glen Publishing Co., 1990.
Anderson Collection	Gordon/Brown/Finley papers, access provided by J. Jay Anderson, Wilkes Community College, Wilkesboro, N.C.
Annals of the War	*The Annals of the War*, Written by Leading Participants North and South. Originally Published in the Philadelphia Weekly Times.
Ashe	Ashe, Samuel A., et. al., eds. *Biographical History of North Carolina: From Colonial Times to the Present*. 8 vols. Greensboro, N.C.: Charles L. Van Noppen, 1917.
AsheCo	A list of Confederate soldiers from Ashe County, taken from John Wheeler Moore's *Roster of North Carolina Troops in the War Between the States* in *The Heritage of Ashe County, North Carolina*, vol. 2. Charlotte, N.C.: Published by the Ashe County Historical Society, 1994, and Printed by Delmar Printing Company, Charlotte.
B&L	Johnson, Robert Underwood, and Clarence Clough Buel, eds. *Battles and Leaders of the Civil War*. 4 vols. New York: 1887–88.
Barringer	"Roster and Sketch of Company F, First Regiment, North Carolina Cavalry, of Cabarrus County, N.C." Unproveniened newspaper article provided by Rufus Barringer, probably from a post-war Concord, N.C. newspaper, *The Times*, circa 1893. The article was prepared by the Committee on Company Records, composed of H.D. Goodman, E.D. McGinnis, R. Barringer, and W.D. Anthony.
Bounty Receipts	Bounty Receipt List, Captain Barringer's Company (F), Courtesy Rufus Barringer.
Cabarrus	*A History of Cabarrus County in the Wars*. Published by the War Records Collection Committee and Sponsored by Cabarrus Co. N.D.
Census	Unless otherwise noted, citations from the U.S. Population, Agriculture, and Slave censuses are for James B. Gordon, Upper Division, Wilkesboro,

Wilkes County, North Carolina. Industry and Social Statistics citations are as noted. All census citations are from Records of the Bureau of the Census, Record Group 29, NA.

CGR	"Confederate Gravestone Records." North Carolina Division, United Daughters of the Confederacy. 1956–1967. 13 volumes, n.p. North Carolina Division of Archives and History.
CMH	Evans, Clement A., ed. *Confederate Military History*. Atlanta: Confederate Publishing Company, 1899.
CSC	*Carolina and the Southern Cross*. Volume 1, Number 6, August 1913. L.V. Archbell, ed. Published in Kinston, N.C.
CSR	Compiled Service Records of Confederate Soldiers Who Served in Organizations from the State of North Carolina, Record Group 109, National Archives, 1960. Microcopy and Roll Number are cited in the text (i.e., CSR 270:1 means Microcopy 270, Roll 1). The names on each roll are in rough alphabetical order.
CSRG	Compiled Service Records for Confederate General and Staff Officers, Record Group 109, National Archives, 1960. Microcopy and Roll Number are cited in the text (i.e., CSRG 270:1 means Microcopy 270, Roll 1). The names on each roll are in rough alphabetical order.
CV	*Confederate Veteran* magazine. Nashville, TN.
Davis	Dedmond, Francis B., ed. "Harvey Davis's Unpublished Civil War 'Diary' and the Story of Company D of the First North Carolina Cavalry." *Appalachian Journal*. Summer 1986: 368–407.
DavisUDC	Mrs. R.E. Davis of the Coltrane-Harris U.D.C., letter to the author, 9/17/96.
Dear Father	Troxler, Beverly Barrier and Billy Dawn Barrier Auciello, eds. *Dear Father: Confederate Letters Never Before Published*. North Billerica, Massachusetts: Beverly B. Troxler and Billy Dawn Barrier Auciello, 1989.
DU	Special Collections Department, William R. Perkins Library, Duke University, Durham, N.C.
Elmira	*List of Confederate Soldiers Buried in Woodlawn Cemetery, Elmira, New York*. Published by the Chemung Historical Society.
Elmwood	"Confederate Soldiers Buried in Elmwood Cemetery, Shepherdstown, West Virginia [Antietam Battlefield]," in Military Collection, Civil War Collection, Box 69, Folder 23, NCSA.
Forsyth	Cook, Jerry. "Forsyth County, N.C. Confederate Soldiers." *The Forsyth County Genealogical Society Journal*, Vol. VII, Summer 1989, Number IV.
FSNMP	Fredericksburg and Spotsylvania National Military Park.
GDAH	Georgia Department of Archives and History, Atlanta, Georgia.
GHM	Greensboro Historical Museum Archives, Greensboro, N.C.
GLP	Carrere, Charlotte, and Robert McAllister. "UDC Gravestone Location Project 1995: Confederate Veteran Grave Locations in North Carolina." NCSA, Raleigh. N.P.
Graves	Adelaide M. Lore, comp. Graveyard Records of the Men in Gray—in Cabarrus County, North Carolina. N.P., Charles A. Cannon Memorial Library, Concord, N.C.

Halifax	Stephen E. Bradley, Jr., comp. *A Roster: Halifax County, North Carolina (1861–1865)*.
Henry	J.L. Henry Letters, PC 587, NCSA.
Hopkins	W.L. Hopkins. Leftwich-Turner Families. 1931. (Reference from R.E.L. Krick, 11/23/96)
Institute Memorial	Charles D. Walker. *Memorial, Virginia Military Institute. Biographical Sketches of the Graduates and Eleves of the Virginia Military Institute Who Fell During The War Between The States.* Philadelphia: J.B. Lippincott & Co., 1875.
Jackson	Hester Bartlett Jackson, ed. *Surry County Soldiers In The Civil War.* Charlotte: Delmar Printing Company for the Surry County Historical Society, 1992.
JBG	James Byron Gordon.
Joyner	Whit Joyner, "Rushed Into Manhood: A Young Tar Heel From Sumter To Appomattox," after an address given to the Confederate Historical Institute, April 1994.
Karchaske	S. Janelle Karchaske, comp. *Mecklenburg County, North Carolina Cemetery Records.* Version 2. Charlotte: Family History Researchers and Publishers, July 1995.
Kittrell	Vance Co. Cemetery Records, List of Confederate Dead, Confederate Cemetery, Kittrell, N.C., according to Louisburg, N.C. Church Register, North Carolina State Archives.
Land We Love	*The Land We Love: A Monthly Magazine Devoted to Literature, Military History, and Agriculture.* 6 vols. Charlotte, N.C.: James P. Irwin and D.H. Hill, Publishers, May 1866–March 1869.
Lore	Adelaide and Eugenia Lore. Cemetery Records Read and Recorded by The Misses Adelaide and Eugenia Lore. N.P., Charles A. Cannon Memorial Library, Concord, N.C.
LC	Manuscripts Division of the Library of Congress, Washington, D.C.
Macon Heritage	Jessie Sutton, ed. *The Heritage of Macon County, North Carolina, 1987.* Macon County Historical Society, in cooperation with Hunter Publishing, Winston-Salem, 1987.
MC	Eleanor S. Brockenbrough Library, The Museum of the Confederacy, Richmond, Virginia.
McNeil	Correspondence with George F. and Joyce McNeil, authors of Wilkes Co., N.C. Cemetery Project.
Medical History	*The Medical and Surgical History of the Civil War.* Wilmington, N.C.: Broadfoot Publishing Company, 1991.
Mizelle	Mizelle, Hazel. "Only Two Living Members of Cabarrus Rangers: This North Carolina Unit Fought Throughout War and was Never Singly Defeated," *The Charlotte Observer*, 7 July 1929.
Monie	John M. Monie, "John Miller Monie." Autobiographical sketch and other papers in Box 71, Folder 31, John Miller Monie Papers, in the Military Collection, Civil War Collection, NCSA, Raleigh, NC.
MVM	Julia Moore Smith [daughter], "Sketch of Captain Martin V. Moore"; Mar-

	tin V. Moore, "Personal and Biographical," both in the Martin V. Moore Papers, #520, SHC, UNC.
NA	National Archives, Washington, D.C.
NC Regts.	Clark, Walter, ed. *Histories of the Several Regiments and Battalions from North Carolina in the Great War 1861–'65.* 5 vols. Goldsboro, N.C.: Nash Brothers, 1901.
NC Troops	Manarin, Louis, and Weymouth Jordan, comps. *North Carolina Troops, 1861–1865: A Roster.* Projected 15 volume series. Raleigh, N.C.: State Department of Archives and History, 1968–1994 ff
NCSA	North Carolina State Archives, North Carolina Division of Archives and History, Raleigh, North Carolina.
NFR	No Further Record.
Occupations	J.K. Rouse. "Occupations of Two Hundred and Seventy Residents of Cabarrus County, North Carolina prior to the War Between the States." N.P. From vertical files, Charles A. Cannon Memorial Library, Concord, N.C.
OR	*The War of the Rebellion: A Compilation of the Official Records of the Union and Confederate Armies.* 70 vols. in 128 parts. Washington: Government Printing Office, 1881–1902.
Our Living and Our Dead	*Our Living and Our Dead: Devoted to North Carolina — Her Past, Her Present, and Her Future.* 4 vols. S.D. Pool, ed. Raleigh, N.C.: North Carolina Branch of the Southern Historical Society, September 1874–August 1876.
Pearce	Pearce, T.H. *They Fought: The Story of Franklin County Men In The Years 1861–1865.* Second Edition. 1969, 1995. Wilmington, NC, Broadfoot Publishing Company.
Powell	Powell, William S., Ed. *Dictionary of North Carolina Biography.* Chapel Hill: UNC Press, 1979.
PL	Beitzell, Edwin W. *Point Lookout Prison Camp For Confederates.* Publ. 1983 by Edwin W. Beitzell with St. Mary's County Historical Society.
Rumple	Rumple, Rev. Jethro. *A History of Rowan County, North Carolina, Containing Sketches of Prominent Families and Distinguished Men. Originally published in 1881.* With new index by Edith M. Clark. Baltimore: Genealogical Publishing Company, 1993.
SHC	The Southern Historical Collection, Wilson Library, University of North Carolina, Chapel Hill, North Carolina.
SHSP	Jones, J. William, et al., eds. *Southern Historical Society Papers.* 52 vols. Richmond: Southern Historical Society, 1876–1959.
6th NC	Jeffrey C. Weaver. *The 5th and 7th Battalions North Carolina Cavalry and the 6th North Carolina Cavalry (65th North Carolina State Troops).* Lynchburg, VA: H.E. Howard, Inc., 1995.
Stepp	Jeff H. Stepp, Project Editor. North Carolina Confederate Burial Locator Project. Database, copies provided April 1996, August 1997.
Stonewall	"Confederate Soldiers Buried in NC Plat, Stonewall Cemetery, Winchester, VA." Military Collection, Civil War Collection, Box 69, Folder 24A, NCSA, Raleigh.

Turner/Baker	National Archives, Office of the Judge Advocate, Record Group 94, Levi Turner and Lafayette Baker Papers, Microcopy 797. (Courtesy Horace Mewborn.)
USAMHI	United States Army Military History Institute. Carlisle, Pennsylvania.
USC	South Carolina Library, University of South Carolina, Columbia, South Carolina.
UVA	Special Collections Department, University of Virginia Library, Charlottesville, Virginia.
VHS	Virginia Historical Society, Richmond, Virginia.
Virginia Democracy	Glass, *Virginia Democracy*, vol. II (1937), p. 106. Ref. R.E.L. Krick to the author, 2/1/97.
VL	Archives, The Library of Virginia, Richmond, Virginia.
WCC	James Larkin Pearson Library, Wilkes Community College, Wilkesboro, N.C.
Winkler Interview	Mrs. Annie F. Winkler, interview with the author, Wilkesboro, N.C. July 20, 1989.
Yadkin	Frances H. Casstevens, *The Civil War and Yadkin County, North Carolina*. Jefferson, NC: McFarland & Company, Inc., 1997.
Zeb. Vance Papers	11/13/63 letter from several 1st N.C. troopers in the NCSA [Zebulon Vance Papers, North Carolina State Archives. courtesy Whit Joyner])

Roster of the 1st North Carolina Cavalry Regiment (9th Regiment North Carolina State Troops)

LATE IN THE NINETEENTH CENTURY, a man by the name of John A. Sloan began working an a book about North Carolina cavalrymen who fought in the Army of Northern Virginia during the Civil War. Although the book itself was apparently never completed, some of Sloan's advance copy appeared in a Concord, North Carolina, newspaper. "North Carolina may well point with pride to the name of [Robert] Ransom and his distinguished comrades of the glorious 'First North Carolina Cavalry,'" he wrote. "It was the thorough organization, drill and discipline of this regiment that lay at the bottom of all the splendid achievements of the North Carolina Cavalry. It was called by Stewart [J.E.B. Stuart] 'a pattern for others.' Its zeal and spirit spread to all of our other cavalry commands. It furnished many of the best officers in other commands, and those officers never ceased to inculcate and enforce the true principals of military duty so admirably taught by Ransom."*

What follows is a roster of those men who fought with the 1st North Carolina Cavalry, the regiment Gordon favored above all others. I began building it during the 1990s and I am proud to at last present it as a part of the second edition of my history of James B. Gordon and his North Carolina cavalry. The basis for this roster is the compiled service records of Confederate soldiers found within the National Archives. I have supplemented that information with multiple other sources: diaries, letters, reminiscences, histories, newspaper accounts, and more. It is as complete as time and research obstacles have allowed it to be, and admittedly those obstacles have been numerous. That includes the fact that the official rolls of the regiment are incomplete — virtually none exist from 1865 — as well as the fact that inaccuracies and inconsistentices plague those records that do exist. Still, the author and compiler hopes that this roster will do justice to the memory of these men.

Abbreviations used in this roster are identified within the abbreviations section.

Abbott, Elias H.: At age 27, enl. in Co. H. 7/11/61 in Goldsboro. PVT, saddler. From Lenoir County. Present until captured while on picket on 2/7/62 near Difficult Run, Va. Exchanged and reported as present from January 1863 through December 1864. Captured at Aberdeen Church 4/3/65. Imprisoned at Point Lookout, where he was described as 5'11" tall, with a dark complexion, dark brown hair, and gray eyes. Released 6/23/65. (CSR 270:1)

Abernathy, Charles P.: Resident of Lenoir, N.C. Also called "Pink." PVT. Enl. 5/11/61, Co. D,

---
*The Concord Register, June 1, 1883.

Boone. Renl. 3/10/64 in Boone, 3/15/64 in Milford, Va.. Admitted G.H. #9, Richmond, 3/26/64. WIA in right arm and side, 8/15/64, along Charles City Rd., near Richmond. Frl. for 60 days from 8/29/64. Reported in a Boone hospital, 9/12/64. (Davis; CSR 270:1; Richmond *Sentinel,* 8/26/64)

Adams, George Finley: B. Sugar Grove, Watauga County, NC, 1843. Enl. Co. D, 7/10/61. PVT. Reported present November 1861 through February 1862, May 1862 through December 1864, except between January 1863 and March 1863 when detailed to secure a horse. Later appointed SGT. Captured and WIA in right thigh, 31 March 1865, Dinwiddie C.H., while carrying a wounded officer from the field. D. 4/22/65, Judiciary Square Hospital, Washington, D.C. Bur. Oakwood Cem., Raleigh. Brother of Tarleton Adams. (CSR 270:1; Adams; Davis; Stepp; CSR 270: 4 for George N. Folk)

Adams, Tarleton P.: B. Boone. Enl. Co. D. Captured "after many months" of service. Imprisoned at Camp Chase, Columbus, OH. After the war, Tarleton walked home from Ohio. (Adams Papers)

Addington, John H.: From Macon County. PVT. Enl. at age 39, Co. K., 3/27/63, Franklin. Detailed to care for horses, July and August 1863. Also absent, probably on same duty, as of 10/31/63. Absent recruiting horses, November and December 1863. Absent January through December 1863, sick since March of that year. (CSR 270:1)

Addington, William M.: Macon County. Enl. 5/16/61, in Co. K. Appointed 1LT., 10/24/61. Present November 1861 through December 1864, except when on detached service in charge of baggage at Gordonsville, January and February 1863. Also absent sick 4/30/64 through 8/31/64. Served as AQM of regiment until resigning, 4/15/62. Prm. CPT, 8/2/62, to command Co. K. (CSR 270:1)

Albright, Calvin H.: Enl. Co. H, 10/1/64, Dinwiddie C.H. PVT. Prl. Greensboro, 5/9/65. (CSR 270:1)

Aldridge, James W.: From Randolph County. At age 21, enl. Asheville, 5/20/61, in Co. G. PVT. Absent sick at Wilson, 5/25/61. Frl. of 45 days beginning 12/3/62. Reported present January 1862, March 1863 through April 1863, September 1863 through 4/1/64. Sick at Richmond hospital, November 1862 through January 1863, July and August 1863. Detailed to buy a horse beginning 5/22/64. Reported sick in Petersburg hospital, October 1864; moved to Raleigh hospital 11/5/64. Reported at Richmond G.H. #9, 1/22/64, and at G.H. #17 to 10/31/62. (CSR 270:1)

Alexander, C.J.: Enl. 11/1/64, Raleigh, in Co. F. PVT. Reported present through December 1864. Reported in Danville hospital, 5/3/65, with a chest ailment. Prl. 5/17/65, Charlotte. Psb. from Iredell Co. (CSR 270:1; Barringer)

Alexander, J.P.: Enl. 6/20/61, Charlotte, in Co. C. SGT. Absent sick in Mecklenburg County, N.C. hospital, beginning 10/15/61. Reported present, May 1862 through October 1862. Detailed to scout, 12/15/62. 2/21/63, detailed to N.C. to buy horses. Present March and April 1863, July 1863 through December 1864. Admitted to Winchester hospital 8/1/64 with illness. Prl. Charlotte, 5/17/65. (CSR 270:1; Alexander)

Alexander, William L.D.: From Concord. At age 23, enl. Co. F 6/15/61. PVT. Reported present November 1861 through February 1862; May 1862 through June 1862; September 1862 through December 1862. Absent on sick frl, July 1863 through December 1863, after being WIA at or near Gettysburg, 7/3 or 7/4/63. Reported present January 1864 through December 1864, including on provost guard at Bowling Green, 3/13/64. Dead as of 1893. (Mizelle; CSR 270:1; Barringer; Cabarrus)

Allen, E.L.: Enl. in Co. G, 9/21/63. PVT. Reported present September 1864 through December 1864. Was in state service prior to joining the regiment. (CSR 270:1)

Allen, John Watson: B. 5/22/46. Enl. in Co. E, 4/16/64, as PVT. Reported present through December 1864. D. 5/9/35. Bur Fairview Cemetery, Warren Co., NC. (CSR 270:1; GLP; CGR: 2)

Allen, Robert M.: Dsh 11/16/61 from Co. F, 14th NC. Enl. 3/12/62, Asheville, in Co. G. From Buncombe County. Reported present May through June 1862; September through October 1862. Absent on detached service with disabled horses, November and December 1862. Reported present January through April 1863; captured and imprisoned at Fort Lookout, July through October 1863. Reported present November 1863 through December 1863; April through December 1864. Captured Ford's Depot, and released 6/22/65. (CSR 270:1; "Rough & Ready Guards," *Asheville Citizen-Times,* 10/9/21.)

Allison, John B.: Farmer before the war. At age 26, enl. Co. K, 6/25/61. PVT. Reported absent, January through February 1862. Wounded in left hand from accidental discharge of pistol shot at White Sulphur Springs, Va. Admitted to hospital in Charlottesville, 3/2/62. Lost 2 fingers, a portion of other fingers as a result. Frl. 3/17/62; dsh at Camp Mars, N.C., 5/10/62. Stood 5'10" with a light complexion, gray eyes, and light hair. (CSR 270:1)

Allman, William C.: Enl. 5/14/61, Co. K, in Franklin, N.C. PVT. Admitted to G.H. #20, Richmond, 10/31/62. Detached to buy a horse in North Carolina, November and December 1863. Reported on horse detail again, April through August 1864. Reported present January through March 1864; September through December 1864. (CSR 270:1)

Almonds, Allen: PVT, Co. K. Macon County, N.C. (CSR 270:1)

Alphin, Jesse Jordan: Farmer, from Duplin County. At age 25, enl. 7/31/63, Kenansville, N.C., in Co. I. PVT. Reported present November 1861 through January 1862; then sick at home in May and June 1862. From September to October 1862, absent. Sick in Richmond G.H. #3, and also Leesburg. 30-day Frl. from 9/30/62 due to diarrhea. Reported present January 1863 through April 1863. In July 1863, received accidental gunshot wound in left forearm, requiring amputation. Frl. from G.H. #9, 9/25/63; reported present September 1864 through October 1864. Detailed November and December 1864 under GEN R.E. Lee's Special Order #274, dated 11/12/64. Placed on guard duty in Lynchburg. Retired 12/6/64, with certificate of disability. Stood 5'11", with a fair complexion, blue eyes, and brown hair. (CSR 270:1)

Alphin, William: Enl. 8/12/61 in Duplin County, N.C., in Co. I. PVT. Rejected. (CSR 270:1)

Alston, George W.: B. 10/15/45. Enl. Raleigh. PVT, Co. E; trn. from Co. B. Reported absent sick on frl., 4/30/64–10/31/64. Reported present November and December 1864. D. 11/8/16. Bur. Cherry Hill Cem., home of the Alstons, Inez, NC. (CSR 270:1; CGR: 6)

Amos, James A.: From Granville County. At age 31, enl. 8/14/61, Co. E. SGT; PVT. Sent to Guilford County to collect sabres, September 1861. Reduced to ranks in November 1861 for neglect of duty. 1/13/62 detailed to be GEN Robert E. Rhodes's bodyguard. Reported present February, May, and June 1862. Captured at Malvern Hill, 8/5/62; Prl. from Fort Wool, 8/26/62. Reported present until Dsh. by furnishing a substitute in November 1862. (CSR 270:1)

Anderson, James: B. Cherokee, N.C. At age 19, in Franklin, enl. 8/31/61 in Co. K. PVT, from Macon County, N.C. Reported present through February 1862. Dsh at Camp Mars, N.C., 5/10/62, from chronic hemorrhoids. Stood 6'1", with a light complexion, black eyes, and dark hair. A farmer before the war. (CSR 270:1)

Anderson, John: B. Buncombe Co. or Alleghany Co., N.C. Farmer before the war. Enl. 6/25/61 in Co. K. PVT. Present from 11/61–2/62, although sick in his quarters during the latter month. Dsh. 5/10/62 due to age, inefficiency, and acute rheumatism. Cns. 11/24/63. Deserted along the Rapidan River, 11/30/63 at age 37. Opposed to secession. Admitted to Kalorama (Eruptive Fever) Hospital, Washington, D.C., on 12/30/63, released 1/25/64. Swore oath of amnesty, 3/22/64. Light complexion, light hair, and grey eyes. (CSR 270:1; Turner/Baker Papers.)

Anderson, Joseph A.: At age 23, enl. in Co. A, 5/23/61. PVT. From Jefferson, N.C. Reported present from November 1861 to February 1862. Captured 10/15/62, in Maryland. Prl. Frederick, Maryland. Frl. during November and December 1862. Reported present from January 1863 through January 1864. Deserted 1/18/64, and New Market. (CSR 270:1; AsheCo)

Anderson, L.D.: Enl. Charlotte, 3/12/62, in Co. C. PVT. Age 39, from Mecklenburg County. Reported present from May through December 1862. Absent on detached service to North Carolina, beginning 1/1/63. Present March through June 1863 until captured at Stephensburg (near Brandy Station), 6/9/63. Held at the Old Capitol Prison. Later, absent again on detached service from 8/7/63 to 4/1/64. (CSR 270:1; Alexander)

Anderton, William J.: From Northampton County. Cns. 7/15/62 in Co. H. PVT. Reported present from January to October 1863. Captured Madison C.H., Va., 9/22/63, and sent to Point Lookout from Old Capitol Prison. D. 2/23/64 of chronic diarrhea; bur. at Point Lookout. (CSR 270:1; PL: 123)

Andrews, Alexander Boyd: B. Franklin County, N.C., 7/23/44. Enl. 5/16/61 as PVT in Co. B. Prm 2LT, Co. E. Prm. 1LT 9/23/61. Prm. CAPT, 7/12/62. Reported present from November 1861 through February 1862. Absent on detached service March and April 1862. During June, July, and part of August, served in N.C. with Companies A and B while the rest of the regiment fought outside Richmond. Reported present Sept.–Oct./62; then absent on detached service through the end of the year. Reported present Jan.–Apr./63. Admitted to a Charlottesville hospital for chronic diarrhea, 7/31/63; returned to duty 8/17/63, but it was considered "special duty." WIA, shot in left lung, at Jack's Shop, 9/22/63, while leading Co. A in a charge. Granted leave 11/3/63; given several extensions, including 1/27/64, 2/25/64, and 5/13/64.

Retired to Invalid Corps, 11/5/64. Patient in a Greensboro hospital when prl, late April or early May 1865. Postwar, Superintendent of Raleigh and Gaston, Raleigh and Augusta, and NC Division of Richmond and Danville R.R. Served as first vice president and on Board of Directors, Southern Railway Corporation, and also as president, Western North Carolina Railroad. Helped establish and maintain Confederate Soldiers Home in Raleigh; member, Protestant Episcopal Church. D. 4/17/15. Bur. Oakwood Cem., Raleigh. (CSR 270:1; *NC Regts.* 1: 447; *Catawba County News,* 6/11/15: 1; Stepp; Pearce 6, 13 says born 7/22, 134; Furlough Papers, Box 42, Folder 17, Military Collection, Civil War Collection, NCSA; Pearce, "Where Cavalry Fought the Navy.")

Angel, Charles: B. Prussia. At age 36, enl. 6/21/61 at Goldsboro, in Co. H. Bugler. From Wayne County. Reported present from November 1861 through February 1862. Captured at Willis Church, Va., 6/29/62, and sent to Fort Delaware. Exd. 8/5/62. Reported AWOL through February 1863. Reported absent sick, March and April, July and August 1863. Absent on detached duty in a Goldsboro hospital, the latter two months as well as September and October 1863. From November 1863 through December 1864, assigned to light duty as a baker or a cook at G.H. #3 in Goldsboro. Stood 5'8", had dark eyes and hair, a fair complexion. (CSR 270:1)

Angel, George W.: Enl. 5/14/61 in Franklin County, N.C., in Co. K. PVT. For 12 months. Reported present from October 1863 until December 1864. Captured at Dinwiddie C.H., 4/2/65, and admitted to a Petersburg hospital 10 days later. (CSR 270:1)

Anthony, Whitmel Hill: B. 8/24/43, Halifax Co. Dismissed from VMI and attended St. Timothy's Hall in Maryland. Volunteered for Palmetto Guard in Charleston, 1/61, participated at Ft. Sumter. 1LT with 12th N.C. Infantry, then after failing reelection at age 18, enl. 7/6/62, in Co. B. PVT. WIA 7/8/63 and sent to Hagerstown, Md. hospital. Present from January through April 1863, and November 1863 through December 1864. Prm. 2LT 8/3/63 to date from 8/1/63, and assumed command of Co. B. Prm 1LT 9/5/63. Prm. CPT 11/5/64. Reported in a Danville hospital, 4/4/65, after being wounded in neck at Chamberlain's Run, 3/31/65. Farmer after the war, and elected to State House of Representatives, 1888. D. 11/1/04; bur. in Scotland Neck Episcopal Cemetery. According to W.H.H. Cowles, "He was a superb soldier, brave as the bravest, true as steel, and an earnest, zealous patriot." (CSR 270:1; Zeb. Vance Papers, NCSA [courtesy Whit Joyner]; Whit Joyner, "Rushed Into Manhood;" Whit Joyner to author, 13 September 1994; CGR: 1; Stepp; "Whitmel Hill Anthony," in Box 70, Folder 4, Military Collection, Civil War Collection, NCSA..

Anthony, William D.: B. 9/24/40. At age 21, at Concord, N.C., enl. 6/15/61 in Co. F. PVT.; Ord. SGT. Present November 1861 through October 1862. Prm. Ord. SGT and trn. to noncommissioned officer staff, 7/27/62. Present November 1862 through April 1863. Absent on detached service, July and August 1863. Reported present September 1863 through December 1864. Resident of Concord, NC, circa 1893. D. 5/26/05. Bur. Mt. Pleasant Lutheran Graveyard, Mt. Pleasant, NC. (CSR 270:1; Mizelle; Barringer; Cabarrus)

Antrice, J.W.: PVT, Co. C. (Alexander)

Antrice, W.M.: PVT, Co. C. Died. (Alexander)

Applewhite, William P.: At age 18, enl. in Co. H, 6/20/61, in Goldsboro, N.C. PVT. Reported present from November 1861 through the end of 1862. After traveling to North Carolina in search of a horse, he was reported present from March to April 1863, until he went horse-seeking again in July and August 1863. Reported present from September to October of the same year, he then went horse searching again in November and December 1863. Reported present from January to February 1864 and from April to December 1864, he was also after horses in the other months of the year. (CSR 270:1)

Archer, William H.: From Warren County, N.C., a member of Co. E. 4CPL. D. 10/10/61 at home, possibly from Typhoid Fever. (CSR 270:1)

Archey, J.W.: PVT, Co. C. (Alexander)

Ardrey, J.W.: Enl. 9/21/63 in Charlotte, at age 17, in Co. C. PVT. Reported present through December 1864. (CSR 270:1; Alexander)

Armfield, David F.: Enl.5/25/61 in Co. A, at age 20. From Union County, N.C. PVT, 2LT. Present, November through December 1861. Assigned to daily duty as courier for General Milledge L. Bonham's Brigade, Jan.–Feb./62. Admitted to a Richmond G.H., 3/24/62. Also present 7/63. Absent scouting beginning Christmas day, 1862, but reported present in Jan.–Feb./63, until frl 2/27/63 to purchase a horse. Elected 2LT, Co. A, 8/2/63. Captured 10/63 at Catleet's Station. Admitted to a G.H. at Point Lookout, 4/30/64, with erysipelas in face and head. Exd. 10/11/64. Commissioned 1LT, 1/6/65, to serve with Co. H. Apptd to board of valuation, 3/21/65. (CSR 270:1; Box 42, Folder 19, Military Collection, Civil War Collection, NCSA)

Armstrong, Nicholas E.: At age 23, volunteered as 2LT in Co. I. From Duplin County. "Never Commissioned." (CSR 270:1)

Arnold, Daniel: Brother of John D. and Jacob Arnold. Enl. in Jefferson, N.C., in Co. A, 3/7/62. PVT. Recruit from E. Tennessee. Detached after a horse, 3/7/62. Reported present September through November 1862. Absent scouting beginning Christmas Day 1862. Reported present January through April 1863, September 1863 through April 1864, and July and August 1864. Declared AWOL beginning 10/12/64. Arrested. (CSR 270:1; AsheCo)

Arnold, Jacob: Brother of John D. and Daniel Arnold. Enl. 3/7/62 in Co. A. PVT, recruit from E. Tennessee. Reported present through July 1863. KIA 8/1/63 at Brandy Station. (CSR 270:1; AsheCo)

Arnold, James J.: Enl. 11/23/61 at age 23 in Co. K, in Franklin, N.C. PVT. Absent sick in Franklin, January and February 1862, then at Weldon hospital May and June 1862. Reported present September 1862 through April 1863. Detailed to buy horses in N.C., July and August 1863. Reported present September 1863 through April 1864. Reported MIA, Hanover C.H., Va., 5/31/64. Captured and held at Point Lookout and Elmira until Exd., 10/11/64. Admitted to a Macon, Ga. hospital with chronic diarrhea, 11/15/64. (CSR 270:1)

Arnold, John D.: Brother of Daniel and Jacob Arnold. Enl. 3/7/62 in Co. A. From E. Tennessee; PVT. Placed on detached service near Winchester beginning 9/5/62. Reported present November 1862 through June 1863. Detached after a horse July and August 1863. Present September 1863 through August 1864. Absent sick beginning 10/27/64; reported present, November and December 1864. (CSR 270:1; AsheCo)

Arnold, John N.: In Franklin, enl. 11/23/61, in Co. K. PVT, from Macon County, age 21. Reported present until absent sick at Manassas, 2/24/62. Present from May 1862 through August 1863. MIA, 9/13/63, at Culpeper C.H. Captured; held at Old Capitol Prison and Elmira until Exd., 3/10/65. (CSR 270:1)

Arnt, Lewis: Enl. in Co. D in Boone, N.C. (Davis)

Arrington, Richard: PVT. Enl. Co. E, 2/13/64. Detached, working with QM Dpt., March and April 1864. At home on "furlough of indulgence," 4/30/64 through October 1864. Absent on detached service to N.C., November and December 1864.(CSR 270:1)

Askew, A.D.: Enl. in Co. E, 4/12/62, at age 17, in Warren County, N.C. Reported present, May through October 1862. Prm. CPL, 6/17/62. Absent on detached service, November and December 1862. Present, January 1863 through April 1863; 6/30/63 through September 1864, except for detached service after a horse to N.C., beginning 8/27/63. Prm. SGT in spring 1863. Horse killed at Buckland, 10/19/64. Captured October 1864, held at Point Lookout. Exd. 11/6/64. (CSR 270:1)

Askew, William H.H.: Enl. 6/26/61 in Co. B. PVT, from Hertford County, N.C. Present November and December 1861; March and April 1862. Detached with the horses, January and February 1862. At home sick, with leave, from 6/1/64 through December 1862. Reported AWOL after 1/1/63; marked deserted. (CSR 270:1)

Autin, W.M.: Enl. 5/29/61, in Co. C, at age 35. From Mecklenburg County, N.C. Reported present November 1861, then absent sick December 1861. Present January 1862, then frl 2/1/62, due to illness. Present May through August 1862. D. 8/8/62, after illness resulting from accidentally shooting himself in his hand. (CSR 270:1)

Autrie, J.W.: At age 30, enl. in Co. C, 6/18/61. PVT. Rejected by LTC Laurence Baker, August 1861. (CSR 270:1)

Averett, D.T.: Enl. 9/14/63 at Raleigh's Camp Holmes, in Co. B. PVT. Absent on horse detail, September and October 1864. Age 43; stood 5'8" with hazel eyes, dark hair, and a dark complexion. (CSR 270:1)

Babbitt, Miles: Enl. 6/7/61 at age 18 in Co. E. PVT, from Warren County, N.C. Present Jan.–Feb./62, May–June/62, 9/62–4/63; 7/63. On detached service in N.C. to purchase a horse, 8/27/63, then present through 3/64. Again detached to N.C. after a horse, 4/1/64. Present 4/30/64–Dec./64. (CSR 270:2)

Bachelor, Blaney W.: Enl. 7/4/61 in Co. I, in Kenansville, N.C. PVT. Age 27, from Duplin County, N.C. Stood 5'8", with auburn hair, blue eyes, and a fair complexion. Present from November 1861 through February 1862. Captured 6/29/62 at Willis Church, Va. Held at Fort Columbus and Fort Delaware. Present from September 1862 through March 1864. D. in camp near Bowling Green, Va., 3/19/64. (CSR 270:1)

Bachelor, W.F.: At age 41, enl. in Co. I, 6/20/61, in Duplin County, N.C. PVT. Rejected. (CSR 270:1)

Bagget, Joseph A.: PVT. Enl. in Co. B, 6/13/61,

in Palenta, N.C. Age 21. Reported present from November 1861 until captured, 2/22/62 while on outpost duty. Reported present January 1863 through April 1863, except when detached to get a horse 2/21/63. WIA Brandy Station, 6/9/63. Suffering from chronic diarrhea in a Richmond hospital as of 7/14/63. On detached service, January and February 1864. Reported present March through April 1864. Listed in infirmary near Stony Creek, 4/30/64 through October 1864. Home on horse detail, November and December 1864. Deserted January 1865. (CSR 270:1)

Bailey, Eason E.: B. Greene County, N.C. 6' 2", with a fair complexion, blue eyes, and light hair. Farmer. Enl. in Co. K 6/29/61 in Goldsboro, N.C. Age 22. Absent sick at home, sent 10/13/61. Suffering from mumps, typhoid fever, an dysentery, Dsh. 5/19/62 for a "completely broken down constitution." (CSR 270:1)

Bailey, Joseph J.: Enl. in Co. E, 6/25/61. Reported present on company muster rolls Jan.–Oct./62, including recruiting service beginning 3/3/62. Prm CPL 2/24/62. Prm. SGT 12/62. Absent on detached service, Jan.–Feb./63. Present, 3/63–2/64. Horse killed near Liberty Mills, 9/25/63. On 3/14/64, admitted to Jackson Hospital, Richmond, with pneumonia. Again reported in a Richmond hospital, 4/1/64. Mar.–Apr./64, absent in N.C. after a horse. WIA severely 8/15 or 8/16/64 along Charles City Rd., near Richmond. At home through October 1864, at home suffering from wound in the leg. (CSR 270:1; Richmond *Sentinel*, 8/26/64)

Bailey, William H.: B. 1842. Enl. 6/27/61 in Co. H. PVT. Absent on detached service during January and February 1862, and also sick in February. At G.H. #4 in Richmond, 11/28/62; trn to smallpox hospital 12/10/62. WIA October 1863 at Culpeper C.H. On extra daily duty, March and April 1864. As of 3/29/64, at a Goldsboro, N.C. hospital. Sick from 4/30/64 through 8/31/64, part of the time at home and also at Jackson Hospital, after being admitted 5/7/64 with a shell wound in the leg and right arm. Reported in a Richmond G.H., Sept.–Dec./64. D. 1/1/94. Bur. Oakwood Cem., Raleigh. (CSR 270:1; Stepp)

Baily, Thomas: A 34-year-old "Recruit from Depot," enl. 5/7/62 at Richmond in Co. K. From Macon County, N.C. PVT. Stood 5' 8", had gray eyes, dark hair, and a dark complexion. Present from May 1862 through July 1863. Captured during the preliminaries to the Gettysburg Campaign, on 5/30/63 at Cedar Run, Va. according to Federal sources. (CSR 270:1)

Baird, J.S.T.: From Buncombe County, N.C. PVT, Co. G. Volunteer. Age 30. (CSR 270:1)

Baird, John H.: At age 19, enl. 5/11/61 in Boone. PVT, Co. D. Reported present from November 1861 through August 1863. Captured near Brandy Station, Va., 8/11/63. Imprisoned at Point Lookout. Exd. 2/10/65. (CSR 270:1)

Baird, John H.: Co. D (Davis)

Baird, Thomas: Co. D (Davis)

Baird, Thomas J.: Enl. at age 19 in Co. B, 7/10/61. PVT, From Watauga County, N.C. Reported absent sick in a Petersburg hospital, November and December 1861. Present January and February 1862, then back in the Petersburg hospital during May and June 1863. Captured at Gettysburg, 7/3/63. Held at Fort Delaware and Point Lookout. Prl 2/18/65. (CSR 270:1; CSR 270: 4 for George N. Folk)

Baisden, James: From Duplin County, N.C., at age 29, enl. in Co. I, 6/17/61. PVT. Present from November 1861 to October 1862. Absent on detached service, November 1862 through February 1863. Present March through July 1863. Captured at Gettysburg, 7/3/63, and imprisoned at Point Lookout. (CSR 270:1)

Baker, George: In Northampton County, N.C., enl. 6/13/61 in Co. B at age 21. PVT. Reported home on sick leave beginning 10/31/61. Present September and October 1862. On detached service the following two months, then present from January to April 1863. Absent with disabled horses, 8/3/63 through December. On detached service, at least part of the time in the infirmary camp, January, February, and March 1864. Thereafter, present through December 1864. (CSR 270:1)

Baker, George: Enl. 3/23/63, in Co. A. From Ashe County, N.C., age 22 at enlistment. PVT. Reported present, March and April 1863. Captured 7/3/63 in Pennsylvania. Incarcerated at Fort Delaware. Suffered from Typhoid Fever while there. (CSR 270:1)

Baker, Hiram: 2LT, Co. A, enl 2/23/62. From Ashe County, N.C., age 21. Resigned 10/3/61. Ren. as PVT. Present from September 1862 through April 1863. On detached service with unserviceable horse, July through October 1863. Present from 11/30/63 through April 1864. Admitted to a Richmond hospital, 5/26/64. Frl. for 60 days, beginning 6/3/64. Reported present, September through December 1864. Admitted to Richmond's Chimborazo hospital, 3/19/65. (CSR 270:1)

Baker, Laurence S.: B. Gates County, N.C., 5/15/30. Graduated USMA, 1851. Entered U.S.

Army as 2LT 7/1/51. Rose to 1LT in Mounted Rifles. When war came, resigned and enl. 5/8/61. Appointed CAPT 7/9/61, to rank from 3/16/61, in Confederate States Army, LTC in Provisional Army dating from 5/16/61. Reported resent November 1861 through June 1862. Prm. COL 3/1/62. Absent during September and October 1862, present November and December of that year. Absent commanding brigade, January through April 1863. Prm BG 23 July 1863 and took command of N.C. Cavalry Brigade; WIA 8/1/63. Lived in Suffolk, VA after the war. D. 4/10/07; buried in Suffolk. (CSR 270:1; Boatner; CMH)

Baker, Shadrick (Shade): Enl. at age 23 in Co. A, 7/13/61 in Raleigh. PVT. Present from November 1861 to December 1862. Absent January and February 1863 with the baggage at Gordonsville. Present from March 1863 through December 1864. (CSR 270:1; AsheCo)

Baker, Simeon: At age 22, enl. 6/12/61 in Co. B. PVT. Reported present from November 1861 through December 1863. Frl. January and February 1864. On detached service at a fishery, March and April 1864. (CSR 270:1; Zeb. Vance Papers, NCSA [courtesy Whit Joyner])

Ball, Alpheus H.: B. Warren County, N.C. Deputy Sheriff there before the war. Stood 5'11", with blue eyes, black hair, and a dark complexion. At age 28, enl. 6/8/61 in Co. E. Reported present January and February 1862, then sick in a Manassas hospital, 3/4/62. Present May and June 1862. Present September 1862 through April 1863. Absent after a horse in N.C. beginning 8/27/63. Present October 1863 to January 1864. Sent to a Richmond hospital (G.H. #9), 1/24/64; admitted to Jackson Hospital, 4/20/64. Experienced paralysis of the left arm after typhoid fever. (CSR 270:1)

Ball, John H.: From Hamptonville, N.C., where he was a clerk. On 5/18/61, enl. in Co. A. Age 22; PVT. Present 11/61–2/62. On detached service in Winchester, Va. beginning 9/11/62. At home on sick frl. beginning 11/25/62 and into December 1862 after being admitted 11/17 to Richmond's G.H. #7 for chronic diarrhea. Jan.–Feb./63, sick in a Gordonsville hospital with erysipelas and pneumonia, then at home on sick frl as of 3/63. July–Aug./63, on detached service to purchase a horse. Present 9/63–10/64. (CSR 270:1; AsheCo; Yadkin)

Ball, Robert D.: B. Warren County, N.C. 5'6" tall, blue eyes, black hair. At age 21, enl. 7/24/61 in Co. E. PVT. Lost arm in accidental shooting, December 1861. Dsh. Admitted to Chimborazo Hospital, Richmond, 3/7/62; Trn. Petersburg hospital, 3/22/62. (CSR 270:1)

Ballance, Daniel: Enl. Co. B, at age 25, 6/12/61, Northampton County, N.C. PVT. Dsh. July 1862. (CSR 270:1)

Ballard, F.A.: Age 21, from Lincoln County, N.C., when enl. 6/10/61 in Co. C. PVT. Present November and December 1861. Absent sick as of 2/26/62 in Petersburg. Present May and June 1862. Captured 9/15/62, Hagerstown, Md. Exd. 11/10/62. Present January through September 1863. Arrested November 1863, and held at Richmond prison, probably for desertion. (CSR 270:1; Alexander)

Ballard, Joseph L.: B. 7/11/43. Enl. 6/10/61 in Co. C at age 19. From Lincoln County, N.C. PVT. Reported present November 1861 through February 1862; May 1862 through March 1863; July through September 1863, except for duty on horse detail as of 8/27/63. Reported AWOL 10/15/63. Present November through January 1864. Held in a Richmond prison, 2/1/64 through February 1864. Present from April to October 1864. Court martialed 11/21/64; trn to Co. G, 33rd Regiment North Carolina State Troops. D. 9/30/24. Bur. in an Iredell Co., NC cem. (CSR 270:1; Alexander; "Burial Places of Confederate Soldiers Whose Descendants are Now Living in Buncombe County," Civil War Clippings File, Pack Memorial Library, Asheville, NC)

Ballew, George M.: From Buncombe County, N.C. Enl. Co. D, February 1862 at age 24. PVT. Absent on horse detail for the rest of the month. Captured 6/29/62 at Willis Church and sent to Fort Delaware. There, he was listed as 5'10", with light hair, blue eyes, and a florid complexion. Present March and April 1863. Present from July 1863 through December 1864. (CSR 270:1; Davis)

Ballew, H.A.: PVT, Co. G, enl. 5/20/61. According to the rolls, deserted 9/16/61 and apparently arrested, but was present 11/28/61 to receive clothing. (CSR 270:1)

Ballew, R. Lee: At age 28, enl. Co. D, 2/22/62 in Asheville. Present May and June 1862. 6/30/62 to 10/31/62, making shoes in Winchester. Present November and December 1862. Absent to purchase a horse, January and February 1862. Present March and April 1863, then absent buying a horse July and August 1863. Afterward, listed on the rolls as AWOL, at home. (CSR 270:1; Davis)

Bancom, Sanders: B. Union County, N.C. Enl. Co. I and Co. G as a PVT 9/16/63 and ren. in June 1864. At age 41, had gray eyes, dark hair, fair complexion, 5'9" tall. Trn. to 16 N.C. Battalion. (CSR 270:1)

Barchett, John L.: Enl. at Camp Beauregard, 8/28/61, in Co. E. PVT, from Warren County, 33. Teamster beginning October 1861. Present Jan.–Feb./62; May–June/62; 9/62–2/62. Appointed blacksmith, 9/1/62. Frl 2/12/63. Present Mar.–Apr./63; 6/30/63–10/31/63, except when detached to N.C. to buy a horse; 11/63–2/64; 4/30/64–Oct./64. Nov.–Dec./64, sent to N.C. to purchase a horse. (CSR 270:1)

Barclay, James A.: B. Lincoln County, N.C. Farmer. At age 39, enl. 9/21/64 in Co. K, at Camp Holmes. PVT. Present until dsh, 12/25/64, due to chronic illnesses such as tuberculosis. 5' 5" tall, dark complexion, hazel eyes, dark hair. (CSR 270:1)

Barden, James W.: Enl. Goldsboro, N.C. in Co. H, 6/20/61. From Wayne County, N.C., age 23. PVT. Present 11/61–2/62. Captured 2/7/62 while on picket near Difficult Run. Present Nov.–Dec./62; absent to buy horse, Jan.–Feb./63. Present Mar.–Apr./63; July–Aug./63; absent on detached service at Gordonsville with unserviceable horses, 9/63–4/64, and also helping with the procurement of horses. Present 4/30–8/31/64. On detached service at Stony Creek, Sept.–Oct./64; present Nov.–Dec./64. Prl. 5/11/65, Greensboro, N.C. (CSR 270:1)

Barden, Joshua J.: B. 1838. From Duplin County, N.C. Enl. 6/17/61 or 6/25/61 in Co. I, at Kenansville, N.C. PVT. Present 11/62–2/62. Appointed 2Bugler 2/1/62. Present May–June/62; Sept.–Dec./62. Absent on detached service, Jan.–Feb./63. Present Mar.–Apr./63. Prm. CPL, 9/12/63. Reported absent 10/7/63, and again 1/1/64–2/64, at Nelson County infirmary camp, on detached service. D. 1897. Bur. in Elmwood Cem., Wayne Co. (CSR 270:1; CGR: 3)

Barden, Samuel James: B. 1834. Enl. in Co. I, 6/17/61, at age 24. PVT. Reported present Nov.–Dec./61. Absent Jan.–Feb./62 on detached service in Warrenton Springs. Present 5/62–6/62; Sept.–Dec./62. Dsh due to diseased eyes, 2/25/63. D. 6/7/09. Bur. Oakwood Cem., Raleigh. (CSR 270:1; Stepp)

Barfield, Solomon J.: Cns. 11/3/64 into Co. H in Raleigh. PVT. Present through 12/64. (CSR 270:1)

Barham, George L.: B. Wake County, N.C. Enl. 7/6/62 in Co. E, at age 25. PVT, farrier. Dsh. 2/5/62 due to organic disease of the digestive organs. 5' 9", fair complexion, blue eyes, sandy hair. (CSR 270:1)

Barker, Edward R.: Enl. 5/23/61, in Co. A, as 3CPL, at Jefferson, N.C. Present 11/61–2/62. WIA at Willis Church, Va., 6/29/62. Present 9/62–4/63. Prm. 2CPL 2/63. Absent at brigade H.Q. 7/63–10/64. Horse killed in battle at Gettysburg, 7/3/63. Prm 1CPL 9/63. Prm 2LT, 10/5/64, after election and confirmation by examining board. (CSR 270:1; AsheCo).

Barnes, G.G.: Resident of Guilford Co. PVT, Co. H. Captured near Salisbury, 4/12/65. Took oath 6/13/65, Camp Chase, Ohio. Stood 5' 9", age 17, had fair complexion, light hair, blue eyes. (CSR 270:2)

Barnes, George W.: In Franklin, N.C, enl. 7/29/61 in Co. K at age 37. PVT. (CSR 270:1) Present 11/61–2/62, although sick in quarters the latter two months. Present 5/62–2/63, except when detached to report to a Lt. Roane, Macon County, N.C., in 12/62. Absent sick 3/4/63. Present July–Aug./63. WIA Jack's Shop, 9/22/63. Deached to recruit horses, 11/63–3/64. Present Apr.–Oct./64. WIA 10/27/64. Appears on an undated POW roll issued by the Army of the Ohio.(CSR 270:1)

Barnes, Godfrey: In Goldsboro, N.C., enl. 6/20/61 at age 37 in Co. H. PVT. Present 11/61–2/62. D. 2/3/62 of disease. (CSR 270:1)

Barnes, H.L.: Enl. 11/17/64, in Raleigh, N.C. PVT. Present through 12/64. (CSR 270:1)

Barnes, William A.: Co. B. (Zeb. Vance Papers, NCSA [courtesy Whit Joyner])

Barnett, T.E.: PVT, Co. C. KIA. (Alexander)

Barrett, J. Monterral: In Asheville, N.C., at age 27, enl. 5/21/61 in Co. G. PVT. 5' 8", light complexion, black eyes, sandy hair. Prewar occupation: farming. Reported present Jan.–Feb./62. Admitted 3/7/62 to a Richmond hospital for dysentery; returned to duty, 4/13/62. Dsh. 5/12/62 for typhoid fever and chronic diarrhea. D. July 1862.

Barrier, Alexander: A farmer before the war. Enl. 2/1/62 in Co. I at age 40. From Stanley County, N.C. PVT. Blacksmith, Mar.–Apr./62. Captured and WIA at Willis Church, 6/29/62. Sent to Fort Delaware. Stood between 5' 6" and 5' 8", with black hair and eyes, sallow complexion. Exd. 8/5/62. Present, 9/62–10/31/63. Kicked by a horse 11/62, fracturing sternum and causing chest infirmity, dropsy of bowels. Dsh. 11/13/62. Ren. Present 1/64–11/64.(CSR 270:1)

Barrier, Caleb C.: Enl. 6/15/61 in Co. F at Concord, N.C. Age 22, PVT. Present 11/61–2/62; May–Dec./62; 7/63. Absent 8/63–12/64, on detached service at Cavalry Division and then Corps H.Q., as wagon master in the ordnance department. Resident of Rowan Co., 1893. (Mizelle; CSR 270:1; Barringer; Cabarrus)

Barrier, Jacob W.: At age 21 in Cabarrus County, N.C., enl. 6/15/61 in Co. F. PVT. 5'11", florid complexion, light hair, blue eyes. Reported present, 11/61–2/62. Admitted to a Richmond hospital with bronchitis, 3/15/62. Released 3/27/62. Present May–June/62; Sept.–Dec./62; 7/63–11/64. Prm SGT, 1863. Elected 2LT, 11/24/64, to rank from 11/9/64. WIA in arm at Bellfield. Awarded leave beginning 1/17/65. Captured at Namozine C.H., 4/3/65. Released on oath from Johnson's Island, 6/18/65. Dead as of 1893. (CSR 270:1; Mizelle; Barringer; Cabarrus)

Barrier, Wiley A.: Enl. Co. I 8/12/61, in Cabarrus County, N.C. Prm. 2LT 9/28/61. Appointed 1LT, 10/1/61. Reported present 11/61–1/62. Absent on detached service, recruiting in N.C., Jan.–Feb./3/62.Present May–June/62; Sept.–Dec./62. Absent recruiting in N.C., Jan.–Feb./63. Present 3/63–4/63. Prm. CAPT 6/20/63. Present 10/31/63; 1/64–12/64. Admitted to the Stuart Hospital, Richmond, 12/3/64. Released 12/23/64. At age 35, tendered resignation 1/11/65. Trn to Salisbury hospital by his request. Wrote W.H. Cheek, "This officer is very deficient in most of the qualities requisite for a good officer." 5'1½", fair complexion, black hair, yellow eyes. (CSR 270:1; Mizelle)

Barrier, Wiley Alexander: B. 7/29/36. Enl. 6/15/61 as 2LT, Co. F. Prm to CPT, Co. I, 9/61. Resigned and trn to 6th N.C. Cavalry. D. 10/6/90. Bur. Mt. Pleasant Lutheran Graveyard, Mt. Pleasant, NC. (Barringer; Cabarrus; Lore: 131)

Barrier, William Lafayette: Enl. 6/15/61 at Concord, N.C., in Co. F. at age 27. 4SG. Present 11/61–2/62; May–June/62; 9/62–7/63. Prm. LT, Co I. Prm. CPT, Co. I. WIA by sabre cut in hand, Gettysburg, 7/3/63. Frl. July–Oct./63. Present Nov.–Dec./63. Absent 2/14/64. WIA near Brook Church, Va., 5/12/64. Minie ball hit his left arm and "passed through elbow joint fracturing inner condyle of humerus." D. 10:50 P.M. 5/17/64 at G.H. #9, Richmond, from erysipelas. Bur. Hollywood Cemetery, Richmond. (CSR 270:1; Mizelle; *The Medical History* 10: 881; 11; 101; *Dear Father,* 123; *Sun,* 3/25/81; Barringer; Cabarrus)

Barringer, Paul A.: B. 1828. From Cabarrus Co. Enl. 4/14/62 in Co. F at age 34. PVT. Reported present May–June/62; 9/62–12/62; 7/63. Sent to procure a horse, 8/27/63. Present 9/63–12/64. D. 4/12/65 from erysipelas of the head at Kittrell Springs, N.C. G.H. Bur. Kittrell Springs Confederate Cem. Had no family; a "pious man" who had been baptized when 5 yrs. old. (CSR 270:1; Kittrell; Barringer; Cabarrus; Stepp)

Barringer, Rufus C.: From Cabarrus County, N.C. Lawyer before the war. At age 39, enl. 4/19/61 in Co. F and elected CPT, 5/16/61. Present, 11/61–2/62; May–June/62; 9/62–6/63. WIA at Brandy Station 6/9/63 from ball fracturing "superior maxilla." Granted leave beginning 6/24/63, rejoined unit 10/12/63. WIA Auburn Mills, 10/14/63. Prm. MAJ 8/26/63; prm. LTC 10/17/63. Absent on detached service, 2/64–5/10/64 in temporary command of the 4th N.C. Cavalry. Prm BG 6/4/64. Commanded N.C. Cavalry Brigade through end of war. WIA at White Oak Swamp, 8/15/64. Captured 4/3/65, Namozine Church, Va. Sent to City Point, Va., Old Captiol Prison in D.C., and Fort Delaware. Released 7/24/65. A resident of Charlotte circa 1893. D. 2/3/1895. Bur. Elmwood Cem., Charlotte. (CSR 270:1; Barringer; Mizelle; Butch Barringer; Cabarrus; *Raleigh Register* 9/2/63).

Barringer, Victor Clay: B. Concord, N.C. 3/29/27. Educated in Concord, NC and at Gettysburg College before graduating from UNC in 1848. Pre-war, served as secretary to his brother, Daniel M. Barringer, U.S. minister to Spain; as a lawyer; and as a professor at Davidson College. Also senator in NC legislature. Enl. 1861 as rgt. MAJ. Resigned 10/61 due to poor health, leaving James B. Gordon as the only rgt. major. Barringer's spot left unfilled since the other rgts raised at that time did not have a second major. Practiced law for remainder of war. Post-war, helped write the first Code of Civil Procedure for NC, then appointed by Pres. Grant to help prepare the *Revised Statutes of the United States,* which is still in use today. Also served 20 years as U.S. representative to the International Court at Alexandria, Egypt. D. 5/27/96. Bur. Rock Creek Cem., Washington, D.C. (Ashe 1: 126; *NC Regts.* 1: 417–18, 485; CSR 270:1; Powell 1: 103)

Barris, E.C.: PVT, Co. C. (Alexander)

Bassett, D.F.: In Asheville, enl. 5/20/61 in Co. B at age 22. 4 SGT. Admitted to G.H. #5 in Richmond, 11/3/61, with measles. Returned to duty 11/8/61. Reported present Jan.–Feb./63, May–June/62, Sept.–Dec./62. Reduced to ranks 12/4/62. Absent Jan.–Feb./63. Present Mar.–Apr./63. Prm. 2LT in Co. F, 5th Tennessee Cavalry, 30 April 1863. Orginally from Buncombe county, N.C. (CSR 270:1)

Bassett, G.W.: 1LT. According to a POW roll dated 4/9/65 at Appomattox, Bassett was an ordinance officer in Barringer's Brigade. Based on ordnance requests in his file, Bassett definitely held that position as of June 1864. Prl. 4/9/65. (CSR 270:1)

Bassett, M.A.: From Buncombe County, N.C. Enl. 5/20/61 at Asheville in Co. G. at age 19. PVT. Present Jan.–Feb./62, May–June/62. Sept.–Oct./62, at G.H. #2, after being admitted 9/9/62. On sick frl, 10/23/62–12/62. Stood 5'11", with a light complexion, dark eyes, and dark hair. Dsh. 1/18/63 due to punctured heel. (CSR 270:1)

Bassett, R.W.: Enl. 5/20/61 at age 20 in Co. B, as PVT, in Asheville. Present Jan.–Feb./62, May–June/62, Sept.–Oct./62. WIA at Barbee's Crossroads, 11/5/62. Reported sick in a Richmond hospital, Nov.–Dec./62. D. January 1863. (CSR 270:1)

Bassett, Thadeus B.: Enl. Co. B as PVT, 5/20/61, in Asheville. Present Jan.–Feb./62 until reported absent sick, then absent with unserviceable horse, 3/62. Present May–June/62, and Sept.–Oct./62. Absent on detached service, Jan.–Dec./62, then present Jan.–Feb./63 and Mar.–Apr./63. Captured near Beverly's Ford, Va., 6/9/63. Present July–Dec./63, 4/1/64, Mar.–Dec./64. Originally from Buncombe County, N.C. (CSR 270:1)

Bastin, Benjamin C.: From Halifax County, age 30, when cns. 7/17/62 as a PVT in Co. I, at Raleigh, N.C. Reported absent, Sept.–Oct./62, then present the remainder of the year. Absent on detached service, Jan.–Feb./63. Present Mar.–Apr./63. Captured at Upperville, Va., 6/21/63; Prl. 6/25/63 from Old Capitol Prison. Present 10/31/63. Prm. CPL 9/1/63. Absent on detached service to remount horses, 1/1/64, but reported present Jan.–Feb./64, Mar.–Dec./64. (CSR 270:1)

Batts, Jesse: B. Duplin County, N.C. At age 22, enl. 6/17/61 in Co. I. PVT. Present 11/61–2/62. D. 2/16/62 at Cantonment W.N. Edwards from accidental gunshot wound. (CSR 270:1)

Batts, Lewis W.: Farmer. Enl. Co. I 6/22/61 at Kenansville, N.C. Reported present, 11/61–2/62. D. 4/4/62 at Manassas, Virginia. (CSR 270:1)

Batts, Thomas: Age 24, from Duplin County, N.C., when enl. in Co. I, 6/20/61, as a PVT, at Kenansville, N.C. Present 11/61–2/62, May–June/62, 9/62–10/62. Absent on detached service, Nov.–Dec./62. Present Jan.–Apr./63. Captured at Upperville, Va. (near Ashby's Gap), 6/21/63. Present 1/1/64–9/64. Reported on detached service, 10/18/64 at Stony Creek, Va. Present Nov.–Dec./64. WIA at Dinwiddie C.H., 3/31/65, with a gunshot wound in both thighs. Took oath, 6/21/65. (CSR 270:1)

Batts, William H.: At Ashville, N.C., enl. 6/17/61 in Co. I as PVT. Age 19, from Duplin County. 5'8", dark hair, blue eyes, florid complexion. Admitted 12/20/61 to G.H. #1, Danville, Va., with pneumonia. Otherwise present 11/61–2/62, May–June/62. Captured at Willis Church, Va., 6/29/62. Reported present 9/62–4/63; 10/31/63; Jan.–Nov./64. Absent on frl., 12/64. (CSR 270:1)

Beam, David: Cns. into Co. H, 9/21/64, in Raleigh, N.C. Reported present through December 1864 (CSR 270:2).

Beare, Felix.: Cns. into Co. H, 9/29/64, in Raleigh, N.C. On detached service with dismounted men, Sept. and Oct. 1864. Reported present through December 1864 (CSR 270:2).

Beaty, Moses: Franklin, N.C. (Macon County.) Enl. 3/11/62, at age 34, in Co. K. PVT. Detailed to cook for officers 1/63–2/63. Sent to hospital sick 8/1/63. Captured Cedar Run, Va. 5/30/63. "Blue eyes, Dark Hair Dark Complexion Height 5 feet 9 inches." Sick at the Wilson, N.C. hospital between 3/30/64 and 8/31/64. Reported present through December 1864. (CSR 270:2).

Beeman, William C.: Jefferson, N.C. Enl. Co. A., 3/5/62, for the war. PVT. Rgt. teamster beginning 2/64. AWOL 8/20/64; deserter (CSR 270:2; AsheCo).

Bell, A.J.: Buncombe County, N.C. At age 25, enl. in Co. G 7/26/61 in Asheville, N.C., for the war. PVT. Deserted near Murfreesboro, N.C. in 6/62 (CSR 270:2).

Bell, Ezekiel Lemuel: Enl. 10/24/61 or 3/21/62 in Co. F., in Concord, Cabarrus County, N.C. Age 18. PVT. Captured, WIA at Barbee's Crossroads, 11/5/62. Frl. 2/2/63 (beginning 1/24/63) for 30 days, and again 11/1/64 to forage in Hampton, Va. by authority of Medical Examination Board, Richmond. Returned April or March 1864. Reported present through December 1864. At some point, Prm to work in commissary dept. Resident of Navarro, TX circa 1893 and also in 1913. After the war, stated that he served about 3 years in the 1st NC Cavalry. (CSR 270:2; Sun, 3/25/81; Barringer; Cabarrus has him as E.L. Bell, and so does his signature in James M. Sloan's "Soldier's Application for a Pension, Texas State Archives, courtesy of Horace Mewborn, so I switched it).

Bell, J.B.: Enl. 10/19/64 at Camp Holmes, in Co. K. PVT. Present through December 64. Psb. Prl. by 10th Michigan Cavalry at Newton, N.C. 4/19/65 (CSR 270:2).

Bell, J.N.: Enl. 2/8/62, Asheville, N.C., in Co. G. Age 37. PVT. Prm. 1CPL, Co. B. Noted on detached service in Charlotte, November 1862–February 1863. At last report, sick in a Raleigh, N.C. hospital, November–December 1864 (CSR 270:2).

Bell, James W.: At age 20, in Clarksville, Northampton County, N.C., enl. 7/13/62, in Co. B. PVT. On detached service, November and December 1862. WIA at Jack's Shop, 9/22/63, and sent home from Hospital #9, Richmond, Va. Reported present through December 1864 (CSR 270:2).

Bell, John W.: Enl. Co. B. 6/12/61 in Northampton County, N.C. PVT. Age 24. Reported absent sick January–February 1862. AWOL June 1862, in Halifax County, N.C. Deserted. (CSR 270:2)

Bell, M.B.: Enl. Ashville, N.C., 5/20/61. Blacksmith. Absent sick in Petersburg, Va. hospital, 4/30/64–8/31/64. Reported present through December 1864 (CSR 270:2).

Bell, Walter Monroe: Enl. in Co. F on 6/15/61, from Concord, N.C. Age 21. PVT. Sent to Barbee's Crossroads 12/28/62. Later prm 1CPL. Prm. 4SGT 11/15/63. Slightly wounded during Bristoe Campaign, after 10/9/63. Prl. Charlotte, N.C. 5/3/65. Dead as of 1893. (Mizelle; CSR 270:2; Barringer; Cabarrus).

Bell, William: PVT, Co. F. (Cabarrus)

Bellew, Hezetiah A.: From Yancey County. Enl. at Asheville, N.C., 5/20/61 in Co. G, at age 24. PVT. Captured at Malvern Hill, 8/5/62. WIA at Upperville, Va., 6/22/63. Shot in left leg. Returned to duty 8/17/63. Reported present through October 1863. AWOL beginning 12/4/63; declared deserted (CSR 270:2).

Benham, Calvin C.: B. 1837. From Jonesville, NC. Son of Dr. Bilson B. Benham and Elizabeth A. Cowles Benham. From Yadkin Co. Enl. as PVT, Co. A, 6/8/61. 9/5/62–10/62, on detached service in Winchester. Jan.–Feb./63, detached with baggage at Gordonsville. Captured 7/4/63 at Gettysburg. Exd. 2/18/65. Bur. Jonesville Cem., Jonesville, NC. (CSR 270:2; AsheCo; Stepp; Yadkin)

Benson, Henry Clay.: From Cabarrus County, N.C. Enl. in Co. F 3/10 or 3/17/62. Prm 3SGT. Reported present through December 1862. Trn. to Co. C, 9th VA Cavalry, 8/22/63. Resident of Richmond, circa 1893. (CSR 270:2; Barringer; Cabarrus).

Bermart, W.: Co. E. PVT. Captured 10/2/64 (CSR 270:2).

Bernhardt, Caleb T.: B. Concord, N.C. Enl. in Co. F., 6/15/61, for the war. PVT. Detailed as nurse to hospital near Upperville, VA., 6/21/63. Captured 7/12/63, Ashby's Gap, Va., by 2nd Mass. Cav., and sent to Point Lookout, Md. Exd. 3/17/64 from City Point, Va. Reported present through December 1864. Sent to buy horses in N.C., 1/1/65. Prl. Salisbury, N.C., 5/30/65. Resident of Rowan Co., circa 1893. (Mizelle; CSR 270:2; Barringer; Rumple: 342; Cabarrus)

Bernhardt, John Crawford: Psb. a schoolmaster before the war. Enl. 6/15/61 in Co. F as a PVT, at age 26. Reported present 11/61–2/62; on detached service beginning 4/22/62. Absent May–June/62. Present 9/62–12/62. Absent 7/20/63 at Camp "Cripple" with dead line horses, through 10/63. Present 11/63–2/64. At home on frl of indulgence, 3/28/64, but also reported present 3/64–11/64. Detached to purchase horse in N.C., 12/64. Prl. Salisbury, N.C., 5/16/65. Resident of Rowan Co., circa 1893. (Mizelle; CSR 270:2; Barringer; Rumple: 342; Cabarrus; Occupations).

Berry, Richard: From Franklin County, N.C. At age 40, cns. 7/16/62 as a PVT in Co. E. Reported present on company muster rolls of 9/62–12/62; absent Nov.–Dec./62. Present Jan.–Feb./63, then on detached service in N.C. to buy a horse, beginning 3/2/63. AWOL as of 8/1/63. Reportedly deserted to Edgecombe County, NC. (CSR 270:2; Pearce: 228)

Berryman, Sanford A.: Enl. as PVT in Co. F 2/3/64. Appears on a clothing receipt, 4/20/64. Reported on the register of Richmond's G.H. #9, 5/28/64, four days after admission, from diarrhea. Admitted again to same hospital on 6/17/64. Also in an unspecified hospital as of 8/22/64. Reported present, Sept.–Dec./64 (CSR 270:2; Cabarrus has him as L.A.).

Best, James J.: From Bertie County, N.C., age 30. Enl. as PVT in Co. E, 4/8/62. Reported present 5/62–6/62. Captured at Malvern Hill, Va., 8/5/62, and exd. 11/10/62. Present 9/62–4/63, 7/63–12/64 (CSR 270:2).

Biddle, James W.: B. 11/28/40. From Craven County, N.C. At age 20, enl. as PVT in Co. H, 7/5/61. Reported present, 11/61–2/62, May–June/62. Appointed QM SGT, 6/10/62. Present Sept.–Dec./62. Absent buying a horse, Jan.–Feb./63, then present Mar.–Apr./63. Absent on detached service buying a horse in N.C., July–Aug./63. Present, 9/63–12/64. Also prm to 2LT, probably on 2/8/65. D. 11/28/14. Bur Cedar Grove Cemetery, New Bern. (CSR 270:1, 270:2; CGR: 1; Stepp)

Biggers, Robert W.: Enl. 2/62 in Co. F as PVT. Age 21. Reported present May–June/62, 9/62–12/62. Trn. to 4th N.C. Cavalry, 5/15/63. Resident of Cabarrus Co., circa 1893. (CSR 270:2; Barringer; Cabarrus)

Billings, Calvin: Cns. 7/11/64 as PVT in Co.

H. Reported present through 8/31/64. Listed as AWOL beginning 9/29/64 (CSR 270:2).

Bird, Lemuel P.: From Jefferson County, Arkansas. PVT, Co. H. Reported present 9/63–1/64. Deserted 2/1/64, received by Army of the Potomac 2/2/64. Held at Old Capitol Prison until he took oath of amnesty, 3/12/64, in Washington, D.C. Released and sent to Philadelphia. Had dark complexion, brown hair, blue eyes, stood 6' tall (CSR 270:2).

Bishop, William T.: At age 32, enl. 5/18/61 as PVT in Co. C. Present 11/61–2/62. Noted on a court martial record, 5/18/62. Present May–Oct./62. Detached to drive baggage, 11/9/62. Present according to rolls of 1/63–4/63, 7/63–12/63. Given frl, 2/25/64. Reported present, 4/1/64. Trn. to the CSA Navy, 5/29/64. (CSR 270:2; Alexander)

Black, James F.: At age 27, enl. from Cabarrus County, N.C. 6/15/61 as PVT in Co. F. Reported present 11/61–2/62, May–June/, Sept.–Dec./62. WIA. Name appears on a clothing receipt, 4/28/63. 7/63, sent to N.C. after a horse. Present 8/27/63–12/64. Living in Mississippi, circa 1893. (CSR 270:2; Mizelle; Barringer; Cabarrus).

Black, Samuel N.: From Mecklenburg County, N.C. At age 25, enl. 5/15 or 5/17/61 as PVT, Co. C. Present 1/62–2/62, May–June/62, Sept.–Dec./62. Absent on detached service, 1/2/63. Present Mar.–Apr./63. Admitted to G.H. in Charlottesville, Va., 5/9/63 with debilitas. Admitted to Richmond G.H. #9, 6/26/63. Frl. July–Aug./63. Present, 9/63–10/64, but also listed as captured at Ford's Depot, 4/3/64. Absent sick, Nov.–Dec./64. 6/24/65, took oath of allegiance. Had dark complexion, black hair, gray eyes, stood 5'8¾" (CSR 270:2; Alexander).

Blackburn, E.G.: From Ashe County, N.C. Enl. at age 21 as PVT in Co. A, 5/28/61. Present Nov.–Dec./61, Jan.–Feb./62. On daily duty as company teamster. Present Sept.–Nov./62. Absent scouting beginning 12/22/62. On frl. to buy a horse, Jan.–Feb./63. Sick at home beginning 2/24/63. Listed as d. On 9/ & 10/63 rolls (CSR 270:2; AsheCo).

Blackburn, William: B. 1839. Farmer. Enl. at age 22 from Ashe County, N.C., in Co. A on 5/25/61. PVT. Absent in Petersburg hospital, Nov.–Dec./61. Admitted to G.H. #1, Danville, Va., 12/19/61, with a fever. On daily duty with the teamsters, Jan.–Mar./62. Dsh. 5/17/62 due to heart disease. Declined rapidly. According to surgeon's certificate, d. 9/27/62 in a Wilson, NC G.H. from the disease. Stood 5'8", had fair complexion, black eyes, light hair. Bur. Maplewood Cem., Wilson. (CSR 270:2; AsheCo; Stepp)

Blackburn, William F.: PVT, Co. K. Enl. 7/6/61, from Macon County, N.C., at age 21. Name appears on a clothing list, 11/28/61. D. Richmond, Va., from pneumonia and typhoid fever, 11/22/61 (CSR 270:2).

Blackwelder, Henry A.: B. 12/7/37. PVT, Co. F, from Cabarrus County, N.C. At age 24, enl. 6/15/61. Present 11/61–2/62, May–June/62, Sept.–Dec./62. Name appears on clothing receipts, 11/28/61, 6/11/64, and 9/25/64. On detached service as teamster to Hampton's Brigade, July–Sept./63. Present 11/63–2/64. On detached service to brigade headquarters, Mar.–Dec./64. D. 2/6/96. Bur. Coldwater Lutheran Church Cem., Cabarrus Co. (CSR 270:2; Mizelle; Barringer; Cabarrus; Lore: 49).

Blackwelder, M.A.: Enl. 6/15/63 as PVT, Co. F. Dsh. (Barringer)

Blackwelder, Nelson: From Cabarrus County, N.C., age 20. Enl. in Co. F., 6/15/61. PVT. Present 11/61–2/62, May–June/62, Sept.–Dec./62. Also present July–Oct./63. Sent to dead line, 11/16/63, and again 2/7/64. D. 7/6/64 in a Petersburg hospital from a 7/4/64 accidental gunshot wound in hand (CSR 270:2; Mizelle; Barringer; Cabarrus).

Blackwelder, Nelson Tobias: B. 6/27/42. Enl. 6/15/61 as PVT in Co. F, at age 19. Resident of Concord, N.C. Present 11/61–2/62, May–June/62, Sept.–Dec./62, July–Aug./63. WIA with right groin flesh wound, in Buckland Races, 10/19/63. Admitted to G.H. #9, 10/24/63. On sick frl, beginning 10/30/63 and extending Nov.–Dec./63. Present Jan.–Dec./64. A great soldier, wrote Fred C. Foard. Resident of Concord, circa 1893. D. 7/1/21. Bur. Bethpage Presbyterian Church Cem., Kannapolis. (CSR 270:2; Barringer; Cabarrus; Stepp; Fred C. Foard to W.G. Means, March 6, 1917, Fred C. Foard Papers, PC 500, NCSA.)

Blackwelder, R.C.: Enl. 5/21/62 as PVT in Co. G. Reported present, Nov.–Dec./64 (CSR 270:2).

Blackwelder, William A.: From Cabarrus County, N.C. Enl. 6/15/61 as PVT, Co. F. Present Nov.–Dec./61. Sent to the hospital, 2/25/62. Present May–June/62. Accidentally shot, 7/9/62. Reported at a Winchester, Va. Hospital, Sept.–Oct./62. Present Nov.–Dec./62, July–Dec./63. 8/2/63, admitted to G.H. #9, Richmond, Va. Sent home on frl, 2/64. Present 2/29/64–4/64. WIA near Ashland or Yellow Tavern, VA, 5/29/64. Admitted to G.H. #9, in Richmond, 6/2/64. D. 7/11/64. Left on person: $57.00 and 2 blankets (CSR 270:2; Mizelle; Sun 3/25/81; Barringer; Cabarrus).

Blackwell, J.P.: PVT, Co. E. Enl. 6/2/64. Registered at G.H. #3, Goldsboro, N.C. Dsh. From hospital, 9/26/64, to return to duty, and present through 12/64 (CSR 270:2).

Blair, Albert W.: From Watauga County. Enl. 3/10/64 as PVT in Co. D. Reported present, Mar.–Apr./64. KIA 6/22/64 (CSR 270:2).

Blair, Elijah S.: Resident of Watauga County. Enl. 5/1/64 as PVT, Co. D. Reported present, 8/31/64. Absent on horse detail, Sept.–Oct./64. Present Nov.–Dec./64. Captured at Southerland Station (Farmville), Va., 4/2/65. On a POW roll at Newport News, Va., 4/23/65. Took oath of allegiance 6/27/65. Had fair complexion, black hair, gray eyes, stood 5'10" (CSR 270:2).

Blair, John C.: From Watauga Co. Enl. 5/16/61 in Co. D as 2LT, to rank from 5/16/61. Absent sick at home, 11/61–2/62. Prm 1LT 2/28/62. Present 3/62. Commissioned CPT, 5/9/62. Present, 6/30/62–7/63. WIA 8/1/63 and sent home. Present 10/31–12/63. 2/29–Apr./64, present on extra daily duty as acting field officer. Captured at Beaver Dam Station, Va., 5/15/64, and sent to various prisons. Held at Morris Island, SC, by Federal authority under Confederate fire from 9/7–10/21/64. Took oath of allegiance and released, 6/16/65. Had dark complexion, dark hair, blue eyes, stood 5'10". (CSR 270:1, 270:2; Davis; SHSP 17: 39)

Blair, William M.: At age 21, enl. 5/11/61 as PVT in Co. D. From Watauga County. Present 11/61–2/62, 5/62–12/62. On detached service, Jan.–Feb./63. Present, Mar.–Apr./63. Admitted 5/15/63 to Charlottesville G.H. with Gonorrhea. Back to duty, 5/26/63. Sent home to buy a horse, July–Aug./63. Present 6/30/63–12/64. Prm. CPL, SGT. Elected 2LT, 11/30/64. Admitted 4/11/65, Point of Rocks hospital, from Petersburg's Post Hospital. (CSR 270:1, 270:2; Davis)

Blake, S.N.: PVT, Co. C. (Alexander)

Blanks, William.: From Granville County, N.C. Enl. as PVT in Co. E, 8/12/61, at age 23. Absent on frl 11/28/61. Present 11/61–2/62, May–June/62, 9/62–7/63. On detached service to Nelson County, Va. with disabled horses, 8/25/63. Absent on frl. In Nelson County, 4/64; present 5/64–8/64. (CSR 270: 2)

Blassingame, John G.: From Buncombe County, N.C. At age 21, enl. 5/16/61 as 2LT in Co. B. Resigned 10/61. Afterward appointed 2LT, 19th N.C. Reported d. at Brandy Station, Va., by 3/64. (CSR 270:1, 270:2)

Blevins, William: Resident of Ashe County, N.C., age 26. Enl. as PVT in Co. A, 5/23/61, from Jefferson, N.C. Reported present 11/61–2/62; Sept.–Oct./62. Under arrest, 11/62–2/63. On daily duty with teamsters, Mar.–Apr./63, 7/63. Captured 8/26/63 at Kelly's Ford, Va. Listed as deserter. Sent to Old Capitol Prison. Took Oath of Allegiance 9/26/63, and sent to Philadelphia two days later. Stood 6' tall, had a light complexion, light hair, and blue eyes. (CSR 270: 2; AsheCo)

Blount, William A.: Appointed ast. surgeon 2/23/62. Absent on detached service, Sept.–Oct./62. Reported present Nov.–Dec./62. On detached service, 2/18/63, then present Mar.–Apr./63, 7/63–2/64. Absent sick, Mar.–Apr./64, but also reported on detached service, 4/1/64. Present May–Aug./64. Commissioned surgeon, 5/1/64. Absent sick at a Wilson, N.C. hospital, 9/23/64, then present Nov.–Dec./64. Prl. at Appomattox, 4/9/65. (CSR 270:1, 270:2)

Blythe, Joseph: Age 21, from Northampton County, N.C. Enl. 6/17/61 as PVT in Co. B. Present 11/61–3/62. Deserted, 4/15/62. (CSR 270:2)

Bobbitt, Miles: B. Warrenton, NC. At age 16, enl. 8/12/61 as PVT, Co. E. On detached service "a good part of the time." WIA slightly 8/15 or 8/16/64 along Charles City Rd., near Richmond. Surrendered at Appomattox C.H., VA. Later wrote that he returned home after the war "without a scratch." (Richmond *Sentinel,* 8/26/64; "Miles Bobbitt," in Military Collection, Civil War Collection, Box 70, Folder 13, NCSA, Raleigh.)

Boggs, Peter F.: PVT, Co. A. Enl. 5/20/61, from Jefferson, N.C. Present 11/61–2/62; 9/62–12/62. Absent scouting beginning 12/25/62. Absent with the horses in N.C., Jan.–Feb./63. Present Mar.–Apr./63, July–Aug./63. WIA 7/3/63 at Gettysburg, Pa. Foot amputated. Retired after frl., 11/13/64. (CSR 270:2; *Medical History* 12: 548; AsheCo)

Bolick, J.J.: PVT, Co. K. Enl. 12/28/63. Present 2/29/64–3/31/64. Absent sick, Apr.–Oct./64. Present 12/64. (CSR 270:2)

Bolick, Mark (Marcus): Age 19, from Caldwell County, N.C. Enl. as bugler in Co. D, 5/11/61 Sick in a Petersburg, Va. hospital, 11/61–2/62. Dsh 12/3/61. (Davis; CSR 270:2)

Bonner, William A.: Enl. 6/18/61 in Co. B. PVT. Age 28, from Martin County, N.C. Present Nov.–Dec./61. As CPL, absent in charge of horses, Jan.–Feb./62. Present Mar.–Apr./62, Sept.–Oct./62. Nov.–Dec./62, absent on detached service. Present Jan.–Apr./63, July–Dec./63. On frl, Jan.–Feb./64. Absent on horse detail, Mar.–Apr./64. Reported present, May–Dec./64. (CSR 270: 2)

Borden, James Cole: B. 6/26/29. From Wayne Co. Enl. in Co. H, 6/24/61, at age 32. SGT. Reported present 9/61–2/62. On sick leave, 3/22/62. Present May–June/62. Prm. 2LT, 6/7/62. Present Sept.–Dec./62. Prm. 1LT 10/22/62. Frl. Jan.–Feb./63. Present Mar.–Apr./63, July–Dec./63. Prm. CPT 7/23/63. Present Jan.–Feb./64. On detached service, Mar.–Apr./64. On leave, 4/30/64–8/31/64. Resigned effective 8/30/64 to become Sheriff of Goldsboro. D. 8/23/85. Bur. Willowdale Cem., Goldsboro. (CSR 270:1, CSR 270: 2; Stepp)

Borders, Mike: PVT, Co. I. Cns. 10/3/64. Present through 12/64. (CSR 270: 2)

Borders, W.R.: PVT, from Shelby, N.C. Cns. 10/3/64 as PVT in Co. I. Present until 12/11/64 when sent to Raleigh, N.C.'s Pettigrew G.H. #13 with a fractured left clavicle. Name appears on a clothing list, 1/24/65. CIA 4/3/65 at Ford's Station, Va. Took Oath of Allegiance, 6/3/65. (CSR 270:2)

Bost, Henry C.: From Cabarrus County, N.C. At age 21, enl. 6/15/61 as in Co. F. PVT. Reported present 11/61–2/62, May–June/62, Nov.–Dec./62. July–Aug./63, after horse KIA at Gettysburg, sent to N.C. to find a replacement. Sept.–Dec./63, present. Appointed 4CPL, 11/15/63. Present 1/64–10/64. Detailed to N.C. after a horse, 12/31/64. Also prm. to 4SGT. Prl. Salisbury, N.C., 1865. WIA. Later a resident of Rowan Co. Dead as of 1893. (CSR 270: 2; Mizelle; Barringer; Rumple: 342; Cabarrus)

Bost, Henry M.: B. 11/10/44. Farmer from Concord, N.C. At age 18, enl. 2/9/63 as PVT, Co. F. Trn. from 4th N.C. Reported present 7/63–3/64. WIA at Ashland, Va., 5/29/64. Admitted to Stuart Hospital in Richmond, 6/2/64. Still there on 7/26/64, "unable to go as he would be injured by being moved." 40-day frl. Beginning 8/15/64. With hospital detachment, 11/64. Dsh. 1/21/65 after gunshot wound that required amputation of right thigh. Stood 5'8", had fair complexion, black eyes, light hair. Resident of Haile Gold Mine, circa 1893. D. 8/30/08. Bur. Cold Springs Methodist Episcopal Church Cem., Cabarrus Co. (CSR 270: 2; Barringer; Cabarrus; Lore: 39)

Bost, J.W.: PVT, Co. F. (Cabarrus)

Bost, Jacob: Pre-war occupation: shoemaker. At age 22, from Cabarrus County, N.C., enl. 6/15/61 in Co. F. PVT. Reported present 11/61–2/62, May–June/62, Sept.–Dec./62. Sent with dead line horses to recuperate, 8/24/63–10/63. Present 11/63–12/64. WIA at Petersburg, 1864. Living in Texas circa 1893. (CSR 270: 2; Mizelle; Barringer; Cabarrus; Occupations)

Bost, Martin Luther: B. 9/25/26. From Cabarrus County, age 35. Enl. as 4CPL in Co. F, 6/15/61. Present 11/61–2/62; May–June/62, Sept.–Dec./62. Dsh and furnished substitute, 5/15/63. Resident of Bost's Mill, circa 1893. D. 12/6/03. Bur. St. Paul's Methodist Church Cem., Cabarrus Co. (CSR 270: 2; Mizelle; Barringer; Cabarrus; Graves)

Bost, Mathisis Jackson: Enl. 2/7/64 as PVT, Co. F. Present 3/64–12/64. Detached to buy a horse in N.C., 1/1/65. (CSR 270: 2; Davis UDC)

Botts, R.M.: From Cleveland County, Va. Cns. 10/3/64 in Co. I, as PVT. Present through 12/64. CIA 4/3/65; prl. 6/23/65. Had light complexion, brown hair, blue eyes, stood 5'8½". (CSR 270: 2)

Bowden, Richard D.: From Warren County, N.C. PVT, Co. E. Enl. 6/25/61 at age 21. D. 2/5/62 at Front Royal hospital, from pneumonia. (CSR 270: 2)

Boyce, John F.: From Northampton County, N.C. At age 18, enl. 3/19/62 as PVT and bugler in Co. B. Listed as sick in quarters, Mar.–Apr./62. D. 5/62 at Kingston. (CSR 270: 2)

Boyd, Alfred D.: Age 22, from Caldwell County, N.C. Enl. 6/18/61 as PVT in Co. D. Present, Nov.–Dec./61. Admitted 1/12/62 to hospital near Manassas, VA with typhoid fever. D. 1/16/62. (CSR 270: 2, Davis)

Boyd, Amos F.: Enl. 2/28/62 as PVT, Co. D. Age 19. Reported absent May–June/62 in a Richmond hospital. Present 6/30/62–4/63, although admitted 7/3/62 to Richmond's G.H. #4 with chronic rheumatism. WIA 6/9/63. D. 6/18/63 or 7/12/63. (CSR 270: 2; Davis)

Boyd, H.H.: Enl. 7/4/61 as PVT, Co. I. Age 33 from Duplin County, N.C. Rejected. (CSR 270:2)

Boyd, James: Enl. 1/26/64 in N.C. and 3/12/64 in Va. as PVT, Co. H. Present Apr.–Dec./64. Prl. Greensboro, N.C., 5/9/65. (CSR 270: 2)

Boyd, Lemual: From Arkansas. Enl. 6/1/61. Deserted at Rapidan River, 2/1/64, at age 31. Reason: wanted to go see his family and then join U.S. heavy artillery at Memphis (Turner/Baker Papers).

Boyd, Perry L.: Resident of Lincoln County, N.C. At age 25, enl. 5/27/62 as PVT, Co. C. Reported present 4/63. Captured at Beverly's Ford, Va., 6/9/63, prl. 6/25/63. Present, 7/63. Detached to N.C. to buy a horse, 8/27/63. Reported present 9/63–12/64. Captured 4/3/65, released from Point Lookout, 6/23/65. Had light complexion, brown hair, gray eyes; stood 6'¾". (CSR 270: 2; Alexander)

Boyd, R.F.: Age 19, from Buncombe County, N.C. enl. As PVT in Co. G, 5/20/61. Present Jan.–

Feb./62, May–June/62, Sept.–Oct./62. On detached service, Nov.–Dec./62. Present Jan.–Feb./63, Mar.–Apr./63. Captured at Rappahannock River, Va., 3/16/63, and exd. 4/2/63. On detached service to buy a horse, July–Aug./63. Present, Sept.–Dec./63. On detached service as a scout for GEN Rufus Barringer, Sept.–Oct./64. Present, Nov.–Dec./64. (CSR 270: 2)

Boyd, W.T.: Age 24, resident of Buncombe County, N.C. Enl. 5/20/61 in Co. G. Reported present Jan.–Feb./62, May–June/62. Admitted to a Charlottesville G.H., 5/8/63. Released 5/11/63. Present 9/62–4/63. KIA, Martinsburg, Va., 7/19/63. (CSR 270: 2)

Boyett, William: B. Duplin County, N.C. At age 18, enl. as PVT in Co. I, 8/23/61. D. 11/5/61 of disease in Fredericksburg, Va. (CSR 270: 2)

Boykin, Robert V: Va. resident. Enl. 4/15/62 as Ast. Chief of Subsistence. Present May–June/62, 9/62–4/63. Regimental ast. chief of subsistence position eliminated by Congress; Boykin to CAPT. Present 6/63–12/63. Frl. Jan.–Feb./64. Present Mar.–Apr./64. On detached service May–June/64, Sept.–Dec./64, acting Ast. Chief of Subsistence for GEN Chambliss' Brigade. (CSR 270:1)

Boyles, Patrick: B. Ireland. Farmer from Duplin County, N.C. At age 32, enl. 6/22/61 as PVT, Co. I. Reported present 11/61–2/62, May–June/62. Dsh. 11/1/62 due to varicose veins. Stood 6' tall, had light complexion, black eyes and hair. (CSR 270: 2)

Bracy, John H.: Age 25, from Northampton County, N.C. Enl. 6/12/61 as PVT in Co. B. Reported present, Nov.–Dec./61. Absent on sick leave, Jan.–Feb./62. Present Mar.–Apr./62. Left at home sick, 7/5/62. Listed as AWOL, Nov.–Dec./62. Present Jan.–Apr./63, 7/63–12/63. Frl., Jan.–Feb./64. In G.H. #1, Danville, Va., with jaundice. Sent to Richmond G.H. Present Mar.–Dec./64. Reported in a Danville G.H., 5/3/65. (CSR 270: 2; Zeb. Vance Papers, NCSA [courtesy Whit Joyner])

Bradford, W.J.: Enl. 10/27/64 as PVT in Co. C. Reported present through 12/64. Prl. 5/24/65, Charlotte, N.C. (CSR 270: 2)

Bradley, John: From Buncombe County, N.C. At age 22, enl. 5/20/61 as PVT, Co. G. D. Centreville, Va., 2/62. (CSR 270: 2)

Bradley, John T.: PVT, Co. D. Present Nov.–Dec./64. (CSR 270: 2)

Bradshaw, B.F.: Co. D, from Tennessee. KIA. (Davis)

Bradshaw, Charles W.: Age 28, from Cabarrus County, N.C. Enl. 6/15/61 as PVT and first bugler, Co. F. Prm. CAPT and/or LTC and trn to 42d N.C., 11/61. Resident of Charlotte, circa 1893. (CSR 270: 2; Mizelle; Barringer; Cabarrus)

Bradshaw, George W.: From Macon County, N.C., age 18. PVT, Co. K. Reported present 11/61–2/62, May–June/62, 9/62–10/63. Absent sick in a hospital, Nov.–Dec./63. Admitted to Richmond's G.H. #24, 12/15/63. Present Jan.–Apr./64. Deserted 4/64. Captured in Green County, TN, 9/27/64. Released from Camp Chase, Ohio, 10/22/64. Enl. U.S. Army, 5/22/65. (CSR 270: 2)

Bradshaw, James H.: Age 28, from Watauga County, N.C. Enl. 8/4/61 as PVT and farrier, Co. D. Present 11/61–2/62, acting as teamster in 2/62. Also present 5/62–12/62, although admitted 7/3/62 to G.H. #4, Richmond, Va., with chronic diarrhea. Reported present, 1/63–4/63. Went home to buy a horse, July–Aug./63, after horse died at Gettysburg, then present through 12/63. WIA 12/31/63. On frl. Jan.–Feb./64. Arrested and confined, Mar.–Apr./64. KIA Reams Station, Va., 8/21/64. (CSR 270: 2; CSR 270: 4 for George N. Folk)

Bradshaw, Josiah P.: From Cherokee County, N.C., age 18. Enl. 6/25/61 in Co. K as CPL. Reported present, 11/61–2/62. Sent to Manassas sick, 2/24/62. Reported present May–June/62, 9/62–4/63. Detached to N.C. to buy a horse, July–Aug./63. Reported present, 10/31/63–3/31/64. Reduced to ranks, 11/8/62. On detached service to brigade H.Q., Mar.–Oct./64, herding cattle for commissary. Present, Nov.–Dec./64.

Branch, William N.: From Franklin County, N.C., age 27. 1SGT, Co. E. Admitted to Richmond's G.H. #3, 10/22/61. D. 12/61 at Manassas of typhoid fever, pneumonia. (CSR 270: 2; Pearce: 15)

Braswell, Henry: Age 32, from Halifax County, N.C. Enl. 7/17/62 as PVT, Co. B. Reported present, 9/62–4/63. On detached service to N.C. after a horse, 8/27/62. Present July–Dec./63. Absent on horse detail, Mar.–Apr./64. Present 4/30/64–10/64. (CSR 270: 2; Zeb. Vance Papers, NCSA [courtesy Whit Joyner]; Halifax, 3)

Braswell, Wilson: Age 25, resident of Northampton County, N.C. Enl. 6/13/61 as PVT, Co. B. Present Nov.–Dec./61. Home on sick leave with bronchitis, Jan.–Feb./62, after discharge from Danville, Va.'s G.H. #1. Present Mar.–Apr./62, 9/62–4/63. WIA at Gettysburg, 7/3/63, and sent to Richmond's G.H. #3 on 7/20/63, then to a Raleigh, N.C. hospital, and then home. Present 11/63–12/63. Admitted 1/19/63 to G.H. #9, Richmond. Present 3/64–8/64. Nov.–Dec./64, at brigade H.Q. as a butcher. Captured at Dinwiddie C.H., Va., 3/31/65, and released 6/24/65 after taking Oath of Amnesty. Had dark complexion, black hair, blue eyes, and stood 5'5". (CSR 270: 2)

Breedlove, Jesse E.: From Macon County, N.C., age 24. Enl. Co. K 6/25/61. PVT. Reported present 11/61–2/62. Reported in a Richmond hospital 3/62, then absent sick at a Wilson, NC hospital, May–June/62. Present 9/62–4/63, 7/63–8/64. On detached service at Stoney Creek, VA, Sept.–Oct./64, and captured there 12/1/64. D. 5/8/65 from pneumonia; bur at Point Lookout. (CSR 270:2; PL: 128)

Breffard, W.J.: PVT, Co. C. (Alexander)

Bremer, David E.: From Washington County, N.C. Enl. 5/1/61 as a PVT in Co. D. Age 20, a volunteer (CSR 270:2).

Bremer, Matthew: A farmer, from Northampton County, N.C. Enl. 6/18/61 as 1SGT in Co. B. Absent November and December 1861 at Richmond hospital. DSH 1/62 at age 48 due to general feeble health, dyspeptic condition of the stomach and other ailments. Stood 5'11", had a fair complexion, blue eyes, grey hair. (CSR 270:2)

Bridges, George W.: From Wayne County, N.C., age 30. PVT, Co. H. Enl. 6/25/61 in Goldsboro, N.C. Reported present November 1861–February 1862; May–June, September–December 1862. Sent to N.C. in January 1863 to obtain a horse. Present March and April 1863, then absent July in August in N.C. again after a horse. Present September 1863 through March 1864, then absent in April 1864 to procure a horse once again. Absent sick 4/30/64 through October; present November and December 1864. Appears on a list of staff officers and men serving at headquarters, Cavalry Corps, Army of Tennessee prl at Greensboro, N.C. 4/65 (CSR 270:2).

Brigman, N. Kelsey: From Buncombe County. At age 22, enl. 5/20/61 as bugler in Co. G. Appears on clothing receipt roll in November 1861. Reported present January and February, although reported sick at home 2/4/62. Reported present May and June, September and October 1862. Absent on detached service November 1862–February 1863. Present July 1863–August 1864. Absent on detached service to procure fresh horse, September and October 1864, then present through December 1864 (CSR 270:2).

Brigman, Robert: Enl.5/20/61 in Co. G., as PVT. Reported present January and February, May and June 1862. Absent September and October that year, at Winchester, by order of Col. Baker. Present November and December 1862. Absent on detached service, January and February 1863, then present March, April, and July 1863 through October 1864. Prm. 4CPL summer 1863, then 3CPL in March or April 1864. Appointed 3SGT 12/1/64 while in middle of November and December 1864 frl. of indulgence. From Buncombe County, N.C., age 20 (CSR 270:2).

Brinegar, E.L.: PVT, Co. A. Prl. Salisbury, N.C., 1865 (CSR 270:2)/

Britt, Lawrence: From Northampton County, N.C., age 19. Enl. as PVT in Co. B, 6/12/61. Absent sick November and December 1861. Present January and February 1862, then absent in a Petersburg hospital from March to June 1862. Reported present September and October 1862; absent on detached service November and December 1862, through February 1863. Detached to procure forage, 2/26/63. Then present through October 1864 (CSR 270:2).

Brittain, W.T.: From Henderson Co., N.C. At age 23, enl. 3/12/62 as PVT in Co. G. Reported present May and June 1862. Absent on detached service at Winchester, Va., September and October 1862. Present November 1862 through April 1863. Absent on detached service to buy a horse, July and August of that year. Present September and October 1863. Trn to Co. K, 11th N.C., in November or December 1863. (CSR 270:2)

Broadhurst W.G.: Enl. 9/8/63? as PVT. Reported present 10/31/63 and 1/1/64. Trn from Co H to Co. I. Received clothing 6/11/64 and 6/16/64. Absent 4/31/64–8/31/64. Appears on a register of a Petersburg hospital, after being admitted 6/21/64. Then trn to a Richmond hospital. WIA 8/21/64, and reported at N.C. hospital. Home on frl October and November 1864. Sick on wounded frl 12/23/64 (CSR 270:2).

Broadnax, W.E.: Co. G. Appointed aide-de-camp 3/1/62. (CSR 270:1)

Broadnax, William E.: From Northampton Co., entered service 10/1/61 at age 30. 2LT, Co. G. Appointed Ransom's aide-de-camp, 10/4/61. Reported present February 1862. In March 1862, trn to GEN Ransoms staff. (CSR 270:2)

Brodie, J.L.: PVT, Co. E. Appears on an April 1865 list of Confederate prisoners who have been paroled not to take up arms against the U.S. Government until regularly exchanged (CSR 270:2).

Brogden, Willis H.: B. August 1839. From Wayne Co. Enl. 6/24/61 in Co. H. as PVT. Reported present 11/61–2/62. Captured at Willis Church, VA, 6/29/62. Held at forts Delaware and Columbus. Stood 5'10", with red hair, hazel eyes, and a pale complexion. Exd. 8/5/62. Reported present Sept.–Oct./62. Absent detached to NC for election, Nov.–Dec./62. Reported present January through April 1863. Absent on detached service to N.C. to buy a horse, July–Aug./63. Present Sept.–Dec./64. Appointed CPL early 1863, then SGT in 1864. D. March 1922. Bur. Willowdale Cem., Goldsboro. (CSR 270:2; Stepp)

Brooks, Solomon: From east Tennessee. Enl. 3/7/62 as PVT in Co. A. Company teamster. Absent on detached service at Winchester, Va., beginning 9/5/62. Present through December 1862. Present January through April 1863. July 1863 through December 1864, present and on extra duty as regimental teamster. (CSR 270:2; AsheCo)

Brosaby, Sims: SGT. Co. not stated. Reported as POW, captured near Madison C.H. 9/23/63. (CSR 270:2)

Brown, Barton R.: From Watauga County, N.C. At age 20, enl. in Co. D 7/19/61 as PVT. Reported present November and December 1861. On extra duty as AQM, January and February, May and June 1862 Appears on a roster as elected 2LT, 5/25/62. Dsh 6/5/62 by prm to 7 NC Battalion as CAPT. Wounded and sent home, 6/30/62 through October 1862 (CSR 270:2).

Brown, Barton Roby: B. circa 1842 in NC. Living in Johnson Co., TN as of 1860. Enl. in Co. D. WIA in MD. Prm CPT, Co. F 7th Bn NC Cavalry, which became Co. A, 6th NC Cavalry. Prl. Nash Co. Reported living in Johnson Co., TN, 1897, working as a stock raiser. Still in Johnson Co. as of 1918. D. circa 1921. Brother of Steven Justice Brown. (CSR 270:1; Davis; 6th NC: 56, 74, 144)

Brown, James W.: From Lenoir County, N.C. Enl. 6/25/61 at age 19. Company not stated. Dsh. (CSR 270:2)

Brown, George Washington: Enl. 4/6/63 or 4/6/64 as PVT, Co. F. Reported present Mar.–Dec./64. Also a member of the 42d Cav. Resident of Concord, circa 1893. D. 2/3/23 at age 77. (CSR 270:2; Barringer; Cabarrus; Graves; DavisUDC)

Brown, John: From Ashe County, N.C. PVT, Co. A. Enl. 3/7/62. Reported present September through December 1862. Absent on frl to buy horse, January and February 1863. At home sick, March and April 1863. Absent on detached service to buy horse, July and August 1863. AWOL beginning 10/29/63. Present 11/30/63–February 1864. On detached service in N.C., March and April 1864. Present through December 1864. WIA in side, Battle of Paynes' Farm (Mine Run Campaign) 11/27/63 or 11/28/63. (CSR 270:2; AsheCo)

Brown, Jonathon H.: B. 12/11/44. PVT, Co. D. Enl. 3/2/64 in Boone, N.C. Present through 12/64. D. 11/16/15. Bur. Brown Cem., Watauga Co. (CSR 270:2; Davis, Stepp)

Brown, Jones M.: PVT. Enl. 11/28/63 at Camp Vance in Co. D. Reported present Sept.–Dec./64. Survived the war only to be KIA 5/65 while fighting renegades at Fort Hamby in Wilkes County, N.C. (CSR 270:2; Hartley)

Brown, Joseph: Enl. 5/11/61 at age 37 as PVT in Co. D. Absent sick at home, in Watauga County, N.C., November and December 1861. Present January and February 1862, then adm. to hospital with pneumonia, 3/8/62. Returned to duty 3/27/62. Present May and June, November and December 1862. On detached service, Jan.–Feb./63. Present 3/63–4/63; 7/63–10/6. Absent at home in search of a horse, Nov.–Dec./63. Present 1/64–4/64. Went home to buy a horse, 8/31/64, but reported present Sept.–Dec./64. Captured Amelia C.H., 5/3/65. Released from Point Lookout after taking Oath of Allegiance, 6/23/65. Had fair complexion, brown hair, hazel eyes, and stood 6' tall (CSR 270:2; Davis).

Brown, Pleasant W.: Enl. as PVT in Co. F, 4/64. Reported present 4/64–10/64. Detailed to buy a horse in N.C., 12/5/64. Adm. 5/3/65 to a Danville hospital with a left chest problem. Frl 4/8/65 for 30 days. Resident of Salisbury, circa 1893. (CSR 270:2; Barringer; Rumple: 342; Cabarrus).

Brown, Stephen J.: From Watauga County, age 17. PVT, Co. D. Enl. 7/19/61. Present 11/61–2/62. Reported at a Richmond hospital, 3/8/62, and dsh from its care 3/27/62. Reported present 5/62–12/62. Adm. to G.H. #10, 12/14/62. Absent to buy a horse, Jan.–Feb./63. Prm SGT in early 1863. Mar.–Apr./63, trn by prm to 2LT to Co. G., 65th N.C. (CSR 270:2; CSR 270:7 for Martin V. Moore).

Brown, Steven Justice: B. 1843 in Watauga Co. Listed on a Johnson Co., TN census, 1860. Enl. in Co. D, 7/19/61. Prm LT Co. F, 7th Bn NC Cavalry, early 1863, which became Co. A, 6th N.C. Cavalry. WIA at Chickamauga. Prl Wakefield, N.C., 4/20/65. Post-war worked as a lawyer in Salisbury, later as a farmer in Johnson Co., TN. Reported living in Johnson Co., 1897. D. 10/8/12. Brother of Barton Roby Brown. (CV XXI [1913]: 175; 6th NC: 56, 74, 144)

Brown, Thomas: Co. D "Big Tom"(Davis)

Brown, Thomas H.: From Watauga County, N.C. At age 18, enl. in Co. D 7/10/61, as PVT. Reported present 11/61–2/62 and 5/62–12/62. Absent to buy a horse, Jan.–Feb./63. Present 3/63–4/63. Prm. CPL, summer 1863. Absent 7/63–8/63 to buy a horse at home, and AWOL there through 10/63. Present 11/63–3/63. Sent home to buy a horse, 3/64–4/64. WIA and sent home, 8/31/64. Reported present Sept.–Dec./64, and prm sgt. (CSR 270:2)

Brown, Thomas, Sr.: Age 21, from Watauga County. Enl. 5/11/61 as PVT. in Co. D. Absent sick, at home, Nov.–Dec./61. Reported present Jan.–Feb./62, 5/62–4/63, 5/63–10/63. Sent home after a horse, Nov.–Dec./63, then reported present 1/64–4/64. Adm. to Jackson Hospital in Richmond, 5/5/64. 2 days later, listed as convalescent patient able to act as nurse. also at G.H. 9, 2/13/64, then at Jackson Hospital with an abscess groin. Returned to duty 2/26/64. Captured near Petersburg, Va., 6/21/64. Held at Point Lookout. Exd 11/1/64. (CSR 270:2)

Brown, William J.: B. England. Enl. at age 26 in Co. G, 5/20/61. Reported present Jan.–Feb./62. Trn. to become musician, 2/1/62. Present 3/62–6/29/62; captured at Willis Church. Sent to Fort Delaware, then exd 8/5/62. Absent sick Sept.–Oct./62; present 11/62–4/63. July–Aug./63, absent with GEN Baker's horse in NC. Present 9/63–4/1/64. Honorably dsh. 7/28/64. From Buncombe County, N.C., stood 5'6", had black hair, dark eyes, and florid complexion. (CSR 270:2)

Brumley, John A.: PVT, Co. F. Enl. 5/64. Reported present 3/64–10/64. Absent Nov.–Dec./64 on detail to work on the railroad. Dead as of 1893. (CSR 270:2; Barringer; Cabarrus)

Bryan, _____: PVT, Co. G. Absent sick, 2/62 (CSR 270:2).

Bryan, Johnson H.: Co. H. R. 10/14/62. (CSR 270:1)

Bryan, Johnson H.: From Craven County, N.C. At age 37, apptd 2LT 8/20/61 in Co. H. Reported present 11/61–12/61. Absent sick Jan.–Feb./62 beginning 1/26/62, and checked into GH #1, Danville, Va. Reported present May–June/62. Resigned due to disability in October or on 11/20/62. (CSR 270:2)

Bryan, Joseph D.: From Watauga County, N.C. PVT, Co. D. At age 19, enl. 5/11/61. Adm. with rheumatism to GH #1, Danville, Va., 1/16/62, then sent to Front Royal hospital. Also reported at home on leave of absence, Jan.–Feb./62. Reported present 5/62–4/63, although probably captured at Willis Church, VA, 6/29/62. Captured near Culpeper C.H., 8/1/63. Sent to Point Lookout, and exd. 2/65 (CSR 270:2; Davis).

Bryant, Andrew J.: From Northampton County, N.C. At age 28, enl. as PVT in Co. B., 6/12/61. Reported present 11/61–12/61. Absent sick, Jan.–Feb./62. In a Petersburg hospital, Mar.–Apr./62. Another report says adm. to Richmond's G.H. #5 with remittent fever, 3/10/62, and returned to duty 3/27/62 (CSR 270:2).

Bryant, Elihu: Enl. as PVT in Co. B, 6/12/61. D. 12/30/61 at Camp W.S. Ashe hospital, from softening of the brain. From Northampton County, N.C. (CSR 270:2).

Bryant, Lorenzo D.: From Northampton County, N.C., age 22. PVT, Co. B. Enl. 7/26/61. Left sick at Camp Beauregaurd, N.C. 10/13/61 when rgt. moved to Va. Reported absent at home on sick leave, Nov.–Dec./61, and still sick Jan.–Feb./62. Dsh March 1862, but present Mar.–Apr./62. Absent on detached service at Winchester, Va., Sept.–Oct./62. Reported present 11/62–4/63. Absent sick at a hospital beginning 6/10/63 through 10/63, then at home sick through April 1864. Appears on a list of Rebel deserters and refugees received at Fort Monroe, 2/7/64, having come into Federal lines at Plymouth N.C. Took Oath of Allegiance, 2/24/64. Had brown hair and fair complexion. Stood 5'11½". (CSR 270:2).

Bryant, William E.: From Northampton County, N.C. PVT, bugler. At age 18, enl. in Co. B., 6/18/61. Reported present, Nov.–Dec./61. Adm. to Moore G.H. #1, in Danville, Va., with diarrhea, 1/2/62. Thereafter at home on sick leave through 2/62. Present Mar.–Apr./62, Sept.–Dec./62; also resent 1/63. Absent, detached as a scout in Fauquier County, Va., 2/63. Present Mar.–Apr./63. Sick in a hospital, July–Aug./63. Present Sept.–Dec./63; Mar.–Apr./64. KIA Ground Squirrel Church, 5/11/64 (CSR 270:2; Zeb. Vance Papers, NCSA [courtesy Whit Joyner]).

Bryant, William Hansel: From Northampton County, N.C., age 22. Enl. as PVT in Co. B., 6/18/61. Reported present 11/61–4/62. Absent and left at home sick, 8/62–10/62. Involved in some unspecified capacity in court martial proceedings, 3/26/63. AWOL Nov.–Dec./62. Present 1/63–4/63, 7/63–12/63, and Mar.–Apr./64. On frl, May–Oct./64 (CSR 270:2; meeting with great-grandson Dr. James H. McCallum, Jr., 1/14/99).

Buckman, Noah: No Co. stated. On a register of prisoners received and disposed of by the PVM GEN, 1/19/65; mis-sent from City Point (CSR 270:2):

Buckner, John: PVT, Co. K, from Macon County, N.C. Age 17. Rejected by Col. Baker (CSR 270:2).

Buckner, W.A.: Co. K, PVT, from Macon County, N.C. Age 25. Rejected by Col. Baker (CSR 270:2).

Bullock, John G.: PVT, Co. E. CNS 3/13/64. Reported present Mar.–Apr./64. Admitted to Richmond's G.H. #9, 5/13/64. Absent on detached service at brigade HQ on provost guard, May–Dec./64 (CSR 270:2).

Bullock, W.A.: PVT, Co. B. Reported absent sick, May–Aug./64. Reported at G.H. #9 in Richmond, 6/17/64. Employed by ward master and detailed in ward, 8/64, and listed at Kittrell Springs, N.C. G.H. #1, 2/15/65, with chronic rheumatism, enlargement of the knee joint. Absent sick, Sept.–Dec./64 (CSR 270:2).

Bundy, _____: Captured at Gettysburg and trn to provost marshal. Complained of being sick; left in hospital there (CSR 270:2).

Bundy, John C.: Enl. 4/27/64 as a PVT in Co. F. Reported present, 4/64–12/64. Living in Montana as of 1893. A great soldier, wrote Fred C. Foard. (CSR 270:2; Barringer; Cabarrus; Fred C. Foard to W.G. Means, March 6, 1917, Fred C. Foard Papers, PC 500, NCSA.)

Burch, Jesse W.: B. Yadkin County, N.C., a farmer. Enl. 10/14/63 as a PVT in Co. D.; trn. from McRae's Battalion. Present Aug.–Dec./64. Age 41, eyes grey, hair black, complexion fair. Stood 6' tall (CSR 270:2).

Burgess, Hugh L.: B. 6/5/31. Enl. in Co. A 5/31/61. PVT, blacksmith. Reported present on company muster rolls of 11/61–2/62, Sept.–Oct./62. 11/62–12/62 present and on extra duty as a blacksmith. Jan.–Feb./63, on frl to purchase horse; Mar.–Apr./63, listed present as staff blacksmith. Absent sick 8/4/63–12/63, and at home in Ashe Co. on sick frl; present 1/64–12/64. Prm 4CPL. D. 9/21/98. Bur. Calloway Family Cem., Beaver Creek, Ashe Co. (CSR 270:2; AsheCo; Stepp).

Burgin, W.B.: From McDowell County, N.C., age 29. Enl. 5/20/61 as a PVT in Co. G. Present Jan.–Feb./62; May–June/62. Admitted to G.H. #24, Richmond, with remittent fever, 7/20/62. D. In a hospital near Hanover, 8/1/62 (CSR 270:2).

Burket, George: Enl. 8/1/62. in Co. A, from Ashe County, N.C. 5SGT. Present 9/62, then on detached service in Winchester, Va., beginning 10/1/62. Present 11/62–4/63. Absent on detached service to buy horse, July–Aug./63. Reported present 9/63–12/64 (CSR 270:2; AsheCo).

Burket, Henry H.: A farmer, resident of Ashe County, N.C. Enl. in Co. A, 7/1/63, as PVT. Reported present, July–Dec./63, but also reported at G.H. #24, in Richmond, admitted 10/3/63 with remittent fever, and returned to duty 10/24/63. Absent on detached service at recruiting camp (infirmary camp) beginning 2/11/64. Present 3/64–4/64; July–Aug./64; on detached service at infirmary camp, Sept.–Oct./64. Captured Stoney Creek, Va., 12/1/64; released 5/15/65. Took Oath of Allegiance at Point Lookout, 6/24/65, and released. Had light complexion, gray eyes, stood 5'7¾" (CSR 270:2; AsheCo).

Burkett, Christian: Age 30, from Ashe Co. Enl. 5/20/61 as PVT, Co. A. Reported present on rolls of 11/61–2/62, and listed as staff teamster. Captured 10/62, near Williamsport, Md. Absent 11/62–2/63. Reported present Mar.–Apr./63. On detached service to buy a horse, July–Aug./63, then present Sept.–Dec./63, Jan.–Apr./64. Pre July–Aug./64 and on extra duty at regimental H.Q. Reported present Sept.–Dec./64 as orderly for Col. Cowles. (CSR 270:2; AsheCo)

Burkett, John: From Ashe Co. Enl. 5/25/61 as PVT, Co. A, at age 22. Reported present on rolls of Nov.–Dec./61. Absent Jan.–Feb./62 at a Manassas hospital, and still sick 3/62. D. 6/1/62. (CSR 270:2; AsheCo)

Burkett, John W.: From Ashe Co. Enl. 5/20/61 as 4SGT, Co. A. Reported present on rolls of 11/61–2/62. Captured 10/15/62 in Md., near the mouth of Monocacy Creek, and exd. 10/31/62. Captors listed him as 6' tall, hazel eyes, dark complexion, dark hair, black whiskers, slimly built, 24 years old. Reported present Nov.–Dec./62. Frl at home beginning 2/15/63, then present Mar.–Apr./63. Prm. 2LT 5/1/63. KIA 8/63, Brandy Station. (CSR 270:2; AsheCo)

Burnett, Alfred: Age 42, from Buncombe Co. Enl. 5/20/61 in Co. G., PVT. (CSR 270:2)

Burnett, James: PVT, Co. E. Prl near Warrenton, 11/62. Also listed as captured in Bristoe Campaign. (CSR 270:2)

Burnett, Jesse J.: From Duplin Co. Enl. 6/20/61 as PVT, Co. I. Age 24. Rejected. (CSR 270:2)

Burnett, Joseph: From Franklin Co. At age 18, enl. 3/26/63 as PVT, Co. E. Reported present on rolls of 6/63–10/14/63. Captured near Auburn, 10/14/63, and suspected KIA. (CSR 270:2; Pearce: 233)

Burnett, M.L.: Enl. 5/22/64 as PVT, Co. G. Reported present through 12/64. Also listed on the roll of a Richmond G.H. dated 8/15/64. (CSR 270:2)

Burnett, Robert: At age 35, this resident of Franklin Co. enl. 3/1/63 as PVT, Co. E. Reported present on rolls of Mar.–Apr./63. On detached service after a horse to N.C., 8/27/63. AWOL beginning 10/1/63. Listed as deserted, 12/15/63. On a list of deserters received at Ft. Monroe 3/27/64, having come into the lines at Washington, N.C. Took oath of amnesty same day. Had light complexion, gray eyes, brown hair, and stood 5'6". (CSR 270:2; Pearce 233)

Burnett, Sidney: From Franklin Co. At age 23, enl. 6/27/61 as PVT, Co. C. Reported present on rolls of Jan.–Feb./62, May–June/62. Sent to G.H. #24, Richmond, in 7/62 with diarrhea and typhoid fever. Frl 8/5/62. Present 11/62–4/63, 7/63–2/64, Mar.–Dec./64. (CSR 270:2; Pearce: 233)

Burnett, T.E.: From Mecklenburg Co. At age 23, enl. 5/14/62 as PVT, Co. E. Reported present May–Oct./62. Absent scouting beginning 12/25/62. Reported present on rolls of Jan.–Mar./63. KIA Upperville, Va., 8/21/63. (CSR 270:2)

Burnett, T.H. From Buncombe Co. At age 20, enl. 5/20/61 as PVT, Co. G. Present according to rolls of Jan.–Feb./62, Sept.–Oct./62. Absent on detached service Nov.–Dec./62. Present Jan.–Apr./63. Absent on detached service with unserviceable horses in Nelson Co., Va., July–Dec./63. KIA 6/21/64. (CSR 270:2)

Burnett, Wiley: From Franklin Co. At age 21, enl. 11/14/61 as PVT, Co. E. Reported present Jan.–Feb./62. Absent sick at a Petersburg hospital, 5/20/62. Reported present on rolls of 9/62–10/63. On register of G.H. #9, Richmond, as admitted 10/2/63 and trn to #24, 10/3. Returned to duty 10/14/63. Present 11/63–9/64. Captured at Chapin's Farm, 10/2/64. Exd. 3/17/65. (CSR 270:2; Pearce: 233)

Burnett, William H.: From Franklin Co. At age 18 enl. 7/22/61 as PVT, Co E. Reported present on rolls of Jan.–Feb./62, May–June/62, 9/62–4/63. On extra duty as a teamster, 2/62. KIA 6/9/63 at Brandy Station. (CSR 270:2; Pearce: 233)

Burreece, James M.: From Macon Co. At age 27, enl . 4/28/61 as PVT, Co. K. Blacksmith. Reported present on rolls of May–June/62. Sept.–Oct./62, guarding wagons at Winchester. Absent Nov.–Dec./62 detached to QM. Present Jan.–Feb./63, Mar.–Apr./63, July–Aug./63, 10/31/63. On detached service to N.C., Nov.–Dec./63. Present Jan.–Oct./64, although also admitted to G.H. #9, 6/7/64. Absent on horse detail, Nov.–Dec./64. (CSR 270:2)

Burris, E.B.: Enl. 3/4/64 as PVT, Co. C. Present Mar.–Dec./64. (CSR 270:2)

Burris, J.T.: B. Stanley Co., 12/19/44. Enl. 3/4/64 as PVT, Co. C. Absent sick at Petersburg and/or Williamsburg hospitals, 7/64, and frl. D. 1/18/27. Bur Midland Baptist Cemetery, Cabarrus Co. (CSR 270:2; Alexander; GLP)

Burton, Blaney W.: Enl. 6/20/61 as PVT, Co. I, at age 30. Rejected. From Duplin Co. (CSR 270:2)

Burton, Dixon: Enl. 6/20/61 as PVT, Co. I, at age 46. Rejected. From Duplin Co. (CSR 270:2)

Burton, Owen K.: At age 24, enl. 6/20/61 as PVT, Co. I. Reported present on rolls of 11/61–2/62, May–June/62. Admitted to G.H. #3, Richmond, 5/28/64, and trn to #5 5/29/64. Present Sept.–Oct./62, Nov.–Dec./62. Absent on detached service Jan.–Feb./63. Reported present Mar.–Apr./63, 10/31/63, 1/1/64–8/31/64. Admitted to Richmond G.H. #5, 5/64 and returned to duty 7/64. On detached service to procure a fresh horse, 10/21/64. Reported as sick in a Raleigh hospital, 11/20/64. From Duplin Co. (CSR 270:2)

Busick, J.P.: Cns 3/3/64 as PVT, Co. H. Reported present on rolls of 4/1/64, Mar.–Aug./64. Absent on horse detail, Sept.–Oct./64. Present Nov.–Dec./64. Prl Greensboro, 4/26/65. (CSR 270:2)

Bustin, William H.: From Halifax Co. PVT, 1SGT, Co. B. At age 23, enl. 4/28/62. Reported present on company muster rolls of 9/62–10/62. Absent on detached service, Nov.–Dec./62. Reported present on company muster roll of 1/63–4/63. Absent on detached service after a horse to NC, beginning 8/27/63. Present 6/30/63–12/63, 3/64–12/64. (CSR 270:2)

Butler, J.T.: From Mecklenburg Co. PVT, Co. C. Enl. 6/25/62, at age 25. Reported present on company muster rolls of 5/62–12/62. Absent to procure a horse in NC, beginning 2/21/63. Reported present July–Aug./63. Absent on detached service beginning 10/15/63. Present 3/64–12/64. Prl Charlotte, 5/12/65. (CSR 270:2; Alexander)

Byrd, Samuel: PVT, Co. H. Cns 3/3/64. Deserted, according to 4/1/64 company muster roll. (CSR 270:2)

Caldwell, Samuel P.: Co. C, Co. D. Appointed 2LT, 5/16/61. Prm 1LT, 9/21/61. Resigned 2/28/62. (CSR 270:1, 2)

Calloway, A.F.: From Ashe Co. PVT, saddler, Co. A. Enl. 2/27/62. Reported absent on detached service as a shoemaker, beginning 10/28/62, according to company muster roll of Sept.–Oct./62. Reported present on muster rolls of 11/62–4/63, 7/63–4/64. Reported in a Richmond G.H. with chronic diarrhea, 5/64; still absent as of July–Aug./64 company muster roll. Trn to Co. A, 26th NC Infantry, 7/19/64. Reported in a Richmond G.H., 8/64. (CSR 270:2; AsheCo)

Calloway, J.C.: Enl. 5/27/61 as PVT, Co. C. Reported present on company muster rolls of 11/61–2/62. Listed sick in a Petersburg G.H. on 3/62 regimental return. Also reported in a Orange C.H. G.H., admitted 3/15/62, with dysentery; apparently died soon thereafter. (CSR 270:2; Alexander)

Campbell, C.H.K.: PVT, Co. A. Enl. 5/22/64. Reported present on muster rolls of July–Oct./64. Absent on detached service in NC baling forage, Nov.–Dec./64. (CSR 270:2; AsheCo)

Campbell, Hugh: Enl. 9/29/64 as PVT, Co. H. Reported present on company muster rolls of Sept.–Dec./64. (CSR 270:2)

Campbell, J.A.: PVT, Co. C. Prl Goldsboro, NC, 5/9/65. (CSR 270:2)

Campbell, R.H.: From Mecklenburg Co. At age 24, enl. 6/3/61 as PVT, Co. C. Reported present on company muster rolls of 11/61–2/62, May–Dec./62. Absent on frl beginning 2/14/62. Reported present Mar.–Apr./63, then absent detailed to NC to buy a horse beginning 8/27/63. Present on company muster rolls of 9/63–12/64. Prl 5/17/65, in Charlotte. (CSR 270:2; Alexander)

Canady, W.E.: From Granville Co. Prm 1LT, Co. E, upon resignation of O.H. Foster. (Promotion Notice, Box 46, Folder 15, Military Collection, Civil War Collection, NCSA.)

Cantrell, A.: PVT, Co. K, age 19. From Macon Co. Rejected by COL Baker. (CSR 270:2)

Carden, P.S.: Appointed 11/29/61 as hospital steward. Reported assigned on 5/17/64 to Chimborazo Hospital, then 5/23/64 to Stuart Hospital, Richmond, but according to a register of the Medical Director's Office, relieved 5/26/64 from duty at Chimborazo and directed to report to a hospital at the Old Fair Grounds, Richmond. Appears on a return of the Stuart hospital, Richmond, 6/64 and 8/64, then relieved from duty there 8/26/64 and ordered to report at a Harrisonburg G.H. 9/17/64, relieved and appointed to a G.H. at Mt. Jackson, VA. Reported there on returns of 10/64 and 12/64. On suggestion of 1/7/65 of the Medical Director, relieved from hospital duty in Va and detailed to report to the 1st NC Cavalry, 2/10/65. Prl 5/9/65. (CSR 270:2)

Carleton, John P.: Enl 9/30/63 as PVT, Co. D. Reported sick in the hospital on company muster roll of 8/31/64. Present 9/64–12/64. (CSR 270:2)

Carlton, Mordecai: Enl. 6/25/61 as PVT, Co. I, at age 22. D. 8/61 at home. From Duplin Co. (CSR 270:2)

Carman, William J.: Enl. 5/25/61 as 5SGT, Co. A. Reported present on company muster rolls of Nov.–Dec./61. Also present Jan.–Feb./62, and on daily duty as a courier. According to regimental return of 2/62, on detached service at GEN Milledge L. Bonham's HQ. On detached service transporting baggage, etc. as of 3/23/62, according to 3/62 return. At home sick beginning 5/25/62. Reduced to ranks due to "being unable for duty." Still absent on sick frl at home, Jan.–Aug./63. Reported present on company muster roll of Sept.–Oct./63. Detailed to unspecified duty in Richmond, 12/63, due to disability. On a return of the post at Camp Lee as cns officer, 2/64. Also listed there as a cns clerk according to company muster rolls of Mar.–Dec./64. Retired 2/14/65 to the Invalid Corps. Also reported assigned to light duty, 2/18/65. Psb. from Wilkes Co., but no Carmans are listed in the County Census of 1850 or 1860, nor is there a burial record for him there. (CSR 270:2; McNeil)

Carole, S.S.: PVT, Co. I. Enl. 6/17/61 at age 18. Rejected by COL Baker. From Duplin Co. (CSR 270:2)

Carpenter, E.L.: PVT, Co. I. Enl 12/21/64; trn from 28th Regiment NC Troops. Reported present on company muster rolls through 12/64. (CSR 270:2)

Carr, Alexander M.: From Lenoir Co. At age 28, enl. 8/16/61 as PVT, Co. H. Absent sick beginning 12/61, in a Mt. Jackson hospital, according to muster rolls of 11/61–2/62. Reported present on company muster rolls of May–June/62, Sept.–Dec./62. Absent on detached service, Jan.–Feb./63. Present Mar.–Apr./63, July–Oct./63. Absent on detached service at brigade HQ, 11/63–12/64, as ambulance driver. (CSR 270:2)

Carraway, Henry J.: Resident of Wayne Co. At age 32, enl 6/20/61 as CPL, Co. H. Reported present on company muster rolls of Nov.–Dec./61. Absent sent to NC recruiting beginning 2/10/62. Reported present May–June/62, Sept.–Oct./62. Absent on scout with MAJ Whitaker, according to muster rolls of Nov.–Dec./62. Present Jan.–Apr./63. Absent on detached service to NC after a horse, July–Aug./63. Present 9/63–2/64. Absent detailed to procure a horse, Mar.–Apr./64. WIA and absent, according to rolls of 4/30–8/31/64. Present Sept.–Dec./64. Captured 4/3/65 at Amelia C.H. Released from Point Lookout on taking oath, 6/26/65. Had fair complexion, brown hair, blue eyes, and stood 5'7¼". (CSR 270:2)

Carrington, Thomas R.: Enl. 11/20/64 as PVT, Co. E. Captured at Hicks Ford, 12/12/64. Exd. 2/13/65. (CSR 270:2)

Carroll, Benegar V.: 1LT, Co. I. Enl. 6/17/61. From Duplin Co., age 30, resident of Magnolia. Never commissioned; resigned 9/28/61. Psb enl in 1 NC Bn. Reported in a Wilmington hospital, 8/19/62, with gonorrhea. Also admitted to a Wilmington hospital, 3/6/64, and returned to duty 3/21/64. Reported in a Wilmington hospital, admitted 5/9/64 and returned to duty 6/3/64. (CSR 270:2)

Carroll, J.H.: Enl 5/25/61 as 3CPL, Co. C. Reported present on muster rolls of Nov.–Dec./61. Absent sick in Petersburg, beginning 1/2/62. Also reported sick on regimental return of 2/62. According to regimental return of 3/62, absent sick in Mecklenburg Co. beginning 1/2/62. Plus, appears on a register of a Danville G.H., admitted 1/2/62 with pneumonia, and sent to Richmond. Absent on detached service beginning 6/12/62. Reported present on company muster rolls of 6/30–12/62. Absent on detached service in Gordonsville, beginning 2/31/63. Reported present, July–Oct./63. Captured near Mine Run, VA, 11/29 or 12/3/63, and exd 3/3/64. Present on company muster rolls of Sept.–Dec./64. (CSR 270:2; Alexander)

Carroll, James: Co. D. (CSR 270: 4 for George N. Folk)

Carroll, Joseph: From Macon Co. At age 23, enl. 5/6/62 as PVT, Co. K. Absent sick in camp according to muster roll of May–June/62. Admitted to a Richmond G.H., 7/8/62, and returned to duty 7/24/62. Present on company muster rolls of 9/62–4/63. Captured 6/9/63 near Beverly's Ford, VA. Absent detailed to NC to buy a horse, July–Aug./63. Reported present on company muster rolls of 11/63–12/64. (CSR 270:2)

Carroll, Smith F.: Resident of Boone. PVT, Bugler, Co. D. Enl. 5/11/61. Reported present on company muster rolls of 11/61–2/62, 5/62–4/63, July–Aug./63. Psb. WIA at Brandy Station, 6/9/63, and captured. WIA, shot in thigh, and admitted to a Richmond hospital, 7/23/63, and returned to duty 8/13/63. WIA by shell explosion and captured near Culpeper CH, 9/13/63. Right leg amputated above the knee in a Washington G.H., 9/23/63. Trn. to prison, 12/7/63; held at Point Lookout. Exd 3/3/64. Admitted 3/6/64 to a Richmond hospital. Applied for an artificial limb. Reported absent and wounded at home according to 8/31/64 company muster roll. Retired 10/19/64, and assigned to Invalid Corps. (CSR 270:2 Davis; Medical History 11: 228)

Carroll, William: Enl. 2/28/62 as PVT, Co. D. Age 38. On a regimental return of 3/62 as on extra duty as a teamster. Reported present on company muster rolls of 5/62–4/63, 11/63–2/64. Psb. deserted, 5/1/63. Subject of a court martial, 3/8/64. Absent under arrest, 2/29/64–10/64, part of that time in a military prison. Released from confinement, 12/1/64. Reported present on company muster rolls of Nov.–Dec./64. (CSR 270:2)

Carson, Andrew M.: PVT, Co. K. From Macon Co., age 30. Rejected by COL Baker. (CSR 270:2)

Carson, J.F.: Cns 3/4/64 as PVT, Co. E. Reported present on company muster rolls of Mar.–Aug./31/64. Absent at home on horse detail, Sept.–Oct./64. Present Nov.–Dec./64. (CSR 270:2)

Carson, Jesse S.: At age 25, enl. 7/20/61 as PVT, Co. K. Reported present on company muster rolls of 11/61–2/62, May–June/62, Sept.–Dec./62. Absent at home to buy a horse, Jan.–Feb./63. Reported present, Mar.–Apr./63, July–Aug./63, 10/31–12/63, Jan.–Mar./31/64. Prm 2SGT. WIA at Blacks and Whites, 6/25/64. On a register of a Danville G.H., 7/27/64, WIA by gunshot in right hand. Frl 7/29/64. From Macon Co. (CSR 270:2)

Carson, John H.: PVT, Co. K. Enl. 6/25/61. Age 28. Reported present on company muster rolls of Nov.–Dec./61. Absent sent to Manassas sick, 2/24/62. Also listed as absent sick on regimental returns of 2/ and 3/62. D. Lynchburg, VA, 3/ or 4/62, of disease. From Macon Co. (CSR 270:2)

Carver, John: Resident of Hendersonville, NC. Enl. 5/20/61 as PVT, Co. G, at age 23. Admitted to a Richmond G.H., 11/3/61, and returned to duty 11/25/61. Reported present on company muster rolls of Jan.–Feb./62, May–June/62, 9/62–4/63, July–Aug./63. WIA at Auburn Mills, 10/14/63. Gunshot wound in toe; toe amputated. May have absorbed as many as 7 wonds there. Absent Nov.–Dec./63 on wounded frl. Reported absent on detached service, 4/1/64. Killed while under arrest and attempting to escape, according to muster roll of Mar.–Apr./64. Bur Mills Point Church, 6 miles west of Hendersonville. (CSR 270:2; CGR: 1; NC Regts. 1: 427)

Carver, Thomas: Enl. 8/1/61 as PVT, Co K. Age 22. Reported present on company muster rolls of 11/61–2/62. Prm blacksmith, 1/1/62. Present May–June/62. Absent on wagon guard at Winchester, Sept.–Oct./62. Present Nov.–Dec./62, then absent to buy a horse at home, Jan.–Feb./63. Reported AWOL beginning on muster rolls of Mar.–Apr./63. From Cherokee Co. (CSR 270:2)

Carvey, J.H.: PVT, Co. E. WIA 8/15 or 8/16/64 along Charles City Rd., near Richmond. (Richmond *Sentinel*, 8/26/64)

Case, _____: Co. D. (Davis)

Case, J.S.: Enl 5/20/61 as SGT, Co. G. Age 21. Reported present on company muster rolls of Jan.–Feb./62, May–June/62, Sept.–Oct./62. Also reported absent on detached service according to 2/62 regimental return. Absent on detached service, Nov.–Dec./62. Present Jan.–Apr./63. Captured at Brandy Station, 8/1/63, and sent to Point Lookout. Exd 3/3/64. Present on company muster rolls of 3/64–12/64, although admitted to and released from a Richmond G.H., 12/64. From Buncombe Co. (CSR 270:2)

Case, Jesse: At age 41, enl. 5/20/61 as CPL, Co. G. Reported present on company muster rolls of Jan.–Feb./62, May–June/62, Sept.–Oct./62. Reduced to PVT, 10/6/62. Absent on detached service, Nov.–Dec./62. Reported present on company muster rolls of Jan.–Apr./63. Absent on detached service as a teamster with the Brigade commissary train, July–Aug./63. Detached with unserviceable horses in Nelson Co, Va., Sept.–Oct./63. Absent with CPT White's dead line, Nov.–Dec./63. Still on detached service, 4/1/64. Reported present, Mar.–Dec./64. Resident of Madison Co. Captured at Amelia C.H., 4/3/65. Released 6/26/65 from Point Lookout on taking oath. Had fair complexion, dark brown hair, blue eyes, and stood 5' 8¾". Still alive in 1889. (CSR 270:2; (*The [Asheville] Daily Citizen*, 7/5/89, copy in Civil War Clippings File, Pack Memorial Library, Asheville, NC.)

Case, Levi H.: Enl. 5/20/61 as PVT, Co. G. Age 18, from Buncombe Co. (CSR 270:2)

Casey, William D.: From Wayne Co. At age 26, enl. 6/20/61 as PVT, Co. H. Absent sick, first at a Petersburg hospital and then at home according to company muster rolls of 11/61–2/62. Present May–June/62, 9/62–4/63, 7/63–8/31/64. On detached service with the provost guard at Brigade HQ, Sept.–Dec./64. Prl 4/20/65. (CSR 270:2)

Cathey, John Archibald: B. 11/15/47. Enl. 11/10/64 as PVT, Co. C. Reported present on company muster rolls of Nov.–Dec./64. D. December 1906. Bur. McKendree Methodist Church Cem., Iredell Co. (CSR 270:2; Alexander; Stepp)

Cawthon, John C.: PVT, Co. E. Enl. 6/4/61, at age 27. Reported present on company muster rolls of Jan.–Feb./62. On a register of a Richmond G.H., admitted 3/9/62 with mumps, and trn to Petersburg 3/24/62. Present May–June/62, 9/62–4/63. Absent on detached service in Nelson Co with disabled horses, beginning 8/63. Reported present on company muster rolls of 11/63–2/64. Absent on detached service in Amherst Co., with disabled horses, 4/1/64. Also reported detailed to NC to buy a horse, Mar.–Apr./64. Present 4/30/64–12/64. On a register of a Petersburg G.H., admitted 8/15/64. From Granville Co. (CSR 270:2; Pearce: 234, calls him Cawthorne.)

Chapman, J.M.: Enl. 5/20/61 as PVT, Co. G. Age 21. Reported present on company muster rolls of Jan.–Feb./62, May–June/62, Sept.–Oct./62. Also reported sick at Richmond on 3/62 regimental return. Captured 11/6/62, and prl. Absent sick in a Richmond hospital, Nov.–Dec./62, and returned to duty, 2/5/63. Reported present, Jan.–Apr./63. Absent on detached service to buy a horse, July–Aug./63. Present Sept.–Oct./63. Trn to Co. B, 1st SC Cavalry, 12/5/63. From Henderson Co. (CSR 270:2)

Charlotte, Cicero: Enl. 8/63 as PVT, Co. H, at age 22. Reported present on company muster roll of July–Aug./63. Captured 9/13/63, at Culpeper CH, and sent to Point Lookout. Hospitalized at Point Lookout for chronic diarrhea, 2/64. Exd 2/13/65. Captured and prl at Raleigh, 5/24/65. (CSR 270:2)

Cheatham, D. Thomas: B. 2/2/38. Enl 10/31/64 as PVT, Co. E. Reported present on company muster rolls of Nov.–Dec./64. D. 12/9/15. Bur. Elmwood Cem., Oxford, NC. (CSR 270:2; Stepp)

Cheatham, James F.: PVT, Co. E. Enl. 10/26/64 as PVT, Co. E. Reported present on company muster rolls of Nov.–Dec./64. Captured 4/3/65 near Petersburg, and released on taking oath 6/26/65. Had light complexion, brown hair, dark gray eyes, and stood 5' 8½". Resident of Granville Co. (CSR 270:2)

Cheek, E.A., Jr.: Enl 10/5/64 as PVT, Co. E. Reported present on company muster rolls of 4/30–12/64. (CSR 270:2)

Cheek, W.H.: Resident of Warrenton, NC. B. 3/18/35. Pre-war profession: lawyer. At age 26, became CPT, Co. E, to rank from 5/16/61. Reported present on company muster rolls of Jan.–Feb./62, May–June/62, Sept.–Oct./62. Absent on detached service, Nov.–Dec./62, Jan.–Feb./63. Also reported present on regimental return of 2/62, then absent on recruiting duty beginning 3/5/62, according to 3/62 return. Present on company muster rolls of Mar.–Apr./63. Absent sick in a Richmond hospital, 8/4/63, then frl 8/25/63 for 15 days. Present according to 6/30–10/31/63 muster rolls. Prm LTC, 9/28/63. Prm COL, 10/17/63. Present Nov.–Dec./63. Absent on special duty, Jan.–Feb./64. Present 4/1/64, Mar.–Apr./64. On a register of a Richmond G.H., admitted 5/13/64 with a gunshot wound in the left arm. WIA 5/11/64 with gunshot wound in the flesh of the shoulder. Frl 5/26/64. Also reported absent on detached service commanding the Brigade, 4/30–8/31/64. Present on field and staff muster rolls of Sept.–Dec./64. Admitted to a Charlottesville G.H. with Syphilis 6/9/63 and returned to duty 7/30/63. Admitted 8/8/63 and 9/12/63 to a Richmond G.H. with syphilis consecutive, and returned to duty 8/29/63 and 9/16/63. Detailed for court, 11/12/63. Captured 4/5/65, near Burkesville, VA. Sent to Johnson's Island. Released on oath and prl, 7/25/65. Had dark complexion, dark hair, black eyes, and stood 5'8". and age listed on oath as 35. Mentioned in special orders regarding leave on 8/27/63, 7/28/64, and 6/2/64. Died three days after finishing piece for Walter Clark on 1st cav. D. Henderson, NC, 3/23/01. Bur. Elmwood Cem., Henderson. (CSR 270:1,2; Stepp to author, 8/8/97, 4/9/98)

Chesson, Hezekiah: At age 18, enl. 8/2/61 as PVT, Co. B. Reported present on company muster rolls of Nov.–Dec./61. Captured 2/22/62 while on outpost duty, according to regimental return of 2/62. On detached service according to company muster roll of Nov.–Dec./62. Reported present Jan.–Apr./63, 6/30/63–12/63, 4/1/64, 3/64–10/64. From Washington Co. (CSR 270:2)

Chesson, Richard B.: At age 33, enl. 8/2/61 as PVT, Co. B. Reported present on company muster rolls of 11/61–4/62, Sept.–Oct./62. On detached service Nov.–Dec./62, then present Jan.–Apr./63. Absent on detached service with disabled horses beginning 8/3/63. Present 6/30–10/31/63, then absent with disabled horses in Nelson Co., VA, Nov.–Dec./63. Reported absent on detached service, Jan.–Feb./64, then absent at the infirmary camp, 4/1/64. Reported present on company muster rolls of Mar.–Dec./64. From Washington Co. (CSR 270:2)

Childress, William: Cns 7/11/64 as PVT, Co. H. Reported present on company muster rolls of 4/30/64–8/31/64. AWOL beginning 9/29/64. (CSR 270:2)

Christenbury, Daniel Robinson: From Mecklenburg Co. Enl. 5/26/61 as PVT, Co. C. Rejected by COL Baker, 8/1/61, at Camp Woodfin. (CSR 270:2)

Christophers, George W.: B. Pitt Co., NC. At age 25, cns 8/1/62 as PVT, Co. I. Reported present on company muster rolls of Sept.–Oct./62. Admitted 11/17/62 to a Richmond G.H. D. 11/25/62 at a Richmond G.H. from disease. From Orange Co., where he was a farmer in feeble health. (CSR 270:2)

Clayton, J.E.: Enl. 11/1/64 as PVT, Co. G. Reported present through December 1864. Appears on a POW roll as captured at Aberdeen C.H., 4/3/65, and released 6/24/65 from Point Lookout. Resident of Forsyth Co., had dark complexion, gray hair, hazel eyes, and stood 5'11". (CSR 270:3)

Clifton, David: From Washington Co., age 21. Enl. 8/2/61 as PVT, Co. B. Reported present on rolls of 11/61–2/62. Listed as deserted, April or May 1862. Also appears on a court martial record, Dept. Of NC, 4/30/62. (CSR 270:3)

Clifton, John T.: From Franklin Co. Served in Co. E. NFR. (Pearce: 236)

Cline, David: Enl. 9/21/64 as PVT, Co. H. Reported present on rolls of Sept.–Dec./64. (CSR 270:3)

Cline, F.M.: Enl. 12/3/64 as PVT, Co. F. Reported present through 12/64. (CSR 270:3)

Cline, Henry: Cns. 9/21/64 as PVT, Co. H. Reported present Sept.–Dec./64. (CSR 270:3)

Cobble, J.D.: B. Rowan Co. Pre–war occupation: carpenter. At age 20, enl. 7/3/61 as PVT, Co. C. Reported present on rolls of Nov.–Dec./61. Absent on frl beginning 2/24/62. Also reported absent sick beginning 5/29/62. Reported absent sick at Winchester beginning 10/15/62. Dsh 12/25/62 from disability. Stood 5'11". had fair complexion, gray eyes. (CSR 270:3; Alexander; Rumple: 342)

Cochan: Caldwell County, N.C. Co. D (Davis)

Cochran, John T.: B. Catawba Co. Pre–war occupation: farmer. Enl. 3/1/64 as PVT, Co. D. Reported present on muster rolls of 8/31/64, Sept.–Dec./64. Age 18, had gray eyes, red hair, a fair complexion, and stood 5'6". (CSR 270:3)

Cochran, Lewis W.: Psb. from Caldwell Co. Enl. 10/1/63 as PVT, Co. D. Reported present on company muster rolls of 8/31/64, Sept.–Dec./64. (CSR 270:3; Davis)

Codie, J.M.: From Jerusalem, in Davie Co. Enl. 10/64 as PVT, Co. B. Reported present on muster rolls of Sept.–Oct./64, then absent at home on horse detail, Nov.–Dec./64. Appears on a register of G.H. #13, Raleigh, 12/4/64. Prl at Salisbury, 5/16/65. (CSR 270:3)

Codie, J.W.: Enl. 9/21/64 as PVT, Co. B. Reported present on muster rolls of Sept.–Dec./64. Listed on a POW Roll as prl at Statesville, 5/26/65. (CSR 270:3)

Coffey, Charles L.: B. 9/18/30. From Caldwell Co. Enl. 2/14/64 as PVT, Co. D. Reported present on muster rolls of Mar.–Apr./64. Went home to buy a horse according to 8/31/64 muster roll. Present Sept.–Dec./64. D. 12/23/16. Bur. Tabernacle

Advent Christian Church Cem., Caldwell Co. (CSR 270:3; Davis; Stepp)

Coffey, Patterson V.: From Caldwell Co. At age 18, enl. 9/20/63 as PVT, Co. D. Reported present on rolls of 6/30/63–4/64, although also reported in a Charlottesville G.H., 12/2–12/15/63. Listed absent sick in a hospital on roll of 8/31/64, and still sick through 10/64. Absent at home on 60-day sick frl, Nov.–Dec./64, beginning 11/5. (CSR 270:3; Davis)

Coleman, Henry S.: Resident of Asheville. Enl. 8/12/61 at age 19. Reported present on muster rolls of May–June/62, 1/63–4/63. Elected and prm 2LT, 5/9/62. On detached service, July–Aug./63, commanding a regimental horse buying detachment. Prm 1LT, 10/5/63. Reported present 9/63–12/63, Mar.–Aug./64. Prm CAPT, 1/7/64. Commanded Co. G. Absent sick in a Goldsboro hospital, Sept.–Oct./64. Reported present on roll of Nov.–Dec./64. Reported AWOL on an inspection report of 2/28/65. Reported absent on an inspection reports of 11/64 and 11/25/64. (CSR 270:1, 3)

Coley, Freeman: From Greene Co. At age 50, enl. 6/61 in Co. H as PVT. Farrier. Reported present on rolls of 11/61–12/61. Absent sent with horses to Warrenton, 2/20/62. Also reported absent sick on regimental return of 2/62. Captured at Willis Church, 6/29/62. Exd 8/5/62. Absent on detached service at Winchester, Sept.–Oct./62. Reported present on muster rolls of Nov.–Dec./62. Absent on detached service, Jan.–Feb./63, then present Mar.–Apr./63, July–Aug./63. Absent on detached service, 9/63–4/64. Dsh at expiration of service, 7/18/64. Stood 5'10½". had black hair, chestnut eyes, fair complexion. (CSR 270:3; *Asheville News*, July 24, 1862)

Coley, Gabriel H.: From Wayne Co. Enl. 6/29/61 at age 24. PVT. (CSR 270:3)

Collins, J.F.: Resident of Beaver Dam, Union Co. Cns. as PVT, Co. I. Reported present on company muster rolls of Mar.–Apr./64, Sept.–Dec./64. Reported in a Raleigh hospital, 1/65. Captured 4/13/65 and took oath 4/22/65. (CSR 270:3)

Coltrane, A.W.: From Randolph Co., age 25; also listed as resident of Greensboro. Enl. 6/3/61 as PVT, Co. C. Farrier. Reported present on rolls of Nov.–Dec./61, Jan.–Feb./62, and May–June/62. Psb. detailed as a nurse for a Richmond hospital, 2/62. Absent sick in a Richmond hospital beginning 10/1/62, psb. suffering from gonorrhea. Reported present Mar.–Apr./63, July–Aug./63. WIA shot in thigh, Jack's Shop, 9/22/63, and sent to a Richmond hospital. Frl for 40 days beginning 10/10/63. Present 11/63–4/63. Absent on detached service beginning 8/13/64. Listed on a record dated 3/8/65, concerning a detail. (CSR 270:3)

Colvard, James W.: B. 1835, Wilkes Co. Son of Wade Hampton and Phoebe Colvard. At age 27, enl. 4/9/63 as PVT, Co. A. Reported present on muster rolls of Mar.–Apr./63. Absent sick July–Aug./63, according to records of a Charlottesville G.H., admitted 8/22 and returned to duty 9/22/63. Present 9/63–4/64. Appears on a register of a Richmond G.H., dated 6/1/64 and 6/2/64, disposition Petersburg. Frl 6/3/64, and reported absent at home sick, July–Aug./64. Reported present on muster rolls of Sept.–Dec./64. KIA 3/31/65 near Dinwiddie C.H., and bur. nearby. (CSR 270:3; McNeil; AsheCo 1: 196–198)

Colvard, Jesse A.: B. 1837, Wilkes Co. Son of Wade Hampton and Phoebe Colvard. At age 23, enl. 2/20/62 as PVT, Co. A. Listed as absent sick in the hospital on a 3/62 regimental return. Reported present on rolls of 9/62–4/63. Captured at Gettysburg, 7/3 or 7/4/63. D. Point Lookout, 9/11/64 or 9/12/64; bur. there. (CSR 270:3; AsheCo; PL: 132; McNeil; AsheCo 1: 196–198)

Colvard, Jesse B.: From Wilkes Co., age 32. Son of Peyton and Jane Colvard. Enl. 5/28/61 in Co. A. 1CPL. Reported present on company muster rolls of Jan.–Feb./62, Sept.–Oct./62. Reduced to ranks, 9/17/62. On a report of 5/25/65 with a severe minie ball wound in the right thigh, at a Petersburg, G.H. Reported present Nov.–Dec./63. Absent Jan.–Feb./63 on frl to purchase a horse. Present Mar.–Apr./63. Absent July–Aug./63 on detached service with unserviceable horses. Reported present Sept.–Oct./63. Listed as AWOL, 11/30–12/31/63, then as present on muster rolls of 1/1/64–4/64. Absent July–Aug./64 on detached service to NC to buy a horse. Reported present on rolls of Sept.–Dec./64. WIA at Dinwiddie C.H., 3/31/65, with gunshot wound in right thigh. Captured 4/3/65 in a Petersburg hospital, and trn to another G.H., 4/30/65. On a POW roll as being confined 5/25/65 and released 5/31/65 after taking the oath. (CSR 270:3; AsheCo)

Colvard, Peyton Monroe: B. 7/6/44. From Wilkes Co. Son of Wade Hampton and Phoebe Colvard. At age 18, enl. 4/9/63 as PVT, Co. A. Reported present on rolls of Mar.–Apr./63, then absent July–Aug./63. Appears on Richmond hospital registers as admitted 9/3/63 and returned to duty 9/23/63. Reported present on rolls of 9/63–2/29/64, save a frl beginning 2/16/64. Present Mar.–Apr./64. Admitted 5/28/64 to a Richmond hospital. Present on rolls of July–Dec./64. D. 9/10/93 in Clay Co., NE. (CSR 270:3; AsheCo; McNeil)

Colvard, Rufus Winfield: B. 8/8/32. Resident of Wilkes Co. Son of Wade Hampton and Phoebe Colvard. Enl. 7/24/61 at age 28 as PVT, Co. A. Company clerk. Reported present on rolls of 11/61–2/62, Sept.–Dec./62. Absent on frl to buy a horse, Jan.–Feb./63. Present Mar.–Apr./63, 7/63–2/29/64. Absent on detached service in N.C. beginning 4/2/64. Reported present on rolls of July–Dec./64. Stood 5'10¾". Had light complexion, dark brown hair, and gray eyes. Took oath 6/24/65, after being captured at Aberdeen Church 4/13/65 and sent to Point Lookout. Post-war, served as Wilkes Co. Commissioner. D. 7/15/91. Bur. in abandoned family graveyard, along White Oak Church Rd., Wilkes Co. (CSR 270:3; McNeil; AsheCo 1: 196–198)

Colvard, Thomas Farrow: From Wilkes Co. Son of Peyton and Jane Colvard. At age 25, enl. 5/23/61 as PVT, Co. A. Reported present on rolls of 11/61–2/62, Sept.–Oct./62. Listed as absent sick at the hospital on regimental return of 3/62. WIA Barbee's Crossroads, 11/5/62, and captured. Prl 11/6/62. Appears on a register of the Richmond Medical Director's Office as admitted 11/17/62 to a Richmond hospital, and trn to Danville 12/26/62. Reported present on company muster rolls of Mar.–Apr./63. Captured at Upperville, 6/21/63, and prl 6/25/63. Absent on detached service, July–Aug./63, to buy a horse. WIA 11/29/63, and admitted 12/1 to a Richmond G.H. Listed as absent on detached service at brigade headquarters, Mar.–Apr./64. Absent on detached service to buy a horse July–Aug./64, then listed as AWOL after 8/30/64. Absent sick beginning 10/27/64, and reported in a Petersburg G.H. with a gunshot wound in the flesh of the right foot, 10/28/64. Trn to a Raleigh hospital, 11/18/64. Reported present on rolls of Nov.–Dec./64. (CSR 270:3; AsheCo; McNeil; Whit Joyner to author, 13 Sept. 1994)

Colvard, Wiley Thomas: B. 12/23/38. From Wilkes Co. Son of Wade Hampton and Phoebe Colvard. At age 23, enl. 3/1/62 as PVT, Co. A. Reported present on company muster rolls of 9/62–4/63, July–Aug./63. Absent on detached service with unserviceable horses, 10/1/63 through 4/1/64. Also listed on detached service in N.C., Mar.–Apr./64. Reported present, July–Dec./64. Married Fannie Severt; psb. lived in Ashe Co. after the war. D. 7/12/08. Bur. Obids Baptist Church Cem., Obids, Ashe Co. (CSR 270:3; McNeil; Stepp)

Colvard, William H.H.: B. 9/2/41. Son of Wade Hampton and Phoebe Colvard, from Wilkes Co. Resident of Pitt Co. Also known as "Buck." At age 23, enl. 2/24/62 as PVT, Co. A. Reported present on muster rolls of 9/62–4/63. Absent on detached service to buy a horse, July–Aug./63. Reported on roll of honor as WIA at Gettysburg, 7/3/63. Present on muster rolls of 11/30/63–4/64, 7/64–12/64. (CSR 270:3; McNeil; AsheCo 1: 196–198)

Conner, C.: Resident of Cleveland Co. Enl. 10/20/64 as PVT, Co. K. Reported present on company muster rolls of Nov.–Dec./64. Appears on a register of a Raleigh hospital as admitted 2/4/65. (CSR 270:3)

Conner, Elijah W.: Age 35, from Northampton Co. Enl. 6/13/61 as PVT, Co. B. Reported present 11/61–4/62, Sept.–Dec./62. Listed on regimental return as on extra duty as a teamster, 2/62. Absent on frl beginning 2/14/63, then present Mar.–Apr./63. Absent on detached service 7/29/63. Reported present on rolls of 6/30/63–10/31/63. Absent at camp of disabled horses in Nelson Co., Va., Nov.–Dec./63. Absent on detached service, psb. at infirmary camp, Jan.–Apr./64. Reported present 4/30–10/64, and on extra duty at the Infirmary Camp from 7/22/64–8/64 as a mechanic. (CSR 270:3)

Connor, S.A.: From Lincoln Co., age 30. Enl. 8/22/61 as PVT, Co. C. Reported present on rolls of Nov.–Dec./61. D. 1/27/62 in camp from pneumonia. (CSR 270:3; Alexander calls him T.A. Conner)

Conrad, J.T.: Enl. 10/26/64 in Co. G. Reported present on muster rolls of Nov.–Dec./64. Appointed 1SGT, 1/26/65. Prl Salisbury, 1865. (CSR 270:3)

Constant, John J.: PVT, Co. K, from Macon Co. Age 24. Rejected by Col. Baker. (CSR 270:3)

Conyers, John R.: From Franklin Co. Enl. 11/9/63 as PVT, Co. B. Later prm CPL. Reported present 4/30–10/64. Listed as admitted to a Petersburg G.H., 8/17/64, and frl 8/27/64. Absent at home on horse detail according to company muster roll of Nov.–Dec./64. (CSR 270:3; Pearce: 237)

Cook, E.L.: Co. E. From Franklin Co. NFR. (Pearce: 238) May be the same man as Eugene J. Cook.

Cook, Eugene J.: B. Franklin Co. Student before the war. Enl. 1/27/64 as PVT, Co. E. Reported present on rolls of 1/64–4/64. On a register of a Richmond hospital, admitted 5/26/64, and trn to Farmville. On register of Farmville G.H., admitted 6/2 or 6/3/64 and returned to duty

6/20/64, with gunshot wound in the right finger. Also listed as absent at Kittrell Springs Hospital, 4/30–Oct./64. Dsh for disability at age 18 due to a heart problem. Had fair complexion, dark eyes, black hair. (CSR 270:3; Pearce: 238) Pearce calls him Cooke. May be the same man as E.L. Cook.

Cook, James M.: Age 40, from Franklin Co. Enl. 8/12/61 as PVT, Co. E. Sent to a Manassas hospital, 2/26/62. D. 3/62 from disease in a Richmond hospital. (CSR 270:3; Pearce: 28, 238)

Cook, Joseph P.: From Cabarrus Co. Enl. 6/15/61 at age 22 as PVT, Co. F. D. Centreville, 12/28/61. (CSR 270:3; Mizelle; Barringer; Cabarrus)

Cook, Richard P.: From Franklin Co. At age 20, enl. 9/28/63 as PVT, Co. E. Reported present on rolls through 10/31/63; also 11/63–2/1/64, 4/1/64. Reported absent on detached service in NC to buy a horse, on rolls of Mar.–Apr./64. Reported present on company muster rolls of 4/30–12/64. (CSR 270:3; Pearce: 238)

Cooke, L.R.: Enl. 7/9/62 as PVT, Co. B. Reported present on rolls of 9/62–12/62. Reported absent, detached to get a horse, 2/21/63. Also absent in N.C. after a horse, 8/27/63. Listed as AWOL on rolls of 6/30–12/63. (CSR 270:3)

Cooley, H.R.: Enl. 10/5/64. Reported present on rolls of 4/30/64–10/64. Absent in N.C. on horse detail, Nov.–Dec./64. (CSR 270:3)

Cooley, Lewis: From Warren Co. Enl. 7/22/61 at age 32 as PVT, Co. E. Reported present on rolls of Jan.–Feb./62, May–June/62. Sent to division hospital 8/20/62. Appears on a register a Richmond hospital as being admitted 9/1/62 and frl 9/30/62 for 30 days. Reported present on muster rolls of 9/62–4/63. On detached service to N.C. after a horse, 8/27/63. Listed as AWOL, 10/63. Present 11/63–2/64, 4/1/64, under arrest. Trn to C.S. Navy, 5/21/64. (CSR 270:3)

Cope, Robert W.: From Cabarrus Co. Enl. 6/15/61 as PVT, Co. F. Reported present on muster rolls of 11/61–2/62. Absent sick as of 6/3/62. Present according to rolls of 9/62–12/62. Absent on sick frl after being WIA at Gettysburg, 7/3/63. On a register of Richmond hospitals, 7/20/63 and 7/21/63. Trn to Raleigh, 7/25/63. Reported present on muster rolls of 9/63–12/64. Resident of Cabarrus Co., circa 1893. (CSR 270:3; Mizelle; Barringer; Cabarrus)

Corbin, E.L.: Age 17, from Macon Co. PVT, Co. K. On a regimental return of 3/62 as a recruit from depot. D. 5/5/62 of disease. (CSR 270:3)

Corbin, Leander: Resident of Macon Co. Enl. 7/27/61 as PVT, Co. K. Reported present on rolls of 11/61–2/62, May–June/62, Sept.–Oct./62. Absent detailed to Macon Co. 11/62–2/63. Present on rolls of Mar.–Apr./64. Captured 7/3/63 at Gettysburg. Stood 5'10". had a sallow complexion, light hair, and dark eyes. Released from Ft. Delaware 6/19/65 after taking oath. (CSR 270:3)

Corn, A.P.: From Henderson Co. At age 26, enl. 5/20/61 as PVT, Co. G. Reported present on rolls of Jan.–Feb./62, May–June/62, 9/62–4/63. On extra duty as a teamster according to regimental return of 3/62. Absent on detached service to buy a horse, July–Aug./63, according to company muster rolls, although also reported prl after being captured at Brandy Station, 6/9/63. Absent sick in a Culpeper hospital, 10/24/63. Reported present on rolls of Nov.–Dec./63, 3/63–12/63. (CSR 270:3)

Corn, F.M.: From Buncombe Co. At age 27, enl. 5/20/61 in Co. G. SGT. Reported present on muster rolls of Jan.–Feb./62, May–June/62, 9/62–4/63, 7/63–10/63. Absent on sick frl, 11/63–12/63, 4/1/64. Listed as AWOL and deserted on muster rolls after Mar.–Apr./64. (CSR 270:3)

Cornel, B.F.: Co. D. (Davis)

Cornett, Francis M.: B. Haywood Co. Farmer. At age 22, enl. in Macon Co. 7/29/61 as PVT, Co. K. Had blue eyes, black hair, a dark complexion, and stood 5'11". Admitted to a Richmond hospital 11/3/61 and returned to duty 11/7/61. Reported present on muster rolls of Nov.–Dec./61. D. of disease, 1/29/ or 1/31/62. (CSR 270:3; Francis M. Cornett Paper, PC 424, NCSA, Raleigh, NC.)

Correll, Benjamin F.: Enl. 5/11/62 from Watauga Co. as PVT, Co. D. Age 21. D. 11/61 of disease in Richmond. (CSR 270:3; Davis)

Correll, William: Co. D. (Davis)

Cottraim, A.W.: PVT, Co. C. (Alexander)

Cottrell, James E.: Enl. 6/6/64 as PVT, Co. D. Reported present on company muster rolls of Sept.–Dec./64. (CSR 270:3)

Council, John M.: From Martin Co. At age 22, enl. 6/12/61 as PVT, Co. B. Reported present on rolls of 11/61–4/62, 9/62–12/62. On a 2/62 regimental return as on extra duty as a teamster. Absent sick in a Petersburg hospital according to a 3/62 regimental return. Absent detached to buy a horse as of 2/21/63. Reported present on rolls of Mar.–Apr./63. Absent on detached service in N.C. to buy a horse as of 8/27/63. Listed as AWOL on rolls of 6/30–10/31/63. Reported present Nov.–Dec./63. Absent on detached service, Jan.–Feb./64, and on detached service at Bowling Green, 4/1/64. Listed as absent on horse detail, Mar.–Apr./64. Reported present on rolls of 4/30–12/64. (CSR 270:3)

Councill, James: From Watauga Co. Enl. in Co. D, 5/16/61. Appointed 2LT to rank from 5/16/61. Listed as absent attending N.C. state convention on roll of Jan.–Feb./62. Listed as present on a regimental return of 3/62. Resigned 5/62. (CSR 270:1, 3)

Councill, Joseph: From Watauga Co. At age 27, enl. as PVT, Co. D, 5/11/61. Reported present on rolls of 11/61–2/62, May–June/62. With extra baggage at Winchester, 6/30–10/31/62. Present Nov.–Dec./62. Absent to buy a horse, Jan.–Feb./63, then present Mar.–Apr./63. Absent at home to buy a horse, July–Aug./63. AWOL beginning 9/27/63; trn as LT to 7th Bn. NC Cavalry, which later became the 6th NC Cavalry. Prl Selma, AL 6/8/65 (CSR 270:3; Davis; 6th NC: 146)

Cowan, William Locke: Resident of Rowan Co. Enl. 6/15/61 as PVT, Co. F. Age 20. D. 12/30/61 at Centreville, from pneumonia. (CSR 270:3; Mizelle; Barringer; Rumple: 342)

Cowart, T.: Trn from state service. Enl. 9/21/64 as PVT, Co. G. Reported present Sept.–Oct./64. Absent detached on horse detail Nov.–Dec./64. (CSR 270:3)

Cowen, John: B. 12/16/19. Farmer. Enl. 10/10/63 as PVT, Co. D; trn from McRae's Bn. Reported present on rolls of 8/31/64–12/64. Had blue eyes, light hair, fair complexion, stood 5'10". D. 12/10/65. Bur. Drusilla Presbyterian Church Cem., McDowell Co. (CSR 270:3; Stepp)

Cowles, William Henry Harrison: B. Hamptonville, Yadkin Co., 4/22/40. Son of Josiah and Nancy Carson Duvall Cowles. At age 21, enl. in Co. A, 5/16/61. Elected 1LT to rank from 5/16/61. Reported present on muster rolls of 11/61–2/62, Sept.–Oct./62, and on regimental returns of 2/62 and 3/62. Prm CPT, 3/1/62. On detached service, Nov.–Dec./62. Present on muster rols of 1/63–4/63. Absent sick according to muster rolls of July–Aug./63. Adm. to a Charlottesville G.H., 7/31/63, and returned to duty 9/12/63. Detailed for court, 9/4/63. Present according to muster rolls of Sept.–Oct./63. WIA by gunshot in abdomen wall at Mine Run, 11/63, and adm. to Richmond's G.H. #4. Remained absent at hospital according to muster rolls of Nov.–Dec./64. Frl beginning 12/31/63 for 60 days; extended 3/4/64. Prm MAJ to rank from 10/17/63. Reported present on muster rolls of 3/64–10/64. Appointed and confirmed LTC 1/19/65, to rank from 6/1/64; accepted 2/27/65. WIA 3/31/65, Chamberlain's Run, with a minie ball to the head. John Allen Smith saved his life in battle. Captured 4/3/65 in the hospital and trn 4/22/65 to Federal hospitals. After the war, worked as a lawyer, Congressman, and in other government capacities. Had 11 children. D. 12/30/01; bur. Wilkesboro Cem., Wilkes Co. (CSR 270:1, 3; CSC: 4; CV 10: 125)

Cox, Gambril: From Burke Co. Enl. at age 24 as PVT, Co. K, 6/25/61. Reported present on company muster rolls of 11/61–2/62, May–June/62, Sept.–Dec./62. Absent on detached service recruiting horses in NC, Jan.–Feb./63. Present and on extra duty as a teamster, Feb.–Mar./62. Present Mar.–Apr./63. WIA, gunshot in thigh (psb. right) that shattered femur, and captured at Brandy Station, 6/9/63. "Had the bloated appearance of a habitual drinker." Leg amputated, 6/9/64. D. 6/24/63 at age 27, after hemorrhage, at an Alexandria, VA hospital. Bur. Alexandria Military Cemetery. (CSR 270:3; Medical History 11: 225, 236; Macon Heritage, 49.)

Cox, John W.: From Lenoir Co. Enl. 6/61 as PVT, Co. H, at age 26. On a 12/61 sick and wounded report with rheumatism. Dsh for disability, 12/22/61. (CSR 270:3)

Cozart, Allen W.: Enl. 8/28/63 as PVT, Co. B. Trn from 16th NC Bn. Reported present on muster rolls of 4/30/64–8/31/64. Had gray eyes, dark hair, and dark complexion, and stood 6'1". Absent on horse detail, Sept.–Oct./64. Captured at Ford's Station, 4/2/65, and sent to Point Lookout. D. 5/28/65 from acute dysentery. Bur. at Point Lookout. (CSR 270:3; PL: 133)

Craige, Kerr: B. Catawba County, 3/14/43. Resident of Salisbury, Rowan Co. Enl. 6/15/61 at age 18 as 5SGT. Prm 2LT, Co. I, to rank from 10/1/61. Reported present on company muster rolls of 11/61–12/61, with Co. I. 1/62–2/62, commanded Co. D. Present according to regimental return of 3/62. Reported present sick on muster rolls of May–June/62, and also present on company muster rolls of 9/62–12/62. Listed as AWOL, Jan.–Feb./63. Present according to company muster rolls of Mar.–Apr./63, 10/31/63. Prm 1LT, 6/20/63. Absent on detached service as volunteer aide to BG James B. Gordon beginning 10/10/63. Absent on frl, Jan.–Feb./64, then present with Co. I according to Mar.–Apr./64 and 4/31–8/31/64 muster rolls. Absent on detached service as acting adjutant for the regiment, 9/64. Present Nov.–Dec./64. Prm CPT, 3/65. Captured 4/3/65 at Namozine Church. Released on oath, 6/18/65. Had dark complexion, light hair, hazel eyes, 6'1". Post-war, Craige served as a lawyer, NC legislator, and in other government and public positions. D. 9/1/04; bur. St. Luke's Episcopal Church Cem., Salisbury. (CSR 270:1, 3; Ashe; Mizelle; Barringer; Cabarrus; Stepp)

Craige, M.F.: From Mecklenburg Co. At age 26, enl. 2/28/62 as PVT, Co. C. Absent scouting beginning 12/25/62. Reported present on company muster roll of 6/30–10/31/62. Absent beginning 5/29/62, according to muster roll of May–June/62. Reported present Sept.–Oct./63, July–Aug./63, Jan.–Apr./63, Nov.–Dec./63, 1/64–12/64. On the register of a Danville G.H. with a gunshot wound in left hand, date 4/3/65 and frl 4/8/65. (CSR 270:3; Alexander)

Crater, S.P.: Enl. 10/28/64 as PVT, Co. B. Reported present on company muster rolls of Sept.–Dec./64. (CSR 270:3)

Crawford, William D.: From Macon Co. Enl. 7/4/61 as bugler, Co. K. Reported present on muster rolls of 11/61–2/62, May–June/62. Guarding the baggage according to 3/62 regimental return. Captured in Maryland, 9/13/62. Exd. 12/8/62. Reported present on company muster rolls of 1/63–4/3. Absent detailed to NC to buy a horse, July–Aug./63. Present, 10/31/63. 11/63–3/31/64. Absent on detached service, Mar.–Apr./64. Absent on detail to care for wounded, 4/30–8/1/64. Present, Sept.–Oct./64, then absent on horse detail, Nov.–Dec./64. (CSR 270:3)

Crawford, William W.: B. in Raleigh, 10/5/34. From Wayne Co. Enl. 6/23/61 at age 26 as PVT, Co. H. Reported present on muster rolls of 11/61–2/62. Sent to a Goldsboro hospital, 4/4/62. Dsh 12/62, unofficially. Stood 5' 6⅞", had dark complexion, brown eyes, dark hair, and was by occupation a merchant. D. 5/29/17. Bur. Willowdale Cem., Goldsboro. (CSR 270:3; GLP; CGR: 3; Stepp)

Creasman, John M.: Resident of Buncombe Co. Age 19, PVT, Co. G. Admitted to a Richmond hospital, 11/14/62, and returned to duty, 2/14/63. Enl. 5/20/61. Reported present on company muster rolls of Jan.–Feb./62, May–June/62, Sept.–Oct./62, 1/63–4/63, July–Oct./63. Absent with unserviceable horses in Nelson Co., Nov.–Dec./63. Absent on detached service, 4/1/64. Listed as AWOL, Mar.–Apr./64 and following. Took oath in Knoxville, Tennessee, 7/28/64, after deserting 5/1/64. Had florid complexion, light hair, light eyes, 6' tall. (CSR 270:3)

Cress, Daniel M.: B. 10/24/40. From Cabarrus Co. Enl. 6/15/61 as PVT, Co. F. Reported present on company muster rolls of 11/61–2/62, May–June/62, 9/62–12/62, 7/63–10/64, although listed in a hospital, 2/25/62, according to regimental return of 2/62. Absent foraging, 12/27/64. D. 1/2/20. Bur. St. John's Lutheran Church Cem., Cabarrus Co. (CSR 270:3; Mizelle calls him Creps, and Cabarrus calls him Crepps; Graves calls him Cress)

Crisp, Joel L.: Enl. 6/25/61 in Co. K at age 18 as 1CPL. Reported present on company muster rolls of Nov.–Dec./61, and present sick in quarters, Jan.–Feb./62. On the register of a Richmond hospital with pneumonia, admitted 3/7/62 and returned to duty 3/27/62. In a Petersburg hospital on 3/11/62 according to a 3/62 regimental return. Reported present May–June/62, Sept.–Dec./62. Prm 5SGT, 12/1/62. Absent sick in a Stephensburg hospital, Jan.–Feb./63. Reported present Mar.–Apr./63, July–Aug./63, 10/31/63. Absent on detached service, Nov.–Dec./63, then reported present 1/64–10/64. Absent on horse detail, Nov.–Dec./64. From Cherokee County. (CSR 270:3)

Crissman, Albert: Enl. 9/2/64 as PVT, Co. H. Reported present Sept.–Oct./64, then absent on horse detail, Nov.–Dec./64. (CSR 270:3)

Critcher, John C.: Enl. 5/11/61 at age 21 as PVT, Co. D. Selected color bearer, 8/1/61. Present Nov.–Dec./61. Absent in a G.H., Jan.–Feb./62. Also listed absent sick on a 2/62 regimental return, and on a 3/62 return as in a Lynchburg hospital. Reported present on company muster rolls of 5/62–12/62. Prm CPL. Absent purchasing a horse, Jan.–Feb./63; also prm SGT. Listed as present, Mar.–Apr./63. D. 8/13/63 at Orange C.H. from wounds received at Brandy Station, 8/1/63. From Watauga Co. (CSR 270:3; Davis)

Crocker, Elijah: B. Johnson, NC. From Franklin Co. Farmer. At age 24, enl. 8/20/61 as PVT, Co. E. Reported present on company muster rolls of Jan.–Feb./62. Absent sick beginning 3/4/62; reported in hospitals thereafter at Manassas, Richmond, and Staunton. Called by rgt. surgeon a "dirt-eating whiner, with a thousand miseries," and dsh 7/30/62 with a "completely broken down constitution." D. 10/16/62; bur. Thornrose Cemetery, Staunton, VA. Stood 5'10", had fair complexion, blue eyes, light hair. (CSR 270:3; Pearce: 239)

Croft, David A.: From Buncombe Co. At age 25, enl. 5/20/61 as PVT, Co. G. Reported present on company muster rolls of Jan.–Feb./62, May–June/62, Sept.–Oct./62. Captured on picket duty at Kelly's Ford, 12/31/62. Reported present Mar.–Apr./63, 7–10/63. Absent to procure a fresh horse in NC, Nov.–Dec./63. Present Mar.–Aug./64, but also appears on a register of a Petersburg G.H., admitted 7/4/64 and returned to duty 7/12/64. Absent on detached service to procure a fresh horse, Sept.–Oct./64. Present Nov.–Dec./64. (CSR 270:3)

Cross, D.M.: Enl. 6/15/61 as PVT, Co. F. Detailed. Resident of Cabarrus Co., circa 1893. (Barringer)

Crouse, Jacob C.: B. 8/18/45. Previously in state service. Enl. 9/29/64 as PVT, Co. G. Reported present on company muster rolls of Sept.–Dec./64. D. 5/26/25. Bur. Antioch Baptist Church Cem., Alleghany Co. (CSR 270:3; Stepp)

Crump, R.H.: Enl. 3/64 as PVT, Co. C. Appears on a company muster roll of Mar.–Apr./64 as courier for GEN Hampton. Also listed absent on detached service on muster roll of 4/30–12/64. Prl Farmville, Va., between 4/11/65 and 4/21/65. (CSR 270:3; Alexander)

Crumpler, James I.: At age 18, enl. 5/25/61 as PVT, Co. A. Reported present on company muster rolls of 11/61–2/62. D. in camp, 3/8/62. (CSR 270:3; AsheCo)

Crumpler, Thomas Newton: B. 2/31 in Rockford, Surry Co. Attended UNC, 1850–1851. Moved to Ashe Co., where he enrolled in law school and then practiced law. Also served in NC Legislature, 1860–61. Apptd. CPT, Co. A, to rank from 5/16/61. Reported present on field and staff muster rolls of Nov.–Dec./61, May–June/62. Absent on recruiting service beginning 2/10/62. Prm. MAJ, 3/1/62. D. 7/11/62 after being WIA at Willis Church, 6/29/62. Known as an "able lawyer and good officer," and as "one of our most noble and brave men." Bur. in Rockford Baptist Church Cemetery, Surry Co. (CSR 270: 1, 3; Jackson, 49–50; AsheCo; W. Randall Crews to the author, March 14, 1997.)

Crunkleton, Joseph W.: B. 2/2/35. Family originally from Greencastle, PA. Enl. 7/20/61 as PVT, Co. K. From Macon Co. Reported present on company muster rolls of Nov.–Dec./61. Absent sent to Manassas sick, 2/26/62. Still absent sick according to 3/62 regimental return. Present May–June/62, Sept.–Dec./62. Absent foraging, Jan.–Feb./63. Present Mar.–Apr./63, July–Aug./63, 10/31/63, 11/63–2/64. Absent on detached service, 2/29–3/31/64. Present, 3/64–12/64. Moved to Georgia in the 1870s, returned to Macon in 1896. D. 5/1/00. Bur. Miller Family Cemetery, near Cliffside, in Macon Co. (CSR 270:3; Macon Heritage, 49, 201; Stepp)

Cruse, M.C.: From Mecklenburg Co. At age 26, enl. 6/14/61 as PVT, Co. C. Psb. in Co. E. Reported present on company muster rolls of Nov.–Dec./61, Jan.–Feb./62, 5/62–4/63. Absent detailed to buy a horse beginning 8/27/63. Reported present 9/63–4/64. Captured 5/5/64. Released from Point Lookout and prl 3/14/65, then finally prl Charlotte, 5/20/65. (CSR 270:3; Alexander)

Cruse, Peter: Enl. 6/15/63 as PVT, Co. F. Dsh. (Barringer)

Cunningham, Harroll A.: From Macon Co. At age 18, enl. 6/25/61 as PVT, Co. K. Reported present on company muster rolls of Nov.–Dec./61, Jan.–Feb./62, May–June/62. Absent on wagon guard at Winchester, Sept.–Oct./62. Present 11/62–4/63, July–Aug./63. Absent on detached service, 10/31/63. Present, Nov.–Dec./63. Listed as AWOL beginning with muster rolls of Mar.–Apr./64. Deserted 2/7/64 and took oath in Tennessee, 2/13/64. (CSR 270:3)

Cunningham, J.M.: At age 25, enl. 2/14/62 as PVT, Co. K. From Macon Co. Reported present on company muster rolls of May–June/62, 9/62–4/63. Absent detailed to NC to buy horses, July–Aug./63. Captured near Brandy Station, 6/9/63. AWOL on roll of 10/31/63. Present on rolls of Nov.–Dec./63, then absent on detached service, Jan.–Mar./64. Present on muster rolls of Mar.–Dec./64. (CSR 270:3)

Cunningham, Jeffrey E.: From Macon Co. At age 20, enl. 6/25/61 as PVT, Co. K. Reported present on muster rolls of 11/61–2/62, May–June/62. Listed on extra duty as a teamster on regimental returns of 2/62 and 3/62. Absent with the wagon guard at Winchester, Sept.–Oct./62. Present Nov.–Dec./62. Absent on detached service recruiting horses in NC, Jan.–Feb./63. Present Mar.–Apr./63, July–Aug./63, 10/31/63, 11/63–3/31/64. POW, 5/27/64. On a roll of POWs at Elmira willing to take the oath, 4/15/65. (CSR 270:3)

Cunningham, Joseph H.: From Granville Co. At age 20, enl. 6/8/61 as PVT, Co. E. Reported present on company muster rolls of Jan.–Feb./62, May–June/62, Sept.–Oct./62. Absent on detached service, Nov.–Dec./62. Present 1/63–4/63, July–Aug./63. Captured near Brandy Station, 6/9/63, and prl 6/11/63. WIA 10/15/63 in Bristoe Campaign. D. 10/16/63. (CSR 270:3)

Cunningham, William A.: At age 18, enl. 6/8/61 as PVT, Co. E. Reported present on company muster rolls of Jan.–Feb./62, May–June/62, 9/62–4/63. WIA in leg and captured near Brandy Station, 6/9/63. Cared for in Alexandria, Washington, and Baltimore hospitals, and prl 8/23/63. Listed ab. in a Petersburg hospital, July–Aug./63, due to a leg wound, then at home 6/30/63–2/64. Reported present on rolls Mar.–Apr./64. Adm. to a Richmond hospital, 5/4/64, with a gunshot wound in the leg; still reported in a Richmond hospital, 5/8/64, and in a Danville G.H., 6/4/64. Trn to Salem, VA, on light duty with the provost guard, according to muster rolls of 4/30/64–10/64 and returns from that post, then reported present on muster rolls of Nov.–Dec./64. On the register of a Danville G.H. of 5/18/65 with a gunshot wound in the leg. From Granville Co. (CSR 270:3)

Curl, Redman: Enl. 6/61 as PVT, Co. B. Reported present on company muster rolls of 11/61–2/62. Absent in a Petersburg hospital, Mar.–Apr./62. Sent home sick from Manassas, 2/20/62 according to muster roll of Sept.–Oct./62. Listed as AWOL on muster roll of Nov.–Dec./62, and as absent sent home sick on roll of 1/63–4/63, July–Aug./63. AWOL thereafter. From Northampton Co. Age 33. Deserted 3/62. (CSR 270:3)

Currin, R.S.: Enl. 7/7/64 as PVT, Co. B. Reported present on muster rolls of Nov.–Dec./64. (CSR 270:3)

Cutrell, Joseph H.: From Northampton Co. At age 18, enl. 6/12/61 as PVT, Co. B. Reported present on company muster rolls of 11/61–4/62, Sept.–Oct./62. Absent on detached service, Nov.–Dec./62. Present 1/63–4/63, 6/30/63–12/63. Absent on detached service, Mar.–Apr./64. Present, 4/30/64–10/64, although in a Danville hospital during part of 6/64. Deserted at Bernard's Mills, Va., with one Colt Revolver, 1/6/65. (CSR 270:3)

Dale, Thomas F.: From Duplin Co. At age 24, enl. 7/4/61 as PVT, Co. I. Rejected. (CSR 270:3)

Dalton, Caleb M.: From Cabarrus Co. At age 36, enl. 6/15/61 as PVT, Co. F. Farrier. Reported present on muster rolls of 11/61–2/62, May–June/62, Sept.–Dec./62. Resigned office of farrier, 12/13/62. Captured at Hanover, PA 6/30/63. Prl and exd, 10/11/64. (CSR 270:3)

Dalton, E.M.: Enl. 9/21/63 as PVT, Co. B. Reported present on muster rolls of 4/30–Oct./64. Absent sick, Nov.–Dec./64. Prl at Statesville, NC, 5/20/65. (CSR 270:3)

Dancy, Menoah: Also called Noah. Brother of Obadiah; had 4 other brothers who died during the war. B. 1846. Enl. 8/14/64 as PVT, Co. A. Reported present on company muster rolls of Sept.–Dec./64. D. 1908. Bur. in Dancy Family Cem., Grassy Creek, Ashe Co. (CSR 270:3; AsheCo; McNeil)

Dancy, Obadiah: B. 10/15/42, Wilkes Co. Brother of Menoah; had 4 other brothers who died during the war. Enl. 3/4/62 as PVT, Co. A. Absent on detached service in Winchester beginning 9/5/62. Reported present on company muster rolls of Nov.–Dec./62, then absent on frl to buy a horse, Jan.–Feb./63. Present Mar.–Apr./63, then absent on detached service to buy a horse, July–Aug./63. Sept.–Oct./63, absent on detached service with unserviceable horses, beginning 8/27/63. Present 11/30–12/31/63. Reported as under arrest, 12/24/63. Mentioned in a court martial record dated 5/2/64. Reported present, 1/1/64–4/64. On detached service to buy a horse, July–Aug./64. Present on Sept.–Dec./64 rolls. According to tombstone, served in 1865 as well. D. 3/24/22. Bur. Old Reddies River Primitive Baptist Church Cem., Wilbar, NC. (CSR 270:3; AsheCo; McNeil; Stepp)

Daniel, A.O.: B. 12/8/38. PVT, Co. I. D. 1/1/62 near Centreville of pneumonia. (*North Carolina Argus*, 2/6/62.)

Daniel, H.: Enl. 11/5/63 as PVT, Co. B. Reported present on muster rolls of 4/30/64–10/64. AWOL on muster rolls of Nov.–Dec./64. (CSR 270:3)

Danner, Joseph W.: From Wayne Co. At age 25, enl. 6/20/61 as PVT, Co. H. Absent sick, Nov.–Dec./61. Reported present on muster rolls of Jan.–Feb./62, May–June/62. Also on regimental returns of 2/62 and 3/62 as on extra duty as a hospital steward. Captured, 10/11/62, and prl. 10/15/62. Reported in a Richmond hospital, admitted 10/27/62 and returned to duty, 1/26/63. On a register of approved frls, dated 10/28/62, as detailed for hospital service. Detailed to a hospital, 1/63–4/63. Captured at Gettysburg, 7/3/63. Prl. and exd. 9/64. Reported in a detachment of prl/exd prisoners at Camp Lee, near Richmond, to 10/31/64. Reported by company muster roll on extra duty with the medical department, Nov.–Dec./64. Prl at Appomattox C.H., 4/9/65. (CSR 270:3)

Davidson, E.C.: Enl. 8/12/64 as PVT, Co. C. Reported present on company muster rolls of Sept.–Dec./64. Prl Charlotte, 5/27/65. (CSR 270:3; Alexander)

Davis, Abner: Resident of Boonville, Yadkin Co. Reported in the 1850 census as a clerk, age 27. Enl. 10/14/63 as PVT, Co. D. Reported absent sick in the hospital according to company muster roll of 8/31/64, having been admitted to a Richmond hospital 8/19/64. Present, Sept.–Oct./64. WIA and absent in the hospital, Nov.–Dec./64. Reported in a Raleigh hospital, 1/65. (CSR 270:3; Yadkin)

Davis, David C.: B. 4/24/37. From Watauga Co. At age 22, enl. 5/11/61. CPL, SGT, Co. D. On company muster rolls of Nov.–Dec./61 reported present, on extra duty attending to sick in hospital. Present Jan.–Feb./62, 5/62–4/63, 6/30/63–3/31/64.

Absent in NC to buy a horse, Mar.–Apr./63. Reported present 8/31–Dec./64. D. 9/11/22. Bur. Zionville Baptist Church Cem., Watauga Co. (CSR 270:3; Davis; Stepp)

Davis, David S.: SGT, Co. H. At age 41, enl. 6/2/0/61. Reported present on company muster rolls of 11/61–2/62. Absent on muster rolls of May–June/62, Sept.–Oct./62, detailed to raise a company. Prm to CPT, Nethercutt's Bn. From Wayne Co. (CSR 270:3)

Davis, Emory: At age 22, enl. 7/62 as PVT, Co. B. Reported present on company muster rolls of 9/62–4/63, 6/30/63–12/63. On frl, Jan.–Feb./64. Reported AWOL beginning 3/9/64. From Northampton Co. (CSR 270:3)

Davis, Harvey A.: B. Catawba Co., 7/17/40. Resident of Watauga Co. At age 20, enl. 5/11/61 as PVT, Co. D. Reported present according to company muster rolls of 11/61–2/62, 5/62–12/62. Reported absent to buy a horse on muster rolls of Jan.–Feb./63 (he left 2/24/63 according to his diary). Reported present, Mar.–Apr./63, July–Aug./63. Captured at Brandy Station, 6/9/63, and prl 6/25/63. WIA at Jack's Shop 9/22/63, shot in left elbow, and frl for 60 days beginning 10/63. Absent at home sick on muster roll of 6/30/63–12/63. Reported present, Jan.–Feb./64, also 2/29–3/31/64 and on extra duty as Provost Guard. Present Mar.–Apr./64; adm. to a Richmond hospital, 5/6/64. Retired 5/15/64. Reassigned to duty in Raleigh with the Invalid Corps. Worked his 110-acre farm after the war. D. 12/29/32; bur. Old Bethany Lutheran Church Cem., Watauga Co. (CSR 270:3; Davis; Stepp)

Davis, J.P.: From Granville Co. At age 24, enl. 2/12/62 as PVT, Co. E. Reported present on company muster rolls of May–June/62, Sept.–Dec./62. Prm CPL, 12/1/62. Also present Jan.–Apr./63, July–Oct./63. Captured near Mine Run, 11/28 or 11/29/63. Hospitalized for diptheria in Washington, 1/31–2/3/64. Prl and exd at Aiken's Landing, Va., 2/24/65. (CSR 270:3)

Davis, James M.: From Cabarrus Co. At age 22, enl. 6/15/61 as PVT, Co. F. Later prm blacksmith. Reported present on company muster rolls of 11/61–2/62, May–June/62, 9/62–12/62. Listed absent at Camp Cripple, in Nelson Co., as of 8/3/63, according to company muster rolls of July–Aug./63. Reported present on rolls of 9/63–12/64. Resident of Rowan Co., circa 1893. (CSR 270:3; Mizelle; Barringer; Cabarrus)

Davis, Jason: From Macon Co. At age 21, enl. 6/25/61 as PVT, Co. K. Reported present on company muster rolls of 11/61–2/62, although listed in a Petersburg hospital in 12/61 with typhoid fever. Sick in quarters, Jan.–Feb./62. Absent sent to Manassas sick on 3/9/62, according to muster roll of May–June/62. D. 3/62 or 4/62 from disease. (CSR 270:3)

Davis, John W.: From Franklin Co. At age 27, enl. 7/26/61 as PVT, Co. E. Reported present on company muster rolls of Jan.–Feb./62, May–June/62, Sept.–Oct./62. Absent on detached service as a courier for GEN J.E.B. Stuart beginning 12/4/62, until Stuart's 5/64 death; then on detached service with GEN W.H.F. Lee 4/30/64–12/64. (CSR 270:3; Pearce: 15, 240)

Davis, M.L.: Enl. 7/4/62 as PVT, Co. C, at age 20. Reported present on company muster rolls of 6/30/62–10/31/62. Absent scouting beginning 12/25/62. Sent to NC to buy a horse beginning 2/21/63. Present, Mar.–Apr./63. Absent sick in NC beginning 6/10/63. Present 9/63–4/64. Absent on detached service beginning 8/15/64, then present, Sept.–Oct./64. Absent on detached service beginning 12/7/64. Psb. prm to non–commissioned officer. From Mecklenburg Co. (CSR 270:3; Alexander)

Davis, Martin: Co. D (Davis)

Davis, Solomon J.: B. 3/20/30. PVT, Co. E. Enl. 8/4/63. Reported present on company muster rolls of 6/30/63–2/64. Absent on detached service in NC to buy a horse, Mar.–Apr./64. Reported present on 4/1/64 roll. WIA severely 8/15, 8/16, or 8/17/64 with gunshot wound in right thigh, along Charles City Rd., near Richmond. Absent in a Farmville and then Richmond hospital through 10/64, then absent at home on 60-day frl. From Granville Co., resident of Williamsboro. D. 4/8/15. Bur. Oakwood Cem., Raleigh. (CSR 270:3; Richmond *Sentinel*, 8/26/64; Stepp)

Davis, Thomas: From Watauga Co. PVT, Co. D. At age 24, enl. 2/28/62. Captured at Willis Church, 6/29/62, and exd. at Aiken's Landing, 8/5/62. Stood 5'9", had light hair, blue eyes, and a fair complexion. Reported present on muster rolls dated 6/30/62–4/63, July–Aug./63. Absent on detached service, 6/30/63–3/31/64. Present, Mar.–Apr./64. Trn to Co B, 37th Regiment NC Troops, 7/21/64, where he was killed (CSR 270:3; Davis)

Davis, Thomas W.P.: From Macon Co. At age 17, enl. 4/11/62 as PVT, Co. K. Reported present on company muster rolls of May–June/62, 9/62–4/63, July–Aug./63. WIA Jack's Shop, 9/22/63. Present 10/31/63, Nov.–Dec./63. AWOL on muster rolls of Jan.–Feb./64, Present 2/29/64–8/31/64.

Absent on detached service at Stoney Creek, Va., Sept.–Oct./64; present Nov.–Dec./64. (CSR 270:3)

Davis, Tyra H.: PVT, Co. K. From Macon Co., age 40. Rejected by COL Baker. (CSR 270:3)

Davis, Wallace E.: From Cabarrus Co. At age 21, enl. 6/15/61 as PVT, Co. F. Reported present on company muster rolls of 11/61–2/62, May–June/62, 9/62–12/62. Absent sent to NC to procure a horse, 8/27/63, on muster roll of July–Aug./63. Reported present 9/63–3/31/64. Trn to Co. E, 4th NC Cavalry, 7/21/64. Dead as of 1893. (CSR 270:3; Mizelle; Barringer; Cabarrus)

Davis, William M.: B. 11/1/38. Enl. 5/11/61 as PVT, Co. D. Reported present on muster rolls of 11/61–2/62, May–June/62. Reported on extra duty as a teamster according to regimental return of 3/62. Absent driving teams at Winchester, 6/30–10/31/62. Present, Nov.–Dec./62, and reported as teamster in the QM dept. Present Jan.–Feb./63, Mar.–Apr./63 and reported as a teamster. Absent on detaced service as a teamster in the QM dept, July–Aug./63; also absent as a teamster, 6/30–10/31/63. Reported present, 11/63–3/31/64, and on extra duty as a teamster. Absent on frl, Mar.–Apr./64. Absent as teamster in QM dept., 8/31/64 muster roll. Absent as a teamster, Sept.–Dec./64. From Watauga Co. D. 4/29/12. Bur. Zionville Baptist Church Cem., Watauga Co. (CSR 270:3; Stepp)

Deal, Sidney: B. 9/26/25. Resident of Watauga Co. Served as sheriff. Psb. enl. 4/15/61 in Co. D, 6th N.C. At age 36, enl. 2/28/62. Co. D, PVT, Blacksmith. Reported present on muster rolls of 5/62–12/62, although sick Nov.–Dec./62. Also present on rolls of 1/63–4/63. WIA 7/10/63, sent to a Richmond hospital, and frl 7/27/63. Reported present 1/64–3/31/64, part of the time on extra duty as provost guard. Absent at home to buy a horse, Mar.–Apr./64. Present 8/31–12/64. Captured 4/15/65 in Lenoir, NC, while on frl collecting men to fight "Tories" at Blowing Rock, NC. Known as a "faithful, headstrong, outspoken Confederate." Released on taking oath, 6/13/65. Had dark complexion, dark hair, hazel eyes, stood 6'3". D. 11/23/96. Bur. Cedar Valley Methodist Church Cem., Caldwell Co. (CSR 270:3; Davis; Stepp; Robert C. Deal to the author, June 8, 1997; R.L. Downs, "Some Incidents of Gen. Stoneman's Raid and other Events of that Period," *Lenoir Topic*,12/17/90–1/14/91)

Deaton, Caleb: Enl. 6/15/61 as Farrier, Co. F. Captured in Maryland, 7/63. Dead as of 1893. (Barringer; Cabarrus)

Deberry, P.P.: Deserter. Arrested 7/64 or 8/64 in Salisbury, NC at his mother's home. Placed in Salisbury Prison. (*Daily Carolina Watchman*, 8/4/64, p. 1, col. 1)

Debnam, T.R.: Resident of Wake Co. PVT, Co. E. Enl. 9/28/64. Reported present on muster rolls of 4/30–Oct./64. Absent in NC on horse detail, Nov.–Dec./64. Captured near Amelia C.H., 4/3/65. Released 6/11/65, on taking the oath. Had dark complexion, dark brown hair, gray eyes, stood 5'10½". (CSR 270:3)

Debnam, Walter: B. Wake Co. Occupation: farmer. Age 24. PVT, Co. E. Enl. 10/13/63. Reported present 4/30–12/64. Psb trn from McRae's Bn., where he served 1 month as 1SGT. Had blue eyes, dark hair, fair complexion, and stood 5'8". (CSR 270:3)

DeHart, J.P.: From Macon Co. Age 30. PVT, Co. K. Rejected by COL Baker. (CSR 270:3)

DeHart, W.J.: From Macon Co. Age 28. PVT, Co. K. Rejected by COL Baker. (CSR 270:3)

Dejernett, C.H.: Enl. 6/15/61 as PVT, Co. F. Dsh 12/61. Dead as of 1893. (Barringer)

Dellinger, A.C.: PVT, Co. K. Enl. 10/31/64. Reported present, Nov.–Dec./64. (CSR 270:3)

Dellinger, Henry S.: B. Lincoln Co. Occupation: farmer. At age 24, enl. 6/15/61 as PVT, Co. F. Accidentally shot in the foot by Henry Fisher, 11/61; crippled for life. Also took typhoid fever. Absent on sick frl, 11/61–2/62. Dsh 5/1/62. Stood 6'¼" tall, had dark complexion and dark hair. Resident of Lincolnton, circa 1893. (CSR 270:3; Mizelle; Barringer; *Concord Register*, June 8, 1883)

Denton, C.D.: PVT, Co. F. (Mizelle; Cabarrus)

Deweese, Jesse: PVT, Co. K, from Macon Co. Age 21. Rejected by COL Baker. (CSR 270:3)

Deweese, John H.: Enl. 4/11/62 as PVT, Co. K. Reported present on muster rolls of May–June/62, 9/62–4/63. Sent to NC to buy horses, July–Aug./63. Reported absent sick on muster roll of 10/31/63, then AWOL to 10/14/63. (CSR 270:3)

Dewey, George Stanley: B. 9/20/41 in New Bern. Fourth child and eldest son of Oliver Stanley Dewey and Matilda (Sparrow) Dewey. Member of Yale College class of 1863 (paternal grandmother Mary Judd Stanley and family lived In Connecticut) but left Yale in 1861 to enlist. Resident of Craven Co. At age 19, enl. 6/29/61 as PVT, Co. H. Reported present on company muster rolls of 11/61–2/62. Also listed on extra duty in the QM dept. on regimental returns of 2/62 and 3/62. Appointed commissary SGT, 5/62 or 6/16/62. Reported present on field and staff muster rolls of May–June/62,

Sept.–Oct./62. Reduced to ranks, 10/24/62. Reported present on company muster rolls of 11/62–4/63, 7/63–12/63. Apptd ADJ, 1/25/64, to rank from 7/23/63. Elected 2LT, Co. H, 8/29/64; prm 1LT and then CPT and took command of Co. H, 8/30/64. Present on field and staff muster rolls of 11/63–8/31/64, and on company muster rolls of Nov.–Dec./64. Apptd to board of valuation, 3/21/65. MAJ. KIA Chamberlain's Run, VA, 3/31/65. Bur. Cedar Grove Cem., New Bern. See letters in SHC. As of Jan 07 Oil on canvas paper likeness of him In the collections of Tryon Palace (CSR 270:1, 3; Stepp; Box 42, Folder 19, Military Collection, Civil War Collection, NCSA; *Carolina Comments* 55 [January 2007: 9])

Dickens, J.M.: From Franklin Co. PVT, Co. E. Enl. 3/8/64. Reported present on company muster rolls of 4/1/64, Mar.–Apr./64. Absent on detached service at Stony Creek, VA, 4/30–10/64. Captured, 12/1/64. Released on taking the oath, 6/4/65. (CSR 270: 3; Pearce: 242)

Dickerson, Alphonso: Listed in 1850 census as age 22, married. Enl. 5/25/61 as PVT, Co. A. Deserted before he was mustered in. Age 22, from Yadkin Co. On 2/15/63, cns in Co. G, 2d Bn NC Infantry. Appointed CPL, 3/23/63; again deserted, 4/26/63. (CSR 270:3; AsheCo; Yadkin)

Dickerson, Chestine: From Warren Co. At age 26, enl. 6/22/61 as a PVT, Co. E. In a Danville hospital with diarrhea, admitted 1/2/62, and trn to Richmond. Sent to a Petersburg hospital, 2/24/62; also reported in a Lynchburg hospital, 2/25/62. Present on muster rolls of May–June/62, 9/62–4/63, 6/30/63–4/64. KIA at Ground Squirrel Church, 5/11/64. (CSR 270:3)

Dickerson, J.R.: From Buncombe Co. At age 30, enl. 5/20/61 as PVT, Co. G. Admitted to a Richmond hospital, 11/3/61, and returned to duty 11/25/61. Reported present on muster rolls of Jan.–Feb./62, May–June/62, 9/62–4/63, July–Aug./63. Listed absent sick on regiment return of 2/62. Absent on detached service with unserviceable horses in Gordonsville, Sept.–Dec./63. Absent on detached service at Stony Creek, VA, 4/30–Aug./64. Absent on detached service to procure a fresh horse, Sept.–Oct./64. Trn to 11th NC Infantry Rgt., 11/ or 12/64. (CSR 270:3)

Dillon, Samuel: Age 30. Enl. 6/20/61 as PVT, Co. H. Reported present on company muster rolls of Nov.–Dec./61. Captured while on picket near Difficult Run, VA, 2/7/62. Prl. Reported present, 11/62–4/63. Absent on detached service, 7/63–2/64, 4/1/64. Reported present, Mar.–Apr./64, then absent sick, 4/30–10/64. Present on rolls of Nov.–Dec./64. From Wayne Co. (CSR 270:3)

Dixon, Alexander: From Ashe Co. Age 20. Enl. 6/6/61 as PVT, Co. A. Reported present on company muster rolls of 11/61–2/62, Sept.–Oct./62. Reported absent scouting, beginning 12/25/62. Present on rolls of 1/63–4/63, 7/63–4/64, 7/64–12/64. (CSR 270:3; AsheCo)

Dixon, James D.: Enl. 6/3/61 as PVT, Co. A. Reported present on company muster rolls of 11/61–2/62, 9/62–4/63, July–Aug./63. Captured 9/13/63 near Culpeper, VA. D. 3/28/65 of chronic diarrhea, at Elmira, NY. Bur. there. (CSR 270:3; AsheCo)

Dixon, James M.: From Ashe Co. At age 22, enl. 6/6/61 as 2CPL, Co. A. Reported present on company muster rolls of 11/61–2/62, Sept.–Oct./62. Absent scouting beginning 12/25/62. Present, 1/63–4/63, July–Oct./63. Prm to SGT, 9/27/63 or 11/1/63. AWOL beginning 12/24/63. Reported present, 1/1/64–8/64. Dsh, 9/21/64, psb on election to a political office. (CSR 270:3; AsheCo)

Dixon, John A.: PVT, Co. A. Enl. 5/23/61, at age 18. Reported present on company muster rolls of 11/61–2/62, 9/62–12/62. Absent on frl to purchase a horse beginning 2/27/63. Reported present, Mar.–Apr./63. Absent on detached service to buy a horse, July–Aug./63. Reported AWOL beginning 10/29/63. Listed as present and under arrest as of 12/10/63. Present, 1/1/64–4/64, 7/64–12/64. From Ashe Co. (CSR 270:3)

Dixon, John F.: From Greene Co. At age 21, enl. 7/4/61 as PVT, Co. H. Reported present on muster rolls of 11/61–2/62, May–June/62, Sept.–Oct./62. Absent detailed on a scout according to Nov.–Dec./62 roll. Absent on frl, Jan.–Feb./63. Present Mar.–Apr./63. Absent on detached service to NC to buy a horse, July–Aug./63. Present, Sept.–Oct./63. KIA 11/27/63 near Orange CH. (CSR 270:3)

Dixon, Josiah: B. Greene Co. PVT, Co. H. Enl. 7/4/61 at age 24. Reported present on company muster roll of Nov.–Dec./61. Absent sent to a Petersburg hospital, 2/20/62. Dsh 5/19/62 due to frequent rheumatism attacks following a bout with typhoid fever. Stood 5' 8¼" tall, had a fair complexion, blue eyes, and dark hair. Occupation: farmer. (CSR 270:3)

Dixon, Noah C.: From Ashe Co. Enl. 7/8/61 as PVT, Co. A. Reported present on company muster rolls of 9/63–4/64, 7/64–12/64. Trn from Co. D, 58th NC. (CSR 270:3; AsheCo)

Dixon, William H.: B. Ashe Co. Occupation: farmer. At age 24, enl. 6/8/61 as PVT, Co. A. Present on muster roll of Nov.–Dec./61. Absent sick, Jan.–Feb./62 on muster rolls, and on 3/10/62 according to 3/62 regimental return. D. 5/10/62. Stood 6'1", had fair complexion, black eyes, and light hair. (CSR 270:3; AsheCo)

Dobson, Franklin: PVT, Co. I. Enl. 6/17/61. From Duplin Co., age 19. Rejected. (CSR 270:3)

Dobson, William P.: PVT, Co. H. Captured 4/3/65 at Aberdeen Church. Released 6/26/65 on taking the oath. Resident of Surry Co. Had light complexion, red hair, hazel eyes, and stood 5'8". (CSR 270:3)

Doherty, William W.: From Mecklenburg Co. At age 21, enl. 6/15/61 as PVT, Co. F. Reported present on company muster rolls of Jan.–Feb./62, May–June/62, Sept.–Dec./62. Prm 2LT, 37th NC Troops or 42d N.C. Infantry, 6/22/63. KIA. (CSR 270:3; Mizelle; Barringer; Cabarrus)

Dove, Jacob: B. 6/12/32 or 6/12/36. From Cabarrus Co. At age 37, enl. 6/15/61 as PVT, Co. F. Reported present on company muster rolls of 11/61–2/62, May–June/62. Reported on extra duty with QM dept. on 2/62 rgt. return; on recruiting service according to 3/62 return. Absent at Winchester with the wagon train, Sept.–Oct./62. Present Nov.–Dec./62, 7/63–2/64. Present 2/29–3/31/64 and on extra duty as wagon master. Reported present Mar.–Dec./64. Absent on extra duty, Nov.–Dec./64. Prl Charlotte, 5/6/65. Resident of Concord, 1893. D. 7/13/01 or 7/13/07. Bur. Center Methodist Church Cem., Cabarrus Co. (CSR 270:3; Mizelle; Barringer; Cabarrus; Lore: 32; Graves)

Dowell, Martin: Resident of Iredell Co. At age 24, enl. 8/15/61 as PVT, Co. K. Reported present on company muster rolls of Nov.–Dec./61. Absent sick at a Manassas G.H., 2/24/62. Present on muster rolls of 9/62–4/63, July–Aug./63, 10/31/63, 11/63–4/30/64. Mentioned in a court martial record of 9/17/63. In hospitals at Richmond and Farmville, admitted 4/64 and returned to duty 7/22/64. Captured at Deep Bottom, 8/18/64. Released 6/12/65 on taking oath. Had dark complexion, dark brown hair, hazel eyes; stood 5'10¼". (CSR 270:3)

Draper, Arodi: B. Northampton Co. Occupation: farmer. Cns 7/15/62 as PVT, Co. H. Reported absent sick at Winchester, Sept.–Oct./62. Dsh 12/10/62. Had fair complexion, blue eyes, red hair; stood 5'6½". (CSR 270:3)

Drew, Mack G.: From Halifax Co. At age 22, enl. 6/12/61 as PVT, Co. B. Reported present on company muster rolls of 11/61–4/62, 9/62–4/63, July–Aug./63, 6/30–12/63, 3/64–12/64. Captured near Dinwiddie C.H. 3/31/65. Released on taking oath, 6/3/65. (CSR 270:3; Halifax: 7)

Dry, J.W.: PVT, Co. F. (Cabarrus)

Dry, John W.: From Cabarrus Co. At age 20, enl. 6/15/61 as PVT, Co. F. Reported present on muster rolls of 11/61–2/62, May–June/62, Sept.–Dec./62. WIA near Funkstown, MD, 7/9/63. Reported present on rolls of 1/64–4/30/64. WIA at Brook Church, 5/12/64, and frl. Adm. to a Richmond hospital, 5/12/64. Also noted on the roll of a Charlotte hospital, Nov.–Dec./64, where he was employed as a guard. Resident of Chattanooga, circa 1893. (CSR 270:3; Mizelle; Barringer; Cabarrus)

Dry, Lawrence W.: From Cabarrus Co., age 23. Enl. 3/1/62 as PVT, Co. F. Reported present on muster roll of May–June/62. Absent making shoes at Winchester, Sept.–Oct./62. Present Nov.–Dec./62, 9/63–8/31/64. Absent sick in the hospital, 9/1/64. Present Nov.–Dec./64. Resident of Cabarrus Co., NC, circa 1893. (CSR 270:3; Barringer; Cabarrus)

Duke, Daniel B.: From Granville Co. At age 20, enl. 6/24/61 in Co. E. Prm to bugler, 7/61. Reported present on rolls of Jan.–Feb./62, May–June/62. On detached service at Winchester, Sept.–Oct./62. Present on rolls of 11/62–4/63, July–Aug./63, 6/30/63–12/64. (CSR 270:3)

Duke, Jordan T.: From Macon Co. At age 29, enl. 6/8/61 as PVT, Co. E. Reported present on company muster rolls of Jan.–Feb./62. D. 2/62 at Manassas Junction of Typhoid Fever. (CSR 270:3)

Duke, W.D.: Resident of Granville Co., age 19. Enl. 6/24/61 as PVT, Co. E. Reported present on company muster rolls of Jan.–Feb./62, May–June/62, Sept.–Dec./62. Absent on detached service, Jan.–Feb./63. Present, Mar.–Apr./63. Reported absent on detached service to NC to buy a horse, 8/27/63. Reported absent at home sick, 10/1/63. Reported present 11/63–4/64. Absent at Stony Creek, VA, 4/30–10/64. Captured there, 12/1/64. Released 6/12/65. Had a dark complexion, dark brown hair, brown eyes, stood 5'11¼". (CSR 270:3)

Dula, George L.: Cns 9/29/64 as PVT, Co. H. Reported present on company muster rolls of 9/12/64. (CSR 270:3)

Dula, John W.: Enl. 4/1/64 as PVT, Co. D. Reported present on muster rolls of Mar.–Apr./64. Absent home buying a horse, 8/31/64–10/64. WIA, broken fibula. Reported in a Danville hospital, 12/64, and frl 12/29/64 for 60 days. (CSR 270:3)

Dula, Thos.: From Caldwell Co., NC. Co. D. Psb. confused with John W. Dula. (Davis)

Dulin, J.M.: Enl. 6/4/61 as PVT, Co. C, at age 25. From Mecklenburg Co. D. 12/25/61 or 12/28/61 of tyhpoid fever. (CSR 270:3; Alexander)

Duncan, C.H.: B. Granville Co. Farmer. At age 41, enl. 8/28/63 as PVT, Co. B. Trn from 16th NC Bn. Absent sick according to muster rolls of 4/30–10/64. Listed as AWOL on Nov.–Dec./64 roll. Had gray eyes, light hair, fair complexion. (CSR 270:3)

Dunkin, W.H.H.: From Rutherford Co. Psb. a resident of Henderson. Enl. 5/20/61 at age 20 as PVT, Co. G. Reported present on company muster rolls of Jan.–Feb./62, May–June/62, 9/62–4/63. Captured in MD, 7/63. Exd 3/17/64. Reported sick in a Raleigh hospital, Mar.–Aug./64; adm. There 8/15/64 and returned to duty 9/13/64. Trn to 25th Rgt NC Troops, 10/13/64. (CSR 270:3)

Dunn, A.R.: Enl. 8/9/64 as PVT, Co. H. Reported present on company muster rolls of 4/30–8/31/64. Trn. to Co. B. Reported present Sept.–Oct./64. Absent sick according to roll of Nov.–Dec./64. (CSR 270:3)

Earley, Abner: Enl. at age 18 as PVT, Co. B, 6/12/61. Dsh. 8/61. From Bertie Co. (CSR 270:4)

Earley, William N.: Resident of Bertie Co. At age 20, enl. 6/61 or 8/61 as PVT, Co. B. Reported present on company muster rolls of 11/61–4/62. D. 7/24 at home, in Clarksville. (CSR 270:4)

Earnhardt, John: Presbyterian minister. Enl. 9/29/63 as PVT, Co. F. Also reported in Co. B. Listed present on company muster rolls of Sept.–Oct./64. Admitted to Kittrell Springs, NC G.H., 12/9/64, and D. there the same month. Bur. at Kittrell Springs Confederate Cem. (CSR 270:4; Kittrell; Barringer)

Earp, Wyatt: Enl. 11/5/63 as PVT, Co. B. Reported absent sick on company muster rolls of 4/30–8/31/64, Sept.–Oct./64. Present Nov.–Dec./64. Prl 5/20/65. (CSR 270:4)

Eaton, J.H.: PVT, Co. G. Trn to 11th N.C. Infantry, according to company muster rolls of Nov.–Dec./64. (CSR 270:4)

Eckard, L.P.: Enl. 10/28/64 as PVT, Co. B. Reported present on company muster rolls of Sept.–Dec./64. Also reported in a Richmond G.H. during 11/64 with pneumonia. Employed on extra duty as a teamster for W.H.F. Lee's cavalry division, 8/64. (CSR 270:4)

Eckard, W.S.: Enl. 9/22/63 as PVT, Co. B. Reported present on company muster rolls of 4/30–10/64. Absent on horse detail according to Nov.–Dec./64 roll. (CSR 270:4)

Eddleman, S.P.: At age 30, enl. 6/17/61 as PVT Co. C. Reported present on company muster rolls of 11/61–2/62, 5/62–4/63, 7/63–12/64. On extra duty as a teamster, according to rgt. returns of 2/62 and 3/62. From Buncombe Co. (CSR 270:4; Alexander calls him T.P. Edleman)

Edmonds, W.: PVT, Co. A. (AsheCo)

Edmondson, Henry R.: From Wayne Co. Enl. 4/17/62 as PVT, Co. H. Reported present on company muster rolls of Mar.–Apr./62. Absent on detached service to buy a horse in NC, July–Aug./63. Present on Sept.–Oct./63 roll. "This young prodigy was only about 17 years old, pretty well grown, prompt in action, wont to read his Bible, which he always carried in his pocket, never known to use profane or ill words, and a kind, obliging, agreeable, and pleasant messmate." Noted for conduct during Gettysburg campaign. Placed on staff of Gen. Hampon as courier. Contracted pneumonia; absent sick in the hospital according to roll of Nov.–Dec./63. D. 12/26/63 at Hanover Junction Hospital. (CSR 270:4; *Wilmington Journal*, 2/18/64.)

Edney, C.W.L.: Co. G. Age 54. Psb. 1SGT who served 5/20–8/20/61. (CSR 270:4)

Edwards, A.J.: From Mecklenburg Co. At age 29, enl. 5/27/61 as PVT, Co. C. Reported present on company muster rolls of Nov.–Dec./61. Absent at Warrenton in charge of the company's horses beginning 2/17/62. Reported present on 5/62–4/63 rolls, and on 7/63–8/31/64 rolls. Absent on detached service beginning 9/25/64, according to rolls of Sept.–Dec./64. (CSR 270:4)

Edwards, E.: B. 1833. From Pitt Co. At age 28, enl. 5/27/61 as PVT, Co. C. Reported present on company muster rolls of 11/61–2/62, 5/62–4/63. Admitted to a Staunton hospital, 3/8/63. Also present on 7/63–8/31/64 rolls. WIA, 10/27/64. D. 11/14/64 at a Wilson, NC G.H. Bur. Maplewood Cem., Wilson. (CSR 270:4; Alexander; Stepp)

Edwards, H.C.: Enl. 6/ or 7/61 as SGT, Co. H. Reported present on company muster rolls of Jan.–Feb./63. Absent on horse detail according to Sept.–Oct./63 rolls. (CSR 270:4)

Edwards, J.T.: PVT, Co. I. Trn from 24th Rgt. NC Troops. Enl. 12/21/64. Reported present on company muster rolls of Nov.–Dec./64. (CSR 270:4)

Edwards, John H: Resident of Edgecombe Co. Cns. 7/16/62 as PVT, Co. E. Reported present on company muster rolls of 9/62–4/63, July–Aug./63. Deserted 9/4/63 along the Rappahannock, and took oath 9/26/63. Forwarded to Philadelphia. Had dark complexion, brown hair, hazel eyes, and stood 5'9". (CSR 270:4)

Edwards, Little B.: From Edgecombe Co. At age 18, cns. 7/16/62 as PVT, Co. E. Reported present on company muster rolls of 9/62–4/63. Absent sick at a G.H., 8/63. Present on rolls of Nov.–Dec./63. Absent in Nelson Co., VA, with disabled horses beginning 2/10/64. POW from Reams Station, 9/29/64. Prl at Point Lookout and exd. at Aiken's Landing, 3/17/65. (CSR 270:4)

Edwards, Royal T.: At age 19, enl. 6/24/61 in Co. E, as PVT. Reported present on company muster rolls of Jan.–Feb./62, May–June/62, 9/62–4/63, July–Aug./63. Prm bugler, 10/1/63. WIA in leg during Bristoe Campaign, 10/20/63, according to muster roll of 6/30–10/31/63. Another report dates the wound to 10/14/63. Admitted to a Richmond G.H., 10/24/63 with a gunshot wound in the right thigh. Frl for 40 days, 10/27/63. Absent at home, Nov.–Dec./63. Present according to Jan.–Dec./64 rolls. From Franklin Co., resident of Louisburg. (CSR 270:4; Pearce: 13, 244 spells it Rial)

Edwards, Samuel D.: From Granville Co. At age 32, enl. 4/63 as PVT, Co. E. Reported present on Mar.–Apr./63 roll. Absent sent to Nelson Co., VA, with disabled horses according to 6/30/63–4/1/64. KIA at Blacks and Whites, 6/23/64. (CSR 270:4)

Edwards, W.H.H.: PVT, Co. A. Enl. 3/3/62. Listed on a 3/62 rgt. return. Admitted to a Richmond G.H., 10/18/62. Reported present on Sept.–Dec./62 rolls. Absent on frl to buy a horse beginning 2/27/63. Present on rolls of Mar.–Apr./63, 7/63–12/63. Absent on frl beginning 2/16/64. Reported present on roll of 4/1/64, and absent on detached service in NC on Mar.–Apr./64 roll. Reported present on 7/64–12/64 rolls. From Ashe Co. (CSR 270:4; AsheCo)

Edwards, William: PVT, Co. A. At age 23, enl. 5/28/61 or 7/23/61. Reported absent sick at Richmond on Nov.–Dec./61 rolls. Dsh. for disability. From Alleghany Co. (CSR 270:4)

Efird, Daniel Cicero: From Bosts Mill, Stanly County. At age 26, enl as PVT, Co. F, on 2/15/62. Reported present on muster rolls of May–June/62. Absent shoemaking at Winchester, Sept.–Oct./62. Present, 11–12/62. Sent to Camp Cripple with horses, 8/24/63. Reported present, 9/63–3/31/64. WIA, shot in the back, near White's Tavern, VA, 8/15/64, and sent to a Richmond hospital. Frl 8/29/64. Also reported on frl on Sept.–Oct./64 muster rolls. Present Nov.–Dec./64. Reported in a Danville hospital 4/3/65 with a gunshot wound in the left index finger; frl 4/8/65. Prl 5/18/65 at Charlotte. Living in Texas as of 1893. (CSR 270:4; Barringer; Richmond *Sentinel*, 8/26/64)

Efird, J.C.: From Stanly Co, age 18. PVT, Co. C. Enl. 7/27/61. Reported present on company muster rolls of Nov.–Dec./61. Absent sick at Petersburg beginning 2/26/62. Also listed as absent sick in Petersburg hospital on regimental returns of 2/ and 3/62. Present May–Oct./62, although also reported in a Danville hospital with rheumatism, 7/62. Absent scouting beginning 12/25/62. Present 1/63–4/63, 7/63–4/64. WIA, gunshot wound in left thigh 8/16/64. D. 8/20/64. (CSR 270:4; Alexander)

Efird, Jacob E.: Enl. 7/27/61 as PVT, Co. C. Reported present on company muster rolls of 11/61–2/62, 5/62–4/63, July–Aug./63. Reported sick in Richmond on 3/62 regimental return. Admitted to a Richmond hospital 3/14/62, then trn to a Farmville hospital, 5/7/62, and returned to duty 6/13/62. Absent on detached service beginning 9/1/63, and at least initially employed as a laborer at HQ Cav Corps. Reportedly remained on detached service through 10/64, although listed as WIA 8/15 or 8/16/64 along Charles City Rd., near Richmond. Admitted to a Raleigh hospital, 9/19/64, and returned to duty 10/2/64. Present, Nov.–Dec./64. From Efird's Mill in Stanly Co. Age 18. Appears on the register of a Greensboro hospital, admitted 4/65. (CSR 270:4; Alexander; Richmond *Sentinel*, 8/26/64; DavisUDC)

Eller, David W.: From Ashe Co. At age 25, enl 5/23/61 or 6/23/61 as PVT, Co. A. Reported present on company muster rolls of 11/61–2/62. Absent on recruiting service beginning 3/2/62, according to 3/62 return. Elected 2LT 6/23/62. Reported in a Lynchburg G.H., for the week ending 11/21/62. Listed as absent on sick leave but on his way to the regiment, Jan.–Feb./63. Present, Mar.–Apr./63, 7/63–4/64. Prm senior 2LT, 2/63. Absent at home on sick frl according to company muster rolls of July–Aug./64, and on inspection reports of 7/64. Mentioned in a leave record dated 8/13/64. Prm 1LT, 10/17/64. Reported present, Sept.–Oct./64. Resigned, 12/5/64. (CSR 270:1, 4; AsheCo)

Eller, Jesse: Enl 9/10/62 as PVT, Co. A. Reported present on company muster rolls of 9/62–4/63. Absent on detached service with unserviceable horses/recruiting camp beginning 8/1/63. Present July–Dec./64. (CSR 270:4; AsheCo)

Eller, John H.: Enl. 2/24/62 as PVT, Co. A. Reported present on company muster rolls of 9/62–4/63. Absent on detached service with unserviceable horses beginning 8/1/63. Present July–Dec./64. (CSR 270:4; AsheCo)

Elliott, E.C.: Of the Baptist faith. Cns. 10/3/64

as PVT, Co. I. Reported present on company muster rolls of Sept.–Oct./64. WIA 12/10/64. Admitted to the G.H. at Kittrell Springs 1/8/65d with severe knee wound. D. 1/12/65 at Kittrell Springs. Bur. Kittrell Springs Confederate Cem. (CSR 270:4; Kittrell; Stepp)

Elliott, James: From Halifax Co. At age 23, enl. 7/62 as PVT, Co. B. Reported present on muster rolls of Sept.–Dec./62. Absent on detached service to buy a horse, Jan.–Feb./63. Present Mar.–Apr./63, then absent on detached service as of 7/12/64. Reported present 6/30–10/31/63. Absent sent to a G.H., 11/63–2/64. Admitted to a Richmond G.H. with syphilis, 12/16/63. Listed in a Richmond G.H. with rubeola, 2/27/64. Returned to duty, 3/25/64. Reported present on company muster rolls of 4/1/64, 4/30–12/64. Absent on horse detail according to muster roll of Mar.–Apr./64. (CSR 270:4)

Elliott, James M.: B. Granville Co. Pre–war occupation: tobacconist. Trn from 16th NC Bn. Enl. 8/26/63 as PVT, Co A. Reported present on company muster rolls of 4/30–12/64. Age 44, had blue eyes, gray hair, and a fair complexion, and stood 5'8" tall. (CSR 270:4)

Elliott, Joseph T.: From Northampton Co. At age 22, enl. 6/18/61 as 1CPL, Co. B. Reported present on company muster rolls of Nov.–Dec./61. Prm 5SGT. Captured, 2/22/62, according to regimental return of 2/62. Reported present, Jan.–Apr./63, July–Aug./63 and 6/30–10/31/63. Elected 2LT, 3/21/63. Reported KIA or severely WIA 7/10/63 at Funkstown and captured at Hagerstown, MD or Williamsport, PA, 7/10/63. Appears on a report of sick and wounded at a Hagerstown Hospital as having a gunshot wound, apparently in the head, and d. 7/28/63. Note: another Elliott of the same or similar name reported absent as POW, Mar.–Apr./64. Reported WIA 9/14/63 and sent to a Richmond hospital. D. 10/4/63. (CSR 270:1, 4; SHSP 27: 248)

Elliott, John H.: From Halifax Co. At age 21, enl. 5/62 as PVT, Co. B. Absent on detached service according to company muster rolls of Nov.–Dec./62. Absent sick beginning 2/18/63. Admitted to a Charlottesville G.H. with diptheria; returned to duty 3/19/63. Admitted to a Staunton hospital, 3/20/63. Beginning 9/63, detailed for hospital guard at Lynchburg. Admitted to a Richmond G.H., 12/5/63. Present, Sept.–Oct./62, 4/1/62, 4/30–12/64. Absent on detached service as a courier for a court martial, Mar.–Apr./64. Admitted to a Charlotte G.H. with syphilis, 4/28/65. Prl there, 5/65. (CSR 270:4)

Elliott, Mack G.: From Halifax Co. At age 18, enl 6/61 as PVT, Co. B. Reported present on company muster rolls of 11/61–4/62, Sept.–Dec./62. Also reported captured, 11/5/62. Reported present on company muster rolls of Jan.–Apr./63. Absent on detached service to NC to buy a horse, beginning 8/27/63. Reported present on rolls of 6/30–10/31/63, Mar.–Aug./31/64. Absent on forage detail, Sept.–Oct./64, then present, Nov.–Dec./64. (CSR 270:4; Zeb. Vance Papers, NCSA [courtesy Whit Joyner])

Elliott, Robert: On a list of persons who have taken the oath at Raleigh, NC, dated 5/24/65. Co. B. Resident of Granville Co. (CSR 270:4)

Ellis, Benjamin P.: Enl. 6/20/61, at age 24, as 1CPL, Co. H. Prm 2LT, Co. K, 10/1/61. Reported present on company muster rolls of 11/61–2/62. According to 2/62 regimental return, absent sick beginning 2/10/62. Died of typhoid fever, 2/25/62 or 3/4/62, at home. (CSR 270:1, 4)

Ellis, Leonard: PVT, Co. D. WIA 8/15 or 8/16/64 along Charles City Rd., near Richmond. (Richmond *Sentinel*, 8/26/64)

Ellis, William: Enl. 10/9/63 as PVT, Co. D. Reported present on company muster rolls of Nov.–Dec./64. (CSR 270:4)

Elrod, William: CPL, Co. A. Captured at Plymouth, 12/9/64. Listed on a Point Lookout, MD POW roll. Released 6/26/65. (CSR 270:4)

Emmett, Nugent T.: At age 25, enl. 1/16/62 as PVT, Co. H. Reported as deserting, 1/28/62. From Lenoir Co. (CSR 270:4)

Ensley, E.L.: At age 23, enl. 7/61 as PVT, Co. G. Reported present on company muster rolls of Jan.–Feb./62, May–June/62, 9/62–4/63. Absent on detached service to buy a horse, July–Aug./63. Reported absent at home sick on company muster rolls of Sept.–Oct./63. Reported AWOL beginning 9/25/64; deserted. From Henderson Co. (CSR 270:4)

Ensley, Joseph A.: At age 21, enl. as PVT, Co. G, 7/61. Reported present on muster rolls of May–June/62, Sept.–Oct./62. Absent on detached service, Nov.–Dec./62. Present, Jan.–Apr./63. Absent on detached service with unserviceable horses in Nelson Co., VA, July–Aug./63. Present, Sept.–Oct./63. Absent in NC to procure a horse, Nov.–Dec./63. Reported present on company muster rolls of Mar.–Dec./64. (CSR 270:4)

Erwin, Charles Harris: B. 3/6/22. Joined Rocky River Presbyterian Church, 9/8/53. Enl. 10/16/64 as PVT, Co. F. Married Virginia Johnson, 1/5/70. D. 10/29/85. Bur. Rocky River Presbyterian

Church Cem., near Concord. (Barringer; DavisUDC; Janet Morrison to author, 9/19/98)

Eskridge, Newton: PVT, Co. K. Reported present on company muster rolls of Nov.–Dec./64. (CSR 270:4)

Eskridge, Samuel: B. 2/14/44. Enl. 5/1/64 or 10/3/64 as PVT, Co. I. WIA, 10/27/64, Boydton Plank Road, and sent to a Weldon, NC hospital. Later sent home on frl. D. 12/14/04. Bur. Zion Baptist Church Cem., Cleveland Co. (CSR 270:4; Stepp; CGR: 4)

Estes, Amos: From Watauga Co. At age 19, enl. 8/19/63 as PVT, Co. D. Reported present on company muster rolls of 6/30/63–3/31/64. Absent at home to buy a horse, Mar.–Apr./64. Reported admitted to a Richmond hospital, 8/19/64. D. of disease, 8/31/64. (CSR 270:4; Davis)

Estes, Lenard N.: From Watauga Co. PVT, Co. D. Enl. 5/11/61. Age 22. Admitted to a Richmond hospital, 12/10/61, and trn to Petersburg. Reported present on company muster rolls of 11/61–2/62, May–Dec./62. Absent on detached service, Jan.–Feb./63. Absent at home to buy a horse, Mar.–Apr./63, July–Aug./63. Present, 6/30/63–3/31/64. Absent at home to buy a horse, according to Mar.–Apr./64 roll. WIA. Admitted to a Richmond hospital, 8/64, with a shell wound in the right shoulder. Sent home on frl, week of 8/27/64. Present, Nov.–Dec./64. Psb from Hickory, NC. (CSR 270:4; Davis)

Estes, Reuben: Enl. 5/1/64 as PVT, Co. D. Absent sick in a hospital, according to company muster roll of 8/31/64. Absent at home sick, Sept.–Oct./64. Present, Nov.–Dec./64. (CSR 270:4; Davis)

Eure, Dempsey: From Northampton Co. B. August 1811. Enl. 1st or 2d qtr. 1862 at age 37, as PVT, Co. B. Reported present on company muster rolls of Sept.–Dec./62. Absent sick beginning 2/16/62. Reported present Mar.–Apr./63, 6/30–12/63, Mar.–Apr./64. Absent assigned to light duty in Salem, VA according to muster rolls of 4/30–8/31/64, Sept.–Oct./64. Also listed on the returns of the Salem post for 10/64, 11/64, 1/65, and 2/65. Reported absent sick, 11/12/64. Prl Farmville, VA, 5/23/65. D. May 1906. Bur. Oakwood Cem., Raleigh. (CSR 270:4; Stepp)

Evans, Robert: From Guilford Co. Cns. 7/15/62 as PVT, Co. A, at age 29. Captured at Gettysburg, 7/3/63. D. 8/30/64 at Point Lookout. (CSR 270:4)

Everett, James H.: From Washington Co. At age 21, enl. 8/2/61 as PVT, Co. B. Reported present on company muster rolls of Nov.–Dec./61. Captured, 2/22/62, according to regimental returns and muster rolls. Reported present on company muster rolls of Jan.–Apr./63, July–Dec./63, Mar.–Oct./64. (CSR 270:4)

Evin, C.: PVT, Co. F. Enl 10/16/64. Reported present on company muster rolls through 12/64. (CSR 270:4)

Exum, Wyatt P.: B. 1/24/34. From Wayne Co. At age 25, enl. 6/25/61 in Co H. 3CPL. On a receipt roll for pay, 11/28/61. Dsh for disability. Cns. 9/9/64 as PVT, Co. H. Reported present on company muster rolls of Nov.–Dec./64. D. 8/7/11. Bur Willowdale Cem., Goldsboro. (CSR 270:4; CGR: 3; Stepp)

Faggert, Elias F.: B. 4/17/33. From Cabarrus Co. At age 28, enl. 6/15/61 as PVT, Co. F. According to company muster rolls, absent on sick frl beginning 12/15/61. Reported present May–June/62, Sept.–Oct./62 (during which time he was listed as being sick), Nov.–Dec./62. WIA at Brandy Station, 8/1/63 or 10/63. Sent to a Richmond hospital, then given sick frl. Present 9/63–10/64. On frl of indulgence, 12/64. Resident of Concord, circa 1893. D. 3/24/12. Bur. Mt. Herman Lutheran Church Cem., Cabarrus Co. (CSR 270:4; Barringer; Cabarrus spells it Faggart; Lore: 115 spells it Faggart)

Faggert, George Ephraim: B. 2/3/31, Cabarrus Co. Farmer. Unmarried; father deceased. At age 29, enl. 6/15/61 as PVT, Co. F. Reported present on company muster rolls of 11/61–2/62. Listed in a Richmond hospital as of 3/17/62. On a sick and wounded report from a Richmond hospital as d. 5/15/62 from chronic diarrhea and/or typhoid fever. Stood 5'9", had a florid complexion, hazel eyes, and dark hair. Bur. St. John's Church Cem., Richmond, VA. (CSR 270:4; Barringer; Mizelle; Cabarrus spells it Faggart; Graves spells it Faggart)

Faggert, Timothy: B. Cabarrus Co. Farmer. At age 39, enl. 6/15/61 as PVT, Co. F. Reported present on company muster rolls of 11/61–2/62, May–June/62. On extra duty with the QM dept, and as a teamster, according to regimental returns of 2/62 and 3/62. Absent at Winchester with the wagon train, Sept.–Oct./62. Present Nov.–Dec./62. Dsh 1/16/63 due to leg difficulties. Stood 5'8" tall, had a florid complexion, blue eyes, sandy hair. "A very faithful soldier," wrote Rufus Barringer. Dead as of 1893. (CSR 270:4; Mizelle; Barringer; Cabarrus spells it Faggart)

Faison, Julian P.: From Duplin Co. At age 36, enl. 7/4/61 as PVT, Co. I. Trn 10/1/61. Also, listed on a receipt roll for pay of 11/28/61 as having been dsh. (CSR 270:4)

Falkner, Joseph B.: From Warren Co. At age 22, enl. 6/20/61 as PVT, Co. E. Reported present on company muster rolls of Jan.–Feb./62, May–June/62, 9/62–4/63, 6/30/63–4/64. Also listed on 3/62 regimental return as being absent sick at Petersburg as of 3/16/62. Absent on detached service at Stony Creek, 4/30–8/31/64, then present Sept.–Dec./64. (CSR 270:4)

Falkner, Sidney: From Franklin Co. At age 25, enl. 7/8/62 as PVT, Co. E. Reported present on company muster rolls of Sept.–Oct./64. Captured at Barbee's Crossroads, 11/5/62. Prl 11/9/62; exd 11/18/62. Present Mar.–Apr./63. Absent on detached service in NC after a horse, beginning 8/27/63. Reported present on company muster rolls of 11/63–12/64. (CSR 270:4; Pearce: 245 spells it Faulkner)

Farder, J.: PVT. Age 25. Amputated right leg at thigh, 6/20/64; amputated left leg, 9/1/64, both due to shot injuries. D. 9/2/64. (*Medical History* 11: 54.)

Farmer, James B.: From Northampton Co. At age 25, enl. 6/15/61 as CPL, Co. B. According to company muster rolls, absent on detached service in charge of horses, Nov.–Dec./61. Present, Jan.–Apr./62, Sept.–Oct./62. Absent on detached service, Nov.–Dec./62. Reported absent sick beginning 2/1/63, according to Jan.–Feb./63 muster roll. Present Mar.–Apr./63. Absent on detached service to NC after a horse, 8/27/63. Present, 6/30–10/31/63. Absent on Provost Guard duty, Nov.–Dec./63. On detached service, Jan.–Feb./64. Listed as absent on horse detail, Mar.–Apr./64, then as on detached service at Milford, 4/1/64. Reported present, 4/30–10/64. Listed as AWOL on Nov.–Dec./64 muster roll. Deserted. (CSR 270:4; Zeb. Vance Papers, NCSA [courtesy Whit Joyner])

Farmer, William: PVT, Co. H. Enl. 6/20/61, at age 25. Dsh for disability. From Greene Co. (CSR 270:4)

Farmer, William H.: From Northampton Co. At age 27, enl. 6/12/61 as PVT, Co. B. Reported present on company muster rolls of Nov.–Dec./61. Absent on sick leave, Jan.–Feb./62. Present, Mar.–Apr./62, Sept.–Oct./62. Absent on detached service, Nov.–Dec./62. According to company muster roll of Jan.–Feb./62, was left 2/10/62 at Stevensburg to work in a hospital. Also listed on regimental return of 2/62 and 3/62 as being absent sick. Reported present Mar.–Apr./63, 6/30–Dec./63, Mar.–Apr./63. Prm SGT, 9/1/63. Absent at the infirmary camp in Lynchburg, 4/30–12/64. Listed on a 2/17/65 report of soldiers on detached service under the AQM in Lynchburg: "In charge of horses of his command. Is indispensable to identify the horses." (CSR 270:4)

Farthing, Thomas B.: B. 2/23/33. From Watauga Co. At age 28, enl. 8/13/61 as PVT, Co. D. Reported present on company muster rolls of 11/61–2/62, 5/62–12/62. Absent at home to buy a horse, Jan.–Feb./63. Reported present, Jan.–Apr./63, 6/30/63–4/64. WIA. Admitted to a Petersburg hospital, 7/14/64, then frl 7/22/64. Absent and at home, 8/31–10/64, then present Nov.–Dec./64. Retired to Invalid Corps, 1/65. Assigned to duty as a nurse at a Richmond hospital 2/65. D. 2/2/86. Bur. Farthing Family Cem., Watauga Co. (CSR 270:4; Davis; Stepp; CSR 270: 4 for George N. Folk)

Farthing, William W.: At age 26, enl 5/11/61 as PVT, Co. D. Reported present on company muster rolls of 11/61–2/62, 5/62–10/31/62. Admitted to a Richmond hospital, 3/7/62, with a gunshot wound. Absent on detached service to procure clothing for the Co., Nov.–Dec./62. Absent to purchase a horse, Jan.–Feb./63. Present Mar.–Apr./63. KIA 6/9/63, Brandy Station. (CSR 270:4; Davis)

Faucett, John S.: PVT, Co. H. Enl 7/11/64. Reported present on company muster rolls of 4/30–10/64. Absent on detached service on horse detail, Nov.–Dec./64. Prl Greensboro, 5/9/65. (CSR 270:4)

Faulkner, Edward T.: From Warren Co. Age 21. PVT, Co. E. Enl. 6/20/61. Reported present on company muster rolls of Jan.–Feb./62, May–June/62, 9/62–4/63, July–Aug./63. Reported in a Richmond hospital with diarrhea, 3/1/62. Trn to and treated in an Amelia C.H. hospital. Released for duty, 5/12/62. Captured at Jack's Shop, 9/22/63. Held at Point Lookout and later at Elmira. Prl and exd, 10/64. Prl Raleigh, 5/25/65. (CSR 270:4)

Felmeth, John M.: From Buncombe Co. At age 43, enl 5/20/61 as CPL, Co. G. Reported present on company muster rolls of Jan.–Feb./62, May–June/62, Sept.–Dec./62. Absent on detached service in 2/62 according to that month's regimental return. Absent on detached service, Jan.–Feb./63. Present Mar.–Apr./63, then absent to buy a horse according to July–Aug./63 rolls. Reported present Sept.–Dec./63, Mar.–Aug./64. Also reported absent in a Richmond hospital, psb. Feb.–Apr./64. Absent on detached service to procure a fresh horse, Sept.–Oct./64. Present, Nov.–Dec./64. (CSR 270:4)

Fenart, James P.: From Duplin Co. At age 32, enl. 7/16/61 as PVT, Co. I. Reported present on company muster rolls of 11/61–2/62, May–June/62,

9/62–4/63. Absent on detached service driving cattle, psb. at corps HQ, beginning 7/63. Still working in that capacity as of 12/64. Admitted to the hospital, 8/25/64. (CSR 270:4)

Ferguson, Bennett D.: From Watauga Co. At age 24, enl. 5/11/61 as PVT, Co. D. Reported present on company muster rolls of 11/61–2/62. Absent sick in a Wilson hospital, beginning 5/28/62. Present, 6/30/62–2/63. "In poor fix for fighting" after drinking whiskey, 9/8/62. Reported under arrest by civil authorities on rolls of Mar.–Apr./63, 6/30–10/31/63. Reported present, Nov.–Dec./63. Absent in the hospital according to rolls of 1/64–3/31/64. Present, Mar.–Apr./64, 8/31–Oct./64. Trn to Co. C, 26th NC, 11/16/64. Bur. Beaver Creek Advent Cem., Wilkes Co. (CSR 270:4; Davis; McNeil)

Ferguson, John D.: From Watauga Co. At age 18, enl. 5/11/61 as PVT, Co. D. Reported present on company muster rolls of Nov.–Dec./61. Absent sick according to regimental returns of 2/62 and 3/62, as well as muster rolls of Jan.–Feb./62. Present, May–Dec./62. Absent on frl, Jan.–Feb./63, then reported present Mar.–Apr./63, 6/30–12/63, 2/29–4/64. Elected 2LT, 6/16/63. WIA with gunshot wound in thigh, 5/64. D. that month in a Richmond hospital. (CSR 270:1, 4; Davis)

Field, William B.: Resident of Charlotte. Enl at age 25 as ORD SGT, 5/27/61, in Co. C. Reported present on company muster rolls of 11/61–2/62. Elected 2LT, to rank from 4/30/62. Captured at Willis Church, 6/29/62. Held at Ft. Warren and also Ft. Columbus. On sick leave in NC, according to rolls, beginning 12/15/62. Again absent on sick leave beginning 6/21/63. Reported admitted to a Richmond G.H., 5/64. Also mentioned in special orders/records in connection with leaves, 8/10/63, 2/6/64, and 7/28/64. 30-Day frl awarded on 8/14/63. Admitted to a Richmond hospital, 1/1/64. Granted a 30-day frl, 1/14/64, due to an "irritable bladder and kidneys." Prm to Sr. 2LT, 8/16/64. Reported present, Sept.–Oct./64. On the register of a Charlotte hospital, 11/14/64. Resigned 11/64. Stood 5'11", had sandy hair, gray eyes, and a florid complexion. (CSR 270:4, 1; Alexander)

Fields, James H.: From Greene Co. PVT, Co. H. At age 22, enl. 7/3/61. Reported present on company muster rolls of 11/61–Feb./62, May–June/62, Sept.–Oct./62. Captured at Barbee's Crossroads, 11/5/62, then prl 11/9/62. Reported absent in NC to buy a horse, Jan.–Feb./63. Present, Mar.–Apr./63. Prm to 2LT, Kinston Provost Guard. Stood about 5'7", had a fair complexion and light hair. Occupation: farmer. (CSR 270:4)

Fields, William: Resident of Alleghany Co. Trn from state service. Enl. 9/29/64 as PVT, Co. G. Reported present on muster rolls of Sept.–Dec./64. Deserted at Bellfield Station, 1/21/65. Swore oath of allegiance, 4/65, and sent north of the Ohio River. Had a fair complexion, dark hair, gray eyes, and stood 6' tall. (CSR 270:4)

Finley, M.R.: From Union Co. At age 21, enl. 5/25/61 as PVT, Co. C. Reported present on company muster rolls of 11/61–2/62, 5/62–4/63, July–Aug./63. Listed in a Richmond and then a Danville hospital, 7/63, and returned to duty 8/18/63. Reported on detached service beginning 10/15/63. Present on rolls of 11/63–2/64. Absent on detached service beginning 3/20/64. Present according to Mar.–Apr./64 rolls. WIA, 8/21/64. Present, Nov.–Dec./64. Retired to Invalid Corps, 1/25/65, and assigned to duty in Richmond. Admitted to a hospital there, 2/9/65. (CSR 270:4; Alexander)

Fisher, Charles H.: B. 5/2/41. Resident of Salisbury. At age 20, enl. 6/15/61 as PVT, Co. F. Reported present on company muster rolls of 11/61–2/62, May–June/62, Sept.–Dec./62, July–Dec./63. Absent at home on frl, 2/64. Also present 2/29–3/31/64. WIA in the left leg near Brandy Station, 8/1/63, and/or White's Tavern/Riddle's Shop, 8/15/64, along Charles City Rd., near Richmond. Admitted to a Richmond hospital. Later frl. Prl Salisbury, 5/65 or 6/65. Resident of Mt. Pleasant, NC, circa 1893. D. 9/14/16. Bur. Mt. Pleasant Lutheran Church Cem., Mt. Pleasant, NC. (CSR 270:4; Barringer; Mizelle; Rumple: 342; Richmond *Sentinel*, 8/26/64; Graves)

Fisher, F.C.: PVT, Co. F. Prl Salisbury, 5/13/65. (CSR 270:4)

Fisher, Jacob Allison: From Cabarrus Co., age 35. 1LT, to rank from 5/16/61. Absent on detached service beginning 1/17/62. Duty: according to 2/62 regimental return, to procure teamsters for regt. service. Reported present on regimental return of 3/62. Also on detached service beginning 4/2/62. Reported present on company muster rolls, Sept.–Dec./62. WIA at Brandy Station, 8/1/63. Thigh gunshot wound. Admitted to a Richmond hospital, 8/2/63, and frl 8/5/63. Prm CPT, 8/26/63. Frl extended into 2/64. On detached service in command of the dead line, 3/12/64. Retired to Invalid Corps, 8/64. Assigned to duty in Greenville, NC. A resident of China Grove, circa 1893. Called CPT by descendents. (CSR 270:1, 4; Mizelle; Barringer; Cabarrus; DavisUDC)

Fisher, Thomas M.: From Cabarrus Co. Enl. 6/15/61 as PVT, Co. F. Reported present on company muster rolls of 11/61–2/62, May–June/62, Sept.–Dec./62. Absent sent to NC to procure a horse, July–Aug./63. Reported present, Sept.–Dec./63. Absent sent to the dead line, 11/15/63. Present Mar.–Aug./64, although listed in a Richmond hospital, admitted 8/15/64. Absent detached to NC after a horse, 10/19/64. Present Nov.–Dec./64. Prl Charlotte, 5/6/65. D. 3/7/82 at age 44. Bur. St. John's Lutheran Church Cem., Cabarrus Co. (CSR 270:4; Mizelle; Barringer; Cabarrus; Graves)

Fisher, William Henry: B. 2/12/47. From Cabarrus Co. Enl. 6/15/61 as PVT, Co. F. WIA. Reported present on company muster rolls of 11/61–2/62, May–June/62. Accidentally wounded mess mate PVT Henry S. Dellinger, 11/61, while on picket duty. Absent in a Lynchburg hospital, 9/10/62. Reported present, Nov.–Dec./62. Absent in NC to procure a horse, 8/27/63. Present, 9/63–12/64. Prm 2 Bugler, 12/25/63. Resident of Arkansas, circa 1893. Later reported living in Tailor, Mississippi, in 1929. D. 11/21/18. (CSR 270:4; Barringer; Mizelle; Cabarrus; Lore: 133 says William Henry, and so does DavisUDC; Concord Register, June 8, 1883)

Fitzgerald, James: PVT, Co. I. Enl. 6/27/61. Deserted. From Duplin Co., age 35. (CSR 270:4)

Fitzgerald, William H.H.: Resident of Concord. Enl. 6/15/61 in Co. F as 1CPL. Prm 1SGT, 10/13/61. Reported present on company muster rolls of 11/61–2/62, May–June/62, Sept.–Dec./62, 7/63–3/64. Elected 2LT, 11/14/63. WIA, gunshot wound in the foot. Reported in the hospital, 8/29/64, and into '65. Prm Sr. 2LT, 8/3/64. Resigned, 1/24/65, due to effects of wound. Resident of Monroe, NC, circa 1893. (CSR 270:1, 4; Mizelle; Barringer; Cabarrus)

Fleming, J.S.: Trn from state service. Enl. 9/21/64 as PVT, Co. G. Reported present on company muster rolls of Sept.–Oct./64. Absent on horse detail, Nov.–Dec./64. Prl at Morganton, NC, 5/13/65. (CSR 270:4)

Fletcher, William F.: From Caldwell Co. At age 40, enl. 7/10/61 as saddler, Co. D. Reported present on company muster rolls of 11/61–2/62, 5/62–2/63. Absent sick at home, Mar.–Apr./63. Present on rolls of 6/30/63–3/31/64. Absent at home to buy a horse, Mar.–Apr./64, then present 8/31–12/64. (CSR 270:4; Davis)

Flow, E.A.: Enl. 8/18/64 as PVT, Co. C. Reported present, Sept.–Dec./64. Prl Charlotte, 5/24/65. (CSR 270:4; Alexander)

Flow, J.M.W.: Enl. 8/18/64 as PVT, Co. C. Reported present, Nov.–Dec./64. WIA. Prl Charlotte, 5/24/65. (CSR 270:4; Alexander)

Flowers, Furney F.: Resident of Wayne Co. At age 19, enl. 6/20/61 as PVT, Co. H. Reported present on company muster rolls of Nov.–Dec./61. Absent at home on sick frl, 2/3/62. Also listed as absent sick on regimental returns of 2/62 and 3/62. Present, May–June/62. Absent on detached service as a shoemaker, Sept.–Oct./62. Reported present on rolls of 11/62–4/63. Absent on detached service to NC to buy a horse, according to July–Aug./63 roll. Present 9/63–12/64. Apptd. 4CPL, 12/1/64. Captured at Ameila CH, 4/3/65. Released from Point Lookout on taking the oath, 6/26/65. Stood 5'10", had a fair complexion, black hair, and hazel eyes. Bur in family cemetery, Brogden Township, about 1 mile NE of Mt Olive, NC. (CSR 270:4; CGR: 3)

Flowers, John J.: B. 1814. From Wayne Co. Occupation: farmer, psb. carpenter as well. Reportedly in bad health before the war. PVT, Co. H. Enl. 5/16/62. Captured at Willis Church, 6/29/62. Exd 8/5/62. Absent on detached service at Winchester, Sept.–Oct./62. Absent in the hospital, according to rolls of 11/62–2/63. Hospital records show admitted 11/17/62 to a Richmond G.H., and trn to a Danville G.H. 12/8/62. Also reported absent sick on muster rolls of Mar.–Apr./63. Frl from a Danville hospital, 5/29/63. Stood 5'11", had black hair, hazel eyes, and a fair complexion. D. 1885. Bur. Bellevue Cem., Wilmington. (CSR 270:4; GLP; Stepp; CGR: 6)

Flowers, William: PVT, Co. C. Resident of Wayne Co. Appears on a POW roll as prl at Goldsboro. NFR. (CSR 270:4)

Flowers, William H.: From Wayne Co. At age 25, enl. 6/20/61 as PVT, Co. H. Reported present on company muster rolls of Nov.–Dec./61. Absent in a Richmond hospital as of 1/10/62, with a fever. Still absent sick according to regimental returns of 2/62 and 3/62. Present on rolls of May–June/62, 9/62–4/63, July–Aug./63. Absent sick and sent to the hospital according to Sept.–Oct./63 rolls. Present, Jan.–Oct./64. Absent on forage detail, Nov.–Dec./64. (CSR 270:4)

Foard, Frederick C.: B. Cabarrus Co. At age 17, enl. Co. A, 20th Regiment NC Troops, 4/19/61. Present our accounted for until WIA in elbow, before Richmond, 7/5/62. Trn to 1st NC Cavalry as PVT, Co. F, 11/4/63. Reported present on company muster rolls of 11/63–3/31/64. Prm to ORD SGT 3/64 or 4/64, and then prm LT and ADC for GEN Barringer, 6/1/64. WIA, captured. Resident of Roanoke, VA, circa 1893. (CSR 270:4; Barringer; NC Troops: 6)

Foard, Noah Partee: Resident of Concord. At age 21, enl. 6/15/61 in Co. F as 2SGT. Prm to 2LT, to rank from 10/61. Reported present on company muster rolls of 11/61–2/62. Also listed present on regimental returns of 2/62 and 3/62. Absent on detached service beginning 6/22/62. Present Sept.–Dec./62, 7/63–10/64. Prm Sr 2LT, 8/62. Prm 1LT, 8/26/63. Absent sick according to Nov.–Dec./64 rolls. Commanded Co. F., beginning summer 1863. Prm CPT, 8/3/64. Trn from a Raleigh hospital and admitted to a Greensboro hospital, 2/25/65. Prl Charlotte, 5/3/65. Resident of Roanoke, VA, circa 1893. (CSR 270:1, 4; Mizelle; Barringer; Cabarrus; Hopkins)

Foard, Robert: Enl. 10/4/64 as PVT, Co. F. Reported present on company muster rolls of Nov.–Dec./64. Dead as of 1893. (CSR 270:4; Barringer; Cabarrus)

Folk, George Nathaniel: Native of VA; resident of Boone. A "brilliant" lawyer who served in the NC legislature, 1856 and 1860. Resigned to organize Co. D in Boone, 5/11/61, and became CPT, to rank from 5/16/61. According to company muster rolls of Jan.–Feb./62, absent in Watauga Co. on recruiting service. Attempted to resign in 1861 but resignation revoked, probably on 12/27/61. Present according to regimental returns of 2/62 and 3/62. A letter of resignation dated 4/28/62 also present in his file. Resigned again 5/9/62 according to a roster of 8/64; accepted 5/12/62, according to rolls of May–June/62. Enl. in 7th Bn. North Carolina Cavalry as LTC and commander, 9/12/62, then became COL when that unit became part of the 6th NC Cavalry. Captured at Kinston, NC, 6/22/64; exd. 12/15/64. Prl. Salisbury, 5/26/65. Post-war, moved to Caldwell Co. and worked as a lawyer. (Davis; CSR 270:1, 4; 6th NC: 1, 56, 79, 151)

Ford, H.H.: PVT, Co. C. Reported present on company muster rolls of Nov.–Dec./64. Psb enl 8/8/64. (CSR 270: 4; Alexander)

Fore, J.C.: From Buncombe Co. Enl 5/20/61 as PVT, Co. G. Reported present on company muster rolls of Jan.–Feb./62, May–June/62, 9/62–4/63. Listed absent on regimental return of 3/62; sick in Richmond. According to a hospital report, was suffering from diarrhea, having been admitted 3/2/62, and trn to Amelia CH 4/11/62. Also admitted to Richmond hospitals 9/30/62 and 10/4/62, and returned to duty 10/10/62. Absent on detached service with unserviceable horses in Nelson Co., VA, July–Dec./63. Present according to muster rolls of Mar.–Dec./64.. Psb. died from pneumonia in a Weldon hospital, 11/15/64 or 2/12/65. (CSR 270:4)

Forrester, John S.: Co. A. Age 25, from Ashe Co. Appointed 2LT to rank from 10/4/61. According to company muster rolls and regimental returns, absent at home on sick frl beginning 10/12/61. Prm 1LT 3/1/62. Resigned 5/12/62. (CSR 270:1, 4)

Foster, Jackson: PVT. Enl. 3/12/62, Co. G. Reported present on company muster rolls of May–June/62. Absent on detached service at Winchester, Sept.–Oct./62. Present on company muster rolls of 11/62–2/63. According to muster rolls of Mar.–Apr./63, trn to Co. I 4/14/63. Reported present, Mar.–Apr./63, 10/31/63. Absent on detached service in Amherst Co., VA, Jan.–Feb./64. Reported present, 1/1/64, Mar.–Aug./31/64. Absent to procure a fresh horse, Sept.–Oct./64. Trn to 20th Regt. NC Troops, 11/16/64, by order dated 10/13/64, because of "taking possession and appropriating to" his own use "the private property of citizens...." (CSR 270:4)

Foster, O.H.: Resigned as 1 LT, Co. E. (Promotion Notice, Box 46, Folder 15, Military Collection, Civil War Collection, NCSA.)

Foster, R.S.: B. Wake Co. Farmer. Enl. 1/64 as PVT, Co. E. Reported present on company muster rolls of 4/30–12/64. Age 18. Stood 6' tall, had gray eyes, light hair, and a fair complexion. (CSR 270:4)

Foster, W.E.: Enl. 2/27/64 as PVT, Co E. Reported present on company muster rolls of Mar.–Apr./1/64. Absent at home on sick frl, 4/30–Oct./64, then reported present on Nov.–Dec./64. (CSR 270:4)

Foulks, John J.: B. Prince Edward Co., VA. From Wayne Co. By occupation a carpenter. PVT, Co. H. At age 45, enl. 6/20/61. Reported in a Richmond hospital as admitted 12/11/61, and trn to Petersburg 12/13/61. Dsh 4/15/62 due to chronic illnesses. Stood 6' had fair complexion, gray eyes, and dark hair. (CSR 270:4)

Franklin, John M.: B. in TN. From Caldwell Co. At age 28, enl. 2/28/62 as PVT, Co. D. Captured at Willis Church, 6/29/62; sent to forts Columbus and Delaware. Exd. 8/5/62. Reported present on company muster rolls of 6/30/62–4/63. Absent on detached service with unserviceable horses, July–Aug./63. Present on 6/30/63–4/64, 8/31–12/64 rolls. Stood 5'10", had light hair, blue eyes, and a fair complexion. (CSR 270:4; Davis)

Frazier, E.R.: Enl. 10/26/63 as PVT, Co. B. Absent sick on 4/30–10/64 rolls. Listed on medical records as admitted to a Petersburg hospital, 7/7/64, and trn to Raleigh 8/11/64. Absent on horse detail according to Nov.–Dec./64 company muster rolls. (CSR 270:4)

Frazier, John D.: From Cabarrus Co. At age 39,

enl. 6/15/61 as 2SGT, Co. F. Reported present on company muster rolls of 11/61–2/62, May–June/62. Absent at Winchester on detached service, Sept.–Oct./62. Present on Nov.–Dec./62, July–Oct./63 rolls. Trn 11/1/63 to CPT H.T. Douglass's Co., 1st Engineer Rgt., Army of Northern Virginia. (Dead as of 1893. CSR 270:4; Barringer; Mizelle; Cabarrus)

Frazier, John McLeod, Jr.: B. 8/5/45. From Watauga Co. At age 18, enl. 5/11/61 as PVT, Co. D. Reported present on company muster rolls of 11/61–2/62, 5/62–10/31/62. Deserted, 11/1/62 at Williamsport, MD. Prl 11/14/62 and requested that he not be exd. D. 5/16/20. Bur. Mariah's Chapel Methodist Cem., Caldwell Co. (CSR 270:4; Davis; Stepp)

Frazier, John McLeod, Sr.: From Watauga Co. At age 44, enl. 2/28/62 as PVT, Co. D. Blacksmith. Present on 5/62–4/63, July–Aug./63 company muster rolls. Absent sick at home on 6/30–10/31/63 rolls. Present according to 11/63–4/64, 8/31/64–12/64 rolls. Bur. Bellevue Cem., Lenoir. (CSR 270:4; Davis; Stepp)

Friend, Valentine: From Duplin Co. At age 27, enl. 6/20/61 as PVT, Co. I. Reported present on 11/61–2/62, May–June/62, Sept.–Oct./62 rolls. Absent on detached service, Nov.–Dec./62. Present, Jan.–Apr./63, 10/31/63, 1/1–Dec./64. Prl Goldsboro, 5/59/65. (CSR 270:4)

Frieze, J.: PVT, Co. F. Enl. 12/4/64, and reported present on company muster rolls of Nov.–Dec./64. (CSR 270:4; Barringer)

Frieze, John: Resident of Cabarrus Co. At age 23, enl. 6/15/61 as PVT, Co. F. Present on Nov.–Dec./61 rolls. Detached from company as musician (bugler), 2/1/62. According to field and staff muster rolls, present Jan.–Apr./62, May–June/62, Sept.–Dec./62. Absent to procure a horse beginning 8/27/63, then present on 9/63–10/64 rolls. Detailed to purchase a horse, 12/5/64. Captured at Dinwiddie C.H., 4/3/65, and released from Point Lookout on taking the oath, 6/26/65. Had a dark complexion, black hair, and blue eyes; stood 5' 9" tall. Resident of Concord, circa 1893. D. 6/16/06 at age 69. Bur. Oakwood Cem., Cabarrus Co. (CSR 270:4; Mizelle; Barringer; Cabarrus; Graves)

Fulford, W.J.: From Granville Co. Farmer. At age 24, enl. 6/8/61 as 3SGT in Co. E. Left at Camp Beauregard sick, 10/13/61, "indefinitely." Dsh 5/27/62 due to pulmonary disease. Stood 6' 2" tall, had a fair complexion, blue eyes, light hair. (CSR 270:4)

Fulghum, Richard Thomas: Enl. 6/28/61 in Co. H at age 19. Appointed SGT MAJ and trn to field and staff, 10/1/61. Reported present on field and staff muster rolls of 11/61–4/62, May–June/62, Sept.–Dec./62. Granted leave of absence, 2/63. Present according to Mar.–Apr./63, July–Aug./63 rolls. Is said to have saved GEN Wade Hampton from capture at Gettysburg. Prm to ADC for GEN Laurence Baker; serving with Baker in 2d District, Dept. of NC and S. Va. From Wayne Co. D. 1885. Bur. Willowdale Cem., Goldsboro. (CSR 270:4; Notes to Elizabeth Collier Diary, #1335-z, SHC; James T. Pugh Papers, #1590, SHC, UNC)

Fuller, James B.: From Franklin Co. At age 22, enl. 6/8/61 as PVT, Co. E. Reported present on company muster rolls of Jan.–Feb./62, May–June/62, 9/62–4/63. Admitted to a Charlottesville hospital, 5/8/63, and trn to Lynchburg, 5/10/63. Reported absent at home sick, beginning 6/29/63. According to rolls beginning 1/64, at a Raleigh hospital. Present on Mar.–Apr./64 rolls. Admitted to a Richmond hospital, 5/5/64. Admitted to a Farmville hospital, 6/3/64, and later trn to Kittrell Springs. Reported in a Lynchburg hospital, 4/30–8/31/64 rolls, then absent at home on sick frl, Sept.–Oct./64. Present, Nov.–Dec./64. Detailed to a Richmond hospital, 1/21/65, then in 2/65 relieved from duty there and directed to report to a Raleigh hospital for assignment. Prl Raleigh, 5/12/65. (CSR 270:4)

Fuller, Jerome H.: From Granville Co. At age 33, enl. 7/16/61 as 2SGT, Co. E. Prm 5SGT, 10/8/61. Reported present on Jan.–Feb./62, May–June/62, 9/62–4/63, 6/30/63–12/63, 4/1/64 rolls. Elected 2LT, 12/21/62. Prm 1LT, 9/28/63, to rank from 7/1/63. Absent on detached service in NC to buy a horse, Mar.–Apr./64. WIA in the thigh, 8/15 or 8/16/64 along Charles City Rd., near Richmond. Admitted to a Richmond hospital, 8/17/64, with a gunshot wound in the upper left thigh. Frl 9/64. Reported absent at home, in Kittrell Springs, Sept.–Dec./64. Still there as of 1/65. Mentioned in a leave record, 2/65. (CSR 270:1, 4 Richmond *Sentinel*, 8/26/64)

Fuller, Milton B.: B. Franklin Co. Farmer. PVT, Co. E. At age 18, enl. 2/27/64. Reported present on company muster rolls of Mar.–Apr./64. Admitted to a Richmond hospital, 5/27/64, and trn to Farmville, 6/2/64, with gonorrhea. Absent at the Kittrells Springs hospital, according to 4/30–Oct./64 rolls. Present, Nov.–Dec./64. Dsh, 1865. Stood 5' 6", had a fair complexion, dark eyes, and black hair. (CSR 270:4)

Fuller, R.M.: From Franklin Co. At age 22, enl.

4/16/63 as PVT, Co. E. Reported present on company muster rolls of Mar.–Apr./63. Absent on detached service to NC to buy a horse beginning 8/27/63. Also reported present on 6/30/63–2/64, 4/1/64 company muster rolls. Absent in NC on frl, Mar.–Apr./64. Present on 4/30–12/64 rolls. (CSR 270:4)

Fulton, J.W.: Cns 10/3/64 as PVT, Co. I. Reported present on company muster rolls of Sept.–Dec./64. (CSR 270:4)

Furr, John: From Cabarrus Co. At age 23, enl. 5/30/61 as PVT, Co. C. Admitted to a Richmond hospital 7/3/62 and a Farmville hospital 7/6/62; returned to duty, 7/29/62. Reported present on company muster rolls of 11/61–2/62, 5/62–2/63. D. 3/63 or 4/63 of disease. (CSR 270:4; Alexander)

Furr, Paul W.: From Cabarrus Co. At age 35, enl. 6/15/61 as PVT, Co. F. Reported present on 11/61–2/62, May–June/62, Sept.–Dec./62, July–Oct./63 rolls. Also listed on extra duty according to 3/62 return. WIA Jack's Shop, 11/21/63. Absent in a Charlottesville G.H. according to Nov.–Dec./63 rolls; admitted 12/2/63 and returned to duty 1/20/64, according to hospital records. Absent home on frl, beginning 2/64. Detached to a fishery, 3/20/64. Present, Mar.–Oct./64. Absent detailed to collect beeves, 12/64. Resident of Concord, circa 1893. (CSR 270:4; Mizelle; Barringer; Cabarrus)

Futrell, Anderson: Resident of Northampton Co. At age 42, enl. 6/61 as 3SGT, Co. B. Reported present on Nov.–Dec./61 rolls. Also present Jan.–Feb./62 but listed as sick in quarters. Present on Mar.–Apr./62, Sept.–Dec./62 rolls. Absent detached with the horses, beginning 1/20/63. Absent at home sick beginning 3/25/63. On detached service in NC after a horse beginning 8/27/63. Present on 6/30–12/63, 4/1/64 rolls. Absent on horse detail, Mar.–Apr./64, then present on 4/30–Dec./64 rolls. Captured near Amelia C.H., 4/3/65, and released from Point Lookout on taking the oath, 6/26/65. Had a dark complexion, grayish hair, hazel eyes, and stood 5' 9½". (CSR 270:4)

Futrell, Bryan B.: From Northampton Co. PVT, Co. B. At age 38, enl. 6/12/61. Present on Nov.–Dec./61 rolls. Admitted to a Danville hospital, 1/1/62, with rheumatism; trn to a Richmond G.H. Absent on sick leave beginning 2/7/62. Dsh 5/62 due to acute rheumatism, as well as pneumonia and an abscess. (CSR 270:4)

Futrell, Bryan G.: From Northampton Co. PVT, Co. B. Enl. 6/15/61 at age 33. Present on Nov.–Dec./61 rolls. Absent at home on sick leave beginning 2/18/62. Also absent sick according to 2/62 and 3/62 regimental returns. WIA in arm and captured near Boonsville and Middletown, MD, 9/62. On a POW roll dated 10/17/62 of prisoners sent to Ft. Monroe, VA for exchange. Prl, 10/62. Admitted 10/23/62 to a Richmond hospital. Arm amputated. Frl for 60 days, 11/62, but reported at home on rolls through 4/1/64. Admitted to a Richmond hospital, 5/6/64, and trn to another Richmond G.H., 5/8/64. (CSR 270:4)

Futrell, Jordan: From Northampton Co. Enl. 4/22/62 as PVT, Co. B. Age 18. Reported present on company muster rolls of 9/62–2/63, although captured 11/5/62 at Barbee's Crossroads and prl 11/9/62. Absent in a Staunton, VA G.H., Mar.–Apr./63. D. 4/9/63, at the Staunton G.H. Another report places a J.H. Futrell of Co. B in a Richmond G.H. as of 5/5/64. (CSR 270:4)

Futrell, Perry: From Northampton Co. Enl. 6/15/61 as PVT, Co. B. Reported present on company muster rolls of Nov.–Dec./61. Also listed on a sick and wounded report at Camp Ashe in 11/61. Dsh due to a hernia 2/3/62 at age 26. Stood 6' 3", had a fair complexion, blue eyes, dark hair. Also, a P.G. Futrell is listed as prl 10/3/62. (CSR 270:4)

Futrell, George: B. Northampton Co. At age 18, enl. 6/15/61 as PVT, Co. B. Reported present on Nov.–Dec./61 rolls. Absent at home on sick leave beginning 2/18/62. Sick absence confirmed by regt returns of 2/62 and 3/62. Dsh 5/3/62. Stood 5' 8½" tall, had dark hair, dark complexion, and hazel eyes. (CSR 270:4)

Futrell, James W.: B. Sussex Co., VA. Occupation: farmer. At age 26, enl. 7/7/61 as PVT, Co. B. Absent at home on sick leave according to Nov.–Dec./61 rolls. Also reported left sick at Camp Beauregard, 10/13/61, on Jan.–Feb./62 rolls. Returned to his company, 4/62, but soon sick again, according to certificate of disability. Reported present, sick in quarters, on Mar.–Apr./62 rolls. Listed as absent sick on 2/62 regimental return. Dsh, 5/5/62, due to "general debility and a weak constitution." Stood 5'11" tall, had a dark complexion, blue eyes, and light hair. (CSR 270:4)

Gadsesen, W.G.: PVT, Co. C. (Alexander)

Gaham, B.C.: PVT, Co. H. On a POW roll as prl 4/20/65. NFR. (CSR 270:5)

Gaines, James L.: From Buncombe Co. On 8/15/61, at age 21, enl. in Co. G. Appointed 2LT to rank from 8/20/61. Appointed Sr. 2LT, 4/62, and adj. (psb AAG), to rank from 10/1/61. According to regimental returns of 2/62 and 3/62, absent on recruiting service beginning 2/20/62. Reported present on field and staff muster rolls of Mar.–Apr./62, and on company and field and staff muster rolls of May–June/62. WIA at Willis Church, 6/29/62. Reported present on field and staff muster rolls of Sept.–Dec./62, Mar.–Apr./63. Also listed here as prm 1LT and adj. of regiment. Absent with leave according to July–Aug./63 rolls, although his horse was KIA at Brandy Station, 8/1/63. Field and staff muster rolls of 6/30–10/31/63 show him as prm CPT and adjutant general or AAG for GEN Laurence Baker's Brigade. Apparently remained with the regt. after Baker's 8/1/63 wound. Later prm LTC. Prl Appomattox C.H., 4/9/65. Also reported in a Farmville hospital between 4/7/65 and 6/15/65 (CSR 270:1, 4)

Galloway, J.C.: PVT, Co. G. Enl. 5/27/61 at age 38. D. 4/9/62 at Petersburg. From Stanly Co. (CSR 270: 4)

Gambill, Jesse A.: Enl. 11/10/63 as PVT in Co. A. Reported present on company muster rolls of Sept.–Dec./64. Reported in a Danville hospital with a gunshot wound in the right leg, 4/4/65. Frl for 40 days 4/8/65. Prl from a Salisbury hospital, 5/2/65. (CSR 270: 4)

Gambill, William J.: B. Ashe Co. Farmer. At age 34, enl. 6/8/61 as PVT, Co. A. When at home on frl, 9/11/61, suffered a broken left forearm while hauling wood. Listed absent at home sick on company muster rolls of 11/61–2/62. Also listed on an 11/61 sick and wounded report with a broken arm. Dsh for disability, 2/6/62, because his limb remained useless. Stood 5'10" tall, had a dark complexion, black eyes, black hair. (CSR 270: 4; AsheCo)

Gamble, J.R.: Enl. 9/21/64 as PVT, Co. K. Reported present on company muster rolls of Sept.–Dec./64. Bur. Cool Springs Cem., Forest City, Rutherford Co., NC. (CSR 270: 4; CGR: 4)

Gamble, Jacob L.: PVT, Co. K. Enl. 9/21/64. Reported present on company muster rolls of Sept.–Dec./64. (CSR 270: 4)

Gardner, A.C.: PVT. Co. A; Co. D. Reference envelope is only record. (CSR 270: 4)

Gardner, Shubal: From Guilford Co. At age 23, enl. 8/2/61 as PVT, Co. A. Reported present on 11/61–2/62, Sept.–Oct./62 rolls. Absent on scout beginning 12/25/62. Absent on frl to purchase a horse, Jan.–Feb./63. Present on Mar.–Apr./63 rolls. Horse KIA in battle at Hunterstown, PA. absent on detached service to purchase a horse, July–Aug./63 rolls. Listed as AWOL on Sept.–Oct./63 company muster rolls beginning 10/29/63. Present, 11/30/63–4/64. (CSR 270: 4; AsheCo)

Garland, J.M.: From Buncombe Co. At age 28, enl. 2/28/62 as PVT, Co. G. Reported present on May–June/62, 9/62–4/63 rolls. Reported in a Richmond hospital, admitted 7/8/62, and trn to Huguenot Springs, 7/26/62. Absent on detached service to purchase a horse, July–Aug./63. Present on Sept.–Dec./63 rolls, then listed absent on detached service, 4/1/64. Present on Mar.–Aug./64 rolls, then absent on detached service as a teamster with the brigade commissary department, Sept.–Dec./64. (CSR 270: 4)

Garrison, W.G.: PVT, Co. C. Enl. 8/18/64. Reported absent sick beginning 10/14/64. In Richmond G.H. with chronic diarrhea, 12/9/64, and returned to duty 1/13/65. Prl Charlotte, 5/12/65. (CSR 270: 4)

Garvey, Harvey: Co. D (Davis)

Garvey, James Harvey: From Watauga Co., a resident of Polin's Creek. Enl. 5/11/61 as PVT, Co. D. Reported present on company muster rolls of 11/61–2/62, May–Oct./62. Absent on detached service in Louisa Co., VA, Nov.–Dec./62. Present on Jan.–Apr./63 rolls. Absent sick in a Richmond hospital according to July–Aug./63 rolls, then present on rolls of 6/30/63–4/64. WIA, 8/15/64. Absent at a Richmond G.H. according to the 8/31/64 muster roll and hospital records. Present Sept.–Oct./64, then absent wounded an in a hospital, Nov.–Dec./64. Listed as admitted to a Richmond hospital, 10/26/64. (CSR 270: 4)

Garvey, John J.: From Ashe Co. At age 22, enl. 5/61 as PVT, Co. A. Reported present in company muster rolls of Nov.–Dec./61. Absent in a Manassas hospital according to Jan.–Feb./62 rolls. Regimental returns of 2/62 and 3/62 show him as absent sick. Absent sick in a Winchester hospital according to Sept.–Oct./62 rolls. Present on Nov.–Dec./62 rolls, then absent on frl to buy a horse beginning 2/27/63. Present on Mar.–Apr./63, July–Aug./63 rolls. WIA at Jack's Shop, 9/22/63, and sent home, according to Sept.–Oct./63 rolls. Admitted to a Richmond hospital, 9/24/63. Listed as AWOL in Mar.–Apr./64 rolls, then present July–Dec./64. On extra duty in commissary department due to a disability, Sept.–Dec./64. (CSR 270: 4; AsheCo)

Garvey, Thomas: PVT, Co. A. Enl. 11/1/63. Reported present on 11/30–12/31/63 rolls. Listed as deserted, 1/18/64, according to muster roll of 1/1–2/29/64. (CSR 270: 4)

Gash, M.M.: SGT, Co. D. Reference envelope only. (Psb the Martin M. Gash who was a member of the 6th NC Cavalry.) (CSR 270: 4)

Gaskins, Joseph: From Franklin Co. Substitute. At age 17, enl. 4/12/62 as PVT, Co. E. Absent sent to a Petersburg hospital, 5/13/62, according to May–June/62 muster rolls. Present on 9/62–4/63, 6/30/63–2/64 rolls. Admitted to a Charlottesville hospital, 5/8/63, and returned to duty 5/11/63. Absent on detached service in NC to buy a horse, according to Mar.–Apr./64 rolls. Reported present on company muster rolls of 4/30–12/64. (CSR 270: 4; Pearce: 247)

Gauldin, J.L.: Enl. 6/21/64 as PVT, Co. G. Reported present on Mar.–Dec./64 company muster rolls. Prl Greensboro, 5/9/65. (CSR 270: 4)

Gaylor, Haywood: From Duplin Co. At age 24, enl. 6/17/61 as PVT, Co. I. Present on Jan.–Feb./62, May–June/62, Sept.–Apr./63 rolls. Listed at times as a waggoneer and a teamster; also listed on extra duty as a teamster on 2/62 and 3/62 regimental returns. Absent on detached service as a teamster according to 10/31/63 roll. Present on 1/1–Dec./64 rolls. (CSR 270: 4)

Gaylor, John Bunyan: From Duplin Co. At age 21, enl. as PVT, Co. I, 6/17/61. Reported present on company muster rolls of 11/61–2/62, May–June/62, Sept.–Dec./62. Absent on detached service, Jan.–Feb./63. Present on Mar.–Apr./63 muster rolls. Arrested as of 9/17/63 according to 10/31/63 muster roll. Present as of 1/1/64 muster roll, then on Jan.–Feb./64 muster roll reported absent in a Confederate prison. Mentioned in a court martial record dated 1/8/64. Trn to 5th NC Cavalry, 7/25/64, or to 51st Regt Infantry, 8/3/64. (CSR 270: 4)

Gaylord, John T.: From Beaufort Co. At age 31, enl. 7/22/61 as PVT, Co. H. Absent sick at home according to Nov.–Dec./61 company muster rolls. Jan.–Feb./62, May–June/62, Sept.–Dec./62 rolls list him as absent, having been sent to a Petersburg hospital 11/28/61. Also listed absent sick on regimental returns of 2/62 and 3/62. Sent to a Wilson, NC G.H. according to Jan.–Feb./63 muster rolls, and reported there through 11/64. Appears on the muster rolls of 10/1/63–5/31/64 for a Wilson, NC G.H. Present on Nov.–Dec./64 company muster rolls. (CSR 270: 4)

Gentry, C.R.: Enl. 11/10/63 as PVT, Co. A. Reported present on company muster rolls of Sept.–Dec./64. (CSR 270: 4)

German, James: B. 1845; resident of Caldwell Co. Cns. 9/29/64 as PVT, Co. H. Reported present on company muster rolls of Sept.–Oct./64. Trn to Co. D, 12/22/64. Reported present on company muster rolls of Nov.–Dec./64. WIA with a minie ball in the right chest/clavicle, 3/31/65, and captured. D. 4/7/65, and apparently originally bur. in Washington, D.C. at age 19. Bur. Oakwood Cem., Raleigh. (CSR 270: 4; Stepp)

German, James C.: Enl. 9/29/64. PVT, Co. D. WIA. (Stepp)

Gettyes, W.S.: Enl. 9/21/64 as PVT, Co. K. Reported present on company muster rolls of Sept.–Dec./64. (CSR 270: 4)

Gettys, Daniel H.: From Macon Co. At age 21, enl. 11/23/61 as PVT, Co. K. Reported present on Nov.–Dec./61 rolls. Absent sent to Manassas sick, 2/26/62, according to muster rolls and regimental returns. D. of disease, 3/9/62. (CSR 270: 4)

Gholson, Joseph: B. 3/10/39, Mecklenburg Co., VA. PVT, Co. E. Enl. 8/20/61, at age 21. Dsh 2/4/62 from chronic diarrhea. Stood 5' 5½" tall. Had a fair complexion, blue eyes, and light hair; by occupation a farmer. D. 9/7/96. Bur. Old Swepson Farm Cem., Mecklenburg Co., VA. CSR 270: 4; CGR: 6)

Gibson, Samuel B.: Resident of Macon Co. At age 19, enl. 6/25/61 as SGT, Co. K. Reported present on company muster rolls of 11/61–2/62, May–June/62, 9/62–4/63. Prm 1SGT 11/1/62. Reported present July–Aug./63. Absent on detached service, Nov.–Dec./63. Reported present 4/30–8/31/64, Sept.–Dec./64. Elected 2LT, 5/1/63, to rank from 4/30/63. Reported AWOL as of 2/28/65 according to an inspection report. On a POW roll in a Petersburg G.H. as captured, 4/3/65; also reported admitted there, 4/8/65, with a severe gunshot wound in the left thigh from a minie ball. Prl 5/1/65. Dsh from Petersburg G.H., 7/12/65. (CSR 270:1, 4)

Gilbert, William: B. Henderson Co. Enl. from Buncombe Co. Occupation: farmer. At age 29, enl. 5/20/61 as PVT, Co. G. Reported present on company muster rolls of Jan.–Feb./62. Listed sick on 2/62 regimental return; listed in a Petersburg G.H., 3/62 regimental return. Stood 5'11", had a dark complexion, blue eyes, dark hair. (CSR 270: 4)

Gill, C.C.: Co. H. Psb. captured at Willis Church, 6/29/62, or at Malvern Hill in 7/62. Exd. Aiken's Landing, VA, 8/5/62, delivered 7/5/62. (CSR 270: 4)

Gillespie, A.M.: Enl. 10/28/64 as PVT, Co. C. Reported present on company muster rolls of Nov.–Dec./64. Prl Charlotte, 5/20/65. (Alexander; CSR 270: 4)

Gillespie, J.M.: Cns 10/3/64 as PVT, Co. I. Reported present on company muster rolls of Sept.–Dec./64. (CSR 270: 4)

Gillespie, Jacob M.: Res. of Lincoln Co. At age 21, enl. 7/4/61, Co. K. 3SGT. Reported present on company muster rolls of 11/61–2/62, May–June/62. WIA and captured at Boonsboro, MD, 9/13/62. Prl 10/3/62 and later exd. Admitted 10/24/62 to a Richmond G.H., and returned to duty 11/14/62. Reported present on rolls of Nov.–Dec./62, Jan.–Apr./63. Absent on detached service in NC to buy a horse, July–Aug./63. Reported present 10/31/63, Nov.–Dec./63. Elected 2LT, 5/1/63. Took command of Co. K. Reported present Jan.–Feb./64, 4/30–8/31/64, Sept.–Dec./64. Also listed on detached service in charge of dismounted men according to 9/25/64 inspection report. Took oath at Nashville, 5/12/65. Stood 6'1", had a fair complexion, light hair, and hazel eyes. (CSR 270:1, 4)

Gillespie, Joseph W.: B. 8/31/46. Enl. 4/12/64 as PVT, Co. C. Reported in a Raleigh G.H. as of 6/30/64. Reported present on company muster rolls of Mar.–Apr./64, 4/30–8/31/64. Absent on detached service beginning 10/2/64, then reported present Nov.–Dec./64. D. 3/23/28. Bur. Mt. Zion Methodist Church Cem., Cornelius. (Stepp; CSR 270: 4)

Gillespie, S.A.: PVT, Co. C. (Alexander)

Gillespie, T.: Enl. 10/24/64 as PVT, Co. C. Reported present on company muster rolls of Nov.–Dec./64. Prl Greensboro, 5/19/65. (CSR 270: 4)

Gillespie, William S.: Resident of Cleveland Co. Cns 10/3/64 as PVT, Co. I. Reported present on company muster rolls of Sept.–Dec./64. Captured at Sutherland's Station, 4/3/65. Released 6/27/65 on taking oath. Stood 6' 4", had a light complexion, brown hair, and blue eyes. (CSR 270: 4)

Gilliam, John: B. 1835. From Wilkes Co. Enl. 5/27 or 5/28/61 as PVT, Co. A. Reported present on company muster rolls of 11/61–2/62, Sept.–Dec./62. Listed on 2/62 regimental return on extra duty as a teamster. Absent on detached service in NC, Jan.–Feb./63. Reported present Mar.–Apr./63. Absent on detached service with unserviceable horses, July–Aug./63. Reported present 9/63–4/64. Absent sick, 8/25/64. D. 9/20/64 in Raleigh, probably from a gunshot wound. Bur. Oakwood Cem., Raleigh. (AsheCo; Stepp; CSR 270: 4; McNeil)

Gillispie, W.L.: Enl. 2/3/64 as PVT, Co. C. Reported present on company muster rolls of Mar.–Apr./64, 4/1/64. Admitted to a Richmond G.H., 6/14/64. D. 6/26/64 in Richmond from disease. (CSR 270: 4)

Glass, James P.: PVT, Co. B. Captured in Monroe Co., TN, 10/20/63. Sent to Camp Chase, OH and Ft. Delaware. (CSR 270: 4)

Glover, Robert W.: From Northampton Co. Enl. 7/61 or 8/61 as PVT, Co. B. Reported present on company muster rolls of Jan.–Feb./62. Admitted to a Richmond G.H., 3/14/62, and returned to duty 4/13/62. Also reported absent on rolls and on regimental returns of 2/62 and 3/62, the latter return mentioning a Petersburg G.H. Reported present 9/62–4/63, 6/30–Dec./63, 4/1/64. Absent on horse detail, Mar.–Apr./64. Reported present 4/30–10/64. (CSR 270: 4)

Goforth, Clement C.: B. Rutherford Co. Occupation: farmer. Enl. 10/63 as PVT, Co. D. Reported present on company muster rolls of 8/31/64–12/64. Captured at Amelia C.H., 4/3/65. Released at age 43 or 44 from Pt. Lookout on taking oath, 6/27/65. Stood about 6' tall, had dark hair and blue eyes. (CSR 270: 4)

Gold, Hill: Cns. 10/3/64 at PVT, Co. I. Reported present on company muster rolls of Sept.–Oct./64. Absent on detached service, 12/23/64, to remount. (CSR 270: 4)

Goode, H.M.: PVT, Co. C. WIA 8/15 or 8/16/64 along Charles City Rd., near Richmond. (Richmond *Sentinel*, 8/26/64)

Goodman, Calvin P.: From Ashe Co. Occupation: farmer. At age 32, enl. 3/1/62 as PVT, Co. A. Absent on detached service in Winchester, beginning 9/5/62. Reported present, Nov.–Dec./62. Detached with the baggage in Gordonsville, Jan.–Feb./63. Reported present Mar.–Apr./63. Absent at home sick, July–Aug./63. Reported present on company muster rolls of Sept.–Oct./63. On detached service in Richmond with a Richmond G.H., 12/29/63–8/64. Absent on sick frl, Sept.–Oct./64. Dsh 9/24/64 at age 35 due to disease. Stood 5'10", had a fair complexion, blue eyes, and light hair. (CSR 270: 4)

Goodman, Harvey: From Ashe Co. Enl. 5/23/61 as PVT, Co. A. D. 12/16/61 at Cantonment W.N. Edwards, from disease. Age 29. (AsheCo; CSR 270: 4)

Goodman, Henry M.: From Cabarrus Co. At age 21, enl. 6/15/61 as PVT, Co. F. Reported present on company muster rolls of 11/61–2/62, May–June/62, Sept.–Dec./62. 1Prm bugler, 2/26/62. WIA at Brandy Station, 8/1/63; admitted to a Richmond G.H., 8/2/63. Afterward absent on sick frl. Reported present 11/63–2/64. Absent sent to the dead line, 3/12/64, according to rolls of 2/29–3/31/64. WIA Atlee's Station. Reported in a Richmond G.H., 3/3/64, with gunshot wound in hand.

Returned to duty, 3/15/64. Reported present Mar.–Dec./64. Resident of Concord, circa 1893. (Barringer; Mizelle; Cabarrus; CSR 270: 4)

Goodman, James D.: Enl. 9/29/63 as PVT, Co. F. WIA, 10/27/64, at Long Creek near Burgess or Bergers Mills on Boydton Plank Rd. D. 10/28/64. (Barringer; CSR 270: 4)

Goodman, John A.: From Ashe Co. Enl. 5/21/61 as PVT, Co. A. Reported present 11/61–2/62. Captured in MD, 10/15/62. Reported present 11/62–4/63, July–Dec./63. Absent sick beginning 1/17/63. Admitted 1/29/64 to a Richmond G.H. with a minie ball wound in the leg. Frl, 2/4/64, for 30 days. Listed AWOL on Mar.–Apr./64 rolls. Reported present 7/12/64. (CSR 270: 4)

Goodman, Joseph Franklin: Served in rgt. NFR. (DavisUDC)

Goodman, Richard B.: From Ashe Co. Enl. 6/62 or 8/62 as PVT, Co. A. Reported present Sept.–Dec./62. Absent on frl to buy a horse, Jan.–Feb./63. Reported present Mar.–Apr./63. On detached service with unserviceable horses, according to July–Oct./63 rolls, beginning 8/1/63. Reported present Nov.–Dec./63. Deserted 1/18/64. (CSR 270: 4)

Goodson, Daniel: B. 1823. PVT, Co. D. Reported present on company muster rolls of Nov.–Dec./64. D. 1884. Bur. St. Luke's Lutheran Church Cem., Lincoln Co. (Stepp; CSR 270: 4)

Goodson, Henry M.: B. 4/11/39. From Lincoln Co. Enl. 5/27/62 as PVT, Co. C. Reported present, May–June/62. Absent on detached service beginning 10/1/62, according to 6/30–Oct./62 rolls. Reported present Nov.–Dec./62. Absent in NC to buy a horse, beginning 2/21/63, according to Jan.–Feb./63 rolls. Reported present Mar.–Apr./63. Absent on detached service to NC to buy a horse, beginning 8/27/63 according to July–Aug./63 rolls. Reported present 9/63–8/64. Absent on detached service, beginning 9/26/64 according to Sept.–Oct./64 rolls. Reported present Nov.–Dec./64. Psb. also served in Co. K, 1st NC Vols. D. 10/4/82. Bur. St. Luke's Lutheran Church Cem., Lincoln Co. (Alexander; Stepp; CSR 270:4)

Goodson, J.H.: From Macon Co. PVT, Co. K. Age 23. Rejected by COL Baker. (CSR 270: 4)

Goodson, Robert: From Buncombe Co. At age 22, enl. 5/20/61 as PVT, Co. G. Reported present Jan.–Feb./62, May–June/62. 2/62 regimental return places him on detached duty in a Richmond hospital. Absent sick at Winchester, Sept.–Oct./62. Reported present 11/62–4/63. Absent sick in a Richmond G.H., July–Aug./63, with gonorrhea.

Reported present Sept.–Dec./63, Mar.–Aug./64. Absent on detached service to buy a horse, Sept.–Oct./64. Reported present Nov.–Dec./64. Prm 3CPL, 12/11/64. (CSR 270: 4)

Gordon, J.L.C.: From Buncombe Co., age 26. Enl. 5/20/61 as PVT, Co. G. Reported present Jan.–Feb./62, May–June/62, 9/62–4/63, July–Aug./63. 3/62 regimental return places him on detached duty in a hospital. According to Sept.–Oct./63 rolls, trn to Co. B, 16th NC Troops on 10/7/63. (CSR 270: 4)

Gordon, James Byron: B. Wilkesboro, Wilkes Co., NC, 11/2/22. Attended Emory & Henry. Businessman, farmer, politician. Enl. 5/1/61 as 1LT in unit that became Co. B, 1st regiment NC State Troops (infantry). Prm CPT, 6/4/61. Prm MAJ and trn to 1st NC Cavalry, 8/61. Reported present on field and staff muster rolls of 11/61–4/62, and on regimental returns of 2/62 and 3/62. Prm LTC, 3/1/62. Reported present on May–June/62, Sept.–Dec./62 rolls. Absent on frl, Jan.–Feb./63. Reported present, Mar.–Apr./63. Absent commanding Hampton's Brigade in Hampton's absence, according to July–Aug./63 rolls. Prm COL, 7/23/63; succeeded Baker in command of rgt., 8/11/63. Prm. BG 9/28/63, and took command of NC Cavalry Brigade. WIA Brook Church, 5/12/64. D. 5/18/64 in a Richmond G.H. from effects of wound and erysipelas. Bur. St. Paul's Episcopal Church Cem., Wilkesboro. (CSR 270:1, 4; *Stuart's Tarheels*)

Gorham, Benjamin C.: From Wake Co. At age 18, enl. 7/1/63 as PVT, Co H. Absent on detached service in NC to procure a horse, July–Aug./63. Reported present 9/63–4/1/64. Absent on detached service to buy a horse, Mar.–Apr./64. Reported present 4/30–Oct./64. Absent on detached service to buy a horse, Nov.–Dec./64. Bur Cross Creek Cem, Fayetteville NC. (CGR: 1; CSR 270: 4)

Goss, Isham: From Ashe Co. Enl. 7/8/63 as PVT, Co. A. Reported present on company muster rolls of 9/63–8/64. Absent on detached service to buy a horse, Sept.–Oct./64. Reported present Nov.–Dec./64. (AsheCo; CSR 270: 4)

Goss, Jesse: Enl. 5/20/61 as PVT, Co. A. Reported present on company muster rolls of 11/61–2/62. Absent in Winchester General Hospital, Sept.–Oct./62. Absent on scout, beginning 12/25/62. Absent on detached service with the baggage at Gordonsville, Jan.–Feb./63. Reported present Mar.–Apr./63. Admitted 7/3/63 to a Charlottesville G.H.; returned to duty 7/9/63. WIA 8/1/63, at Brandy Station. D. 8/24/63. (CSR 270: 4)

Goss, R.C.: PVT, Co. A. (AsheCo)

Grady, Durham: From Duplin Co. At age 18, enl. 8/5/61 as PVT, Co. I. Reported present on company muster rolls of 11/61–2/62, May–June/62, Sept.–Dec./62. Absent on detached service, Jan.–Feb./63. Reported present Mar.–Apr./63, 10/31/63, 1/1/64–2/64. Prm CPL, 7/15/64. Captured 8/25/64, Ream's Station. Held at Point Lookout. Exd. 3/65. (CSR 270:5)

Grady, Elisha: From Onslow Co. At age 27, enl. 7/4/61 as PVT, Co. I. Dsh; furnished substitute. (CSR 270:5)

Grady, L.C.: From Duplin Co. At age 18, enl. 7/4/61 as PVT, Co. I. Rejected. (CSR 270:5)

Grady, Lewis: From Duplin Co. At age 22, Enl. 3/22/63 as PVT, Co. I. Reported present Mar.–Apr./63. WIA 6/21/63 at Upperville. Admitted to a Richmond G.H., 7/21/63. Frl 7/22/63. Remained absent on frl as of 10/31/63 and 1/1/64. Reported present on company muster rolls of Jan.–Feb./64. Absent on detached service to remount, Mar.–Apr./64. Reported present 4/31–Dec./64. (CSR 270:5)

Grady, William G.: From Duplin Co. At age 23, enl. 6/17/61 as 3SGT, Co. I. Reported present on company muster rolls of 11/61–2/62, May–June/62. Reported present on company muster rolls of Sept.–Dec./62. Prm 2LT, 9/62 (elected). Reported present and under arrest, Jan.–Feb./63; reported present, Mar.–Apr./63. Mentioned in court martial orders of 5/25/63. Prm Sr. 2LT, 6/20/63. KIA 10/19/63 near Buckland. "He was a brave and good man." (CSR 270:1, 5)

Grady, Winfrey: From Duplin Co. At age 36, enl. 7/4/61 as PVT, Co. I. Reported present on company muster rolls of 11/61–2/62. Captured at Willis Church, 6/29/62; sent to forts Columbus and Delaware. According to POW list, stood 5'7", had light hair, blue eyes, and a florid complexion. Exd. 8/5/62. Reported present Sept.–Dec./62. Absent on detached service, Jan.–Feb./63. Absent sick in Campbell Co., Mar.–Apr./63. Reported present 10/31/63, 1/1/64–2/64. WIA 8/22/64 and sent to a Petersburg G.H. reported present, Nov.–Dec./64. Captured near Goldsboro, 3/28/65. Sent to Hart's Island in New York Harbor. D. 4/25/65 from typhoid fever. (CSR 270:5)

Gragg, John Shelby: B. 5/26/42 in Buncombe Co. Psb. resided in Caldwell Co. Occupation: farmer. Enl. 7/10/61 as PVT, Co. D. Reported present Nov.–Dec./61, and on extra duty attending to the sick in the hospital. Reported present on company muster rolls of Jan.–Feb./62, May–10/31/62. According to regimental return of 2/62, on extra duty as a teamster. Reported present Nov.–Dec./62 and on extra duty as a teamster in the QM Dept. Absent to procure a horse, Jan.–Feb./63. Reported present Mar.–Apr./63. Captured 7/5/63 in PA. Released 1/29/64 on taking the oath; joined the Union army for a three-year stint. D. 10/4/29. Bur. Pleasant Grove Union Church Cem., Buncombe Co. (Stepp; CSR 270:5; Davis)

Gragg, Posy: According to trooper Harvey Davis, Posy Gragg of Co. D was "discharged at Burnsville. Carried out on a rail." (Davis)

Gragg, William Waitsdel/Waightstill: From Watauga Co. At age 28, enl. 2/28/62 as PVT, Co. D. Captured at Willis Church, 6/29/62. According to a Federal report, Gragg was age 22, stood 6' tall, and had fair hair, blue eyes, and a light complexion. Held at forts Delaware and Columbus. Exd. 8/5/62. Reported present on company muster rolls of 6/30/62–4/63. Absent at home to procure a horse according to July–Aug./63 rolls; reported present on 6/30/63–12/64 rolls. WIA and captured 3/28/65 while home on frl (Davis; CSR 270:5; *Watauga Democrat*, June 14, 1999)

Graham, Adelbert J. B. New York. From Watauga Co. Psb. has other ties to Buncombe Co. At age 18, enl. 7/10/61 as PVT, Co. D. Reported present on company muster rolls of Nov.–Dec./61. Absent in a G.H., Jan.–Feb./62, according to muster rolls and to the 2/62 regimental return. Captured at Willis Church, 6/29/62. Exd. 8/5/62. According to Federal POW record, stood 5'11", had light hair, blue eyes, and a pale complexion. Reported present 6/30–10/31/62. Absent sick, Nov.–Dec./62, and Jan.–Feb./63 in a Gordonsville G.H. Reported in a Lynchburg G.H., Mar.–Apr./63. At home, 6/30–10/31/63. Reported present, Nov.–Dec./63. Absent on detached service, Jan.–Feb./64. Reported present on extra duty, 2/29–3/31/64. Absent to procure a horse, Mar.–Apr./64. Trn Co. A, 37th Rgt. NC Troops, 7/21/64. Admitted to a Petersburg G.H., 7/28/64, and psb sent to Goldsboro, 8/4/64. NFR. (Davis; CSR 270:5)

Graham, J.R.: Enl. 2/12/62 as PVT, Co. C. Reported present 11/63–8/31/64. On detached service beginning 10/14/64, according to Sept.–Oct./64 rolls. Reported present Nov.–Dec./64. Captured according to a POW roll of 4/22/65. (Alexander; CSR 270:5)

Graham, Joel A.: From Rowan Co. Enl. 9/21/64 or 10/9/64 as PVT, Co. F. Reported present on company muster rolls of Sept.–Oct./64. Absent Nov.–Dec./64 (beginning 12/5/64) in NC to purchase a horse. Prl Salisbury, 5/13/65; oath dated 5/31/65. Resident of China Grove, circa 1893. (CSR 270:5; Barringer)

Graham, W.A.: Enl. 11/5/64 as PVT, Co. A. Reported present on company muster rolls of Nov.–Dec./64. NFR. (AsheCo; CSR 270:5)

Grant, J.T.: PVT, Co. B. Admitted 3/20/64 to a Richmond G.H. Absent sick according to 4/1/64 roll. Listed as trn by order on same roll, and Mar.–Apr./64 rolls. On a sick and wounded report as D. 4/11/64 from erysipelas. (CSR 270:5)

Grant, John Lewis: B. Duplin Co., 6/6/31. Enl. 7/9/61 as PVT, Co. I. According to Jan.–Feb./62 rolls, absent sick beginning 1/10/62. Initially admitted that day to a Danville Hospital, then sent to a Richmond G.H. Also listed absent sick on Rgt Return of 2/62. KIA 6/29/62 at Willis Church. (CSR 270:5; Bob Krick to the author, March 4, 2002)

Grant, William H.H.: From Yadkin Co. At age 18, enl. 12/1/62 as PVT, Co. A. Reported present on company muster rolls of Jan.–Apr./63. Captured 7/4/63. Exd 5/3/64. Admitted 5/8/64 to a Richmond G.H. with chronic diarrhea. Frl for 30 days beginning 5/20/64. Reported present on company muster rolls of July–Aug./64. Absent on detached service to buy a horse, according to Sept.–Oct./64 rolls. Reported present on rolls of Nov.–Dec./64. (AsheCo; CSR 270:5)

Green, Andrew Heartsfield: From Franklin Co. At age 24, enl. 9/5/63 as PVT, Co. B. Trn from 16th NC Bn. Reported present on rolls of 4/30–Oct./64. Absent on horse detail, Nov.–Dec./64. (CSR 270:5; Pearce: 250)

Green, Bartlett: From Watauga Co. At age 33, enl. 7/10/61 as PVT, Co. D. Reported present on Nov.–Dec./61 rolls. Admitted to a Danville G.H. with a heart condition, 1/12/62, then trn to Richmond. Reported absent sick in a Richmond G.H. on Jan.–Feb./62 rolls; also listed as absent sick on 2/62 Rgt Return. Absent on detached service, May–June/62. Reported present 6/30/62–4/63. Absent on detached service with unserviceable horses, 6/30–10/31/63. Reported present on rolls of 11/63–4/64, 8/31/64–12/64. (Davis; CSR 270: 4 for George N. Folk; CSR 270:5)

Green, Calvin: Enl. 8/12/64 as PVT, Co. D. Reported present on company muster rolls of Sept.–Dec./64. (CSR 270:5)

Green, Daniel M.: B. Watauga Co. Pre-war occupation: farmer. At age 25, enl. 7/10/61 as PVT, Co. D. According to Nov.–Dec./61 rolls, absent sick in a Petersburg G.H. Jan.–Feb./62, absent sick at home. Rgt Return of 2/62 confirms illness absence; return of 3/62 reports him at home sick since 11/8/61. Reported present May–June/62. Absent sick at Winchester according to rolls of 6/30–10/31/63. Admitted 9/26/62 to a Culpeper hospital, and returned to duty 9/30/62. Dsh 12/10/62 for chronic rheumatism. Had a fair complexion, blue eyes, light hair. Stood 5' 9" or 5'11", (Davis; CSR 270:5)

Green, David V.: From Macon Co. At age 21, enl. 7/25/61 as PVT, Co. K. Reported present on company muster rolls of 11/61–2/62, May–June/62, 9/62–4/63. Prm 4CPL, 12/1/62. Absent on detached service to buy a horse in NC, July–Aug./63. Reported present on 10/31/63–3/31/64 rolls. KIA at Brook Church, 5/12/64. (Macon Heritage, 49; CSR 270:5)

Green, Elbert J.: From Watauga Co. At age 20, enl. 5/11/61 as PVT, Co. D. Reported present on company muster rolls of Nov.–Dec./61. Absent sick according to rolls of Jan.–Feb./62 and Rgt Return of 2/62. Admitted to a Charlottesville G.H. 2/27/62 with chronic rheumatism. Returned to duty 3/17/62. D. of disease, probably on 4/8/62. (Davis; CSR 270:5)

Green, Elisha: B. NC. From Watauga Co. At age 33, enl. 5/11/61 as SGT, Co. D. Reported present on company muster rolls of Nov.–Dec./61, and on extra duty attending sick in a G.H. Absent Jan.–Feb./62 on recruiting service in Watauga Co. 2/62 Rgt Return also lists him as on detached service. Captured at Willis Church, 6/29/62. Exd 8/5/62. Reported absent making shoes in Winchester, 6/30–10/31/62. First reported AWOL, 11/62. Deserted. According to a U.S. POW report: age 34, stood 6' tall, had light hair, blue eyes, and a fair complexion. (Davis; CSR 270:5)

Green, Isaac: From Watauga Co. Enl. 5/11/61 as PVT, Co. D. Reported present on company muster rolls of Nov.–Dec./61. Absent Jan.–Feb./62 in a G.H.; also listed absent sick on 2/62 Rgt Return, and sick in a Lynchburg hospital on 3/62 Rgt Return. Reported present May–June/62. Captured 10/12/62, and absent through 10/31/62. Described on a 10/14/62 POW list as a slimly-built 5' 8", with a sandy complexion, hazel eyes, no whiskers, and 22 years old. Exd 10/31/62. Reported present 11/62–4/63, July–Aug./63. Captured at Jack's Shop, 9/22/63. Joined U.S. service, 1/26/64. (Davis; CSR 270:5)

Green, James N.: Resident of Franklin Co. Cns 3/1/64 as PVT, Co. E. Reported present Mar.–Apr./64. Absent on detached service at Stony Creek,

VA, 4/30–Oct./64. Reported present on company muster rolls of Nov.–Dec./64. Captured 4/3/65 at Aberdeen C.H., VA. Released on taking the oath, 6/27/65. Had a fair complexion, blue eyes, and stood 5' 9½". (CSR 270:5; Pearce: 250)

Green, John: Enl. 7/25/64 as PVT, Co. E. Reported present on company muster rolls of 4/30/64–10/64. Absent sick in a Wake Forest, NC G.H., according to Nov.–Dec./64 rolls. (CSR 270:5)

Green, John Enzor: From Watauga Co. At age 19, enl. 5/11/61 as PVT, Co. D. Reported present on company muster rolls of 11/61–2/62, 5/62–4/63, 6/30/63–3/31/64. Absent at home to buy a horse according to Mar.–Apr./64 rolls. Reported present 8/31/64–12/64. On a Knoxville, TN POW register of Rebel deserters as confined 4/17/65. (Davis; CSR 270:5)

Green, Leander: Resident of Watauga Co. Enl. 5/1/64 as PVT, Co. D. Company muster rolls of 8/31/64 show him absent at home after a horse. The Sept.–Oct./64 rolls show him absent and in a G.H. after being WIA. Reported present, Nov.–Dec./64. Deserted at Bellfield, VA, 1/30/65. On a Knoxville, TN POW register of Rebel deserters as being confined and taking the oath, probably on 4/17/65. Had a fair complexion, dark hair, blue eyes, and stood 5'11". (Davis; CSR 270:5)

Green, Lott: From Watauga Co. At age 29, enl. 5/11/61 as SGT, Co. D. Reported present on company muster rolls of Nov.–Dec./61, and on extra duty superintending the shoeing of horses. Reported present Jan.–Feb./62, reduced to ranks, and confined by sentence of a General Court Martial. According to 3/62 Rgt Return, absent sick in a Richmond G.H. Possibly admitted 3/18/62 with diarrhea, and released 3/27/62. Reported present 5/62–4/63, 6/30/63–4/31/64. Reported absent to buy a horse, Mar.–Apr./64; also listed absent for the same reason, 8/31/64. Reported present Sept.–Dec./64. Deserted at Bellfield, VA, 1/1/65. On a Knoxville, TN POW register of Rebel deserters as being confined and taking the oath in 4/65. Had a fair complexion, dark hair, blue eyes, and stood 6' tall. Admitted to a Louisville, KY post hospital, 7/3/65, and released 7/6/65. (CSR 270:5)

Green, Lott W.: B. 7/6/33. From Watauga Co. Enl. 5/16/61 as PVT, Co. D. Reported present on company muster rolls of 11/61–2/62, 5/62–12/62. Absent at home on frl, Jan.–Feb./63. Prm CPL. Reported present Mar.–Apr./63. Admitted 6/10/63 with a gunshot wound to a Charlottesville G.H. Frl for 40 days beginning 7/10/63. Prm SGT. Reported present Jan.–Apr./64. On an Invalid Corps register as "totally disqualified" and retiring, 9/1/64. D. 9/22/05. Bur. Stony Fork Baptist Church Cem., Watauga Co. (Davis; Stepp; CSR 270: 4 for George N. Folk; CSR 270:5)

Green, Plummer W.: Enl. 3/14/64 as PVT, Co. E. Reported present on company muster rolls of 3/64–12/64, although also found a the register of a Richmond G.H. as being admitted 5/13/64. (CSR 270:5)

Green, Robert F.: Cns 4/1/64 as PVT, Co. E. Reported present Mar.–Apr./64. Absent on detached service at Stony Creek, VA, 4/30/64–10/64. Captured 12/1/64; exd 1/17/65. (CSR 270:5)

Green, Robert H.: From Caldwell Co. At age 18, enl. 5/25/61 as PVT, Co. D. Reported present on company muster rolls of 11/61–2/62, 5/62–4/63, 7/63–3/31/64. Absent on frl, Mar.–Apr./64. According to 8/31/64 roll, absent at home after a horse. Present Sept.–Dec./64. Prm CPL, 11/ or 12/64. (CSR 270:5)

Green, Thomas: From Watauga Co. Enl. 5/11/61 as PVT, Co. D. Reported present on company muster rolls of 11/61–2/62, 5/62–4/63. On detached service with unserviceable horses, 6/30–10/31/63. Absent at a recruiting camp, Nov.–Dec./63. Absent on detached service, 1/64–3/31/64. Reported present on Mar.–Apr./64 and Sept.–Dec./64 rolls. Possibly KIA in 1865. (Davis; CSR 270:5)

Green, W.H.: Cns 10/3/64 as PVT, Co. I. Reported present on company muster rolls through 12/64. (CSR 270:5)

Green, William A.: Cleveland Co. resident. At age 18, enl. 8/6/61 as PVT, Co. E. Reported present on company muster rolls of Jan.–Feb./62, May–June/62, Sept.–Oct./62. Captured at Malvern Hill, VA, 8/5/62. Prl 8/26/62. Absent on detached service, Nov.–Dec./62. Reported present Jan.–Apr./63, 6/30/63–10/64. Nov.–Dec./64, on detached service in NC baling forage. Captured at Amelia C.H., 4/3/65. Took oath, 6/27/65. Had a dark complexion, grayish hair, gray eyes, and stood 5'11¼". (CSR 270:5)

Greenfield, William J.: From Caldwell Co. At age 34, enl. 2/28/62 as PVT, Co. D. Reported present on company muster rolls of 5/62–4/63. Absent on detached service as a teamster in the quartermaster dept., 6/30/63–10/31/63. Reported present 11/63–2/64. Absent on detached service, 2/29–4/64. Reported AWOL on 8/31/64 roll, then listed as presently for duty on Sept.–Dec./64 rolls. Trn to Co. I, 26th NC, 12/30/64. (Davis; CSR 270:5)

Greenway, John E.: B. Granville Co. Blacksmith before the war. Trn from 16th NC Bn. Enl.

8/28 or 9/4/63 as PVT, Co. B. Reported present on company muster rolls of 4/30–10/64. Age 33 as of 6/2/64. Absent sick, Nov.–Dec./64. Had gray eyes, dark hair, and a fair complexion; stood 6' tall. (CSR 270:5)

Greer, J.E.: From Lenoir, NC. Enl. 7/26/61 as PVT, Co. B. Reported present on company muster rolls of Nov.–Dec./64. Enlisted for one year. (CSR 270:5)

Greer, Larkin E.: Age 20, from Watauga Co. Enl. 6/27/61 as PVT, Co. A. Reported present on company muster rolls of 11/61–2/62, Sept.–Dec./62. According to Jan.–Feb./63 rolls, absent on frl to buy a horse beginning 2/27/63. Mar.–Apr./63 rolls list him as still absent and arrested for a misdemeanor. Confined in jail at Floyd C.H., VA. Still incarcerated as of Mar.–Apr./64 rolls. Possibly a member of Co. D at some point. (AsheCo; CSR 270:5; Davis)

Gregg, W.H.: Co. G. (*The* [Asheville] *Daily Citizen*, 7/5/89, copy in Civil War Clippings File, Pack Memorial Library, Asheville, NC.)

Gregory, C.A.: Enl. 11/5/64 as PVT, Co. E. Reported present on company muster rolls of Nov.–Dec./64. (CSR 270:5)

Grier, John Laban: B. 1/21/31, Mecklenburg Co. Enl. 6/15/61 as 1SGT, Co. F. Prm 2LT, 10/1/61. Reported present on company muster rolls of Nov.–Dec./61. Absent on detached service beginning 2/26/62, according to muster rolls of Jan.–Feb./62. Rgt. Returns of 2/62 and 3/62 show him absent on recruiting service. D. Hanover C.H., VA, from typhoid fever, 8/24/62. Bur Steele Creek Presbyterian Church Burying Ground, Charlotte. (CSR 270:1, 5; Mizelle; Barringer; GLP; Karchaske; Cabarrus)

Griffin, J.T.: PVT, Co. A. Admitted 6/27/62 to a Richmond G.H. with a gunshot wound in the arm and elbow joint. Frl for 30 days, beginning 7/7/62. D. 3/20/63 in Lynchburg, from pneumonia. (CSR 270:5 misfiled in the CSRs of Jesse and John C. Griffin)

Griffin, Jesse: Cns. 6/2/64 as PVT, Co. I. Admitted to a Richmond G.H., 7/29/64, with erysipelas. Frl for 60 days beginning 8/18/64. Reported present Nov.–Dec./64. Retired to the Invalid Corps, 1/12/65. (CSR 270:5)

Griffin, John C.: From Lenoir Co., age 22. Enl. 6/61 as PVT, Co. C. Reported present on company muster rolls of 11/61–2/62. Reported absent May–June/62 after being WIA in a skirmish, 6/29/62. In a Richmond G.H. Also absent 9/62–4/63. Deserted. On a POW prl as captured near Kinston, 12/14/62. (CSR 270:5)

Griggs, William: From Buncombe Co. At age 22, enl. 5/20/61 as PVT, Co. G. Reported present on company muster rolls of Jan.–Feb./62, May–June/62, 9/62–4/63, July–Dec./63, 4/1/64. On detached service at Division HQ, Mar.–Apr./64. Reported present 4/30–8/64. On detached service as a teamster with W.H.F. Lee's Division QM Dept., Sept.–Dec./64, and possibly also July–Aug./64. (CSR 270:5)

Grim, J.A.: PVT, Co. F. On a muster roll of officers and men prl Salisbury, 5/3/65. (CSR 270:5)

Grisham, Charles: Enl. 7/21/62 as PVT, Co. I. Trn from a CPT Ward's NC Cavalry. Reported present on company muster rolls of 9/62–4/63, 10/31/63, 1/1/64, Jan.–Feb./64. On detached service in NC to remount, Mar.–Apr./64. Reported present, 4/31/64–12/64. From Duplin Co. Age 25. Originally enl 4/15/61. (CSR 270:5)

Grisham, John W.: From Duplin Co. At age 20, enl. 6/20/61 as PVT, Co. I. Reported present on company muster rolls of 11/61–2/62, May–June/62. WIA Willis Church, 6/29/62. Reported present Sept.–Dec./62. Also present Jan.–Feb./63 and under arrest; present Mar.–Apr./63. Roll of 10/31/63 also reports him under arrest as of 10/20/63. Reported present Jan.–Feb./64. Trn 8/64 to either the 38th or 18th Rgt NC Troops. (CSR 270:5)

Grissom, Robert D.: From Granville Co. At age 24, enl. 6/8/61 as PVT, Co. E. Absent Jan.–Feb./62 sent to a Petersburg G.H. on 2/25/62. Rgt Returns of 2/62 and 3/62 confirm his absence, the later return showing him in a Lynchburg G.H. Reported present on company muster rolls of May–June/62, Sept.–Dec./62. Admitted 2/63 to a Charlottesville G.H. with chronic bronchitis; returned to duty 3/16/63. Reported present Mar.–Apr./63, 6/30/63–2/64, 3/64–8/31/64. Absent on extra duty with the ambulance corps, Sept.–Oct./64. Reported present Nov.–Dec./64. Prl Appomattox C.H., 4/9/65. (CSR 270:5)

Grissom, Thomas W.: From Granville Co. At age 22, enl. 6/24/61 as PVT, Co. E. Reported absent Jan.–Feb./62; admitted with a fever to a Danville G.H.; sent to a Richmond G.H. D. 2/62 in the hospital. (CSR 270:5)

Gums, William: From Northampton Co. At age 17, enl. 6/61 as PVT, Co. B. Reported present on company muster rolls of Nov.–Dec./61. Captured 2/22/62. Reported present Jan.–Apr./63, 6/30–Dec./63. Absent sick in a Lynchburg G.H., Mar.–Apr./64. Involved in court martial proceedings, 3/26/63. Absent on detached service in an infirmary camp, 4/1/64. Absent sick 4/30–12/64. (CSR 270:5)

Gunter, J.C.: Enl. 10/10/64 as PVT, Co. K. Reported present on company muster rolls of Sept.–Dec./64. (CSR 270:5)

Gurganis, Lewis: From Onslow Co. At age 24, enl. 7/4/61 as PVT, Co. I. Rejected. (CSR 270:5)

Gurley, Lewis: From Wayne Co. At age 26, enl. 9/19/61 as PVT, Co. H. Reported present on company muster rolls of 11/61–2/62, May–June/62, 9/62–4/63, July–Aug./63. Admitted 7/19/63 to a Richmond G.H., then trn to another G.H. 8/15/63, with gonorrhea. Captured 9/63 at Kelly's Ford. Prl 5/3/64. Admitted to a Richmond G.H., 5/8/64, then frl 5/12/64. Reported present 4/30–Dec./64. (CSR 270:5)

Gurley, Nelson: From Ashe Co. At age 18, enl. 5/24/61 as PVT, Co. A. Reported present on company muster rolls of 11/61–2/62, 9/62–4/63. WIA 7/63 near Williamsport, MD. Admitted to a Richmond G.H., 7/28/63. Absent, July–Oct./63. Roll of Mar.–Apr./64 reports him at home sick since 3/4/64. Reported present, July–Dec./64. (AsheCo; CSR 270:5)

Gurley, Nestor H.: B. Wayne Co. At age 21, enl. 6/20/61 as PVT, Co. H. Reported present on company muster rolls of 11/61–2/62. Absent May–June/62, WIA by 2 minie balls, one lacerating a muscle near the right nipple and the other striking the right thigh, 6/29/62 at Willis Church. Dsh 12/25/62; "can raise hand only a few inches from body. Arm disabled." Stood 5'10", had fair complexion, black eyes, and black hair. Pre-war occupation: clerk. (CSR 270:5)

Guy, Albert: From Macon Co. At age 19, enl. 1/17/62 as PVT, Co. K. Reported present on company muster rolls of May–June/62, Sept.–Dec./62. Absent at home on detached service to buy a horse, Jan.–Feb./63. Absent at home sick, Mar.–Apr./63. Reported absent sick in NC, July–Aug./63. Also listed absent sick on rolls of 10/31/63, 11/63–2/64, 2/29–3/31/64. Subsequently deserted to E. TN. (CSR 270:5)

Guy, Andrew J.: From Macon Co. At age 21, enl. 3/5/62 as PVT, Co. K. Reported present on company muster rolls of May–June/62, 9/62–4/63. Absent on detached service to NC to purchase horses, July–Aug./63. Reported present 10/31/63–10/64. Absent detailed to bale forage for the QM, Nov.–Dec./64. (CSR 270:5)

Guy, George W.: From Macon Co. At age 24, enl. 3/5/62 as PVT, Co. K. Reported present on company muster rolls of May–June/62, 9/62–4/63, 7/63–3/31/64. Listed as MIA, 5/9/64. According to Federal POW records, captured at Spotsylvania C.H., 5/12/64. Released, 6/7/65. (CSR 270:5)

Guy, Henry E.: From Macon Co. At age 25, enl. 3/5/62 as PVT, Co. K. Reported present and sick in quarters on rolls of May–June/62. D. Richmond, 7/4/62. (CSR 270:5)

Guy, Lewis G.: Resident of Duplin Co. At age 21, enl. 7/61 as PVT, Co. I. Reported present on company muster rolls of 11/61–2/62. WIA at Willis Church, 6/29/62. Reported present Sept.–Dec./62. Absent on detached service, Jan.–Feb./63. Also absent on detached service, attending sick in Campbell Co., Mar.–Apr./63. Listed on a hospital muster roll of July–Aug./63 at Scottsville, VA. Listed as present on rolls of 10/31/63, 1/1/64, Jan.–Aug./31/64. On frl 11/3/64, and also reported present Nov.–Dec./64. Captured at Amelia C.H., 4/3/65. Released on taking the oath, 6/27/65. Had a dark complexion, black hair, blue eyes, and stood 5'10½". (CSR 270:5)

Hadges, J.J.: Co. D. (CSR 270: 4 for George N. Folk)

Hagan, Thomas: Cns. 7/11/64 as PVT, Co. H. Reported present on company muster rolls of 4/30–8/31/64. AWOL beginning 9/29/64, according to company muster rolls of Sept.–Dec./64. (CSR 270:5)

Haggard, Hixon E.: From Northampton Co. Brother of Jesse Haggard. At age 36, enl. 6/18/61 as SGT, Co. B. Reported present on company muster rolls of Nov.–Dec./61. Absent Jan.–Feb./62 on detached service scouting, beginning 2/3/62. Rgt return of 2/62 reports him on detached service, and 3/62 return lists him absent sick. Reported present Mar.–Apr./62. Absent "left home 8/10" according to rolls of Sept.–Oct./62. Reported AWOL on rolls of Nov.–Dec./62. Prm CPT, Miller's BN, 9/62. (CSR 270:5)

Haggard, Jesse: From Northampton Co. Brother of Hixon Haggard. At age 37, enl. 6/12/61 as PVT, Co. B. Reported present on company muster rolls of 11/61–4/62. Absent at home sick beginning 8/1/62 according to Sept.–Oct./62 rolls. Listed as AWOL, 11/62–2/63. Officially listed as deserter, 4/28/63. Trn to 12th Bn, Co. A, 10/62. (Whit Joyner to author, 13 September 1994; CSR 270:5)

Hagler, Jacob: Enl. 6/15/61 as PVT, Co. F. Captured at Ream's Station, 8/23/64.

Hagler, Jacob: From Cabarrus Co. At age 39, enl. 6/15/61 as PVT, Co. F. Reported present on company muster rolls of Nov.–Dec./61, Jan.–Feb./62, May–June/62. Absent sick in a Lynchburg

G.H., 9/20/62, per Sept.–Dec./62 company muster rolls. Also reported admitted 11/1/62 to a Richmond G.H., then returned to duty, 11/27/62. According to July–Oct./63 rolls, absent sent to a G.H., 8/26/63. Admitted to a Richmond G.H., 7/14/63 with chronic diarrhea. Frl 7/25/63 for 30 days. Also reported admitted 9/22/63 to a Richmond G.H. Reported present on hospital muster rolls, Richmond, to 10/31/63. Absent on detached service at brigade HQ, 12/1/63–3/31/64. Captured near Reams Station/Malone's Crossing, according to rolls of 3/64–12/64. According to Federal POW records, captured 8/25/64, and exd. 3/1/65. Admitted to a Richmond G.H., 3/18/65. Frl 3/24/65 for 30 days. Dead as of 1893. (Barringer; Cabarrus; CSR 270:5)

Hagler, Joel A.: Enl. 2/6/64 as PVT, Co. F. Reported present Mar.–Dec./64. Resident of Saw, NC, circa 1893. (Barringer; Cabarrus; CSR 270:5)

Hale, David D.: PVT, Co. A. (AsheCo)

Hale, David L. From Guilford Co. At age 25, enl. 6/8/61 as PVT, Co. A. Reported present on company muster rolls of Nov.–Dec./61. Also reported present and acting as rgt. teamster, Jan.–Feb./62, 9/62–2/63. Rgt Return for 2/62 and 362 list him as on extra duty as a teamster. Reported present Mar.–Apr./63 as staff wagoner. AWOL July–Aug./63. According to roll of Sept.–Oct./63, absent on detached service at the company shops, NC, since 6/27/63. Absent on detached service at Fayetteville, NC Foundry beginning 7/27/63. Otherwise accounted for 11/30/63–4/64, July–Dec./64. (CSR 270:5; AsheCo as David L. Hall)

Hall, Anderson J.: From Northampton Co. At age 18, enl. 1862 as PVT, Co. B. Reported present 9/62–4/63, 6/30–Dec./63, 4/1–8/31/64. Absent with Provost Guard at Brigade HQ, Sept.–Dec./64. (CSR 270:5)

Hall, Charles M.: B. Sampson Co. Co. G. Age 38, stood 6'6", had dark hair, gray eyes, and a light complexion. Dsh for disability, 8/19/61. (CSR 270:5)

Hall, Cornelius: From Northampton Co. Farmer. At age 22, enl. 1862 as PVT, Co. B. Reported present Sept.–Oct./62. Absent sent to a Gordonsville G.H., 11/15/62. Admitted to a Richmond G.H., 11/17/62; admitted again to a Richmond G.H., 12/10/62. Reported present on company muster rolls of Jan.–Apr./63. Absent on detached service to purchase a horse in NC, 8/27/63. Captured at Catlett's Station, 10/14/63. Exd. 2/65. (CSR 270:5)

Hall, Ed: Co. B. (Zeb. Vance Papers, NCSA [courtesy Whit Joyner]; first name also listed as Ad)

Hall, J.B.: Enl. 2/24/64 as PVT, Co. E. Reported present on company muster rolls of Mar.–Apr./64. According to roll of 4/30–8/31/64, prm to aide-de-camp on the staff of Laurence Baker, 7/15/64. (CSR 270:5)

Hall, John: From Northampton Co. At age 20, enl. 7/62 as PVT, Co. B. Absent sent to a Winchester G.H., Sept.–Oct./62. Reported present on company muster rolls of 11/62–4/63. Absent on detached service to purchase a horse in NC, 8/27/63. Reported AWOL on rolls of 6/30–10/31/63. Reported present Nov.–Dec./63, Mar.–Oct./64. NFR. (CSR 270:5)

Hall, William S.: Enl. 7/62 as saddler, Co. B. Absent on detached service in Winchester, VA, according to Sept.–Oct./62 company muster rolls. Beginning 2/21/63, absent on detached service to make shoes at Gordonsville, VA, according to Jan.–Feb./63 rolls. Absent sick in a Gordonsville G.H. as of 2/10/63 according to Mar.–Apr./63 rolls. On July–Aug./63 rolls, listed on detached service to NC after a horse, beginning 8/27/63. Reported present on company muster rolls of 6/30–10/31/63 rolls. Reported absent at home sick on 11/63–2/64, 4/1/64 rolls. Absent on detached service making shoes at corps HQ, Mar.–Apr./64. Reported present, 4/30–Oct./64. (CSR 270:5)

Halsey, Frank B.: From Alleghany Co. At age 22, enl. 6/6/61 as PVT, Co. A. Reported present on company muster rolls of 11/61–2/62. Reported absent on Sept.–Oct./62 rolls as on detached service at Winchester beginning 9/5/62. Nov.–Dec./62 rolls report him absent scouting since 12/25/62. Jan.–Feb./63 rolls, absent on frl beginning 2/15/63. Reported present Mar.–Apr./63. Listed AWOL on July–Aug./63 rolls, beginning either 6/27 or 7/27/63. Reported present Jan.–Aug./64. Absent sick beginning 10/27/64, according to Sept.–Oct./64 rolls. Reported admitted to a Petersburg G.H. with a gunshot wound in the left hand, 10/28/64. Trn to Raleigh, 11/11/64. Reported present Nov.–Dec./64. (AsheCo; CSR 270:5)

Ham, Henry B.: From Wayne Co. At age 29, enl. 6/20/61 as PVT, Co. H. Reported present Nov.–Dec./61. According to Jan.–Feb./62 rolls, captured on picket near Difficult Run, VA, 2/7/62. Reported present on company muster rolls of Nov.–Dec./62. Absent on horse detail, Jan.–Feb./63. Reported present Mar.–Apr./63. Absent on detached service to procure a horse, July–Aug./63, after horse was KIA 8/1/63. Listed as AWOL, Sept.–Dec./63; also listed as dsh, 12/31/63. Also mentioned in Jan.–Feb./64 records. (CSR 270:5)

Ham, Jacob: B. Ashe Co. Farmer. Enl. 3/7/62 as PVT, Co. A. Reported present on company muster rolls of Sept.–Dec./62. Absent Jan.–Feb./63 on frl to buy a horse. Reported present Mar.–Apr./63. WIA 6/9/63 in right shoulder joint. Operated on 6/10/63; head and neck incised. Admitted 7/3/63 to a Charlottesville G.H., then frl 7/17/63, initially for 60 days. At home recuperating afterwards. Admitted to a Richmond G.H., 5/22/64, with a gunshot wound in right shoulder joint. Returned to duty, 6/2/64. Dsh at age 38, 2/14/65, due to infection from wound. Stood 5'8", had a fair complexion, blue eyes, and auburn hair.(*Medical History* 10: 532; AsheCo; CSR 270:5)

Ham, Joseph H.: From Franklin Co. At age 23, enl. 6/61 or 7/61 as PVT, Co. E. Reported present on company muster rolls of May–June/62, 9/62–4/63. Absent on detached service in NC to procure a horse beginning 8/27/63 (according to July–Aug./63 rolls). Reported present 6/30/63–12/64. (Pearce: 253; CSR 270:5)

Hamilton, Franklin F.: B. Washington Co., NC. Enl. 8/2/61 as PVT, Co. B. Absent at a Culpeper C.H. G.H., Nov.–Dec./61. Reported present on company muster rolls, Jan.–Apr./62. Dsh 5/5/62 at age 30 due to a broken down constitution from winter exposure. Stood 5'8" tall, had a florid complexion and blue eyes. (CSR 270:5)

Hamilton, Josiah: Cns 6/2/64 as PVT, Co. I, after trn from 16th NC Bn. Reported present on company muster rolls through 12/64. (CSR 270:5)

Hamilton, William H.: Resident of Ashe Co. Enl. 11/10/64 as PVT, Co. A, after trn from McRae's Bn, 10/7/64. Reported present on company muster rolls of Sept.–Dec./64. Captured at Five Forks, VA, 4/1/65. Released on taking the oath, 6/27/65. Stood 5'10¼", had a dark complexion, black hair, and hazel eyes. (AsheCo; CSR 270:5)

Haney, Charles: From McDowell Co. At age 44, enl. 6/20/61 as PVT, Co. G. Reported present on company muster rolls of Jan.–Feb./62, May–June/62. Reported in a Richmond G.H., 10/4/62. Reported present Sept.–Oct./62. Dsh 12/28/62 or 1/31/63. D. 5/20/63. (CSR 270:5)

Hanley, George J.: From Chatham Co. At age 19, enl. 7/7/62. Reported present on company muster rolls of Sept.–Oct./62. Absent on detached service on a scout, Jan.–Feb./63. Reported present Mar.–Apr./63, July–Aug./63. AWOL beginning 9/63. (CSR 270:5)

Hanrahan, Walter S.: From Pitt Co. At age 32, enl. 6/25/61 as QM SGT, Co. H. Admitted to a G.H., 12/17/61, and trn. Reported absent sick at home on company muster rolls of Nov.–Dec./61. Captured 2/7/62 while on picket along Difficult Run, VA. Elected 2LT, 11/20/62, to rank from 10/26/62. Resigned 5/63. (CSR 270:5)

Hardin, A.P.: From Henderson Co. At age 24, enl. 5/20/61 as PVT, Co. G. Reported present on company muster rolls of Jan.–Feb./62, May–June/62, Sept.–Oct./62. Absent on detached service, 11/62–2/63. Reported AWOL, Mar.–Apr./63. Captured (listed as a J.P. Harding) 5/63 at Thompson's Crossroads, and prl. Absent July–Aug./63 on prl. Reported present Sept.–Dec./63. AWOL beginning 2/64 according to 4/1/64 roll. According to Mar.–Apr./64 roll, absent under the sentence of a General Court Martial. Still absent, in Salisbury, NC, 4/30–Aug./64. Reported present on company muster rolls of Sept.–Dec./64. (CSR 270:5)

Hardin, Frank: Resident of Jefferson. At age 22, enl 5/21/61. 3SGT., Co. A. Reported present on company muster rolls of Jan.–Feb./62, 9/62–4/63. Admitted 5/9/63 to a Charlottesville G.H. with syphilis. Returned to duty, 6/6/63. Absent on detached service after a horse, July–Aug./63. Reported present 9/63–2/29/64. Absent on detached service to buy a horse, 2/29/64. Reported present 4/1/64, 7–8/64, then absent on detached service to again procure a horse, Sept.–Oct./64. Reported present, Nov.–Dec./64. Admitted to a Raleigh G.H., 9/17/64, and returned to duty, 9/23/64. (AsheCo; CSR 270:5)

Hardin, Henry W.: From Ashe Co. B. 12/29/21. Enl. 5/25/61. 1SGT, Co. A. Reported present on company muster rolls of 11/61–2/62, Sept.–Oct./62. According to Nov.–Dec./62 roll, absent scouting beginning 12/25. Absent on detached service with the baggage at Gordonsville, Jan.–Feb./63. Reported present on company muster rolls of Mar.–Apr./63. Trn 6/63 to Co. D, 58th N.C. D. 9/11/04. Bur. Boone City Cem., Boone. (AsheCo; Stepp; CSR 270:5)

Hardin, Martin: From Ashe Co. At age 23, enl. 6/8/61 as PVT, Co. A. Reported present on company muster rolls of 11/61–2/62. Absent on detached service at Winchester, beginning 9/17/62, according to Sept.–Oct./62 roll. Absent on detached service, Nov.–Dec./62. Absent on sick frl, Jan.–Feb./63. Reported present, Mar.–Apr./63. Trn 6/63 to Co. D, 58th N.C. (AsheCo; CSR 270:5)

Hardin, Samuel N.: From Henderson Co. At age 17, enl. 5/20/61 as PVT, Co. G. Reported present on company muster rolls of Jan.–Feb./62, May–June/62. Absent sick in camp at Winchester, VA, Sept.–Oct./62. Reported present 11/62–4/63. Absent on detached service to procure a horse, July–Aug./63. Reported present, Sept.–Dec./63, Mar.–Oct./64. (CSR 270:5)

Hardy, Andrew J.: B. in NC. From Onslow Co. At age 40, enl. 7/61 as PVT, Co. I. Reported present on company muster rolls of 11/61–2/62. Captured at Willis Church, 6/29/62. Stood 5'8", had dark hair, blue eyes, and a sallow complexion. Absent in camp at Winchester, VA, Sept.–Oct./62. Reported present 11/62–4/63, 10/31/63, Jan.–Dec./64. Captured 4/25/65 at New Bern. Prl 5/65 and released to Duplin Co. (CSR 270:5)

Hardy, Lemuel H.: From Onslow Co. At age 18, enl. 5/62 as PVT, Co. I. Reported present on company muster rolls of May–June/62, 11/62–4/63, 10/31/63, Jan.–Aug./64. Reported on detached service with Provost Guard at brigade HQ, Sept.–Dec./64. (CSR 270:5)

Hargett, F.M.: From Mecklenburg Co. At age 19, enl. 5/25/61 as PVT, Co. C. D. 12/61 in Camp W.S. Ashe of either pneumonia or typhoid fever. (CSR 270:5; Alexander)

Hargett, H.M.: From Mecklenburg Co. At age 30, enl. 5/25/61 as PVT, Co. C. Reported absent sick on company muster rolls of 11/61–2/62, beginning 11/4/61 in Petersburg. Also listed absent sick on rgt return of 2/62. Reported present 5/62–10/31/62. Absent sent to NC "to take charge of horses purchased for the regiment," 12/25/62, Jan.–Feb./63. Reported present Mar.–Apr./63. According to July–Aug./63 rolls, absent on detached service since 8/7/63. Reported absent sick as of 9/1/63 on Sept.–Oct./63 rolls. On a register of a Charlottesville G.H. as admitted 8/22/63 and trn 9/21/63. Reported present 11/63–2/64. Listed on 4/1/64 as on detached service as of 3/15/64. Reported present Mar.–Aug./31/64. Absent on detached service as of 10/14/64, according to Sept.–Oct./64. Reported present, Nov.–Dec./64. Admitted 1/30/65 to a Charlotte G.H. (Alexander; CSR 270:5)

Hargett, Harrison: From Mecklenburg Co. At age 35, enl. 5/25/61 as PVT, Co. C. Absent sick, Nov.–Dec./61. D. 1/17/62 in Petersburg. (Alexander; CSR 270:5)

Hargett, Osborne: From Mecklenburg Co. At age 33, enl. 7/30/61 as PVT, Co. C. Reported present on company muster rolls of 11/61–2/62, 5/62–4/63. Admitted to a Richmond G.H., 7/29/64. Reported present July–Aug./63. According to Sept.–Oct./63 rolls, captured 9/22/63. Prl, 4/27/64. Admitted 5/1/64 to a Richmond G.H. with chronic diarrhea. Frl 5/2/64; also frl from a G.H., 8/11/64. Absent sick, 4/30–8/31/64. Absent on detached service beginning 10/20/64 according to Sept.–Oct./64 rolls. Reported present, Nov.–Dec./64 rolls. (Alexander; CSR 270:5)

Harkey, B.C.: PVT. Co. unknown. According to a register of POWs at Camp Hamilton, VA, captured 5/30/65; released 5/31/65. (CSR 270:5)

Harkey, B.M.: Admitted 5/4/64 to Richmond G.H. with shrapnel wound in shoulder. Admitted to Danville G.H., 5/18/64. Retired to Invalid Corps, 8/11/64. (CSR 270:5 for David M. Harkey) May be the same man as David M. Harkey.

Harkey, David M.: B. 8/29/26. From Cabarrus Co. Enl. 6/15/61 as PVT, Co. F. Reported present on company muster rolls of 11/61–2/62, May–June/62, Sept.–Dec./62. WIA Upperville, 6/21/63. Absent on sick frl, according to July–Aug./63 rolls. Reported present Jan.–Mar./31/64. Absent on sick frl, Mar.–Dec./64. Resident of Charlotte, circa 1893. D. 1/17/06. Bur. Oakwood Cem., Raleigh. (Barringer; Mizelle; Cabarrus; Stepp; CSR 270:5) May be the same man as B.M. Harkey.

Harkey, John Michael: Enl. 10/4/64 as PVT, Co. F. Reported present on company muster rolls of Sept.–Oct./64. Dead as of 1893. (CSR 270:5; Barringer)

Harkey, P.C.: From Mecklenburg Co. At age 32, enl. 5/28/61 as 4SGT, Co. C. Reported present on company muster rolls of 11/61–2/62, May–10/31/62. Absent sent to NC for clothing, 11/21/62. Reported present on company muster rolls of Jan.–Apr./63, July–Oct./63. Absent on detached service as of 12/28/63 according to Nov.–Dec./63. Reported present on company muster rolls of Jan.–Dec./64. WIA by minie ball at Dinwiddie C.H., 3/31/65. Sent to a Federal G.H. with a gunshot wound in the right side. (CSR 270:5; Alexander)

Harkey, S.B.: From Mecklenburg Co. At age 31, 5/25/61 as PVT, Co. C. According to a pay receipt roll, d. 10/61. Place of death: Ridgeway, NC, according to a claim. (CSR 270:5; Alexander calls him T.B.)

Harrell, A.J.: B. 1/12/41. Cns. 10/12/64 as PVT, Co. I. Absent sick in a Richmond G.H. beginning 10/26/64, according to company muster rolls of Sept.–Oct./64. Returned to duty, 11/10/64. Reported present Nov.–Dec./64. D. 7/23/07. Bur. Willowdale Cem., Goldsboro, NC. (Stepp; CSR 270:5)

Harrell, David: From Martin Co. At age 29, enl. 7/8/62 as PVT, Co. B. Reported present on company muster rolls of 4/62–4/63, July–Dec./63, Mar.–Dec./64. (CSR 270:5; Zeb. Vance Papers, NCSA [courtesy Whit Joyner])

Harrell, James H.: Resident of Green County, NC. At age 27, enl. 8/16/61 as PVT, Co. H. Volunteered "because every one else did." Reported present on company muster rolls of 11/61–2/62, May–June/62, Sept.–Dec./62. Absent to procure a horse, Jan.–Feb./63. Reported present on company muster rolls of Mar.–Apr./63. Absent sent to a G.H., 6/63, according to July–Oct./63 rolls. Reported present Nov.–Dec./63. According to Jan.–Feb./64 rolls, deserted 2/1/64, at the Rapidan River. Took oath of allegiance, 3/12/64, and sent to Philadelphia. Had light complexion, brown hair, blue eyes, and stood 5' 9¾". (Turner/Baker Papers; CSR 270:5).

Harrill, A.S.: Cns. 6/2/64 as PVT, Co. I. Reported present through 12/64. Rolls of Mar.–Apr./64, dated 9/7/64, also lists him as on detached service in NC to remount horses. NFR. (CSR 270:5)

Harrington, L.: PVT, Co. G. WIA. At age 34, 4" excision taken from left humerus, 4/2/65. D. 5/18/65 from exhaustion. (*Medical History* 10: 683)

Harris, James H.: From Warren Co. At age 26, enl. 6/27/61 as PVT, Co. E. On detached service as a courier with GEN Stuart's Bodyguard, beginning 11/15/61. Also reported absent on Jan.–Feb./62 rolls. Rgt returns of 2/62 and 3/62 also report him as on detached service with Stuart's H.Q. Reported present, May–June/62, Sept.–Oct./62. Beginning with Nov.–Dec./62 rolls, on detached service with Stuart beginning 11/5/62. Continued on detached service with Stuart through 10/31/63. Captured 8/1/63, according to Nov.–Dec./63 rolls. Exd 10/30/64. (CSR 270:5)

Harris, John: From Buncombe Co. At age 22, enl. 5/20/61 as PVT, Co. G. Reported present on company muster rolls of Jan.–Feb./62. Rgt Return of 2/62 reports him on extra duty as a teamster. According to May–June/62 rolls, deserted near Murfreesboro, NC, 6/62. (CSR 270:5)

Harris, Richard W.: From Warren Co. At age 25, enl. 6/14/61 as PVT, Co. E. Absent sick beginning 10/13/61. Rgt Return of 2/62 lists him as absent sick. Reported present May–June/62, Sept.–Dec./62. Absent on detached service, Jan.–Feb./63. Reported present on company muster rolls of Mar.–Apr./63. Captured 6/21/63 at Upperville, VA, according to July–Aug./63 rolls. Nov.–Dec./63 rolls list him as KIA at Upperville. (CSR 270:5)

Harris, Wade: Res. of Franklin Co. At age 23, enl. 8/6/61 as PVT, Co. E. Reported present on company muster rolls of Jan.–Feb./62, May–June/62. Reported in a G.H., 9/8/62, according to Sept.–Oct./62 rolls. Also admitted 10/23/62 to a Richmond G.H. with diarrhea. Returned to duty from the Danville G.H., 11/6/62. Reported present 11/62–4/63, July–Oct./31/63. Absent on detached service in Nelson Co., VA, with disabled horses, 11/63–2/64. Absent on frl in NC, Mar.–Apr./64. Reported present 4/30–Oct./64. Captured 12/10/64 at Armstrong Mills, VA; reported absent as a POW on Nov.–Dec./64 company muster rolls. Released 6/27/65 on taking the oath. Had fair complexion, dark brown hair, and blue eyes, and stood 5' 9¼". (Pearce: 255; CSR 270:5)

Harrison, George W.: Cns 2/6/64 as PVT, Co. E. Reported present on company muster rolls of 4/1/64, Mar.–Dec./64. WIA; admitted to a Richmond G.H., 5/25/64, with a gunshot wound in the scalp. Returned to duty 6/2/64. (CSR 270:5)

Hartis, A.L.: B. 1840. From Mecklenburg Co. At age 28, enl. 3/8/62 as PVT, Co. C. Reported present on company muster rolls of 5/62–4/63, 7/63–12/64. Prl in Charlotte, NC, 5/17/65. D. 2/22/05. Bur. Elmwood Cem., Charlotte. (Alexander; Stepp; CSR 270:5)

Hartis, M.A.: From Mecklenburg Co. At age 23, enl. 5/10/62 as PVT, Co. C. Reported present on company muster rolls of 5/62–4/63, July–Aug./63. According to Sept.–Oct./63 and Nov.–Dec./63 rolls, on detached service beginning 10/8/63 and 12/1/63. Reported present Jan.–Apr./64. Absent sick 4/30–8/31/64. Reported present Sept.–Oct./64. Admitted 7/16/64 to a Petersburg G.H. and again on 8/13/64 with syphilis. Returned to duty from a Farmville G.H., 9/27/64. Absent on frl beginning 12/22/64, according to Nov.–Dec./64 rolls. On a POW list in Raleigh, NC, 4/13/65. (Alexander; CSR 270:5)

Hartley, Elbert: Co. D (Davis)

Hartley, F.E.: SGT, Co. D. On a register of POWs at Knoxville, TN, as captured 3/28/65 at Boone, NC. (CSR 270:5; Davis lists him as "Fin")

Hartley, Harrison: Resident of Boone, NC. Enl. 9/1/63 as PVT, Co. D. Reported present on company muster rolls of 11/63–4/64, 8/31–Dec./64. Captured 3/28/65 at Boone, NC. Released on taking the oath, 6/16/65. Had dark complexion, dark hair, and dark eyes, and stood 5' 3". Excellent horseman. (CSR 270:5; Jim Grant to the author, July 10, 1990)

Hartley, Lewis H.: B. 10/30/45. Enl. 12/20/63 as PVT, Co. D. Reported present on company muster rolls of Jan.–Apr./64. Company muster rolls list him as absent sick in a G.H., 8/31/64, Sept.–

Oct./64. Admitted 8/15/64 to a Petersburg G.H. and deserted from there, 9/14/64. According to a Danville G.H. register, frl 10/26/64 for 30 days after a bout with chronic diarrhea. Reported on sick frl, Nov.–Dec./64. D. 7/7/20. Bur. Laurel Fork Baptist Church Cem., Watauga Co. (Stepp; CSR 270:5)

Hartley, Rubin: Co. D (Davis)

Hartman, Enoch: Enl. 9/6/64 as PVT, Co. K. Deserted 10/64 and took the oath. (CSR 270:5)

Hartzog, James: B. 9/2/26. Enl. 9/29/64 as PVT, Co. K. Reported absent sick on company muster rolls of Nov.–Dec./64. Admitted 12/16/64 to a Richmond G.H. Frl for 60 days, 1/18/65. D. 6/22/01. Bur. Calloway Family Cem., Beaver Creek, Ashe Co. (Stepp; CSR 270:5)

Haskins, H.: PVT, Co. A. Admitted 3/24/65 to a Richmond G.H. Frl for 30 days, 3/27/65. Prl Goldsboro, 5/13/65. (CSR 270:5)

Haurishea, Walter S.: Co. H. R. May 1863. (CSR 270:1)

Hauser, D.H.: Cns 10/3/64 as PVT, Co. I. Reported present on company muster rolls of Sept.–Dec./64. (CSR 270:5)

Hauser, I.: PVT, Co. H. Middle 3d of leg amputated, 7/1/63. D. 4/2/64. (*Medical History* 12: 557)

Hawks, Frederick A.: B. 1840. From Warren Co. At age 21, enl. 6/4/61 as PVT, Co. E. Reported present on company muster rolls of Jan.–Feb./62. Rgt Return of 3/2 lists him absent sick in a Richmond G.H. beginning 3/23/62. Reported present May–June/62, 9/62–2/63. Absent at a Staunton G.H. beginning 4/1/63 according to Mar.–Apr./63 rolls. Listed as convalescent on a Staunton G.H. hospital roll to 4/30/63. Also reported absent sick on rolls of July–Aug./63. Admitted to a Richmond G.H., 7/31/63. Reported present 6/30–10/31/63. Absent on frl, Nov.–Dec./63. Reported present Jan.–Apr./64. Absent on detached service at Stony Creek, VA, 4/30–10/64. Captured 12/1/64 at Wilkinson Bridge. Reported absent as a POW, Nov.–Dec./64. Released on taking the oath, 6/14/65. Had a florid complexion, brown hair, gray eyes, and stood 6'1¼". D. 1913. Bur. Wise Baptist Church Cem., Warren Co. (CSR 270:5; CGR: 6)

Hawks, James H.: From Warren Co. At age 18, enl. 8/61 as PVT, Co. E. Reported present on company muster rolls of Jan.–Feb./62, May–June/62. Captured at Williamsport, MD, 9/20 or 9/21/62. Exd, 10/6/62. Admitted to a Richmond G.H., 10/9/62. Frl 11/1/62. On a register of approved frl, dated 10/18/62. Listed as AWOL, Jan.–Feb./63. Reported present Mar.–Apr./63. According to July–Aug./63, absent on detached service in NC to procure a horse beginning 8/27/63. Reported present 6/30/63–2/64, 4/1/64. Absent on detached service in NC to buy a horse, Mar.–Apr./64. Reported present 4/30–Oct./64. Trn to the infantry according to Nov.–Dec./64 roll.

Hayes, C.W.: From Franklin Co. At age 27, enl. 6/11/61 as PVT, Co. E. Reported present on company muster rolls of Jan.–Feb./62, May–June/62. Captured at Malvern Hill, 8/5/62, and prl 8/26/62. Reported present 9/62–4/63. Rgt return of 3/62 lists him as sick in Culpeper beginning 1/2/62. D. 4/4/63. (CSR 270:5)

Hayes, James H.: From Granville Co. or Warren Co. At age 21, enl. 6/61 as PVT, Co. E. According to Jan.–Feb./62 company muster rolls, absent at a Manassas G.H. beginning 2/26/62. Rgt returns of 2/62 and 3/62 list him as absent sick. Admitted 3/2/62 to a G.H. with chronic diarrhea. Trn to a Petersburg G.H., 4/19/62. Reported present May–June/62, Sept.–Oct./62. Absent on detached service Nov.–Dec./62. Absent on detached service with COL Baker, Mar.–Apr./63. Absent on detached service with COL/GEN Gordon as courier beginning 8/20/63, according to July–Aug./63 rolls, and remained in that position through 4/64. Reported present, 4/30/64–10/64. Absent in a Raleigh G.H., Nov.–Dec./64; admitted 11/22/64 with chronic rheumatism. Trn to Kittrell's, 1/1/65. (CSR 270:5)

Hayes, John W.: Co. H. KIA. (Monie)

Hayes, John H.: From Wayne Co. Enl. 6/20/61 as CPL, Co. H. Reported present Nov.–Dec./61. Absent home on sick frl beginning 2/3/62, according to company muster rolls of Jan.–Feb./62. Rgt returns of 2/62 and 3/62 show him absent sick beginning 2/3/62. Reported present May–June/62. Absent on detached service at Winchester, VA, Sept.–Oct./62. On detached service as a scout with MAJ Whitaker, Nov.–Dec./62. Reported present, Jan.–Apr./63. Absent on detached service to procure a horse, July–Aug./63. Elected 2LT, 8/1/63. Reported present 9/63–4/64. Resigned 7/13/64 due to ill health and age. (CSR 270:1; CSR 270:5)

Hayes, Wyatt: Co. D. Trn. to 37th North Carolina. (Davis)

Hayman, William: From Wilson Co. At age 45, cns. 7/62 as PVT, Co. I. Reported present on company muster rolls of Sept.–Dec./62. Absent on detached service, Jan.–Feb./63. Reported present Mar.–Apr./63. Captured at Hagerstown, MD, 7/12/63. Dsh 12/17/64 on taking the oath. Had a dark complexion, black hair, and gray eyes, and stood 5' 6½". (CSR 270:5)

Hazell, A.S.: Cns. 11/26/64 as PVT, Co. H. Reported present on company muster rolls of Nov.–Dec./64. (CSR 270:5)

Hazell, M.C.: Enl. 1/26/64 as PVT, Co. H. Reported present on company muster rolls of Mar.–Apr./64, 4/1/64. Admitted to a Richmond G.H. with a gunshot wound, 6/14/64. Frl for 30 days, 6/30/64. Reported absent on frl, 4/30–12/64. (CSR 270:5)

Hearn, Reuben M.: From Pitt Co. At age 19, enl. 4/7/62 as PVT, Co. H. WIA 6/29/62 at Willis Church and sent to the G.H., according to May–June/62 rolls. Also absent, 4/1/64. Reported present on extra or daily duty, Mar.–Apr./64. Medical examining board ordered him to light duty with Invalid Corps in Tarboro, NC, 5/7/64, due to a gunshot wound in the "cranium right parietal bone, loss of bone." On rolls of 4/30–10/64, listed absent on light duty at Tarboro. Admitted to a Richmond G.H., 11/5/64, and returned to duty 11/9/64. According to Nov.–Dec./64 rolls, retired by examining board 12/2/64. (CSR 270:5)

Heatherly, Moses: From Henderson Co. Enl. 5/20/61 as PVT, Co. G. Reported present on company muster rolls of Jan.–Feb./62, May–June/62. Absent in camp at Winchester on detached service, Sept.–Oct./62. Reported present 11/62–4/63. Absent on detached service to procure a horse, July–Aug./63. Absent sick at home, Sept.–Dec./63. Listed AWOL, 4/1/64. Deserted. (CSR 270:5)

Heavlin, Robert A.: B. 1/36. Enl. 10/27/64 as PVT, Co. E. Absent on frl of indulgence, Nov.–Dec./64. D. 5/31/16. Bur. Oakwood Cem., Raleigh. (Stepp; CSR 270:5)

Helms, H.M.: From Union Co. At age 18, enl. 10/21/61 as PVT, Co. C. Reported present on company muster rolls of 11/61–2/62, 5/62–4/63, July–Aug./63. Captured 9/22/63, at Jack's Shop. Prl 10/11/64 and exd 10/29/64. Psb. d from chronic diarrhea at Elmira Prison. (Alexander; CSR 270:5)

Helms, J.A.: From Union Co. At age 26, enl. 5/25/61 as PVT, Co. C. Reported present on company muster rolls of 11/61–2/62, 5/62–4/63. Absent on detached service since 8/24/63 according to July–Aug./63 rolls. Absent Sept.–Oct./63. Reported present 11/63–4/64. WIA and admitted 6/64 to a Richmond or Petersburg G.H. D. 6/22/64 from effects of gunshot wound. (Alexander; CSR 270:5)

Helms, J.W.: From Union Co. At age 20, enl. 5/25/61 as PVT, Co. C. Reported present on company muster rolls of 11/61–2/62, 5/62–10/62. Admitted 7/4/62 to a Richmond G.H. with a back contusion; trn to a Petersburg G.H. Absent scouting beginning 12/25/62, according to Nov.–Dec./62 rolls. Reported present Jan.–Apr./63, July–Oct./63. Absent on detached service beginning 12/28/63, according to Nov.–Dec./63 rolls. Reported present Jan.–Dec./64. (Alexander; CSR 270:5)

Helms, Manoah: Age 41. Born in Union Co. Enl. 9/16/63 in 16th NC Bn. Cns. 6/2/64 as PVT, Co. I. Reported present on company muster rolls of Mar.–Apr./64, 4/31–8/31/64. On detached service at Stony Creek, VA, beginning 10/1/64, according to Sept.–Oct./64 rolls. Absent on detached service beginning 12/8/64 to remount, according to Nov.–Dec./64 rolls. Had gray eyes, black hair, a fair complexion, and stood 5/8 1/2." (CSR 270:5)

Hemphill, W.A.: From Buncombe Co. At age 21, enl. 7/26/61 as PVT, Co. G. Reported present on company muster rolls of Jan.–Feb./62. According to rgt returns of 2/62 and 3/62. Reported present May–June/62, Sept.–Dec./62. Absent on detached service, Jan.–Apr./63. Listed as AWOL, July–Aug./63. Deserted, 4/5/63. (CSR 270:5)

Henderson, W.M.F.: From Mecklenburg Co. At age 24, enl. 5/8/62 as PVT, Co. C. Reported present on company muster rolls of May–Dec./62. Absent on detached service in NC to procure a horse beginning 2/21/63, according to Jan.–Feb./63 rolls. Reported present Mar.–Apr./63, 7/63–4/64. Absent on detached service beginning 8/15/64, according to 4/30–8/31/64 roll. Reported present on Sept.–Oct./64. According to Nov.–Dec./64 roll, "dropped by order." Prl Charlotte, 5/24/65. (Alexander; CSR 270:5)

Hendrix, Floyd F.: From Watauga Co. At age 24, enl. 5/11/61 as PVT, Co. D. Reported present on company muster rolls of 11/61–2/62, 5/62–2/63. "In poor fix for fighting" after drinking whiskey, 9/8/62. Absent at home sick, Mar.–Apr./63. Absent at home to procure a horse, July–Aug./63. Prm CPL. Reported present 6/30/63–2/64. Absent 2/29–3/31/64. Absent at home to buy a horse, Mar.–Apr./64. WIA and absent at home according to rolls of 8/31/64. Reported present Sept.–Dec./64. (Davis; CSR 270:5)

Hendrix, William: Co. D. WIA. Admitted 7/16/64 to a Petersburg G.H. with a gunshot wound. Trn to Salisbury, NC, 7/27/64. (CSR 270:5)

Hendrix, William B.: From Wilkes Co. At age 21, enl. 7/10/61 as PVT, Co. D. Reported present on company muster rolls of Nov.–Dec./61. D. in camp, 2/17 or 2/19/62, from pneumonia

(Davis; CSR 270: 4 for George N. Folk; CSR 270:5)

Henry, James F.: From Macon Co. At age 24, enl. 7/23/61 as PVT, Co. K. Absent on company muster rolls of 11/61–2/62, at home suffering from a broken leg. Rgt return of 2/62 reports him absent sick. Prm 4CPL, spring 1862. Reported present May–June/62, 9/62–4/63. Prm 2CPL according to Nov.–Dec./62 rolls. Absent on detached service in NC to procure a horse, July–Aug./63. Prm 1CPL according to Nov.–Dec./63 rolls. Reported present 10/31/63–831/64. Admitted to a Richmond G.H., 7/29/64, with pleuritis. Returned to duty, 8/15/64. Absent on detached service to bale forage for CPT White, AQM, Sept.–Oct./64. (CSR 270:5)

Henry, James L.: From Buncombe Co. Age 23. Reported present on Field and Staff rolls of 11/61–2/62. According to those rolls, commissioned adj 10/24/62. Reported present on company muster rolls as 1LT and commanding Co. G, Jan.–Feb./62. Rgt Return of 2/62 shows him present as adj; 3/62 return shows him absent sick beginning 3/4/62. Acted as adj until 4/15/62, when James L. Gaines took the position. Absent with GEN Ransom's staff, May–June/62, Sept.–Oct./62. Absent as brigade inspector according to Jan.–Feb./63 rolls. Absent detailed to GEN Hampton's staff, Mar.–Apr./63. Absent detached on a general court martial at Culpeper C.H., according to July–Aug./63 rolls. Served as Judge Advocate for Stuart's Division, 8/26–Oct./9/63. Effective 10/5/63, resigned as commander, Co. G, to take command of a home defense cavalry company as CPT in the NC mountains for state defense. (CSR 270:1, 5; one record in John S. Henry CSR; Henry)

Henry, John S.: From Macon Co. At age 28, enl. as PVT, Co. K, 7/25/61. Reported present on company muster rolls of 11/61–2/62, May–June/62, 9/62–4/63, July–Aug./63, 10/31/63–12/64. Prm 4 CPL according to Nov.–Dec./63 rolls. Prm 5SGT, 10/1/64. (CSR 270:5)

Henry, R.A.: From Macon Co. At age 18, enl. 2/16/63 as PVT, Co. K. Reported present on company muster rolls of Mar.–Apr./63. KIA 6/23 or 6/27/63, at Fairfield Station, VA. (CSR 270:5)

Henry, William W.: From Macon Co. At age 24, enl. 5/6/62 as PVT, Co. K. Reported present on company muster rolls of May–June/62, 9/62–4/63, July–Aug./63, 10/31/63. Absent sick in a G.H., Nov.–Dec./63. Reported present Jan.–Oct./64. Absent Nov.–Dec./64 guarding forage at Bellfield, VA. (CSR 270:5)

Henson, John W.: B. 5/13/19 in Surry Co. From Watauga Co. Farmer. Enl. 2/28/62 or 3/1/62 as PVT, Co. D. Absent sick according to company muster rolls of May–June/62, in a G.H. at Wilson, NC beginning 4/28/62. Reported present 6/30–10/31/62. Dsh due to "testis" problem. Stood 6' tall, had blue eyes, light hair. D. 10/21/05. Bur. Henson's Chapel Cem., Watauga Co. (Stepp; CSR 270:5)

Herndon, William H.: B. 5/16/46. Cns. 10/3/64 as PVT, Co. I. Reported present on company muster rolls of Sept.–Dec./64. D. 6/7/03. Bur. Bethlehem Baptist Church Cem., Cleveland Co. (Stepp; CSR 270:5)

Herring, Abiah: B. Wayne Co. At age 24, enl. 6/20/61 as PVT, Co. H. Reported present on company muster rolls of 11/61–2/62. Reported absent sick on rgt return of 2/62. Reported present on rolls of May–June/62, Sept.–Oct./62. Stood 5' 8¾", had fair complexion, blue eyes, and light hair. D. from disease 12/16/62 at Culpeper C.H. (CSR 270:5)

Hess, W.: PVT, Co. E. According to Federal records, captured 12/10/64. Sent to City Point, 12/11/64. (CSR 270:5)

Hester, William: From Macon Co. Age 18. PVT, Co. I. Rejected by COL Baker. (CSR 270:5)

Hestilo, Elias: Resident of Asheville. At age 18, enl. 5/20/61 as PVT, Co. G. Admitted 11/3/61 to a Richmond G.H. with the measles. Returned to duty, 11/8/61. Reported present on company muster rolls of Jan.–Feb./62. Admitted 3/18/62 to a Richmond G.H. with diarrhea. Returned to duty 3/22/64. Reported present May–June/62, 9/62–4/63, July–Aug./63. Absent on detached service in the QM Dept. at Brandy Station, Sept.–Oct./63. Reported with the Div. Q.M., Nov.–Dec./63. Reported absent on detached service, 4/1/64. Absent sick in a Petersburg G.H., Mar.–Aug./64. Admitted 8/20/64 to a Petersburg G.H. with chronic diarrhea. Trn to Danville, VA, 9/30/64. Reported present on company muster rolls of Sept.–Oct./64. Trn to 16th NC, 12/2/64, according to Nov.–Dec./64 rolls. (CSR 270:5)

Hestlow, J.A.: From Buncombe Co. At age 19, enl. 5/20/61 as PVT, Co. G. Reported present on company muster rolls of Jan.–Feb./62, May–June/62, 9/62–4/63. Absent on detached service in Nelson Co., VA, with unserviceable horses, July–Oct./63. Absent Nov.–Dec./63 on provost duty at Orange C.H. Admitted 1/12/64 to a Charlottesville G.H. Trn to Lynchburg, 1/14/64. Reported present 4/1/64. Admitted 4/3/64 to a Richmond G.H. with pleurisy. Returned to duty 4/18/64 Reported present 4/30–Aug./64. Absent on detached service as a teamster with the rgt's wagons, Sept.–Oct./64. Reported present Nov.–Dec./64. (CSR 270:5)

Hicks, A.: PVT, Co. B. On a POW Register, Knoxville, TN, as captured in Boone, NC, 3/28/65. (CSR 270:5)

Hicks, Benjamin W.: Resident of Granville Co. Enl. 10/25/64 as PVT, Co. E. Reported present on company muster rolls of Nov.–Dec./64. Captured 4/4/65 at Namozine Church. Took oath, 6/14/65. Had a light complexion, brown hair, and gray eyes, and stood 6' tall. (CSR 270:5)

Hicks, Calvin B.: B. 3/9/33. From Wayne Co. At age 28, enl. 6/20/61 as PVT, Co. H. According to Roll of Honor, "Rejected on account of health." D. 3/30/95. Bur Willowdale Cem, Goldsboro. (CGR: 3; Stepp; CSR 270:5)

Hicks, Romeo: Enl. 9/21/64 as PVT, Co. K. Reported present on company muster rolls of Sept.–Dec./64. (CSR 270:5)

Hickson, Jesse: Co. E. Deserted after trn to Co. A, 12th Bn (Whit Joyner to author, 13 September 1994)

Higdon, Joseph Hoffman: B. 7/25/39. From Macon Co. Enl. 7/23/61 as SGT, Co. K. Reported present on company muster rolls of Nov.–Dec./61. According to Jan.–Feb./62 rolls and 2/62 rgt return, absent sick at a Manassas G.H. beginning 2/24/62. Reported present May–June/62, Sept.–Dec./62. Absent on frl beginning 2/14/63, according to Jan.–Feb./63 rolls. Reported present 3/4/63, July–Aug./63, 10/31/63–12/64. D. 1/1/09. Bur. Sugar Fork Baptist Church Cem., Macon Co. (Stepp; CSR 270:5)

Higdon, William Washington: B. 1843. From Macon Co. Enl. 5/6/62 as PVT, Co. K. Reported present on company muster rolls of May–June/62, 9/62–4/63. Absent detailed to buy a horse in NC, July–Aug./63. Reported present 10/31/63–3/31/64. Absent sick, 4/30–Oct./64. Admitted 8/64 to a Richmond G.H. per hospital register and rolls of Mar.–Apr./64. Issued a passport for frl, 9/16/64, destination Wallhalla, NC. Reported present Nov.–Dec./64. D. 5/8/11. Bur. Sugar Fork Baptist Church Cem., Macon Co. (Stepp; CSR 270:5)

Hight, Reddin: From Franklin Co. At age 26, enl. 6/8/61 as 2CPL, Co. E. Reported present on company muster rolls of Jan.–Feb./62, May–June/62, 9/62–4/63. Prm 1CPL according to May–June/62 rolls. Prm SGT 5/62: to 5SGT according to Sept.–Oct./62 rolls, and 4SGT according to Nov.–Dec./62 rolls. Absent on detached service in NC to procure a horse beginning 8/27/63, according to July–Aug./63 rolls. Reported present 6/30/63–4/64. Absent on detached service with dismounted men, 4/30–Oct./64. Reported present Nov.–Dec./64. Prl Appomattox, 4/9/65. (Pearce: 13, 213; CSR 270:5)

Higlar, Ja___: Co. F. PVT (Mizelle)

Hill, Calhoun: Enl. 7/4/61 as PVT, Co. I. Reported present on company muster rolls of Nov.–Dec./61; appointed hospital steward and psb prm to SGT. Reported present Jan.–Feb./62. May–June/62 absent Sept.–Oct./62 detailed at Shepherdstown G.H. Reported absent on detached service, 11/62–2/63. Absent on detached service at Hanover Junction, VA, Mar.–Apr./63. Company muster rolls of 10/31/63 lists him on detached service as of 9/17/63. Reported absent on detached service Jan.–Feb./64. Psb also a member of Huger's Bty. (CSR 270:5)

Hill, Edmund H.: From Cabarrus Co. At age 27, enl. 2/15/62 as PVT, Co. F. According to company muster rolls of May–June/62, absent sick beginning 5/26/62. Reported present Sept.–Dec./62, July–Aug./63. KIA at Jack's Shop, 9/22/63. (Barringer; Cabarrus; CSR 270:5)

Hilliard, James H.: From Buncombe Co. At age 25, enl. 7/26/61 as PVT, Co. G. Listed on receipt roll for pay of 11/28/61. NFR. (CSR 270:5)

Hilliard, W.L.: From Buncombe Co. According to field and staff muster rolls of 11/61–2/62, commissioned surgeon, 10/24/61, to rank from 5/16/61. Rgt returns of 2/62 and 3/62 show him present. Reported present on field and staff muster rolls of May–June/62. Reported absent with live on Sept.–Oct./62 rolls. Trn to a G.H. in the Dept. Of Tennesee, 8/62. (CSR 270:1, 5)

Hilton, S.H.: From Mecklenburg Co. At age 19, enl. 2/24/62 as PVT, Co. C. Listed as presented on 3/62 rgt return. Reported present on company muster rolls of May–Dec./62. Absent on detached service beginning 2/26/63, according to Jan.–Feb./63 roll. Reported present Mar.–Apr./63, July–Oct./63. Reported absent scouting as of 12/23/63, according to Nov.–Dec./63 roll. Also reported scouting on rolls of Jan.–Feb./64 and 4/1/64. Captured near Petersburg, 6/64. Prl 11/64. Reported present on company muster rolls of Nov.–Dec./64. Prl Charlotte, 5/20/65. (CSR 270:5; Alexander)

Hodges, Elbert: From Tennessee. At age 30, enl. 5/29/61 as PVT, Co. A. Reported present on company muster rolls of 11/61–2/62, Sept.–Oct./62. According to Nov.–Dec./62 rolls, absent scouting beginning 12/25/62. Absent on frl to procure a horse, Jan.–Feb./63, and again beginning 2/24/63 according to Mar.–Apr./63 rolls. Admitted to a Charlottesville G.H., 6/10/63, and returned to duty

6/18/63. WIA at Brandy Station, 8/1/63, and therefore listed absent from regt on July–Aug./63 rolls. Admitted to a Richmond G.H., 8/2/63. Reported present Sept.–Oct./63, 11/1/63, and prm 3CPL. Reported present 11/30/63–2/29/64. Reported in confinement beginning 2/28/64, according to 4/1/64 roll. Reported present Mar.–Apr./64, July–Dec./64. (AsheCo; CSR 270:5)

Hodges, Thomas M.: B. Ashe Co., from Tennessee. At ge 23, enl. 5/29/61 as PVT, Co. A. Reported present on company muster rolls of Nov.–Dec./61. Absent Jan.–Feb./62 at a Manassas G.H. According to rgt return of 2/62, absent sick beginning 2/24/62. According to sick and wounded reported, d. 3/5/62 of typhoid fever. (CSR 270:5; AsheCo calls him L.M. Hodges)

Hodges, William: From Watauga Co. At age 26, enl. 2/28/62 as PVT, Co. D. Reported present on company muster rolls of 5/62–Apr./63, July–Aug./63. Absent at home sick according to rolls of 6/30–10/31/63. Reported present 11/63–Apr./64. Absent at home to procure a horse as of 8/31/64. Reported present Sept.–Dec./64. (CSR 270:5; Davis)

Holbrooks, Allison: From Lincoln Co. Enl. 5/13/62 as PVT, Co. C. Reported present on company muster rolls of May–Dec./62. Absent in NC to procure a horse beginning 2/21/63, according to Jan.–Feb./63 rolls. Reported present Mar.–Apr./63, July–Oct./63. According to Nov.–Dec./63 rolls, listed as AWOL beginning 12/24 or 12/25/63. Deserted. Received in Federal lines and took the oath, 11/64. (Alexander; CSR 270:5)

Holcombe, James: From Buncombe Co. Enl. as PVT, Co. G. Reported present on company muster rolls of Jan.–Feb./62, May–June/62, 9/62–4/63. Absent on detached service to procure a horse, July–Aug./63. Absent at home sick, Sept.–Oct./63. Captured 10/16/63 in Madison Co., TN. D. 3/20/64 at Rock Island Barracks, Ill. (CSR 270:5; also spelled Holcrombe)

Holden, E.M.: From Mecklenburg Co. At age 31, enl. 7/22/61 as PVT, Co. C. Reported present on company muster rolls of 11/61–2/62, May–June/62. Rgt return of 3/62 lists him sick in a Petersburg G.H. beginning 3/23/62. Also listed as admitted 3/22/62 to a Petersburg G.H. and returned to duty 3/31/62. According to 6/30–10/31/62 rolls, d. 8/10/62. D. at Richmond from typhoid fever. (Alexander; CSR 270:5)

Holdsclaw, J.W.: From Watauga Co. At age 21, enl. 5/11/61 as PVT, Co. D. Reported present on company muster rolls of 11/61–2/62, May–Dec./62. Absent Jan.–Feb./63 as an orderly for a general court martial at Charlottesville. Reported present Mar.–Apr./63. Absent at home to procure a horse, July–Aug./63. Listed AWOL, 6/30–Dec./63. Reported present Jan.–Apr./64. Admitted to a Petersburg G.H., 6/64. Absent at home to procure a horse according to 8/31/64 rolls, then reported present Sept.–Dec./64. Captured in Boone, NC, 3/28/65. Took the oath, 6/10/65. Had a florid complexion, dark hair, gray eyes, and stood 5'6". (Davis says Holisclaw; CSR 270:5)

Holdsclaw, William: From Watauga Co. At age 29, enl. 5/11/61 as PVT, Co. D. Reported present on company muster rolls of 11/61–2/62. Rgt returns of 2/62 list him on recruiting service in NC; 3/62 return lists him on extra duty as a teamster. Reported present May–10/31/62. Also reported present Nov.–Dec./62 as a teamster in the Q.M. Dept., Jan.–Feb./63, and again present as a teamster Mar.–Apr./63. Absent July–Aug./63 on detached service as a teamster in the Q.M. Dept., and absent 6/30–10/31/63 as a teamster with a MAJ Briggs. Reported present 11/63–2/64, and reported present 2/29–3/31/64 on extra duty as a teamster. Absent Mar.–Apr./64 as a teamster in the ordnance dept. Absent at home to procure a horse, 8/31/64. Also reported on extra duty as a teamster on rolls of Apr.–June/64, 8/1–9/30/64. According to company muster rolls, absent in a G.H., Sept.–Dec./64. Admitted 10/28/64 to a Petersburg G.H. with a gunshot wound in the left leg. Returned to duty, 11/30/64, then admitted to a Raleigh G.H. 12/7/64. Returned to duty, 1/2/65. (Davis says Holisclaw; CSR 270:5)

Holemon, Thomas: From Watauga Co. At age 23, enl 6/8/61 as PVT, Co. A. Reported present on company muster rolls of 11/61–2/62, Sept.–Oct./62. Also listed as admitted 1/16/62 with fever to a Danville G.H. and sent to Front Royal. Absent scouting beginning 12/25/62 according to Nov.–Dec./62 rolls. Reported present Jan.–Apr./63. Absent sick beginning 6/9/63 according to July–Aug./63 rolls. Rolls of Mar.–Apr./64 lists him as D in a Lynchburg G.H. Psb admitted 7/11/63 to a Richmond G.H., and d. 7/15/63 from continued fever. (AsheCo says Hollemon; CSR 270:5)

Holland, Anthony: From Macon Co. At age 37, enl. 2/16/63 as PVT, Co. K. Reported present on company muster rolls of Mar.–Apr./63. Absent in NC on frl, July–Aug./63. Absent wounded, 10/31/63. Reported sick at home Nov.–Dec./63, and also reported absent wounded, Jan.–Feb./64. Reported present 2/29–3/31/64. Retired due to a disability according to Mar.–Apr./64 rolls. Admitted 5/4/64 to a Richmond G.H. with chronic rheumatism. Later entered a Raleigh G.H., and returned to duty 5/24/64. Retired to Invalid Corps, 7/15/64. (CSR 270:5)

Holliday, Titus T.: From Greene Co. At age 24, enl. 7/5/61 as PVT, Co. H. Reported present on company muster rolls of Nov.–Dec./61. According to Jan.–Feb./62 rolls, d. 2/23/62. On 2/62 rgt return, listed as d. 2/24/62 from typhoid fever. Also noted as d. 2/23/62. (CSR 270:5)

Hollinsworth, W.J.: From Henderson Co. At age 23, enl. 5/20/61 as PVT, Co. G. Reported present on company muster rolls of Jan.–Feb./62, May–June/62, Sept.–Oct./62. Absent on detached service, Nov.–Dec./62. Reported present Jan.–Apr./63. WIA 6/9/63 at Brandy Station. Home on frl July–Oct./63. Absent with the brigade ambulance train, Nov.–Dec./63. Absent on detached service, 4/1/64; also reported absent Mar.–Apr./64. Reported present 4/30–Oct./64. Absent doing detached service on provost guard at brigade HQ, Nov.–Dec./64. (CSR 270:5)

Holloway, W.S.: Enl. 11/10/64 as PVT, Co. E. According to company muster rolls of Nov.–Dec./64, absent at Belfield on provost guard. (CSR 270:5)

Hollowell, Augustus Bright: B. 1847. Enl. 4/1/64 as PVT, Co. H. Reported present on company muster rolls of Mar.–Apr./64. Absent at a G.H., 4/30–8/31/64. Reported present Sept.–Dec./64. D. 1911. Bur. Willowdale Cem., Goldsboro. (Stepp; CSR 270:5)

Hollowell, William H.: From Northampton Co. At age 27, enl. 7/26/61 as PVT, Co. B. Reported present on company muster rolls of Nov.–Dec./61. Absent at a G.H., Jan.–Apr./62. Rgt return of 2/62 lists him absent sick; rgt return of 3/62 lists him absent sick at a Petersburg G.H. Absent Sept.–Oct./62, sent home from Manassas sick. Deserted. (CSR 270:5)

Holyfield, John H.: Enl. 9/2/64 as PVT, Co. H. Absent wounded according to Sept.–Dec./64 rolls. (CSR 270:5)

Hooper, Chance: From Henderson Co. At age 22, enl. 5/20/61 as PVT, Co. G. Reported present on company muster rolls of Jan.–Feb./62, 9/62–4/63. Absent on detached service with the provost guard at Culpeper C.H., July–Aug./63. Reported present Sept.–Dec./63, 4/1/64, Mar.–Aug./64. AWOL Sept.–Dec./64. (CSR 270:5)

Hoover, S.S.: Enl. 8/18/64 as PVT, Co. C. Reported present on company muster rolls of Sept.–Dec./64. Prl in Charlotte, 5/15/65. (CSR 270:5)

Hopkins, P.: From Stanly Co. At age 27, enl. 5/27/61 as PVT, Co. C. Reported present on company muster rolls of Nov.–Dec./61. According to Jan.–Feb./62 rolls, absent sick at Petersburg beginning 2/26/62. Rgt return of 2/62 also lists him absent sick, and hospital records list him as admitted 1/3/62 to a Danville G.H. with bronchitis and sent to Front Royal. Absent sick beginning 5/29/62 according to May–June/62 rolls. Absent on detached service at Winchester as of 10/28/62 according to 6/30–10/31/62 rolls. Reported present Nov.–Dec./62. Reported present Mar.–Apr./63. Absent on detached service as of 7/28/63 according to rolls of July–Dec./63. According to Jan.–Feb./64 rolls, POW in Greene Co, VA since 10/11/63. Mar.–Oct./64 rolls list him as absent under arrest since 11/63. Admitted 5/26/64 to a Richmond G.H., and trn to Lynchburg 7/8/64. Absent sick, Nov.–Dec./64. (Alexander; CSR 270:5)

Horne, Jesse: B. NC. From Duplin Co. At age 27, enl. 2/5/62 as PVT, Co. I. Captured at Willis Church, VA, 6/29/62. Exd 8/5/62. Stood 5'8", had fair hair, blue eyes, and a fair complexion. Reported present on company muster rolls of 9/62–4/63. Reported present Mar.–Apr./63 on extra duty cooking for wagoners. Admitted 8/18/63 to a Charlottesville G.H., then returned to duty on 8/21/63. Reported present 10/31/63, 1/1–10/64. Also listed as admitted to a Richmond G.H., 6/19/64. According to Nov.–Dec./64 rolls, trn to 43d NC, 10/29/64 or 11/64. (CSR 270:5)

Horton, Jonathan F.: From Watauga Co. At age 25, enl. 6/6/61 as PVT, Co. A. Reported present on company muster rolls of Nov.–Dec./61. Absent at Manassas G.H., Jan.–Feb./62. According to rgt return of 2/62, absent sick beginning 2/24. According to 3/62 rgt return, d. 3/2/62 in camp, from disease. Surgeon's Certificate lists gastritis as the cause of death. (AsheCo; CSR 270:5)

Horton, Nathan: From Watauga Co. Farmer by occupation. At age 31, enl. 6/6/61 as PVT, Co. A. Reported present on company muster rolls of Nov.–Dec./61. Absent Jan.–Feb./62 at a Manassas G.H. Rgt return of 2/62 shows him absent sick as of 2/24/62. Admitted 3/27/62 to a Richmond G.H. with jaundice. Also sent to a Petersburg G.H., 3/62. Reported present Sept.–Oct./62. Dsh as PVT, 12/17/62. Prm LT, 37th NC, according to Nov.–Dec./62 rolls. According to Roll of Honor, prm dated 12/1/62. Stood 5'10", had fair complexion, blue eyes, chesnut hair. (AsheCo; CSR 270:5)

Hoskins, David A.: Res. of Guilford Co. At age 20, cns 7/16/62. Reported present Sept.–Dec./62.

Absent on detached service as a nurse at a Stevensburg, VA G.H., Jan.–Feb./63. Reported present, Mar.–Apr./63. Reported present July–Aug./63. Deserted 9/4/63, according to 6/30–10/31/63 rolls. In Federal records, reported as deserting near Rappahannock River and thereafter being sent to Philadelphia. Took oath, 9/10/63 or 9/27/63. Had light complexion, brown hair, blue eyes, and stood 5'9". (CSR 270:5)

Houpe, James F.: Enl. 3/10/64 as PVT, Co. D. Reported present on company muster rolls of Mar.–Apr./64. Absent at home to procure a horse according to rolls of 8/31/64. On horse detail, Sept.–Oct./64. Reported present Nov.–Dec./64. (CSR 270:5)

Houston, A.A.: Enl. 9/10/64 as PVT, Co. C. Reported present on company muster rolls of Sept.–Dec./64. Prl Charlotte, 5/27/65. (CSR 270:5)

Houston, Edward S.: From Duplin Co. At age 27, enl. 6/17/61 as PVT, Co. I. Reported present on company muster rolls of 11/61–2/62, May–June/62, Sept.–Dec./62. Captured at Barbee's Crossroads, 11/5/62, and prl that same month. Absent on detached service, Jan.–Feb./63. Reported present Mar.–Apr./63. Absent on detached service in Nelson Co., VA, 10/7/63, according to 10/1/63 rolls. Rolls of 1/1/64 list him absent on detached service in a Nelson Co., VA infirmary camp since 11/7/63. Absent Jan.–Feb./64 on detached service in Amherst Co., VA since 11/7/63. Absent sick Mar.–Oct./64 at home on sick frl. Reported present Nov.–Dec./64.

Houston, William J.: From Duplin Co. Age 33. Elected 1LT, 8/20/61; later prm CPT, Co. I, to rank form 5/16/61. Reported present, commanding company, on company muster rolls of Nov.–Dec./61. Reported present and sick in camp, Jan.–Feb./62. Rgt return of 2/62 lists him present. Rgt return of 3/62 lists him absent on recruiting service since 3/2/62. Reported present May–June/62, Sept.–Oct./62. Captured 11/6/62; horse killed. Prl 11/9/62. WIA and absent, Nov.–Dec./62. Reported present Jan.–Feb./63, Mar.–Apr./63. KIA 6/21/63 near Upperville, VA. Bur. Middleburg, VA Cem. Described as "brave, kind, and generous...." (CSR 270:1, 5; O'Neill, *Aldie, Middleburg, and Upperville*, 123)

Howard, Allen: Enl. 9/22/63 as PVT, Co. B. Reported present on company muster rolls of 4/30–Oct./64. Absent sick according to rolls of Nov.–Dec./64. (CSR 270:5)

Howerton, Albertus W.: From Rowan Co. Enl. 6/15/61 as PVT, Co. F, at age 27. Reported absent on sick frl, Nov.–Dec./61. Sources disagree as to exact date, but dsh 1/62 or 2/62. (Mizelle; Barringer; Rumple: 342; CSR 270:5)

Howington, William W.: From Watauga Co. At age 24, enl. 5/25/61 as PVT, Co. D. Absent sick in a Petersburg G.H. according to Nov.–Dec./61 rolls. Rolls of Jan.–Feb./62 list him dsh from a Petersburg G.H., 1/16/62. A register of payments to dsh soldiers lists him as dsh 12/16/61. Prm in 58 NC. (Davis; CSR 270:5)

Hoyle, James R.: B. 8/11/31. Resident of Pitt Co. Enl. 4/62 as PVT, Co. H. Reported present on company muster rolls of May–June/62, 9/62–4/63. One month's pay suspended by a rgt court martial, 1/24/63, according to rolls of Jan.–Feb./63. Absent on detached service, July–Aug./63. Reported present, Sept.–Oct./63. Absent sick and sent to a G.H., 12/18/63, according to Nov.–Dec./63 rolls. Admitted 12/21/63 to a Richmond G.H. Frl 1/5/64. Reported present Jan.–Feb./64. Absent sent to a G.H. sick, 4/1/64. On extra daily duty, 3–4/64. Admitted 3/22/64 to a Richmond G.H., and returned to duty, 4/20/64. Reported present 4/30–8/31/64. Dropped from company muster rolls as a deserter, Sept.–Oct./64. Captured at Weldon RR, 9/4/64, with horse, saddle, and bridle. Took oath, 9/9/64. Had dark complexion, dark hair, and black eyes, stood 6' tall. D. 9/19/23. Bur. Oakwood Cem., Raleigh. (Stepp; CSR 270:5)

Hudson, J.A.: PVT, Co. F. Trn to 10th VA Cavalry, 1862. (Rumple: 410)

Hudson, John H.: From Mecklenburg Co. At age 26, enl. 5/28/61 as PVT, Co. C. Reported present on company muster rolls of 11/61–2/62, 5/62–4/63, 7/63–12/64. (Alexander; CSR 270:5)

Huffman, D.M.: Cns. 2/11/64 as PVT, Co. H. Reported present on company muster rolls of Mar.–Apr./64, 4/1/64, 4/30–Dec./64. Prl Greensboro, NC, 5/10/65. (CSR 270:5)

Hughes, William F.: From Greene Co. At age 23, enl. 7/3/61 as PVT, Co. H. Reported present on company muster rolls of Nov.–Dec./61. Captured at Difficult Run, VA, 2/7/62. Rgt return of 2/62 confirms that he was captured on outpost duty, 2/7/62. Prl according to Nov.–Dec./62 rolls. Absent procuring a horse, Jan.–Feb./63. Reported present Mar.–Apr./63, July–Aug./63. According to Sept.–Oct./63 rolls, captured 10/14/63. Federal records report the capture at Warrenton Junction/Catlett's Station, VA area. Prl 2/18/65. Exd 2/23/65. (CSR 270:5)

Hughey, R.W.C.: From Buncombe Co. At age 21, enl. 5/20/61 or 7/26/61 as PVT, Co. G. Reported present on company muster rolls of Jan.–Feb./62. Rgt return of 2/62 lists him on extra duty as a teamster. Reported present May–June/62, 9/62–4/63. Absent on detached service with the unserviceable horses in Nelson Co., VA, July–Aug./63. Reported present Sept.–Oct./63. Absent on provost duty at Orange C.H., Nov.–Dec./63. Reported present 4/1/64. Rolls of Mar.–Apr./64 list him as deserted. (CSR 270:5)

Hunt, James: Enl. 9/21/64 as PVT, Co. K. Reported present on company muster rolls of Sept.–Dec./64. Rgt return of 2/62 lists him on extra duty as a teamster.

Hunt, James D.: B. 9/1/45. Enl. 10/5/63 as PVT, Co. D. Reported present on company muster rolls of Sept.–Dec./64. On a register of a Danville, VA G.H. with a gunshot wound in the left forearm. Frl 4/9/65 for 60 days. D. 4/11/94. Bur. Old Bethel Methodist Church Cem., Roaring River, Wilkes Co., N.C. (McNeil; Stepp; CSR 270:5)

Hunter, H. Holmes.: From Gates Co. Surgeon, to rank from 5/25/63. According to field & staff muster rolls of July–Aug./63, absent sick in NC. Relieved 9/22/63. (CSR 270:1, 5)

Hunter, Henry B.: B. 1845. Psb. trn from 3d VA Cavalry. Enl. 6/1/63 as PVT, Co. E. Reported present on company muster rolls of 4/30–12/64. D. 1923. Bur. Fairview Cem., Warrenton, NC. (CGR: 6; CSR 270:5)

Hunter, J.W.: From Mecklenburg Co. At age 30, enl. 5/8/62 as PVT, Co. C. Reported present on company muster rolls of May–June/62. WIA. Reported absent sick in Charlotte, NC beginning 7/1/62 according to rolls of 6/30–Oct./64. According to rolls of Nov.–Dec./64, retired by medical examining board. Invalid Corps register has him retiring on 12/29/64. (Alexander; CSR 270:5)

Hurston, A.W.: PVT, Co. C. (Alexander)

Hurt, John C.: B. Surry Co. Farmer. Age 18. Trn from McRae's Bn. Enl. 10/5/63 as PVT, Co. D. Reported present on company muster rolls of 8/31–Dec./64. Captured near Dinwiddie C.H., 4/3/65. Released 6/13/65 on taking the oath. Had a florid complexion, dark brown hair, hazel eyes, stood 5' 8". (CSR 270:5)

Hutchinson, David S.: B. 1830. From Mecklenburg Co. At age 30, enl. 6/24/61 as SGT, Co. C. Reported present on company muster rolls of Nov.–Dec./61. Admitted 1/12/62 with a fever to a Danville G.H., and sent to Richmond. Absent sick in Petersburg as of 1/12/62, according to Jan.–Feb./62 rolls. Rgt return of 2/62 lists him absent sick. 3/62 rgt return lists him on detached service on recruiting service in NC since 3/23/62. Reported present May–June/62 absent on detached service in Winchester, VA, beginning 10/1/62, according to Sept.–Oct./62 rolls. Reported present 11/62–4/63. Beginning 8/27/63, absent in NC to procure a horse, according to rolls of July–Aug./63. Reported present 9/63–4/64. KIA 8/15/64 along Charles City Rd., and/or Boydton Plank Rd., near Richmond. Bur. Sugaw Creek Presbyterian Church Cem., Mecklenburg Co. (Richmond *Sentinel*, 8/26/64; Alexander; Stepp; CSR 270:5)

Hutton, George: From Craven Co. At age 18, enl. 5/21/63 as PVT, Co. H. Reported present on company muster rolls of July–Aug./63. Absent sick in a G.H., Sept.–Oct./63. Absent sick and sent to a G.H. on 12/28/63, according to company muster rolls of Nov.–Dec./63. Absent sick and sent to a G.H. according to rolls of Jan.–Aug./31/64. Admitted 6/17/64 to a Richmond G.H. Absent on detached service packing fodder in NC, Sept.–Dec./64. Prl Greensboro, 5/4/65. (CSR 270:5)

Ingle, J.P.: From Buncombe Co. At age 18, enl. 5/20/61 as PVT, Co. G. Reported present on company muster rolls of Jan.–Feb./62. Rgt return of 2/62 lists him as on extra duty as a teamster. Reported present May–June/62, Sept.–Oct./62. Captured at Barbee's Crossroads, 11/5/62. Prl 11/62. Reported present Mar.–Apr./63. Absent on detached service to procure a horse, July–Aug./63. Absent sick at home, Sept.–Oct./63. Reported AWOL, 9/64. (CSR 270:5)

Ingram, Joseph A.: B. Johnston Co. Farmer. At age 41, enl. 6/20/61 as CPL, Co. H. Admitted 12/11/62 to a Richmond G.H. and trn 12/13/62 to Petersburg. As a result, reported absent on company muster rolls of 11/61–2/62. Rgt return of 2/62 lists him as absent sick. 3/62 rgt return reports him absent in a Petersburg G.H. since 12/10/62. Dsh 5/19/62 due to age, broken down health, chronic liver disease, and back problems. Stood 6'½", had fair complexion, blue eyes, gray hair. (CSR 270:5)

Iredell, Cadwallader J.: Resident of Raleigh. 2LT, Co. E, to rank from 10/4/61. Reported present on company muster rolls of Jan.–Feb./62. Rgt return of 2/62 lists him as present, and 3/62 rgt return reports him absent detached in charge of recruits beginning 3/25/62. Reported present on company muster rolls of May–June/62. Admitted 9/8/62 to a Richmond G.H. with dysentery. Reported present Sept.–Oct./62. Absent on detached service, Nov.–Dec./62. Prm Sr 2LT, 12/21/62. Reported present and on extra duty as acting adjutant, Jan.–Apr./63, July–Aug./63. Prm 1LT,

7/3/63. Reported present 6/30–10/31/63. According to rolls of Nov.–Dec./63, reported present and prm CPT, taking command of Co. E. Prm CPT, 9/28/63. Reported present Jan.–Aug./31/64. Admitted 5/14/64 to a Richmond G.H. with a gunshot wound to the leg. According to a medical director's office report, also had gunshot wound in right breast, arm. Frl 5/19/64. Admitted 10/4/64 to a Raleigh G.H. On company muster rolls, listed absent in a Raleigh G.H., Sept.–Oct./64. Also reported absent on inspection reports of 9/25/64 and 11/30/64. Reported present Nov.–Dec./64. Listed in a Danville G.H., 4/4/65, with a gunshot wound in the left thigh. Prl 4/26/65 from a Thomasville, NC G.H. (CSR 270:1, 5; *Raleigh Register*, 9/2/63)

Israel, Ed M.: Resident of Buncombe Co. At age 18, enl. 5/20/61 as PVT, Co. G. Admitted 1/10/62 to a Danville G.H with a fever, and sent to a Richmond G.H. Reported present on company muster rolls of Jan.–Feb./62. Rgt return of 2/62 lists him absent sick. Reported present May–June/62, 9/62–4/63. Absent sick in a Richmond G.H., July–Aug./63. Absent home on sick frl, Sept.–Oct./63. Reported present Nov.–Dec./63, Mar.–Aug./64. Absent on detached service to procure a horse, Sept.–Oct./64. Rolls of Nov.–Dec./64 list him as deserted. Took oath 12/8/64. Had dark complexion, black hair, brown eyes, and stood 5'5". (CSR 270:5)

Jacks, William H.H.: From Ashe Co. Enl. 2/27/62 as PVT, Co. A. Reported present on company muster rolls of Sept.–Oct./62. Absent scouting beginning 12/25/62, according to Nov.–Dec./62 rolls. Reported present Jan.–Apr./63, July–Aug./63. According to Sept.–Oct./63 rolls, captured at Jack's Shop, 9/22/63. Federal records say he was exd 10/29/64 and prl 10/11/64, and d. 11/4/64 at Ft. Monroe. According to Nov.–Dec./64 rolls, d. at City Point, 10/12/64. (AsheCo; CSR 270:6)

Jackson, George A.: From Lenoir Co. At age 23, enl. 6/29/61 as PVT, Co. H. Reported present on company muster rolls of 11/61–2/62. Listed on 2/62 regimental return as on extra duty as a teamster. Rolls of May–June/62 list him as captured at Willis Church, 6/29/62. Exd 8/5/62. Absent on detached service in Winchester, Sept.–Oct./62. Reported present on company muster rolls of Nov.–Dec./62. Absent on detached service, Jan.–Feb./63. Reported present Mar.–Apr./63, then again absent on detached service to procure a horse, July–Aug./63. Reported present on company muster rolls of 9/63–2/64, 4/1/64. Absent to procure a horse, Mar.–Apr./64. Reported present 4/30–12/64. WIA. According to Federal records, b. VA. Stood 5'7", had dark hair, dark eyes, and a dark complexion. (CSR 270:6)

Jacobs, Bazel P.: From Macon Co. At age 23, enl. 5/14/61 as PVT, Co. K. Reported present on company muster rolls of 10/31/63. Absent detailed to NC to procure a horse, Nov.–Dec./63. Reported present 1/64–3/31/64. According to company muster rolls of Mar.–Apr./64, WIA 6/25/64. Frl from a Danville G.H., 9/22/64. (CSR 270:6)

Jarrett, John A.: From Buncombe County, NC. At age 26, enl. as PVT, Co. D, on 2/22/62. Reported present on company muster rolls of 5/62–4/63. Absent captured beginning 7/5/63 according to rolls of July–Aug./63. Federal records list him as captured 7/3/63 and exd 2/13/65. (Davis; CSR 270:6)

Jenkins, Coleman O.: Cns 9/10/62 as PVT, Co. H, in Urbana, MD. Reported present on company muster rolls of 9/62–4/63, 7/63–4/64. Absent on detached service to procure a horse, 4/30–8/31/64. Reported present Sept.–Oct./64. Absent on detached service with horse detail, 11/12/64. (CSR 270:6)

Jenkins, F.M.: From Macon Co. PVT, Co. K. Age 16. Rejected by LTC Baker. (CSR 270:6)

Jenkins, John T.: Probably from Henderson, NC. Enl. 9/4/63 as PVT, Co. B. Absent sick, 4/30–12/64. Admitted to a Richmond G.H., 8/19/64. (CSR 270:6)

Jenkins, Robert: From Yadkin Co. Enl. 11/1/63 as PVT, Co. H. Reported present on company muster rolls of Nov.–Dec./63. Reported present on extra daily duty, Jan.–Feb./64, 4/1/64. Reported present on company muster rolls of Mar.–Apr./64. WIA and absent according to rolls of 4/30–8/31/64. Admitted 6/14/64 to a Richmond G.H. with a gunshot wound. Absent in Kittrell Springs G.H., Sept.–Oct./64. Also reported as admitted 9/15/64 to a Raleigh G.H. with syphilis. Retired, 10/2/64. Absent on detached service with the QM Dept., Nov.–Dec./64. (CSR 270:6)

Jenkins, William L.: B. 11/19/28. PVT, Co. D. D. 8/7/80. Bur. Fourth Creek Presbyterian Church Cem., Statesville. (Stepp)

Jenkins, William T.: From Macon Co. Age 18. Enl. 6/25/61 as PVT, Co. K. Reported present on company muster rolls of Nov.–Dec./61. Absent sick at Manassas beginning 2/24/62. 2/62 regimental return confirms absence due to illness. 3/62 regimental return lists him in a G.H. as of 2/24/62. Reported present on company muster rolls of May–

June/62, Sept.–Oct./62, Nov.–Dec./62. Prm to 3CPL on 12/1/62, according to company muster rolls. Reported present Jan.–Apr./63, July–Aug./63, 10/31/63, 11/63–12/64. Prm 3CPL after 10/31/63 according to rolls. (CSR 270:6)

Jennings, C.J.: From Mecklenburg Co. At age 21, enl. 5/28/61 as PVT, Co. C. Reported present on company muster rolls of 11/61–2/62, but also reported as admitted to a Danville G.H., 1/4/62. Reported present May–10/31/62. Absent detailed to shell corn as of 12/28/62, according to rolls of Nov.–Dec./62. Reported present on company muster rolls of 1–/4/63. Absent detailed to procure a horse in NC beginning 8/27/63, according to July–Aug./63 rolls. Reported present on company muster rolls of 9/63–12/64. (Alexander; CSR 270:6)

John, W.J.: PVT, Co. A. (AsheCo)

Johnson, Daniel: From Macon Co. At age 37, enl 7/6/61 as PVT, Co. K. Reported present on company muster rolls of 11/61–2/62, May–June/62, Sept.–Oct./62. Absent according to company muster rolls of Nov.–Dec./62. Jan.–Feb./63, absent and detached to report to Lt. Roane in Macon Co as of 12/27/62. Reported present on company muster rolls of Mar.–Apr./63. Absent on detached service, July–Aug./63. Reported present 10/31/63. Rolls of Nov.–Dec./63 list him as detailed to NC to procure a horse. Reported present Jan.–Mar./31/64. Absent after being WIA 5/12/64, according to rolls of 4/30–Oct./64. Admitted 5/12/64 to a Richmond G.H. Reported present on company muster rolls of Nov.–Dec./64. (CSR 270:6)

Johnson, James H.: From Macon Co. At age 18, enl. 7/10/63 as PVT, Co. K. Reported present on company muster rolls of 10/31/63, 11/63–3/31/64. Reported absent sick, 4/30–Oct./64; also listed as sent to a G.H. as of 8/19/64 or 8/20/64. Frl to SC, 8/27/64. Reported present Nov.–Dec./64. (CSR 270:6)

Johnson, James M.: From Northampton Co. Age 37. Enl. 6/61 as PVT, Co. B. Reported present on company muster rolls of 11/61–4/62. Absent sick according to regimental return of 2/62. Reported present Sept.–Dec./62. Absent sent to a G.H., 2/1/63, according to Jan.–Feb./63 rolls. Reported present Mar.–Apr./63, 6/30–10/31/63. According to rolls of July–Aug./63, absent on detached service in NC to procure a horse beginning 8/27/63. Reported present Nov.–Dec./63. Absent on detached service 4/1/64. On detached service at a fishery, Mar.–Apr./64. Reported present on company muster rolls of 4/30–Dec./64. (Zeb. Vance Papers, NCSA [courtesy Whit Joyner]; CSR 270:6)

Johnson, Miles W.: Or Johnston. From Cabarrus Co. At age 40, enl. 6/15/61 as 2LT, Co. F. Resigned 10/1/61. Re-enl. 9/63 as PVT, Co. F. Reported present on company muster rolls of Sept.–Dec./64. Resident of Concord circa 1893. D. 4/27/97. Bur. Oakwood Cem., Cabarrus Co. (Barringer; Barringer calls him Johnston and says enl in '64; Mizelle; Cabarrus; Graves calls him Milas Johnston; CSR 270:6)

Johnson, R.W.: Enl. 5/10/62 as PVT, Co. G. reported present on company muster rolls of Nov.–Dec./64. (CSR 270:6)

Johnson, Samuel: From Halifax Co. At age 23, enl. 6/61 as PVT, Co. B. Reported present on company muster rolls of Nov.–Dec./61. Absent sick, Jan.–Feb./62. Reported present Mar.–Apr./62, Sept.–Oct./62. Absent on detached service, Nov.–Dec./62. Absent on detached service with baggage at Gordonsville beginning 2/20 or 2/21/62 according to company muster rolls of Jan.–Apr./63. Reported present July–Aug./63. Absent sick at Gordonsville, 6/30–10/31/63. Reported present Nov.–Dec./63. Absent sick on company muster rolls of Mar.–Apr./64. Reported present 4/30–Dec./64; also reported admitted to a Richmond G.H., 5/6/64. (Halifax, 12; CSR 270:6)

Johnson, Thomas: B. Ashe Co. Farmer. Enl. 6/3/61 as PVT, Co. A. Absent at home sick according to company muster rolls of 11/61–Feb./62. Regimental returns of 2/62 list him as absent sick beginning 12/10; 3/62 returns list him absent sick in a hospital as of 3/10/62. Absent on detached service at Winchester beginning 9/11/62 according to rolls of Sept.–Oct./62. According to rolls of Nov.–Dec./62, dsh for disability, 12/25/62. At age 23, dsh on 12/24/62 or 1/1/63 due to sciatica causing partial loss of use and diminution in right leg. Stood 5'10", had a fair complexion, blue eyes, fair hair. (AsheCo; CSR 270:6)

Johnson, W.P.: PVT, Co. C. Held at Morris Island, SC, by Federal authority under Confederate fire from 9/7–10/21/64. (Alexander; SHSP 17: 40)

Johnson, William H.H.: From Ashe Co. At age 20, enl. 5/23/61 as PVT, Co. A. Reported present on company muster rolls of 11/61–2/62. Absent captured at Williamsport, MD, 10/27/62, according to rolls of Sept.–Oct./62. Absent on prl, Nov.–Dec./62. Jan.–Feb./63, at home as prl POW since 12/20/63. Reported present on company muster rolls of Mar.–Apr./63. Absent on detached service to procure a horse, July–Aug./63. Reported present Sept.–Dec./31/63. Deserted 1/18/64 according to 1/1/64–2/29/64 rolls. (CSR 270:6)

Johnston, Cyrus A.: Enl. 11/1/64 as PVT, Co. F. Reported present on company muster rolls of Nov.–Dec./64. Captured at Dinwiddie C.H., 4/3/65. Released 6/8/65. Resident of Mooresville, NC, circa 1893. Also listed as C.J. Johnson. (Barringer; CSR 270:6)

Johnston, James F.: Enl. 4/61 w/23d NC Infantry. Applied in 8/63 to raise cavalry co. to be attached to GEN Richard Ewell's HQ as scouts, guides, couriers. Recommended by Ewell, Stephen D. Ramseur, others. Not accepted. Enl. 4/7/64 as PVT, Co. C. Reported present on company muster rolls of Mar.–Apr./64. Absent on detached service as PVT, 4/30–8/31/64, psb. serving as commissary for brigade of Robert D. Johnston, former commander of 23d. Highly recommended by Hampton, Barringer, others to serve permanently in position. Also cited for valor by Barringer at Blacks and Whites, 6/23/64. Absent on detached service as PVT Sept.–Oct./64, beginning 6/23/64, serving as aide to GEN Barringer. Appointed 2LT, 11/15/64. Reported present as 2LT, Nov.–Dec./64. Admitted 4/18/65 to a Charlotte G.H. with a gunshot wound in the lower extremities. Prl as CPT in Charlotte, 5/13/65. (CSR 270:1, 6; Alexander spells name "Johnson")

Johnston, James G.: From Rowan Co. At age 22, enl. 6/15/61 as 4CPL, Co. F. Reported present on company muster rolls of Nov.–Dec./61. Absent sent to a G.H., 2/25/62, according to Jan.–Feb./62 rolls. Regimental returns of 2/62 also list him absent sick, and 3/62 as absent sent to a G.H. as of 2/25. Reported present on company muster rolls of May–June/62. Reported present Sept.–Dec./62 as 2CPL. WIA Brandy Station, 1863. Absent July–Aug./63 as 1CPL on detached service in NC to procure a horse. Reported present 9/63–2/64. Appointed 3SGT, 11/15/63. Rolls of 2/29–3/31/64 list him absent on pvst gd in Bowling Green. WIA 5/29/64 at Ashland and on sick frl through 12/64. Admitted 6/64 to a Richmond G.H. and then to a Danville G.H. with a gunshot wound. Dead as of 1893. Bur. At Poplar Tent Presbyterian Church Cem., Cabarrus Co. (Barringer; Mizelle; Rumple: 343; Cabarrus; Graves calls him James C.; CSR 270:6)

Johnston, Nathaniel: B. 5/1/34. Enl. 6/15/61 as PVT, Co. F. Absent on sick frl, 11/61–2/62, beginning 12/8/61. Regimental returns list him as absent sick, 2/62, and absent sick 3/62 beginning 12/21/61. Reported present on company muster rolls of May–June/62, Sept.–Dec./62. Absent July–Aug./63 in NC to procure a horse, beginning 8/27/63. Reported present 9/63–12/64. Resident of Cabarrus Co., circa 1893. D. 4/4/00. Bur. Gilwood Presbyterian Church Cem., Cabarrus Co. (Barringer; Cabarrus; Lore: 66; CSR 270:6)

Johnston, W.P.: From Mecklenburg Co. and/or Guilford Co. At age 18, enl. 5/28/61 as PVT, Co. C. Reported present on company muster rolls of 11/61–2/62, 5/62–10/31/62. Absent scouting beginning 12/25/62, according to rolls of Nov.–Dec./62. Absent on detached service, Jan.–Feb./63. Reported present Mar.–Apr./63. Absent on detached service beginning 8/13/63 according to July–Aug./63 rolls. Reported present Sept.–Oct./63. According to Federal records, captured at Bristoe Station, 11/25/63, and reported to be a LT and one of John Mosby's men, although he later claimed to be only a PVT while imprisoned. Released 6/12/65. Had dark complexion, brown hair, and blue eyes, and stood 5'10" (CSR 270:6)

Johnston, William S.: B. Duplin Co. At age 34, enl 6/22/61 as PVT, Co. I. Reported present on company muster rolls as 5SGT, Nov.–Dec./61. Also reported present Jan.–Feb./62. Reported present as PVT, May–June/62. Sept.–Oct./62, absent sick at Winchester. Absent sick in a G.H., Nov.–Dec./62, Jan.–Feb./63. According to company muster rolls of Mar.–Apr./63, d. in a G.H. Other records list him as d. 1/15/63 in Lynchburg. (CSR 270:6)

Jones, _____: From Sparta, NC. KIA at Gettysburg. "Not on roster." (Monie)

Jones, A.J.: From Buncombe Co. At age 25, enl. 5/20/61 as PVT, Co. G. Reported present on company muster rolls of Jan.–Feb./62, May–June/62, Sept.–Oct./62. Absent as a POW, Nov.–Dec./62. Prl 11/9/62. Reported present on company muster rolls of Jan.–Apr./63. Rolls of July–Aug./63 list him as KIA. Actually WIA and captured at Funkstown, MD, 7/63. Admitted 7/18/63 to a U.S. G.H. in Frederick, MD, with a gunshot wound in the neck. Admitted 11/16/63 to a Richmond G.H. Rolls of Nov.–Dec./63 list him as absent wounded and on frl, and dropped from the rolls for some time due to mistakes. Reported present 4/1/64. Admitted to a Richmond G.H., 5/5/64, with a gunshot wound in the face or mouth. Absent at a Danville G.H., according to company muster rolls of Mar.–Aug./64. Frl from Danville G.H., 9/29/64. Absent on sick frl, Sept.–Oct./64. Nov.–Dec./64, on detached service and light duty in Richmond. Retired to Invalid Corps, 12/6/64. Family thought him dead and attempted to file claims. Listed as a member of Bates's Invalid Bn at Appomattox, where he surrendered. (CSR 270:6; SHSP 15: 462)

Jones, Alexander S.: From Warren Co. At age 18, Cns 8/61 or 7/63 or 8/63 as PVT, Co. E. Reported present on company muster rolls of 6/30–10/31/63. Prm to regimental SMJ, according to rolls of Nov.–Dec./63. Reported present on Field and Staff rolls of Jan.–Feb./63, 4/1/64, Mar.–Apr./64, Sept.–Dec./64. (CSR 270:6)

Jones, Allen: Cns 9/29/64 as PVT, Co. H. Reported present on company muster rolls of Sept.–Dec./64. (CSR 270:6)

Jones, Arthur: Bur Hastings Cem, Fork Township, Wayne Co., NC. D while at Ft Fisher, where he was stationed while home visiting with family. (CGR: 3)

Jones, Craven: From Lenoir Co. At age 35, enl. 7/4/61 as PVT, Co. H. Reported present on company muster rolls of 11/61–2/62, May–June/62. Admitted 7/8/62 to a Richmond G.H. w/diarrhea. Returned to duty 7/10/62. Reported present Sept.–Dec./62. Absent on detached service, Jan.–Feb./63. Reported present Mar.–Apr./63. Absent on detached service in NC to procure a horse, July–Aug./63. Reported present Sept.–Oct./63. Absent on detached service with unserviceable horses, Nov.–Dec./63, Jan.–Feb./64, 4/1/64. Reported present Mar.–Apr./64. Absent sick according to rolls of 4/30–8/31/64. Absent sick in Goldsboro, Sept.–Oct./64. Reported present on company muster rolls of Nov.–Dec./64. (CSR 270:6)

Jones, Frederick A.: B. 7/31/32. From Wayne Co. Enl. 6/29/61 as PVT, Co. H. Reported present on company muster rolls of Nov.–Dec./61. Captured 2/7/62 at Difficult Run. Exd. Absent on rolls of Nov.–Dec./62, detailed to City Point. Served as a clerk and courier for COL Robert Ould, judge and agent/commissioner for exchange of prisoners. Absent on detached service 1/63–12/64 at City Point Admitted 11/26/64 to a Richmond G.H. with a fever. Returned to duty, 1/26/65. Prl Greensboro, 5/1/65. D. 10/6/67. Bur. Cedar Grove Cem., New Bern. (Stepp; CSR 270:6)

Jones, James: Enl. 9/22/63 as PVT, Co. B. Reported present on company muster rolls of 4/30/64–12/64. (CSR 270:6)

Jones, John T.: From Warren Co. Cns. 8/12/63 as PVT, Co. E. Reported present on company muster rolls of 6/30–Dec./63. Absent on detached service in NC to procure a horse, Mar.–Apr./64. Absent on detached service on pvst duty in Bowling Green according to rolls of 4/1/64. On detached service in NC, 4/30–8/31/64. Reported present on company muster rolls of Sept.–Oct./64. On detached service in NC bailing forage, Nov.–Dec./64. (CSR 270:6)

Jones, Lewis: From Duplin Co. At age 29, re-enl. 2/5/62 as PVT, Co. I. Reported present on company muster rolls of May–June/62, Sept.–Oct./62. Absent sick at a G.H., Nov.–Dec./62. Also reported absent sick on Jan.–Feb./63 rolls. D. 4/18/63, Campbell Co., VA. (CSR 270:6)

Jones, Samuel C.: Resident of Duplin Co. At age 31, enl. 6/22/61 as PVT, Co. I. Reported present on company muster rolls of Nov.–Dec./61, and listed as appointed CPL on 11/13/61. Absent Jan.–Feb./62 on recruiting service in NC, beginning 2/3/62. According to regimental returns, absent on detached service in 2/62 and on recruiting service in 3/62. Reported present on company muster rolls of May–June/62 and listed as 5SGT; also present Sept.–Oct./62. Absent on detached service as 2SGT, according to Nov.–Dec./62 rolls. Reported present Jan.–Apr./63. According to 10/31/63 company muster rolls, prm LT 10/24/63. Elected. Reported present Jan.–Dec./64. Medical report lists him with broken rib on 4/2/64 and frl for 30 days to his residence in Wilmington. Prm 1LT, 3/1/65. (CSR 270:1, 6)

Jones, William: From Watauga Co. or Ashe Co. At age 23, enl. 5/11/61 as CPL, Co. D. Reported present on company muster rolls of 11/61–2/62, 5/62–4/63. According to rolls of Jan.–Feb./63, prm SGT. Reported present 6/30/63–4/64. Captured at Hanover Junction, 5/27/64. Absent captured, 8/31/64–12/64. Exd. 10/29/64. (CSR 270:6; Davis says from Ashe, perhaps enl there)

Jones, William D.: From Louisiana. Asst. Surgeon. Assigned to regt by order of Wade Hampton. Reported present on company muster rolls of Sept.–Oct./62, Jan.–Feb./63. Absent with sick men, Mar.–Apr./63. Reported present July–Aug./63, 6/30/63–4/1/64. (CSR 270:1, 6)

Jones, William S.: Resident of Lenoir Co. At age 23, enl. 7/22/61 as PVT, Co. H. Reported present on company muster rolls of 11/61–2/62, May–June/62, Sept.–Oct./62. Absent detailed to report to BGD commissary, Nov.–Dec./62. Absent at home to procure a horse, Jan.–Feb./63. Reported present Mar.–Apr./63. Absent on detached service to procure a horse, July–Aug./63. Reported AWOL, Sept.–Oct./63. Reported present on company muster rolls of 11/63–8/31/64. Admitted 9/15/64 to a Raleigh G.H. with gonorrhea. Returned to duty, 9/23/64. Absent on detached service at Stony Creek, Sept.–Oct./64. Captured at Stony Creek, 12/3/64. Had hazel eyes, fair complexion, light brown hair, and stood 5'10" tall. (CSR 270:6; Monie)

Jordan, Benjamin F.: From Guilford Co. At age

19, enl. 9/3/63 as PVT, Co. C. Reported present on company muster rolls of 9/63–8/31/64. Absent on detached service beginning 9/24/64, according to rolls of Sept.–Oct./64. Reported present Nov.–Dec./64. Prl Greensboro, 1865. (Alexander; CSR 270:6)

Jordan, Daniel P.: B. 10/6/22. Farmer, from Wayne Co. At age 39, enl. 6/20/61 as PVT, Co H. Absent sick at home according to company muster rolls of Nov.–Dec./61. Absent sent to NC by COL Ransom beginning 11/5/61 according to rolls of Jan.–Feb./62. According to 2/62 regimental return, absent sick. 3/62 regimental return lists him on detached service beginning 11/5/61. Dsh 4/21/62 due to a disability (chronic rheumatism). Stood 6'2", had a fair complexion, blue eyes, light hair. D. 5/15/90. Bur. Eureka Christian Churchyard, Grantham Township, Wayne Co., NC. (CGR: 3 lists him as Jordon; CSR 270:6)

Jordan, Elisha B.: From Wayne Co. At age 27, enl. 6/20/61 as CPL, Co. _____. Reported present on company muster rolls of 11/61–2/62. According to regimental return of 3/62, _____. Absent sent to Goldsboro on recruiting service, May–June/62, 9/62–2/63. Reported present Mar.–Apr./63. Absent on detached service in NC to procure a horse, July–Aug./63. Reported AWOL Sept.–Oct./63 as 4SGT. Reported present Nov.–Dec./63. Absent on frl 1/64–4/1/64. Absent detailed on a horse, Mar.–Apr./64, reported present 4/30–12/64. (CSR 270:6)

Jordan, Joel: From Wayne Co. Mechanic. In poor health before the war. At age 23, enl. 6/20/61 as PVT, Co. H. Absent sick at home, Nov.–Dec./61. Reported present on company muster rolls of Jan.–Feb./62. According to regimental return of 2/62, absent sick. Reported present May–June/62, Sept.–Oct./62. Admitted 11/17/62 to a Richmond G.H. with rheumatism. Absent sent to a Gordonsville G.H. according to rolls of Nov.–Dec./62. Frl for 30 days, 12/3/62. Reported present, Jan.–Apr./63. Absent sent to recruit horses, July–Aug./63. Absent on detached service, Sept.–Oct./63. Reported present, Nov.–Dec./63. According to Jan.–Feb./64 rolls, KIA 1/28/64. (CSR 270:6)

Jordan, William: From Buncombe Co. At age 31, enl. 3/10/62 as PVT, Co. G. Reported present on company muster rolls of May–June/62, Sept.–Dec./62. Absent on detached service, Jan.–Feb./63. Reported present Mar.–Apr./63, July–Dec./63, Mar.–Aug./64. Also reported on extra duty at Orange C.H. as laborer, 11/27/63–12/16/63. Absent on detached service with unserviceable horses at Stony Creek, Sept.–Oct./64. According to rolls of Nov.–Dec./64, trn to Co. C, 25th NC Infantry. (CSR 270:6)

Justice, David: B. 11/18/23. Cns. 10/3/64 as PVT, Co. I. Reported present on company muster rolls of Sept.–Dec./64. Admitted to a Danville G.H., 4/4/65, with a gunshot wound in the leg. Frl. 4/8/65. D. 3/31/10. Bur. Ros Grove Baptist Church Cem., Cleveland Co. (Stepp; CSR 270:6)

Justice, M.S.: From Henderson Co. At age 17, enl. 3/62 as PVT, Co. G. Reported present on company muster rolls of May–June/62, Sept.–Oct./62. Absent on detached service, Nov.–Dec./62. Reported present on company muster rolls of Jan.–Apr./63. Captured 6/9/63, Beverly Ford. Prl 6/11/63. Absent on detached service to buy a horse, July–Aug./63. Reported present Sept.–Dec./63, 4/1/64. Absent on detached service to buy a horse, Mar.–Aug./64. Reported present Sept.–Dec./64. (CSR 270:6)

Justus, A.C.: Trn from state service. Enl. 9/21/64 as PVT, Co. G. Reported present on company muster rolls of Sept.–Dec./64. (CSR 270:6)

Keaton, S.M.: PVT, Co. A. On a Federal report as a deserter who surrendered in the Dept. of W. VA, 4/65. Stood 6'2", 24 years old, had a dark complexion, gray eyes, dark hair. Farmer before the war. Took the oath and went North, 4/1/65. (CSR 270:6)

Keiser, George A.: From Cabarrus Co. At age 28, enl. 6/15/61 as PVT, Co. F. Reported present on company muster rolls of 11/61–2/62, May–June/62, Sept.–Dec./62. Trn to Co. E, 5th NC Cavalry, 4/63 or 5/63. (CSR 270:6; Mizelle; Cabarrus; Barringer spells it Kizer and lists him as trn to 4th N.C. Cavalry)

Keistler, Daniel E.: From Lincoln Co. At age 21, enl. 5/20/61 as PVT, Co. A. reported present on company muster rolls of Nov.–Dec./61. Absent Jan.–Feb./62 at a Manassas G.H. Reported admitted to a Charlottesville G.H., 2/27/62, and returned to duty 3/17/62. Regimental returns for 2/62 list him absent sick beginning 2/24/62. Regimental returns for 3/62 report him in a G.H. as of 3/10/62. Reported present Sept.–Dec./62. According to Jan.–Feb./63 rolls, d. 1/20/63 in camp. Other records report him as accidentally shot, 1/24/63. (CSR 270:6; AsheCo lists him as "Kistler")

Keith, Arnold: From Buncombe Co. At age 24, enl. 5/20/61 in Co. G. Artificer. Reported present on company muster rolls of Jan.–Feb./62, May–June/62. Absent on detached service making shoes in Winchester, Sept.–Oct./62. Reported present

Nov.–Dec./62. Absent on detached service, Jan.–Feb./63. Reported present on company muster rolls of Mar.–Apr./63, July–Aug./63. Absent on detached service with unserviceable horses near Gordonsville, Sept.–Oct./63. Reported present Nov.–Dec./63, Mar.–Aug./64. Admitted 6/3/64 to a Petersburg G.H. with a gunshot wound in the left shoulder, then trn to a Raleigh G.H. 6/3/64. Also listed as admitted 6/64 to a Richmond G.H. On the register of a Raleigh G.H. as on frl as of 6/23/64. Absent on detached service to procure a horse, Sept.–Oct./64. Listed as AWOL, Nov.–Dec./64. (CSR 270:6)

Keith, E.H.: Enl. 4/29/61 as PVT, Co. G. Absent sick at Richmond according to regimental returns of 3/62. Reported present on company muster rolls of Sept.–Dec./63. Listed as deserted while on picket, 4/1/64. Admitted 6/3/64 to a Petersburg G.H. with a gunshot wound in the left shoulder. (CSR 270:6)

Kennedy, Jesse C.: B. Lenoir Co. Farmer. At age 19, enl. 7/22/61 as PVT, Co. H. Absent sick at home, Nov.–Dec./61. Dsh 2/3/62 according to Jan.–Feb./63 rolls and dsh certificate. Dsh due to consumption. Stood 5'10", had a fair complexion, blue eyes, dark hair. (CSR 270:6)

Kennedy, William B.: B. 1836. From Hallsville, Duplin Co. At age 24, enl. 6/22/61 as PVT, Co. I. Reported present on company muster rolls of 11/61–2/62. Absent on detached service, May–June/62. Reported present Sept.–Oct./62. Absent on detached service, 11/62–2/63. Reported present on company muster rolls of Mar.–Apr./63, 10/31/63, 1/1/64–8/31/64. According to Sept.–Dec./64 rolls, WIA 8/27/64. Also reported as WIA Boydton Plank Rd., 10/27/64. Admitted to Kittrell Springs, NC G.H. Left leg amputated due to gangrened thigh. D. 12/29/64 at Kitrell Springs G.H. from diarrhea. Bur. Kittrell Springs Confederate Cem. (CSR 270:6; Kittrell; Stepp)

Kent, Elisha: PVT. On a 2/18/64 Federal register of prisoners received and disposed of by PVST Marshall. Listed as a deserter. Had horse and saddle with him when he deserted. (CSR 270:6)

Kilpatrick, William F.: From Duplin Co. At age 20, enl. 6/24/61 as PVT, Co. I. Reported present on company muster rolls of 11/61–2/62, May–June/62, Sept.–Dec./62. Absent on detached service, Jan.–Apr./63. Absent in a Lynchburg G.H. beginning 10/12/63, according to 10/31/63 rolls. Rolls of 1/1/64 list him as absent in Lynchburg beginning 10/15/63. Reported present Jan.–Oct./64. (CSR 270:6)

Kincade, J.W.: PVT, Co. B. According to company muster rolls of Sept.–Oct./64, exd for PVT R.H. Powell of the 3rd NC Cavalry. Trn to Co. G, 3rd NC Cavalry, 10/26/64. (CSR 270:6)

King, H.J.: PVT, Co. G. On a list of Confederate POWs captured in a Raleigh G.H., 4/13/65. (CSR 270:6)

King, John Wiley: From Macon Co. or Cherokee Co. At age 18, enl. as PVT, Co. K, 6/25/61. Reported present on company muster rolls of Nov.–Dec./61. Beginning 2/19/62, absent detailed to care for horses at White Sulphur Springs, VA, according to rolls of Jan.–Feb./62. Regimental returns of 2/62 list him as on detached service. Reported present May–June/62. Absent WIA and captured at Boonsboro, MD, 9/13/62, according to Sept.–Oct./62 roll. Also listed as 2QM SGT. Prl & exd, 10/62. Admitted 10/24/62 to a Richmond G.H. with a wound in the left thigh. 11/6/62, frl for 30 days. Rolls of Nov.–Dec./62 report his capture as occurring at Middleton, MD.; listed as 2SGT. Rolls of Jan.–Feb./63 list him as home on frl. Reported present Mar.–Apr./63, July–Aug./63, 10/31/63–10/64. Listed as 1SGT beginning with Mar.–Apr./63 rolls. Absent on horse detail according to rolls of Nov.–Dec./64. (CSR 270:6)

King, Martin Van Buren: B. 9/1/40, Cabarrus Co. Enl. 3/31/62 as PVT, Co. F. reported present on company muster rolls of May–June/62, Sept.–Dec./62. According to pension application, WIA in the forehead at Gettysburg. According to company muster rolls of July–Aug./63, at Camp Cripple, Nelson Co., beginning 8/3/63. Still absent with dead line horses, Sept.–Oct./63. Also absent Nov.–Dec./63 with dead line in Botetourt Co., VA. Absent at home on frl, Jan.–Feb./64, beginning 2/64. Reported present on company muster rolls of 2/29/64–12/64. Admitted to a Richmond G.H., 5/26/64, due to a debility. Returned to duty, 6/2/64. Absent detached as a courier, Nov.–Dec./64. Prl Charlotte, 5/24/65. After the war, married Eliza R. McLellan and had 3 sons and 4 daughters. Resident of Hickory Grove Community, Mecklenburg Co. Served as an officer of Hickory Grove Methodist Church. Suffered from epilepsy later in life, perhaps as a result of his Gettysburg wound. D. 1/21/21. (CSR 270:6; Barringer; Cabarrus; Janet Morrison to the author, 9/10/98)

King, R.R.: B. 1/19/28. Enl. 2/14/62 as PVT, Co. C. Reported present on company muster rolls of 4/30–Dec./64. Prl in Charlotte, 5/24/65. D. 11/19/08. Bur. Amity Presbyterian Church Cem., Charlotte. (Alexander; Karchaske; CSR 270:6)

King, Virgil T.: From Buncombe Co. At age 24, enl. 5/20/61 as PVT, Co. G. Reported present on company muster rolls of Jan.–Feb./62, May–June/62. Absent on detached service at Winchester, Sept.–Oct./62. Reported present Nov.–Dec./62. Absent on detached service, Jan.–Feb./63. Reported present Mar.–Apr./63. Absent on detached service with brigade QM train, July–Aug./63. WIA slightly 10/10/63. Admitted 10/14/63 to a Richmond G.H. Absent WIA at home on frl according to rolls of 9/63–4/1/64. Reported AWOL afterward. Captured 4/5/65 at Aberdeen C.H. Released 6/28/65 on taking the oath. Stood 5'10", with blond complexion and dark brown hair. (CSR 270:6)

Kinnamon, George: PVT, Co. ____. Captured at Willis Church, 6/28/62. Exd 8/5/62. (CSR 270:6)

Kinsland, L.H.: Enl. 12/28/63 as PVT, Co. K. Reported present on company muster rolls of 2/29–12/64. (CSR 270:6)

Kinsland, William: From Macon Co. At age 20, enl. 7/61 as PVT, Co. K. Reported present on company muster rolls of Nov.–Dec./61. Admitted 1/1/62 to a Danville G.H. with a fever, and sent to a Richmond G.H. According to rolls of Jan.–Feb./62, absent sent to Manassas sick beginning 2/24/62. According to regimental return of 2/62, absent sick. Reported present May–June/62, 9/62–4/63. Absent detached to buy a horse in NC, July–Aug./63. Reported present on rolls of 10/31/63–3/31/64. WIA 5/9/64 according to rolls of Mar.–Apr./64. Admitted to a Richmond G.H., 5/64, with a gunshot wound in the right arm. Frl for 60 days, 6/3/64. Reported present Sept.–Dec./64. (CSR 270:6)

Kinyann, L.G.: PVT, Co. E. Reported present on company muster rolls of 4/30–Dec./64. (CSR 270:6)

Kirby, Allen: From Caldwell Co. At age 36, enl. 2/28/62 as PVT, Co. D. According to company muster rolls of May–June/62, absent in a Lynchburg G.H. Admitted 7/3/62 to a Richmond G.H. with chronic rheumatism. Reported present on rolls of 6/30/62–4/63. WIA 6/21/63 and absent at home afterward according to July–Aug./63 rolls. Roll of Honor reports him WIA 6/22/63. Admitted 7/20/63 to a Richmond G.H. with a gunshot wound in the left ankle. Trn 7/24/63 to a Raleigh G.H. Reported present on company muster rolls of 9/63–2/64. Dsh 3/9/64, according to a register of payments to dsh soldiers. (Davis; CSR 270:6)

Kirkpatrick, J.M.: PVT. On a Federal records as deserting in the Bermuda Hundred area either 2/14 or 2/21/65. Took the oath and sent to Philadelphia. (CSR 270:6)

Kirksey, James S.: B. Iredell Co. Resident of Cabarrus Co. Farmer. At age 32, enl. 6/15/61 as PVT, Co. F. Reported present on company muster rolls of 11/61–2/62. According to 3/62 regimental return, in a G.H. beginning 3/10. Another report list him as admitted 3/8/62 to a Richmond G.H. with bronchitis, and returned to duty 3/27/62. Absent on sick frl beginning 5/7/62 according to rolls of May–June/62. Rolls of Sept.–Oct./62 list him absent at Winchester with the wagon train. Dsh 11/20/62, according to rolls of Nov.–Dec./62, due to a hereditary pulmonary condition. Stood 5'10¼", and had a dark complexion, hazel eyes, and dark hair. Dead as of 1893. Some sources list him as James L. Kirksey. (Barringer; CSR 270:6; Mizelle & Cabarrus list him as James L.)

Kizziah, J.W.: From Mecklenburg Co. At age 19, enl. 6/3/61 in Co. C as 2 Bugler. Reported present on company muster rolls of 11/61–2/62, May–10/31/62. Rolls of Nov.–Dec./62 list him absent scouting beginning 12/25/62. Reported present Jan.–Apr./63, July–Aug./63. Absent on detached service beginning 10/10/63, according to rolls of 9/63–2/64. Reported present Mar.–Dec./64. (CSR 270:6; Alexander lists him as a non–commissioned officer)

Klapp, John A.: Enl. 1/26/64 as PVT, Co. H. Reported present on company muster rolls of Mar.–Apr./64. KIA 6/13/64 at White Oak Swamp. (CSR 270:6)

Klutts, Julius Caesar: B. 1/1/29. From Cabarrus Co. Enl. 6/15/61 as PVT, Co. F. Admitted 12/20/61 to a Danville G.H., and sent to Mt. Jackson. Company muster rolls of Nov.–Dec./61 report him absent in a Petersburg G.H. Rolls of Jan.–Feb./62 list him as in a G.H. since 12/21/61. Regimental return of 2/62 lists him as absent sick. Reported present May–June/62, Sept.–Dec./62. Reported in a Richmond G.H., 5/10/63. According to rolls of July–Aug./63, absent in NC to procure a horse. Reported present 9/63–3/31/64. Trn to Co. E, 4th NC Cavalry, 7/21/64. Resident of Cabarrus Co., circa 1893. D. 5/15/17. Bur. Bethel Methodist Episcopal Church Cem., Cabarrus Co. (CSR 270:6 in John L. Knight file; Barringer; Cabarrus; Lore: 13; Mizelle's spelling is different)

Klutts, Leonard P.: From Cabarrus Co. Farmer; in good health. At age 20, enl. 6/15/61 as PVT, Co. F. Reported present on company muster rolls of 11/61–2/62, May–June/62, Sept.–Dec./62. WIA 11/5/62, Barbee's Crossroads. Admitted 11/17/62 to a Richmond G.H. with a wound in the right side of his head. Frl 11/25/62 for 30 days. WIA at Upperville, 6/21/63, and absent on sick frl beginning July–Aug./63. Reported present 2/29–3/31/64. Absent on frl according to company muster rolls of Mar.–Dec./64. Reported admitted to a Richmond G.H. 5/64, with a gunshot wound in his hip. In a Raleigh G.H., 5/27/64, and then trn to Salisbury, NC. Retired to the Invalid Corps, 9/13/64, and detailed to Charlotte by a Medical Examining Board. Took the oath in Salisbury, 6/26/65. Living in Missouri, circa 1893. (CSR 270:6; Barringer; Cabarrus)

Klutts, S.P.: PVT, Co. F. Stood 6' tall. Had a fair complexion, blue eyes, and light hair. Retired 3/17/65. Detailed to Charlotte. (CSR 270:6 in csr of Leonard P. Klutts; Mizelle also has a P. Klutts)

Knight, John L.: From Macon Co. Farmer. Enl. 7/27/61 as PVT, Co. K. Admitted 11/17/62 to a Richmond G.H., and frl 11/17/62. Reported present on company muster rolls of 11/61–2/62, May–June/62, Sept.–Oct./62. Absent after being WIA at Gaines's Crossroads, 11/7/62. Sent to a G.H. from Madison C.H., 11/15/62, according to rolls of Nov.–Dec./62. Admitted 1/17/63 to a Richmond G.H and trn to Danville. Reported present Mar.–Apr./63. Listed as deserted 3/27, but with a gunshot wound in the side. Captured 7/12/63 at Funkstown, MD, according to rolls of July–Aug./63. Listed in a Danville G.H., 6/4/64, with a gunshot wound in his face. Trn 6/21/64. Rolls of Sept.–Oct./64 list him as a deserter. (CSR 270:6)

Knoble, J.C.: SGT, Co. B. Listed as frl to Tarboro, 9/26/64. Information found in John E. Knowles file. (CSR 270:6)

Knowles, John E.: From Washington Co. At age 19, enl. 8/2/61 as PVT, Co. B. Reported present 11/61–4/62, 9/62–4/63. WIA and captured near Funkstown, MD, 7/10/63, according to rolls of July–Aug./63 and according to Federal records. Rolls of 4/30–8/31/64 and Sept.–Dec./64 list him as absent sick. Exd. 9/18/64. Admitted 2/16/65 to a Richmond G.H. with a gunshot wound in the leg. Frl 2/24/65 for 60 days, to Tarboro. Admitted 4/65 to a Greensboro G.H. Prl 5/1/65 from a High Point G.H. (CSR 270:6)

Kornegay, G.W.: At age 26, enl. 7/4/61 as PVT, Co. I. Rejected. (CSR 270:6)

Kornegay, William F.: B. 6/18/32. From Wayne Co. Age 29. Co. H. Apptd 2LT to rank from 5/16/61. Absent sick at home, Nov.–Dec./61. Also reported home at sick, Jan.–Feb./62, since 10/23/61. Rgt returns list him as absent sick, Feb.–Mar./62, since 10/23/61. Resigned due to disability, R. 1/27/62 or 4/62. D 10/31/01. Bur Willowdale Cem, Goldsboro. (CSR 270:1, 6; CGR: 3; Stepp)

Kuykendall, E. Jackson: From Buncombe Co. At age 27, enl. 2/22/62 as PVT, Co. G. Reported present on company muster rolls of May–June/62, Sept.–Dec./62. Absent on detached service, Jan.–Apr./63. Absent on detached service to purchase a horse, July–Aug./63. Reported present Sept.–Dec./63, 4/1/64, Mar.–Aug./64. AWOL, Sept.–Oct./64. Reported present Nov.–Dec./64 and prm to 2LT. Elected 2LT, 10/21/64. Apptd to a board of valuation, 3/21/65. (Box 42, Folder 19, Military Collection, Civil War Collection, NCSA; CSR 270:1, 6; other name spellings include Kuykendall, Kurkendall, Kingkendall; csr is Kirkendall; I went with his signature)

Kuykendall, E. Jackson: From Buncombe Co. At age 27, enl. 2/22/62 as PVT, Co. G. Reported present on company muster rolls of May–June/62, Sept.–Dec./62. Absent on detached service, Jan.–Apr./63. Absent on detached service to purchase a horse, July–Aug./63. Reported present Sept.–Dec./63, 4/1/64, Mar.–Aug./64. AWOL, Sept.–Oct./64. Reported present Nov.–Dec./64 and prm to 2LT. Elected 2LT, 10/21/64. Apptd to a board of valuation, 3/21/65. (Box 42, Folder 19, Military Collection, Civil War Collection, NCSA; CSR 270:1, 6; other name spellings include Kuykendall, Kurkendall, Kingkendall; csr is Kirkendall; I went with his signature)

Kuykendall, J.R.: Trn from state service. Enl. 9/21/64 as PVT, Co. G. Reported present on company muster rolls of Sept.–Oct./64. Absent on detached service with a horse detail, Nov.–Dec./64. Captured 4/3/65 at Aberdeen C.H. (CSR 270:6)

Laird, J.C.: Captured at Front Royal. On a list of non–commissioned officers and PVTs as exd at Aiken's Landing, 8/5/62. (CSR 270:6)

Lambert, Reubin A.: Enl. 9/2/64 as PVT, Co. K. Reported present on company muster rolls of Sept.–Dec./64. (CSR 270:6)

Lambeth, Thomas L.: B. 11/21/48. PVT. D 11/8/01. Bur Salem Cem., Winston-Salem. (GLP; CGR: 6)

Lane, Amos: From Northampton Co. At age 25, enl. 3/12/62 as PVT, Co. B. Reported present on company muster rolls of Mar.–Apr./62. According to rolls of Sept.–Dec./62, deserted 8/18/62. (CSR 270:6)

Lane, Hardy B.: B. in NC. From Craven Co. At age 32, enl. 6/20/61 as SGT, Co. H. Reported present on company muster rolls of 11/61–2/62.

Captured at Willis Church, 6/29/62, according to company muster rolls of May–June/62. Exd, 8/5/62. According to Federal records, age 33, stood 5'11½", had dark hair, gray eyes, and a sallow complexion. Reported present Sept.–Oct./62. According to rolls of Nov.–Dec./62, absent detached to take prisoners to Richmond. Prm and trn to 3d NC Infantry, according to rolls of Jan.–Feb./63. (CSR 270:6)

Lane, Harvey W.: From Bertie Co. At age 25, enl. 3/10/62 as PVT, Co. E. Reported present on company muster rolls of May–June/62, Sept.–Dec./62, Mar.–Apr./63. According to rolls of 6/30–10/31/63, said to have deserted to Bertie Co., 10/31/63. Rolls of July–Aug./63 report him as AWOL since 8/1/63. (CSR 270:6)

Lane, William B.: B. Craven Co. Farmer. Enl. 7/5/61 as PVT, Co. H. Reported present on company muster rolls of Nov.–Dec./61. Rolls of Jan.–Feb./62 list him as captured 2/7/62 at Difficult Run. 2/62 regimental returns agree, listing him as captured 2/7/62 while on outpost duty. Listed as prl and absent, May–June/62, Sept.–Oct./62. Reported present 11/62–4/63. Absent WIA and sent to a G.H. according to rolls of 7/63–4/64. Admitted 7/21/63 to a Richmond G.H. Detailed 4/27/64. Also listed as absent sick, 4/30–8/31/64. According to company muster rolls of Sept.–Dec./64, absent on light duty as a clerk in Goldsboro. Prm CPL. Dsh 12/64 upon election to NC House of Commons, representing Craven Co. Age 32, stood 5'9", had a fair complexion, blue eyes, and dark hair. (CSR 270:6)

Lane, William P.: From Wayne Co. At age 19, enl. 6/20/61 as PVT, Co. H. According to company muster rolls of Nov.–Dec./61, trn to Cpt James Lane's NC Artillery Co, 12/5/61, and prm LT. (CSR 270:6)

Lanier, David J.: B. Duplin Co. Enl. 4/15/61 in CPT Ward's NC Cavalry. Trn and Enl. 7/21/62 as PVT, Co. I. Company muster rolls of Nov.–Dec./62 report him as absent on detached service. Reported present Jan.–Feb./63. According to rolls of Mar.–Apr./63, D. 3/26 or 3/27/63 in Rockingham Co., VA. (CSR 270:6)

Lanier, Jesse: B. 1844. From Duplin Co. Enl. 6/20/61 as Bugler, Co. I. Reported present on company muster rolls of 11/61–2/62, May–June/62, 9/62–4/63. Rolls of Mar.–Apr./63 list him as absent sick in Rockingham Co., VA. Reported present 10/31/63, 1/1/64, Jan.–Dec./64. Admitted 7/29/64 to a Richmond G.H. Returned to duty, 8/8/64. Captured 4/25/65 in Hamilton, VA. Released on prl 5/1/65. Bur. Faison Family Cem./Old Town Cem., Faison, Duplin Co, NC. (GLP; CGR: 2; Stepp; CSR 270:6)

Lassiter, Godwin C.M.: From Northampton Co. At age 20, enl. 6/12/61 as PVT, Co. B. Absent at home on sick leave according to company muster rolls of Nov.–Dec./61. Rolls of Jan.–Feb./62 list him as D. 2/12 in camp. On a 2/62 sick and wounded report with chronic dysentery; d. 2/13. Regimental return of 2/62 also reports him as D. 2/12/62. D. at Cantonment W.N. Edwards. (CSR 270:6)

Lassiter, James P.: Enl. 6/12/61 as 2SGT, Co. unknown. Reported present on company muster rolls of 11/61–4/62, Sept.–Dec./62. Prm 1SGT, 10/62. Absent Jan.–Feb./63 on detached duty to buy a horse, beginning 2/21. Reported present Mar.–Apr./63, 6/30–Dec./63. Reported present 4/1/64. Absent Mar.–Apr./64 on horse detail. Absent with dismounted men, 4/30–10/64. Trn to Co. H., 2nd NC Cavalry, 11/8/64. (CSR 270:6)

Lassiter, Moses N.: From Northampton Co. At age 33, enl. 6/18/61 as PVT, Co. B. According to company muster rolls of Nov.–Dec./61, absent at home on sick leave. Rolls of Jan.–Feb./62 report him left sick at Camp Beaureagard, 10/15/61. 2/62 Regimental return lists him as absent sick. Reported present on company muster rolls of Mar.–Apr./62. Rolls of Sept.–Oct./62 list him as dsh, 8/3/62. (CSR 270:6)

Lassiter, Stephen L.: From Northampton Co. At age 22, enl. 6/12/61. According to company muster rolls of Nov.–Dec./61, absent at home on sick leave. Rolls of Jan.–Feb./62 report him left sick at Camp Beaureagard, 10/15/61. Regimental return of 2/62 reports him absent sick. Reported present on company muster rolls of Mar.–Apr./62, Sept.–Oct./62. Admitted to a Richmond G.H. with a fever, 9/13/62. Returned to duty 10/18/62 after bout with typhoid fever. Absent on detached service, Nov.–Dec./62. Reported present, Jan.–Apr./63. Absent on detached service in NC to procure a horse beginning 8/27/63, according to rolls of July–Aug./63. Reported present 6/30–10/31/63, Nov.–Dec./63, Mar.–Apr./64. D. 5/15/64, Brook Church. (CSR 270:6)

Laston, T.J.: PVT, Co. A. (AsheCo)

Latham, David: Enl. 3/7/62 as PVT, Co. A. Reported present on company muster rolls of Sept.–Oct./62. Reported present as company teamster, Nov.–Dec./62. According to rolls of Jan.–Feb./63, absent on frl to buy a horse beginning 2/27/63. Rolls of Mar.–Apr./63 list him as sick at home. Trn 6/63 to Co. D., 58th NC Infantry. (AsheCo; CSR 270:6)

Latham, Jacob: From Ashe Co. PVT, Co. A. 25. D. 9/25/61 of disease. (AsheCo; CSR 270:6)

Laughter, S.L.: Trn from state service. Enl. 9/21/64 as PVT, Co. G. Reported present on company muster rolls of Sept.–Dec./64. (CSR 270:6)

Laurie, James: From Lenoir Co. At age 25, enl. 7/61 as PVT, Co. H. Reported present on company muster rolls of 11/61–2/62, May–June/62, 9/62–4/63. Absent according to rolls of July–Aug./63; deserted. (CSR 270:6)

Lawrence, J.G.: Enl. 5/10/64 as PVT, Co. A. Reported present on company muster rolls of July–Dec./64. (AsheCo; CSR 270:6)

Lawrance, Sam A.: Enl. 10/9/64 as PVT, Co. F. Reported present on company muster rolls of Sept.–Dec./64. Prl 5/29/65 in Salisbury. Resident of Mooresville, NC, circa 1893. (CSR 270:6 also lists him as enl 9/29/63; Mizelle spells it Lawrence; Barringer spells it Lowrance)

Laxton, Thomas J.: Enl. 2/27/62 as PVT, Co. A. According to company muster rolls of Sept.–Dec./62, absent sent home on sick frl beginning 8/5/62. Absent Nov.–Dec./62. Reported present on company muster rolls of Jan.–Feb./63. Reported present Mar.–Apr./63 as regimental teamster. Reported present July–Aug./63. According to rolls of Sept.–Oct./63, captured 9/13/63. Prl 3/9/64 and exd 3/10/64. Absent July–Aug./64. Trn to Co. A, 26th NC Infantry, but listed as AWOL and at home on frl, Sept.–Oct./64. (CSR 270:6)

Leach, Frank: From Macon Co. Age 40. 2LT, Co. K. Resigned due to health reasons. (CSR 270:6).

League, L.L.: PVT. According to Federal records, captured at Brandy Station, 8/1/63.

Leak, James R.: From Northampton Co. At age 25, enl. 6/12/61 as 4CPL, Co. B. reported present of company muster rolls of Nov.–Dec./61. Company muster rolls of Jan.–Feb./62 list him as 2CPL and present but sick in quarters. Regimental return of 3/62 list him absent on recruiting service. Reported present Mar.–Apr./62, Sept.–Oct./62. Absent on detached service, Nov.–Dec./62. According to rolls of Jan.–Feb./63, absent detached to procure a horse beginning 2/26. Also listed as 5SGT. Reported present Mar.–Apr./63, 6/30–Dec./63, 4/1/64. Listed as 4SGT beginning on rolls of July–Aug./63. Absent on horse detail as 4SGT, Mar.–Apr./64. Trn 4/27/64 to Co. A, 12th NC Bn Cavalry. (CSR 270:6)

Leak, John M.: B. 10/30/47. PVT. D. 12/15/24. (Personal Observation.)

Leath, George: Enl. 3/3/64 as PVT, Co. H. reported present on company muster rolls of 4/1/64, Mar.–Oct./64. Absent detached on horse detail, Nov.–Dec./64. (CSR 270:6)

Ledford, Alexander J.: Enl. 11/23/61 as PVT, Co. K. Reported present on company muster rolls of 11/61–2/62, May–June/62, Sept.–Oct./62. Absent Nov.–Dec./62 detached to bring clothing from Macon Co., GA, beginning 11/8/62. Absent on detached service, Jan.–Feb./63. Reported present Mar.–Apr./63, July–Aug./63, 10/63–3/31/64. Absent on detached service with signal corps as operator, 4/25/64–10/64. (CSR 270:6)

Ledford, Leander T.: From Macon Co. At age 20, enl. 11/23/61 as PVT, Co. K. Reported present on company muster rolls of Nov.–Dec./61. According to rolls of Jan.–Feb./62, d. of measles 1/25/62 at Cantonment W.N. Edwards. Another report lists him as d. 1/26/62 of bronchitis. (CSR 270:6)

Lee, William: From Watauga Co. Age 31. PVT, Co. D. D. of pneumonia at Cantonment W.N. Edwards, 12/6/61. (Davis; CSR 270:6)

Lee, William H.: B. 5/3/37. From Cabarrus Co. At age 24, enl. 6/15/61 as PVT, Co. F. Reported present on company muster rolls of 11/61–2/62. Regimental return of 2/62 lists him on extra duty as a teamster. Reported present May–June/62, Sept.–Dec./62, July–Dec./63. Absent at home on frl, 2/64, according to rolls of Jan.–Feb./64. Reported present 2/29/64–12/64. D. 8/1/21. Bur. Rocky Ridge Cem., Cabarrus Co. (CSR 270:6; Mizelle lists him as W.M. Lee; Barringer says dead as of 1893; Cabarrus; Lore: 168)

Lefler, Peter A.: From Cabarrus Co. At age 22, enl. 6/15/61 as PVT, Co. F. Reported present on company muster rolls of 11/61–2/62, May–June/62, Sept.–Dec./62. KIA Brandy Station, 6/9/63. (Barringer; Mizelle; Cabarrus; CSR 270:6)

Lemon, William H.: From Craven Co. At age 20, enl. 6/20/61 as PVT, Co. H. Reported present on company muster rolls of Nov.–Dec./61. Regimental returns of 2/62 list him as trn 2/1/2. According to field and staff muster rolls of Jan.–Feb./62, trn from Co. H 2/1/62 to regimental staff. Company muster rolls of Jan.–Feb./62 report him as trn to regimental band, 2/27/62. According to rolls of Jan.–Feb./63, absent on detached service. Federal records list him as captured 3/63 at Catlett's Station. Absent on prl after being captured according to rolls of Mar.–Apr./63. Absent on detached service, July–Aug./63, to procure a horse in NC. AWOL according to rolls of Sept.–Oct./63. Absent on detached service as a scout, Nov.–Dec./63. Federal records report him as captured 1/12/64, Fairfax Co., VA. Absent captured according to rolls of Mar.–Apr./64. Exd, 2/24/65. Prl, 3/10/65. (CSR 270:6)

Lentz, William A.: B. 1/3/35. Resident of Cabarrus Co. Enl. 6/15/61 as PVT, Co. F. Reported present on company muster rolls of 11/61–2/62. Regimental return of 2/62 lists him as on extra duty as a teamster. Reported present May–June/62, Sept.–Dec./62. Rolls of July–Aug./63 list him absent on sick frl after being WIA at Upperville, VA, 6/21/63. Admitted 7/23/63 to a Richmond G.H. with a gunshot wound in the shoulder. Frl for 30 days, 7/29/63. Reported present Jan.–Mar./31/64. Admitted 5/5/64 to a Richmond G.H. with a minie ball wound in the shoulder. Trn from a Raleigh G.H., 5/28/64. Absent on frl Mar.–Oct./64. Reported present Nov.–Dec./64, and disabled. Retired 1/6/65 to the Invalid Corps. 1/11/65, ordered to report for light duty. 2/13/65, detailed to report to the surgeon in charge at a Richmond G.H. Captured in Richmond, 4/6/65. Took oath and released, 6/28/65. Had a light complexion, light brown hair, and blue eyes, and stood 6' tall. Resident of Concord, circa 1893. D. 9/23/13. Bur St. John's Lutheran Church Cem., Cabarrus Co. (Barringer; Mizelle; Cabarrus; Graves; CSR 270:6)

Lester, Isaac S.: Enl. 3/12/64 as PVT, Co. H. Reported present on company muster rolls of 4/30–8/31/64. Absent Sept.–Oct./64 in Kittrell Springs, NC G.H. Reported present Nov.–Dec./64. Prl Greensboro, 1865, prb on 4/26. Living in Dyer, AK in 1916; requested names and addresses of 1st NC Cavalry survivors, especially those of Co. H. (CSR 270:6; CV 24 [1916]: 287)

Lester, James T.: From Northampton Co. At age 21, enl. 6/21/61 as PVT, Co. B. Reported present on company muster rolls of 11/61–4/62. Regimental return of 2/62 lists him as on extra duty as a teamster. Return of 3/62 listed him as absent sick in a Petersburg G.H. Reported present Sept.–Oct./62. Absent on detached service, Nov.–Dec./62. Absent detached to secure a horse, beginning 2/21/63 according to Jan.–Feb./63 rolls. Reported present Mar.–Apr./63. Absent on detached service with the ordnance wagons, July–Aug./63. Reported present on company muster rolls of 6/30–Dec./63. POW, Jan.–Feb./64. Reported present, 4/1/64. Absent detached to secure a horse, Mar.–Apr./64. Trn to Co. D, 43rd NC Infantry, 8/27/64. (CSR 270:6)

Lewellyn, J.: From Randolph Co. At age 39, enl. 6/3/61 as PVT, Co. C. Reported present on company muster rolls of 11/61–2/62, May–June/62. Prm CPL, 3/1/62. Reported present 4/63–6/30/63, July–Aug./63. Absent Sept.–Oct./63 due to a 9/14/63 wound. Reported present 11/63–12/64. Prl Greensboro, NC, 5/16/65. (CSR 270:6; Alexander; alternate spellings include Lewallen and Lewallyn)

Lewis, J.C.: From Mecklenburg Co. At age 22, enl. 5/25/61 as PVT, Co. C. Reported present on company muster rolls of 11/61–2/62, 5/62–4/63. Absent on detached service to by a horse beginning 8/27/63, according to rolls of July–Aug./63. Reported present 9/63–12/64. (CSR 270:6; Alexander lists him as C.J.)

Lewis, James M.: From Mecklenburg Co. At age 30, enl. 2/28/62 as PVT, Co. C. Reported present on company muster rolls of May–June/62. WIA and absent sick at Charlotte beginning 7/1/62 according to rolls of 6/30–10/31/63. Trn to a Richmond G.H., 12/1/63. Reported present Nov.–Dec./63. Absent Jan.–Feb./64. Reported as detailed 1/28/64. Admitted 2/10/64 to a Richmond G.H. with a gunshot wound to the face. Reported present 4/1/64. Absent WIA according to rolls of Mar.–Apr./64. Also reported as returned to duty, 3/14/64. Admitted 5/5/64 to a Richmond G.H. with a gunshot wound to the face. A 5/20/64 register of the Medical Directors Office lists him as retired due to a gunshot wound in his face. Rolls of Nov.–Dec./64 declare him retired by the Medical Examining Board. Admitted 3/65 to a Greensboro G.H. (Alexander; CSR 270:6)

Lewis, William R.: Resident of Watauga Co. At age 17, enl. 5/11/61 as PVT, Co. D. Also listed as bugler. Reported present on company muster rolls of 11/61–2/62. Also listed as orderly for COL Baker. Regimental return of 2/62 lists him on daily duty as Baker's orderly. 3/62 regimental return lists him sick in a Petersburg hospital beginning 3/29/62. Reported present May–Dec./62. Absent to buy a horse, Jan.–Feb./63. Reported present Mar.–Apr./63. Absent at home to procure a horse, July–Aug./63. Reported present on company muster rolls of 6/30/63–3/31/64. Absent at home to buy a horse, Mar.–Apr./64. WIA 8/15/64 along Charles City Rd., near Richmond. Admitted 8/15/64 to a Richmond G.H. with a gunshot wound in the left hand. Returned to duty, 8/25/64. Reported present 8/31/64. Absent on horse detail, Sept.–Oct./64. Reported present Nov.–Dec./64. PVT, Co. E. Captured Watauga Co., 3/28/65. Took the oath, 6/10/65. Had a florid complexion, black hair and eyes, stood 5'9". (Richmond *Sentinel*, 8/26/64; Davis; CSR 270:6)

Lilly, James M.: From Montgomery Co. Cns

7/28/62 or 8/21/62 as PVT, Co. H. Reported present on company muster rolls of 9/62–4/63. Absent on detached service in the Assistant Commissary of Subsistence Dept., July–Aug./63. Reported present Sept.–Dec./63. Reported present Jan.–Feb./64 on extra duty in the Commissary Department. 4/1/64, reported present and on extra daily duty. Mar.–Apr./64, absent detached to procure a horse. KIA, 8/21/64, according to rolls of 4/30–8/31/64. (CSR 270:6 also lists him as James H.)

Lindsay, William B.: From Cabarrus Co. At age 26, enl. 6/15/61 as PVT, Co. F. Reported present on company muster rolls of 11/61–2/62, May–June/62, Sept.–Dec./62. Absent July–Aug./63 in Loudoun Co. to procure a horse, beginning 8/4/63. Reported present Sept.–Oct./63. Absent Nov.–Dec./63. Captured 12/3/63 near Mine Run. Prm scout. Prl 3/14/65. Resident of Loudon Co., VA, circa 1893. (Barringer; Mizelle; Cabarrus; CSR 270:6)

Linebarger, F.H.: Enl. 9/22/63 as PVT, Co. B. Reported present on company muster rolls of 4/30–Dec./64. (CSR 270:6)

Link, William A.: Res. Person Co. PVT. Deserted and entered Federal lines at Edenton, NC, 9/1/64. Took the oath, 9/23/64. Had a dark complexion, light hair, light eyes, and stood 5'5¾". (CSR 270:6)

Lipe, Edmund G.: B. 1/18/39. From Cabarrus Co. Enl. 6/15/61 as PVT, Co. F or Co. G. Reported present on company muster rolls of 11/61–2/62, May–June/62, Sept.–Dec./62. Appointed Farrier, 12/15/62. Absent in NC to procure a horse, 8/27/63, according to rolls of July–Aug./63. Reported present, 9/63–2/64. WIA at Atlee's Station, 3/2/64, and absent 2/29–3/31/64. Admitted 3/2/64 to a Richmond G.H. with a pistol ball wound in his right side. Frl beginning 4/24/64. Remained on frl through 12/64. Resident of Concord, circa 1893. D. 11/20/10. Bur. Coldwater Lutheran Church Cem., Cabarrus Co. (Barringer; Mizelle; Cabarrus; Lore: 51; Graves; CSR 270:6)

Lippard, Charles W.: B. 9/8/30. From Watauga Co. Enl. 5/11/61 as SGT, Co. D. Reported present on company muster rolls of Nov.–Dec./61. Reported present Jan.–Feb./62. Admitted to a Richmond G.H., 3/8/62, and returned to duty 3/27/62. Reported present May–June/62 as 1SGT. Also reported present on rolls of 6/30–10/31/62. Elected 2LT, 11/20/62. Absent sick, Nov.–Dec./62. Prm Sr. 2LT, 12/25/62. Absent sick at home on a frl, Jan.–Feb./63. Reported present on company muster rolls of Mar.–Apr./63. Submitted resignation letter 5/27/63 and it was accepted 6/16/63, due to ill health. D. 12/11/74. Bur. Howell Cem., NC 194, Watauga Co. (Davis; Stepp; CSR 270:6)

Litaker, Henry: From Cabarrus Co. Known as "Little Henry." At age 22, enl. 6/15/61 as 2Bugler, Co. F. Reported present on company muster rolls of 11/61–2/62, May–June/62, Sept.–Dec./62. Prm Chief (regimental) Bugler, 12/62 or 12/63. On detached service beginning 2/24/63 according to Field and Staff muster rolls of Jan.–Feb./63. Reported present on Field and Staff muster rolls of Mar.–Apr./63. Absent on detached service, July–Aug./63. Reported present 6/30–12/63, Mar.–Aug./31/64. Admitted 6/18/64 to a Richmond G.H. Horse KIA at Jack's Shop, 9/22/63. On frl of indulgence beginning 10/28/64 according to rolls of Sept.–Oct./64. Reported present on rolls of Nov.–Dec./64. Dead as of 1893. (Mizelle; Barringer; Cabarrus; Sun, 3/25/81; CSR 270:6)

Livitzer, R.P.: Saddler. Co. A. From Ashe Co. (AsheCo)

Lomax, Adolphus W.: From Macon Co. At age 20, enl. 6/25/61. Reported present on company muster rolls of 11/61–2/62. Rgt returns of 3/62 list him in a G.H. Admitted 3/14/62 to a Richmond G.H. with diarrhea; returned to duty 3/27/62. Absent sent home to Kinston 6/1/62, according to company muster rolls of May–June/62. According to rolls of Jan.–Feb./63, D. 2/14/63 at Stevensburg, VA after being WIA in a skirmish at Rappahannock Bridge, 2/7/63. (Macon Heritage, 49; CSR 270:6)

London, Carlos L.: B. 1/21/45. Resident of Cleveland Co. Cns 9/29/64 as PVT, Co. H. reported present on company muster rolls of Sept.–Dec./64. Captured at Sutherland's Station, 4/3/65. Released on taking the oath, 6/28/65. D. 4/4/85. Bur. New Bethel Baptist Church Cem., near Lawndale, NC. (CGR: 4; CSR 270:6 lists him as Charles)

London, James: B. 11/3/18. Cns 9/29/64 as PVT, Co. H. Reported present on company muster rolls of Sept.–Dec./64. D. 5/21/03. Bur. New Bethel Baptist Church Cem., near Lawndale, NC. (CGR: 4; CSR 270:6)

Long, Edwin: Cns 4/12/64 as PVT, Co. H. Reported present on company muster rolls of Mar.–Apr./64, 4/30–8/31/64. Trn to 5th N.C. Cavalry, 7/11/64. (CSR 270:6)

Long, Henry A.: B. 3/15/31. From Cabarrus Co. Enl. 6/15/61 as PVT, Co. F. Reported absent in the Camp Ashe hospital, according to company muster rolls of Nov.–Dec./61. Reported present on company muster rolls of Jan.–Feb./62, May–June/62,

Sept.–Dec./62. Absent in NC to procure a horse beginning 8/27/63, according to rolls of July–Aug./63. Reported present 9/63–10/64. Absent detailed to collect forage, 12/64, according to rolls of Nov.–Dec./64. Prl Salisbury, 5/15/65. Resident of Concord, NC, circa 1893. D. 9/14/98. Bur. Mt. Carmel Methodist & New Gilead Church Graveyard, Cabarrus Co. (Mizelle; Bounty Receipts; Barringer; Cabarrus; Lore: 110; CSR 270:6)

Long, William M.: From Cabarrus Co. At age 22, enl. 6/15/61 as PVT, Co. F. Reported present on company muster rolls of 11/61–2/62, May–June/62, Sept.–Dec./62. Absent on sick frl after being WIA at Gettysburg, 7/3/63. According to July–Aug./63 rolls, admitted 7/15/63 to a G.H. with a gunshot wound. Frl 8/1/63. Reported present on company muster rolls of Sept.–Oct./63. Absent sent to the dead line, beginning 11/15/63, according to rolls of Nov.–Dec./63. Reported present Mar.–Oct./64. Absent 12/64 to collect forage, according to rolls of Nov.–Dec./64. Prl in Salisbury, NC, 5/16/65. Resident of Concord, circa 1893. D. 5/25/02, at age 62 yrs 11 mos 29 days. Bur Mt Carmel Methodist & New Gilead Church Graveyard, Cabarrus Co. (Mizelle; Bounty Receipts; Barringer; GLP; Cabarrus; Lore: 110; CSR 270:6)

Lonkbill, Franklin: PVT, Co. B. Captured in Boone, N.C., 3/28/65, and sent to Chattanooga, TN 4/12/65. (CSR 270:6)

Lookabill, J.W.: From Watauga Co. At age 26, enl. 5/16/61 as CPL, Co. D. Prm SGT. D. of pneumonia at Camp W.S. Ashe near Centerville, VA, 12/25/61 (according to sick and wounded report) or 1/62. (Davis; CSR 270:6)

Lookabill, W.H.: Enl. 3/16/63 as PVT, Co. I. Reported absent sick in Campbell Co., VA, Mar.–Apr./63. Reported present on company muster rolls of 10/31/63. Rolls of 1/1/64 list him as deserted, beginning 11/10/63. According to Federal records, received 11/9/63. May have been captured. Age 21, stood 6' tall, with light hair. Took the oath of allegiance, 5/65. From either Davie or Davidson Co. (CSR 270:6)

Louder, Archibald J.: From Cabarrus Co. At age 19, enl. 6/15/61 as PVT, Co. F. Admitted 11/3/61 to a Richmond G.H. Returned to duty, 12/9/61. Reported present on company muster rolls of 11/61–2/62, May–June/62, Sept.–Dec./62, 7/63–3/31/64. Prm to scout. WIA 8/23/64, Old Stage Road. D. 8/24/64. (Mizelle; Bounty Receipts; Barringer; Cabarrus; CSR 270:6; alternate spelling is Lowder)

Love, Thomas: From Union Co. At age 25, enl. 6/15/61 as PVT, Co. F. Reported present on company muster rolls of 11/61–2/62, May–June/62, Sept.–Dec./62. Prm QM Sgt for Co. F, 5/63. Reported present on company muster rolls of July–Aug./63. Absent with dead line horses beginning 10/5/63, according to rolls of Sept.–Oct./63. Reported present 11/63–12/64. Prm QM SGT, 5/63. Resident of Union Co., circa 1893. (Mizelle; Bounty Receipts; Barringer; Cabarrus; CSR 270:6)

Lovelace, William: Cns 6/2/64 as PVT, Co. I. According to company muster rolls of Mar.–Apr./64, on detached service in NC to remount beginning 9/6/64. Reported present on company muster rolls of 4/31–12/64. (CSR 270:6)

Loveless, W.W.: From McDowell Co. At age 19, enl. 5/20/61 as PVT, Co. G. Reported present on company muster rolls of Jan.–Feb./62, May–June/62, 9/62–4/63. Absent on detached service to buy a horse according to rolls of July–Aug./63. Reported present Sept.–Dec./63. Absent on detached service on provost duty at Bowling Green, VA, probably in early 1864. Reported present on company muster rolls of Mar.–Oct./64. According to rolls of Nov.–Dec./64, trn to 55th NC Infantry 12/3/64. (CSR 270:6)

Lovesey, Thomas W.: From Granville Co. At age 21, enl. 7/61 as PVT, Co. E. Reported present on company muster rolls of Jan.–Feb./62, May–June/62, Sept.–Dec./62, Mar.–Apr./63, July–Aug./63, 6/30–12/63. Absent on frl, Jan.–Feb./64. Reported present on rolls of 4/1/64, Mar.–Dec./64. (CSR 270:6)

Lovin, Joel H.: From Cherokee Co. At age 23, enl. 6/25/61 as PVT, Co. K. Reported present on company muster rolls of 11/61–2/62, May–June/62. Captured 9/62. Absent after being captured at Boonsboro, MD, 9/13/62, according to rolls of Sept.–Oct./62. Exd. Prl 10/3/62. Admitted 11/2/62 to a Richmond G.H. According to rolls of Nov.–Dec./62, absent sick in a Richmond G.H. beginning 11/8/62. Still absent in a Richmond G.H. beginning Jan.–Feb./63. Listed as admitted to a Richmond G.H., 2/19/63. Reported present on company muster rolls of Mar.–Apr./63, July–Aug./63, 10/31/63, 11/63–12/64. Post-war, involved in a moonshine disagreement between Macon Co. and Moccasin, Ga called the Moccasin War. (CSR 270:6; Macon Heritage, 49)

Lowdermilk, G.W.: From Macon Co. Age 37. PVT, Co. K. Rejected by COL Baker. (CSR 270:6)

Lucas, James Samuel: B. Beaufort Co. From Hyde Co. Student before the war. At age 22, enl. 7/6/62 as PVT, Co. E. Reported present on company muster rolls of Sept.–Dec./62. Prm 1LT, 64th

NC Infantry. Stood 5'8", had a fair complexion, blue eyes, and light hair. (CSR 270:6)

Luckey, Samuel: From Macon Co. Age 34. PVT, Co. K. Rejected by COL Baker. (CSR 270:6)

Luhn, Gustave J.: B. Berlin, Prussia. From Rowan Co. Bookkeeper before the war. At age 22, enl. 6/15/61 as PVT, Co. F. Reported present on company muster rolls of Nov.–Dec./61. Prm chief bugler. Dsh 12/61 or 1/62. Stood 5' 6½", had a dark complexion, black eyes, and dark hair. (Mizelle; Barringer; Rumple: 343; CSR 270:6)

Lunsford, Arthur: From Buncombe Co. At age 23, enl. 2/25/62 as PVT, Co. G. Reported present on company muster rolls of May–June/62, 9/62–4/63. Absent sick in a Staunton, VA G.H., according to rolls of July–Aug./63. Rolls of Sept.–Oct./63 list him on provost guard dty at Culpeper C.H., VA. Rolls of Nov.–Dec./63 also list him as absent on provost duty. Absent on detached service, 4/1/64; absent on provost duty, 3–4/64. Company muster rolls of 4/30–Dec./64 list him absent on detached service at corps H.Q. with the provost guard. Prl Appomattox C.H., 4/9/65. (CSR 270:6)

Lunsford, E.M.: From McDowell Co. At age 24, enl. 5/20/61 as PVT, Co. G. Reported present on company muster rolls of Jan.–Feb./62, May–June/62. Absent sick at Winchester according to rolls of 9/62–4/63. Rolls of July–Aug./63 report him missing in action at or near Funkstown, MD, as of 7/63. According to Federal records, captured 7/10 or 7/11/63. D. while a prisoner of war. Bur. at Point Lookout. (PL: 151; CSR 270:6)

Lunsford, James G.: From Buncombe Co. At age 29, enl. 3/1/62 as PVT, Co.G. Reported present on company muster rolls of May–June/62, 9/62–4/63, July–Dec./63. Absent on detached service at Bowling Green with the provost guard, probably during Jan.–Apr./64. Reported absent without leave on rolls of 4/1/64. According to rolls of Mar.–Oct./64, absent on sick leave after being wounded in action. Reported present, Nov.–Dec./64. (CSR 270:6)

Luther, W.A.: From Buncombe Co. At age 18, enl. 5/20/61 as PVT, Co. G. Reported present on company muster rolls of Jan.–Feb./62, May–June/62. Reported present Sept.–Oct./62 and prm to CPL, 10/6/62. Also reported present on company muster rolls of 11/62–4/63, July–Dec./63, 4/1/64, Mar.–Aug./64. Absent in the trenches with the dismounted men from the brigade, according to rolls of Sept.–Oct./64. Rolls of Nov.–Dec./64 list him as trn to the 11th NC Infantry. (CSR 270:6)

Lyda, J.W.: Enl. 9/25/63 as PVT, Co. G. Reported present on company muster rolls of Nov.–Dec./63. Absent on detached service according to rolls of 4/1/64. Reported present Mar.–Oct./64. Rolls of Nov.–Dec./64 list him as absent on detached service on horse detail. (CSR 270:6)

Lyda, Jacob R.: From Buncombe Co. At age 32, enl. 3/13/63 as PVT, Co. G. Reported present on company muster rolls of May–June/62, 9/62–4/63. Absent on detached service as a teamster with the brigade commissary train, July–Dec./63. Absent on detached service with brigade HQ, Mar.–Apr./64. Absent on detached service as a teamster with the brigade commissary train, 4/30–8/31/64. According to rolls of Sept.–Oct./64, absent on detached service as a teamster with the regiment's wagons in NC. Absent on detached service in NC to forage, Nov.–Dec./64. (CSR 270:6)

Lyles, Eli: Cns. 6/2/64 as PVT, Co. I. Absent sick according to company muster rolls of 4/30–8/31/64. Reported sick in a G.H., 8/11/64. Rolls of Sept.–Oct./64 list as D. 8/20 or 8/22/64 at a Wilson G.H. from chronic diarrhea. Bur. Maplewood Cem., Wilson. (Stepp; CSR 270:6)

Lynch, Needham B.: From Wayne Co. At age 23, enl. 7/6/61 as PVT, Co. H. Federal records list him as captured at White Oak Swamp, VA, 8/5/62, and prl 8/26/62. Reported present on company muster rolls of 11/61–2/62, May–June/62, Sept.–Oct./62. According to rolls of Nov.–Dec./62, absent on detached service with MAJ Whitaker. Reported present on rolls of Jan.–Apr./63, 7/63–10/64. Absent Nov.–Dec./64 on detached service with the provost guard at Belfield. (CSR 270:6)

Mabry, S.G.: B. Warren Co. Farmer before the war. Trn from 16th NC Bn. Enl. 10/20/63 as PVT, Co. B. Reported present on company muster rolls of 4/30–Dec./64. Age 39. Had gray eyes, dark hair, and a dark complexion, and stood 5' 8½". (CSR 270:6)

Malone, Charles Daniel: B. 7/29/45 in Louisburg, Franklin Co., NC. Attended Louisburg Academy. Enl. as PVT, Co. E, 9/20/63. Reported present on company muster rolls of 6/30/63–2/64, 4/1/64. Absent on frl in NC, according to rolls of Mar.–Apr./64. Reported present on company muster rolls of 4/30–Oct./64. According to rolls of Nov.–Dec./64, absent on horse detail in NC. Declined election to rank; courier to Hampton and Stuart. Often commanded company. WIA in right hand, Hatcher's Run. Mason. Post-war, mercantilist, teacher, Protestant Episcopal missionary. Fathered 7 children. D. Henderson, NC 6/17/27. Bur. Oakwood Cem., Louisburg. (CV 35 [1927]: 344; Stepp; Pearce: 267; CSR 270:6)

Maney, L.M.: From Macon Co. PVT, Co. K. Age 35. Rejected by COL Baker. (CSR 270:6)

Mangum, William C.: Enl. 11/20/63 as PVT, Co. B. Reported absent sick on company muster rolls of 4/30–Oct./64. (CSR 270:6)

Manly, Harrison: From Macon Co. At age 34, enl. 8/10/61 as PVT and blacksmith, Co. K. Reported present on company muster rolls of 11/61–2/62, May–June/62, Sept.–Dec./62. Absent on detached service at home to purchase a horse according to rolls of Jan.–Feb./63. Reported present Mar.–Apr./63, July–Aug./63. Trn to Co. H, 16th NC Infantry, 9/19/63. (CSR 270:6)

Marcus, William Alphonso: From Macon Co. At age 21, enl. 7/61 as PVT, Co. K. Reported present on company muster rolls of 11/61–2/62, May–June/62, 9/62–4/63, July–Aug./63. Trn 10/6/63 to Co. H, 16th NC Infantry. (CSR 270:6)

Mareddy, Benjamin B.: From Duplin Co. At age 18, enl. 7/21/62 as PVT, Co. I. Trn from CPT Ward's NC Cavalry. Reported present on company muster rolls of Sept.–Oct./62. Absent on detached service according to rolls of Nov.–Dec./62. Reported present Jan.–Apr./63, 10/31/63, 1/1/64, Jan.–Feb./64. Prm CPL. According to rolls of Mar.–Apr./64 dated 9/7/64, KIA 5/11/64 near Richmond, VA. (CSR 270:6)

Marlow, Joseph: From Watauga Co. At age 18, enl. 9/20/63 as PVT, Co. D. Reported present on company muster rolls of 6/30/63–4/64. Admitted 5/25/64 to a Richmond G.H. with a gunshot wound to the chest. Frl 6/6/64 for 40 days. Reported present on rolls of 8/31/64. According to rolls of Sept.–Oct./64, retired 9/12/64. An Invalid Corps register lists him as retiring 9/19/64. (CSR 270:6)

Marriet, J.A.: Co. I. D. 7/8/63. Bur. NC Plat, Stonewall Cem., Winchester, VA. (Stonewall)

Marsh, J.L.: From Buncombe Co. At age 37, enl. 7/26/61 as PVT, Co. G. Dsh 8/30/61 "by order of the governor of North Carolina." (CSR 270:6)

Martin, Edward: At age 22, enl. 9/2/61 as PVT, Co. C. Deserted 10/1/61. (Alexander; CSR 270:6)

Martin, John A.: From Yadkin Co. At age 22, enl. 5/25/61 as PVT, Co. A. Reported present on company muster rolls of 11/61–2/62, Sept.–Oct./62. Absent on detached service to procure corn according to rolls of Nov.–Dec./62. Rolls of Jan.–Feb./63 list him absent on frl to buy a horse beginning 2/27/63. Reported present on company muster rolls of Mar.–Apr./63, July–Dec./31/63. Rolls of Jan.–Feb./64 list him absent on frl since 2/25/64. Reported present 4/1/64. Absent on detached service in North Carolina, Mar.–Apr./64. Reported present, July–Dec./64. (AsheCo; Yadkin; CSR 270:6)

Martin, Martin: From Montgomery Co. Cns. 7/28/62 as PVT, Co. H. Absent detached as a wagoner for the general conscript, Sept.–Dec./62. Also reported on extra dty as a teamster with Hampton's Brigade, Oct.–Dec./62. Rolls of Jan.–Apr./63 list him as absent as a wagoner for GEN Wade Hampton. Reported present on company muster rolls of July–Aug./63. Rolls of Sept.–Oct./63 list him as wounded and absent sent to a G.H. as of 10/10/63. Reported admitted to a Richmond G.H., 10/14/63. Severely wounded in Bristoe Campaign. Absent on sick frl, Mar.–Apr./64. Reported present on company muster rolls of 4/30–Dec./64. (CSR 270:6)

Martin, Martin Stanback: Cns. 3/15/64 at age 17 as PVT, Co. H. Reported present on company muster rolls of 4/1/64, Mar.–Dec./64. Gave "brilliant service to his country." D. at age 84, having built well "a noble edifice of character." (CV 38 [1930]: 236; CSR 270:6)

Martin, William Lee: B. 12/24/29. From Yadkin Co. Enl. 5/25/61 as PVT, Co. A. Reported present on company muster rolls of 11/61–2/62. Prm QM SGT, 6/1/62. Reported present 9/62–4/63. Rolls of July–Aug./63 list him as absent captured. According to Federal records, captured at Gettysburg, 7/3/63. Exd. 2/13/65. Admitted 2/19/65 to a Richmond G.H. D. 3/18/09. Bur. Flat Rock Baptist Church Cem., Yadkin Co. (Stepp; CSR 270:6 AsheCo lists him as W.H.)

Mast, Daniel P.: Resident of Watauga Co. At age 18, enl. as a PVT, Co. D, 5/11/61. Reported present on company muster rolls of Nov.–Dec./61. Reported present on company muster rolls of Nov.–Dec./61. Also reported present Jan.–Feb./62, and appointed to fill J.W. Lookabill's vacancy as CPL, 1/28/62. Reported present on company muster rolls of May–June/62, 6/30/62–4/63. Prm SGT of Nov.–Dec./62 rolls. Elected 2LT, 12/25/62. Reported present July–Aug./63, 6/30–10/31/63 and reported as acting adjutant. Reported present Nov.–Dec./63. Prm Sr 2LT, 6/16/63. Reported present on rolls of 2/29–3/31/64 and listed on extra duty as brigade provost marshal. Reported present on company muster rolls of Mar.–Apr./64, 8/31–Dec./64. Signs roll as commanding Co. D, Nov.–Dec./64. Wounded by a bullet in the leg at Dinwiddie C.H., 3/31/65. Captured in a Petersburg G.H., 4/3/65. Also reported admitted 4/26/65 to a Petersburg G.H. Took the oath and prl, 6/27/65. (Davis; CSR 270:6)

Mast, David H.: From Watauga Co. At age 21,

enl. 6/1/61 as PVT, Co. D. Reported present on company muster rolls of Nov.–Dec./61. Absent on sick leave according to rolls of Jan.–Feb./62. According to 2/62 regimental return, at home sick beginning 2/10/62. Regimental return of 3/62 also lists him as absent sick. Reported present on company muster rolls of May–Dec./62. Absent on horse detail, Jan.–Feb./63. Reported present Mar.–Apr./63. Absent at home on horse detail, July–Aug./63. Reported present on company muster rolls of 6/30/63–3/31/64. On frl at home according to rolls of Mar.–Apr./64. Reported present on company muster rolls of 8/31/64, Sept.–Dec./64. WIA Chamberlain's Run, 1865. Reportedly spent 5 months in a Petersburg prison at some point. Reported prl at Salisbury, NC, 5/20/65, and also from a Petersburg G.H., 6/28/65. Lived in Winston-Salem after the war. D. 1/11/11. (Davis; Forsyth: 34; CSR 270:6)

Mast, P.H.: From Panther Creek, Forsyth Co. At age 20, enl. 5/61 as PVT, Co. D. Captured in Morganton, 1865, and prl. D. 1/11/11. (Forsyth: 34)

Mathis, Aaron: From Cherokee Co. Age 18. PVT, Co. K. Rejected by COL Baker. (CSR 270:6)

Mathis, David W.: From Duplin Co. Enl. 6/17/61 as Farrier, Co. I. According to company muster rolls of Jan.–Feb./62, sick at Petersburg beginning 12/11/61. Rolls of May–June/62 list him as absent wounded at a Richmond G.H. According to regimental returns of 2/62, absent sick. WIA at Willis Church, VA, 6/29/62. On a sick and wounded report for July 1862. Dsh 7/19/62 due to effects from a gunshot wound in the head and neck and a broken arm. Age 34, stood 5'8", had a fair complexion, dark eyes, and black hair. Farmer before the war. (CSR 270:6)

Matthews, J.S.: 1LT, Co. D. Captured 5/18/65, at Hartwell, GA. Prl. (CSR 270:6)

Matthews, John: Resident of NC. PVT, Co. H. Deserted, possibly on 5/8/65 in TN. Reportedly prl 4/26/65 and took the oath in Chattanooga, TN, 5/4/65. Pledged to remain in the North. Had a light complexion, light hair, and hazel eyes, and stood 5'6". Had no family. (CSR 270:6)

Matthews, William: From Cherokee Co. Age 21. PVT, Co. K. Rejected by COL Baker. (CSR 270:6)

Matthias, Thomas L.: From Buncombe Co. At age 18, enl. 5/20/61 as 1SGT, Co. G. Reported present on company muster rolls of Jan.–Feb./62, May–June/62, Sept.–Oct./62. Absent on detached service, Nov.–Dec./62. Absent on frl, Jan.–Feb./63. Reported present according to rolls of Mar.–Apr./63. Elected 2LT, 5/10/63. Reported present on rolls of July–Aug./63, and listed as 2LT commanding the company. Rolls of Sept.–Dec./63 list him as present as well. Prm Sr 2LT, 10/5/63. Prm 1LT, 1/7/64. Reported present and listed as 1LT on rolls of Mar.–Dec./64. (CSR 270:1, 6)

Maxwell, John H.: From Duplin Co. At age 18, enl. 6/23/61 as PVT, Co. I. Reported present on company muster rolls of 11/61–2/62, May–June/62, Sept.–Dec./62. On detached service according to rolls of Jan.–Feb./63, then listed present on rolls of Mar.–Apr./63. Admitted 7/19/63 to a Richmond G.H. Reported present, 10/31/63. Deserted or captured 11/9/63 near Culpeper C.H., VA. Age 26, stood 5'10", had dark hair. Took oath 4/10/65. (CSR 270:6)

Maxwell, Robert H.: Resident of Charlotte. Enl. 5/16/61 in Co. C. Appointed 2LT on 8/20/61, to rank from 5/16/61. Prm Sr 2LT, 9/21/61. Reported present on company muster rolls of Nov.–Dec./61. Absent on recruiting duty in NC beginning 2/4/62, according to rolls of Jan.–Feb./62. Prm 1LT, 2/6/62. Regimental returns of 2/62 list him as absent on recruiting service beginning 2/9/62. 3/62 regimental returns list him as present. Reported present on company muster rolls of May–Oct./62 and listed as 1LT. On detached service with GEN Stuart in Pa., 10/62. According to rolls of Nov.–Dec./62, absent in NC to purchase a horse beginning 12/16/62. Still absent on detached service according to rolls of Jan.–Feb./63. Reported present on company muster rolls of Mar.–Apr./63. Also reported present and commanding the company, July–Aug./63. Admitted to a Richmond G.H. with a gunshot wound in the right arm, 9/17/63. Frl beginning 10/63; leave subsequently extended. Listed as WIA 9/13/63 and absent beginning on rolls of Sept.–Oct./63. Also listed as absent sick beginning with rolls of Mar.–Apr./64. Retired according to rolls of Sept.–Oct./64. Retired 8/30/64. Took the oath, 5/15/65. (CSR 270:1, 6; Alexander)

Maxwell, Thomas R.: From Watauga Co. At age 19, enl. 5/11/61 as PVT, Co. D. D. 12/9/61 from pneumonia near Centerville, VA. Co D (Davis; CSR 270:6)

May, Thomas M.: From Franklin Co. B. 8/31/31. Cns. 3/4/64 as PVT, Co. E. Reported present on company muster rolls of Mar.–Apr./64, 4/1/64. Absent on detached service at Stony Creek, VA, 4/30–Oct./64. Admitted to a Richmond G.H., 5/19/64. According to a receipt roll, grinding corn 4/30–8/31/64. Reported present on company muster rolls of 12/64. D. 11/6/11, in Raleigh, NC.

Bur. Oakwood Cem., Raleigh. (Stepp; Pearce: 268; CSR 270:6)

END ROLL 6

McBrayer, D.O.: Cns. 10/3/64 as PVT, Co. I. Reported present Sept.–Dec./64. (CSR 270:7)

McBrayer, David B.: B. 3/30/44. Cns. 4/30/64 as PVT, Co. I. Reported present Sept.–Dec./64. D. 6/7/35. Bur. McBrayer Family Cem., Boiling Springs, Cleveland Co. (Stepp; CSR 270:7)

McBride, Barzilla C.: From Watauga Co. At age 35, enl. 5/11/61 as PVT, Co. D. Reported present 11/61–2/62. Absent as a POP May–June/62 after being captured at Willis Church, 6/29/62. Federal records list him as B. NC, age 32, stood 6' tall, had dark hair, dark eyes, and florid complexion. Exd 8/5/62. Reported present 6/30–10/31/62. Rolls of Nov.–Dec./62 report him as prm to SGT. Reported present Jan.–Feb./63. Absent sick according to rolls of Mar.–Apr./63. Reported present 6/30–10/31/63. Reduced to ranks as PVT, 12/1/63, according to rolls of Nov.–Dec./63. The same rolls list him as absent on detached service with the brigade QM. Absent 2/29–3/31/64 on detached service with the QM Dept. Reported present Mar.–Apr./64. Admitted 5/5/64 to a Richmond G.H. with a wound. Reported on extra duty as of 6/30/64 as forage master. Absent on detached service with the QM department at corps HQ, 8/31/64. Reported present Sept.–Dec./64. (Davis; CSR 270:7)

McCall, J.A.: From Mecklenburg Co. At age 35, enl. 7/7/62 as PVT, Co. C. Reported present 7/63–2/64, 4/1/64. Trn to Co. I, 48th NC, 4/27/64. (Alexander; CSR 270:7)

McCall, J.M.: PVT, Co. C. (Alexander)

McCall, Joseph: From Macon Co. At age 18, enl. 7/25/61 as PVT, Co. K. Reported present 11/61–2/62. Absent sent sick to Manassas on 2/24/62 according to rolls of Jan.–Feb./62. Regimental returns of 2/62 list him as absent sick. Reported present May–June/62. Absent Sept.–Oct./62 after being WIA and captured at Boonsboro, MD, 9/13/62. Prl 10/31/62. Admitted 10/24/62 to a Richmond G.H. with a fracture of the left arm. Frl 11/23/62. Absent according to rolls of Nov.–Dec./62 , frl to Macon Co. Absent through Mar.–Apr./64, then reported present 4/30–Dec./64. Retired to Invalid Corps 12/1/64. Prl Newton, NC, 4/19/65. (CSR 270:7)

McCall, S.M.: From Mecklenburg Co. At age 36, enl. 5/25/61 as PVT, Co. C. Reported present 11/61–2/62, 5/62–4/63, 7/63–12/64. (CSR 270:7)

McCall, William: B. 1841. Enl. 5/25/61 as PVT, Co. C. D. Prm 2CPL. DSH 9/24/61 for disability. D. 1906. Bur. Amity Presbyterian Church Cem., Charlotte. (Alexander; Karchaske; CSR 270:7)

McCarver, Alexander: From S.C. At age 23, enl. 5/9/61 as PVT, Co. C. NFR. (Alexander; CSR 270:7)

McCarver, James: From S.C. At age 23, enl. 6/9/61 as PVT, Co. C. Absent sick Nov.–Dec./61. Also reported In a Richmond G.H. as of the 4th quarter of 1861, admitted 12/11/61. Returned to duty 2/24/62. Reported present Jan.–Feb./62. Deserted 4/6/62. (Alexander; CSR 270:7)

McClure, James: Enl. 6/3/61. Rejected 8/1/61 by mustering officer, Col. Baker. (CSR 270:7 for James M. Miller)

McCoy, H.H. Pinkney: From Macon Co. At age 22, enl. 6/25/61 as PVT, Co. K. Reported present 11/61–2/62, May–June/62, Sept.–Dec./62, Mar.–Apr./63. Absent MIA as of 7/12/63 at Funkstown according to rolls of July–Aug./63. On Federal POW rolls as captured at Antietam Bridge, 7/10/63. Exd 3/17/64. Rolls of Sept.–Oct./64 list him as trn; other records confirm Trn 10/21/64 to Co. H., 16th NC. (CSR 270:7)

McCullin, William S.: From Wayne Co. Student. At age 19, enl. 6/20/61 as PVT, Co. H. Reported present 11/61–2/62. Absent on rolls of Jan.–Feb./62 at home on sick frl beginning 2/22/62. Regimental returns of 2/62 list him as absent sick, and returns of 3/62 list him as absent on sick leave as of 2/22/62. Reported present May–June/62. Rolls of Sept.–Oct./62 report him as D. 8/21/62. Cause of death: disease. Stood 5'9½", had a fair complexion, hazel eyes, and dark hair. Died at Horn Quarter in King William County, Va.; buried in the cemetery there. (CSR 270:7; R.E.L. Krick to the author, January 12, 2005)

McDaniel, Andrew: From Northampton Co. At age 20 or 22, enl. 6/18/61 as PVT, Co. B. Reported present, 11/61–2/62. Absent on detached service with the horses of the rgt according to rolls of Mar.–Apr./62. Reported present, Sept.–Dec./62. Rolls of Jan.–Feb./63 list him as absent detached in charge of the horses. Reported present Mar.–Apr./63. Rolls of July–Aug./63 report him as KIA near Upperville, Va. "He fell in the front rank of the head of his company," the records say. Bur. Upperville, VA Cem. (Personal Knowledge; CSR 270:7)

McDaniel, Augustus: From Northampton Co. At age 20, enl. 6/24/61 as PVT, Co. B. Reported present 11/61–2/62. Absent at a Petersburg H.G. as of 4/2/62, according to rolls of Mar.–Apr./62. Rolls of Sept.–Oct./62 list him as absent left for home and sick since 8/10/62. Reported AWOL on rolls of Nov.–Dec./62. Admitted 11/12/62 to a Farmville G.H. and returned to duty 1/13/63. Reported present Jan.–Apr./63. Absent on detached service to NC to buy a horse as of 8/27/63, according to rolls of July–Aug./63. Reported present 6/30–12/63, 4/1/64. Absent on horse detail, Mar.–Apr./64. Absent 4/30–12/64 on for age detail. (Zeb. Vance Papers, NCSA [courtesy Whit Joyner]; CSR 270:7)

McDaniel, Elisha: From Northampton Co. At age 24, enl. 3/13/62 or 4/22/62 as PVT, Co. B. Reported present Mar.–Apr./62, 9/62–4/63, 6/30–12/63, Mar.–Apr./64. Absent at an infirmary camp near Stony Creek, 4/30–10/64. Reported present Nov.–Dec./64. (CSR 270:7)

McDoughall/McDougall, Malcom: From Mecklenburg Co. At age 27, enl. 6/20/61 as PVT and bugler, Co. C. Prm chief bugler, 10/1 or 11/1/61. Reported present Nov.–Dec./61, Jan.–June/62, Sept.–Oct./62. Admitted 7/8/62 to a Richmond G.H. with debilitas, returned to duty 7/10/62. Also listed as trn from Cpt Wade's Co., 2nd NC Infantry. (Alexander; CSR 270:7)

McDowell, Arthur: From Macon Co. At age 21, enl. 11/23/61 as PVT, Co. K. Reported present 11/6102/62, May–June/62, 9/62–4/63, July–Aug./63, 10/31/63, Nov.–Dec./63. Absent on detached service, Jan.–Apr./64. WIA, minie ball In knee, In skirmish near Hanover Junction, 5/24/64. Admitted to a Richmond G.H., 5/25/64. D. 6/16/64. (Macon Heritage, 49; CSR 270:7)

McDowell, Thomas R.: From Macon Co. At age 28, enl. 2/16/63 as PVT, Co. K. Reported present Mar.–Apr./63. Absent on detached service July–Aug./63, 10/31/63, Nov.–Dec./63 on detached service recruiting horses. Also listed absent on detached service Jan.–Mar./31/64. Reported present Mar.–Aug./31/64. Absent on detached service at Stony Creek, VA, Sept.–Oct./64. Reported present Nov.–Dec./64. (CSR 270:7)

McEwen, E.C.R.: From TN. Enl. 3/7/62 as PVT, Co. A. Regimental returns of 3/62 list him as a recruit from the depot. Reported present on rolls of 9/62–4/63. Absent on detached service to procure a horse, July–Aug./63. Rolls of Sept.–Oct./63 report him as AWOL since 10/29. Reported present 11/30/63–4/64, July–Aug./64, Nov.–Dec./64. Absent on detached service to procure a horse, Sept.–Oct./64. One record lists him as D. 4/15/63 but appears to be a clerical error. (AsheCo; CSR 270:7)

McEwen, James E.L.: From TN. Middle initials also given as E.T.L. Enl. 3/7/62 as PVT, Co. A. Reported present 9/62–2/63. Rolls of Mar.–Apr./63 list him as absent sick at a Staunton G.H. Rolls of July–Aug./63 list him as D. 3/1/63. Another report says he entered the G.H. on 3/12/63 and was improving as of 4/7/63. Register of deaths report him as d. 4/9/63 at Staunton G.H. (AsheCo; CSR 270:7)

McEwen, T.M.R.: From TN. Enl. 2/27/62 as PVT, Co. A. Reported present 9/012/62. Absent on frl to procure a horse as of 2/27/63 according to rolls of Jan.–Feb./63. Reported present Mar.–Apr./63. Rolls of July–Aug./63 list him as absent as a POW as of 7/4/63. Rolls of Sept.–Oct./64 report him as D. Pt. Lookout, 8/15/64. Date of death also given as 6/25/64. Bur. Point Lookout. (AsheCo; PL: 152; CSR 270:7)

McGalliard, Waitsel A.: From Caldwell Couny, NC. Enl. 3/3 or 3/12/64 as PVT, Co. D. Reported present on rolls of 2/29–4/64. Admitted 6/14/64 to a Richmond G.H. with enteritis. Rolls of 8/31/64 list him as D. 6/30/64 in a Richmond G.H. from a gunshot wound. May also have been in a Danville G.H. (Davis; CSR 270:7)

McGinnis, E. Decatur: From Mecklenburg Co. Enl. 6/15/61 as PVT, Co. F. Prm SGT. Reported present 11/61–2/62, May–June/62. Absent on detached service as of 6/4/62. Reported present Sept.–Dec./62. Rolls of July–Aug./63 list him as absent in NC to procure a horse starting 8/27/63. Reported present 9/63–3/31/64. Absent on detached service with the dead line beginning 5/4/64 according to rolls of 4/30–8/1/64. Reported present Sept.–Dec./64. WIA Chamberlain's Run, 1865. Reported In a Danville G.H. as of 4/6/65 with a gunshot wound In the left thigh; frl 4/8/65. Resident of Charlotte, circa 1893. (Barringer; Mizelle; CSR 270:7)

McGinnis, John: From Mecklenburg Co. At age 17, enl. 8/20/63 as PVT, Co. C. Reported present 11/63–8/31/64. Absent on detached service as of 10/14/64 according to rolls of Sept.–Oct./64. Reported present, Nov.–Dec./64. (Alexander; CSR 270:7)

McGowns, William C.: From Pitt Co. At age 33, CNS 7/15/62 as PVT, Co. I. Reported present Sept.–Dec./62. Absent on detached service Jan.–Feb./63. Reported present Mar.–Nov./63, 10/31/63, Jan.–Feb./64. Admitted 2/5/64 to a Richmond G.H., and returned to duty 2/25/64. Reported present and listed as 3CPL on rolls of Mar.–Apr./64 (dated 9/7/64). WIA near Reams Station, 8/25/64. Prm CPL 7/15/64 and at home on frl. Reported AWOL 3/27/65. (CSR 270:7)

McKinney, Joseph A.: Enl. 9/21/64 as PVT, Co. K. Reported present Sept.–Oct./64. Reported absent on horse detail, Nov.–Dec./64. (CSR 270:7)

McKinney, Thomas J.: Enl. 9/21/64 as PVT, Co. K. Reported present Sept.–Oct./64. Absent on horse detail, Nov.–Dec./64. (CSR 270:7)

McKoy, James L.: From TN. Enl. 4/13/63 as PVT, Co. H. Trn from the 18th NC Infantry. Reported present Mar.–Apr./63, 7/63–4/64. Absent WIA according to rolls of 4/30–8/31/64. Suffered gunshot wound in the left hand around 6/29/64. On a Danville G.H. register as frl 7/6/64. Frl extended 9/2/64. Reported present Sept.–Oct./64. On extra duty as mail carrier per rolls of Nov.–Dec./64. (CSR 270:7)

McLeod, John M.: B. 1826. From Mecklenburg Co. At age 40, enl. 5/13/62 as PVT, Co. C. Other records say enl. 8/10/63. Reported present May–June/62. Absent on detached service at Winchester 10/1/62 per rolls of 6/30–10/31/62. Reported present 11/62–4/63. Absent on detached service to procure a horse as of 8/27/63 per rolls of July–Aug./63. Reported present 9/63–10/64. Absent per Nov.–Dec./64 rolls, WIA 12/10/64. D. 1/7/65. Bur. Sardis Presbyterian Church Cem., Charlotte. (Alexander; Stepp; CSR 270:7)

McLeod, Marcus D.L.: Resident of Mecklenburg Co. Apptd 1LT, Co. C, 5/16/61. Appointed commissary SGT/Ast. Chief of Subsistence, 8/20/61. Reported present Nov.–Dec./61; reappointed Ast. Chief of Subsistence and commissioned 10/22/61 or 10/24/61. Reported present Nov.–Dec./62. Reported present on regimental returns of 2/62 and 3/62. Absent on detached service with the horses as of 4/9/62 according to rolls of Mar.–Apr./62. According to rolls of May–June/62, trn to Co. C and prm CPT, 4/62. Also listed as commissioned CPT, Co. C, 2/6/62. Reported present 5/62–4/63, July–Aug./63. Absent according to rolls of Sept.–Oct./63 after being WIA 9/13. Admitted 9/15/63 to a Richmond G.H. with a gunshot wound in the right arm. Frl 9/20/63. Reported present sick Nov.–Dec./63. Reported present Jan.–Dec./64. Detailed to serve in court, 4/18/64. Prm MAJ., 1/19/65, to rank from 6/1/64. Admitted to a Danville G.H. 4/4/65 with a gunshot wound in the left jaw. "With all his goodness and amiability, he is no qualified to take command of a Regt." (CSR 270:1; Alexander; CSR 270:7; James B. Gordon to Rufus Barringer, 9/1/63, Rufus Barringer Papers, Notre Dame ["With all his goodness"])

McMillan, A.J.: From Ashe Co. At age 23, enl. 6/3/61 as PVT, Co. A. Reported present 11/61–2/62, although reported as courier for 4th Division Jan.–Feb./62. Regimental returns of 2/62 list him as on detached duty at BG Milledge Bonham's HQ. Regimental returns of 3/62 list him as absent sick at a hospital as of 3/10/62. D. 4/15/63. (AsheCo; CSR 270:7)

McMillan, James B.: From Ashe Co. At age 25, enl. 7/24/61 as PVT, Co. A. Reported present 11/61–2/62. Returns of 3/62 report him as absent with the unserviceable horses. Reported present Sept.–Dec./62. Prm 4CPL 11/8/62. Reported absent on frl to procure a horse as of 2/27, according to rolls of Jan.–Feb./63. Reported present Mar.–Apr./63, July–Aug./63. Absent according to rolls of Sept.–Oct./63 after being captured 9/22 at Jack's Shop. Exd 5/3/64. Admitted 5/8/64 to a Richmond G.H. with rheumatism; frl 5/12. Absent on rolls of Sept.–Dec./64 on detached service at the infirmary camp. On a 2/17/65 report of soldiers on detached service in Lynchburg under Walter Coles, AQM, as "In charge of horses ... indispensable to identify the horses." (AsheCo; CSR 270:7)

McNeely, Theodore Newton: B. 4/3/30. From Mecklenburg Co. Enl. 7/13/61 as PVT, Co. C. Reported present Nov.–Dec./61. Admitted to a Danville G.H. 1/12/62 with diarrhea. Absent sick since 1/12/62 in Petersburg according to rolls of Jan.–Feb./62. Regimental returns of 2/62 list him as absent sick. Returns of 3/62 list him as sick in Petersburg since 1/12/62. Reported present 5/62–12/62. Absent on detached service in NC starting 1/20/63 according to rolls of Jan.–Feb./63. Reported present Mar.–Apr./63. Absent on detached service in NC to procure a horse as of 8/27/63 according to rolls of July–Aug./63. Reported present 9/63–2/64. Absent 4/1/64 after being WIA 3/2/64. Admitted 3/2/64 to a Richmond G.H. Also reported admitted 3/3/64 to a Richmond G.H. with a minie ball wound to the thigh. Frl 3/12/64. Reported present Mar.–Apr./64, 4/30–12/64. Reported at a Danville G.H. 4/3/65 with a gunshot wound in the left arm. D. 6/12/15. Bur. Hopewell Presbyterian Church Cem., Mecklenburg Co. (Alexander; Stepp; CSR 270:7)

McRorie, Thomas H.: PVT, Co. D. D. 6/2/62. Bur. Fourth Creek Presbyterian Church Cem., Statesville. (Stepp)

Means, John McK. Wilson/William: B. 1834. From Cabarrus Co. Prewar occupation: miller. Enl. 6/15/61 as PVT, Co. F. Reported present 11/61–2/62, May–June/62, Sept.–Dec./62. Rolls of July–Oct./63 list him as absent sick at a hospital after being WIA at Brandy Station, 8/1/63. Admitted 8/2/63 to a Richmond G.H. Absent on sick frl, Sept.–Oct./64. Reported present 11/63–2/64. Absent sent to the deadline, 3/12/64, per rolls of 2/29–3/31/64. Reported present Mar.–Dec./64. D. 11/3/89, at age 55. Bur. Rocky River Presbyterian Church Cem., Cabarrus Co. (Mizelle; Bounty Papers; Barringer; Cabarrus; Lore: 187; Occupations; Graves; CSR 270:7)

Medlin, Frank: B. 3/25/22. From Macon Co. Enl. 6/25/61 as PVT, Co. K. Reported present 11/61–2/62, May–June/62, Sept.–Oct./62. Rolls of Nov.–Dec./62 report him as absent detached to bring clothing from Macon Co as of 11/8/62. Absent on detached service to procure horses, Jan.–Feb./63. Reported present Mar.–Apr./63, July–Aug./63, 10/31/63. Absent on detached service, Nov.–Dec./63. Absent on leave, Jan.–Feb./64. AWOL from 3/24/64 according to rolls of 2/29–3/31/64. Rolls of Mar.–Apr./64 list him as deserted from Cherokee Co. to E. TN. Rolls of 4/30–8/31/64 list him as dropped as a deserter to date from 8/27/64. D. 3/11/08. Bur. Panther Creek Cem., Judson, Graham Co. (Stepp; CSR 270:7)

Medlin, James H.: From Macon Co. Age 19. PVT, Co. K. Rejected by Col. Baker. Named in register of claims of deceased officers and soldiers from NC, filed by his father on 6/13/63. D. Cumberland Gap. (CSR 270:7)

Medlin, Thomas F.: From Macon Co. At age 16, enl. 6/25/61 as PVT, Co. K. Reported present Nov.–Dec./61. Absent Jan.–Feb./62 at Manassas sick since 2/24/62. Regimental returns of 2/62 list him as absent sick. Returns of 3/62 place him in a G.H. as of 2/24/62. Reported present May–June/62, 9/62–4/63, July–Aug./63, 10/31/63–3/31/64. Absent on horse detail, Mar.–Aug./31/64. Reported present Sept.–Oct./64 and prm 4CPL as of 10/1. Reported present Nov.–Dec./64. (CSR 270:7)

Melton, Berry B.: Enl 9/21/64 as PVT, Co. K. Reported present, Sept.–Dec./64. (CSR 270:7)

Melton, John: From Buncombe Co. At age 25, enl. 5/20/61 as PVT, Co. G. Reported present Jan.–Feb./62, May–June/62, 9/62–4/63, July–Oct./63. Rolls of Nov.–Dec./63 list him as absent sick with leave. Reported present 4/1/64. Absent on detached service at brigade HQ Mar.–Apr./64; also absent on detached service as a teamster at brigade HQ from 4/30–8/31/64. Rolls of July–Aug./64 list him as absent on detached service at brigade HQ. Rolls of Sept.–Dec./64 list him as AWOL. (CSR 270:7)

Mendenhall, W.H.H.: From Ashe Co. At age 21, enl. 6/8/61 as PVT, Co. A. Reported present 11/61–2/62. On 2/62 regimental returns as extra duty as a teamster. Reported present Sept.–Dec./62. Absent on frl to procure a horse since 2/27/63 according to rolls of Jan.–Feb./63. Reported present Mar.–Apr./63. Absent on detached service to buy a horse according to rolls of July–Aug./63, after horse was KIA at Hunterstown, PA 7/3/63. Rolls of Sept.–Oct./63 list him as AWOL since 10/29/63. Rolls of 11/30–12/31/63 report him as under arrest since 12/29. Reported present Jan.–Dec./64. (AsheCo; CSR 270:7)

Mercer, Job: From Duplin Co. At age 30, enl. 2/15/62 as PVT, Co. I. Reported present May–June/62, Sept.–Oct./62, Jan.–Apr./63. Absent as of 10/31/63 as a POW in MD. Reported absent 1/1/64 as a POW captured 7/4 or 7/5/63. Rolls of Mar.–Apr./64 report him as d. in a Federal G.H., 10/20/63. Federal records list him as captured 7/3/63 and D. 9/25/63 at Ft. Delaware fro acute dysentery. Bur. Ft. Delaware. (CSR 270:7)

Mercer, John: From Duplin Co. PO Buena Vista. At age 31, enl. 6/22 or 6/24/61 as PVT, Co. I. Reported present 11/61–2/62. Absent at St. Charles G.H. in Richmond, May–June/62, after being WIA. Admitted 7/5/62 to a Richmond G.H. with a chest wound, and frl 30 days beginning 8/21/62. Reported present 9/62–4/63. WIA 7/29/63. Admitted 9/28/62 to a Richmond G.H. and returned to duty 9/30/62. Reported present 10/31/63, Jan.–Dec./64. Admitted 2/10/65 to a Raleigh G.H. with rheumatism and anemia, retired 2/18/65. (CSR 270:7)

Mercer, John William: B. Circa 1834. Farmer. From Duplin Co. At age 27, enl. 6/25/61 as PVT, Co. I. Reported present 11/61–2/62. Absent on rolls of May–June/62 at a Richmond GH. WIA 6/29/62 at Willis Church. Absent on rolls of Sept.–Oct./62 sick at home from the effects of his wound. Also absent for the same reason 11/62–2/63. Reported present Mar.–Apr./63. Rolls of 10/31/63 report him as dsh 6/8/63. According to dsh records, stood 6' tall, had a light complexion, gray eyes, black hair; dsh due to "gunshot wound in right palm of hand and wrist resulting in anychlosis." Rifle ball exited from elbow. Ambrotype of Mercer in possession of family today (*Military Images*, Sept.–Oct./94, vol. XVI #2, p. 30; CSR 270:7).

Mercer, Joseph Hill: From Duplin Co. At age 35, enl. 4/21/62 as PVT, Co. I. Reported present May–June/62 but WIA 6/29/62 at Willis Church. Reported present Sept.–Oct./62. Absent on detached service Jan.–Feb./63. Reported present Mar.–Apr./63, 10/31/63, Jan.–Apr./64. Absent on detached service 7/1/64, 4/31–8/31/64 on provost guard at brigade HQ. Reported present Sept.–Oct./64. Absent beginning 12/8/64 according to rolls of Nov.–Dec./64 to mount a fresh horse. (CSR 270:7)

Merriman, Lewis: From Ashe Co. At age 25, enl. 5/25/61 as PVT, Co. A. Rolls of Nov.–Dec./61 list him as D. 12/28/61 at Catonment W.N. Edwards. On a 12/61 sick and wounded report with typhoid pneumonia. (CSR 270:7; AsheCo lists him as Lewis Merryan)

Merriman, Wade C.: From Wilkes Co. At age 23, enl. 5/23/61 as PVT, Co. A. Reported present 11/61–2/62, Sept.–Oct./62. Absent on detached service to procure clothing according to Nov.–Dec./62 rolls. Reported present Jan.–Apr./63. Absent sick on rolls of July–Aug./63. Rolls of Sept.–Oct./63 report him as absent sick since 9/7 at Richmond but may also have been procuring a horse. Admitted 9/22/63 to a Richmond G.H. Reported present 11/30/63–12/64. Related to the Colvards. (AsheCo; McNeil; CSR 270:7; alternate spelling to last name is Merryman)

Merritt, Benajah C.: B. 1838. From Duplin Co. Enl. 6/17/61 as PVT, Co. I. Reported present Nov.–Dec./61 and appointed SGT 11/13/61. Reported present Jan.–Feb./62, May–June/62. WIA 7/16/62. Reported in a Richmond G.H., 9/1/62. Absent Nov.–Dec./62 at home after being WIA. Reported present Jan.–Feb./63. Rolls of Mar.–Apr./63 report him as D. 3/27/63 or 3/28/63 at Rockingham, VA. Another record states he d. 3/18/63 at Richmond. "He was always at his post." Bur. Merritt Family Cem., Sampson Co. (Stepp; CSR 270:7)

Merritt, James W.: B. NC. From Duplin Co. At age 32, enl. 6/20/61 as PVT, Co. I. Reported present 11/61–2/62. Rolls of May–June/62 list him as captured 6/29/62. Stood 6' tall, had dark hair, blue eyes, and a dark complexion. Exd 8/5/62. Reported present 9/62–4/63, 10/31/63, Jan.–Apr./64. List as PVT as of rosters of Mar.–Apr./64 (dated 9/7/64). Later prm SGT. (CSR 270:7)

Merritt, John A.: From Duplin Co. At age 21, enl. 6/20/61 as PVT, Co. I. Reported present 11/61–2/62, May–June/62, 9/62–4/63. Absent at a GH as of 6/26/63 "supposed to be dead but no official report of it," according to 10/31/63 rolls. Rolls of 1/1/64 state that he d. at Jordan Springs G.H. near Winchester, 7/8/63. (CSR 270:7)

Merritt, Tillinghast W.: From Duplin Co. At age 20, enl. 6/17/61 as CPL, Co. I. Reported present as 2CPL 11/61–2/62. Rolls of May–June/62 list him as WIA 6/29/62 but reported present. Absent Sept.–Oct./62 detailed to make shoes. Reported present and listed as 4CPL 11/62–4/63. Rolls of 10/31/63 report him as present and prm SGT 9/1/63. Reported present 1/1/64, Jan.–Feb./64. Absent sick at a GH on rolls of Mar.–Apr./64 (dated 9/7/64), 4/31–8/31/64. Admitted 5/5/64 to a Richmond G.H. with a minie ball wound in the right leg or left thigh. Reported present Sept.–Oct./64. Rolls of Nov.–Dec./64 list him as retired 11/17/64. Other records list him as retired 11/23/64 to Invalid Corps. (CSR 270:7)

Merritt, Timothy W.: Resident of Magnolia, Duplin Co., NC. At age 20, enl. 3/1/62, 4/1/62, or 5/1/62 as PVT, Co. I. Regimental returns of 3/62 place him in a GH as of 3/23/62. Reported absent sick at Petersburg on rolls of May–June/62. Reported present Sept.–Oct./62. Absent on detached service Nov.–Dec./62. Reported present Jan.–Apr./63. Roll of 10/31/63 report him absent after WIA near Buckland, 10/19/63. After suffering a gunshot wound in the flesh of the right thigh, rl from a Richmond G.H. for 40 days beginning 11/13/63. Still on frl as of Jan.–Feb./64. Reported present Mar.–Dec./64. (CSR 270:7)

Michel, James A.: Co. B. (Zeb. Vance Papers, NCSA [courtesy Whit Joyner])

Miller, Andrew J.: From Ashe Co. At age 40, enl. 6/8/61 as PVT, Co. A. Reported present 11/61–2/62. Absent on rolls of Sept.–Oct./62 as a POW, captured near Williamsport, MD, 10/29/62. Rolls of 11/62–2/63 report him absent on prl. Reported present Mar.–Apr./63. Absent July–Aug./63 on detached service to buy a horse. Rolls of Sept.–Oct./63 list him as AWOL since 10/29/63. Reported present 11/30–12/31/63. Rolls of 1/1–2/29/64, 4/1/64 report him as absent in confinement In Richmond since 2/9/64. Reported present Mar.–Apr./64, July–Dec./64. (AsheCo; CSR 270:7)

Miller, Andrew J. ("Buck"): From Watauga Co. At age 23, enl. 5/11/61 as PVT, Co. D. Reported present 11/61–2/62, May–June/62. Rolls of 6/30–10/31/62 list him as absent at Winchester sick. Reported present 11/62–2/63. Reported present Mar.–Apr./63 and listed as a teamster. Absent on detached service as a teamster In the QM Dept, 6/30–10/31/63. Reported present Nov.–Dec./63. Absent on detached service, Jan.–Feb./64. Name on a court martial record, 1/27/64. Absent 2/29–Apr./64 on detached service as a teamster with the QM Dept. Absent 8/31/64 as a teamster in Nelson Co., VA. Reported present, Sept.–Oct./64. Absent at home on frl, Nov.–Dec./64. (Davis; CSR 270:7)

Miller, David: From Ashe Co. At age 21, enl.

5/25/61 as PVT, Co. A. Reported present 11/61–2/62. Absent at a Manassas G.H., Jan.–Feb./62. Regimental returns of 2/62 list him as absent sick since 2/24. Reported present Sept.–Dec./62. Absent Jan.–Feb./63 on frl to procure a horse beginning 2/27/63. Reported present Mar.–Apr./63, July–Aug./63, and Sept.–Oct./63, the latter rolls listing him as prm to blacksmith 9/1/63. Reported present 11/30–12/31/63. Absent on frl 2/16/64 per rolls of 1/1–2/29/64. Reported present 4/1/64. Absent on detached service in NC, Mar.–Apr./64. Reported present July–Dec./64. (AsheCo; CSR 270:7)

Miller, Edmond: From Watauga Co. Age 19. PVT, Co. D. D. 11/24/61 at Camp Ashe, Ridgeway, NC of measles and pneumonia. First death in Co. D. (Davis; CSR 270:7)

Miller, G.W.: Co. D. (CSR 270: 4 for George N. Folk)

Miller, George: PVT, Co. A. Admitted to a Charlottesville G.H. with chronic rheumatism 11/21/62, and also reported sent to a Lynchburg G.H. 11/21. Admitted 10/19/64 to a Richmond G.H., and returned to duty 11/7/64. Note: records may belong to G.W. Miller of Co. D but exact identification no longer possible. (AsheCo; CSR 270:7)

Miller, George W.: From Duplin Co., age 22. Company not stated but likely was Company I. Reported present Jan.–Feb./62, May–June/62, Sept.–Dec./62. Absent on leave, Jan.–Feb./63. Reported present 3–4/63. On hospital muster rolls of a Richmond G.H. as present in the 2nd, 3rd, and 4th quarters of 1863 (July–December). According to rolls of 10/31/63, WIA 10/19/63 near Warrenton. Admitted to a Richmond G.H., 10/19/63. Reported present Mar.–Aug./31/64. Retired 9/9/64, according to rolls of Sept.–Oct./64. (CSR 270:7)

Miller, Henry: From Ashe Co. At age 22, enl. 6/3/61 as PVT, Co. A. Reported present 11/61–2/62. Regimental returns of 3/62 list him as sick in a Richmond G.H. as of 3/15/62. Absent at home on frl beginning 8/6 according to rolls of Sept.–Oct./62. Reported present 11/62–2/63. Absent sick Mar.–Apr./63. Admitted 4/1/63 to a Richmond G.H., then 4/21/63 to a Staunton G.H. According to hospital muster rolls, had typhoid fever and "improving slowly." Absent as a POW, July–Aug./63. Federal records report him as captured at Gettysburg 7/4/63 or Waynesboro 7/6/63. Absent on sick frl at home beginning 9/15/63 per rolls of Sept.–Oct./63. Absent sick per 11/30/63–5/1/64 rolls. AWOL as of 8/20/64 per July–Aug./64 rolls. Reported present Sept.–Dec./64. (CSR 270:7; AsheCo)

Miller, Henry G.: From Rowan Co. At age 25, enl. 3/20/62 or 3/21/62 as PVT, Co. F. Reported present May–June/62, 9/62–12/62. Absent In NC on horse detail as of 8/27/63 per rolls of July–Aug./63. Reported present 9/63–2/64. Reported present but on extra duty, 2/29–3/31/64. Reported present Mar.–Aug./1/64. Absent In detached service In NC to procure a horse as of 10/19/64 per rolls of Sept.–Oct./64. Absent on detached service to collect for age as of 12/64 per Nov.–Dec./64. Detailed. WIA at Blacks and Whites. Prl at Salisbury, 5/3/65. Took oath, 6/14/65. Resident of Rowan Co., circa 1893. (Barringer; Rumple: 343; CSR 270:7)

Miller, James: From Ashe Co. At age 19, enl. 5/13/61 as PVT, Co. A. Reported present, 11/61–2/62. Regimental returns of 3/62 list him as on extra duty as a teamster. Reported present, Sept.–Oct./62. Absent scouting as of 12/25 per rolls of Nov.–Dec./62. Absent on frl to procure a horse as of 2/27 per rolls of Jan.–Feb./63. Reported present Mar.–Apr./63. Captured at Gettysburg, 7/3/63. Absent as a POW per rolls of July–Aug./63 following. Exd 2/18/65. (AsheCo; CSR 270:7)

Miller, James M.: From Mecklenburg Co. Appointed CPT, Co. C, to rank from 5/16/61. Reported present Nov.–Dec./61. Rolls of Jan.–Feb./62 and regimental returns list him as resigning 2/6/62. Accepted 2/6/62, and dsh 2/12/62. (CSR 270:1; Alexander; CSR 270:7)

Miller, John: From Ashe Co. At age 25, enl. 6/3/61 as PVT, Co. A. Reported present 11/61–2/62. Regimental returns of 3/62 list him in a G.H. as of 3/10/62. D. from disease 5/13/62. (AsheCo; CSR 270:7)

Miller, John: Enl. 5/1/64 as PVT, Co. A. Absent as a POW as of 6/1/64 per rolls of May–Dec./64. (CSR 270:7)

Miller, John Richard: From Dublin Co. At age 26, enl. 4/16, 4/20, or 4/22/62 as PVT, Co. I. Absent as a POW after being captured 6/29/62 per rolls of May–June/62. Federal records: born In NC, age 28, stood 6', had dark hair, black eyes, and a dark complexion. Exd 8/5/62. Reported present Sept.–Oct./62. Absent on detached service Nov.–Dec./62. Reported present Jan.–Apr./63, 10/31/63, Jan.–Aug./31/64. Absent on detached service with the provost guard at Milford, 2/5/64, per rolls of Jan.–Feb./64. Absent on detached service at Stony Creek, 10/30/64. Absent on detached service to procure a horse per rolls of Nov.–Dec./64. Later served in the NC House of Representatives. According to Miller, he escaped capture and was not exchanged. *(Sinclair, General Assembly (Raleigh: 1889) FIND THIS;* CSR 270:7)

Miller, Robert C.: Resident of Caldwell Co. Enl. 11/10/64 as PVT, Co. D. Reported present, Nov.–Dec./64. Captured 4/3/65. Released 6/29/65. Federal records: light complexion, brown hair, blue eyes, and stood 5'9". (CSR 270:7)

Miller, S.J.: Age 18. Rejected by Col. Baker. (CSR 270:7)

Miller, Simeon W.: Enl. 10/8/62 as PVT, Co. A. Reported present, Sept.–Oct./62. Rolls of Nov.–Dec./62 report him as KIA 11/5/62. (CSR 270:7)

Miller, Thomas J.: From Watauga Co. At age 22, enl. 5/11/61 as PVT, Co. D of disease at Camp W.S. Ashe near Centerville, VA, 11/61. Claim filed 5/18/63. (Davis)

Miller, W.H.: Cns. 10/3/64 as PVT, Co. I. Reported present, Sept.–Oct./64. Rolls of Nov.–Dec./64 list him as absent on detached service to procure a fresh horse. Prm CPL. (CSR 270:7)

Miller, William: From Watauga Co. At age 46, enl. 5/20/61 as PVT, Co. D. Reported present 11/61–2/62. Rolls of Jan.–Feb./62 and regimental returns of 2/62 list him as dsh 2/16/62 at Manassas. On a sick and wounded report of 2/62 as dsh 2/6. Dsh for age. Upon dsh, age 46, stood 5'7", dark complexion, blue eyes, black hair, farmer, but with a "broken-down constitution," chronic rheumatism, and general dropsy. Also listed as dsh 2/15. Afterward served in the 58th NC. (CSR 270:7; Davis; CSR 270: 4 for George N. Folk)

Miller, William A.: B. 12/12/42. From Ashe Co. Enl. 5/23/61 as PVT, Co. A. Reported present, Nov.–Dec./61. Absent Jan.–Feb./62 at a Manassas G.H. Regimental returns of 2/62 confirm he was absent sick as of 2/24, while the 3/62 returns say absent sick at a G.H. since 3/10/62. Richmond G.H. records say admitted 3/7/62 with typhoid fever and trn 3/24/62 to a Petersburg G.H. Reported present, Sept.–Dec./62. Absent on frl to procure a horse, Jan.–Feb./63. Reported present, Mar.–Apr./63. Absent per rolls of July–Aug./63 and after being captured 7/4 at or near Gettysburg. According to Federal records, a resident of Ashe Co., with a fair complexion, dark hair, blue eyes, and stood 5'7". Released 6/19/65 on taking the oath. D. 2/18/10. Bur. Calloway Family Cem., Ashe Co. (AsheCo; Stepp; CSR 270:7)

Miller, William G.: PVT, Co. K. Reported present Nov.–Dec./61. NFR. (CSR 270:7)

Miller, William H.: From Watauga Co. At age 22, enl. 5/11/61 as PVT, Co. D. Reported present 11/61–2/62, 5/62–4/63. Absent on rolls of July–Aug./63 at home to procure a horse. Absent AWOL per rolls of 6/30–10/31/63. Reported present 11/63–2/64. Reported AWOL 2/29–3/31/64. Reported present Mar.–Apr./64, 8/31/64, Sept.–Dec./64. (CSR 270:7)

Miller, W.W.: PVT, Co. C. Captured 11/12/64. Sent to City Point 11/13/64 and Point Lookout 11/24/64. (CSR 270:7)

Miller, Willis: Co. F. KIA 5/64 in the Wilderness. "And one of the most touching scenes I ever witnessed was Captain John R. Erwin writing next morning to the boy's father of his death." (Means, "Additional Sketch Sixty-Third Regiment (Fifth Cavalry)," *NC Regts.* 3: 594.)

Mills, C.B.: Enl. 5/22/64 as PVT, Co. G. Absent at a Petersburg G.H. per rolls of Mar.–Oct./64. Frl 8/15/64 to Spartanburg, S.C. Reported present Nov.–Dec./64. (CSR 270:7)

Mills, F.M.: PVT, Co. I. Age 24, right arm amputated 10/27/64. Dsh. (*Medical History* 10: 799)

Mills, Henry J.: From Pitt Co. At age 28, cns 7/15/62 or 7/17/62 as PVT, Co. I. Rolls of Sept.–Oct./62 confirm that he was a cns requested from the depot and sick at Winchester. Absent on detached service per rolls of Nov.–Dec./62. Reported present Mar.–Apr./63. Rolls of 10/31/63 list him as KIA 6/9/63 at Brandy Station. "He was a brave and gallant soldier." (CSR 270:7)

Mills, James H.: From Pitt Co. At age 26, ens 7/15/62 as PVT, Co. I. Per rolls of Sept.–Oct./62, cns from the depot but absent sick at Winchester. Absent on detached service per rolls of 11/62–2/63. Reported present Mar.–Apr./63. Rolls of 10/31/63 place him as captured 6/29 or 6/30/63 in PA. According to Federal records, captured at Hanover, PA on 6/20/63 or 6/30/63. Rolls thru 12/64 report him as absent. Exd 2/18/65. Reported on muster rolls of prl/exd POW's of 2/23/65. (CSR 270:7)

Mills, R.H.: Enl. 4/4/65 or 4/5/65 as PVT, Co. G. Reported present, Mar.–Aug./31/64, July–Dec./64. (CSR 270:7)

Mills, William F.: B. Pitt Co., NC. Farmer. Cns 7/17/62 as PVT, Co. I. According to rolls of Sept.–Oct./62, cns from the depot and reported present. Absent on detached service Jan.–Feb./63. Reported present, Mar.–Apr./63, 10/31/63, Jan.–Feb./64. On detached service to remount as of 9/6/64, per rolls of Mar.–Apr./64. Reported present, 4/31–8/31/64. Absent after being WIA on Boydton Plank Road, 10/27/64. Arm amputated. Rolls of Nov.–Dec./64 report him as absent at home on frl. Dsh 1/19/65 due to wound in and amputation of right arm. At dsh, age 23 or 24, 5' 8" tall, light complexion, gray eyes, light hair. (CSR 270:7)

Mills, William N.: From Pitt Co. At age 23, cns 7/15/62 or 7/17/62 as PVT, Co. I. Listed on muster rolls of Sept.–Oct./62 as cns from the depot. Received in a Richmond G.H., 10/4/62. Reported present, Nov.–Dec./62. Absent on detached service, Jan.–Feb./63. Reported present Mar.–Apr./63, 10/31/63, 1/1/64. Rolls of Mar.–Apr./64 (dated 9/7/64) and 4/30–8/31/64 report him as deserted 6/30/64. (CSR 270:7)

Millsapps, William M.: From Watauga Co. At age 19, enl. 5/11/61 as PVT, Co. D. Reported present on rolls of Nov.–Dec./61, Jan.–Feb./62, 5/62–4/63. Rolls of July–Aug./63 report him as WIA 6/9/63 at Brandy Station. Admitted 7/3/63 to a Charlottesville G.H., and frl 7/24/63 for 30 days. Absent at home sick on rolls of 6/30–10/31/63, Nov.–Dec./63, Jan.–Apr./64. Admitted 7/25 or 7/30/64 to a Richmond G.H. with a gunshot wound in the right and left thigh. Frl 7/26/63. Detailed 8/29/64. Absent reported In a G.H., 8/31/64. Returned to duty, 10/10/64. Reported present Sept.–Oct./64. Rolls of Nov.–Dec./64 list him as retired. Retired to Invalid Corps, 11/23/64. Also listed on a register of the Invalid Corps as retired 12/23/64. Living at Beach Creek, Watauga Co., in 1890. (Almsay: 227, which spells his name as "Millsepse"; CSR 270:7; Davis spells his name "Milsap.")

Milton, Jule A.: Enl. 9/21/64 as PVT, Co. K. Absent after being WIA 10/27/64, according to rolls of Sept.–Oct./64. Reported present Nov.–Dec./64. (CSR 270:7)

Minton, Thomas G.: From Watauga Co. At age 18, enl. 5/11/61 as PVT, Co. D. Reported present on rolls of Nov.–Dec./61. Absent sent to a G.H. per rolls of Jan.–Feb./62. Absent sick at a Hanover C.H. G.H. on rolls of 6/30–10/31/62. Admitted 10/7/62 to a G.H., and frl 10/27/62. Absent at home sick, Nov.–Dec./62. Reported present, Jan.–Apr./63. KIA 8/1/63 at Brandy Station, per rolls of July–Aug./63. (Davis; CSR 270:7)

Misenheimer, Edward: From Cabarrus Co. At age 21, enl. 6/15/61 as PVT, Co. F. Reported present 11/61–2/62, May–June/62, Sept.–Dec./62, 7/63–3/31/64. Per rolls of Mar.–Apr./64 (dated 4/30/64), in a G.H. after being WIA near White's Tavern on Charles City Rd. near Richmond, 8/15/64 or 8/16/64. Admitted 8/16/64 to a Richmond G.H with a gunshot wound in the left foot. Frl 8/27/64 to Concord, but also reported still in G.H., thru 10/64. Frl Nov.–Dec./64. D. 11/20/64. (Richmond *Sentinel*, 8/26/64; Bounty Receipts; Barringer; Cabarrus; CSR 270:7)

Misenheimer, Isam/Isham: B. 3/4/18. Occupation: farmer. From Stanly Co. At age 45, enl. 3/1/62 as PVT, Co. I. Reported present, 9/62–2/63. Reported present Mar.–Apr./63 and on extra duty as a teamster. Rolls of 10/31/63 report him absent on detached service to 2/63. Rolls of 1/1/64, Jan.–Feb./64 list him as absent on detached service driving an ambulance at brigade HQ as of 12/22/63. Reported present 3/64–10/64. Rolls of Nov.–Dec./64 list him as trn 11/21 or 11/29/64 to the 8th NC Infantry. D. 2/17/97. Bur. Marvin Methodist Church Cem., Alexander Co. (Stepp; CSR 270:7)

Misenheimer, Jacob W.: From Cabarrus Co. At age 21, enl. 6/15/61 as PVT, Co. F. Reported present on rolls of 11/61–2/62. Regimental returns of 2/62 list him as a teamster. Absent on detached service 4/2/62 per rolls of May–June/62. Reported present Sept.–Oct./62. Admitted 4/26/63 to a Richmond G.H. Admitted 5/8/63 to a Richmond G.H. with debilities and returned to duty 5/15/63. Absent in NC to procure a horse 8/27/63 per rolls of July–Aug./63. Reported present 9/63–4/64. Admitted 5/5/64 to a Richmond G.H. with a fever. Per rolls of Mar.–Apr./64 (dated 4/20/64), on frl after being WIA at Canon's Landing, VA, 5/21/64. Admitted 5/25 or 5/26/64 with diarrhea and frl for 30 days, 6/6/64. Admitted to a G.H. 6/2/64 with diarrhea and returned to duty 6/12/64. Frl continued thru 10/64. Rolls of Nov.–Dec./64 say he was prm 2CPL 7/21/64. Another source says he was WIA along the James River, 6/63. Captured 2/6/65 near Petersburg, released 6/30/65. Resident of Rowan Co., circa 1893. (Mizelle; Bounty Receipts; Barringer; Cabarrus; CSR 270:7)

Mitchell, Alexander: From Northampton Co. At age 20, enl. 4/12/62 or 7/18/62. Reported present, 9/62–4/63. Absent Mar.–Apr./63 detached to take the horse of a sick LT to him in the country. Absent July–Aug./63 sick at a Staunton G.H., 6/22/63. Absent sent to a Staunton G.H., 8/1/63, per rolls of Nov.–Dec./63. Absent Jan.–Feb./64, 4/1/64. D. 8/1/63 from chronic diarrhea, per surgeon's certificate. (CSR 270:7)

Mitchell, James A.: Enl. 6/18/61 as PVT, Co. B. Reported present, Nov.–Dec./61. Absent sick, Jan.–Feb./62. Admitted 2/27/62 to a Charlottesville G.H., and returned to duty 3/11/62. Regimental returns of 2/62 list him on detached service. Reported present, Mar.–Apr./62, Sept.–Dec./62. Absent on detached service to bring horses for the regiment, 2/1, per rolls of Jan.–Feb./63. Reported present, Mar.–Apr./63. Absent on detached service to NC to procure a horse, 8/27, per rolls of July–Aug./63. Reported present 6/30–10/31/63. Reported present Nov.–Dec./63, 4/1/64. Absent on horse detail, Mar.–Apr./64. Reported present, 4/30–12/64. Admitted to a Richmond G.H., 8/15/64. (CSR 270:7)

Mizell, Adolphus: Enl. 7/11/62 as PVT, Co. B. Reported present, Sept.–Dec./62. Absent on detached service 2/21 per rolls of Jan.–Feb./62. Reported present Mar.–Apr./63, 4/1/63, 6/30–Dec./63. Absent on horse detail, Mar.–Apr./64. Reported present 4/30–Dec./64. Prl Appomattox C.H., 4/9/65. (CSR 270:7)

Mizell, Silas: B. Bertie Co. Enl. 7/11/62 as PVT, Co. B. Reported present Sept.–Dec./62. Absent Jan.–Feb./63 at a G.H. 2/1. Rolls of Mar.–Apr./63 list him as dsh. Admitted 3/26/63 with debilitas to a Charlottesville G.H. Dsh 4/7/63. Dsh 3/15/63 due to chronic bronchitis: age 30, 6', red complexion, gray eyes, light hair, farmer. (CSR 270:7)

Monie, John Miller: B. 12/31/41 in Kilmarnock, Ayrshire, Scotland. Attended school there. Moved to live with his uncle in New Bern, NC, in the late 1850s. From Lenoir Co. Enl. 7/22/61 as PVT, Co. H. Reported present 11/61–12/61. Absent Jan.–Feb./62 at home on sick frl as of 2/11/62. Per regimental returns of 2/62, absent sick. Reported present May–June/62, Sept.–Oct./62. Absent on scout with Maj. Whitaker per rolls of Nov.–Dec./62. Reported present Jan.–Apr./63, 7/63–12/64. Rolls of Jan.–Feb./64 list him as prm to 3CPL; rolls of Sept.–Oct./64 list him as prm to 2CPL. Ordered to assume duties of a LT with Co. H, 3/31/65. WIA severely with a gunshot wound in the upper third of the right thigh, a flesh wound, and captured at Dinwiddie C.H., VA, 3/31/65. Took oath at Lincoln G.H. in Washington, D.C., 6/12/65. Listed as resident of Iredell Co., with a ruddy complexion, auburn hair, gray eyes, 5'10". Released 6/14/65. (Monie; CSR 270:7)

Monroe, J.L.: Co. C. L. D. 8/30/64. (CSR 270:1)

Montague or — s, H.W.: Co. B. KIA 8/15 or 8/16/64 along Charles City Rd., near Richmond. (Richmond *Sentinel*, 8/26/64)

Montgomery, William P.: From Franklin Co. At age 18, enl. 5/15/62 as PVT, Co. E. Reported present May–June/62, Sept.–Oct./62. Absent on detached service, Nov.–Dec./62. Reported present Mar.–Apr./63. WIA and captured at Brandy Station, 6/9/63. Exd. 6/30/63. Admitted 6/30/63 to a Petersburg G.H. and frl for 60 days. Absent per rolls of July–Aug./63 at a Petersburg G.H. after being WIA. Absent 6/30–Dec./63 at home with a leg wound. Reported present Jan.–Feb./64. Admitted 2/9/64 to a Richmond G.H. Absent on sick frl 4/1/64. Absent on detached service with the division ambulance train Mar.–Apr./64. Reported present 4/30–Oct./64. Absent on horse detail in NC, Nov.–Dec./64. On a register of a Danville G.H. as WIA 4/3/65 and frl 4/8/65 for 40 days, 4/8/65. (Pearce: 270; CSR 270:7)

Moore, J.T.: Enl. 10/26/64 as PVT, Co. G. Reported present, Nov.–Dec./64. (CSR 270:7)

Moore, James D.: Trn 7/23/64 from 26th NC to PVT, Co. D. Absent on horse detail, Sept.–Oct./64. Reported present, Nov.–Dec./64. (CSR 270:7)

Moore, John W.: From Mecklenburg Co. At age 19, enl. 5/28/61 as 1BGL, Co. C. Reported present 11/61–2/62, May–June/62, 6/30–Dec./62. Rolls of Jan.–Feb./63 list him as absent on sick frl since 2/14/63. Reported present Mar.–Apr./63. Absent detailed to NC to procure a horse, 8/27/63, per rolls of July–Oct./63. Reported present, 11/63–4/64. Admitted 2/1/64 to a Richmond G.H. with an illness, returned to duty 2/12/64. Absent on detached service 6/9/64 per rolls of 4/30/64–12/64. Admitted 11/4/64 to a Raleigh G.H. with chronic diarrhea, returned to duty 11/17/64. Prl Charlotte, 5/18/65. (Alexander; CSR 270:7)

Moore, Martin Van Buren: B. Shown's Cross Roads, Johnson Co., TN, 4/12/37. From Watauga Co. Pre–war, worked as farmer, educator, and businessman. In 1861, helped raise infantry company in Watauga Co., NC, but when that unit was not accepted into the state service he enl. 8/21/61 as PVT, Co. D. Reported present 11/61–2/62; orderly for MAJ James B. Gordon. Returns of 2/62 list him on detached service as a Gordon's orderly. Admitted 3/14/62 with the mumps to a Richmond G.H., and trn to a Petersburg G.H. 3/24. Returns of 3/62 report him as absent sick at home as of 3/25/62. Absent on detached service, May–June/62. Reported present 6/30–10/31/62. Rolls of Nov.–Dec./62 and other records list him as dsh 11/20/62 and prm 2LT in the 37th NC but declined to accept 12/2/62 prm as CPT, AQM, and later QM, 65th N.C. (7th Bn. NC Cavalry), later part of the 6th NC Cavalry Rgt. Surrendered and took oath at Camden, SC, 6/19/65. Post–war, worked as a businessman, postal official, and writer/contributor to dozens of publications such as the *Philadelphia Weekly Times*, *Maine Bugle*, Atlanta *Constitution*, *Harper's*, and

Ladies Home Journal. Prepared history of the 6th NC Cavalry for John W. Moore's *Roster of North Carolina Troops in the War Between the States.* D. Auburn, Alabama, in 1900. Bur. Belleview Cem., Lenoir, NC. (CSR 270: 4 for George N. Folk; Davis; 6th NC: 56, 87, 162; MVM; CSR 270:7)

Moore, Ransom S.: From Duplin Co. At age 37, enl. 9/30/61 as 3CPL, Co. I. Reported present 11/61–2/62. Absent sick at Goldsboro, May–June/62. Reported present, Sept.–Dec./62. Absent on detached service, Jan.–Feb./63. Reported present Mar.–Apr./63 (prm to 2CPL). Reported present 10/31/63 (prm to 1CPL). Reported present Jan.–Feb./64 (prm to 3SGT). Rolls of Mar.–Apr./64 (dated 9/17/64) list him as captured 7/21/64 at Col. Wyatt's. Rolls of 4/31–8/31/64 following place the capture on 8/21/64. Released on taking the oath, 3/22/65, and transportation furnished to Dublin, Indiana. (CSR 270:7)

Moretz, Alfred Jacob: B. 10/19/39 in Watauga Co. Enl. 5/11/61 as PVT, Co. D. Reported present 11/61–2/62, May–June/62, 6/30–4/63. Absent July–Aug./63 at home to procure a horse. Reported present 6/30/63–3/31/64. Reported present 6/30/63–3/31/64. Absent at home to procure a horse, Mar.–Apr./64. Reported present 8/31–12/64 and prm CPL. D. 8/10/16. Bur. Old Bethany Lutheran Church Cem., Watauga Co. (Davis; Stepp; CSR 270:7)

Moretz, Daniel: B. 9/24/12 in Randolph Co. Occupation: millwright. From Watauga Co. Enl. 5/11/61 as PVT, Co. D. Reported present 11/61–2/62. Regimental returns of 2/62: absent sick. Reported present, May–June/62. Absent sick at Winchester, 6/30/62–4/63. According to rolls of Nov.–Dec./62, dsh. due to disability. Dsh 11/20/62 or 11/30/62. At dsh, stood 5'10", had a dark complexion, gray eyes, dark hair. Reason for dsh: "general dropsy and old age." Captured 3/28/65 in Boone. According to Federal records, age 49, stood 5'10", had a dark complexion, gray eyes, dark hair. D. 9/12/68. Bur. Old Bethany Lutheran Church Cem., Watauga Co. (Davis; Stepp; CSR 270:7; Some records misfiled under "Moritz, D." in CSR 270:7)

Moretz, Jonathon: B. 1842. Occupation: farmer. From Watauga Co. Enl. 5/11/61 as PVT, Co. D. Absent on rolls of Nov.–Dec./61 on detached service at White Sulphur Springs tending to horses. Absent Jan.–Feb./62 tending horses at Warrenton Springs, Va. Rolls of May–June/62 list him as absent after being captured at Willis Church, 6/29/62. According to Federal records, stood 5'7", had light hair, light eyes, and pale complexion. Exd 8/5/62. Rolls of 11/62 state he was dsh due to disability from a broken-down constitution, but he was also reported present 11/63–12/64. At dsh, listed as 5'7" with a fair complexion, blue eyes, and auburn hair. D. 1926. Bur. Old Bethany Lutheran Church Cem., Watauga Co. (Davis; Stepp; CSR 270: 4 for George N. Folk; CSR 270:7)

Moretz, Timothy: B. 1841. From Watauga Co. Enl. 5/11/61 as PVT, Co. D. Reported present 11/61–2/62, 5/62–4/63, 6/30–10/31/63. Absent sick at a G.H., Nov.–Dec./63. In a Richmond G.H. per 12/31/63 roll. Reported present Jan.–Feb./64. Absent sick on detached service 2/29–3/31/64. Absent on detached service Mar.–Apr./64 at fishery. Admitted 8/20/64 to a Richmond G.H., then frl from a Richmond G.H. to Hickory, 8/27/64. Absent 8/31/64 sick in a G.H. Absent Sept.–Oct./64 on horse detail. Reported present, Nov.–Dec./64. WIA Jack's Shop, R. Ford. D. 3/18/15. Bur. Old Bethany Lutheran Church Cem., Watauga Co. (Davis; Stepp; CSR 270:7)

Morgan, J. Riley: Resident of Franklin. Enl. 4/62 as PVT, Co. K. Reported present May–June/62, 9/62–4/63, July–Aug./63. Debility & fever first appeared 8/26/63; frl 10/7/63. Absent sick 10/31/63. Admitted 9/15/63 or 9/16/63 to a Richmond G.H. with remittent fever. On frl, 10/8/63. Reported present, Nov.–Dec./63, Jan.–Feb./64. Absent on detached service per rolls of 2/29–3/31/64. Reported present Mar.–Apr./64, 4/30–10/64. Absent sick at a G.H., Nov.–Dec./64. D. 1/26/65 in the hospital. (CSR 270:7)

Morgan, Joseph: From Macon Co. At age 23, enl. as PVT, Co. K. Rejected by Col. Baker. (CSR 270:7)

Morgan, Lorenzo D.: From Macon Co. At age 26, enl. 6/25/61 as PVT, Co. K. Reported present 11/61–2/62. Admitted 11/9/61 to Orange C.H. G.H. and returned to duty 11/27/61. On a register of a Farmville G.H., 11/27/61, and returned to duty. Reported present May–June/62, 9/62–4/63. Absent detached to buy a horse in NC per rolls of July–Aug./63. Reported present 10/31/63–12/64. (CSR 270:7)

Morphew, Levi: B. 6/13/21. From Watauga Co. Enl. 5/11/61 as PVT, Co. D. Reported present 11/61–2/62, May–June/62. Absent per rolls of 6/30–10/31/62 driving a team at Winchester. Reported present Nov.–Dec./62 driving a team in the Q.M. Dept. Reported present Jan.–Feb./63, Mar.–Apr./63 (listed as a teamster on the latter rolls). Absent on detached service as a teamster with the

Q.M. Dept. per rolls of 6/30–10/31/63. Reported present Nov.–Dec./63, 2/29–Dec./64. D. 5/24/14. Bur. Morphew Cem., Hardin Rd., Watauga Co. (Davis; Stepp; CSR 270:7)

Morris, G.C.: Enl. 8/64 as PVT, Co. C. Reported present 4/30–8/31/64. Absent sick since 9/20 per rolls of Sept.–Oct./64. Reported present Nov.–Dec./64. Prl Charlotte, 5/13/65. (Alexander; CSR 270:7)

Morrison, John Harris: B. Mecklenburg Co., 8/2/33. Enl. 9/29/63 or 10/9/64 as PVT, Co. F. Reported present Sept.–Oct./64. Absent on detached service in NC to buy a horse as of 12/27 per rolls of Nov.–Dec./64. Served as deacon at Poplar Tent Presbyterian Church. Twice married. Had 5 children with his first wife and 1 with his second. D. 1/1/92. Bur. Poplar Tent Presbyterian Church Cem., Cabarrus Co. (Barringer; Cabarrus; Lore: 155; Graves; DavisUDC; Janet Morrison to author, 9/19/98; CSR 270:7)

Morrow, James L.: Resident of Mecklenburg Co. At age 25, enl. 8/12/61 in Co. C. Appointed 2LT, to rank from 10/1/61. Reported present Nov.–Dec./61 as BVT 2LT. Reported present Jan.–Feb./62 and signs roll as commanding the company. Appointed Sr 2LT 2/6/62. Reported present on regimental returns of 2/62, then absent on 3/62 returns recruiting since 3/23/62 per G.O. #15. Reported present May–10/31/62. Rolls of Nov.–Dec./62 say he is absent on detached service. Rolls of Jan.–Feb./63 also list him as absent on detached service in Virginia 2/26/63. Reported present Mar.–Apr./63, 9/63–4/64 (and commanding the company). Rolls of 4/30–8/31/64 report him KIA. KIA 8/15 or 8/16/64 along Charles City Rd., near Richmond. (Richmond *Sentinel*, 8/26/64; Alexander; CSR 270:7)

Moses, Hosea: B. Macon Co. At age 22, enl. 7/25/61 as PVT, Co. K. Absent 11/61–2/62 In a Petersburg G.H. 10/21/61. Regimental returns of 2/62 list him as absent sick, and 3/62 say he has been in a Petersburg G.H. since 10/24/61. Dsh 5/5/62 due to debility and prostration stemming from measles, typhoid fever, pneumonia, and bronchitis. Stood 6'1", had a dark complexion, gray eyes, black hair. Farmer. Enl. in 6th North Carolina Cavalry (65th Regiment NC Troops) on 3/10/63; dsh 5/9/63. (CSR 270:7)

Moses, Larkin J.: From Macon Co. At age 26, enl. 11/23/61 as PVT, Co. K. Reported present Nov.–Dec./61. Rolls of Jan.–Feb./62 list him as D. of disease 2/5 at Cantonment W.N. Edwards. Regimental returns of 2/62 say he D. 1/5/62. Report of sick and wounded states he died 2/5/62 of typhoid fever. (CSR 270:7)

Moss, Benjamin L.: From Nash Co. At age 26, Enl. 8/10/61 as PVT, Co. E. Absent sick beginning 10/13/61. Regimental returns of 2/62 list him as absent sick and 3/62 as absent at home sick since 10/13/61. Reported present May–June/62. Admitted 7/12/62 to a Richmond G.H., his forefinger having been shot off. Frl 7/14/62. Absent sent to a Richmond G.H. 7/18/62 per rolls of May–June/62. Rolls of Mar.–Apr./63 report him as identified a deserter by Maj. Whitaker "from continued absence." Reported deserted 6/63. Reported present Nov.–Dec./63 and "in arrest with charges." Inn a Richmond G.H. with pneumonia, 2/12/64. Absent Jan.–Apr./64 under arrest in Richmond under sentence of a court martial awaiting action. Reported in Castle Thunder, "death sentence commuted hard labor," 5/7/64. Rolls of 4/30–8/31/64 list him as retired by disability, 8/10/64. On a list of POWs confined in prison who volunteered in the Winder Legion to defend against Sheridan's 1864 raid and were prl, 8/3/64. Retired to invalid corps, 8/1/64 or 8/3/64. (CSR 270:7)

Moss, Milton: Enl. 9/21/64 as PVT, Co. K. Reported present Sept.–Dec./64. NFR. (CSR 270:7)

Moss, Thomas H.: From Nash Co. At age 27, enl. 8/12/61 as PVT, Co. E. Prm Bugler, 8/61. Reported present Jan.–Feb./64, May–June/62, Sept.–Oct./62. KIA at Barbee's Crossroads, 11/5/62. (CSR 270:7)

Moten, N.D.: Enl. 11/20/64 as PVT, Co. E. Reported present, Nov.–Dec./64. (CSR 270:7)

Mull, J.A.: Cns 9/21/64 as PVT, Co. H. Reported present, Nov.–Dec./64. (CSR 270:7)

Mull, William: Cns 9/21/64 as PVT, Co. H. Reported present, Nov.–Dec./64. (CSR 270:7)

Muncey, R.T.: PVT, Co. B. On a register of POWs at Knoxville, TN, as captured 3/24/65 in Lee County, VA, and sent to Chattanooga, TN 5/3/65. (CSR 270:7)

Munger, Jerome B.: From Franklin Co. At age 25, enl. 6/24/61 as PVT, Co. E. Rolls of Jan.–Feb./62 state that he d. in camp, 2/22/62. Regimental returns list him as d. 1/22/62. On a 2/62 sick and wounded report as d. 2/22/62 from pneumonia. Another report says he died 1/62 from typhoid fever. (CSR 270:7)

Murphey, Patrick B.: From Northampton Co. At age 23, enl. 6/61 as PVT, Co. B. Reported present 11/61–4/62. Regimental returns of 2/62 list him as on detached service. Absent at home sick 8/10 per Sept.–Oct./62 rolls. Rolls of Nov.–Dec./62 list him as absent at a Richmond G.H. Admitted 11/1/62 to a Richmond G.H. and returned to duty 2/9/63. Reported present Jan.–Feb./63. Absent on detached service in NC to procure a horse 8/27 per rolls of July–Aug./63. Reported present, Mar.–Apr./63. Reported present 6/30–10/31/63 and prm to 4CPL 9/1/63. Reported present Nov.–Dec./63, Mar.–Oct./64. Admitted 11/9/64 to a Raleigh G.H. Absent sick Nov.–Dec./64. Returned to duty 1/24/65. Alternative spellings: Patric Murphrey. (Zeb. Vance Papers, NCSA [courtesy Whit Joyner]; CSR 270:7)

Murphy, James J.: From Franklin Co. Dsh for disability, 9/61. At age 25, enl. 7/8/62 as PVT, Co. E. Reported present Sept.–Dec./62, Mar.–Apr./63, 6/30/63–12/64. May also have reenlisted in 1863. (Pearce: 15; CSR 270:7)

Murphy, Mal: From Buncombe Co. At age 23, enl. 5/20/61 as PVT, Co. G. Admitted to a Richmond G.H., 11/3/61, and returned to duty 11/8/61. Reported present Jan.–Feb./62. Regimental returns of 2/62 and 3/62 list him on extra duty as a teamster. Reported present, May–June/62, 9/62–4/63, July–Dec./63. Absent on detached service Jan.–Feb./64, 4/1/64 at brigade HQ. Reported present, Mar.–Dec./64. (CSR 270:7)

Murray, Joseph J.: From Franklin Co. Age 22. PVT, Co. E. Reported present 9/62–4/63. Absent on detached service in NC to buy a horse 8/27 per rolls of July–Aug./63. Reported present 6/30–10/31/63. Rolls of Nov.–Dec./63 trn to 14th NC. Admitted 11/27/63 to a Richmond G.H. Trn CPT Lawrence's Co., 44th NC, 12/5/63. (CSR 270:7)

Murray, Robert K.: B. Duplin Co. At age 22, enl. 6/20/61 as PVT, Co. I. Rolls of Jan.–Feb./62 report him sick at home, left camp 1/3/62. RAdmitted 1/2/62 to a Danville G.H. and sent to a Richmond G.H. regimental returns of 2/62 list him as absent sick; returns of 3/62 say sick at home 1/6/62. Absent after being captured at Willis Church 6/29/62, per rolls of May–June/62. D. Ft Delaware, 8/2 or 8/18/62, according to Federal records: age 22, stood 5'11", had black hair, black eyes, and a dark complexion. (CSR 270:7)

Murray, U.D. (*The [Asheville] Daily Citizen*, 7/5/89, copy in Civil War Clippings File, Pack Memorial Library, Asheville, NC.)

Murray, Ulysses D.: Resident of Buncombe Co. At age 22, enl. 5/20/61 as PVT, Co. G. Reported present Jan.–Feb./62, May–June/62. Rolls of Sept.–Oct./62 report him as WIA and left at Dranesville, 9/62. Prl 10/2/62. Absent on rolls of Nov.–Dec./62 in a Dranesville G.H. Admitted 12/2/62 to a Chancellorsville G.H. with a gunshot wound. Absent Jan.–Feb./63 at a N.C. G.H. Rolls of Mar.–Apr./63, July–Aug./63 report him at home, WIA in the foot accidentally. Reported present, Sept.–Oct./63. Detailed 12/3/63. Absent on provost duty at Greenville, 11/63–4/1/64. Reported present, Mar.–Dec./64. Admitted 4/6/64 for duty at a Richmond G.H. Captured 4/3/65 and took the oath 6/29/65. Had a light complexion, dark brown hair, gray eyes, and stood 5'7". (CSR 270:7)

Murry, Joseph Jonah: 27. From Franklin Co. Served in Co. E, also in Co. K, 24th NC. D. Orange Co., VA, 2/22/64. (Pearce: 273)

Musgrave, Samuel Allen: From Watauga Co. At age 25, enl. 4/1/63 as PVT, Co. D. Reported present Mar.–Apr./63. Captured 6/9/63. Absent AWOL 6/30/63–12/63. Reported present Jan.–Apr./64. Admitted 5/12/64 to a Richmond G.H. D. 5/31/64 in a G.H. per 8/31/64 rolls. On a register as D. 7/14/64 at a Richmond G.H. (CSR 270:7; Davis)

Mustien, John D.: From Warren Co. At age 22, enl. 6/12/61 as PVT, Co. E. Absent left Co. B sick 10/31/61, per rolls of Jan.–Feb./62. Returns of 2/62 list him as absent sick; returns of 3/62 list him as at home sick since 10/31/62. Absent at a Petersburg G.H. 5/13/62 per rolls of May–June/62. Absent Sept.–Dec./62 sent to a Petersburg G.H. 6/13/62. Rolls of Mar.–Apr./63 list him as D. Liberty G.H., 6/21/63. Another record says he D. 1/4/63 from heart disease at Dinwiddie C.H. (CSR 270:7)

Neal, A.F.: Cns 9/21/64 as PVT, Co. H. Reported present Sept.–Dec./64. Captured 4/3/65. D. 4/25/65 from a severe gunshot wound in the right knee. Bur. Petersburg Fairgrounds Hospital Cemetery. (CSR 270:7)

Neal, John B.B.: From Gates Co. At age 21, appt 2LT to rank from 10/4/61, Co. I. Reported present 11/61–2/62 and commanding Co. I. Reported present on regimental returns of Feb.–Mar./62. Prm AQM 4/15/62. Commissioned QM 4/15/62 and reported present per rolls of May–June/62. Reported present 9/62–4/63, July–Aug./63. Received a leave order, 1/63. Per rolls of 6/30–10/31/63, prm Brigade QM 6/23/63. Prm MAJ and QM, 7/23/63. (CSR 270:7; CSR 270:1)

Neal, John R.: From Orange Co. PVD, Co. D. According to roll of honor, D. 6/62 at Richmond. (Possibly a member of the 1st NC Infantry rather than cavalry). (CSR 270:7)

Neaves, William: Enl. 9/29/64 as PVT, Co. G. Reported present Sept.–Dec./64. Trn from state service. (CSR 270:7)

Neil, James C.: From Cabarrus Co. At age 20, enl. 6/15/61 as PVT, Co. F. Reported present 11/61–2/62. Regimental return of 3/62 reports him in a G.H., 2/25/62. Reported present May–June/62, 9/62–12/62, 7/63–12/64. WIA Williamsport, MD. On a court martial record of 5/2/64. Prl. Charlotte, 5/19/65. Resident of Coddle Creek, NC, circa 1893. Last name also spelled Neal, Niel, or Neill, and middle initial sometimes given as G. (Barringer; Mizelle; Cabarrus; CSR 270:7; Bounty Receipts)

Neill, Thomas D.: B. 1827. From Buncombe Co. Enl. 2/24/62 as PVT, Co. G. Reported present May–June/62, Sept.–Oct./62. Absent on detached service per rolls of Jan.–Feb./63. Reported present Mar.–Apr./63, July–Oct./63. Absent on pvst guard duty at Orange C.H., Nov.–Dec./63. Absent on detached service with the brigade ambulance train, probably Jan.–Feb./64 although rolls unclear.; Absent on detached service 4/1/64. Absent on detached service with the brigade HQ with the ambulance train, Mar.–Dec./64. Prm SGT, date unknown. D. 1904. Bur. Newton Academy Cem., Asheville. Alternative spelling of last name: Neil. (Stepp; CSR 270:7)

Nelson, Samuel: From Northampton Co. At age 23, enl. 6/15/61 as PVT, Co. B. Reported present 11/61–4/62, 9/62–4/63. Absent on detached service with disabled horses 8/3 per July–Aug./63 rolls. Reported present 6/30/63–12/63. Reported AWOL Jan.–Feb./64. Rolls of 4/1/64 list him as AWOL since 2/20/64. Other records list him as deserted 3/12/64. Entered Federal lines near Plymouth, NC. Took oath of amnesty 3/20/64. Federal records list him as having a light complexion, brown hair, blue eyes, and stood 5' 8½". (CSR 270:7)

Nelson, Thomas R.: Enl. 3/30/64 or 9/29/64 as PVT, Co. E. Reported present on rolls of 4/30–10/64. Rolls of Nov.–Dec./64 list him as trn Co. D. Reported present, Nov.–Dec./64. (CSR 270:7; Davis)

Newson, H.B.: Enl. 9/25/63 as PVT, Co. G. Was in state service. Absent at Weldon G.H., Mar.–Apr./64. Absent sick at a Richmond G.H. 4/30–8/31/64. Absent at a Weldon G.H., July–Oct./64. Reported present Nov.–Dec./64. (CSR 270:7)

Newsom, Henry T.: From Northampton Co. At age 19, enl. 6/12/61 as PVT, Co. B. Reported present on rolls of 11/61–2/62, Mar.–Apr./62, Sept.–Oct./62. Absent on detached service, 11/62–2/63 in charge of horses. Reported present Mar.–Apr./63, 6/30–12/63, 4/1/64. Absent sick at a G.H., Mar.–Apr./64. Admitted 4/25/64 to a Richmond G.H. with scabies, trn 4/30 to Farmville, and returned to duty 5/15 or 5/18/64. Reported present 4/30–12/64. Alternate spelling of last name: Newsome (Zeb. Vance Papers, NCSA [courtesy Whit Joyner]; CSR 270:7)

Newsom, William T.: From Northampton Co. At age 23, enl. 6/18/61 as PVT, Co. B. Reported present 11/61–2/62. Reported present but sick in quarters on rolls of Mar.–Apr./63. Reported present 9/62–4/63. Absent on detached service with wagons sent from the regiment 7/29, per rolls of July–Aug./63. Absent 6/30–10/31/63 sent to a G.H. in Lynchburg 9/20. Admitted to a Richmond G.H., 10/10/63. Reported present Nov.–Dec./63, Mar.–Aug./31/64. Returned to duty 5/17/64 from a Farmville G.H. Absent as a teamster at BG HQ, Sept.–Dec./64. (CSR 270:7)

Noles, A.J.: From Mecklenburg Co. At age 20, enl. 6/17/61. Co. not reported but probably Co. C. Reported present 11/61–2/62. Admitted 1/3/62 to a Danville G.H. with jaundice and sent to Front Royal. Regiment return of 3/62 lists him as sick at a Petersburg G.H. 3/23/62. D. 4/15/62 at a Petersburg G.H. (CSR 270:7; Alexander calls him A.T. Noles)

Noles, W.A.: From Mecklenburg Co. At age 28, enl. 5/14/62 as PVT, Co. C. Reported present on company muster rolls of 5/62–12/62. Absent Jan.–Feb./63 on detached service in NC since 1/20. Reported present Mar.–Apr./63, 7/63–12/64. (Alexander; CSR 270:7)

Norwood, Robert G.: From Granville Co. At age 21, enl. 6/3/61 as PVT, Co. E. Reported present Jan.–Feb./62. Absent May–June/62 at home sick since 5/6/62. Absent on detached service at Winchester, Sept.–Oct./62. Reported present 11/62–4/63, and prm 4CPL per rolls of Mar.–Apr./63. Rolls of July–Aug./63 list him as prm 3CPL and on detached service in NC to procure a horse. Reported present 6/30–10/31/63. Absent on detached service guarding baggage at Orange C.H. 11/20/63 per rolls of Nov.–Dec./63. Reported present Jan.–Feb./64. Reported present 4/1/64 but under arrest. Absent on detached service in NC to procure a horse, Mar.–Apr./64. Reported present 4/30–12/64. Prm 2CPL per rolls of 4/30–8/31/64. Prm 5SGT per rolls of Sept.–Oct./64. (CSR 270:7)

O'Brien, Augustus: B. Franklin Co. From Granville Co. At age 32, enl. 3/3/62 as CPL, Co. E. Reported present May–June/62 (as 3CPL), Sept.–Oct./62 (as 2CPL). D. after being WIA 11/7/62 at Amissville, per rolls of Nov.–Dec./62. Other records say WIA at Gaines's Crossroads,

11/7/62. D. 11/11/62 at B.H. Spilman's residence in Rappahannock County, VA. (Bob Krick email to the author, 7/13/06; CSR 270:7).

O'Brien, Hugh: From Granville Co. At age 28, enl. 5/15/61 as PVT, Co. E. Reported present May–June/62, Sept.–Oct./62. Absent captured near Gaines's Crossroads 11/1/62 per rolls of Nov.–Dec./62. Other records say captured 11/5/62 and prl 11/62. Prm CPL 12/62. Reported present Jan.–Apr./63. Absent in NC to procure a horse 8/27/63 per rolls of July–Aug./63. Reported present 6/30–Oct./64. Absent in NC on horse detail, Nov.–Dec./64. Reported in a Danville G.H. 4/3/65 with a gunshot wound in the right hand. Frl 4/8/65. (CSR 270:7)

O'Brien, M.: B. Franklin Co. Enl. 5/15/62 as PVT, Co. E. Reported present on company muster rolls of May–June/62. D. 8/19/62 from pneumonia at Hanover C.H. (CSR 270:7)

O'Daniel, Alexander: B. Duplin Co. At age 22, enl. 6/25/61 as PVT, Co. I. D. in quarters at Cantonment W.N. Edwards 1/1/62 per rolls of 11/61–2/62 and 2/62 regimental returns. A sick and wounded report dates his death 1/2/62. (CSR 270:7)

Ogburn, C.B.: B. Forsyth Co. Farmer. Enl. 9/25/63 as PVT, Co. G. Reported present on rolls of Mar.–Dec./64. Prl Salisbury, 6/15/65. Per descriptive list, age 44, blue eyes, black hair, dark complexion, and stood 58" tall. Forsyth County resident after the war. (Forsyth: 35; CSR 270:7)

Ogburn, M.H.: B. Forsyth Co. Farmer. After spending 1 year in home guards, trn to/enl. 9/25/63 as PVT, Co. G. Other records date enlistment to 5/64. Reported present Mar.–Dec./64. 6/4/64 descriptive list says he is 26, 5'7", and had black eyes, dark hair, and a fair complexion. After going home to remount in Winston-Salem, rejoined command around Petersburg. Had horse shot from under him, 4/3/65. Went home to remount when surrender occurred. Prl Greensboro, 5/20/65. Post-war resident of Winston-Salem. Age 76 and still living in 1914. (CV XXII[1914]: 233; Forsyth: 36; CSR 270:7)

Ogburn, Mat L.: From Forsyth Co. Enl. 6/24/64 as PVT, Co. G. Reported present Mar.–Aug./64. Absent Sept.–Oct./64 at a Petersburg G.H. after being WIA. Admitted 10/28/64 to a Petersburg G.H. with a gunshot wound in the flesh of the left thigh. Trn to Greensboro, 11/13/64. Absent sick on frl, Nov.–Dec./64. Prl Greensboro, 5/9/65. Took oath at Salisbury, 6/15/65. (CSR 270:7)

O'Hagen, Charles J.: From Pitt Co. Commissioned 5/16/61 as Asst. Surgeon. Reappointed 10/24/61. Reported present Nov.–Dec./61, Jan.–Apr./62. Also reported present on regimental returns of Feb.–Mar./62. Per rolls of May–June/62, trn to 35th NC, 5/8/62, and succeeded by William A. Blount. Other records state he was trn. to 38th NC and prm surgeon. (CSR 270:1, 7)

Oliver, John T.: From Wayne Co. Enl. 6/20/61 as PVT, Co. H. Rejected by Col. Ransom due to health. (CSR 270:7)

Oliver, William Milton: From Watauga Co. At age 28, enl 2/28/62 as PVT, Co. D. Reported present 5/62–4/63, 6/30–10/31/63. Absent sick in a G.H. 11/63–2/64 per company muster rolls. Admitted 1/18/64 to a Richmond G.H. Reported admitted to a Richmond G.H. sick, 2/5/64. Frl 2/29/64 for 30 days. Reported at home sick, 2/29/64–4/64. Rolls of 8/31/64 say he d. in the hospital, 8/15/64. (Davis; CSR 270:7)

Orr, D.K.: From Mecklenburg Co. At age 22, enl. 6/12/61 as PVT, Co. C. Reported present 11/61–2/62. Regiment returns of 3/62 list him as absent recruiting in Mecklenburg 3/23/62. Reported present May–June/62, 6/30–10/31/62. Absent scouting 12/25/62 per rolls of Nov.–Dec./62. Reported present Jan.–Apr./63. Absent detailed to NC to buy a horse per rolls of July–Aug./63. Reported present 9/63–4/64. Absent WIA 7/23/64 per rolls of 4/30–8/31/64, Sept.–Dec./64. Admitted 7/27/64 to a Danville G.H. with a gunshot wound in both feet. Frl 8/6/64 from a Danville G.H. Admitted 2/8/65 to a Charlotte G.H. with a gunshot wound. Returned to duty 2/13/65. Prm CPL, date unknown. Retired to Invalid Corps, 2/22/65. Admitted 4/65 to a Greensboro G.H. Prl Charlotte, 5/30/65. (Alexander; CSR 270:7)

Orr, J.I.: From Mecklenburg Co. At age 21, enl. 7/29/61 as PVT, Co. C. Reported present 11/61–2/62, 5/62–10/31/62. Absent sent to NC to take charge of horses purchased by Lt. Maxwell, 12/25/62. Still reported in NC per rolls of Jan.–Feb./63. Reported present Mar.–Apr./63. KIA Brandy Station per rolls of July–Aug./63. (CSR 270:7; Alexander lists as J.A. or J.J. Orr)

Orr, J.N.: From Mecklenburg Co. At age 30, enl. 2/28/62 as PVT, Co. C. Regimental return of 3/62 lists him as a recruit from depot. Reported present May–June/62, Nov.–Dec./62, Jan.–Apr./63, July–Aug./63. Absent on detached service at Winchester 10/28 per rolls of 6/30–10/31/62. KIA 9/22/63 at Jack's Shop per rolls of Sept.–Oct./63. (CSR 270:7; Alexander lists as J.A. or J.J. Orr)

Orr, N.D.: Enl. 4/4/64 as PVT, Co. C. Reported present 4/30–12/64. WIA. (Alexander; CSR 270:7)

Osborn, Frank: Enl. 8/14/64 as PVT, Co. A. Reported present Sept.–Dec./64. (CSR 270:7)

Osborn, George: Enl. 8/14/64 as PVT, Co. A. Reported present July–Dec./64. (CSR 270:7; AsheCo)

Osborn, Landin C.: From Tennessee. Enl. 3/7/62 as PVT, Co. A. Reported present 9/62–4/63. Absent July–Aug./63 on detached service to procure a horse. Reported present 9/63–4/1/64. Absent on detached service in NC Mar.–Apr./64. Reported present July–Dec./64. (AsheCo; CSR 270:7)

Osburn, Jesse: Enl. 9/29/64 as PVT, Co. G. Trn from state service. Reported present Sept.–Dec./64. (CSR 270:7)

Osgood, Frank: B. 1838. From Craven Co. Enl. 6/29/61 as PVT, Co. H. Absent sick at a Petersburg G.H., Nov.–Dec./61. Admitted 12/17/61 to a Richmond and also reported at a Danville G.H. the same day. Trn to a Petersburg G.H., 12/17. Reported present Jan.–Feb./62. Regimental return of Feb.–Mar./62 list him on extra duty with the QM Dept. Absent after being captured at Willis Church, 6/29/62, per rolls of May–June/62. Exd 8/5/62. Absent Sept.–Oct./62 on detached service at Winchester. Absent detailed to NC for clothing, Nov.–Dec./62. Reported present Jan.–Apr./63. Stood 5' 6½" had black hair and eyes and a pale complexion. D. of disease. Marker in Cedar Grove Cem., New Bern, says he is bur. in unknown grave in Tarboro, NC. (Stepp; CSR 270:7)

Outlaw, Britton: From Bertie Co. At age 24, enl. 3/26/62 as PVT, Co. E. Reported present May–June/62. Admitted 9/9/62 to a Richmond G.H. with typhoid fever. Frl 9/21/62. Absent on rolls of Sept.–Dec./62 sent to a G.H. 9/8/62. According to medical director's office records, returned to duty 3/28/63. Admitted 3/25/63 with strangulated hernia. List as AWOL on rolls of Mar.–Apr./63. Dropped as a deserter. See Troops and Addenda. (CSR 270:7)

Overby, J.J.: Enl. 6/1/63 as PVT, Co. B. Absent sick per rolls of 4/30/64–1064. List as AWOL on rolls of Nov.–Dec./64. (CSR 270:7)

Owen, Alfred: B. 1818. From Rowan Co. Enl. 6/15/61 as PVT, Co. F. Absent per rolls of Nov.–Dec./61 at Camp W.S. Ashe G.H. Reported present Jan.–Feb./62. Regimental returns of 2/62 list him as on detached duty as a mail carrier; 3/62 returns list him as on detached duty with the staff dept. Reported present May–June/62. Absent at Winchester with the wagon train, Sept.–Oct./62. Reported present Nov.–Dec./62, 7/63–2/64. Rolls of 2/29–3/31/64 list him as present and on extra duty as a mail carrier. Reported present 4/30–12/64. Prm to mail carrier. Dead as of 1893. Bur. Owen Family Cem., near Lexington, NC. (Mizelle; Bounty Receipts; Barringer; Stepp; CSR 270:7)

Owenby, Sims S.: From Watauga Co. At age 26, enl. 2/22/62 as PVT, Co. D. Reported present May–Dec./62. Absent buying horses Jan.–Feb./63, and prm CPL. Reported present Mar.–Apr./63, July–Aug./63, and prm SGT. Horse KIA at Upperville, VA. Absent after being captured at Madison C.H., VA, 9/22/63, per rolls of 6/30–10/31/63. Rolls of 1/63–4/64 list him as absent as a POW. Rolls of 8/31/64 list him as WIA and captured 6/30/63, and having taken the oath. According to Federal records, captured 9/22/63, and joined the U.S. service 2/25/64. (Davis; CSR 270:7)

Owens, Anderson: Enl. 2/25/64 or 9/25/64 as PVT, Co. F. Reported present Mar.–Dec./64. Dead as of 1893. (Barringer; CSR 270:7)

Page, E.M.: From Stanly Co. At age 21, enl. 8/22/61 as PVT, Co. C. Reported present 11/61–2/62. Regimental returns of 3/62 list him as sick at a Petersburg G.H. 10/23/61. Reported present May–June/62. Absent 6/30–10/31/62 on detached service at Winchester 10/1/62. Reported present 11/62–4/63. Absent after being captured 7/3/63 per rolls of July–Aug./63. Per rolls of Sept.–Oct./64, d. at Ft. Delaware. (Alexander; CSR 270:7)

Page, Hardy: Enl. 2/5/62 as PVT and blacksmith, Co. I. Rolls of May–June/62 list him as absent as a POW 6/29/62. Exd 8/5/62. Reported present Sept.–Oct./62. Absent as a POW per rolls of Nov.–Dec./62. Prl 11/9/62. According to Federal records, B. NC, age 25, stood 5' 7", had black hair, gray eyes, and sallow complexion. Reported present Jan.–Apr./63, 10/31/63, Jan.–Dec./64. (CSR 270:7)

Parham, Jamie: Enl. 10/27/64 as PVT, Co. E. Reported present, Nov.–Dec./64. (CSR 270:7)

Park, Andrew Jackson: PVT, Co. A. Captured 6/18/64 "near Liberty" by Hunter's forces in Rockbridge Co., VA. Per Federal records, age 27, 5'10" tall, dark complexion, brown eyes, black hair, carpenter. Released from confinement on taking the oath, 12/13/64. (CSR 270:7)

Parker, Britton T.: From Northampton Co. At age 23, enl. 7/9/62 or 7/12/62 as PVT, Co. B. Reported present 9/62–4/63. Absent on detached service In NC to procure a horse as of 8/27 per rolls of July–Aug./63. Reported present 6/30–

12/63, 4/1/64. Absent on horse detail Mar.–Apr./64. Reported present 4/30–10/64. Absent Nov.–Dec./64 on horse detail. Per Federal records, received 2/27/65 as a deserter, took the oath, and transportation furnished to Indiana. (Zeb. Vance Papers, NCSA [courtesy Whit Joyner]; CSR 270:7)

Parker, Cornelius: Resident of Northampton Co. At age 23, enl. 6/12/61 as PVT, Co. B. Regimental returns of 2/62 list him as n extra duty with the QM Dept. 3/62 returns say absent sick at a Petersburg G.H. Reported present 11/61–4/62, 9/62–4/63, 6/30–12/63, 4/1/64. Absent Mar.–Apr./64 on horse detail. Deserted and received New Bern 9/1/64. Other records say came into Federal lines near Edenton, NC. Had brown eyes, brown hair, and a dark complexion, and stood 5'8". Took the oath 9/23/64. (Zeb. Vance Papers, NCSA [courtesy Whit Joyner]; CSR 270:7)

Parker, J.F.: B. Union Co. Enl. 9/16/64, and trn from 16th NC Bn. Cns. 6/2/64 as PVT, Co. I. Reported present Mar.–Apr./64 (dated 9/7/64), 4/31–10/64. Absent on detached service 12/8/64 to mount a fresh horse per rolls of Nov.–Dec./64. Age 18, gray eyes, black hair, fair complexion, 5'10½", farmer. (CSR 270:7)

Parker, Solomon: From Northampton Co. At age 28, enl. 6/15/61 as PVT, Co. B. Reported present 11/61–4/62, Sept.–Dec./62. Absent on frl 2/14 per rolls of Jan.–Feb./63. Reported present Mar.–Apr./63. Absent on detached service in NC to buy a horse 8/27 per rolls of July–Aug./63. Reported present 6/30–12/63. On detached service Jan.–Feb./64. Absent on detached service at infirmary camp, Mar.–Apr./64, and prm CPL. Deserted 2/65, but also reported admitted 2/23 or 2/24/65 to a Richmond G.H. (Zeb. Vance Papers, NCSA [courtesy Whit Joyner]; CSR 270:7)

Parks, C.C.: Co. A. R. 2/21/63. (CSR 270:1)

Parks, Dewitt C.: From Iredell or Wilkes Co. At age 30, enl. 5/28/61 as a musician, Co. A. Reported present, Nov.–Dec./61. Trn 2/1/62 to field and staff and reported present, Jan.–Feb./62. Regimental return of 2/62 lists him as on detached duty learning music, and 3/62 lists him as trn to field and staff. Reported present Mar.–Apr./62. Rolls of May–June/62 list him WIA in the leg and hand 6/29/62. Elected 2LT, Co. A, 7/22/62. Absent sick from wounds, Sept.–Dec./62 and listed as 2LT. Reported present, Jan.–Feb./63. Per rolls of Mar.–Apr./63, resigned 2/21/63. Other records say he resigned 2/14/63 from wounds. Per letter of resignation, dated 2/8/63, due to gunshot wound in the left hand received 6/29/62 at Willis Church and rendered him unfit for duty due to abscesses there, and his hands and fingers contracted and contorted. Bur. Union Baptist Church Cem., Somers Township, Wilkes Co. (McNeil; CSR 270:7)

Parks, Henry: B. 1835. D. 1902. Co. I, 9th NC Cav. Bur Jim Woods Cem, Wayne Co., NC. (CGR: 3)

Parks, Henry: B. Wayne Co. At age 26, enl. 6/25/61 in Co. H. Reported present 11/61–2/62. Per regimental returns of 3/62, D. 3/9/62 in Richmond of disease. Farmer. Stood 5'7" tall, had fair complexion, hazel eyes, and black hair. (CSR 270:7)

Parks, John L.: B. 6/25/22. Resident of Park's Store, NC. Enl. 9/23/64 as PVT, Co. C. Captured at Armstrong's Mill, 12/10/64. Exd 1/17/65. Admitted 1/22/65 to a Richmond G.H. with intermittent fever. Reported in a Richmond G.H. as of 1/31/65 with emaciation and fever. Frl 2/5/65. D. 3/6/06. Bur. Hopewell Presbyterian Church Cem., Mecklenburg Co. (Alexander; Stepp; CSR 270:7)

Parks, William P.: From Ashe Co and/or Iredell Co. At age 18, enl. 5/25 or 6/8/61 as PVT and 2Bugler, Co. A. Reported present on company muster rolls as a musician, 11/61–2/62. Regimental returns of 2/62 list him as on detached duty learning music. 3/62 regimental returns list him as trn to regimental band on 2/1/62. Trn 2/1/62 to field and staff. Absent at home sick Mar.–Apr./62. Reported present May–June/62, Sept.–Dec./62. Apparently trn back to his company as reported absent detached scouting with Co. A, Jan.–Feb./63. Listed as AWOL Mar.–Apr./63. Absent on detached service scouting July–Aug./63. Reported present 9/63–4/1/64. Absent on detached service In NC Mar.–Apr./64. Reported present July–Aug./64. Reported on detached service scouting Sept.–Dec./64. (AsheCo; CSR 270:7)

Parsons, Calloway: From Wilkes Co. Apparently b. 1840 to either John and Massey Church Parsons or Michael and Jane Norris Parsons, both of whom had a son of that name. At age 21, enl. 5/27/61 as PVT, Co. A. Reported present Nov.–Dec./61, and Jan.–Feb./62 as a regimental teamster. Regimental returns of 2/62 list him on detached service 12/28/61; 3/62 returns say he is on extra duty as a teamster. Reported present 9/62–4/63. Absent on detached service to procure a horse, July–Aug./63. Reported present 9/63–4/1/64. Absent Mar.–Apr./64 on detached service in NC. Returned to duty from a Richmond G.H., 2/5/64. Reported present July–Dec./64. (AsheCo; McNeil; CSR 270:7)

Parsons, John S.: From Alleghany Co. At age

23, enl. 7/31/61 as PVT, Co. A. Reported present 11/61–2/62. Regimental return of 3/62 lists him as absent sick at a G.H. 3/10/62. Absent Sept.–Oct./62 after being captured at Williamsport, MD, 10/29. Reported on prl Nov.–Dec./62. Admitted 12/30/62 to a Petersburg G.H., and returned to duty 2/25/63. Rolls of July–Aug./63 and Sept.–Oct./63 list him as AWOL since 7/27. Reported present Jan.–Feb./64. Absent on prl sick in a G.H. then at home sick since 3/4 per rolls of Mar.–Apr./64. Reported AWOL since 3/19/64 per rolls of Mar.–Dec./64. Deserted. (AsheCo; CSR 270:7)

Parsons, Jonathon Frank: From Wilkes Co. At age 29, enl. 4/7 or 4/8/63 as PVT, Co. D. Reported present Mar.–Apr./63. Captured at Beverly Ford near Brandy Station, 6/9/63. Absent at home to buy a horse, July–Aug./63. Reported present 6/30/63–12/64. Prl. Appomattox 4/9/65. (Davis; CSR 270:7)

Parsons, L.C.: PVT, Co. A. (AsheCo)

Parsons, Solomon C.: From Alleghany Co. At age 24, enl. 6/12/61 as PVT, Co. A. Reported present Nov.–Dec./61. Absent In charge of unserviceable horses Jan.–Feb./62. Regimental returns of 3/62 list him as absent since at a G.H. 3/10/62. Absent as a POW after being captured near Williamsport, MD 10/29 per rolls of Sept.–Oct./62. Rolls of Nov.–Dec./62 list him as absent on prl. Reported present Jan.–Apr./63. AWOL since 7/27 per rolls of July–Dec./63. Reported present Jan.–Dec./64. (AsheCo; CSR 270:7)

Parsons, William G.: From Alleghany Co. At age 27, enl. 6/3/61 as PVT, Co. A. Reported present 11/61–2/62, Sept.–Oct./62. Rolls of Nov.–Dec./62 say he d. 11/9/62 after being WIA at Barbee's Crossroads 11/5/62. (AsheCo; CSR 270:7)

Parsons, William R.: From Wilkes Co. Enl. 3/7/62 as PVT, Co. A. Reported present 9/62–2/63. Admitted 3/31/63 to a Staunton G.H. Rolls of Mar.–Apr./63 list him as absent sick at Staunton. Rolls of July–Aug./63 say he d. 3/2/63. Other records say he D. 5/2/63 at a Staunton G.H., or on 5/10/63 of disease. (AsheCo; McNeil; CSR 270:7; unable to locate grave in Wilkes)

Pasley, James H.: PVT, Co. A. (AsheCo)

Pasley, John C.: B. Ashe Co. Farmer. At age 35, enl. 9/1/61 as PVT, Co. A. Reported present 11/61–2/62. Regimental returns of 3/62 list him as absent sick in a G.H., 3/10/62. Absent on detached service since 9/5 in Winchester per rolls of Sept.–Oct./62. Reported present Nov.–Dec./62. Absent Jan.–Feb./63 on detached service with the baggage at Gordonsville. Reported present Mar.–Apr./63. Trn 5/23 per rolls of July–Aug./63. Also listed as dsh 12/31/62. Dsh by prm — false certificate — AWOL. Stood 5'11", had a fair complexion, blue eyes, dark hair. (CSR 270:7)

Pasley, Wiley: B. Ashe Co. At age 23, enl. 6/8/61 as PVT, Co. A. Reported present Nov.–Dec./61. Absent on sick frl, Jan.–Feb./62. Regimental return of 2/62 says AWOL and returns of 3/62 report him absent sick in a G.H. 3/10/62. Reported present Sept.–Dec./62. Absent on detached service with the baggage at Gordonsville, Jan.–Feb./63. Reported present Mar.–Apr./63. Rolls of July–Aug./63 report he trn 5/23/63. Other records state dsh by prm but "since discovered to be false cut." Stood 5'10½ tall, had dark complexion, blue eyes, and dark hair. (AsheCo; CSR 270:7)

Passmore, Travis: From Macon Co. At age 19, enl. 4/5/62 as PVT, Co. K. Reported present on company muster rolls of May–June/62, 9/62–4/63. Absent on detached service July–Aug./63. Absent sick 10/31/63, 11/63–2/64. Reported present 2/29–23/31/64. Rolls of Mar.–Apr./64 dated 4/30/64 list him as WIA 5/9/64. Admitted 5/16/64 to a Richmond G.H. with a gunshot wound and fractured arm, which was amputated. Frl 6/29/64 for 60 days. Absent until 12/64 and retired. (CSR 270:7)

Paten, John: PVT, Co. A. (AsheCo)

Patten, W.B.: Co. C. Bur. Elmwood Cem., Shepherdstown, W. VA. (Elmwood)

Patterson, David Atlas: B. Orange County, NC. D. Salisbury Hospital. (Conversation with a member of the Durham SCV.)

Patterson, E.S.: From Buncombe Co. Enl. 2/27/62 as PVT, Co. G. Reported present, Jan.–Feb./62, May–June/62, 9/62–4/63, July–Aug./63, Sept.–Oct./63. Absent as a POW as of 9/13/63. Prm SGT. Rolls of 4/1/64 list him as captured at Jack's Shop, 9/23/63. Federal records list him as a SGT from Buncombe Co., captured 9/14/63 and D. 3/14/64. Rolls of Mar.–Apr./64 report him as D while a POW at Point Lookout. SGT, Bur. at Point Lookout. Middle initial also given as L. (PL: 157; CSR 270:7)

Patterson, J.H.: B. Mecklenburg Co. Farmer. Enl. 8/28/63 as PVT, Co. B. Reported present 4/30–12/64. Age 44, blue eyes, dark hair, fair complexion, stood 5' 9½". (CSR 270:7)

Patterson, John Alex: From Cabarrus Co. At age 43, enl. 6/15/61 as PVT, Co. F. Reported present 11/61–2/62. Regimental returns of 3/62 list him as in a G.H. 2/25/62. Reported present May–June/62. Absent at Winchester with wagon trains, Sept.–Oct./62. Reported present Nov.–Dec./62.

Absent at Camp Cripple in Nelson Co., VA as of 8/3/63 per rolls of July–Aug./63. Also reported absent 8/3/63 on detached service with dead line horses per rolls of 9/63–12/64. Commissary Dept. Prl Charlotte, 5/6/65. Dead as of 1893. (Barringer; Cabarrus; CSR 270:7)

Patterson, John M.: Co. F. PVT (Mizelle)

Patterson, John Potts: B. 1840. Resident of Davidson College in Mecklenburg Co. Enl. 4/2/62 or 4/14/62 as PVT, Co. F. Reported present on company muster rolls of May–June/62, Sept.–Dec./62. WIA Upperville with a gunshot wound in the hand, 6/21/63, per rolls of July–Oct./63. Admitted 6/28/63 to a Richmond G.H. Middle and ring finger amputated. Absent on frl for 40 days beginning 7/14/63. Reported present 11/63–3/31/64. On detached service in NC 8/13/64 per rolls of Mar.–Aug./64. Reported present Sept.–Oct./64. Prl Charlotte, 5/17/65. Absent on extra duty at regimental HQ, Nov.–Dec./64. Resident of Coddle Creek, NC, circa 1893. D. 4/18/08. Bur. Bethel Lutheran Church Cem., Mecklenburg Co. (Barringer; Stepp; CSR 270:7)

Patton, George W.: From Macon Co. At age 25, enl. 2/16/63 as PVT, Co. K. Reported present Mar.–Apr./63. Absent sick in NC, July–Aug./63. Absent on detached service 10/31/63, 11/62–2/64. Reported present 2/29/64–8/31/64. Absent sick Sept.–Oct./64. Reported present Nov.–Dec./64. (CSR 270:7)

Paschall, R.D.: From Warren Co. At age 25, enl. 8/8/61 as PVT, Co. E. Admitted 1/17/62 to a Danville G.H. with typhoid fever, and sent to Richmond. Rolls of Jan.–Feb./62 list him as d. at a Richmond G.H., 1/29/62, and a Richmond G.H. register agrees with that date. Regimental returns of 2/62 say he d. 1/27. Other records say he d. 2/63 at Front Royal. (CSR 270:7)

Peach, H.: From Stanly Co. At age 29, enl. 5/25/61 as PVT, Co. C. Reported present Nov.–Dec./61. Rolls of Jan.–Feb./62 report him as deserted from the picket line, 1/15/62. (Alexander; CSR 270:8)

Peacock, Richard M.: From Washington Co. At age 18, enl. 8/2/61 as PVT, Co. B. Reported present 11/61–2/62. Absent in a Petersburg G.H., Mar.–Apr./62. Regimental return of 3/62 lists him as absent sick in a Petersburg G.H. Reported present 9/62–4/63, July–Aug./63, 6/30–12/63, 4/1/64, Mar.–Dec./64. (Zeb. Vance Papers, NCSA [courtesy Whit Joyner]; CSR 270:8)

Pearce, Sampson: From Duplin Co. At age 22, enl. 6/20/61 as PVT, Co. I. Reported present Nov.–Dec./61 and appointed blacksmith. Reported present Jan.–Feb./62. Absent sick at Petersburg per May–June/62 rolls. Reported present Sept.–Oct./62. Reported present and in confinement under arrest, 11/62–2/63. Named in Court Martial case G.O. #41, 3/7/63. Reported present Mar.–Apr./63 and on extra daily duty as a blacksmith. Absent at home on frl after being WIA 6/21/63 per rolls of 10/31/63. WIA at Upperville, VA; right leg amputated. Reported at home on frl through 10/64. Retired by medical examining board in Wilson, NC, per rolls of Nov.–Dec./64. (CSR 270:8)

Pearcey, Joshua J.: B. Warren Co. Farmer. At age 24, enl. 8/11/61 as PVT, Co. E. Absent per rolls of Jan.–Feb./62 on detached service indefinitely near Warrenton, 2/16/62. Regimental returns of 2/62 list him as absent sick. Dsh 5/6/62, listed as age 24, 5' 8½", with dark complexion, blue eyes, dark hair. "Physically and mentally incapable of performing the duties of the soldier ..., a worthless sort of fellow." (CSR 270:8)

Pearson, Charles W.: From Rowan Co. At age 22, enl. 6/15/61 in Co. B, 10th VA Cavalry. Trn 10/27/62 to Co. F as PVT. Reported present Nov.–Dec./62. Prm 2LT, 5th NC Cavalry, 2/63. Prm CPT, 7/64. Resident of Millrose, NC, circa 1893. (Barringer; Rumple: 343; CSR 270:8)

Peele, Joseph W.: From Northampton Co. At age 26, Appointed 2LT, Co. B, on 8/20/61 to rank from 5/16/61. Regimental returns of 2/62 list him as absent recruiting 2/9/62. Reported absent at Scotland Neck in charge of unserviceable horses. Prm Sr 2LT 7/12/62. Prm 1LT to rank from 10/25/62. Reported present and commanding Co. B per rolls of Nov.–Dec./62. Absent Jan.–Feb./63 on detached service in NC with dead line horses. Reported present Mar.–Apr./63, July–Aug./63. Absent per rolls of 6/30–10/31/63 after being WIA 9/22 and sent to Gordonsville. Also listed as WIA 9/13 or 9/16/63 at Raccoon Ford, VA, and admitted 9/17/63 to a Richmond G.H. with a gunshot wound in the left thigh. D. 10/4/63 of pyaemia per surgeon's certificate. Also listed as KIA 10/5/63. May have served as assistant QM. (CSR 270:1, 8)

Pelve, J.W.: PVT, Co. C. Admitted to U.S. G.H. at Ft. Monroe, 5/17/65, with a gunshot wound and left arm fracture suffered at Dinwiddie C.H. on 4/2/65. Left arm amputated mid–third. (CSR 270:8, filed with Joseph W. Peele)

Penland, David H.: Resident of Buncombe Co. At age 24, enl. 5/20/61 as PVT, Co. G. Reported present Jan.–Feb./62. Regimental returns of 2/62 list him as absent sick. 3/62 returns list him as deserted absent sick "having recovered was ordered to report." Reported present, May–June/62, 9/62–4/63, July–Oct./63. Absent Nov.–Dec./63 with unserviceable horses at Stony Creek Depot. Absent as a POW, Nov.–Dec./64. Captured at Stony Creek, 12/1/64. Released from Pt. Lookout 6/16/65 upon taking the oath. Had light complexion, dark hair, and hazel eyes, stood 5'9". (CSR 270:8)

Penly, Adolphus W.: Enl. 9/1/63 as PVT, Co. D. Reported present Nov.–Dec./63. Absent on detached service Jan.–Feb./64. Reported present 2/29–3/31/64. Absent at home to procure a horse, 3/4/64. Reported present 8/31/64. Absent on horse detail Sept.–Oct./64. Reported AWOL Nov.–Dec./64. (Davis; CSR 270:8)

Pennel, N.C.: 1LT, Co. B. On roll of POWs of Johnston's army as prl at Morganton, NC, 5/13/65. (CSR 270:8)

Penninger, Daniel H.: B. 12/22/19. From Rowan Co. Enl. 10/5/63 or 5/30/64 as PVT, Co. F. Reported present Nov.–Dec./64. Prl Salisbury, 6/17/65. D. 12/13/00. Bur. Unity Presbyterian Church Cem., Woodleaf, Rowan Co. (Barringer; Stepp; CSR 270:8)

Perkinson, James H.: From Warren Co. At age 17, enl. 6/18/61 as PVT, Co. E. Reported present Jan.–Feb./62, May–June/62, Sept.–Oct./62. absent on detached service Nov.–Dec./62. Reported present Jan.–Apr./63. Absent on detached service in NC to procure a horse as of 8/27/63 per rolls of July–Aug./63. Reported present 6/30–10/31/63. Absent on detached service doing provost duty at Milford Station, 12/23/63 per rolls of Nov.–Dec./63 and Jan.–Apr./64. Reported present 4/30–12/64. (CSR 270:8)

Perry, R.: B. Franklin Co. Farmer. Enl. 11/19/63 as PVT, Co. B. Reported present 4/30–12/64. Age 43, with blue eyes, dark hair, fair complexion, stood 5'11½". Also served in Co. D, McRae's BN. (Pearce: 279; CSR 270:8)

Person, Benjamin T.: From either Greene Co. or Robeson in Pitt Co. At age 28, enl. as PVT, Co. H, 3/17/62. According to rolls of May–June/62 appointed hospital steward 6/1/62. Reported present May–June/62. Rolls of Sept.–Oct./62 report him as detached to Winchester and prm 10/24 to 2LT, Co. H. Also reported as prm 2LT 10/21/62. Absent on detached service Nov.–Dec./62. Prm. SR 2LT 11/20/62. Reported present Jan.–Apr./63. Listed on a court martial record of 3/26/63. Reported present July–Aug./63. Prm 1LT 7/23/63. Admitted 8/6/63 to a Charlottesville G.H. with hepatitis, and returned to duty 8/25/63. Reported present 9/63–2/64. Resigned 2/10/64 or 2/29/64 to join Co. D, 2nd NC Cavalry. (CSR 270:1, 8)

Person, Jesse H.: From Franklin Co. Age 19. Co. E. Reported present Jan.–Feb./62 and prm 2LT. Other records list him as prm Sr 2LT 10/10/61. Regimental returns of 2/62 list him as reported present near Centerville; 3/62 list him as present at Weldon. Reported present, May–June/62, Sept.–Dec./62. Prm 1LT according to rolls of Nov.–Dec./62. Other records confirm Prm 1LT on 12/21/62. Absent on detached service in NC, Jan.–Feb./63. Reported present, Mar.–Apr./63. Rolls of July–Aug./63 list him as KIA 7/3/63 at Gettysburg. Other records report him as KIA Hanover, Pa., 7/1/63. (CSR 270:1; Pearce: 6, 279)

Person, Matthew Pressley: B. 10/7/34. From Franklin Co. Enl. 3/3/62 or 5/4/62 as PVT, Co. E. Absent May–June/62 at a Petersburg G.H., 5/21/62. Prm farrier 6/62. Reported present Sept.–Dec./62. Absent on detached service with Lt. Person 2/63 per Jan.–Feb./63 rolls. Reported present Mar.–Apr./63. Rolls of July–Aug./63 report him as absent July–Aug./63 sent to Nelson Co. with the disabled horses, 8/1/63. Still there per rolls of 6/30–10/31/63. Reported present 11/63–2/64, 4/1/64. Absent on detached service in NC, Mar.–Apr./64. Reported present 4/30–10/64. Trn to Brigade Band per rolls of Nov.–Dec./64. D. 4/2/98. Bur. Oakwood Cem., Louisburg, NC. (Stepp; CSR 270:8)

Person, Thomas B.: From Franklin Co. At age 18, enl. 7/20/63 as PVT, Co. E. Reported present, July–Aug./63. Per rolls of 6/30–10/31/63, D in Warrenton on 10/20 after being WIA at Auburn, 10/14/63. (CSR 270:8)

Perviance, David Harvey: From Cabarrus Co. At age 22, enl. 6/15/61 as PVT, Co. F. Reported present 1161–2/62, May–June/62, 9/62–12/62, July–Aug./63. Admitted 7/15/63 to a Richmond G.H. with a gunshot wound, and returned to duty 8/18/63. Per rolls of Sept.–Oct./63 following, captured 9/13 near Culpeper at Raccoon Ford. Federal records report him as captured 9/14/63. Dead as of 1893. (Mizelle; Bounty Receipts; Barringer; Cabarrus; CSR 270:8)

Perviance, William A.: B. 12/6/41. Enl. 6/15/61 as PVT, Co. F. Reported present Nov.–Dec./61. Rolls of Jan.–Feb./62 list him as on detached service as a musician 2/1/62 and trn from Co. F. to Field and Staff. Regimental returns of 2/62 also list him as trn. Reported present as a musician Mar.–Apr./62. absent on rolls of May–June/62 after being captured 6/29/62. Rolls of Sept.–Oct./62 list him as captured in MD, 9/10/62. Exd 11/10/62 and listed as B in NC, age 20, 5'7½" brown hair, hazel eyes, sallow complexion. Reported present Nov.–Dec./62. D. Charlottesville, 4/5/62 (tombstone) or 4/5/63 (Barringer). Also reported as admitted 2/19/63 to a Charlottesville G.H. and D. from chronic rheumatism 4/5/63. Bur. Bethel Methodist Episcopal Church Cem., Cabarrus Co. (Mizelle; Bounty Receipts; Barringer; Cabarrus; Lore: 15; CSR 270:8)

Petrea, David H.: From Cabarrus Co. At age 23, enl. 6/15/61 as PVT, Co. F. Dsh 10/4/61. Dead as of 1893. (CSR 270:8; Mizelle; Bounty Receipts; Barringer; Cabarrus. Alternate name spellings are Petre and Petrea)

Pettit, William: From Buncombe Co. At age 22, enl. 2/11, 2/18, or 2/24/62 as PVT, Co. B. Reported present, May–June/62, Sept.–Dec./62. Absent under arrest at Charlottesville, Jan.–Feb./63. Reported present, Mar.–Apr./63. Listed in a court martial G.O., 3/26/63. Absent MIA 7/9/63 in MD per rolls of July–Aug./63. Reported absent as a POW on rolls of 9/63–12/64. According to Federal records, captured at Antietam Bridge, MD, 7/10/63 and exd 11/1/64. (CSR 270:8)

Petty, Felix W.: Enl. 10/5/63 as PVT, Co. D. Reported present Sept.–Dec./64. (CSR 270:8)

Pfaff, F.W.: Res. Forsyth Co. PVT. Had dark complexion, dark brown hair, gray eyes, and stood 5'6". Took oath at Pt. Lookout, MD 6/30/65. (CSR 270:8)

Pharr, John M.: From Cabarrus Co. At age 32, enl. 6/15/61 as CPL, Co. F. Reported present, 11/61–2/62. Regimental returns of 3/62 list him as in a G.H. 3/17/62. Reported present, May–June/62. Rolls of Sept.–Oct./62 report him as 9/2 or 9/3/62 at Fairfax C.H. Other records give date as 9/6/62. (Bounty Receipts; Barringer; Cabarrus; CSR 270:8)

Pharr, Roland (Rolin) W.: B. 3/12/38 or 1844 (tombstone). From Cabarrus Co. Farmer. Enl. 6/15/61 as PVT, Co. F. Sick with measles, 10/61, then pneumonia, then feeble all winter. Reported present 11/61–2/62. Relapsed and returned to the hospital in 3/62. Dsh 4/26/62, and listed as age 18, 6' tall, with a dark complexion and dark hair. D. 5/12/62 (per tombstone) or 11/28/63 (per records). Bur. Rocky River Pres. Church Cem., Cabarrus Co. (Bounty Receipts; Barringer; Cabarrus; Lore: 194; Janet Morrison to author, 9/19/98; CSR 270:8)

Phelan, John: Enl. 2/17/63 as PVT, Co. C. Absent per rolls of Jan.–Feb./64 sick since 2/2/64. Reported in a Richmond G.H. as admitted 1/31/64 and returned to duty 3/21/64. Reported present 4/1/64, Mar.–Apr./64. Absent on detached service 8/25/64, per rolls of 4/30–8/31/64. Absent per rolls of Sept.–Oct./64 on detached service since 10/22/64. Reported present Nov.–Dec./64. Prl Charlotte 5/15/65. (CSR 270:8)

Phifer, M.D.: From Union Co. At age 23, enl. 10/15/61 as PVT, Co. A. Reported present, 11/61–2/62. Regimental return of 3/62 list him as absent sick in a G.H. since 3/10/62. Also reported as admitted 3/9/62 to a Richmond G.H. with debilitas and returned to duty 3/24/62. Reported present, Sept.–Oct./62. Absent scouting 12/25/62 per rolls of Nov.–Dec./62. Absent Jan.–Feb./63 on detached service with horses in NC. Reported present Mar.–Apr./63. Rolls of July–Aug./63 report him as KIA at Brandy Station, 8/1. (AsheCo; CSR 270:8)

Phifer, William H.: From Union Co. At age 18, enl. 8/2/61 as PVT, Co. A. Reported present 11/61–2/62. Regimental returns of 3/62 list him as absent sick in a G.H. 3/10/62. Reported present Sept.–Oct./62. Absent scouting since December per rolls of Nov.–Dec./62. absent on frl to procure a horse, Jan.–Feb./63. Reported present, Mar.–Apr./63. Absent as a POW per rolls of 7/4/63–12/64. Horse killed at Hunterstown, PA, 7/3/63. According to Federal records, captured at Gettysburg 7/3/63. Exd 2/18/65. Reported present 2/23/65 In detachment of prl/exd prisoners at Camp Lee, Richmond. (AsheCo; CSR 270:8)

Phillips, E.E.: From Ashe Co. At age 26, enl. 5/23/61 as PVT, Co. A. Reported present Nov.–Dec./61. Absent at Manassas G.H. Jan.–Feb./62. Regimental returns of 2/62 place him absent sick since 2/24, while returns of 3/62 list him absent sick 3/10/62. Reported present Sept.–Dec./62. Absent on frl to procure a horse, Jan.–Feb./63. Reported present, Mar.–Apr./63. Absent on detached service at brigade HQ, July–Aug./63, Sept.–Oct./63, through 8/64, since 7/25/63. Reported present, Sept.–Dec./64. (AsheCo; CSR 270:8)

Phillips, Eli: From Tennessee. Enl. 3/7/62 as PVT, Co. A. Absent on detached service 9/17 at Winchester per rolls of Sept.–Oct./62. Reported present 11/62–4/63. Admitted 7/25/63 to a Richmond G.H. Rolls of July–Aug./63 list him as absent sick after being WIA in Pa. WIA 7/3/63 at Gettysburg in leg or foot, which was amputated. Rolls of Sept.–Oct./63 list him as sent home after his foot was amputated on 7/4/63. Absent sick, 11/30–4/31/64. As of 5/1/64, listed as AWOL and a deserter on rolls of Mar.–Dec./64. (AsheCo; CSR 270:8)

Phillips, John: Enl. 3/7/62 or 5/7/62 as PVT, Co. A. According to rolls of Sept.–Oct./62, D. 7/1/62. Another record list him as d. 7/2/62 from disease. (AsheCo; CSR 270:8)

Philpot, S.R.: PVT, Co. E. Prl. Appomattox, 4/9/65. (CSR 270:8)

Pholan, J.: PVT, Co. C. (Alexander)

Pickens, S.V.: From Buncombe Co. At age 25, enl. 5/20/61 as PVT, Co. G. Reported present Jan.–Feb./62. Regimental returns of 3/62 list him as sick in Richmond. Reported present, May–June/62. Reported AWOL at Sheperdstown, MD, per Sept.–Oct./62 rolls. Prl Sheperdstown, 9/30/62. Reported present Nov.–Dec./62, Jan.–Apr./63, July–Aug./63. Absent on pvst duty at Orange C.H., Nov.–Dec./63. (CSR 270:8)

Pierce, Ephraim: From Johnson Co. At age 22, enl. 6/20/61 or 7/28/61 as PVT, Co. H. Absent sick at home per rolls of Nov.–Dec./61. Rolls of Jan.–Feb./62 list him as absent sent home on sick frl 10/13/62. Regimental returns of 2/62 list him as absent sick, and returns of 3/62 report him on sick leave since 10/13/61. Reported present, May–June/62. Absent Sept.–Dec./62 after being sent to a Richmond G.H. 7/2/62. Reported present Mar.–Apr./63. Absent sent with horses to recruit, July–Aug./63. Absent on detached service Sept.–Oct./63. Reported present 11/63–2/64. Absent on detached service, 4/1/64. Reported present 3/64–8/31/64. (CSR 270:8)

Pinnell, Green. Co. E. From Franklin Co. (Pearce: 280)

Pinnell, Jackson. From Franklin Co. Enl. 6/3/61 as PVT, Co. E. Dsh 11/61 after furnishing a substitute. (Pearce: 280; CSR 270:8)

Pitchford, Robert D.: From Warren Co. At age 22, enl. 8/8/61 as PVT, Co. E. Other records put him in Co. D. Absent per rolls of Jan.–Feb./62 sent to a G.H. sick, 2/26/62. Regimental returns of 2/62 list him as absent sick, and 3/63 list him as sick at Manassas, 2/26/62. Reported present May–June/62, 9/62–4/63, July–Aug./63. Absent on detached service at Gordonsville with disabled horses, 10/15/63, per rolls of 6/30–10/31/63. Absent on detached service in Nelson Co. with disabled horses, Nov.–Dec./63, 4/1/64. Reported present, Mar.–Apr./64. Absent after being captured per rolls of 4/30/64 following. According to Federal records, captured at Cold Harbor, 6/1/64, or near Totopotomoy Creek, VA, 6/4/64. D. 7/15/64 in a railroad accident near Shohola, PA. Bur. there, then moved to an unidentified grave at Woodlawn Cemetery, Elmira, NY. (Elmira: 1, 12; CSR 270:8)

Pittman, John W.: B. Duplin Co. At age 26, enl. 6/17/61 as blacksmith and artificer, Co. I. According to rolls of Nov.–Dec./61, D. 12/8/61 from disease at Manassas. According to a sick and wounded report, d. 12/6 of pneumonia. (CSR 270:8)

Pitts, Caleb: Enl. 4/29/? as PVT, Co. C. Reported present, Mar.–Apr./64 and trn from 20th North Carolina Infantry, 4/18/64. Reported present, 4/30–8/31/64. Absent after being WIA 9/22/64 per rolls of Sept.–Oct./64. Reported present, Nov.–Dec./64. Prl Charlotte, 5/3/65. (CSR 270:8)

Pitts, George A.: From Cabarrus Co. At age 29, enl. 6/15/61 as PVT, Co. F. Reported present 11/61–2/62. Regimental returns of 2/62 list him as on extra duty as a teamster, and 3/62 on sick frl since 3/4/62. Reported present May–June/62, Sept.–Dec./62, 7/63–2/64. Rolls of 2/29/64–3/31/64 list him as on extra daily duty as a teamster. Reported present Mar.–Oct./64. Detailed to QM Dept. Living in eastern NC, circa 1893. (Mizelle; Barringer; Cabarrus; CSR 270:8)

Pleasants, Ellis P.: B. Warren Co. From Franklin Co. or Granville Co. At age 23, enl. 6/8/61 as PVT, Co. E. Prm CPL, SGT. Reported present as 5SGT, 1–2/62. Reported absent as 4SGT at a Petersburg G.H. sick, 5/17/62, per rolls of May–June/62. Rolls of Sept.–Oct./62 list him as 3SGT and D. of typhoid pneumonia home. According to an affidavit, he D. 9/2/62 at home. Stood 5'10¾", had a dark complexion, blue eyes, light hair; farmer. (CSR 270:8)

Pledger, James W.: From Northampton Co. At age 18, enl. 7/26/61 as PVT, Co. B. Reported present Nov.–Dec./61, Jan.–Apr./62. Absent as 4CPL and on detached service with horses at Winchester, Sept.–Oct./62. Rolls of Nov.–Dec./62 report him present and 2LT. Elected 2LT, 11/20/62. Reported present Jan.–Feb./63. Absent left sick at Campbell Co., VA, 4/22/63, per rolls of Mar.–Apr./63. KIA 6/21/63 "while gallantly leading his company in the charge" at Upperville. Listed on a Federal WIA list from Upperville with carbine ball wounds to the arm and breast. (CSR 270:1, 8)

Plummer, G.W.: Enl. 11/10/63 as PVT, Co. A. Reported present, Sept.–Dec./64. (AsheCo; CSR 270:8)

Plummer, Henry Falkener: B. 1/31/46, in Mecklenburg Co. Enl. 8/30/63 as PVT, Co. E. Reported present, 4/30–10/64. Absent Nov.–Dec./64 on a frl of indulgence. May also have served in Co. A, 3d Va. Cavalry. Married Lucy Davis Henderson. D. 2/25/11, Newport News, Va. (CSR 270:8; Virginia Democracy)

Plummer, J.C.: Enl. 5/1/64 as PVT, Co. A. Absent on detached service to buy a horse, Sept.–Oct./64. Reported present Nov.–Dec./64. (AsheCo; CSR 270:8)

Plummer, J.K.: Enl. 1/22/64 as PVT, Co. E. Absent at home on frl of indulgence, 4/30–10/64. Reported present, Nov.–Dec./64. Trn 3 VA Cavalry. (CSR 270:8)

Plummer, Jesse R.: From Ashe Co. At age 23, enl. 7/13/61 as PVT, Co. A. Reported present, Nov.–Dec./61. Reported present Jan.–Feb./62 as "courier for 4th Division." Regimental returns of 2/62 place him on daily duty at BG Milledge L. Bonham's HQ. Returns of 3/62 report him absent sick at a G.H., 3/10/62. Per rolls of Sept.–Dec./62, sent home on sick frl 3/9. AWOL Jan.–Feb./63 but on his way to the regiment. Reported present Mar.–Apr./63. Absent on detached service to buy a horse, July–Aug./63. Reported present Sept.–Oct./63. Absent on detached service 11/30/63–2/29/64 at brigade HQ since 11/29/63. Reported present 4/1/64. Absent on detached service in NC, Mar.–Apr./64. AWOL July–Aug./64. Reported present Sept.–Dec./64. (AsheCo; CSR 270:8)

Plummer, John: Enl. 6/10/64? as PVT, Co. A. Reported AWOL on rolls of July–Aug./64. NFR. (CSR 270:8)

Plummer, W.E.: Enl. 9/24/64 as PVT, Co. G, after being reassigned from state service. Reported present, Sept.–Dec./64. (CSR 270:8)

Pollock, John C.: From Duplin Co. At age 23, enl. 6/25/61 as PVT, Co. I. Rejected. (CSR 270:8)

Poteete, Henry: Enl. 10/1/63 as PVT, Co. D. From Caldwell County, NC. KIA 8/15, 8/16/64, or 8/17/64 at White Oak Swap or along Charles City Rd., near Richmond. Alternate last name spelling: Poteat. (Davis; Richmond *Sentinel*, 8/26/64)

Potter, John: From Ashe Co. At age 22, enl. 5/23/61 as PVT, Co. A. Reported present 11/61–2/62, and reported on rolls of Jan.–Feb./62 as regimental teamster. Per regimental returns of 2/62 on extra duty as a teamster. Regimental returns of 3/62 report him absent sick at a G.H., 3/10/62. Also reported present 9/62–4/63. Absent July–Aug./63 on detached service to buy a horse. Reported present 9/63–2/64, 4/1/64. Absent on detached service in NC Mar.–Apr./64. Reported present July–Dec./64. (CSR 270:8)

Potter, John B.: Enl. 2/28/62 as PVT, Co. D. Reported present, May–10/31/62. Rolls of Nov.–Dec./63 plus other records list him as deserting 11/1/62 at Williamsport, MD. Prl 11/11/62. (Davis; CSR 270:8)

Potts, C.A.: PVT, Co. C. (Alexander)

Potts, T.E.: Enl. 8/10/64 as PVT, Co. C. Absent on detached service 10/25/64 per rolls of Sept.–Oct./64. Reported present, Nov.–Dec./64. Admitted 12/3/64 to a Charlotte G.H., and returned to duty 12/20/64. (Alexander; CSR 270:8)

Potts, William M.: From Mecklenburg Co. At age 18, enl. 3/14/62 as PVT, Co. F. (Some records say he enl 6/15/63.) Regimental returns of 3/62 list him as on extra duty as a teamster. Reported present May–June/62, Sept.–Dec./62. KIA Upperville, VA, 6/21/63. (Barringer; CSR 270:8)

Powell, Godwin M.: From Northampton Co. At age 19, enl. 4/22/62 as PVT, Co. B. Admitted 10/31/62 to a Richmond G.H. Reported present, 9/62–4/63. Absent on detached service in NC to buy a horse, 8/27/63, per rolls of July–Aug./63. Reported present 6/30–Dec./63, 4/1/64, Mar.–Apr./64. (Zeb. Vance Papers, NCSA [courtesy Whit Joyner]; CSR 270:8)

Powell, Henry H.: From Northampton Co. At age 23, enl. 6/12, 7/12, or 7/19/62 as PVT, Co. B. Reported present 9/62–4/63, 6/30–12/63. On detached service, Jan.–Feb./64. Reported present, Mar.–Apr./64, 4/1/64. Absent as a POW, 4/30/64–12/64. Per Federal records, captured near Petersburg, 10/27/64. D. 3/1/65 at Pt. Lookout and buried in the POW graveyard. (Zeb. Vance Papers, NCSA [courtesy Whit Joyner]; PL: 159; CSR 270:8)

Powell, John R.: From Halifax Co. At age 25, enl. 6/20/61 as PVT, Co. H. Reported present, 11/61–2/62. Regimental return of 3/62 lists him on sick leave as of 3/29/62. Absent as a POW after being captured at Willis Church, 6/29/62, per rolls of May–June/62. Per Federal records, B. NC, age 26, 5'5½", black hair, chestnut eyes, fair complexion, and exd 8/5/62. Listed AWOL on rolls of Sept.–Oct./62. Absent detached on a scout with MAJ Whitaker, Nov.–Dec./62. Reported present, Jan.–Apr./63. Absent on detached service in NC to buy a horse, July–Aug./63. Reported present 9/63–2/64, 4/1/64. Absent Mar.–Apr./64 on horse detail. Reported present 4/30–12/64. (Halifax, 18; CSR 270:8)

Powell, Mills B.: From Northampton Co. At age 25, enl. 6/15/61 as PVT, Co. B. Reported present 11/61–4/62, Sept.–Oct./62. Absent on detached service, Nov.–Dec./62. Reported present, Jan.–Apr./63, July–Aug./63 Captured at Upperville, 6/21/63. Absent WIA 10/14/63 and sent to a G.H. per rolls of 6/30–10/31/63. Absent at home after being WIA per rolls of Nov.–Dec./63. WIA in the hand at Auburn. Admitted 10/21/63 to a Richmond G.H. Reported present 4/1/64, Mar.–Apr./64. KIA Ground Squirrel Church, 5/11/64. (CSR 270:8)

Powell, R.H.: Enl. 10/16/63 as PVT, Co. B. Reported present, 4/30/64–12/64. Unanimously elected 2LT, 12/6/64. (CSR 270:1, 8)

Powell, Randolph A.: From Halifax Co. At age 18, enl. 6/20 or 6/23/61 as PVT, Co. H. Reported present, Nov.–Dec./61. Per rolls of Jan.–Feb./62, D. 2/14/62. Regimental returns of 2/62 list him as D. 2/62. D. of disease. Stood 5'11¾", had a fair complexion, blue eyes, and light hair. Farmer. Compare Silas G. Carter, PVT, Co. G, 44th NC. (Halifax, 18; CSR 270:8)

Presson, Thomas J.: B. Va. From Lenoir Co. At age 28, enl. 6/20/61 as PVT, Co. H. Reported present, 11/61–2/62, May–June/62. Absent on detached service at Winchester, Sept.–Oct./62. Dsh due to disability, 12/25/62. Leg problems. Stood 5'10¾", had a dark complexion, black eyes and hair. Carpenter. (CSR 270:8)

Preston, William: Pvt., Co. G. Enl. 1861. (eBay listing, February 2004, copy in author's possession.)

Price, Benajah: From Wayne Co. At age 37, enl. 7/22/61 as PVT, Co. H. Absent with the wagons, Nov.–Dec./61. Reported present, Jan.–Feb./62. Regimental returns of Feb.–Mar./62 list him as on extra duty as a teamster. Absent May–June/62 after being WIA at Willis Church. Admitted 7/27/62 to a Richmond G.H. with a gunshot wound to the lungs. Per rolls of Sept.–Oct./62, D. 8/14/62. (CSR 270:8; Monie also referred to a "Bengale" Price that was KIA 6/29/62.)

Price, John: From Ashe Co. Enl. 3/1/62 as PVT, Co. A. D. 5/15/62 from disease. (AsheCo; CSR 270:8)

Price, Nathaniel: B. 1826. Resident of Ashe Co., near Creston. Married, had a son and daughter when he volunteered. Enl. 5/20/61 as PVT, Co. A. Reported present Nov.–Dec./61. Absent recruiting 2/10/62 per rolls of Jan.–Feb./62. Regimental returns of 2/62 report him on detached service as of 2/10, and returns of 3/62 list him as absent sick as of 3/23/62. Reported present, Sept.–Oct./62. Per company muster rolls of Nov.–Dec./62, reported present and prm 3CPL, 11/8. Reported present Jan.–Feb./63 and listed as 5SGT. Reported present Mar.–Apr./63. Absent on detached service to procure a horse, July–Aug./63. Reported present, 9/63–4/64. Admitted 5/25 or 5/27/64 to a Richmond G.H. Frl 7/17/64 due to a gunshot wound in the thigh. Absent at home on sick frl, July–Aug./64. Rolls of Sept.–Oct./64 list him as AWOL since 10/12/64. Rolls of Nov.–Dec./64 list him as a deserter. Said to have saved General Hampton's life at Gettysburg, and Hampton remembered that by giving him a deed to a mountain farm in Jackson County where he lived the rest of his days. D. 1892. Bur. Webster Cem., Jackson Co. (AsheCo, 19; Stepp; CSR 270:8)

Pridgen, James W.: From Greene Co. At age 21, enl. 6/20/61 as PVT, Co. H. D. 12/25/61 or 12/27/61 at Camp W.S. Ashe of typhoid pneumonia. (CSR 270:8)

Primrose, John William: B. 1838. From Craven Co. Enl. 6/24/61 as PVT, Co. H. Reported present 11/61–2/62. Frl 2/24/62. Regimental returns of 3/62 report him on leave of absence as of 3/23/62. May–June/62, 9/62–4/63. Absent on detached service in NC to buy a horse per rolls of July–Aug./63. Absent Sept.–Oct./63 at a Richmond G.H. Reported present, Nov.–Dec./63. Admitted to a Richmond G.H., 1/29/64. Absent at a Richmond G.H. Jan.–Feb./64 and listed as 2SGT. Reported present 4/1/64. Rolls of Mar.–Apr./64 list him as sick in quarters. Reported present 4/30–8/31/64. Sept.–Oct./64 on extra duty as regimental commissary SGT. Absent on detached service on horse detail, Oct.–Dec./64. Appointed CPT and Ast. Chief of Subsistence, 3/1/65. D. 1907. Bur. Washington Co., Mississippi. (CSR 270:1, 8; R.E.L. Krick to author, 11/5/1998)

Privette, Burkette Morris: B. 3/18/39. From Wayne Co. Enl. 8/8/61 as bugler, Co. H. Reported present 11/61–4/62, Sept.–Oct./62. Absent detailed as a scout with MAJ Whitaker, Nov.–Dec./62. Reported present, Jan.–Apr./63, July–Aug./63. Absent WIA and sent to the hospital per rolls of Sept.–Dec./63. WIA 10/19/63 in chin and shoulder. After being wounded, "he was complimented publicly for gallant conduct." Admitted 10/24/63 to a Richmond G.H. Prl for 30 days, 10/30/63. Reported present Jan.–Feb./64, 4/1/64. Absent on frl, Mar.–Apr./64. Reported present 4/30–12/64. Captured at Burkeville, 4/5/65. Released 6/16/65. Per Federal records, a resident of Goldsboro with a fair complexion, brown hair, gray eyes, and stood 5'7¼" tall. D. 10/27/95. Bur. Willowdale Cem, Goldsboro. (GLP; CGR: 3; Stepp; CSR 270:8)

Proctor, J.A.: PVT, Co. K. Admitted 2/24/65 to a Richmond G.H. (CSR 270:8; card filed with Mansfield Proctor)

Proctor, Mansfield: From Cherokee Co. At age 18, enl. 6/25/61 as PVT Co. K. Reported present 11/61–2/62, May–June/62, 9/62–4/63. Rolls of

July–Aug./63 report him as detached to NC to buy horses. Rolls of 10/31/63 as KIA 9/22/63 at Jack's Shop. (CSR 270:8; Macon Heritage, 49 lists KIA name as J.A. Proctor)

Proctor, Moses: Enl. 7/11/61 as PVT, Co. K. Absent sick in a hospital, Nov.–Dec./61. Absent Jan.–Feb./62 at a Manassas G.H., 2/26/62. Regimental returns of 2/62 list him as absent sick; returns of 3/62 say he D. 3/3 in camp. D. of disease. Another record says he D. 3/6/62 of typhoid fever at Manassas. (CSR 270:8; cards filed with Proctor, Mansfield and Proctor, M)

Proffit, David: From Watauga Co. At age 26, enl. 2/28/62 as PVT, Co. D. Reported present, May–June/62. Rolls of 6/30–10/31/62 report him as D Hanover C.H., 8/4/62. D. from disease. According to diarist Davis, he D. 11/62 at Occoquan. (Davis; CSR 270:8)

Proffit, James: From Watauga Co. At age 33, enl. 5/11/61 as PVT, Co. D. Reported present, Nov.–Dec./61. Absent sent to a G.H., Jan.–Feb./62. Regimental returns of 2/62 list him as absent sick; returns of 3/62 place him in a Lynchburg G.H. as of 2/24/62. Reported present, May–Dec./62. Absent on detached service, Jan.–Feb./63. Reported present Mar.–Apr./63, 7/63–4/64. Admitted 5/25/64 to a Richmond G.H. with a gunshot wound to the flesh of the right arm. Frl for 40 days, 6/9/64. Absent at home 8/31/64, Sept.–Oct./64 due to his wounds. Reported present, Nov.–Dec./64. Also on register of Invalid Corps as retired 11/25/64 and assigned to the Medical Director of the Army of Northern Virginia, 1/7. Mentioned in Special Orders #293/5, Department of the Army of Northern Virginia, to report for assignment to Gen. Lee. Captured at Dinwiddie C.H., 4/3/65. Released 6/17/65 on taking the oath. Resident of Watauga Co., fair complexion, brown hair, hazel eyes, stood 5' 8⅓". (Davis; CSR 270:8)

Proffit, Thomas: From Buncombe Co. At age 28, enl. 5/11/61 as PVT, Co. D. D from typhoid pneumonia at Cantonment W.N. Edwards, 12/15/61. According to the diarist Davis, he D. at Camp W.S. Ashe near Centerville, VA, 12/61. (Davis; CSR 270:8)

Propst, E.A., Jr.: From Concord. Enl. 10/20/64 or 10/30/4 as PVT, Co. F. WIA 12/9/64 and frl. Prl Salisbury, 6/14/65. Dead as of 1893. (Barringer; Cabarrus; CSR 270:8)

Pruitt, William H: From Granville Co. At age 38, Enl. 7/17/61 as PVT, Co. E. Absent per company muster rolls of Jan.–Feb./62 sent near Warranton 12/27/61. Regimental returns of 2/62 list him as absent sick. Absent May–June/62 at a Petersburg G.H. sick as of 5/13/62. Rolls of Sept.–Oct./62 place him on detached service at Winchester. Reported present, 11/62–4/63. Absent July–Aug./63 on detached service in NC after a horse as of 8/27/63. Reported present, 6/30/63–12/64. Buried at Kittrell Springs, NC. Confederate cemetery. (CSR 270:8)

Pucket, P.: PVT. Captured at Harrison's Landing, 6/27/62. Exd at Aiken's Landing, 8/5/62. (CSR 270:8)

Pugh, James A.: No Unit specified. Cav, Co. K. Bur Scotland Neck Episcopal, Halifax Co., NC. May have been in a VA unit. (GLP)

Pugh, James M.: B. Orange Co. Carpenter before the war. At age 35, enl. 6/3/61 as SGT, Co. C. Rolls of Nov.–Dec./61 list him as absent sick. Reported present Jan.–Feb./62. Regimental returns of 3/62 list him as sick at a Petersburg G.H., 3/23/62. Reported present 5/62–4/63. Absent July–Dec./63 on detached service as of 8/7/63. Reported present Jan.–Feb./64. Absent on detached service 4/1/64, Mar.–Dec./64 on detached service 8/7/63. As of 1/1/64–6/30/64, on duty at recruiting camp in Lynchburg. SGT, 35, blue eyes, light hair, ruddy complexion, stood 5'10½", On a report dated 2/17/65 of soldiers on detached service in the employ of Walter Coles, AQMD, at Lynchburg "in charge of horses of his command. Is indispensable to identify the horses of his command." Prl Raleigh, 5/10/65. (Alexander; James T. Pugh Papers, #1590, SHC, UNC; CSR 270:8)

Puryear, W.H.: Enl. 10/25/64 as PVT, Co. B, in Raleigh. Reported present Nov.–Dec./64. (CSR 270:8)

Quinn, Ed. C.: Cns 10/3/64 as PVT, Co. I. Reported present on company muster rolls of Sept.–Dec./64. (CSR 270:8)

Quinn, William Franklin: B. Duplin Co. At age 24, enl. 7/21/62 as PVT, Co. I. Trn from CPT Ward's Cav. Reported present Sept.–Dec./62. Rolls of Jan.–Feb./63 list him as dsh due to disability 2/22/63. Listed as 6' tall with a dark complexion, black eyes, and hair. Admitted 2/25/63 to a Richmond G.H. with debilitas. Deserted 4/22/63. (CSR 270:8)

Ragan, John: B. 3/3/34 in Watauga Co. Occupation: farmer. Enl. 5/11/61 as PVT, Co. D. Went on sick list 10/6/61. Absent in a Petersburg G.H., 11/61–2/62. Regimental returns of 2/62 list him as absent sick. One report lists him as dsh 1/17/62 due to chronic tonsillitis, but also reported present 5/62–4/63. Absent at home to buy a horse, July–

Aug./63. Reported present, 6/30/63–3/31/64. Absent at home to buy a horse, Mar.–Apr./64. Reported present 8/31/64, Sept.–Dec./64. Stood 5'11" tall, had a fair complexion, blue eyes, auburn hair. D. 11/2/99. Bur. Meat Camp Baptist Church Cem., Watauga Co. (Davis; Stepp; CSR 270:8)

Ragan, William: Enl. 9/1/63 as PVT, Co. D. Reported present 6/30/63–12/63. Absent on detached service, Jan.–Mar./64. Reported present, 13–4/64. Admitted 5/12/64 to a Richmond G.H. According to 8/31/64 company muster rolls, d. 5/17/64 in G.H. According to surgeon's certificate, d. 5/18/64 due to febris typhoidis. According to Davis, D. 11/62. (Davis; CSR 270:8)

Ransom, Robert, Jr.: B. 2/12/28. From Warren Co. Appointed COL, to rank from 5/16/61. Entered state service 5/8 or 8/12/61 and Confederate service 10/21/61. Reported present 11/61–2/62. Reported present on regimental returns of 2/62. Prm BG, 11/1/62. Prm MAJ GEN, 5/26/63. D. 1/14/92. Bur. Cedar Grove Cem., New Bern, NC. (CSR 270:1; Stepp; CSR 270:8)

Rasberry, Willis J.: From Greene Co. At age 29, enl. 6/29/61 as PVT, Co. H. Reported present Nov.–Dec./61. Absent Jan.–Feb./62 as an escort for GEN Stuart, 1–2/62. Regimental return of 2/62 lists him as on detached service. Absent May–June/62, Sept.–Oct./62 detached to raise a company. Prm 2LT, Netercutt's Bn. (CSR 270:8)

Ratliff, William: Cns. 6/29/61 as PVT, Co. H. Absent on detached service, Sept.–Oct./64. Trn to Col D, 5th NC Cavalry, 11/1/64 per rolls of Nov.–Dec./64. (CSR 270:8)

Rawls, Isaiah: From Craven Co, but also claimed to be resident of VA. At age 28, enl. 6/20/61 as PVT, Co. H. Reported present 11/61–2/62. Regimental returns of 2/62 list him as on extra duty as a teamster. Regimental returns of 3/62 show him in a Richmond G.H. 3/23/62. Reported present May–June/62. Absent Sept.–Oct./62 sick sent to Winchester. Absent Nov.–Dec./62 sent to a Gordonsville G.H., 12/30/62. Absent Jan.–Feb./63 sent to a Petersburg G.H. sick. Absent sick Mar.–Apr./63. Absent on detached service to recruit horses, July–Aug./63, Sept.–Oct./63. Rolls of Nov.–Dec./63 list him on detached service as provost guard at Division H.Q. Admitted 1/29/64 to a Richmond G.H. Absent Jan.–Feb./64 on detached duty. Absent detailed by the QM at Richmond, 4/1/64, Mar.–Apr./64. Employed as a carpenter by MAJ. J.B. Harvis, QM at Richmond, per report dated 6/11/64; age given as 31. Also reported as carpenter and on light duty in a report dated 8/64, detached 1/21/64. Absent on light duty, 4/30–8/31/64, and Sept.–Oct./64 in Richmond. Absent on detached service in Richmond, Nov.–Dec./64. (CSR 270:8)

Ray, Addison (Ad): Enl. 8/11/63 as PVT, Co. D. Reported present, 11/63–12/64. (Davis; CSR 270:8)

Ray, Farrow: From Ashe Co. At age 18, enl. 7/8/61 as PVT, Co. D, 58th NC. Trn to Co. A, 6/6/63. Absent AWOL Sept.–Oct./63. (CSR 270:8; AsheCo lists him as Harrow)

Ray, George W.: From Ashe Co. At age 33, enl. 5/27/61 as PVT, Co. A. Reported present 11/61–2/62. Absent on detached service as a shoemaker since 10/28 per rolls of Sept.–Oct./62. Absent on detached service Nov.–Dec./62. Reported present and under arrest, 1–2/63. Reported present Mar.–Apr./63, July–Aug./63, Sept.–Oct./63 and prm saddler 9/1/63. Reported present 11/30/63–2/29/64, 4/1/64. Deserted 3/20/64. Received by Army of the Potomac, 3/23, took oath, and sent to Washington, D.C. 3/25/64. (AsheCo; CSR 270:8)

Ray, Henry H.: From Ashe Co. At age 24, enl. 5/27/61 as PVT, Co. A. Reported present, 11/61–2/62, Sept.–Dec./62. Absent on detached service with shoemakers for the regiment, Jan.–Feb./63. On a Staunton G.H. roll for 2/28/63 as admitted 3/7/63 with typhoid fever and convalescing. Reported present Mar.–Apr./63. Reported AWOL, July–Aug./63. Reported present, Sept.–Dec./63. On a court martial record, 1/27/64. Absent in confinement at Richmond since 2/9 per rolls of 1/1–2/29/64, 4/1/64. Reported present Mar.–Apr./64. AWOL 8/30/64 per rolls of July–Aug./64. Reported present, Sept.–Dec./64. (AsheCo; CSR 270:8)

Ray, J.F.: PVT, Co. A. (AsheCo)

Ray, James: From Ashe Co.; resident of Jefferson. At age 30, enl. 5/24/61 as PVT, Co. A. Reported present, 11/61–2/62. Admitted 3/8/62 to a Richmond G.H. with rheumatism, and returned to duty 3/27/62. Absent as a POW after being captured near Williamsport, MD 10/29 per rolls of Sept.–Oct./62. Absent on prl per rolls of Nov.–Dec./62; absent as a prl POW at home, Jan.–Feb./63. Reported present, Mar.–Apr./63. Absent on detached service to buy a horse, July–Aug./63. AWOL 10/29 per rolls of Sept.–Oct./63. Reported AWOL 10/22 per rolls of 11/30–Dec./31/63. Per rolls of 1/1/64–2/29/64, under arrest since 2/14. Reported present 4/1/54, Mar.–Apr./64. Frl from a Richmond G.H. 7/11/64 after suffering a broken tibia and fibula 5/12/64. Frl 60 days. Absent at home on sick frl per rolls of July–Aug./64; AWOL Sept.–Dec./64. Listed as a deserter. (AsheCo; CSR 270:8)

Ray, Jesse: From Ashe Co. At age 18, enl. 5/25/61 as PVT, Co. A. Reported present, 11/61–2/62, Sept.–Oct./62, 11/62–4/63. Reported AWOL on rolls of July–Aug./63. Reported present, 9/63–8/64. Reported AWOL Sept.–Oct./64. Reported present, Nov.–Dec./64. (AsheCo; CSR 270:8)

Ray, John A.: From Ashe Co. At age 18, enl. 3/27, 4/9, or 4/27/63 as PVT, Co. A. Reported present Mar.–Apr./63, 7/63–8/64. Admitted 2/12/64 to a Richmond G.H. Listed as AWOL Sept.–Oct./64; reported present, Nov.–Dec./64. (AsheCo; CSR 270:8)

Ray, John H.: From Ashe Co. At age 20, enl. 5/1/61 as PVT, Co. D, 58th NC. Trn to Co. A, 6/6/63. Reenl 7/8/63 as 2LT. Absent on detached service to buy a horse, July–Aug./63. Reported present, 9/63–2/64. Admitted 2/13/64 to a Richmond G.H., and returned to duty 2/20/64. Reported present, 4/1/64. Rolls of Mar.–Apr./64 list him as absent on detached service in NC. Reported present, July–Dec./64. (AsheCo; CSR 270:8)

Ray, John M.: From Ashe Co. At age 25, enl. 5/24/61 as PVT, Co. A. Absent according to rolls of Nov.–Dec./61 at a Richmond G.H. Absent Jan.–Feb./62 in charge of unserviceable horses. Regimental returns of 2/62 list him on detached service 12/28/61. Returns of 3/62 list him as absent sick at a G.H. 3/10/62. Admitted 3/19/62 to a Richmond G.H. with diarrhea and returned to duty 3/27/62. Absent on detached service at Winchester since 10/15/62 per rolls of Sept.–Oct./62. Absent on detached service, Nov.–Dec./62. Absent on detached service at Gordonsville, Jan.–Feb./63. Absent Mar.–Apr./63 after a horse since 3/4. Rolls of July–Aug./63 list him as trn 6/15. Trn to 58th NC Infantry. Other records say trn 6/6/63. (AsheCo; CSR 270:8)

Ray, John S.: Res. of Cleveland Co. PVT, Co. I. Captured at Amelia C.H., 4/3/65, and sent to Pt. Lookout. Released 6/17/65 on taking the oath. Had dark complexion, dark brown hair, blue eyes, stood 5' 6¾". (CSR 270:8)

Ray, Joseph I.: Enl. 7/8/62 or 63 as PVT, Co. A. Reported present 11/30/63–2/29/64, 4/1/64. Absent on detached service in NC Mar.–Apr./64. Reported present July–Aug./64. On detached service to purchase a horse Sept.–Oct./64. Reported present, Nov.–Dec./64. Inquiry regarding his record from Oklahoma Board of Pensions came to ADJ GEN office dated 6/30/1915 (CSR 270:8)

Ray, Leonidas: Enl. 10/10/64 as PVT, Co. K. Reported present, Sept.–Dec./64. (CSR 270:8)

Ray, Samuel: From Ashe Co. At age 36, enl. 7/31/61 as PVT, Co. A. Reported present as a blacksmith, Nov.–Dec./61. Absent sent home on detail with sick, Jan.–Feb./62. Regimental return of 2/62 lists him as absent sick; 3/62 as absent sick at a G.H. 3/10/62. Detailed as wagoner 3/15/62. Absent Sept.–Oct./62 as a wagon master at Winchester since 9/5/62. Reported present as assistant wagon master 4/62–4/63, July–Aug./63. Reported present, Sept.–Oct./63. On extra duty per rolls of 11/30–12/31/63. Reported present on extra duty as a wagon master since 4/15/62 per rolls of Jan.–Feb./29/64. Reported present on extra duty since 3/15/62 per rolls of 4/1/64. On extra duty assisting the wagon master, Mar.–Apr./64. ON extra duty as rgt forage master, July–Aug./64. Reported present, Sept.–Oct./64. Absent on frl of indulgence, Nov.–Dec./64. (AsheCo; CSR 270:8)

Ray, William: From Ashe Co. At age 20, enl. 5/24/61 as PVT, Co. A. Reported present 11/61–2/62, 9/62–4/63. Captured since 10/1/62; prl 11/9/62. Admitted 11/24/62 to a Petersburg G.H. and returned to duty 12/9/62. Reported AWOL July–Aug./63. Listed on a court martial record dated 1/8/64. Reported present 9/63–4/64, July–Aug./64. Absent sick Sept.–Oct./64. Admitted 9/17/64 to a Raleigh G.H. and returned to duty 9/23/64. Reported present Nov.–Dec./64. Captured 4/13 or 4/18/65 at Watauga Co. and sent to Chattanooga 5/7/65. Took oath 6/16/65 and released at Louisville, KY. Had dark complexion, dark hair, dark eyes, stood 5' 8½". (AsheCo; CSR 270:8)

Ray, William: Resident of Macon Co. At age 24, Enl. 3/1/62 as PVT, Co. K. Reported present May–June/62, 9/62–4/63. Absent on detached service per rolls of July–Aug./63. Reported missing near Martinsburg and assumed a POW per rolls of 10/31/63, 11/63–12/64. Per Federal records, enl. 3/13/61 and captured 7/19/63 near Martinsburg In Berkley Co., VA., stood 5'10", had a fair complexion, dark eyes, dark hair, and a farmer. Released 6/19/65 on taking the oath. (CSR 270:8)

Rea, D.B.: From Mecklenburg Co. At age 28, enl. 6/25/62 or 7/4/62 as PVT, Co. C. Reported present, 6/30/62–12/62. Absent in NC to buy a horse, 2/21/63, per rolls of Jan.–Apr./63. Per rolls of July–Aug./63, trn to Co. F, 5th NC Cavalry, 6/13/63 or 8/8/63. In 1863, published *Sketches of Hampton's Cavalry in the Summer, Fall, and Winter Campaigns of '62, Including Stuart's Raid into Penn-*

sylvania, and Also, in Burnside's Rear. (Alexander; CSR 270:8)

Rea, J.M.: From Mecklenburg Co. At age 22, enl. 5/25/61 as PVT, Co. C. Reported present 11/61–2/62, May–10/31/62. Absent scouting 12/25 per rolls of Nov.–Dec./62. Reported present Jan.–Apr./63, July–Oct./63. Absent on detached service 11/1 per rolls of Nov.–Dec./63. Reported present Jan.–Oct./64. Absent on detached service 12/1/64 per rolls of Nov.–Dec./64. (Alexander; CSR 270:8)

Rea, John Lee: From Mecklenburg Co. Enl. 5/25/61, but rejected by Col. Baker, 8/1/61. Enl. 10/27/64 as PVT, Co. C. Reported present Nov.–Dec./64. Farrier. Dsh. Later lived in Union Co. (Alexander; CSR 270:8)

Rea, R.R.: Enl. 10/28/64 as PVT, Co. C. Reported present, Nov.–Dec./64. Prl Charlotte, 5/15/65. (Alexander; CSR 270:8)

Rea, Robert: Enl. 10/28/64 as PVT, Co. C. Reported present, Nov.–Dec./64. (Alexander; CSR 270:8)

Rea, William A.: Resident of Mecklenburg Co. Enl. 2/28/62 as PVT, Co. C. Regimental return lists him as a recruit from Depot in 3/62. Reported present May–Oct./62. Absent in NC 12/25 to take care of horses purchased by LT Maxwell, Nov.–Dec./62. Absent Jan.–Feb./63 on detached service in NC since 12/21/62. Reported present as PVT and farrier on rolls of Mar.–Apr./63, 7/63–12/64. Captured at Ford's Depot, 4/3/65, and released 6/17/65 on taking the oath. Had dark complexion, black hair, and hazel eyes. (Alexander; CSR 270:8)

Reaves, John: Co. K. KIA Reams Station. (Macon Heritage, 49.)

Reavis, William A.: From Granville Co. At age 18, enl. 6/8/61 as PVT, Co. E. Absent on detached service with GEN Rodes' body guard indefinitely beginning 1/15/62 per rolls of Jan.–Feb./62. Regimental return of 2/62 lists him as on detached service. Reported present May–June/62, Sept.–Dec./62. Absent on detached service Jan.–Feb./63. Reported present Mar.–Apr./63. Absent on detached service in NC to procure a horse 8/27/63, per rolls of July–Aug./63, and listed as prm 4CPL. Reported present 6/30/63–4/64. Absent at home on frl of indulgence 4/30–10/64, and prm 3CPL and then 2CPL per Sept.–Oct./64. Reported present Nov.–Dec./64. (CSR 270:8)

Redman, Thomas W.: Enl. 9/22/63 as PVT, Co. B. Reported present 4/30–12/64. (CSR 270:8)

Redmond, S.M.: From Buncombe Co. At age 24, enl. 5/20/61 as PVT, Co. G. Later prm CPL. Reported present Jan.–Feb./62, May–June/62, Sept.–Oct./62. Absent as a POW Nov.–Dec./62. Prl 11/62. Reported present Jan.–Apr./63, 7/63–8/64. Listed as AWOL on rolls of Sept.–Dec./64. (CSR 270:8)

Reeves, Charles: From Ashe Co. At age 28, enl. 7/8/62 as PVT. Reported AWOL on rolls of Sept.–Oct./63, and joined by trn. Trn 6/6/63 from Co. D, 59th NC Infantry. Rolls of 11/30/63–2/29/64 list him as AWOL since 11/1. Also reported AWOL 4/1/64, Mar.–Apr./64, July–Oct./64, since 10/27/63. Rolls of Nov.–Dec./64 list him as deserted. (AsheCo; CSR 270:8)

Reeves, Cicero: Enl. 11/10/63 at Jefferson as PVT, Co. A. Reported present Sept.–Dec./64. (AsheCo; CSR 270:8)

Reeves, John: From Macon Co. At age 31, enl. 8/15/61 as PVT, Co. K. Reported present 11/61–2/62, May–June/62, 9/62–4/63. Absent sick in NC July–Aug./63. Reported present 10/32/63, 11/63–3/31/64. Admitted 1/4/64 to a Richmond G.H. Rolls of Mar.–Apr./64 list him as WIA 8/30/64. Rolls of 4/30–8/31/64 list him as absent WIA. Rolls of Sept.–Oct./64 say he D. from wounds. D. Petersburg G.H. 9/5/64 due to gunshot wound. (CSR 270:8)

Reinhardt, John Franklin: B. 5/14/44. From Lincoln Co. Enl. 4/25/61 as PVT, Co K, 1st NC Vols. Enl. 5/3/62 as PVT, Co. C. Reported present May–June/62, 6/30/62–4/63. Absent detached in NC on horse detail 8/27/63 per rolls of July–Aug./63. Horse KIA Martinsburg, 7/19/63. Absent Sept.–Oct./63 as courier for GEN James B. Gordon 10/15. Absent 11/63–2/64 as a courier for GEN Wade Hampton 12/1/63. Also absent as a courier for GEN Hampton 4/1/64, Mar.–Apr./64. Absent on detached service 4/30–8/31/64. Absent on detached service 12/1/63 per rolls of Sept.–Dec./64. Prl Greensboro, 4/29/65, and listed as a member of the Army of Tennessee Cavalry Corps HQ staff. D. 6/9/13. Bur. New Hope Methodist Church Cem., Lincoln Co. (Stepp; Alexander lists as "Reenhardt."; CSR 270:8)

Revel, James H.: B. Ashe Co. From Macon Co. Farmer. At age 25, enl. 6/25/61 as PVT, Co. K. Absent sick at a Petersburg G.H., Nov.–Dec./61. Absent on 27-day sick leave and frl 1/30/62, per rolls of Jan.–Feb./62. Regimental returns of 2/62 list him as absent sick and 3/62 returns list him as on sick leave 1/30/62. Absent May–June/62, Sept.–Oct./62. Absent Nov.–Dec./62 sick sent to a G.H. from Madison C.H. 11/12/62 and 11/14/62. Admitted 11/13/62 to a Richmond G.H. and returned to duty 11/27/62. Absent Jan.–Feb./63. Absent at home sick

Mar.–Apr./63. Absent July–Aug./63 detached to buy a horse in NC. Reported at a Charlottesville G.H. 10/6/63 to draw clothes. Absent sick 10/31/63. Dsh per rolls of Nov.–Dec./63. Dsh 11/14/63 due to chronic rheumatism. Age 27, stood 6' tall, had a dark complexion, black eyes and hair. (CSR 270:8)

Reynolds, Israel Henry: Enl. 5/22/64 as PVT, Co. G. Reported present Mar.–Apr./64 thru 10/64. absent on detached service on a horse detail, Nov.–Dec./64. Bur. Riverside Cem., Asheville. (Stepp; CSR 270:8 also gives first initial as J)

Rhea, J.M.: Enl. 4/29/61 as PVT, Co. G. Reported present Sept.–Oct./63. Absent to procure a horse per rolls of Nov.–Dec./63. AWOL Jan.–Feb./64, 4/1/64. Rolls of Mar.–Apr./64 and July–Aug./64 list him as KIA by stories while on detached service. (CSR 270:8)

Rhine, J.W.: PVT. On a register of deserters as received by the provost marshall general in Washington, D.C., 3/13/65. Took the oath and transported to Boston. (CSR 270:8)

Rice, J.W.: Enl. 10/25/64 at Raleigh as PVT, Co. B. Reported present, Nov.–Dec./64. (CSR 270:8)

Rice, W.F.: B. Granville Co. Farmer. Enl. 6/21/63 or 11/21/63 as PVT, Co. B. Reported present 4/30–12/64. Per descriptive list, age 38, blue eyes, gray hair, florid complexion, stoof 5' 8½". (CSR 270:8)

Rich, Phil: Identified by Fred C. Foard as a 1st NC Cav trooper; although Foard's letter is inaccurate in many respects. (Fred C. Foard to W.G. Means, March 6, 1917, Fred C. Foard Papers, PC 500, NCSA.)

Rickman, Phillip R.: From Macon Co. Farmer. At age 25, enl. 6/25/61 as PVT, Co. K. Reported present 11/61–2/62. Dsh at Camp Mars due to disability. Dsh 5/19/62 due to chronic bronchitis; stood 6'1", had a light complexion, blue eyes, sandy hair. (CSR 270:8)

Rickman, William C.: From Macon Co. At age 23, enl. 6/25/61 as PVT, Co. K. Reported present Nov.–Dec./61. Absent Jan.–Feb./62 sent to a Manassas G.H. sick on 2/24/62. Regimental return 2/62 lists him as absent sick. Reported present May–June/62, Sept.–Oct./62. Per rolls of Nov.–Dec./62, detached to report to Lt. Roane in Macon Co. 12/27/62. Absent on detached service with Lt Roane, Jan.–Feb./63. Absent on detached service, Mar.–Apr./63. Rolls of July–Aug./63 list him as absent MIA as of 7/19. Reported present 10/31/63. Admitted 12/1/63 to a Richmond G.H. Absent Nov.–Dec./63, Jan.–Oct./64 after being WIA 11/29/63. Admitted 1/30/64 to a Richmond G.H. with a gunshot wound in the left thigh. Frl 2/17/64.

Reported present Nov.–Dec./64. On a register of the Invalid Corps as retired 12/1/64. Reported 3/3/65 at a Richmond G.H. (CSR 270:8)

Riggs, Lot: B. 1828. From Wilkes Co. Enl. 3/7/62 as PVT, Co. A. Regimental return of 3/62 lists him as a recruit from the depot. Reported present 9/62–4/63. Absent July–Aug./63 with unserviceable horses. Reported present 9/63–4/64. Absent sick July–Aug./64. Listed in a Statesville G.H. for the period ending 8/27/64, or may have frl or trn. Reported present Sept.–Dec./64. D. 1869. Bur. Faw-McNeil-Riggs graveyard, near intersection of NC 16 and Pleasant Home Church Rd., Wilkes Co. (AsheCo; McNeil; CSR 270:8; Blake Lovette)

Riggs, Thomas: PVT, Co. A. (AsheCo)

Riley, Hugh: From Wayne Co. At age 35, enl. 6/20/61 as blacksmith, Co. H. Reported present 11/61–2/62. Absent left at Greensboro sick as of 4/3/62 per rolls of May–June/62. Reported present Sept.–Oct./62, 11/62–4/63, 7/63–12/64. (CSR 270:8)

Riley, Phillip G.: B. Ireland. From Wayne Co. At age 19, enl. 6/23/61 as PVT, Co. H. Reported present Nov.–Dec./61. Rolls of Jan.–Feb./62 list him as trn to the regimental band 2/27/62. Reported present Jan.–Feb./62 as a musician and trn to the bank 2/1/62. Regimental return of 2/62 lists him as trn 2/1. Reported present Mar.–Apr./62. Absent captured 6/29/62 per rolls of May–June/62. Exd 8/5/62 after being delivered 7/12/62. Reported as age 20, stoof 5'7¾", with red hair, dark eyes, light freckled complexion. Listed as AWOL, Sept.–Oct./62. Reported present 11/62–4/63, July–Aug./63. Per Federal records, captured near Culpeper, 9/13/63. Captured Sept.–Oct./63 and listed as a POW through 12/64. Prl 3/10/65. (CSR 270:8)

Rinehardt, Caleb Mark: B. Cabarrus Co. At age 18, enl. 6/15/61 as PVT, Co. F. Reported present, Nov.–Dec./61. Absent at a G.H. 2/29/62 per rolls of Jan.–Feb./62. Regimental return of 2/62 lists him as absent sick; returns of 3/62 list him as D. Lynchburg 3/8/62. Other records say he D. 3/7/62 or 5/7/62 in Lynchburg. D. of gastritis. (Mizelle; Barringer; Cabarrus; CSR 270:8; alternative spelling is Reinhardt; Barringer calls him Mark)

Ring, Jack: Was in state service before assigned by Col. Mallet to regiment. Enl. 9/25/63 as PVT, Co. G. Absent at a Richmond G.H. per rolls of Mar.–Apr./64. Absent sick at a Weldon G.H. per rolls of 4/30–8/31/64. Absent July–Oct./64 sick in a Richmond G.H. Admitted 8/15/64 to a Petersburg G.H. and trn 9/23/64 to Raleigh. Admitted 9/28/64 to a Raleigh G.H. with chronic rheumatism. Trn

10/28/64 to Greensboro from Winston. Reported absent sick in a Greensboro G.H. per company muster rolls of Nov.–Dec./64. (CSR 270:8)

Ritch, Philemon M.: From Mecklenburg Co. At age 21, enl. 6/15/61 as PVT, Co. F. Reported present Nov.–Dec./61. Absent at a G.H. 2/25/62 per rolls of Jan.–Feb./62. Absent sick per rgt returns of 2/62. Reported present May–June/62, Sept.–Dec./62. Absent in NC to procure a horse 8/27/63 per rolls of July–Aug./63. Reported present 9/63–12/64. WIA 12/3/64. Resident of Charlotte, circa 1893. (Mizelle; Bounty Receipts; Barringer; CSR 270:8; name also spelled Philomon)

Ritch, Thomas L.: From Mecklenburg Co. At age 23, enl. 6/15/61 as PVT, Co. F. Absent on detached service, Nov.–Dec./61. Absent Jan.–Feb./62 as body guard of GEN Stuart, 11/7/61. Regimental return of 2/62 lists him as on detached service, and 3/62 lists him as on detached service 3/2/62. Reported present May–June/62. Absent with GEN Stuart, Sept.–Dec./62. Prm to courier for GEN Stuart. Absent as a courier 8/62–8/31/64. Reported present, Sept.–Dec./64. Resident of Charlotte, circa 1893. (Mizelle; Barringer; CSR 270:8)

Roan, William H.: From Northampton Co. At age 18, enl. 6/18/61 as PVT, Co. B. Reported present 11/61–12/61. D. 2/25/62 in camp per rolls of Jan.–Feb./62 and regimental returns of 2/62. D. Centerville. Per a sick and wounded report, D. 2/25 from typhoid fever. (CSR 270:8)

Roane, William H.: Resident of Macon Co. Enl. in state service as 2LT, Co. K. Enl. in Confederate service, 10/21/61. Reported present Nov.–Dec./62. Absent on recruiting service at Franklin, NC as of 2/3/62 per rolls of Jan.–Feb./62. Regimental returns of 2/62 list him as absent on recruiting service since 2/10 per special orders #10 dated 2/9/62. Rolls of 3/62 list him as present at Weldon. Reported present May–June/62, Sept.–Oct./62. Prm 1LT, 8/2/62. Absent 11/62–2/63 on detached service to buy a horse in western NC. Reported present Mar.–Apr./63 and reported as 1LT. Trn 6/13/63 from a Richmond G.H. to a Salisbury G.H. Absent sick July–Aug./63, 10/31/63–8/31/64. Resigned per rolls of Sept.–Oct./64. Resigned 6/28/64, 9/8/64, or 9/18/64 as 1LT, Co. K. Per 8/29/64, surgeon Wm. A. Blount certified Roane as permanently disabled. (CSR 270:1, 8)

Roaney, William: Cns. 9/21/64 as PVT, Co. H. Reported present Sept.–Oct./64. Absent on detached service with a horse detail, Nov.–Dec./64. (CSR 270:8)

Roark, William B.: B. Dec. 1835. From Ashe Co. Enl. 5/24/61 as PVT, Co. A. Absent at home sick per rolls of 11/61–2/62. Regimental return of 2/62 lists him as absent sick 12/11. Also reported absent sick at a G.H. 3/10/62. Reported present 9/62–4/63, 7/63–12/64. D. July 1907. Bur. Oakwood Cem., Raleigh. (Stepp; CSR 270:8; AsheCo spells last name as Roork)

Roberson, D.D.: Enl. 9/21/64 as PVT, Co. E. Reported present, 4/30–10/64. Absent at a Bellfield, VA G.H., Nov.–Dec./64. (CSR 270:8)

Roberson, J.W.: PVT, Co. A. (AsheCo)

Roberson, Jasper: From Watauga Co. At age 20, enl. 5/11/62 as PVT, Co. D. D. of disease. NFR. (CSR 270:8)

Roberts, Charles M.: Resident of Granville Co. At age 25, enl. 8/3/61 as PVT, Co. E. Prm CPL 10/10/61. Prm 1SGT 12/62. Reported present Jan.–Feb./62. Absent sent to a hospital sick 3/15/62 per rolls of May–June/62. Regimental return of 3/62 lists him as sick in a Petersburg G.H., 3/15/62. Reported present, Sept.–Oct./62. Absent on detached service, Nov.–Dec./62. Absent Jan.–Feb./63 on detached service sent to NC after a horse, 2/63. Reported present Mar.–Apr./63. Horse KIA Gettysburg, 7/3/63. Absent July–Aug./63 in NC to procure a horse, 8/27/63. Reported present 6/30/63–4/64. Rolls of 4/30/64–8/31/64 list him as prm 2LT, Co. B. Commissioned 2LT, 4/14/64. Absent sick on company muster rolls of 4/30/64–10/64. Admitted to a Richmond G.H., 6/4/64. Admitted 6/5/64 to a Richmond G.H. Admitted 6/17/64 with diarrhea to a Richmond G.H. Returned to duty 6/21. Not stated, Nov.–Dec./64. WIA 8/15 along Charles City Rd., near Richmond. Right leg amputated at thigh, 8/15/64. Admitted to a Richmond G.H., 8/16/64. Right leg amputated. Frl. 9/9/64 or 9/13/64. 60 day frl to residence in Williamsboro, NC. (CSR 270:1; Medical History 11: 328; Richmond *Sentinel*, 8/26/64; CSR 270:8)

Roberts, Gaines W.: From Buncombe Co. At age 49, enl. 3/12/62 as PVT, Co. G. Reported present May–June/62. Absent on detached service at Winchester, Sept.–Oct./62. Reported present, Nov.–Dec./62. Absent detailed to NC, Jan.–Feb./63. Reported present Mar.–Apr./63, July–Dec./63, 4/1/64. Reported AWOL and deserted on rolls of Mar.–Dec./64. (CSR 270:8)

Roberts, John E.: PVT, Co. D. Captured Loudoun Co., 3/25/64. Per Federal records, captured 3/24/64 at Edward's Ferry, a deserter. D. 6/24/64 at Richmond according to a register of killed and wounded. Another report says D. 6/25/64 from a gunshot wound. (CSR 270:8)

Roberts, John E.: Resident of Cleveland Co. Cns 10/3/64 as PVT, Co. I. Reported present Sept.–Oct./64. Absent on frl, 12/15/64. Captured at Amelia C.H., 4/3/65, and released 6/19/65 on taking the oath. Had a light complexion, light hair, gray eyes, and stood 5' 6½". (CSR 270:8)

Robertson, J.M.: From Warren Co. At age 26, enl. 6/14 or 6/18/61 as PVT, Co. E. Reported present Jan.–Feb./62, May–June/62, Sept.–Oct./62, 11/62–4/63. Absent on detached service to procure a horse in NC, 8/27/63. Reported present 6/30–10/31/63. Absent as a POW at Locust Grove 11/27, 11/28, or 11/29/63, per rolls of 11/63–4/64. Per Federal records, captured 11/28/63 at Mine Run. Absent on detached service at Stony Creek, VA per rolls of 4/30–10/64. Absent Nov.–Dec./64 in NC on horse detail. (CSR 270:8)

Robertson, John W.: From Ashe Co. Enl. 2/27/62 as PVT, Co. A. Absent left sick near Warrenton on 8/30/62 per rolls of Sept.–Oct./62. Absent sick Nov.–Dec./62. Absent sick at a G.H., Jan.–Feb./63. Per rolls of Mar.–Apr./63, D. 3/1 Marion, VA. Other records state he D. 3/25/63 or disease. (CSR 270:8)

Robinson, William F.: From Montgomery Co. Cns. 7/28/62 as PVT, Co. F. Reported present, Sept.–Dec./62. Absent on horse detail, Jan.–Feb./63. Reported present Mar.–Apr./63, 7/63–2/64. Absent on frl, 4/1/64. Reported present Mar.–Apr./64, 4/30–12/64. WIA. NFR. (CSR 270:8)

Robson, George M.: From Mecklenburg Co. At age 40, enl. 3/15/62 as PVT, Co. C. Reported present 5/62–10/31/62. Absent scouting 12/25 per rolls of Nov.–Dec./62. Reported present Jan.–Apr./63, 7/63–12/64. Prm 2SGT per rolls of Sept.–Oct./64. Captured at Amelia CH, 4/6/65. Released on oath but also listed as ill, 6/4/65. (Alexander; CSR 270:8)

Rochelle, Quincy V.B.: Resident of Angola, NC. From New Hanover Co. At age 27, enl. 6/24/61 as PVT, Co. I. Reported present Nov.–Dec./61. Admitted 12/17/61 to a Danville G.H. and sent to Richmond. Absent sick at home, having left camp 12/20/61, per rolls of Jan.–Feb./62. Regimental return of 2/62 lists him as absent sick, while 3/62 return lists him sick at home as of 1/6/62. Reported present May–June/62, 9/62–4/63, 10/31/63. Absent WIA 11/27/63 near Plank Road and Orange Co Hospital Road per rolls of 1/1/64. Frl 1/5/64 for 60 days due to a shell wound under the ball of the right great toe received 11/27/63. Absent 12/64. Retired to Invalid Corps, 1/19/65, to Raleigh. (CSR 270:8)

Rodgers, Thomas D.: From Macon Co. Enl. 3/5/62 as PVT, Co. K. Reported present, May–June/62. Absent sick at Winchester, Sept.–Oct./62. Absent sick 11/12/62 at a G.H., 11/12/62 per rolls of Nov.–Dec./62. Per rolls of Jan.–Feb./63, D. 11/24/62 at a Gordonsville G.H. D. of disease. D. of typhoid fever, 11/24/62, at a Gordonsville G.H., per sick and wounded report. However, also listed on a register of a Wilmington G.H., 10/24/64, with debilitas. (CSR 270:8)

Rodgers, Woodson M.: From Catawba Co. At age 22, enl. 3/21/62 as PVT, Co. F. Reported present May–June/62, 9/62–12/62, July–Aug./63. Absent MIA 9/22/63 per rolls of Sept.–Oct./63. Captured at Jack's Shop. Reported present Nov.–Dec./64 but also reported as prl 3/10/65. (CSR 270:8)

Rodwell, T.D.: Enl. 10/25/64 as PVT, Co. E. Absent in NC on a horse detail per rolls of Nov.–Dec./64. (CSR 270:8)

Rogers, J.S.: From Macon Co., age 22. PVT, Co. K. Rejected by COL Baker. (CSR 270:8)

Rogers, James M.: Enl. 6/15/63 or 9/29/63 as PVT, Co. F. Captured at Jack's Shop, 11/63. Reported present, Sept.–Oct./64. (Barringer; CSR 270:8; name in records also spelled Rodgers)

Rogers, James M.: B. 5/8/24. Enl. 10/9/64 as PVT, Co. F. Reported present, Nov.–Dec./64. Resident of Rowan Co, circa 1893. D. 1/23/00. Bur. Shiloh Methodist Church Cem., Cabarrus Co. (Barringer; Graves; CSR 270:8)

Rogers, Joe W.: Enl. 10/1/64 as PVT, Co. F. Reported present, Nov.–Dec./64. KIA Chamberlain's Run, 3/65. (Barringer; CSR 270:8)

Rogers, John H.: From Macon Co. At age 24, enl. 3/5/62 as PVT, Co. K. Reported present, May–June/62. Absent on wagon guard at Winchester per rolls of Sept.–Oct./62. Reported present, Nov.–Dec./62. Absent on detached service to guard baggage at Gordonsville, Jan.–Feb./63. Reported present, Mar.–Apr./63. Absent July–Aug./63 detached to buy a horse in NC. Absent on detached service 10/31/63, 11/63–3/31/64. Reported present, Mar.–Dec./64. (CSR 270:8)

Roland, Abner: From Watauga Co. Enl. 5/11/62 as PVT, Co. D. On a payroll receipt of 11/28/61, but also reported as D. in Petersburg, 11/61. (Davis; CSR 270:8; alternate name spellings Rolland and Rowland, and middle initial either B or S)

Rominger, E.A.: B. Forsyth Co. Farmer. Trn from Mallet's Bn. At age 43, enl. 9/25/63 as PVT, Co. G. Reported present, Mar.–Oct./64. Rolls of Nov.–Dec./64 list him as absent to bale forage in

NC. Had gray eyes, black hair, a dark complexion, and stood 5'10". (CSR 270:8)

Rose, E.D.: From Northampton Co. At age 20, enl. 4/20/62 as PVT, Co. B. Reported present 9/62–4/63. Absent sick at a Staunton G.H. 6/15 per rolls of July–Aug./63. Reported present 6/30–12/63, Mar.–Apr./64, 4/1/64. Absent on a forage detail 4/30–12/64. Admitted 8/15/64 to a Richmond G.H. Returned to duty 9/14/64. (CSR 270:8)

Rose, Jacob M.: From Jackson Co. At age 21, enl. 6/25/61 as PVT. Prm CPL. Reported present 11/61–2/62, May–June/62, 9/62–4/63, July–Aug./63. Rolls of 10/31/63 list him as on detached service. Rolls of Nov.–Dec./63 list him as a SGT and absent recruiting service. Also absent on detached service Jan.–Mar./64. Reported AWOL, Mar.–Dec./64. Reduced to PVT, 10/1/64. (CSR 270:8)

Rose, James T.: Cns 7/15/62 as PVT, Co. H. Reported present 11/62–4/63, July–Oct./63. Rolls of Nov.–Dec./63 list him as KIA 11/29/63. Also reported absent on detached service at Winchester, Sept.–Oct./64. (CSR 270:8)

Rose, L. Rowan: From Cabarrus Co. At age 33, enl. 5/15/63 as PVT, Co. F. Reported present July–Aug./63. Rolls of Sept.–Oct./63 list him as appointed hospital steward 10/7/63. Reported present 6/30/63–12/63, 4/1/64, Mar.–Dec./64. Prl Salisbury, 1865. Resident of Mt. Pleasant, NC, circa 1893. (CSR 270:8; Cabarrus; Barringer lists him as D.L. Rose)

Rose, Nathan: From Northampton Co. At age 25, enl. 6/18/61 as PVT, Co. B.D. 11/22/61 at Camp W.S. Ashe. D. 12/61 at Manassas. Per a sick and wounded report, D. from meningitis at Camp Ashe 11/18/61. (CSR 270:8)

Rose, Quilla L.: From Macon Co. Age 18. PVT, Co. K. Rejected by COL Baker. (CSR 270:8)

Rose, Robert: Enl. 9/18/63 as PVT, Co. F. Per rolls of Mar.–Apr./64, in a G.H. as of 6/12/64. Rolls of Sept.–Oct./64 list him as in a G.H. as of 6/12/64. Admitted 6/30/64 to a Richmond G.H. Returned to duty, 11/5/61. Reported present on rolls of Nov.–Dec./64. Prl Salisbury, 1865. Dead as of 1893. (Barringer; CSR 270:8)

Rosier, Q.: PVT, Co. I. Admitted 12/17/61 to a Richmond G.H., and trn to Petersburg 12/19/61. (CSR 270:8; cards incorrectly filed with Quilla L. Rosier)

Ross, Allen: Cns. 3/9/64 as PVT, Co. I. Rolls of Mar.–Apr./64 list him as on detached service to remount horse, 9/6/64. Admitted 5/25/64 to a Richmond G.H. Reported present 4/31–8/31/64. Rolls of Sept.–Oct./64 list him as absent on detached service 10/7/64 on guard duty at the Commissary HQ. (CSR 270:8)

Rouse, John L.: From Wayne Co. Age 17 at enl. PVT, Co. H. Dsh for disability. (CSR 270:8)

Rowles, Marshall: From Chatham Co. At age 22, enl. 6/25/61 as PVT, Co. H. Reported present 11/61–2/62. Regimental return of 3/62 lists him as on extra duty as a teamster. Reported present, May–June/62. Absent on detached service as a shoemaker at Winchester, Sept.–Oct./62. Reported present, Nov.–Dec./62. Absent to procure a horse, Jan.–Feb./63. Reported present, Mar.–Apr./63. Absent on detached service in NC to procure a horse, July–Aug./63. AWOL per rolls of Sept.–Oct./63. Reported present, Nov.–Dec./63. Absent on detached service with unserviceable horses, Jan.–Feb./64, 4/1/64. Absent on detached service as a teamster at Lynchburg, Mar.–Apr./64. Absent on detached service to procure a horse, 4/30–8/31/64. Reported present, Sept.–Oct./64. Absent as a POW, 12/10/64. Captured 12/10/64 at Armstrong's Mills. Released 5/13/65. (CSR 270:8)

Royal, Thomas: From Ashe Co. At age 21, enl. 6/13/61 as PVT, Co. A. Absent 11/61–2/62 at a Manassas G.H. Admitted 1/1/62 to a Danville G.H. with rheumatism. Regimental returns of 2/62 lists him as absent sick as of 2/24. 3/62 returns report him absent sick in a G.H. as of 3/10/62. Reported present 9/62–4/63. Absent on detached service to buy a horse, July–Aug./63. Reported present, 9/63–2/29/64, 4/1/64. Absent on detached service in NC, Mar.–Apr./64. Reported present, July–Dec./64. (AsheCo; CSR 270:8)

Royster, H.T.: From Warren Co. At age 22, enl. 9/22/61 as PVT, Co. E. Absent on detached service recruiting, 2/5/62, per rolls of Jan.–Feb./62. Regimental return of 2/62 lists him as on detached service. Reported present May–June/62 and prm from CPL to 5SGT, 6/7/62. Reported present as 4SGT, Sept.–Oct./62. Absent on detached service as 3SGT, Nov.–Dec./62. Prl 11/9/62. On the register of the Williamsburg G.H. as admitted 12/19/62 with intermittent fever and "sent to guard house" 12/17/62. Absent Jan.–Feb./63 on detached service in NC to procure a horse, Jan.–Feb./63. Reported present, Mar.–Apr./63. Absent on detached service in NC to procure a horse as a 2SGT as of 8/27/63 per rolls of July–Aug./63. Horse KIA at Brandy Station and appraised for $550. Reported present 6/30/63–2/64 and listed Jan.–Feb./64 as 3SGT. Absent 4/1/64 on provost duty at Bowling

Green. Absent Mar.–Apr./64 on detached service on a fishing detail. Reported present, 4/30–10/64, and listed as a PVT on rolls of Sept.–Oct./64. Absent in NC on a horse detail, Nov.–Dec./64. (CSR 270:8)

Royster, Iowa M.: From Wake Co. At age 22, enl. 3/13/62 as PVT or SGT, Co. E. Later listed as SGT. Reported present, May–June/62, 9/62–4/63. Prm 2LT, Co. G, 37th NC Infantry. (CSR 270:8)

Rudd, Thomas H.: Cns. 4/10/64 as PVT, Co. H. Absent sick 4/30–8/31/64, Sept.–Dec./64. Trn to Co. B, 34th NC Infantry, 1/24/65. (CSR 270:8)

Ruffin, Etheldred F.: B. in Franklin Co. Dred for short. Farmer. At age 31, enl. 6/23/61 as PVT, Co. H. Later prm Ordinance SGT. Absent sick per rolls of Nov.–Dec./61. Rolls of Jan.–Feb./62 list him as being at home on sick frl since 11/27/61. absent sick per regimental returns of 2/62. Returns of 3/62 lists him as on sick frl since 11/27/61. Absent sent to a Goldsboro G.H. 4/15, 4/19, or 4/24/62, per rolls of May–June/62, 9/62–12/63. Dsh. Admitted 1/19/64 to a Richmond G.H. Dsh due to disability, 2/4/64, with rheumatism and joint and stomach problems. Stood 6' 3" tall, had a fair complexion, black eyes and hair. (Pearce: 283; CSR 270:8)

Ruffin, Thomas C.: B. 9/9/20. From Wayne Co. At age 40, enl. 5/16/61 as CAPT, Co. F. Apptd CAPT, Co. F, 8/20/61. Reported present 11/61–2/62. Regimental rolls of 3/62 lists him as absent on recruiting service, 3/23/62. Rolls of May–June/62 lists him as absent after being captured at Willis Church, 6/28/62. POW records gives age as 41, height 6'1½" black eyes, black hair, florid complexion and B. in NC. Released for exchange, 7/31/62. Reported present, 9/62–4/63. Prm MAJ 6/29/63. Prm LTC, 7/23/63. Received sabre wound in head; admitted to G.H. #4, Richmond, 7/22/63. Frl. 7/29/63. Absent per rolls of July–Aug./63 sick in NC. Per report of 7/29/63, given leave. Per report of 9/14/63, leave extended. 10/3/62, detailed for court. Co. H. On a court of inquiry, 2/25/63. Prm COL 9/28/63. WIA and captured near Bristoe Station, 10/14/63. On a roll of POWs at 2d Division U.S. G.H. in Alexandria as captured 10/14/63 and received a gunshot wound in the scalp or head. Admitted 10/15/63 to an Alexandria, VA hospital. Admitted to 2d Division (U.S.) Hospital, Alexandria, VA. Hit in skull and remained conscious but delirious. D. 10/17/63 or 10/18/63. Per record of death and interment, bur. in a Citizens Cemetery, Alexandria. Later moved and bur. Oakwood Cem., Louisburg, NC. "He was beloved as a gallant and skillful officer [and] died in the hands of the enemy." (CSR 270:1, 8; *Medical History* 7: 12, 204; Stepp; *Raleigh Register*, 9/2/63)

Ruggles, Thomas C.: From New Hanover Co. At age 20, enl. 7/1/61 as PVT, Co. H. Absent sick at a Richmond G.H., Nov.–Dec./61. Sent to a Richmond G.H. 11/27/61 per rolls of Jan.–Feb./62. Admitted 11/29/61 with syphilis. Frl for 10 days in Feb. Regimental returns of 2/62 list him as absent sick; 3/62 as in a Richmond G.H. since 11/27/61. Reported present May–June/62, Sept.–Oct./62. D. 7/8/62 from disease. Per another report, admitted to Chimborazo G.H. in Richmond, 3/8/62, with typhoid fever. (CSR 270:8)

Russell, J.G.: From Macon Co. Age 17. PVT, Co. K. Rejected by COL Baker. (CSR 270:8)

Russell, Robert: Enl. 7/8 or 7/12/62 as PVT, Co. B. Reported present 11/62–4/63, 6/30/63–12/63, Mar.–Oct./64. Absent on forage detail per rolls of Nov.–Dec./64. Deserted, per a 3/4/65 list of deserters at Suffolk, VA. (Zeb. Vance Papers, NCSA [courtesy Whit Joyner]; CSR 270:8)

Russell, Willis: From Ashe Co. At age 33, enl. 5/25/61 as PVT, Co. A. Reported present, Nov.–Dec./61. Reported present Jan.–Feb./62 as company blacksmith. Reported present 9/62–4/63. Rolls of July–Aug./63 list him as deserted 8/25 or 8/26. On a Federal register of POWs received and disposed of by the Army of the Potomac's Provost Marshall dated 8/26/63; a deserter. Per Federal records, captured at Kelly's Ford, 8/26/63 and took the oath 9/27. Reported as a resident of Ashe, with dark complexion, black hair, blue eyes, and stood 6'1". Admitted 9/6/63 to a Washington, D.C. G.H. and released 9/20. Released and sent to Philadelphia, 9/28/63. (AsheCo; misfiled in Thomas C. Ruffin's file; CSR 270:8)

Ryan, David S.: From Warren Co. At age 21, enl. 6/25/61 as PVT, Co. H. Absent Nov.–Dec./61 on detached service. Absent Jan.–Feb./62 in Richmond was a telegraph operator since 11/27. Regimental returns of 2/62 list him on detached service; 3/62 list him on detached service sent to the Richmond telegraph office. Absent on detached service with the telegraph office, May–June/62, 9/62–2/63. Per rolls of Mar.–Apr./63, prm LT of 10th NC Bn. Also mentioned as dsh 11/62, but not likely. May have been on duty as assistant superintendent/military telegraphist with the Army of Tennessee when prl at Greensboro, 4/65. (CSR 270:8)

Safrit, Jackson: Enl. 2/14/64 as PVT, Co. F. Dead as of 1893. (Barringer)

Saine, Anderson: Enl. 9/6/64 as PVT, Co. K. Reported present, Sept.–Dec./64. (CSR 270:8)

Sanders, W.H.: From Mecklenburg Co. At age 20, enl. 7/25/61 as PVT, Co. C. Absent sick Nov.–Dec./61. Absent sick Jan.–Feb./62 since 10/31/61 in Mecklenburg Co. Regimental return of 2/62 lists him as absent sick. Reported present, May–June/62. Absent sick since 7/1/62 in Charlotte, NC 6/30–10/31/62. Reported present 11/61–4/63. Absent as a POW after being captured 7/3/63 per rolls of July–Aug./63 and following. Per Federal records, captured at Franklin, MD 7/3/63. Exd 3/3/64. Admitted 6/25/64 to a Richmond G.H. Admitted 8/15/64 to a Petersburg G.H. and returned to duty 9/5/64. Absent on detached service 10/14/64 per rolls of Sept.–Oct./64. Reported present, Nov.–Dec./64. Prl 5/18/65 at Greensboro. (Alexander; CSR 270:8)

Sandlin, William: Res. of Duplin Co. At age 25, enl. 6/25/61 as PVT, Co. I. Reported present, 11/61–2/62. Prm to CPL, 5/62. Reported present, May–June/62, although WIA 6/29/62. Reported present Sept.–Oct./62, Nov.–Dec./62. Absent on leave, Jan.–Feb./63. Reported present Mar.–Apr./63, 10/31/63, 1/64–8/31/64. Absent on detached service at Stony Creek, 10/18/64. Reported present, Nov.–Dec./64. Captured at Amelia C.H., 4/3/65. Released 6/20/65 on taking the oath. Listed as having a light complexion, brown hair, gray eyes, and stood 5'10". (CSR 270:8)

Sapp, J.S.: Res. of Forsyth Co. Trn from state service and assigned to the rgt by COL Mallett. Enl. 5/63 or 5/64 as PVT, Co. G. Absent at a Richmond G.H., Mar.–Apr./64. Absent sick at a Richmond G.H., 4/30–8/31/64. Admitted 8/15/64 to a Richmond G.H. Admitted 8/16/64 to a Richmond G.H. with a fever; returned to duty 10/6/64. Reported present, Sept.–Dec./64. Had a light complexion, "grayish" hair, hazel eyes, stood 5'7", Captured 4/3/65 at Aberdeen C.H. Released 6/20/65. (CSR 270:8)

Sapp, Thomas H.: From Cabarrus Co. At age 24, enl. 6/15/61 as PVT, Co. F. Reported present Nov.–Dec./61. Absent at a G.H., 2/25/62 per rolls of Jan.–Feb./62. Regimental return of 2/62 lists him as absent sick. Regimental return of 3/62 lists him as absent sick at a G.H. since 2/25/62. Reported present May–June/62, Sept.–Dec./62, 7/63–12/64. Dead as of 1893. (Mizelle; Barringer; Cabarrus)

Saudlin, Jesse: From Duplin Co. Age 20. Enl. 7/4/61 as PVT, Co. I. Rejected. (CSR 270:8)

Sauls, Henry J.: B. 1835. From Wayne Co. At age 26, enl. in Wayne Co. 6/25/61 as PVT, Co. H. Reported present 11/61–2/62, May–June/62, 9/62–4/63, 7/63–2/64. Prm CPL per rolls of Sept.–Oct./63 and prm 2CPL per rolls of Jan.–Feb./64. Absent on detached service, 4/1/64. Reported present, Mar.–Apr./64. Absent after being WIA per rolls of 4/30–8/31/64. Reported present, Sept.–Dec./64. Commissioned 2LT, 9/21/64. Elected and passed examining board, 11/64. On leave as of 1/15/65. Absent 1/21/65 per the Medical Examining Board Inspection Report dated 2/28/65. Reported in Kittrell Springs G.H., 4/7/65. D. 1902. Bur Eureka Methodist Churchyard, Eureka, NC. (CSR 270:1, 8; Monie; alternate spelling is Sausl; CGR: 3)

Sauls, James V.: From Northampton Co. Enl. 6/18/61 as PVT, Co. B. Reported present, 11/61–2/62. Absent sick per regimental return of 2/62. Absent sick at a Petersburg G.H. per regimental returns of 3/62. Absent at home sick per rolls of Mar.–Apr./62. Absent sent home from Weldon 4/1 per rolls of Sept.–Oct./62. Rolls of Nov.–Dec./62 report him AWOL. Prm 1LT, Wheeler's Bn., 9/62. (CSR 270:8)

Saunders, Peter: From Ashe Co. At age 20, enl. 5/23/61 as PVT, Co. A. Reported present, 11/61–2/62. Regimental returns of 3/62 list him with unserviceable horses. Absent on detached service as a shoemaker, 10/28 per rolls of Sept.–Oct./62. Reported present, Nov.–Dec./62. Absent on frl to buy a horse 2/27 per rolls of Jan.–Feb./63. Reported present Mar.–Apr./63. Absent sick July–Aug./63. Reported present Sept.–Dec./63. Rolls of 1/1–2/29/64 list him as deserted 1/18. (AsheCo; CSR 270:8)

Savage, William: From Buncombe Co. Age 25. PVT, Co. G. On a 5/16/61 court martial record. (CSR 270:8)

Scales, George B.: From Warren Co. At age 26, enl. 6/3/61 as PVT, Co. E. Reported present Jan.–Feb./62 and on extra duty as a teamster. Regimental returns of Mar.–62 and 3/62 list him as on extra duty as a teamster. Reported present May–June/62, Sept.–Oct./62, Nov.–Dec./62 and on extra duty as a teamster. Absent on frl Jan.–Feb./63. Reported present Mar.–Apr./63. Absent on G.H. 8/31/63 per rolls of July–Aug./63. Reported present 6/30–10/31/63 and on extra duty as an ambulance driver 10/30. Admitted 9/2/63 to a Richmond G.H. with a form of syphilis and returned to duty 10/10. Reported present Nov.–Dec./63 and on extra duty as a regimental wagoner. Absent on frl Jan.–Feb./64. Reported present, Mar.–Aug./64. Absent on extra duty as a teamster per rolls of Sept.–Oct./64. Absent Nov.–Dec./64 in NC driving a wagon. (CSR 270:8)

Scarborough, E.O.: From Duplin Co. At age 43, enl. 7/16/61 as PVT, Co. I. Rejected. (CSR 270:8)

Schneider, Gustaf H.: From Mecklenburg Co. At age 31, enl. 5/27/61 as PVT, Co. C or G. Reported present, 1–2/62. Regimental returns of 2/62 and 3/62 list him as on extra duty with the commissary dept. Reported present May–June/62, 6/30/62–4/63. Absent detached in NC to buy a horse 8/27/63 per rolls of July–Aug./63. Rolls of Sept.–Oct./63 list him as trn 10/9/63 to government works at Salisbury, NC. Detailed to work in government shops 10/9/63. Rolls of Nov.–Dec./64 list him as absent on detached service since 9/63. Admitted to a Charlotte G.H. 2/14/65 and returned to duty 2/8/65. Listed on a hospital muster roll or medical purveying dept., Charlotte, Nov.–Dec./63, Sept.–Oct./63, Jan.–Feb./64, Nov.–Dec./64, and assigned by surgeon gen., 10/9/63. Detailed in orders dated 10/9/63 and 11/18/64. (CSR 270:8; Alexander)

Scott, William R.: From Cabarrus Co., P.O. Mt. Pleasant. At age 32, enl. 6/15/61 as QM SGT, Co. F. Reported present Nov.–Dec./61. Absent on detached service 2/10/62 per rolls of Jan.–Feb./62. Regimental return of 2/62 lists him on detached service. 3/62 returns place him on recruiting service 2/10/62. Reported present and elected 2LT 9/10/62 per rolls of Sept.–Oct./62. Prm 2LT, 9/1/62. Reported present Nov.–Dec./62. Absent sick at Hanover Junction 8/8/63 per rolls of July–Oct./63. Absent at a Raleigh G.H. 8/8/63 per rolls of Nov.–Dec./63. Reported on leave, 9/15/63. Absent Jan.–Apr./64 detached as an enrolling/recruiting officer in Cabarrus, NC. Reported in Gaston Co., NC, 4/30–Dec./64. Leave extended, 2/26/64. Per 7/64 inspection report, on light duty as enrolling officer. Prm 1LT 8/3/64. Retired 3/13 or 4/13/65. Resident of Arkansas, circa 1893. (CSR 270:1, 8; Mizelle; Barringer; Cabarrus)

Seahome, A.C.: Cns. 12/29/64 as PVT, Co. I. Reported present Nov.–Dec./64. (CSR 270:8)

Seahorn, J.A.: Enl. 6/15/63 as PVT, Co. F. Dsh. (Barringer)

Segle, Lewis M.: From Buncombe Co. Enl. 5/20/61 as PVT, Co. G. Reported present Jan.–Feb./62, May–June/62, Sept.–Dec./62, Jan.–Apr./63. Absent WIA 8/1/63 at Brandy Station and sent to Hanover C.H. per rolls of July–Aug./63. Absent at home on frl after being WIA at home per rolls of Sept.–Dec./63. Admitted 8/2/63 to a Richmond G.H. AWOL Jan.–Feb./64. Absent on detached service 4/1/64. Admitted 5/5/64 to a Richmond G.H. after being WIA with a minie ball wound to the right arm and/or shoulder. Returned to duty, 6/14/64. Reported present 5/7/64 as a convalescent, serving as a nurse at a Richmond G.H. Reported present Mar.–Aug./64. Absent on detached service to buy a horse Sept.–Oct./64. Reported present, Nov.–Dec./64. (CSR 270:8)

Setzer, Frank: Co. D (Davis)

Sevard, Henry: From Ashe Co. At age 31, enl. 5/23/61 as PVT, Co. A. Per company rolls of Nov.–Dec./61, D. 12/1 at Camp W.S. Ashe. Other reports list him as D. 11/28/62 of disease. On a sick and wounded report as D. 12/1/61 at Camp Ashe from typhoid fever. (AsheCo — spells as Severt; CSR 270:8)

Shackleford, John M.: B. 1827. From Buncombe Co. Enl. 3/1/62 as PVT, Co. G, at age 35. D. from disease in a Goldsboro, NC hospital, 5/5/62. Bur. Willowdale Cem., Goldsboro. (CSR 270:9; Stepp)

Sharpe, James B.: Enl. 5/10/64 as PVT in Co. A. Present July–Dec./64. Name appears on a clothing receipt roll, 7/15/64 and 9/15/64. Prl. Appomattox, Va., 4/9/64. (CSR 270:9; AsheCo)

Shaver, Ed W.: Enl. 10/1/64 as PVT, Co. F. Captured at Burgess Mill, 10/9/64. Resident of Salisbury, circa 1893. (Barringer)

Shaver, Ervin: Enl. 10/1/64 in Co. F. PVT. Captured 10/27/64, Plank Road, Va. Sent to Point Lookout. Released on taking Oath of Allegiance, 12/3/64. (CSR 270:9)

Shaw, Robert J.: Resident of Franklin Co., N.C. At age 28, enl. 5/16/61 in Co. E. 1LT; served as acting AQM. Detached on recruiting service, 2/5/62. Present 3/62. Reported in Raleigh settling accounts with quartermaster department, beginning 5/25/62. Sick at home, Sept.–Oct./62. Resigned 12/5/62, and died soon thereafter. (CSR 270:1,9; Pearce: 6, 13, 284)

Shearer, Thomas H.: Residence, Watauga Co., N.C. At age 24, enl. 5/11/61 in Co. D. PVT. Present Nov.–Dec./61, Jan.–Feb./62. Reported in Lynchburg hospital, 2/24/62. Adm. To G.H. #5, Richmond, with rheumatism, and returned to duty 3/27/62. D. 5/4/62 in a Petersburg hospital from disease. (CSR 270:9; Davis)

Sherrill, Alfred R.: CNS 9/21/64 into Co. H. PVT. Present through 12/64. (CSR 270:9)

Shields, Andrew J.: From Macon Co., N.C. At age 43, enl. 6/25/61 as PVT in Co. K. Present Nov.–Dec./61. 1/1/62, prm. Farrier. Present Jan.–

Feb./62, May–June/62. Detached to guard baggage at Manchester, Sept.–Dec./62. Went home to buy a horse, Jan.–Feb./63. Absent sick at home, Mar.–Apr./63. Reported present July–Aug./63, Nov.–Dec./63. On detached service recruiting horses, Jan.–Feb./64; also detached Feb.–Mar./64. Dsh 7/25/64 due to age. (CSR 270:9)

Shields, Ashbel: From Macon Co., N.C. At age 17, enl. 4/5/62 in Co. K. PVT. Present May–June/62, 9/62–4/63. Absent sick in a hospital, July–Aug./63. Received at Richmond's G.H. #9, 11/10/63. Present 10/31/63, 11/63–3/64. AWOL Apr.–Aug./64. Absent sick Nov.–Dec./64. (CSR 270:9)

Shields, William W.: Enl. at age 22 6/25/61 in Co. K. PVT. Adm. to G.H. #1, Richmond with Rubeola, 11/3/61; adm. 12/9/61 and released 12/17/61 from Petersburg hospital. Reported present 11/61–2/62, May–June/62, 9/62–4/63. Detached to buy horse in N.C., July–Aug./63; on detached service, 10/31/63–3/31/64. Present 3/64–10/31/64, but also reported absent sick Sept.–Oct./64. Present Nov.–Dec./64, although reported in a Richmond hospital 11/18/64. (CSR 270:9)

Shipman, J.A.: From Henderson Co., N.C., age 18. Enl. 5/20/61 as PVT in Co. G. Name appears on a clothing receipt, 11/28/61. Reported present Jan.–Feb./62, May–June/, Sept.–Oct./62. Absent on detached service, Nov.–Dec./62. Present Jan.–Apr./63. WIA 7/15/63 or 7/19/63 at Martinsburg, Va. D. 7/22/63 or 8/22/63. (CSR 270:9)

Shipman, J.K.P.: From Buncombe Co., N.C. At age 16, enl. 5/20/61 in Co. G. CPL, SGT. Present Jan.–Mar./62. Apr.–June/62, at home on sick frl. Reported Sept.–Oct./62. Absent on detached service, Nov.–Dec./62. Present Jan.–Apr./63, July–Aug./63. Captured 9/22/63 at Jack's Shop, Va. Sent to Pt. Lookout, via Old Capitol Prison. Trn Elmira, 8/64. D. 10/22/64, from chronic diarrhea. Buried at Pt. Lookout. (CSR 270:9; PL: 163)

Shook, F.R.: Enl. 9/21/64 in Co. H. PVT. Present Sept.–Oct./64. Absent on horse detail, Nov.–Dec./64. According to records of the 10th Mich. probably prl. 4/19/65, Newton, N.C. (CSR 270:9)

Shull, Noah J.: Age 21, from Watauga Co. Enl. 7/10/61, Co. D. PVT, SGT. Name appears on a clothing roll, 11/28/61. Reported present Nov.–Dec./61, Jan.–Feb./62, May–June/62. Captured in Md., 9/13/62. Reported present 1/63–4/63, 6/30–10/31/63. Horse KIA, Monterey, PA 7/4/63. Prm. To CPL by 2/63, SGT by 10/63. Captured 11/28/63, Mine Run, Va. Sent to Pt. Lookout; exd 2/24/65. (CSR 270:9; Davis; CSR 270: 4 for George N. Folk)

Sides, Mathias: Residence, Stanley Co., N.C. At age 39, enl. 3/20/62 as PVT, Co. I. Reported present May–June/62, Sept.–Dec./62. Absent sick Jan.–Feb./63. Present Mar.–Apr./63, but reported in a Staunton Hospital with pneumonia 3/15/63 and 4/7/63 and noted as "improving." Present 10/31/63, 1/1/64–12/64. On detached service in N.C. 12/28/64, "baling forage." (CSR 270:9)

Sides, Reuben A.: From Rowan Co., N.C., where he was a farmer. At age 21, enl. 6/15/61 as PVT in Co. F. Reported present 11/61–2/62. Name appears on a clothing receipt roll, 11/28/61. Admitted to a Danville G.H., 1/16/62, with erysipelas; later sent to Front Royal. Dsh 5/1/62 due to arm being in a "swollen and sensitive" condition from erysipelas. Stood 5'6", had a fair complexion, blue eyes, and sandy hair. (CSR 270:9; Barringer; Mizelle; Bounty Receipts; Rumple: 343)

Siler, James W.: From Macon Co., N.C. At age 23, enl. 7/14/61 as PVT in Co. K. Reported present 11/61–2/62. D. of disease, 4/8/62 in Petersburg. (CSR 270:9)

Siler, Jesse W.: Co. K. Reported present May–June/, Sept.–Oct./62. Elected 5/4/62 and prm to 2LT 8/2/62. KIA Gaines Crossroads, 11/7/62, and his men wept at the sight of his body lying in the snow. (CSR 270:1, 9; Rea, 61, Macon Heritage, 49.)

Siler, Thaddeus P.: From Macon Co. Enl. 5/16/61 in Co. K. CPT, Co. K commanding officer, to rank from 5/16/61. Reported present Nov.–Dec./61, Jan.–Feb./62. Absent on scouting service, 3/23/62. Present May–June/62. Captured Boonsboro, MD, 9/13/62. Prb. WIA. Exd. 10/18/62. Reported in Petersburg G.H., 12/10/62, and frl. 40 days beginning 12/18/62. Resigned and trn to 7th Bn. NC Cavalry, which later became the 6th NC Cavalry. D. mid-1890s in Macon Co. (CSR 270:1, 9; 6th NC: 56, 92, 98, 169)

Siler, Thomas Summerfield: Macon Co., N.C. resident and farmer. At age 27, enl. 7/4/61. SGT, Co. K. Reported present Nov.–Dec./61, May–June/62. Absent sick beginning 2/11/62, with acute rheumatism. Dsh at Harrison C.H., 8/17/62, from rheumatism, dyspepsia, and chronic diarrhea. Stood 6'2¾", red complexion, blue eyes, red hair. (CSR 270:9)

Siler, William Theodore: Macon Co., N.C. resident. At age 24, enl. 7/4/61 in Co. K. SGT, QM SGT. Reported present 11/61–2/62. Adm.to a G.H. 3/6/62. Present May–June/62. D. 8/10/62 or 8/15/62 of disease. (CSR 270:9)

Siler, Willie P.: From Macon Co., N.C. Enl. at

age 17 6/18/63 as PVT, Co. K. Reported present 10/31/63, 11/63–12/64. Name appears on clothing receipts for 2d and 3d quarters of 1864. Prl. Charlotte, N.C. 5/30/65. (CSR 270:9)

Simmer, H.H.: D. 10/16/62. Bur. NC Plat, Stonewall Cem., Winchester, VA. (Stonewall)

Simmonds, Thomas J.: Macon Co., N.C. resident, age 24. Enl. 6/25/61 as PVT in Co. K. Reported present 11/61–2/62, May–June/62, 9/62–4/63. On detached service July–Aug./63. Captured Cedar Run, Va., 5/30/63 by Michigan cavalry. Stood 6'2", with dark complexion and hair and blue eyes. Trn. Co. H. 16Th N.C. 10/16/63. Reported on ordnance duty in Cheatham's Division at Dalton, Ga., 12/15/63. (CSR 270:9)

Simmonds, William R.: Resident of Macon Co., N.C. Enl. 3/11/62 as PVT in Co. K. Reported present May–June/62. Guarding baggage at Winchester, Sept.–Oct./62. Reported present Nov.–Dec./62. On detached service in N.C. in search of horses, Jan.–Feb./63. Guarding baggage at Gordonsville, Mar.–Apr./63. Captured Cedar Run, Va., 5/30/63 by 7th Mich. Cav. Dark complexion, gray hair, blue eyes. Absent sick 10/31/63–2/64. Reported present 2/29–3/31/64. On detached service Mar.–Apr./64. 4/30–Dec./64, reported herding cattle for the commissary dpt. (CSR 270:9)

Simmons, James H.: Enl. At Camp Holmes, 11/21/64. PVT, Co. K. Present Nov.–Dec./64. (CSR 270:9)

Simms, John M.: Resident of Ridgeway, N.C. Cns. 3/13/64 as PVT, Co. E. Reported present Mar.–Oct./64, although adm. to Richmond G.H. 5/13 or 5/28/64 and frl. 6/17 or 6/19/64 with a problem in the forearm or wrist. Name appears on clothing roll, 4/20/64. (CSR 270:9)

Simpler, Owen: Enl. Co. B. 3/29/62 as PVT. Deserted 4/13/62. (CSR 270:9)

Sims, J.S.: Polk Co., N.C. resident. Trn. From 16th N.C. 2/10/62 as PVT in Co. G. 3/64–10/64 on sick frl. Reported present Nov.–Dec./64. At age 25, WIA 4/9/65 at Appomattox C.H., Va.; gunshot fractured right humerus just above elbow joint. Captured; listed at age 43. Portion of right arm amputated, 4/9/65 or 4/10/65. Released, 6/10/65. Sent to City Point, Va., then Washington, D.C. Took Oath of Allegiance 6/12/65 and released 6/14/65. Had fair complexion, light hair, blue eyes. (CSR 270:9; *Medical History* 10: 731)

Sippard, _____. R.: Co. D. Retired 6/16/63. (CSR 270:1)

Sitrewalt, T.L.: Enl. 10/4/64 as PVT, Co. F. Resident of Rowan Co., circa 1893. (Barringer)

Sitzer, Frank: Enl. 10/6/63 as PVT in Co. D. Reported present 8/31/64. Absent on horse detail, Sept.–Oct./64. Present Nov.–Dec./64. On payment rolls, 7/15/64 and 9/25/64. (CSR 270:9)

Slagle, Sidney R.: Macon Co., N.C. resident. At age 24, enl. 7/4/61 in Co. K. PVT, saddler. Reported present Nov.–Dec./61. Absent on recruiting service, 2/11/62. Present May–June/62. Absent shoe making at Winchester, Va., Sept.–Oct./62. Reported present Nov.–Dec./62. On detached service making shoes, Jan.–Feb./63. Present Mar.–Apr./63, July–Aug./63. Reported MIA 10/31/63, after being captured 10/14/64 at Catlett's Station, Va. Sent to Old Capitol Prison and then Pt. Lookout. Exd. 3/14/65. (CSR 270:9)

Sloan, Edwin R.: Cabarrus Co., N.C. resident. Enl. 6/15/61 as PVT in Co. F. at age 26. Reported present 11/61–2/62. On extra duty as teamster in 2/62. Present May–June/62, Sept.–Dec./62, July–Aug./63. KIA near Raccoon Ford/Culpeper C.H., Va., 9/13/63. (CSR 270:9; Mizelle; Barringer; Cabarrus)

Sloan, James McKnight: B. Cabarrus Co., N.C. Enl. 6/15/61 at age 18 in Co. F as PVT. Reported present Nov.–Dec./61, Jan.–Feb./62, May–June/62, Sept.–Dec./62. Prm to scout for Hampton. Sent on scout into Fauquier Co., Va. 8/1/63. Present 7/63, 9/63. Scouting again in Fauquier, 10/27/63 and 12/18/63. Detached there as independent scout, 1/1/63. Captured Catlett's Station, 6/9/63, and held in Old Capitol Prison. Escaped from Point Lookout, 9/4/63. Absent 1/64–3/31/64. On detached service in NC 3/31/64–8/10/64 to buy a horse. Detached as a scout in U.S. lines, 9/23/64–12/64. Late in the war captured in Fredericksburg along with another scout and sent by water to a guard boat near Fort Monroe; escaped, and went on to ambush and kill 19 Yankees while on the way back to their lines. Had light complexion, gray eyes, brown hair. Surrendered at Greensboro, NC, 4/20/65. Moved to TX in October 1883, and became a Dallas resident in 1908, where he worked as a teamster. D. 3/9/1920 of complications from hepatitis at the Dallas home of his daughter. Bur. Grone? Hill Cem., Dallas. (CSR 270:9; Mizelle; Bounty Receipts; Barringer; Cabarrus; *Land We Love* 3: 350 calls him "Swan," but 4: 164 corrects it; Soldier's Application for a Pension, 8/30/1913, Texas State Archives, courtesy of Horace Mewborn; Pension file says enl 4/61, but statement of EL Bell in file says June 1861)

Slocumb, Thomas W.: From Craven Co., N.C. Enl. 4/21/63 as PVT in Co. H. Reported present

4/63. Adm. To G.H. #9, 8/5/63. 3/64–4/64, reported on sick frl. On light duty on detached service in Goldsboro, N.C. as of 4/1/64, then 4/30–12/64. Dsh 12/21/64 and prm AAG of N.C., to rank from 11/27/64. (CSR 270:9)

Smiley, John: Resident of Macon Co., N.C., age 17. PVT, Co. K. Rejected by Col. Baker. (CSR 270:9)

Smith, A.S.: From Rutherford Co., N.C. At age 19, enl. 5/20/61 as PVT in Co. G. Reported present Jan.–Feb./62, May–June/62. Absent sick in Richmond, Sept.–Dec./62, having been admitted to G.H. #2, 9/9/62. Present 1/63–4/63; 2/63–10/63. Trn to Co. B, 6th Rgt. NC Troops. (CSR 270:9)

Smith, A.W.: Enl. 6/10/61 as PVT in Co. E. Absent Jan.–Feb./62, and sent to Manassas hospital 2/26/62 "indefinitely;" adm. 3/2/62 to G.H. #18 in Richmond "indefinitely" with a case of jaundice. Returned to duty 3/8/62. D. at home of dysentery, 7/6/62. (CSR 270:9)

Smith, Ahaseurus: Resident of Duplin Co., N.C. At age 23, enl. 7/14/61 as PVT in Co. I. Reported present 11/61–2/62. D. 4/9/62 at Kinston, N.C. Family collected $134.00 in back pay, 9/63. (CSR 270:9)

Smith, Alfred: Resident of Duplin Co., N.C., and Ahaseurus Smith's brother. Enl. 6/20/61 as PVT in Co. I. D. 11/22/61 in Petersburg, Va. (CSR 270:9)

Smith, Andrew J.: Resident of Duplin Co., N.C. Enl. in Co. I, 6/25/61. Age 21. PVT, CPL. Reported present 11/61–2/62; May–June/62; Sept.–Oct./62, Mar.–Apr./63, 10/31/63, and 1/1/64. Absent on detached service 11/62–2/63, and again absent, taking care of cattle, 1/20/64–2/64. Reported present 3/64–12/64. (CSR 270:9)

Smith, B.: SGT. According to unclear POW records, captured 6/28/62 near Richmond and sent to Ft. Delaware, 7/9/62. However, *Asheville News* account of Willis Church battle lists a SGT Z. Smith as captured at Willis Church on 6/29/62. NFR. (CSR 270:9; *Asheville News*, July 24, 1862)

Smith, Benjamin Franklin: B. 6/1/39. From Duplin Co. Enl. 6/17/61 as PVT, Co. I. Reported present on company muster rolls of 11/61–2/62; May–June/62; Sept.–Dec./62. Absent on detached service Jan.–Feb./63. Reported present 3/63–4/63, 10/31/63, Jan.–Aug./31/64. Absent on detached service at Stony Creek, Va., 10/18/64 and 12/8/64 to mount fresh horses. D. 8/24/21. Bur. B.F. Smith Cem., along NC 111 in Duplin Co. (CSR 270:9; Stepp)

Smith, Caleb Franklin: B. 12/6/45 (?). Resident of Mt. Pleasant, N.C. Enl. 6/15/61 as PVT, Co. F. Reported present 11/61–2/62; May–June/, Sept.–Dec./62. WIA at Upperville, Va., 6/21/63, with gunshot wound in flesh of leg. Adm. To G.H. #9, Richmond, 7/22/63. Reported on 40-day sick frl. after being released from G.H. #24, 7/25/63. apparently placed on detached service 7/63–3/64 on detached service in Raleigh, N.C. Prm CPL. On register of Invalid Corps, 12/5/64, as being assigned to command conscripts in NC. Post-war, served as Justice of the Peace. Resident of Cabarrus Co., circa 1893. D. 12/25/15. Bur. Mt. Herman Lutheran Church Cem., Cabarrus Co. Kept shell in his wound the rest of his life. (CSR 270:9; Mizelle; Barringer; Cabarrus; Lore: 116; Conversation with Ray Smith, 1-704-873-8580)

Smith, George: PVT, Co. I. Enl. 4/19/64. Reported present on rolls of 3/64–12/64. (CSR 270:9)

Smith, George L.: B. 2/14/45. Enl. 5/15/63 as PVT, Co. F. WIA 8/15 or 8/16/64 along Charles City Rd., near Richmond. Reported present on rolls of 3/64–12/64. Resident of Coddle Creek, NC, circa 1893. D. 5/14/93. Bur. Coddle Creek A.R.P. Graveyard, Iredell Co. (CSR 270:9; Barringer; Richmond *Sentinel*, 8/26/64; Cabarrus; Lore: 38)

Smith, Hugh: From Ashe Co., where he was a farmer. At age 34, enl. 5/25/61 in Co. A as PVT. Later prm to 2SGT. Reported present 11/61–2/62. Absent sick at Winchester, Va., 3/29/62 until 11/16/62; reported admitted to G.H. #7 in Richmond, 11/17/62, with chronic bronchitis, and frl. 11/25/62. Reported at home sick through December. D. at home, 3/63. (CSR 270:9; AsheCo)

Smith, J.: PVT. Captured near Richmond, 6/28/62, psb. at Willis Church on 6/29/62. Sent to Ft. Delaware, 7/9/62. Age 20, stood 5'9", had gray hair, blue eyes, and dark complexion. (CSR 270:9)

Smith, J.M.: Enl. as PVT, Co. I, 8/13/64. Reported present 3/30/64–12/64. Prl. Charlotte, N.C. 5/13/65. (CSR 270:9)

Smith, J.W.: PVT, Co. C. (Alexander)

Smith, Jacob J.: Resident of Duplin Co., N.C. Enl. 7/15/62 as PVT in Co. I. Reported present Jan.–Feb./64. Admitted to G.H. #9, 8/15/64, and to G.H. #24 the next day. Frl. 8/23/ or 8/25/64 with chronic diarrhea and a fever. Reported present Nov.–Dec./64.On detached service to procure a fresh horse, 10/18/64, but reported at a Danville hospital the same day. D. 11/3/64 of typhoid fever at G.H. #13, Richmond. (CSR 270:9)

Smith, Jacob James, Sr.: B. 11/27/41. Enl.

2/25/62 at age 24. PVT, Co. I. Captured 6/29/62 near Richmond, and exd. At Aiken's Landing, 8/25/62. Reported present 9/62–4/63; 10/31/63; 1/1/64, Mar.–Dec./64. D. 3/9/12. Bur. Stumpy Field Cem., Duplin Co. (CSR 270:9; Stepp)

Smith, James E.: PVT. Appears on an undated roll of POWs at the Provost Marshal's Office, Goldsboro, N.C.

Smith, James G: From Ashe Co., N.C. Enl. 3/5/62 as PVT in Co. A. Reported present Sept.–Dec./62. Absent to buy a horse, 2/27/63. Reported present 3/63–4/63. Captured 7/4/63 and sent to Point Lookout. Exd. 2/65. Adm. 2/19/65 to G.H. #9, Richmond; also on a Petersburg hospital register, 6/24/64. (CSR 270:9; AsheCo)

Smith, John Allen: B. 4/5/35. From Cabarrus Co., N.C. At age 26, enl. 6/15/61 as PVT in Co. F. Absent Nov.–Dec./61 in a hospital. Reported present Jan.–Feb./62, May–June/62, Sept.–Dec./62. On extra duty as a teamster, Oct.–Dec./62 with HQ of Hampton's Brigade. Reported present 7/63–12/64. Prm. CPL 7/1/64. Saved W.H.H. Cowles's life in battle. D. 1/19/89. Bur St. Martin's Lutheran Church Cem., Cabarrus Co. (CSR 270:9; Mizelle; *Wilkesboro Chronicle* 7/22/91; Barringer; GLP; Cabarrus; Lore: 212)

Smith, John E.: A farmer, from Wayne Co., N.C. At age 26, enl. 6/25/61 as PVT in Co. H. Reported present Nov.–Dec./61. Sent home on sick frl., 2/22/62. Mortally WIA 6/29/62 at Willis Church, and D. 7/1/62. Stood 5'7¼", had fair complexion, blue eyes, and light hair. (CSR 270:9; Monie calls him John W.)

Smith, John Gordon: B. 1/30/38. From Duplin Co., N.C., age 25. Enl. 4/10/62 as PVT in Co. I. Reported present May–June/62. Absent as brigade teamster, Sept.–Oct./62. On detached service 11/62–4/63, driving a wagon at brigade H.Q. Also reported on detached service, 9/5/63. Reported present 1/64–12/64. D. 8/12/17. Bur. Hebron Presbyterian Church Cem., Duplin Co. (CSR 270:9; Stepp)

Smith, John L.: B. 7/9/33. From Alleghany Co., N.C., but a resident of Mocksville. Enl. 8/12/61. Appointed 2LT, Co. A, 10/8/61. Reported present 11/61–3/62. Prm. 1LT, 5/12/62. Present 9/62–10/62. On detached service, Nov.–Dec./62. Leave of absence, Jan.–Feb./63. Reported present 3/63–4/63, July–Aug./63. WIA 9/12/63 near Culpeper, with gun shot wound in right arm that fractured the humerus. Admitted to G.H. #4, Richmond, 9/15/63, and frl. 10/31/63 for 60 days. Prm. CPT 10/17/63 and given command of Co. A. Absent in the recruiting camp, Mar.–Apr./64. Reported present 7/64–12/64. WIA 9/12/64 and reported in a Richmond hospital. Reported still at home on 2/28/65, in Mocksville, according to an inspection report. Left arm amputated at a Petersburg G.H. 3/8/65. Trn. 3/22/65. Admitted to Fair Ground Post Hospital, Petersburg, 4/8/65, then sent to G.H. 4/11/65. Listed on a roll of POWs at Fair Ground Post Hospital, captured there 5/3/65. D. 9/5/99. Bur. Shiloh Methodist Church Cem., Alleghany Co. (CSR 270:1, 9; Stepp)

Smith, John Thomas: From Northampton Co., N.C. Enl. at age 23 3/12/62 as PVT in Co. B. Listed on detached service to procure a horse, 2/21/63; reported present Mar.–Apr./63. Absent on detached service to procure a horse, July–Aug./63. Present 6/30/63–10/31/63. Absent sick in the hospital, Nov.–Dec./63. Absent on horse detail, Mar.–Apr./64. Reported present, 4/1/64. Trn to Co. D., 43d Regt. N.C. Troops, 8/27/64, then to McGregor's battery of horse artillery, 9/16/64. (CSR 270:9)

Smith, John Ufford: From Hyde Co., N.C., age 30. PVT, Co. H. Enl. 5/21/62. Reported present Sept.–Dec./62. On detached service at Gordonsville, Va., Jan.–Apr./63; on detached service to N.C. to procure a horse, July–Aug./63. Reported present, 9/63–12/63. Bur Cedar Grove Cemetery, New Bern, NC. (CSR 270:9; CGR: 1)

Smith, Jones Robert: B. 6/27/39. From Duplin Co. Enl. as PVT, 6/25/61, in Co. I. Reported present 11/61–2/62, May–June/62, 9/62–4/63. Reported present 10/31/63; 1/1/64–2/64. WIA 8/19/64 near Petersburg, Va., and sent to a Petersburg G.H. Listed with a fracture of the lower tibia. Trn. to a Danville, Va. hospital, and listed in a hospital register there, 10/2/64, with a hurt right leg. Frl. 10/18/64 for 60 days. D. 11/14/19. Bur. Hebron Presbyterian Church Cem., Duplin Co. (CSR 270:9; 'Stepp)

Smith, Jordan: Enl. 7/11/62 as PVT in Co. B. Absent on detached service at Winchester, Va., 9/10/62. Absent Jan.–Feb./63, detached to make shoes at Gordonsville. Reported present Mar.–Apr./63. (CSR 270:9)

Smith, Mark H.: Age 23, from Gaston Co., N.C. Enl. 3/21/62 as PVT in Co. F. Reported present May–June/62, Sept.–Dec./62; 7/63–3/64. WIA at Blacks and Whites, 6/23/64, and sent to the hospital. Reported present Sept.–Dec./64. Dead as of 1893. (CSR 270:9; Barringer; Cabarrus gives name as Mark A.)

Smith, Richard W.: From Northampton Co., N.C., age 21. Enl. 6/12/61 as PVT in Co. B. Left sick at Camp Beauregard, 10/13/61. Absent at home on sick leave, Nov.–Dec./61. Absent 1/62–4/62. Admitted to G.H. #2, Richmond, 3/17/62, and trn. To Petersburg, 3/22/62, but also reported at Culpeper sick, 3/18/62. Reported present 9/62–4/63, July–Oct./63. Detailed as a butcher at brigade H.Q. commissary, 11/63–3/1/64. Trn. 10/16/64 to McGregor's battery of horse artillery. Absent on horse detail, Mar.–Apr./64. Deserted 3/6/65. Took oath and sent to Wilmington, N.C. (CSR 270:9)

Smith, Robert O.: From Franklin Co. Resident of Kittrell's Depot, N.C. At age 20, enl. 6/18/61 or 8/12/61as PVT in Co. E. Later promoted to CPL. Reported present 1/62–2/62. Admitted to G.H. #18, 3/1/62, with diarrhea. Returned to duty 5/20/62, and reported present 5/62–6/62, 9/62–2/63. Absent on detached service Jan.–Feb./63; Mar.–Apr./63 on detached service at Gordonsville with baggage. WIA in left foot, 6/9/63, with compound fracture of the metacarpal bone. Sent to G.H. #25 in Richmond, and frl. Reported absent at home until 4/64. Admitted 5/4/64 to G.H. #9 with a left foot problem, then 5/5/64 to Jackson Hospital in Richmond. Reported in a Danville, Va. G.H., 5/18/64 and 6/17/64, and trn. On detached service with brigade H.Q. guarding wagons, 4/30/64–8/31/64. Also absent on detached service at brigade H.Q., Sept.–Oct./64. Assigned to light duty Nov.–Dec./64. Retired/detailed to Invalid Corps, 12/5/64. On register of Richmond's G.H. #9, 1/18/65, then listed as admitted to Moore Hospital, G.H. #24, in Richmond with lumbago, 1/19/65. Frl. 3/2/65. (CSR 270:9; Pearce: 284)

Smith, Seth D.: From Duplin Co., N.C. At age 18, enl. 4/10/62 as PVT in Co. D. Captured at Willis Church, 6/29/62, and sent to Fort Delaware. Exd. 8/5/62 at Aiken's Landing. Reported present 9/62–4/63, 10/31/63. On detached service as guard at Milford Station, 12/24/63, then back with unit by 1/1/64. Reported present Jan.–Dec./64. Prl. 4/25/65 and sent home. Stood 5' 6" tall, had black hair, dark eyes, sallow complexion. (CSR 270:9)

Smith, Solomon S.: Age 28, from Northampton Co., N.C. Enl. in Co. B., 6/12/61. Bugler, PVT. Reported present 11/61–2/62. Admitted to G.H. #2 in Richmond, 3/17/62, and trn to a Petersburg hospital, 3/22/62. Reported at home sick the same month. Reported AWOL, Nov.–Dec./62. Reported present Jan.–Apr./63, but admitted 3/12/63 to a Staunton, VA hospital, and "improving very slowly" as of 4/7/63. Present June–Dec./63, 4/1/64. Absent with HQ detachment, Mar.–Apr./64. On a report of sick and wounded in N.C. hospitals, 11/64. D. 11/7/64 at Wilson, NC G.H. #12 from gunshot wound. Bur. Maplewood Cem., Wilson. (CSR 270:9; Zeb. Vance Papers, NCSA [courtesy Whit Joyner]; Stepp)

Smith, W.J.: PVT, Co. B. Shoemaker. Made petition to Gov. Vance, 11/13/63, for discharge due to "weak constitution," but Vance could not discharge him. "Honest, sober, upright, industrious." (Zeb. Vance Papers, NCSA [courtesy Whit Joyner])

Smith, William H.: From Northampton Co., N.C. At age 20, enl. 2/62 as PVT in Co. B. Reported present Mar.–Apr./62, Sept.–Oct./62. Captured 11/5/62. On a prl. of POWs at a Warrenton camp, 11/9/62, then still reported as confined at City Point, 11/14/62. Reported present 1/63–4/63. Absent on detached service to N.C. after a horse, 8/27/63, then absent at home sick until 4/64. (CSR 270:9)

Smith, William J.: Enl. 7/61 at age 30 as PVT in Co. B. Saddler. Absent on detached service, Nov.–Dec./62. On detached service to N.C. after a horse, 8/27/63. Absent sick at home, 10/31/63, then reported present 11/63–12/63. Reported present 4/1/64, then sent on horse detail later in the month. Absent at home, 4/30–12/64. From Northampton Co., N.C. (CSR 270:9)

Smith, Zacheus: B. 12/21/11. From Duplin Co., N.C. At age 48, enl. 7/14/61 in Co. I. SGT. Reported present on Nov.–Dec./61 roll. On detached service, patrolling, on Jan.–Feb./62 roll. Listed as on recruiting service on a 3/3/62 regimental return. Captured at Willis Church, 6/29/62. Exd. 8/5/62, and listed by captors as being age 45, 6½" tall, with black eyes, dark hair, and florid complexion. In camp at Winchester on Sept.–Oct./62 roll. Reported present in confinement Nov.–Dec./62 roll, and under arrrest on Jan.–Feb./63 roll, for a court martial on 3/17/63. Reported present on July–Aug./63, 10/31/63, Jan.–Feb./64 rolls. Dsh 7/16/64 and elected to House of Commons, 8/64. Bur. Zacheus Smith Cem., along NC 111, Duplin Co. (CSR 270:9; Stepp)

Solomon, Henry C.: B. 1838. From either Cabarrus or Stanley Co., N.C. PVT, blacksmith. Enl. 6/15/61 in Co. B or Co. F. Trn. to either Co. B or Co. F 8/61. Reported present on rolls Nov.–Dec./61, Jan.–Feb./62, Mar.–Apr./62, Sept.–Oct./62. On detached service Nov.–Dec./62. Reported present on rolls, 1/63–4/63, 6/30/63–12/63, Mar.–Apr./64. Listed as on forage detail, Sept.–Dec./64. WIA in jaw 8/15 or 8/16/64 along Charles City Rd., near Richmond. Reported at G.H. #9, Richmond, with gunshot wound in left side at being admitted 8/16/64. Frl for 30 days beginning 8/27/64. Prl in Albemarle, N.C., 5/19/65. Resident of Montgomery Co., circa

1893. Bur. Stoney Fork Cem., Montgomery Co. (CSR 270:9; Mizelle; Bounty Receipts; Barringer; Richmond *Sentinel*, 8/26/64; Cabarrus; Stepp)

Souther, J.B.: At age 20, from Henderson Co., N.C., enl. 3/11/62 as PVT in Co. G. Reported present on rolls of May–June/62, Sept.–Dec./62, Jan.–Apr./63. Captured at Beverly's Ford, Va.., 6/9/63, and prl 6/25/63. On detached service July–Aug./63. Listed as AWOL 10/25/63. Reported present Nov.–Dec./63, 3/64–8/64. On detached service Sept.–Oct./64, then listed as AWOL Nov.–Dec./64. (CSR 270:9)

Sparrow, J. Stewart: Enl. 5/23/63 as PVT in Co. C. Reported present on rolls of July–Aug./63. Absent WIA, 9/22/63. Admitted to G.H. #9, Richmond, 9/24/63, and listed on hospital rolls until 2/29/64. However, reported present on regimental rolls of Nov.–Dec./63. Admitted to Jackson Hospital, Richmond, with pistol ball in leg, 2/8/64. On the morning report of that hospital listed as returned to duty 3/15/64. Reported present on rolls of 3/64–12/64. Captured 4/1/65 near Five Forks, and released from Point Lookout 6/3/65. (CSR 270:9; Alexander)

Spears, James F.G.: From Cabarrus Co. At age 22, enl. 6/15/61 or 3/1/62 as PVT in Co. F. Reported present on rolls of May–June/62, Sept.–Dec./62, July–Aug./63, 9/63–3/31/64. On detached service at brigade H.Q., June–Dec./64. Joined Rocky River Presbyterian Church 11/30/66. Living in Mississippi, circa 1893. (CSR 270:9; Barringer; Cabarrus; Janet Morrison to author, 9/19/98)

Speed, Henry Goodridge: B. at Roseland, Granville Co., 8/19/45. After attending Belmont Select School, he entered VMI in 1862. Enl. as PVT, Co. E., 9/18/63. Also served in the 3d VA Cavalry. D. at Poplar Spring Church near Petersburg, 8/21/64, from shrapnel wound to the heart. Speed was "ready and anxious for any adventure which promised fun and amusement, provided there was a little danger so much the better." (CSR 270:9; Institute Memorial: 482–84)

Speers, R.H.: Enl. 11/22/64 in Co. F, PVT. Reported present on rolls through 12/64. Prl. Charlotte, 5/17/65. In 1929, living in Forest City, Arkansas. (CSR 270:9; Mizelle; Barringer; alternative name spelling is Spearse or Speers)

Speight, Abram L.: Enl. 12/30/63 as PVT, Co. H. Reported present on rolls of Jan.–Feb./64. On detached service, 3–4/64. Reported present on rolls of 4/30/64–12/64. Trn to brigade band, 12/22/64. (CSR 270:9)

Spivey, John W.: From Northampton Co. At age 25, enl. 4/20 or 4/22/62 in Co. B, as PVT. Absent in a Winchester hospital, 9/20/62–12/62. Reported present on rolls of Nov.–Dec./63, Jan.–Feb./63, 3/63–10/63. Trn 1/ or 2/64. (CSR 270:9)

Springs, James A.: From Buncombe Co., age 18. Enl. 3/1/62 as PVT in Co. G. On extra duty as a teamster, 3/62. Reported present May–June/62, Sept.–Oct./62. Absent on detached service Nov.–Dec./62. Reported in a Charlottesville hospital on roll of Jan.–Feb./63. Admitted there 2/11/63, returned to duty 3/7/63. Reported present Mar.–Apr./63, July–Aug./63. D. Auburn, 10/14/63. (CSR 270:9)

Springs, W.L.: Age 16, from Buncombe Co., N.C. Substitute. Enl. 5/16/63 as PVT in Co. G. Absent on detached service to buy a horse, July–Aug./63. Reported present on rolls of Sept.–Oct./63, 4/30–10/64. Nov.–Dec./63, reported sick in a Lynchburg hospital. 4/1/64, reported under arrest at Gordonsville. Admitted to Richmond's G.H. #9, 6/2/64. Reported deserted on rolls of Nov.–Dec./64. Received 12/6/64 by U.S. troops, took oath on 12/8. Had a dark complexion, black hair, brown eyes, stood 5' 9", (CSR 270:9)

Springs, William: Age 39. PVT, Co. G, from Buncombe Co. Enl. 5/20/61. Reported present on rolls of Jan.–Feb./62, May–June/62, Sept.–Dec./62, Jan.–Apr./63. Furnished a substitute. (CSR 270:9)

Staakes, Andrew W.: Duplin Co., age 22. Enl. 6/22/61 as PVT in Co. I. Reported present on rolls of Nov.–Dec./61. Reported sick at Petersburg after leaving camp 2/21/62. Admitted to G.H. #18, 3/2/62, and D. 3/6 or 3/8/62 "in convulsions." (CSR 270:9)

Stalcup, John Thaddeus: Of Macon Co. At age 17, enl. 3/27/63 as PVT in Co. K. Reported present on rolls of Mar.–Apr./63. Reported sick, 8/63, at a Charlottesville hospital, and trn to a Lynchburg hospital, 9/63. On sick frl Nov.–Dec./63, Jan.–Dec./64. (CSR 270:9)

Stallcup, William R.: Macon Co. Enl. at age 19 on 6/25/61 as PVT in Co. K. Reported present on rolls of 11/61–2/62, May–June/62. Feb.–Mar./62 on extra duty as a teamster. Absent sick in a Petersburg hospital, 10/62–2/63. At home sick, Mar.–Apr./63. Captured 6/9/63 at Beverly's Ford. Reported present on rolls of July–Aug./63, 10/31/63, Nov.–Dec./63. AWOL Jan.–Feb./64. Reported present on rolls of 2/29–12/64. (CSR 270:9)

Stamper, Creede: CNS. 9/29/64 as PVT in Co. H. Reported present on rolls through 12/64. (CSR 270:9)

Stanis, J.B.: PVT, Co. C. (Alexander)

Stanley, Samuel W.: Craven Co. Enl. 5/20/61 or 6/20/61 as PVT in Co. H. Later CPL. Reported present on rolls of 11/61–2/62. Captured Willis Church, 6/29/62, and exd 8/5/62. Reported present on rolls of Sept.–Oct./62, Jan.–Feb./63. Absent sick Mar.–Apr./63. On detached service to N.C., July–Aug./63. Reported present on rolls of 9/63–2/64. Absent on detached service Mar.–Apr./64, then reported present 4/30–8/31/64. On extra duty as adj. clerk, Sept.–Oct./64. On leave, Nov.–Dec./64. Admitted to a Danville hospital, 5/4/65, with a wrist wound. Deserted 5/7/65. Prl Greensboro, 5/9/65. Stood 5' 9¾", had light hair, light eyes, and light complexion. (CSR 270:9)

Starns, Clark R.: Enl. 5/17/61 as PVT in Co. C. Age 19 from Mecklenburg Co. Reported present on rolls of 11/61–2/62, May–Oct./62. Scouting, 12/25/62. Reported present on rolls of Jan.–Feb./63, Mar.–Apr./63. Captured 6/30/63 at Hanover or 7/3/63 at Gettysburg. Had dark complexion, brown hair, and gray eyes, stood 5' 9". Released 6/19/65 after taking oath. (CSR 270:9; Alexander)

Starns, J.B.: From Mecklenburg Co. At age 24, enl. Co. C., 6/12/61, as CPL and blacksmith. Reported present on rolls of 11/61–1/62. Absent in N.C. recruiting, beginning 2/4/62. Reported present May–Oct./62. Absent on scout, 12/25/62. Reported present on rolls of 1/63–4/63, 7/63–12/64. Prl Charlotte, 5/27/65. (CSR 270:9; Alexander spells it Stearns)

Staton, Alfred: B. Halifax Co.; farmer. Cns. 7/16/62 as PVT in Co E. Absent on detached service to Winchester, Sept.–Oct./62. 11/15/62, sent to a Richmond hospital "indefinitely." Listed on 11/17/62 register of G.H. #7, Richmond, with chronic rheumatism. Absent until dsh due to disability, 8/7/63. Age 31 at dsh. Stood 5' 5", had fair complexion, gray eyes, dark hair. (CSR 270:9)

Steel, Hugh A.: Resident of Patterson, N.C. Enl. 6/25/63 as PVT in Co. D. CPL. Reported present July–Aug./63. WIA Jack's Shop, 9/22/63. Admitted 9/24/63 to B.H. #9 and 9/25/63 to G.H. #24, Richmond. On 40-day home frl beginning 10/10/63. Reported present on rolls of 1/64–4/64, 8/31–12/64. Listed on register of Danville G.H., admitted 4/3/65 with gunshot wound in right breast. Frl. 4/9/65. (Davis; CSR 270:9)

Steel, Manlius D.: Resident of Charlotte, age 23. Enl. 5/13/62 as PVT, Co. C. Reported present on rolls of 5/62–12/62. Prm Ord. SGT, 6/1/62. Reported present on rolls of 1/63–4/63, 7/63–8/63. WIA Jack's Shop, 9/22/63. Admitted to G.H. #9, Richmond, 9/24/63. On frl 10/7/63 from G.H. #24 for 60 days. Leave extended, 3/6/64. Reported present 3/64–12/64, although reported in Winder G.H., Richmond, 10/26/64 and returned to duty 11/1/64. Elected 2LT and passed exam, 1/9/65. On register of Danville G.H. with gunshot wound in head, 4/4/65. (CSR 270:1, 9; Alexander)

Steele, Henry: Enl. 8/16/63 as PVT in Co. D. Reported present 8/31/64–12/64. (CSR 270:9)

Steele, W.G.: Age 19, from South Carolina. Enl. 5/13/62 as PVT, Co. C. Reported present on rolls of May–June/62. On detached service to Winchester, 10/1/62. Reported scouting, 12/25/62. 2/21/63, went to N.C. to buy a horse. Reported present on rolls of Mar.–Apr./63, July–Aug./63. Captured Jack's Shop, 9/22/63. Exd. 10/24/64. Reported present Nov.–Dec./64. (CSR 270:9; Alexander)

Stellman, A.: Enl. from Edgecombe Co. at age 23 on 7/16/62 as PVT, Co. E. Reported present on rolls of 9/62–4/63, July–Aug./63. Deserted 9/4/63, took oath of allegiance. Gives residence as Germany. Had light complexion, brown hair, blue eyes, stood 5/9." (CSR 270:9)

Stepp, Jackson: Buncombe Co., age 34. Enl. 5/20/61 as PVT, Co. G. Reported present on rolls of 1/62–2/62, May–June/62, and Sept.–Oct./62, much of it on extra duty as teamster. Reported present on rolls of 11/62–2/63. Absent sick at home, Mar.–Apr./63; on detached service to buy a horse, July–Aug./63. Reported present Sept.–Dec./63, Mar.–Aug./64. AWOL Sept.–Oct./64, reported present on rolls of Nov.–Dec./64. Still living in Buncombe Co. as of 1890. (CSR 270:9; Almsay: 31)

Stepp, Lewis L.: At age 20, enl. 5/20/61 as PVT, Co. G. D. 2/62. From Buncombe Co. (CSR 270:9)

Stetson, William H.: At age 40, enl. 6/20/61. Saddler, Co. I. Reported present on rolls of 11/61–2/62. Captured Willis Church, 6/29/62, and exd. 8/5/62. Absent making shoes, Sept.–Oct./62. Reported present Nov.–Dec./62, Jan.–Apr./63, 10/31/63, 1/1/64, Jan.–Feb./64. WIA 5/1/64. Admitted to a Petersburg hospital, 7/30/64, and sent home on frl, 8/19/64 through 12/64. On register of POWs at Hamilton Military Prison, 5/65. Prl to Duplin Co. Had fair complexion, fair hair, blue eyes, stood 5'11", (CSR 270:9)

Stiller, Charles M.: Farmer, Rowan Co. Age 24. Enl. as PVT in Co. F, 6/15/61. Reported present 11/61–2/62, May–June/62, Sept.–Dec./62, July–Dec./63. Appointed CPL 11/15/63. Reported present 1/64–3/31/64. D. 5/20/64 after being WIA 5/11/64, psb. at Verdiersville. 6' tall, sallow complexion, gray eyes, dark hair. (Mizelle; CSR 270:9; Barringer; Rumple: 343)

Stirewall, H.L.: Enl. 9/64 or 10/64 as PVT, Co. F. Reported present on rolls of Sept.–Oct./64. Absent to buy a horse in N.C., 12/15/64. (CSR 270:9)

Stirewalt, J.C.: Enl. 10/31/64 as PVT, Co. F. Later WIA. Reported present through 12/64. Resident of Rowan Co., circa 1893. (CSR 270:9; Barriner)

Stirewalt, John R.: B. 1841. Farmer from Cabarrus Co. Enl. 6/15/61 as PVT, Co. F. Reported present on rolls of Nov.–Dec./61, Jan.–Feb./62, May–June/62, Sept.–Oct./62. Absent on sick frl, 11/25/62. WIA in left thigh 11/5/62, Barbee's Crossroads. Admitted 11/17/62 to G.H. #7, and frl. For 30 days 11/25/62. Absent July–Aug./63 to purchase a horse. Reported present on rolls of Sept.–Dec./63, Jan.–Apr./64. KIA near Concord Church, 6/29/64 during Wilson's Raid, at age 25 years 5 months. Bur. Poplar Tent Presbyterian Church Cem., Cabarrus Co. (Mizelle; Bounty Receipts; CSR 270:9; Sun 3/25/81; Barringer; Cabarrus; Lore: 158; Stepp)

Stocker, Christian: Age 27, from Mecklenburg Co. Enl. 5/28/61 as PVT in Co. C. Deserted 10/23/61. (CSR 270:9)

Stokes, James W.: B. 7/7/38. Resident of Duplin Co. At age 20, enl. 6/25/61 as PVT in Co. I. Reported present on rolls of 11/61–2/62. Captured at Willis Church, 6/29/62. Exd. 8/5/62. Reported present on rolls of 11/62–4/63 and 1/1/64–12/64, but also listed as captured 5/3/64 at Amelia C.H. Released 6/20/65 after taking oath. Stood 5'9", had light complexion, dark brown hair, hazel eyes. D. 4/18/87. Bur. Stokes Family Cem., Duplin Co. (CSR 270:9; Stepp)

Stone, Henry W.: Age 22, from Granville Co. Enl. 6/8/61 as SGT, Co. E. Reported present on rolls of Jan.–Feb./62 (on extra duty in Commissary Dept.); May–June/62. Reduced to PVT, 6/7/62. On detached service at Winchester, Sept.–Oct./62. Prm Commissary SGT, 10/62. Reported present Jan.–Feb./63, Mar.–Apr./63, July–Dec./63 as Commissary SGT. Reported present Jan.–Oct./64. On register of a Danville hospital, 4/3/64, with gunshot wound in left arm. Frl. 60 days, 4/8/64. Reduced to ranks, 4/15/64. Admitted to G.H. Camp Winder, 6/4/64. On horse detail to N.C., Nov.–Dec./64. (CSR 270:9)

Stone, S.W.: PVT, Co. F. (Mizelle; Cabarrus)

Story, Lemuel H.: From Northampton Co. Enl. 6/61 as PVT. Bugler. Reported present on rolls of 11/61–2/62, Mar.–Apr./62, Sept.–Oct./62. Also reported absent sick on 3/62 regimental return. On detached service, Nov.–Dec./62, then present on rolls of Jan.–Apr./63, July–Dec./63, Mar.–Oct./64. Absent on horse detail, Nov.–Dec./64. (CSR 270:9)

Stovall, Drury M.: Resident of Granville Co. PVT. On POW roll at Point Lookout as captured at Amelia C.H., 4/3/65. Took oath, 4/13/65. Dark complexion, brown hair, blue eyes, stood 6'1". (CSR 270:9)

Stowe, Washington: From Cabarrus Co. Enl. 6/15/61 as PVT, Co. F, at age 24. Reported present on rolls of 11/61–2/62. On sick frl, 5/29/62. Reported present Sept.–Dec./62, July–Aug./63. Captured in Maryland, 9/22/63. Admitted to U.S. small pox hospital, Point Lookout, 11/22/63. D. with chronic diarrhea 1/31/65 at Point Lookout, and buried there. (Mizelle; Bounty Receipts; CSR 270:9; Barringer; PL: 166)

Stradley, John A.: From Buncombe Co. At age 26, enl. '61 in Co. G. On regimental return, 3/62. Reported absent sick in a Petersburg hospital, 6/13/62, through 12/62. Reported present on rolls of Jan.–Apr./63. Captured 7/5/63 and sent to Point Lookout. Exd. 3/3/64. Mar.–Apr./64 on detached service to buy a horse, and again 8/11–10/64. (CSR 270:9)

Strain, James L.: Age 19, from Macon Co. Enl. 8/3/61 as PVT, Co. K. Reported present on rolls of 11/61–2/62, May–June/62, 9/62–4/63. Absent at a G.H. according to 3/62 regimental return. On detached service July–Aug./63, and WIA slightly 8/1/63. Reported present 10/1/63, then absent on detached service 11/63–3/31/64. AWOL 4/1/64–12/64. On a register of deserters, Knoxville, 2/20/65 and released 2/21/65. (CSR 270:9)

Strickland, Levi: B. Wayne Co. Age 29. Enl. 6/20/61 as PVT, Co. H. Absent on detached service, Nov.–Dec./61. Sent to Warrenton with horses, 12/28/61–2/62. Dsh 6/14/62. According to COL Baker, Strickland was "timid" and "inactive" and found "wanting." At G.H. Camp Winder with chronic diarrhea, admitted 9/28/63 and frl 12/31/63 for 30 days. (CSR 270:9)

Strum, William A.E.: B. Granville Co. Age 28. Enl. 7/25 or 8/12/61 as PVT, Co. E. Admitted 1/1/62 to G.H. #1, Danville, with a fever, and sent to Richmond. D. at a Petersburg hospital, 1/8/62. (CSR 270:9)

Stucker, Christian: PVT, Co. C. (Alexander)

Sturgill, George: B. 8/3/39. From Ashe Co., age 20. Enl. 6/8/61 as PVT, Co. A. Reported present on rolls of 11/61–2/62, 9/62–4/63, July–Dec./63.

Frl 2/29/64, and reported present Mar.–Apr./64. AWOL, 8/30/64, but present Sept.–Dec./64. D. 5/6/17. Bur. Mt. Zion Methodist Church Cem., Alleghany Co. (CSR 270:9; AsheCo; Stepp)

Sturgill, James: From Ashe Co., N.C., age 23. Enl. 6/8/61 as PVT, Co. A. Reported present Nov.–Dec./61, then absent in a Manassas hospital, Jan.–Feb./62. Also reported absent sick in regimental returns of 2/24/62 and 3/62. Reported present 9/62–4/63. Captured 7/4/63; exd. 2/23/65. (CSR 270:9; AsheCo)

Sugg, John: Resident of Greene Co., age 30. Enl. 6/20/61 as PVT, Co. H. Reported present Nov.–Dec./61. Captured 2/7/62, Difficult Run. Reported present 11/62–12/62. Jan.–Feb./63, absent after a horse. Reported present Mar.–Apr./63, then absent July–Aug./63 to recruit horses. Reported present on rolls of Sept.–Dec./63. Absent on frl, Jan.–Feb./64. Reported present on rolls of Mar.–Aug./64. On detached service at Stony Creek, Sept.–Oct./64. Captured 12/64, at Stony Creek. Had fair complexion, dark brown hair, blue eyes, stood 5'9". Released 6/20/65. (CSR 270:9; Monie)

Sumner, Richard R.: B. Green Co. TN; Resident of Buncombe Co. Enl. 8/8/61 in Co. G. Bugler, Farrier. Reported present on rolls of Jan.–Feb./62. Captured at Middletown, MD 9/12/62. Exd. 11/10/62. Reported present 11/62–4/63. Captured at Carlisle, 7/5/63. Declined exchange; may have deserted. Released on taking oath, 5/12/65. Sandy complexion, brown hair, hazel eyes, 6' tall. May have also served in 7th N.C. Cav. (CSR 270:9)

Sumner, W.W.: Enl. 10/1/62 as PVT in Co. B. Reported present on rolls of 4/30/64–10/64. Deserted at Norfolk, 1/16/65, and took oath, 1/18/65. Moved to Randolph Co., Ind. (CSR 270:9)

Sutherland, Andrew: From Ashe Co. Brother of Joseph and Harrison Sutherland. Enl. 2/27/62 as PVT in Co. A. Reported present on rolls of Sept.–Oct./62. Absent scouting on rolls of 12/25/62. Reported present on Jan.–Apr./63 rolls. On detached service on rolls of 7/63–4/64, herding cattle. Reported present on rolls of July–Dec./64. (CSR 270:9; AsheCo; Noe, *Civil War in Appalachia*, 55–56.)

Sutherland, Harrison: From Ashe Co. Enl. 1862. Brother of Joseph and Andrew Sutherland. D. from anemia at Ft. Delaware, 8/64. (Noe, *Civil War in Appalachia*, 55–56.)

Sutherland, Joseph: From Ashe Co. Born 1846. Brother of Andrew and Harrison Sutherland. Enl. 8/14/64 as PVT in Co. A. Reported present on rolls of July–Dec./64. On a sick and wounded report, G.H. #1, Weldon, 3/65, with typhoid fever. D. 3/19/65. (CSR 270:9; AsheCo; Noe, *Civil War in Appalachia*, 55–56.)

Sutton, William T.: B. 1824. From Lenoir Co. Enl. 7/6/61 as PVT, Co. H. Reported present Nov.–Dec./61, Jan.–Feb./62, May–June/62, Sept.–Dec./62. Also reported abs sick on 2/62 regimental return. On detached service Jan.–Apr./63, 7/63–2/64, Mar.–Apr./64 in ord. Dept., brigade H.Q. On detached service at cavalry corps H.Q., rolls of Sept.–Oct./64, with dismounted men. Nov.–Dec./64, on horse detail. D. 1896. Bur. Oakwood Cem., Raleigh. (CSR 270:9; Stepp)

Swan, Franklin M.: From Buncombe Co., age 17. Enl. 5/20/61 as PVT, Co. G. Reported present on rolls of Jan.–Feb./62, May–June/62, Sept.–Oct./62, 11/62–4/63, July–Aug./63. Also reported abs sick on 2/62 regimental return. Absent on frl, Sept.–Oct./63. Sick at home, Nov.–Dec./63. Reported AWOL 4/1/64, but listed as present on rolls of 4/64–12/64. (CSR 270:9)

Swan, James W.: PVT, Co. B. Listed on POW roll of Camp Chase, Ohio, as arrested 10/20/63 in Monroe Co., TN. Trn to Fort Delaware, 2/29/ or 3/4/64. (CSR 270:9)

Swearingin, J.W.: Enl. 8/18/64 as PVT, Co. C. Reported present on rolls of Sept.–Dec./64. (CSR 270:9)

Swift, Samuel: Resident of Watauga Co. At age 30, enl. 5/11/61 as PVT, Co. D. (CSR 270:9)

Swinson, James W.: B. Duplin Co. Mechanic. Enl. 6/17/61 as PVT, Co. I. Reported present Nov.–Dec./61. At age 30, dsh 2/12/62 for disability with disease in legs and arms and "utter demorilization" of character; addicted to "opium eating." Stood 6,' had dark complexion, black hair, blue eyes. (CSR 270:9)

Swinson, John W.: Enl. at age 24 on 3/5/62 as PVT, Co. I. Reported present on rolls of May–June/62. Listed sick at Winchester, Sept.–Oct./62. Reported present Nov.–Dec./63, then absent on detached service on rolls of Jan.–Feb./63. Absent sick in Campbell Co., Va., Mar.–Apr./63. Present 10/31/63. Trn 11/18 or 11/19/63 to 55th N.C. Troops, Co. H. From Onslow Co. (CSR 270:9)

Switzer, Bev. P.: Enl. 6/3/61 as saddler, Co. A. Present 11/61–2/62, Sept.–Dec./62. Absent on detached service with baggage at Gordonsville, Jan.–Feb./63. Reported present on rolls of Mar.–Apr./63. Also reported as trn Co. D, 58th N.C. Troops, 6/62. (CSR 270:9)

Tappscott, J.M.: PVT, Co. H. Enl. 3/12/64. Reported present on rolls of Mar.–Oct./64. Listed as AWOL, Nov.–Dec./64. (CSR 270:9)

Tappscott, T.J.: Enl. 3/12/54 as PVT, Co. H. Reported present on rolls of Mar.–Oct./64. Absent on horse detail, Nov.–Dec./64. (CSR 270:9)

Taylor, A.W.: Montgomery Co., N.C. Enl. 5/28/61 as PVT, Co. C. Reported present Nov.–Dec./61. Absent sick at Petersburg beginning 2/26/62. Captured 7/3/63, and took oath, 7/7/63. Reported deserted, Sept.–Oct./64. (CSR 270:9)

Taylor, A.W.: PVT, Co. C. (Alexander)

Taylor, Art: PVT, Co. C. Deserted. (Alexander)

Taylor, George: B. New Bern. Clerk. At age 24, enl. 8/21/63 as PVT, trn from 35th N.C.. Reported present 8/63. Captured and WIA at Culpeper, 9/18/63. Left leg, broken from fall of horse, amputated below knee. Stood 5'11", had dark complexion, dark eyes, and dark hair. (CSR 270:9)

Taylor, George H.: PVT, Co. H. Age 22. Psb WIA 8/63. Broke left tibia and fibula by fall of horse, 9/23/63. Amputated leg and trn.to prison duty. (Medical History 12: 675; Monie)

Taylor, J.A.: Age 23, from Anson Co. Enl. 8/21/61 as PVT, Co. C. Dsh 12/6/61. Absent sick at Petersburg, 11/30/61–2/62, and also absent sick 5/29/62–12/62, in various hospitals. D. Richmond, 12/25/62 or 1/25/63. (CSR 270:9; Alexander)

Taylor, J.C.: From Mecklenburg Co. PVT, Co. C. Enl. 7/27/61. Reported present, 11/61–2/62. Captured at Willis Church, 6/29/62 and exd. 8/5/62. Also reported present on rolls of 6/62–4/63, July–Aug./63. Absent sick, 9/21/63. Absent on detached service, 11/13/63. Reported present on rolls of Jan.–Feb./64. On detached service 4/1/64, then reported present Mar.–Dec./64. Stood 6'1", had dark hair and complexion, hazel eyes. (CSR 270:9; Alexander)

Taylor, J.H.: Enl. 6/2/64 as PVT, Co. E. Reported present on all rolls through 12/64. (CSR 270:9)

Taylor, J.M.: From Union Co., age 22. Enl. 5/18/61 as PVT, Co. C. Listed on sick and wounded report of 12/61 with acute dysentery, measles. D. 12/6/61 in Camp W.S. Ashe of typhoid fever. (CSR 270:9; Alexander)

Taylor, James: Age 16, from Buncombe Co. Enl. 5/20/61 as PVT, Co. G. Reported present on rolls of Jan.–Feb./62, May–June/62, 9/62–4/63, July–Oct./63. Absent on frl, Nov.–Dec./63. 4/1/64, absent on detached service. Reported present 4/30/6–12/64. (CSR 270:9)

Taylor, Morgan: Buncombe Co., age 20. Enl. 5/20/61 as CPL, Co. G. Reported present on rolls of Jan.–Feb./62, May–June/62, Sept.–Oct./62. Listed as captured, Nov.–Dec./62. Also listed on a roll of POWs prl at Warrenton, 11/9/62. Reported present on rolls of 1/63–4/63. Absent on detached service with unserviceable horses in Nelson Co. Reported present Sept.–Dec./63. Mar.–Oct./64, on detached service with horse detail. Appointed 4CPL 12/1/64. (CSR 270:9)

Taylor, N.L.: Co. G. (*The [Asheville] Daily Citizen*, 7/5/89, copy in Civil War Clippings File, Pack Memorial Library, Asheville, NC.)

Taylor, Robert: Buncombe Co., age 20. Enl. 5/20/61 as PVT, Co. G. Reported present on rolls of 1/62–2/62, May–June/62. Captured at Malvern Hill, 8/5/62, and exd. 8/26/62. Present Sept.–Dec./62,1–Apr./63. Absent on detached service to buy a horse, July–Aug./63. Reported present 9/63–12/63. Present Mar.–Aug./64. Sept.–Oct./64 on detached service in trenches with dismounted men. Nov.–Dec./64 present. (CSR 270:9)

Taylor, W.F.: Age 28, from Mecklenburg Co. Enl. 3/12/62 as PVT, Co. C. Reported present on rolls of May–June/62. Absent sick at Warrenton, 9/15/62. Present Nov.–Dec./62, Jan.–Apr./63, July–Dec./63. With provost guard at Milford, Jan.–Apr./64, then present–Dec./64. (CSR 270:9; Alexander)

Taylor, W.M.: Enl. 5/15/64 in Co. K. Present through 12/64. (CSR 270:9)

Teague, Loss L.: Age 19, from Buncombe Co. Enl. 5/20/61 as PVT, Co. G. Reported present 11/61–2/62. On sick leave, 3/30/62. Present on rolls of May–June/62, 9/62–4/63. Captured 8/1/63, Brandy Station. D. 12/26/63, Point Lookout, and is bur. there. (CSR 270:9; PL: 167)

Thigpen, Allen: Age 21, from Duplin Co. Enl. 6/20/61 as PVT in Co. I. Reported present on rolls of 11/61–2/62. Admitted to a Danville hospital, 1/3/62 with a skin disease; sent to Front Royal. Absent sick at home, May–June/62. Reported present 9/62–4/63. Arrested 9/12/63. Present 1/1/64. Name appears on a court martial record, 1/8/64. Trn to 5th N.C., 8/31/64. (CSR 270:9)

Thompson, J.N.: Enl. 6/3/61 as PVT, Co. C. Reported present Nov.–Dec./61. Absent sick at Petersburg 2/26/62–3/62. Appears on a sick and wounded report of 3/62, Lynchburg. D. Lynchburg, 3/14/62, age 35, from pneumonia. (CSR 270:9; Alexander)

Thompson, James H.: From Wayne Co., age 24. Enl. 6/20/61 as PVT, Co. H. (CSR 270:9)

Thompson, Louis: B. 1826. From Mecklenburg Co. At age 36, enl. 5/25/61 in Co. C. Dsh 8/1/61 with deformed hand. Stood 5'10½," had light gray eyes, brown complexion, dark hair. D. 3/30/98. Bur. Elmwood Cem., Charlotte. (CSR 270:9; Stepp)

Thompson, R.G.: Age 39, from Mecklenburg Co. PVT, Co. C. Enl. 6/25/62. Reported present on rolls of May–June/62, 6/30–10/31/62. Absent 12/25/62 scouting. Reported present 1/63–4/63, 7/63–12/64. Admitted 10/10/63 to a Charlottesville G.H. with chronic rheumatism, trn 11/9/63 to G.H. #24, Richmond. (CSR 270:9; Alexander)

Thompson, Waitman: Enl. 6/24/61 as PVT, Co. H. From Wayne Co., age 18. Dsh. (CSR 270:9)

Thornton, William R.: B. Warren Co. Farmer. Enl. 7/26/61. CPL, Co. E. Accidentally shot in left hand with pistol; most of hand removed. Dsh 2/6/62 at age 37. Stood 5' 8¾", had light complexion, blue eyes, black hair. (CSR 270:9)

Tipton, A.J.: From Macon Co., age 18. PVT, Enl. 7/20/61 in Co. K. Listed in 12/61 sick and wounded report at Camp W.N. Edwards. On 12/27/61, D. In Centreville hospital, with typhoid fever. (CSR 270:9)

Todd, James: Co. D. R. 1863. KIA. (CSR 270:1; Davis)

Todd, James I.: Watauga Co., age 18. Enl. 5/11/61 as PVT, Co. D. Reported present on rolls of 11/61–2/62, May–Dec./62. Absent on detached service, Jan.–Feb./63. Present Mar.–Apr./63. WIA 7/3/63 and sent home. Listed as absent on detached service, Nov.–Dec./63, then present Jan.–Dec./64. Listed as courier for "Genl Lee," 8/31/64. NFR. (CSR 270:9)

Todd, John C.: Enl. 8/31/64 as PVT, Co. D, in Boone. Reported present through 12/64. (CSR 270:9)

Todd, Joseph B.: At age 28, from Watauga Co., enl. 5/16/61 in Co. D. 1LT. Resigned 9/61. (CSR 270:1, 9; Davis)

Todd, Joseph W.: B. 1839. Lawyer. Enl. 5/11/61 as SGT, Co. D. From Watauga Co. Reported present on rolls of Nov.–Dec./61, Jan.–Feb./62, May–June/62, 6/30/62–12/62, Jan.–Feb./63. Present Mar.–Apr./63, 7/63–12/63, Jan.–Mar./64. Mar.–Apr./64, absent on detached service. Present 8/31/64–12/64. 1LT J.W. Elected to 2LT 4/30/62 and prm 1LT 5/9/62. Also in file information on a man from Mecklenburg Co. who entered into service 4/30/62, prm 1LT 5/9/62. Also Meck roll of honor, 5/9/62 enl. prm 2LT 4/30/62 and to 1LT 5/9/62. Post-war reported living in Jefferson, N.C. D. 1909. Bur. Jefferson Town Cem., Ashe Co. Gravestone gives rank as CPT. (CSR 270:9; Davis; CV 16 [1908]: 319; Stepp; Davis)

Tolliver, Creed: Trn. from state service. Enl. 9/29/64 as PVT, Co. G. Reported present through 12/64. (CSR 270:9)

Tomberlin, E.M.: From Mecklenburg Co. At age 30, enl. 5/29/61 as PVT, Co. C. Reported present on rolls of 11/61–2/62, May–June/62, 6/30/62–12/62, 1/63–4/63, 7/63–4/64. Absent after being WIA, 7/23/64. On a 7/21/64 register of a Danville G.H. with gunshot wound in arm, and frl 7/23/64 according to the same register. Retired by medical board according to roll of Nov.–Dec./64. On a register of the Invalid Corps as retired 12/15/64. (CSR 270:9; Alexander)

Tomlin, J.: From Union Co., age 21. Enl. 2/10/62 as PVT, Co. C. On regimental return of 3/62. Reported present May–June/62. Admitted to G.H. Camp Winder in Richmond, 7/8/62, and returned to duty 8/4/62. Absent on detached service beginning 10/1/62 at Winchester. Present on rolls of Nov.–Dec./62, Jan.–Apr./63, 7/63–12/63. Frl 2/25/64, then reported present on roll of 4/1/64. Trn Co. B, 20th regt NCT, 4/19/64. (CSR 270:9; Alexander)

Toms, James M.: PVT, Co. K. Reported present on company muster rolls of Nov.–Dec./64. (CSR 270:9)

Torrans, Samuel C.: B. 1838. From Duplin Co. Enl. 7/20/61 as PVT, Co. I. Reported present on rolls of 11/61–2/62, May–June/62, Sept.–Oct./62. Appointed SGT 10/62. Absent on detached service, Nov.–Dec./62, Jan.–Apr./63. WIA at Upperville, 6/21/63. D. 6/27/63. Bur. Torrans Family Cem., Duplin Co. Name spelled Torrance in service records. Also a man named S. Tarrains bur. Upperville, VA cem. (CSR 270:9; Stepp; Personal Knowledge)

Tow, Shadrack: From Buncombe Co. At age 36, enl. 5/20/61 as PVT, Co. G. Reported present on rolls of Jan.–Feb./62, although absent sick according to regimental returns of 2/62 and 3/62. Present May–June/62, 9/62–4/63. Under arrest at Culpeper C.H., July–Oct./63. Listed as deserted, 8/63. (CSR 270:9)

Tredennick, J.P.: B. 1/25/46. From Mecklenburg Co., age 18. Enl. 3/26/63 as PVT, Co. C. Reported present Mar.–Apr./63, 7/63–10/64. Absent on detached service beginning 12/7/64. D. 1/5/06. Bur. Sardis Creek Presbyterian Church Cem., Charlotte. (CSR 270:9; Karchaske; Alexander calls him N.P. & spells it Tredermick)

Tredennick, J.R.: Farrier, PVT, Co. C. At age 25, enl. 2/18/62. Present 5/62–10/62. Absent scouting beginning 12/25/62. Absent 2/21/63 in NC to buy a horse. Present Mar.–Apr./63, 7/63–12/64. From Mecklenburg Co. (CSR 270:9; Alexander)

Tredennick, W.S.: PVT, Co. C. Enl. at age 22 on 2/28/62. On a regimental return of 3/62. Reported present May–Dec./62, Jan.–Apr./63, 7/63–8/31/64. Absent on detached service beginning 9/23/64. Listed as killed accidentally, probably on 12/1/64. From Mecklenburg Co. (CSR 270:9; Alexander)

Triplett, Franklin Clayton: B. Caldwell Co. Farmer. Enl. 12/10/63 as PVT, Co. D. Reported present on rolls of 1/64–4/64. Absent sick, 8/31/64. Appears on a register of Pettigrew G.H. #13, Raleigh, as admitted 8/29/64 and returned to duty 9/13/64. Present Sept.–Oct./64. Dsh 11/8/64. Stood 5'7", had fair complexion, blue eyes, light hair. (CSR 270:9)

Triplett, Joel: Resident of Watauga Co. At age 34, enl. 2/28/62 as PVT, Co. D. Reported present on rolls of May–Dec./62. Absent to buy a horse, Jan.–Feb./63. Reported present Mar.–Apr./63. Went home to buy a horse, July–Aug./63. AWOL 6/30–10/31/63. Present Nov.–Dec./63. Absent on frl, Jan.–Feb./64. Present 2/29–Apr./64, 8/31–12/64. Captured at Ford's Depot, 4/3/65. Released on taking oath, 6/21/65. Had a dark complexion, dark brown hair, blue eyes, stood 5'11". Horses killed at Auburn, 10/63, and Ground Squirrel Church, 5/64. (CSR 270:9; Davis)

Triplett, Nimrod: From Watauga Co. At age 37, enl. 5/11/61 as PVT, Co. D. Reported present on rolls of Nov.–Dec./61. Absent sick at home Jan.–Feb./62. Reported absent sick in a Petersburg hospital, May–June/62. Reported present, 6/30/62–12/62. Absent to buy a horse, Jan.–Feb./63. Present Mar.–Apr./63. Described as "brave" and "gallant." KIA 7/10/63 near Funkstown, Md. (CSR 270:9; Davis)

Triplett, Tolbert: Psb. a resident of Wilkes Co., but more likely from Ashe. Enl. in Ashe Co. on 3/7/62 as PVT, Co. A. Absent sick at Winchester, Sept.–Oct./62. Reported present on rolls of 11/62–4/63, July–Aug./63. AWOL Sept.–Oct./63. Reported present on rolls of 11/30/63–2/29/64. Present 4/1/64, but also listed as absent on detached service in N.C., Mar.–Apr./64. Present 7/64–12/64. On a roll of POWs as captured at Amelia C.H., 4/3/65, and released 6/21/65 on taking oath. Had dark complexion, dark brown hair, blue eyes, and stood 6'¾", (CSR 270:9; AsheCo; McNeil)

Truehart, James: PVT, Co. I. On a list of staff officers serving at H.Q. Cav. Corps, Army of Tennessee, and prl in Greensboro, N.C. 4/26/65. (CSR 270:9)

Tucker, James P.: From Wayne Co. At age 25, enl. in Co. H as PVT, 7/1/61. Reported present on rolls of Nov.–Dec./61, Jan.–Feb./62, May–June/62, Sept.–Oct./62, Jan.–Apr./63. WIA near Boonsboro, Md. and sent to a Richmond hospital, July–Aug./63. Present 9/63–2/64. Also present Mar.–Apr./64 and listed on extra or daily duty. Present 4/30/64–10/64. Listed on extra duty as commissary SGT, Nov.–Dec./64. (CSR 270:9)

Turner, H.G.: PVT, Co. A. (AsheCo)

Turner, Hugh C.: From Ashe Co. Enl. 3/5/62 as PVT, Co. A. Reported present on rolls of 11/62–12/62. Detached in care of baggage at Gordonsville, Jan.–Feb./63–4/63. Present July–Oct./63. Prm 4CPL 11/1/63. According to muster roll of 11/30–12/31/63, absent on detached service with unserviceable horses beginning 11/1/63. Listed at recruiting camp beginning 11/15/63 on muster rolls of 1/1/64–2/29/64. Listed on detached service at infirmary camp since 11/15/63 on roll of 4/1/64. Absent on detached service in N.C. to remount himself on rolls of Mar.–Apr./64 and July–Aug./64. Present 9/64–12/64. Captured near Williamsport, MD 9/19/62 and prl the same month. On a register of a Charlottesville G.H., admitted 11/20/63 and returned to duty 11/28/63. Also on a list of casualties in Gordon's Brigade during the Bristoe Campaign as wounded slightly. (CSR 270:9; AsheCo)

Turner, John: Identified by Fred C. Foard as a 1st NC Cav trooper; although Foard's letter is inaccurate in many respects. (Fred C. Foard to W.G. Means, March 6, 1917, Fred C. Foard Papers, PC 500, NCSA.)

Turner, John Smith: B. 12/12/39. From Cabarrus Co. At age 21, enl. as PVT, Co. F, 6/15/61. Reported present on rolls of 11/61–2/62, May–June/62, 9/62–12/62, July–Aug./63, 9/63–12/64. Prm to CPL 7/1/64. Prm LT for gallantry at Chamberlain's Run, 4/65. On a list of POWs prl between 4/11 and 4/21/65 by the PVM, Army of the Potomac. Resident of Smith's Ford, circa 1893. D. 3/24/26. Bur. Mt. Pleasant Methodist Church Cem., Cabarrus Co. (CSR 270:9; Mizelle; Bounty Receipts; Barringer; Cabarrus calls him John L.; Graves calls him John Smith)

Turner, Nicholas G.: From Ashe Co., resident of Jefferson. Enl. 2/24/62 in Co. A. PVT, 1SGT. Reported present on rolls of Sept.–Dec./62, and listed as Assistant QM SGT. Present Jan.–Feb./63, and also Mar.–Apr./63 on daily duty service in the QM department. Absent on detached service to buy a horse, July–Aug./63. On the register of a Raleigh G.H. as admitted 9/30/63 and returned to duty 10/8/64. Reported present on rolls of 9/63–2/29/64, 4/1/64. Absent on detached service to NC to buy a fresh horse according to Mar.–Apr./64 roll. Present July–Dec./64. Prm 2LT. Captured at Dinwiddie C.H., 4/3/65, and also listed as captured in a Richmond hospital the same day. (CSR 270:9; AsheCo)

Turnmire, Larkin G.: From Watauga Co. At age 22, enl. as PVT, Co. D, 2/28/62. Reported present on rolls of 5/62–4/63. Absent on detached service as a teamster in the ordnance department, 6/63–2/64. Listed present on extra duty, 2/29–3/31/64. Present Mar.–Apr./64. Trn to Co. C., 37th N.C. troops, 7/21/64. (CSR 270:9; Davis)

Tuthero, Silas: PVT, Co. K. Enl. 6/25/61. From Macon Co., age 21. Reported present on rolls of 11/61–2/62, May–June/62, 9/62–4/63, 7/63–8/63, 10/31/63, and 11/63–3/31/64. Absent on horse detail, 3/64–8/31/64. Present Sept.–Dec./64. Also listed as slightly wounded in the Bristoe Campaign. (CSR 270:9)

Tutherow, A.M.: PVT, Co. K, from Macon Co., age 23. Dsh for disability. (CSR 270:9)

Tutherow, John: PVT, Co. K. From Macon Co., age 27. Rejected by Col. Baker. (CSR 270:9)

Tuttle, B. Marcus: Enl. 8/27/63 as PVT, Co. D. Reported present on rolls of Sept.–Oct./64. Listed absent as courier at relay post, Nov.–Dec./64. (CSR 270:9)

Twitty, Robert Cheek: B. 1838. Enl. 2/3/64 as PVT, Co. E. Reported present 4/1/64. On rolls of Mar.–Apr./64, listed as absent on detached service in N.C. to buy a horse. On rolls of 4/30–8/31/64, reported at home on frl, also Sept.–Oct./64. Dsh and prm to regimental ADJ, 11/28/64. Still serving in that position as of 3/21/65. D. 1903. Bur Twitty Cem, Manson, Warren Co., NC. (CSR 270:1, 9; GLP; CGR: 2; Box 42, Folder 19, Military Collection, Civil War Collection, NCSA)

Tye, W.B.: From Union Co. Enl. 6/3/61 as PVT, Co. C. Reported present on rolls of 11/61–2/62, 5/62–4/63. Absent detailed to NC to buy a horse, 8/27/63. Reported present on rolls of 9/63–12/63. Deserted 1/18/64 according to muster rolls. (CSR 270:9; Alexander)

Tyra, Alfred: From Watauga Co., age 24. Enl. 5/11/61 as PVT, Co. D. Reported present on rolls of 11/61–2/62, 5/62–6/62. Listed as missing and captured in Pennsylvania, 10/10/62, and later declared killed. (CSR 270:9; Davis)

Ualle, P.O.: PVT, Co. C. (Alexander)

Underwood, S.M.: From Union Co. At age 22, enl. 5/25/61 as PVT, Co. C. Reported present on company muster rolls of 11/61–2/62. Absent sick beginning 5/29/62, according to rolls of May–June/62. Reported present on company muster rolls of 6/30/62–4/63, 7/63–12/64. (Alexander; CSR 270:10)

Underwood, William H.: From Northampton Co. At age 35, enl. 6/27/61 as PVT, Co. B. D. 11/13/61 at a Fredericksburg G.H. (CSR 270:10)

Upchurch, A.J.: From Franklin Co. At age 22, enl. 8/61 as PVT, Co. E. Reported present on company muster rolls of Jan.–Feb./62. Also reported admitted to a Danville G.H. with diarrhea, 1/2/62. Sent to a Richmond G.H. Rolls of May–June/62 list him as absent sick in a Goldsboro, NC G.H. beginning 5/1/62. Still reported absent on rolls of 12/62. Reported present on company muster rolls of Jan.–Apr./63. KIA 6/9/63 at Brandy Station, VA. (Pearce: 291; CSR 270:10)

Upchurch, J.N.: From Franklin Co. At age 19, enl. 8/11/61 as PVT, Co. E. Reported present on company muster rolls of Jan.–Feb./62. Absent sick in a Petersburg G.H. as of 5/13/62. Reported present on rolls of Sept.–Dec./62. Absent on detached service, Jan.–Feb./63. Reported present on company muster rolls of Mar.–Apr./63, July–Aug./63, 6/30/63–12/64. Horse KIA at Buckland, VA, 10/19/63. Prm CPL. Captured near Petersburg, 4/3/65. D. 4/18/65, from pneumonia according to Federal records. Bur. at Point Lookout. (PL: 169; Pearce: 292; CSR 270:10)

Uzzell, James: B. 3/8/33. From Wayne Co. Fair complexion, blue eyes, dark hair, farmer. PVT, Co. H. Enl. 6/20/61. Reported present Nov.–Dec./61. Absent Jan.–Mar./62, and reported on sick frl as of 2/3/62. Diagnosed with typhoid fever and varicose veins that prevent him from riding and marching. Dsh 5/19/62. D. 11/6/18. Bur in family cem, New Hope Township, Wayne Co., NC. Co. H. (CGR: 3; CSR 270:10)

Uzzell, Joshua: B. 1841 In Wayne County. Enl 6/20/61 as PVT, Co. H. Reported present 11/61–2/62. D. 4/12/62 from unspecified disease, possibly in Wilmington. Unmarried, no children. Bur in family cem, New Hope Township, Wayne Co., NC. Co. H. (CGR: 3; CSR 270:10)

Uzzell, Major D. Wayne County native. At age 20, enl 6/20/61 as PVT, Co. H. Reported present 11/61–2/62. Listed on report of sick and wounded at Manassas G.H. as dying 1/10/62 from typhoid fever. Also reported admitted 1/1/62 to a Danville G.H., and "left without our knowledge." (CSR 270:10)

Vail, Thomas L.: From Wayne County. Age 33. 1 LT, Co. H. Appointed either 8/20/61 or 10/2/61 to rank from 5/16/61. Reported present 11/61–3/62,

May–June/62. Reported admitted to Danville G.H. with pneumonia, 1/3/62, and transferred to Charlottesville. Rosters of Sept.–Oct./62 list him as resigned and accepted on 10/14/62. Reason: "my health is much impaired." R. 10/14/62. Later listed as on light duty as a conscript. Took oath at Charlotte, 5/29/65. (CSR 270:1, 10)

Vance, J.C.: From Mecklenburg Co. Enl. 3/12/62 as PVT, Co. C. Reported absent on May–June/62 rosters as sick since 5/15/62. Rosters of 6/30–10/31/62 listed him as dying on 7/7/62. Died at Wilson G.H., leaving $5.35. (Alexander; CSR 270:10)

Vanhoy, Norman H.: Enl. 9/22/63 as PVT, Co. B. Reported present, 4/30/64–12/64. (CSR 270:10)

Vann, James Henry.: From Northampton Co. At age 18, enl. 6/18/61 as PVT, Co. B. Reported present, 11/61–2/62. According to rolls of Mar.–Apr./62, left absent sick at Orange C.H. on 3/21/62. Listed on regimental return of 2/62 as being on detached service. Returns of 3/62 report him absent sick at Petersburg G.H. Also reported admitted 3/18/62 to Richmond G.H., then given a 30 day frl as of 4/24/62. D. 3/62. (CSR 270:10)

Vann, William: From Northampton Co. At age 25, enl. 6/12/61 as PVT, Co. B. Reported present, 11/61–4/62. Returns of 2/62 list him as on extra duty with the quartermaster's dept. Reports of Sept.–Oct./62 listed him as absent sick at home beginning 8/10/62. Prm to 2LT with Wheeler's Bn, 9/62. Listed as AWOL, Nov.–Dec./62. D. 6/23/64, according to a report of sick and wounded in NC hospitals. (CSR 270:10)

Van Pelt, J.N.: From Mecklenburg Co. At age 22, enl. 5/25/61 as PVT, Co. C. Reported present 11/61–2/62. Admitted to Orange C.H. G.H. 11/9/61 with remittent fever. Returned to duty on 12/3/61. Rolls of May–June/62 list him as absent as a POW beginning 6/29/62 (Willis Church). Reported present on rolls of 6/30/62–4/63. Absent on detached service as a courier for Gen. J.E.B. Stuart beginning in 8/63 and continuing Jan.–Feb./64 and Jan.–Feb./64. Reported present, Mar.–Dec./64. (Alexander; CSR 270:10; note: records intermingled with J.W. Van Pelt's.)

Van Pelt, J.W.: PVT, Co. C. Records from the Petersburg G.H. and elsewhere indicate that his left arm or a portion of it amputated, apparently due to a minie ball wound, on 3/31/65. Captured 4/3/65. Later admitted to the Ft. Monroe G.H., then prl on taking the oath 6/29/65. Age 25. According to Federal records, stood 5'8" tall, had light hair and dark eyes, and born in N.C. (*Medical History* 10: 731; CSR 270:10; note: records intermingled with J.N. Van Pelt's)

Vaughan, Richard M.: From Northampton Co. At age 25, enl. 6/20/61 as PVT, Co. B. Reported present 11/61–2/62, May–June/62. Absent at home sick since 8/10 according to rolls of Sept.–Oct./62. AWOL Nov.–Dec./62. Rolls of Jan.–Feb./63 listed him as absent in a hospital beginning 2/1. Reported present Mar.–Apr./63, 6/30/12/63, 4/1/64. Absent on frl according to rolls of Mar.–Apr./64, then reported present 4/30–10/64. (CSR 270:10)

Vaughn, Elisha T.: From Northampton Co. At age 19, enl. 6/18/61 as PVT, Co. B. Reported present 11/61–4/62, 9/62–4/63, July–Aug./63. Regimental returns of 3/62 list him as in charge of horses. KIA at Jack's Shop, 9/22/63. "He was a good man and brave soldier," reports the Roll of Honor. (CSR 270:10).

Vaughn, James: From Northampton Co. At age 17, enl. 6/18/61 as PVT, Co. B. Reported absent to home on sick leave, 11/61–2/62. Reported present Mar.–Apr./62, Sept.–Oct./62. Absent on detached service Nov.–Dec./62. Reported present, Jan.–Apr./63. Listed as AWOL 6/30–10/31/63, but also listed as absent on detached service in NC procuring horses as of 8/27, and as absent at home sick Nov.–Dec./63. (CSR 270:10)

Vaughn, John T.: From Northampton Co. At age 23, enl. 6/61 as PVT, Co. B. Reported present, 11/61–4/62, Sept.–Oct./62. Absent on detached service, Nov.–Dec./62. Reported present, Jan.–Apr./63. Absent on detached service with Maj. Biggs of the Commissary Dept., July–Aug./63. Reported present, 6/30–10/31/63. Absent at home on frl, Nov.–Dec./63. Reported present on rolls of Mar.–Apr./64 and 4/1/64. Admitted 5/19/64 to a Richmond G.H. and 5/23 to a Danville G.H. with a gunshot wound in the arm; frl 6/20/64. Listed absent as a POW from 4/30–10/64. Captured at Reams Station, 9/29/64, and exd in 3/65. (Zeb. Vance Papers, NCSA [courtesy Whit Joyner]; CSR 270:10)

Vauldin, John V.: Co G. Listed in the Mansion House Hotel in Salisbury on 5/9/65. (Mansion House Register)

Vickers, Andrew Jackson: From Cabarrus Co. At age 20, enl. 6/15/61 as PVT, Co. F. Reported present, 11/61–2/62, May–June/62, Sept.–Dec./62., KIA Upperville, VA, 6/21/63. (Barringer; Mizelle; Cabarrus; CSR 270:10)

Vincent, J.W.: Enl 1/26/64 as PVT, Co. H. Reported present, Mar.–Oct./64. Absent on detached service, Nov.–Dec./64. (CSR 270:10)

Wade, John W.: From Northampton Co. At age 26, enl 6/12/61 as PVT, Co. B. Reported present, Nov.–Dec./61. Absent sick in a hospital, Jan.–Feb./62. Also listed as absent sick on regimental return of 2/62. Reported present Mar.–Apr./64, 9/62–4/63, 6/30–12/63, Mar.–Oct./64. (CSR 270:10)

Walker, Albert H.: From Charlotte. At age 20, enl. 6/25/61 as PVT, Co. K. Reported present 11/61–2/62, May–June/62, Sept.–Oct./62. Absent 11/62–2/63 detailed to report to a Lt. Roane in Macon Co., beginning 12/26/62. Reported present Mar.–Apr./63, July–Aug./63, and 10/31/63, and promoted to 4CPL 7/1/63. Absent detached on horse duty In NC and also listed as 3CPL, Nov.–Dec./63. Reported absent on detached service, Jan.–Feb./64. Reported present, 2/29–10/64. Absent on horse detail, Nov.–Dec./64. (CSR 270:10)

Walker, Henry C.: Enl. 9/29/63 or 10/9/64 as PVT, Co. F. Reported present, Sept.–Oct./64. Not stated Nov.–Dec./64 but listed as detached to NC to buy a horse as of 1/1/65. (Barringer; CSR 270:10)

Walker, J.B.: From Mecklenburg Co. At age 27, enl. 5/8/62 as PVT, Co. C. Listed absent sick on rolls of May–June/62 since 5/29/62. Rolls of 6/30–10/31/62 list him as detached as of 7/1/62. (Alexander; CSR 270:10)

Walker, James H.: B. 1826. Enl. 6/15/61 as PVT, Co. F. Reported present 11/6102/62. Regimental return of 3/62 lists him as absent in a G.H. as of 2/25/62. Prm. 3CPL. Receipt roll dated Hanover Junction lists him as dying 4/28/63. Other records confirm that he D. 4/7/62 at a Petersburg G.H. Unmarried and no children. Stood 6' 3", had a dark complexion, blue eyes, and dark hair. Farmer. Bur. Rocky River Presbyterian Church Cem., near Concord. (Barringer; Mizelle; Janet Morrison to the author, 9/19/98; CSR 270:10)

Walker, James J.: 3CPL (Cabarrus)

Walker, S.W.: From Wake Co. At age 19, enl 7/2/61 as PVT, Co. E. Absent on rolls of Jan.–Feb./62 at Culpeper G.H. since 1/2/62. Other reports list him as admitted 1/4/62 to Danville G.H. with diarrhea, and sent to Culpeper. Reported present May–June/62, 9/62–4/63. Absent sick at a G.H. since 6/9/63 according to rolls of July–Aug./63. Reported present 6/30/63–4/1/64. Absent on detached service in NC after horses, Mar.–Apr./64. Reported present, 4/30–12/64. Prm 4CPL according to rolls of Sept.–Oct./64. (CSR 270:10)

Wallace, John A.: PVT, Co. C. On Point Lookout POW roll as captured at Ford's Depot, 4/3/65. Arrived at Point Lookout 4/13/65. Released on taking the oath, 6/3/65. (CSR 270:10)

Wallace, M.L.: From Mecklenburg Co. At age 28, enl. 5/14/62 as PVT, Co. C. Reported present May–June/62. Absent on detached service at Winchester beginning 10/1/62 according to rolls of 6/30–10/31/62. Absent on a scout beginning 12/25/62 according to rolls of Nov.–Dec./62. Rolls of Jan.–Feb./63 list him as absent In NC buying a horse as of 2/21/63. Reported present Mar.–Apr./63, 7/63–10/64. KIA 12/10/64. (Alexander; CSR 270:10)

Wallace, William: From Mecklenburg Co. At age 37, enl. 3/30/63 as PVT, Co. C. Reported present, Mar.–Apr./63. KIA at Upperville, VA, dated to 8/21/63. (Alexander; CSR 270:10)

Walls, P.P.: From Mecklenburg Co. At age 25, enl. 5/28/61 as PVT, Co. C. Absent sick according to rolls of Nov.–Dec./61. Reported present, Jan.–Feb./62, 5/62–4/63. Regimental returns of 3/62 list him as on the sick roll at a Petersburg G.H., 3/23/62. Absent on detached service beginning 8/1/63 or 8/7/63 according to rolls of July–Aug./63, 9/63–2/64, 4/1/64, 8/1/64. Reported present, Mar.–Apr./64. On a 7/64 muster roll of Co. B, Ward's Confederate Bn, as a prisoner at Lynchburg having deserted. (CSR 270:10)

Walston, Rufus: From Greene Co. At age 21, enl. 7/9/61 as PVT, Co. H. Reported present 11/61–2/62, May–June/62,–Dec./62. Absent on frl, Jan.–Feb./63. Reported present Mar.–Apr./63. Absent July–Aug./63 after being captured near Beverly Ford (during the Battle of Brandy Station) on 6/9/63. Prl 6/11/63. Reported present 9/63–8/31/64. Reported AWOL while on frl, Sept.–Oct./64. Reported present Nov.–Dec./64. Middle initial given as either S., T., or F. (CSR 270:10)

Walter, Paul: From Cabarrus Co. At age 32, enl. 6/15/61 as PVT, Co. F. Reported present Nov.–Dec./61. Reported admitted 1/3/62 to a Danville G.H. with bronchitis and transferred to a Front Royal G.H. Reported absent on rolls of Jan.–Feb./62 after being sent to a GH as of 2/25/62. Also reported sick on regimental returns of 2/62. Reported present May–June/62, Sept.–Dec./62, July–Aug./63. Rolls of Sept.–Oct./63 list him as KIA at Jack's Shop on 9/22/63. Other reports list him as d. 10/1/63 from wounds. Middle initial given as either M. or A. (CSR 270:10; Barringer; Mizelle; Cabarrus)

Ward, John: Enl. 5/4/64 as PVT, Co. D. Reported present on rolls of Sept.–Dec./64. (CSR 270:10)

Ward, Josiah: Born in Martin Co. Farmer by trade. At age 40, enl. 6/20/61 as PVT, Co. H. Reported present on rolls of 11/61–2/62. D. of disease,

4/19/62. Stood 5' 9½", had a fair complexion, gray eyes, and light hair. (CSR 270:10)

Warle, W.: PVT., Col B. Listed on register of sick and wounded at the U.S. Smallpox Hospital, Point Lookout, MD, as admitted 12/12 after being captured 7/5. Also listed at returned to duty on 12/15. Not dated. NFR. (CSR 270:10)

Warlick, Pinckney D.: From Northampton Co. At age 40, enl. 10/2/64 at Camp Holmes. Reported present Nov.–Dec./64. NFR. (CSR 270:10)

Warren, James C.: Enl. /12/61 as PVT, Co. B. Reported absent at home on sick leave, Nov.–Dec./61, absent sick in a G.H. Jan.–Apr./62. Regimental returns also report him sick in a G.H. at Petersburg. On the register of a Danville G.H. as admitted 1/17/62 and sent to Ward #8. 1/62 report of sick and wounded report him as having pneumonia. DSH 3/62. (CSR 270:10)

Warren, Jesse B.: From Northampton Co. At age 35, enl. 7/26/61 as PVT, Co. B. Reported present Nov.–Dec./61. Rosters of Jan.–Feb./62 report him as D. at Moore G.H. in Manassas Junction on 1/25/62. Another report lists him as D. 1/20. Alternate middle initial is P. (CSR 270:10)

Wasson, F.A.: Enl. 9/22/63 as PVT, Co. B. Reported present on rolls of 4/30–12/64. (CSR 270:10)

Waterbury, William: PVT, Co. H. DSH 9/1/61 per S.O. 149 A.G.O. 1861, Par. 9. (CSR 270:10)

Waters, Elisha: Enl. 9/21/64 as PVT, Co. G. Reported present Sept.–Dec./64. On rosters of Nov.–Dec./64, reported in state service before being assigned to the rgt by a Col. Mallett. (CSR 270:10)

Waters, Owen T.: From Beaufort Co. At age 42, enl. 6/26/61 as PVT, Co. I. Reported present 11/61–2/62, May–June/62. Reports of 9/62–4/63, 8/1/63, and 1/1/64–8/31/64 list him as absent on detached service at brigade HQ driving a wagon/serving as a teamster. Rosters of Sept.–Oct./64 list him as dsh due to age, having turned 45. (CSR 270:10)

Watkins, J.A.: Enl. 10/3/64 as PVT, Co. B. Reported present Nov.–Dec./64. (CSR 270:10)

Watkins, R.C.: Enl. 9/22/63 as PVT, Co. B. Reported present 4/30/64–12/64. (CSR 270:10)

Watson, J.W.: Co. E. Admitted 3/31/63 to a Staunton G.H. (CSR 270:10)

Watson, Lewis N.: Enl. 3/14/64 as PVT, Co E. Reported present on rolls of Mar.–Dec./64. Horse listed as KIA at Ground Squirrel Church. On register of a Petersburg G.H. as admitted 7/4/64 with dysentery. Frl for 60 days on 7/16/64. Bur Fairview Cem, Warrenton, N.C. B. 11/20/34, D. 6/10/11. (CSR 270:10; CGR: 2)

Watson, Noah: Co. E. Reported in a G.H., 5/28/62. Name listed on a record of dead soldiers' property. (CSR 270:10)

Watson, W.A.: Born Chester, South Carolina. At age 32, enl. 5/28/61 as PVT, Co. C. Reported present 11/61–2/62, 5/62–10/31/62. Absent in NC on 12/25/62 to take charge of horses purchased by Lt. Maxwell, Nov.–Dec./62. Also listed on detached service Jan.–Feb./63. According to rolls of Mar.–Apr./63 and 7/63–4/1/64, absent sick since 4/1/63. Other records report him as admitted 5/4/64 to a Richmond G.H. with bronchitis. Also admitted 8/14/64 to a Richmond G.H. Rolls of Sept.–Oct./64 list him as absent sick since 5/5/64. Admitted 10/64 to a Richmond G.H., then frl 10/21/64 for 60 days. Reported present Nov.–Dec./64. Diagnosed with disease of the lungs; dsh 1/25/65. Had a mild complexion, blue eyes, and light hair. A carpenter by trade. (Alexander; CSR 270:10)

Watson, William A.: B. 3/22/32. Enl. 5/25/61 as PVT, Co. D. D. 4/1/18. Bur. Lexington City Cem., Lexington, NC. (Stepp)

Watson, William J.: B. in Sampson Co. From Duplin Co. At age 27, enl. 6/17/61 as PVT, Co. I. Reported present, 11/61–2/62. KIA 6/29/62. (CSR 270:10)

Watts, William: From Boone. Enl. 3/10/64 as PVT, Co. D. Reported present Mar.–Apr./64. Absent at home to procure a horse, 8/31/64. Reported present, Sept.–Dec./64. Prl at Appomattox C.H., 4/9/65. (CSR 270:10)

Waycaster, John N.: B. Yancey Co. From Macon Co. At age 20, enl. 6/25/61 as PVT, Co. K. Reported present 11/61–2/62, May–June/62. Rolls of Sept.–Dec./62 list him absent wounded in action and sent to a Richmond G.H. as of 8/1/62. Reported on 10/62 sick and wounded report with a gunshot wound. Dsh 10/24/62. Right foot amputated due to gunshot wound, 7/1/62. Also listed as absent on rolls of Jan.–Feb./63. Had a dark complexion, black eyes, and hair. (CSR 270:10)

Wayman, J.W.: Enl. 9/22/63 as PVT, Co. B. Absent sick, 4/30–12/64. (CSR 270:10)

Weaver, J.D.: Resident of Polk Co. Enl. 9/21/64 as PVT, Co. G. Reported present, Sept.–Dec./64. Was in state service prior to being assigned to the regiment by Col. Mallett. Had a dark complexion, brown hair, gray eyes. Stood 5' 6". Captured at Amelia C.H., 4/3/65. Took the oath on 6/21/65 and released. (CSR 270:10)

Weaver, J.L.: Enl. 5/9/61 as PVT, Co. G. Reported present, Nov.–Dec./64. (CSR 270:10)

Webb, Alfred: From Buncombe Co. At age 41, enl. 3/62 as PVT, Co. G. Reported present, May–June/62, Sept.–Dec./62. Absent on detached service Jan.–Feb./63. Absent on detached service at Gordonsville according to rolls of Mar.–Apr./63. Reported present, July–Oct./63. Absent at home on sick frl, Sept.–Dec./63. Absent on detached service at Bowling Green according to 4/1/64 rolls. Rolls of Mar.–Apr./64 list him as absent on detached service at brigade HQ. Rolls of 4/30–8/31/64 report him absent guarding the commissary train. Also listed as absent on detached service July–Dec./64. Admitted 3/25/64 to a Richmond G.H. for duty. Probably prl by 10th Michigan Cavalry Regiment at Newton, NC on 4/19/65. (CSR 270:10)

Webb, Joseph W.: Enl. 5/64 as PVT, Co. D. Reported present 8/31/64. Absent on horse detail, Sept.–Oct./64. Reported present on rolls of Nov.–Dec./64. (CSR 270:10)

Webb, William H.: From Johnson Co. At age 24, enl. 6/27/61 as PVT, Co. H. Reported present 11/61–2/62. Regimental returns of 3/62 show him in a G.H. 3/1/62; also reported admitted to a Richmond G.H. 3/14/62 with a gunshot wounded in the thigh. Frl to 6/2/62. Reported present May–June/62, 9/62–4/63, 7/63–12/64. (CSR 270:10)

Webster, William M.: Enl. 9/21/64 as PVT, Co. K. Reported present, Sept.–Dec./64. (CSR 270:10)

Weir, Philip: PVT, Co. G. NFR. May also have been Philip Ware, 9th Virginia Infantry. (CSR 270:10)

Welch, James A.C.: B. Cabarrus Co. At age 23, enl. 6/15/61 as PVT, Co. F. Rolls of 11/61–2/62 list him as absent in a Petersburg H.G. as of 11/5/6.' Regimental return of 2/62 list him as absent sick; 3/62 returns report him as on frl since 11/14/62. Dsh 4/22/62. Spinal disease. Stood 5' 8½" tall, had a fair complexion, blue eyes, dark hair. Farmer. (CSR 270:10; Barringer; Mizelle)

Welch, John T.L.: From Cherokee Co. At age 27, enl. 6/25/61 as PVT, Co. K. Reported present 11/61–2/62. Regimental return lists him as in a Richmond G.H. as of 3/11. Reported present May–June/62, 9/62–4/63, July–Aug./63, 10/31/63–3/31/64. Assigned role of artificer, 10/31/63. Absent sick at a G.H., Mar.–Dec./64. Also reported admitted to a Richmond G.H., 6/10/64. May also have served in the 5th NC Cavalry Regiment. (CSR 270:10)

Welch, Mandes J.: Enl. 8/64 as PVT, Co. K. Reported present, Sept.–Dec./64. (CSR 270:10)

Welch, Robert W.: From Macon Co. At age 19, enl. 7/11/61 as PVT, Co. K. Reported present 11/61–2/62. Regimental return lists him in a Richmond G.H. as of 3/11/62. D. 4/7/62 from disease, at Petersburg. (CSR 270:10)

Wells, Daniel D.: From Duplin Co. 2LT, Co. I. One record says commissioned 6/17/61 but another says he was never commissioned. Resigned; accepted 9/28/61. (CSR 270:10)

Werner, L.: From Mecklenburg Co. At age 25, enl. 5/30/61 as PVT, Co. C. Muster rolls of Nov.–Dec./61 lists him as deserting 10/23/61 at Richmond. (Alexander; CSR 270:10)

Wesson, Josephus: From Northampton Co. At age 29, enl. 7/8/61 as PVT, Co. B. Reported absent at a Petersburg G.H. as of 11/29/61 according to rolls of Nov.–Dec./61. Also reported absent sick on rolls Jan.–Feb./62. Rolls of Mar.–Apr./62 list him as D 12/22/61 at a Richmond G.H, while regimental return of 3/62 report him D 12/20/61. (CSR 270:10)

West, W.P.: PVT, Co. A. Confined at Knoxville, TN as a deserter on 11/8/64. Given a certificate of loyalty and released. May have been a member of the 9th Bn NC Infantry, not the 1st NC Cavalry. (CSR 270:10)

West, W.R.: From Buncombe Co. Enl. 5/16/61 as 1LT, Co. G. Resigned 8/61. (CSR 270:10)

Whaley, Amos H.: From Duplin Co. At age 22, enl. 7/4/61 as PVT, Co. I. Reported present Jan.–Feb./62, May–June/62. Absent sick at a Richmond G.H. according to rolls of Sept.–Oct./62. Admitted 9/30/62 to a Richmond G.H.; still in the hospital on 11/18/62. Absent on detached service according to rolls of Nov.–Dec./62. Reported present Jan.–Apr./63, 10/31/63, Jan.–Feb./64. Rolls of Mar.–Apr./64 (dated 9/7/64) and 4/31–8/31/64 reported him as KIA on either 5/13 or 5/15/64 near Richmond. (CSR 270:10)

Whaley, J.J.: Enl. 4/18/64 as PVT, Co. I. Trn from 3rd NC Infantry Regiment. Reported present on rolls of Mar.–Apr./64 (dated 9/7/64), 4/31–8/31/64, and Sept.–Dec./64. D. Claim on 2/20/65 for effects of Jason Whaley. (CSR 270:10)

Wheless, E.L.: From Louisburg. Enl. 7/2/61 as PVT, Co. E. Reported present, Mar.–Apr./63. Reported In a Liberty, VA G.H., May–June/63. Rolls of July–Aug./63 list him on detached service In Nelson Co., VA with disabled horses as of 8/25/63. Reported present 6/30–Dec./63. Absent on frl, Jan.–Dec./64. (CSR 270:10)

Wheless, Elijah J.: From Franklin Co. At age 25, Enl. 7/2/61 as PVT, Co. E. Reported present 1/02/62, May–June/62, Sept.–Dec./62. (Pearce: 293; CSR 270:10)

Wheless, James H.: From Franklin Co. At age

26, enl. 7/8/62 as PVT, Co. E. Absent on detached service at Winchester according to rolls of Sept.–Oct./62. Reported present, 11/6204/63. WIA 7/3/63 at Gettysburg according to rolls of July–Aug./63. Reported present on rolls of 6/30–12/63. Absent In Amherst Co., VA., with disabled horses according to rolls of Jan.–Feb./64 and 4/1/64. Reported present Mar.–Dec./64, although admitted to a Richmond G.H. with bronchitis on 5/5/64. WIA slightly 8/15 or 8/16/64 along Charles City Rd., near Richmond. (Pearce: 293; CSR 270:10; Richmond *Sentinel*, 8/26/64)

Wheless, William J.: From Franklin Co. At age 30, enl. 7/8/62 as PVT, Co. E. Absent on detached service with the Commissary Dept. according to rolls of 9/012/62. Absent Jan.–Feb./63. Reported present, Mar.–Apr./63, July–Aug./63, 6/30/63–4/1/64 on extra duty with the regimental QM. Absent on detached service in NC to procure a horse according to rolls of Mar.–Apr./64. Reported present, 4/30–12/64. Admitted 9/11/64 and 10/19/64 to a Raleigh G.H. with chronic diarrhea. (Pearce: 293; CSR 270:10)

Whitaker, H.A.: From Mecklenburg Co. At age 35, enl. 2/28/62 as PVT, Co. C. Regimental return of 3/62 lists him as a recruit from depot. Reported present, May–June/62. Absent sick at Warrenton since 9/13/62 according to rolls of 6/30–10/31/62. Reported present, 11/62–4/63. KIA 7/3/63 at Gettysburg. (Alexander; CSR 270:10)

Whitaker, John Henry: From Northampton Co. At age 35, enl. 5/16/61 in Co. B. Apptd. CPT Co. B, 8/20/61. Reported present, 11/61–4/62, and also reported present on regimental returns of Feb.–Mar./62. Apptd MAJ, 7/12/62. Reported present, Sept.–Oct./62. Detailed for court, 10/3/62. Granted leave, 12/24/62. Reported present, Jan.–Apr./63. Prm COL. KIA 6/29/63 at Fairfax Station. (CSR 270: 1, 10)

Whitaker, William H.: B. Halifax Co. John H. Whitaker's younger brother. Graduate of UNC. Lived in California where he practiced law. A "noble looking handsome figure with the earnest eyes." At age 23, enl. 1/1/62 in Co. B. Reported present Jan.–Feb./62 but sick in quarters. Prm 1SGT 2/1/62. Also reported present Mar.–Apr./62. Absent at home sick beginning 6/1 per rolls of Sept.–Oct./62. In a small engagement "he was complimented specially by his General." Exposure to picket duty broke down his constitution. Sent home to recuperate, but came down with pneumonia and D. 10/22/62 in Orange Co. "Died at Chapel Hill where he had done very well at UNC." Reportedly he said to his doctor, "If only I could fall on the Battle field, and could strike one more blow for my country." (Whit Joyner to author, 13 September 1994; Halifax, 23; "William Whitaker," in William Whitaker Papers, PC 1033, NCSA; CSR 270:10).

White: LT. Bur. Middleburg, VA cem. Not known if he was 1st. (Personal Knowledge)

White, Frederick: Enl. 9/22/63 as PVT, CO. B. Reported present, 4/30–12/64. (CSR 270:10)

White, J.S.: PVT, Co. C. (Alexander)

White, J.T.: Enl. 8/10/64 as PVT, Co. C. Reported present Sept.–Dec./64. (CSR 270:10)

White, John B.: At age 24, enl. 5/20/61 as PVT, Co. G (Buncombe Rangers). Regimental rolls of Jan.–Feb./62 and returns of 3/62 list him as D. in a Richmond G.H. of typhoid fever. Different sources give his date of death as either 3/17/62 or 3/24/62. People were "greatly esteemed by his acquaintance." (*Asheville News*, 4/12/62, p. 1, col. 3; CSR 270:10)

White, Marshall Lindley: B. 1841 In Cabarrus Co. Joined Rocky River Presbyterian Church, 9/8/53. Enl. 6/15/61 as PVT, Co. F. Prm to courier for LTC Baker. Regimental return place him on detached duty as the colonel's orderly. KIA Willis Church, 6/29/62. Rolls of May–June/62 list him absent as a POW, but Sept.–Oct./62 list him as KIA. Stood 6' 2" plus, had a fair complexion, gray eyes, and sandy hair. Farmer. Bur. Rocky River Presbyterian Church Cem., near Concord. In 1/65, account settled with his father, David White, providing $50 bounty. (Barringer; Mizelle; Cabarrus; Janet Morrsion to the author, 9/19/98; CSR 270:10)

White, Noah: B. Caldwell Co. At age 41, enl. 9/10/64 as PVT, Co. D. Trn from McRae's Bn. Reported present 8/31/64. Rosters of Sept.–Dec./64 report him wounded in a Raleigh G.H. Register of a Petersburg G.H. list him with a gunshot wound in the flesh, right side, having been admitted 10/28/64 and transferred to a Raleigh G.H. on 11/10/64. Stood 5' 9", had gray eyes, black hair, and a fair complexion. Farmer. (CSR 270:10)

White, R.C.: From Bertie Co. At age 22, enl. as PVT, Co. E. Dates for enl vary, include 3/20/62, 3/26/62, and 5/25/62. Reported present May–June/62, Sept.–Oct./62. absent on detached service, Nov.–Dec./62. Reported present, Mar.–Apr./63. Admitted 7/18/62 to a Richmond G.H. with bronchitis; frl 7/30/62. Listed absent on rolls of July–Aug./63, in North Carolina to procure horses, beginning 8/22/63. Reported present 6/30–10/31/63. Rolls of Nov.–Dec./63 list him as absent on detached service guarding baggage at Orange C.H. Absent Jan.–Feb./64 at Milford Station on Provost Guard. Reported present 4/1/64, although reported absent on detached service In North Carolina after a horse on rolls of Mar.–Apr./64. Absent 4/30–8/31/64 on detached service In North Carolina; also listed absent Sept.–Oct./64 on detached service at Clarksville Junction, NC. Absent Nov.–Dec./64 bailing forage. (CSR 270:10)

White, W.H.: Enl. 10/27/64 as PVT, Co. E. Reported present, Nov.–Dec./64. (CSR 270:10)

White, William Jones: B. 10/7/42. Resident of Warren Co. Enl. 8/27/61 in Co. E. QMSGT. Reported present, 11/61–6/62, Sept.–Dec./62. On rolls of Nov.–Dec./62, listed as hospital steward and also prm 2SGT. Trn to Field & Staff and reported present Jan.–Feb./63, but also still listed as hospital steward. Reported present Mar.–Apr./63, July–Aug./63. According to rolls of July–Aug./63, elected 2LT on 7/3/63. On rolls of 6/30–Dec./63, listed as acting QM of the regiment. 1/02/64 listed as dsh and prm CPT and QM of the regiment, with commission to date from 11/4/63. Reported present Jan.–Feb./64. Absent on detached service, Mar.–Apr./64. Reported present 430–12/64. D. 9/23/03. Bur Fairview Cem, Warrenton, NC. (CSR 270:1; CGR: 2, 6; CSR 270:10)

Whiteside, Francis P.: From Buncombe Co. At age 17, enl. 2/26/62 as PVT, Co. G. Reported present May–June/62. Captured at Malvern Hill, 8/5/62; frl and dsh, 8/26/62. Reported present Sept.–Dec./62, Jan.–Apr./63, July–Dec./63, Mar.–Aug./64. Listed as 4 CPL on rolls of July–Aug./63, as 3CPL on rolls of Sept.–Oct./63, and 2SGT beginning with rolls of Mar.–Apr./64. Absent on detached service to buy a horse, Sept.–Oct./64. Reported present, Nov.–Dec./64. Fought throughout the war, and "left the field, with others," on 4/9/65 after the surrender. His widow, probably living in Amarillo, TX, tried to get a badly-needed pension about 1918. (CV 26 [1918]: 327; CSR 270:10).

Whitesides, Charles D.: From Buncombe Co. At age 18, enl. 5/20/61 as PVT, Co. G. Reported present Jan.–Feb./62. Regimental returns of 3/62 place him In a Petersburg hospital. Reported present May–June/62. Admitted 7/4/62 to a Richmond hospital with bronchitis. Returned to duty 7/12/62. Reported present, Sept.–Oct./62. Listed absent sick in a hospital 11/62–2/63. Employed as a teamster, 12/27/62–4/23/63. Reported present, Mar.–Apr./63. Captured 6/21/63 at Upperville. Absent on detached service to buy a horse, July–Aug./63. Reported present Sept.–Oct./63. Rolls of Nov.–Dec./63 listed him as absent sick in a Hanover Junction hospital. D. 1/8/64 at that hospital from typhoid fever. (CSR 270:10)

Whitesides, James: From Buncombe Co. At age 20, enl. 5/20/61 as PVT, Co. G. Reported present Jan.–Feb./62. Regimental returns of 2/62 and 3/62 list him as absent sick at White Sulphur Springs. A report dated 4/10/62 lists him at a Warrenton Springs G.H., too sick to be moved. Admitted to a Charlottesville G.H. 3/31/62 due to dropsy and sent 4/23/62 to a Lynchburg G.H. Reported present May–June/62. Admitted 7/4/62 to a Richmond G.H. and returned to duty 7/12/62. Reported present 9/62–4/63. Absent after being wounded and captured according to rolls of 7/63 following. Wounded with a carbine call in the flesh of both the right and left thigh and through the scrotum. Captured near Upperville, VA, 6/21/63, 6/22/63, or 7/27/63. Listed as POW on rolls of 12/64. Reported present on muster roll of prl/exd POWs at Camp Lee, VA near Richmond, 2/17/65. (CSR 270:10)

Whitfield, Benjamin F.: From Lenoir Co. At age 17, enl. 7/22/61 as PVT, Col. H. Reported present Nov.–Dec./61. Admitted to a Danville G.H. with diarrhea, 1/2/62. Absent at a Petersburg G.H. 1/10/62 according to rolls of 1/02/62. Regimental returns of 2/62 list him as absent sick. Reported present on rolls of May–June/62, 9/62–4/63, July–Aug./63. Absent captured 9/13/63 at Kelly's Ford according to rolls of Sept.–Oct./63 following. Prl 2/25/65. (CSR 270:10)

Whitfield, Bryan: Resident of Wayne Co. At age 19, enl. 8/14/61 as PVT, Co. H. Reported present, Nov.–Dec./61. Regimental returns of 2/62 list him as absent sick and returns of 3/62 list him as on sick leave since 1/17/62. Absent at home on sick frl as of 2/17/62 according to rolls of Jan.–Feb./62. Reported present on rolls of May–June/62 and appointed CPL as of 5/20/62. Reported present 9/62–4/63. Also reported present on rolls of July–Aug./63 and listed as a 2LT. Prm 2LT 8/14/63; prm SR2LT 7/14/64. Rolls of Sept.–Oct./63 list him as absent captured on 9/13/63. Family history also reports him as WIA. Exd 2/25/65. In 1865, married Ellen P. White and had 10 children. D. At New Haven, CT. (CSR 270:1; E.M. Whitfield, *Whitfield Family*, vol. 1, present. 150. Ref. R.E.L. Krick to the author, 2/1/97; Monie; CSR 270:10)

Whitmire/Whitman, John: PVT, Co. B and/or Co. H. Captured 9/13/63. Prl at Elmira, 3/10/65. A John Whitman captured 8/13/63 and trn for ex, 3/10/65. (CSR 270:10)

Whittington, William W.F.: From Watauga Co. At age 24, enl. 8/19/61 as PVT, Co. D. Reported present Nov.–Dec./61. Reported admitted to a Richmond G.H. 1/2/62 with bronchitis. Absent at home on sick leave according to rolls of Jan.–Feb./62. Regimental returns of 2/62 list him as absent sick, and 3/62 report him as absent sick at home as of 12/28/62. Reported present May–Dec./62. Absent to procure a horse according to rolls of Jan.–Feb./63. Reported present Mar.–Apr./63, 6/30–10/31/63. Absent to procure a horse according to rolls of Nov.–Dec./63. Reported present Jan.–Mar./31/64. Mar.–Apr./64 rolls list him as absent after a horse. Reported present 8/31–Dec./64. (CSR 270:10)

Wiggins, Tapley: From Cabarrus Co. At age 24, enl. 6/15/61 as blacksmith, Co. F. Reported present 11/61–2/62, May–June/62, Sept.–Dec./62, 7/63–12/64. Resident of Rowan Co., circa 1893. (CSR 270:10; Barringer; Mizelle; Cabarrus calls him "Turphy")

Wiggs, James H.: B. 3/25/37. From Wayne Co. Goldsboro resident, clerk. Enl. 6/20/61 as PVT, Co. H. Reported absent sick In a Richmond G.H., Nov.–Dec./61. Reported present on rolls of Jan.–Feb./62, May–June/62, Sept.–Oct./62, Jan.–Apr./63, July–Oct./63. Reported absent at home on frl on rolls of Nov.–Dec./63. Reported present on extra daily duty on rolls of Jan.–Apr./64 beginning 12/10/63. According to Federal records, captured 12/10/64 "before Petersburg, on the Vaughn road, near Armstrong's Mill." Took the oath and released 5/65. Reported himself to "have always been opposed to secession." D. 10/15/90. Bur Willow Dale Cem, Goldsboro, NC. Co. I. (GLP; CGR: 3; CSR 270:10)

Wilburn, Stephen: PVT. On 11/30/64 register of oaths and deserters as having taken the oath and given transportation to Cincinnati. (CSR 270:10)

Wild, Joseph W.: CPL, Co. E. On POW rolls as arrested in Monroe Co., TN, 10/20/63. Exd 2/27/65. (CSR 270:10)

Wiliams, Albert Franklin: B. Duplin Co. A farmer from Greene Co. At age 19, enl. 6/22/61 as PVT, Co. I. Listed on the accounts of a Richmond G.H., 12/20/62–1/63. Reported present, Jan.–Feb./62. Rolls of May–June/62 list him as captured on 6/29/62. According to Federal records, age 20, stood 5/8," had light hair, blue eyes, and fair complexion. Confederate records estimate him at 5'10", Exd at Aiken's Landing, 8/5/62. Reported absent in camp at Winchester, Sept.–Oct./62. Absent on detached service, 11/62–2/63. Dsh 3/15/ or 3/29/63 or 4/4/63 on furnishing a substitute. Settled in Duplin Co., married and raised five children; d. 1926. (CSR 270:10; "A.F. Williams Diary, 1862," *Lower Cape Fear Historical Society Bulletin* XVII (3) April 1974.

Wilkerson, James: Enl. 10/24/61 as PVT, Co. F. Prm shoemaker. Dead as of 1893. (Barringer)

Wilkes, James O.: From Macon Co. Enl. 4/29/62 as PVT, Co. K. Reported present and attending to officers' horses, May–June/62, Sept.–Dec./62, Jan.–Feb./63. Also reported present Mar.–Apr./63, July–Aug./63, 10/31/63–8/64. Absent detached Sept.–Oct./64 shucking corn near Stony Creek. Absent Nov.–Dec./64 baling for age for the Q.M. (CSR 270:10)

Wilkison, J.S.: From Cabarrus Co. Enl. 10/24/64 as PVT, Co. F. Reported present Nov.–Dec./64. Reported AWOL in 3/65 and 4/65. (CSR 270:10)

Williams, B.H.: At age 21, enl. 6/21/61 as PVT, Co. I. Rejected. (CSR 270:10)

Williams, Branch: From Duplin Co. At age 30, enl. 4/20/62 as PVT, Co. I. Reported present, May–June/62, Sept.–Dec./62. Absent on detached service, Jan.–Feb./63. Absent on detached service Mar.–Apr./63 guarding baggage at Gordonsville, Va. Reported present 10/31/63, 1/1–8/31/64. Absent on detached service to procure a horse, Sept.–Oct./64. Reported present Nov.–Dec./64. (CSR 270:10)

Williams, Edwards: From Duplin Co. Age 34. PVT, Co. I. According to roster of May–June/62, absent captured on 6/29/62. According to Federal POW records, stood 5'6" tall, had gray hair, black eyes, and a dark complexion. Exd 8/5/62. Reported present Sept.–Dec./62. Absent on detached service, Jan.–Feb./63. Reported present Mar.–Apr./63, 10/31/63. Absent on detached service as a hospital guard, 12/29/63, according to rolls of 1/1/64 and Jan.–Feb./64. Absent Mar.–Oct./64. Trn 4/29/64 to 3d NC according to rolls of Nov.–Dec./64. Also listed in other records as trn to the 38th NC on 11/21/64. (CSR 270:10)

Williams, Hansley E.: From Duplin Co. At age 46, enl. 3/15/63 as PVT, Co. I. Reported present Mar.–Apr./63 and listed as a substitute for A. Williams. On hospital muster rolls of July–Aug./63 (dated 9/18/63), which also say he enlisted in 1/63. Reported present 10/31/63, Jan.–Feb./64. Captured at Snow Hill, NC, 3/17/65 or 3/28/65. Released 6/19/65. Had a fair complexion, dark hair, gray eyes, and stood 5'5" tall. (CSR 270:10)

Williams, Hiram N.: Enl. 12/28/63 as PVT, Co. K. Reported present on rolls of 2/29–3/31/64,

Mar.–Aug./31/64. Rolls of Sept.–Oct./64 list him as on detached service at Stony Creek. Rolls of Nov.–Dec./64 report him as absent after being captured 12/1/64. On a roll of sick prisoners who took the oath as released, 6/8/65. (CSR 270:10)

Williams, J.G.: From Buncombe Co. At age 30, enl. 2/20/62 as PVT, Co. G. Reported present May–June/62, Sept.–Dec./62. Absent on detached service, Jan.–Feb./63. Reported present, Mar.–Apr./63. Absent on detached service to buy a horse according to rolls of July–Aug./63. Rolls of Sept.–Oct./63 and 4/1/64 list him as AWOL since 6/25/63. Reported present Mar.–Aug./64. Absent on detached service with unserviceable horses at Stoney Creek according to rolls of Sept.–Oct./64. Rolls of Nov.–Dec./64 report him as trn to Co. K, 25th NC Infantry, on 12/3/64. (CSR 270:10)

Williams, J.M.: From Bertie Co. At age 27, enl. 4/15/62 as PVT, Co. C. Absent sick since 5/15/62 according to rolls of May–June/62. Reported present, 6/30–10/31/62. Absent scouting since 12/25/62 according to rolls of Nov.–Dec./62. Reported present Jan.–Apr./63. Absent on detached service beginning 8/27/63 to buy a horse according to rolls of July–Aug./63. Reported present, 9/63–12/64. (Alexander; CSR 270:10)

Williams, Jerry P.: From Duplin Co. At age 24, enl. 6/17/61 as PVT, Co. I. Reported present 11/61–2/62. According to rolls of May–June/62, absent as a POW after being captured 6/29/62. Federal records say he was b. in NC, age 20, stood 5'8", had light hair, gray eyes, and a sallow complexion. Exd 8/5/62. Reported present 9/62–4/63, 10/31/63, 1/1–12/64. (CSR 270:10)

Williams, Jesse K.: From Macon Co. At age 24, enl. 7/27/61 as PVT, Co. K. Reported present Nov.–Dec./61. According to rolls of Jan.–Feb./62, absent sick sent to Manassas on 2/26/62. Regimental returns of 2/62 list him as absent sick. Returns of 3/62 report him as sick in a G.H. beginning 2/26/62. Reported present May–June/62. Absent Sept.–Oct./62 after being captured at Boonsboro, MD, on 9/13/62. Reported present Nov.–Dec./62. Absent on detached service to procure a horse according to rolls of Jan.–Feb./63. Reported present, Mar.–Apr./63. Absent on rolls of July–Aug./63 after being captured 6/21/63 at Upperville, VA. Listed as AWOL as of 10/64 according to rolls of 10/31/63–10/64. Reported present Nov.–Dec./64. (CSR 270:10)

Williams, John D.: From Martin Co. At age 27, enl. 7/8/62 as PVT, Co. B. Reported present Sept.–Dec./62. Absent on detached service to buy a horse starting 2/21 according to rolls of Jan.–Feb./63. Reported present Mar.–Apr./63. Absent sent to a G.H. sick on 8/12/63 according to rolls of July–Aug./63. Reported present 6/30–12/63, 4/1/64. Absent on horse detail, Mar.–Apr./64. Reported present, 4/30–12/64. In a Charlottesville G.H. as of 4/3/65 with a gunshot wound in the left thigh. Also listed on a Danville G.H. register about the same time. (CSR 270:10)

Williams, Joseph F.: From Macon Co. At age 28, enl. 7/23/61 as PVT, Co. K. Reported present, Nov.–Dec./61. Absent sent sick to Manassas on 2/24/62 according to rolls of Jan.–Feb./62. Regimental returns of 2/62 also list him as absent sick. Reported present, May–June/62. Absent at a Winchester, VA G.H. according to rolls of Sept.–Oct./62. Listed as 1SGT. Rolls of Nov.–Dec./62 report him as D of disease at Winchester on 10/31/62. (CSR 270:10)

Williams, Starkey: From Duplin Co. At age 19, enl. as PVT, Co. I. Rejected. (CSR 270:10)

Williams, Thomas: Enl. 10/25/64 as PVT, Co. B, at Raleigh. Absent sick according to rolls of Nov.–Dec./64. NFR. (CSR 270:10)

Wilson, J.: Co. H. Admitted 7/3/62 to a Richmond G.H. and 7/6/62 to a Farmville G.H. with debility. Admitted 7/6/62 to a Farmville G.H. with a gunshot wound. Returned to duty 7/19/62. Admitted 6/64 to a Petersburg or Richmond G.H. (CSR 270:10; records may belong to John Wilson of Co. C.)

Wilson, John: From Union Co. At age 20, enl. 6/16/61 as PVT, Co. C. Reported present, 11/61–2/62, 5/62–4/63, 7/63–4/64. Absent WIA 6/21/64 according to rolls of Nov.–Dec./64. (CSR 270:10)

Wilson, John: Enl. 11/1/64 as PVT, Co. E. Reported present, Nov.–Dec./64. (CSR 270:10)

Wilson, John N.D.: From Mecklenburg Co. Resident of Cabarrus Co. At age 30, enl. 6/15/61 as PVT, Co. F. Reported present, Nov.–Dec./61. According to rolls of Jan.–Feb./62, absent sent to a G.H., 2/25/62. Regimental return of 2/62 lists him as absent sick; return of 3/62 places him in a G.H. as of 2/25. Reported present May–June/62, Sept.–Dec./62. Absent in NC to procure a horse beginning 8/27/63 according to rolls of July–Aug./63. Reported present 9/63–10/64. Absent on detached service Nov.–Dec./64 as a guard at Walker's Mill, VA. Captured at Dinwiddie C.H., 4/3/65. Released on taking the oath, 6/21/65. Had light complexion, dark brown hair, blue eyes, and stood 5'11½". (CSR 270:10)

Williams, W.R.T.: Co. B. 2LT, R. 10/15/62 (CSR 270:1)

Williamson, J.A.: PVT, Co. C. (Alexander)

Williford, T.F.: B. 1840. PVT, Co. C. Bur. Concord, NC. (Alexander; Graves)

Wilson, J.G.: PVT, Co. F. (Cabarrus)

Wilson, John N.D.: Enl. 6/15/61 as 2CPL, Co. F. Prm SGT, 1863. Captured at Namozine Church, 4/3/65. Joined Rocky River Presbyterian Church, near Concord, 11/23/78. D. 1886. (Barringer; Mizelle; Cabarrus; Janet Morrison to the author, 9/19/98)

Wilson, John: PVT, Co. C. (Alexander)

Wimbith, J.H.: Enl. 8/30/63 as PVT, Co. E. Reported present, 4/30–12/64. (CSR 270:10)

Winberger, D.H.: On an undated roll of rebel deserters as oath administered, 6/2/63. Lists dated 4/29/63 and 5/30/63 list him as a rebel deserter who reported to the Washington, D.C. provost marshal's office. (CSR 270:10)

Winders, William H.: From Duplin Co. At age 20, enl. 6/25/61 as PVT, Co. I. Reported present 11/61–2/62, May–June/62, Sept.–Dec./62. Absent on detached service, Jan.–Feb./63. Reported present Mar.–Apr./63, 10/3/63, 1/1/64. Absent on detached service in Amherst Co., VA, Jan.–Feb./64. Also reported on detached service on rolls of Mar.–Apr./64 (dated 9/7/64) as absent in NC to remount beginning 9/6/64. Reported present 4/31–10/64. Absent on detached service beginning 12/21/64 according to Nov.–Dec./64 rolls. Listed as 1CPL on rolls until the Jan.–Feb./63 roll. Prm Sgt 3/18 (not dated). (CSR 270:10)

Winebarger, Marcus D.: B. 12/25/39. From Watauga Co. Enl. 5/11/61 as Bugler, Co. D. Reported present, 11/61–2/62, 5/62–4/63. Deserted 5/25/63. According to Federal records, prl to go to Washington, D.C. on 5/27/63. D. 3/10/28. Bur. Howell Family Cem., along NC 194 N. in Watauga Co. (Davis; Stepp; CSR 270:10)

Wolfe, Artemus J.: Resident of SC. Asst. Surgeon. Commission dated 4/1/64. Reported present on rolls of 3/64–8/31/64. Absent on 60-day sick frl since 9/13/64 according to rolls of Sept.–Oct./64. Reported present, Nov.–Dec./64. (CSR 270:10; CSR 270:1 gives middle initial as A)

Wood, John M.: From Buncombe Co. At age 36, enl. 2/22/62 as PVT, Co. D. Reported present, May–June/62, 6/30–10/31/62. Reported absent sick in a G.H. on rolls of Nov.–Dec./62. Reported present on rolls of Jan.–Apr./63. Absent on detached service with unserviceable horses, 6/30–10/31/63. Rolls of 11/63–4/64 list him absent under arrest in Lynchburg. According to rolls of 8/31/64, trn to 37th NC 9/21/64. D. later in the war. (CSR 270:10)

Wood, W.W.: From Ashe Co. At age 18, enl. 6/18/61 as Bugler, Co. A. Reported present, 11/61–2/62. May have been WIA 8/28/62; record in William R. Wood's file of a PVT from Co. A. Rolls of Sept.–Oct./62 list him as absent on detached service at Winchester since 9/5. Rolls of Nov.–Dec./62 report him absent scouting beginning 12/25. Rolls of Jan.–Feb./63 list him absent on detached service with the baggage at Gordonsville. Reported present, Mar.–Apr./63. Absent on detached service to procure a horse, July–Aug./63. Reported present 9/63–4/64. Admitted 9/17/64 to a Raleigh G.H. with gonorrhea and returned to duty 9/28/64. Listed as from Jonesville, NC. Rolls of Nov.–Dec./64 report him trn to the rgt band. (AsheCo; CSR 270:10)

Wood, William R.: From Halifax Co. At age 25 or 26, enl as 1 LT in Co. B. Prm CPT, Co. G, 9/23/61. Regimental returns of 3/62 and other records list him as present and appointed CPT, 10/10/61, to rank from 6/6/61. Reported present as CPT, Co. G, May–June/62, Sept.–Dec./62. Detailed for court, 1/31/63, and reported absent at brigade court martial Jan.–Feb./63. Reported present Mar.–Apr./63. According to rolls of July–Aug./63, absent at home after being wounded at Upperville, 6/22/63. Other records list him as severely wounded at Upperville, on either 6/21 or 6/22/63, with a severe fracture of the humorous by a shell and his right arm paralyzed. Rolls of Sept.–Dec./63 list him as absent sick. Resigned 1/7/64. On extended leave, 1/64. (CSR 270:10; CSR 270:1; Halifax, 25)

Woodard, William H.: B. Wayne Co. From Johnson Co. Trader. At age 34, enl. 6/20/61 as PVT, Co. H. Absent sick at home, Nov.–Dec./61. Reported present 11/61–2/62. Regimental returns of 3/62 list him on ED with the adjutant's office. Reported present May–June/62. Absent on detached service at Winchester, Sept.–Oct./62. Rolls of Nov.–Dec./62 list him as dsh on a disability on 12/10/62. Had mumps and chronic inflammation and enlargement of the testis, which caused him difficulty when riding or walking. At dsh age 35, stood 5'11½", had a fair complexion, blue eyes, and dark hair. (CSR 270:10)

Woodfin, John W.: From Buncombe Co. Age 41. Enl. 5/16/61. Apptd CPT, Co. G, to rank from 5/16/61. Prm MAJ, 2nd NC Cavalry Regiment, 10/10/61. Resigned on 8/24/62 from 2nd NC Cavalry due to "ill-health;" endorsement by Surgeon J.G. Thomas states, "unable to perform his regular duties." (CSR 270:1; CSR 270:10)

Woodfin, Nicholas W.: Older brother of John W. Woodfin. B. 1/29/10. Served in NC legislature of 1844, 1848, 1850. Farmer, slave owner, and lawyer. Represented Buncombe Co. at secession convention. D. 5/23/76. (Biographical file of Nicholas W. Woodfin, Pack Memorial Library, Asheville, NC)

Wooding, William: From Watauga Co. At age 19, enl 5/16/61 as PVT, Co. D. D. of disease on 11/28/61 according to payroll. (CSR 270:10)

Woodlief/Woodliff, John B.: B. Franklin Co. Farmer. At age 26, enl. 6/15/61 in Co. E. Reported present Jan.–Feb./62, May–June/62. On detached service in Winchester, VA, per rolls of Sept.–Oct./62. Also reported absent on detached service, Nov.–Dec./62. Reported present Mar.–Apr./63. Absent on detached service In NC to procure a horse beginning 8/27/63, according to rolls of July–Aug./63. Rolls of 6/30–10/31/63 list him as absent sent to a GH beginning 10/28/63. Absent Nov.–Dec./63 at a Lynchburg G.H., and again listed absent Jan.–Feb./64 at a Richmond G.H. Also reported admitted to a Richmond G.H. 1/25 or 1/29/64 with a gunshot wound (minie ball) in the left knee. Returned to duty 3/15/64. Reported present 4/1/64, but then absent on rolls of Mar.–Apr./64 in a Richmond G.H., still suffering from his leg wound. Admitted 4/20/64 to a Richmond G.H. and trn 4/30/64 from a Richmond G.H. to Farmville. Admitted there 5/1/64, then sent back to a Richmond G.H. on 5/17. Reported present 4/30–10/64. Admitted 6/9/64 to a Richmond G.H. with a leg problem; frl 6/17/64. Admitted 10/1/64 to a Raleigh G.H, external turpentine application given; returned 10/15/64. Dsh due to a sore leg according to rolls of Nov.–Dec./64. Other records say dsh due to a large ulceration of the leg. Dsh date probably 12/28/64 (records say 12/28/61). Stood 5'7½", had a dark complexion, blue eyes, black hair. (Pearce: 298; CSR 270:10)

Woodliss, J.B.: PVT, Co. E. Had malaria, 10/2/64, and returned to duty 10/15/64. (*Medical History* 5: 187).

Woodring, Jacob L.: From Watauga Co. At age 22, enl. 5/11/61 as PVT, Co. D. Reported present 11/61–2/62, May–Dec./62. Absent sick at Gordsonville according to rolls of Jan.–Feb./63. Absent on detached service guarding baggage at Gordonsville according to rolls of Mar.–Apr./63. Rolls of July–Aug./63 list him as absent on detached service driving beeves, and rolls of 6/30/62–2/64 also list him absent on detached service. Rolls of 2/29–3/31/64 report him absent on detached service with the commissary department, and rolls of Mar.–Apr./64 list him as absent on detached service driving cattle. Reported present 8/31–12/64. (CSR 270:10; Davis)

Woodring, John A.: From Watauga Co. At age 22, enl. 5/11/61 as PVT, Co. D. Reported present 11/61–2/62. Rolls of May–June/62 list him as absent captured at Willis Church, 6/29/62. Federal records: B. NC, age 21, stood 5'8" tall, had light hair, dark eyes, and florid complexion. Exd 8/5/62. Reported present 6/30/62–4/63, July–Aug./63, 6/30–12/63. Absent on frl Jan.–Feb./64. Reported present 2/29–3/31/64. Absent Mar.–Apr./64 at home to procure a horse. Reported present 8/31/64. Absent on horse detail, Sept.–Oct./64. Reported present, Nov.–Dec./64. (Davis)

Woodring, William: Co. D. D. 12/10/61. (Davis)

Woodruff, William A.: Cns at PVT, Co. H, 7/15/62. Listed absent sick at Winchester on rolls of Sept.–Oct./62. Absent Nov.–Dec./62 sent to a hospital sick. According to rolls of Jan.–Feb./63, absent ill at a hospital as of 12/10/62. "Very sick" when he left the regiment. Rolls of Mar.–Apr./63 list him as D. 9/12/62 In Lynchburg but unit not informed until 4/25/63. (CSR 270:10)

Wooten, Bryant H.: From New Hanover Co. At age 28, enl. 3/20/62 as PVT, Co. I. Reported present May–June/62, 9/62–4/63, 10/31/63, 1/64–8/31/64. On a Richmond G.H. hospital muster roll to 10/31/62 dated 12/1/62. Medical Director's office list him as returned to duty, 12/6/62. Absent on a detached service horse detail beginning 10/21/64, according to rolls of Sept.–Oct./64. Rolls of Nov.–Dec./64 list him as trn 12/6/64 to 11th NC Infantry. (CSR 270:10)

Worley, Francis M.: From Duplin Co. At age 18, enl. 6/25/61 as PVT, Co. I. Rejected. (CSR 270:10)

Worsely, John B.: B. Green Co. From Pitt Co. At age 21, enl. 7/22/61 as PVT, Co. H. Reported present 11/61–2/62, May–June/62, 9/62–4/63. Rolls of July–Aug./63 report him as sent to the hospital that July. Admitted 7/3/64 to a Williamsburg G.H. Reported present 9/63–4/64. Absent sick according to rolls of 4/30–8/31/64. Absent on detached service with the dismounted men, Sept.–Oct./64. Vaccinated 9/4/64. Reported present, Nov.–Dec./64. Trn to 3rd NC Cavalry, 9/4/64. Also reported in Troop H., 6th SC Cavalry. (*The [Asheville] Daily Citizen*, 7/5/89, copy in Civil War Clippings File, Pack Memorial Library, Asheville, NC.)

Wray, George W.: Cns 10/3/64 as PVT, Co. I. Reported present Sept.–Dec./64. (CSR 270:10)

Wray, John Simpson: Cns 10/3/64 as PVT, Co. I. Reported present, Sept.–Oct./64. Rolls of Nov.–Dec./64 list him as absent on detached service after a fresh horse as of 12/23/64. (CSR 270:10)

Wray, John Stanhope: Co. I. Bur Sunset Cem, Cleveland Co, NC. B 1/20/47, D 5/12/27. (GLP; CGR: 2)

Wren, John A.: From Buncombe Co. At age 24, enl 5/20/61 as PVT, Co. G. On a receipt roll for pay, 11/28/61. NFR. (CSR 270:10)

Wright, Albert: From Buncombe Co. At age 24, enl. 2/22/63 as PVT, Co. D. Reported present, May–June/62. Absent driving a team at Winchester, 6/30–10/31/62. Reported present as a teamster in the Q.M. Dept, Nov.–Dec./62. Reported present Jan.–Feb./63, also Mar.–Apr./63 and listed in the latter months as a teamster. Absent on horse detail, July–Aug./63, after his horse was KIA at Brandy Station on 8/1/63. AWOL according to rolls of 6/30–10/31/63. Reported present 11/63–4/64. On a register of a Richmond G.H. as admitted with a gunshot wound, 5/17/64, and sent on a 60-day frl 6/3/64. Rolls of 8/31/64 list him as absent and gone home after being WIA. Reported present Sept.–Oct./64; rolls of Nov.–Dec./64 report him as retired. Retired to invalid corps, 11/1/64. (CSR 270:10)

Wright, Alexander: Co. D. Psb. from Wilkes Co., but he is not listed in the County Census of 1850 or 1860, nor is there a burial record for him there. (Davis; McNeil)

Wright, Buckner L.H.: B. Carroll Co., MS. From Wayne Co. Farmer. At age 25, enl. 6/20/61 as PVT, Co. H. Reported present 11/61–2/62. Absent at home on sick frl as of 1/10/62 according to rolls of Jan.–Feb./62. Regimental returns of 2/62 list him as absent sick; returns of 3/62 list him as on sick leave as of 1/10/62. Admitted to a Danville G.H. with a fever, 1/10/62. Rolls of May–June/62 report him as dsh 6/14/62. Ankle injury. Stood 5'11½" tall, had a fair complexion, hazel eyes, dark hair. (CSR 270:10)

Wright, J.H.: Cns. 9/21/64 as PVT, Co. H. Reported present on rolls of Sept.–Dec./64. (CSR 270:10)

Wright, Philip M.: From Duplin Co. At age 27, enl. 7/24/61 as PVT, Co. I. Bugler. Reported present on rolls of 11/61–2/62. Absent on detached service, May–June/62. Reported present, Sept.–Oct./62. Absent sick according to rolls of 11/62–1/63. Admitted 11/17/62 to a Richmond G.H. Trn to private quarters, 12/3/62; pass expired, 12/10/62. Trn 12/24. Admitted 12/25/62 to a Richmond G.H. Returned to duty from Richmond G.H., 3/11/63. Reported present, Mar.–Apr./63. Absent after being captured 7/9/63 at Hagerstown, MD, according to 10/31/63 rolls. Federal records list him as captured on 7/12/63. Prl from Pt. Lookout for exchange, 3/16/64. Rolls of Mar.–Apr./64 (dated 9/7/64) report him as prm SGT, 7/15/64. Reported present, 4/31–12/64. On a 4/4/65 register of a Danvile G.H. with a gunshot wound in the right breast; frl 4/9/65. Prl Greensboro, NC, 5/11/65. (CSR 270:10)

Wyont, John T.: From Macon Co. At age 21, enl. 7/4/61 as PVT, Co. K. Bugler. Rolls of Nov.–Dec./61 list him as absent sick at a G.H. Rolls of Jan.–Feb./62 report him as absent sent to Manassas sick as of 2/24/62. Regimental returns of 2/62 list him as absent sick. Reported present May–June/62. Absent Sept.–Oct./62 at Winchester making shoes. Reported present 11/62–4/63, July–Aug./63, 10/31/63–3/31/64. Rolls of Mar.–Apr./64 list him as on detached service at brigade HQ. Absent as a teamster according to rolls of 4/30–8/31/64 and Nov.–Dec./64. Reported present, Sept.–Oct./64.(CSR 270:10)

Yancey, George H.: Resident of Warren Co. At age 21, enl in Co. E. Commissary SGT, 2 LT. Reported present Nov.–Dec./61. Trn from company to serve as commissary SGT, 10/1/61, and reported present Jan.–Apr./62. Rolls of May–June/62 report him as reduced to ranks and returned to Co. E, 6/17/62. Reported present May–June/62. Admitted 7/18/62 with intermittent fever. Reported present Sept.–Oct./62 and prm to 4CPL. Rolls of Nov.–Dec./62 list him as 3CPL and absent serving as a courier for Gen. Ransom as of 11/7/62. Reported present Jan.–Feb./64. Elected 2LT, 1/25/64, but not formally commissioned until 2/14/65. Reported present Mar.–Dec./64. Admitted 6/4/64 to a Richmond G.H. with chronic diarrhea. (CSR 270:1; CSR 270:10)

Yandle, James B.: B. 1835. From Mecklenburg Co. At age 26, enl. 5/25/61 as PVT, Co. C. D. 7/18/61 of disease. Bur. Mt. Harmony Baptist Church Cem., Mecklenburg Co. (CSR 270:10; Alexander; Stepp shows as in Co. D.)

Yandle, W.A.: Born Mecklenburg Co. Carpenter. At age 24, enl. 5/25/61 as PVT, Co. C. Rolls of Nov.–Dec./61 report him as absent sick. Reported present Jan.–Feb./62, 5/62–4/63. Dsh 6/8/63 due to disability from a gunshot wound In the left hand, which caused the losses of the top middle finger. Stood 5'7", had a brown complexion, hazel eyes, dark hair. (Alexander; CSR 270:10)

Yandle, W.H.: From Mecklenburg Co. At age 19, enl. 5/25/61 as PVT, Co. C. Admitted 12/11/61 to a Richmond G.H. Absent sick Nov.–Dec./61. Also reported absent sick since 11/6/61 at Petersburg according to Jan.–Feb./62 rolls. Regimental returns of 2/62 list him as absent sick. Returned to duty 3/22/62. Reported present May–June/62, 6/30/62, 4/63, 7/63–12/64. (CSR 270:10; Alexander)

Yeargan, Leonidas H.: From Chatham Co. At age 25, enl. 3/22/62 as PVT, Co. H. Reported present May–June/62, Sept.–Oct./62, 1/63–4/63, July–Aug./63. Absent with unserviceable horses, Sept.–Oct./63. Admitted to a Richmond G.H. 1/29/64. Reported present 11/63–2/64, 4/1/64. Absent on horse detail Mar.–Apr./64. Admitted to a Richmond G.H. 6/7/64. Reported present, 4/30–8/31/64. Absent on horse detail Sept.–Oct./64, then reported present Nov.–Dec./64. (CSR 270:10)

Young, John W.: From Franklin Co. At age 22, enl. 5/20/61 as PVT, Co. E. Rolls of Jan.–Feb./62 list him as trn 2/1/62 to the regimental band. Absent sick according to rolls of Mar.–Apr./62, May–June/62, Sept.–Oct./62. D. 2/62 or 3/9/62 from illness, either at Manassas Junction or Richmond. (Pearce: 28; CSR 270:10)

Young, W.A.: PVT, Co. E. Trn to serve as a musician on 2/1/62 according to rolls of Jan.–Feb./62. NFR. (CSR 270:10)

Yount, F.W.: Cns 9/21/64 as PVT, Co. H. Reported present, Sept.–Dec./64. (CSR 270:10)

Appendix I:
J.E.B. Stuart's Brigade and Divisional Commanders*

Generals, showing pre-war training and rank upon entering Confederate service

Laurence S. Baker	USMA 1851; Reg. Army	Lieutenant Colonel
Matthew C. Butler	South Carolina College	Captain
John R. Chambliss	USMA 1853; Reg. Army	Colonel
James B. Gordon	Emory & Henry, 1843	First Lieutenant
Wade Hampton	Planter/Legislator	Colonel
William E. Jones	Emory & Henry; USMA 1848; Reg. Army	Major
Fitzhugh Lee	USMA 1856; Reg. Army	First Lieutenant
W. H. F. Lee	Harvard; Regular Army	Captain
Lunsford L. Lomax	USMA 1856; Reg. Army	Captain
Beverly Robertson	USMA 1849; Reg. Army	Colonel
Williams Wickham	Virginia; Vol. Cavalry	Captain
P. M. B. Young	Ga. Military Academy; attended USMA	Second Lieutenant

*Here are listed only those men who were brigade and, in some cases, division commanders reporting to Stuart. Two other brigadiers, Albert G. Jenkins and John D. Imboden, only served in Stuart's organization during the invasion of Pennsylvania. Jenkins, a Harvard graduate, was promoted to brigadier general on August 5, 1862. Veteran of fighting in western Virginia, Jenkins's unit served in a mostly independent role in Pennsylvania. Jenkins himself was wounded the day before his unit reported to Stuart (*OR,* vol. 27, pt. 2, 698; [Shurict], "Jenkins' Brigade in the Gettysburg Campaign," *SHSP* 24: 344). Imboden, a graduate of Washington College, entered the war by organizing the Staunton Artillery. He was appointed brigadier general on October 11, 1862. Following service in western Virginia, Imboden's Brigade covered the army's left flank and subsequently its retreat int he Gettysburg Campaign.

Appendix II: Gordon and His Farm*

Land & Equipment

	1850	1860	Change
Acres (Improved)	250	325	30%
Acres (Unimproved)	1,565	1,650	5%
Land Value	$8,000	$15,000	88%
Farm Implements & Machinery Value	$300	$340	13%

Livestock

	1850	1860	Change
Horses	6	4	-33%
Asses & Mules	0	3	-
Milch Cows	8	9	13%
Oxen, "Other Cattle"	46	29	-37%
Sheep	35	25	-29%
Swine	180	225	25%
Livestock Value	$1,371	$1,800	31%
Animals slaughtered	30	110	267%

Crop (In Bushels)

	1850	1860	Change
Wheat	190	570	200%
Rye	150	100	-33%
Indian Corn	3,625	3,500	-4%
Oats	200	275	38%
Peas & Beans	0	10	-
Irish Potatoes	30	10	-40%
Sweet Potatoes	40	0	-
Tobacco	0	14,000	-

Other

	1850	1860	Change
Value of orchard products	0	$10	-
Butter	40 lbs.	50 lbs.	25%
Home mfr. goods	$15	$10	-33%
Beeswax & honey	110 lbs.	0	-

*1850 Agriculture Census for Wilkes County (Schedule 4), p. 343, line 1362; 1860 Agriculture Census for Wilkes County (Schedule 4), p. 29, line 21, both from Records of the Bureau of the Census, Record Group 29, NA.

Appendix III: Gordon's Printed House Documents

WHILE SERVING AS A REPRESENTATIVE in the North Carolina General Assembly in 1850 and 1851, James B. Gordon introduced several bills for consideration to the House of Commons. The following are the texts of two of those legislative pieces: "A Bill to Facilitate the Collection of the Public Revenue and Economize the Mode Thereof," and "A Bill to Incorporate Yadkin Navigation Company." The bills, which display not only his thinking but also his political agenda, are quoted here in full just as the state's official publisher printed them in 1851.*

A Bill to Facilitate the Collection of the Public Revenue and Economize the Mode Thereof

November 30, 1850. Introduced by Mr. J. B. Gordon. Read first time and passed, and referred to the Committee on Finance. December 27, 1850. Read second time and on motion of Mr. S. J. Person, laid on the table and ordered to be printed.

I. *Be it enacted by the General Assembly of the State of North Carolina, and it is hereby enacted by the authority of the same,* That it shall be the duty of the Clerks of the several County Courts in this State to make the return of the list of taxable property in their counties to the comptroller, on or before the first day of September in each and every year; including in said list the returns now by law to be made to them by the several Sheriffs of their counties, of the amount received from taxes imposed on merchants, retailers of spirituous liquors, stage players, sleight of hand performers, rope dancers, circus riders, equestrian performers, and all exhibitors of natural and artificial curiosities, and from all other sources of revenue now by law established.

II. *Be it further enacted,* That the several Clerks of the County Courts, shall have the same power to administer oaths to the several Sheriffs, as by law now the Comptroller has, and also to make the same allowances for insolvents, and it shall be the duty of the Clerks, also to transmit the revenue of the Sheriff, and the sureties to his bond for the collection of the Public Taxes, and his nearest and usual place of residence; and the nearest Bank of either of the State, Bank of Cape Fear, or other safe and solvent Institutions.

III. *And be it further enacted,* That it shall be the duty of the Comptroller to make up the accounts of said Sheriff's, from said list as by law he is now required to do; and report the same to the Treasurer, and transmit a duplicate of the same to the Sheriff whose accounts he has comptrolled and settled, and it shall be the duty of the Treasurer to direct said Sheriff to deposit the said amount thus due, (without charge or expense to the State) in the nearest Bank as the Treasurer

---

*House and Senate Documents Printed for the General Assembly of North Carolina at the Session of 1850–1851 (Raleigh: Thomas J. Lemay, Printer to the State, 1851), p. 135, 325–33, 493–96.

may direct; which deposit shall be made in the months of July, August, and September, in each and every year; and the said Sheriff shall transmit to the Treasurer and Comptroller, duplicate certificates of said deposit, by mail or some safe hand, which certificate shall be a discharge of said Sheriff and his sureties for amount due to the State, and the Comptroller shall forthwith charge the Treasurer the amount thus collected.

IV. *Be it further enacted,* That it shall be the duty of the Treasurer when he shall receive from said Sheriff, the said certificates of deposit, to credit said Sheriff on the Books of the Treasury, and transmit to him duplicate receipts countersigned by the Comptroller for the amount paid by said Sheriff.

V. *Be it further enacted,* That should any Sheriffs fail to deposit the several amounts due and transmit certificates of the same, to Treasurer and Comptroller, on or before the first day of November, in each and every year, they shall be liable to the same fines and penalties, that they are now liable by law, to be recovered in any Superior Court of Law in this State, on motion of the Public Treasurer.

VI. *Be it further enacted,* That all laws and clauses of laws coming within the meaning and purview of this act are hereby repealed.

A Bill to Incorporate Yadkin Navigation Company

House of Commons, December 12, 1850. Introduced by Mr. J. B. Gordon. Read first time and passed, and on motion of Mr. Gordon referred to the Committee on Internal Improvements, and ordered to be printed.

I. *Be it enacted by the General Assembly of the State of North Carolina, and it is hereby enacted by the authority of the same,* That for the purpose of effecting a communication by Steamboat navigation upon the Yadkin River from that point where the North Carolina Rail Road shall pass over the said River to the town of Wilkesboro' in the county of Wilkes, the formation of a corporate Company, with a capital stock of Three Hundred thousand Dollars, is hereby authorized; to be called "the Yadkin Navigation company," and when formed in compliance with the conditions hereinafter prescribed, to have a corporate existence as a body politic for fifty years.

II. That for the purpose of creating the capital stock of said Company, the following persons be and the same are hereby appointed and constituted a board of commissioners, (to wit:) Hamilton C. Jones of the county of Rowan, Thales McDonald of the county of Davidson, Peter Hairston* of the county of Davie, _____ of the county of Surry, and _____ of the county of Wilkes; whose duty it shall be to direct the opening of books for subscription of stock, at such times and places and under the direction of such persons as they or a majority of them may designate; and the said board of commissioners shall appoint a chairman of their body, Treasurer and all other officers, and in the name of the Board to sue for and recover all sums of money that ought, under this Act, to be received by them.

III. That all persons who may hereafter be authorized to open books for the subscription of stock to said company, by the Board of Commissioners herein before appointed for that purpose, shall open books at any time after the ratification of this Act, ten days previous notice being given in some one or more of the public newspapers in this State; and that said books, when opened, shall be kept open for the space of ten days at least, and as long thereafter as the Board of Commissioners above named, shall direct; that all subscriptions of stock shall be in shares of one hundred dollars, the subscriber paying at the time of making such subscription, five dollars on each share

---

*Peter Wilson Hairston (1819–1886) was a prominent planter who owned Cooleemee, a plantation that still stands beside the Yadkin River in Davie County. Hairston and Gordon knew each other, probably through Hairston's brother-in-law, who had studied under Peter Ney, and through Hairston's second wife, Fanny McCoy Caldwell Hairston. During the Civil War, Hairston served briefly with Jeb Stuart, Hairston's relative and brother-in-law through his first marriage. Later he joined the staff of another relative, Jubal Early. See Hairston, *Cooleemee Plantation.*

thus subscribed, to the person or persons authorized to receive such subscription; and in case of failure to pay said sum, all such subscriptions shall be void, but only at the option of the said Board of Commissioners or of the Company after it shall have been formed, who may, if they choose, treat the same as valid and sue for and recover the said sum; and upon closing the books, all such sums as shall have been thus received of subscribers on the first cash installment, shall be paid over to the said Board of Commissioners by the persons receiving them; and for failure thereof such person or persons shall be personally liable to said Board of Commissioners before the organization of said company and to the company itself after its organization, to be recovered in the Superior Court of Law within this State, in the county where such delinquent resides, or if he resides in any other State, then in any of the Superior Courts of Law in either of the Counties of Rowan, Davidson, Davie, Surry, or Wilkes: And the said Board of Commissioners shall have power to call on and require all persons empowered to receive subscriptions of stock, at any time and from time to time, as a majority of them may think proper, to make a return of the stock by them respectively received and to make payment of all sums of money made by the subscribers; That all persons receiving subscriptions of stock shall pass a receipt to the subscriber or subscribers for the payment of the first installment, as heretofore required to be paid; and upon their settlement with the Board of Commissioners as aforesaid, it shall be the duty of the said Board in like manner to pass their receipt for all sums thus received, to the persons from whom received; and such receipts shall be taken and held to be good and sufficient vouchers to the persons holding them.

IV. It shall be the duty of said Board of Commissioners to direct and authorize the opening of books for the subscription of stock in the manner above described, until the sum of one hundred thousand dollars shall have been subscribed to the capital stock of the company; and as soon as such sum shall have been subscribed and the installment of five dollars per share on said sum shall have been received by the Board, said Company shall be regarded as formed; and the said Board of Commissioners or a majority of them, shall sign and seal a duplicate declaration to that effect, with the names of the subscribers appended, and cause one of the said duplicates to be deposited in the office of Secretary of State, and thence forth, from the closing of the books of subscription as aforesaid, the subscribers to the stocks shall form one body politic and corporate, in deed and in law, for the purposes aforesaid, by the name and style of the "Yadkin Navigation Company."

V. That whenever the sum of one hundred thousand dollars shall have been thus subscribed, the subscribers, their executors, administrators and assigns, shall be, and they are hereby declared to be incorporated into a company by the name and style of the "Yadkin Navigation Company," and by that name shall be capable in Law and Equity of purchasing, holding, selling, leasing and conveying estates, real, personal and mixed, and of acquiring the same by gift or devise, so far as shall be necessary for the purposes embraced within the scope, object and intent of their charter and no further; and shall have perpetual succession, and by their corporate name may sue and be sued, plead and be impleaded in any Court of Law or Equity in the State of North Carolina; and may have and use a common seal, which they may alter and renew at their pleasure; and shall have and enjoy all other rights and immunities which other corporate bodies may and of right do exercise; and may make all such by-laws, rules, and regulations, as are necessary for the government of the corporation, for effecting the object for which it is created, not inconsistent with the Constitution and laws of this State or of the United States.

VI. That notice of process served upon any of the Directors of said Company, shall be taken and deemed lawful notice of service of process upon the Company, so as to bring it before any Court within this State.

VII. That as soon as the sum of one hundred thousand dollars shall have been subscribed as aforesaid, it shall be the duty of said Board of Commissioners to appoint a time for the stockholders to meet at Mocksville in Davie County, which they shall cause to be previously published for the space of twenty days in one or more newspapers in this State; at which time and place the said Stockholders, in person or by proxy, shall proceed to elect the directors of said Company, and to enact all such regulations and by-laws as may be necessary for the government of the corporation and the transaction of its business; The persons elected Directors at this meeting, shall serve such period, not exceeding one year, as the stockholders may direct; and at this meeting the stockholders shall fix on the day and place or places where the subsequent election of Directors shall be held; and such elections shall henceforth be annually made, but if the day for the annual election should pass without any election of Directors, the corporation shall not be thereby dissolved, but it shall be lawful on any other day to hold and make such election in such manner as may be prescribed by a by-law of the corporation.

VIII. That at such first general meeting of stockholders, a majority of all the shares subscribed shall be represented before proceeding to business; and if a sufficient number do not appear on the day appointed, those who do attend shall have power to adjourn from time to time until a regular meeting shall be thus formed; and at such meeting the stockholders may provide by a by-law as to the number of stockholders and the amount of stock to be held by them which shall constitute a quorum at all subsequent meetings of stockholders or directors.

IX. That at all elections, and upon all votes taken at any meeting of the stockholders, each share of stock shall be entitled to one vote, and any stockholder in said company may vote by proxy, and proxies may be verified in such manner as the by-laws of the company may proscribe.

X. That the affairs of the company shall be managed by twelve Directors, to be elected annually from among the stockholders, by ballot, and a majority of the stock represented; who shall have power to fill vacancies in their number.

XI. That the President of the company shall be elected by the Directors from among their number in the manner prescribed by the by-laws of the corporation.

XII. That the said Board of Commissioners shall make their return of the shares of stock subscribed for, at the first general meeting of the stockholders, and shall at the same time pay over all sums of money by them received to the Company's Agent, and for failure so to do, shall be personally liable at the suit of said Company.

XIII. That all contracts and agreements, authenticated by the President and Secretary of the Board of Directors, shall be binding on the company without a seal, and such mode of authentication may be used as the regulations of the company may prescribe.

XIV. That the said Board of Directors may call for the payment of the sums subscribed as stock in said company, in such installments as the interest of said company may in their opinion require; the call for each payment shall be published in one or more newspapers in this State for the space of one month before the day of payment; and on failure of any stockholder to pay such installment as thus required, the Directors may sell at public auction, on a previous notice of ten days, for cash, all the stock subscribed for in said company by such stockholder, and convey the same to the purchaser at said sale; and if said sale of stock do [sic] not produce enough to pay off the incidental expenses of the sale, and the entire amount by such stockholder to the company for such subscription of stock, then and in that case the whole of such balance shall be held and taken as due at once to the company, and may be recovered of such stockholder or his executors, administrators and assigns, at the suit of said company, either by summary motion in any Court of Superior jurisdiction in the county where the delinquent resides, on a previous notice of ten days to such subscriber, or by the action of assumpsit in any Court of competent jurisdiction, or by a warrant before a justice of the peace, where the sum claimed does not exceed one hundred dollars; and in all cases of the assignment of stock, before the whole amount has been paid to the company, then for all sums due on such stock, both the original subscribers, and the first and all subsequent assignees shall be liable to the company, and the same may be recovered as above described.

XV. That said company shall issue certificates of stock to its members, which shall be transferable in such manner as may be prescribed by the regulations of the corporation; and the said company shall have power to increase their capital at any time to an amount not exceeding three hundred thousand dollars, either by opening books for the subscription of stock or by selling such new stock.

XVII. That the said company be and they are hereby authorized to open and construct works in and upon the Yadkin River, for the purpose of effecting navigation by Steamboat and otherwise upon said River from that point where the North Carolina Rail Road shall pass over the same to the town of Wilkesboro' in the county of Wilkes; and to this end shall have power to contract with any person or persons, for and on behalf of the company, for constructing said work and building all such locks, dams, canals, and other structures which they may deem necessary to carry out and effectuate the objects and intent of this Act of incorporation; And to appoint a Clerk, Treasurer and all such other officers as they may think necessary and proper, and to transact all the business of the company during the intervals between the general meetings of the stockholders.

XVIII. That the said President and Directors, their officers and servants, shall have full power and authority to enter upon all lands and tenements through which they may desire to conduct their works, and to lay out the same according to their pleasure, so that the mill house, yard, and other buildings of any person be not invaded without his consent; and they shall have power to enter on and lay out such contiguous land, as they may desire to occupy, as sites for depots, store houses, ware houses, toll houses, and other buildings for the necessary accommodation of their officers, agents, and servants, their horses, mules, and cattle, and for the protection of the property of the company: *Provided*, that the land so laid out for these latter purposes shall not exceed two acres in any one parcel.

XIX. That if the President and Directors cannot agree with the owner or owners of the land so entered upon and laid out by them, as to the terms of purchase, it shall be lawful for them to apply to the Court of Pleas and Quarter Sessions of the county in which a part of said land lies; and upon such application the Court shall appoint five discreet freeholders, to assess the damages to the owners from the condemnation of the land aforesaid: That no such appointment, however, shall be made unless it appear to the Court that ten days previous notice of the application shall have been given to the owner of the land, or to the guardian if the owner be an infant, or the Committee if the owner be a lunatic or *non compos mentis*, if such owner, guardian, or Committee reside in the State; but if they or any of them shall reside out of the State, then publication of an intention to make such application shall be made for the space of one month in some one or more newspapers within this State: A day for the meeting of said freeholders, to perform the duty assigned them, shall be designated in the order appointing them; and any one or more of them attending on that day may adjourn from time to time until their business shall be finished; and of the five freeholders any three or more of them may act; after having been duly sworn or solemnly affirmed before some justice of the peace that they will impartially and justly ascertain the damages which will be sustained by the proprietors of the land from the condemnation thereof, and that they will truly certify their proceedings thereupon to the Court of the said county making the appointment.

XX. It shall be the duty of the said freeholders, in pursuance of the order appointing them, to assemble on the land proposed to be condemned, and after surveying the same and hearing such proper evidence as the party may offer, they shall ascertain as nearly as may be the damages which the proprietors of the land will sustain by the condemnation thereof, all the attendant circumstances being considered; and when they shall have agreed upon the amount of damages, they shall make an accurate report thereof to the Court appointing them, which report shall also contain a description of the location and quantity of the land so condemned; and appended thereto a certificate of the magistrate before whom they were qualified, of such due qualification.

XXI. When said report shall be returned, unless good cause be shewn at that time, the same shall be confirmed and spread upon the record: but if said report should be disaffirmed, or if the said freeholders being unable to agree, should report their disagreement, or for any other cause they should fail to report within a reasonable time after their appointment, the Court may supersede them and appoint others in their stead.

XXII. The said Court of Pleas and Quarter Sessions may upon the confirmation of the report of said freeholders, award judgment and execution against said company for the amount of damages so assessed; and when the said judgment shall be paid and discharged, the title of the land for which such damages are assessed, shall be vested in the company in the same manner as if the proprietor had sold and conveyed it to them; and the said Court shall then order the report of the freeholders to be registered in the county for which the court sits, and the same shall be read in evidence as in cases of registered deeds for the conveyance of land.

XXIII. The said President and Directors for the purpose of constructing their work aforesaid and the works necessarily conducted therewith, or of repairing the same, after they shall have been made, or of enlarging or otherwise altering the same, shall be at liberty, by themselves, their officers, agents or servants, at any time, to enter upon any adjacent land and to cut, quarry, dig, take, and carry away therefrom, and wood, stone, gravel or earth which they may deem necessary: *Provided*, however, that they shall not, without the consent of the owner, cut down any fruit trees, or any tree preserved in any lot of field for shade or for ornament, nor take any timber, gravel or stone constituting any part of any fence or building; and for all such wood, stone, and gravel thus taken the said President and Directors shall pay to the owner or owners thereof a reasonable compensation to be by them agreed upon; and in case of their failure to agree upon the value of said articles, then the same shall be valued by three freeholders appointed by any justice of the peace of the county where the stone &c. may be situated, upon the application of the owner thereof, after a previous notice of ten days to the other party; and in case either party shall be dissatisfied with their determination, an appeal to the County Court shall be allowed and sent up by the said justice.

XXIV. That all acts and clauses of acts coming in conflict with the purview and meaning of this act, or which give rights, privileges and franchises at variance with those given by this act, but which rights, privileges and franchises have not as yet been used and enjoyed, or have been abandoned, be and they are hereby repealed.

XXV. The said President and Directors, shall have power to purchase with the funds of the company, and place on the river after it shall have been improved, boats of any description, which they may deem suited to the transportation of persons and property, and they may if they think proper, contract with other persons for the transportation of persons and property upon said River, and said company or those with whom they contract to carry on such transportation, shall be deemed and take common carriers and as such be liable.

XXVI. That said company and all its works shall be exempt from taxation by the State or any county for the space of fifteen years, and after that time the State may impose a tax not to exceed twenty five cents per annum upon the share of stock in said company.

XXVII. So soon as any portion of the said River shall be in readiness for transportation, it shall be lawful for the said President and Directors, to transport by their officers and agents, or by contractors under them, persons and property on the same; and they shall have power to charge for the transportation of persons, goods, produce, merchandise and other articles of property, any sum not exceeding the following rates, (to wit:) on persons, not exceeding six cents per mile for each person; for the transportation of goods, produce, merchandise and other articles, not exceeding an average of ten cents per ton per mile, and for the transportation of the mail, such sums as they may agree for; and they shall also be allowed to receive for storage and weighing, the usual rates in such cases, and they shall be allowed to divide the net profits of the company among the stockholders in proportion to the stock held by them respectively.

XXVIII. The stock in said company shall be transferable under such rules and regulations as their by-laws may prescribe, and all stock shall be evidenced by certificates to be issued by the said President and Directors.

XXIX. If any person or persons shall willfully, injure, impair or destroy any of the works of said company or any part thereof, or shall place any obstruction in said River, such person or persons shall be deemed guilty of a misdemeanor, and on conviction thereof shall be fined or imprisoned at the discretion of the Court, and shall moreover be liable, at suit of said company, in damages.

XXX. That this act shall be in force from and after its ratification, and so continue for the space of fifty years.

Notes

Abbreviations used in the Notes appear at the beginning of Part II: The Roster

Chapter 1

1. "General James B. Gordon," typewritten MS., James Gordon Hackett Collection, NCSA; Forester, "William Lenoir," *Heritage of Wilkes*, 315–16; Messick, *Kings Mountain*, 131 ff.; "Fairmount," *Heritage of Wilkes*, 33.

2. Hayes, *Land of Wilkes*, 6; Van Noppen and Van Noppen, *Western North Carolina*, 4.

3. Hickerson, *Happy Valley*, 8; Winkler Interview; Young, *North Carolina*, 24.

4. Lefler and Newsome, *North Carolina*, 33, 156–57, 182–83; Mitchell, "The Granville District and Its Land Records," *North Carolina Historical Review*, April 1993, 103.

5. Finley, "Address on James B. Gordon," copy provided by Annie Finley Winkler.

6. "General James B. Gordon," typewritten MS., James Gordon Hackett Collection, NCSA; Eckert, *John Brown Gordon*, 6.

7. Leyburn, *The Scotch-Irish*, 157 ff; Cowles, *CSC*, 19; Cowles, "Life and Services," 8; McBride, *Gordon Kinship*, 159.

8. Leyburn, *The Scotch-Irish*, 199, 213; Finley, "Address on James B. Gordon," copy provided by Annie Finley Winkler. The latter source says the Gordons came to Wilkes in 1775. George's tombstone in St. Paul's Episcopal Church cemetery in Wilkesboro says Gordon arrived in 1770.

9. Absher, ed., *Heritage of Wilkes County*, v; McBride, *Gordon Kinship*, 159; "General James B. Gordon," typewritten MS., James Gordon Hackett Collection, NCSA. The original title of the town, "Wilkesborough," followed herein, changed to Wilkesboro as the "ugh" gradually dropped from usage.

10. Lefler and Newsome, *North Carolina*, 243 ff; Forester, "William Lenoir," *Heritage of Wilkes*, 315–16; "General James B. Gordon," typewritten MS., James Gordon Hackett Collection, NCSA; Harper, *Fort Defiance*.

11. Lefler and Newsome, *North Carolina*, 249–50; Higgenbotham, *War Of American Independence*, 364.

12. McBride, *Gordon Kinship*, 159; "General James B. Gordon," typewritten MS., James Gordon Hackett Collection, NCSA. George Gordon died in 1800.

13. Anderson, *Wilkes County Sketches*, 30.

14. Hayes, 468, 84, 88. According to Ashe, et. al., eds., *Biographical History* 8: 27–28, Nathaniel Gordon served in the General Assembly in 1819, 1821–23, 1825–1828. According to Index to Compiled Service Records of Volunteer Soldiers Who Served during the War of 1812, Microcopy 602, Roll 83, NA, Nathaniel Gordon served in the Seventh Regiment (Pearson's) North Carolina Militia.

15. Cowles, *CSC*, 22; Cowles, "Life and Services," 16. Sarah was born on October 6, 1798.

16. Sarah Brown to Allen Brown, February 19 and 20, 1860, Brown Family Letters, GHM; Sarah Gordon Brown to Allen Brown, April 1, 1855, James G. Hackett Papers, DU; Aurelia Halsey to Sarah Brown, June 28, 1864, Aurelia Halsey Correspondence, GHM.

17. Harper, *Fort Defiance*, 12; Hickerson, *History and Genealogy*, 20.

18. Winkler Interview; Hickerson, *History and Genealogy*, 20.

19. Hickerson, *History and Genealogy*, 20; Simpson, ed., *Heritage of Wilkes County* 2, 75; Diary of Elisha Mitchell, July 1828, in Anderson, "Early Wilkes Schools," *The Journal-Patriot*, October 28, 1976. According to Elizabeth C. Finley, "Brigadier General James B. Gordon," *Heritage of Wilkes*, 228, and *Heritage of Wilkes* 2: 75, the school was held in Wilkesborough's old courthouse until a new one was built in 1825.

20. Cowles, *CSC*, 19; Cowles, "Life and Services," 6; James Foote, "Reminiscences of Peter Steuart Ney," n.p., Peter Stewart Ney Papers, NCSA; Weston, *Historic Doubts*, 135, 146.

21. JBG to Sarah Gordon Brown, September 7, 1833, Hickerson, *History and Genealogy*, 6.

22. Weston, *Historic Doubts*, 136; James Foote, "Reminiscences of Peter Steuart Ney," n.p., Peter Stewart Ney Papers, NCSA. Marshal Ney was supposedly shot in Paris in 1815; Peter Ney died in 1846 (Keever, *Iredell*, 207). See also James Foote, "Reminiscences of Peter Steuart Ney," n.p., Peter Stewart Ney Papers, NCSA. A student there in 1837 and 1838, Foote said he was told this story by a Civil War general who had also been a pupil of Ney's.

23. Cowles, *CSC*, 19; Cowles, "Life and Services," 7; Keever, *Iredell*, 206; JBG to Sarah Gordon Brown, May 11, 1834, Hickerson, *History and Genealogy*, 23, and Gordon-Hackett Papers, SHC.

24. Cowles, *CSC*, 19; Cowles, "Life and Services," 6; Hickerson, *History and Genealogy*, 128.

25. Cowles, *CSC*, 19; Cowles, "Life and Services," 7; JBG to his mother, May 11, 1834, Gordon-Hackett Papers, SHC.

26. Hayes, 80, 88; Winkler Interview. Brown was also a trustee of Wilkesborough Academy (*Heritage of Wilkes* 2: 75). During the War of 1812, Brown served in the 18th Infantry Regiment. In 1823, he assumed command of the upper regiment of Wilkes County Militia (Hamilton Brown Papers, SHC).

27. In 1834, Brown bought a lot in Wilkesboro and built a home there ("Brown House One of Oldest In Wilkes County," *The Journal-Patriot*, October 28, 1976). Letters indicate that the family lived at Oakland after JBG became its legal owner. Family tradition has it that the Browns lived at both homes (Winkler Interview). Brown also owned property near Brown's Ford west of town. Most likely, Brown did move

his family to the new home, but he watched Oakland when JBG was absent. Apparently, the Brown home was not completed until late in the 1850s; in JBG to Tom Brown, 31 January 1858, James G. Hackett Papers, DU, JBG wrote, "I am very busy getting lumber to build a house."

28. Hugh Thomas Brown Diary, 13 October 1857, Hamilton Brown Papers, SHC.

29. Stevenson, *History of Emory & Henry*, 52.

30. Stevenson, *History of Emory & Henry*, 148.

31. Cowles, *CSC*, 19; Cowles, "Life and Services," 7; Stevenson, *History of Emory & Henry*, 166. Fire destroyed the records of early Emory & Henry college students. Those that exist state only that JBG of Wilkes County, N.C., attended Emory & Henry from 1841 to 1843 (Ramona Woodson, letter to author, September 1, 1989, in the author's possession).

32. Stevenson, *History of Emory & Henry*, 70; "General James B. Gordon," typewritten MS., James Gordon Hackett Collection, NCSA. Among Emory & Henry's students were J. E. B. Stuart and William E. Jones, both future Confederates. Jones was a year behind JBG; Stuart came about five years after JBG left.

33. W. L. Van Eaton to JBG, n.d.; A. J. Fleming to JBG, January 15, 1845; both in Gordon-Hackett Papers, SHC.

34. JBG to Caroline Gordon, November 21, 1843, James Gordon Hackett Collection, NCSA.

35. Ibid.

Chapter 2

1. J. G. Hackett, untitled MS., Gordon-Hackett Papers, SHC; Crouch, *Sketches of Wilkes*, 47–48. Crouch identified the trees as cedars; Hackett called them sycamores.

2. Sallie Anderson, "'Oakland,' Old Home of Gen. Gordon, Being Razed for New Wilkes Hospital," unprovenienced article from *The Journal-Patriot*, copy provided by Annie Finley Winkler; Winkler Interview; 1850 Agriculture Census for Wilkes County, microcopy 432, roll 649, p. 343, line 1362, NA; 1860 Agriculture Census for Wilkes County, p. 29, line 21, NA, (F.2.112 N, 1860 Agriculture Census for Lenoir-Yancey Counties, Winston-Salem Public Library Copy from North Carolina Division of Archives and History copy of NA census records). Anderson wrote of the hill on which Oakland stood: "A state-erected marker ... bears the information that the birth-place of the general stands 300 yards north. It is only a slight exaggeration to add that it is also 300 yards almost straight up in the air."

3. 1850 Agriculture Census; 1860 Agriculture Census; JBG to Caroline Gordon Hackett, May 9, 1859, James G. Hackett Papers, DU.

4. 1850 Agriculture Census, 1860 Agriculture Census. In 1860, seven tanneries and one tobacco factory operated in the county, and employed only twenty-one men (1860 Industry Census for Wilkes County, North Carolina, Record Group 29, p. 1, NA [F.2.113 N, 1860 Industry Census for Alamance-Yancey Counties, Winston-Salem Public Library Copy from North Carolina Division of Archives and History copy of NA census records]).

5. Inscoe, "Mountain Masters," 158.

6. Inscoe, "Mountain Masters," *The North Carolina Historical Review*, 145; 1850 Social Statistics Census for Wilkes County, Group 29, NA, p. 316–326 (F.2.108 N, 1850 Social Statistics Census for Alamance-Yancey Counties, Winston-Salem Public Library Copy from North Carolina Division of Archives and History copy of NA census records). Wilkes County had a total population of 12,069 in 1850. See also McKinney, "Women's Role," *North Carolina Historical Review*, 38 ff.

7. 1850 Slave Census, Microcopy 432, roll 656, p. 1109, line 33, NA; 1860 Slave Census, Microcopy 653, roll 927, p. 6, line 22, NA; Cowles, *CSC*, 19; Cowles, "Life and Services," 7; Bess Gordon Finley Grier, untitled MS. reminiscences of James B. Gordon (May 7, 1934, n.p.), 3. This document, written by a descendant of one of JBG's sisters, was supplied by Annie Finley Winkler.

8. JBG to Allen Brown, January 5, 1854, Hamilton Brown Papers, SHC.

9. JBG to Allen Brown, December 11, 1852, in Hickerson, *Echoes*, 40–41.

10. Sarah Gordon Brown to Allen Brown, April 1, 1855, James G. Hackett Papers, DU; JBG to Allen Brown, December 11, 1852, in Hickerson, *Echoes*, 40–41.

11. JBG to Allen Brown, January 5, 1854, Hamilton Brown Papers, SHC.

12. JBG to Caroline Gordon, September 13, 1853, in Hickerson, *History and Genealogy*, 131.

13. JBG to Allen Brown, January 18, 1854, Hamilton Brown Papers, SHC.

14. Allen Brown Diary, July 31, 1855, Hamilton Brown Papers, SHC.

15. JBG to Allen Brown, December 11, 1852, in Hickerson, *Echoes*, 40–41; JBG to Caroline Gordon, September 13, 1853, in Hickerson, *History and Genealogy*, 131.

16. JBG to Allen Brown, December 11, 1852, in Hickerson, *Echoes*, 40–41; James Gwyn Diary, August 3, 1859, August 22, 1859, James Gwyn Papers, SHC; Hugh Thomas Brown Diary, September 13, 1857, Hamilton Brown Papers, SHC.

17. Hugh Thomas Brown Diary, December 16, 1857, October 13, 1857, Hamilton Brown Papers, SHC; Hickerson, *Echoes*, 51. William Makepeace Thackeray was a British novelist who lived from 1811–1863.

18. JBG to Tom Brown, January 31, 1858, James G. Hackett Papers, DU; James Gordon Hackett Collection, NCSA; Tom Brown to JBG, May 12, 1860, in James Gordon Hackett Papers, DU; Hugh Thomas Brown Diary, Hamilton Brown Papers, SHC.

19. Hayes, 271; 1860 Slave Census. In JBG to Caroline Gordon, September 13, 1853, Hickerson, *History and Genealogy*, 131, JBG writes that Augustus "will clear over $1,000 on his cattle." Fairmount stood on Kensington Heights where the North Wilkesboro Post Office is today (1996). Fairmount itself is a private residence, resting a few yards down the hill from where it once stood.

20. JBG to Caroline Gordon, August 6, 1843, Gordon-Hackett Papers, SHC; Elizabeth C. Finley, "Richard Nathaniel Hackett," *Heritage of Wilkes*, 234; Hayes, 71, 131; Hubbard, *Physicians in Wilkes County*, 9.

21. Kate Cameron Finley, "John Tate Finley Family," *Heritage of Wilkes*, 206.

22. Jane C. Ogburn, "Preface," in Anderson, *North Wilkesboro*, xii; Eckert, *John B. Gordon*, 7.

23. Winkler Interview. For more on John B. Gordon, see the Epilogue.

24. Hickerson, *History and Genealogy*, 10; J. G. Hackett, "Colonel Hamilton Allen Brown," *CSC*, 3.

25. Tom Brown to JBG, May 12, 1860, in James Gordon Hackett Papers, DU.

26. Crouch, *Sketches of Wilkes*, 45; Leyburn, *The Scotch-Irish*, 199.

27. Various receipts, Anderson Collection; JBG to "Campbell," April 5, 1857, Atwood & Co. Collection, SHC.

28. Various receipts, Anderson Collection.

29. George W. Reed & Company Receipt, Anderson Collection.

30. [?] to JBG, December 9, 1858, Anderson Collection.

31. Atwood & Co. to JBG, April 4, 1859, Anderson Collection.

32. Sarah Gordon Brown to Allen Brown, February 22, 1853, in Hickerson, *Echoes*, 41. JBG later ran the store by himself when John and Ann moved to Cherokee County, Alabama in the 1850s. (JBG to Allen Brown, January 5, 1854, Hamilton Brown Papers, SHC). After JBG's death, the Finleys returned to Wilkesborough.

33. Sarah Gordon Brown to Carrie Gordon, August 5, 18?, James G. Hackett Papers, DU; Sarah Brown to Allen

Brown, February 19 and 20, 1860, Brown Family Letters, GHM.

34. Calvin J. Cowles to his wife, October 4, 1850, Calvin J. Cowles Papers, SHC; Various receipts, Anderson Collection.

35. Crouch, *Sketches of Wilkes,* 29–30.

36. Thackeray, *The Newcomes,* 7–13, 25–26; Kerr Craige, "General James B. Gordon," CV 6 (1898): 216; Hayes, 158.

37. Kruman, *Parties and Politics,* 7, 28.

38. Leyburn, *The Scotch-Irish,* 319; Minutes, the Wilkes County Board of the Superintendents of Common Schools, 1841–1853, NCSA. The minutes are incomplete, but JBG was noted as present at meetings in 1849, 1850, 1853, and 1857. In 1850, 5,339 children attended Wilkes County's common schools.

39. Hickerson, *History and Genealogy,* 19; Crouch, *Sketches of Wilkes,* 45; Kruman, *Parties and Politics,* 40–41.

40. D. Little, J. T. Asbury, and H.A. Oxford to JBG, n.d., James Gordon Hackett Collection, NCSA.

41. Crouch, *Sketches of Wilkes,* 45; Hayes, *Land of Wilkes,* 85; Kruman, *Parties and Politics,* 17, 40.

42. *Raleigh Register,* October 2, 1850, p. 3, col. 3; Cowles, *CSC,* 19; Cowles, "Life and Services," 7; JBG to Carrie, November 24, 1850, James Gordon Hackett Papers, NCSA.

43. *North Carolina Standard,* November 20, 1850, p. 3, col. 3.

44. *North Carolina Standard,* November 27, 1850, p. 1, col. 3; *Raleigh Register,* November 20, 1850, p. 2, col. 4; November 27, 1850, p. 1, col. 2, col. 5.

45. *House Documents,* 135; JBG to Carrie, November 24, 1850, James Gordon Hackett Papers, NCSA.

46. *Raleigh Register,* November 27, 1850, p. 4, col. 1-col. 2; p. 4, col. 2; cols. 4–5; February 12, 1851, p. 4, col. 5.

47. Kruman, *Parties and Politics,* 11, 91.

48. *House Documents,* 55; *North Carolina Standard,* January 22, 1851, p. 4, col. 4; ibid., col. 6.

49. *North Carolina Standard,* 4 December 1850, p. 2, col. 4; *House Documents,* 135, 494. For the complete text of this and other of Gordon's bills, see Appendix III.

50. *North Carolina Standard,* January 29, 1851, p. 4, col. 3.

51. *House Documents,* 327, 335.

52. JBG to Carrie, December 10, 1850, James Gordon Hackett Collection, NCSA; *North Carolina Standard,* January 22, 1851, p. 2, col. 2; February 5, 1851, p. 4, col. 5.

53. *Raleigh Register,* December 25, 1850, p. 3, col. 5–6; *Journals of the Senate and House of Commons,* 689. See also *North Carolina Standard,* December 25, 1850, p. 2, col. 4.

54. JBG to Lytle Hickerson, December 8, 1850, James Gwyn Papers, SHC.

55. *Raleigh Register,* December 18, 1850, p. 1, col. 7; *House Journals,* 718, 717, 561. See also *House Journals,* 708.

56. *North Carolina Standard,* December 25, 1850, p. 2, col. 2; *Raleigh Register,* January 1, 1851, p. 1, col. 1.

57. Caroline Gordon to JBG, January 4, 1851, James B. Gordon Papers, NCSA.

58. JBG to Carrie, December 10, 1850, James Gordon Hackett Collection, NCSA.

59. JBG to Carrie, November 24, 1850, James Gordon Hackett Collection, NCSA; *House Documents,* 265.

60. *Raleigh Register,* January 12, 1851, p. 4, col. 5; Kruman, *Parties and Politics,* 130 ff. *House Documents,* 255 ff. See also the *Raleigh Register,* January 8, 1851, p. 1, col. 4; p. 3, col. 3. JBG voted in favor of white suffrage, a vote seen as a "stab" to the hopes of the west.

61. Hays, 155.

62. M. S. Stokes to JBG, April 28, 1847, James Gordon Hackett Collection, NCSA.

63. Ibid.

64. *The Carolina Watchman,* January 2, 1851, p. 2, col. 2; *North Carolina Standard,* January 22, 1851, p. 3, col. 3; p. 4, col. 4.

65. *Raleigh Register,* February 5, 1851, p. 1, col. 3, col. 2.

66. Various receipts, Anderson Collection.

67. JBG to Caroline Gordon, May 29, 1856, James Gordon Hackett Collection, NCSA.

68. Ashe, et al., eds., *Biographical History* 1: 245 ff; *North Carolina Standard,* June 11, 1856, p. 1, col. 1; Warner and Yearns, *Biographical Register,* 63–64. Craige is also spelled "Craig" in many sources.

69. James G. Hackett Papers, DU; JBG to Caroline Gordon, May 29, 1856, James Gordon Hackett Collection, NCSA. The Hackett Papers contain a handwritten invitation to JBG, at Brown's Hotel, inviting him "to dine" with the president.

70. JBG to R. F. Hackett, June 4, 1856, James Gordon Hackett Collection, NCSA.

71. *Raleigh Register,* July 9, 1856, p. 2, col. 3; June 11, 1856, p. 1, col. 4.

72. *Raleigh Register,* June 11, 1856, p. 1, col. 4.

73. *North Carolina Standard,* June 11, 1856, p. 1, col. 1; *Raleigh Register,* June 11, 1856, p. 1, col. 4.

74. *Raleigh Register,* June 18, 1856, p. 4, col. 5.

75. Freidel, *The Presidents,* 35; *Raleigh Register,* June 18, 1856, p. 4, col. 5; Boatner, *Civil War Dictionary,* 660.

76. JBG to R.F. Hackett, June 4, 1856, James Gordon Hackett Collection, NCSA; Freidel, *The Presidents,* 36.

77. JBG to Caroline Gordon, June 7, 1856, Hackett Collection; *Raleigh Register,* June 18, 1856, p. 4, col. 5.

78. McKinney, "Women's Role," 42; *History of Alleghany County,* 16.

79. James H. Parks, et. al., to JBG, April 28, 1859, Bess Gordon Finley Grier MS.

80. McKenzie Interview.

81. Original St. Paul's Parish Register in Boston M. Lacey and Frank McKenzie, "St. Paul's Episcopal Old, Beautiful Church," *The Journal-Patriot,* October 28, 1976; McKenzie Interview.

82. "St. Paul's Episcopal Old, Beautiful Church." The church, renovated in 1995, is still in use today, and its cemetery contains the graves of JBG, his father and mother, Hamilton Brown, Allen Brown, Dr. R. F. Hackett, and other family members. See also the *Winston-Salem Journal,* September 24, 1995, B1, B6.

83. 1860 Social Statistics Census for Wilkes County, North Carolina, Record Group 29, NA (F.2.114 N, 1860 Social Statistics Census for Alamance-Yancey Counties, Winston-Salem Public Library Copy from North Carolina Division of Archives and History copy of NA census records), not paginated.

84. JBG to Caroline Gordon, September 13, 1853, in Hickerson, *History and Genealogy,* 131.

85. Allen Brown to Hamilton Brown, November 20, 1852, Hamilton Brown Papers, SHC; JBG to R. F. Hackett, May 21, 1860, James Gordon Hackett Collection, NCSA; ? to JBG, February 14, 1857, James B. Gordon Letters, Brown Family Letters, GHM. For JBG's view on Salisbury, see JBG to Tom Brown, January 31, 1858, James G. Hackett Papers, DU.

86. ? to JBG, February 14, 1857, James B. Gordon Letters, Brown Family Letters, GHM; Mrs. James Harvey Gordon to Caroline Gordon, November 4, 1854, Hickerson, *History and Genealogy,* 133; Sarah Brown to Allen Brown, February 19 and 20, 1860, Brown Family Letters, GHM.

87. JBG to Caroline Gordon, July 12, 1853, James Gordon Hackett Collection, NCSA; Caroline Gordon to JBG, January 4, 1851, James B. Gordon Papers, NCSA.

88. Tom Brown to JBG, May 12, 1860, James G. Hackett Papers, DU; JBG to R. F. Hackett, May 21, 1860, James Gordon Hackett Collection, NCSA.

89. Winkler Interview; JBG to Caroline Gordon, September 13, 1853, in Hickerson, *History and Genealogy,* 131; JBG to Caroline Gordon, July 12, 1853, James Gordon Hackett Collection, NCSA.

90. Tom Brown to Caroline Gordon Hackett, May 2, 1861, James Gordon Hackett Collection, NCSA.

91. JBG to Caroline Gordon, August 6, 1843, Gordon-Hackett Collection, SHC; Anderson Collection.
92. James Gwyn Diary, February 1, 1855, James Gwyn Papers, SHC; Calvin J. Cowles to his wife, October 4, 1850, Calvin J. Cowles Papers, SHC; Rufus L. Patterson to JBG, April 28, 1852, James G. Hackett Papers, DU. Marie Morehead Patterson died in 1862. Patterson (1830–1879) later married Mary Fries of Salem.
93. 1860 Population Census of Wilkes County, microcopy 653, roll 918, p. 141, line 1045, NA); 1850 Agriculture Census; 1860 Agriculture Census.
94. JBG to "Campbell," April 5, 1857, Atwood & Company Papers, SHC; Tax Receipts, Hamilton Brown Papers, SHC. JBG told Campbell in May 1857 that he was planning to invest in some land in "the northwest." JBG called St. Louis a "beautiful city," and said the region was a "wonderful country" that had much business, enterprise, and was experiencing rapid growth (JBG to Caroline Gordon, May 15, 1857, James Gordon Hackett Collection, NCSA).
95. Hamilton Brown Collection, SHC; JBG to Tom Brown, January 31, 1858, James G. Hackett Papers, DU. In Sarah Gordon Brown to Allen Brown, May 1, 1855, James Gordon Hackett Papers, DU, Mrs. Brown noted that JBG had volunteered to take Mr. Brown north for the eye operation.
96. Leyburn, *The Scotch-Irish*, 99.
97. H. T. Brown to Carrie Hackett, February 25, 1861, Gordon-Hackett Papers, SHC.

Chapter 3

1. Cowles, *CSC*, 18; Cowles, "Life and Services," 5–6; H. T. Brown to Caroline Gordon Hackett, May 2, 1861, James Gordon Hackett Collection, NCSA.
2. Kruman, *Parties and Politics*, 106–107; *OR*, vol. 1, p. 486; Barrett, *Civil War*, 15–16; Warner and Yearns, *Biographical Register*, 64.
3. "An Ordinance to Dissolve the Union Between the State of North Carolina...," Bryan Grimes Papers, NCSA.
4. Calvin J. Cowles to Andrew Cowles, May 1, 1861, Calvin J. Cowles Papers, NCSA; James Gwyn Diary, May 1, 1861, James Gwyn Papers, SHC.
5. W. H. Proffit Journal, May 1, 1861; Starr, *Union Cavalry* 1: 88–89, 91; Gwyn Diary, May 4, 1861, James Gwyn Papers, SHC. According to the CSR for James B. Gordon, First North Carolina Cavalry Regiment (Ninth North Carolina State Troops), Microcopy 270, Roll 4, JBG entered the service on May 8, 1861. The Official Commission in the James B. Gordon Papers, NCSA, notes JBG's rank dates from May 9.
6. Calvin J. Cowles to John W., May 17, 1861 and Calvin J. Cowles to Calvin Benham, May 27, 1861, Calvin J. Cowles Papers, NCSA; Gwyn Diary, May 14, 1861, James Gwyn Papers, SHC. See also Calvin J. Cowles Papers, SHC.
7. JBG to W. M. Barber, July 10, 1861, Bess Gordon Finley Grier MS, copy in the author's possession. JBG noted that there was a balance due on the subscription list of $91.90. He had apparently spent $674.24 already.
8. Calvin J. Cowles to John W., May 17, 1861, Calvin J. Cowles Papers, NCSA; see also Calvin J. Cowles Papers, SHC; Gwyn Diary, May 14, 1861, James Gwyn Papers, SHC. The hill is known today as Barricks Hill.
9. Spainhour, "Incidents," *CSC*, 5. For the weather see Gwyn Diary, May 6, May 15, and May 20, 1861, James Gwyn Papers, SHC.
10. JBG to Augustus W. Finley, August 18, 1863; JBG to Augustus Finley, July 18, 1863, typewritten MS. courtesy J. Jay Anderson, WCC; R. A. Spainhour, "History of Company B, First North Carolina Regiment," *CSC*, 9.
11. Proffit Journal, May 28–29, 1861; *Carolina Watchman*, May 30, 1861, p. 2, col. 4; W. H. Proffit to his parents, in Hancock, *Four Brothers*, 5. *Raleigh Register*, May 22, 1861, recorded that Governor Ellis established a military camp west of Statesville, near the railroad, as a rendezvous point for volunteers from western counties. The men may have assembled there while waiting for the train.
12. *Carolina Watchman*, May 30, 1861, p. 2, col. 4; Proffit Journal, May 29, 1861.
13. Proffit Journal, May 31, June 10, 1861; Official Commission Document, James B. Gordon Papers, NCSA.
14. JBG to his mother, June 5, 1861, James B. Gordon Collection, NCSA.
15. Harrison Proffit to his parents, in Hancock, *Four Brothers*, 5; Samuel J. Ginings to S. Johnson, July 9, 1861, Calvin J. Cowles Papers, SHC. For a description of a captain's duties, see Blackford, comp., *Letters*, 154.
16. JBG to Sarah Gordon Brown, June 17, 1861, James B. Gordon Letters, Brown Family Letters, GHM; Samuel J. Ginings to S. Johnson, July 9, 1861, Calvin J. Cowles Papers, SHC; Proffit Journal, July 4, 1861.
17. JBG to W. M. Barber, July 10, 1861, Bess Gordon Finley Grier MS, copy in the author's possession; Samuel J. Ginings to S. Johnson, July 9, 1861, Calvin J. Cowles Papers, SHC.
18. Proffit Journal, 5–6; Zebulon Vance[?] to Sarah Gordon Brown, July 8, 1864, James B. Gordon Papers, Brown Family Letters, GHM.
19. Samuel J. Ginings to S. Johnson, July 9, 1861, Calvin J. Cowles Papers, SHC; Proffit Journal, 5–6.
20. Winkler interview; JBG to Sarah Gordon Brown, August 14, 1861, James B. Gordon Papers, NCSA.
21. *NC Troops* 2: 1; Barringer, "Ninth Regiment (First Cavalry)," *NC Regts.* 1: 417. The details of JBG's transfer are not known. The North Carolina legislature organized the 1st N.C. Cavalry Regiment under "An Act To Raise Ten Thousand State Troops." Under this act, which was ratified on May 8, 1861, the regiment was the ninth raised (The 1st N.C. Infantry Regiment being the first), so its line number made the 9th Regiment North Carolina State Troops. The 1st North Carolina Cavalry was the unit's common name in service of the Confederacy, but it was still referred to at times as the 9th. Cf. *OR*, vol. 51, pt. 2, 377.
22. James B. Gordon to Sarah Gordon Brown, June 17, 1861, James B. Gordon Letters, Brown Family Letters, GHM.
23. Dedmond, "Davis's 'Diary,'" *Appalachian Journal*, 383; *Richmond Dispatch*, September 22, 1861.
24. Barringer, "Ninth Regiment (First Cavalry)," *NC Regts.* 1: 417; M. V. M., "Gen. James B. Gordon," *The Daily Confederate*, May 25, 1864, p. 2, col. 1.
25. Cowles, *CSC*, 19; Cowles, "Life and Services," 9; James B. Gordon Papers, NCSA.
26. CSR for James B. Gordon, First North Carolina Cavalry Regiment (Ninth North Carolina State Troops), Microcopy 270, Roll 4; Official Commission Document, James B. Gordon Papers, NCSA. JBG's rank dated from June 17.
27. *CMH* 5: 345–46.
28. *Richmond Dispatch*, October 18, 1861, p. 3, col. 1; Colonel Wharton J. Green, "Ransom Address," 11. See also "North Carolina Women of the Confederacy," *CV* 38 (1930): 419, for more on Mrs. Ransom.
29. JBG to his mother, August 14, 1861, James Gordon Hackett Collection, NCSA. By saying that a cavalry officer "never rides any way only in a race," JBG might be referring to one of J. E. B. Stuart's cavalry maxims. In Stuart's words, "... a gallop is a gait unbecoming a soldier, unless he is going toward the enemy.... We gallop toward the enemy, and trot away, always" (Eggleston, *Rebel's Recollections*, 114).
30. Green, "Ransom Address," 15, 18; Dowdey, *The Seven Days*, 160; Opie, *Rebel Cavalryman*, 238.
31. Kerr Craige Address, MS., n.d., copy provided by Craige's grandson, Mr. Archibald Craige, Keswick, Va., copy in the author's possession.
32. *NC Troops* 2: xii, 7–8; Dedmond, "Davis's 'Diary,'" 383; Wm. L. Barrier to his father, July 9, 1861, Troxler and Auciello, eds., *Dear Father*, 81.

33. *NC Troops* 2: 1; *CV* 38 (1930): 419.
34. Gordon, "Organization of Troops," *NC Regts.* 1: 1–2.
35. *Richmond Dispatch,* August 3, 1861.
36. Journal of various subjects, Hamilton Brown Papers; *Richmond Enquirer,* October 19, 1861, p. 3, col. 4; *Raleigh Register,* October 23, 1861, p. 3, col. 3.
37. Green, "Ransom Address," 20; Barringer, "Ninth Regiment (First Cavalry)," *NC Regts.* 1: 417; Dedmond, "Davis's 'Diary,'" 383.
38. *Richmond Dispatch,* September 26, 1861.
39. *CMH* 5: 291; Thomas, *Bold Dragoon,* 202.
40. Curtis, "Journal," *Our Living and Our Dead* 2: 41; JBG to Caroline Gordon, July 12, 1853, NCSA; E. C. Finley, "William Henry Harrison Cowles and Family," Calvin J. Cowles Papers, SHC; J. B. Armfield, "Colonel William H. H. Cowles," *CSC,* 4.
41. Freeman, *Lee's Lieutenants* 2: 327. The disparity in "sabres" and "men" results from those assigned to wagon duty. The latter did not wield a sabre. Dedmond, "Davis's 'Diary,'" 383, notes that the regiment numbered 881 enlisted men, forty-three officers, and two doctors; the *Richmond Dispatch* of September 26, 1861, noted that the regiment contained 879 men and 964 horses.
42. *Richmond Dispatch,* September 26, 1861.
43. H. T. Brown to Caroline Gordon Hackett, May 2, 1861, James Gordon Hackett Collection, NCSA.
44. Mary Cunningham to Sarah Gordon Brown, August 25, 1861, Mary Cunningham Letters, Brown Family Letters, GHM; *OR,* vol. 3, 121, 123–24. Miss Cunningham, Tom's fiancee, said he lived ten minutes after receiving the fatal wound. His last words, "Lord have mercy," were uttered as a smile settled onto his dying face. He was buried in the Cunningham family burial ground in Van Buren (D. C. Williams to Sarah Gordon Brown, August 23, 1864, D. C. Williams Letters, Brown Family Letters, GHM). For a probable reference to Brown, see Snead, "First Year," *B&L* 1: 270–71.
45. JBG to Allen Brown, August 19, 1861, James Gordon Hackett Collection, NCSA; Warner and Yearns, *Biographical Register,* 63–64.
46. JBG to Allen Brown, August 19, 1861, James Gordon Hackett Collection, NCSA.
47. JBG to Allen Brown, August 19, 1861, James Gordon Hackett Collection, NCSA; Warner and Yearns, *Biographical Register,* 236–37. In addressing his letter, JBG incorrectly noted that Camp Beauregard was in Virginia.
48. *OR,* vol. 4, 649.
49. *OR,* vol. 51, pt. 2, 301, 336. See also Barringer, "Ninth Regiment (First Cavalry)," *NC Regts.* 1: 417–18; *NC Troops* 1: 1.
50. Starr, *Union Cavalry* 1: 212; Wm. L. Barrier to his father, October 4, 1861, Troxler and Auciello, eds., *Dear Father,* 83.
51. *The People's Press,* October 25, 1861, p. 2, col. 4.
52. *Raleigh Register,* October 23, 1861, p. 1, col. 6; *The People's Press,* October 25, 1861, p. 2, col. 4.
53. ; Dedmond, "Davis's 'Diary,'" 383; *Richmond Enquirer,* October 19, 1861, p. 3 col. 4.
54. *The People's Press,* October 25, 1861, p. 2, col. 4; *Richmond Dispatch,* October 18, 1861, p. 3 col. 1; *Raleigh Register,* October 23, 1861, p. 3, col. 2.
55. *The People's Press,* October 25, 1861, p. 2, col. 4; Dedmond, "Davis's 'Diary,'" 383.
56. Dedmond, "Davis's 'Diary,'" 383.
57. *The Petersburg Express,* quoted in *Raleigh Register,* October 23, 1861, p. 3, col. 1; Dedmond, "Davis's 'Diary,'" 383.
58. Wm. L. Barrier to his father, October 26, 1861, Troxler and Auciello, eds., *Dear Father,* 84.
59. Dedmond, "Davis's 'Diary,'" 383. Davis wrote incorrectly that the regiment arrived in Petersburg on October 18.
60. *Richmond Enquirer,* October 19, 1861, p. 3 col. 4; October 22, 1861, p. 3, col. 6; *Richmond Dispatch,* October 19, 1861; *Raleigh Register,* October 23, 1861, p. 3, col. 2.
61. *Richmond Enquirer,* October 19, 1861, p. 3 col. 4; *Raleigh Register,* October 23, 1861, p. 3, col. 2.

62. Dedmond, "Davis's 'Diary,'" 383; *Raleigh Register,* October 23, 1861, p. 3, col. 2.
63. *OR,* Series 1, vol. 51, part 2, 350; *OR,* Series 1, vol. 5, 909.
64. Barringer, "Ninth Regiment (First Cavalry)," *NC Regts.* 1: 419; Dedmond, "Davis's 'Diary,'" 383.
65. *The People's Press,* October 25, 1861, p. 2, col. 4; *Richmond Enquirer,* October 19, 1861, p. 3 col. 4; *Richmond Dispatch,* October 22, 1861; Barringer, "Ninth Regiment (First Cavalry)," *NC Regts.* 1: 419. See also Mizelle, "Cabarrus Rangers," *The Charlotte Observer,* July 7, 1929. In Dedmond, "Davis's 'Diary,'" 383, trooper Davis quotes "a publication" written by President Davis which said that "N.C. can boast of the finest, as well as the first regt. of Cav in the Confederate service."
66. Wm. L. Barrier to his father, October 26, 1861, Troxler and Auciello, eds., *Dear Father,* 84–85.
67. Davis, *Stuart,* 394; *Richmond Dispatch,* October 25, 1861. *Raleigh Register,* October 23, 1861, p. 3, col. 2 noted that the regiment had about thirty wagons; *The Fredericksburg Recorder,* quoted in *Raleigh Register,* November 6, 1861, p. 2, col. 3, recorded that the regiment had about forty-five wagons; and the *Richmond Dispatch,* quoted in the *Carolina Watchman,* April 7, 1862, p. 3, col. 1, reported that the train had between forty and fifty. For an analysis of the appropriate number of regimental wagons, see Starr, *Union Cavalry* 1: 28.
68. *The Land We Love,* vol. 1, no. 4 (October 1866), 417; *The Fredericksburg Recorder,* quoted in *Raleigh Register,* November 6, 1861, p. 2, col. 3. According to this source, the regiment was forced to leave a few men who were sick in a Fredericksburg hospital.
69. *The Land We Love,* vol. 1, no. 4 (October 1866), 417; vol. 2, no. 1 (November 1866), 25.
70. Dedmond, "Davis's 'Diary,'" 383; Barringer, "Ninth Regiment (First Cavalry)," *NC Regts.* 1: 484.
71. Dedmond, "Davis's 'Diary,'" 383; Barringer, "Ninth Regiment (First Cavalry)," *NC Regts.* 1: 419; Freeman, *Lee's Lieutenants* 1: xlix; Mitchell, ed., *The Letters of Major General James E. B. Stuart,* 157.
72. Blackford, *War Years,* 31, 41.
73. Dedmond, "Davis's 'Diary,'" 383; J. R. Gibbons, "The Origin of Company Q," *CV* 22 (1914): 320.
74. J. W. Biddle to "Pa," December 16, 1861, Samuel S. Biddle Papers, DU; Barringer, "Ninth Regiment (First Cavalry)," *NC Regts.* 1: 419; Gibbons, "Company Q," *CV* 22 (1914): 320.
75. J. H. Person to his sister, December 6, 1861, Presley Carter Person Papers, DU; J. W. Biddle to "Pa," December 16, 1861, Samuel S. Biddle Papers, DU; *Raleigh Register,* December 11, 1861, p. 2, col. 4.
76. Dedmond, "Davis's 'Diary,'" 383–84.
77. *Concord Register,* June 8, 1883.
78. Gibbons, "Company Q," *CV* 22 (1914): 320; J. W. Biddle to "Pa," December 16, 1861, Samuel S. Biddle Papers, DU.
79. Gibbons, "Company Q," *CV* 22 (1914): 320.
80. Jacob A. Fisher to Father and Mother, December 8, 1861, Civil War Miscellaneous Collection, USAMHI; *Richmond Dispatch,* December 6, 1861.
81. Gibbons, "Company Q," *CV* 22 (1914): 320; Wm. L. Barrier to his father, December 4, 1861, Troxler and Auciello, eds., *Dear Father,* 86; *OR,* vol. 5, 446. One member of the regiment, apparently a participant, wrote a letter that was printed in the December 6, 1861 *Richmond Dispatch,* p. 2, col. 5, concerning the scout. It was reprinted in the *Raleigh Register* on December 11, 1861, p. 2, cols. 4 and 5.
82. Jeb Stuart to Mrs. Stuart, November 24, 1861, in *The Letters of General J. E. B. Stuart,* 226; *Raleigh Register,* December 11, 1861, p. 2, col. 4. According to historian Horace Mewborn, Ransom was incorrect when he called the mill "Hockhurst's Mill" in his report. The proper spelling is related in the text.
83. *OR,* vol. 5, 446; Cooke, *Wearing of the Gray,* 380–381.
84. *OR,* vol. 5, 446.

85. Ibid.
86. *OR,* vol. 5, 446; *Raleigh Register,* December 11, 1861, p. 2, col. 4.
87. *OR,* vol. 5, 446; *Raleigh Register,* December 11, 1861, p. 2, col. 4; Dedmond, "Davis's 'Diary,'" 384.
88. Rawle, et. al., *Third Pennsylvania,* 24–25; Rufus Barringer to V. C. Barringer, January 27, 1866, Rufus Clay Barringer Papers, SHC; *OR,* vol. 5, 446; *Raleigh Register,* December 11, 1861, p. 2, col. 4.
89. JBG to Caroline Gordon Hackett, December 3, 1861, James Gordon Hackett Collection, NCSA; Dedmond, "Davis's 'Diary,'" 384.
90. *OR,* Vol. 5, 444; *Raleigh Register,* December 11, 1861, p. 2, col. 4; JBG to Caroline Gordon Hackett, December 3, 1861, James Gordon Hackett Collection, NCSA.
91. Freeman, *Lee's Lieutenants* 2: 328; *OR,* vol. 5, 446.
92. *Raleigh Register,* December 11, 1861, p. 2, col. 4; JBG to Caroline Gordon Hackett, December 3, 1861. JBG added that the "Col was kind enough in making out his report to headquarters to mention my name very kindly and flatteringly with the affair." Ransom wrote that the charge was "most gallantly led by Gordon" and added that "I do no injustice in mentioning particularly Major Gordon, whom I directed to lead the charge" (*OR,* vol. 5, 446–47).
93. *Raleigh Register,* December 11, 1861, p. 2, col. 4. The newspaper claims that JBG killed two Yankees, but Ransom reported only one enemy dead. The confirmed dead man was said to be a Lieutenant Lane from Philadelphia.
94. *OR,* vol. 5, 446–47; *Raleigh Register,* December 11, 1861, p. 2, col. 4.
95. *OR,* vol. 5, 446; Starr, *Union Cavalry* 1: 243; *Raleigh Register,* December 11, 1861, p. 2, col. 4; Rawle, *Third Pennsylvania,* 24–25; General Orders #5, December 3, 1861, J. E. B. Stuart Papers, DU. Federal reports offer no casualty figures; Confederate sources differ slightly.
96. *Raleigh Register,* December 11, 1861, p. 2, col. 4; Rawle, *Third Pennsylvania,* 24–25; Mizelle, "Cabarrus Rangers," *The Charlotte Observer,* July 7, 1929; D.C. Williams to JBG, December 19, 1861, James B. Gordon Letters, Brown Family Letters, GHM.
97. *OR,* vol. 5, 446. Other Confederate cavalry units in Virginia had already fought with Federal infantry, but until Vienna Stuart's men had not squared off with Federal cavalry.
98. JBG to Caroline Gordon Hackett, December 3, 1861; J. W. Biddle to "Pa," December 16, 1861, Samuel S. Biddle Papers, DU.
99. J. W. Biddle to "Pa," December 16, 1861, Samuel S. Biddle Papers, DU; JBG to Sarah Gordon Brown, December 23, 1861, James Gordon Hackett Collection, NCSA.
100. JBG to Caroline Gordon Hackett, December 3, 1861, James Gordon Hackett Collection, NCSA; *Johnston's Narrative,* 69, in Freeman, *Lee's Lieutenants* 1: 111.
101. J. W. Biddle to Rosa, December 5, 1861, Samuel S. Biddle Papers, DU; J. W. Biddle to "Pa," December 16, 1861, Samuel S. Biddle Papers, DU.
102. J. W. Biddle to Rosa, December 5, 1861; J. W. Biddle to "Pa," December 16, 1861, both in Samuel S. Biddle Papers, DU.
103. *OR,* vol. 5, 490; McClellan, *Stuart,* 43.
104. J. W. Biddle to Pa, December 25, 1861, Samuel S. Biddle Papers, DU; McClellan, *Stuart,* 43; Thomas, *Bold Dragoon,* 98.
105. *Raleigh Register,* December 25, 1861, p. 2, col. 4; *OR,* vol. 5, 474, 490–91; JBG to Sarah Gordon Brown, December 23, 1861, James Gordon Hackett Collection, NCSA.
106. JBG to Sarah Gordon Brown, December 23, 1861, James Gordon Hackett Collection, NCSA. Actually, the Federal unit had been ordered up by Brigadier-General George A. McCall. The objectives: to drive back the enemy's pickets "which have recently advanced within four or five miles of our lines ... and carried off two good Union men, and threatened others; and, secondly, to procure a good supply of forage" (*OR,* vol. 5, 480; McClellan, *Stuart,* 43).
107. McClellan, *Stuart,* 44; *OR,* vol. 5, 491.
108. McClellan, *Stuart,* 44.
109. *OR,* vol. 5, 491–92. For more on these soldiers' difficulties, see the *Richmond Dispatch,* quoted in *The People's Press,* January 3, 1862, p. 2, col. 6, and *OR,* vol. 5, 483.
110. JBG to Sarah Gordon Brown, December 23, 1861, James Gordon Hackett Collection, NCSA; *OR,* vol. 5, 493.
111. JBG to Sarah Gordon Brown, December 23, 1861, James Gordon Hackett Collection, NCSA; *OR,* vol. 5, 493.
112. McClellan, *Stuart,* 45.
113. J. W. Biddle to Pa, December 25, 1861, Samuel S. Biddle Papers, DU; JBG to Sarah Gordon Brown, December 23, 1861, James Gordon Hackett Collection, NCSA; JBG to Allen Brown, December 30, 1861, James B. Gordon Letters, Brown Family Letters, GHM.
114. Barringer, "Ninth Regiment (First Cavalry)," *NC Regts.* 1: 419–20.
115. J. W. Biddle to Pa, December 25, 1861, Samuel S. Biddle Papers, DU; Stuart, *McClellan,* 45.
116. JBG to Allen Brown, December 30, 1861, James B. Gordon Letters, Brown Family Letters, GHM; Wm. L. Barrier to his father, December 25, 1861, Troxler and Auciello, eds., *Dear Father,* 88; Various receipts, Anderson Collection.
117. J. W. Biddle to Pa, December 25, 1861, S. S. Biddle Papers, DU; Cowles, *CSC,* 20; Cowles, "Life and Services," 10; JBG to Allen Brown, December 30, 1861, James B. Gordon Letters, Brown Family Letters, GHM.

Chapter 4

1. CSR for James B. Gordon, First North Carolina Cavalry Regiment (Ninth North Carolina State Troops), Microcopy 270, Roll 4; Dedmond, "Davis's 'Diary,'" 385.
2. JBG to Sarah Gordon Brown, February 3, 186[2], James B. Gordon Letters, Brown Family Letters, GHM; George F. Adams to Alfred and Betsy Adams, January 6, 1862, Adams Papers; J.W. Biddle to his father, February 9, 1862, Simpson and Biddle Family Papers, NCSA.
3. JBG to Sarah Gordon Brown, February 3, 186[2], James B. Gordon Letters, Brown Family Letters, GHM; Requisition for Captain Folk's Company D, February 13, 1862, George Stanley Dewey Papers, SHC; JBG to Sarah Gordon Brown, February 3, 186[2], James B. Gordon Letters, Brown Family Letters, GHM. For the weather, see also J. E. B. Stuart to Laura Ratcliffe January 30, February 3, 1862, LC.
4. Dedmond, "Davis's 'Diary,'" 385; W. L. Barrier to his father, February 10, 1862, Troxler and Auciello, eds., *Dear Father,* 90; JBG to Sarah Gordon Brown, January 16, 1862, James B. Gordon Letters, Brown Family Letters, GHM.
5. George F. Adams to Alfred and Betsy Adams, Adams Papers.
6. *OR,* vol. 5, 506; *NC Troops* 2: 1; J.W. Biddle to his father, February 9, 1862, Simpson and Biddle Family Papers, NCSA.
7. Mamie Barber, "Colonel William Morgan Barber," *CSC* 6. Barber was captured at Gettysburg and later exchanged. He was mortally wounded on September 30, 1864 and died October 3, 1864. Barber was buried near JBG. The traditional spelling for his name is Barbour.
8. Ashe, *Biographical History* 1: 252; Barrett, *Civil War,* 98; Brawley, *Lawrence O'Bryan Branch,* 133 ff.
9. J. W. Biddle to Pa, February 3, 1862, S.S. Biddle Papers, DU; *OR,* vol. 9, 55.
10. *NC Troops* 2: 1; *OR,* vol. 51, pt. 2, 474; vol. 9, 164.
11. *OR,* vol. 9, 56; Jeb Stuart to Mrs. Stuart, March 2, 1862, in *The Letters of Major General J.E.B. Stuart,* 252; J. W. Biddle to Pa, February 3, 1862, S.S. Biddle Papers, DU.
12. Foote, *The Civil War* 1: 238; Freeman, *Lee's Lieutenants* 1: 135, 140.
13. JBG to Sarah Gordon Brown, March 7, 1862, James B. Gordon Papers, NCSA.
14. Ibid.

15. Starr, *Union Cavalry* 1: 249–50.
16. Freeman, *Lee's Lieutenants* 1: 140.
17. Dedmond, "Davis's 'Diary,'" 386. Harvey Davis, who was not present, wrote that the 1st North Carolina destroyed this historical bridge. E. P. Alexander, in Alexander, *Fighting For The Confederacy,* 72, claimed that he and one other person destroyed the bridge.
18. *OR*, vol. 51, pt. 2, 512; *NC Troops* 2: 1; Dedmond, "Davis's 'Diary,'" 386. R. E. Lee wrote in *OR*, vol. 51, pt. 2, 541: "It was intended that [the regiment] should go to Goldsborough....." Upon the unit's arrival, Brigadier General J. R. Anderson was to "order it to such point on the line as in your judgment stands in most need of this arm of the service."
19. J. W. Biddle to Pa, February 3, 1862, S. S. Biddle Papers, DU; Eggleston, *Rebel's Recollections,* 124; Dedmond, "Davis's 'Diary,'" 386.
20. *OR,* vol. 51, part 2, 474; Freeman, *R. E. Lee* 2: 8; *The People's Press,* March 28, 1862, p. 2, col. 3.
21. Dedmond, "Davis's 'Diary,'" 386; *The Petersburg Express,* quoted in the *Carolina Watchman,* April 7, 1862, p. 3, col. 1.
22. Dedmond, "Davis's 'Diary,'" 386; W. L. Barrier to his father, n.d., Troxler and Auciello, *Dear Father,* 91; *OR,* vol. 9, 453; CSR for James B. Gordon, First North Carolina Cavalry Regiment (Ninth North Carolina State Troops), Microcopy 270, Roll 4.
23. J. H. Person to his sister, April 1, 1862, Presley Carter Person Papers, DU; *OR,* vol. 51, pt. 2, 541; Brooks, *Butler and His Cavalry,* 384.
24. Dedmond, "Davis's 'Diary,'" 386; W. L. Barrier to his father, n. d., Troxler and Auciello, *Dear Father,* 91.
25. Boatner, *Dictionary,* 40; *CMH* 5: 291–92; McSwain, *Crumbling Defenses,* 58. On March 6, Ransom was promoted and given the task of organizing the cavalry of Generals Johnston and Beauregard in the West and Southwest. However, upon the fall of New Bern, he was ordered to duty in eastern North Carolina (*CMH* 5: 346; Green, "Ransom Address," 13–14).
26. CSR for James B. Gordon, First North Carolina Cavalry Regiment (Ninth North Carolina State Troops), Microcopy 270, Roll 4; Official Commission Document, James B. Gordon Papers, NCSA.
27. Dedmond, "Davis's 'Diary,'" 386; W. L. Barrier to his father, n.d., Troxler and Billy Auciello, *Dear Father,* 91.
28. *CSC,* 15; Dedmond, "Davis's 'Diary,'" 386; *NC Troops* 2: 1; CSR for James B. Gordon, First North Carolina Cavalry Regiment (Ninth North Carolina State Troops), Microcopy 270, Roll 4.
29. W. A. Graham, Nineteenth Regiment (Second Cavalry)," *NC Regts.* 2: 82; Curtis, "Journal," *Our Living and Our Dead* 2: 42–3; W. L. Barrier to his father, n.d., Troxler and Auciello, *Dear Father,* 91.
30. *OR,* vol. 9, 453; J. Pugh to Sarah Heck, April 26, 1862, James T. Pugh Papers, SHC.
31. *OR.,* vol. 9, 379; Barrett, *Civil War,* 122.
32. *OR,* vol. 9, 381. Burnside had 16,528 men present for duty.
33. J. Pugh to Sarah Heck, April 26, 1862, James T. Pugh Papers, SHC; JBG to R.F. Hackett, April 19, 1862, James Gordon Hackett Collection, NCSA.
34. *OR,* vol. 9, 453; JBG to R.F. Hackett, April 19, 1862, James Gordon Hackett Collection, NCSA.
35. JBG to R.F. Hackett, April 19, 1862, James Gordon Hackett Collection, NCSA; *CSC,* 15.
36. JBG to R.F. Hackett, April 19, 1862, James Gordon Hackett Collection, NCSA.
37. Dedmond, "Davis's 'Diary,'" 386.
38. CSR for James Anderson, First North Carolina Cavalry Regiment (Ninth North Carolina State Troops), Microcopy 270, Roll 1; CSR for John Anderson, First North Carolina Cavalry Regiment (Ninth North Carolina State Troops), Microcopy 270, Roll 1.
39. JBG to R.F. Hackett, May 11, 1862, James Gordon Hackett Collection, NCSA.
40. Ibid.
41. *NC Troops* 2: 1.
42. Dedmond, "Davis's 'Diary,'" 386.
43. Dedmond, "Davis's 'Diary,'" 386–87.
44. *NC Troops* 2: 1.
45. J. H. Person to his mother, May 12, 1862, Presley Carter Person Papers, DU.
46. Graham, "Nineteenth Regiment (Second Cavalry)," *NC Regts.* 2: 82–83.
47. Barrett, *Civil War,* 125. Ransom leveled the charges after Holmes ordered him to investigate. General Lee concurred in the findings but decided the regiment needed drill, not punishment. See also Graham, "Nineteenth Regiment (Second Cavalry)," *NC Regts.* 2: 82.
48. Freeman, *Lee's Lieutenants* 1: 211–12.
49. Freeman, *R. E. Lee* 2: 63.
50. Hill, "Forty-first Regiment (Third Cavalry)," *NC Regts.* 2: 768.
51. Robins, "Stuart's Ride," *B&L* 2: 271.
52. Ibid.
53. Dedmond, "Davis's 'Diary,'" 387.
54. Barrett, *Civil War,* 131–32; Cheek, "Additional Sketch Ninth Regiment (First Cavalry)," *NC Regts.* 1: 446–48; Pearce, "Where Cavalry Fought the Navy," *The State,* 7–9. For another adventure of these detached companies, see *OR,* vol. 51, pt. 2, 568.
55. Dedmond, "Davis's 'Diary,'" 387; *OR,* vol. 11, pt. 2, 525.
56. J.W. Biddle to Rosa, June 28, 1862, Simpson and Biddle Family Papers, NCSA; *Carolina Watchman,* August 4, 1862, p. 2, col. 5.
57. *OR,* vol. 11, pt. 2, 525 contradicts the arrival date recorded in *NC Troops* 2: 1–2, and Dedmond, "Davis's 'Diary,'" 387. The later two sources hold that the regiment arrived on June 27.
58. Dedmond, "Davis's 'Diary,'" 387.

Chapter 5

1. JBG to R.F. Hackett, May 11, 1862, James Gordon Hackett Collection, NCSA; J. H. Person to his sister, June 15, 1862, S. S. Biddle Papers, DU; Haile Diary, June 13, 1862, MC; CSR for James B. Gordon, First North Carolina Cavalry Regiment (Ninth North Carolina State Troops), Microcopy 270, Roll 4.
2. Haile diary, June 15, 1862, MC.
3. *OR,* vol. 11, part 2, 514; Cooke, *Wearing of the Gray,* 22–23; McClellan, *Stuart,* 54; Haile diary, June 15, 1862, MC; Thomas, *Bold Dragoon,* 127.
4. *OR,* vol. 11, part 1, 1038, 1037.
5. Freeman, *Lee's Lieutenants* 1: 299.
6. Robins, "Stuart's Ride," *B&L* 2: 275; *OR,* vol. 11, pt. 1, 1042.
7. McClellan, *Stuart,* 53; *The Land We Love* 2: 369. The latter account could refer to John B. Gordon. It says the J.B. Gordon in the anecdote was afterward a lieutenant general, but neither JBG nor John B. Gordon attained that rank. In any case, if the man in the story was related to one, he would have been related to both.
8. McClellan, *Stuart,* 67; J.W. Biddle to Rosa, June 28, 1862, Simpson and Biddle Family Papers, NCSA.
9. *OR,* vol. 11, pt. 2, 525.
10. *B&L* 2: 317.
11. *OR,* vol. 11, pt. 3, 645, 534. Only two months before, Stuart had commanded a total of 1,289 men.
12. Thomas, *Bold Dragoon,* 131.
13. *OR,* vol. 11, part 2, 521, 525; *NC Troops* 2: 2; McClellan, *Stuart,* 72.
14. *OR,* vol. 11, part 2, 499, 513. The 10th Virginia cavalry was in reserve on Nine Mile road. *NC Troops* 2: 1, records that Baker's five newly-arrived companies of the 1st were placed in reserve on Phillips's Farm once they reached Vir-

ginia. *OR,* vol. 11, pt. 2, 520 indicates that units of the 1st were not placed in reserve there until after the Battle of Malvern Hill.

15. E. C. Finley, "William Henry Harrison Cowles and Family," Calvin J. Cowles Papers, SHC.

16. Freeman, *Lee's Lieutenants* 1: 514–515.

17. Wheeler, *Reminiscences,* 469.

18. Dowdey, *The Seven Days,* 251.

19. McClellan, *Stuart,* 72; *OR,* vol. 11, part 2, 515.

20. Beale, *History of the Ninth Virginia,* 24–25.

21. Longstreet, *Manassas to Appomattox,* 148; Freeman, *R. E. Lee* 2: 132; Hill, *Bethel To Sharpsburg,* 2: 126.

22. *OR,* vol. 11, pt. 2, 523; Averell, "With the Cavalry," *B&L* 2: 429.

23. *OR,* vol. 11, pt. 2, 523. Stuart addressed this to Colonel Tom Rosser three days before Baker arrived at Richmond.

24. *OR,* vol. 11, pt. 2, 513, 525; *NC Troops* 2: 2. Baker, in his report, mistakenly wrote that Lee ordered him into the field on the night of June 29. The mission actually took place during the daylight hours of June 29, as is confirmed in *OR,* vol. 11, pt. 2, 526 and 532, and McClellan, *Stuart,* 79. Stuart also incorrectly recorded the date in *OR,* vol. 11, pt. 2, 521.

25. Freeman, *R. E. Lee* 2: 176; *OR,* vol. 11, pt. 2, 235, 525; Sears, *To The Gates of Richmond,* 265. Baker did not mention JBG's detachment as taking part in his mission. Davis, in Dedmond, "Davis' Diary,'" 387, recalled that Baker's force during this movement was "the regiment." In light of this contradictory information, it cannot be known with certainty if JBG's force took part in the scout along the Willis' Church Road. However, it appears from the extant information that Baker only retained his portion of the regiment; JBG worked along the Darbytown and Osborne roads. In D. H. Hill, *Bethel To Sharpsburg,* 2: 126, it is stated that JBG and three companies went with Stuart to the White House, but Stuart's report indicates otherwise.

26. Rawle, *Third Pennsylvania,* 86; *OR,* vol. 11, pt. 2, 525.

27. Barringer, "Ninth Regiment (First Cavalry)," *NC Regts.* 1: 420; Averell, "With the Cavalry," *B&L* 2: 431; Dedmond, "Davis's 'Diary,'" 387.

28. Barringer, "Ninth Regiment (First Cavalry)," *NC Regts.* 1: 420; Rufus Barringer to V. C. Barringer, January 27, 1866, Rufus Clay Barringer Papers, SHC.

29. *Concord Register,* June 8, 1883.

30. For the different casualty estimates, see *OR,* vol. 11, pt. 2, 507; Barringer, "Ninth Regiment (First Cavalry)," *NC Regts.* 1: 420; Averell, "With the Cavalry," *B&L* 2: 431; *NC Troops* 2: 2; and Hill, *Bethel To Sharpsburg,* 2: 126.

31. Mizelle, "Cabarrus Rangers," *The Charlotte Observer,* July 7, 1929; Rawle, *Third Pennsylvania,* 86; *OR,* vol. 11, part 2, 235. For Crumpler, see *People's Press,* July 25, 1862, p. 2, col. 2; *Carolina Watchman,* August 4, 1862, p. 2, col. 5.

32. Barringer, "Ninth Regiment (First Cavalry)," *NC Regts.* 1: 420; Dedmond, "Davis' Diary,'" 387; Hill, *Bethel To Sharpsburg* 2: 126.

33. *OR,* vol. 11, pt. 2, 235, 202; Averell, "With the Cavalry," *B&L* 2: 431; Dedmond, "Davis' Diary,'" 387.

34. Rawle, *Third Pennsylvania,* 86; Barringer, "Ninth Regiment (First Cavalry)," *NC Regts.* 1: 420; *OR,* vol. 11, pt. 2, 532.

35. *NC Troops* 2: 2; Freeman, *R. E. Lee* 2: 180.

36. McClellan, "Peninsular Campaign, *B&L* 2: 185–86.

37. Freeman, *R. E. Lee* 2: 182; McClellan, "Peninsular Campaign, *B&L* 2: 186.

38. *OR,* vol. 11, pt. 2, 525, 527. Colonel Goode, commanding the 3d Virginia, wrote that "an advance guard from my regiment, thrown out by Colonel Baker, reported that both sides of the road leading to Jackson's left, which road was exceedingly narrow and thickly wooded on either side, was occupied in force by the enemy's sharpshooters. It was deemed impracticable to make the connection with Jackson's command, and we encamped that night at Gatewood's farm" (ibid., 527). Rosser, colonel of the 5th Virginia Cavalry, wrote that the 1st North Carolina and the 3d and 5th regiments moved to the left to support Magruder's attack (ibid., 533).

39. Cowles, *CSC,* 21; Cowles, "Life and Services," 13; Winkler Interview.

40. Cooke, *Wearing of the Gray,* 530.

41. Averell, "With the Cavalry," *B&L* 2: 433; Freeman, *R. E. Lee* 2: 210; Longstreet, *Manassas to Appomattox,* 144.

42. Freeman, *R. E. Lee* 2: 237–38.

43. Cooke, *Wearing of the Gray,* 530.

44. W. L. Barrier to his father, August 13, 1862, Troxler and Auciello, *Dear Father,* 95.

45. Freeman, *R. E. Lee* 2: 232, 237–38.

46. *OR,* vol. 11, pt. 2, 519, 525; McClellan, *Stuart,* 82; Dedmond, "Davis' 'Diary,'" 388.

47. Freeman, *Lee's Lieutenants* 1: 640; J. E. B. Stuart to Flora Stuart, July 5, 1862, quoted in Freeman, *Lee's Lieutenants* 1: 642; McClellan, *Stuart,* 82 ff.

48. *OR,* vol. 11, pt. 2, 521; Davis, 150; *The Concord Sun,* March 25, 1881, p. 1, col. 3.

49. Blackford, *War Years,* 87–88.

50. Von Borcke, *Memoirs,* 1: 83–85.

51. D. B. Rea, *Sketches,* 6; *Daily Confederate,* May 25, 1864, p. 1, cols. 1–2. David B. Rea, author of *Sketches,* was a private in Company C of the 1st until June 1863, when he was transferred to the 5th North Carolina Cavalry. The writer of the second source, an M. V. M., also served with JBG during the war's early days, and then wrote an obituary of JBG in May 1864.

52. Dedmond, "Davis' 'Diary,'" 388; Freeman, *R. E. Lee* 2: 256.

53. Dedmond, "Davis' 'Diary,'" 388–89; J. H. Person to his mother, July 27, 1862, S. S. Biddle Papers, DU; Cad. J. Iredell to Miss Mattie, May 14, 1862, Cadwallader Jones Iredell Papers, SHC. The shell landed near W. H. Cheek, a future commander of the 1st North Carolina. He escaped unharmed.

54. Cooke, *Wearing of the Gray,* 167; Dedmond, "Davis's 'Diary,'" 388; Cad. J. Iredell to Miss Mattie, July 15, 1862, Cadwallader J. Iredell Papers, SHC.

55. J. W. Biddle to Rosa, August 3, 1862, S. S. Biddle Papers, DU.

56. Freeman, *R. E. Lee* 2: 257; Dedmond, "Davis's 'Diary,'" 389.

57. *OR,* vol. 11, pt. 3, 657; Barringer, "Ninth Regiment (First Cavalry)," *NC Regts.* 1: 420–21; McClellan, *Stuart,* 86.

58. *CMH,* vol. 4, 622–23; Freeman, *R. E. Lee* 2: 257; Nichols, *Fitz Lee,* 10–11, 18.

59. Cooke, *Wearing of the Gray,* 52.

60. Wells, *Hampton and His Cavalry,* 36–40; Freeman, *Lee's Lieutenants* 1: 93; Boatner, *Dictionary,* 370.

61. Rea, *Sketches,* 5–6.

62. Freeman, *R. E. Lee* 2: 261.

63. Martha Lenoir Gordon Finley to Sarah J. Lenoir, July 31, 1862, copy in James Gwyn Papers, SHC.

64. Dedmond, "Davis's 'Diary,'" 389; Rea, *Sketches,* 6; J. W. Biddle to Rosa, August 3, 1862, S. S. Biddle Papers, DU.

65. Rea, *Sketches,* 6.

66. *OR,* vol. 11, pt. 2, 952.

67. *OR,* vol. 11, pt. 2, 951. McClellan called it a reconnaissance.

68. Freeman, *R. E. Lee* 2: 269–70.

69. Rea, *Sketches,* 6–7.

70. Via P. M. B. Young and Wade Hampton. *OR,* vol. 11, pt. 2, 956; Freeman, *R. E. Lee* 2: 269–70.

71. Dedmond, "Davis' 'Diary,'" 389; *OR,* vol. 11, pt. 2, 951, 953; Rea, *Sketches,* 7. The presence of Baker's force did discourage the advance of a cavalry scout under Captain George A. Custer. The Federal cavalry scout, which had helped capture the White Oak Swamp Bridge from pickets of the 10th Virginia, returned to camp. For the full story of the reoccu-pation of Malvern Hill, see *OR,* vol. 11, pt. 2, 951–964.

72. Freeman, *R. E. Lee* 2: 269–70; Sears, *To the Gates of Richmond*, 354.
73. *OR,* vol. 12, pt. 3, 958.
74. J. W. Biddle to Pa, August 15, 1862, S. S. Biddle Papers, DU; *OR,* vol. 12, pt. 3, 942.
75. *OR,* vol. 12, pt. 2, 725; McClellan, *Stuart,* 89.
76. *OR,* vol. 11, pt. 2, 507, 952. Other than the 1st's sixty-one casualties, the 1st Virginia lost one man killed and the 4th Virginia lost one killed and four wounded.
77. *OR,* vol. 12, pt. 3, 931.
78. Dedmond, "Davis's 'Diary,'" 389; Rea, *Sketches,* 8.
79. J. W. Biddle to Pa, August 15, 1862, S. S. Biddle Papers, DU; Rea, *Sketches,* 8–9; Dedmond, "Davis's 'Diary,'" 389.
80. Rea, *Sketches,* 9–10. The message was signed simply, "First Illinois Cavalry." According to Sears, *To the Gates of Richmond,* 383–85, the Illinois horse units present were the 8th Illinois, the McClellan Dragoons, and the Sturgis Rifles.
81. Rea, *Sketches,* 11; Dedmond, "Davis's 'Diary,'" 389.
82. Dedmond, "Davis's 'Diary,'" 389. The last army corps had left Harrison's Landing on the morning of August 16, leaving only a cavalry rear guard. For the details of this rear guard's withdrawal, plus mention of skirmishing with Confederate cavalry that may have been the 1st, see *OR,* vol. 11, pt. 2, 964–67. For Confederate information gathering, see also Mosby, *War Reminiscences,* 243–44.
83. Dedmond, "Davis's 'Diary,'" 389.
84. In *OR,* vol. 11, pt. 3, 657–58, dated July 29, 1862, Lee's assistant adjutant general told D. H. Hill, commanding the Department of North Carolina, that the army had previously requested the return of the two companies without success. The squadron had been detained "south of the river" for an unspecified "cause." Hill sent them back to Virginia right away.
85. Dedmond, "Davis's 'Diary,'" 389; "Sidelights," *CSC,* 15.

Chapter 6

1. *OR,* vol. 12, pt. 3, 942.
2. Ibid., 941–42.
3. *OR,* vol. 12, pt. 3, 944; vol. 12, pt. 2, 744. Lee also requested the 2d North Carolina Cavalry, but it was retained in North Carolina.
4. Dedmond, "Davis's 'Diary,'" 389–90; *NC Troops* 2: 2.
5. Von Borcke, *Memoirs,* 1: 173; McClellan, *Stuart,* 109.
6. *OR,* vol. 12, pt. 2, 181 ff.; *OR,* vol. 12, pt. 3, 934; McDonald, *Laurel Brigade,* 81. Robertson's brigade had been formed around the command of Turner Ashby, the cavalryman of Shenandoah Valley fame.
7. Davis, *Stuart,* 189; *OR,* vol. 19, pt. 1, 660, 810. Stuart's returns for October 10 report 6,378 aggregate present and 10,298 aggregate present and absent. Cf. *OR,* vol. 19, pt. 1, 453; pt. 2, 713.
8. Sears, *Landscape Turned Red,* 91.
9. *OR,* vol. 12, pt. 2, 814; vol. 19, pt. 1, 822; vol. 12, pt. 2, 744; Von Borcke, *Memoirs,* 1: 173; McClellan, *Stuart,* 109.
10. Rea, *Sketches,* 13.
11. Rea, *Sketches,* 13–15; *OR,* vol. 19, pt. 1, 822.
12. *OR,* vol. 19, pt. 1, 822.
13. *OR,* vol. 19, pt. 1, 822; Rea, *Sketches,* 15; Dedmond, "Davis's 'Diary,'" 390.
14. Dedmond, "Davis's 'Diary,'" 390–91; Von Borcke, *Memoirs,* 1: 175; *OR,* vol. 12, pt. 2, 744.
15. Channing Price to Mrs. Thomas R. Price, September 5, 1862, R. Channing Price Papers, SHC.
16. *OR,* vol. 19, pt. 1, 814, 822; Dedmond, "Davis's 'Diary,'" 391; Von Borcke, *Memoirs,* 1: 177, 179.
17. Dedmond, "Davis's 'Diary,'" 391; Rea, *Sketches,* 17; Neese, *Three Years,* 111.
18. Channing Price to Mrs. Thomas R. Price, September 10, 1862, Price Papers, SHC; Rea, *Sketches,* 17–18; Dedmond, "Davis's 'Diary,'" 391.
19. *OR,* vol. 19, pt. 1, 814–15; Dedmond, "Davis's 'Diary,'" 391.
20. *NC Troops* 2: 2; *OR,* vol. 19, pt. 1, 822.
21. *OR,* vol. 19, pt. 1, 815; Von Borcke, *Memoirs,* 1: 191; McClellan, *Stuart,* 110.
22. McClellan, *Stuart,* 110–11.
23. Von Borcke, *Memoirs,* 1: 188; Blackford, *War Years,* 140; J. H. Person to his mother, September 27, 1862, Presley Carter Person Papers, DU.
24. Channing Price to Mrs. Thomas R. Price, September 10, 1862, Price Papers, SHC; Davis, *Stuart,* 196; Von Borcke 1: 196; Dedmond, "Davis's 'Dairy,'" 391. Freeman, *Lee's Lieutenants* 2: 158, n. 18, surmised that 3d Indiana Cavalry and the 8th Illinois Cavalry fought the 1st North Carolina.
25. Dedmond, "Davis's 'Diary,'" 391; Von Borcke, *Memoirs,* 1: 196; Sears, *Landscape Turned Red,* 96–97.
26. *OR,* vol. 19, pt. 1, 815; Jeb Stuart to Mrs. Stuart, September 12, 1862, in *The Letters of Major General J. E. B. Stuart,* 265; Channing Price to Mrs. Thomas R. Price, September 10, 1862, Price Papers, SHC; Sears, *Landscape Turned Red,* 93.
27. *OR,* vol. 19, pt. 1, 815; Von Borcke, *Memoirs,* 1: 200; Channing Price to Mrs. Thomas R. Price, September 10, 1862, Price Papers, SHC. McClellan, *Stuart,* 114 records that Stuart withdrew his cavalry on September 12 due to a general advance "along his whole line."
28. *OR,* vol. 19, pt. 1, 822; Freeman, *R. E. Lee* 2: 366; Von Borcke, *Memoirs,* 1: 202.
29. *OR,* vol. 19, pt. 1, 822.
30. Cox, "Forcing Fox's Gap," *B&L* 2: 583–84; *OR,* vol. 19, pt. 1, 822; Sears, *Landscape Turned Red,* 121.
31. Cox, "Forcing Fox's Gap," *B&L* 2: 584; Rea, *Sketches,* 21.
32. Cox, "Forcing Fox's Gap," *B&L* 2: 584; *OR,* vol. 19, pt. 1, 822; Rea, *Sketches,* 21–22; McClellan, *Stuart,* 114.
33. Rea, *Sketches,* 23.
34. "The Beau Sabreur," *SHSP* 25: 147.
35. D. H. Hill, "The Battle of South Mountain" *B&L* 2: 565.
36. Sears, *Landscape Turned Red,* 131–32.
37. Sears, *Landscape Turned Red,* 113.
38. General Orders No. 26, Cavalry Tactics, July 30, 1863, *The Letters of Major General J. E. B. Stuart,* 332.
39. *OR,* vol. 19, pt. 1, 816; McClellan, *Stuart,* 114.
40. Von Borcke, *Memoirs,* 1: 204, 209; Rea, *Sketches,* 22–24.
41. *OR,* vol. 19, pt. 1, 816; D.H. Hill, "The Battle of South Mountain," *B&L* 2: 560.
42. Rea, *Sketches,* 23.
43. *OR,* vol. 19, pt. 1, 816; Rea, *Sketches,* 23.
44. Rea, *Sketches,* 24; *OR,* vol. 19, pt. 1, 817, 824. Hampton added in his report, that the 1st North Carolina lost eight wounded and three missing at Catoctin.
45. Rea, *Sketches,* 25; *OR,* vol. 19, pt. 1, 817.
46. McClellan, *Stuart,* 115; Von Borcke, *Memoirs,* 1: 209.
47. Rea, *Sketches,* 25; Channing Price to Mrs. Thomas R. Price, September 18, 1862, Price Papers, SHC.
48. Von Borcke, *Memoirs,* 1: 209; Rea, *Sketches,* 25.
49. Rea, *Sketches,* 25; Von Borcke, *Memoirs,* 1: 210.
50. Rea, *Sketches,* 25.
51. *OR,* vol. 19, pt. 1, 817.
52. Hill, "The Battle of South Mountain," *B&L* 2: 560.
53. Sears, *Landscape Turned Red,* 139. Compare Freeman, *R. E. Lee* 2: 369, n. 72, and *Lee's Lieutenants* 2: 173.
54. *OR,* vol. 19, pt. 2, 607.
55. *OR,* vol. 19, pt. 2, 607; *OR,* vol. 19, pt. 1, 817. Specifically, Hampton was dispatched to Burkittsville, a village at the eastern base of South Mountain between Crampton's Gap and Brownsville Gap. At Crampton's Munford's command consisted of only three regiments; both the 6th Virginia and the 17th Virginia Battalion were on detached service (McClellan,

Stuart, 110.) A battery and three regiments of infantry under Colonel William A. Parham were with Munford (Freeman, *Lee's Lieutenants* 2: 189).

56. McClellan, *Stuart*, 115.
57. *OR*, vol. 19, pt. 1, 818; *SHSP* 25: 148; *OR*, vol. 19, pt. 1, 817, 824.
58. McClellan, *Stuart*, 116; Rea, *Sketches*, 26; "The Beau Sabreur," *SHSP* 25: 147. Young would soon thereafter be promoted to colonel, to date from November 1 (Official Commission Document, December 29, 1862, Pierce M. B. Young Collection, GDAH).
59. McClellan, *Stuart*, 116; Neese, *Three Years,* 119.
60. Rea, *Sketches*, 26; *OR*, vol. 19, pt. 1, 818.
61. McClellan, *Stuart*, 118; Sears, *Landscape Turned Red,* 161.
62. Sears, *Landscape Turned Red,* 162–63; *OR*, vol. 19, pt. 1, 818; McClellan, *Stuart*, 120.
63. McClellan, *Stuart*, 124 ff.
64. Dedmond, "Davis's 'Diary,'" 392; *OR*, vol. 19, 519.
65. Sears, *Landscape Turned Red,* 166–67.
66. Rea, *Sketches*, 29; J. Pugh to Sarah Keck, September 15, 1862, James T. Pugh Papers, SHC.
67. Rea, *Sketches,* 31; Stuart, *McClellan,* 127; *OR*, vol. 19, pt. 1, 819.
68. Blackford, *War Years,* 149; McClellan, *Stuart,* 133. According to Von Borcke, *Memoirs,* 1: 231, Robertson's Brigade, under Munford, was detached to the army's extreme right flank, while Fitz Lee and Wade Hampton's brigades remained in reserve on the army's extreme left flank along the Potomac.
69. Rea, *Sketches,* 31; Blackford, *War Years,* 147.
70. McClellan, *Stuart,* 129.
71. *OR*, vol. 19, pt.1, 821; Dedmond, "Davis's 'Diary,'" 392.
72. Channing Price to Mrs. Thomas R. Price, September 18, 1862, Price Papers, SHC.
73. Sears, *Landscape Turned Red,* 321.
74. McClellan, *Stuart,* 132.
75. *OR*, vol. 19, pt. 1, 820.
76. Blackford, *War Years,* 152. According to Cheek ("Additional Sketch Ninth Regiment (First Cavalry)," *NC Regts.* 1: 482, pickets from the 1st were also the last to be withdrawn from the Antietam battlefield.
77. Barringer, "Ninth Regiment (First Cavalry)," *NC Regts.* 1: 421; *OR*, vol. 19, pt. 1, 820.
78. Blackford, *War Years,* 152–53.
79. Barringer, "Ninth Regiment (First Cavalry)," *NC Regts.* 1: 422; Rea, *Sketches,* 36.
80. *OR*, vol. 19, pt. 1, 824; Davis, *Stuart,* 208.
81. Blackford, *War Years,* 154; Von Borcke, *Memoirs,* 1: 252–53.
82. *OR*, vol. 19, pt. 1, 824; Von Borcke, *Memoirs,* 1: 253–54.
83. Dedmond, "Davis's 'Diary,'" 393; Barringer, "Ninth Regiment (First Cavalry)," *NC Regts.* 1: 422.
84. Von Borcke, *Memoirs,* 1: 255–56.
85. Von Borcke, *Memoirs,* 1: 255–56; Dedmond, "Davis's 'Diary,'" 393.
86. Z. B. Vance to G. W. Randolph, September 15, 1862, CSRG for James B. Gordon, Microcopy 331, Roll 109.
87. Hill, "Forty-first Regiment (Third Cavalry)," *NC Regts.* 2: 769; *NC Troops* 2: 178. Baker was appointed November 17, 1862, to rank from September 3. Prior to its concentration, the 3d assisted in the defense of North Carolina.
88. Blackford, *War Years,* 154; Opie, *Rebel Cavalryman,* 95; Von Borcke, *Memoirs,* 1: 258.
89. Rea, *Sketches,* 37.
90. Von Borcke, *Memoirs,* 1: 258. Von Borcke mistakenly called JBG a major.
91. W. L. Barrier to his father, October 7, 1862, Troxler and Auciello, *Dear Father,* 97. Barrier added that only three hundred horses were then fit for duty in the 1st. At the time, John B. B. Neal was Acting Quartermaster and Robert V. Boykin was Acting Commissary of Subsistence (*NC Troops* 2: 8).

Chapter 7

1. Rea, *Sketches,* 38; Freeman, *Lee's Lieutenants* 2: 286.
2. Channing Price to Mrs. Thomas R. Price, October 15, 1862, R. Channing Price Papers, SHC.
3. *OR*, vol. 19, pt. 2, 55–56; McClellan, *Stuart,* 137; Brooks, *Butler and His Cavalry,* 80.
4. Blackford, *War Years,* 164; *OR*, vol. 19, pt. 2, 57.
5. Rea, *Sketches,* 38; Channing Price to Mrs. Thomas R. Price, October 15, 1862, R. Channing Price Papers, SHC.
6. R. Channing Price to Mrs. Thomas R. Price, October 15, 1862, R. Channing Price Papers, SHC; *OR*, vol. 19, pt. 2, 55; Freeman, *Lee's Lieutenants* 2: 284.
7. *OR*, vol. 19, pt. 2, 56, 55.
8. Von Borcke, *Memoirs,* 1: 298.
9. Rea, *Sketches,* 37; McClellan, *Stuart,* 138.
10. *Concord Register,* June 29, 1883; Rea, *Sketches,* 39; *OR*, vol. 19, part 2, 57.
11. McClellan, *Stuart,* 139.
12. *OR*, vol. 19, pt. 2, 52; Channing Price to Mrs. Thomas R. Price, October 15, 1862, R. Channing Price Papers, SHC.
13. Blackford, *War Years,* 165; McClellan, *Stuart,* 139.
14. Rea, *Sketches,* 41; Blackford, *War Years,* 166; Channing Price to Mrs. Thomas R. Price, October 15, 1862, R. Channing Price Papers, SHC.
15. Davis, *Stuart,* 218.
16. Davis, *Stuart,* 218; Rea, *Sketches,* 41.
17. Blackford, 165, 166, 167; *OR*, vol. 19, pt. 2, 52.
18. McClellan, *Stuart,* 139–40; Channing Price to Mrs. Thomas R. Price, October 15, 1862, R. Channing Price Papers, SHC; Rea, *Sketches,* 42.
19. McClellan, *Stuart,* 140.
20. Channing Price to Mrs. Thomas R. Price, October 15, 1862, R. Channing Price Papers, SHC; *OR*, vol. 19, pt. 2, 52; Rea, *Sketches,* 42, 43. Hampton (*OR*, vol. 19, pt. 2, 57) reported that his brigade entered Mercersburg "without opposition."
21. Rea, *Sketches,* 44; Channing Price to Mrs. Thomas R. Price, October 15, 1862, Price Papers, SHC; *OR*, vol. 19, pt. 2, 57; Boatner, *Dictionary,* 820.
22. *OR*, vol. 19, pt. 2, 52; McClellan, *Stuart,* 141; Channing Price to Mrs. Thomas R. Price, October 15, 1862, R. Channing Price Papers, SHC.
23. *OR*, vol. 19, pt. 2, 52, 57. Lee and his escort, bearing a "dirty rag" on a stick, entered the town around 7:00 P.M. (McClure, *Lincoln,* 371).
24. Channing Price to Mrs. Thomas R. Price, October 15, 1862, R. Channing Price Papers, SHC; *OR*, vol. 19, pt. 2, 57; McClure, *Lincoln,* 372).
25. Stuart, *McClellan,* 141; Rea, *Sketches,* 44; Channing Price to Mrs. Thomas R. Price, October 15, 1862, R. Channing Price Papers, SHC; McClure, *Lincoln,* 372.
26. *Concord Register,* June 29, 1883;
27. Stuart, *McClellan,* 141; Brooks, *Butler and His Cavalry,* 81.
28. *OR*, vol. 19, pt. 2, 57; *The Philadelphia Inquirer,* quoted in *The People's Press,* October 24, 1862, p. 3, col. 1.
29. *The Philadelphia Inquirer,* quoted in *The People's Press,* October 24, 1862, p. 3, col. 1; *OR*, vol. 19, pt. 2, 52.
30. *OR*, vol. 19, pt. 2, 52.
31. Channing Price to Mrs. Thomas R. Price, October 15, 1862, R. Channing Price Papers, SHC; Rea, *Sketches,* 44.
32. *OR*, vol. 19, pt. 2, 52; McClellan, *Stuart,* 147.
33. Rea, *Sketches,* 44; *OR*, vol. 19, pt. 2, 58; *The Philadelphia Inquirer,* quoted in *The People's Press,* October 24, 1862, p. 3, col. 1.
34. *OR*, vol. 19, pt. 2, 52–53, 59; *The Philadelphia Inquirer,* quoted in *The People's Press,* Salem, N.C., October 24, 1862, p. 3, col. 1. According to McClellan, *Stuart,* 148–49, Butler commanded the rear-guard and lit the fuse that set off the explosion. Leaving Chambersburg at 9:00 A.M., Butler and Cowles rejoined the command at Cashtown.

35. Blackford, *War Years,* 169; *OR,* vol. 19, pt. 2, 53; McClellan, *Stuart,* 148.
36. McClellan, *Stuart,* 149; Rea, *Sketches,* 48; *Concord Register,* June 29, 1883.
37. Rea, *Sketches,* 50; McClellan, *Stuart,* 150–51, 149.
38. *OR,* vol. 19, pt. 2, 53; Rea, *Sketches,* 50.
39. McClellan, *Stuart,* 152, 155; *OR,* vol. 19, pt. 2, 53; Freeman, *Lee's Lieutenants* 2: 291.
40. Davis, *Stuart,* 229; Barringer, "Ninth Regiment (First Cavalry)," *NC Regts.* 1: 422.
41. *CMH,* 295; Barringer, *Natural Bent,* 115; Rufus Barringer to President Andrew Johnson, June 14, 1865, "Case Files of Applications From Former Confederates for Presidential Pardons (Amnesty Papers)," Microcopy 1003, Roll 38, Group I, NA; "General Rufus Barringer," *CV* 9 (1901): 69.
42. McClellan, *Stuart,* 153; Rea, *Sketches,* 50; Brooks, *Butler and His Cavalry,* 231; *OR,* vol. 19, pt. 2, 53.
43. *OR,* vol. 19, pt. 2, 53; Blackford, *War Years,* 174; McClellan, *Stuart,* 153.
44. Blackford, *War Years,* 170; Douglas, *I Rode With Stonewall,* 188.
45. Blackford, *War Years,* 171; *OR,* vol. 19, pt. 2, 53. For more on Stoneman, see the Epilogue.
46. *OR,* vol. 19, pt. 2, 58.
47. McClellan, *Stuart,* 155; *OR,* vol. 19, pt. 2, 53.
48. *OR,* vol. 19, pt. 2, 53; McClellan, *Stuart,* 155–56.
49. Blackford, *War Years,* 175; McClellan, *Stuart,* 156.
50. McClellan, *Stuart,* 158; Blackford, *War Years,* 175; *OR,* vol. 19, pt. 2, 53.
51. Blackford, *War Years,* 176; Douglas, *I Rode With Stonewall,* 188.
52. *OR,* vol. 19, pt. 2, 58.
53. *OR,* vol. 19, pt. 2, 58; McClellan, *Stuart,* 158.
54. McClellan, *Stuart,* 159; Blackford, *War Years,* 177.
55. Blackford, 178; Longacre, *Mounted Raids,* 43. It should be noted here that there is no mention of Butler's near-disaster in the official reports by either Stuart, whom Blackford portrayed as being very moved by the potential of losing Butler's men, or by Hampton, Butler's immediate commander. Hampton, in his report, did single out Cowles as his rear-guard commander.
56. *OR,* vol. 19, pt. 2, 58; E. C. Finley, "William Henry Harrison Cowles and Family," Calvin J. Cowles Papers, SHC; Brooks, *Butler and His Cavalry,* 82–83. In his official report, Hampton mentioned that Captain Cowles rendered "most important services." Cowles may have been the last man to cross the river (Cheek, "Additional Sketch Ninth Regiment [First Cavalry]," *NC Regts.* 1: 480).
57. Brooks, *Butler and His Cavalry,* 84.
58. McClellan, *Stuart,* 160; *OR,* vol. 19, pt. 2, 53.
59. Rea, *Sketches,* 56; Blackford, *War Years,* 178; Channing Price to Mrs. Thomas R. Price, October 15, 1862, R. Channing Price Papers, SHC.
60. Blackford, *Letters From Lee's Army,* 128.
61. Wade Hampton to Fisher, October 24, 1862, Hampton Family Papers, USC; M. V. M., "General James B. Gordon," May 25, 1864, *The Daily Confederate,* p. 1, col. 1.
62. Blackford, *War Years,* 181; CSR for James B. Gordon, First North Carolina Cavalry Regiment (Ninth North Carolina State Troops), Microcopy 270, Roll 4; CSR for Laurence Baker, First North Carolina Cavalry Regiment (Ninth North Carolina State Troops), Microcopy 270, Roll 1.
63. CSRG for James B. Gordon, Microcopy 331, Roll 109. The report did not include the horses of commissioned officers because they were personal property, but list the non-commissioned staff and band with 71 horses.
64. Cooke, *Wearing of the Gray,* 512; "Charles Daniel Malone," *CV* 35 (1927): 344.
65. John Esten Cooke Diary, December 15, 1863, UVA.
66. Von Borcke, *Memoirs,* 1: 321.
67. *OR,* vol. 19, pt. 2, 103.
68. Ibid., 104. Dedmond, "Davis's 'Diary,'" 393, contradicted this, stating that the 1st North Carolina had been on "the shortest rations of any time during the war," eating only one full meal per day while at Martinsburg.
69. Von Borcke, *Memoirs,* 1: 322; *OR,* vol. 19, pt. 2, 140–41; *NC Troops* 2: 2.
70. *OR,* vol. 19, pt. 2, 141; McClellan, *Stuart,* 169–73; Freeman, *Lee's Lieutenants* 2: 310. Stuart added that Lee's brigade was "impaired by the 'greased heel' and sore tongue, at that time prevailing among the horses." Colonel W. H. F. Lee, who normally would have commanded in Fitz Lee's absence, had yet to recover from the injuries he had received at Boonsboro.
71. Blackford, *War Years,* 183.
72. *OR,* vol. 19, pt. 2, 142.
73. Dedmond, "Davis's 'Diary,'" 393; Rea, *Sketches,* 58.
74. Rea, *Sketches,* 58; *OR,* vol. 19, pt. 2, 143.
75. *OR,* vol. 19, pt. 2, 143.
76. *OR,* vol. 19, pt. 2, 143; Von Borcke, *Memoirs,* 2: 39, 43. Beale, *History of the Ninth Virginia,* 51, 52.
77. *OR,* vol. 19, pt. 2, 144; Rea, *Sketches,* 58. Stuart's report and Rea's account of the Confederate dispositions differ somewhat.
78. Rea, *Sketches,* 58; *OR,* vol. 19, pt. 2, 117.
79. Field And Staff muster rolls, in CSR for Laurence Baker, First North Carolina Cavalry Regiment (Ninth North Carolina State Troops), Microcopy 270, Roll 1, record that Baker was absent during September and October. He was probably on his way to rejoin the brigade during the first days of November.
80. *The Land We Love,* vol. 1, no. 3 (July 1866), 208–9; Rea, *Sketches,* 58.
81. Beale, *History of the Ninth Virginia,* 52.
82. *OR,* vol. 19, pt. 2, 144, 126.
83. *OR,* vol. 19, pt. 2, 144, 126.
84. Beale, *History of the Ninth Virginia,* 52; Von Borcke, *Memoirs,* 2: 47.
85. *OR,* vol. 19, pt. 2, 145–46.
86. *OR,* vol. 19, pt. 2, 146.
87. Dedmond, "Davis's 'Diary,'" 394; *OR,* vol. 19, pt. 2, 146.
88. *OR,* vol. 19, pt. 2, 146; Dedmond, "Davis's 'Diary,'" 394.
89. *OR,* vol. 19, pt. 2, 126; Starr, *Union Cavalry* 1: 321–22.
90. *OR,* vol. 19, pt. 2, 146. The conversation is reconstructed from JBG's report. In Dedmond, "Davis's 'Diary,'" 394, Davis writes of the charge, "why Col. Gordon done so [ordered the charge] is hard to tell for on getting over the hill the charging column found a stone fence over which it was impossible to pass cavalry."
91. *OR,* vol. 19, pt. 2, 146. Hampton filed no report. JBG wrote his on November 22, 1862.
92. Ibid.
93. *OR,* vol. 19, pt. 2, 146.
94. Ibid.
95. *OR,* vol. 19, pt. 2, 146. Stuart, in ibid., 144, reported that the 1st "suffered a good deal."
96. *OR,* vol. 19, pt. 2, 146.
97. Ibid., 126.
98. Cooke, *Surry of Eagle's Nest,* 348–49; Ms. Peggy Vogtsberger, letter to the author, July 8, 1994. Ms. Vogtsberger points out that Cooke's account may have confused this action with the gallant stand of two Southern pieces on November 4, or Cooke may simply have taken literary license with this account. See McClellan, *Stuart,* 181.
99. *OR,* vol. 19, pt. 2, 146.
100. *OR,* vol. 19, pt. 2, 146; Rea, *Sketches,* 60.
101. *OR,* vol. 19, pt. 2, 117; Rea, *Sketches,* 60–61; *The Land We Love,* vol. 1, no. 3 (July 1866), 208–9. Pleasonton wrote that the fight lasted six hours. Stuart reported that the fight opened at 9:00 A.M.
102. *OR,* vol. 19, pt. 2, 126; for some of the casualties in Company F of the First, see *The Concord Sun,* March 25, 1881, p. 1, col. 3.

103. Starr, *Union Cavalry* 1: 322.
104. *OR*, vol. 19, pt. 2, 144. The 2d North Carolina (Nineteenth Regiment North Carolina State Troops) consisted of only ten companies at this time. The other two were on detached duty along the Roanoke River. The regiment, under the temporary command of Lieutenant Colonel W. H. Payne, had arrived at Warrenton on October 12 (Graham, "Nineteenth Regiment North Carolina State Troops [Second Cavalry]," *NC Regts.* 2: 87). According to McClellan, *Stuart*, 186, the regiment operated between Warrenton and Fredericksburg under the overall command of Colonel John R. Chambliss, who also directed the 13th Virginia and the 15th Virginia.
105. Longstreet, "The Battle of Fredericksburg," *B&L* 3: 70.
106. *OR*, vol. 19, pt. 2, 712–13.
107. War Notes, March 8, 1863, John Esten Cooke Papers, DU; Von Borcke 2: 49. "I shall never get over it," Stuart told Cooke. "It is irreparable."
108. *OR*, vol. 19, part 2, 144; Rea, *Sketches*, 61.
109. *OR*, vol. 19, part 2, 144; Rea, *Sketches*, 61; *NC Troops* 2: 89. In his report, Stuart mentioned a fight "near Gaines' Cross-Roads" but does not identify the units involved. The "portion of Hampton's command" that fought there "behaved with great gallantry," Stuart reported.
110. Ibid.

Chapter 8

1. Von Borcke, *Memoirs*, 2: 60.
2. Freeman, *R. E. Lee* 2: 430.
3. Blackford, *War Years*, 186–87; Von Borcke, *Memoirs*, 2: 79. "Grumble" Jones's brigade was on duty in the Shenendoah Valley (*OR*, vol. 21, 544).
4. *CMH* 4: 625–27; Freeman, *R. E. Lee* 2: 485, n. 68.
5. Barringer, "Ninth Regiment (First Cavalry)," N.C. Regts. 1: 422; Dedmond, "Davis's 'Diary,'" 394; CSR for James B. Gordon, First North Carolina Cavalry Regiment (Ninth North Carolina State Troops), Microcopy 270, Roll 4. The regiment assumed this position on November 22, 1862 after leaving Brandy Station.
6. Freeman, *Lee's Lieutenants* 2: 397–98.
7. *OR*, vol. 21, 15.
8. McClellan, *Stuart*, 188; *OR*, vol. 21, 14, 16.
9. Channing Price to Mrs. Thomas R. Price, November 30, 1862, R. Channing Price Papers, SHC. The picket included elements of the 5th U.S.
10. *OR*, vol. 21, 15; Freeman, *Lee's Lieutenants* 2: 398–99.
11. A. E. Adams to Tarleton Adams, December 10, 1862, Alfred Adams Papers, DU.
12. *OR*, vol. 21, 690; Dedmond, "Davis's 'Diary,'" 394. The regiment moved there on November 29, 1862.
13. *OR*, vol. 21, 690.
14. A. E. Adams to Tarleton Adams, December 10, 1862, Alfred Adams Papers, DU; McClellan, *Stuart*, 189.
15. *OR*, vol. 21, 691; A. E. Adams to Tarleton Adams, December 10, 1862, Alfred Adams Papers, DU.
16. *OR*, vol. 21, 690; Brooks, *Butler and His Cavalry*, 85.
17. *OR*, vol. 21, 690.
18. Brooks, *Butler and His Cavalry*, 51–54.
19. *OR*, vol. 21, 690; Brooks, *Butler and His Cavalry*, 85; *The Land We Love*, vol. 3, no. 2 (June 1867), 159–60.
20. *OR*, vol. 21, 690, 689. Hampton reported that two sutlers' wagons were destroyed in the town and five broke down afterward. All told, Hampton returned with seventeen captured wagons.
21. *OR*, vol. 21, 690. The Telegraph Road led generally south to Fredericksburg.
22. McClellan, *Stuart*, 188–89; *OR*, vol. 21, 691.
23. J. H. Person to his mother, December 25, 1862, Presley Carter Person Papers, DU.
24. Freeman, *Lee's Lieutenants* 2: 398.
25. *OR*, vol. 21, 695–97; Channing Price to Mrs. Thomas R. Price, December 23, 1862, R. Channing Price Papers, SHC.
26. Davis, *Stuart*, 261; Channing Price to Mrs. Thomas R. Price, January 2, 1863, R. Channing Price Papers, SHC.
27. *OR*, vol. 21, 731, 735–36; McClellan, *Stuart*, 196 ff.
28. *OR*, vol. 21, 734; Barringer, "Ninth Regiment (First Cavalry)," *NC Regts.* 1: 422; Dedmond, "Davis's 'Diary,'" 394.
29. Rea, *Sketches*, 66; *OR*, vol. 21, 735.
30. *OR*, vol. 21, 736.
31. Heros Von Borcke to R. Channing Price, July 29, 1862, R. Channing Price Papers, SHC; CSR for Laurence Baker, First North Carolina Cavalry Regiment (Ninth North Carolina State Troops), Microcopy 270, Roll 1.
32. *Raleigh Register*, March 11, 1863, p. 2, col. 4.
33. Calvin J. Cowles to his father, May 6, 1861, Calvin J. Cowles Papers, NCSA.
34. JBG to Augustus Finley, January 27, 1863, manuscript courtesy J. Jay Anderson, WCC, copy in the author's possession. For more on disloyalty in western North Carolina, see *OR*, vol. 18, 897–98.
35. Freeman, *Lee's Lieutenants* 2: 428; *OR*, vol. 21, 1101.
36. *OR*, vol. 25, pt. 1, 650.; Von Borcke, *Memoirs*, 2: 191–92. Reports note 11,532 aggregate present and absent, although one regiment was not accounted for.
37. Dedmond, "Davis's 'Diary,'" 394; W. L. Barrier to his father, January 12, 1863, Troxler and Auciello, *Dear Father*, 101. The 1st moved to these camps on 4 January 1863.
38. *The People's Press*, January 14, 1863; Von Borcke, *Memoirs*, 2: 170–71, 179; McClellan, *Stuart*, 204.
39. Wade Hampton to Mary F. Hampton, January 27, 1863, Hampton Family Papers, USC.
40. *OR*, vol. 25, pt. 1, 7–9.
41. Von Borcke, *Memoirs*, 2: 179, 183; Davis, *Stuart*, 267. The 1st North Carolina withdrew on February 16, 1863 (Dedmond, "Davis's 'Diary,'" 395).
42. Von Borcke, *Memoirs*, 2: 194; CSR for James B. Gordon, First North Carolina Cavalry Regiment (Ninth North Carolina State Troops), Microcopy 270, Roll 4. Information in the James B. Gordon Papers, NCSA, Raleigh, N.C., differs on the details of the leave. There, JBG's leave is said to be of thirty-day duration beginning February 13. The official rolls are followed in the text.
43. Dedmond, "Davis's 'Diary,'" 395. Harvey Davis recorded that when Fitz Lee's men took over the regiment pulled out of their camps and marched in the mud and snow to Orange Court House and Gordonsville. Davis was then himself furloughed to purchase a horse.
44. *CMH* 5: 313; Cowles, *CSC*, 20; Cowles, "Life and Services," 10–11.
45. *NC Troops* 2:3; CSR for James B. Gordon, First North Carolina Cavalry Regiment (Ninth North Carolina State Troops), Microcopy 270, Roll 4, Field and Staff Muster Rolls; *Carolina Watchman*, May 11, 1863. In Barringer, "Ninth Regiment (First Cavalry)," *NC Regts.* 1: 422, it is noted that the camp of Hampton's brigade during this period was located "near Stevensburg."
46. *OR*, vol. 25, pt. 1, 1047; J. Pugh to Sarah Keck, March 17, 1862, SHC. Stuart wrote that the brigade was south of the James, recruiting. Lee notes Hampton's whereabouts in ibid., *OR*, vol. 25, pt. 1, 795. Dedmond, "Davis's 'Diary,'" 374, suggested that the regiment was "effectively 'disbanded'" during these months, but Pugh, writing from Rockingham County, added that many in the infantry were on furlough so the cavalry had to stay to keep the Yankees back.
47. Gilmor, *Four Years*, 72; Cooke, *Wearing of the Gray*, 118. Barringer, in "Ninth Regiment (First Cavalry)," *NC Regts.* 1: 422, suggests that the 1st North Carolina Cavalry fought at Kelly's Ford. Baker, still temporarily commanding the brigade, did participate, and miscellaneous detached Tarheels may have as well, but the regiment as a whole did not.

48. *OR,* vol. 25, pt. 1, 139, 104, 108, 139, 528, 536, 139.
49. Jeb Stuart to James A. Seddon, February 22, 1863, *The Letters of Major General James E. B. Stuart,* 294–95; E. L. Dabney to "My Dearest Betty," May 1, 1863, Saunders Family Papers, VHS; CSR for James B. Gordon, First North Carolina Cavalry Regiment (Ninth North Carolina State Troops), Microcopy 270, Roll 4; CSRG for James B. Gordon, Microcopy 331, Roll 109. Apparently, JBG also served as regiment commander in early April. Baker was commanding the brigade because Hampton was absent (J. H. Person to his sister, April 11, 1863, Presley Carter Person Papers, DU).
50. Thomas, *Bold Dragoon,* 202, CSR for Laurence Baker, First North Carolina Cavalry Regiment [Ninth North Carolina State Troops], Microcopy 270, Roll 1.
51. Von Borcke, *Memoirs,* 2: 173–74; Freeman, *Lee's Lieutenants* 2: 431; J. H. Person to his mother, April 21, 1863, Presley Carter Person Papers, DU. Person was later killed during the Gettysburg Campaign.
52. E. L. Dabney to "My Dearest Betty," May 1, 1863, Saunders Family Papers, VHS. Cheek, actually a company commander at the time, was not promoted to lieutenant colonel until September 1863.
53. Von Borcke, *Memoirs,* 2: 152–53; J. H. Person to his mother, April 21, 1863, Presley Carter Person Papers, DU; *Raleigh Register,* April 29, 1863, p. 1, col. 1. Freeman, *Lee's Lieutenants* 2: 430, wrote that the natives believed that winter was not unusually severe.
54. J. H. Person to Dear sister Martha, and J. H. Person to his mother, April 21, 1863, Presley Carter Person Papers, DU; *OR,* vol. 25, pt. 1, 711, 737, 738.
55. Blackford, *War Years,* 203; *OR,* vol. 25, pt. 2, 782.
56. Starr, *Union Cavalry* 1: 365; Freeman, *R. E. Lee* 3: 4; Couch, "Chancellorsville Campaign," *B&L* 3: 155.
57. *OR,* vol. 25, pt. 2, 771; George S. Dewey to his mother, May 4, 1863, George Stanley Dewey Papers, SHC.
58. *OR,* vol. 25, pt. 2, 772.
59. Ibid.
60. *OR,* vol. 25, pt. 2, 772; George S. Dewey to his mother, May 4, 1863, George Stanley Dewey Papers, SHC.
61. *OR,* vol. 25, pt. 2, 772.
62. Ibid., 774.
63. *OR,* 25, pt. 2, 789; Boatner, *Dictionary,* 803; Starr, *Union Cavalry* 1: 357; Wade Hampton to Miss Mary Hampton, May 13, 1863, copy in Wade Hampton Papers, SHC.
64. Freeman, *Lee's Lieutenants* 3: 1; *OR,* vol. 25, pt. 2, 825, 823; Jesse Person to Dear Mother, June 2, 1863, Presley Carter Person Papers, DU. As such, the total strength of the regiment, 873 officers and men, was 89.6 percent of the September, 1861 strength of 974 men reported in *OR,* vol. 5, 446–47.
65. Myers, *The Comanches,* 139, 150, 180; Boatner, *Dictionary,* 423; Freeman, *Lee's Lieutenants* 2: 709–10; Freeman, *R. E. Lee* 3: 14.
66. Boatner, *Dictionary,* 435; Freeman, *Lee's Lieutenants* 2: 708; Freeman, *R. E. Lee* 3: 14.
67. McClellan, *Stuart,* 261.
68. Galloway, "Sixty-third Regiment (Fifth Cavalry)," *NC Regts.* 3: 530; Freeman, *Lee's Lieutenants* 2: 476, 708–9; Jeb Stuart to Mrs. Stuart, October 21, 1861 and September 12, 1862, *The Letters of General J. E. B. Stuart,* 221, 266.
69. Galloway, "Sixty-third Regiment (Fifth Cavalry)," *NC Regts.* 3: 530; Jeb Stuart to R. H. Chilton, in *The Letters of General J. E. B. Stuart,* 319–20.
70. *OR,* vol. 25, pt. 2, 825; Myers, *The Comanches,* 160–61. Officially, Robertson's brigade also included the 3d North Carolina (the unit JBG had almost commanded via Governor Vance's 1862 recommendation), the 7th Confederate, and the 62d Georgia. Those units were on detached duty. Jenkins's brigade was not detailed in the report.
71. *OR,* vol. 25, pt. 2, 836.
72. Ibid., 837, 836.
73. Freeman, *Lee's Lieutenants* 2: 712–13; Freeman, *R. E. Lee* 3: 28; *OR,* vol. 25, pt. 2, 844, quoted in Freeman, *Lee's Lieutenants,* vol. 2, 714.
74. Freeman, *R. E. Lee* 3: 25; Davis, *Stuart,* 300; Wade Hampton to Miss Mary Hampton, May 13, 1863, copy in Wade Hampton Papers, SHC; Tom Rosser to Bettie, May 12, 1863, Rosser Papers, UVA.
75. JBG to Augustus Finley, May 12, 1863, transcript courtesy J. Jay Anderson; Davis, *Stuart,* 299.
76. JBG to Augustus Finley, May 12, 1863, transcript courtesy J. Jay Anderson. Cf. Hickerson, *Echoes,* 95.
77. Freeman, *R. E. Lee* 3: 24; *OR,* vol. 25, pt. 1, 849–50.

Chapter 9

1. Blackford, *War Years,* 212. Blackford recorded that many men lost their hats during mock charges. Actually, Lee had forbidden charges during the review (Freeman, *Lee's Lieutenants* 3: 4).
2. Freeman, *Lee's Lieutenants* 3: 3–4; Cooke, *Wearing of the Gray,* 305–6.
3. Neese, *Three Years,* 168; McDonald, *Laurel Brigade,* 131; Shaw, "Fifty-ninth Regiment (Fourth Cavalry)," *NC Regts.* 3: 460.
4. Blackford, *War Years,* 212; Coltrane, *Memoirs,* 11; McDonald, *Laurel Brigade,* 132.
5. Freeman, *Lee's Lieutenants* 3: 4; Cooke, *Wearing of the Gray,* 305–6.
6. Freeman, *R. E. Lee* 3: 30; Blackford, *War Years,* 212–13.
7. Black, *Crumbling Defenses,* 18; Galloway, "Sixty-third Regiment (Fifth Cavalry)," *NC Regts.* 3: 531.
8. Myers, *The Comanches,* 180; McDonald, *Laurel Brigade,* 131.
9. Moffet, "Battle of Brandy Station," *CV* 14 (1906): 74; Cadwallader J. Iredell to ?, May 30, 1863, Cadwallader J. Iredell Papers, SHC; Cowles, *CSC,* 20; Cowles, "Life and Services," 9.
10. Freeman, *R. E. Lee* 3: 31; Robert Lee to Mrs. Lee, quoted in Davis, *Stuart,* 305.
11. McClellan, *Stuart,* 262; Freeman, *Lee's Lieutenants* 3: 5; Hall, "Brandy Station," *Civil War Times Illustrated,* 34.
12. Blackford, *War Years,* 210. McClellan, in "The Battle of Fleetwood," *Annals of the War,* 394, estimates that Stuart's available force during the Battle of Brandy Station did not exceed six thousand men. Many troopers were absent on special duty, such as "horse details."
13. J. Pugh to Sarah Keck, May 12, 1863, James T. Pugh Papers, SHC.
14. Hall, "Brandy Station," 33; McClellan, *Stuart,* 262.
15. McClellan, *Stuart,* 262; *OR,* vol. 27, part 2, 680. The 4th North Carolina camped near the farm of John Minor Botts and picketed the lower fords of the Rappahannock (Shaw, "Fifty-ninth Regiment [Fourth Cavalry]," *NC Regts.* 3: 460).
16. Cooke, *Wearing of the Gray,* 512.
17. Blackford, *War Years,* 213; Myers, *The Comanches,* 181; *OR,* vol. 27, pt. 2, 680, 737 ff.
18. *OR,* vol. 27, pt. 2, 721.
19. *OR,* vol. 27, pt. 2, 732; Barringer, "Ninth Regiment (First Cavalry)," *NC Regts.* 1: 423.
20. Moffet, "Battle of Brandy Station," *CV* 14 (1906): 74; McClellan, *Stuart,* 266; Mosby, *Stuart's Cavalry,* 18.
21. *OR,* vol. 27, pt. 2, 748–49; 772; Neese, *Three Years,* 171.
22. *OR,* vol. 27, pt. 2, 680; pt. 1, 906; Starr, *Union Cavalry* 1: 378, n. 37; 372.
23. Hall, "Brandy Station," 34–35; McClellan, *Stuart,* 264; Mosby, *Stuart's Cavalry,* 5. Pleasonton had assumed corps command when Stoneman took leave because of ill health. Stoneman was appointed Chief of the Cavalry Bureau on July 28 (Freeman, *Lee's Lieutenants* 3: 7, n. 20; Starr, *Union Cavalry* 1: 367–68).
24. Hall, "Brandy Station," 36; McClellan, *Stuart,* 263.
25. Hall, "Brandy Station," 35; *OR,* vol. 27, pt. 2, 749.

26. Graham, "Nineteenth Regiment (Second Cavalry)" *NC Regts.* 2: 90–91, 95; J. Emory M____, "Grave of Col. Williams," *Our Living and Our Dead* 1: 138.
27. *OR*, vol. 27, pt. 2, 680, 749, 732.
28. McClellan, *Stuart*, 263; Hall, "Brandy Station," 37; McClellan, *Stuart*, 267; Opie, *Rebel Cavalryman*, 152.
29. *OR*, vol. 27, pt. 2, 721, 732; W. L. Barrier to his father, June 10, 1863, Troxler and Auciello, *Dear Father*, 110. The sharpshooters were from the Cobb Legion.
30. W. L. Barrier to his father, June 10, 1863, Troxler and Auciello, *Dear Father*, 110; Hall, "Brandy Station," 37.
31. W. A. Graham, "Nineteenth Regiment (Second Cavalry)" *NC Regts.* 2: 91; McClellan, *Stuart*, 267.
32. *OR*, vol. 27, pt. 2, 683, 733–36; Shaw, "Fifty-ninth Regiment (Fourth Cavalry)," *NC Regts.* 3: 460–61.
33. *OR*, vol. 27, pt. 2, 680; McClellan, *Stuart*, 269; Davis, *Stuart*, 307; Jeb Stuart to Robert E. Lee, October 24, 1862, in *The Letters of General J. E. B. Stuart*, 271; Myers, *The Comanches*, 183.
34. Blackford, *War Years*, 215; Davis, *Stuart*, 307; Myers, *The Comanches*, p. 183.
35. McClellan, *Stuart*, 269; *OR*, vol. 27, pt. 2, 680–81; Brooks, *Butler and His Cavalry*, 173.
36. McClellan, *Stuart*, 269–70.
37. McClellan, *Stuart*, 270.
38. McClellan, *Stuart*, 271; *OR*, vol. 27, pt. 2, 681.
39. Hall, "Brandy Station," 37; *OR*, vol. 27, 732.
40. *OR*, vol. 27, 721; Robertson, "Reminiscence," 20; *Wilkesboro Chronicle*, July 22, 1891, p. 1, col. 2.
41. McClellan, *Stuart*, 271; Hall, "Brandy Station," 39; *OR*, vol. 27, pt. 2, 721.
42. McClellan, *Stuart*, 271–72; McClellan, "The Battle of Fleetwood," *Annals of the War*, 398; *OR*, vol. 27, pt. 2, 683.
43. McClellan, *Stuart*, 272; Myers, *The Comanches*, 183–85; *OR*, vol. 27, pt. 2, 683.
44. Myers, *The Comanches*, 185; Blackford, *War Years*, 215.
45. McClellan, *Stuart*, 274, 276.
46. J. E. B. Stuart to W. H. Taylor, June 1, 1863, *The Letters of General J. E. B. Stuart*, 322–23.
47. *OR*, vol. 27, pt. 2, 722, 732; Blackford, *War Years*, 215. The Cobb Legion was ordered to strike the enemy "to his front and right." The courier from Stuart was probably Blackford. Stuart, Blackford recalled, "turned to me and ordered me to gallop along the line and order every commanding officer of a regiment to move on Fleetwood at a gallop" (Blackford, *War Years*, 215).
48. Blackford, *War Years*, 215; Hall, "Brandy Station," 40.
49. McClellan, *Stuart*, 277; Hall, "Brandy Station," 40; Davis, *Stuart*, 309.
50. Crouch, *Sketches of Wilkes*, 31; *CMH* 5: 292; *OR*, vol. 27, pt. 2, 726, 682.
51. Blackford, *War Years*, 216; *OR*, vol. 27, pt. 2, 722; McClellan, *Stuart*, 277.
52. Blackford, *War Years*, 216; Moffet, "Battle of Brandy Station," *CV* 14 (1906): 74; Galloway, "Sixty-third Regiment (Fifth Cavalry)," *NC Regts.* 3: 532.
53. *OR*, vol. 27, pt. 2, 726, 733; Barringer, "Ninth Regiment (First Cavalry)," *NC Regts.* 1: 423; McClellan, *Stuart*, 277.
54. *Concord Register*, June 22, 1883.
55. Galloway, "Sixty-third Regiment (Fifth Cavalry)," *NC Regts.* 1: 532; Von Borcke, *Memoirs*, 2: 26.
56. *OR*, vol. 27, pt. 2, 726, 718, 723; Rufus Barringer to V. C. Barringer, January 27, 1866, Rufus Clay Barringer Papers, SHC; "Nicholas P. Tredenick," *CV* 14 (1906): 132.
57. *OR*, vol. 27, pt. 2, 726; Crouch, *Sketches of Wilkes*, 31; Opie, *Rebel Cavalryman*, 154.
58. Hall, "Brandy Station," 40; Freeman, *Lee's Lieutenants* 3: 11; *OR*, vol. 27, pt. 2, 682. The Federals retired before Robertson, the 5th North Carolina in the advance, arrived on the scene (*OR*, vol. 27, pt. 2, 736).
59. *OR*, vol. 27, pt. 2, 682, 723; "Colonel W. H. Cowles," *CV* 10 (1902): 125; Crouch, *Sketches of Wilkes*, 31; *OR*, vol. 27, pt. 2, 726.
60. *OR*, vol. 27, pt. 2, 682, 736. Unable to use his full force "at the very moment they could have reaped the fruits of victory they so brilliantly won," Hampton took up position in protection of the hill.
61. *OR*, vol. 27, pt. 2, 683; Starr, *Union Cavalry* 1: 386–87; Brooks, *Butler and His Cavalry*, 171.
62. Von Borcke, *Memoirs*, 2: 280; McClellan, *Stuart*, 291; Brooks, *Butler and His Cavalry*, 133.
63. Freeman, *Lee's Lieutenants* 3: 12; Starr, *Union Cavalry* 1: 387.
64. *OR*, vol. 27, pt. 2, 682, 736; Galloway, "Sixty-third Regiment (Fifth Cavalry)," *NC Regts.* 3: 532.
65. *OR*, vol. 27, pt. 2, 722.
66. *OR*, vol. 27, pt. 2, 683.
67. Graham, "Nineteenth Regiment (Second Cavalry)," *NC Regts.* 2: 93; Freeman, *R. E. Lee* 3: 32; J. Emory M____, "Grave of Col. Williams," *Our Living and Our Dead* 1: 138. Graham's account of Williams's death differs with McClellan, *Stuart*, 283. In the latter, Williams participated in the charge after begging permission to join. He was buried in Hilliardstown, in Nash County, North Carolina.
68. Hall, "Brandy Station," 42; Blackford, *War Years*, 217; W. L. Barrier to Father, June 10, 1863, Troxler and Auciello, *Dear Father*, 110.
69. *OR*, vol. 27, pt. 2, 723. (For the "fine" morning reference, see W. L. Barrier to his father, June 10, 1863, Troxler and Auciello, *Dear Father*, 110.)
70. *OR* Series I, vol. 27, pt. 2, 720, 726, 723; W. L. Barrier to his father, June 10, 1863, Troxler and Auciello, *Dear Father*, 110.
71. J. W. Biddle to Rosa, June 16, 1863, S. S. Biddle Papers, DU.
72. W. L. Barrier to his Father, June 10, 1863, Troxler and Auciello, *Dear Father*, 110.
73. Archibald Craige to the author, April 17, 1994.

Chapter 10

1. JBG to "Campbell," April 5, 1857, Atwood & Co. Collection, SHC.
2. Myers, *The Comanches*, 187–88; Freeman, *Lee's Lieutenants* 3: 20; Freeman, *R. E. Lee* 3: 29, 32.
3. Freeman, *R. E. Lee* 3: 32–33; *OR*, vol. 27, pt. 2, 687.
4. *OR*, vol. 27, pt. 2, 687. The 15th Virginia Cavalry of W. H. F. Lee's brigade was also left on the lower Rappahannock to cooperate with A. P. Hill.
5. *OR*, vol. 27, pt. 2, 689; Von Borcke, *Memoirs*, 2: 285. According to Longstreet, *Manassas to Appomattox*, 340–41, the First Corps marched north along the east base of the Blue Ridge. By June 19, the corps was between Ashby's Gap and Snicker's Gap. The Third Corps passed through the valley.
6. Von Borcke, *Memoirs*, 2: 284; Mosby, *Stuart's Cavalry*, 61.
7. *OR*, vol. 27, pt. 2, 739–41; McClellan, *Stuart*, 297.
8. McClellan, *Stuart*, 301; Starr, *Union Cavalry* 1: 402; *OR*, vol. 27, pt. 2, 741.
9. *OR*, vol. 27, pt. 2, 688; Coltrane, *Memoirs*, 12–13; McClellan, *Stuart*, 303–4.
10. Means, "Additional Sketch Sixty-third Regiment (Fifth Cavalry)," *NC Regts.* 3: 563; Galloway, "Sixty-third Regiment (Fifth Cavalry)," *NC Regts.* 3: 532–33.
11. Means, "Additional Sketch Sixty-third Regiment (Fifth Cavalry)," *NC Regts.* 3: 563; Galloway, "Sixty-third Regiment (Fifth Cavalry)," *NC Regts.* 3: 532–33.
12. Coltrane, *Memoirs*, 13; *OR*, vol. 27, pt. 2, 688; McClellan, *Stuart*, 296–97.
13. *OR*, vol. 27, pt. 2, 689; Shaw, "Fifty-ninth Regiment (Fourth Cavalry)," *NC Regts.* 3: 456; O'Neill, *Aldie, Middleburg, and Upperville*, 105; Von Borcke, *Memoirs*, 2: 289–90.

14. *OR*, vol. 27, pt. 2, 689; Brooks, *Butler and His Cavalry*, 172.
15. Freeman, *R. E. Lee* 3: 38; Mosby, *Stuart's Cavalry*, 67.
16. *OR*, vol. 27, pt. 2, 689; McClellan, *Stuart*, 306; Black, *Crumbling Defenses*, 22. Pleasonton told army headquarters at 5:00 A.M. on June 18: "I send, this morning early, one of Buford's brigades to Thoroughfare Gap, to ascertain all the facts, and assist Duffie, if it is needed. I am also sending a brigade, with a couple of guns, to Snicker's Gap, to scout the valley, and send parties toward Winchester, Harper's Ferry, and Sperryville" (*OR*, pt. 1, vol. 27, 907).
17. *OR*, vol. 27, pt. 2, 689. Hampton probably battled with the "party" Pleasonton sent toward Sperryville (*OR*, vol. 27, pt. 1, 907).
18. Brooks, *Butler and His Cavalry*, 172.
19. Von Borcke, *Memoirs*, 2: 290; *OR*, vol. 27, pt. 2, 689; pt. 1, 908.
20. Von Borcke, *Memoirs*, 2: 291–93; *OR*, vol. 27, pt. 2, 689; McClellan, *Stuart*, 307; Starr, *Union Cavalry* 1: 405.
21. *OR*, vol. 27, pt. 2, 690.
22. *OR*, vol. 27, pt. 2, 690; Coltrane, *Memoirs*, 13; McClellan, *Stuart*, 307.
23. *OR*, vol. 27, pt. 1, 911; Brooks, *Butler and His Cavalry*, 174.
24. McClellan, *Stuart*, 308.
25. *OR*, vol. 27, pt. 2, 690; O'Neill, "The Fight for the Loudoun Valley," *Blue & Gray*, 50; O'Neill, *Aldie, Middleburg, and Upperville*, 121, 123; Brooks, *Butler and His Cavalry*, 176.
26. *OR*, vol. 27, pt. 2, 690; McClellan, *Stuart*, 309; Brooks, *Butler and His Cavalry*, 177.
27. Coltrane, *Memoirs*, 13–14; Brooks, *Butler and His Cavalry*, 177. At one point, the assistant surgeon of the 1st North Carolina went to the assistance of the wounded Black (Black, *Crumbling Defenses*, 29).
28. Graham, "Nineteenth Regiment (Second Cavalry)," *NC Regts*. 2: 96; *OR*, vol. 27, pt. 2, 691; McClellan, *Stuart*, 309.
29. McClellan, *Stuart*, 311, 314; Shaw, "Fifty-ninth Regiment (Fourth Cavalry)," *NC Regts*. 3: 461–62; Brooks, *Butler and His Cavalry*, 174. In a reference to an earlier part of the day, Brooks placed part of Hampton's brigade north of the pike. McClellan said it was entirely to the pike's south.
30. Shaw, "Fifty-ninth Regiment (Fourth Cavalry)," *NC Regts*. 3: 461–62; McClellan, *Stuart*, 311.
31. McClellan, *Stuart*, 311–13; *CMH* 5: 292–93; *Philadelphia Weekly Times*, July 20, 1878, in McClellan, *Stuart*, 311–12.
32. Cooke, *Wearing of the Gray*, 18; *Philadelphia Weekly Times*, July 20, 1878, in McClellan, *Stuart*, 311–12; Cadwalader J. Iredell to Shaw, July 9, 1863, Robert J. Brake Collection, USAMHI.
33. Cooke, *Wearing of the Gray*, 26.
34. *Philadelphia Weekly Times*, July 20, 1878, in McClellan, *Stuart*, 311–12.
35. Galloway, "Sixty-third Regiment (Fifth Cavalry)," *NC Regts*. 3: 529, 535–36; Means, "Additional Sketch Sixty-third Regiment (Fifth Cavalry)," *NC Regts*. 3: 567.
36. Galloway, "Sixty-third Regiment (Fifth Cavalry)," *NC Regts*. 3: 529, 533–36; Shaw, "Fifty-ninth Regiment (Fourth Cavalry)," *NC Regts*. 3: 462; Means, "Additional Sketch Sixty-third Regiment (Fifth Cavalry)," *NC Regts*. 3: 567, 587; McClellan, *Stuart*, 312; *NC Troops* 2: 372. Evans died on July 24.
37. Means, "Additional Sketch Sixty-third Regiment (Fifth Cavalry)," *NC Regts*. 3: 559; *OR*, vol. 27, pt. 2, 712–13. Losses at Upperville totaled 209 Union and 180 Confederate (Boatner, *Dictionary*, 862).
38. *OR*, vol. 27, pt. 2, 912; Starr, *Union Cavalry* 1: 412.
39. *NC Troops* 2: 93, 101, 266; Robertson, "Reminiscence," 23; W. A. Graham, "Nineteenth Regiment (Second Cavalry)," *NC Regts*. 2: 93. Cantwell had been promoted to lieutenant colonel on October 10, 1862, to rank from September 28, making him JBG's junior in rank. Payne initially commanded the 2d from March 20 to early June before giving way to Williams. Thereafter, both Graham, an Orange County native who had been promoted to captain on November 8, 1862, and Captain James W. Strange served as temporary commanders, Strange immediately following Williams's death and Graham after June 30. Graham assumed command when Payne was captured at Hanover (*NC Troops* 2: 101; Boatner, *Dictionary*, 625; *CMH* 4: 646–47).
40. Galloway, "Sixty-third Regiment (Fifth Cavalry)," *NC Regts*. 3: 534.
41. Means, "Additional Sketch Sixty-third Regiment (Fifth Cavalry), *NC Regts*. 3: 567; Galloway, "Sixty-third Regiment (Fifth Cavalry)," *NC Regts*. 3: 534; Coltrane, *Memoirs*, 14.
42. Galloway, "Sixty-third Regiment (Fifth Cavalry), *NC Regts*. 3: 529–31; Means, "Additional Sketch Sixty-third Regiment (Fifth Cavalry), *NC Regts*. 3: 545, 549–57.
43. *CMH* 4: 656–57; Jeb Stuart to R. H. Chilton, *The Letters of General J. E. B. Stuart*, 319–20; Galloway, "Sixty-third Regiment (Fifth Cavalry), *NC Regts*. 3: 530; Coltrane, *Memoirs*, 7.
44. Shaw, "Fifty-ninth Regiment (Fourth Cavalry)," *NC Regts*. 3: 456. For a list of delegates to the North Carolina secession convention of June 1861, see "An Ordinance to Dissolve the Union Between the State of North Carolina..," copy in the Bryan Grimes Papers, NCSA.
45. *OR*, vol. 27, pt. 1, 912; Galloway, "Sixty-third Regiment (Fifth Cavalry)," *NC Regts*. 3: 534; *OR*, vol. 27, pt. 2, 691.
46. *OR*, vol. 27, pt. 2, 692.
47. Longstreet, *Manassas to Appomattox*, 343; McClellan, *Stuart*, 319; Freeman, *R. E. Lee* 3: 550. Freeman said the division of forces was actually not equal. Mosby, in *Stuart's Cavalry*, 172, believed that General Lee decided which brigades stayed to watch the gaps.
48. *OR*, vol. 27, pt. 3, 923, 927–28.
49. *OR*, vol. 27, pt. 3, 927.
50. *OR*, vol. 27, pt. 2, 692. Salem Depot is known today as Marshal.
51. Cooke, *Wearing of the Gray*, 9; *OR*, vol. 27, pt. 2, 692.
52. Notecard, "Robertson and Gettysburg," D. S. Freeman Papers, Personal Papers Collection (Accession 23682), VL; *OR*, vol. 27, pt. 2, 692; McClellan, *Stuart*, 318–19.
53. Galloway, "Sixty-third Regiment (Fifth Cavalry)," *NC Regts*. 3: 534.
54. *OR*, vol. 27, pt. 2, 751; "Map 8," *B&L* 3: 264; Mosby, "Confederate Cavalry," *B&L* 3: 252.
55. *OR*, vol. 27, pt. 3, 927; Mosby, *Stuart's Cavalry*, 216. Mosby, in *Stuart's Cavalry*, 195–201, argues that Robertson did not leave the gaps because of orders from Lee to remain there until otherwise directed. On the authority of both Robertson and Harry Heth, Mosby claims that Robertson and Lee maintained daily communication with each other. Contradicting that is Freeman, in *R.E. Lee* 3: 59, 63, 147, who states that Lee did not know why Robertson, a man with whom he had not worked closely, had been delayed in rejoining the army.
56. Freeman, *R. E. Lee* 3: 29, 43.
57. McClellan, *Stuart*, 323; *OR*, vol. 27, pt. 2, 693. A portion of the 1st North Carolina, probably under Lieutenant Robert H. Maxwell of Company C, was cut off from Stuart's main body during the raid. This contingent and other stray troopers served under Colonel John Black during part of the campaign (Black, *Crumbling Defenses*, 32).
58. *OR*, vol. 27, pt. 3, 923; Freeman, *R. E. Lee* 3: 60; McClellan, *Stuart*, 334–35.
59. *OR*, vol. 27, pt. 2, 708; pt. 1, 913, 926; Freeman, *R. E. Lee* 3: 63–64; Mosby, *War Reminiscences*, 181 ff.
60. *OR*, vol. 27, pt. 2, 751–52, 760; *OR*, vol. 27, pt. 3, 927; Mosby, *Stuart's Cavalry*, 196; Neese, *Three Years*, 185.
61. *OR*, vol. 27, pt. 3, 927; Robertson, "Confederate Cav-

alry," *B&L* 3: 253; Neese, *Three Years,* 185; Opie, *Rebel Cavalryman,* 171–72.

62. Blackford, *War Years,* 229; Freeman, *R.E. Lee* 3: 550; Harry Heth and Beverly Robertson in Mosby, *Stuart's Cavalry,* 195–96, 200–1; *OR,* vol. 27, pt. 1, 913. See also Mosby, *War Reminiscences,* 181 ff.

63. *OR,* vol. 27, pt. 2, 321; Robertson, "Confederate Cavalry," *B&L* 3: 253; *OR,* vol. 27, pt. 2, 760. John Mosby, in "Confederate Cavalry," *B&L* 3: 252 disagreed; he said the courier met Robertson at the gaps in the mountains. The dispatch has not survived.

64. Myers, *The Comanches,* 195; Neese, *Three Years,* 186; Coltrane, *Memoirs,* 15; *OR,* vol. 27, pt. 3, 943. Coltrane later recounted this passage differently: "Remember, we do not make war upon women and children and property."

65. Galloway, "Sixty-third Regiment (Fifth Cavalry)," *NC Regts.* 3: 535; *OR,* vol. 27, pt. 2, 760.

66. Shaw, "Fifty-ninth Regiment (Fourth Cavalry)," *NC Regts.* 3: 462–63; Coltrane, *Memoirs,* 15; Hopkins, *Bull Run to Appomattox,* 97.

67. Neese, *Three Years,* 186.

68. *OR,* vol. 27, pt. 2, 760; Neese, *Three Years,* 186.

69. Shaw, "Fifty-ninth Regiment (Fourth Cavalry)," *NC Regts.* 3: 462; Robertson, "The Confederate Cavalry in the Gettysburg Campaign," *B&L* 3: 253; Mosby, "Confederate Cavalry," *B&L* 3: 252.; McClellan, *Stuart,* 336. Many postwar accounts conflict as to the timing of this march. The correct sequence of events can only be found in the reports of Jones's regiment commanders (*OR,* vol. 27, pt. 2, 759–60).

70. Shaw, "Fifty-ninth Regiment (Fourth Cavalry)," *NC Regts.* 3: 462; *OR,* vol. 27, pt. 2, 760.

71. *OR,* vol. 27, pt. 2, 752; Shaw, "Fifty-ninth Regiment (Fourth Cavalry)," *NC Regts.* 3: 463; McClellan, *Stuart,* 347; Myers, *The Comanches,* 200.

72. Shaw, "Fifty-ninth Regiment (Fourth Cavalry)," *NC Regts.* 3: 463; Galloway, "Sixty-third Regiment (Fifth Cavalry)," *NC Regts.* 3: 535; Neese, *Three Years,* 188. Galloway's article suggests that the 5th was present at Gettysburg, but the evidence is conclusive that the unit was not. Instead, Galloway's text should be associated with the 5th's work around Cashtown and Fairfield.

73. *OR,* vol. 27, pt. 2, 752; McDonald, *Laurel Brigade,* 154; Robertson, "Confederate Cavalry," *B&L* 3: 253. According to Jones, in *OR,* vol. 27, pt. 2, 752, the trains at Fairfield were those of the cavalry division.

74. Galloway, "Sixty-third Regiment (Fifth Cavalry)," *NC Regts.* 3: 535; Neese, *Three Years,* 188.

75. *OR,* vol. 27, pt. 2, 752; Stuart, *McClellan,* 347.

76. *OR,* vol. 27, pt. 2, 752, 756; Opie, *Rebel Cavalryman,* 173.

77. Galloway, "Sixty-third Regiment (Fifth Cavalry)," *NC Regts.* 3: 535; Opie, *Rebel Cavalryman,* 54; McDonald, *Laurel Brigade,* 135; *OR,* vol. 27, pt. 2, 760.

78. *OR,* vol. 27, pt. 2, 752; McClellan, *Stuart,* 348.

79. McDonald, *Laurel Brigade,* 155; *OR,* vol. 27, pt. 2, 756; pt. 1, 943, 993; Opie, *Rebel Cavalryman,* 172–73. This Union action was probably part of General Wesley Merritt's effort to annoy the Confederate "right and rear."

80. Shaw, "Fifty-ninth Regiment (Fourth Cavalry)," *NC Regts.* 3: 463; Galloway, "Sixty-third Regiment (Fifth Cavalry)," *NC Regts.* 3: 535; *OR,* vol. 27, pt. 2, 751 ff.

81. Galloway, "Sixty-third Regiment (Fifth Cavalry)," *NC Regts.* 3: 535.

82. Freeman, *Lee's Lieutenants* 3: 195; Black, *Crumbling Defenses,* 45.

83. Imboden, "Confederate Retreat," *B&L* 3: 423; *OR,* vol. 27, pt. 2, 699; Hopkins, *Bull Run to Appomattox,* 103; Wittenberg and Petruzzi, "Thunder on the Mountain," 26.

84. *OR,* vol. 27, pt. 2, 311, 322; 699; Freeman, *R. E. Lee* 3: 135.

85. *OR,* vol. 27, pt. 2, 699; Wittenberg and Petruzzi, "Thunder on the Mountain," 26.

86. Shaw, "Fifty-ninth Regiment (Fourth Cavalry)," *NC Regts.* 3: 463.

87. Coltrane, *Memoirs,* 17; *OR,* vol. 27, pt. 2, 699–700, 753; vol. 27, pt. 1, 991–93; McDonald, *Laurel Brigade,* 157. The force actually consisted of about 3,500 men.

88. Opie, *Rebel Cavalryman,* 173; McDonald, *Laurel Brigade,* 157.

89. McClellan, *Stuart,* 352–55; *OR,* vol. 27, pt. 1, 993–94; pt. 2, 753.

90. McClellan, *Stuart,* 352–55; *OR,* vol. 27, pt. 1, 993–94; pt. 2, 753; Wittenberg and Petruzzi, "Thunder on the Mountain," 28.

91. McClellan, *Stuart,* 352–55; *OR,* vol. 27, pt. 2, 753; W. P. Shaw, "Fifty-ninth Regiment (Fourth Cavalry)," *NC Regts.* 3: 463.

92. McClellan, *Stuart,* 352–55; *OR,* vol. 27, pt. 1, 917, 994; pt. 2, 753; W. P. Shaw, "Fifty-ninth Regiment (Fourth Cavalry)," *NC Regts.* 3: 463; Hamlin, *Old Bald Head,* 156–57; Freeman, *Lee's Lieutenants* 3: 208; Freeman, *R. E. Lee* 3: 137; Wittenberg and Petruzzi, "Thunder on the Mountain," 29.

93. *OR,* vol. 27, pt. 1, 994; Means, "Additional Sketch Sixty-third Regiment (Fifth Cavalry), *NC Regts.* 3: 569–70.

94. Means, "Additional Sketch Sixty-third Regiment (Fifth Cavalry), *NC Regts.* 3: 569–70.

95. Coltrane, *Memoirs,* 14; Means, "Additional Sketch Sixty-third Regiment (Fifth Cavalry), *NC Regts.* 3: 569–70, 588; *OR,* vol. 27, pt. 1, 988. The officer Cahill shot died that night in the regimental surgeon chair of the 5th North Carolina. In *Old Bald Head,* 157, Hamlin described Ewell's losses in trains as minimal.

96. Means, "Additional Sketch Sixty-third Regiment (Fifth Cavalry), *NC Regts.* 3: 569–70; Galloway, "Sixty-third Regiment (Fifth Cavalry)," *NC Regts.* 3: 535.

97. Freeman, *R. E. Lee* 3: 137; Means, "Additional Sketch Sixty-third Regiment (Fifth Cavalry), *NC Regts.* 3: 569–70.

98. *OR,* vol. 27, pt. 2, 701; McClellan, *Stuart,* 356.

99. Freeman, *R. E. Lee* 3: 136; Coltrane, *Memoirs,* 17.

100. *OR,* vol. 27, pt. 1, 995; pt. 2, 581, 701; McClellan, *Stuart,* 359; "Jenkins' Brigade in the Gettysburg Campaign," *SHSP* 24: 347.

101. Coltrane, *Memoirs,* 18.; *OR,* vol. 27, pt. 2, 581, 702; McClellan, *Stuart,* 359–60.

102. *OR,* vol. 27, pt. 2, 702.

103. Means, "Additional Sketch Sixty-third Regiment (Fifth Cavalry), *NC Regts.* 3: 570; *OR,* vol. 27, pt. 2, 702.

104. *OR,* vol. 27, pt. 2, 702.

105. *OR,* vol. 27, pt. 1, 928, 995; pt. 2, 702; McClellan, *Stuart,* 360–61; Freeman, *Lee's Lieutenants* 3: 166; Imboden, "Confederate Retreat," *B&L* 3: 425 ff.

106. *OR,* vol. 27, pt. 2, 715.

107. Freeman, *R. E. Lee* 3: 137; Freeman, *Lee's Lieutenants* 3: 166.

108. Means, "Additional Sketch Sixty-third Regiment (Fifth Cavalry)," *NC Regts.* 3: 570; Opie, *Rebel Cavalryman,* 236; *OR,* vol. 27, pt. 2, 697–98, 703. For Jenkins's wounding, see "Jenkins' Brigade in the Gettysburg Campaign," *SHSP* 24: 344.

109. Cadwalader J. Iredell to Shaw, July 9, 1863, Robert J. Brake Collection, USAMHI. By this point, Iredell wrote, the regiment's horses were nearly broken down.

110. *OR,* vol. 27, pt. 2, 703; Freeman, *R. E. Lee* 3: 140.

111. Longstreet, *Manassas to Appomattox,* 428; *OR,* vol. 27, pt. 2, 704, 716.

112. "Jenkins' Brigade in the Gettysburg Campaign," *SHSP* 24: 349; *OR,* vol. 27, pt. 2, 704–5; pt. 3, 994–95.

113. Freeman, *R. E. Lee* 3: 138; McClellan, *Stuart,* 363–64; JBG to his mother, July 27, 1863, James B. Gordon Papers, NCSA. JBG had been sick for four or five days before he complained about his thinness.

114. *OR,* vol. 27, pt. 2, 704–5. News of the loss of Vicksburg spread through the cavalry this day ("Jenkins' Brigade in the Gettysburg Campaign," *SHSP* 24: 349.

115. *OR*, vol. 27, pt. 2, 323, 699, 705; Blackford, *War Years*, 234–35; Freeman, *R. E. Lee* 3: 142, 144.
116. Official Commission document, June 18, 1863, James B. Gordon Papers, NCSA; Roberts, "Additional Sketch Nineteenth Regiment (Second Cavalry)," *NC Regts.* 2: 99. The commission was authored in Raleigh.
117. McClellan, *Stuart*, 328; Graham, "Nineteenth Regiment (Second Cavalry)," *NC Regts.* 2: 98.
118. Freeman, *R. E. Lee* 3: 143; Coltrane, *Memoirs*, 19. Coltrane added, "You can only understand the joke if a minie ball has passed your ear."
119. *OR*, vol. 27, pt. 2, 704–5; Freeman, *Lee's Lieutenants* 3: 166–67; Galloway, "Sixty-third Regiment (Fifth Cavalry)," *NC Regts.* 3: 535; Longstreet, *Manassas to Appomattox*, 429–30.
120. *OR*, vol. 27, pt. 2, 705; Shaw, "Fifty-ninth Regiment (Fourth Cavalry)," *NC Regts.* 3: 457; Means, "Additional Sketch Sixty-third Regiment (Fifth Cavalry)," *NC Regts.* 3: 570; JBG to his mother, July 27, 1863, James B. Gordon Papers, NCSA. JBG told his mother that he had recently experienced a similar illness.
121. *OR*, vol. 27, pt. 2, 706; Freeman, *R. E. Lee* 3: 144.
122. Cooke, *Wearing of the Gray*, 252; *OR*, vol. 27, pt. 2, 323–24, 706; Freeman, *R. E. Lee* 3: 144–45.
123. For the contradictory references, compare Barringer, "Ninth Regiment (First Cavalry)," *NC Regts.* 1: 425–26; Roberts, "Additional Sketch Nineteenth Regiment (Second Cavalry)," *NC Regts.* 2: 99; Shaw, "Fifty-ninth Regiment (Fourth Cavalry)," *NC Regts.* 3: 464–65, Galloway, "Sixty-third Regiment (Fifth Cavalry)," *NC Regts.* 3: 535; *NC Troops* 2: 4; Coltrane, *Memoirs*, 19; and JBG's letters of July 18 and 27 quoted in the text.
124. JBG to Augustus Finley, July 18, 1863, in Hickerson, *Echoes*, 95; typewritten manuscript courtesy J. Jay Anderson, Wilkes Community College.
125. JBG to his mother, July 27, 1863, James B. Gordon Papers, NCSA.
126. *OR*, vol. 27, pt. 1, 932; *Richmond Enquirer*, quoted in the *People's Press*, August 13, 1863, p. 2, col. 6; Black, *Crumbling Defenses*, 56; Grimsley, *Battles In Culpeper*, 14.
127. *OR*, vol. 27, pt. 1, 932; pt. 2, 324; *People's Press*, August 6, 1863, p. 2, col. 5; August 13, 1863, p. 2, col. 6; Black, *Crumbling Defenses*, 56–57; Henderson, *Bristoe Station*, 20–21.
128. *OR*, vol. 27, pt. 1, 932; pt. 2, 324, 609; pt. 3, 827; *People's Press*, August 6, 1863, p. 2, col. 5; August 13, 1863, p. 2, col. 6; Neese, *Three Years*, 203; Henderson, *Bristoe Station*, 20–23.
129. Brooks, *Butler and His Cavalry*, 171; *OR*, vol. 27, pt. 2, 311. According to Brooks, *Butler and His Cavalry*, 171, Baker was the first officer to fall, so brigade command devolved on Young. When Young was wounded, Black took command of the brigade; then he was hit, and Colonel T. J. Lipscomb of the 2d South Carolina took over. Then Lipscomb was wounded. Lieutenant Colonel Rich of the Phillips Legion was the last to command the brigade during the battle.
130. Address on Laurence S. Baker, Given by Judge Jas. C. MacRae, Raleigh, N.C., 1907. N.P., copy in the author's possession; *OR*, vol. 27, pt. 1, 725–26; *People's Press*, August 6, 1863, p. 2, col. 5; August 13, 1863, p. 2, col. 6; *CMH* 5: 293; Black, *Crumbling Defenses*, 58.
131. Freeman, *Lee's Lieutenants* 3: 210, n. 24; Thomas, *Bold Dragoon*, 202.
132. *OR*, vol. 27, pt. 3, 1069; CSR for James B. Gordon, First North Carolina Cavalry Regiment (Ninth North Carolina State Troops), Microcopy 270, Roll 4; Official Commission document, James B. Gordon Papers, NCSA. On the back of the document is written: "...Cavalry in line of battle at Hagerstown, Maryland July 13 1863. This commission received on the above day. It was not accepted. I was soon after commissioned col. of the 1 No C Cavalry. J. B. Gordon."
133. Black, *Crumbling Defenses*, 59–62, 65; *OR*, vol. 51, pt. 2, 748. There is a misconception in much of the literature that Baker was wounded on September 22 at Jack's Shop, not on August 1.
134. CSR for James B. Gordon, First North Carolina Cavalry Regiment (Ninth North Carolina State Troops), Microcopy 270, Roll 4. The August 1863 field and staff muster roll for the First North Carolina reports JBG as "absent comd'g Brigade."

Chapter 11

1. Freeman, *R. E. Lee* 3: 145; *OR*, vol. 27, pt. 2, 324; Freeman, *Lee's Lieutenants* 3: 206.
2. Henderson, *Bristoe Station*, 27; JBG to his mother, July 27, 1863, James B. Gordon Papers, NCSA.
3. James Pugh to Sarah Keck, July 12, 1863, Pugh Papers, SHC; Myers, *The Comanches*, 205.
4. George S. Dewey to his sister, July 31, 1863, George Stanley Dewey Papers, SHC.
5. George S. Dewey to his sister, July 31, 1863, George Stanley Dewey Papers, SHC; Barrett, *Civil War*, 171; James Gwyn Diary, March 20, 1863, James Gwyn Papers, SHC; Van Noppen, *Stoneman's Last Raid*, 13.
6. Julia P. Gwyn to "My Dear Uncle," July 25, 1863, James Gwyn Papers, SHC; James Gwyn Diary, September 1, 1863, James Gwyn Papers, SHC.
7. Calvin J. Cowles to President Andrew Johnson, July 29, 1865, "Case Files of Applications From Former Confederates for Presidential Pardons (Amnesty Papers)," Microcopy 1003, Roll 38, Group I, NA. W. W. Holden urged immediate action on Cowles's amnesty application because "Mr. Cowles is, and has been a strong Union man...."
8. JBG to Augustus W. Finley, August 18, 1863, typewritten manuscript courtesy J. Jay Anderson, WCC; Anderson, *Wilkes County Sketches*, 51.
9. James Pugh to Sarah Keck, September 18, 1863, Pugh Papers, SHC; Various subscription receipts, Anderson Collection; *People's Press*, August 20, 1863, p. 2, col. 4; *Raleigh Register*, September 2, 1863, p. 4, cols. 2–3.
10. JBG to Augustus W. Finley, August 18, 1863, typewritten manuscript courtesy J. Jay Anderson, WCC; JBG to Augustus W. Finley, July 18, 1863, in Hickerson, *Echoes*, 95; ibid., typewritten manuscript courtesy J. Jay Anderson, WCC.
11. Peter W. Hairston to Mrs. Fanny Hairston, October 30, 1863, Peter W. Hairston Papers, SHC; JBG to Augustus W. Finley, August 18, 1863, typewritten MS. courtesy J. Jay Anderson, WCC; ibid., in Hickerson, *Echoes*, 96. "We are in camp," wrote one soldier, "and have been for a good bit their is no talk of any more fighting here at this time" (James Pugh to Sarah Keck, August 29, 1863, Pugh Papers, SHC).
12. James Pugh to Sarah Keck, September 18, 1863, Pugh Papers, SHC; McClellan, Stuart, 372–74; Henderson, *Bristoe Station*, 33 ff; Grimsley, *Battles In Culpeper*, 17. Pugh's casualty estimate appears high, but in the absence of reports his statement stands. See also Neese, *Three Years*, 208 ff.
13. Shaw, "Fifty-ninth Regiment (Fourth Cavalry)," *NC Regts.* 3: 464; Freeman, *R. E. Lee* 3: 144.
14. *OR*, vol. 29, pt. 1, 452; pt. 2, 665; Freeman, *R. E. Lee* 3: 251–52; Davis, *Stuart*, 357–58.
15. Graham, "Nineteenth Regiment (Second Cavalry)," *NC Regts.* 2: 79; McClellan, *Stuart*, 257–61; Opie, *Rebel Cavalryman*, 335.
16. James Pugh to B. S. White, October 8, 1863, Pugh Papers, SHC; George S. Dewey to his sister, July 31, 1863, George Stanley Dewey Papers, SHC.
17. CSRG for James B. Gordon, Microcopy 331, Roll 109; McClellan, *Stuart*, 257–61.
18. General Orders #26, July 30, 1863, in *The Letters of Major General James E. B. Stuart*, 329–33; JBG to his mother, July 27, 1863, James B. Gordon Papers, NCSA; James Pugh to Sarah Keck, August 12, 1863, Pugh Papers, SHC.

19. *OR,* vol. 27, pt. 2, 705; pt. 3, 1006–7; *CMH* 4: 658; Galloway, "Sixty-third Regiment (Fifth Cavalry)," *NC Regts.* 3: 535–36.
20. *OR,* vol. 27, pt. 3, 1068; Freeman, *Lee's Lieutenants* 3: 209.
21. JBG to Augustus W. Finley, August 18, 1863, typewritten manuscript courtesy J. Jay Anderson, WCC, and in Hickerson, *Echoes,* 96; James Pugh to Sarah Keck, August 29, 1863, Pugh Papers, SHC. *OR,* vol. 29, pt. 2, 707–8; McClellan, *Stuart,* 371–72. The order was dated September 9, 1863. This was technically not a corps because Stuart was not promoted to lieutenant general, the appropriate rank of a Confederate corps commander (Freeman, *Lee's Lieutenants* 3: 211). According to one soldier, Stuart "seems very surprised he has not been made Lt. General. I told him Gen'l Lee had complained about the Pennsylvania confusion" (Peter W. Hairston to Mrs. Fanny Hairston, October 30, 1863, Peter W. Hairston Papers, SHC).
22. McClellan, *Stuart,* 371–72; Roberts, "Additional Sketch Nineteenth Regiment (Second Cavalry)," *NC Regts.* 2: 99.
23. *CMH* 7: 458–59; Freeman, *Lee's Lieutenants* 3: 215; J. E. B. Stuart to P. M. B. Young, August 10, 1863, September 10, 1863, Pierce M. B. Young Collection, GDAH.
24. Freeman, *Lee's Lieutenants* 3: 213–14. Rosser's rank was dated October 10, 1863.
25. "Paper B," October 24, 1862, and Stuart to Flora Stuart, November 6, 1862, *The Letters of Major General James E. B. Stuart,* 275; Freeman, *Lee's Lieutenants* 3: 212–13 and n. 35; *CMH* 4: 658–59.
26. Tom Rosser to "My dear wife," August 31, September 15, September 16, September 27, 1863, Thomas Lafayette Rosser Papers (#1171), Papers of the Gordon and Rosser Families, UVA.
27. *CMH* 4: 628–29; Boatner, 489; Stuart to Flora Stuart, July 30, 1857, *The Letters of Major General James E. B. Stuart,* 167.
28. *CMH* 4: 685–86; Blackford, *Letters,* 144.; Jeb Stuart to R. H. Chilton, February 4, 1863, *The Letters of Major General James E. B. Stuart,* 292. On the eve of one battle Wickham said, "If I am killed tomorrow it will be for Virginia, the land of my fathers, and not for the damned secession movement."
29. Wade Hampton to Louis Wigfall, February 16, 1863, VHS, in Thomas, *Bold Dragoon,* 201–2; Wade Hampton to Miss Mary Hampton, May 13, 1863, copy in Wade Hampton Papers, SHC.
30. "Deeds of valor" quoted in W. H. Cheek, "Additional Sketch Ninth Regiment (First Cavalry)," *NC Regts.* 1: 448; Barrett, *Civil War In North Carolina,* 187; *OR,* Series 4, vol. 2, 114–15. Vance also wanted the 5th North Carolina to return to North Carolina (James Seddon to Zebulon Vance, September 17, 1863, Zebulon B. Vance Papers, NCSA).
31. R. Ransom to S. Cooper, September 22, 1863, CSRG for James B. Gordon, Microcopy 331, Roll 109.
32. *OR,* vol. 29, pt. 2, 902; J. E. B. Stuart to P. M. B. Young, August 10, 1863, Pierce M. B. Young Collection, GDAH; W. H. Cheek, "Additional Sketch Ninth Regiment (First Cavalry)," *NC Regts.* 1: 449, 451. Gordon commanded Hampton's brigade from August 1 to September 9.
33. Cheek, "Additional Sketch Ninth Regiment (First Cavalry)," *NC Regts.* 1: 448–49; McClellan, *Stuart,* 374. Cheek's article quotes extensively a "communication written to the Fayetteville Observer about the time by an officer of the regiment...."
34. Untitled reminiscences of Fred Foard, aide of Brigadier General Rufus Barringer, p. 1, Fred C. Foard Papers, NCSA.
35. Cheek, "Additional Sketch Ninth Regiment (First Cavalry)," *NC Regts.* 1: 452–53.
36. McClellan, *Stuart,* 374; Coltrane *Memoirs,* 20; Cheek, "Additional Sketch Ninth Regiment (First Cavalry)," *NC Regts.* 1: 449, 452–53.

37. Coltrane, *Memoirs,* 20; Means, "Additional Sketch Sixty-third Regiment (Fifth Cavalry)," *NC Regts.* 3: 572–73.
38. Coltrane, *Memoirs,* 20; Means, "Additional Sketch Sixty-third Regiment (Fifth Cavalry)," *NC Regts.* 3: 573; Cheek, "Additional Sketch Ninth Regiment (First Cavalry)," *NC Regts.* 1: 450. Coltrane apparently wrote his memoirs while referring to Means's *NC Regts.* article, although the second quote appeared only in Coltrane's memoirs.
39. McClellan, *Stuart,* 374–75; Means, "Additional Sketch Sixty-third Regiment (Fifth Cavalry)," *NC Regts.* 3: 573–74; Cheek, "Additional Sketch Ninth Regiment (First Cavalry)," *NC Regts.* 1: 451. Stuart made no report of this action.
40. Means, "Additional Sketch Sixty-third Regiment (Fifth Cavalry)," *NC Regts.* 3: 573; Cheek, "Additional Sketch Ninth Regiment (First Cavalry)," *NC Regts.* 1: 451.
41. Boatner, *Dictionary,* 679; Freeman, *Lee's Lieutenants* 3: 327–28, 699, 710; *CMH* 5: 346–47; *OR,* vol. 27, pt. 3, 1003; Green, "Ransom's Address," 13 ff.
42. Green, "Ransom Address," 13; Boatner, 679; Freeman, *Lee's Lieutenants* 3: 4, 327–28, 699, 710. Mrs. Ransom once wrote Lee's headquarters asking that Ransom be promoted. Stuart wrote his brother-in-law, "I don't see how you can avoid ... Ransom...." (Jeb Stuart to John R. Cooke, February 28, 1863, in Thomas, *Bold Dragoon,* 203.) For an event that reflected poorly on Ransom, see Jordan, "'Yankees and Rebels," *North Carolina Historical Review,* 207 ff.
43. R. Ransom to JBG, September 22, 1863, James B. Gordon Papers, NCSA. Ransom added that his wife and another lady friend sent JBG their "kind regards." As for the Unionist sympathies in North Carolina, Ransom wrote, "Success in our great battles will kill it & nothing else will."
44. Green, "Ransom Address," 16; R. Ransom to S. Cooper, September 22, 1863, CSRG for James B. Gordon, Microcopy 331, Roll 109.
45. R. E. Lee to Jefferson Davis, September 26, 1863, CSRG for James B. Gordon, Microcopy 331, Roll 109.
46. Rufus Barringer to D.H. Hill, July 22, 1864, D.H. Hill Papers, SHC.
47. Freeman, *Lee's Lieutenants* 3: 215; Official Commission, September 28, 1863, James B. Gordon Papers, NCSA; CSR for James B. Gordon, First North Carolina Cavalry Regiment (Ninth North Carolina State Troops), Microcopy 270, Roll 4. Freeman described JBG as "distinguished for bravery and intelligent leadership...."
48. James B. Gordon to J. E. B. Stuart, October 3, 1863, H. B. McClellan Papers, VHS. According to Tom Rosser, Stuart recommended that Rosser's commission date from September 28 so that he would rank JBG. (Tom Rosser to "My dear wife," October 5, 1863, Thomas Lafayette Rosser Papers, Papers of the Gordon and Rosser Families, UVA.)
49. Register of Appointments, CSRG for James B. Gordon, Microcopy 331, Roll 109; Freeman, *Lee's Lieutenants* 3: 210; Cowles, *CSC,* 20; Cowles, "Life and Services," 11. In the opinion of John Galloway, "Sixty-third Regiment (Fifth Cavalry)," *NC Regts.* 3: 536, "... no promotion was ever better deserved than this." For an example of the congratulations JBG received on his promotion, see A. Foster to R. F. Hackett, March 9, 1864, James Gordon Hackett Papers, NCSA.
50. E. L. Dabney to "My Dearest Betty," August 4, 1863, October 25, 1863, Saunders Family Papers, VHS; Trout, *They Followed The Plume,* 94–99, 331; John Esten Cooke Diary (#5925), September 29, 1863, UVA; "War Notes," February 12, 1864, John Esten Cooke Papers, DU; J.E.B. Stuart to Mrs. Peter Saunders, quoted in *Writings of Maud Carter Clement,* 8.
51. *NC Troops* 2: 7, 61; Crute, *Confederate Staff Officers,* 72; Carr, "The Gordon-Barringer Brigade," *NC Regts.* 4: 582; *Our Living and Our Dead* 2: 182.
52. Warner and Yearns, *Biographical Register,* 63–64. Burton Craige turned down the opportunity to run for the Regular Congress.
53. Ashe, *Biographical History* 1: 250–51; *CV* 6 (1898): 228; Burton Craige to Thomas F. Hickerson, January 14,

1941, in Hickerson, *Echoes*, 138. See Kerr Craige to Sarah Brown, February 22, 1864, James B. Gordon Letters, Brown Family Letters, GHM. "Dear Madam," Craige wrote, "Enclosed is a dispatch, received to-day from Genl. Gordon, which will explain the purpose of my writing."

54. William L. Barrier to his father, November 5, 1863, Troxler and Auciello, *Dear Father*, 114; Cowles, *CSC*, 20; Cowles, "Life and Services," 11.

55. Barringer, "Ninth Regiment (First Cavalry)," *NC Regts*. 1: 426; Roberts, "Additional Sketch Nineteenth Regiment (Second Cavalry)," *NC Regts*. 2: 99; *NC Troops* 2: 104; *OR*, vol. 29, pt. 2, 902. Robinson was promoted colonel September 9, 1863, to rank from July 23. His date of exchange is unknown, but he was probably not present when JBG took command of the brigade. Andrews had been a major since September 6, 1862 and would be promoted to Lieutenant Colonel in February 1864.

56. Cheek, "Additional Sketch Ninth Regiment (First Cavalry)," *NC Regts*. 1: 449.

57. Graham, "Nineteenth Regiment (Second Cavalry)," *NC Regts*. 2: 97; Roberts, "Additional Sketch Nineteenth Regiment (Second Cavalry)," *NC Regts*. 2: 99; *NC Regts*. 3: 456 ff.

58. Tom Brown to Caroline Gordon Hackett, May 2, 1861, James Gordon Hackett Collection, NCSA; Cowles, *CSC*, 20; Cowles, "Life and Services," 11.

59. Freeman, *R. E. Lee* 3: 168; Cooke, *Wearing of the Gray*, 253.

60. Freeman, *Lee's Lieutenants* 3: 239–41; *R. E. Lee* 3: 169–71, 174; *OR* Series I, vol. 29, pt. 1, 408–9.

61. *Philadelphia Weekly Times*, February 7, 1880, in McClellan, *Stuart*, 379; *OR*, vol. 29, pt. 1, 439.

62. Freeman, *Lee's Lieutenants* 3: 249; *OR*, vol. 29, pt. 1, 439; McClellan, *Stuart*, 376.

63. *OR*, vol. 29, pt. 1, 460, 455, 439; McClellan, *Stuart*, 378–79; *OR*, vol. 29, pt. 1, 440, 457–60, 460; Cooke, *Wearing of the Gray*, 253. After JBG's temporary stint in command, Young commanded Butler's old brigade in this campaign as a colonel. Williams C. Wickham, injured by a fall of his horse, also missed much of this campaign, so his brigade was commanded by Colonel Thomas Owen.

64. Garnett, *Riding With Stuart*, 13.

65. Coltrane, *Memoirs*, 21; *OR*, vol. 29, pt. 1, 440, 460; McClellan, *Stuart*, 376–77; John Esten Cooke Diary, October 25, 1863, UVA.

66. Cooke, *Wearing of the Gray*, 254; *OR*, vol. 29, pt. 1, 440, 460. Young and JBG captured over 87 prisoners and between 75 and 100 "excellent arms."

67. *OR*, vol. 29, pt. 1, 440; McClellan, *Stuart*, 377; *OR*, vol. 29, pt. 1, 440, 460.

68. McClellan, *Stuart*, 377; *OR*, vol. 29, pt. 1, 440, 460; Cooke, *Wearing of the Gray*, 255. In *OR*, vol. 29, pt. 1, 455, Funsten reported that the 11th Virginia joined JBG's brigade in the fight.

69. McClellan, *Stuart*, 377; *OR*, vol. 29, pt. 1, 440; Freeman, *R. E. Lee* 3: 172; John Esten Cooke Diary, October 25, 1863, UVA. Cooke's horse was named Buck.

70. Cooke, *Wearing of the Gray*, 255; John Esten Cooke Diary, October 25, 1863, UVA. On p. 348 of his part-fiction part-history book *Surry of Eagle's Nest*, Cooke called JBG one of his best friends.

71. *OR*, vol. 29, pt. 1, 440; McClellan, *Stuart*, 379; Cooke, *Wearing of the Gray*, 254–55. McClellan called 1,500 "an extreme estimate."

72. *OR*, vol. 29, pt. 1, 440–41, 445, 460; McClellan, *Stuart*, 378–79; Cooke, *Wearing of the Gray*, 256–57. Stuart also dispatched the 11th Virginia Cavalry to strike the Warrenton road to Rixeyville to ascertain if the enemy was retreating in that direction (*OR*, vol. 29, pt. 1, 441).

73. Coltrane, *Memoirs*, 21; Cooke, *Wearing of the Gray*, 257.

74. *OR*, vol. 29, pt. 1, 441, 460; McClellan, *Stuart*, 378–79; Shaw, "Fifty-ninth Regiment (Fourth Cavalry)," *NC Regts*. 3: 465; Cooke, *Wearing of the Gray*, 257.

75. Grimsley, *Battles In Culpeper*, 19; Galloway, "Sixty-third Regiment (Fifth Cavalry)," *NC Regts*. 3: 536; Means, "Additional Sketch Sixty-third Regiment (Fifth Cavalry), *NC Regts*. 3: 575.

76. *OR*, vol. 29, pt. 1, 441; Shaw, "Fifty-ninth Regiment (Fourth Cavalry)," *NC Regts*. 3: 465; Cooke, *Wearing of the Gray*, 257.

77. *OR*, vol. 29, pt. 1, 441–42, 460; McClellan, *Stuart*, 379. The two regiments of infantry supporting Fitz Lee had halted at Stone-House Mountain.

78. John Esten Cooke Diary, October 25, 1863, UVA.

79. *OR*, vol. 29, pt. 1, 442–43, 460; McClellan, *Stuart*, 379–80; Means, "Additional Sketch Sixty-third Regiment (Fifth Cavalry), *NC Regts*. 3: 576. Lee could not tell friend from foe because of the distance.

80. Opie, *Rebel Cavalryman*, 196.

81. John Esten Cooke Diary, October 25, 1863, UVA.

82. *OR*, vol. 29, pt. 1, 443; Freeman, *Lee's Lieutenants* 3: 250.

83. *OR*, vol. 29, pt. 1, 443, 455; Means, "Additional Sketch Sixty-third Regiment (Fifth Cavalry), *NC Regts*. 3: 576; Neese, *Three Years*, 232. The Botts home was known as "Auburn."

84. Coltrane, *Memoirs*, 22; Means, "Additional Sketch Sixty-third Regiment (Fifth Cavalry), *NC Regts*. 3: 576.

85. *OR*, vol. 29, pt. 1, 443, 460; McClellan, *Stuart*, 379–80; Coltrane, *Memoirs*, 22; Means, "Additional Sketch Sixty-third Regiment (Fifth Cavalry), *NC Regts*. 3: 576. JBG and Coltrane agreed that the 18th Pennsylvania Cavalry had been the flanking force; McClellan thought it was a battalion of the 5th New York Cavalry. *OR*, vol. 29, pt. 1, 386 also suggests that the unit was the 18th Pennsylvania.

86. *OR*, vol. 29, pt. 1, 443; McClellan, *Stuart*, 380; Freeman, *Lee's Lieutenants* 3: 251.

87. Means, "Additional Sketch Sixty-third Regiment (Fifth Cavalry), *NC Regts*. 3: 577.

88. *OR*, vol. 29, pt. 1, 443; Coltrane, *Memoirs*, 22.

89. Cooke, *Wearing of the Gray*, 257.

90. *OR*, vol. 29, pt. 1, 443–44; McClellan, *Stuart*, 382–83.

91. Coltrane, *Memoirs*, 22; Means, "Additional Sketch Sixty-third Regiment (Fifth Cavalry), *NC Regts*. 3: 577; *OR*, vol. 29, pt. 1, 442, 460.

92. Freeman, *R. E. Lee* 3: 173–74.

93. *OR*, vol. 29, pt. 1, 444–47, 460. Rosser, who had been left at Fleetwood with the 5th Virginia, was attacked there by three Federal infantry corps and a cavalry division on October 12. When Young's brigade came up from James City, the Confederates held Culpeper against larger enemy forces. As a result, Lee's position and movements were not discovered (McClellan, *Stuart*, 383–84).

94. Freeman, *Lee's Lieutenants* 3: 239; Cooke, *Wearing of the Gray*, 260; Means, "Additional Sketch Sixty-third Regiment (Fifth Cavalry), *NC Regts*. 3: 578. Means correctly writes that the brigade actually crossed the Hedgeman River at sunset, not the Hazel as JBG reported in *OR*, vol. 29, pt. 1, 460. Means also claimed that contrary to Stuart's report, the 5th North Carolina played an important part in the 12th Virginia's charge at Warrenton Sulphur Springs (*OR*, vol. 29, pt. 1, 445).

95. McClellan, *Stuart*, 387; *OR*, vol. 29, pt. 1, 447.

96. McClellan, *Stuart*, 387; W. H. H. Cowles in Cheek, "Ninth Regiment (First Cavalry)," *NC Regts*. 1: 454; *OR*, vol. 29, pt. 1, 461. Auburn was also called Auburn Mills.

97. Blackford, 238; McClellan, *Stuart*, 387.

98. *OR*, vol. 29, pt. 1, 447; McClellan, *Stuart*, 387–88; Coltrane, *Memoirs*, 23; W. H. H. Cowles in Cheek, "Ninth Regiment (First Cavalry)," *NC Regts*. 1: 454–55. The officer did not reach Lee in time for the Confederates to capitalize on this intelligence (*OR*, vol. 29, pt. 1, 447).

99. *OR*, vol. 29, pt. 1, 447, 461; Cooke, *Wearing of the Gray*, 260; Cheek, "Ninth Regiment (First Cavalry)," *NC Regts*. 1: 455.

100. *OR,* vol. 29, pt. 1, 447; Coltrane, *Memoirs,* 23.
101. McClellan, *Stuart,* 387; W. H. H. Cowles in Cheek, "Ninth Regiment (First Cavalry)," *NC Regts.* 1: 455.
102. *OR,* vol. 29, pt. 1, 447; McClellan, *Stuart,* 387–88. Federal forces had apparently diverged from the main line of withdrawal at Warrenton Junction, intending to rejoin it at Bristoe (Freeman, *Lee's Lieutenants* 3: 255).
103. *OR,* vol. 29, pt. 1, 447–48, 461; Coltrane, *Memoirs,* 22, 23; Cowles, *CSC,* 21; Cowles, "Life and Services," 12.
104. *OR,* vol. 29, pt. 1, 447–48; Freeman, *Lee's Lieutenants* 3: 256.
105. Blackford, 238–39; Coltrane, *Memoirs,* 24.
106. Means, "Additional Sketch Sixty-third Regiment (Fifth Cavalry), *NC Regts.* 3: 579; Cooke, *Wearing of the Gray,* 261; Coltrane, *Memoirs,* 24.
107. *Coltrane Memoirs,* 22; Means, "Additional Sketch Sixty-third Regiment (Fifth Cavalry), *NC Regts.* 3: 580; *Concord Register,* July 6, 1883.
108. Rankin, "Sketch of Fifth Regiment North Carolina Cavalry," unprovenienced article in the author's possession; *OR,* vol. 29, pt. 1, 448; Cooke, *Wearing of the Gray,* 261; Cowles, *CSC,* 21; Cowles, "Life and Services," 12.
109. *OR,* vol. 29, pt. 1, 461, 448; Cowles, *CSC,* 21; Cowles, "Life and Services," 12.
110. *OR,* vol. 29, pt. 1, 448; McClellan, *Stuart,* 391; Coltrane, *Memoirs,* 24; Blackford, *War Years,* 240; Means, "Additional Sketch Sixty-third Regiment (Fifth Cavalry), *NC Regts.* 3: 580.
111. *OR,* vol. 29, pt. 1, 448; McClellan, *Stuart,* 390, 392.
112. *OR,* vol. 29, pt. 1, 448, 461; Means, "Additional Sketch Sixty-third Regiment (Fifth Cavalry), *NC Regts.* 3: 580; Coltrane, *Memoirs,* 24.
113. *OR,* vol. 29, pt. 1, 448; McClellan, *Stuart,* 392–93.
114. Whit H. Anthony, "Cavalry Fight at Bucklands, Va.," Peter Evans Smith Papers, SHC; *OR,* vol. 29, pt. 1, 448; McClellan, *Stuart,* 392; *Charlotte Observer,* March 3, 1893.
115. Means, "Additional Sketch Sixty-third Regiment (Fifth Cavalry), *NC Regts.* 3: 581; McClellan, *Stuart,* 392; *OR,* vol. 29, pt. 1, 448; Whit H. Anthony, "Cavalry Fight at Bucklands, Va.," Peter Evans Smith Papers, SHC; *Charlotte Observer,* March 3, 1893; *Concord Register,* July 6, 1883. W. H. H. Cowles in Cheek, "Additional Sketch Ninth Regiment (First Cavalry)," *NC Regts.* 1: 456, remembered that purpose of Ruffin's charge was "a diversion so that our remaining troops could debouch into the open road and pass in rear of the enemy's column."
116. *OR,* vol. 29, pt. 1, 448, 461; Cowles, *CSC,* 21; Cowles, "Life and Services," 13; *Concord Register,* July 6, 1883. JBG called Ruffin "gallant and accomplished;" Stuart described him as "a model of worth, devotion, and heroism."
117. *OR,* vol. 29, pt. 1, 448; W. H. H. Cowles in Cheek, "Additional Sketch Ninth Regiment (First Cavalry)," *NC Regts.* 1: 455–56; Barringer, "Ninth Regiment (First Cavalry)," *NC Regts.* 1: 427; Whit H. Anthony, "Cavalry Fight at Bucklands, Va.," Peter Evans Smith Papers, SHC; *Observer,* March 3, 1893
118. *OR,* vol. 29, pt. 1, 448; McClellan, *Stuart,* 392. According to *Medical And Surgical History Of The Civil War* 7: 204, which recorded a vivid description of the wound, Ruffin lived until October 18.
119. W. H. H. Cowles in Cheek, "Additional Sketch Ninth Regiment (First Cavalry)," *NC Regts.* 1: 456. Stuart reported that Cowles "nobly seconded" JBG's example of bravery and ability (*OR,* vol. 29, pt. 1, 448).
120. W. H. H. Cowles in Cheek, "Additional Sketch Ninth Regiment (First Cavalry)," *NC Regts.* 1: 456; Blackford, *War Years,* 240; *Concord Register,* July 6, 1883. An alternate wording, from Cowles, *CSC,* 21, and "Life and Services, 13, is "It is nothing but a scratch...."
121. Cowles, *CSC,* 21; Cowles, "Life and Services," 13. The quotes and events recorded in Cowles's accounts in *CSC,* 21 and "Life and Services," 13 and in Cheek, "Additional Sketch Ninth Regiment (First Cavalry)," *NC Regts.* 1: 454–57 differ somewhat. Cowles gave his address in 1887 and wrote his account for Cheek's *NC Regts.* article around 1900. The later account, however, is more detailed and appears to be accurate. As for the retreat, according to Means, 589, D. B. Coltrane, a "first-class fighting private," was "among the foremost and most helpful men in the dangerous and difficult task of bringing out from that triangle the heavy ordnance wagons of Gordon's Brigade...."
122. *OR,* vol. 29, pt. 1, 448. Cowles, in *CSC,* 21 and "Life and Services," 13, differed with Stuart's report by recording that JBG guarded the rear during the withdrawal from Cedar Run valley. Stuart's report, being the contemporary account, is followed in the text.
123. *OR,* vol. 29, pt. 1, 448–49; Freeman, *Lee's Lieutenants* 3: 241–47, 260.
124. Freeman, *Lee's Lieutenants* 3: 259–60; Rufus Barringer to V. C. Barringer, January 27, 1866, Rufus Clay Barringer Papers, SHC. Barringer received a minor thigh wound during the action.
125. Barringer, "Ninth Regiment (First Cavalry)," *NC Regts.* 1: 427; *NC Troops* 2: 63; Peter W. Hairston to Mrs. Fanny Hairston, October 30, 1863, Peter W. Hairston Papers, SHC; *Charlotte Observer,* March 3, 1893. For more on Hairston, see Appendix III.
126. Freeman, *R. E. Lee* 3: 185; *OR,* vol. 29, pt. 1, 406–9, 449, 448.
127. Cowles, *CSC,* 21; Cowles, "Life and Services," 13; Blackford, *War Years,* 240; *OR,* vol. 29, pt. 1, 449–50, 461; John Esten Cooke Diary, December 15, 1863, UVA. Fitz Lee came up to support JBG late in the day, but darkness prevented him from joining the battle.
128. Rawle, *Third Pennsylvania,* 346–47.
129. Ibid., 347–48.
130. Ibid., 348–49.
131. Ibid., 349–51, 356.
132. John Esten Cooke Diary, December 15, 1863, UVA; *OR,* vol. 29, pt. 1, 450, 461; Cooke, *Wearing of the Gray,* 263–64; Means, "Additional Sketch Sixty-third Regiment (Fifth Cavalry), *NC Regts.* 3: 582.
133. Cooke, *Wearing of the Gray,* 266; *OR,* vol. 29, pt. 1, 450–51.
134. Means, "Additional Sketch Sixty-third Regiment (Fifth Cavalry), *NC Regts.* 3: 582; McClellan, *Stuart,* 393; *OR,* vol. 29, pt. 1, 451, 461.
135. Means, "Additional Sketch Sixty-third Regiment (Fifth Cavalry), *NC Regts.* 3: 583; W. H. H. Cowles in Cheek, "Additional Sketch Ninth Regiment (First Cavalry), *NC Regts.* 1: 457; Blackford, *War Years,* 241; Whit H. Anthony, "Cavalry Fight at Bucklands, Va.," Peter Evans Smith Papers, SHC; Blackford, *War Years,* 241.
136. *OR,* vol. 29, pt. 1, 451, 461; Cooke, *Wearing of the Gray,* 266; Barringer, "Ninth Regiment (First Cavalry)," *NC Regts.* 1: 427.
137. *OR,* vol. 29, pt. 1, 461; W. H. H. Cowles in Cheek, "Additional Sketch Ninth Regiment (First Cavalry)," *NC Regts.* 1: 457–58.
138. Barringer, "Famous Regiment," 7; Barringer, "Ninth Regiment (First Cavalry)," vol. 1, 427. Cowles and Barringer's *NC Regts.* accounts differ slightly. Cowles, for example, remembered JBG's words here as "Charge with the First North Carolina!" (Cheek, "Additional Sketch Ninth Regiment [First Cavalry]," *NC Regts.* 1: 458).
139. Whit H. Anthony, "Cavalry Fight at Bucklands, Va.," Peter Evans Smith Papers, SHC; *Charlotte Observer,* March 3, 1893.
140. *Carolina Watchman,* October 26, 1863, p. 2, col. 3.
141. Barringer, "Ninth Regiment (First Cavalry)," *NC Regts.* 1: 427; Cowles in Cheek, "Additional Sketch Ninth Regiment (First Cavalry)," *NC Regts.* 1: 458; Whit H. Anthony, "Cavalry Fight at Bucklands, Va.," Peter Evans Smith Papers, SHC; Barringer, "Famous Regiment," 7; *Charlotte Observer,* March 3, 1893.
142. Cowles in Cheek, "Additional Sketch Ninth Regi-

ment (First Cavalry)," *NC Regts.* 1: 458; McClellan, *Stuart,* 394–95; Blackford, *War Years,* 241; *Concord Register,* July 6, 1883. Cowles did not mention Barringer's part in the action.

143. *OR,* vol. 29, pt. 1, 451; Barringer, "Ninth Regiment (First Cavalry)," *NC Regts.* 1: 428; Whit H. Anthony, "Cavalry Fight at Bucklands, Va.," Peter Evans Smith Papers, SHC.

144. McClellan, *Stuart,* 394–95; Barringer, "Ninth Regiment (First Cavalry)," *NC Regts.* 1: 428; Cowles in Cheek, "Additional Sketch Ninth Regiment (First Cavalry)," *NC Regts.* 1: 458; Whit H. Anthony, "Cavalry Fight at Bucklands, Va.," Peter Evans Smith Papers, SHC.

145. *OR,* vol. 29, pt. 1, pt. 1, 461; Coltrane, *Memoirs,* 25–26; *OR,* vol. 29, pt. 1, 452, 461. Coltrane wrote, "This was one day it was my privilege to ride by the side of General Stuart for quite a while."

146. *OR,* vol. 29, pt. 1, 461; Cowles in Cheek, "Additional Sketch Ninth Regiment (First Cavalry)," *NC Regts.* 1: 459; Rufus Barringer to V. C. Barringer, January 27, 1866, Rufus Clay Barringer Papers, SHC; Whit H. Anthony, "Cavalry Fight at Bucklands, Va.," Peter Evans Smith Papers, SHC; *Charlotte Observer,* March 3, 1893

147. John Esten Cooke Diary, December 15, 1863, UVA.

148. McMahon, "Gettysburg to Grant," *B&L* 4: 85; Cooke, *Wearing of the Gray,* 266; Means, "Additional Sketch Sixty-third Regiment (Fifth Cavalry)," *NC Regts.* 3: 584; Cowles in Cheek, "Additional Sketch Ninth Regiment (First Cavalry)," *NC Regts.* 1: 459; *Charlotte Observer,* March 3, 1893.

149. *OR,* vol. 29, pt. 1, 452–53, 454; McClellan, *Stuart,* 396; Freeman, *Lee's Lieutenants* 3: 262–63.

150. *OR,* vol. 29, pt. 1, 414, 454, 461, 462. On November 23, the army's medical director reported 6 killed and 47 wounded in JBG's brigade. On December 10, it was reported that the brigade had lost 5 killed, 56 wounded, and 8 missing. In his report of December 10, JBG estimated 125 total casualties.

151. *OR,* vol. 29, pt. 1, 448; Freeman, *Lee's Lieutenants* 3: 262; Davis, *Stuart,* 367.

152. Jeb Stuart to Mrs. Flora Stuart, February 8, 1864, J. E. B. Stuart Letters, UVA. Stuart dated his Bristoe report February 13, 1864 (*OR,* vol. 29, pt. 1, 439).

Chapter 12

1. Freeman, *R. E. Lee* 3: 189; *People's Press,* December 3, 1863, p.1, col. 5; Neese, *Three Years,* 233–34.

2. Myers, *The Comanches,* 234; Freeman, *R. E. Lee* 3: 189; *People's Press,* December 3, 1863, p.1, col. 5; Neese, *Three Years,* 233–34.

3. John Esten Cooke Diary, November 5, 1863, UVA; William L. Barrier to his father, November 5, 1863, Troxler and Auciello, eds., *Dear Father,* 114; Jeb Stuart to Nannie, November 13, 1863, *The Letters of Major General James E. B. Stuart,* 354–55. For JBG's height, estimated to be 6'3" or 6'4," see Fred Foard to Prof. D. H. Hill, November 23, 1916, Fred C. Foard Papers, NCSA

4. Jeb Stuart to Nannie, November 13, 1863, *The Letters of Major General James E. B. Stuart,* 354–55.

5. Means, "Additional Sketch Sixty-third Regiment (Fifth Cavalry)," *NC Regts.* 3: 583.

6. Coltrane, *Memoirs,* 26; Joseph F. Waring to W. W. Gordon, November 12, 1863, Joseph F. Waring Papers, SHC; Barringer, "Ninth Regiment (First Cavalry)," *NC Regts.* 1: 428; Means, "Additional Sketch Sixty-third Regiment (Fifth Cavalry)," *NC Regts.* 3: 584.

7. Black, *Crumbling Defenses,* 18; Smith, ed., "The Civil War Diary of Peter W. Hairston, Volunteer Aide to Major General Jubal A. Early, November 7–December 4, 1863," *North Carolina Historical Review* LXVII, 77, 79; Means, "Additional Sketch Sixty-third Regiment (Fifth Cavalry)," *NC Regts.* 3: 584–85. This may have been the incident described in Myers, *The Comanches,* 235.

8. Hairston Diary, 83. JBG's brigade may have been camped at Orange Springs at this point (*OR,* vol. 51, pt. 2, 785).

9. *OR,* vol. 29, pt. 1, 898; Freeman, *Lee's Lieutenants* 3: 274; McClellan, *Stuart,* 397–99; Blackford, *War Years,* 242–43.

10. *NC Troops* 2: 7, 44; Cheek, "Additional Sketch Ninth Regiment (First Cavalry)," *NC Regts.* 1: 454. Cheek was appointed captain to rank from May 16, 1861; appointed lieutenant colonel to rank from September 28, 1863; and to colonel to rank from October 17, 1863.

11. *OR,* vol. 29, 820; Graham and Skoch, *Mine Run,* 47; Hairston Diary, 84.

12. Cowles, *CSC,* 21; Cowles, "Life and Services," 13–14; Graham and Skoch, *Mine Run,* 49.

13. *OR,* vol. 29, pt. 1, 898–899; McClellan, *Stuart,* 397–99; Blackford, *War Years,* 242–43; Graham and Skoch, *Mine Run,* 49; Hairston Diary, 84; Freeman, *Lee's Lieutenants* 3: 269–70, 274.

14. Hairston Diary, 84–85; *OR,* vol. 29, pt. 1, 899.

15. *OR,* vol. 29, pt. 1, 899, 901–2, 906. See Freeman, *Lee's Lieutenants* 3: 278–79 for an analysis of Stuart's micromanagement of this situation.

16. Rawle, et. al., *Third Pennsylvania,* 370; *OR,* vol. 29, pt. 1, 899–900, 902, 905; Myers, *The Comanches,* 237.

17. *OR,* vol. 29, pt. 1, 900, 902–3; Garnett, *Riding With Stuart,* 19–20; Means, "Additional Sketch Sixty-third Regiment (Fifth Cavalry)," *NC Regts.* 3: 586.

18. *OR,* vol. 29, pt. 1, 903.

19. *OR,* vol. 29, pt. 1, 900, 902–3; CSRG for James B. Gordon, Microcopy 331, Roll 109.

20. William L. Barrier to his father, December 20, 1863, Troxler and Auciello, *Dear Father,* 116.

21. *OR,* vol. 29, pt. 1, 901, 903; Graham and Skoch, *Mine Run,* 49. Captured Confederates from Hampton's division, including troopers from the 1st and 5th, estimated Rosser's brigade at 1,100 men strong, while JBG's and Young's brigades were thought to be weaker (*OR,* vol. 29, pt. 2, 526).

22. *OR,* vol. 29, pt. 1, 900, 907; Blackford, 243; McClellan, *Stuart,* 398–99; J. W. Biddle to Pa, December 6, 1863, S. S. Biddle Papers, DU; Black, *Crumbling Defenses,* 68. Fitz Lee's command was on duty around Morton's and Raccoon fords between November 26 and December 3.

23. *OR,* vol. 29, pt. 1, 900–903; J. W. Biddle to Pa, December 6, 1863, S. S. Biddle Papers, DU.

24. *Biblical Recorder,* December 3, 1863.

25. Crouch, *Sketches of Wilkes,* 31; *OR,* vol. 29, pt. 1, 900, 901, 903; vol. 51, pt. 2, 792–93. As a result of Cowles's wound, Stuart wrote, "...the cavalry on that road was left without the skillful leadership and direction which otherwise would have been supplied."

26. Rufus Barringer to Victor Barringer, January 27, 1866, Rufus Clay Barringer Papers, SHC; Means, "Additional Sketch Sixty-Third Regiment (Fifth Cavalry)," *NC Regts.* 3: 586; *NC Troops* 2: 5; Roberts, "Additional Sketch Nineteenth Regiment (Second Cavalry)," *NC Regts.* 2: 99–100; *Richmond Examiner,* January 8, 1864, p. 1, col. 6.

27. Joseph F. Waring Diary, January 6, 1864, Joseph F. Waring Papers, SHC.

28. *OR,* vol. 33, p. 19; Coltrane, *Memoirs,* 27. Coltrane identified the general in this incident as Rufus Barringer, but if it occurred when he said it did JBG would have still been brigade commander.

29. *OR,* vol. 29, pt. 1, 460–61; 902–3; George F. Adams to his parents, January 8, 1864, Adams Papers; *NC Troops* 2: 9, 41.

30. Rufus Barringer to Zebulon Vance, September 26, 1863, Zebulon Baird Vance Papers, NCSA; Jeb Stuart to James A. Seddon, February 22, 1863, *The Letters of Major General James E. B. Stuart,* 294–95.

31. Rufus Barringer to Victor Barringer, January 27, 1866, Rufus Clay Barringer Papers, SHC; Barringer, *Natural Bent,* 116. Dr. Paul B. Barringer was Rufus Barringer's son.

32. Freeman, *R. E. Lee* 3: 251–52; Freeman, *Lee's Lieutenants*, 316; *OR*, vol. 33, 1118–19; E. L. Wells, *Hampton and His Cavalry*, 83; Black, *Crumbling Defenses*, 70.

33. *OR*, vol. 33, 1118.

34. *OR*, vol. 33, 1140; CSRG for James B. Gordon, Microcopy 331, Roll 109.

35. *OR*, vol. 29, pt. 2, 862–63; vol. 33, 1100, 1119, 1132, 1143; Black, *Crumbling Defenses*, 18.

36. *OR*, vol. 33, 1100; Means, "Additional Sketch Sixty-Third Regiment (Fifth Cavalry)," *NC Regts.* 3: 586; Thomas, *Bold Dragoon*, 278.

37. C. J. Iredell to Private W. P. Montgomery, December 12, 1863, Presley Carter Person Papers, DU. This furlough extension document shows the chain of command at work. It was approved and forwarded by, in order, Iredell (Company E commander), Barringer (commanding the First N.C.), JBG, Hampton, Stuart, and W. H. Taylor, one of Lee's staff officers.

38. *OR*, vol. 33, 1119; George F. Adams to his parents, January 8, 1864, Adams Papers; Roberts, "Additional Sketch Nineteenth Regiment (Second Cavalry)," *NC Regts.* 2: 99–100. JBG apparently recruited his dismounted men, many of them doubtless members of the 2d Horse, at Orange Court House. Hampton reported 75 to 100 there on January 30 (*OR*, vol. 33, 1132).

39. *OR*, vol. 33, 1088–89, 1100; Rufus Barringer to Victor Barringer, January 27, 1866, Rufus Clay Barringer Papers, SHC. Lee disapproved Hampton's plan to replace JBG's pickets with nearby infantry on the grounds that "small infantry pickets, as proposed, could be easily cut off. Nothing less than two brigades would be safe such a distance from support."

40. Major James Paxton to Brig. Genl. Gordon, April 28, 1864, James B. Gordon Papers, NCSA; Rufus Barringer to Victor Barringer, January 27, 1866, Rufus Clay Barringer Papers, SHC.

41. Galloway, "Sixty-third Regiment (Fifth Cavalry)," *NC Regts.* 3: 536; Means, "Additional Sketch Sixty-Third Regiment (Fifth Cavalry)," *NC Regts.* 3: 586, 591; Major James Paxton to Brig. Genl. Gordon, April 28, 1864, James B. Gordon Papers, NCSA. Norman FitzHugh was the quartermaster of the cavalry (Freeman, *Lee's Lieutenants* 3: 411); see also *OR*, vol. 33, 1100, 1143.

42. Myers, *The Comanches*, 240; Black, *Crumbling Defenses*, 70; JBG to J. M. Pugh, February 4, 1864, James T. Pugh Papers, SHC. The results of this expedition are unclear.

43. Opie, *Rebel Cavalryman*, 183–86.

44. Joseph F. Waring Diary, January 6, January 13, January 22, January 25, 1864, Joseph F. Waring Papers, SHC; Jeb Stuart to James A. Seddon, February 22, 1863; Jeb Stuart to R. H. Chilton, April 9, 1863, both in *The Letters of Major General James E. B. Stuart*, 294–95, 311–12.

45. M. P. Person to Dear Father, January 2, 1864, Presley Carter Person Papers, DU.

46. *Journal of the Congress of the CSA*, 531, 809; Hickerson, *History and Genealogy*, 99. Baker's brigadier general commission, to date from July 23, was also submitted.

47. Fred C. Foard to W.G. Means, March 6, 1917, Fred C. Foard Papers, NCSA.

48. Cooke, *Wearing of the Gray*, 258–59; *OR*, vol. 29, pt. 1, 446; Freeman, *Lee's Lieutenants* 3: 251–52.

49. Galloway, "Sixty-third Regiment (Fifth Cavalry)," *NC Regts.* 3: 537–38; P. M. B. Young to Mrs. Alsop, June 30, 1864, Wynne Family Papers, VHS.

50. *The Land We Love*, October 1866, vol. 1, no. 6, 434.

51. John Esten Cooke Diary, December 15, 1863, UVA.

52. Cooke, *Wearing of the Gray*, 512–13.

53. Roberts, "Additional Sketch Nineteenth Regiment (Second Cavalry)," *NC Regts.* 2: 100; Galloway, "Sixty-third Regiment (Fifth Cavalry)," *NC Regts.* 3: 536.

54. Joseph F. Waring Diary, January 8, 1864, Joseph F. Waring Papers, SHC; Joseph F. Waring to W. W. Gordon, November 12, 1863, Joseph F. Waring Papers, SHC; JBG to Aurelia Halsey, March 26, 1864, James B. Gordon Papers, NCSA.

55. Joseph F. Waring Diary, January 24, January 25, 1864, Joseph F. Waring Papers, SHC; E. L. Wells, *Hampton and His Cavalry*, 124–25; Jeb Stuart to James A. Seddon, February 27, 1864, *The Letters of Major General James E. B. Stuart*, 375.

56. Coltrane, *Memoirs*, 26.

57. Cooke, *Wearing of the Gray*, 512; *CV* 6 (1898): 268. This event took place in the fall of 1863, but the article identifies Rufus Barringer, not JBG, as the brigade commander. Actually, Barringer did not assume command until 1864.

58. George F. Adams to his parents, January 8, 1864, Adams Papers; Freeman, *R. E. Lee* 3: 253, 255–56. Lee refused to allow troops from Florida, Alabama, and Texas to go home unless replacements were sent. Those who did receive furloughs found extensions difficult to obtain, and met with stern discipline if they dawdled.

59. J. E. B. Stuart to his wife, January 27, 1864; J. E. B. Stuart Letters, UVA; "War Notes," February 12, 1864, John Esten Cooke Papers, DU; Wilmington Journal, February 18, 1864.

60. Special Orders Number 44, James B. Gordon Papers, NCSA; J. E. B. Stuart to his wife, January 27, 1864; J. E. B. Stuart Letters, UVA; "War Notes," February 12, 1864, John Esten Cooke Papers, DU.

61. Winkler Interview. As of 1989, the Winkler family still owned two of these beds.

62. *OR*, vol. 33, 201–202; McClellan, *Stuart* 399–405; Barringer, "Ninth Regiment (First Cavalry)," *NC Regts.* 1: 428–29; Cheek, "Additional Sketch Ninth Regiment (First Cavalry)," *NC Regts.* 1: 459–64; Wells, *Hampton and His Cavalry*, 107 ff; *SHSP* 24: 280. See also J. W. Biddle to Pa, March 4, 1864, S. S. Biddle Papers, DU. The Carolinians present were mostly members of the 1st North Carolina Cavalry, along with a few men from the 2d Horse.

63. Hairston Diary, 62–3, 82. The units in question were Major William J. Pfohl's 21st North Carolina and Major Rufus W. Wharton's battalion of North Carolina Sharpshooters, both of Hoke's Brigade.

64. Calvin J. Cowles to Zebulon Vance, September 26, 1863, Zebulon B. Vance Papers, NCSA.

65. Cowles, *CSC*, 21; Cowles, "Life and Services," 14; Winkler Interview.

66. Cowles, *CSC*, 21; Cowles, "Life and Services," 14–15.

67. JBG to his mother, n. d. James B. Gordon Letters, Brown Family Letters, GHM; Wilkes County Will Records, Book 5, p. 388, NCSA. This will may have been written before JBG's furlough. The date cannot be fixed with certainty. It was recorded in the Wilkes County Will Records in August 1864.

68. Hickerson, *Echoes*, 138; Cooke, *Wearing of the Gray*, 530; Elizabeth Maxwell (Alsop) Wynne Diary, April 11, 1864, Wynne Family Papers, VHS. Miss Wynne wrote, "We formed some new acquaintences, amongst whom were Genl. Stuart & Genl. Gordon. The latter I thought very pleasant but did not see enough of him to like or dislike him." See also her entry of May 20, 1864, where she mentioned, "Genl. Gordon and Johnston entertained us very agreeably the whole way up to Taylorsville...." For more on Mrs. Alsop's and Stuart's cavalry, see J. E. B. Stuart to Mrs. Alsop, n. d., and P. M. B. Young to Mrs. Alsop, June 30, 1864, Wynne Family Papers, VHS.

69. Aurelia Halsey to Sarah Brown, December 31, 1864, Aurelia Halsey Correspondence, GHM; JBG to Aurelia Halsey, March 26, 1864, James B. Gordon Papers, NCSA. Aurelia had been born on August 31, 1846 (Meem, ed., *John Gaw Meem*, 4). A Gordon, probably James B. as John was married, apparently frequented parties in Richmond (Harrison, *Recollections*, 178).

70. See brief note of Aurelia Halsey dated March 22, 1864 in the Aurelia Halsey Correspondence, GHM; and card, n.d.,

in James B. Gordon Papers, NCSA. For JBG's camps in Campbell County, see Aurelia Halsey to JBG, March 28, 1864, James B. Gordon Papers, NCSA.
  71. Morris and Foutz, *Lynchburg in the Civil War,* 45; 1850 Population Census, Lynchburg, Campbell County, Virginia, Microcopy 432, Roll 938, P. 83B; 1860 Population Census, Lynchburg, (P.O. Castle Craig) Campbell County, Virginia, Microcopy 653, Roll 1338, page 435; *The News,* March 2, 1939. For more on Don P. Halsey, see *SHSP* 31: 193 ff., and Runge, ed., *Four Years,* 126.
  72. Aurelia Halsey to James B. Gordon, April 27, 1864, James B. Gordon Papers, NCSA.
  73. JBG to Aurelia Halsey, March 26, 1864, James B. Gordon Papers, NCSA; Aurelia Halsey to JBG, March 28, 1864, James B. Gordon Papers, NCSA. Aurelia referred to a "General I." in her letter, and feared that he considered her "inconsistent." In her April 27 letter to JBG (James B. Gordon Papers, NCSA), she recorded how a General Williams called and said that "reports" about her had alarmed Aurelia's friends in his command.
  74. Aurelia Halsey to Sarah Brown, June 28, 1864; Aurelia Halsey to James B. Gordon, April 6, 1864, both in Aurelia Halsey Correspondence, GHM.
  75. Aurelia Halsey to JBG, April 20, 1864, Aurelia Halsey Correspondence, GHM. According to this letter, Aurelia's confirmation had taken place on April 20, 1863.
  76. Jones, *Christ in the Camp,* 341; *Biblical Recorder,* January 16, 1864.
  77. Aurelia Halsey to Sarah Brown, June 28, 1864, Aurelia Halsey Correspondence, GHM. See also JBG to Aurelia Halsey, March 26, 1864, James B. Gordon Papers, NCSA.
  78. Williams, ed., Mary B. Chesnut, *A Diary From Dixie,* 394. There is a possibility that the Gordon Mrs. Chesnut saw was John B. Gordon instead of James B. Gordon. However, the evidence presented by Cowles, and inferred from the dates of JBG's furloughs, makes it likely that JBG was present. John Gordon was probably at his headquarters along the Rapidan near Clark's Mountain (Gordon, *Reminiscences of the Civil War,* 229).
  79. Cowles, *CSC,* 22; Cowles, "Life and Services," 16; Ramage, *Rebel Raider,* 206; Freeman, *R. E. Lee* 3: 261. Lee and Davis met on Monday, March 14. Another source, *Daily Confederate,* May 25, 1864, p. 1, cols. 1–2, recorded that Stuart and JBG were called together to Richmond to welcome Morgan "and make the trio of cavalry chieftains of the South."
  80. Cowles, *CSC,* 22; Cowles, "Life and Services," 16–17. Cowles's otherwise reliable work erroneously claimed that at this point JBG had already arranged to be married.
  81. J. W. Biddle to Pa, December 1, 1863, S. S. Biddle Papers, DU; "Glimpses of Army Life in 1864," *SHSP* 18: 408.
  82. Freeman, *R. E. Lee* 3: 223; Tucker, *Zeb Vance,* 337–38.
  83. "Glimpses of Army Life in 1864," *SHSP* 18: 407–408; JBG to Aurelia Halsey, March 26, 1864, James B. Gordon Papers, NCSA.
  84. Joseph F. Waring Diary, April 4, 1864, Joseph F. Waring Papers, SHC; J. W. Biddle to Pa, April 11, 1864, S. S. Biddle Papers, DU. For more details on Vance's visit, see Tucker, *Zeb Vance,* 337 ff.
  85. Leave of Absence Request, April 14, 1864, Cadwallader J. Iredell Papers, SHC; H. B. McClellan to JBG, April 21, 1864, James B. Gordon Papers, NCSA.
  86. Joseph F. Waring Diary, April 4, April 15, April 16, April 25, May 3, 1864; Jeb Stuart to JBG, April 13, 1864, Jeb Stuart Letter, GHM. Concerning JBG's advice, Waring wrote, "I believe not in that way of doing."
  87. M. P. Person to Sam, March 16, 1864, Presley Carter Person Papers, DU.
  88. Roberts, "Additional Sketch Nineteenth Regiment (Second Cavalry)," *NC Regts.* 2: 99–100; *OR,* vol. 36, pt. 1, 1027; Jeb Stuart to JBG, April 13, 1864, Jeb Stuart Letter, GHM.
  89. Jeb Stuart to JBG, April 13, 1864, Jeb Stuart Letter, GHM.
  90. *OR,* vol. 33, 1306; vol. 36, pt. 2, 958; Rufus Barringer to Victor Barringer, January 27, 1866, Rufus Clay Barringer Papers, SHC; W. P. Shaw, "Fifty-ninth Regiment (Fourth Cavalry)," *NC Regts.* 3: 465–66.
  91. *NC Regts.* 2: 773; *OR,* vol. 36, pt. 2, 940; vol. 33, 1306; Rufus Barringer to Zeb Vance, May 4, 1864, Zeb Vance Papers, NCSA; Barringer, "Ninth Regiment (First Cavalry)," *NC Regts.* 1: 429.
  92. Galloway, "Sixty-third Regiment (Fifth Cavalry)," *NC Regts.* 3: 536; Means, "Additional Sketch Sixty-Third Regiment (Fifth Cavalry)," *NC Regts.* 3: 586, 591; *OR,* vol. 36, pt. 2, 940.
  93. Freeman, *R. E. Lee* 3: 217, 262, 262, n. 17; Freeman, *Lee's Lieutenants* 3: 411; *CMH* 4: 627. Lee's rank was issued as of April 23, 1864.
  94. J. E. B. Stuart to Samuel Cooper, March 23, 1864; J. E. B. Stuart to James A. Seddon, May 2, 1864, *The Letters of Major General James E. B. Stuart,* 377, 387–89; Black, *Crumbling Defenses,* 18.
  95. *OR,* vol. 36, pt. 2, 954.
  96. Chesnut, *Diary,* 395; Thomas, *Bold Dragoon,* 281; *OR,* vol. 36, pt. 2, 953. In a dispatch dated May 5, Hampton wrote: "One North Carolina regiment here [at Milford], one on picket, one [the Fifth] marching from Richmond."
  97. Joseph F. Waring Diary, May 5, 1864, Joseph F. Waring Papers, SHC.
  98. *OR,* vol. 36, pt. 1, 1027; Freeman, *Lee's Lieutenants* 3: 339, 411.
  99. JBG to Aurelia Halsey, March 26, 1864, James B. Gordon Papers, NCSA.
  100. Aurelia Halsey to JBG, April 27, 1864, James B. Gordon Papers, NCSA.
  101. Ibid. JBG had planned to visit Aurelia on April 26.

Chapter 13

  1. *Daily Confederate,* May 25, 1864, p. 1, cols. 1–2. This article, entitled "Gen. James B. Gordon, In Memoriam," was a lengthy obituary signed by "M. V. M."
  2. Hopkins, *Bull Run to Appomattox,* 143; Humphreys, *Virginia Campaign,* 2; George F. Adams to his parents, January 8, 1864, Adams Papers, copy in the author's possession.
  3. Freeman, *Lee's Lieutenants* 3: 348.
  4. Humphreys, *Virginia Campaign,* 18.
  5. Aurelia Halsey to JBG, April 27, 1864, James B. Gordon Papers, NCSA.
  6. Cowles, *CSC,* 22; Cowles, "Life and Services," 17; *OR,* vol. 36, pt. 2, 952–53; *NC Troops,* vol. 2, 5.
  7. *OR,* vol. 51, pt. 2, 888; Rhea, *Wilderness,* 80. Only about two hundred of the 1st's troopers were actually picketing the fords (*The Daily Confederate,* February 22, 1865.)
  8. "Nicholas P. Tredenick," *CV* 14: 132; *The Daily Confederate,* February 22, 1865; *OR,* vol. 51, pt. 2, 888; McClellan, *Stuart,* 406.
  9. William L. Barrier to his father, May 8, 1864, Troxler and Auciello, eds., *Dear Father,* 122; Cadwallader J. Iredell to Mattie, May 7, 1864, Cadwallader J. Iredell Papers, SHC.
  10. J. D. Ferguson, Entry for May 4, "[Diary] Memoranda of the itinerary and operations of Major General Fitz Lee's Cavalry Division of the Army of Northern Virginia from May 4th to October 1864, inclusive," Munford-Ellis Family Papers, DU. Ferguson was major and assistant adjutant general of Lee's Division.
  11. McClellan, *Stuart,* 407; *OR,* vol. 36, pt. 2, 952, 954–55, 1028; Rhea, *Wilderness,* 123; Freeman, *Lee's Lieutenants* 3: 349–50. Tredenick captured a horse from a Yankee this day ("Nicholas P. Tredenick," *CV* 14: 132).
  12. *OR,* vol. 36, pt. 2, 952, 955, 1028; *Daily Confederate,* February 22, 1865.
  13. *OR,* vol. 36, pt. 2, 961. Legend has it that on the move of Confederate forces from Mine Run to Spotsylvania Courthouse, JBG's brigade made a sixty-six mile trip in twenty-

three hours without rest or sleep. They reached Spotsylvania about sunset and drove the Federals before sleeping (Crouch, *Sketches of Wilkes*, 46).

14. *OR*, vol. 36, pt. 2, 961–62; Freeman, *Lee's Lieutenants* 3: 368–72; Rhea, *Wilderness*, 404–405, 409.

15. Humphreys, *Virginia Campaign*, 52; Matter, *If It Takes All Summer*, 5.

16. Matter, *If It Takes All Summer*, 36–37, 41.

17. Garnett, *Riding With Stuart*, 56–57; Matter, *If It Takes All Summer*, 36–37, 41.

18. Joseph F. Waring Diary, May 7, 1864, Joseph F. Waring Papers, SHC.

19. Galloway, "Sixty-third Regiment (Fifth Cavalry)," *NC Regts*. 3: 536; Matter, *If It Takes All Summer*, 36–37, 41; *The Daily Confederate*, February 22, 1865. See Sheridan's report, *OR*, vol. 36, pt. 2, 515–16.

20. Garnett, *Riding With Stuart*, 57.

21. *OR*, vol. 36, pt. 2, 970–71; vol. 51, pt. 2, 898.

22. Freeman, *Lee's Lieutenants* 3: 377–79; *OR*, vol. 36, pt. 2, 968; Matter, *If It Takes All Summer*, 25, 28. JBG received official orders to join Fitz Lee's brigade while near White Hall on May 8 (Means, "Additional Sketch Sixty-Third Regiment [Fifth Cavalry]," *NC Regts*. 3: 595).

23. Rufus C. Barringer to V. C. Barringer, January 27, 1866, Rufus Clay Barringer Papers, SHC.

24. Noble J. Brooks Diary, May 8, 1864, Noble J. Brooks Papers, SHC.

25. McClellan, *Stuart*, 407–409.

26. Coltrane, *Memoirs*, 28; Means, "Additional Sketch Sixty-Third Regiment (Fifth Cavalry)," *NC Regts*. 3: 594; Crouch, *Sketches of Wilkes*, 46; *The Daily Confederate*, February 22, 1865. Means recalled the death here of Company F's Willis Miller. Wrote Means: "And one of the most touching scenes I ever witnessed was Captain John R. Erwin writing next morning to the boy's father of his death."

27. "Nicholas P. Tredenick," *CV* 14: 132.

28. Matter, *If It Takes All Summer*, 82; Brooks, *Butler and His Cavalry*, 327. According to Brooks, "Hold your ground there, you damned scoundrels," was one of Young's mildest expressions.

29. *SHSP* 16: 452; *OR*, vol. 36, pt. 1, 787; Phil Sheridan, *Memoirs*, 154–55; Matter, *If It Takes All Summer*, 81; Rodenbough, "Sheridan's Richmond Raid," *B&L* 4: 189; *OR*, vol. 36, pt. 1, 789.

30. *OR*, vol. 36, pt. 1, 789; Sheridan, *Memoirs*, 155.

31. *OR*, pt. 1, vol. 36, pt. 1, 787; McMahon, "From Gettysburg to the Coming of Grant," *B&L* 4: 94. Merritt assumed command of the First Division on May 7.

32. McClellan, *Stuart*, 410; *OR*, vol. 36, pt. 1, 209, 776, 789; vol. 51, pt. 2, 905–906. Field returns for June 1 listed 12,420 Federal cavalrymen present for duty in Sheridan's Cavalry Corps. A year after the fact, Sheridan claimed ten thousand effectives (*OR*, pt. 1, vol. 36, pt. 1, 787).

33. McClellan, *Stuart*, 410; E. P. Alexander, *Fighting For The Confederacy*, 374; Nichols, *Fitz Lee*, 67; *Daily Confederate*, May 23, 1864, p. 2, col. 4, and February 22, 1865; *CV* 19 (1911) 575–76.

34. Longacre, *Mounted Raids*, 263.

35. McClellan, *Stuart*, 409–10; *OR*, vol. 36, pt. 1, 789, 853, 857.

36. *OR*, vol. 36, pt. 1, 776–77, 789–90; *OR*, vol. 51, pt. 2, 908; William Campbell, "Autobiographical Sketch," *William and Mary College Quarterly Historical Magazine*, April 1929, 105.

37. *Daily Confederate*, May 23, 1864, p. 2, col. 4; February 22, 1865. The squadron from the 1st reportedly captured some three hundred men, as well as much arms and equipment, during their detached duty.

38. McClellan, *Stuart*, 410; Judith McGuire, *Diary of a Southern Refugee*, 269–70, in Davis, *Stuart*, 388. Garnett, *Riding With Stuart*, 62, recounts this story as well but records Stuart's words a bit differently. See also J. D. Ferguson Diary, Entry for May 9, Munford-Ellis Family Papers, DU. McClellan said Stuart had between four and five thousand men. Barringer, in "Ninth Regiment (First Cavalry)," *NC Regts*. 1: 429, guessed about four thousand men.

39. Garnett, *Riding With Stuart*, 62; McClellan, *Stuart*, 410; *OR*, vol. 36, pt. 1, 789–90.

40. Garnett, *Riding With Stuart*, 62.

41. Ibid., 62–3. Garnett wrote that this meeting occurred early on May 10, but in all likelihood it took place in the evening of May 9.

42. *OR*, vol. 36, pt. 1, 777, 790, 817, 826, 853; vol. 51, pt. 2, 909, 910; Longacre, *Mounted Raids*, 267. The prisoners had been captured in the Wilderness.

43. *OR*, vol. 36, pt. 1, 789–90, 853.

44. Davis, *Stuart*, 389; *Daily Confederate*, May 23, 1864, p. 2, col. 4, and February 22, 1865; Rodenbough, "Sheridan's Richmond Raid," *B&L* 4: 189.

45. *Daily Confederate*, May 23, 1864, p. 2, col. 4; *OR*, vol. 36, pt. 1, 817; Miller, "Yellow Tavern," *Civil War History* 2: 64.

46. *OR*, vol. 36, pt. 1, 790, 817, 853, 878–79.

47. Coltrane, *Memoirs*, 29.

48. *OR*, vol. 51, pt. 2, 911.

49. *OR*, vol. 51, pt. 2, 911; Longacre, *Mounted Raids*, 265. The Mountain Road was also called Three Notch Road or the Louisa Road.

50. McClellan, *Stuart*, 410–11; Series I, vol. 51, pt. 2, 913; Andrew Reid Venable to Fitz Lee, June 7, 1888, VHS.

51. Eggleston, *Rebel's Recollections*, 123.

52. McClellan, *Stuart*, 410; Freeman, *Lee's Lieutenants* 3: 416; Andrew Reid Venable to Fitz Lee, June 7, 1888, VHS. Venable had recently joined Stuart's staff as assistant inspector general.

53. Opie, *Rebel Cavalryman*, 90–91. Opie used the saying when describing how Stuart sent him racing cross-country at top speed to deliver some orders. "Up hill and down, over fences and ditches, I did go 'a-kiting,' sure enough, never once halting or drawing reign...."

54. *OR*, vol. 36, pt. 1, 790; vol. 51, pt. 2, 912; *CV* 19 (1911) 575–76.

55. *OR*, vol. 51, pt. 2, 913.

56. *OR*, vol. 36, pt. 1, 790.

57. McClellan, *Stuart*, 411; *OR*, vol. 51, pt. 2, 914, 912; Andrew Reid Venable to Fitz Lee, June 7, 1888, VHS.

58. "Civil War Experiences of Leiper M. Robinson," typescript copy, VHS; Cowles, *CSC*, 22; Cowles, "Life and Services," 18; Andrew Reid Venable to Fitz Lee, June 7, 1888, VHS. Venable does not mention the dispatch to JBG, but Cowles was with JBG and can be counted as a reliable witness on this point. However, the complete text of Stuart's dispatch to JBG has not survived.

59. *SHSP* 29: 227–29.

60. McClellan, *Stuart*, 411.

61. *OR*, vol. 51, pt. 2, 916; Jeb Stuart to Braxton Bragg, May 11, 1864, in *The Letters of Major General James E. B. Stuart*, 391.

62. Cheek, "Additional Sketch Ninth Regiment (First Cavalry)," *NC Regts*. 1: 465; Galloway, "Sixty-third Regiment (Fifth Cavalry)," *NC Regts*. 3: 537; Coltrane, *Memoirs*, 29.

63. *OR*, vol. 36, pt. 1, 790, 857; vol. 51, pt. 2, 917; Longacre, *Mounted Raids*, 270; McClellan, Stuart, 411.

64. *OR*, vol. 36, pt. 1, 790, 857. Davies reported that he marched all night, rejoined the column and then crossed the railroad at the junction of the Brook Road, which was near Allen's Station.

65. Jeb Stuart to Braxton Bragg, May 11, 1864, in *The Letters of Major General James E. B. Stuart*, 392.

66. McClellan, *Stuart*, 411.

67. *OR*, vol. 51, pt. 2, 918; *CV* 39 (1939) 98–100; Braxton Bragg to J. B. Sale, May 11, 1864, in *The Letters of Major General James E. B. Stuart*, 393; McClellan, *Stuart*, 412; *SHSP* 29: 228–229.

68. Cheek, "Additional Sketch Ninth Regiment (First Cavalry)," *NC Regts*. 1: 465.

69. Means, "Additional Sketch Sixty-third Regiment (Fifth Cavalry)," *NC Regts.* 3: 596–97.
70. Means, "Additional Sketch Sixty-third Regiment (Fifth Cavalry)," *NC Regts.* 3: 596–97; *OR*, vol. 36, pt. 1, 864.
71. Cheek, "Additional Sketch Ninth Regiment (First Cavalry)," *NC Regts.* 1: 465.
72. Means, "Additional Sketch Sixty-third Regiment (Fifth Cavalry)," *NC Regts.* 3: 597; *Daily Confederate,* May 23, 1864, p. 2, col. 4.
73. Cheek, "Additional Sketch Ninth Regiment (First Cavalry)," *NC Regts.* 1: 465; *OR*, vol. 36, pt. 1, 864.
74. Cheek, "Additional Sketch Ninth Regiment (First Cavalry)," *NC Regts.* 1: 465. The Daily Confederate of February 22, 1865 places this fight along the Fredericksburg Railroad, not far from Ten Mile Branch.
75. Roberts, "Additional Sketch Nineteenth Regiment (Second Cavalry)," *NC Regts.* 2: 100–101; *NC Troops* 2: 104. Roberts was not specific as to the battle this anecdote applies to, but *NC Troops* dates Worth's death on May 11, the same date as the fight described in the text. The *Daily Confederate* of May 23, 1864, p. 2, col. 4, which is somewhat garbled in chronology, may also refer to this attack.
76. Cheek, "Additional Sketch Ninth Regiment (First Cavalry)," *NC Regts.* 1: 465–66; *NC Troops* 2: 7. After the war, Cheek added, he met a Federal officer who saw this fight and stated that the 1st North Carolina was considered the best Confederate regiment of cavalry.
77. Means, "Additional Sketch Sixty-third Regiment (Fifth Cavalry)," *NC Regts.* 3: 597–98.
78. Galloway, "Sixty-third Regiment (Fifth Cavalry)," *NC Regts.* 3: 537.
79. Samuel A. Ashe, et al., eds., *Biographical History* 1: 251. The writer of this article incorrectly recorded that Kerr Craige's horse troubles occurred on May 8.
80. Means, "Additional Sketch Sixty-third Regiment (Fifth Cavalry)," *NC Regts.* 3: 600–601; *Daily Confederate,* May 23, 1864, p. 2, col. 4.
81. McClellan, *Stuart,* 412–13; Freeman, *Lee's Lieutenants* 3: 420; Andrew Reid Venable to Fitz Lee, June 7, 1888, VHS; *CV* 17 (1909): 76–77.
82. Longacre, *Mounted Raids,* 271; *OR*, vol. 36, pt. 1, 813. For the time, see Freeman, *Lee's Lieutenants* 3: 420, n. 38.
83. "Civil War Experiences of Leiper M. Robinson," typescript copy, VHS.
84. McClellan, *Stuart,* 412; *OR*, vol. 36, pt. 1, 818; "Civil War Experiences of Leiper M. Robinson," typescript copy, VHS.
85. Andrew Reid Venable to Fitz Lee, June 7, 1888, VHS; McClellan, *Stuart,* 412.
86. *OR*, vol. 36, pt. 1, 834.
87. McClellan, *Stuart,* 412–13. See also copies of dispatches from Stuart to Bragg in Davis, *Stuart,* 398–99. At the time, fourteen infantry brigades of varying sizes were posted at Drewry's Bluff, Richmond, and Petersburg. One cavalry brigade and an abundance of artillery was also available (Freeman, *R. E. Lee* 3: 333).
88. Garnett, *Riding With Stuart,* 68.
89. William P. Roberts, "Additional Sketch Nineteenth Regiment (Second Cavalry)," *NC Regts.,* vol. 2, 100; Thomas F. Hickerson, *Echoes of Happy Valley,* 130; Cowles, *CSC,* 23; Cowles, "Life and Services," 18; *CV* 19 (1911) 575–76. Cowles wrote that Stuart made this comment "during a lull in the action which preceded the final struggle in which Stuart fell, on the receipt of a message from Gordon...." The *CV* account of Garnett solidifies this. "During the battle, he [Stuart] deplored the absence of Gordon's North Carolina brigade, who were attacking Sheridan's rear far away on the Mountain Road."
90. Jeb Stuart to Braxton Bragg, May 11, 1864, in *The Letters of Major General James E. B. Stuart,* 394.
91. Von Borcke, *Memoirs,* 2: 311; *CV* 17 (1909): 76–77.
92. *OR*, vol. 36, pt. 1, 790, 818, 879.

93. *OR*, vol. 36, pt. 1, 818; *CV* 17 (1909): 76–77; Andrew Reid Venable to Fitz Lee, June 7, 1888, VHS; McClellan, *Stuart,* 413–14; *CV* 19 (1911): 531.
94. McClellan, *Stuart,* 415; *OR*, vol. 36, pt. 1, 818, 777, 791; vol. 51, pt. 2, 923; *CV* 17 (1909): 76–77.
95. "Civil War Experiences of Leiper M. Robinson," typescript copy, VHS; *SHSP* 36: 121–24.
96. "Civil War Experiences of Leiper M. Robinson," typescript copy, VHS; *OR*, vol. 36, pt. 1, 777, 791, 862.
97. *OR*, vol. 36, pt. 1, 853, 791; *Richmond Dispatch,* May 12, 1864, p. 1, col. 2.
98. *OR*, vol. 36, pt. 1, 777, 791.
99. *SHSP* 16: 453; Von Borcke, *Memoirs,* 2: 308.
100. *OR*, vol. 36, pt. 1, 791, 879; "Brook Church Fight," *SHSP* 29: 139; Longacre, *Mounted Raids,* 276; Pitts, "Landmarks," 16.
101. *OR*, vol. 36, pt. 1, 819.
102. Longacre, *Mounted Raids,* 277–80; *OR*, vol. 36, pt. 1, 878–79, 791; Pitts, "Landmarks," 16.
103. Rodenbough, "Sheridan's Richmond Raid," *B&L* 4: 188; Longacre, *Mounted Raids,* 278–79.
104. *Richmond Examiner,* May 13, 1864, p. 1, col. 1; May 14, 1864, p. 1, col. 4; Pitts, "Landmarks," 12. According to Pitts, Brook Church, which stood on the southwest corner of Brook Road and the Military Road (today's Azalea Avenue), was accidentally burned by Confederate troops in July 1864.
105. Means, "Additional Sketch Sixty-third Regiment (Fifth Cavalry)," *NC Regts.* 3: 603–604; "Brook Church Fight," *SHSP* 29: 139; Crouch, *Sketches of Wilkes,* 32; *OR*, vol. 36, pt. 1, 854. The account by Means and the article in *SHSP* are, except for a few word changes, almost identical, although the *SHSP* article does not cite Means. The text quotes the earlier *NC Regts.* article.
106. Cowles, *CSC,* 21, 23; Cowles, "Life and Services," 15, 19; *OR*, vol. 36, pt. 1, 854.
107. Coltrane, *Memoirs,* 29. Coltrane wrote: "We heard very soon that he [Stuart] was wounded, but news of his death didn't reach us for several days."
108. Means, "Additional Sketch Sixty-third Regiment (Fifth Cavalry)," *NC Regts.* 3: 602–603; "Brook Church Fight," *SHSP* 29: 140.
109. Means, "Additional Sketch Sixty-third Regiment (Fifth Cavalry)," *NC Regts.* 3: 602–603; "Brook Church Fight," *SHSP* 29: 140; *The Land We Love,* vol. 2, no. 3, 223. A third account, Galloway, "Sixty-third Regiment (Fifth Cavalry)," *NC Regts.* 3: 537, recorded that JBG was reconnoitering near a bridge when he was wounded. See also Coltrane, *Memoirs,* 30, for an abbreviated version of Means's account.
110. *Richmond Dispatch,* May 13, 1864, p. 1, col. 1; *OR*, vol. 36, pt. 1, 854, 791. The Virginia regiments were the 32d, the 19th, and probably the 14th, although the cited newspaper source is unclear. The 19th arrived at noon and attempted to relieve the 14th, but the latter regiment declined the offer. These units were probably part of General Archibald Gracie's brigade (McClellan, *Stuart,* 416).
111. Means, "Additional Sketch Sixty-third Regiment (Fifth Cavalry)," *NC Regts.* 3: 603; "Brook Church Fight," *SHSP* 29: 140; *Daily Confederate,* May 23, 1864, p. 2, col. 4. See also J. D. Ferguson Diary, Entry for May 13, Munford-Ellis Family Papers, DU.
112. *Daily Dispatch,* May 13, 1864, p. 1, col. 1; *OR*, vol. 36, pt. 1, 791.
113. *Richmond Examiner,* May 14, 1864, p. 1, col. 1; *OR*, vol. 36, pt. 1, 791.
114. *The Land We Love,* vol. 2, no. 3, 223.
115. *CV* 19 (1911): 575–76; Garnett, *Riding With Stuart,* 72.
116. Waitt, *Confederate Military Hospitals,* 11–12; *Richmond Examiner,* May 13 1864, p. 3, col. 3. For Read's full name, see various references in *Medical and Surgical History of the Civil War,* among them vol. 7: 54, 98–99, 11: 69, 101,

111, 116, 118–19, 391. This building, wrote Waitt, stood until the Richmond Female Institute merged with the University of Richmond in 1914. It was replaced — again, ironically for the education-minded JBG — by the Virginia Mechanics Institute Building at 1000 E. Marshall Street.

117. M. J. Derlosset to Col. Brown, May 25, 1864, copy furnished by J. Jay Anderson. The condyle is a rounded process at the end of the bone, forming a ball and socket joint with the hollow part of another bone.

118. *Richmond Dispatch,* May 13, 1864, p. 1, col. 1; Richmond Examiner, May 13, 1864, p. 3, col. 3; *Richmond Whig,* May 13, 1864, p. 1, col. 3; p. 1, col. 1.

119. Aurelia Halsey to JBG, May 16, 1864, James B. Gordon Papers, NCSA.

120. Aurelia Halsey to Sarah Brown, June 28, 1864, Aurelia Halsey Correspondence, GHM; M. J. Derlosset to Col. Brown, May 25, 1864, copy furnished by J. Jay Anderson; Daily Dispatch, May 20, 1864, p. 1, col. 5; *The Medical and Surgical History of the Civil War* 6: 664.

121. R. Gibbon to Sarah Brown, May 18, 1864, James B. Gordon Papers, NCSA.

122. M. J. Derlosset to Col. Brown, May 25, 1864, copy furnished by J. Jay Anderson.

123. M. J. Derlosset to Col. Brown, May 25, 1864, copy furnished by J. Jay Anderson; *The Medical and Surgical History of the Civil War* 6: 664, 663; *Dorland's Medical Dictionary,* 460; *Good Housekeeping Guide,* 328. Derlosset wrote JBG realized his condition "about 12 hours before he died."

124. R. Gibbon to Sarah Brown, May 18, 1864, James B. Gordon Papers, NCSA.

125. *Richmond Examiner,* May 19, 1864, p. 1, col. 3; *The Medical and Surgical History of the Civil War* 10: 881; R. Gibbon to Sarah Brown, May 18, 1864, James B. Gordon Papers, NCSA. For Barrier, who died on May 16, in Richmond, see Mrs. S. I. Epps to M. Barrier, May 17, 1864, Troxler and Auciello, eds., *Dear Father,* 123.

126. R. Gibbon to Sarah Brown, May 18, 1864, James B. Gordon Papers, NCSA; *Richmond Examiner,* May 20, 1864, p. 1, col. 2; *Richmond Dispatch,* May 20. 1864, p. 1, col. 5; Winkler Interview; *The Medical and Surgical History of the Civil War* 6: 666.

127. Fred Foard to Prof. D. H. Hill, November 23, 1916, Fred C. Foard Papers, NCSA; R. Gibbon to Sarah Brown, May 18, 1864, James B. Gordon Papers, NCSA. For references to Dr. Gibson, see *The Medical and Surgical History of the Civil War* 10: 578, 581, 601.

128. R. Gibbon to Sarah Brown, May 18, 1864, James B. Gordon Papers, NCSA.

129. Elizabeth Maxwell (Alsop) Wynne Diary, May 20, 1864, Wynne Family Papers, VHS. Mrs. Wynne added, "Genl. Gordon too has 'fought his last battle,' he was a gallant officer, but I fear, a worldly man."

130. R. Gibbon to Sarah Brown, May 18, 1864, James B. Gordon Papers, NCSA; Elizabeth Maxwell (Alsop) Wynne Diary, May 20, 1864, Wynne Family Papers, VHS. Miss Alsop wrote, "I do not know when I have felt more about the death of one with whom I was so little acquainted. There is something so lonely, so touching in him laying himself down to die, just as if he was going to sleep."

Conclusion

1. *Richmond Dispatch,* May 20, 1864, p. 1, col. 5; *Richmond Examiner,* May 20, 1864, p. 1, col. 2; Finley, "Address on James B. Gordon," 13. Osborne was "a brother of Judge Frank Osborne of Charlotte." Both Osborne and Craige were "intimate friends" of JBG.

2. Aurelia Halsey to Sarah Brown, June 28, 1864, Aurelia Halsey Correspondence, GHM; *Daily Confederate,* May 25, 1864, p. 1, cols. 1–2; Joseph F. Waring Diary, May 19, 1864, May 11, 1864, Joseph F. Waring Papers, SHC.

3. *Richmond Whig,* May 20, 1864, p. 1, col. 2; CSRG for James B. Gordon, Microcopy 331, Roll 109. Many of JBG's original army comrades did survive the war. Of the one hundred or so original members of the Wilkes Valley Guards, about forty were still alive in 1895 (*The Chronicle,* September 19, 1895, p. 1, col. 2).

4. Fred Foard to Prof. D. H. Hill, November 23, 1916, Fred C. Foard Papers, NCSA. There is no record that JBG ever was promoted to major general.

5. Fred Foard to Prof. D. H. Hill, November 23, 1916, Fred C. Foard Papers, NCSA; Hickerson, *Echoes,* 138; Hickerson, *History and Genealogy,* 20. According to a letter from Burton Craige, Kerr Craige's son, to Hickerson, JBG's sword was afterward stolen by "General Clingman's crowd" and lost to history.

6. Arthur Cowles to his mother, May 24, 1864, Calvin J. Cowles Papers, SHC; *Carolina Watchman,* May 23, 1864, p. 2 col. 5. In Hillsboro Arthur Cowles wrote, "I regret the death of Gen Gordon who distinguished himself before his death by his gallant conduct on the field His body was expected to pass through here on 22 I never learned whether it did so or not." Burton Craige died on December 30, 1875 (Jethro Rumple, *Rowan County,* 243).

7. Bess Gordon Finley Grier MS, copy in author's possession.

8. Zebulon Vance(?) to Mrs. Sarah Brown, Brown Family Letters, July 8, 1864, GHM.

9. Wilkes County Estate Records, 1777–1945, entries for J. B. Gordon, 1878 and 1864, NCSA. At least three hundred acres of the disputed land was located along Hunting Creek in Wilkes County.

10. "General James B. Gordon's Monument." Unpublished MS, James Gordon Hackett Papers, DU.

11. Winkler Interview; Hartley, "War's Last Cavalry Raid," 19–20; Phillips, *The Last Ninety Days,* 197.

12. Calvin J. Cowles to W. J. Palmer, October 1, 1870, Calvin J. Cowles Papers, NCSA.

13. *OR,* vol. 36, pt. 2, 931; Kerr Craige Address, Ms., n.d., copy provided by Craige's grandson, Mr. Archibald Craige, Keswick, Va.; Cowles, *CSC,* 23; Cowles, "Life and Services," 19. See also Special Orders No. 118, May 21, 1864, Pierce M. B. Young Collection, GDAH.

14. Carr, "The Gordon-Barringer Brigade," *NC Regts.* 4: 581–82; Rufus C. Barringer to V. C. Barringer, January 27, 1866, Rufus Clay Barringer Papers, SHC. Later promoted to major general, Young helped defend against Sherman's march to Savannah and then through the Carolinas. After the war, he served in Congress and as a delegate to several Democratic national conventions. He also was appointed commissioner to the Paris exposition and to the West Point Board of Visitors. Young was later sent to St. Petersburg, Russia as counsel-general, and was appointed minister to Guatemala and Honduras. He died in 1896 (*CMH* 7: 459–60; Boatner, *Dictionary,* 953).

15. James B. Gordon letters, CSR for Rufus Barringer, Microcopy 270, Roll 1.

16. "Battle At Reams Station," *SHSP* 19: 113 ff.; Cheek, "Additional Sketch Ninth Regiment (First Cavalry)," *NC Regts.* 1: 470; *OR,* vol. 51, pt. 2, 962.

17. M. P. Person to Sallie, June 9, 1864, Presley Carter Person Papers, DU.

18. Cheek, "Additional Sketch Ninth Regiment (First Cavalry)," *NC Regts.* 1: 476; Rufus Barringer to V. C. Barringer, January 27, 1866, Rufus Clay Barringer Papers, SHC; Roberts, "Additional Sketch Nineteenth Regiment (Second Cavalry)," *NC Regts.* 2: 107.

19. Coltrane, *Memoirs,* 41–42; Rufus Barringer to V. C. Barringer, January 27, 1866, Rufus Clay Barringer Papers, SHC; Rufus Barringer to Chiswell Dabney, May 8, 1865, Saunders Family Papers, VHS; Rufus Barringer Journal, April 1, 1865, Rufus C. Barringer Papers, SHC.

20. The story of the Halsey family can be pieced together from the *Lynchburg Virginian,* August 23, 1864, p. 1, col. 4; *Lynchburg News,* January 2, 1883, from Lynchburg, Virginia

Obituaries Clippings, Vol. 6, Jones Memorial Library, Lynchburg; Yancey, *Lynchburg And Its Neighbors,* 123–24; *The News,* March 2, 1939; Krick, *Lee's Colonels,* 156. Seth, Aurelia's father, died in 1875. Alex Halsey, one of Aurelia's brothers, died in July 1864, near Leetown, at the Battle of Smithfield while commanding Company I of the 21st Virginia Cavalry. Don, another brother, was a post-war lawyer who died at forty-eight on New Year's Day 1883 from a stroke. Stephen, another brother, was wounded at Woodstock on October 9, 1864 and twice at the Battle of Lynchburg. He survived the war and his brothers and sister. Living until the age of ninety-five, he worked as a bander and in tobacco. Still called major, he died in 1939.

21. *Lynchburg Virginian,* April 24, 1873, p. 3, col. 2; J. Lawrence Meem, ed., *John Gaw Meem and His Descendants,* 4.

22. Meem, ed., *John Gaw Meem and His Descendants,* 4.

23. *Lynchburg Virginian,* August 24, 1883, p. 3. cols. 1–2; August 13, 1883, p. 3, col. 1; August 14, 1883, p. 3, col. 3. After Aurelia's death, Meem sold Mount Airy and moved to Washington, D. C., where he worked for the Treasury Department. An engineer by trade, he is said to have drawn the plans and supervised the construction of the Bureau of Engraving and Printing. Meem also worked as an auditor in the War Department until his death in 1908 (John Meem Payne, "Recollections of Mount Airy," and James C. Meem II, "Brief Notes on Some Meem Ancestors — A Listing of Descendants of John Gaw Meem II," both in Meem, *John Gaw Meem and His Descendants,* 4).

24. H. A. Brown to Steuart, February 18, 1864, Hamilton Brown Letters, MC; "Colonel Hamilton Allen Brown," *CSC* 2–3; Hickerson, *Echoes,* 138. For reference to a visit, see *The Chronicle,* July 28, 1892, p. 4, col. 1. Kerr Craige married General L. O'B. Branch's daughter in 1873, had seven children, became a lawyer in Salisbury, and joined the North Carolina legislature. He later became Third Assistant Postmaster General under President Benjamin Cleveland, a trustee of the University of North Carolina and the president of the First National Bank of Salisbury. Nominated to Congress, Craige turned it down because of declining health. He died in 1904. (Ashe et. al., *Biographical History,* vol. 1, 252; *CV* 6 [1898], 228; unprovenienced article courtesy of Archibald Craige, copy in the author's possession.)

25. Opie, *A Rebel Cavalryman with Lee, Stuart and Jackson,* 316; Foard Reminiscences, 16, Fred C. Foard Papers, NCSA. Crouch, *Sketches of Wilkes,* 32–33, gives a somewhat different story of Cowles's wounding.

26. *The Journal-Patriot,* July 1, 1968, clipping in Calvin J. Cowles Papers, SHC; Crouch, *Sketches of Wilkes,* 32; *CV* 10 (1902): 125; E. C. Finley, "William Henry Harrison Cowles and Family," Calvin J. Cowles Papers, SHC.

27. *The Chronicle,* July 22, 1891, p. 1, col. 3; April 22, 1891, p. 4, col. 1; May 18, 1893, p. 1, col. 1; June 1, 1893, p. 4, col. 3; Calvin J. Cowles Papers, SHC.

28. *The Chronicle,* July 20, 1893, p. 4, col. 3; Hickerson, *Echoes,* 121. The quoted letter was dated September 6, 1882.

29. J. Jay Anderson, *North Wilkesboro: The First 100 Years,* 251–52, 78, 76, 88; Hickerson, *History and Genealogy,* 20; *The Chronicle,* December 3, 1890, p. 4, col. 1; December 10, 1890, p. 1, col. 2; July 1, 1891, p. 1 col. 3; October 5, 1893, p. 4, col. 3. In 1891, the Gordon Hotel Company sold the Gordon Hotel to several investors who expected to lease control to an experienced "hotelest" (*The Chronicle,* June 10, 1891, p. 4, col. 2). North Wilkesboro is today located on land that once belonged to the Finleys. *The Chronicle* of June 3, 1891 also spoke of JBG's bravery: "No braver heart e'er beat, no knightlier sword ever waved, than his."

30. John B. Gordon, *Reminiscences,* 152–53.

31. Winkler Interview; *The Chronicle,* November 26, 1892, p. 1, col. 3.

32. Edward A. Pollard, *The Lost Cause,* 752, 751; William M. S. Rasmussen, "Making the Confederate Murals: Studies by Charles Hoffbauer," *The Virginia Magazine of History and Biography,* 436; Seippel, *Gordon Chapter.* At this writing (1996), the UDC Chapter is still in existence and the Sons of Confederate Veterans Camp is being rechartered.

33. Cowles, *CSC,* 23; Cowles, "Life and Services," 19–20.

34. *Daily Confederate,* May 25, 1864, p. 1, cols. 1–2.

35. *Daily Confederate,* May 25, 1864, p. 1, cols. 1–2; Winkler Interview. For Waring, see Chapter 12.

36. Kerr Craige Address, Ms., n.d., copy provided by Craige's grandson, Mr. Archibald Craige, Keswick, Va, copy in the author's possession.; Galloway, "Sixty-third Regiment (Fifth Cavalry)," *NC Regts.* 3: 538. The National Archives' files of letters received by the Confederate War Department contains no letters from JBG.

37. Cooke, *Wearing of the Gray,* 255; Rufus Barringer to V. C. Barringer, January 27, 1866, Rufus Clay Barringer Papers, SHC; *Daily Confederate,* May 25, 1864, p. 1, cols. 1–2.

38. Fred C. Foard Reminiscences, 16–17, NCSA. See also T. B. Kingsbury, "North Carolina Generals," *Our Living and Our Dead* 3: 751.

39. J. E. B. Stuart's Autograph Album, copy of the original, in the Jeb Stuart Papers, VHS.

Bibliography

Manuscript Sources

Duke University, Special Collections Library, Durham, North Carolina.
  Alfred Adams Papers.
  Samuel S. Biddle Papers.
  John Esten Cooke Papers.
  James G. Hackett Papers.
  Munford-Ellis Family Papers.
  Presley Carter Person Papers.
  J. E. B. Stuart Papers.

Georgia Department of Archives and History, Atlanta.
  Pierce M. B. Young Collection.

Greensboro Historical Museum, Greensboro, North Carolina.
  Brown Family Letters.
  J. E. B. Stuart Letter.

Library of Congress, Manuscript Division, Washington, D.C.
  J. E. B. Stuart Papers.

Museum of the Confederacy, Eleanor S. Brockenbrough Library, Richmond, Virginia.
  Hamilton [Allen] Brown Letters.
  Robert G. Haile Diary.

North Carolina State Archives, North Carolina Division of Archives and History, Raleigh.
  Calvin J. Cowles Papers.
  Fred C. Foard Papers.
  James B. Gordon Papers.
  Bryan Grimes Papers.
  James G. Hackett Collection.
  Military Collection, Civil War Collection
  Robert Ransom Papers.
  Simpson and Biddle Family Papers.
  Mrs. Gordon Smith Letter.
  Zebulon Baird Vance Papers.
  William Whitaker Papers.

Private Collections.
  Alfred T. Adams, Boone, North Carolina.
    Adams Papers.
  Rufus Barringer, Rocky Mount, North Carolina.
    Address on Laurence S. Baker. Given by Judge Jas. C. MacRae, Raleigh, N.C., 1907.
  Archibald Craige, Keswick, Virginia.
    Kerr Craige Address.
  Meneta W. Proffit Henderson, Wilkesboro, North Carolina.
    W. H. Proffit Journal.
  Annie Finley Winkler, Houston, Texas.
    Bess Gordon Finley Grier MS.
    T.B. Finley. "Address to the James B. Gordon Chapter of the United Daughters of the Confederacy."

University of North Carolina at Chapel Hill, Southern Historical Collection, Chapel Hill.
  Rufus Clay Barringer Papers.
  Noble J. Brooks Papers.
  Hamilton Brown Papers.
  Calvin J. Cowles Papers.
  George Stanley Dewey Papers.
  James Gwyn Papers.
  Peter W. Hairston Papers.
  Wade Hampton Papers.
  D.H. Hill Papers
  Cadwallader J. Iredell Papers.
  Jones-Patterson Papers.
  Patterson-Lenoir Papers.
  R. Channing Price Papers.
  James T. Pugh Papers.
  Peter Evans Smith Papers.
  Joseph F. Waring Papers.

University of South Carolina, South Caroliniana Library, Columbia.
  Hampton Family Papers.

University of Virginia, Alderman Library, Special Collections Department, Charlottesville.
  John Esten Cooke Diaries (Clifton Waller Barrett Library).
  Thomas Lafayette Rosser Papers (in Papers of the Gordon and Rosser Families).
  J. E. B. Stuart Letters.

U.S. Army Military History Institute, Carlisle, Pennsylvania.

Robert J. Brake Collection (Cadwalader J. Iredell letter).
Civil War Miscellaneous Collection (Jacob A. Fisher letters and notes).

Virginia Historical Society, Richmond.
H. B. McClellan Papers.
Leiper M. Robinson Papers (typescript copy).
Saunders Family Papers.
J. E. B. Stuart Papers.
Andrew Reid Venable Letter.
Wynne Family Papers.

Virginia State Library and Archives (The Library of Virginia), Richmond.
Douglas Southall Freeman Papers, Personal Papers Collection.
Jacob Yoder Diaries, Personal Papers Collection.

Wilkes Community College, James Larkin Pearson Library, Wilkesboro, North Carolina.
Anderson Collection (Gordon/Brown/Finley Papers), access provided by J. Jay Anderson.

Periodicals

Carolina Watchman (Salisbury, N.C.). 1851; 1861–1864
The [Charlotte] *Daily Bulletin.* 1863.
Concord [N.C.] *Sun.* 1881.
The Daily Confederate (Raleigh, N.C.). 1864–1865.
The Journal-Patriot (North Wilkesboro, N.C.). 1976.
Lynchburg Virginian. 1883.
North Carolina Argus. 1861–1864.
North Carolina Standard (Raleigh). 1850–1851; 1856; 1861–1864.
The [North Wilkesboro, N.C.] *Chronicle.* 1890–1895.
People's Press (Salem, N.C.). 1861–1863.
Raleigh Register. 1850–1851; 1856; 1861–1864.
Richmond Daily Dispatch. 1861–1864.
Richmond Daily Examiner. 1861–1864.
Richmond Daily Whig. 1861–1864.
Richmond Enquirer. 1861–1864.
Wilmington Journal, 1864.

Articles and Speeches

"A.F. Williams Diary, 1862." *Lower Cape Fear Historical Society Bulletin* XVII (April 1974), 1–6.
Armfield, J. B. "Colonel William H. H. Cowles." *CSC*, 4–5.
Averell, William W. "With the Cavalry on the Peninsula." *B&L* 2: 429–33.
Barber, Mamie. "Colonel William Morgan Barber." *CSC*, 6.
Barringer, Rufus. "Cavalry Sketches." *The Land We Love* 4 (November 1867): 1–6.
———. "The First North Carolina Cavalry: A Famous Cavalry Regiment." Written for Confederate Veterans Association. NA.
———. "Ninth Regiment (First Cavalry)." *NC Regts.* 1: 417–43.
"The Beau Sabreur of Georgia: A Fitting Tribute to the Gallant General P. M. B. Young, C. S. A." *SHSP* 25: 146–151.

"Brook Church Fight, and Something About the Fifth North Carolina Cavalry." *SHSP* 29: 139–44.
Burgess, W. W. "Soldier's Story of J.E.B. Stuart's Death." *SHSP* 36: 121–24.
Campbell, William. "Autobiographical Sketch." *William and Mary College Quarterly Historical Magazine.* Vol. 9, no. 2 (April 1929): 88–109.
[Carlton, P. C.] "Colonel W. H. Cowles." *CV* 10 (1902): 125.
Carr, Julian S. "The Gordon-Barringer Brigade." *NC Regts.* 4: 581–82.
"Charles Daniel Malone." *CV* 35 (1927): 344.
Cheek, W. H., with William H. H. Cowles. "Additional Sketch Ninth Regiment (First Cavalry)." *NC Regts.* 1: 445–87.
Clark, Walter. "Generals from North Carolina." *NC Regts.* 1: xi–xiv.
Cowles, William H. H. "The Life and Services of General James B. Gordon." Raleigh: Edwards, Broughton & Co., Power Printers and Binders, 1887.
———. "Oration on James B. Gordon." *CSC,* 17–23.
Couch, Darius N. "The Chancellorsville Campaign." *B&L* 3: 154–171.
Cox, Jacob D. "Forcing Fox's Gap and Turner's Gap." *B&L* 2: 583–90.
Curtis, W. A. "A Journal of Reminiscences of the War, From May 1, 1861, to January 1, 1862." *Our Living and Our Dead* 2: 36–44.
"The Death of General J. E. B. Stuart," *B&L* 4: 194.
Dedmond, Francis B., ed. "Harvey Davis's Unpublished Civil War 'Diary' and the Story of Company D of the First North Carolina Cavalry." *Appalachian Journal* (Summer 1986): 368–407.
Dorsey, Frank. "Gen. J. E. B. Stuart's Last Battle." *CV* 17 (1931) 76–77.
Finley, Thomas B. "Address on James B. Gordon." Speech presented to the James B. Gordon Chapter of the United Daughters of the Confederacy. Winston-Salem, N.C.: n.d.
Galloway, John M. "Sixty-Third Regiment (Fifth Cavalry)." *NC Regts.* 3: 529–43.
Garnett, Theodore S. "The Dashing Gen. J. E. B. Stuart." *CV* 19 (1911): 575–76.
"General Rufus Barringer." *CV* 9 (1901): 69–70.
Gibbons, J. R. "The Origin of Company Q." *CV* 22 (1914): 320.
"Glimpses of Army Life in 1864." *SHSP* 18: 407–422.
Gordon, Major A. "Organization of Troops." *NC Regts.* 1: 3–49.
Graham, W. A. "Nineteenth Regiment (Second Cavalry)." *NC Regts.* 2: 79–98.
Green, Wharton J. "Address on General Robert Ransom." Delivered before the Ladies Memorial Association, May 10, 1899. Suffolk, VA: Robert Hardy, 1987.
Hall, Clark B. "The Battle of Brandy Station." *Civil War Times Illustrated* 29 (May/June 1990): 32–45.
Hartley, Chris. "War's Last Cavalry Raid." *America's Civil War* 2 (January 1990): 19–25.
Hill, D. H. "The Battle of South Mountain, or Boonsboro: Fighting for Time at Turner's and Fox's Gaps." *B&L* 2: 559–81.
Hill, Joshua B. "Forty-First Regiment (Third Cavalry)." *NC Regts.* 2: 767–87.

Imboden, John D. "The Confederate Retreat from Gettysburg." *B&L* 3: 420–29.
Inscoe, John C. "Mountain Masters: Slaveholding in Western North Carolina." *North Carolina Historical Review* LXI (April 1984): 143–73.
Jordan, Weymouth T., Jr., "'Drinking Pulverized Snakes and Lizards:' Yankees and Rebels in Battle at Gum Swamp." *North Carolina Historical Review* LXXI (April 1994): 207–31.
Kingsbury, T. B. "North Carolina Generals." *Our Living and Our Dead* 3: 749–752.
Longstreet, James. "The Battle of Fredericksburg." *B&L* 3: 70–85.
M_____, J. Emory. "Over the Grave of Colonel Sol. Williams." *Our Living and Our Dead* 1: 138.
McClellan, George B. "The Peninsular Campaign." *B&L* 2: 160–87.
McClellan, H. B. "The Battle of Fleetwood." *Annals of the War*, 392–403.
McCormick, Cyrus. "How Gallant Stuart Met His Death." *CV* 39 (1931): 98–100.
McKinney, Gordon B. "Women's Role in Civil War Western North Carolina." *North Carolina Historical Review* LXIX (January 1992): 37–56.
McMahon, Martin T. "From Gettysburg to the Coming of Grant." *B&L* 4: 81–94.
McRae, J. C. "List of Confederate Soldiers in the General Assembly of North Carolina." *Our Living and Our Dead* 2: 180–83.
Means, Paul B. "Additional Sketch Sixty-Third Regiment (Fifth Cavalry)." *NC Regts.* 3: 545–657.
Miller, Samuel H. "Yellow Tavern." *Civil War History* 2 (1956): 57–81.
Mitchell, Thornton W. "The Granville District and Its Land Records." *North Carolina Historical Review* LXX (April 1993): 103–128.
Mizelle, Hazel. "Only Two Living Members of Cabarrus Rangers: This North Carolina Unit Fought Throughout War and was Never Singly Defeated." *The Charlotte Observer*, July 7, 1929.
Moffet, George H. "Battle of Brandy Station." *CV* 14 (1906): 74–5.
Mosby, John S. "The Confederate Cavalry in the Gettysburg Campaign." *B&L* 3: 251–52.
"Nicholas P. Tredenick." *CV* 14 (1906): 132.
"The North Carolina Cavalry." *The Concord* [N.C.] *Register*. May 25, June 1, June 15, June 22, June 29, July 6, July 13, July 27, August 3, and August 10, 1883.
"North Carolina Women of the Confederacy." *CV* 38 (1930): 419–20.
Oliver, J. R. "J.E.B. Stuart's Fate at Yellow Tavern." *CV* 19 (1911): 531.
O'Neill, Robert F., Jr. "The Fight for the Loudoun Valley: Aldie, Middleburg, and Upperville, Va." *Blue & Gray* (October 1993): 12–21, 46–60.
Pearce, N. B. "Arkansas Troops in the Battle of Wilson's Creek." *B&L* 1: 298–303.
Pearce, T.H. "Where Cavalry Fought the Navy. *The State* 40 (June 15, 1972), 7–9.
Pitts, Dr. H. Douglas. "Landmarks of Sheridan's Raid." 20 pp. Unpublished MS, 1995.
Rankin, N.P. "Sketch of Fifth Regiment North Carolina Cavalry." Unprovenienced article in the author's possession.
Rasmussen, William M. S. "Making the Confederate Murals: Studies by Charles Hoffbauer." *The Virginia Magazine of History and Biography* 101 (July 1993): 433–456.
Roberts, William P. "Additional Sketch Nineteenth Regiment (Second Cavalry)." *NC Regts.* 2: 99–109.
[Roberts, William P.] "Paroles of the Army of Northern Virginia." *SHSP* 18: 386–88.
Robertson, Beverly H. "The Confederate Cavalry in the Gettysburg Campaign." *B&L* 3: 253.
Robertson, Frank S. "Reminiscence of the Years 1861–1865." Edited by L. C. Angle, Jr., and Edwin T. Hardison. *The Historical Society of Washington County, Va. Bulletin*, series II, no. 23 (1986): 6–39.
Robins, W. T. "Stuart's Ride Around McClellan." *B&L* 2: 271–75.
Rodenbough, Theo. F. "Sheridan's Richmond Raid." *B&L* 4: 188–193.
[Schurict, Hermann.] "Jenkins' Brigade in the Gettysburg Campaign: Extracts From the Diary of Lieutenant Hermann Schurict, 14th Virginia Cavalry." *SHSP* 24: 339–50.
Shaw, W. P. "Fifty-ninth Regiment (Fourth Cavalry)." *NC Regts.* 3: 455–72.
Smith, Everard H, ed. "The Civil War Diary of Peter W. Hairston, Volunteer Aide to Major General Jubal A. Early, November 7–December 4, 1863." *North Carolina Historical Review* LXVII (January 1990): 59–86.
Snead, Thomas L. "The First Year of the War in Missouri." *B&L* 1: 262–77.
Spainhour, R. A. "History of Company B, First North Carolina Regiment." *CSC*, 9–11.
_____. "Incidents of Confederate War, Funny and Otherwise." *CSC,* 5.
[Steadman, Charles M.] "Battle at Reams Station." *SHSP* 19: 113–120.
Wittenberg, Eric J., and J. David Petruzzi. "Thunder on the Mountain: The Battle of Monterey Pass, July 4–5, 1863." *Blue & Gray Magazine* 26: 26–32.

Records, Interviews, and Correspondence

Case Files of Applications from Former Confederates for Presidential Pardons (Amnesty Papers). Microcopy 1003, Roll 38, Group I, National Archives.
Church Records, 1847–1861. St. Paul's Episcopal Church, Wilkesboro, NC.
Compiled Service Record of James Anderson, First North Carolina Cavalry Regiment (Ninth North Carolina State Troops), Microcopy 270, Roll 1. From Compiled Service Records of Confederate Soldiers Who Served in Organizations from the State of North Carolina, Record Group 109, National Archives, 1960.
Compiled Service Record of James B. Gordon, First North Carolina Cavalry Regiment (Ninth North Carolina State Troops), Microcopy 270, Roll 4. From Compiled Service Records of Confederate Soldiers Who Served in Organizations from the State

of North Carolina, Record Group 109, National Archives, 1960.
Compiled Service Record of James B. Gordon, Microcopy 331, Roll 109. From Compiled Service Records for Confederate General and Staff Officers, Record Group 109, National Archives, 1960.
Compiled Service Record of John Anderson, First North Carolina Cavalry Regiment (Ninth North Carolina State Troops), Microcopy 270, Roll 1. From Compiled Service Records of Confederate Soldiers Who Served in Organizations from the State of North Carolina, Record Group 109, National Archives, 1960.
Compiled Service Record of Laurence S. Baker, First North Carolina Cavalry Regiment (Ninth North Carolina State Troops), Microcopy 270, Roll 1. From Compiled Service Records of Confederate Soldiers Who Served in Organizations from the State of North Carolina, Record Group 109, National Archives, 1960.
Compiled Service Record of Rufus Barringer, First North Carolina Cavalry Regiment (Ninth North Carolina State Troops), Microcopy 270, Roll 1. From Compiled Service Records of Confederate Soldiers Who Served in Organizations from the State of North Carolina, Record Group 109, National Archives, 1960.
House and Senate Documents Printed for the General Assembly of North Carolina at the Session of 1850–1851. Raleigh: Thomas J. Lemay, Printer to the State, 1851.
Index to Compiled Service Records of Volunteer Soldiers Who Served during the War of 1812. Microcopy 602, Roll 83, National Archives.
Journal of the Congress of the Confederate States of America: 1861–1865. Washington, D.C.: Government Printing Office, 1904.
Journals of the Senate and House of Commons of the General Assembly of the State of North Carolina at the Session of 1850–51. Raleigh: Seaton Gales, Printer for the State, 1851.
McKenzie, Frank, Rector. Interview with the author. Wilkesboro, N.C., July 20, 1989.
Minutes, Wilkes County Board of Superintendents of Schools. 1841–1853. North Carolina State Archives, Raleigh.
United States Census for Wilkes County, North Carolina. 1830, 1840, 1850, 1860. Record Group 29, National Archives.
Vogtsberger, Peggy (John Pelham Historical Association). Letter to author, July 8, 1994.
Winkler, Annie F. Interview with the author. Wilkesboro, N.C., July 20, 1989.
Woodson, Ramona (Emory and Henry College). Letter to author, September 1, 1989.

Books and Published Addresses

Absher, W. O., ed. *The Heritage of Wilkes County: 1982.* Winston-Salem, N.C.: Wilkes Genealogical Society, with Hunter Publishing, 1982.
Alexander, Edward Porter. *Fighting for the Confederacy: The Personal Recollections of General Edward Porter Alexander.* Gary Gallagher, ed. Chapel Hill: University of North Carolina Press, 1989.
Anderson, J. Jay. *North Wilkesboro: The First Hundred Years.* Charlotte, NC: Delmar, 1990.
_____. *Wilkes County Sketches.* Wilkesboro, N.C.: Wilkes Community College, 1976.
Ashe, Samuel A., et al., eds. *Biographical History of North Carolina: From Colonial Times to the Present.* 8 vols. Greensboro, NC: Charles L. Van Noppen, 1917.
Barrett, John G. *The Civil War in North Carolina.* Chapel Hill: University of North Carolina Press, 1963.
Barringer, Paul. *The Natural Bent.* Chapel Hill: University of North Carolina Press, 1949.
Beale, R. L. T. *History of the Ninth Virginia Cavalry in the War Between the States.* Richmond: B. F. Johnson Publishing Company, 1899.
Black, John Logan. *Crumbling Defenses, or Memoirs and Reminiscences of John Logan Black.* Eleanor D. McSwain, ed. Macon, GA: Eleanor D. McSwain, 1960.
Blackford, Susan L., comp. *Letters from Lee's Army, Or Memoirs of Life In and Out of the Army in Virginia During the War Between the States.* Ed. and abridged by Charles M. Blackford III. New York: A. S. Barnes, 1962.
Blackford, W. W. *War Years with J.E.B. Stuart.* New York: Charles Scribner's Sons, 1945.
Boatner, Mark Mayo III. *The Civil War Dictionary,* rev. ed. New York: David McKay, 1988.
Brawley, James Shober. *The Public and Military Career of Lawrence O'Bryan Branch.* Master's thesis, University of North Carolina at Chapel Hill, 1951.
Chesnut, Mary Boykin. *A Diary from Dixie.* Ben Ames Williams, ed., with a foreword by Edmund Wilson. Cambridge, MA: Harvard University Press, 1980.
Clement, Maud Carter. *Writings of Maud Carter Clement.* Salem, WV: Walsworth Publishing for the Pittsylvania Historical Society, 1982.
Coltrane, Daniel Branson. *The Memoirs of Daniel Branson Coltrane.* Raleigh, NC: Edwards and Broughton, 1956.
Cooke, John Esten. *Surry of Eagle's Nest, or the Memoirs of a Staff-Officer Serving In Virginia, Edited from the MSS. of Colonel Surry.* New York: G. W. Dillingham Co., Publishers, 1866.
_____. *Wearing of the Gray: Being Personal Portraits, Scenes, and Adventures of the War.* Philip Van Doren Stern, ed. Bloomington: Indiana University Press, 1959.
Crouch, John. *Historical Sketches of Wilkes County.* Wilkesboro, NC: Wilkes Genealogical Society, 1902.
Crute, Joseph H., Jr. *Confederate Staff Officers: 1861–1865.* Powhatan, VA: Derwent, 1982.
Davis, Burke. *Jeb Stuart: The Last Cavalier.* New York: Fairfax, 1988.
Dorland's Illustrated Medical Dictionary. 26th ed. Philadelphia: W.B. Saunders, 1981.
Douglas, Henry Kyd. *I Rode with Stonewall.* New York: Ballantine, 1961.
Dowdey, Clifford. *The Seven Days: The Emergence of Robert E. Lee.* New York: Fairfax, 1978.
Eckert, Ralph Lowell. *John Brown Gordon: Soldier, Southerner, American.* Baton Rouge: Louisiana State University Press, 1989.
Eggleston, George Cary. *A Rebel's Recollections.* Bloomington: Indiana University Press, 1959.

Foote, Shelby. *The Civil War: A Narrative*. 3 vols. New York: Vintage, 1974.

Freeman, Douglas Southall. *Lee's Lieutenants*. 3 vols. New York: Charles Scribner's Sons, 1942–44.

_____. *R. E. Lee: A Biography*. 4 vols. New York: Charles Scribner's Sons, 1951.

Freidel, Frank. *The Presidents of the United States of America*. Washington, D. C.: White House Historical Association, 1964.

Garnett, Theodore Stanford. *Riding with Stuart: Reminiscences of an Aide-de-Camp*. Robert J. Trout, ed. Shippensburg, PA: White Mane, 1994.

Gilmor, Harry. *Four Years in the Saddle*. New York: Harper and Brothers, Publishers, 1866; rpt. Butternut and Blue.

Good Housekeeping Family Health and Medical Guide. New York: Hearst, 1979.

Gordon, John Brown. *Reminiscences of the Civil War*. New York: Charles Scribner's Sons, 1918.

Graham, Martin F., and George F. Skoch. *Mine Run: A Campaign of Lost Opportunities*. Lynchburg, VA: H. E. Howard, 1987.

Grimsley, Daniel A. *Battles In Culpeper County, Virginia, 1861–1865*. Culpeper, VA: Raleigh Travers Green, 1900.

Hairston, Peter W. *The Cooleemee Plantation and its People*. Lexington, NC: Davidson County Community College, 1986.

Hamlin, Percy Gatling. *Old Bald Head: The Portrait of a Soldier*. Strasburg, VA: Shenandoah, 1940.

Hancock, Mary Alice. *Four Brothers in Gray*. Wilkesboro, NC: Wilkes Community College, 1975.

Harper, Margaret E. *Fort Defiance and the General*. Hickory, NC: Clay, 1976.

Harrison, Constance Cary. *Recollections Grave and Gay*. New York: Charles Scribner's Sons, 1912.

Hartley, Chris J. *To Restore the Old Flag: A Brief History of Wilkes County and the Civil War*. Wilkesboro, NC: Old Wilkes, 1990.

Hassler, William W. *Colonel John Pelham: Lee's Boy Artillerist*. Richmond, VA: Garrett and Massie, 1960.

Hayes, Johnson J. *The Land of Wilkes*. Wilkesboro, NC: Wilkes County Historical Society, 1962.

Henderson, William D. *The Road to Bristoe Station: Campaigning With Lee and Meade, August 1–October 20, 1863*. Lynchburg, VA: H. E. Howard, 1987.

Hickerson, Thomas F. *Echoes of Happy Valley*. Chapel Hill, NC: Thomas F. Hickerson, 1962.

_____. *Happy Valley: History and Genealogy*. Chapel Hill, NC: Thomas F. Hickerson, 1940.

Higgenbotham, Don. *The War of American Independence: Military Attitudes, Policies, and Practice, 1763–1789*. Boston: Northeastern University Press, 1983.

Hill, Daniel Harvey. *Bethel to Sharpsburg*. 2 vols. Raleigh: Edwards and Broughton, 1926.

History of Alleghany County, 1589 through 1976. Winston-Salem, NC: Hunter, 1976.

Hopkins, Luther W. *From Bull Run to Appomattox: A Boy's View*. Baltimore: Fleet-McGinley, 1908.

Horton, Clarence E., Jr. *An Historical Sketch of Olde Concord, 1796–1860*. Charlotte: Clarence E. Horton, Jr., and Delmar Printing., 1994.

Hubbard, Fred C. *Physicians, Medical Practice, and the Development of Hospitals in Wilkes County, 1830 to 1975*. Wilkesboro, NC: Fred C. Hubbard, 1978.

Humble, Richard. *Napoleon's Peninsular Marshals: A Reassessment*. New York: Taplinger, 1974.

Humphreys, Andrew A. *The Virginia Campaign of '64 and '65: The Army of the Potomac and the Army of the James*. New York: Charles Scribner's Sons, 1883, rpt. Broadfoot, 1989. Campaigns of the Civil War series, introduction by Chris Calkins.

Jones, J. William. *Christ in the Camp, or Religion in the Confederate Army*. New York: B.F. Johnson and Company, 1887; rpt. Harrisonburg, VA: Sprinkle, 1986.

Keever, Homer H. *Iredell: Piedmont County*. Brady Printing with Iredell County Bicentennial Commission, 1976.

Krick, Robert K. *Lee's Colonels: A Biographical Register of the Field Officers of the Army of Northern Virginia*. Dayton, OH: Morningside, 1979.

Kruman, Marc W. *Parties and Politics in North Carolina: 1836–1865*. Baton Rouge: Louisiana State University Press, 1983.

Lefler, Hugh Talmage, and Albert Ray Newsome. *North Carolina: The History of a Southern State*. Chapel Hill: University of North Carolina Press, 1954.

Leyburn, James G. *The Scotch-Irish: A Social History*. Chapel Hill: University of North Carolina Press, 1962.

Livermore, Thomas L. *Numbers and Losses in the Civil War in America, 1861–65*. Dayton, OH: Morningside, 1986.

Longacre, Edward G. *Mounted Raids of the Civil War*. South Brunswick, N.J., and New York: A. S. Barnes, 1975.

Longstreet, James. *From Manassas to Appomattox: Memoirs of the Civil War in America*. Secaucus, NJ: Blue and Gray, 1985.

Matter, William D. *If It Takes All Summer: The Battle of Spotsylvania*. Chapel Hill: University of North Carolina Press, 1988.

McBride, Nancy S. *Gordon Kinship*. McClure, 1973.

McClellan, H. B. *I Rode With Jeb Stuart: The Life and Campaigns of Major-General J.E.B. Stuart*. Boston and New York: Houghton, Mifflin and Company, 1885, rpt. Eagle, 1991.

McClure, A. K. *Abraham Lincoln and Men of War-Times: Some Personal Recollections of War and Politics During the Lincoln Administration*. Philadelphia: The Times Publishing Company, 1892.

McDonald, William N. *A History of the Laurel Brigade: Originally the Ashby Cavalry of the Army of Northern Virginia and Chew's Battery*. Bushrod C. Washington, ed. Baltimore: Sun, 1907.

The Medical and Surgical History of the Civil War. Wilmington, NC: Broadfoot, 1991.

Meem, J. Lawrence, Jr., ed. *John Gaw Meem and His Descendants*. Charlottesville, VA: J. L. Meem, 1985.

Messick, Hank. *Kings Mountain*. Boston: Little, Brown, 1976.

Mitchell, Adele H., ed. *The Letters of Major General James E. B. Stuart*. Stuart-Mosby Historical Society, 1990.

Morris, George S., and Susan L. Foutz. *Lynchburg in

the Civil War: The City, the People, the Battle. Lynchburg: H. E. Howard, 1984.

Mosby, John S. *Mosby's War Reminiscences (and) Stuart's Cavalry Campaigns*. New York: Pageant, 1958.

———. *Stuart's Cavalry in the Gettysburg Campaign*. New York: Moffat, Yard, 1908, rpt. Olde Soldier Books, 1987.

Myers, Frank M. *The Comanches: A History of White's Battalion, Virginia Cavalry, Laurel Brigade, Hampton Division, A. N. V., C. S. A*. Baltimore: Kelly, Piet and Company, Publishers, 1871; rpt. with introduction and notes by Lee A. Wallace, Jr., by Butternut Press, 1987.

Neese, George M. *Three Years in the Confederate Horse Artillery*. New York and Washington: Neale, 1911.

Nichols, James L. *General Fitzhugh Lee: A Biography*. Lynchburg, VA: H. E. Howard, 1989.

O'Neill, Robert, Jr. *The Cavalry Battles of Aldie, Middleburg and Upperville: Small but Important Riots*. Lynchburg, VA: H. E. Howard, 1993.

Opie, John N. *A Rebel Cavalryman with Lee Stuart and Jackson*. Chicago: W.B. Conkey Company, 1899.

Phillips, Cornelia Spencer. *The Last Ninety Days of the War in North Carolina*. New York: Watchman Publishing Company, 1866.

Pollard, Edward A. *The Lost Cause; A New Southern History of the War of the Confederates*. New York: E. B. Treat and Company, Publishers, 1867.

Ramage, James A. *Rebel Raider: The Life of General John Hunt Morgan*. Lexington: University Press of Kentucky, 1986.

Rawle, William Brook, William E. Miller, James W. McCorkell, Andrew J. Speese, and John C. Hunterson (The Regimental History Committee). *History of the Third Pennsylvania Cavalry, Sixteenth Regiment Pennsylvania Volunteers, In the American Civil War, 1861–1865*. Philadelphia: Franklin, 1905.

Rea, D. B. *Sketches of Hampton's Cavalry in the Summer, Fall, and Winter Campaigns of '62, Including Stuart's Raid into Pennsylvania, and Also, in Burnside's Rear*. Raleigh, NC: Strother and Company, Steam Book and Job Printers, 1863.

Rhea, Gordon C. *The Battle of the Wilderness, May 5–6, 1864*. Baton Rouge: Louisiana State University Press, 1994.

Rumple, Jethro. *A History of Rowan County, North Carolina*. Baltimore: Genealogical, 1990.

Runge, William H., ed. *Four Years in The Confederate Artillery: The Diary of Private Henry Robinson Berkely*. Richmond: Virginia Historical Society, 1991.

Sears, Stephen W. *Landscape Turned Red: The Battle of Antietam*. New York: Poplar, 1983.

———. *To the Gates of Richmond*. New York: Ticknor and Fields, 1992.

Seippel, Janet Blum. *James B. Gordon Chapter, United Daughters of the Confederacy, March 30, 1898–1973*. Winston-Salem, NC: James B. Gordon Chapter of the United Daughters of the Confederacy, 1973.

Sheridan, Philip. *Civil War Memoirs*. Paul Andrew Hutton, ed. New York: Bantam, 1991.

Simpson, Nancy W., ed. *The Heritage of Wilkes County: Volume II, 1990*. Charlotte, NC: Wilkes Genealogical Society, with Delmar Printing, 1990.

Starr, Stephen Z. *The Union Cavalry in the Civil War*. 3 vols. Baton Rouge: Louisiana State University Press, 1979.

Stevenson, George J. *Increase in Excellence: A History of Emory and Henry College 1836–1963*. New York: Appleton-Century-Crofts, 1963.

Thackeray, William M. *The Newcomes: Memoirs of a Most Respectable Family*. Arthur Pendennis, ed. London: Macmillian, 1926.

Thomas, Emory M. *Bold Dragoon: The Life of J. E. B. Stuart*. New York: Harper and Row, 1986.

Trout, Robert J. *They Followed the Plume: The Story of J. E. B. Stuart and His Staff*. Mechanicsburg, PA: Stackpole, 1993.

Troxler, Beverly Barrier, and Billy Dawn Barrier Auciello, eds. *Dear Father: Confederate Letters Never Before Published*. North Billerica, MA: Beverly B. Troxler and Billy Dawn Barrier Auciello, 1989.

Tucker, Glenn. *Zeb Vance: Champion of Personal Freedom*. Indianapolis: Bobbs-Merrill, 1965.

Van Noppen, Ina W. *Stoneman's Last Raid*. Raleigh: North Carolina State University Print Shop, 1961.

——— and John J. Van Noppen. *Western North Carolina Since the Civil War*. Boone, NC: Appalachian Consortium Press, 1973.

Von Borcke, Heros. *Memoirs of the Confederate War*. 2 vols. Dayton, OH: Morningside, 1985.

Waitt, Robert W. *Confederate Military Hospitals in Richmond*. Richmond, VA: Richmond Civil War Centennial Committee, 1964.

Warner, Ezra J., and W. Buck Yearns. *Biographical Register of the Confederate Congress*. Baton Rouge: Louisiana State University Press, 1975.

Wells, Edward L. *Hampton and His Cavalry in '64*. Richmond, VA: Owens, 1991.

Weston, James A. *Historic Doubts as to the Execution of Marshal Ney*. New York: Thomas Whittaker, 1895.

Wheeler, John H. *Reminiscences and Memoirs of North Carolina and Eminent North Carolinians*. Baltimore: Genealogical, 1966.

Yancey, Rosa Faulkner. *Lynchburg and Its Neighbors*. Richmond, VA: J. W. Ferguson and Sons, 1935.

Young, Joanne. *North Carolina: The First Two Hundred Years*. Birmingham, AL: Oxmoor House, 1975.

Index

Adams, George F. 52, 109–200, 207
Alabama infantry regiment: Tenth 48
Aldie, Va., battle of 140
Alexander, Edward Porter 213
Alexander, Ham 178
Alleghany County, N.C. 29
Alsop, Elizabeth Maxwell 230
Anderson, James 58
Anderson, John 58
Anderson, Richard H. 88, 212
Andrews, Clinton M. 173, 205, 227, 234
Annapolis, Md. *see* U.S. Naval Academy
Anthony, Whit 188
Arkansas infantry regiment: Third 40
Armfield, R.F. 236
Army of Northern Virginia 5, 66, 75, 79, 86, 89, 90, 91, 103, 121, 139, 142, 143, 146, 149, 153, 156, 157, 158, 163, 189, 203, 204, 206, 209, 212, 214
Army of Tennessee 174
Army of the Potomac 47, 53, 64–66, 70, 79, 84, 89, 90, 98, 103, 112, 116, 117–118, 120, 142, 148, 149, 158, 174, 181, 190, 193, 194, 207, 212
Army of Virginia (Federal) 73
Atwood & Company 21
Auburn, Va. 180–183
Averell, W.W. 68–69, 123

Baker, John A. 92, 225, 234
Baker, Laurence S. 52, 58, 59, 62, 65, 67–69, 72, 74–75, 76, 78, 79, 84, 85, 86, 91, 92, 102, 104, 109, 116, 120, 121, 122, 124, 127, 130, 133–134, 135, 136, 137, 138, 144, 145, 146, 152, 157, 158, 159, 160, 161–162, 166, 168, 171, 172, 204, 239
Banks, Nathaniel P. 60
Barbee's Crossroads, battle of 103, 109, 128
Barbour (Barber), William Morgan 53, 58
Barker, Theo 205
Barlow, Francis 237
Barrier, William L. 35, 39, 42, 92, 94, 208, 229
Barringer, Rufus C. 46, 67–68, 92, 98–99, 120, 131, 135, 171, 174–175, 182, 183, 186–187, 188, 195, 197, 210, 232, 234, 239, 240

Beauregard, P.G.T. 36, 47, 73, 205, 223
Beckham, Robert F. 128, 184, 190
Bell, Charles A. 46
Benjamin, Judah P. 53
Biddle, J.W. 194
Black, John L. 130, 134, 137, 162, 197
Blackford, W.W. 89, 98, 101, 104, 127, 134, 135, 136, 182, 186
Blackwelder, W.A. 71
Boone, Daniel 7
Bragg, Braxton 203, 205, 216, 218, 220, 221, 222, 223, 225
Branch, Lawrence O'Bryan 53
Brandy Station, Va., battle of 128–138
Brandy Station, Va., second battle of 161–162, 167
Brandy Station, Va., third battle of 177–179
Breathed, James 127, 222
Bristoe, Va., campaign 174–188
Bristoe Station, Va., battle of 183
Brook Church, Va., battle of 225–227
Brown, Allen *see* Brown, Hamilton Allen
Brown, Frank 220
Brown, Hamilton 12–13, 17, 20, 21, 31, 32, 38, 40, 201, 202, 235
Brown, Hamilton Allen 12, 17–18, 20, 24, 32, 34, 37, 38, 65–66, 160, 161, 201, 235–236
Brown, Hugh Thomas 12–13, 18–19, 20, 31, 32, 33, 39–40, 51
Brown, John 8
Brown, Sarah Gordon 10–12, 17, 18, 21, 40, 31, 73, 160–161, 200, 201, 232, 235
Buchanan, James 29
Buckland, Va. Races 186–188
Buena Vista, battle of 27
Buford, John 123, 129, 131, 136, 137, 143–144, 157, 161, 169, 170, 184, 185
Bull Run, first battle of *see* Manassas, first battle of
Bull Run, second battle of *see* Manassas, second battle of
Burnside, Ambrose E. 52–53, 56–57, 61, 73, 83, 85, 89, 109, 111, 112, 114, 116, 117–118, 208
Burt (slave) 39, 51, 52, 54, 58, 125, 193
Butler, Benjamin 223

Butler, Matthew C. 2, 94, 95, 97, 100, 101, 113–114, 128, 136, 166, 167, 227
Butler's Brigade 168, 169–170, 196, 205, 206
Buzzard's Roost 15

Cahill, John 155
Caldwell, Baxter 155
Camp Ashe 44, 45, 47, 50, 52
Camp Beauregard 36, 37, 40, 41
Camp Cripple 45
Camp Discipline 76, 77, 78
Camp Edwards 35–36
Camp Johnston 44
Camp Mars 58, 62
Campbell, William 9
Cantonment W.N. Edwards 52, 54, 79
Cantwell, Edward 142, 146
Carson, T.M. 235
Carteret, Sir George 8
Carver, John 183
Cedar Mountain, Va., battle of 73, 75
Chamberlain's Run, Va., battle of 234
Chambersburg, Pa.: capture of 95–98; raid 93–101
Chambliss, John R. 140, 141, 144, 149, 153, 156, 160, 167, 205
Chambliss's Brigade 156, 206, 213
Chancellorsville, battle of 121–122, 125
Chapman, George H. 222
Chapman, James 8
Chapman, Mary *see* Gordon, Mary Chapman
Cheek, William H. 2, 28, 121, 169, 190–191, 197, 198, 200, 204, 210, 219, 234
Chickamauga, battle of 174
Clark, Henry T. 37, 40, 41
Cleveland, Benjamin 8, 9
Clingman, Thomas L. 27, 146
Cobb, Thomas R.R. 66, 167
Cobb Legion *see* Georgia cavalry units
Coltrane, Daniel B. 147, 151, 155, 159, 169, 195, 199, 234
Conscription Act 56, 117
Cooke, John Esten 1, 2, 102, 108, 120, 128, 145, 176, 178, 184, 188, 189, 198, 199, 200, 201

431

Cooke, Philip St. George 64
Cooper, Samuel 40, 42, 170
Copeland, Virginius 194
Cornwallis, Charles 9, 10, 135
Couch, Darius N. 69, 91
Cowles, Calvin J. 117, 164, 232–233
Cowles, Caroline Elizabeth 236
Cowles, Miles 65
Cowles, William H.H. 39, 45, 65, 91, 97–98, 101, 108, 117, 120, 135, 136, 172, 173, 177, 182, 186, 187, 192, 194, 195, 201, 208, 209, 210, 219, 233–234, 236, 238, 240
Cox, Jacob 78, 83, 84, 85, 86, 88, 94, 98
Craige, Burton *see* Craige, Francis Burton
Craige, Francis Burton 28, 33, 40, 173, 232
Craige, Kerr 2, 28, 53, 138, 173, 201, 220, 225, 230, 231–232, 227, 228, 229, 233, 235, 239
Crowden (overseer) 16, 59, 117
Crumpler, Thomas N. 38, 61, 68
Custer, George A. 6, 187, 188, 215, 221, 222, 224–225

Dabney, Chiswell 2, 172, 176, 188
Dabney, Elizabeth 121
Dahlgren, Ulric 200
Daters & Company 21
Davies, Henry E. 187, 218
Davis, Benjamin F. ("Grimes") 88, 106, 107–108, 128
Davis, Burke 239
Davis, Harvey 42, 44, 55, 59, 69, 116
Davis, Jefferson 2, 42, 61, 75, 78, 82, 121, 123, 162, 166, 171, 200, 204, 225, 236
Dearing, James A. 205
Delony, William G. 108
Devin, Thomas C. 130, 131, 132, 221
Dobbin, James C. 18, 23, 27
Dorsey, G.W. 222
Douglas, Stephen A. 29
Dove, Jacob 50
Dranesville, Va., battle of 48–51, 80
Duffie, Alfred 130

Eagle Mills 21
Early, Jubal 190, 194
Elkin Manufacturing Company 21
Ellis, John W. 36, 37–38
Emack, George M. 154
Emancipation Proclamation 121, 164
Emory & Henry 13, 18, 94, 123, 202
Enfield Rifles 124
Erwin, J.R. 227
Erysipelas 228–229
Evans, Peter G. 144, 145–146, 168, 191
Evans, Stephen B. 160, 173, 197, 205
Ewell, Richard S. 73, 125, 139, 149, 150, 153, 154, 158, 160, 174, 180, 183, 207, 208, 209, 210

Fairfield, Pa., battle of 151–152
"Fairmount" 19
Falling Waters 159
Farley, Will 136
Farming 16–17
Ferebee, Dennis 146, 147, 152, 154, 157, 168, 171, 173, 177, 191, 197, 205
Ferguson, M.J. 157

Ferguson, Patrick 7, 9
Finley, Augustus Washington 19, 66, 104, 117, 160, 164, 200, 235
Finley, John Tate 19, 20, 21, 200, 235
Finley, Martha Lenoir Gordon 10, 66, 19, 104, 200, 235
Finley, Sarah Ann Gordon 10, 19, 26, 200
Finley, Thomas Brown 104, 236
Fisher, Henry 44
Fisher, Jacob A. 45
Foard, Fred 230–231
Foard, Noah P. 169, 198
Folk, George 39
Fontaine, Edmund 216
Fort Macon, battle of 57
Fortress Monroe 73
Franklin, William B. 84, 87–88
Frayser's Farm, battle of *see* Glendale, Va., battle of
Fredericksburg, Va., battle of 114
Fredericksburg, Va., campaign 103–118
Freeman, Douglas S. 148, 239
Frémont, John C. 60
French, Samuel G. 92
Funsten, Oliver R. 174, 177, 178, 180, 184
Funsten's Brigade 180, 183, 184

Gaines, James L. 135–136, 162, 172–173
Gaines's Crossroads, Va., battle of 109–110
Gaines's Mill, Va., battle of 66
Galloway, John B. 215, 219–220
Garland, Samuel 222
Garnett, Theodore S. 174, 210, 214, 221, 227–228
Gay, Abner 11
George W. Reed & Company 21
Georgia artillery unit: Sumter Flying Artillery 48
Georgia cavalry units: Cobb Legion 65, 66, 67, 72, 74, 84, 87, 106, 107, 108, 109, 124, 130, 166, 267, 170, 210; Phillips Legion 100, 101, 104, 124
Georgia Military Institute 167
Gettysburg, Pa., battle of 151–152
Gettysburg, Pa., campaign 139–162, 166, 170
Gibbon, Mr. 229–230
Gibson, Charles Bell 229–230
Gillett's Farm, N.C., skirmish at 60
Ginnings, Samuel, 36
Gist, Christopher 7
Glendale, Va. (Frayser's Farm), battle of 66
Goodall's Tavern, Va., battle of 6, 218–219
Gordon, Caroline *see* Hackett, Caroline Louisa Gordon
Gordon, Caroline Gwyn 20, 31
Gordon, Chapman 7
Gordon, Charles 7–9, 19–20
Gordon, George 7–9, 15
Gordon, James Byron 32, 41, 42, 45, 52, 53, 54, 58–59, 60, 61, 71, 72, 74, 75, 76, 77, 102, 111, 116–117, 121, 124, 125, 127, 128, 143, 163, 165, 166, 174, 184–185, 189, 194–195, 196, 197–199, 204–205;

Alleghany County 29; analyzes Rufus Barringer 234; appearance of 6, 22, 23, 58, 194, 199, 201, 207; Auburn, Va. 160–163, 188; Barbee's Crossroads, Va. 103–109; birth of 9; Brandy Station, Va. 128, 130–131, 133–134, 135, 137–138; Bristoe, Va., campaign 174–183; Brook Church, Va. 225–227; brothers 17–19, 40, 203; brothers-in-law 19, 232; Buckland, Va., races 186–188; burial of 231–232; business activities of 20–22, 139; career of 1–3, 238–240; Chambersburg, Md., raid 93–102; commands Fifth N.C. Cavalry 139, 142, 143, 144–145, 146, 147, 148, 150, 151, 152, 153–155, 156, 157, 158, 159, 160, 162; Conscription Act, opinion of 58; Craige, Burton 28, 33, 40; death of 226–230, 231–232, 233; death of Tom Brown 40; Democratic Presidential Convention 27–29; Dranesville, Va. 48–51; educational background of 11–14; enlists 33–34; equips Wilkes Valley Guards 34; farming 16–17; Fredericksburg, Va., campaign 103–109, 112–114, 116, 118; furloughs of 119, 200–201; Gaines's Crossroads, Va. 109–110; Gettysburg, Pa., campaign 139, 142, 143, 144–145, 146, 147, 148, 150, 151, 152, 153–155, 156, 157, 158, 159, 160, 162; Goodall's Tavern, Va. 6, 218–219; Gordon, John B. 58, 236–237; Ground Squirrel Church, Va. 6, 219–220; Hagerstown, Md. 156–157; Halsey, Aurelia 202–203, 204, 206, 228, 231, 235; health of 12, 159; Jack's Mountain, Pa. 153–155; Jack's Shop, Va. 169–170; Malvern Hill 70–71; Maryland campaign 79, 80, 81, 82, 85–86, 89–90, 91–92; memory of 236–240; military influences of 26–27; Mine Run, Va., campaign 190–193; mother 10, 202, 203, 229–230; N.C. General Assembly 23–27; "Oakland" 15–17, 201; Parker's Store, Va. 192–193; Peninsula campaign 63–71; political career of 22–29; promotions of 2, 37, 56, 91–92, 158–159, 162, 168–169, 171–172, 198; relationship with J.E.B. Stuart 5–6, 47, 48, 127, 199, 239, 240; religion 29–31, 203, 229–230; secession of N.C. 33; sisters 10, 19–20, 203; slavery issue 26–27; slaves 17, 164–165, 201, 232; staff of 172–173, 195; transfers to cavalry 36–37; Vienna, Va. 45–47; wealth of 32; Wilderness 208–212; Wilkes Valley Guards 34–36; women 31–32, 176, 188, 198, 201–202; wounded 183–184, 226–227; Yellow Tavern, Va., campaign 5–6, 213–220, 221–227; youth of 9–14
Gordon, John 9
Gordon, Mrs. John B. 189
Gordon, John Brown 2, 20, 209, 236–237

Index

Gordon, John George 8
Gordon, Martha Lenoir *see* Finley, Martha Lenoir Gordon
Gordon, Mary Chapman 8
Gordon, Melinda 20
Gordon, Nathaniel 9–10, 11, 12, 15
Gordon, Sarah Ann *see* Finley, Sarah Ann Gordon
Gordon, Sarah Gwyn *see* Brown, Sarah Gordon
Gordon, Sarah Herndon 8, 13, 135
Gordon, Zechariah Herndon 20
Gordon Springs, Ga. 19–20, 174
Gracie, Archibald 225
Graham, W.A. 159
Grant, Ulysses S. 5, 207, 210, 211–212, 233
Granville, Earl 8
Gregg, David M. 105, 129, 132, 137, 142, 143–144, 208, 212, 215, 218, 223, 225, 227
Gregory, Ed S. 235
Ground Squirrel Church, Va., battle of 6, 219–220
Gwyn, James 33, 34, 164
Gwyn, Julia P. 164
Gwyn, Martha Lenoir 10, 11
Gwyn, Richard R. 10

Hackett, Caroline Louisa Gordon 10, 18, 19, 20, 25–26, 31–32, 58, 73–74, 104, 200, 201, 235, 236
Hackett, Florence 104
Hackett, James Gordon 236
Hackett, Robert F. 19, 22, 58, 104, 200, 235, 236
Hagerstown, Md., battle of 156–157
Hairston, Peter W. 183, 190, 200
Halsey, Alex 202
Halsey, Aurelia 202–203, 204, 206, 208, 228, 231, 235
Halsey, Don 202
Halsey, Julia 202
Halsey, Seth 202
Halsey, Stephen 202
Hampton, Frank 137
Hampton, Preston 87, 136
Hampton, Wade 73, 74–75, 76, 80, 83, 84, 85, 86, 91, 92, 93, 94, 95, 96, 97, 99, 100, 101, 102–103, 104, 106, 107, 108, 109, 112–116, 118, 120, 122, 123, 125, 128, 130, 132, 133, 134, 135, 136, 137, 138, 144–145, 160, 162, 166, 168, 172, 190, 192, 196, 199, 200, 205–206, 209, 210
Hampton's Brigade 72, 73, 75–76, 78, 79, 80, 82, 83, 85, 87, 88, 89, 90–91, 93, 94, 95, 100, 102–103, 104–109, 111, 112, 113, 114, 116, 118–119, 120, 121, 122, 123, 124, 125, 127, 128, 130, 132–133, 134–135, 136, 137, 142, 143, 144, 146, 148, 149, 153, 157, 158, 161–162, 163, 165, 167, 171,
Hampton's Division 166, 174, 189, 192, 193, 194, 196, 199, 205, 206
Harper, Samuel Finley 198
Harrison's Landing, Va. 71, 73, 75
Hartwood Church, Va., skirmish at 112
Henry, Patrick 72
Hill, A.P. 73, 75, 89, 90, 122, 125, 139, 142, 149, 153, 158, 160, 174, 183, 190, 192, 207, 208, 209
Hill, D.H. 2, 64, 78, 85, 86–87, 88, 98–99, 104, 108, 170, 233
Hillsboro (N.C.) Military Academy 232
Hoke, Robert F. 200–201, 203
Holden, W.W. 27, 33, 164
Holmes, Theophilus 55, 56, 60
Hood, John Bell 126
Hooker, Joseph 73, 88, 121–122, 125, 129, 142, 148, 149,
Horse Artillery *see* Stuart Horse Artillery
Houston, William 144
Hubbard, Fred C. 237
Huey, Pennock 154
Huger, Benjamin 53

Illinois cavalry regiment: Eighth 108
Imboden, John D. 123, 149, 150, 153
Imboden's Brigade 123, 150, 157
Indiana cavalry regiment: Third 108
Iredell, Cadwallader 208
Iverson, Alfred 156

Jack's Mountain, Pa., battle of 153–155
Jack's Shop, Va., battle of 169–170
Jackson, Thomas Jonathan ("Stonewall") 60–61, 65, 66, 70, 71, 73, 75, 76, 79, 84, 87, 90, 99, 103, 111, 114, 122, 125
Jackson College 18
Jefferson Medical College 19
Jenkins, Albert G. 123, 124, 150, 157
Jenkins's Brigade 124, 139, 156, 167
John, Lord Carteret 8
Johnson, Bradley T. 217, 222
Johnson, Edward 209
Johnson, L.A. 159
Johnston, Joseph E. 36, 42, 44, 47, 53, 60, 61
Jones, William D. 120
Jones, William E. ("Grumble") 94, 97, 100, 103, 109, 123, 127, 130, 132, 133, 136, 144, 154, 160, 166, 174
Jones's Brigade 109, 127, 128, 130, 132, 133, 136, 139, 140, 143, 148, 153, 156, 157, 161–162, 169, 174, 177, 178, 180, 183

Kansas-Nebraska Act of 1854 29
Kelly's Ford, Va., battle of 120
Kentucky infantry regiment (Confederate): First 48, 49
Kilpatrick, Hugh Judson 134, 154, 156, 157, 170, 176, 177, 178, 185, 186, 200
Kilpatrick-Dahlgren Raid 213
Kings Mountain, S.C., battle of 7, 9, 27

Latane, William 63
Laurel Brigade 167, 197
Lee, Fitzhugh 5, 66, 72–73, 79, 90, 103, 109, 120, 124, 126, 149, 153, 158, 160, 166, 167, 168, 177, 185, 186, 187, 205, 210, 211, 212, 214, 215, 216, 222, 223, 225, 227, 231, 234
Lee, Robert E. 2, 5, 37, 55, 60, 61, 63, 64, 66, 67, 70, 71, 72, 73, 74, 75, 77, 78, 82, 84, 88, 89, 90, 91, 93, 94, 102, 109, 118, 121, 122, 123, 124–125, 126, 127, 138, 147–148, 150, 152–153, 158, 159–160, 162, 163, 165, 166, 171, 172, 174, 177, 180, 181, 183, 189, 191, 192, 193, 195–196, 200, 203, 204, 205, 206, 207, 208, 210, 213, 216–217, 234
Lee, Thomas C. 96
Lee, W.H.F. ("Rooney") 66, 94, 100, 101, 112, 124, 128, 130, 131, 132, 137, 149, 167, 205, 206, 234
Lee's (Fitz) Brigade 81, 83, 90, 103, 104, 108, 109, 112, 119, 120, 124, 127, 137, 139–140, 143, 149, 158
Lee's (Fitz) Division 167, 174, 180, 184, 189, 190, 205, 206, 208, 210–212, 213, 216, 217, 218, 227, 234
Lee's (W.H.F.) Brigade 94, 100, 101, 109, 112, 124, 127, 128, 130, 131, 132, 137, 140, 142, 149, 159, 167
Lefler, P.A. 131
Lenoir's Rangers 7
Letcher, John 189
Lincoln, Abraham 33, 73, 109, 111, 121, 160
Litaker, Henry ("Little") 187
Lomax, Lunsford L. 5, 136, 167, 168, 180, 189, 205, 221, 222
Lomax's Brigade 167, 183, 221, 206, 214, 216, 217, 221
Longstreet, James 74, 76, 84, 88, 103, 110, 111, 125, 136, 139, 148, 149, 153, 158, 160, 174, 196, 203, 207, 208, 209, 212
Lords Proprietors 7, 8
Lost Cause 237

Magruder, John B. 60
Mahone, William 162, 212
Maine cavalry regiment: First 134, 218–219
Malone, Charles D. 102
Malvern Hill, Va., battle of 70–71
Manassas, first battle of 36, 43, 52, 73
Manassas, second battle of 76, 78
Manly, Charles 23, 24
Manson, Otis Frederic 229–230
Martin, James G. 41
Martin, William T. 66, 84, 85, 113, 114
Maryland campaign 80–91
Maryland cavalry battalion (Confederate): First 167, 215
Maryland cavalry regiment (Federal): First 133
Massachusetts cavalry regiment: First 218
Massachusetts infantry regiment: Seventh 69
Matthews, George H. 213
McBride, B.C. 195
McClellan, George B. 47, 53, 56–57, 67, 70, 71, 75, 76, 81, 84, 88, 89, 90, 92, 98, 99, 103
McClellan, H.B. 53, 59, 60, 61, 63, 66, 71, 73, 90, 109, 132, 217, 218, 220, 221
McClennahan, John M. 215
McDowell, Irvin 36, 60, 61
McDowell, Va., battle of 58–59

McLaws, Lafayette 74, 78, 84, 87, 88
McRae, J.C. 173
Meade, George G. 149, 150, 160, 161, 165, 174, 176, 177, 180, 181, 183, 188, 190, 192, 194, 207, 212
Meadow Bridges, Va., battle of 223–225
Means, Paul B. 173, 219, 225–226
Mechanicsville, Va. (Beaver Dam Creek), battle of 65
Meem, Erna R. 235
Meem, James L., II 235
Meem, John Gaw 235
Meem, Julia H. 235
Meem, Stephen H. 235
Merritt, Wesley 212, 213, 218, 224, 225, 227
Mexican War 26–27
Michigan cavalry regiment: Fifth 215
Middleburg, Va., battle of 140–142
Miles, Dixon S. 88
Miller, Calvin 11
Miller, J.M. 39
Milroy, Robert 58
Mine Run, Va., campaign 190–194
Mississippi cavalry unit: Jeff Davis Legion 63, 65, 66, 72, 84, 85, 87, 113, 114, 124, 130, 134, 135, 144, 145, 161, 166, 192, 197, 199, 210
Moor, Augustus 83, 84
Moore, John 226, 227
Morehead, J. Turner 177
Morehead, John M. 32
Morgan, John Hunt 203–204
Mosby, John S. 130, 142
"Mount Airy" 235
Mount Vernon 32
Munford, Thomas T. 79, 87, 127, 137, 139–140, 143
Murat, Joachim 2, 229

Namozine Church, Va., battle of 234
Neese, George 80, 151, 152
New Bern, battle of 53
New York cavalry regiments: Second 134; Sixth 215, 221; Eighth 88, 105, 106, 107–108; Tenth 134, 135, 136
New York Herald 136
Newcome, Colonel 19, 22, 198
The Newcomes: The Story of a Most Respectable Family 19, 22, 198
Ney, Peter S. 11–12, 27, 160, 239
North Carolina cavalry brigade 124, 168, 171–173, 184–185, 189, 190, 194–195, 196–197, 198, 199, 200, 204, 205, 228, 233–234, 239; Appomattox, Va. 234; Auburn, Va. 180–183; Bristoe, Va., campaign 174–188; Brook Church, Va. 225–227; Buckland Va. Races 186–188; Chamberlain's Run, Va. 234; creation of 166, 168; Goodall's Tavern, Va. 218–219; Ground Squirrel Church, Va. and 219–220; Jack's Shop, Va. and 169–170; Mine Run, Va., campaign 190–194; Parker's Store, Va. and 192–193; war's end and 233–234; Wilderness and 208–212;

winter quarters and 200; Yellow Tavern, Va., campaign 5–6, 213–220, 221–227
North Carolina cavalry regiments: First 36, 40–41, 42, 43, 47, 48, 52, 53, 54–55, 59–60, 61–62, 71, 72, 76–77, 102, 118, 119, 120, 121, 122, 123, 124, 125–127, 160, 163, 164, 165, 166, 171, 173, 182, 195, 196, 197, 200, 203, 234; Barbee's Crossroads 103–109; Brandy Station 128, 130, 131, 133, 134, 135, 137; Bristoe Station, Va., campaign 177–188; Brook Church Va. 225; Buckland Races 186–188; Chambersburg, Md. Raid 93–102; Dranesville, Va. 48–51; drilling of 39; estimates of 41–43 equipment of 38–39; Fredericksburg campaign 109–110, 112–114, 116; Gaines's Crossroads, Va. 109–110; Gettysburg, Pa., campaign 140, 142, 143, 144–145, 146, 152, 159, 160, 162; Goodall's Tavern, Va. 219; Ground Squirrel Church, Va. 220; gunboats 62; Hartwood Church Va. skirmish 112; horses of 120, 200; Jack's Shop, Va. 169–170; Malvern Hill, Va. 70–71; Maryland campaign 78–91; Mine Run, Va., campaign 190–191, 192; N.C. service 52–62; organization of 38; Parker's Store, Va. 193; Peninsula campaign 63–65, 67–71; picket duty 44, 45, 52; reviews of 42; Vienna, Va. 45–47; Wilderness 208, 209–212; Willis Church, Va. 87–89; winter quarters 52, 119; Yellow Tavern, Va., campaign 213, 219, 220, 221; Second 38, 56, 57, 60, 61, 108–109, 124, 130, 131, 137, 146, 147, 159, 169, 161, 162, 167, 173, 180, 182, 191, 193, 194, 196, 197, 200, 205, 208, 209, 212, 215, 219, 225, 227, 234; Third 56, 61, 92, 205, 234; Fourth 123–124, 132, 137, 140–141, 142, 144, 146, 149, 152, 154, 157, 159, 166, 167, 173, 174, 177, 178, 182, 191, 196–197, 205, 234; Fifth 123–124, 136–137, 140–141, 144, 145, 146–148, 150–159, 166, 167, 169, 177–178, 191, 193, 196–197, 205, 208, 210, 212, 214, 215, 217, 218, 219, 225–226, 227, 234
North Carolina home front 163–164
North Carolina infantry regiments: First 35–36, 65–66, 235; Thirteenth 64; Thirty-seventh 53; Forty-eighth 90
North Carolina Railroad 35
North Wilkesboro, N.C. 236

"Oakland" 10, 12, 13, 15–17, 201, 233, 237
Officers' Hospital 228–230
Ohio cavalry regiment: Sixth 215
Ord, E.O.C. 48

Parker's Store, Va., battle of 192–193
Pate, Henry C. 221
Patterson, Rufus L. 32, 33
Patterson, Samuel F. 11, 32

Payne, W.H.F. 146, 147, 159
Pearce, N. Bart 40
Pegram, R.S. 137
Pelham, John 66, 79–80, 82, 92, 100, 101, 108, 114, 120
Pendleton, Alexander S. 190
Peninsula campaign 57, 60–62, 75
Pennsylvania cavalry units: First 133; Third 46, 69, 184; Fifth 52; Sixth 220; Eighth 105; Eighteenth 188, 190
Pennsylvania infantry units: First Reserves 48
Perry, Edward 162
Perry, Tom *see* University of North Carolina, still an admirer of
Person, Jesse 121
Person, Matthew 234
Pettigrew, James J. 159
Phillips Legion *see* Georgia cavalry units
Phillips's Farm 71
Pickens, Francis 114
Pickett, George 223
Pierce, Franklin 28, 29
Pitzer, Andrew L. 48
Pleasonton, Alfred 84, 98, 100, 101, 103, 104, 108, 123, 129, 130, 143, 144, 147, 148, 150
Pollard, Edward A. 237
Pollocksville, N.C., skirmish at 59
Pope, John 73, 76
Porter, Fitz John 65, 66
Presidential convention of 1856 (Democratic) 27–29
Price, Channing 93, 95, 112
Price, Sterling 29
Proffit, W. Harrison 33, 35
Pugh, J.M. 56, 57–58, 119, 127, 163, 164, 165, 197

Ramseur, Stephen 202
Randolph, George W. 92
Ransom, Robert 37–39, 40, 41, 42, 43, 45–47, 48, 50, 54–55, 69, 92, 170–171, 239
Ransom, Mrs. Robert 38, 41
Rappahannock Bridge, battle of 190
Rea, D.B. 98
Read, James Bond 228, 229
Ream's Station, Va., battle of 234
Reese, Randall H. 194
Reid, David S. 26
Reno, Jesse L. 88
Rhode Island cavalry regiment: First 140
Rhode Island infantry regiment: Second 69
Rich, Jerry E. 113
Ripley, Roswell S. 74
Roanoke Island, N.C., battle of 52
Roberts, William Paul 196, 219, 234, 240
Robertson, Beverly H. 81, 124, 128, 131–132, 140, 140–141, 144, 145, 147, 148, 149, 150, 151–152, 154, 156, 157, 158, 166, 167
Robertson, James M. 212–213
Robertson's Brigade 81, 83, 124, 127, 128, 131–132, 135, 136, 139, 140–141, 142, 143, 145, 146, 148, 150, 151, 152, 153, 156, 157, 158, 159, 169, 166

Index 435

Robinson, Leiper M. 221, 223
Robinson, William G. 173, 191
Robinson's Show 22
Ross, Fitzgerald 196
Rosser, Thomas L. 65, 67, 70, 104, 108, 109, 112, 127, 167, 168, 186, 189, 190, 192–193, 194, 196, 198, 209
Rosser's Brigade 189, 192–193, 194, 198, 206, 212, 213
Ruffin, Thomas 38, 169, 173, 177–178, 182

Sackett, Belcher & Company 21
St. Paul's Episcopal Church 30–31, 117, 232
Salem College 19
Savage's Station, Va., battle of 66
Scales, Alfred H. 64
Scammon, Eliakim 83
Seddon, James 122–123
Seven Days *see* Peninsula campaign
Sevier, John 9
Sharpsburg, Md., battle of 89–90
Shaw, E.F. 227
Shelby, Isaac 9
Sheridan, Philip H. 5–6, 212–227, 233
Shoup, Jacob G. 152
Shoup, John C. 152
Sigel, Franz 114, 115
Siler, Jesse W. 108, 110
Siler, Thaddeus P. 86
Slocum, Henry Warner 88
Smith, Kirby 235
Smith, Peter Evans 186–187
South Carolina cavalry regiments: First 109, 113, 124, 130, 137, 161, 162, 167, 175, 197; Second 83, 94, 107, 108, 109, 113, 124, 128, 132, 145, 161, 162, 166
South Carolina College 113, 177
South Carolina infantry regiment: Sixth 48, 49
South Carolina unit: Hampton Legion 65, 72, 73
South Mountain, Md., battle of 85–88, 167
Speese, Andrew 184–185
Spruill, S.B. 60
Staley, Esley 22
Starr, Samuel H. 152
Stevens, Thaddeus 90
Stokes, Montford Sidney 26–27, 33, 34, 59, 66, 76
Stoneman, George 99, 121, 122
Stoneman's Raid (1865) 233
Stuart, Flora 125, 147, 188, 216
Stuart, James Ewell Brown 2, 11, 43–44, 45–47, 53, 54, 55, 61, 71, 73, 77, 103, 104, 106, 109, 110, 114, 118, 119, 120, 123, 124, 126–127, 160, 165, 166, 172, 174, 184, 185, 189, 190, 195, 200, 201, 203, 204, 205; Auburn, Va. and 180–183; Brandy Station, Va. and 128, 131–138; Bristoe, Va., campaign and 174–188; Buckland, Va. Races and 186–188; Catlett's Station, Va. raid and 76; Chambersburg, Md. Raid and 93–102, 151–57; death of 363, 365; Dranesville, Va. and 48–51; evaluates First N.C. Cavalry 127; Fredericksburg, Va., campaign and 103–114; Gettysburg campaign and 139–140, 141–150, 152, 153, 156–157, 159, 162; Jack's Shop, Va. and 169–170; Maryland campaign and 78–80, 82–92; Mine Run, Va., campaign and 190–194; Peninsula campaign and 63–64, 66–67, 69, 71; promotion of 72; relationship with James B. Gordon 5, 47, 127, 172, 186, 227–228, 240; reorganization of cavalry 109, 123–124, 166–168, 205–206; Wilderness 208, 209–212; wounded 222, 227–228; Yellow Tavern, Va., battle of 5–6, 220–223; Yellow Tavern, Va., campaign and 15–16, 212–227
Stuart Horse Artillery 132, 133, 154, 156, 170, 184, 190, 222
Sumner, Edwin V. 79
Sweeney, Sam 200

Taylor, Zachary 26
Thackeray, William M. 19, 22, 198
Thomason, Hugh F. 40
Tredenick, Nicholas P. 135, 208
Twiggs, J.D. 113

United Confederate Veterans 237
United Daughters of the Confederacy 230, 237
U.S. cavalry regiments: First 37; Second 72; Third 56; Sixth 105, 152
U.S. Military Academy 37, 56, 72, 121, 147, 167, 168
U.S. Naval Academy 18, 34
University of North Carolina 18, 147, 28, 173; *see also* Perry, Tom
University of Virginia 202
Upperville, Va., battle of 143–146

Vance, Zebulon B. 59, 91–92, 117, 163, 168, 204, 205, 232
Venable, Andrew Reid 102, 185, 216, 217, 221, 222
Vienna, Va., skirmish at 45–47
Virginia artillery unit: Chew's Battery 132, 133, 154
Virginia cavalry battalions: Fifteenth 68; Seventeenth 109; Thirty-fifth 109, 124, 133, 139, 166
Virginia cavalry regiments: First 63, 65, 66, 72, 109, 124, 167, 220, 222; Second 79, 109, 124, 167, 202, 218; Third 65, 67, 70, 72, 109, 124, 167, 213; Fourth 63, 65, 66, 72, 109, 124, 131, 147, 167, 168, 215, 216; Fifth 65, 69, 70, 72, 109, 124, 167, 221; Sixth 109, 124, 133, 149, 152, 154, 166; Seventh 109, 124, 149, 152, 166, 178; Ninth 63, 65, 66, 67, 72, 109, 124, 167; Tenth 65, 72, 100, 101, 109, 124, 167; Eleventh 127, 136, 149, 157, 167, 168, 178; Twelfth 109, 124, 133, 166, 178; Thirteenth 167, 124; Fifteenth 109, 124, 167; Twenty-first 202
Virginia infantry unit: (Richmond) City Battalion 227
Von Borcke, Heros 79, 91, 106, 118, 120, 135, 143, 222

Walker, John 84
Waring, Joseph 135, 137, 197, 199, 204, 205, 206, 210, 231, 239
Wells, Edward L. 2
West Point *see* U.S. Military Academy
Whitaker, John H. 112, 116, 120, 136, 149
White, B.S. 160
White, Elijah 139
White, M.L. 68
Wickham, Williams C. 5, 66, 103, 132, 167, 168, 172, 213, 214, 221
Wickham's Brigade 5, 167, 205, 206, 213, 216, 217, 220, 221, 222
Wigwam 200
Wilderness campaign 208–212
Wiley, William J. 155
Wilkes County, N.C. 8, 17, 22, 24, 116–117, 119, 163–164
Wilkes General Hospital 237
Wilkes Regional Medical Center 237–238
Wilkes Valley Guards 33–37, 65–66
Wilkesboro, N.C. 8, 9, 24, 26, 33, 116–117, 119
Wilkesborough Academy 11
Williams, Solomon 60, 130, 137, 146
Willis Church, Va., battle of 67–69
Wilson, James H. 208, 212, 215, 218, 223–224, 225, 227
Wilson's Creek, Mo., battle of 40
Wofford, William T. 157
Worth, Subal G. 219

Yadkin County, N.C. 25
Yadkin Navigation Company 24
Yellow Tavern, Va. 5–6, 220–223
Yellow Tavern, Va., battle of 6, 218, 220–223
Yellow Tavern, Va., campaign 5–6, 212–227
Young, P.M.B. 74, 84, 87, 134, 135, 137, 162, 167, 169, 175, 176, 179, 186, 189, 192, 193, 194, 198–199, 203, 204, 210, 234
Young, Samuel 12
Young's Brigade 175, 176, 185, 189, 192, 193, 194, 196, 198–199, 205, 206, 210, 212, 213

www.ingramcontent.com/pod-product-compliance
Lightning Source LLC
Chambersburg PA
CBHW081532300426
44116CB00015B/2604